# TABLES OF THE MOON.

---

AMERICAN EPHEMERIS

AND

NAUTICAL ALMANAC.

# TABLES

# OF THE MOON;

CONSTRUCTED FOR THE USE OF

## THE AMERICAN EPHEMERIS AND NAUTICAL ALMANAC.

BY

PROFESSOR BENJAMIN PEIRCE, LL.D.

PUBLISHED BY AUTHORITY OF THE SECRETARY OF THE NAVY.

---

BUREAU OF NAVIGATION,
WASHINGTON.
1865.

University Press:
Welch, Bigelow, and Company,
Cambridge.

# PREFACE

## TO THE SECOND EDITION.

---

One of the first steps in the preparation of the American Ephemeris and Nautical Almanac, founded by Congress in March, 1849, was the collection of materials for new Tables of the Moon. The work was completed, and the first edition of the American Tables was published in 1853.

Since this preliminary step, however indispensable, unavoidably delayed the appearance of the Almanac, I am very solicitous to make known, here and elsewhere, the great obligations which American astronomical science is under to Hon. John P. Kennedy, then the Secretary of the Navy, for his just estimate of the magnitude and importance of this work. Although the processes by which it was conducted had formed no part of his study, its objects and value were perfectly understood by a scholar who had already adorned the literature of his own country by his writings.

The American Tables, as is stated in the title-page of the first edition, are "constructed from Plana's theory, with Airy's and Longstreth's corrections, Hansen's two inequalities of long period arising from the action of Venus, and Hansen's values of the secular variations of the mean motion and the motion of the perigee."

The formulas of Plana's theory were taken, not from Plana's own work, but from pages lxxiv.–lxxx. of the Introduction to the Reduction of the Observations of the Moon, made at the Royal Observatory, at Greenwich, from 1750 to 1830.

These formulas were adopted because they claimed to be corrected by Plana himself, and, what is of more importance, because they had been compared with observation, and formed the basis of Airy's corrections of the elements of the Moon.

The term $0''.8 \sin [23]$, which occurs in that formula, is very different from the corresponding term $3''.3 \sin [23]$, which is originally given by Plana; but it appears from the remarks given on page lxxxi. of the Introduction to the Lunar Observations, that this correction was adopted with the assent of Plana, and it was, therefore, attributed to Plana in the American Tables.

Airy's corrections of the Lunar elements were adopted from his Memoir in Vol. XVII. of the Memoirs of the Royal Astronomical Society. In making these corrections, the two inequalities given at that time by Hansen, and produced by the disturbing force of Venus, were introduced in the comparison. Therefore it was necessary to introduce these terms also into the American Tables, in order to have the theory which had been verified by observation. Very different values of these terms have since been given by Hansen, and are introduced into his Tables. A new set of corrections of the Lunar elements has also been made by Airy; but these corrections were published several years after the appearance of the American Tables.

Just before the final preparation of the American Tables, and when the first volume of the American Ephemeris was on the eve of completion, Longstreth's empirical corrections of Plana's formula for the Moon's longitude were communicated to me by their author; they were accompanied by a table of comparisons (published in the Memoirs of the American Philosophical Society for 1853) which sufficiently attest their value and propriety, and the forthcoming volume of the Ephemeris was delayed until the corresponding changes were computed and applied.

The present edition of the American Tables of the Moon is the same as the first, with the exception of the correction of typographical errors; the substitution of the Tables of the Moon's Parallax constructed from Walker's and Adams's formulas, in the place of the original Parallax Tables; and the addition of a Table adapted to a convenient modification of the method of computing the latitude, by Professor J. D. Runkle.

A third edition will shortly be issued, of which the basis will still be Plana's theory, while the Tables will be corrected to conform to the new Solar Parallax, and the corrected elements of the Moon's orbit.

WASHINGTON, Navy Department,
March, 1865.

C. H. DAVIS,
*Rear-Admiral, and Chief of the Bureau of Navigation.*

# INTRODUCTION.

## I. CONSTRUCTION OF THE TABLES.

THESE tables are constructed from the theory of PLANA, modified by the theoretical investigations of HANSEN, and the empirical corrections of AIRY and LONGSTRETH.

The moon's mean longitude is also to be corrected by the two terms of long period, arising from the action of Venus, which were discovered by HANSEN, and printed in the *Astronomische Nachrichten*, No. 597, and which are expressed by

$\delta_{\text{h.}}\,\theta =$ the correction of the mean longitude of the moon arising from the action of Venus.

The following notation is adopted,

$\theta =$ the mean longitude of the moon,
$\varpi =$ the longitude of the moon's perigee,
$\eta =$ the longitude of the moon's node,
$\theta_{s.} =$ the mean longitude of the sun,
$\varpi_{s.} =$ the longitude of the sun's perigee.
$\theta', \theta'_{s.}, \varpi'_{s.}$, and $\eta' =$ the respective daily motions of $\theta, \varpi, \theta_{s.}, \varpi_{s.}$, and $\eta$.
$\theta_0, \varpi_0, \theta_{s.0}, \varpi_{s.0}, \eta_0 =$ the values of $\theta, \varpi, \theta_{s.}, \varpi_{s.}$, and $\eta$ at any assumed epoch, as the beginning of the nineteenth century.

The values of $\theta$, $\varpi$, &c., at any number of days $i$ from this epoch are, from the formulæ of PLANA, with the corrections given by HANSEN in the *Astronomische Nachrichten*, No. 597,

$$
\begin{aligned}
\theta &= \theta_0 + \theta' i + 8''.598\,(10)^{-9}\, i^2 + 3''.6483\,(10)^{-16}\, i^3 + \delta_{\text{h.}}\,\theta, \\
\varpi &= \varpi_0 + \varpi' i - 27''.217\,(10)^{-9}\, i^2 - 13''.750\,(10)^{-16}\, i^3, \\
\theta_{s.} &= \theta_{s.0} + \theta'_{s.}\, i + 0''.91584\,(10)^{-9}\, i^2 + 0''.03879\,(10)^{-16}\, i^3, \\
\varpi_{s.} &= \varpi_{s.0} + \varpi'_{s.}\, i + 0''.91584\,(10)^{-9}\, i^2 + 0''.03879\,(10)^{-16}\, i^3, \\
\eta &= \eta_0 + \eta' i + 6''.0355\; 10^{-9}\, i^2 + 2''.3744\,(10)^{-16}\, i^3.
\end{aligned}
$$

The values of $\theta_0$, $\varpi_0$, &c., and of $\theta'_0$, $\varpi'_0$, &c., derived, for the mean noon of Washington of the date 1801, Jan. 0, from the values obtained by AIRY in his Memoir upon the *Corrections of the Elements of the Moon's Orbit*, published in the *Memoirs of the Royal Astronomical Society*, Vol. XVII., and from BESSEL's Tables of the Sun, are

$$
\begin{aligned}
\theta_0 &= 107^\circ\; 55'\; 40''.5, & \theta' &= 13^\circ\; 635''.02808897, \\
\varpi_0 &= 266\;\; 4\; 51.3, & \varpi' &= 0\;\; 401.05783886, \\
\theta_{s.0} &= 279\; 52\; 44.3, & \theta'_{s.} &= 0\; 3548.32999304, \\
\varpi_{s.0} &= 279\; 31\; 10.4, & \varpi'_{s.} &= 0\;\; 0.16947241, \\
\eta_0 &= 13\; 55\; 52.6, & \eta' &= -0\;\; 190.63366070.
\end{aligned}
$$

# INTRODUCTION.

The assumed Western Longitude of Greenwich from Washington is $18^{h.}\ 51^{m.}\ 48^{s.}$.
The notation

$g''$ = the mean anomaly of Venus,
$z$ = the mean anomaly of the sun $= \theta_{s.} - \varpi_{s.}$,
$u$ = the uncorrected mean longitude of the moon $= \theta - \delta_{h.}\ \theta$,
$x$ = the mean anomaly of the moon $= \theta - \varpi$,
$y$ = the mean argument of the latitude $= \theta - \eta$,
$t$ = the argument of variation $= \theta - \theta_{s.}$,
$\breve{u}$ = the true longitude of the moon,
$\breve{y}$ = the true argument of the latitude,
♀ = the mean heliocentric longitude of Venus,
⊕ = the mean heliocentric longitude of the earth $= 180° + \theta_{s.}$,
♃ = the mean heliocentric longitude of Jupiter,
$H = 8g'' - 13z + 315°\ 30'$,
$H' = 18g'' - 16z - x + 35°\ 20'.2$,

gives the following formulæ for the longitude, latitude, and horizontal parallax of the moon.

In writing these formulæ, most of the arguments are expressed by numbers, in which the digit occupying the place of units is the coefficient of $x$, that in the place of tens is the coefficient of $t$, that in the place of hundreds is the coefficient of $z$, that in the place of thousands is the coefficient of $y$, and that in the place of tens of thousands is the coefficient of $u$. The accents upon the numbers indicate that the coefficient is negative. Thus the number of the argument [14′ 253′] denotes

$$u - 4y + 2z + 5t - 3x.$$

The form of the formula of the longitude is modified simply by substituting the term dependent upon the true arguments of the latitude, instead of the equivalent terms. This is accomplished by adding to the formula of longitude the equation,

$$\begin{aligned} 0 = & -416''.7 \sin 2\breve{y} + 411''.7 \sin 2y + 4''.1 \sin (2y + 2x), \\ & + 0''.9 \sin (2y - 2x) - 46''.0 \sin (2y - x) + 45''.2 \sin (2y + x), \\ & + 0''.3 \sin (2y + 3x) - 9''.3 \sin (2y + x - 2t) + 8''.8 \sin (2y - x + 2t), \\ & + 0''.9 \sin (2y + x + 2t) + 0''.1 \sin (2y - x - 2t) - 0''.4 \sin (2y + 2x - 2t), \\ & - 0''.5 \sin (2y - 2x + 2t) + 5''.7 \sin (2y + 2t) - 3''.8 \sin (2y - 2t), \\ & - 0''.4 \sin (2y - x + z) - 0''.4 \sin (x + z - 2y) - 0''.2 \sin (2y - 4t + x), \\ & + 1''.0 \sin (2y - t) - 0''.7 \sin (2y + z) + 1''.3 \sin (2y - z), \\ & - 0''.4 \sin (x - 2t + z + 2y) + 0''.3 \sin (2t + 2y - z) + 0''.3 \sin (2t - z - 2y). \end{aligned}$$

The form of the formula for latitude is modified in a way which is evident from inspection of the formula, and which is designed to obviate the necessity of correcting the arguments for the change from mean to true longitude. The formula of parallax is retained in PLANA's form.*

The terms of the various equations are given in the *first column* of the following tables of the formulæ united with the constants which are employed in the construction of the tables. The *second column* contains the initial letter of the authority for the corresponding coefficients of the equation, whether PLANA, AIRY, or LONGSTRETH. The letter is accented when the value of the coefficient is modified by the present form of the tables. The *third column* contains the period of the argument expressed in mean solar days. The *fourth column* contains the number of the argument. The *fifth column* contains the number of the table which gives the values of the equation.

* See Formula, page 305.

| EQUATION. | AUTHORITY. | PERIOD. | ARGUMENT. | TABLE. |
|---|---|---|---|---|
| ā = the moon's true longitude. | | | | |
| = nutation | | | | |
| + u — 8° 3135″.2 | A. | | | 2 |
| +22655″.226 | | d. | | 6 |
| +22639.2 sin [1] | A. | 27.55455245 | 1 | 6 |
| + 769.5 sin [2] | P. | | | 6 |
| + 36.7 sin [3] | P. | | | 6 |
| + 2.0 sin [4] | P. | | | 6 |
| + 0.1 sin [5] | P. | | | 6 |
| + 4587.4 | | | | 7 |
| + 4586.9 sin [21′] | A. | 31.81193574 | 2 | 7 |
| + 31.2 sin [42′] | L. | | | 7 |
| + 2457.02 | | | | 8 |
| — 122.1 sin [10] | P. | 29.53058800 | 3 | 8 |
| + 2371.0 sin [20] | A. | | | 8 |
| + 0.9 sin [30] | P. | | | 8 |
| + 14.4 sin [40] | P. | | | 8 |
| + 670.5 | | | | 9 |
| — 670.3 sin [100] | A. | 365.259687 | 4 | 9 |
| — 7.9 sin [200] | P. | | | 9 |
| + 225.3 | | | | 10 |
| + 18.0 sin [1′1] | P. | 411.78517 | 5 | 10 |
| — 212.4 sin [2′2] | P. | | | 10 |
| + 206.9 | | | | 11 |
| + 206.9 sin [1′21′] | L. | 34.84689 | 6 | 11 |
| + 192.1 | | | | 12 |
| + 192.1 sin [21] | P. | 9.61372 | 7 | 12 |
| + 165.9 | | | | 13 |
| + 165.9 sin [1′20] | P. | 15.38731 | 8 | 13 |
| + 148.1 | | | | 14 |
| + 148.1 sin [1′01] | P. | 29.80283 | 9 | 14 |
| + 110.0 | | | | 15 |
| — 110.0 sin [101] | L. | 25.62170 | 10 | 15 |
| + 85.0 | | | | 16 |
| — 85.0 sin [2001′] | L′. | 26.87829 | 11 | 16 |
| + 58.7 | | | | 17 |
| — 58.7 sin [202′0] | P′. | 173.31006 | 12′ | 17 |
| + 38.0 | | | | 18 |
| + 38.0 sin [41′] | P. | 10.08460 | 13 | 18 |
| + 28.8 | | | | 19 |
| — 28.8 sin [121′] | P. | 29.26328 | 14 | 19 |
| + 25.0 | | | | 20 |
| — 25.0 sin [120] | L. | 14.19161 | 15 | 20 |
| + 21.0 | | | | 21 |
| — 8.2 sin [11] | P. | 14.25418 | 16 | 21 |
| + 14.1 sin [22] | P. | | | 21 |
| + 17.2 | P. | | | 22 |
| + 17.2 sin [110] | P. | 27.32168 | 17 | 22 |
| + 14.0 | | | | 23 |
| + 14.0 sin [1′21] | P. | 9.87359 | 18 | 23 |
| + 12.8 | | | | 24 |
| — 12.8 sin [2′3] | P. | 24.30220 | 19 | 24 |
| + 9.6 | | | | 25 |
| + 9.6 sin [1′02] | P. | 14.31731 | 20 | 25 |
| + 9.2 | | | | 26 |
| — 9.2 sin [12′2] | L. | 131.67112 | 21 | 26 |
| + 8.1 | | | | 27 |
| — 0.4 sin [1′10] | P. | 32.12809 | 22 | 27 |
| + 7.8 sin [2′20] | P. | | | 27 |
| + 9.8 | | | | 28 |
| — 9.8 sin [202′1] | L′. | 23.77463 | 23 | 28 |
| + 7.3 | | | | 29 |
| — 7.3 sin [102] | P. | 13.27650 | 24 | 29 |
| + 2.9 | | | | 30 |
| — 2.9 sin [121] | P. | 9.36717 | 25 | 30 |
| + 1.9 | | | | 31 |
| + 1.9 sin [41] | L. | 5.82261 | 26 | 31 |
| + 1.6 | | | | 32 |

| EQUATION. | AUTHORITY. | PERIOD. | ARGUMENT. | TABLE. |
|---|---|---|---|---|
| Equations of Longitude continued. | | d. | | |
| + 0″.8 sin [1′2] | P. | 25.82638 | 27 | 32 |
| — 0.9 sin [2′4] | P. | | | 32 |
| + 7.5 | | | | 33 |
| + 7.5 sin [2′21′] | P. | 38.52204 | 28 | 33 |
| + 6.3 | | | | 34 |
| — 6.3 sin [2′021] | P′. | 32.76364 | 29 | 34 |
| + 3.8 | | | | 35 |
| + 3.8 sin [1′41′] | P. | 10.37093 | 30 | 35 |
| + 3.0 | | | | 36 |
| — 3.0 sin [31′] | P. | 15.31442 | 31 | 36 |
| + 3.0 | | | | 37 |
| + 3.0 sin [1′42′] | L. | 16.63016 | 32 | 37 |
| + 2.1 | | | | 38 |
| + 2.1 sin [2′01] | P. | 32.45058 | 33 | 38 |
| + 2.0 | | | | 39 |
| — 2.0 sin [221′] | P. | 27.09271 | 34 | 39 |
| + 1.2 | | | | 40 |
| — 1.2 sin [201] | P. | 23.94223 | 35 | 40 |
| + 1.0 | | | | 41 |
| + 1.0 sin [111] | P. | 13.71881 | 36 | 41 |
| + 0.5 | | | | 42 |
| + 0.5 sin [43′] | P. | 37.62533 | 37 | 42 |
| + 0.4 | | | | 43 |
| — 0.4 sin [12] | P. | 9.39439 | 38 | 43 |
| + 0.6 | | | | 44 |
| — 0.6 sin [32′] | P. | 34.47528 | 39 | 44 |
| + 0.4 | | | | 45 |
| + 0.4 sin [1′03] | P. | 9.42177 | 40 | 45 |
| + 0.4 | | | | 46 |
| — 0.4 sin [103] | P. | 8.95955 | 41 | 46 |
| + 0.3 | | | | 47 |
| + 0.3 sin [2′21] | P. | 10.14791 | 42 | 47 |
| + 0.6 | | | | 48 |
| + 0.6 sin [1′22] | P. | 7.26893 | 43 | 48 |
| + 0.3 | | | | 49 |
| — 0.3 sin [12′3] | P. | 22.78614 | 44 | 49 |
| + 0.2 | | | | 50 |
| — 0.2 sin [2021] | P′. | 5.63335 | 45 | 50 |
| + 0.4 | | | | 51 |
| — 0.4 sin [2′101] | P′. | 29.01328 | 46 | 51 |
| + 1.3 | | | | 52 |
| + 1.3 sin [21′00] | P′. | 14.13256 | 47 | 52 |
| + 0.5 | | | | 53 |
| — 0.5 sin [2′022] | P. | 14.96709 | 48 | 53 |
| + 0.2 | | | | 54 |
| — 0.2 sin [202′2] | P′. | 12.76271 | 49 | 54 |
| + 0.4 | | | | 55 |
| — 0.4 sin [2101′] | P′. | 25.03597 | 50 | 55 |
| + 0.2 | | | | 56 |
| — 0.2 sin [2001] | P′. | 9.10846 | 51 | 56 |
| + 1.0 | | | | 57 |
| + 1.0 sin [201′0] | P′. | 25.23137 | 52 | 57 |
| + 2.6 | | | | 58 |
| — 2.6 sin [212′0] | P′. | 117.53942 | 53 | 58 |
| + 1.2 | | | | 59 |
| + 1.2 sin [1′40] | P. | 7.53494 | 54 | 59 |
| + 0.9 | | | | 60 |
| — 0.9 sin [141′] | P. | 9.81365 | 55 | 60 |
| + 0.7 | | | | 61 |
| — 0.7 sin [2100] | P′. | 13.11748 | 56 | 61 |
| + 0.8 | | | | 62 |
| + 0.8 sin [23] | P. | 5.66247 | 57 | 62 |
| + 0.5 | | | | 63 |
| — 0.5 sin [142′] | P. | 15.24221 | 58 | 63 |
| + 0.6 | | | | 64 |
| — 0.6 sin [204′1] | P′. | 38.96397 | 59 | 64 |

| EQUATION. | AUTHORITY. | PERIOD. | ARGUMENT. | TABLE. |
|---|---|---|---|---|
| Equations of Longitude continued. | | | | |
| + 0″.4 | | | | 65 |
| — 0.4 sin [212′1] | P′. | d. 22.32171 | 60 | 65 |
| + 0.4 | | | | 66 |
| + 0.4 sin [4000] | P′. | 6.80305 | 61 | 66 |
| + 0.3 | | | | 67 |
| + 0.3 sin [21′20] | P′. | 7.22100 | 62 | 67 |
| + 0.3 | | | | 68 |
| + 0.3 sin [11000] | P. | 13.63340 | 63 | 68 |
| + 0.3 | | | | 69 |
| — 0.3 sin [2′1′21] | P. | 35.99212 | 64 | 69 |
| + 0.2 | | | | 70 |
| — 0.2 sin [140] | P. | 7.23638 | 65 | 70 |
| + 0.2 | | | | 71 |
| — 0.2 sin [2′030] | P′. | 35.59582 | 66 | 71 |
| + 1.0 | | | | 72 |
| — 1.0 sin [1′1001] | A. | 27.44332 | 67 | 72 |
| + 0.7 | | | | 73 |
| + 0.7 sin [11′001] | A. | 27.66669 | 68 | 73 |
| + 2.2 | | | | 74 |
| — 2.2 sin [1′2′2] | L. | 471.89326 | 69 | 74 |
| + 1.5 | | | | 75 |
| + 1.5 sin [21′2′0] | P. | 329.79056 | 70 | 75 |
| + 1.3 | | | | 76 |
| — 1.1 sin (♀−⊕) | | 583.921 | 71 | 76 |
| + 0.4 sin 2 (♀−⊕) | | | | 76 |
| + 0.8 | | | | 77 |
| + 0.7 sin (⊕−♃) | | 398.884 | 72 | 77 |
| — 0.2 sin 2 (⊕−♃) | | | | 77 |
| + 2.0 | | | | 78 |
| + 2.0 sin [2002′] | P′. | 1095.1653 | 73′ | 78 |
| + 0.5 | | | | 79 |
| + 0.5 sin [111′] | P. | 3232.8202 | 74 | 79 |
| + 53.2 | | | | 80 |
| + 23.2 sin *H*. | | 84753.24 | 75 | 80 |
| + 65 65 | | | | 81 |
| + 27.4 sin *H′*. | | 95489.94 | 76 | 81 |
| —416.9 sin 2 $\bar{y}$. | | | 77 | 82 |
| + 6.38 sin $(u-y)$ | | | | 81A. |
| — 0.97 cos $(u-y)$ | | | | 81A. |

*The Moon's Latitude = + *A* sin $\bar{y}$ + *B* cos $\bar{y}$ *

| EQUATION. | AUTHORITY. | PERIOD. | ARGUMENT. | TABLE. |
|---|---|---|---|---|
| — 60″. | | | | |
| + 15.8 | | | | 92 |
| + 15.8 sin [102′1] | P. | d. 188.2015 | 78 | 92 |
| + 22.2 | | | | 93 |
| + 14.4 sin [1001′] | P. | 2190.3306 | 73 | 93 |
| + 0.6 | | | | 94 |
| — 0.6 sin [101′0] | P. | 346.6201 | 12‴ | 94 |
| + 0.2 | | | | 95 |
| — 0.2 sin [1′101] | P. | 438.3608 | 79 | 95 |
| + 0.1 | | | | 96 |
| — 0.1 sin [1101′] | P. | 313.0547 | 80 | 96 |
| + 0.7 | | | | 97 |
| + 0.7 sin [112′1] | P. | 124.2046 | 81 | 97 |
| + 1.8 | | | | 98 |
| + 1.8 sin [1′021] | P. | 14.8655 | 82 | 98 |
| + 0.7 | | | | 99 |
| + 0.7 sin [1′2′20] | P. | 39.2116 | 83 | 99 |
| + 0.6 | | | | 100 |
| — 0.6 sin [1002] | P′. | 9.5717 | 84 | 100 |
| + 0.5 | | | | 101 |
| — 0.5 sin [1′011] | P. | 29.9342 | 48 | 101 |
| + 0.4 | | | | 102 |
| + 0.4 sin [302′0] | P′. | 23.5193 | 85 | 102 |
| + 0.3 | | | | 103 |
| + 0.3 sin [1′042′] | P. | 38.2830 | 86 | 103 |

| EQUATION. | AUTHORITY. | PERIOD. | ARGUMENT. | TABLE. |
|---|---|---|---|---|
| Equations of Latitude continued. | | | | |
| + 0″.2 | | | | 104 |
| — 0.2 sin [1021] | P. | d. 7.1041 | 87 | 104 |
| + 0.2 | | | | 105 |
| + 0.2 sin [1021′] | P. | 14.6664 | 88 | 105 |
| + 0.2 | | | | 106 |
| + 0.2 sin [1′022] | P. | 9.6561 | 89 | 106 |
| + 0.2 | | | | 107 |
| — 0.2 sin [1′021] | P. | 32.2808 | 90 | 107 |
| + 6.2 | | | | 108 |
| — 6.18 sin 3 $\bar{y}$ | P. | | 77 | 108 |
| + 9.1 | | | | 109 |
| + 2.17 cos $\bar{u}$ | A. | | | 109 |
| — 8.80 sin $\bar{u}$ | A. | | | 109 |

In which the values of *A*. and *B*. are given by the following formulæ:

| EQUATION. | AUTHORITY. | PERIOD. | ARGUMENT. | TABLE. |
|---|---|---|---|---|
| *A* = 17600″.0 | A′. | | | |
| + 846.0 | | | | |
| + 527.5 cos [20′20] | P. | d. 173.31006 | 12″ | 83 |
| + 25.7 | | | | |
| + 25.7 cos [2002′] | P. | 1095.1653 | 73‴ | 84 |
| + 22.1 | | | | |
| — 22.1 cos [212′0] | P. | 117.5394 | 53′ | 85 |
| + 1.3 | | | | |
| — 1.3 cos [1] | P. | 27.5546 | 1′ | 86 |
| + 10.3 | | | | |
| — 10.3 cos [21′2′0] | P. | 329.7906 | 70′ | 87 |
| + 6.63 | | | | |
| — 1.3 cos [100] | P′. | 365.2597 | 4 | 89 |
| + 4.7 | | | | |
| + 4.7 cos [2′2] | P. | 205.8926 | 5′ | 90 |
| *B* = —1000. | | | | |
| + 846.0 | | | | |
| — 527.5 sin [202′0] | P. | 173.31006 | 12′ | 83 |
| + 25.7 | | | | |
| — 25.7 sin [2002′] | P. | 1095.1653 | 73″ | 84 |
| + 22.1 | | | | |
| — 22.1 sin [212′0] | P. | 117.5394 | 53 | 85 |
| + 1.3 | | | | |
| — 1.3 sin [1] | P. | 27.5546 | 1 | 86 |
| + 10.3 | | | | |
| + 10.3 sin [21′2′0] | P. | 329.7906 | 70 | 87 |
| + 88.9 | | | | |
| + 48.9 sin [100] | P′. | 365.2597 | 4 | 88 |
| + 4.7 | | | | |
| + 4.7 sin [2′2] | P. | 205.8926 | 5 | 90 |
| + 1.0 | | | | |
| — 1.0 sin [1′1] | P′. | 411.7852 | 5 | 91 |

*The Moon's Equatorial Horizontal Parallax = *

| EQUATION. | AUTHORITY. | PERIOD. | ARGUMENT. | TABLE. |
|---|---|---|---|---|
| 3000″. | | | | |
| + 348.0 | | | | 110 |
| + 186.8 cos [1] | P. | d. 27.55455 | 1″ | 110 |
| + 10.3 cos [2] | P. | | | 110 |
| + 0.6 cos [3] | P. | | | 110 |
| + 28.6 | | | | 111 |
| — 0.9 cos [10] | P. | 29.53059 | 3 | 111 |
| + 27.6 cos [20] | P. | | | 111 |
| + 0.1 cos [40] | P. | | | 111 |
| + 34.2 | | | | 112 |
| + 33.9 cos [21′] | P. | 31.81194 | 2 | 112 |
| + 0.3 cos [42′] | P. | | | 112 |

* See Table cxxxvii.

* See Formula, page 305.

| EQUATION. | AUTHORITY. | PERIOD. | ARGUMENT. | TABLE. |
|---|---|---|---|---|
| The Moon's Equatorial Horizontal Parallax continued. | | | | |
| + 1″.4 | | | | 113 |
| + 1.4 cos [1′21′] | P. | d. 36.8469 | 6 | 113 |
| + 3.1 | | | | 114 |
| + 3.1 cos [21] | P. | 9.6137 | 7 | 114 |
| + 2.2 | | | | 115 |
| + 2.2 cos [1′20] | P. | 15.3873 | 8 | 115 |
| + 1.2 | | | | 116 |
| + 1.2 cos [101] | P. | 29.8028 | 9 | 116 |
| + 0.9 | | | | 117 |
| — 0.9 cos [1′01] | P. | 25.6217 | 10 | 117 |
| + 1.2 | | | | 118 |
| + 1.2 cos [2001′] | P. | 26.8783 | 11 | 118 |
| + 0.5 | | | | 119 |
| + 0.5 cos [41′] | P. | 10.0846 | 13 | 119 |
| + 0.2 | | | | 120 |
| — 0.2 cos [121′] | P. | 29.2633 | 14 | 120 |
| + 0.6 | | | | 121 |

| EQUATION. | AUTHORITY. | PERIOD. | ARGUMENT. | TABLE. |
|---|---|---|---|---|
| The Moon's Equatorial Horizontal Parallax continued. | | | | |
| — 0″.6 cos [120] | P. | d. 14.1916 | 15 | 121 |
| + 0.3 | | | | 122 |
| + 0.3 cos [22] | P. | 7.1271 | 16 | 122 |
| + 0.2 | | | | 123 |
| + 0.2 cos [1′21] | P. | 9.8736 | 18 | 123 |
| + 0.1 | | | | 124 |
| + 0.1 cos [2′2] | P. | 24.3022 | 19′ | 124 |
| + 0.4 | | | | 125 |
| — 0.4 cos [100] | P. | 365.2597 | 4 | 125 |
| + 0.2 | | | | 126 |
| + 0.2 cos [22′] | P. | 205.8926 | 5 | 126 |
| + 0.2 | | | | 127 |
| — 0.2 cos [20′20] | P. | 173.3101 | 12′ | 127 |
| The Moon's Equatorial Semidiameter = The Horizontal Parallax. × 0.272274 | B. | | | 128 |

This value of the Moon's Semidiameter is that deduced by Burckhardt from eclipses and occultations, and should be used for the computation of these phenomena. But for Meridian Observations it seems to vary with the telescope ranging from 2″ to 3″ greater than the value here given.

The Principal Terms of the Second and Fourth Differences of the Longitude for a Quarter of a Day are given in the following formulæ.

| EQUATION. | ARGUMENT. | TABLE. |
|---|---|---|
| Second Difference of the Longitude for a Quarter of a Day = | | |
| —130″. | | |
| + 76.0 | | 6″ |
| — 73.563 sin [1] | 1 | 6″ |
| — 9.993 sin [2] | | 6″ |
| — 1.071 sin [3] | | 6″ |
| — 0.104 sin [4] | | 6″ |
| — 0.008 sin [5] | | 6″ |
| + 11.2 | | 7″ |
| — 11.180 sin [21′] | 2 | 7″ |
| — 0.304 sin [42′] | | 7″ |
| + 31.16 | | 8″ |
| + 0.345 sin [10] | 3 | 8″ |
| — 20.808 sin [20] | | 8″ |
| — 0.023 sin [30] | | 8″ |
| — 0.650 sin [40] | | 8″ |
| + 0.42 | | 11″ |
| — 0.42 sin [1′21′] | 6 | 11″ |
| + 5.12 | | 12″ |
| — 5.117 sin [21] | 7 | 12″ |
| + 1.73 | | 13″ |
| — 1.727 sin [21′] | 8 | 13″ |
| + 0.41 | | 14″ |
| — 0.411 sin [1′01] | 9 | 14″ |
| + 0.41 | | 15″ |
| + 0.413 sin [101] | 10 | 15″ |
| + 0.29 | | 16″ |
| + 0.288 sin [2001′] | 11 | 16″ |
| + 0.92 | | 18″ |
| — 0.920 sin [41′] | 13 | 18″ |
| + 0.08 | | 19″ |
| + 0.083 sin [121′] | 14 | 19″ |
| + 0.31 | | 20″ |
| + 0.306 sin [120] | 15 | 20″ |
| + 0.80 | | 21″ |
| + 0.100 sin [11] | 16 | 21″ |
| — 0.680 sin [22] | | 21″ |
| + 0.06 | | 22″ |
| — 0.057 sin [110] | 17 | 22″ |

| EQUATION. | ARGUMENT. | TABLE. |
|---|---|---|
| Second Difference, continued. | | |
| + 0″.35 | | 23″ |
| — 0.354 sin [1′21] | 18 | 23″ |
| + 0.05 | | 24″ |
| + 0.054 sin [2′3] | 19 | 24″ |
| + 0.11 | | 25″ |
| — 0.115 sin [1′02] | 20 | 25″ |
| + 0.07 | | 27″ |
| — 0.074 sin [2′20] | 22 | 27″ |
| + 0.10 | | 29″ |
| + 0.102 sin [102] | 24 | 29″ |
| + 0.08 | | 30″ |
| — 0.081 sin [121] | 25 | 30″ |
| + 0.14 | | 31″ |
| — 0.137 sin [41] | 26 | 31″ |
| + 0.19 | | 35″ |
| — 0.087 sin [1′41′] | 30 | 35″ |
| Fourth Difference of the Longitude for a Quarter of a Day = | | |
| — 1″.00 | | |
| + 0.45 | | 6^IV. |
| + 0.239 sin [1] | 1 | 6^IV. |
| + 0.130 sin [2] | | 6^IV. |
| + 0.031 sin [3] | | 6^IV. |
| + 0.005 sin [4] | | 6^IV. |
| + 0.03 | | 7^IV. |
| + 0.027 sin [21′] | 2 | 7^IV. |
| + 0.003 sin [42′] | | 7^IV. |
| + 0.31 | | 8^IV. |
| + 0.303 sin [20] | 3 | 8^IV. |
| + 0.006 sin [30] | | 8^IV. |
| + 0.029 sin [40] | | 8^IV. |
| + 0.14 | | 12^IV. |
| + 0.136 sin [21] | 7 | 12^IV. |
| + 0.02 | | 13^IV. |
| + 0.018 sin [21′] | 8 | 13^IV. |
| + 0.02 | | 18^IV. |
| + 0.022 sin [41′] | 13 | 18^IV. |
| + 0.03 | | 21^IV. |
| + 0.033 sin [22] | 16 | 21^IV. |

## INTRODUCTION.

Since HANSEN's inequalities of long period, arising from the action of Venus, affect the mean longitude of the moon, they must be applied to the several arguments contained in Tables V*a*. or V*b*., and to render these corrections always additive the arguments in Tables II*a*. and II*b*. have been diminished by the following constants: —

| | |
|---|---|
| Arg. 1 by 0.001859, | Arg. 8 by 0.0012, |
| Arg. 2 by 0.001410, | Arg. 9 by 0.0012, |
| Arg. 3 by 0.001214, | Arg. 10 by 0.0010, |
| Arg. 6 by 0.0013, | Arg. 11 by 0.0011, |
| Arg. 7 by 0.0011, | Arg. 13 by 0.0012. |

And Tables V*a*. and V*b*. have been constructed by the formulæ, —

| | TABLE V*a*. | TABLE V*b*. |
|---|---|---|
| Corr. Arg. 1 | 0.00050 + 0.0004933 sin $H$ | + 0.001359 + 0.0005826 sin $H'$, |
| Corr. Arg. 2 | 0.00060 + 0.000569 sin $H$ | + 0.00081 + 0.000673 sin $H'$, |
| Corr. Arg. 3 | 0.00053 + 0.000529 sin $H$ | + 0.000684 + 0.000624 sin $H'$, |
| Corr. Arg. 6 | 0.0006 + 0.00062 sin $H$ | + 0.0007 + 0.00074 sin $H'$, |
| Corr. Arg. 7 | 0.0002 + 0.00017 sin $H$ | + 0.0009 + 0.00021 sin $H'$, |
| Corr. Arg. 8 | 0.0003 + 0.00028 sin $H$ | + 0.0009 + 0.00033 sin $H'$ |
| Corr. Arg. 9 | 0.0005 + 0.00053 sin $H$ | + 0.0007 + 0.00053 sin $H'$, |
| Corr. Arg. 10 | 0.0005 + 0.00046 sin $H$ | + 0.0005 + 0.00054 sin $H'$, |
| Corr. Arg. 11 | 0.0005 + 0.00048 sin $H$ | + 0.0006 + 0.00056 sin $H'$, |
| Corr. Arg. 13 | 0.0002 + 0.00018 sin $H$ | + 0.0010 + 0.00021 sin $H'$. |

## II. DESCRIPTION OF THE TABLES.

TABLES I*a*., I*b*., and I*c*. are Tables of Astronomical Dates in mean solar days reckoned from the beginning of the Julian Period, from which the date of any event can be reduced to days and decimals of a day when it is originally given in the usual form with reference to the Christian Era.

Tables II*a*. and II*b*. contain the values of the mean longitude, the negative of the longitude of the node, and all the arguments for the mean Washington noon of every thousandth day from 2300000 to 2500000.

Tables III*a*. and III*b*. contain the motions of the mean longitude, and of the longitude of the node for every interval of days and fractions of a day less than 1000 days, and the first ten multiples of all the periods.

Table IV. contains the constants by which the mean longitude, and the longitude of the node, and the various arguments, can be reduced, from the interval from 2400000 to 2500000 days to any previous time after the commencement of the Julian Period.

Tables V*a*. and V*b*. contain the corrections of the various arguments for HANSEN's term of long period in the action of Venus.

Tables VI. to LXXXII. inclusive contain the different equations of the moon's longitude.

Tables VI″. to XXXVII″. inclusive contain the second differences for a quarter of a day of the moon's longitude.

Tables VI.$^{IV.}$ to XVI.$^{IV.}$ inclusive contain the fourth differences for a quarter of a day of the moon's longitude.

Tables LXXXIII. to CIX. inclusive contain the terms of the moon's latitude.

Tables CX. to CXXVII. inclusive contain the terms of the moon's horizontal parallax.

Table CXXVIII. contains the table for the moon's semidiameter.

## III. USE OF THE TABLES.

1. Reduce the instant for which the moon's place is to be computed to its date in days and decimals of a day from Washington mean noon, by means of Tables I*a*., I*b*., and I*c*. The number of days for the beginning of the year is to be found in Table I*a*., that for the day of the year in Table I*b*., and the decimal of the day in Table I*c*.

2. Find the longitudes and arguments for the date from Tables II*a*., II*b*., III*a*., III*b*., V*a*., and V*b*.

*If the date is contained within the interval* 2300000 *to* 2500000 *days,*

Find the value of the longitude or argument for the preceding thousandth day in Table II*a*. or II*b*., in the column headed with the name of the longitude or argument; multiply the number which is contained in the column headed with the accented name of the longitude or argument by one thousandth part of the excess of the date over that of the preceding thousandth day. Find in Table III*a*. the motion of the longitude for this excess of days.

The sum of the three numbers thus found for each longitude is the mean longitude for the date, and the sum of the two numbers for each argument and of the excess of the date over that of the preceding thousandth day is the argument for the date. The argument thus found must be reduced by substituting as many entire multiples of the period of the argument as it contains, and Table III*b*. will facilitate this process of reduction. Finally, correct the argument by the addition of the corrections contained in Tables V*a*. and V*b*.

*If the date is less than* 2300000 *days,*

Change the hundred thousands of the date to 24; find the longitude and arguments by the preceding process for the changed date, with the exception of the corrections contained in Tables V*a*. and V*b*. Take from Table IV. the constants of longitude and argument which correspond to the hundred-thousandth day next preceding the given date. Multiply the excess of the date over the next preceding hundred-thousandth day by the accented number of which the logarithm is given in the column of Table IV. next following the longitude or argument to which it corresponds when it is of sufficient magnitude to be noticed. Multiply the square of this excess by the doubly accented number of which the logarithm is given in the column of Table IV. next following that of the singly accented number, when it is of sufficient magnitude to be noticed. The sum of these two products, added to the constant, and corrected by the addition of the correction of Tables V*a*. and V*b*. is the total addition to be made to the longitude or argument obtained by the preceding process.

3. Find, by means of the several arguments, the equations of longitude contained in the Tables VI. – LXXXI*A*. inclusive, and add their sum to the value of $u$ already obtained.

It is to be observed, in entering Tables XVII., LIII., and LXXVIII., that

Arg. 12′ = Arg. 12, but that the period is half as long.
Arg. 48′ = Arg. 48 — $6^{d}.26$, and it has a half-period.
Arg. 73′ = Arg. 73 + $173^{d}.792$, and it has a half-period.

4. To the sum of $u$ and the equations of longitude add the value of $y - u$ already obtained, and this sum is $\bar{y}$, which is the argument with which Table LXXXII. is to be entered for the final equation of longitude, which is to be added to the sum of $u$ and the other equations in order to obtain the true longitude, $\bar{u}$, of the moon.

5. Find the value of $A$ by entering

| | | d. |
|---|---|---|
| Table LXXXIII. with the Arg. $12''$ | $=$ Arg. 12 — | 43.3275, |
| Table LXXXIV. with the Arg. $73'''$ | $=$ Arg. 73 + | 47.5826, |
| Table LXXXV. with the Arg. $53'$ | $=$ Arg. 53 — | 29.38, |
| Table LXXXVI. with the Arg. $1'$ | $=$ Arg. 1 + | 6.89, |
| Table LXXXVII. with the Arg. $70'$ | $=$ Arg. 70 — | 82.45, |
| Table LXXXIX. with the Arg. 4 | | |
| Table XC. with the Arg. $5'$ | $=$ Arg. 5 + | 51.47. |

The value of $A$ is the sum of the equations thus obtained increased by $17600''$.

6. Find the value of $B$ by entering Tables LXXXIII. to XCI. inclusive (excepting Table LXXXIX.) with the arguments respectively written above them.

The sum of the equations thus obtained diminished by $1000''$ is the value of $B$.

7. Find the remaining equations of the moon's latitude by entering Tables XCII. to CIX. inclusive with the arguments respectively written above them.

The sum of the equations thus obtained, diminished by $60''$, and added to the sum of the products of $A$ by sin $\bar{y}$, and of $B$ by cos. $\bar{y}$, is the moon's latitude.

8. The moon's equatorial horizontal parallax is found by entering tables CX. to CXXVII. inclusive with their respective arguments, and adding $3000''$ to the sum of the equations thus obtained.

9. The moon's equatorial semidiameter is found by multiplying the equatorial horizontal parallax by 0.272274, which product may be readily obtained by means of Table CXXVIII.

This value is to be used for the computation of eclipses, but in the reduction of meridian observations it should be increased by $2''.5$ in the case of a telescope for which no special investigation has been made, or by whatever constant may be found suitable by a special investigation for each telescope.

10. *Directions for the Computation of an Ephemeris.* The longitude, exclusive of nutation and the equation of Table LXXXII., should be found for each successive noon; and also the second and fourth differences of the equations for a quarter of a day from the Tables VI.$^{\text{II.}}$ to XXI.$^{\text{IV.}}$ inclusive.

If then the following notation is adopted,

$u_t$ $=$ the longitude for the time $t$ in days, exclusive of nutation and the equation of Table LXXXII.

$A_t$ $=$ the sum of all those equations for which tables of second differences are given.

$A'_t$ $=$ the sum of all those equations for which tables of second differences are not given.

$B_t$ $=$ the sum of all the tabular second differences from those tables for which tables of fourth differences are given.

$B'_t$ $=$ the sum of all the tabular second differences from those tables for which tables of fourth differences are not given.

$B''_t = B_t + B'_t$.

$C_t$ $=$ the sum of all the tabular fourth differences for all the equations for which they are given.

$\Delta^n\, V_t$ $=$ the $n$th differences of the series of $n+1$ numbers

$$V_{t-\frac{1}{8}n},\quad V_{t-\frac{1}{8}n+\frac{1}{4}},\ V_{t-\frac{1}{8}n+\frac{1}{2}},\ V_{t-\frac{1}{8}n+\frac{3}{4}},\ \&c.,$$
$$V_{t+\frac{1}{8}n-\frac{3}{4}},\ V_{t+\frac{1}{8}n-\frac{1}{2}},\ V_{t+\frac{1}{8}n-\frac{1}{4}},\ V_{t+\frac{1}{8}n},$$

of which the first corresponds to the date preceding the date $t$ by $\frac{1}{8}n$ days, and the last corresponds to the date which follows the date $t$ by $\frac{1}{8}n$ days, and the intermediate numbers are at intervals of a quarter of a day apart.

$\Delta'^n\, V_t$ $=$ the $n$th quarter difference of the values of the $n+1$ numbers

$$V_{t-\frac{1}{2}n},\quad V_{t-\frac{1}{2}n+1},\ V_{t-\frac{1}{2}n+2},\ V_{t-\frac{1}{2}n+3},\ \&c.,$$
$$V_{t+\frac{1}{2}n-3},\ V_{t+\frac{1}{2}n-2},\ V_{t+\frac{1}{2}n-1},\ V_{t+\frac{1}{2}n},$$

of which the first corresponds to the date which precedes the date $t$ by $\frac{1}{2}n$ days, and the last corresponds to the date which follows the date $t$ by $\frac{1}{2}n$ days, the intermediate numbers occurring at intervals of a day. In taking these quarter differences, all the terms of each order of difference are to be divided by four, before their quarter differences are obtained in the same way.

In the following computations it will be sufficiently accurate to put

$$\Delta^4\ V_t = \Delta'^4\ V_t,$$
$$\Delta^2\ V_t = \Delta'^2\ V_t - \tfrac{5}{4}\,\Delta'^4\ V_t.$$

Find for each noon and interpolate by differences for every six hours

$$\Delta^4 u_t = C_t + \Delta^2 B_t + \Delta^4\ A'_t - 1''.$$

Test the accuracy of $B_t$ by the formula

$$\Delta^2 B_t = C_t + \tfrac{5}{4}\,\Delta^2\ C_t - 1''.$$

Find for each noon

$$\Delta^2 u_t = B''_t + \Delta^2\ A'_t - 130''.$$

Find for each day and for the instant $\frac{3}{8}$ths of a day after the noon

$$\Delta^3 u_{t+\frac{3}{8}} = \Delta\ B''_{t+\frac{1}{2}} + \Delta^3\ A'_{t+\frac{1}{2}} + \tfrac{1}{3}\,\Delta^4\ u_{t+\frac{1}{2}}.$$

Interpolate the remaining third differences of $u_t$ by means of the fourth differences, being careful to adopt a judicious distribution of the small changes which are required in the fourth differences to accomplish this interpolation.

Interpolate the second differences of $u_t$ with a similar regard to changes of the third differences.

Test the accuracy of $A_t$ by the formula

$$\Delta^2 A_t = B''_t + \tfrac{5}{4}\ C_t + \tfrac{5}{4}\,\Delta^2\ B'_t - 130'',$$

Find for each day and the instant $\frac{3}{8}$ths of a day after the noon

$$\Delta\ u_{t+\frac{3}{8}} = 3^{0}\ 1058''.757 + \Delta\ A_{t+\frac{1}{2}} + \Delta\ A'_{t+\frac{1}{2}} + \tfrac{1}{3}\,\Delta^2\ u_{t+\frac{1}{2}} - \tfrac{1}{4}\,\Delta^4\ u_{t+\frac{1}{2}}.$$

Interpolate the first differences of $u_t$ by the aid of the second differences, and by them interpolate the values of $u_t$.

The values of $\bar{y}$ should be obtained for each quarter of a day, and thence the equations from Table LXXXII.

The various terms of the latitude and horizontal parallax need only be found for each noon, except $A.$ sin $\bar{y}$, which, after the interpolation of $A.$, should be computed for each quarter of a day.

### 11. *Example.*

Find the moon's longitude, latitude, equatorial horizontal parallax for the date B. C. 413, August 27, at 6 o'clock in the afternoon, mean solar time at Athens.

*Solution.* The western longitude of Athens from Washington being 17$^{h.}$ 16$^{m.}$ 53$^{s.}$, the given date is in Washington time —413 August 26$^{d.}$ 23$^{h.}$ 16$^{m.}$ 53$^{s.}$. This is reduced to the Julian date in days by Tables I*a.*, I*b.*, and I*c.*

| | |
|---|---|
| —500 years is in Julian date in days | 1538798. |
| 13 *B.* | 31777. |
| Aug. 26 | 238. |
| 23$^{h.}$ | 0.958333333 |
| 16$^{m.}$ | 0.011111111 |
| 53$^{s.}$ | 0.000613426 |
| —413 Aug. 26$^{d.}$ 23$^{h.}$ 16$^{m.}$ 53$^{s.}$ | 1570813.970057870 |

By substituting 2400000 for the 1500000, the date becomes 2470813.970057870, whence from Tables II. to V. inclusive the arguments are obtained as follows:

| | u | y-u | Argument 1. | 2. | 3. |
|---|---|---|---|---|---|
| From Table II*b*., for 2470000, | 22° 2502″.58 | 132° 758″.5 | 10.9057714 | 21.243406 | 8.500660 |
| Correction × .81397, | 1.29 | —0.9 | 1142 | —58 | 263 |
| From Table III*a*., or the excess of date, | 285 692.60 | 43 370.1 | 813.9700579 | 813.970058 | 813.970058 |
| From Table IV. for 1500000, | 4 2708.83 | 220 1207.8 | 14.9092506 | 22.915317 | 3.859920 |
| Accented No. × 70813.97, | —1035.81 | 730.4 | —909656 | 57954 | —20960 |
| Doubly accented No. × (70813.97)², | —4.94 | 3.2 | —5031 | 340 | —112 |
| Correction from Table V*a*., | | | 335 | 61 | 30 |
| Correction from Table V*b*., | | | 16989 | 1202 | 1048 |
| Greatest Multiple of Period for Subtraction, | | | 826.6365734 | 827.110329 | 797.325876 |
| Mean Longitude or Argument for date, | 312 1264.55 | 35 3069.1 | 13.0588844 | 31.077951 | 28.985031 |

| Argument | 4. | 5. | 6. | 7. | 8. | 9. | 10. |
|---|---|---|---|---|---|---|---|
| From Table II*b*., for 2470000, | 281.3878 | 316.3339 | 5.6456 | 9.3725 | 4.7758 | 26.1947 | 23.6165 |
| Correction × .81397, | 0 | 13 | 0 | 0 | 0 | 0 | 0 |
| The excess of date, | 813.9701 | 813.9701 | 813.9701 | 813.9701 | 813.9701 | 813.9701 | 813.9701 |
| From Table IV., | 365.1276 | 168.9847 | 25.1207 | 7.7149 | 4.0279 | 16.1365 | 13.8541 |
| Accented No. × 70813.97, | 0 | —1.0665 | 656 | —454 | —219 | —984 | —846 |
| Doubly acc. No. × (70813.97)², | 0 | —60 | 8 | —2 | —1 | —5 | —5 |
| Correction from Table V*a*., | 0 | 0 | 0 | 0 | 0 | 0 | 1 |
| Correction from Table V*b*., | 0 | 0 | 11 | 10 | 11 | 10 | 8 |
| Gr. Mult. of Period for Subtr., | 1095.7791 | 1235.3555 | 836.3254 | 826.7797 | 815.5275 | 834.4791 | 845.5160 |
| Argument for date, | 364.7064 | 62.8620 | 8.4785 | 4.2332 | 7.2254 | 21.7243 | 5.8405 |

| Argument | 11. | 12. | 13. | 14. | 15. | 16. | 17. |
|---|---|---|---|---|---|---|---|
| From Table II*b*., for 2470000, | 0.9587 | 20.6699 | 3.2232 | 5.760 | 5.577 | 4.931 | 15.347 |
| The excess of date, | 813.9701 | 813.9701 | 813.9701 | 813.970 | 813.970 | 813.970 | 813.970 |
| From Table IV., | 19.0676 | 171.4161 | 9.9006 | 21.068 | 3.704 | 9.575 | 3.560 |
| Accented No. × 70813.97, | 761 | 1642 | 51 | 59 | —21 | —61 | —21 |
| Doubly acc. No. × (70813.97)², | 4 | 9 | 0 | 0 | 0 | 0 | 0 |
| Correction from Table V*a*., | 0 | 0 | 0 | 0 | 0 | 0 | 0 |
| Correction from Table V*b*., | 9 | 0 | 11 | 0 | 0 | 0 | 0 |
| Gr. Mult. of Period for Subtr., | 833.2270 | 693.2402 | 826.9369 | 819.372 | 823.113 | 826.743 | 819.650 |
| Argument for date, | 0.8468 | 312.9810 | 0.1632 | 21.485 | 0.117 | 1.672 | 13.206 |

| Argument | 18. | 19. | 20. | 21. | 22. | 23. | 24. | 25. |
|---|---|---|---|---|---|---|---|---|
| From Table II*b*., for 2470000, | 4.364 | 3.891 | 1.139 | 69.94 | 28.372 | 17.824 | 1.155 | 4.760 |
| The excess of date, | 813.970 | 813.970 | 813.970 | 813.97 | 813.970 | 813.970 | 813.970 | 813.970 |
| From Table IV., | 7.935 | 8.791 | 1.178 | 108.02 | 4.212 | 12.603 | 1.086 | 7.516 |
| Accented No. × 70813.97, | —50 | —207 | —101 | —73 | —24 | —60 | —94 | —47 |
| Gr. Mult. of Period for Subtr., | 819.508 | 826.275 | 816.087 | 921.70 | 835.330 | 832.112 | 809.866 | 824.311 |
| Argument for date, | 6.711 | 0.170 | 0.099 | 69.50 | 11.200 | 12.225 | 6.251 | 1.888 |

| Argument | 26. | 27. | 28. | 29. | 30. | 31. | 32. | 33. |
|---|---|---|---|---|---|---|---|---|
| From Table II*b*., for 2470000, | 3.087 | 0.34 | 24.849 | 21.477 | 1.760 | 9.15 | 11.01 | 15.34 |
| The excess of date, | 813.970 | 813.97 | 813.970 | 813.970 | 813.970 | 813.97 | 813.97 | 813.97 |
| From Table IV., | 0.368 | 24.56 | 27.863 | 18.084 | 10.182 | 13.03 | 7.35 | 17.58 |
| Accented No. × 70813.97, | —38 | —16 | —78 | —149 | 5 | 2 | 7 | —12 |
| Gr. Mult. of Period for Subtr., | 815.165 | 826.44 | 847.484 | 851.855 | 819.304 | 826.98 | 831.51 | 843.72 |
| Argument for date, | 2.222 | 12.27 | 19.120 | 1.527 | 6.613 | 9.19 | 0.89 | 3.05 |

| Argument | 34. | 35. | 36. | 37. | 38. | 39. | 40. | 41. |
|---|---|---|---|---|---|---|---|---|
| From Table II*b*., for 2470000, | 25.51 | 18.42 | 12.65 | 36.4 | 17.71 | 13.1 | 16.26 | 7.35 |
| The excess of date, | 813 97 | 813.97 | 813.97 | 814.0 | 813.97 | 814.0 | 813.97 | 813.97 |
| From Table IV., | 19.51 | 12.93 | 9.22 | 33.9 | 2.17 | 10.7 | 4.65 | 4.39 |
| Accented No. × 70813.97, | 5 | —8 | —5 | 3 | —10 | —2 | 11 | 11 |
| Gr. Mult. of Period for Subtr., | 839.87 | 837.98 | 823.13 | 865.4 | 826.71 | 827.4 | 829.12 | 824.28 |
| Argument for date, | 19.17 | 7.26 | 12.66 | 19.2 | 7.04 | 10.2 | 5.87 | 1.54 |

| Argument | **42.** | **43.** | **44.** | **45.** | **46.** | **47.** | **48.** | **49.** |
|---|---|---|---|---|---|---|---|---|
| From Table II*b*., for 2470000, | 4.08 | 3.31 | 0.5 | 6.42 | 5.3 | 11.98 | 26.58 | 2.2 |
| The excess of date, | 813.97 | 813.97 | 814.0 | 813.97 | 814.0 | 813.97 | 813.97 | 814.0 |
| From Table IV., | 8.11 | 9.77 | 8.2 | 11.54 | 20.4 | 3.54 | 1.51 | 1.2 |
| Accented No. × 70813.97, | —5 | —6 | 0 | 0 | 0 | 0 | —12 | 0 |
| Gr. Mult. of Period for Subtr., | 821.98 | 814.12 | 820.3 | 828.10 | 812.4 | 819.69 | 838.16 | 816.8 |
| Argument for date, | 4.13 | 12.87 | 2.4 | 3.83 | 27.3 | 9.80 | 3.78 | 0.6 |

| Argument | **50.** | **51.** | **52.** | **53.** | **54.** | **55.** | **56.** | **57.** |
|---|---|---|---|---|---|---|---|---|
| From Table II*b*., for 2470000, | 20.9 | 8.23 | 16.97 | 15.27 | 5.10 | 12.40 | 12.36 | 2.93 |
| The excess of date, | 814.0 | 813.97 | 813.97 | 813.97 | 813.97 | 813.97 | 813.97 | 813.97 |
| From Table IV., | 17.6 | 7.20 | 3.04 | 116.22 | 3.93 | 9.63 | 3.25 | 10.20 |
| Accented No. × 70813.97, | 0 | —4 | 0 | 12 | 0 | 0 | 0 | 0 |
| Gr. Mult. of Period for Subtr., | 851.2 | 819.76 | 832.64 | 940.32 | 813.77 | 824.35 | 826.40 | 815.40 |
| Argument for date, | 1.3 | 9.60 | 1.34 | 5.26 | 9.23 | 11.65 | 3.18 | 11.70 |

| Argument | **58.** | **59.** | **60.** | **61.** | **62.** | **63.** | **64.** | **65.** |
|---|---|---|---|---|---|---|---|---|
| From Table II*b*., for 2470000, | 11.51 | 32.28 | 14.74 | 0.26 | 7.82 | 0.35 | 20.93 | 12.82 |
| The excess of date, | 813.97 | 813.97 | 813.97 | 813.97 | 813.97 | 813.97 | 813.97 | 813.97 |
| From Table IV., | 6.71 | 28.49 | 11.84 | 3.40 | 11.09 | 8.73 | 19.88 | 3.83 |
| Accented No. × 70813.97, | 0 | 0 | 0 | 0 | 0 | 0 | 0 | 0 |
| Gr. Mult. of Period for Subtr., | 823.08 | 857.21 | 825.90 | 816.37 | 823.19 | 818.00 | 827.82 | 824.95 |
| Argument for date, | 9.11 | 17.53 | 14.65 | 1.26 | 9.69 | 5.05 | 26.96 | 5.67 |

| Argument | **66.** | **67.** | **68.** | **69.** | **70.** | **71.** | **72.** | **73.** |
|---|---|---|---|---|---|---|---|---|
| From Table II*b*., for 2470000, | 26.4 | 27.20 | 6.94 | 281.5 | 61.7 | 201.5 | 179.3 | 1231.1 |
| The excess of date, | 814.0 | 813.97 | 813.97 | 814.0 | 814.0 | 814.0 | 814.0 | 814.0 |
| From Table IV., | 5.1 | 4.21 | 25.69 | 387.5 | 0.4 | 406.6 | 281.4 | 184.3 |
| Accented No. × 70813.97, | 0 | —8 | —11 | —26 | —3 | 0 | 0 | 7.2 |
| Gr. Mult. of Period for Subtr., | 818.7 | 823.30 | 830.00 | 1415.7 | 659.6 | 1167.8 | 1196.7 | 2190.2 |
| Argument for date, | 26.8 | 22.00 | 16.49 | 64.7 | 216.2 | 254.3 | 78.0 | 46.4 |

| Argument | **74.** | **75.** | **76.** | **78.** | **79.** | **80.** | **81.** | **82.** |
|---|---|---|---|---|---|---|---|---|
| From Table II*b*., for 2470000, | 1691 | 54809 | 77263 | 60.489 | 282.2 | 68.3 | 14.23 | 10.000 |
| The excess of date, | 814 | 814 | 814 | 813.970 | 814.0 | 814.0 | 813.97 | 813.970 |
| From Table IV., | 1905 | 32286 | 52991 | 170.305 | 401.3 | 26.2 | 112.35 | 2.633 |
| Accented No. × 70813.97, | 9 | 0 | 0 | —.427 | 0 | 0 | —28 | 0 |
| Gr. Mult. of Period for Subtr., | 3233 | 84753 | 95490 | 941.008 | 1315.1 | 626.1 | 869.43 | 817.603 |
| Argument for date, | 1186 | 3156 | 35578 | 103.329 | 182.4 | 282.4 | 70.84 | 9.000 |

| Argument | **83.** | **84.** | **85.** | **86.** | **87.** | **88** | **89.** | **90.** |
|---|---|---|---|---|---|---|---|---|
| From Table II*b*., for 2470000, | 12.80 | 17.33 | 9.53 | 24.78 | 1.01 | 4.42 | 1.92 | 15.3 |
| The excess of date, | 813.97 | 813.97 | 813.97 | 813.97 | 813.97 | 813.97 | 813.97 | 814.0 |
| From Table IV., | 24.97 | 8.28 | 14.44 | 31.21 | 4.82 | 5.08 | 4.68 | 20.4 |
| Accented No. × 70813.97, | 0 | 0 | 0 | 0 | 0 | 0 | 0 | 0 |
| Gr. Mult. of Period for Subtr., | 823.44 | 823.17 | 823.18 | 842.22 | 809.87 | 821.32 | 811.11 | 839.3 |
| Argument for date, | 28.30 | 16.41 | 14.76 | 27.74 | 9.93 | 2.15 | 9.46 | 10.4 |

HENCE:

| | | |
|---|---|---|
| Arg. 12′ = 139.6709 | Arg. 73′ = 220.2 | Arg. 1′ = 19.95 |
| Arg. 12″ = 96.3434 | Arg. 73″ = 367.8 | Arg. 70′ = 133.7 |
| Arg. 48′ = 12.49 | Arg. 73‴ = 94.0 | Arg. 5′ = 114.33 |
| Arg. 12‴ = 292.9810 | Arg. 53′ = 93.42 | |

| TABLE. | EQUATION. | TABLE. | EQUATION. |
|---|---|---|---|
| VI. | 45193″.81 | XLV. | 0″.04 |
| VII. | 71.73 | XLVI. | 0.02 |
| VIII. | 1655.54 | XLVII. | 0.04 |
| IX. | 1340.46 | XLVIII. | 0.13 |
| X. | 206.06 | XLIX. | 0.26 |
| XI. | 176.80 | L. | 0.04 |
| XII. | 360.58 | LI. | 0.40 |
| XIII. | 323.57 | LII. | 2.59 |
| XIV. | 170.69 | LIII. | 0.25 |
| XV. | 130.22 | LIV. | 0.22 |
| XVI. | 169.81 | LV. | 0.41 |
| XVII. | 45.31 | LVI. | 0.01 |
| XVIII. | 4.56 | LVII. | 0.92 |
| XIX. | 23.67 | LVIII. | 5.14 |
| XX. | 48.53 | LIX. | 2.16 |
| XXI. | 37.54 | LX. | 0.45 |
| XXII. | 34.12 | LXI. | 1.39 |
| XXIII. | 20.49 | LXII. | 0.55 |
| XXIV. | 25.40 | LXIII. | 0.03 |
| XXV. | 0.51 | LXIV. | 0.04 |
| XXVI. | 0.00 | LXV. | 0.38 |
| XXVII. | 10.81 | LXVI. | 0.30 |
| XXVIII. | 0.02 | LXVII. | 0.59 |
| XXIX. | 0.45 | LXVIII. | 0.10 |
| XXX. | 4.33 | LXIX. | 0.20 |
| XXXI. | 3.16 | LXX. | 0.36 |
| XXXII. | 1.78 | LXXI. | 0.13 |
| XXXIII. | 14.92 | LXXII. | 0.10 |
| XXXIV. | 0.49 | LXXIII. | 1.19 |
| XXXV. | 2.05 | LXXIV. | 4.40 |
| XXXVI. | 0.16 | LXXV. | 2.93 |
| XXXVII. | 0.13 | LXXVI. | 1.49 |
| XXXVIII. | 0.02 | LXXVII. | 1.33 |
| XXXIX. | 0.03 | LXXVIII. | 1.55 |
| XL. | 2.38 | LXXIX. | 0.50 |
| XLI. | 1.35 | LXXX. | 31.26 |
| XLII. | 0.99 | LXXXI. | 81.62 |
| XLIII. | 0.56 | LXXXI*A*. | —4.52 |
| XLIV. | 0.73 | | |

| | ° | ″ |
|---|---|---|
| Sum of Equations of Longitude, | 0 | 50222.76 |
| or, | 13 | 3422.76 |
| Mean Longitude, | 312 | 1264.55 |
| Longitude in Orbit, | 326 | 1087.31 |
| $y - u$, | 35 | 3069.1 |
| $\bar{y}$, | 2 | 556.4 |
| Table LXXXII., | | —31.33 |
| Nutation of Equinox, | | 10.54 |
| $\bar{u}$ = true Longitude = | 326 | 1066.52 |

| TABLE. | *A*. | *B*. |
|---|---|---|
| LXXXIII. | 1359″.62 | 725″.75 |
| LXXXIV. | 0.72 | 31.78 |
| LXXXV. | 26.83 | 43.69 |
| LXXXVI. | 1.07 | 0.01 |
| LXXXVII. | 13.42 | 20.11 |
| LXXXVIII. | | 40.00 |
| LXXXIX. | 6.66 | |
| XC. | 0.00 | 4.73 |
| XCI. | | 2.00 |
| Constant, | 17600. | —1000. |
| | $A$ = 19008.32 | $B$ = — 131.93 |

| TABLE. | EQUATION. | TABLE. | EQUATION. |
|---|---|---|---|
| XCII. | 31″.50 | CI. | 0″.98 |
| XCIII. | 7.90 | CII. | 0.47 |
| XCIV. | 0.67 | CIII. | 0.39 |
| XCV. | 0.23 | CIV. | 0.00 |
| XCVI. | 0.11 | CV. | 0.00 |
| XCVII. | 0.77 | CVI. | 0.39 |
| XCVIII. | 3.44 | CVII. | 0.26 |
| XCIX. | 0.87 | CVIII. | 5.50 |
| C. | 0.90 | CIX. | 15.79 |

| | | |
|---|---|---|
| Constant, | | —60. |
| Sum, | | 10.17 |
| $A \sin \bar{y}$, | | 714.62 |
| $B \cos \bar{y}$, | | —131.83 |
| ☽'s Latitude = | | 592.96 |
| = | 9′ | 52.96 |

| TABLE. | EQUATION. | TABLE. | EQUATION. |
|---|---|---|---|
| CX | 367″.08 | CXXIII. | 0″.17 |
| CXI. | 57.27 | CXXIV. | 0.03 |
| CXII. | 28.73 | CXXV. | 0.14 |
| CXIII. | 2.88 | CXXVI. | 0.08 |
| CXIV. | 4.57 | CXXVII. | 0.01 |
| CXV. | 2.51 | CXXVIII. | 0.09 |
| CXVI. | 0.02 | CXXIX. | 0.07 |
| CXVII. | 0.02 | CXXX. | 0.06 |
| CXVIII. | 0.67 | CXXXI. | 0.11 |
| CXIX. | 0.31 | CXXXII. | 0.40 |
| CXX. | 0.46 | CXXXIII. | 0.63 |
| CXXI. | 0.42 | CXXXIV. | 0.01 |
| CXXII. | 0.21 | | |

| | |
|---|---|
| Constant, | 3000. |
| sin ☽'s Horizontal Parallax = | 3466.95 |
| Table CXXXV., | 0.16 |
| ☽'s Horizontal Parallax, | 3467.11 |

# TABLE I*a*.

Date of Jan. 0 in Common Years,
and of Jan. 1 in Bissextile Years.

| Year. | Date in Mean Solar Days. | Year. | Date in Mean Solar Days. | YEAR IN THE CENTURY. | | Days from previous Centennial Date. | YEAR IN THE CENTURY. | | Days from previous Centennial Date. |
|---|---|---|---|---|---|---|---|---|---|
| | | | | If Negative. | If Positive. | | If Negative. | If Positive. | |
| —4713*B*. | 0 | —1000 | 1356173 | 100 | 1 | 0 | 50 | 51 | 18262 |
| —4712 | 365 | — 900 | 1392698 | 99 | 2 | 365 | 49*B*. | 52*B*. | 18628 |
| —4711 | 730 | — 800 | 1429223 | 98 | 3 | 730 | 48 | 53 | 18993 |
| —4710 | 1095 | — 700 | 1465748 | 97*B*. | 4*B*. | 1096 | 47 | 54 | 19358 |
| —4709*B*. | 1461 | — 600 | 1502273 | 96 | 5 | 1461 | 46 | 55 | 19723 |
| —4708 | 1826 | — 500 | 1538798 | 95 | 6 | 1826 | 45*B*. | 56*B*. | 20089 |
| —4707 | 2191 | — 400 | 1575323 | 94 | 7 | 2191 | 44 | 57 | 20454 |
| —4706 | 2556 | — 300 | 1611848 | 93*B*. | 8*B*. | 2557 | 43 | 58 | 20819 |
| —4705*B*. | 2922 | — 200 | 1648373 | 92 | 9 | 2922 | 42 | 59 | 21184 |
| —4704 | 3287 | — 100 | 1684898 | 91 | 10 | 3287 | 41*B*. | 60*B*. | 21550 |
| —4703 | 3652 | 1 | 1721423 | 90 | 11 | 3652 | 40 | 61 | 21915 |
| —4702 | 4017 | 101 | 1757948 | 89*B*. | 12*B*. | 4018 | 39 | 62 | 22280 |
| —4701*B*. | 4383 | 201 | 1794473 | 88 | 13 | 4383 | 38 | 63 | 22645 |
| —4700 | 4748 | 301 | 1830998 | 87 | 14 | 4748 | 37*B*. | 64*B*. | 23011 |
| —4600 | 41273 | 401 | 1867523 | 86 | 15 | 5113 | 36 | 65 | 23376 |
| —4500 | 77798 | 501 | 1904048 | 85*B*. | 16*B*. | 5479 | 35 | 66 | 23741 |
| —4400 | 114323 | 601 | 1940573 | 84 | 17 | 5844 | 34 | 67 | 24106 |
| —4300 | 150848 | 701 | 1977098 | 83 | 18 | 6209 | 33*B*. | 68*B*. | 24472 |
| —4200 | 187373 | 801 | 2013623 | 82 | 19 | 6574 | 32 | 69 | 24837 |
| —4100 | 223898 | 901 | 2050148 | 81*B*. | 20*B*. | 6940 | 31 | 70 | 25202 |
| —4000 | 260423 | 1001 | 2086673 | 80 | 21 | 7305 | 30 | 71 | 25567 |
| —3900 | 296948 | 1101 | 2123198 | 79 | 22 | 7670 | 29*B*. | 72*B*. | 25933 |
| —3800 | 333473 | 1201 | 2159723 | 78 | 23 | 8035 | 28 | 73 | 26298 |
| —3700 | 369998 | 1301 | 2196248 | 77*B*. | 24*B*. | 8401 | 27 | 74 | 26663 |
| —3600 | 406523 | 1401 | 2232773 | 76 | 25 | 8766 | 26 | 75 | 27028 |
| —3500 | 443048 | 1501 | 2269298 | 75 | 26 | 9131 | 25*B*. | 76*B*. | 27394 |
| —3400 | 479573 | 1583 | 2299238 | 74 | 27 | 9496 | 24 | 77 | 27759 |
| —3300 | 516098 | 1584*B*. | 2299604 | 73*B*. | 28*B*. | 9862 | 23 | 78 | 28124 |
| —3200 | 552623 | 1585 | 2299969 | 72 | 29 | 10227 | 22 | 79 | 28489 |
| —3100 | 589148 | 1586 | 2300334 | 71 | 30 | 10592 | 21*B*. | 80*B*. | 28855 |
| —3000 | 625673 | 1587 | 2300699 | 70 | 31 | 10957 | 20 | 81 | 29220 |
| —2900 | 662198 | 1588*B*. | 2301065 | 69*B*. | 32*B*. | 11323 | 19 | 82 | 29585 |
| —2800 | 698723 | 1589 | 2301430 | 68 | 33 | 11688 | 18 | 83 | 29950 |
| —2700 | 735248 | 1590 | 2301795 | 67 | 34 | 12053 | 17*B*. | 84*B*. | 30316 |
| —2600 | 771773 | 1591 | 2302160 | 66 | 35 | 12418 | 16 | 85 | 30681 |
| —2500 | 808298 | 1592*B*. | 2302526 | 65*B*. | 36*B*. | 12784 | 15 | 86 | 31046 |
| —2400 | 844823 | 1593 | 2302891 | 64 | 37 | 13149 | 14 | 87 | 31411 |
| —2300 | 881348 | 1594 | 2303256 | 63 | 38 | 13514 | 13*B*. | 88*B*. | 31777 |
| —2200 | 917873 | 1595 | 2303621 | 62 | 39 | 13879 | 12 | 89 | 32142 |
| —2100 | 954398 | 1596*B*. | 2303987 | 61*B*. | 40*B*. | 14245 | 11 | 90 | 32507 |
| —2000 | 1090923 | 1597 | 2304352 | 60 | 41 | 14610 | 10 | 91 | 32872 |
| —1900 | 1127448 | 1598 | 2304717 | 59 | 42 | 14975 | 9*B*. | 92*B*. | 33238 |
| —1800 | 1163973 | 1599 | 2305082 | 58 | 43 | 15340 | 8 | 93 | 33603 |
| —1700 | 1200498 | 1600*B*. | 2305448 | 57*B*. | 44*B*. | 15706 | 7 | 94 | 33968 |
| —1600 | 1237023 | 1601 | 2305813 | 56 | 45 | 16071 | 6 | 95 | 34333 |
| —1500 | 1273548 | 1701 | 2342337 | 55 | 46 | 16436 | 5*B*. | 96*B*. | 34699 |
| —1400 | 1210073 | 1801 | 2378861 | 54 | 47 | 16801 | 4 | 97 | 35064 |
| —1300 | 1246598 | 1901 | 2415385 | 53*B*. | 48*B*. | 17167 | 3 | 98 | 35429 |
| —1200 | 1283123 | | | 52 | 49 | 17532 | 2 | 99 | 35794 |
| —1100 | 1319648 | | | 51 | 50 | 17897 | 1*B*. | 100*B*. | 36160 |
| —1000 | 1356173 | | | 50 | 51 | 18262 | | 100 | 36159 |

# TABLE Ib.

Number of Days from Jan. 0 in Common Years, and Jan. 1 in Bissextile Years.

| Day of Month. | JANUARY. Common Year. | JANUARY. Bissextile Year. | FEBRUARY. Common Year. | FEBRUARY. Bissextile Year. | MARCH. | APRIL. | MAY. | JUNE. | JULY. | AUGUST. | SEPTEMBER. | OCTOBER. | NOVEMBER. | DECEMBER. | 1582. OCTOBER. | 1582. NOVEMBER. | 1582. DECEMBER. |
|---|---|---|---|---|---|---|---|---|---|---|---|---|---|---|---|---|---|
| 1 | 1 | 0 | 32 | 31 | 60 | 91 | 121 | 152 | 182 | 213 | 244 | 274 | 305 | 335 | 274 | 295 | 325 |
| 2 | 2 | 1 | 33 | 32 | 61 | 92 | 122 | 153 | 183 | 214 | 245 | 275 | 306 | 336 | 275 | 296 | 326 |
| 3 | 3 | 2 | 34 | 33 | 62 | 93 | 123 | 154 | 184 | 215 | 246 | 276 | 307 | 337 | 276 | 297 | 327 |
| 4 | 4 | 3 | 35 | 34 | 63 | 94 | 124 | 155 | 185 | 216 | 247 | 277 | 308 | 338 | 277 | 298 | 328 |
| 5 | 5 | 4 | 36 | 35 | 64 | 95 | 125 | 156 | 186 | 217 | 248 | 278 | 309 | 339 | | 299 | 329 |
| 6 | 6 | 5 | 37 | 36 | 65 | 96 | 126 | 157 | 187 | 218 | 249 | 279 | 310 | 340 | | 300 | 330 |
| 7 | 7 | 6 | 38 | 37 | 66 | 97 | 127 | 158 | 188 | 219 | 250 | 280 | 311 | 341 | | 301 | 331 |
| 8 | 8 | 7 | 39 | 38 | 67 | 98 | 128 | 159 | 189 | 220 | 251 | 281 | 312 | 342 | | 302 | 332 |
| 9 | 9 | 8 | 40 | 39 | 68 | 99 | 129 | 160 | 190 | 221 | 252 | 282 | 313 | 343 | | 303 | 333 |
| 10 | 10 | 9 | 41 | 40 | 69 | 100 | 130 | 161 | 191 | 222 | 253 | 283 | 314 | 344 | | 304 | 334 |
| 11 | 11 | 10 | 42 | 41 | 70 | 101 | 131 | 162 | 192 | 223 | 254 | 284 | 315 | 345 | | 305 | 335 |
| 12 | 12 | 11 | 43 | 42 | 71 | 102 | 132 | 163 | 193 | 224 | 255 | 285 | 316 | 346 | | 306 | 336 |
| 13 | 13 | 12 | 44 | 43 | 72 | 103 | 133 | 164 | 194 | 225 | 256 | 286 | 317 | 347 | | 307 | 337 |
| 14 | 14 | 13 | 45 | 44 | 73 | 104 | 134 | 165 | 195 | 226 | 257 | 287 | 318 | 348 | | 308 | 338 |
| 15 | 15 | 14 | 46 | 45 | 74 | 105 | 135 | 166 | 196 | 227 | 258 | 288 | 319 | 349 | 278 | 309 | 339 |
| 16 | 16 | 15 | 47 | 46 | 75 | 106 | 136 | 167 | 197 | 228 | 259 | 289 | 320 | 350 | 279 | 310 | 340 |
| 17 | 17 | 16 | 48 | 47 | 76 | 107 | 137 | 168 | 198 | 229 | 260 | 290 | 321 | 351 | 280 | 311 | 341 |
| 18 | 18 | 17 | 49 | 48 | 77 | 108 | 138 | 169 | 199 | 230 | 261 | 291 | 322 | 352 | 281 | 312 | 342 |
| 19 | 19 | 18 | 50 | 49 | 78 | 109 | 139 | 170 | 200 | 231 | 262 | 292 | 323 | 353 | 282 | 313 | 343 |
| 20 | 20 | 19 | 51 | 50 | 79 | 110 | 140 | 171 | 201 | 232 | 263 | 293 | 324 | 354 | 283 | 314 | 344 |
| 21 | 21 | 20 | 52 | 51 | 80 | 111 | 141 | 172 | 202 | 233 | 264 | 294 | 325 | 355 | 284 | 315 | 345 |
| 22 | 22 | 21 | 53 | 52 | 81 | 112 | 142 | 173 | 203 | 234 | 265 | 295 | 326 | 356 | 285 | 316 | 346 |
| 23 | 23 | 22 | 54 | 53 | 82 | 113 | 143 | 174 | 204 | 235 | 266 | 296 | 327 | 357 | 286 | 317 | 347 |
| 24 | 24 | 23 | 55 | 54 | 83 | 114 | 144 | 175 | 205 | 236 | 267 | 297 | 328 | 358 | 287 | 318 | 348 |
| 25 | 25 | 24 | 56 | 55 | 84 | 115 | 145 | 176 | 206 | 237 | 268 | 298 | 329 | 359 | 288 | 319 | 349 |
| 26 | 26 | 25 | 57 | 56 | 85 | 116 | 146 | 177 | 207 | 238 | 269 | 299 | 330 | 360 | 289 | 320 | 350 |
| 27 | 27 | 26 | 58 | 57 | 86 | 117 | 147 | 178 | 208 | 239 | 270 | 300 | 331 | 361 | 290 | 321 | 351 |
| 28 | 28 | 27 | 59 | 58 | 87 | 118 | 148 | 179 | 209 | 240 | 271 | 301 | 332 | 362 | 291 | 322 | 352 |
| 29 | 29 | 28 | | 59 | 88 | 119 | 149 | 180 | 210 | 241 | 272 | 302 | 333 | 363 | 292 | 323 | 353 |
| 30 | 30 | 29 | | | 89 | 120 | 150 | 181 | 211 | 242 | 273 | 303 | 334 | 364 | 293 | 324 | 354 |
| 31 | 31 | 30 | | | 90 | | 151 | | 212 | 243 | | 304 | | 365 | 294 | | 355 |

# TABLE Ic.

To Reduce Hours, Minutes, and Seconds of Time to Decimals of a Day.

| Hours and Minutes. | Decimal of a Day. | Minutes. | Decimal of a Day. | Minutes and Seconds. | Decimal of a Day. | Seconds. | Decimal of a Day. |
|---|---|---|---|---|---|---|---|
| h. | | m. | | m. | | s. | |
| 1 | .041666667 | 13 | .009027778 | 50 | .034722222 | 23 | .000266204 |
| 2 | .083333333 | 14 | .009722222 | 51 | .035416667 | 24 | .000277778 |
| 3 | .125000000 | 15 | .010416667 | 52 | .036111111 | 25 | .000289352 |
| 4 | .166666667 | 16 | .011111111 | 53 | .036805556 | 26 | .000300926 |
| 5 | .208333333 | 17 | .011805556 | 54 | .037500000 | 27 | .000312500 |
| 6 | .250000000 | 18 | .012500000 | 55 | .038194444 | 28 | .000324074 |
| 7 | .291666667 | 19 | .013194444 | 56 | .038888889 | 29 | .000335648 |
| 8 | .333333333 | 20 | .013888889 | 57 | .039583333 | 30 | .000347222 |
| 9 | .375000000 | 21 | .014583333 | 58 | .040277778 | 31 | .000358796 |
| 10 | .416666667 | 22 | .015277778 | 59 | .040972222 | 32 | .000370370 |
| 11 | .458333333 | 23 | .015972222 | 60 | .041666667 | 33 | .000381944 |
| 12 | .500000000 | 24 | .016666667 | | | 34 | .000393519 |
| 13 | .541666667 | 25 | .017361111 | | | 35 | .000405093 |
| 14 | .583333333 | 26 | .018055556 | | | 36 | .000416667 |
| 15 | .625000000 | 27 | .018750000 | | | 37 | .000428241 |
| 16 | .666666667 | 28 | .019444444 | s. 1 | .000011574 | 38 | .000439815 |
| 17 | .708333333 | 29 | .020138889 | 2 | .000023148 | 39 | .000451389 |
| 18 | .750000000 | 30 | .020833333 | 3 | .000034722 | 40 | .000462963 |
| 19 | .791666667 | 31 | .021527778 | 4 | .000046296 | 41 | .000474537 |
| 20 | .833333333 | 32 | .022222222 | 5 | .000057870 | 42 | .000486111 |
| 21 | .875000000 | 33 | .022916667 | 6 | .000069444 | 43 | .000497685 |
| 22 | .916666666 | 34 | .023611111 | 7 | .000081019 | 44 | .000509259 |
| 23 | .958333333 | 35 | .024305556 | 8 | .000092593 | 45 | .000520833 |
| 24 | 1.000000000 | 36 | .025000000 | 9 | .000104167 | 46 | .000532407 |
| | | 37 | .025694444 | 10 | .000115741 | 47 | .000543981 |
| m. 1 | .000694444 | 38 | .026388889 | 11 | .000127315 | 48 | .000555556 |
| 2 | .001388889 | 39 | .027083333 | 12 | .000138889 | 49 | .000567130 |
| 3 | .002083333 | 40 | .027777778 | 13 | .000150463 | 50 | .000578704 |
| 4 | .002777778 | 41 | .028472222 | 14 | .000162037 | 51 | .000590278 |
| 5 | .003472222 | 42 | .029166667 | 15 | .000173611 | 52 | .000601852 |
| 6 | .004166667 | 43 | .029861111 | 16 | .000185185 | 53 | .000613426 |
| 7 | .004861111 | 44 | .030555556 | 17 | .000196759 | 54 | .000625000 |
| 8 | .005555556 | 45 | .031250000 | 18 | .000208333 | 55 | .000636574 |
| 9 | .006250000 | 46 | .031944444 | 19 | .000219907 | 56 | .000648148 |
| 10 | .006944444 | 47 | .032638889 | 20 | .000231481 | 57 | .000659722 |
| 11 | .007638889 | 48 | .033333333 | 21 | .000243056 | 58 | .000671296 |
| 12 | .008333333 | 49 | .034027778 | 22 | .000254630 | 59 | .000682870 |
| 13 | .009027778 | 50 | .034722222 | 23 | .000266204 | 60 | .000694444 |

# TABLE IIa.

Epochs and Arguments for each Thousandth Day, from 2300000 to 2400000.

For Washington Mean Noon.

| Day of Julian Period. | u | u′ | y-u | (y-u′) | Arg. 1. | 1′. | 2. | 2′. |
|---|---|---|---|---|---|---|---|---|
| | ° ″ | ″ | ° ″ | ″ | d. | 0.000 | d. | 0.000 |
| 2300000 | 315 909.18 | −1.34 | 130 248.9 | +0.9 | 22.4927509 | −1188 | 24.229050 | +079 |
| 2301000 | 171 2335.93 | 1.32 | 183 83.5 | 0.9 | 2.9741917 | 1173 | 6.247185 | 078 |
| 2302000 | 28 162.69 | 1.30 | 235 3518.1 | 0.9 | 11.0101863 | 1158 | 20.077254 | 077 |
| 2303000 | 244 1589.47 | 1.29 | 288 3352.7 | 0.9 | 19.0461825 | 1143 | 2.095387 | 076 |
| 2304000 | 100 3016.27 | 1.27 | 341 3187.2 | 0.9 | 27.0821802 | 1128 | 15.925454 | 075 |
| 2305000 | 317 843.09 | 1.26 | 34 3021.8 | 0.9 | 7.5636269 | 1113 | 29.755521 | 074 |
| 2306000 | 173 2269.92 | 1.24 | 87 2856.4 | 0.8 | 15.5996276 | 1097 | 11.773650 | 073 |
| 2307000 | 30 96.77 | 1.22 | 140 2690.9 | 0.8 | 23.6356298 | 1082 | 25.603715 | 072 |
| 2308000 | 246 1523.64 | 1.21 | 193 2525.4 | 0.8 | 4.1170810 | 1067 | 7.621843 | 071 |
| 2309000 | 102 2950.52 | 1.19 | 246 2359.9 | 0.8 | 12.1530862 | 1052 | 21.451905 | 070 |
| 2310000 | 319 777.42 | 1.17 | 299 2194.4 | 0.8 | 20.1890929 | 1037 | 3.470031 | 069 |
| 2311000 | 175 2204.34 | 1.15 | 352 2028.9 | 0.8 | 0.6705487 | 1022 | 17.300092 | 068 |
| 2312000 | 32 31.27 | 1.13 | 45 1863.4 | 0.8 | 8.7065584 | 1007 | 31.130151 | 067 |
| 2313000 | 248 1458.23 | 1.12 | 98 1697.8 | 0.8 | 16.7425697 | 0992 | 13.148273 | 066 |
| 2314000 | 104 2885.19 | 1.10 | 151 1532.3 | 0.8 | 24.7785824 | 0977 | 26.978331 | 065 |
| 2315000 | 321 712.18 | 1.09 | 204 1366.7 | 0.8 | 5.2600442 | 0962 | 8.996451 | 064 |
| 2316000 | 177 2139.18 | 1.07 | 257 1201.1 | 0.7 | 13.2960600 | 0946 | 22.826507 | 063 |
| 2317000 | 33 3566.20 | 1.05 | 310 1035.6 | 0.7 | 21.3320773 | 0931 | 4.844626 | 062 |
| 2318000 | 250 1393.24 | 1.04 | 3 870.0 | 0.7 | 1.8135436 | 0916 | 18.674680 | 061 |
| 2319000 | 106 2820.29 | 1.02 | 56 704.4 | 0.7 | 9.8495639 | 0901 | 0.692797 | 060 |
| 2320000 | 323 647.37 | 1.00 | 109 538.6 | 0.7 | 17.8855856 | 0886 | 14.522848 | 059 |
| 2321000 | 179 2074.45 | 0.98 | 162 373.0 | 0.7 | 25.9216089 | 0871 | 28.352899 | 058 |
| 2322000 | 35 3501.56 | 0.96 | 215 207.4 | 0.7 | 6.4030813 | 0856 | 10.371013 | 057 |
| 2323000 | 252 1328.68 | 0.95 | 268 41.7 | 0.7 | 14.4391077 | 0841 | 24.201061 | 056 |
| 2324000 | 108 2755.82 | 0.93 | 320 3476.0 | 0.7 | 22.4751355 | 0826 | 6.219173 | 055 |
| 2325000 | 325 582.98 | 0.92 | 13 3310.4 | 0.7 | 2.9566124 | 0811 | 20.049220 | 054 |
| 2326000 | 181 2010.15 | 0.90 | 66 3144.7 | 0.6 | 10.9926433 | 0795 | 2.067329 | 053 |
| 2327000 | 37 3437.34 | 0.88 | 119 2979.0 | 0.6 | 19.0286756 | 0780 | 15.897374 | 052 |
| 2328000 | 254 1264.55 | 0.87 | 172 2813.2 | 0.6 | 27.0647095 | 0765 | 29.727418 | 051 |
| 2329000 | 110 2691.77 | 0.85 | 225 2647.5 | 0.6 | 7.5461925 | 0750 | 11.745524 | 050 |
| 2330000 | 327 519.02 | 0.83 | 278 2481.8 | 0.6 | 15.5822294 | 0735 | 25.575566 | 049 |
| 2331000 | 183 1946.28 | 0.81 | 331 2316.0 | 0.6 | 23.6182678 | 0720 | 7.593671 | 048 |
| 2332000 | 39 3373.55 | 0.79 | 24 2150.3 | 0.6 | 4.0997553 | 0705 | 21.423711 | 047 |
| 2333000 | 256 1200.85 | 0.78 | 77 1984.5 | 0.6 | 12.1357967 | 0690 | 3.441814 | 046 |
| 2334000 | 112 2628.16 | 0.76 | 130 1818.7 | 0.6 | 20.1718397 | 0675 | 17.271851 | 045 |
| 2335000 | 329 455.48 | 0.75 | 183 1652.9 | 0.6 | 0.6533317 | 0660 | 31.101888 | 044 |
| 2336000 | 185 1882.83 | 0.73 | 236 1487.1 | 0.5 | 8.6893777 | 0644 | 13.119988 | 043 |
| 2337000 | 41 3310.19 | 0.71 | 289 1321.3 | 0.5 | 16.7254252 | 0629 | 26.950023 | 042 |
| 2338000 | 258 1137.57 | 0.70 | 342 1155.4 | 0.5 | 24.7614742 | 0614 | 8.968121 | 041 |
| 2339000 | 114 2564.96 | 0.68 | 35 989.6 | 0.5 | 5.2429723 | 0599 | 22.798153 | 040 |
| 2340000 | 331 392.38 | 0.66 | 88 823.7 | 0.5 | 13.2790243 | 0584 | 4.816249 | 039 |
| 2341000 | 187 1819.81 | 0.64 | 141 657.8 | 0.5 | 21.3150778 | 0569 | 18.646280 | 038 |
| 2342000 | 43 3247.25 | 0.62 | 194 491.9 | 0.5 | 1.7965804 | 0554 | 0.664373 | 037 |
| 2343000 | 260 1074.72 | 0.61 | 247 326.0 | 0.5 | 9.8326370 | 0538 | 14.494402 | 036 |
| 2344000 | 116 2502.20 | 0.59 | 300 160.1 | 0.4 | 17.8686951 | 0523 | 28.324430 | 035 |
| 2345000 | 333 329.70 | 0.58 | 352 3594.2 | 0.4 | 25.9047547 | 0508 | 10.342521 | 034 |
| 2346000 | 189 1757.21 | 0.56 | 45 3428.3 | 0.4 | 6.3862634 | 0493 | 24.172546 | 033 |
| 2347000 | 45 3184.75 | 0.54 | 98 3262.3 | 0.4 | 14.4223261 | 0478 | 6.190635 | 032 |
| 2348000 | 262 1012.30 | 0.53 | 151 3096.3 | 0.3 | 22.4583902 | 0462 | 20.020659 | 031 |
| 2349000 | 118 2439.86 | 0.51 | 204 2930.4 | 0.3 | 2.9399035 | 0447 | 2.038746 | 030 |
| 2350000 | 335 267.45 | −0.49 | 257 2764.4 | +0.3 | 10.9759706 | −0432 | 15.868767 | +029 |

# TABLE II*a*.

Epochs and Arguments for each Thousandth Day, from 2300000 to 2400000.

For Washington Mean Noon.

| Day of Julian Period. | u | u′ | y-u | (y-u′) | Arg. 1. | 1′. | 2. | 2′. |
|---|---|---|---|---|---|---|---|---|
| | ° ″ | ″ | ° ″ | ″ | d. | 0.000 | d. | 0.000 |
| 2350000 | 335 267.45 | −0.49 | 257 2764.4 | +0.3 | 10.9759706 | −0432 | 15.868767 | +029 |
| 2351000 | 191 1695.05 | 0.47 | 310 2598.4 | 0.3 | 19.0120393 | 0417 | 29.698788 | 028 |
| 2352000 | 47 3122.67 | 0.45 | 3 2432.4 | 0.3 | 27.0481095 | 0402 | 11.716872 | 027 |
| 2353000 | 264 950.30 | 0.44 | 56 2266.4 | 0.3 | 7.5296288 | 0387 | 25.546891 | 026 |
| 2354000 | 120 2377.96 | 0.42 | 109 2100.3 | 0.3 | 15.5657021 | 0372 | 7.564973 | 025 |
| 2355000 | 337 205.63 | 0.41 | 162 1934.3 | 0.3 | 23.6017769 | 0357 | 21.394990 | 024 |
| 2356000 | 193 1633.31 | 0.39 | 215 1768.2 | 0.2 | 4.0833007 | 0341 | 3.413069 | 023 |
| 2357000 | 49 3061.02 | 0.37 | 268 1602.2 | 0.2 | 12.1193785 | 0326 | 17.243084 | 022 |
| 2358000 | 266 888.74 | 0.36 | 321 1436.1 | 0.2 | 20.1554579 | 0311 | 31.073098 | 021 |
| 2359000 | 122 2316.48 | 0.34 | 14 1270.0 | 0.2 | 0.6369863 | 0296 | 13.091175 | 020 |
| 2360000 | 339 144.23 | 0.32 | 67 1103.9 | 0.2 | 8.6730686 | 0281 | 26.921186 | 019 |
| 2361000 | 195 1572.01 | 0.30 | 120 937.8 | 0.2 | 16.7091525 | 0266 | 8.939261 | 018 |
| 2362000 | 51 2999.80 | 0.28 | 173 771.6 | 0.2 | 24.7452379 | 0251 | 22.769271 | 017 |
| 2363000 | 268 827.60 | 0.27 | 226 605.5 | 0.2 | 5.2267724 | 0235 | 4.787344 | 016 |
| 2364000 | 124 2255.43 | 0.25 | 279 439.3 | 0.2 | 13.2628608 | 0220 | 18.617351 | 015 |
| 2365000 | 341 83.27 | 0.24 | 332 273.2 | 0.2 | 21.2989508 | 0205 | 0.635422 | 014 |
| 2366000 | 197 1511.13 | 0.22 | 25 107.0 | 0.1 | 1.7804898 | 0190 | 14.465428 | 013 |
| 2367000 | 53 2939.00 | 0.20 | 77 3540.8 | 0.1 | 9.8165828 | 0175 | 28.295432 | 012 |
| 2368000 | 270 766.90 | 0.19 | 130 3374.6 | 0.1 | 17.8526773 | 0159 | 10.313500 | 011 |
| 2369000 | 126 2194.81 | 0.17 | 183 3208.4 | 0.1 | 25.8887734 | 0144 | 24.143503 | 010 |
| 2370000 | 343 22.73 | 0.15 | 236 3042.2 | 0.1 | 6.3703184 | 0129 | 6.161569 | 009 |
| 2371000 | 199 1450.68 | 0.13 | 289 2875.9 | 0.1 | 14.4064175 | 0114 | 19.991569 | 008 |
| 2372000 | 55 2878.64 | 0.11 | 342 2709.7 | 0.1 | 22.4425181 | 0099 | 2.009633 | 007 |
| 2373000 | 272 706.62 | 0.10 | 35 2543.4 | 0.1 | 2.9240678 | 0083 | 15.839632 | 006 |
| 2374000 | 128 2134.62 | 0.08 | 88 2377.2 | 0.1 | 10.9601715 | 0068 | 29.669629 | 005 |
| 2375000 | 344 3562.63 | 0.06 | 141 2210.9 | +0.1 | 18.9962766 | 0053 | 11.687650 | 004 |
| 2376000 | 201 1390.66 | 0.04 | 194 2044.6 | 0.0 | 27.0323833 | 0037 | 25.517686 | 003 |
| 2377000 | 57 2818.71 | 0.02 | 247 1878.3 | 0.0 | 7.5139391 | 0022 | 7.535745 | 002 |
| 2378000 | 274 646.77 | −0.01 | 300 1711.9 | 0.0 | 15.5500488 | −0007 | 21.365738 | +001 |
| 2379000 | 130 2074.85 | +0.01 | 353 1545.6 | 0.0 | 23.5861601 | +0008 | 3.383795 | 000 |
| 2380000 | 346 3502.95 | 0.03 | 46 1379.2 | 0.0 | 4.0677204 | 0024 | 17.213787 | −001 |
| 2381000 | 203 1331.07 | 0.05 | 99 1212.9 | 0.0 | 12.1038347 | 0039 | 31.043777 | 002 |
| 2382000 | 59 2759.20 | 0.07 | 152 1046.5 | 0.0 | 20.1399505 | 0054 | 13.061831 | 003 |
| 2383000 | 276 587.35 | 0.08 | 205 880.1 | 0.0 | 0.6215154 | 0070 | 26.891820 | 004 |
| 2384000 | 132 2015.52 | 0.10 | 258 713.7 | 0.0 | 8.6576343 | 0085 | 8.909872 | 005 |
| 2385000 | 348 3443.71 | 0.11 | 311 547.3 | 0.0 | 16.6937547 | 0100 | 22.739858 | 006 |
| 2386000 | 205 1271.91 | 0.13 | 4 380.9 | −0.1 | 24.7298766 | 0115 | 4.757908 | 007 |
| 2387000 | 61 2700.13 | 0.15 | 57 214.5 | 0.1 | 5.2114476 | 0130 | 18.587893 | 008 |
| 2388000 | 278 528.37 | 0.16 | 110 48.0 | 0.1 | 13.2475726 | 0146 | 0.605940 | 009 |
| 2389000 | 134 1956.62 | 0.18 | 162 3481.6 | 0.1 | 21.2836990 | 0161 | 14.435923 | 010 |
| 2390000 | 350 3384.89 | 0.20 | 215 3315.1 | 0.1 | 1.7652747 | 0176 | 28.265904 | 011 |
| 2391000 | 207 1213.18 | 0.22 | 268 3148.6 | 0.1 | 9.8014042 | 0191 | 10.283949 | 012 |
| 2392000 | 63 2641.49 | 0.24 | 321 2982.1 | 0.1 | 17.8375353 | 0206 | 24.113929 | 013 |
| 2393000 | 280 469.81 | 0.25 | 14 2815.6 | 0.1 | 25.8736679 | 0222 | 6.131972 | 014 |
| 2394000 | 136 1898.15 | 0.27 | 67 2649.1 | 0.2 | 6.3552496 | 0237 | 19.961949 | 015 |
| 2395000 | 352 3326.51 | 0.28 | 120 2482.6 | 0.2 | 14.3913852 | 0252 | 1.979990 | 016 |
| 2396000 | 209 1154.88 | 0.30 | 173 2316.1 | 0.2 | 22.4275224 | 0268 | 15.809965 | 018 |
| 2397000 | 65 2583.27 | 0.32 | 226 2149.5 | 0.2 | 2.9091087 | 0283 | 29.639940 | 019 |
| 2398000 | 282 411.68 | 0.33 | 279 1983.0 | 0.3 | 10.9452489 | 0299 | 11.657978 | 020 |
| 2399000 | 138 1840.11 | 0.35 | 332 1816.4 | 0.3 | 18.9813907 | 0314 | 25.487950 | 021 |
| 2400000 | 354 3268.55 | +0.37 | 25 1649.8 | −0.3 | 27.0175339 | +0329 | 7.505986 | −022 |

# TABLE IIa.

Epochs and Arguments for each Thousandth Day, from 2300000 to 2400000.

For Washington Mean Noon.

| Day of Julian Period. | Arg. 3. | 3′. | 4. | 5. | 5′. | 6. | 7. | 8. | 9. |
|---|---|---|---|---|---|---|---|---|---|
| | d. | 0.0000 | d. | d. | 0.00 | d. | d. | d. | d. |
| 2300000 | 16.095387 | −27 | 127.1421 | 383.5901 | −14 | 23.6328 | 8.7464 | 3.8010 | 21.5098 |
| 2301000 | 12.055368 | 27 | 31.3631 | 148.2332 | 14 | 13.0730 | 8.9197 | 3.6257 | 8.2136 |
| 2302000 | 8.015349 | 27 | 300.8437 | 324.6615 | 14 | 2.5132 | 9.0931 | 3.4504 | 24.7202 |
| 2303000 | 3.975330 | 26 | 205.0647 | 89.3046 | 14 | 26.8004 | 9.2663 | 3.2750 | 11.4240 |
| 2304000 | 29.465900 | 26 | 109.2856 | 265.7329 | 14 | 16.2406 | 9.4395 | 3.0997 | 27.9306 |
| 2305000 | 25.425882 | 26 | 13.5065 | 30.3761 | 14 | 5.6808 | 9.6128 | 2.9244 | 14.6345 |
| 2306000 | 21.385865 | 25 | 282.9872 | 206.8044 | 13 | 29.9679 | 0.1724 | 2.7491 | 1.3383 |
| 2307000 | 17.345848 | 25 | 187.2081 | 383.2328 | 13 | 19.4081 | 0.3457 | 2.5738 | 17.8449 |
| 2308000 | 13.305831 | 24 | 91.4290 | 147.8760 | 13 | 8.8483 | 0.5190 | 2.3984 | 4.5487 |
| 2309000 | 9.265815 | 24 | 360.9097 | 324.3044 | 13 | 33.1354 | 0.6922 | 2.2231 | 21.0554 |
| 2310000 | 5.225799 | 24 | 265.1306 | 88.9476 | 13 | 22.5756 | 0.8655 | 2.0478 | 7.7592 |
| 2311000 | 1.185783 | 23 | 169.3515 | 265.3761 | 12 | 12.0158 | 1.0388 | 1.8725 | 24.2659 |
| 2312000 | 26.676355 | 23 | 73.5725 | 30.0193 | 12 | 1.4560 | 1.2121 | 1.6972 | 10.9697 |
| 2313000 | 22.636340 | 23 | 343.0531 | 206.4478 | 12 | 25.7431 | 1.3853 | 1.5218 | 27.4763 |
| 2314000 | 18.596325 | 22 | 247.2741 | 382.8763 | 12 | 15.1833 | 1.5586 | 1.3465 | 14.1801 |
| 2315000 | 14.556311 | 22 | 151.4950 | 147.5196 | 12 | 4.6235 | 1.7319 | 1.1712 | 0.8840 |
| 2316000 | 10.516297 | 22 | 55.7159 | 323.9482 | 12 | 28.9106 | 1.9052 | 0.9959 | 17.3906 |
| 2317000 | 6.476284 | 21 | 325.1966 | 88.5915 | 11 | 18.3508 | 2.0785 | 0.8206 | 4.0945 |
| 2318000 | 2.436270 | 21 | 229.4175 | 265.0201 | 11 | 7.7910 | 2.2517 | 0.6452 | 20.6011 |
| 2319000 | 27.926845 | 21 | 133.6384 | 29.6635 | 11 | 32.0781 | 2.4250 | 0.4699 | 7.3050 |
| 2320000 | 23.886833 | 20 | 37.8594 | 206.0923 | 11 | 21.5183 | 2.5983 | 0.2946 | 23.8116 |
| 2321000 | 19.846820 | 20 | 307.3400 | 382.5209 | 11 | 10.9585 | 2.7716 | 15.5066 | 10.5154 |
| 2322000 | 15.806809 | 20 | 211.5609 | 147.1644 | 10 | 0.3987 | 2.9449 | 15.3313 | 27.0221 |
| 2323000 | 11.766797 | 19 | 115.7819 | 323.5930 | 10 | 24.6858 | 3.1182 | 15.1560 | 13.7260 |
| 2324000 | 7.726786 | 19 | 20.0028 | 88.2365 | 10 | 14.1260 | 3.2915 | 14.9807 | 0.4298 |
| 2325000 | 3.686775 | 19 | 289.4835 | 264.6652 | 10 | 3.5662 | 3.4648 | 14.8053 | 16.9365 |
| 2326000 | 29.177352 | 18 | 193.7044 | 29.3087 | 10 | 27.8533 | 3.6380 | 14.6300 | 3.6403 |
| 2327000 | 25.137342 | 18 | 97.9253 | 205.7374 | 10 | 17.2934 | 3.8113 | 14.4547 | 20.1470 |
| 2328000 | 21.097332 | 18 | 2.1463 | 382.1662 | 09 | 6.7336 | 3.9846 | 14.2794 | 6.8508 |
| 2329000 | 17.057323 | 17 | 271.6269 | 146.8098 | 09 | 31.0207 | 4.1579 | 14.1041 | 23.3575 |
| 2330000 | 13.017314 | 17 | 175.8478 | 323.2386 | 09 | 20.4609 | 4.3312 | 13.9288 | 10.0613 |
| 2331000 | 8.977305 | 16 | 80.0688 | 87.8822 | 09 | 9.9011 | 4.5045 | 13.7535 | 26.5680 |
| 2332000 | 4.937296 | 16 | 349.5494 | 264.3110 | 09 | 34.1882 | 4.6778 | 13.5782 | 13.2719 |
| 2333000 | 0.897288 | 16 | 253.7703 | 28.9547 | 09 | 23.6283 | 4.8511 | 13.4029 | 29.7785 |
| 2334000 | 26.387869 | 15 | 157.9913 | 205.3835 | 08 | 13.0685 | 5.0244 | 13.2276 | 16.4824 |
| 2335000 | 22.347861 | 15 | 62.2122 | 381.8124 | 08 | 2.5087 | 5.1977 | 13.0522 | 3.1863 |
| 2336000 | 18.307854 | 15 | 331.6929 | 146.4561 | 08 | 26.7958 | 5.3710 | 12.8769 | 19.6930 |
| 2337000 | 14.267847 | 14 | 235.9138 | 322.8850 | 08 | 16.2360 | 5.5443 | 12.7016 | 6.3968 |
| 2338000 | 10.227841 | 14 | 140.1347 | 87.5288 | 08 | 5.6761 | 5.7176 | 12.5263 | 22.9035 |
| 2339000 | 6.187835 | 14 | 44.3557 | 263.9577 | 07 | 29.9632 | 5.8909 | 12.3510 | 9.6074 |
| 2340000 | 2.147829 | 13 | 313.8363 | 28.6015 | 07 | 19.4034 | 6.0642 | 12.1757 | 26.1141 |
| 2341000 | 27.638412 | 13 | 218.0572 | 205.0305 | 07 | 8.8436 | 6.2375 | 12.0004 | 12.8179 |
| 2342000 | 23.598407 | 13 | 122.2782 | 381.4595 | 07 | 33.1306 | 6.4108 | 11.8251 | 29.3246 |
| 2343000 | 19.558402 | 12 | 26.4991 | 146.1033 | 07 | 22.5708 | 6.5841 | 11.6498 | 16.0285 |
| 2344000 | 15.518398 | 12 | 295.9797 | 322.5323 | 07 | 12.0110 | 6.7574 | 11.4745 | 2.7324 |
| 2345000 | 11.478394 | 12 | 200.2007 | 87.1762 | 06 | 1.4511 | 6.9307 | 11.2991 | 19.2391 |
| 2346000 | 7.438391 | 11 | 104.4216 | 263.6053 | 06 | 25.7382 | 7.1041 | 11.1238 | 5.9429 |
| 2347000 | 3.398387 | 11 | 8.6426 | 28.2492 | 06 | 15.1784 | 7.2774 | 10.9485 | 22.4496 |
| 2348000 | 28.888973 | 11 | 278.1232 | 204.6783 | 06 | 4.6185 | 7.4507 | 10.7732 | 9.1535 |
| 2349000 | 24.848970 | 10 | 182.3441 | 381.1074 | 06 | 28.9056 | 7.6240 | 10.5979 | 25.6602 |
| 2350000 | 20.808968 | −10 | 86.5651 | 145.7514 | −05 | 18.3457 | 7.7973 | 10.4226 | 12.3641 |

# TABLE IIa.

Epochs and Arguments for each Thousandth Day, from 2300000 to 2400000.

For Washington Mean Noon.

| Day of Julian Period. | Arg. 3. | 3′. | 4. | 5. | 5′. | 6. | 7. | 8. | 9. |
|---|---|---|---|---|---|---|---|---|---|
| | d. | 0.0000 | d. | d. | 0.00 | d. | d. | d. | d. |
| 2350000 | 20.808968 | −10 | 86.5651 | 145.7514 | −05 | 18.3457 | 7.7973 | 10.4226 | 12.3641 |
| 2351000 | 16.768966 | 10 | 356.0457 | 322.1805 | 05 | 7.7859 | 7.9706 | 10.2473 | 28.8708 |
| 2352000 | 12.728965 | 09 | 260.2666 | 86.8245 | 05 | 32.0730 | 8.1439 | 10.0720 | 15.5747 |
| 2353000 | 8.688963 | 09 | 164.4876 | 263.2537 | 05 | 21.5131 | 8.3172 | 9.8967 | 2.2786 |
| 2354000 | 4.648963 | 08 | 68.7085 | 27.8977 | 05 | 10.9533 | 8.4905 | 9.7214 | 18.7853 |
| 2355000 | 0.608962 | 08 | 338.1891 | 204.3270 | 05 | 0.3934 | 8.6638 | 9.5460 | 5.4892 |
| 2356000 | 26.099550 | 08 | 242.4101 | 380.7562 | 04 | 24.6805 | 8.8372 | 9.3707 | 21.9959 |
| 2357000 | 22.059550 | 07 | 146.6310 | 145.4003 | 04 | 14.1207 | 9.0105 | 9.1954 | 8.6998 |
| 2358000 | 18.019551 | 07 | 50.8520 | 321.8296 | 04 | 3.5608 | 9.1838 | 9.0201 | 25.2065 |
| 2359000 | 13.979552 | 07 | 320.3326 | 86.4737 | 04 | 27.8479 | 9.3571 | 8.8448 | 11.9104 |
| 2360000 | 9.939553 | 06 | 224.5536 | 262.9030 | 04 | 17.2880 | 9.5304 | 8.6695 | 28.4172 |
| 2361000 | 5.899555 | 06 | 128.7745 | 27.5472 | 04 | 6.7282 | 0.0900 | 8.4942 | 15.1211 |
| 2362000 | 1.859557 | 06 | 32.9954 | 203.9765 | 03 | 31.0152 | 0.2633 | 8.3189 | 1.8250 |
| 2363000 | 27.350147 | 05 | 302.4760 | 380.4059 | 03 | 20.4554 | 0.4366 | 8.1436 | 18.3317 |
| 2364000 | 23.310150 | 05 | 206.6970 | 145.0501 | 03 | 9.8955 | 0.6100 | 7.9683 | 5.0356 |
| 2365000 | 19.270153 | 05 | 110.9179 | 321.4795 | 03 | 34.1825 | 0.7833 | 7.7930 | 21.5424 |
| 2366000 | 15.230156 | 04 | 15.1389 | 86.1238 | 03 | 23.6227 | 0.9566 | 7.6177 | 8.2463 |
| 2367000 | 11.190160 | 04 | 284.6195 | 262.5532 | 02 | 13.0628 | 1.1300 | 7.4424 | 24.7530 |
| 2368000 | 7.150164 | 04 | 188.8404 | 27.1975 | 02 | 2.5030 | 1.3033 | 7.2671 | 11.4569 |
| 2369000 | 3.110169 | 03 | 93.0614 | 203.6270 | 02 | 26.7900 | 1.4766 | 7.0918 | 27.9636 |
| 2370000 | 28.600762 | 03 | 362.5420 | 380.0565 | 02 | 16.2302 | 1.6499 | 6.9165 | 14.6676 |
| 2371000 | 24.560767 | 03 | 266.7629 | 144.7008 | 02 | 5.6703 | 1.8232 | 6.7412 | 1.3715 |
| 2372000 | 20.520772 | 02 | 170.9839 | 321.1303 | 02 | 29.9573 | 1.9965 | 6.5659 | 17.8783 |
| 2373000 | 16.480778 | 02 | 75.2048 | 85.7747 | 01 | 19.3975 | 2.1699 | 6.3906 | 4.5822 |
| 2374000 | 12.440784 | 01 | 344.6854 | 262.2043 | 01 | 8.8376 | 2.3432 | 6.2153 | 21.0889 |
| 2375000 | 8.400791 | 01 | 248.9064 | 26.8487 | 01 | 33.1246 | 2.5165 | 6.0400 | 7.7929 |
| 2376000 | 4.360798 | 01 | 153.1273 | 203.2783 | 01 | 22.5648 | 2.6899 | 5.8648 | 24.2996 |
| 2377000 | 0.320805 | 00 | 57.3483 | 379.7079 | −01 | 12.0049 | 2.8632 | 5.6895 | 11.0035 |
| 2378000 | 25.811401 | −00 | 326.8289 | 144.3524 | 00 | 1.4450 | 3.0366 | 5.5142 | 27.5103 |
| 2379000 | 21.771409 | +00 | 231.0498 | 320.7820 | 00 | 25.7321 | 3.2099 | 5.3389 | 14.2142 |
| 2380000 | 17.731417 | 01 | 135.2708 | 85.4265 | 00 | 15.1722 | 3.3832 | 5.1636 | 0.9181 |
| 2381000 | 13.691425 | 01 | 39.4917 | 261.8562 | 00 | 4.6123 | 3.5565 | 4.9883 | 17.4249 |
| 2382000 | 9.651434 | 01 | 308.9723 | 26.5007 | 00 | 28.8993 | 3.7299 | 4.8130 | 4.1288 |
| 2383000 | 5.611444 | 02 | 213.1933 | 202.9305 | 00 | 18.3395 | 3.9032 | 4.6377 | 20.6356 |
| 2384000 | 1.571454 | 02 | 117.4142 | 379.3602 | +01 | 7.7796 | 4.0766 | 4.4624 | 7.3395 |
| 2385000 | 27.062052 | 02 | 21.6352 | 144.0048 | 01 | 32.0666 | 4.2499 | 4.2871 | 23.8463 |
| 2386000 | 23.022062 | 03 | 291.1158 | 320.4346 | 01 | 21.5067 | 4.4232 | 4.1118 | 10.5502 |
| 2387000 | 18.982073 | 03 | 195.3367 | 85.0792 | 01 | 10.9469 | 4.5966 | 3.9365 | 27.0570 |
| 2388000 | 14.942084 | 03 | 99.5577 | 261.5090 | 01 | 0.3870 | 4.7699 | 3.7612 | 13.7610 |
| 2389000 | 10.902095 | 04 | 3.7786 | 26.1537 | 01 | 24.6740 | 4.9433 | 3.5859 | 0.4649 |
| 2390000 | 6.862107 | 04 | 273.2592 | 202.5835 | 02 | 14.1141 | 5.1166 | 3.4106 | 16.9717 |
| 2391000 | 2.822119 | 04 | 177.4802 | 379.0134 | 02 | 3.5542 | 5.2899 | 3.2353 | 3.6757 |
| 2392000 | 28.312720 | 05 | 81.7011 | 143.6581 | 02 | 27.8413 | 5.4633 | 3.0600 | 20.1824 |
| 2393000 | 24.272733 | 05 | 351.1817 | 320.0880 | 02 | 17.2814 | 5.6366 | 2.8847 | 6.8864 |
| 2394000 | 20.232746 | 05 | 255.4027 | 84.7327 | 02 | 6.7215 | 5.8100 | 2.7094 | 23.3932 |
| 2395000 | 16.192759 | 06 | 159.6236 | 261.1627 | 03 | 31.0085 | 5.9833 | 2.5341 | 10.0971 |
| 2396000 | 12.152773 | 06 | 63.8446 | 25.8075 | 03 | 20.4486 | 6.1566 | 2.3589 | 26.6039 |
| 2397000 | 8.112788 | 06 | 333.3252 | 202.2374 | 03 | 9.8887 | 6.3300 | 2.1836 | 13.3078 |
| 2398000 | 4.072802 | 07 | 237.5461 | 378.6674 | 03 | 34.1757 | 6.5033 | 2.0082 | 0.0118 |
| 2399000 | 0.032817 | 07 | 141.7671 | 143.3123 | 03 | 23.6158 | 6.6767 | 1.8330 | 16.5186 |
| 2400000 | 25.523420 | +08 | 45.9880 | 319.7423 | +03 | 13.0559 | 6.8500 | 1.6577 | 3.2226 |

# TABLE IIa.

Epochs and Arguments for each Thousandth Day, from 2300000 to 2400000.

For Washington Mean Noon.

| Day of Julian Period. | Arg. 10. | 11. | 12. | 13. | 14. | 15. | 16. | 17. |
|---|---|---|---|---|---|---|---|---|
| | d. | d. | d. | d. | d. | d. | d. | d. |
| 2300000 | 23.5709 | 6.1437 | 211.1477 | 9.3568 | 25.412 | 6.884 | 0.337 | 10.837 |
| 2301000 | 24.3246 | 11.6470 | 171.2876 | 0.8971 | 1.197 | 13.471 | 2.544 | 27.256 |
| 2302000 | 25.0784 | 17.1504 | 131.4274 | 2.5220 | 6.246 | 5.866 | 4.751 | 16.355 |
| 2303000 | 0.2104 | 22.6538 | 91.5673 | 4.1470 | 11.295 | 12.454 | 6.958 | 5.451 |
| 2304000 | 0.9642 | 1.2788 | 51.7072 | 5.7719 | 16.343 | 4.849 | 9.165 | 21.871 |
| 2305000 | 1.7179 | 6.7822 | 11.8470 | 7.3968 | 21.392 | 11.437 | 11.371 | 10.969 |
| 2306000 | 2.4716 | 12.2856 | 318.6070 | 9.0217 | 26.440 | 3.832 | 13.578 | 0.067 |
| 2307000 | 3.2254 | 17.7890 | 278.7469 | 0.5620 | 2.226 | 10.419 | 1.531 | 16.486 |
| 2308000 | 3.9791 | 23.2923 | 238.8867 | 2.1870 | 7.274 | 2.815 | 3.738 | 5.584 |
| 2309000 | 4.7329 | 1.9174 | 199.0266 | 3.8119 | 12.323 | 9.402 | 5.945 | 22.005 |
| 2310000 | 5.4866 | 7.4208 | 159.1665 | 5.4368 | 17.371 | 1.798 | 8.152 | 11.101 |
| 2311000 | 6.2403 | 12.9242 | 119.3063 | 7.0617 | 22.420 | 8.385 | 10.359 | 0.199 |
| 2312000 | 6.9941 | 18.4276 | 79.4462 | 8.6866 | 27.468 | 0.781 | 12.566 | 16.619 |
| 2313000 | 7.7478 | 23.9309 | 39.5860 | 0.2269 | 3.254 | 7.368 | 0.519 | 5.717 |
| 2314000 | 8.5016 | 2.5560 | 346.3460 | 1.8519 | 8.303 | 13.955 | 2.726 | 22.136 |
| 2315000 | 9.2553 | 8.0593 | 306.4858 | 3.4768 | 13.351 | 6.351 | 4.933 | 11.234 |
| 2316000 | 10.0091 | 13.5627 | 266.6257 | 5.1017 | 18.400 | 12.938 | 7.140 | 0.332 |
| 2317000 | 10.7629 | 19.0661 | 226.7655 | 6.7267 | 23.448 | 5.334 | 9.347 | 16.752 |
| 2318000 | 11.5166 | 24.5694 | 186.9053 | 8.3516 | 28.497 | 11.921 | 11.554 | 5.849 |
| 2319000 | 12.2704 | 3.1945 | 147.0451 | 9.9765 | 4.282 | 4.316 | 13.761 | 22.269 |
| 2320000 | 13.0241 | 8.6978 | 107.1850 | 1.5168 | 9.330 | 10.905 | 1.714 | 11.366 |
| 2321000 | 13.7779 | 14.2011 | 67.3248 | 3.1417 | 14.379 | 3.299 | 3.921 | 0.464 |
| 2322000 | 14.5316 | 19.7045 | 27.4646 | 4.7666 | 19.428 | 9.886 | 6.128 | 16.884 |
| 2323000 | 15.2854 | 25.2078 | 334.2246 | 6.3915 | 24.476 | 2.282 | 8.335 | 5.982 |
| 2324000 | 16.0391 | 3.8329 | 294.3644 | 8.0165 | 0.262 | 8.869 | 10.542 | 22.401 |
| 2325000 | 16.7929 | 9.3362 | 254.5042 | 9.6414 | 5.310 | 1.265 | 12.749 | 11.499 |
| 2326000 | 17.5467 | 14.8396 | 214.6440 | 1.1817 | 10.359 | 7.852 | 0.702 | 0.597 |
| 2327000 | 18.3004 | 20.3429 | 174.7838 | 2.8067 | 15.407 | 0.248 | 2.909 | 17.016 |
| 2328000 | 19.0542 | 25.8463 | 134.9236 | 4.4316 | 20.456 | 6.835 | 5.116 | 6.114 |
| 2329000 | 19.8079 | 4.4713 | 95.0634 | 6.0565 | 25.505 | 13.422 | 7.323 | 22.534 |
| 2330000 | 20.5617 | 9.9746 | 55.2032 | 7.6814 | 1.290 | 5.817 | 9.530 | 11.631 |
| 2331000 | 21.3155 | 15.4780 | 15.3430 | 9.3063 | 6.338 | 12.405 | 11.737 | 0.729 |
| 2332000 | 22.0693 | 20.9813 | 322.1029 | 0.8466 | 11.387 | 4.800 | 13.944 | 17.149 |
| 2333000 | 22.8231 | 26.4847 | 282.2427 | 2.4715 | 16.435 | 11.388 | 1.897 | 6.247 |
| 2334000 | 23.5768 | 5.1097 | 242.3825 | 4.0965 | 21.484 | 3.785 | 4.104 | 22.666 |
| 2335000 | 24.3306 | 10.6130 | 202.5223 | 5.7214 | 26.532 | 10.370 | 6.311 | 11.764 |
| 2336000 | 25.0844 | 16.1164 | 162.6621 | 7.3463 | 2.318 | 2.766 | 8.518 | 0.862 |
| 2337000 | 0.2164 | 21.6197 | 122.8018 | 8.9713 | 7.366 | 9.355 | 10.725 | 17.282 |
| 2338000 | 0.9702 | 0.2447 | 82.9416 | 0.5116 | 12.415 | 1.749 | 12.932 | 6.379 |
| 2339000 | 1.7240 | 5.7481 | 43.0814 | 2.1365 | 17.464 | 8.336 | 0.885 | 22.799 |
| 2340000 | 2.4778 | 11.2513 | 3.2212 | 3.7614 | 22.512 | 0.732 | 3.092 | 11.897 |
| 2341000 | 3.2316 | 16.7547 | 309.9811 | 5.3863 | 27.560 | 7.319 | 5.299 | 0.995 |
| 2342000 | 3.9854 | 22.2580 | 270.1209 | 7.0112 | 3.346 | 13.906 | 7.506 | 17.414 |
| 2343000 | 4.7392 | 0.8830 | 230.2606 | 8.6361 | 8.394 | 6.302 | 9.713 | 6.512 |
| 2344000 | 5.4930 | 6.3863 | 190.4004 | 0.1764 | 13.443 | 12.889 | 11.920 | 22.932 |
| 2345000 | 6.2467 | 11.8897 | 150.5402 | 1.8013 | 18.491 | 5.285 | 14.127 | 12.029 |
| 2346000 | 7.0005 | 17.3930 | 110.6799 | 3.4263 | 23.540 | 11.872 | 2.080 | 1.127 |
| 2347000 | 7.7543 | 22.8963 | 70.8197 | 5.0512 | 28.588 | 4.267 | 4.287 | 17.547 |
| 2348000 | 8.5081 | 1.5213 | 30.9594 | 6.6761 | 4.375 | 10.855 | 6.494 | 6.645 |
| 2349000 | 9.2619 | 7.0246 | 337.7193 | 8.3010 | 9.422 | 3.250 | 8.701 | 23.064 |
| 2350000 | 10.0157 | 12.5279 | 297.8590 | 9.9259 | 14.471 | 9.837 | 10.908 | 12.162 |

# TABLE II*a*.

Epochs and Arguments for each Thousandth Day, from 2300000 to 2400000.

For Washington Mean Noon.

| Day of Julian Period. | Arg. **10.** | **11.** | **12.** | **13.** | **14.** | **15.** | **16.** | **17.** |
|---|---|---|---|---|---|---|---|---|
| | d. | d. | d. | d. | d. | d. | d. | d. |
| 2350000 | 10.0157 | 12.5279 | 297.8590 | 9.9259 | 14.471 | 9.837 | 10.908 | 12.162 |
| 2351000 | 10.7695 | 18.0313 | 257.9988 | 1.4662 | 19.519 | 2.233 | 13.115 | 1.260 |
| 2352000 | 11.5233 | 23.5346 | 218.1385 | 3.0911 | 24.568 | 8.820 | 1.068 | 17.679 |
| 2353000 | 12.2771 | 2.1596 | 178.2782 | 4.7160 | 0.353 | 1.216 | 3.275 | 6.777 |
| 2354000 | 13.0309 | 7.6629 | 138.4180 | 6.3410 | 5.401 | 7.805 | 5.482 | 23.197 |
| 2355000 | 13.7847 | 13.1662 | 98.5577 | 7.9659 | 10.450 | 0.199 | 7.690 | 12.295 |
| 2356000 | 14.5385 | 18.6695 | 58.6974 | 9.5908 | 15.498 | 6.786 | 9.897 | 1.393 |
| 2357000 | 15.2923 | 24.1728 | 18.8372 | 1.1311 | 20.547 | 13.374 | 12.104 | 17.812 |
| 2358000 | 16.0461 | 2.7978 | 325.5970 | 2.7561 | 25.595 | 5.769 | 0.057 | 6.910 |
| 2359000 | 16.7999 | 8.3011 | 285.7367 | 4.3810 | 1.381 | 12.357 | 2.264 | 23.329 |
| 2360000 | 17.5537 | 13.8044 | 245.8764 | 6.0059 | 6.429 | 4.752 | 4.470 | 12.427 |
| 2361000 | 18.3075 | 19.3077 | 206.0161 | 7.6308 | 11.478 | 11.339 | 6.677 | 1.525 |
| 2362000 | 19.0613 | 24.8110 | 166.1558 | 9.2557 | 16.526 | 3.734 | 8.885 | 17.945 |
| 2363000 | 19.8151 | 3.4360 | 126.2956 | 0.7960 | 21.575 | 10.322 | 11.091 | 7.043 |
| 2364000 | 20.5690 | 8.9393 | 86.4353 | 2.4209 | 26.623 | 2.717 | 13.299 | 23.462 |
| 2365000 | 21.3228 | 14.4426 | 46.5750 | 4.0458 | 2.409 | 9.304 | 1.252 | 12.560 |
| 2366000 | 22.0766 | 19.9459 | 6.7147 | 5.6708 | 7.457 | 1.700 | 3.459 | 1.658 |
| 2367000 | 22.8305 | 25.4492 | 313.4745 | 7.2957 | 12.506 | 8.287 | 5.666 | 18.077 |
| 2368000 | 23.5843 | 4.0742 | 273.6142 | 8.9206 | 17.554 | 0.683 | 7.873 | 7.175 |
| 2369000 | 24.3381 | 9.5774 | 233.7539 | 0.4609 | 22.603 | 7.270 | 10.080 | 23.595 |
| 2370000 | 25.0919 | 15.0807 | 193.8936 | 2.0858 | 27.651 | 13.858 | 12.287 | 12.693 |
| 2371000 | 0.2240 | 20.5840 | 154.0333 | 3.7107 | 3.437 | 6.253 | 0.240 | 1.790 |
| 2372000 | 0.9778 | 26.0873 | 114.1729 | 5.3356 | 8.485 | 12.841 | 2.447 | 18.210 |
| 2373000 | 1.7317 | 4.7123 | 74.3126 | 6.9605 | 13.534 | 5.236 | 4.654 | 7.308 |
| 2374000 | 2.4855 | 10.2156 | 34.4523 | 8.5855 | 18.582 | 11.825 | 6.861 | 23.727 |
| 2375000 | 3.2393 | 15.7188 | 341.2121 | 0.1258 | 23.631 | 4.219 | 9.068 | 12.825 |
| 2376000 | 3.9932 | 21.2221 | 301.3518 | 1.7507 | 28.679 | 10.806 | 11.275 | 1.923 |
| 2377000 | 4.7470 | 26.7254 | 261.4914 | 3.3757 | 4.464 | 3.201 | 13.482 | 18.343 |
| 2378000 | 5.5009 | 5.3504 | 221.6311 | 5.0006 | 9.513 | 9.789 | 1.435 | 7.440 |
| 2379000 | 6.2547 | 10.8536 | 181.7708 | 6.6255 | 14.561 | 2.184 | 3.642 | 23.860 |
| 2380000 | 7.0085 | 16.3569 | 141.9104 | 8.2504 | 19.610 | 8.772 | 5.849 | 12.958 |
| 2381000 | 7.7623 | 21.8602 | 102.0501 | 9.8753 | 24.659 | 1.167 | 8.056 | 2.056 |
| 2382000 | 8.5162 | 0.4852 | 62.1897 | 1.4156 | 0.444 | 7.755 | 10.263 | 18.475 |
| 2383000 | 9.2700 | 5.9884 | 22.3294 | 3.0405 | 5.492 | 0.150 | 12.470 | 7.573 |
| 2384000 | 10.0239 | 11.4917 | 329.0892 | 4.6654 | 10.541 | 6.737 | 0.423 | 23.993 |
| 2385000 | 10.7777 | 16.9950 | 289.2288 | 6.2903 | 15.589 | 13.325 | 2.630 | 13.091 |
| 2386000 | 11.5316 | 22.4983 | 249.3685 | 7.9153 | 20.638 | 5.720 | 4.837 | 2.188 |
| 2387000 | 12.2855 | 1.1232 | 209.5081 | 9.5402 | 25.686 | 12.308 | 7.044 | 18.608 |
| 2388000 | 13.0393 | 6.6265 | 169.6477 | 1.0805 | 1.472 | 4.703 | 9.252 | 7.706 |
| 2389000 | 13.7932 | 12.1298 | 129.7874 | 2.7054 | 6.520 | 11.291 | 11.458 | 24.125 |
| 2390000 | 14.5470 | 17.6330 | 89.9270 | 4.3303 | 11.569 | 3.686 | 13.665 | 13.223 |
| 2391000 | 15.3008 | 23.1363 | 50.0666 | 5.9552 | 16.617 | 10.273 | 1.618 | 2.321 |
| 2392000 | 16.0547 | 1.7612 | 10.2063 | 7.5801 | 21.666 | 2.669 | 3.826 | 18.741 |
| 2393000 | 16.8086 | 7.2645 | 316.9660 | 9.2050 | 26.714 | 9.256 | 6.033 | 7.839 |
| 2394000 | 17.5624 | 12.7677 | 277.1056 | 0.7453 | 2.499 | 1.652 | 8.240 | 24.258 |
| 2395000 | 18.3163 | 18.2710 | 237.2453 | 2.3702 | 7.548 | 8.239 | 10.447 | 13.356 |
| 2396000 | 19.0702 | 23.7743 | 197.3849 | 3.9952 | 12.596 | 0.635 | 12.654 | 2.454 |
| 2397000 | 19.8240 | 2.3992 | 157.5245 | 5.6201 | 17.645 | 7.222 | 0.607 | 18.873 |
| 2398000 | 20.5779 | 7.9025 | 117.6641 | 7.2450 | 22.693 | 13.810 | 2.814 | 7.971 |
| 2399000 | 21.3317 | 13.4057 | 77.8037 | 8.8699 | 27.742 | 6.205 | 5.021 | 24.391 |
| 2400000 | 22.0856 | 18.9090 | 37.9433 | 0.4102 | 3.527 | 12.792 | 7.228 | 13.489 |

# TABLE IIa.

Epochs and Arguments for each Thousandth Day, from 2300000 to 2400000.

For Washington Mean Noon.

| Day of Julian Period. | Arg. 18. | 19. | 20. | 21. | 22. | 23. | 24. | 25. | 26. |
|---|---|---|---|---|---|---|---|---|---|
| | d. | d. | d. | d. | d. | d. | d. | d. | d. |
| 2300000 | 7.892 | 22.048 | 4.908 | 57.34 | 18.074 | 6.402 | 6.714 | 0.194 | 5.702 |
| 2301000 | 0.786 | 1.356 | 2.696 | 3.97 | 22.104 | 7.868 | 10.976 | 7.274 | 4.214 |
| 2302000 | 3.553 | 4.966 | 0.484 | 82.27 | 26.133 | 9.333 | 1.963 | 4.987 | 2.725 |
| 2303000 | 6.320 | 8.576 | 12.589 | 28.90 | 30.162 | 10.799 | 6.225 | 2.699 | 1.237 |
| 2304000 | 9.086 | 12.185 | 10.378 | 107.20 | 2.063 | 12.264 | 10.487 | 0.412 | 5.572 |
| | | | | | | | | | |
| 2305000 | 1.980 | 15.795 | 8.166 | 53.83 | 6.093 | 13.730 | 1.474 | 7.491 | 4.083 |
| 2306000 | 4.747 | 19.405 | 5.954 | 0.46 | 10.122 | 15.196 | 5.736 | 5.204 | 2.595 |
| 2307000 | 7.513 | 23.014 | 3.742 | 78.76 | 14.152 | 16.661 | 9.999 | 2.916 | 1.107 |
| 2308000 | 0.407 | 2.322 | 1.530 | 25.39 | 18.181 | 18.127 | 0.985 | 0.629 | 5.441 |
| 2309000 | 3.174 | 5.932 | 13.635 | 103.70 | 22.210 | 19.592 | 5.247 | 7.708 | 3.953 |
| | | | | | | | | | |
| 2310000 | 5.942 | 9.542 | 11.423 | 50.33 | 26.239 | 21.058 | 9.510 | 5.422 | 2.465 |
| 2311000 | 8.708 | 13.151 | 9.211 | 128.63 | 30.268 | 22.524 | 0.495 | 3.134 | 0.977 |
| 2312000 | 1.602 | 16.761 | 6.999 | 75.26 | 2.170 | 0.215 | 4.758 | 0.847 | 5.311 |
| 2313000 | 4.369 | 20.371 | 4.787 | 21.89 | 6.199 | 1.680 | 9.021 | 7.926 | 3.823 |
| 2314000 | 7.136 | 23.981 | 2.575 | 100.19 | 10.228 | 3.146 | 0.007 | 5.639 | 2.335 |
| | | | | | | | | | |
| 2315000 | 0.029 | 3.288 | 0.363 | 46.82 | 14.258 | 4.612 | 4.269 | 3.352 | 0.847 |
| 2316000 | 2.796 | 6.898 | 12.468 | 125.12 | 18.287 | 6.077 | 8.532 | 1.064 | 5.181 |
| 2317000 | 5.563 | 10.508 | 10.256 | 71.75 | 22.316 | 7.543 | 12.794 | 8.144 | 3.693 |
| 2318000 | 8.330 | 14.117 | 8.044 | 18.38 | 26.346 | 9.008 | 3.780 | 5.857 | 2.204 |
| 2319000 | 1.224 | 17.727 | 5.832 | 96.69 | 30.375 | 10.474 | 8.042 | 3.569 | 0.716 |
| | | | | | | | | | |
| 2320000 | 3.991 | 21.337 | 3.620 | 43.32 | 2.277 | 11.940 | 12.305 | 1.282 | 5.051 |
| 2321000 | 6.758 | 0.644 | 1.408 | 121.62 | 6.305 | 13.406 | 3.292 | 8.361 | 3.563 |
| 2322000 | 9.525 | 4.254 | 13.513 | 68.25 | 10.335 | 14.871 | 7.554 | 6.074 | 2.074 |
| 2323000 | 2.419 | 7.864 | 11.301 | 14.88 | 14.364 | 16.337 | 11.816 | 3.786 | 0.586 |
| 2324000 | 5.186 | 11.474 | 9.090 | 93.18 | 18.393 | 17.802 | 2.803 | 1.499 | 4.921 |
| | | | | | | | | | |
| 2325000 | 7.952 | 15.084 | 6.878 | 39.81 | 22.423 | 19.268 | 7.065 | 8.579 | 3.432 |
| 2326000 | 0.846 | 18.693 | 4.666 | 118.11 | 26.452 | 20.734 | 11.327 | 6.291 | 1.944 |
| 2327000 | 3.613 | 22.305 | 2.454 | 64.74 | 30.481 | 22.199 | 2.314 | 4.004 | 6.279 |
| 2328000 | 6.380 | 1.611 | 0.242 | 11.37 | 2.382 | 23.665 | 6.576 | 1.717 | 4.790 |
| 2329000 | 9.146 | 5.221 | 12.347 | 89.67 | 6.412 | 1.355 | 10.838 | 8.796 | 3.302 |
| | | | | | | | | | |
| 2330000 | 2.041 | 8.830 | 10.135 | 36.30 | 10.441 | 2.821 | 1.825 | 6.509 | 1.814 |
| 2331000 | 4.808 | 12.440 | 7.923 | 114.61 | 14.471 | 4.287 | 6.088 | 4.221 | 0.326 |
| 2332000 | 7.574 | 16.050 | 5.711 | 61.24 | 18.500 | 5.753 | 10.350 | 1.934 | 4.660 |
| 2333000 | 0.468 | 19.660 | 3.499 | 7.87 | 22.529 | 7.218 | 1.336 | 9.014 | 3.172 |
| 2334000 | 3.235 | 23.269 | 1.287 | 86.17 | 26.558 | 8.684 | 5.599 | 6.727 | 1.684 |
| | | | | | | | | | |
| 2335000 | 6.002 | 2.577 | 13.392 | 32.80 | 30.588 | 10.150 | 9.861 | 4.439 | 0.196 |
| 2336000 | 8.769 | 6.187 | 11.180 | 111.10 | 2.489 | 11.615 | 0.847 | 2.151 | 4.530 |
| 2337000 | 1.663 | 9.797 | 8.969 | 57.73 | 6.518 | 13.081 | 5.110 | 9.231 | 3.041 |
| 2338000 | 4.430 | 13.407 | 6.757 | 4.36 | 10.547 | 14.546 | 9.372 | 6.944 | 1.554 |
| 2339000 | 7.196 | 17.016 | 4.545 | 82.66 | 14.577 | 16.012 | 0.358 | 4.656 | 0.065 |
| | | | | | | | | | |
| 2340000 | 0.090 | 20.626 | 2.333 | 29.29 | 18.606 | 17.478 | 4.621 | 2.369 | 4.400 |
| 2341000 | 2.857 | 24.236 | 0.121 | 107.60 | 22.636 | 18.944 | 8.884 | 0.082 | 2.912 |
| 2342000 | 5.624 | 3.544 | 12.226 | 54.23 | 26.665 | 20.410 | 13.146 | 7.161 | 1.423 |
| 2343000 | 8.391 | 7.154 | 10.014 | 0.86 | 30.694 | 21.875 | 4.132 | 4.874 | 5.758 |
| 2344000 | 1.285 | 10.765 | 7.803 | 79.16 | 2.595 | 23.341 | 8.395 | 2.586 | 4.270 |
| | | | | | | | | | |
| 2345000 | 4.052 | 14.375 | 5.591 | 25.79 | 6.625 | 1.032 | 12.657 | 0.299 | 2.781 |
| 2346000 | 6.818 | 17.985 | 3.379 | 104.09 | 10.654 | 2.497 | 3.644 | 7.379 | 1.293 |
| 2347000 | 9.585 | 21.595 | 1.167 | 50.72 | 14.683 | 3.963 | 7.906 | 5.091 | 5.628 |
| 2348000 | 2.479 | 0.900 | 13.272 | 129.03 | 18.713 | 5.428 | 12.168 | 2.804 | 4.139 |
| 2349000 | 5.246 | 4.510 | 11.061 | 75.66 | 22.742 | 6.894 | 3.155 | 0.517 | 2.651 |
| 2350000 | 8.013 | 8.120 | 8.848 | 22.29 | 26.771 | 8.360 | 7.417 | 7.596 | 1.163 |

# TABLE II*a*.

Epochs and Arguments for each Thousandth Day, from 2300000 to 2400000.

For Washington Mean Noon.

| Day of Julian Period. | Arg. 18. | 19. | 20. | 21. | 22. | 23. | 24. | 25. | 26. |
|---|---|---|---|---|---|---|---|---|---|
| | d. | d. | d. | d. | d. | d. | d. | d. | d. |
| 2350000 | 8.013 | 8.120 | 8.848 | 22.29 | 26.771 | 8.360 | 7.417 | 7.596 | 1.163 |
| 2351000 | 0.907 | 11.730 | 6.636 | 100.59 | 30.801 | 9.826 | 11.679 | 5.309 | 5.498 |
| 2352000 | 3.674 | 15.340 | 4.424 | 47.22 | 2.702 | 11.292 | 2.666 | 3.021 | 4.010 |
| 2353000 | 6.441 | 18.950 | 2.212 | 125.52 | 6.731 | 12.757 | 6.929 | 0.734 | 2.521 |
| 2354000 | 9.208 | 22.560 | 0.000 | 72.15 | 10.761 | 14.223 | 11.191 | 7.814 | 1.033 |
| 2355000 | 2.102 | 1.868 | 12.106 | 18.78 | 14.790 | 15.689 | 2.177 | 5.526 | 5.368 |
| 2356000 | 4.869 | 5.478 | 9.894 | 97.09 | 18.819 | 17.154 | 6.440 | 3.239 | 3.879 |
| 2357000 | 7.636 | 9.088 | 7.682 | 43.72 | 22.849 | 18.620 | 10.702 | 0.951 | 2.391 |
| 2358000 | 0.530 | 12.697 | 5.470 | 122.02 | 26.878 | 20.085 | 1.688 | 8.031 | 0.903 |
| 2359000 | 3.297 | 16.307 | 3.258 | 68.65 | 30.907 | 21.551 | 5.951 | 5.744 | 5.238 |
| 2360000 | 6.064 | 19.917 | 1.046 | 15.28 | 2.809 | 23.017 | 10.214 | 3.457 | 3.749 |
| 2361000 | 8.830 | 23.527 | 13.151 | 93.58 | 6.838 | 0.708 | 1.200 | 1.169 | 2.261 |
| 2362000 | 1.724 | 2.835 | 10.940 | 40.20 | 10.867 | 2.174 | 5.463 | 8.250 | 0.773 |
| 2363000 | 4.491 | 6.445 | 8.728 | 118.51 | 14.897 | 3.639 | 9.725 | 5.961 | 5.107 |
| 2364000 | 7.258 | 10.055 | 6.516 | 65.14 | 18.926 | 5.105 | 0.711 | 3.674 | 3.619 |
| 2365000 | 0.152 | 13.665 | 4.304 | 11.78 | 22.955 | 6.571 | 4.974 | 1.387 | 2.131 |
| 2366000 | 2.919 | 17.274 | 2.092 | 90.08 | 26.984 | 8.036 | 9.236 | 8.466 | 0.643 |
| 2367000 | 5.686 | 20.884 | 14.197 | 36.71 | 31.014 | 9.502 | 0.223 | 6.179 | 4.977 |
| 2368000 | 8.452 | 0.192 | 11.985 | 115.01 | 2.915 | 10.967 | 4.485 | 3.892 | 3.489 |
| 2369000 | 1.347 | 3.803 | 9.774 | 61.64 | 6.944 | 12.433 | 8.748 | 1.604 | 2.001 |
| 2370000 | 4.113 | 7.412 | 7.562 | 8.27 | 10.974 | 13.899 | 13.010 | 8.684 | 0.513 |
| 2371000 | 6.880 | 11.022 | 5.350 | 86.57 | 15.003 | 15.365 | 3.997 | 6.396 | 4.847 |
| 2372000 | 9.647 | 14.632 | 3.138 | 33.20 | 19.032 | 16.831 | 8.259 | 4.109 | 3.359 |
| 2373000 | 2.541 | 18.242 | 0.926 | 111.51 | 23.062 | 18.296 | 12.521 | 1.822 | 1.871 |
| 2374000 | 5.308 | 21.852 | 13.031 | 58.14 | 27.091 | 19.762 | 3.508 | 8.901 | 0.383 |
| 2375000 | 8.075 | 1.160 | 10.819 | 4.77 | 31.120 | 21.228 | 7.770 | 6.614 | 4.717 |
| 2376000 | 0.969 | 4.770 | 8.607 | 83.07 | 3.022 | 22.693 | 12.033 | 4.327 | 3.229 |
| 2377000 | 3.736 | 8.379 | 6.396 | 29.70 | 7.051 | 0.384 | 3.019 | 2.039 | 1.741 |
| 2378000 | 6.503 | 11.989 | 4.184 | 108.00 | 11.080 | 1.849 | 7.282 | 9.119 | 0.253 |
| 2379000 | 9.270 | 15.599 | 1.972 | 54.63 | 15.110 | 3.315 | 11.544 | 6.831 | 4.587 |
| 2380000 | 2.164 | 19.209 | 14.077 | 1.27 | 19.139 | 4.781 | 2.531 | 4.544 | 3.099 |
| 2381000 | 4.931 | 22.819 | 11.865 | 79.57 | 23.168 | 6.247 | 6.793 | 2.257 | 1.611 |
| 2382000 | 7.697 | 2.127 | 9.653 | 26.20 | 27.198 | 7.713 | 11.055 | 9.337 | 0.123 |
| 2383000 | 0.591 | 5.737 | 7.442 | 104.50 | 31.227 | 9.178 | 2.042 | 7.049 | 4.457 |
| 2384000 | 3.358 | 9.347 | 5.230 | 51.13 | 3.128 | 10.644 | 6.305 | 4.762 | 2.969 |
| 2385000 | 6.125 | 12.957 | 3.018 | 129.43 | 7.158 | 12.110 | 10.568 | 2.475 | 1.481 |
| 2386000 | 8.892 | 16.567 | 0.806 | 76.06 | 11.187 | 13.575 | 1.555 | 0.187 | 5.815 |
| 2387000 | 1.786 | 20.177 | 12.911 | 22.70 | 15.216 | 15.041 | 5.816 | 7.267 | 4.327 |
| 2388000 | 4.553 | 23.787 | 10.699 | 101.00 | 19.245 | 16.506 | 10.078 | 4.980 | 2.839 |
| 2389000 | 7.319 | 3.095 | 8.487 | 47.63 | 23.275 | 17.972 | 1.065 | 2.692 | 1.351 |
| 2390000 | 0.214 | 6.705 | 6.276 | 125.93 | 27.304 | 19.438 | 5.327 | 0.405 | 5.685 |
| 2391000 | 2.981 | 10.315 | 4.064 | 72.56 | 31.334 | 20.904 | 9.590 | 7.484 | 4.197 |
| 2392000 | 5.748 | 13.925 | 1.852 | 19.19 | 3.235 | 22.370 | 0.576 | 5.197 | 2.709 |
| 2393000 | 8.514 | 17.535 | 13.957 | 97.50 | 7.264 | 0.060 | 4.839 | 2.910 | 1.221 |
| 2394000 | 1.408 | 21.145 | 11.745 | 44.13 | 11.294 | 1.526 | 9.102 | 0.622 | 5.555 |
| 2395000 | 4.175 | 0.453 | 9.534 | 122.43 | 15.323 | 2.992 | 0.088 | 7.702 | 4.067 |
| 2396000 | 6.942 | 4.063 | 7.322 | 69.06 | 19.352 | 4.457 | 4.350 | 5.415 | 2.579 |
| 2397000 | 9.709 | 7.673 | 5.110 | 15.69 | 23.381 | 5.923 | 8.613 | 3.127 | 1.090 |
| 2398000 | 2.603 | 11.283 | 2.898 | 93.99 | 27.411 | 7.388 | 12.875 | 0.840 | 5.425 |
| 2399000 | 5.370 | 14.893 | 0.686 | 40.62 | 31.440 | 8.854 | 3.862 | 7.920 | 3.937 |
| 2400000 | 8.137 | 18.503 | 12.791 | 118.93 | 3.342 | 10.320 | 8.124 | 5.633 | 2.449 |

# TABLE II*a*.

Epochs and Arguments for each Thousandth Day, from 2300000 to 2400000.

For Washington Mean Noon.

| Day of Julian Period. | Arg. 27. | 28. | 29. | 30. | 31. | 32. | 33. | 34. | 35. |
|---|---|---|---|---|---|---|---|---|---|
| | d. | d. | d. | d. | d. | d. | d. | d. | d. |
| 2300000 | 15.42 | 22.494 | 32.009 | 2.076 | 14.53 | 4.53 | 23.94 | 5.18 | 8.26 |
| 2301000 | 8.19 | 20.922 | 16.336 | 6.466 | 3.78 | 6.72 | 17.97 | 2.75 | 2.69 |
| 2302000 | 0.96 | 19.350 | 0.662 | 0.486 | 8.34 | 8.91 | 12.00 | 0.32 | 21.06 |
| 2303000 | 19.56 | 17.778 | 17.753 | 4.877 | 12.91 | 11.10 | 6.04 | 24.98 | 15.48 |
| 2304000 | 12.33 | 16.205 | 2.080 | 9.267 | 2.15 | 13.29 | 0.07 | 22.55 | 9.91 |
| 2305000 | 5.10 | 14.633 | 19.171 | 3.287 | 6.71 | 15.48 | 26.55 | 20.12 | 4.34 |
| 2306000 | 23.70 | 13.061 | 3.497 | 7.678 | 11.28 | 1.04 | 20.58 | 17.69 | 22.70 |
| 2307000 | 16.47 | 11.488 | 20.588 | 1.697 | 0.52 | 3.23 | 14.61 | 15.26 | 17.13 |
| 2308000 | 9.24 | 9.916 | 4.915 | 6.087 | 5.09 | 5.42 | 8.65 | 12.83 | 11.56 |
| 2309000 | 2.01 | 8.344 | 22.006 | 0.107 | 9.65 | 7.61 | 2.68 | 10.40 | 5.98 |
| 2310000 | 20.61 | 6.772 | 6.332 | 4.498 | 14.22 | 9.80 | 29.16 | 7.97 | 0.41 |
| 2311000 | 13.38 | 5.200 | 23.424 | 8.888 | 3.46 | 11.99 | 23.19 | 5.54 | 18.78 |
| 2312000 | 6.15 | 3.628 | 7.750 | 2.908 | 8.02 | 14.18 | 17.22 | 3.11 | 13.21 |
| 2313000 | 24.75 | 2.055 | 24.841 | 7.299 | 12.59 | 16.37 | 11.25 | 0.68 | 7.63 |
| 2314000 | 17.52 | 0.483 | 9.168 | 1.318 | 1.83 | 1.93 | 5.29 | 25.34 | 2.06 |
| 2315000 | 10.29 | 37.433 | 26.259 | 5.709 | 6.40 | 4.12 | 31.77 | 22.91 | 20.43 |
| 2316000 | 3.06 | 35.860 | 10.585 | 10.099 | 10.96 | 6.31 | 25.78 | 20.48 | 14.85 |
| 2317000 | 21.66 | 34.288 | 27.676 | 4.119 | 0.21 | 8.50 | 19.81 | 18.05 | 9.28 |
| 2318000 | 14.43 | 32.715 | 12.003 | 8.509 | 4.77 | 10.69 | 13.84 | 15.62 | 3.70 |
| 2319000 | 7.20 | 31.143 | 29.094 | 2.529 | 9.33 | 12.88 | 7.88 | 13.19 | 22.07 |
| 2320000 | 25.80 | 29.571 | 13.421 | 6.919 | 13.90 | 15.07 | 1.91 | 10.76 | 16.50 |
| 2321000 | 18.57 | 27.999 | 30.511 | 0.939 | 3.14 | 0.63 | 28.41 | 8.33 | 10.93 |
| 2322000 | 11.34 | 26.427 | 14.838 | 5.329 | 7.71 | 2.82 | 22.44 | 5.90 | 5.35 |
| 2323000 | 4.11 | 24.854 | 31.929 | 9.720 | 12.28 | 5.01 | 16.47 | 3.47 | 23.72 |
| 2324000 | 22.71 | 23.282 | 16.256 | 3.740 | 1.52 | 7.20 | 10.51 | 1.04 | 18.15 |
| 2325000 | 15.48 | 21.710 | 0.582 | 8.130 | 6.08 | 9.39 | 4.54 | 25.70 | 12.57 |
| 2326000 | 8.25 | 20.137 | 17.673 | 2.149 | 10.64 | 11.58 | 31.02 | 23.27 | 7.00 |
| 2327000 | 1.02 | 18.565 | 2.000 | 6.540 | 15.21 | 13.77 | 25.05 | 20.84 | 1.42 |
| 2328000 | 19.62 | 16.992 | 19.091 | 0.560 | 4.46 | 15.96 | 19.08 | 18.41 | 19.79 |
| 2329000 | 12.39 | 15.420 | 3.418 | 4.951 | 9.02 | 1.52 | 13.12 | 15.98 | 14.22 |
| 2330000 | 5.16 | 13.848 | 20.509 | 9.341 | 13.59 | 3.72 | 7.15 | 13.55 | 8.65 |
| 2331000 | 23.76 | 12.276 | 4.835 | 3.361 | 2.83 | 5.91 | 1.18 | 11.12 | 3.07 |
| 2332000 | 16.53 | 10.704 | 21.926 | 7.751 | 7.39 | 8.10 | 27.66 | 8.69 | 21.44 |
| 2333000 | 9.30 | 9.132 | 6.253 | 1.771 | 11.95 | 10.29 | 21.69 | 6.26 | 15.87 |
| 2334000 | 27.90 | 7.559 | 23.344 | 6.161 | 1.20 | 12.48 | 15.72 | 3.83 | 10.29 |
| 2335000 | 20.67 | 5.987 | 7.671 | 0.181 | 5.77 | 14.67 | 9.76 | 1.40 | 4.72 |
| 2336000 | 13.44 | 4.415 | 24.763 | 4.572 | 10.33 | 0.23 | 3.79 | 26.06 | 23.08 |
| 2337000 | 6.21 | 2.842 | 9.088 | 8.962 | 14.90 | 2.42 | 30.27 | 23.63 | 17.51 |
| 2338000 | 24.80 | 1.270 | 26.179 | 2.982 | 4.14 | 4.61 | 24.30 | 21.20 | 11.94 |
| 2339000 | 17.58 | 38.220 | 10.506 | 7.372 | 8.70 | 6.80 | 18.33 | 18.77 | 6.37 |
| 2340000 | 10.35 | 36.648 | 27.597 | 1.392 | 13.27 | 8.99 | 12.37 | 16.34 | 0.79 |
| 2341000 | 3.12 | 35.076 | 11.924 | 5.782 | 2.51 | 11.18 | 6.40 | 13.91 | 19.16 |
| 2342000 | 21.71 | 33.504 | 29.015 | 10.173 | 7.08 | 13.37 | 0.43 | 11.48 | 13.59 |
| 2343000 | 14.49 | 31.931 | 13.342 | 4.193 | 11.64 | 15.56 | 26.91 | 9.05 | 8.01 |
| 2344000 | 07.26 | 30.359 | 30.433 | 8.583 | 0.89 | 1.12 | 20.94 | 6.62 | 2.44 |
| 2345000 | 0.02 | 28.787 | 14.760 | 2.603 | 5.45 | 3.31 | 14.98 | 4.19 | 20.81 |
| 2346000 | 18.62 | 27.214 | 31.850 | 6.993 | 10.01 | 5.50 | 9.01 | 1.76 | 15.24 |
| 2347000 | 11.40 | 25.642 | 16.178 | 1.013 | 14.58 | 7.69 | 3.04 | 26.42 | 9.66 |
| 2348000 | 4.17 | 24.069 | 0.504 | 5.403 | 3.82 | 9.88 | 29.52 | 23.99 | 4.09 |
| 2349000 | 22.76 | 22.497 | 17.595 | 9.794 | 8.39 | 12.07 | 23.55 | 21.56 | 22.45 |
| 2350000 | 15.54 | 20.925 | 1.922 | 3.814 | 12.95 | 14.26 | 17.59 | 19.13 | 16.88 |

# TABLE IIa.

Epochs and Arguments for each Thousandth Day, from 2300000 to 2400000.

For Washington Mean Noon.

| Day of Julian Period. | Arg. 27. | 28. | 29. | 30. | 31. | 32. | 33. | 34. | 35. |
|---|---|---|---|---|---|---|---|---|---|
| | d. | d. | d. | d. | d. | d. | d. | d. | d. |
| 2350000 | 15.54 | 20.925 | 1.922 | 3.814 | 12.95 | 14.26 | 17.59 | 19.13 | 16.88 |
| 2351000 | 8.31 | 19.353 | 19.013 | 8.204 | 2.20 | 16.45 | 11.62 | 16.70 | 11.31 |
| 2352000 | 1.08 | 17.780 | 3.340 | 2.224 | 6.76 | 2.01 | 5.65 | 14.27 | 5.73 |
| 2353000 | 19.67 | 16.208 | 20.431 | 6.614 | 11.32 | 4.20 | 32.13 | 11.84 | 24.10 |
| 2354000 | 12.45 | 14.635 | 4.757 | 0.634 | 0.57 | 6.39 | 26.16 | 9.41 | 18.53 |
| 2355000 | 5.23 | 13.063 | 21.848 | 5.024 | 5.13 | 8.58 | 20.20 | 6.98 | 12.96 |
| 2356000 | 23.81 | 11.491 | 6.175 | 9.415 | 9.70 | 10.77 | 14.23 | 4.55 | 7.38 |
| 2357000 | 16.58 | 9.918 | 23.266 | 3.435 | 14.26 | 12.96 | 8.26 | 2.12 | 1.81 |
| 2358000 | 9.36 | 8.346 | 7.593 | 7.825 | 3.51 | 15.15 | 2.29 | 26.78 | 20.18 |
| 2359000 | 2.13 | 6.773 | 24.684 | 1.845 | 8.07 | 0.71 | 28.77 | 24.35 | 14.60 |
| 2360000 | 20.72 | 5.201 | 9.011 | 6.235 | 12.64 | 2.90 | 22.81 | 21.92 | 9.03 |
| 2361000 | 13.50 | 3.629 | 26.102 | 0.255 | 1.88 | 5.09 | 16.84 | 19.49 | 3.46 |
| 2362000 | 6.27 | 2.057 | 10.429 | 4.645 | 6.44 | 7.28 | 10.87 | 17.06 | 21.82 |
| 2363000 | 24.86 | 0.484 | 27.520 | 9.036 | 11.01 | 9.47 | 4.90 | 14.63 | 16.25 |
| 2364000 | 17.63 | 37.434 | 11.846 | 3.056 | 0.25 | 11.66 | 31.38 | 12.20 | 10.68 |
| 2365000 | 10.41 | 35.862 | 28.938 | 7.446 | 4.82 | 13.85 | 25.42 | 9.77 | 5.10 |
| 2366000 | 3.18 | 34.289 | 13.265 | 1.466 | 9.38 | 16.04 | 19.45 | 7.34 | 23.47 |
| 2367000 | 21.77 | 32.717 | 30.355 | 5.856 | 13.95 | 1.60 | 13.48 | 4.91 | 17.90 |
| 2368000 | 14.54 | 31.144 | 14.682 | 10.247 | 3.19 | 3.79 | 7.51 | 2.48 | 12.32 |
| 2369000 | 7.32 | 29.572 | 31.773 | 4.266 | 7.75 | 5.99 | 1.54 | 0.05 | 6.75 |
| 2370000 | 0.08 | 28.000 | 16.100 | 8.657 | 12.32 | 8.18 | 28.03 | 24.71 | 1.18 |
| 2371000 | 18.68 | 26.428 | 0.427 | 2.676 | 1.56 | 10.37 | 22.06 | 22.28 | 19.55 |
| 2372000 | 11.46 | 24.856 | 17.518 | 7.067 | 6.13 | 12.56 | 16.09 | 19.85 | 13.97 |
| 2373000 | 4.23 | 23.283 | 1.845 | 1.087 | 10.69 | 14.75 | 10.12 | 17.42 | 8.40 |
| 2374000 | 22.82 | 21.711 | 18.936 | 5.477 | 15.26 | 0.31 | 4.15 | 14.99 | 2.82 |
| 2375000 | 15.59 | 20.139 | 3.263 | 9.868 | 4.50 | 2.50 | 30.64 | 12.56 | 21.19 |
| 2376000 | 8.37 | 18.566 | 20.354 | 3.887 | 9.06 | 4.69 | 24.67 | 10.13 | 15.62 |
| 2377000 | 1.14 | 16.994 | 4.682 | 8.278 | 13.63 | 6.88 | 18.70 | 7.70 | 10.04 |
| 2378000 | 19.73 | 15.421 | 21.772 | 2.298 | 2.87 | 9.07 | 12.73 | 5.27 | 4.47 |
| 2379000 | 12.50 | 13.849 | 6.099 | 6.688 | 7.44 | 11.26 | 6.76 | 2.84 | 22.84 |
| 2380000 | 5.28 | 12.277 | 23.190 | 0.708 | 12.00 | 13.45 | 0.80 | 0.41 | 17.27 |
| 2381000 | 23.87 | 10.705 | 7.516 | 5.098 | 1.25 | 15.64 | 27.28 | 25.07 | 11.69 |
| 2382000 | 16.64 | 9.132 | 24.608 | 9.489 | 5.81 | 1.20 | 21.31 | 22.64 | 6.12 |
| 2383000 | 9.42 | 7.560 | 8.934 | 3.508 | 10.37 | 3.39 | 15.34 | 20.21 | 0.54 |
| 2384000 | 2.19 | 5.987 | 26.026 | 7.899 | 14.94 | 5.58 | 9.37 | 17.78 | 18.91 |
| 2385000 | 20.78 | 4.415 | 10.352 | 1.918 | 4.19 | 7.77 | 3.41 | 15.35 | 13.34 |
| 2386000 | 13.55 | 2.843 | 27.444 | 6.309 | 8.75 | 9.96 | 29.89 | 12.92 | 7.77 |
| 2387000 | 6.33 | 1.270 | 11.770 | 0.329 | 13.31 | 12.15 | 23.92 | 10.49 | 2.19 |
| 2388000 | 24.92 | 38.220 | 28.861 | 4.719 | 2.56 | 14.34 | 17.95 | 8.06 | 20.56 |
| 2389000 | 17.69 | 36.647 | 13.188 | 9.110 | 7.12 | 16.53 | 11.98 | 5.63 | 14.99 |
| 2390000 | 10.47 | 35.075 | 30.279 | 3.129 | 11.68 | 2.09 | 6.02 | 3.20 | 9.41 |
| 2391000 | 3.24 | 33.503 | 14.606 | 7.520 | 0.93 | 4.28 | 0.05 | 0.77 | 3.84 |
| 2392000 | 21.83 | 31.931 | 31.697 | 1.539 | 5.49 | 6.47 | 26.53 | 25.43 | 22.21 |
| 2393000 | 14.61 | 30.358 | 16.024 | 5.930 | 10.06 | 8.66 | 20.56 | 23.00 | 16.63 |
| 2394000 | 7.38 | 28.786 | 0.351 | 10.321 | 14.62 | 10.85 | 14.59 | 20.57 | 11.06 |
| 2395000 | 0.14 | 27.214 | 17.442 | 4.340 | 3.87 | 13.04 | 8.63 | 18.14 | 5.49 |
| 2396000 | 18.74 | 25.641 | 1.769 | 8.731 | 8.43 | 15.23 | 2.66 | 15.71 | 23.85 |
| 2397000 | 11.52 | 24.069 | 18.860 | 2.750 | 13.00 | 0.79 | 29.14 | 13.28 | 18.28 |
| 2398000 | 4.29 | 22.496 | 3.187 | 7.141 | 2.24 | 2.98 | 23.17 | 10.85 | 12.71 |
| 2399000 | 22.88 | 20.924 | 20.278 | 1.161 | 6.80 | 5.17 | 17.20 | 8.42 | 7.13 |
| 2400000 | 15.66 | 19.352 | 4.605 | 5.551 | 11.37 | 7.36 | 11.24 | 5.99 | 1.56 |

# TABLE IIa.

Epochs and Arguments for each Thousandth Day, from 2300000 to 2400000.

For Washington Mean Noon.

| Day of Julian Period. | Arg. 36. | 37. | 38. | 39. | 40. | 41. | 42. | 43. | 44. |
|---|---|---|---|---|---|---|---|---|---|
| | d. | d. | d. | d. | d. | d. | d. | d. | d. |
| 2300000 | 2.44 | 27.6 | 18.63 | 10.6 | 3.86 | 5.90 | 1.84 | 8.97 | 7.8 |
| 2301000 | 0.96 | 11.8 | 4.04 | 10.8 | 5.14 | 2.43 | 7.34 | 5.86 | 5.3 |
| 2302000 | 13.21 | 33.5 | 8.23 | 11.0 | 6.44 | 16.88 | 2.70 | 2.74 | 2.7 |
| 2303000 | 11.74 | 17.6 | 12.42 | 11.2 | 7.73 | 13.41 | 8.20 | 14.18 | 0.1 |
| 2304000 | 10.26 | 1.8 | 16.62 | 11.5 | 9.03 | 9.94 | 3.56 | 11.06 | 20.3 |
| 2305000 | 8.79 | 23.5 | 2.02 | 11.7 | 10.32 | 6.47 | 9.06 | 7.95 | 17.7 |
| 2306000 | 7.32 | 7.6 | 6.22 | 11.9 | 11.61 | 3.01 | 4.43 | 4.83 | 15.1 |
| 2307000 | 5.84 | 29.4 | 10.41 | 12.2 | 12.91 | 17.45 | 9.92 | 1.72 | 12.5 |
| 2308000 | 4.37 | 13.5 | 14.61 | 12.4 | 14.20 | 13.98 | 5.29 | 13.15 | 9.9 |
| 2309000 | 2.90 | 35.2 | 0.01 | 12.6 | 15.49 | 10.51 | 0.64 | 10.04 | 7.3 |
| 2310000 | 1.42 | 19.3 | 4.21 | 12.8 | 16.78 | 7.05 | 6.15 | 6.92 | 4.7 |
| 2311000 | 13.67 | 3.4 | 8.40 | 13.0 | 18.07 | 3.58 | 1.51 | 3.81 | 2.1 |
| 2312000 | 12.20 | 25.2 | 12.60 | 13.2 | 0.52 | 0.11 | 7.00 | 0.70 | 22.4 |
| 2313000 | 10.72 | 9.3 | 16.79 | 13.4 | 1.82 | 14.55 | 2.37 | 12.13 | 19.8 |
| 2314000 | 9.25 | 31.0 | 2.19 | 13.7 | 3.11 | 11.08 | 7.87 | 9.01 | 17.2 |
| 2315000 | 7.78 | 15.2 | 6.39 | 13.9 | 4.40 | 7.61 | 3.23 | 5.90 | 14.6 |
| 2316000 | 6.30 | 36.9 | 10.58 | 14.1 | 5.70 | 4.14 | 8.73 | 2.79 | 12.0 |
| 2317000 | 4.83 | 21.0 | 14.78 | 14.4 | 6.99 | 0.67 | 4.10 | 14.23 | 9.4 |
| 2318000 | 3.36 | 5.1 | 0.18 | 14.6 | 8.29 | 15.12 | 9.59 | 11.10 | 6.8 |
| 2319000 | 1.88 | 26.9 | 4.38 | 14.8 | 9.58 | 11.65 | 4.95 | 7.99 | 4.2 |
| 2320000 | 0.41 | 11.0 | 8.57 | 15.0 | 10.87 | 8.19 | 0.31 | 4.88 | 1.6 |
| 2321000 | 12.66 | 32.7 | 12.77 | 15.2 | 12.16 | 4.72 | 5.82 | 1.77 | 21.8 |
| 2322000 | 11.18 | 16.8 | 16.96 | 15.4 | 13.45 | 1.25 | 1.17 | 13.19 | 19.2 |
| 2323000 | 9.71 | 1.0 | 2.37 | 15.6 | 14.74 | 15.70 | 6.68 | 10.08 | 16.6 |
| 2324000 | 8.23 | 22.7 | 6.56 | 15.9 | 16.04 | 12.22 | 2.04 | 6.97 | 14.1 |
| 2325000 | 6.76 | 6.8 | 10.76 | 16.1 | 17.33 | 8.75 | 7.53 | 3.86 | 11.5 |
| 2326000 | 5.29 | 28.6 | 14.95 | 16.3 | 18.62 | 5.28 | 2.90 | 0.75 | 8.9 |
| 2327000 | 3.82 | 12.7 | 0.35 | 16.6 | 1.08 | 1.81 | 8.39 | 12.17 | 6.3 |
| 2328000 | 2.34 | 34.4 | 4.55 | 16.8 | 2.37 | 16.26 | 3.76 | 9.06 | 3.7 |
| 2329000 | 0.87 | 18.5 | 8.75 | 17.0 | 3.66 | 12.79 | 9.26 | 5.95 | 1.1 |
| 2330000 | 13.12 | 2.6 | 12.94 | 17.2 | 4.95 | 9.33 | 4.62 | 2.84 | 21.3 |
| 2331000 | 11.64 | 24.4 | 17.13 | 17.4 | 6.24 | 5.86 | 10.12 | 14.27 | 18.7 |
| 2332000 | 10.17 | 8.5 | 2.54 | 17.6 | 7.53 | 2.39 | 5.48 | 11.15 | 16.1 |
| 2333000 | 8.69 | 30.2 | 6.73 | 17.8 | 8.82 | 16.84 | 0.84 | 8.04 | 13.5 |
| 2334000 | 7.22 | 14.4 | 10.93 | 18.0 | 10.12 | 13.37 | 6.35 | 4.93 | 10.9 |
| 2335000 | 5.75 | 36.1 | 15.12 | 18.3 | 11.41 | 9.90 | 1.70 | 1.82 | 8.3 |
| 2336000 | 4.28 | 20.2 | 0.53 | 18.5 | 12.70 | 6.43 | 7.20 | 13.24 | 5.8 |
| 2337000 | 2.80 | 4.3 | 4.72 | 18.7 | 14.00 | 2.96 | 2.56 | 10.13 | 3.2 |
| 2338000 | 1.33 | 26.1 | 8.91 | 18.9 | 15.29 | 17.41 | 8.06 | 7.02 | 0.6 |
| 2339000 | 13.58 | 10.2 | 13.12 | 19.1 | 16.58 | 13.94 | 3.43 | 3.91 | 20.8 |
| 2340000 | 12.10 | 31.9 | 17.31 | 19.3 | 17.87 | 10.47 | 8.94 | 0.79 | 18.2 |
| 2341000 | 10.63 | 16.0 | 2.71 | 19.5 | 0.32 | 7.00 | 4.29 | 12.22 | 15.6 |
| 2342000 | 9.15 | 0.2 | 6.90 | 19.7 | 1.61 | 3.53 | 9.79 | 9.11 | 13.0 |
| 2343000 | 7.68 | 21.9 | 11.10 | 19.9 | 2.91 | 0.06 | 5.15 | 6.00 | 10.4 |
| 2344000 | 6.21 | 6.0 | 15.29 | 20.2 | 4.20 | 14.51 | 0.51 | 2.88 | 7.8 |
| 2345000 | 4.73 | 27.8 | 0.70 | 20.4 | 5.49 | 11.04 | 6.01 | 14.32 | 5.2 |
| 2346000 | 3.26 | 11.9 | 4.89 | 20.6 | 6.78 | 7.57 | 1.37 | 11.20 | 2.6 |
| 2347000 | 1.79 | 33.6 | 9.09 | 20.9 | 8.07 | 4.10 | 6.87 | 8.09 | 0.0 |
| 2348000 | 0.31 | 17.7 | 13.28 | 21.1 | 9.37 | 0.63 | 2.23 | 4.97 | 20.3 |
| 2349000 | 12.56 | 1.9 | 17.48 | 21.3 | 10.66 | 15.08 | 7.73 | 1.86 | 17.7 |
| 2350000 | 11.09 | 23.6 | 2.88 | 21.5 | 11.95 | 11.61 | 3.09 | 13.29 | 15.1 |

# TABLE II*a*.

Epochs and Arguments for each Thousandth Day, from 2300000 to 2400000.

For Washington Mean Noon.

| Day of Julian Period. | Arg. **36.** | **37.** | **38.** | **39.** | **40.** | **41.** | **42.** | **43.** | **44.** |
|---|---|---|---|---|---|---|---|---|---|
| | d. | d. | d. | d. | d. | d. | d. | d. | d. |
| 2350000 | 11.09 | 23.6 | 2.88 | 21.5 | 11.95 | 11.61 | 3.09 | 13.29 | 15.1 |
| 2351000 | 9.61 | 7.7 | 7.07 | 21.7 | 13.24 | 8.14 | 8.59 | 10.18 | 12.5 |
| 2352000 | 8.14 | 29.4 | 11.27 | 21.9 | 14.53 | 4.67 | 3.96 | 7.06 | 9.9 |
| 2353000 | 6.67 | 13.6 | 15.46 | 22.1 | 15.83 | 1.20 | 9.45 | 3.95 | 7.3 |
| 2354000 | 5.19 | 35.3 | 0.87 | 22.4 | 17.12 | 15.65 | 4.82 | 0.84 | 4.7 |
| 2355000 | 3.72 | 19.4 | 5.06 | 22.6 | 18.41 | 12.17 | 0.18 | 12.27 | 2.1 |
| 2356000 | 2.25 | 3.5 | 9.26 | 22.8 | 0.86 | 8.70 | 5.68 | 9.15 | 22.3 |
| 2357000 | 0.77 | 25.3 | 13.45 | 23.1 | 2.15 | 5.23 | 1.04 | 6.04 | 19.7 |
| 2358000 | 13.02 | 9.4 | 17.65 | 23.3 | 3.45 | 1.76 | 6.54 | 2.93 | 17.1 |
| 2359000 | 11.55 | 31.1 | 3.05 | 23.5 | 4.74 | 16.21 | 1.90 | 14.37 | 14.5 |
| 2360000 | 10.07 | 15.2 | 7.25 | 23.7 | 6.03 | 12.74 | 7.40 | 11.24 | 12.0 |
| 2361000 | 8.60 | 37.0 | 11.44 | 23.9 | 7.32 | 9.27 | 2.76 | 8.13 | 9.4 |
| 2362000 | 7.13 | 21.1 | 15.64 | 24.1 | 8.61 | 5.80 | 8.26 | 5.02 | 6.8 |
| 2363000 | 5.65 | 5.2 | 1.04 | 24.3 | 9.91 | 2.33 | 3.62 | 1.91 | 4.2 |
| 2364000 | 4.18 | 27.0 | 5.23 | 24.5 | 11.20 | 16.78 | 9.12 | 13.34 | 1.6 |
| 2365000 | 2.71 | 11.1 | 9.43 | 24.8 | 12.49 | 13.31 | 4.49 | 10.22 | 21.8 |
| 2366000 | 1.24 | 32.8 | 13.62 | 25.0 | 13.78 | 9.84 | 9.98 | 7.11 | 19.2 |
| 2367000 | 13.48 | 17.0 | 17.82 | 25.2 | 15.07 | 6.37 | 5.35 | 4.00 | 16.6 |
| 2368000 | 12.01 | 1.1 | 3.22 | 25.4 | 16.37 | 2.90 | 0.70 | 0.89 | 14.0 |
| 2369000 | 10.53 | 22.8 | 7.42 | 25.6 | 17.66 | 17.35 | 6.21 | 12.31 | 11.4 |
| 2370000 | 9.06 | 6.9 | 11.61 | 25.8 | 0.11 | 13.88 | 1.57 | 9.20 | 8.8 |
| 2371000 | 7.59 | 28.7 | 15.81 | 26.0 | 1.40 | 10.41 | 7.06 | 6.09 | 6.2 |
| 2372000 | 6.11 | 12.8 | 1.21 | 26.2 | 2.69 | 6.94 | 2.43 | 2.98 | 3.7 |
| 2373000 | 4.64 | 34.5 | 5.41 | 26.4 | 3.99 | 3.47 | 7.93 | 14.41 | 1.1 |
| 2374000 | 3.17 | 18.6 | 9.60 | 26.7 | 5.28 | 0.00 | 3.29 | 11.29 | 21.3 |
| 2375000 | 1.69 | 2.8 | 13.80 | 26.9 | 6.57 | 14.45 | 8.79 | 8.18 | 18.7 |
| 2376000 | 0.22 | 24.5 | 17.99 | 27.1 | 7.86 | 10.98 | 4.15 | 5.07 | 16.1 |
| 2377000 | 12.47 | 8.6 | 3.40 | 27.4 | 9.15 | 7.51 | 9.65 | 1.96 | 13.5 |
| 2378000 | 11.00 | 30.4 | 7.59 | 27.6 | 10.45 | 4.04 | 5.01 | 13.38 | 10.9 |
| 2379000 | 9.52 | 14.5 | 11.78 | 27.8 | 11.74 | 0.57 | 0.37 | 10.27 | 8.3 |
| 2380000 | 8.05 | 36.2 | 15.98 | 28.0 | 13.03 | 15.02 | 5.88 | 7.16 | 5.7 |
| 2381000 | 6.57 | 20.3 | 1.38 | 28.2 | 14.32 | 11.55 | 1.23 | 4.05 | 3.1 |
| 2382000 | 5.10 | 4.4 | 5.58 | 28.4 | 15.61 | 8.08 | 6.73 | 0.94 | 0.5 |
| 2383000 | 3.63 | 26.2 | 9.77 | 28.6 | 16.91 | 4.61 | 2.10 | 12.36 | 20.8 |
| 2384000 | 2.15 | 10.3 | 13.97 | 28.9 | 18.20 | 1.14 | 7.59 | 9.25 | 18.2 |
| 2385000 | 0.68 | 32.0 | 18.16 | 29.1 | 0.65 | 15.59 | 2.96 | 6.14 | 15.6 |
| 2386000 | 12.93 | 16.2 | 3.57 | 29.3 | 1.94 | 12.12 | 8.46 | 3.03 | 13.0 |
| 2387000 | 11.46 | 0.3 | 7.76 | 29.6 | 3.23 | 8.65 | 3.82 | 14.46 | 10.4 |
| 2388000 | 9.98 | 22.0 | 11.95 | 29.8 | 4.53 | 5.18 | 9.32 | 11.34 | 7.8 |
| 2389000 | 8.51 | 6.1 | 16.15 | 30.0 | 5.82 | 1.71 | 4.68 | 8.23 | 5.2 |
| 2390000 | 7.03 | 27.9 | 1.56 | 30.2 | 7.11 | 16.16 | 0.04 | 5.12 | 2.6 |
| 2391000 | 5.56 | 12.0 | 5.75 | 30.4 | 8.40 | 12.69 | 5.55 | 2.00 | 0.0 |
| 2392000 | 4.09 | 33.7 | 9.95 | 30.6 | 9.69 | 9.22 | 0.90 | 13.43 | 20.2 |
| 2393000 | 2.62 | 17.8 | 14.14 | 30.8 | 10.99 | 5.75 | 6.41 | 10.32 | 17.6 |
| 2394000 | 1.14 | 2.0 | 18.34 | 31.0 | 12.28 | 2.28 | 1.76 | 7.21 | 15.0 |
| 2395000 | 13.39 | 23.7 | 3.74 | 31.3 | 13.57 | 16.73 | 7.26 | 4.09 | 12.4 |
| 2396000 | 11.92 | 7.8 | 7.93 | 31.5 | 14.86 | 13.25 | 2.63 | 0.98 | 9.9 |
| 2397000 | 10.44 | 29.6 | 12.13 | 31.7 | 16.15 | 9.79 | 8.12 | 12.41 | 7.3 |
| 2398000 | 8.97 | 13.7 | 16.32 | 31.9 | 17.45 | 6.32 | 3.49 | 9.30 | 4.7 |
| 2399000 | 7.49 | 35.4 | 1.73 | 32.1 | 18.74 | 2.85 | 8.99 | 6.18 | 2.1 |
| 2400000 | 6.02 | 19.5 | 5.92 | 32.3 | 1.19 | 17.30 | 4.35 | 3.07 | 22.3 |

# TABLE IIa.

Epochs and Arguments for each Thousandth Day, from 2300000 to 2400000.

For Washington Mean Noon.

| Day of Julian Period. | Arg. 45. | 46. | 47. | 48. | 49. | 50. | 51. | 52. | 53. |
|---|---|---|---|---|---|---|---|---|---|
| | d. | d. | d. | d | d. | d. | d. | d. | d. |
| 2300000 | 3.87 | 23.2 | 12.49 | 22.74 | 1.5 | 15.1 | 8.53 | 0.73 | 94.82 |
| 2301000 | 6.77 | 7.7 | 9.08 | 4.98 | 6.0 | 13.7 | 6.60 | 16.70 | 36.96 |
| 2302000 | 9.66 | 21.2 | 5.67 | 17.15 | 10.4 | 12.2 | 4.67 | 7.45 | 96.65 |
| 2303000 | 12.56 | 5.8 | 2.25 | 29.32 | 2.2 | 10.8 | 2.74 | 23.42 | 38.79 |
| 2304000 | 15.46 | 19.3 | 12.97 | 11.56 | 6.7 | 9.3 | 0.81 | 14.17 | 98.48 |
| 2305000 | 1.46 | 3.9 | 9.56 | 23.73 | 11.3 | 7.9 | 17.09 | 4.92 | 40.62 |
| 2306000 | 4.36 | 17.4 | 6.15 | 5.97 | 3.0 | 6.5 | 15.16 | 20.89 | 100.20 |
| 2307000 | 7.25 | 2.0 | 2.74 | 18.14 | 7.5 | 5.0 | 13.23 | 11.64 | 42.45 |
| 2308000 | 10.15 | 15.5 | 13.46 | 0.38 | 12.1 | 3.6 | 11.30 | 2.38 | 102.13 |
| 2309000 | 13.05 | 0.0 | 10.05 | 12.55 | 3.7 | 2.1 | 9.37 | 18.36 | 44.28 |
| 2310000 | 15.95 | 13.6 | 6.64 | 24.73 | 8.3 | 0.7 | 7.44 | 9.10 | 103.96 |
| 2311000 | 1.95 | 27.1 | 3.23 | 6.96 | 0.0 | 24.3 | 5.51 | 25.08 | 46.11 |
| 2312000 | 4.84 | 11.7 | 13.95 | 19.14 | 4.5 | 22.9 | 3.58 | 15.83 | 105.79 |
| 2313000 | 7.74 | 25.2 | 10.54 | 1.37 | 9.0 | 21.4 | 1.65 | 6.57 | 47.94 |
| 2314000 | 10.64 | 9.8 | 7.13 | 13.55 | 0.8 | 20.0 | 17.93 | 22.55 | 107.62 |
| 2315000 | 13.54 | 23.3 | 3.72 | 25.72 | 5.3 | 18.5 | 15.99 | 13.29 | 49.77 |
| 2316000 | 16.44 | 7.8 | 0.31 | 7.96 | 9.8 | 17.1 | 14.07 | 4.04 | 109.45 |
| 2317000 | 2.43 | 21.4 | 11.03 | 20.13 | 1.5 | 15.7 | 12.14 | 20.01 | 51.60 |
| 2318000 | 5.33 | 5.9 | 7.62 | 2.37 | 6.0 | 14.2 | 10.21 | 10.76 | 111.28 |
| 2319000 | 8.23 | 19.5 | 4.21 | 14.54 | 10.5 | 12.8 | 8.28 | 1.50 | 53.42 |
| 2320000 | 11.13 | 4.0 | 0.79 | 26.71 | 2.3 | 11.4 | 6.35 | 17.48 | 113.11 |
| 2321000 | 14.03 | 17.5 | 11.51 | 8.95 | 6.8 | 10.0 | 4.42 | 8.23 | 55.26 |
| 2322000 | 0.02 | 2.1 | 8.10 | 21.12 | 11.3 | 8.5 | 2.49 | 24.20 | 114.94 |
| 2323000 | 2.92 | 15.6 | 4.69 | 3.36 | 3.1 | 7.1 | 0.56 | 14.95 | 57.09 |
| 2324000 | 5.82 | 0.2 | 1.28 | 15.53 | 7.6 | 5.6 | 16.84 | 5.69 | 116.77 |
| 2325000 | 8.72 | 13.7 | 12.00 | 27.70 | 12.1 | 4.2 | 14.91 | 21.67 | 58.92 |
| 2326000 | 11.62 | 27.3 | 8.59 | 9.94 | 3.8 | 2.8 | 12.98 | 12.41 | 1.06 |
| 2327000 | 14.51 | 11.8 | 5.18 | 22.11 | 8.3 | 1.3 | 11.05 | 3.16 | 60.74 |
| 2328000 | 0.51 | 25.3 | 1.77 | 4.35 | 0.1 | 24.9 | 9.12 | 19.14 | 2.89 |
| 2329000 | 3.41 | 9.9 | 12.48 | 16.52 | 4.6 | 23.4 | 7.19 | 9.88 | 62.57 |
| 2330000 | 6.31 | 23.4 | 9.08 | 28.70 | 9.1 | 22.0 | 5.26 | 0.63 | 4.72 |
| 2331000 | 9.21 | 8.0 | 5.66 | 10.94 | 0.8 | 20.6 | 3.33 | 16.60 | 64.41 |
| 2332000 | 12.10 | 21.5 | 2.25 | 23.11 | 5.3 | 19.1 | 1.40 | 7.35 | 6.55 |
| 2333000 | 15.00 | 6.1 | 12.97 | 5.35 | 9.9 | 17.7 | 17.68 | 23.32 | 66.23 |
| 2334000 | 0.99 | 19.6 | 9.56 | 17.52 | 1.6 | 16.2 | 15.75 | 14.07 | 8.38 |
| 2335000 | 3.90 | 4.1 | 6.15 | 29.69 | 6.1 | 14.8 | 13.82 | 4.81 | 68.06 |
| 2336000 | 6.80 | 17.7 | 2.74 | 11.93 | 10.5 | 13.4 | 11.89 | 20.79 | 10.21 |
| 2337000 | 9.69 | 2.2 | 13.46 | 24.10 | 2.4 | 11.9 | 9.96 | 11.54 | 69.89 |
| 2338000 | 12.59 | 15.8 | 10.05 | 6.34 | 6.9 | 10.5 | 8.03 | 2.28 | 12.04 |
| 2339000 | 15.49 | 0.3 | 6.64 | 18.51 | 11.4 | 9.0 | 6.10 | 18.26 | 71.72 |
| 2340000 | 1.49 | 13.8 | 3.23 | 0.75 | 3.1 | 7.6 | 4.17 | 9.00 | 13.87 |
| 2341000 | 4.38 | 27.4 | 13.95 | 12.92 | 7.6 | 6.2 | 2.24 | 24.98 | 73.55 |
| 2342000 | 7.28 | 11.9 | 10.54 | 25.09 | 12.2 | 4.8 | 0.31 | 15.72 | 15.70 |
| 2343000 | 10.18 | 25.5 | 7.12 | 7.33 | 3.9 | 3.3 | 16.59 | 6.47 | 75.38 |
| 2344000 | 13.08 | 10.0 | 3.71 | 19.50 | 8.4 | 1.9 | 14.67 | 22.44 | 17.53 |
| 2345000 | 15.98 | 23.6 | 0.30 | 1.74 | 0.1 | 0.4 | 12.73 | 13.19 | 77.21 |
| 2346000 | 1.97 | 8.1 | 11.02 | 13.91 | 4.6 | 24.0 | 10.80 | 3.94 | 19.36 |
| 2347000 | 4.87 | 21.6 | 7.61 | 26.08 | 9.2 | 22.6 | 8.87 | 19.91 | 79.04 |
| 2348000 | 7.77 | 6.2 | 4.20 | 8.32 | 0.9 | 21.1 | 6.94 | 10.66 | 21.19 |
| 2349000 | 10.67 | 19.7 | 0.79 | 20.49 | 5.4 | 19.7 | 5.01 | 1.40 | 80.87 |
| 2350000 | 13.57 | 4.3 | 11.51 | 2.73 | 9.9 | 18.3 | 3.08 | 17.38 | 23.02 |

# TABLE IIa.

Epochs and Arguments for each Thousandth Day, from 2300000 to 2400000.

For Washington Mean Noon.

| Day of Julian Period. | Arg. 45. | 46. | 47. | 48. | 49. | 50. | 51. | 52. | 53. |
|---|---|---|---|---|---|---|---|---|---|
| | d. | d. | d. | d. | d. | d. | d. | d. | d. |
| 2350000 | 13.57 | 4.3 | 11.51 | 2.73 | 9.9 | 18.3 | 3.08 | 17.38 | 23.02 |
| 2351000 | 16.46 | 17.8 | 8.10 | 14.91 | 1.7 | 16.9 | 1.15 | 8.12 | 82.70 |
| 2352000 | 2.46 | 2.4 | 4.69 | 27.08 | 6.2 | 15.4 | 17.43 | 24.10 | 24.85 |
| 2353000 | 5.36 | 15.9 | 1.28 | 9.32 | 10.6 | 14.0 | 15.50 | 14.84 | 84.53 |
| 2354000 | 8.26 | 0.4 | 11.99 | 21.49 | 2.4 | 12.5 | 13.58 | 5.59 | 26.68 |
| 2355000 | 11.16 | 14.0 | 8.58 | 3.73 | 6.9 | 11.1 | 11.64 | 21.57 | 86.36 |
| 2356000 | 14.05 | 27.5 | 5.17 | 15.90 | 11.5 | 9.7 | 9.71 | 12.31 | 28.50 |
| 2357000 | 0.05 | 12.0 | 1.76 | 28.07 | 3.2 | 8.2 | 7.78 | 3.06 | 88.19 |
| 2358000 | 2.95 | 25.6 | 12.48 | 10.31 | 7.7 | 6.8 | 5.85 | 19.03 | 30.33 |
| 2359000 | 5.85 | 10.1 | 9.07 | 22.48 | 12.2 | 5.3 | 3.92 | 9.78 | 90.02 |
| 2360000 | 8.75 | 23.7 | 5.66 | 4.72 | 4.0 | 3.9 | 1.99 | 0.55 | 32.17 |
| 2361000 | 11.64 | 8.2 | 2.25 | 16.89 | 8.5 | 2.5 | 0.06 | 16.50 | 91.85 |
| 2362000 | 14.54 | 21.8 | 12.97 | 29.06 | 0.2 | 1.1 | 16.34 | 7.24 | 33.99 |
| 2363000 | 0.54 | 6.3 | 9.56 | 11.30 | 4.7 | 24.6 | 14.42 | 23.22 | 93.68 |
| 2364000 | 3.44 | 19.9 | 6.15 | 23.47 | 9.2 | 23.2 | 12.49 | 13.97 | 35.82 |
| 2365000 | 6.34 | 4.5 | 2.74 | 5.71 | 1.0 | 21.7 | 10.56 | 4.71 | 95.51 |
| 2366000 | 9.23 | 17.9 | 13.46 | 17.88 | 5.5 | 20.3 | 8.63 | 20.69 | 37.65 |
| 2367000 | 12.13 | 2.5 | 10.05 | 0.12 | 9.9 | 18.9 | 6.70 | 11.43 | 97.34 |
| 2368000 | 15.03 | 16.0 | 6.64 | 12.29 | 1.7 | 17.4 | 4.77 | 2.18 | 39.48 |
| 2369000 | 1.03 | 0.6 | 3.22 | 24.47 | 6.2 | 16.0 | 2.84 | 18.16 | 99.17 |
| 2370000 | 3.92 | 14.1 | 13.94 | 6.71 | 10.7 | 14.6 | 0.91 | 8.90 | 41.31 |
| 2371000 | 6.82 | 27.7 | 10.53 | 18.88 | 2.5 | 13.2 | 17.19 | 24.87 | 101.00 |
| 2372000 | 9.72 | 12.2 | 7.12 | 1.12 | 7.0 | 11.7 | 15.26 | 15.62 | 43.14 |
| 2373000 | 12.62 | 25.7 | 3.71 | 13.29 | 11.6 | 10.3 | 13.34 | 6.37 | 102.83 |
| 2374000 | 15.52 | 10.3 | 0.30 | 25.46 | 3.3 | 8.8 | 11.41 | 22.34 | 44.97 |
| 2375000 | 1.51 | 23.8 | 11.02 | 7.70 | 7.8 | 7.4 | 9.47 | 13.09 | 104.66 |
| 2376000 | 4.41 | 8.4 | 7.61 | 19.87 | 12.3 | 6.0 | 7.54 | 3.83 | 46.80 |
| 2377000 | 7.31 | 21.9 | 4.20 | 2.11 | 4.0 | 4.5 | 5.61 | 19.81 | 106.49 |
| 2378000 | 10.21 | 6.5 | 0.79 | 14.28 | 8.5 | 3.1 | 3.68 | 10.55 | 48.63 |
| 2379000 | 13.11 | 20.0 | 11.51 | 26.45 | 0.3 | 1.6 | 1.75 | 1.30 | 108.32 |
| 2380000 | 16.00 | 4.5 | 8.10 | 8.69 | 4.8 | 0.2 | 18.03 | 17.28 | 50.46 |
| 2381000 | 2.00 | 18.1 | 4.68 | 20.87 | 9.3 | 23.8 | 16.10 | 8.02 | 110.15 |
| 2382000 | 4.90 | 2.6 | 1.27 | 3.10 | 1.0 | 22.3 | 14.18 | 24.00 | 52.29 |
| 2383000 | 7.80 | 16.2 | 11.99 | 15.28 | 5.6 | 20.9 | 12.25 | 14.74 | 111.98 |
| 2384000 | 10.70 | 0.7 | 8.58 | 27.45 | 10.0 | 19.4 | 10.32 | 5.49 | 54.12 |
| 2385000 | 13.59 | 14.2 | 5.17 | 9.69 | 1.8 | 18.0 | 8.38 | 21.46 | 113.81 |
| 2386000 | 16.49 | 27.8 | 1.76 | 21.86 | 6.3 | 16.6 | 6.45 | 12.21 | 55.95 |
| 2387000 | 2.49 | 12.3 | 12.48 | 4.10 | 10.8 | 15.1 | 4.52 | 2.95 | 115.64 |
| 2388000 | 5.39 | 25.9 | 9.07 | 16.27 | 2.6 | 13.7 | 2.59 | 18.93 | 57.78 |
| 2389000 | 8.29 | 10.4 | 5.66 | 28.44 | 7.1 | 12.2 | 0.66 | 9.68 | 117.47 |
| 2390000 | 11.18 | 24.0 | 2.25 | 10.68 | 11.6 | 10.8 | 16.94 | 0.42 | 59.61 |
| 2391000 | 14.08 | 8.5 | 12.97 | 22.85 | 3.3 | 9.4 | 15.02 | 16.40 | 1.76 |
| 2392000 | 0.08 | 22.0 | 9.56 | 5.09 | 7.8 | 8.0 | 13.09 | 7.14 | 61.44 |
| 2393000 | 2.98 | 6.6 | 6.14 | 17.26 | 12.4 | 6.5 | 11.16 | 23.12 | 3.59 |
| 2394000 | 5.88 | 20.1 | 2.73 | 29.43 | 4.1 | 5.1 | 9.23 | 13.86 | 63.27 |
| 2395000 | 8.77 | 4.7 | 13.45 | 11.67 | 8.6 | 3.6 | 7.29 | 4.61 | 5.42 |
| 2396000 | 11.67 | 18.2 | 10.04 | 23.84 | 0.3 | 2.2 | 5.36 | 20.59 | 65.10 |
| 2397000 | 14.57 | 2.8 | 6.63 | 6.08 | 4.9 | 0.8 | 3.43 | 11.33 | 7.25 |
| 2398000 | 0.57 | 16.3 | 3.22 | 18.25 | 9.4 | 24.3 | 1.50 | 2.08 | 66.93 |
| 2399000 | 3.46 | 0.8 | 13.94 | 0.49 | 1.1 | 22.9 | 17.78 | 18.05 | 9.08 |
| 2400000 | 6.36 | 14.4 | 10.53 | 12.67 | 5.6 | 21.5 | 15.85 | 8.80 | 68.76 |

# TABLE II*a*.

Epochs and Arguments for each Thousandth Day, from 2300000 to 2400000.

For Washington Mean Noon.

| Day of Julian Period. | Arg. 54. | 55. | 56. | 57. | 58. | 59 | 60. | 61. | 62. |
|---|---|---|---|---|---|---|---|---|---|
| | d. | d. | d. | d. | d. | d. | d. | d. | d. |
| 2300000 | 8.49 | 4.41 | 1.74 | 12.90 | 7.94 | 32.07 | 16.92 | 8.62 | 4.61 |
| 2301000 | 13.88 | 3.42 | 4.81 | 10.64 | 1.95 | 19.01 | 12.44 | 1.76 | 8.11 |
| 2302000 | 4.20 | 2.43 | 7.88 | 8.39 | 11.21 | 5.95 | 7.96 | 8.52 | 11.61 |
| 2303000 | 9.59 | 1.43 | 10.96 | 6.13 | 5.22 | 31.85 | 3.49 | 1.67 | 0.67 |
| 2304000 | 14.98 | 0.44 | 0.91 | 3.87 | 14.47 | 18.78 | 21.33 | 8.42 | 4.17 |
| | | | | | | | | | |
| 2305000 | 5.29 | 19.08 | 3.98 | 1.61 | 8.49 | 5.72 | 16.85 | 1.57 | 7.67 |
| 2306000 | 10.68 | 18.09 | 7.05 | 16.35 | 2.50 | 31.62 | 12.38 | 8.32 | 11.17 |
| 2307000 | 1.00 | 17.09 | 10.13 | 14.09 | 11.76 | 18.56 | 7.90 | 1.47 | 0.24 |
| 2308000 | 6.39 | 16.10 | 0.08 | 11.83 | 5.77 | 5.50 | 3.42 | 8.22 | 3.74 |
| 2309000 | 11.77 | 15.11 | 3.15 | 9.58 | 15.03 | 31.40 | 21.27 | 1.37 | 7.24 |
| | | | | | | | | | |
| 2310000 | 2.09 | 14.12 | 6.22 | 7.32 | 9.04 | 18.33 | 16.79 | 8.12 | 10.74 |
| 2311000 | 7.49 | 13.13 | 9.29 | 5.06 | 3.06 | 5.27 | 12.31 | 1.27 | 14.24 |
| 2312000 | 12.87 | 12.14 | 12.37 | 2.80 | 12.31 | 31.17 | 7.83 | 8.02 | 3.30 |
| 2313000 | 3.18 | 11.14 | 2.32 | 0.54 | 6.33 | 18.11 | 3.36 | 1.18 | 6.80 |
| 2314000 | 8.57 | 10.15 | 5.39 | 15.28 | 0.34 | 5.05 | 21.20 | 7.93 | 10.30 |
| | | | | | | | | | |
| 2315000 | 13.96 | 9.16 | 8.46 | 13.02 | 9.60 | 30.95 | 16.72 | 1.08 | 13.81 |
| 2316000 | 4.28 | 8.17 | 11.54 | 10.76 | 3.61 | 17.88 | 12.25 | 7.83 | 2.88 |
| 2317000 | 9.66 | 7.18 | 1.49 | 8.51 | 12.87 | 4.82 | 7.77 | 0.98 | 6.37 |
| 2318000 | 15.05 | 6.18 | 4.56 | 6.25 | 6.88 | 30.72 | 3.29 | 7.73 | 9.87 |
| 2319000 | 5.37 | 5.19 | 7.63 | 3.99 | 0.90 | 17.66 | 21.14 | 0.88 | 13.37 |
| | | | | | | | | | |
| 2320000 | 10.76 | 4.20 | 10.71 | 1.73 | 10.15 | 4.59 | 16.66 | 7.63 | 2.44 |
| 2321000 | 1.07 | 3.21 | 0.66 | 16.47 | 4.17 | 30.49 | 12.18 | 0.78 | 5.94 |
| 2322000 | 6.46 | 2.21 | 3.73 | 14.21 | 13.42 | 17.43 | 7.70 | 7.54 | 9.44 |
| 2323000 | 11.85 | 1.21 | 6.80 | 11.95 | 7.44 | 4.37 | 3.23 | 0.68 | 12.94 |
| 2324000 | 2.17 | 0.23 | 9.88 | 9.69 | 1.45 | 30.27 | 21.07 | 7.44 | 2.00 |
| | | | | | | | | | |
| 2325000 | 7.55 | 18.86 | 12.95 | 7.44 | 10.71 | 17.21 | 16.59 | 0.59 | 5.50 |
| 2326000 | 12.94 | 17.87 | 2.90 | 5.18 | 4.72 | 4.14 | 12.12 | 7.34 | 9.01 |
| 2327000 | 3.26 | 16.88 | 5.97 | 2.92 | 13.97 | 30.04 | 7.64 | 0.49 | 12.51 |
| 2328000 | 8.65 | 15.89 | 9.05 | 0.66 | 7.99 | 16.98 | 3.16 | 7.24 | 1.57 |
| 2329000 | 14.03 | 14.89 | 12.12 | 15.40 | 2.00 | 3.92 | 21.01 | 0.39 | 5.07 |
| | | | | | | | | | |
| 2330000 | 4.35 | 13.90 | 2.07 | 13.14 | 11.26 | 29.82 | 16.53 | 7.14 | 8.57 |
| 2331000 | 9.74 | 12.91 | 5.14 | 10.88 | 5.27 | 16.76 | 12.05 | 0.29 | 12.07 |
| 2332000 | 0.06 | 11.92 | 8.21 | 8.62 | 14.53 | 3.69 | 7.58 | 7.05 | 1.14 |
| 2333000 | 5.44 | 10.92 | 11.29 | 6.37 | 8.54 | 29.59 | 3.10 | 0.19 | 4.64 |
| 2334000 | 10.83 | 9.93 | 1.24 | 4.11 | 2.56 | 16.53 | 20.94 | 6.95 | 8.14 |
| | | | | | | | | | |
| 2335000 | 1.14 | 8.94 | 4.31 | 1.85 | 11.81 | 3.47 | 16.47 | 0.10 | 11.64 |
| 2336000 | 6.54 | 7.95 | 7.38 | 16.58 | 5.83 | 29.37 | 11.99 | 6.85 | 0.70 |
| 2337000 | 11.92 | 6.96 | 10.46 | 14.32 | 15.08 | 16.31 | 7.51 | 0.00 | 4.20 |
| 2338000 | 2.24 | 5.96 | 0.41 | 12.07 | 9.10 | 3.24 | 3.04 | 6.75 | 7.70 |
| 2339000 | 7.63 | 4.97 | 3.48 | 9.81 | 3.11 | 29.14 | 20.88 | 13.51 | 11.21 |
| | | | | | | | | | |
| 2340000 | 13.02 | 3.98 | 6.55 | 7.56 | 12.36 | 16.08 | 16.40 | 6.65 | 0.27 |
| 2341000 | 3.33 | 2.99 | 9.62 | 5.30 | 6.38 | 3.02 | 11.93 | 13.41 | 3.77 |
| 2342000 | 8.72 | 2.00 | 12.70 | 3.04 | 0.39 | 28.92 | 7.45 | 6.55 | 7.27 |
| 2343000 | 14.11 | 1.00 | 2.65 | 0.78 | 9.65 | 15.85 | 2.97 | 13.31 | 10.77 |
| 2344000 | 4.43 | 0.01 | 5.72 | 15.51 | 3.66 | 2.79 | 20.82 | 6.46 | 14.27 |
| | | | | | | | | | |
| 2345000 | 9.81 | 18.65 | 8.79 | 13.26 | 12.92 | 28.69 | 16.34 | 13.21 | 3.34 |
| 2346000 | 0.13 | 17.66 | 11.87 | 11.00 | 6.93 | 15.63 | 11.86 | 6.36 | 6.84 |
| 2347000 | 5.52 | 16.67 | 1.82 | 8.74 | 0.95 | 2.57 | 7.38 | 13.12 | 10.34 |
| 2348000 | 10.91 | 15.67 | 4.89 | 6.49 | 10.20 | 28.47 | 2.91 | 6.26 | 13.84 |
| 2349000 | 1.22 | 14.68 | 7.96 | 4.23 | 4.22 | 15.40 | 20.75 | 13.02 | 2.90 |
| 2350000 | 6.61 | 13.69 | 11.04 | 1.97 | 13.47 | 2.34 | 16.27 | 6.16 | 6.40 |

# TABLE II*a*.

Epochs and Arguments for each Thousandth Day, from 2300000 to 2400000.

For Washington Mean Noon.

| Day of Julian Period. | Arg. 54. | 55. | 56. | 57. | 58. | 59 | 60. | 61. | 62. |
|---|---|---|---|---|---|---|---|---|---|
| | d. | d. | d. | d. | d. | d. | d. | d. | d. |
| 2350000 | 6.61 | 13.69 | 11.04 | 1.97 | 13.47 | 2.34 | 16.27 | 6.16 | 6.40 |
| 2351000 | 12.00 | 12.70 | 0.99 | 16.70 | 7.49 | 28.24 | 11.80 | 12.92 | 9.90 |
| 2352000 | 2.32 | 11.71 | 4.07 | 14.45 | 1.50 | 15.18 | 7.32 | 6.06 | 13.41 |
| 2353000 | 7.70 | 10.71 | 7.13 | 12.19 | 10.75 | 2.11 | 2.84 | 12.82 | 2.47 |
| 2354000 | 13.09 | 9.72 | 10.21 | 9.93 | 4.77 | 28.02 | 20.69 | 5.97 | 5.97 |
| 2355000 | 3.41 | 8.73 | 0.16 | 7.68 | 14.02 | 14.95 | 16.21 | 12.72 | 9.47 |
| 2356000 | 8.80 | 7.74 | 3.23 | 5.42 | 8.04 | 1.89 | 11.73 | 5.87 | 12.97 |
| 2357000 | 14.18 | 6.75 | 6.30 | 3.16 | 2.06 | 27.79 | 7.26 | 12.63 | 2.03 |
| 2358000 | 4.50 | 5.75 | 9.38 | 0.90 | 11.31 | 14.73 | 2.78 | 5.77 | 5.53 |
| 2359000 | 9.89 | 4.76 | 12.45 | 15.63 | 5.33 | 1.66 | 20.62 | 12.53 | 9.04 |
| 2360000 | 0.21 | 3.77 | 2.40 | 13.38 | 14.58 | 27.56 | 16.15 | 5.67 | 12.54 |
| 2361000 | 5.60 | 2.78 | 5.47 | 11.12 | 8.59 | 14.50 | 11.67 | 13.43 | 1.60 |
| 2362000 | 10.98 | 1.78 | 8.54 | 8.86 | 2.61 | 1.44 | 7.19 | 5.57 | 5.10 |
| 2363000 | 1.30 | 0.79 | 11.62 | 6.61 | 11.86 | 27.34 | 2.71 | 12.33 | 8.60 |
| 2364000 | 6.69 | 19.43 | 1.57 | 4.35 | 5.88 | 14.28 | 20.56 | 5.48 | 12.10 |
| 2365000 | 12.07 | 18.43 | 4.64 | 2.09 | 15.13 | 1.21 | 16.08 | 12.23 | 1.17 |
| 2366000 | 2.39 | 17.44 | 7.71 | 16.82 | 9.15 | 27.11 | 11.60 | 5.38 | 4.67 |
| 2367000 | 7.78 | 16.45 | 10.79 | 14.57 | 3.16 | 14.05 | 7.13 | 12.14 | 8.17 |
| 2368000 | 13.17 | 15.46 | 0.74 | 12.31 | 12.42 | 0.99 | 2.65 | 5.28 | 11.67 |
| 2369000 | 3.48 | 14.46 | 3.81 | 10.05 | 6.43 | 26.89 | 20.49 | 12.04 | 0.73 |
| 2370000 | 8.87 | 13.47 | 6.88 | 7.79 | 0.45 | 13.82 | 16.02 | 5.18 | 4.23 |
| 2371000 | 14.26 | 12.48 | 9.95 | 5.54 | 9.70 | 0.76 | 11.54 | 11.94 | 7.73 |
| 2372000 | 4.58 | 11.49 | 13.03 | 3.28 | 3.72 | 26.66 | 7.06 | 5.08 | 11.24 |
| 2373000 | 9.96 | 10.49 | 2.98 | 1.02 | 12.97 | 13.60 | 2.59 | 11.84 | 0.30 |
| 2374000 | 0.28 | 9.50 | 6.05 | 15.75 | 6.99 | 0.54 | 20.43 | 4.98 | 3.80 |
| 2375000 | 5.67 | 8.51 | 9.12 | 13.50 | 1.00 | 26.44 | 15.95 | 11.74 | 7.30 |
| 2376000 | 11.06 | 7.52 | 12.20 | 11.24 | 10.26 | 13.37 | 11.48 | 4.89 | 10.80 |
| 2377000 | 1.37 | 6.53 | 2.15 | 8.98 | 4.27 | 0.31 | 7.00 | 11.64 | 14.30 |
| 2378000 | 6.76 | 5.53 | 5.22 | 6.73 | 13.52 | 26.21 | 2.52 | 4.79 | 3.37 |
| 2379000 | 12.15 | 4.54 | 8.29 | 4.47 | 7.54 | 13.15 | 20.37 | 11.55 | 6.87 |
| 2380000 | 2.47 | 3.55 | 11.37 | 2.21 | 1.55 | 0.08 | 15.89 | 4.69 | 10.37 |
| 2381000 | 7.86 | 2.56 | 1.32 | 16.94 | 10.81 | 25.98 | 11.41 | 11.45 | 13.87 |
| 2382000 | 13.24 | 1.57 | 4.39 | 14.69 | 4.82 | 12.92 | 6.94 | 4.59 | 2.93 |
| 2383000 | 3.56 | 0.57 | 7.46 | 12.43 | 14.08 | 38.82 | 2.46 | 11.35 | 6.43 |
| 2384000 | 8.95 | 19.21 | 10.54 | 10.17 | 8.09 | 25.76 | 20.30 | 4.49 | 9.93 |
| 2385000 | 14.33 | 18.22 | 0.49 | 7.91 | 2.11 | 12.70 | 15.83 | 11.25 | 13.44 |
| 2386000 | 4.65 | 17.23 | 3.56 | 5.66 | 11.36 | 38.59 | 11.36 | 4.40 | 2.50 |
| 2387000 | 10.04 | 16.24 | 6.63 | 3.40 | 5.38 | 25.53 | 6.87 | 11.15 | 6.00 |
| 2388000 | 0.36 | 15.24 | 9.71 | 1.14 | 14.63 | 12.47 | 2.40 | 4.30 | 9.50 |
| 2389000 | 5.74 | 14.25 | 12.78 | 15.87 | 8.65 | 38.37 | 20.24 | 11.06 | 13.00 |
| 2390000 | 11.13 | 13.26 | 2.73 | 13.62 | 2.66 | 25.31 | 15.76 | 4.20 | 2.06 |
| 2391000 | 1.45 | 12.27 | 5.80 | 11.36 | 11.91 | 12.24 | 11.29 | 10.96 | 5.56 |
| 2392000 | 6.84 | 11.28 | 8.87 | 9.10 | 5.93 | 38.14 | 6.81 | 4.10 | 9.07 |
| 2393000 | 12.22 | 10.28 | 11.95 | 6.85 | 15.18 | 25.08 | 2.33 | 10.86 | 12.57 |
| 2394000 | 2.54 | 9.29 | 1.90 | 4.59 | 9.20 | 12.02 | 20.18 | 4.00 | 1.63 |
| 2395000 | 7.93 | 8.30 | 4.97 | 2.33 | 3.21 | 37.92 | 15.70 | 10.76 | 5.13 |
| 2396000 | 13.32 | 7.31 | 8.04 | 0.07 | 12.47 | 24.86 | 11.22 | 3.90 | 8.63 |
| 2397000 | 3.63 | 6.32 | 11.12 | 14.80 | 6.48 | 11.79 | 6.74 | 10.66 | 12.13 |
| 2398000 | 9.02 | 5.32 | 1.07 | 12.55 | 0.50 | 37.69 | 2.27 | 3.81 | 1.20 |
| 2399000 | 14.41 | 4.33 | 4.14 | 10.29 | 9.75 | 24.63 | 20.11 | 10.56 | 4.70 |
| 2400000 | 4.73 | 3.34 | 7.21 | 8.03 | 3.77 | 11.57 | 15.63 | 3.71 | 8.20 |

# TABLE IIa.

Epochs and Arguments for each Thousandth Day, from 2300000 to 2400000.

For Washington Mean Noon.

| Day of Julian Period. ARG. | 63. | 64. | 65. | 66. | 67. | 68. | 69. | 70. | 71. |
|---|---|---|---|---|---|---|---|---|---|
| | d. | d. | d. | d. | d. | d. | d. | d | d. |
| 2300000 | 8.80 | 11.71 | 9.97 | 32.1 | 11.13 | 18.74 | 163.0 | 233.6 | 122.6 |
| 2301000 | 13.57 | 3.93 | 11.36 | 35.4 | 23.17 | 22.74 | 219.2 | 244.2 | 538.6 |
| 2302000 | 4.69 | 32.14 | 12.74 | 3.1 | 7.76 | 26.74 | 275.4 | 254.8 | 370.8 |
| 2303000 | 9.45 | 24.36 | 14.12 | 6.4 | 19.80 | 3.07 | 331.7 | 265.5 | 203.0 |
| 2304000 | 0.58 | 16.58 | 1.01 | 9.7 | 4.40 | 7.07 | 387.9 | 276.1 | 35.1 |
| 2305000 | 5.34 | 8.80 | 2.39 | 13.1 | 16.44 | 11.07 | 444.1 | 286.8 | 451.2 |
| 2306000 | 10.11 | 1.02 | 3.77 | 16.4 | 1.04 | 15.07 | 28.4 | 297.4 | 283.4 |
| 2307000 | 1.23 | 29.23 | 5.14 | 19.7 | 13.08 | 19.06 | 84.6 | 308.0 | 115.5 |
| 2308000 | 6.00 | 21.46 | 6.52 | 23.0 | 25.12 | 23.06 | 140.8 | 318.7 | 531.6 |
| 2309000 | 10.77 | 13.68 | 7.90 | 26.3 | 9.71 | 27.06 | 197.0 | 329.3 | 363.8 |
| 2310000 | 1.89 | 5.89 | 9.28 | 29.6 | 21.76 | 3.39 | 253.2 | 10.1 | 195.9 |
| 2311000 | 6.65 | 34.11 | 10.66 | 32.9 | 6.35 | 7.39 | 309.4 | 20.7 | 28.1 |
| 2312000 | 11.42 | 26.33 | 12.05 | 0.6 | 18.39 | 11.39 | 365.7 | 31.3 | 444.1 |
| 2313000 | 2.54 | 18.55 | 13.43 | 4.0 | 2.99 | 15.39 | 421.9 | 42.0 | 276.3 |
| 2314000 | 7.30 | 10.77 | 0.33 | 7.3 | 15.03 | 19.39 | 6.2 | 52.6 | 108.5 |
| 2315000 | 12.07 | 2.99 | 1.70 | 10.6 | 27.08 | 23.39 | 62.4 | 63.3 | 524.5 |
| 2316000 | 3.19 | 31.20 | 3.08 | 13.9 | 11.67 | 27.39 | 118.6 | 73.9 | 356.7 |
| 2317000 | 7.96 | 23.42 | 4.46 | 17.2 | 23.71 | 3.72 | 174.8 | 84.5 | 188.9 |
| 2318000 | 12.72 | 15.64 | 5.84 | 20.6 | 8.30 | 7.72 | 231.0 | 95.2 | 21.0 |
| 2319000 | 3.85 | 7.87 | 7.22 | 23.9 | 20.34 | 11.72 | 287.2 | 105.8 | 437.1 |
| 2320000 | 8.61 | 0.09 | 8.60 | 27.2 | 4.94 | 15.72 | 343.4 | 116.4 | 269.2 |
| 2321000 | 13.38 | 28.30 | 9.98 | 30.5 | 16.98 | 19.72 | 399.7 | 127.0 | 101.4 |
| 2322000 | 4.50 | 20.52 | 11.37 | 33.8 | 1.58 | 23.72 | 455.9 | 137.6 | 517.5 |
| 2323000 | 9.26 | 12.74 | 12.74 | 1.6 | 13.62 | 0.05 | 40.2 | 148.3 | 349.6 |
| 2324000 | 0.39 | 4.96 | 14.12 | 4.9 | 25.67 | 4.05 | 96.4 | 158.9 | 181.8 |
| 2325000 | 5.15 | 33.17 | 1.02 | 8.2 | 10.26 | 8.05 | 152.6 | 169.6 | 13.9 |
| 2326000 | 9.91 | 25.39 | 2.40 | 11.5 | 22.30 | 12.05 | 208.8 | 180.2 | 430.0 |
| 2327000 | 1.04 | 17.61 | 3.78 | 14.8 | 6.90 | 16.05 | 265.0 | 190.8 | 262.2 |
| 2328000 | 5.80 | 9.83 | 5.15 | 18.2 | 18.94 | 20.04 | 321.2 | 201.5 | 94.3 |
| 2329000 | 10.57 | 2.05 | 6.53 | 21.5 | 3.53 | 24.04 | 377.4 | 212.1 | 510.4 |
| 2330000 | 1.69 | 30.26 | 7.91 | 24.8 | 15.57 | 0.37 | 433.7 | 222.7 | 342.6 |
| 2331000 | 6.46 | 22.49 | 9.29 | 28.1 | 0.17 | 4.37 | 18.0 | 233.3 | 174.7 |
| 2332000 | 11.23 | 14.71 | 10.67 | 31.4 | 12.21 | 8.37 | 74.2 | 243.9 | 6.9 |
| 2333000 | 2.35 | 6.93 | 12.06 | 34.7 | 24.25 | 12.37 | 130.4 | 254.6 | 423.0 |
| 2334000 | 7.11 | 35.14 | 13.44 | 2.4 | 8.85 | 16.37 | 186.6 | 265.2 | 255.1 |
| 2335000 | 11.88 | 27.36 | 0.33 | 5.8 | 20.89 | 20.37 | 242.8 | 275.8 | 87.3 |
| 2336000 | 3.00 | 19.58 | 1.71 | 9.1 | 5.49 | 24.37 | 299.0 | 286.4 | 503.4 |
| 2337000 | 7.76 | 11.80 | 3.09 | 12.4 | 17.53 | 0.70 | 355.2 | 297.0 | 335.5 |
| 2338000 | 12.53 | 4.02 | 4.47 | 15.7 | 2.12 | 4.70 | 411.5 | 307.7 | 167.7 |
| 2339000 | 3.65 | 32.23 | 5.85 | 19.0 | 14.16 | 8.70 | 467.7 | 318.3 | 583.7 |
| 2340000 | 8.42 | 24.45 | 7.23 | 22.3 | 26.21 | 12.70 | 52.0 | 328.9 | 415.9 |
| 2341000 | 13.18 | 16.67 | 8.61 | 25.6 | 10.80 | 16.70 | 108.2 | 9.7 | 248.1 |
| 2342000 | 4.31 | 8.90 | 9.99 | 28.9 | 22.84 | 20.70 | 164.4 | 20.3 | 80.2 |
| 2343000 | 9.07 | 1.12 | 11.38 | 32.3 | 7.44 | 24.70 | 220.6 | 31.0 | 496.3 |
| 2344000 | 0.20 | 29.33 | 12.76 | 0.0 | 19.48 | 1.03 | 276.8 | 41.6 | 328.5 |
| 2345000 | 4.96 | 21.55 | 14.13 | 3.3 | 4.08 | 5.03 | 333.0 | 52.3 | 160.6 |
| 2346000 | 9.72 | 13.77 | 1.03 | 6.6 | 16.12 | 9.03 | 389.3 | 62.9 | 576.7 |
| 2347000 | 0.85 | 5.99 | 2.41 | 9.9 | 0.71 | 13.03 | 445.5 | 73.5 | 408.9 |
| 2348000 | 5.61 | 34.20 | 3.79 | 13.3 | 12.75 | 17.03 | 29.8 | 84.2 | 241.0 |
| 2349000 | 10.37 | 26.42 | 5.17 | 16.6 | 24.80 | 21.03 | 86.0 | 94.8 | 73.2 |
| 2350000 | 1.50 | 18.64 | 6.55 | 19.9 | 9.39 | 25.03 | 142.2 | 105.4 | 489.3 |

# TABLE II*a*.

Epochs and Arguments for each Thousandth Day, from 2300000 to 2400000.

For Washington Mean Noon.

| Day of Julian Period. | ARG. **63.** | **64.** | **65.** | **66.** | **67.** | **68.** | **69.** | **70.** | **71.** |
|---|---|---|---|---|---|---|---|---|---|
| | d. | d. | d. | d. | d. | d. | d. | d. | d. |
| 2350000 | 1.50 | 18.64 | 6.55 | 19.9 | 9.39 | 25.03 | 142.2 | 105.4 | 489.3 |
| 2351000 | 6.26 | 10.86 | 7.93 | 23.2 | 21.43 | 1.36 | 198.4 | 116.0 | 321.4 |
| 2352000 | 11.03 | 3.09 | 9.31 | 26.5 | 6.04 | 5.36 | 254.6 | 126.6 | 153.6 |
| 2353000 | 2.16 | 31.30 | 10.68 | 29.9 | 18.08 | 9.35 | 310.9 | 137.3 | 569.6 |
| 2354000 | 6.92 | 23.52 | 12.07 | 33.2 | 2.67 | 13.36 | 367.1 | 147.9 | 401.8 |
| 2355000 | 11.69 | 15.74 | 13.45 | 0.9 | 14.71 | 17.36 | 423.3 | 158.6 | 234.0 |
| 2356000 | 2.81 | 7.96 | 0.35 | 4.2 | 26.76 | 21.36 | 7.6 | 169.2 | 66.1 |
| 2357000 | 7.57 | 36.17 | 1.73 | 7.5 | 11.35 | 25.35 | 63.8 | 179.8 | 482.2 |
| 2358000 | 12.34 | 28.39 | 3.10 | 10.9 | 23.39 | 1.68 | 120.0 | 190.5 | 314.4 |
| 2359000 | 3.46 | 20.61 | 4.48 | 14.2 | 7.99 | 5.68 | 176.2 | 201.1 | 146.5 |
| 2360000 | 8.22 | 12.83 | 5.86 | 17.5 | 20.02 | 9.68 | 232.5 | 211.7 | 562.6 |
| 2361000 | 12.99 | 5.05 | 7.24 | 20.8 | 4.62 | 13.68 | 288.7 | 222.3 | 394.8 |
| 2362000 | 4.11 | 33.27 | 8.62 | 24.1 | 16.66 | 17.68 | 344.9 | 232.9 | 226.9 |
| 2363000 | 8.88 | 25.49 | 9.99 | 27.5 | 1.26 | 21.68 | 401.1 | 243.6 | 59.1 |
| 2364000 | 0.01 | 17.71 | 11.38 | 30.8 | 13.30 | 25.68 | 457.3 | 254.2 | 475.1 |
| 2365000 | 4.77 | 9.93 | 12.76 | 34.1 | 25.35 | 2.01 | 41.6 | 264.9 | 307.3 |
| 2366000 | 9.53 | 2.15 | 14.14 | 1.8 | 9.94 | 6.01 | 97.8 | 275.5 | 139.5 |
| 2367000 | 0.66 | 30.36 | 1.04 | 5.1 | 21.98 | 10.01 | 154.0 | 286.1 | 555.5 |
| 2368000 | 5.42 | 22.58 | 2.41 | 8.4 | 6.57 | 14.01 | 210.3 | 296.8 | 387.7 |
| 2369000 | 10.18 | 14.80 | 3.79 | 11.8 | 18.61 | 18.01 | 266.5 | 307.4 | 219.9 |
| 2370000 | 1.31 | 7.02 | 5.17 | 15.1 | 3.21 | 22.01 | 322.7 | 318.0 | 52.0 |
| 2371000 | 6.07 | 35.23 | 6.55 | 18.4 | 15.25 | 26.01 | 378.9 | 328.6 | 468.1 |
| 2372000 | 10.84 | 27.46 | 7.93 | 21.7 | 27.30 | 2.34 | 435.1 | 9.4 | 300.2 |
| 2373000 | 1.96 | 19.68 | 9.31 | 25.0 | 11.89 | 6.34 | 19.4 | 20.1 | 132.4 |
| 2374000 | 6.73 | 11.90 | 10.69 | 28.3 | 23.93 | 10.34 | 75.7 | 30.7 | 548.5 |
| 2375000 | 11.50 | 4.12 | 12.07 | 31.7 | 8.53 | 14.34 | 131.9 | 41.4 | 380.6 |
| 2376000 | 2.62 | 32.33 | 13.45 | 35.0 | 20.57 | 18.34 | 188.1 | 52.0 | 212.8 |
| 2377000 | 7.38 | 24.55 | 0.35 | 2.7 | 5.16 | 22.34 | 244.3 | 62.6 | 44.9 |
| 2378000 | 12.15 | 16.77 | 1.73 | 6.0 | 17.20 | 26.34 | 300.5 | 73.3 | 461.0 |
| 2379000 | 3.27 | 8.99 | 3.11 | 9.3 | 1.80 | 2.67 | 356.7 | 83.9 | 293.2 |
| 2380000 | 8.03 | 1.21 | 4.49 | 12.6 | 13.84 | 6.67 | 412.9 | 94.5 | 125.4 |
| 2381000 | 12.80 | 29.43 | 5.87 | 15.9 | 25.89 | 10.67 | 469.1 | 105.1 | 541.4 |
| 2382000 | 3.92 | 21.65 | 7.25 | 19.2 | 10.48 | 14.67 | 53.5 | 115.7 | 373.6 |
| 2383000 | 8.68 | 13.87 | 8.63 | 22.6 | 22.52 | 18.67 | 109.7 | 126.4 | 205.7 |
| 2384000 | 13.45 | 6.09 | 10.01 | 25.9 | 7.12 | 22.67 | 165.9 | 137.0 | 37.9 |
| 2385000 | 4.58 | 34.30 | 11.39 | 29.3 | 19.16 | 26.67 | 222.1 | 147.7 | 454.0 |
| 2386000 | 9.34 | 26.52 | 12.77 | 32.6 | 3.75 | 2.99 | 278.3 | 158.3 | 286.1 |
| 2387000 | 0.47 | 18.74 | 14.15 | 0.3 | 15.79 | 6.99 | 334.5 | 168.9 | 118.3 |
| 2388000 | 5.23 | 10.96 | 1.05 | 3.6 | 0.39 | 11.00 | 390.7 | 179.6 | 534.4 |
| 2389000 | 9.99 | 3.19 | 2.43 | 6.9 | 12.43 | 15.00 | 446.9 | 190.2 | 366.5 |
| 2390000 | 1.12 | 31.40 | 3.81 | 10.2 | 24.48 | 18.99 | 31.3 | 200.8 | 198.7 |
| 2391000 | 5.88 | 23.62 | 5.19 | 13.5 | 9.07 | 22.99 | 87.5 | 211.4 | 30.9 |
| 2392000 | 10.65 | 15.84 | 6.57 | 16.8 | 21.13 | 26.99 | 143.7 | 222.0 | 446.9 |
| 2393000 | 1.77 | 8.06 | 7.95 | 20.2 | 5.71 | 3.32 | 199.9 | 232.7 | 279.1 |
| 2394000 | 6.53 | 0.28 | 9.33 | 23.5 | 17.75 | 7.32 | 256.1 | 243.3 | 111.2 |
| 2395000 | 11.30 | 28.49 | 10.70 | 26.8 | 2.35 | 11.32 | 312.3 | 254.0 | 527.3 |
| 2396000 | 2.43 | 20.71 | 12.09 | 30.1 | 14.39 | 15.32 | 368.5 | 264.6 | 359.5 |
| 2397000 | 7.19 | 12.94 | 13.47 | 33.4 | 26.43 | 19.32 | 424.8 | 275.2 | 191.6 |
| 2398000 | 11.96 | 5.16 | 0.37 | 1.2 | 11.02 | 23.32 | 9.1 | 285.9 | 23.8 |
| 2399000 | 3.08 | 33.37 | 1.75 | 4.5 | 23.06 | 27.32 | 65.3 | 296.5 | 439.8 |
| 2400000 | 7.84 | 25.59 | 3.13 | 7.8 | 7.66 | 3.65 | 121.5 | 307.1 | 272.0 |

# TABLE IIa.

Epochs and Arguments for each Thousandth Day, from 2300000 to 2400000.

For Washington Mean Noon.

| Day of Julian Period. | Arg. 72. | 73. | 74. | 75. | 76. | 78. | 79. | 80. | 81. |
|---|---|---|---|---|---|---|---|---|---|
| | d. | d. | d. | d. | d. | d. | d. | d. | d. |
| 2300000 | 103.9 | 2077.0 | 3031 | 54315 | 2766 | 6.448 | 366.2 | 57.0 | 50.32 |
| 2301000 | 306.2 | 886.7 | 798 | 55315 | 3766 | 65.440 | 51.1 | 117.8 | 56.68 |
| 2302000 | 109.5 | 1886.7 | 1798 | 56315 | 4766 | 124.432 | 174.4 | 178.7 | 63.04 |
| 2303000 | 311.7 | 696.4 | 2798 | 57315 | 5767 | 183.424 | 297.7 | 239.5 | 69.41 |
| 2304000 | 115.1 | 1696.4 | 565 | 58315 | 6767 | 54.214 | 420.9 | 300.3 | 75.77 |
| 2305000 | 317.3 | 506.1 | 1565 | 59315 | 7767 | 113.206 | 105.9 | 48.1 | 82.13 |
| 2306000 | 120.7 | 1506.1 | 2565 | 60315 | 8768 | 172.198 | 229.1 | 109.0 | 88.49 |
| 2307000 | 322.9 | 315.8 | 332 | 61315 | 9768 | 42.988 | 352.4 | 169.8 | 94.85 |
| 2308000 | 126.2 | 1315.8 | 1332 | 62315 | 10769 | 101.981 | 37.3 | 230.6 | 101.22 |
| 2309000 | 328.5 | 125.5 | 2332 | 63315 | 11769 | 160.972 | 160.6 | 291.5 | 107.58 |
| 2310000 | 131.8 | 1125.5 | 99 | 64315 | 12769 | 31.763 | 283.9 | 39.2 | 113.94 |
| 2311000 | 334.1 | 2125.5 | 1099 | 65315 | 13769 | 90.755 | 407.2 | 100.1 | 120.30 |
| 2312000 | 137.4 | 935.2 | 2099 | 66315 | 14769 | 149.747 | 92.1 | 160.9 | 2.46 |
| 2313000 | 339.6 | 1935.2 | 3099 | 67315 | 15770 | 20.538 | 215.3 | 221.7 | 8.83 |
| 2314000 | 143.0 | 744.8 | 867 | 68315 | 16770 | 79.530 | 338.6 | 282.6 | 15.19 |
| 2315000 | 345.2 | 1744.8 | 1867 | 69315 | 17770 | 138.522 | 23.5 | 30.4 | 21.55 |
| 2316000 | 148.6 | 554.5 | 2867 | 70315 | 18771 | 9.312 | 146.8 | 91.2 | 27.92 |
| 2317000 | 350.8 | 1554.5 | 634 | 71315 | 19771 | 68.304 | 270.1 | 152.0 | 34.28 |
| 2318000 | 154.1 | 364.1 | 1634 | 72315 | 20772 | 127.296 | 393.4 | 212.8 | 40.65 |
| 2319000 | 356.4 | 1364.1 | 2634 | 73315 | 21772 | 186.288 | 78.3 | 273.7 | 47.01 |
| 2320000 | 159.7 | 173.9 | 401 | 74315 | 22772 | 57.079 | 201.6 | 21.5 | 53.37 |
| 2321000 | 361.9 | 1173.9 | 1401 | 75315 | 23772 | 116.071 | 324.8 | 82.3 | 59.73 |
| 2322000 | 165.3 | 2173.9 | 2401 | 76315 | 24773 | 175.064 | 9.8 | 143.2 | 66.09 |
| 2323000 | 367.5 | 983.6 | 168 | 77315 | 25773 | 45.854 | 133.0 | 204.0 | 72.46 |
| 2324000 | 170.9 | 1983.6 | 1168 | 78315 | 26773 | 104.846 | 256.3 | 264.8 | 78.82 |
| 2325000 | 373.1 | 793.3 | 2168 | 79315 | 27774 | 163.838 | 379.6 | 12.6 | 85.18 |
| 2326000 | 176.5 | 1793.3 | 3168 | 80315 | 28774 | 34.628 | 64.5 | 73.4 | 91.55 |
| 2327000 | 378.7 | 602.9 | 935 | 81315 | 29774 | 93.620 | 187.8 | 134.3 | 97.91 |
| 2328000 | 182.0 | 1602.9 | 1935 | 82315 | 30775 | 152.613 | 311.1 | 195.1 | 104.28 |
| 2329000 | 384.3 | 412.6 | 2935 | 83315 | 31775 | 23.403 | 434.3 | 255.9 | 110.64 |
| 2330000 | 187.6 | 1412.6 | 703 | 84315 | 32775 | 82.395 | 119.3 | 3.8 | 117.00 |
| 2331000 | 389.8 | 222.3 | 1703 | 562 | 33775 | 141.387 | 242.5 | 64.6 | 123.36 |
| 2332000 | 193.2 | 1222.3 | 2703 | 1562 | 34775 | 12.178 | 365.8 | 125.4 | 5.52 |
| 2333000 | 395.4 | 32.0 | 470 | 2562 | 35775 | 71.170 | 50.7 | 186.3 | 11.89 |
| 2334000 | 198.8 | 1032.0 | 1470 | 3562 | 36776 | 130.162 | 174.0 | 247.1 | 18.25 |
| 2335000 | 2.1 | 2032.0 | 2470 | 4562 | 37776 | 0.952 | 297.3 | 307.9 | 24.61 |
| 2336000 | 204.4 | 841.7 | 237 | 5562 | 38776 | 59.945 | 420.6 | 55.7 | 30.98 |
| 2337000 | 7.7 | 1841.7 | 1237 | 6562 | 39776 | 119.937 | 105.5 | 116.5 | 37.34 |
| 2338000 | 209.9 | 651.3 | 2237 | 7562 | 40777 | 177.929 | 228.8 | 177.4 | 43.71 |
| 2339000 | 13.3 | 1651.3 | 4 | 8562 | 41777 | 48.719 | 352.0 | 238.2 | 50.07 |
| 2340000 | 215.5 | 461.0 | 1004 | 9562 | 42777 | 107.712 | 36.9 | 299.1 | 56.43 |
| 2341000 | 18.9 | 1461.0 | 2004 | 10562 | 43777 | 166.704 | 160.2 | 46.9 | 62.79 |
| 2342000 | 221.1 | 270.7 | 3004 | 11562 | 44777 | 37.495 | 283.5 | 107.7 | 69.15 |
| 2343000 | 24.4 | 1270.7 | 771 | 12562 | 45777 | 96.487 | 406.8 | 168.6 | 75.52 |
| 2344000 | 226.7 | 80.4 | 1771 | 13562 | 46777 | 155.479 | 91.7 | 229.4 | 81.88 |
| 2345000 | 30.0 | 1080.4 | 2771 | 14562 | 47778 | 26.270 | 215.0 | 290.2 | 88.24 |
| 2346000 | 232.2 | 2080.4 | 539 | 15562 | 48778 | 85.262 | 338.3 | 38.0 | 94.61 |
| 2347000 | 35.6 | 890.1 | 1539 | 16562 | 49778 | 144.254 | 23.2 | 98.9 | 100.97 |
| 2348000 | 237.8 | 1890.1 | 2539 | 17562 | 50778 | 15.045 | 146.4 | 159.7 | 107.34 |
| 2349000 | 41.2 | 699.7 | 306 | 18562 | 51778 | 74.037 | 269.7 | 220.5 | 113.70 |
| 2350000 | 243.4 | 1699.7 | 1306 | 19562 | 52778 | 133.029 | 393.0 | 281.3 | 120.06 |

# TABLE II*a*.

Epochs and Arguments for each Thousandth Day, from 2300000 to 2400000.

For Washington Mean Noon.

| Day of Julian Period. | ARG. 72. | 73. | 74. | 75. | 76. | 78. | 79. | 80. | 81. |
|---|---|---|---|---|---|---|---|---|---|
| | d. | d. | d. | d. | d. | d. | d. | d. | d. |
| 2350000 | 243.4 | 1699.7 | 1306 | 19562 | 52778 | 133.029 | 393.0 | 281.3 | 120.06 |
| 2351000 | 46.8 | 509.4 | 2306 | 20562 | 53778 | 3.820 | 77.9 | 29.1 | 2.22 |
| 2352000 | 249.0 | 1509.4 | 73 | 21562 | 54778 | 62.812 | 201.2 | 90.0 | 8.58 |
| 2353000 | 52.3 | 319.1 | 1073 | 22562 | 55778 | 121.805 | 324.5 | 150.8 | 14.95 |
| 2354000 | 254.6 | 1319.1 | 2073 | 23562 | 56778 | 180.797 | 9.4 | 211.6 | 21.31 |
| 2355000 | 57.9 | 128.7 | 3073 | 24562 | 57778 | 51.588 | 132.7 | 272.5 | 27.67 |
| 2356000 | 260.1 | 1128.7 | 840 | 25562 | 58779 | 110.580 | 255.9 | 20.3 | 34.04 |
| 2357000 | 63.5 | 2128.7 | 1840 | 26562 | 59779 | 169.572 | 379.2 | 81.1 | 40.40 |
| 2358000 | 265.7 | 938.4 | 2840 | 27562 | 60779 | 40.363 | 64.1 | 141.9 | 46.77 |
| 2359000 | 69.1 | 1938.4 | 607 | 28562 | 61779 | 99.355 | 187.4 | 202.8 | 53.13 |
| 2360000 | 271.3 | 748.1 | 1607 | 29562 | 62779 | 158.347 | 310.7 | 263.6 | 59.49 |
| 2361000 | 74.7 | 1748.1 | 2607 | 30562 | 63779 | 29.138 | 434.0 | 11.4 | 65.85 |
| 2362000 | 276.9 | 557.8 | 374 | 31562 | 64779 | 88.131 | 118.9 | 72.2 | 72.21 |
| 2363000 | 80.2 | 1557.8 | 1374 | 32562 | 65779 | 147.123 | 242.2 | 133.1 | 78.58 |
| 2364000 | 282.5 | 367.5 | 2374 | 33562 | 66779 | 17.914 | 365.5 | 193.9 | 84.94 |
| 2365000 | 85.8 | 1367.5 | 142 | 34562 | 67779 | 76.906 | 50.4 | 254.7 | 91.30 |
| 2366000 | 288.0 | 177.1 | 1142 | 35562 | 68779 | 135.898 | 173.6 | 2.5 | 97.67 |
| 2367000 | 91.4 | 1177.1 | 2142 | 36562 | 69779 | 6.689 | 296.9 | 63.4 | 104.03 |
| 2368000 | 293.6 | 2177.1 | 3142 | 37562 | 70779 | 65.682 | 420.2 | 124.2 | 110.40 |
| 2369000 | 97.0 | 986.8 | 909 | 38562 | 71779 | 124.674 | 105.1 | 185.0 | 116.76 |
| 2370000 | 299.2 | 1986.8 | 1909 | 39562 | 72779 | 183.666 | 228.4 | 245.8 | 123.12 |
| 2371000 | 102.6 | 796.5 | 2909 | 40562 | 73779 | 54.457 | 351.7 | 306.7 | 5.28 |
| 2372000 | 304.8 | 1796.5 | 676 | 41562 | 74779 | 113.450 | 36.6 | 54.5 | 11.64 |
| 2373000 | 108.1 | 606.1 | 1676 | 42562 | 75779 | 172.442 | 159.9 | 115.3 | 18.01 |
| 2374000 | 310.4 | 1606.1 | 2676 | 43562 | 76779 | 43.233 | 283.2 | 176.1 | 24.37 |
| 2375000 | 113.7 | 415.8 | 443 | 44562 | 77779 | 102.225 | 406.4 | 237.0 | 30.73 |
| 2376000 | 315.9 | 1415.8 | 1443 | 45562 | 78779 | 161.217 | 91.3 | 297.8 | 37.09 |
| 2377000 | 119.3 | 225.5 | 2443 | 46562 | 79779 | 32.008 | 214.6 | 45.6 | 43.45 |
| 2378000 | 321.5 | 1225.5 | 210 | 47562 | 80779 | 91.000 | 337.9 | 106.4 | 49.82 |
| 2379000 | 124.9 | 35.1 | 1210 | 48562 | 81779 | 149.992 | 22.8 | 167.3 | 56.18 |
| 2380000 | 327.1 | 1035.1 | 2210 | 49562 | 82779 | 20.784 | 146.1 | 228.1 | 62.54 |
| 2381000 | 130.4 | 2035.1 | 3210 | 50562 | 83779 | 79.777 | 269.4 | 288.9 | 68.90 |
| 2382000 | 332.7 | 844.8 | 978 | 51562 | 84779 | 138.769 | 392.7 | 36.7 | 75.26 |
| 2383000 | 136.0 | 1844.8 | 1978 | 52562 | 85779 | 9.560 | 77.6 | 97.6 | 81.63 |
| 2384000 | 338.3 | 654.5 | 2978 | 53562 | 86779 | 68.552 | 200.9 | 158.4 | 87.99 |
| 2385000 | 141.6 | 1654.5 | 745 | 54562 | 87778 | 127.545 | 324.1 | 219.2 | 94.35 |
| 2386000 | 343.8 | 464.2 | 1745 | 55562 | 88778 | 186.537 | 9.0 | 280.1 | 100.72 |
| 2387000 | 147.2 | 1464.2 | 2745 | 56562 | 89778 | 57.328 | 132.3 | 27.9 | 107.08 |
| 2388000 | 349.4 | 273.8 | 512 | 57562 | 90778 | 116.321 | 255.6 | 88.7 | 113.45 |
| 2389000 | 152.8 | 1273.8 | 1512 | 58562 | 91778 | 175.313 | 378.9 | 149.5 | 119.81 |
| 2390000 | 355.0 | 83.5 | 2512 | 59562 | 92778 | 46.105 | 63.8 | 210.4 | 1.97 |
| 2391000 | 158.3 | 1083.5 | 279 | 60562 | 93778 | 105.097 | 187.1 | 271.2 | 8.33 |
| 2392000 | 360.6 | 2083.5 | 1279 | 61562 | 94778 | 164.090 | 310.4 | 19.0 | 14.69 |
| 2393000 | 163.9 | 893.2 | 2279 | 62562 | 288 | 34.881 | 433.6 | 79.8 | 21.06 |
| 2394000 | 366.2 | 1893.2 | 46 | 63562 | 1288 | 93.873 | 118.6 | 140.6 | 27.42 |
| 2395000 | 169.5 | 702.8 | 1046 | 64562 | 2288 | 152.866 | 241.8 | 201.5 | 33.78 |
| 2396000 | 371.7 | 1702.8 | 2046 | 65562 | 3287 | 23.657 | 365.1 | 262.3 | 40.15 |
| 2397000 | 175.1 | 512.5 | 3046 | 66562 | 4287 | 82.649 | 50.0 | 10.1 | 46.51 |
| 2398000 | 377.3 | 1512.5 | 813 | 67562 | 5287 | 141.642 | 173.3 | 70.9 | 52.88 |
| 2399000 | 180.7 | 322.1 | 1813 | 68562 | 6287 | 12.433 | 296.6 | 131.8 | 59.24 |
| 2400000 | 382.9 | 1322.1 | 2813 | 69562 | 7287 | 71.425 | 419.9 | 192.6 | 65.60 |

# TABLE II*a*.

Epochs and Arguments for each Thousandth Day, from 2300000 to 2400000.

For Washington Mean Noon.

| Day of Julian Period. | Arg. 82. | 83. | 84. | 85. | 86. | 87. | 88. | 89. | 90. |
|---|---|---|---|---|---|---|---|---|---|
| | d. | d. | d. | d. | d. | d. | d. | d. | d. |
| 2300000 | 11.905 | 34.45 | 10.79 | 7.32 | 1.08 | 2.19 | 2.97 | 6.79 | 5.9 |
| 2301000 | 1.051 | 14.95 | 15.33 | 19.50 | 5.72 | 7.62 | 5.65 | 2.56 | 5.2 |
| 2302000 | 5.062 | 34.65 | 0.74 | 8.17 | 10.37 | 13.05 | 8.34 | 17.64 | 4.5 |
| 2303000 | 9.073 | 15.15 | 5.28 | 20.36 | 15.01 | 4.27 | 11.02 | 13.41 | 3.8 |
| 2304000 | 13.084 | 34.86 | 9.82 | 9.03 | 19.65 | 9.69 | 13.70 | 9.18 | 3.1 |
| 2305000 | 2.229 | 15.36 | 14.37 | 21.22 | 24.30 | 0.91 | 1.72 | 4.94 | 2.4 |
| 2306000 | 6.241 | 35.07 | 18.91 | 9.89 | 28.94 | 6.34 | 4.40 | 0.71 | 1.6 |
| 2307000 | 10.252 | 15.56 | 4.31 | 22.08 | 33.59 | 11.76 | 7.08 | 15.79 | 0.9 |
| 2308000 | 14.263 | 35.27 | 8.85 | 10.74 | 38.23 | 2.98 | 9.77 | 11.56 | 0.2 |
| 2309000 | 3.408 | 15.77 | 13.39 | 22.93 | 4.59 | 8.40 | 12.45 | 7.33 | 31.8 |
| 2310000 | 7.420 | 35.48 | 17.93 | 11.60 | 9.23 | 13.83 | 0.47 | 3.10 | 31.1 |
| 2311000 | 11.431 | 15.98 | 3.33 | 0.27 | 13.87 | 5.05 | 3.15 | 18.18 | 30.4 |
| 2312000 | 0.577 | 35.69 | 7.88 | 12.45 | 18.52 | 10.47 | 5.83 | 13.94 | 29.7 |
| 2313000 | 4.588 | 16.18 | 12.42 | 1.12 | 23.16 | 1.69 | 8.52 | 9.71 | 29.0 |
| 2314000 | 8.599 | 35.89 | 18.96 | 13.31 | 27.80 | 7.12 | 11.20 | 5.48 | 28.3 |
| 2315000 | 12.610 | 16.39 | 2.36 | 1.98 | 32.45 | 12.54 | 13.88 | 1.25 | 27.6 |
| 2316000 | 1.756 | 36.10 | 6.91 | 14.17 | 37.09 | 3.76 | 1.90 | 16.33 | 26.9 |
| 2317000 | 5.767 | 16.60 | 11.45 | 2.83 | 3.44 | 9.18 | 4.58 | 12.10 | 26.2 |
| 2318000 | 9.778 | 36.31 | 15.99 | 15.02 | 8.09 | 0.40 | 7.26 | 7.86 | 25.5 |
| 2319000 | 13.789 | 16.80 | 1.39 | 3.69 | 12.74 | 5.83 | 9.95 | 3.63 | 24.8 |
| 2320000 | 2.935 | 36.51 | 5.93 | 15.88 | 17.38 | 11.25 | 12.63 | 18.71 | 24.1 |
| 2321000 | 6.946 | 17.01 | 10.48 | 4.55 | 22.03 | 2.47 | 0.65 | 14.48 | 23.4 |
| 2322000 | 10.957 | 36.72 | 15.02 | 16.73 | 26.67 | 7.90 | 3.33 | 10.25 | 22.7 |
| 2323000 | 0.103 | 17.22 | 0.42 | 5.40 | 31.32 | 13.32 | 6.01 | 6.02 | 22.0 |
| 2324000 | 4.114 | 36.93 | 4.96 | 17.59 | 35.96 | 4.54 | 8.70 | 1.78 | 21.3 |
| 2325000 | 8.125 | 17.42 | 9.50 | 6.26 | 2.32 | 9.96 | 11.38 | 16.86 | 20.6 |
| 2326000 | 12.136 | 37.13 | 14.05 | 18.45 | 6.96 | 1.18 | 14.06 | 12.63 | 19.8 |
| 2327000 | 1.282 | 17.63 | 18.59 | 7.11 | 11.61 | 6.61 | 2.08 | 8.40 | 19.1 |
| 2328000 | 5.293 | 37.34 | 3.99 | 19.30 | 16.25 | 12.03 | 4.76 | 4.17 | 18.4 |
| 2329000 | 9.304 | 17.83 | 8.53 | 7.97 | 20.89 | 3.25 | 7.45 | 19.25 | 17.7 |
| 2330000 | 13.315 | 37.55 | 13.07 | 20.16 | 25.53 | 8.67 | 10.13 | 15.02 | 17.0 |
| 2331000 | 2.461 | 18.04 | 17.62 | 8.83 | 30.18 | 14.10 | 12.81 | 10.79 | 16.3 |
| 2332000 | 6.472 | 37.75 | 3.02 | 21.02 | 34.82 | 5.32 | 0.83 | 6.55 | 15.6 |
| 2333000 | 10.483 | 18.25 | 7.56 | 9.68 | 1.18 | 10.74 | 3.51 | 2.32 | 14.9 |
| 2334000 | 14.494 | 37.96 | 12.10 | 21.87 | 5.83 | 1.96 | 6.19 | 17.40 | 14.2 |
| 2335000 | 3.640 | 18.46 | 16.64 | 10.54 | 10.47 | 7.39 | 8.88 | 13.17 | 13.5 |
| 2336000 | 7.651 | 38.16 | 2.04 | 22.73 | 15.11 | 12.81 | 11.56 | 8.94 | 12.8 |
| 2337000 | 11.662 | 18.66 | 6.59 | 11.40 | 19.75 | 4.03 | 14.24 | 4.71 | 12.1 |
| 2338000 | 0.808 | 38.37 | 11.13 | 23.58 | 24.40 | 9.45 | 2.26 | 0.47 | 11.4 |
| 2339000 | 4.819 | 18.87 | 15.67 | 12.25 | 29.04 | 0.67 | 4.94 | 15.55 | 10.7 |
| 2340000 | 8.831 | 38.58 | 1.07 | 0.92 | 33.69 | 6.10 | 7.63 | 11.32 | 10.0 |
| 2341000 | 12.842 | 19.08 | 5.61 | 13.11 | 0.05 | 11.52 | 10.31 | 7.09 | 9.3 |
| 2342000 | 1.987 | 38.78 | 10.16 | 1.78 | 4.69 | 2.74 | 12.99 | 2.86 | 8.6 |
| 2343000 | 5.999 | 19.28 | 14.70 | 13.96 | 9.33 | 8.16 | 1.01 | 17.94 | 7.9 |
| 2344000 | 10.010 | 38.99 | 0.10 | 2.63 | 13.98 | 13.59 | 3.69 | 13.71 | 7.2 |
| 2345000 | 14.021 | 19.49 | 4.64 | 14.82 | 18.62 | 4.81 | 6.37 | 9.47 | 6.5 |
| 2346000 | 3.167 | 39.20 | 9.18 | 3.49 | 23.26 | 10.23 | 9.06 | 5.24 | 5.8 |
| 2347000 | 7.178 | 19.69 | 13.73 | 15.68 | 27.91 | 1.45 | 11.74 | 1.01 | 5.1 |
| 2348000 | 11.189 | 0.19 | 18.27 | 4.34 | 32.55 | 6.88 | 14.42 | 16.09 | 4.4 |
| 2349000 | 0.335 | 19.90 | 3.67 | 16.53 | 37.19 | 12.30 | 2.44 | 11.86 | 3.7 |
| 2350000 | 4.346 | 0.40 | 8.21 | 5.20 | 3.55 | 3.52 | 5.12 | 7.63 | 3.0 |

# TABLE II*a*.

Epochs and Arguments for each Thousandth Day, from 2300000 to 2400000.

For Washington Mean Noon.

| Day of Julian Period. | Arg. 82. | 83. | 84. | 85. | 86. | 87. | 88. | 89. | 90. |
|---|---|---|---|---|---|---|---|---|---|
| | d. | d. | d. | d. | d. | d. | d. | d | d. |
| 2350000 | 4.346 | 0.40 | 8.21 | 5.20 | 3.55 | 3.52 | 5.12 | 7.63 | 3.0 |
| 2351000 | 8.357 | 20.11 | 12.76 | 17.39 | 8.20 | 8.94 | 7.81 | 3.40 | 2.3 |
| 2352000 | 12.368 | 0.61 | 17.30 | 6.06 | 12.84 | 0.16 | 10.49 | 18.48 | 1.6 |
| 2353000 | 1.514 | 20.31 | 2.70 | 18.25 | 17.48 | 5.59 | 13.17 | 14.24 | 0.9 |
| 2354000 | 5.525 | 0.81 | 7.24 | 6.91 | 22.13 | 11.01 | 1.19 | 10.01 | 0.2 |
| 2355000 | 9.536 | 20.52 | 11.78 | 19.10 | 26.77 | 2.23 | 3.87 | 5.78 | 31.8 |
| 2356000 | 13.548 | 1.02 | 16.33 | 7.77 | 31.41 | 7.66 | 6.55 | 1.55 | 31.0 |
| 2357000 | 2.693 | 20.73 | 1.73 | 19.96 | 36.05 | 13.08 | 9.24 | 16.63 | 30.3 |
| 2358000 | 6.704 | 1.22 | 6.27 | 8.63 | 2.42 | 4.30 | 11.92 | 12.40 | 29.6 |
| 2359000 | 10.716 | 20.93 | 10.81 | 20.81 | 7.06 | 9.72 | 14.60 | 8.16 | 28.9 |
| 2360000 | 14.727 | 1.43 | 15.35 | 9.48 | 11.70 | 0.94 | 2.62 | 3.93 | 28.2 |
| 2361000 | 3.872 | 21.14 | 0.75 | 21.67 | 16.35 | 6.37 | 5.30 | 19.01 | 27.5 |
| 2362000 | 7.884 | 1.64 | 5.30 | 10.34 | 20.99 | 11.79 | 7.99 | 14.78 | 26.8 |
| 2363000 | 11.895 | 21.35 | 9.84 | 22.53 | 25.63 | 3.01 | 10.67 | 10.55 | 26.1 |
| 2364000 | 1.041 | 1.84 | 14.38 | 11.19 | 30.28 | 8.43 | 13.35 | 6.32 | 25.4 |
| 2365000 | 5.052 | 21.55 | 18.92 | 23.38 | 34.92 | 13.86 | 1.37 | 2.08 | 24.7 |
| 2366000 | 9.063 | 2.05 | 4.32 | 12.05 | 1.28 | 5.08 | 4.05 | 17.16 | 24.0 |
| 2367000 | 13.074 | 21.76 | 8.87 | 0.72 | 5.92 | 10.50 | 6.74 | 12.93 | 23.3 |
| 2368000 | 2.220 | 2.26 | 13.41 | 12.91 | 10.57 | 1.72 | 9.42 | 8.70 | 22.6 |
| 2369000 | 6.231 | 21.97 | 17.95 | 1.57 | 15.21 | 7.15 | 12.10 | 4.47 | 21.9 |
| 2370000 | 10.242 | 2.46 | 3.35 | 13.76 | 19.86 | 12.57 | 0.12 | 0.24 | 21.2 |
| 2371000 | 14.253 | 22.17 | 7.89 | 2.43 | 24.50 | 3.79 | 2.80 | 15.32 | 20.5 |
| 2372000 | 3.399 | 2.67 | 12.44 | 14.62 | 29.14 | 9.22 | 5.48 | 11.09 | 19.8 |
| 2373000 | 7.410 | 22.38 | 16.98 | 3.29 | 33.78 | 0.43 | 8.17 | 6.85 | 19.1 |
| 2374000 | 11.422 | 2.88 | 2.38 | 15.48 | 0.15 | 5.86 | 10.85 | 2.62 | 18.4 |
| 2375000 | 0.567 | 22.59 | 6.93 | 4.14 | 4.79 | 11.28 | 13.53 | 17.70 | 17.7 |
| 2376000 | 4.579 | 3.08 | 11.46 | 16.33 | 9.43 | 2.50 | 1.55 | 13.47 | 16.9 |
| 2377000 | 8.590 | 22.79 | 16.01 | 5.00 | 14.08 | 7.93 | 4.23 | 9.24 | 16.2 |
| 2378000 | 12.601 | 3.29 | 1.41 | 17.19 | 18.72 | 13.35 | 6.92 | 5.01 | 15.5 |
| 2379000 | 1.747 | 23.00 | 5.95 | 5.86 | 23.36 | 4.57 | 9.60 | 0.77 | 14.8 |
| 2380000 | 5.758 | 3.50 | 10.49 | 18.04 | 28.01 | 10.00 | 12.28 | 15.85 | 14.1 |
| 2381000 | 9.769 | 23.20 | 15.03 | 6.71 | 32.65 | 1.21 | 0.30 | 11.62 | 13.4 |
| 2382000 | 13.780 | 3.70 | 0.43 | 18.90 | 37.29 | 6.64 | 2.98 | 7.39 | 12.7 |
| 2383000 | 2.926 | 23.41 | 4.98 | 7.57 | 3.65 | 12.06 | 5.66 | 3.16 | 12.0 |
| 2384000 | 6.937 | 3.91 | 9.52 | 19.76 | 8.30 | 3.28 | 8.35 | 18.24 | 11.3 |
| 2385000 | 10.949 | 23.62 | 14.06 | 8.42 | 12.94 | 8.71 | 11.03 | 14.01 | 10.6 |
| 2386000 | 0.094 | 4.12 | 18.61 | 20.61 | 17.58 | 14.12 | 13.71 | 9.78 | 9.9 |
| 2387000 | 4.106 | 23.82 | 4.00 | 9.28 | 22.23 | 5.35 | 1.73 | 5.54 | 9.2 |
| 2388000 | 8.117 | 4.32 | 8.55 | 21.47 | 26.87 | 10.78 | 4.41 | 1.31 | 8.5 |
| 2389000 | 12.128 | 24.03 | 13.09 | 10.14 | 31.51 | 2.00 | 7.10 | 16.39 | 7.8 |
| 2390000 | 1.274 | 4.53 | 17.63 | 22.32 | 36.16 | 7.42 | 9.78 | 12.16 | 7.1 |
| 2391000 | 5.285 | 24.24 | 3.03 | 10.99 | 2.52 | 12.84 | 12.46 | 7.93 | 6.4 |
| 2392000 | 9.296 | 4.74 | 7.58 | 23.18 | 7.16 | 4.06 | 0.48 | 3.70 | 5.7 |
| 2393000 | 13.307 | 24.45 | 12.12 | 11.85 | 11.80 | 9.49 | 3.16 | 18.78 | 5.0 |
| 2394000 | 2.453 | 4.95 | 16.66 | 0.52 | 16.45 | 0.70 | 5.84 | 14.54 | 4.3 |
| 2395000 | 6.464 | 24.65 | 2.06 | 12.70 | 21.09 | 6.13 | 8.53 | 10.31 | 3.6 |
| 2396000 | 10.476 | 5.15 | 6.60 | 1.37 | 25.73 | 11.55 | 11.21 | 6.08 | 2.8 |
| 2397000 | 14.487 | 24.86 | 11.15 | 13.56 | 30.38 | 2.77 | 13.89 | 1.85 | 2.1 |
| 2398000 | 3.633 | 5.36 | 15.69 | 2.23 | 35.02 | 8.20 | 1.91 | 16.93 | 1.4 |
| 2399000 | 7.644 | 25.07 | 1.09 | 14.42 | 1.38 | 13.62 | 4.59 | 12.70 | 0.7 |
| 2400000 | 11.655 | 5.56 | 5.63 | 3.09 | 6.02 | 4.84 | 7.28 | 8.47 | 0.0 |

# TABLE IIb.

Epochs and Arguments for each Thousandth Day, from 2400000 to 2500000.

For Washington Mean Noon.

| Day of Julian Period. | u | u′ | y-u | (y-u′) | Arg. 1. | 1′. | 2. | 2′. |
|---|---|---|---|---|---|---|---|---|
| | ° ″ | ″ | ° ″ | ″ | d. | 0.000 | d. | 0.000 |
| 2400000 | 354 3268.55 | +0.37 | 25 1649.8 | −0.3 | 27.0175339 | +0329 | 7.505986 | −022 |
| 2401000 | 211 1097.01 | 0.39 | 78 1483.2 | 0.3 | 7.4991263 | 0344 | 21.335956 | 023 |
| 2402000 | 67 2525.49 | 0.41 | 131 1316.6 | 0.3 | 15.5352726 | 0359 | 3.353990 | 024 |
| 2403000 | 284 353.99 | 0.42 | 184 1149.9 | 0.3 | 23.5714205 | 0375 | 17.183959 | 025 |
| 2404000 | 140 1782.50 | 0.44 | 237 983.3 | 0.3 | 4.0530174 | 0390 | 31.013926 | 026 |
| 2405000 | 356 3211.03 | 0.46 | 290 816.7 | 0.3 | 12.0891684 | 0405 | 13.031957 | 027 |
| 2406000 | 213 1039.58 | 0.48 | 343 650.0 | 0.4 | 20.1253208 | 0421 | 26.861922 | 028 |
| 2407000 | 69 2468.14 | 0.50 | 36 483.3 | 0.4 | 0.6069224 | 0436 | 8.879951 | 029 |
| 2408000 | 286 296.72 | 0.51 | 89 316.6 | 0.4 | 8.6430779 | 0452 | 22.709914 | 030 |
| 2409000 | 142 1725.32 | 0.53 | 142 149.9 | 0.4 | 16.6792349 | 0467 | 4.727941 | 031 |
| 2410000 | 358 3153.94 | 0.55 | 194 3583.2 | 0.4 | 24.7153935 | 0482 | 18.557902 | 032 |
| 2411000 | 215 982.57 | 0.57 | 247 3416.5 | 0.4 | 5.1970011 | 0497 | 0.575927 | 033 |
| 2412000 | 71 2411.22 | 0.59 | 300 3249.8 | 0.4 | 13.2331628 | 0512 | 14.405886 | 034 |
| 2413000 | 288 239.89 | 0.60 | 353 3083.0 | 0.4 | 21.2693259 | 0528 | 28.235845 | 035 |
| 2414000 | 144 1668.57 | 0.62 | 46 2916.3 | 0.4 | 1.7509382 | 0543 | 10.253866 | 036 |
| 2415000 | 0 3097.28 | 0.63 | 99 2749.5 | 0.4 | 9.7871044 | 0558 | 24.083823 | 037 |
| 2416000 | 217 926.00 | 0.65 | 152 2582.7 | 0.5 | 17.8232722 | 0574 | 6.101842 | 038 |
| 2417000 | 73 2354.73 | 0.67 | 205 2415.9 | 0.5 | 25.8594414 | 0589 | 19.931797 | 039 |
| 2418000 | 290 183.49 | 0.68 | 258 2249.1 | 0.5 | 6.3410598 | 0605 | 1.949814 | 040 |
| 2419000 | 146 1612.26 | 0.70 | 311 2082.3 | 0.5 | 14.3772322 | 0620 | 15.779767 | 041 |
| 2420000 | 2 3041.05 | 0.72 | 4 1915.5 | 0.5 | 22.4134060 | 0635 | 29.609718 | 042 |
| 2421000 | 219 869.85 | 0.74 | 57 1748.6 | 0.5 | 2.8950290 | 0650 | 11.627732 | 043 |
| 2422000 | 75 2298.68 | 0.76 | 110 1581.8 | 0.5 | 10.9312059 | 0665 | 25.457682 | 044 |
| 2423000 | 292 127.52 | 0.77 | 163 1414.9 | 0.5 | 18.9673844 | 0681 | 7.475694 | 045 |
| 2424000 | 148 1556.38 | 0.79 | 216 1248.0 | 0.5 | 27.0035644 | 0696 | 21.305642 | 046 |
| 2425000 | 4 2985.25 | 0.80 | 269 1081.1 | 0.5 | 7.4851935 | 0711 | 3.323652 | 047 |
| 2426000 | 221 814.14 | 0.82 | 322 914.2 | 0.6 | 15.5213766 | 0727 | 17.153597 | 048 |
| 2427000 | 77 2243.05 | 0.84 | 15 747.3 | 0.6 | 23.5575612 | 0742 | 30.983542 | 049 |
| 2428000 | 294 71.98 | 0.85 | 68 580.4 | 0.6 | 4.0391949 | 0758 | 13.001549 | 050 |
| 2429000 | 150 1500.93 | 0.87 | 121 413.5 | 0.6 | 12.0753826 | 0773 | 26.831491 | 051 |
| 2430000 | 6 2929.89 | 0.89 | 174 246.5 | 0.6 | 20.1115718 | 0788 | 8.849497 | 052 |
| 2431000 | 223 758.87 | 0.91 | 227 79.5 | 0.6 | 0.5932101 | 0803 | 22.679437 | 053 |
| 2432000 | 79 2187.86 | 0.93 | 279 3512.6 | 0.6 | 8.6294024 | 0819 | 4.697440 | 054 |
| 2433000 | 296 16.88 | 0.94 | 332 3345.6 | 0.7 | 16.6655962 | 0834 | 18.527379 | 055 |
| 2434000 | 152 1445.91 | 0.96 | 25 3178.6 | 0.7 | 24.7017915 | 0850 | 0.545380 | 056 |
| 2435000 | 8 2874.96 | 0.97 | 78 3011.6 | 0.7 | 5.1834360 | 0865 | 14.375316 | 057 |
| 2436000 | 225 704.02 | 0.99 | 131 2844.5 | 0.7 | 13.2196344 | 0880 | 28.205251 | 058 |
| 2437000 | 81 2133.10 | 1.01 | 184 2677.5 | 0.7 | 21.2558343 | 0896 | 10.223250 | 059 |
| 2438000 | 297 3562.20 | 1.02 | 237 2510.5 | 0.8 | 1.7374834 | 0911 | 24.053183 | 060 |
| 2439000 | 154 1391.32 | 1.04 | 290 2343.4 | 0.8 | 9.7736864 | 0927 | 6.071179 | 061 |
| 2440000 | 10 2820.46 | 1.06 | 343 2176.3 | 0.8 | 17.8098910 | 0942 | 19.901110 | 062 |
| 2441000 | 227 649.61 | 1.08 | 36 2009.2 | 0.8 | 25.8460971 | 0957 | 1.919104 | 063 |
| 2442000 | 83 2078.78 | 1.10 | 89 1842.1 | 0.8 | 6.3277523 | 0972 | 15.749033 | 064 |
| 2443000 | 299 3507.97 | 1.11 | 142 1675.0 | 0.8 | 14.3639615 | 0988 | 29.578961 | 065 |
| 2444000 | 156 1337.17 | 1.13 | 195 1507.9 | 0.8 | 22.4001722 | 1003 | 11.596952 | 066 |
| 2445000 | 12 2766.39 | 1.15 | 248 1340.8 | 0.8 | 2.8818320 | 1018 | 25.426878 | 067 |
| 2446000 | 229 595.63 | 1.17 | 301 1173.6 | 0.9 | 10.9180457 | 1034 | 7.444867 | 068 |
| 2447000 | 85 2024.89 | 1.19 | 354 1006.5 | 0.9 | 18.9542611 | 1049 | 21.274791 | 069 |
| 2448000 | 301 3454.16 | 1.20 | 47 839.3 | 0.9 | 26.9904779 | 1065 | 3.292778 | 070 |
| 2449000 | 158 1283.45 | 1.22 | 100 672.1 | 0.9 | 7.4721439 | 1080 | 17.122700 | 071 |
| 2450000 | 14 2712.76 | +1.24 | 153 504.9 | −0.9 | 15.5083639 | +1095 | 30.952622 | −072 |

# TABLE II*b*.

Epochs and Arguments for each Thousandth Day, from 2400000 to 2500000.

For Washington Mean Noon.

| Day of Julian Period. | u | u′ | y-u | (y-u′) | Arg. 1. | 1′. | 2. | 2′. |
|---|---|---|---|---|---|---|---|---|
| | ° ″ | ″ | ° ″ | ″ | d. | 0.000 | d. | 0.000 |
| 2450000 | 14 2712.76 | +1.24 | 153 504.9 | −0.9 | 15.5083639 | +1095 | 30.952622 | −072 |
| 2451000 | 231 542.09 | 1.26 | 206 337.7 | 0.9 | 23.5445853 | 1110 | 12.970606 | 073 |
| 2452000 | 87 1971.43 | 1.28 | 259 170.5 | 0.9 | 4.0262559 | 1126 | 26.800525 | 074 |
| 2453000 | 303 3400.79 | 1.29 | 312 3.3 | 0.9 | 12.0624804 | 1141 | 8.818507 | 075 |
| 2454000 | 160 1230.17 | 1.31 | 4 3436.0 | 0.9 | 20.0987065 | 1157 | 22.648424 | 076 |
| 2455000 | 16 2659.56 | 1.32 | 57 3268.8 | 0.9 | 0.5803817 | 1172 | 4.666404 | 077 |
| 2456000 | 233 488.97 | 1.34 | 110 3101.5 | 1.0 | 8.6166109 | 1187 | 18.496319 | 078 |
| 2457000 | 89 1918.40 | 1.36 | 163 2934.2 | 1.0 | 16.6528416 | 1203 | 0.514296 | 079 |
| 2458000 | 305 3347.85 | 1.37 | 216 2766.9 | 1.0 | 24.6890738 | 1218 | 14.344209 | 080 |
| 2459000 | 162 1177.32 | 1.39 | 269 2599.6 | 1.0 | 5.1707552 | 1234 | 28.174121 | 081 |
| 2460000 | 18 2606.80 | 1.41 | 322 2432.3 | 1.0 | 13.2069906 | 1249 | 10.192097 | 082 |
| 2461000 | 235 436.30 | 1.43 | 15 2265.0 | 1.0 | 21.2432275 | 1264 | 24.022007 | 083 |
| 2462000 | 91 1865.82 | 1.45 | 68 2097.6 | 1.0 | 1.7249134 | 1280 | 6.039980 | 084 |
| 2463000 | 307 3295.35 | 1.46 | 121 1930.3 | 1.0 | 9.7611534 | 1295 | 19.869887 | 085 |
| 2464000 | 164 1124.90 | 1.48 | 174 1762.9 | 1.0 | 17.7973949 | 1311 | 1.887858 | 086 |
| 2465000 | 20 2554.47 | 1.49 | 227 1595.6 | 1.0 | 25.8336379 | 1326 | 15.717764 | 087 |
| 2466000 | 237 384.05 | 1.51 | 280 1428.2 | 1.1 | 6.3153300 | 1341 | 29.547669 | 088 |
| 2467000 | 93 1813.66 | 1.53 | 333 1260.8 | 1.1 | 14.3515761 | 1357 | 11.565637 | 089 |
| 2468000 | 309 3243.28 | 1.54 | 26 1093.4 | 1.1 | 22.3878238 | 1372 | 25.395539 | 090 |
| 2469000 | 166 1072.92 | 1.56 | 79 925.9 | 1.1 | 2.8695206 | 1388 | 7.413505 | 091 |
| 2470000 | 22 2502.58 | 1.58 | 132 758.5 | 1.1 | 10.9057714 | 1403 | 21.243406 | 092 |
| 2471000 | 239 332.25 | 1.60 | 185 591.0 | 1.1 | 18.9420237 | 1418 | 3.261370 | 093 |
| 2472000 | 95 1761.94 | 1.62 | 238 423.6 | 1.1 | 26.9782775 | 1434 | 17.091268 | 094 |
| 2473000 | 311 3191.65 | 1.63 | 291 256.1 | 1.1 | 7.4599805 | 1449 | 30.921166 | 095 |
| 2474000 | 168 1021.37 | 1.65 | 344 88.6 | 1.1 | 15.4962374 | 1465 | 12.939127 | 096 |
| 2475000 | 24 2451.11 | 1.67 | 36 3521.1 | 1.1 | 23.5324959 | 1480 | 26.769022 | 097 |
| 2476000 | 241 280.87 | 1.69 | 89 3353.6 | 1.2 | 4.0142035 | 1496 | 8.786981 | 099 |
| 2477000 | 97 1710.65 | 1.71 | 142 3186.1 | 1.2 | 12.0504650 | 1512 | 22.616874 | 100 |
| 2478000 | 313 3140.44 | 1.72 | 195 3018.6 | 1.2 | 20.0867281 | 1527 | 4.634831 | 101 |
| 2479000 | 170 970.26 | 1.74 | 248 2851.0 | 1.2 | 0.5684403 | 1543 | 18.464723 | 102 |
| 2480000 | 26 2400.09 | 1.76 | 301 2683.4 | 1.2 | 8.6047066 | 1558 | 0.482677 | 103 |
| 2481000 | 243 229.94 | 1.78 | 354 2515.9 | 1.2 | 16.6409743 | 1573 | 14.312566 | 104 |
| 2482000 | 99 1659.80 | 1.80 | 47 2348.3 | 1.2 | 24.6772436 | 1589 | 28.142454 | 105 |
| 2483000 | 315 3089.69 | 1.81 | 100 2180.7 | 1.3 | 5.1589620 | 1604 | 10.160406 | 106 |
| 2484000 | 172 919.59 | 1.83 | 153 2013.1 | 1.3 | 13.1952344 | 1620 | 23.990294 | 107 |
| 2485000 | 28 2349.50 | 1.84 | 206 1845.5 | 1.3 | 21.2315084 | 1635 | 6.008243 | 108 |
| 2486000 | 245 179.44 | 1.86 | 259 1677.8 | 1.3 | 1.7132314 | 1651 | 19.838127 | 109 |
| 2487000 | 101 1609.39 | 1.88 | 312 1510.2 | 1.4 | 9.7495084 | 1667 | 1.856075 | 110 |
| 2488000 | 317 3039.36 | 1.89 | 5 1342.5 | 1.4 | 17.7857870 | 1682 | 15.685956 | 111 |
| 2489000 | 174 869.35 | 1.91 | 58 1174.9 | 1.4 | 25.8220671 | 1698 | 29.515837 | 112 |
| 2490000 | 30 2299.35 | 1.93 | 111 1007.2 | 1.4 | 6.3037963 | 1713 | 11.533782 | 113 |
| 2491000 | 247 129.37 | 1.95 | 164 839.5 | 1.4 | 14.3400795 | 1728 | 25.363662 | 114 |
| 2492000 | 103 1559.41 | 1.97 | 217 671.8 | 1.4 | 22.3763642 | 1744 | 7.381605 | 115 |
| 2493000 | 319 2989.47 | 1.98 | 270 504.1 | 1.4 | 2.8580981 | 1759 | 21.211481 | 116 |
| 2494000 | 176 819.54 | 2.00 | 323 336.3 | 1.4 | 10.8943860 | 1775 | 3.229422 | 117 |
| 2495000 | 32 2249.63 | 2.02 | 16 168.6 | 1.5 | 18.9306754 | 1790 | 17.059297 | 118 |
| 2496000 | 249 79.74 | 2.04 | 69 0.8 | 1.5 | 26.9669663 | 1805 | 30.889171 | 119 |
| 2497000 | 105 1509.87 | 2.06 | 121 3433.1 | 1.5 | 7.4487064 | 1821 | 12.907108 | 120 |
| 2498000 | 321 2940.01 | 2.07 | 174 3265.3 | 1.5 | 15.4850004 | 1836 | 26.736981 | 121 |
| 2499000 | 178 770.17 | 2.09 | 227 3097.5 | 1.5 | 23.5212960 | 1852 | 8.754916 | 122 |
| 2500000 | 34 2220.35 | +2.11 | 280 2929.7 | −1.5 | 4.0030408 | +1867 | 22.584786 | −123 |

# TABLE II*b*.

Epochs and Arguments for each Thousandth Day, from 2400000 to 2500000.

For Washington Mean Noon.

| Day of Julian Period. | Arg. 3. | 3′. | 4. | 5. | 5′. | 6. | 7. | 8. | 9. |
|---|---|---|---|---|---|---|---|---|---|
| | d. | 0.0000 | d. | d. | 0.00 | d. | d. | d. | d. |
| 2400000 | 25.523420 | +08 | 45.9880 | 319.7423 | +03 | 13.0559 | 6.8500 | 1.6577 | 3.2226 |
| 2401000 | 21.483436 | 08 | 315.4686 | 84.3872 | 04 | 2.4961 | 7.0233 | 1.4824 | 19.7294 |
| 2402000 | 17.443452 | 08 | 219.6896 | 260.8172 | 04 | 26.7831 | 7.1967 | 1.3071 | 6.4334 |
| 2403000 | 13.403468 | 09 | 123.9105 | 25.4621 | 04 | 16.2232 | 7.3700 | 1.1319 | 22.9401 |
| 2404000 | 9.363485 | 09 | 28.1314 | 201.8922 | 04 | 5.6633 | 7.5434 | 0.9566 | 9.6441 |
| 2405000 | 5.323502 | 09 | 297.6121 | 378.3224 | 04 | 29.9503 | 7.7167 | 0.7813 | 26.1509 |
| 2406000 | 1.283520 | 10 | 201.8330 | 142.9673 | 05 | 19.3904 | 7.8901 | 0.6060 | 12.8549 |
| 2407000 | 26.774125 | 10 | 106.0540 | 319.3975 | 05 | 8.8305 | 8.0634 | 0.4307 | 29.3617 |
| 2408000 | 22.734144 | 10 | 10.2749 | 84.0425 | 05 | 33.1175 | 8.2368 | 0.2555 | 16.0657 |
| 2409000 | 18.694162 | 11 | 279.7555 | 260.4727 | 05 | 22.5576 | 8.4101 | 0.0802 | 2.7696 |
| 2410000 | 14.654181 | 11 | 183.9765 | 25.1177 | 05 | 11.9977 | 8.5835 | 15.2922 | 19.2765 |
| 2411000 | 10.614200 | 11 | 88.1974 | 201.5479 | 05 | 1.4377 | 8.7569 | 15.1169 | 5.9805 |
| 2412000 | 6.574220 | 12 | 357.6780 | 377.9782 | 06 | 25.7247 | 8.9302 | 14.9416 | 22.4873 |
| 2413000 | 2.534239 | 12 | 261.8990 | 142.6233 | 06 | 15.1648 | 9.1036 | 14.7664 | 9.1912 |
| 2414000 | 28.024848 | 12 | 166.1199 | 319.0535 | 06 | 4.6049 | 9.2769 | 14.5911 | 25.6981 |
| 2415000 | 23.984868 | 13 | 70.3408 | 83.6987 | 06 | 28.8919 | 9.4503 | 14.4158 | 12.4021 |
| 2416000 | 19.944889 | 13 | 339.8215 | 260.1290 | 06 | 18.3320 | 0.0100 | 14.2405 | 28.9088 |
| 2417000 | 15.904910 | 13 | 244.0424 | 24.7742 | 07 | 7.7721 | 0.1833 | 14.0652 | 15.6127 |
| 2418000 | 11.864932 | 14 | 148.2634 | 201.2045 | 07 | 32.0591 | 0.3567 | 13.8900 | 2.3168 |
| 2419000 | 7.824954 | 14 | 52.4843 | 377.6349 | 07 | 21.4992 | 0.5300 | 13.7147 | 18.8237 |
| 2420000 | 3.784977 | 15 | 321.9649 | 142.2801 | 07 | 10.9393 | 0.7034 | 13.5394 | 5.5277 |
| 2421000 | 29.275587 | 15 | 226.1859 | 318.7105 | 07 | 0.3793 | 0.8768 | 13.3641 | 22.0345 |
| 2422000 | 25.235610 | 15 | 130.4068 | 83.3557 | 07 | 24.6663 | 1.0501 | 13.1888 | 8.7385 |
| 2423000 | 21.195634 | 16 | 34.6277 | 259.7862 | 08 | 14.1064 | 1.2235 | 13.0136 | 25.2454 |
| 2424000 | 17.155657 | 16 | 304.1084 | 24.4315 | 08 | 3.5465 | 1.3969 | 12.8383 | 11.9494 |
| 2425000 | 13.115681 | 16 | 208.3293 | 200.8620 | 08 | 27.8335 | 1.5702 | 12.6630 | 28.4562 |
| 2426000 | 9.075706 | 17 | 112.5502 | 377.2924 | 08 | 17.2735 | 1.7436 | 12.4877 | 15.1602 |
| 2427000 | 5.035731 | 17 | 16.7712 | 141.9378 | 08 | 6.7136 | 1.9170 | 12.3124 | 1.8642 |
| 2428000 | 0.995756 | 17 | 286.2518 | 318.3683 | 08 | 31.0006 | 2.0903 | 12.1372 | 18.3710 |
| 2429000 | 26.486369 | 18 | 190.4728 | 83.0137 | 09 | 20.4407 | 2.2637 | 11.9619 | 5.0750 |
| 2430000 | 22.446395 | 18 | 94.6937 | 259.4443 | 09 | 9.8807 | 2.4371 | 11.7866 | 21.5819 |
| 2431000 | 18.406421 | 18 | 364.1743 | 24.0897 | 09 | 34.1677 | 2.6105 | 11.6113 | 8.2859 |
| 2432000 | 14.366448 | 19 | 268.3953 | 200.5203 | 09 | 23.6078 | 2.7838 | 11.4360 | 24.7928 |
| 2433000 | 10.326475 | 19 | 172.6162 | 376.9509 | 09 | 13.0479 | 2.9572 | 11.2608 | 11.4968 |
| 2434000 | 6.286502 | 19 | 76.8371 | 141.5964 | 10 | 2.4879 | 3.1306 | 11.0855 | 28.0036 |
| 2435000 | 2.246530 | 20 | 346.3178 | 318.0270 | 10 | 26.7749 | 3.3039 | 10.9102 | 14.7076 |
| 2436000 | 27.737146 | 20 | 250.5387 | 82.6725 | 10 | 16.2150 | 3.4773 | 10.7349 | 1.4117 |
| 2437000 | 23.697174 | 21 | 154.7596 | 259.1032 | 10 | 5.6550 | 3.6507 | 10.5596 | 17.9185 |
| 2438000 | 19.657203 | 21 | 58.9806 | 23.7488 | 10 | 29.9420 | 3.8240 | 10.3844 | 4.6225 |
| 2439000 | 15.617232 | 21 | 328.4612 | 200.1795 | 10 | 19.3821 | 3.9974 | 10.2091 | 21.1294 |
| 2440000 | 11.577261 | 22 | 232.6822 | 376.6103 | 11 | 8.8221 | 4.1708 | 10.0338 | 7.8335 |
| 2441000 | 7.537291 | 22 | 136.9031 | 141.2559 | 11 | 33.1091 | 4.3442 | 9.8585 | 24.3403 |
| 2442000 | 3.497321 | 22 | 41.1240 | 317.6866 | 11 | 22.5491 | 4.5176 | 9.6832 | 11.0443 |
| 2443000 | 28.987940 | 23 | 310.6047 | 82.3323 | 11 | 11.9892 | 4.6910 | 9.5080 | 27.5512 |
| 2444000 | 24.947970 | 23 | 214.8256 | 258.7631 | 11 | 1.4292 | 4.8643 | 9.3327 | 14.2552 |
| 2445000 | 20.908002 | 23 | 119.0465 | 23.4087 | 12 | 25.7162 | 5.0377 | 9.1574 | 0.9593 |
| 2446000 | 16.868033 | 24 | 23.2675 | 199.8396 | 12 | 15.1562 | 5.2111 | 8.9822 | 17.4661 |
| 2447000 | 12.828065 | 24 | 292.7481 | 376.2705 | 12 | 4.5963 | 5.3844 | 8.8069 | 4.1702 |
| 2448000 | 8.788097 | 24 | 196.9690 | 140.9162 | 12 | 28.8833 | 5.5578 | 8.6317 | 20.6770 |
| 2449000 | 4.748130 | 25 | 101.1900 | 317.3471 | 12 | 18.3233 | 5.7312 | 8.4564 | 7.3811 |
| 2450000 | 0.708163 | +25 | 5.4109 | 81.9929 | +12 | 7.7634 | 5.9046 | 8.2811 | 23.8880 |

# TABLE II*b*.

Epochs and Arguments for each Thousandth Day, from 2400000 to 2500000.

For Washington Mean Noon.

| Day of Julian Period. | Arg. 3. | 3′. | 4. | 5. | 5′. | 6. | 7. | 8. | 9. |
|---|---|---|---|---|---|---|---|---|---|
| | d. | 0.0000 | d. | d. | 0.00 | d. | d. | d. | d. |
| 2450000 | 0.708163 | +25 | 5.4109 | 81.9929 | +12 | 7.7634 | 5.9046 | 8.2811 | 23.8880 |
| 2451000 | 26.198784 | 25 | 274.8916 | 258.4238 | 13 | 32.0503 | 6.0780 | 8.1058 | 10.5921 |
| 2452000 | 22.158818 | 26 | 179.1125 | 23.0696 | 13 | 21.4904 | 6.2514 | 7.9305 | 27.0989 |
| 2453000 | 18.118852 | 26 | 83.3334 | 199.5006 | 13 | 10.9304 | 6.4248 | 7.7553 | 13.8030 |
| 2454000 | 14.078886 | 27 | 352.8141 | 375.9316 | 13 | 0.3705 | 6.5982 | 7.5800 | 0.5070 |
| 2455000 | 10.038921 | 27 | 257.0350 | 140.5774 | 13 | 24.6574 | 6.7716 | 7.4047 | 17.0139 |
| 2456000 | 5.998956 | 27 | 161.2559 | 317.0084 | 13 | 14.0975 | 6.9449 | 7.2295 | 3.7180 |
| 2457000 | 1.958991 | 28 | 65.4769 | 81.6543 | 14 | 3.5375 | 7.1183 | 7.0542 | 20.2248 |
| 2458000 | 27.449615 | 28 | 334.9575 | 258.0854 | 14 | 27.8245 | 7.2917 | 6.8790 | 6.9289 |
| 2459000 | 23.409651 | 28 | 239.1784 | 22.7313 | 14 | 17.2645 | 7.4651 | 6.7037 | 23.4358 |
| 2460000 | 19.369687 | 29 | 143.3994 | 199.1625 | 14 | 6.7045 | 7.6385 | 6.5284 | 10.1399 |
| 2461000 | 15.329724 | 29 | 47.6203 | 375.5936 | 14 | 30.9915 | 7.8119 | 6.3531 | 26.6467 |
| 2462000 | 11.289761 | 29 | 317.1010 | 140.2396 | 15 | 20.4315 | 7.9853 | 6.1779 | 13.3508 |
| 2463000 | 7.249799 | 30 | 221.3219 | 316.6707 | 15 | 9.8716 | 8.1587 | 6.0026 | 0.0549 |
| 2464000 | 3.209837 | 30 | 125.5428 | 81.3167 | 15 | 34.1585 | 8.3321 | 5.8274 | 16.5618 |
| 2465000 | 28.700463 | 30 | 29.7638 | 257.7479 | 15 | 23.5985 | 8.5055 | 5.6521 | 3.2659 |
| 2466000 | 24.660502 | 31 | 299.2444 | 22.3940 | 15 | 13.0386 | 8.6789 | 5.4768 | 19.7728 |
| 2467000 | 20.620541 | 31 | 203.4653 | 198.8252 | 15 | 2.4786 | 8.8523 | 5.3016 | 6.4768 |
| 2468000 | 16.580580 | 32 | 107.6863 | 375.2564 | 16 | 26.7655 | 9.0257 | 5.1263 | 22.9837 |
| 2469000 | 12.540620 | 32 | 11.9072 | 139.9025 | 16 | 16.2056 | 9.1991 | 4.9511 | 9.6878 |
| 2470000 | 8.500660 | 32 | 281.3878 | 316.3339 | 16 | 5.6456 | 9.3725 | 4.7758 | 26.1947 |
| 2471000 | 4.460700 | 33 | 185.6088 | 80.9800 | 16 | 29.9325 | 9.5459 | 4.6005 | 12.8988 |
| 2472000 | 0.420741 | 33 | 89.8297 | 257.4113 | 16 | 19.3725 | 0.1056 | 4.4253 | 29.4057 |
| 2473000 | 25.911370 | 33 | 359.3104 | 22.0575 | 17 | 8.8126 | 0.2790 | 4.2500 | 16.1098 |
| 2474000 | 21.871411 | 34 | 263.5313 | 198.4889 | 17 | 33.0995 | 0.4524 | 4.0748 | 2.8139 |
| 2475000 | 17.831453 | 34 | 167.7522 | 374.9202 | 17 | 22.5395 | 0.6258 | 3.8995 | 19.3208 |
| 2476000 | 13.791495 | 34 | 71.9732 | 139.5665 | 17 | 11.9796 | 0.7993 | 3.7242 | 6.0249 |
| 2477000 | 9.751538 | 35 | 341.4538 | 315.9979 | 17 | 1.4196 | 0.9727 | 3.5490 | 22.5318 |
| 2478000 | 5.711581 | 35 | 245.6747 | 80.6441 | 17 | 25.7065 | 1.1461 | 3.3737 | 9.2359 |
| 2479000 | 1.671624 | 35 | 149.8957 | 257.0756 | 18 | 15.1465 | 1.3195 | 3.1985 | 25.7428 |
| 2480000 | 27.162255 | 36 | 54.1166 | 21.7220 | 18 | 4.5865 | 1.4929 | 3.0232 | 12.4470 |
| 2481000 | 23.122299 | 36 | 323.5972 | 198.1534 | 18 | 28.8734 | 1.6663 | 2.8479 | 28.9539 |
| 2482000 | 19.082343 | 36 | 227.8182 | 374.5849 | 18 | 18.3135 | 1.8397 | 2.6727 | 15.6580 |
| 2483000 | 15.042388 | 37 | 132.0391 | 139.2313 | 18 | 7.7535 | 2.0131 | 2.4974 | 2.3621 |
| 2484000 | 11.002433 | 37 | 36.2601 | 315.6628 | 19 | 32.0404 | 2.1865 | 2.3222 | 18.8690 |
| 2485000 | 6.962478 | 38 | 305.7407 | 80.3092 | 19 | 21.4804 | 2.3599 | 2.1469 | 5.5731 |
| 2486000 | 2.922524 | 38 | 209.9616 | 256.7408 | 19 | 10.9204 | 2.5334 | 1.9716 | 22.0800 |
| 2487000 | 28.413158 | 38 | 114.1826 | 21.3872 | 19 | 0.3604 | 2.7068 | 1.7964 | 8.7841 |
| 2488000 | 24.373205 | 39 | 18.4035 | 197.8188 | 19 | 24.6473 | 2.8802 | 1.6211 | 25.2911 |
| 2489000 | 20.333251 | 39 | 287.8841 | 374.2504 | 19 | 14.0874 | 3.0536 | 1.4459 | 11.9952 |
| 2490000 | 16.293298 | 39 | 192.1051 | 138.8970 | 20 | 3.5274 | 3.2270 | 1.2706 | 28.5021 |
| 2491000 | 12.253346 | 40 | 96.3260 | 315.3287 | 20 | 27.8143 | 3.4004 | 1.0953 | 15.2063 |
| 2492000 | 8.213394 | 40 | 0.5470 | 79.9752 | 20 | 17.2543 | 3.5738 | 0.9201 | 1.9104 |
| 2493000 | 4.173442 | 40 | 270.0276 | 256.4069 | 20 | 6.6943 | 3.7472 | 0.7448 | 18.4173 |
| 2494000 | 0.133490 | 41 | 174.2485 | 21.0534 | 20 | 30.9812 | 3.9207 | 0.5696 | 5.1215 |
| 2495000 | 25.624127 | 41 | 78.4695 | 197.4851 | 20 | 20.4212 | 4.0941 | 0.3943 | 21.6284 |
| 2496000 | 21.584177 | 41 | 347.9501 | 373.9169 | 21 | 9.8612 | 4.2675 | 0.2191 | 8.3325 |
| 2497000 | 17.544226 | 42 | 252.1710 | 138.5635 | 21 | 34.1481 | 4.4410 | 0.0439 | 24.8395 |
| 2498000 | 13.504276 | 42 | 156.3920 | 314.9953 | 21 | 23.5881 | 4.6144 | 15.2559 | 11.5436 |
| 2499000 | 9.464326 | 43 | 60.6129 | 79.6419 | 21 | 13.0281 | 4.7878 | 15.0807 | 28.0505 |
| 2500000 | 5.424377 | +43 | 330.0935 | 256.0737 | +21 | 2.4681 | 4.9612 | 14.9054 | 14.7547 |

# TABLE II*b*.

Epochs and Arguments for each Thousandth Day, from 2400000 to 2500000.

For Washington Mean Noon.

| Day of Julian Period. | Arg. **10.** | **11.** | **12.** | **13.** | **14.** | **15.** | **16.** | **17.** |
|---|---|---|---|---|---|---|---|---|
| | d. | d. | d. | d. | d. | d. | d. | d. |
| 2400000 | 22.0856 | 18.9090 | 37.9433 | 0.4102 | 3.527 | 12.792 | 7.228 | 13.489 |
| 2401000 | 22.8395 | 24.4122 | 344.7031 | 2.0351 | 8.575 | 5.188 | 9.435 | 2.587 |
| 2402000 | 23.5934 | 3.0372 | 304.8427 | 3.6600 | 13.624 | 11.775 | 11.642 | 19.006 |
| 2403000 | 24.3473 | 8.5404 | 264.9823 | 5.2849 | 18.672 | 4.171 | 13.849 | 8.104 |
| 2404000 | 25.1011 | 14.0436 | 225.1219 | 6.9098 | 23.721 | 10.758 | 1.802 | 24.524 |
| 2405000 | 0.2333 | 19.5469 | 185.2615 | 8.5347 | 28.769 | 3.153 | 4.010 | 13.621 |
| 2406000 | 0.9872 | 25.0501 | 145.4010 | 0.0751 | 4.555 | 9.741 | 6.217 | 2.719 |
| 2407000 | 1.7410 | 3.6751 | 105.5406 | 1.7000 | 9.604 | 2.136 | 8.424 | 19.139 |
| 2408000 | 2.4949 | 9.1783 | 65.6802 | 3.3249 | 14.652 | 8.724 | 10.631 | 8.237 |
| 2409000 | 3.2488 | 14.6815 | 25.8198 | 4.9498 | 19.700 | 1.119 | 12.838 | 24.657 |
| 2410000 | 4.0027 | 20.1848 | 332.5795 | 6.5747 | 24.749 | 7.706 | 0.791 | 13.754 |
| 2411000 | 4.7566 | 25.6880 | 292.7191 | 8.1996 | 0.534 | 0.102 | 2.998 | 2.852 |
| 2412000 | 5.5105 | 4.3129 | 252.8586 | 9.8245 | 5.582 | 6.689 | 5.205 | 19.271 |
| 2413000 | 6.2644 | 9.8162 | 212.9982 | 1.3648 | 10.631 | 13.277 | 7.412 | 8.369 |
| 2414000 | 7.0183 | 15.3194 | 173.1378 | 2.9897 | 15.679 | 5.672 | 9.619 | 24.789 |
| 2415000 | 7.7721 | 20.8226 | 133.2774 | 4.6146 | 20.728 | 12.260 | 11.826 | 13.887 |
| 2416000 | 8.5260 | 26.3259 | 93.4169 | 6.2396 | 25.776 | 4.655 | 14.033 | 2.985 |
| 2417000 | 9.2799 | 4.9508 | 53.5565 | 7.8645 | 1.561 | 11.243 | 1.986 | 19.404 |
| 2418000 | 10.0338 | 10.4540 | 13.6961 | 9.4894 | 6.610 | 3.638 | 4.193 | 8.502 |
| 2419000 | 10.7877 | 15.9572 | 320.4557 | 1.0297 | 11.658 | 10.225 | 6.401 | 24.922 |
| 2420000 | 11.5416 | 21.4605 | 280.5952 | 2.6546 | 16.707 | 2.621 | 8.608 | 14.020 |
| 2421000 | 12.2955 | 0.0854 | 240.7348 | 4.2795 | 21.755 | 9.208 | 10.815 | 3.117 |
| 2422000 | 13.0494 | 5.5886 | 200.8743 | 5.9044 | 26.804 | 1.604 | 13.022 | 19.537 |
| 2423000 | 13.8033 | 11.0918 | 161.0139 | 7.5293 | 2.589 | 8.191 | 0.975 | 8.635 |
| 2424000 | 14.5572 | 16.5950 | 121.1534 | 9.1542 | 7.638 | 0.587 | 3.182 | 25.055 |
| 2425000 | 15.3111 | 22.0983 | 81.2930 | 0.6945 | 12.686 | 7.174 | 5.389 | 14.152 |
| 2426000 | 16.0650 | 0.7232 | 41.4325 | 2.3195 | 17.735 | 13.762 | 7.596 | 3.250 |
| 2427000 | 16.8189 | 6.2264 | 01.5720 | 3.9444 | 22.783 | 6.157 | 9.803 | 19.670 |
| 2428000 | 17.5728 | 11.7296 | 308.3317 | 5.5693 | 27.831 | 12.745 | 12.010 | 8.768 |
| 2429000 | 18.3267 | 17.2328 | 268.4712 | 7.1942 | 3.617 | 5.140 | 14.217 | 25.188 |
| 2430000 | 19.0806 | 22.7360 | 228.6107 | 8.8191 | 8.665 | 11.727 | 2.171 | 14.285 |
| 2431000 | 19.8345 | 1.3609 | 188.7503 | 0.3594 | 13.713 | 4.123 | 4.378 | 3.383 |
| 2432000 | 20.5884 | 6.8641 | 148.8898 | 1.9843 | 18.762 | 10.710 | 6.585 | 19.802 |
| 2433000 | 21.3423 | 12.3673 | 109.0293 | 3.6092 | 23.810 | 3.106 | 8.792 | 8.900 |
| 2434000 | 22.0963 | 17.8706 | 69.1688 | 5.2341 | 28.859 | 9.693 | 10.999 | 25.320 |
| 2435000 | 22.8502 | 23.3738 | 29.3083 | 6.8590 | 4.644 | 2.088 | 13.206 | 14.418 |
| 2436000 | 23.6041 | 1.9987 | 336.0679 | 8.4840 | 9.693 | 8.676 | 1.159 | 3.516 |
| 2437000 | 24.3581 | 7.5019 | 296.2075 | 0.0243 | 14.741 | 1.071 | 3.366 | 19.935 |
| 2438000 | 25.1120 | 13.0051 | 256.3470 | 1.6492 | 19.790 | 7.659 | 5.573 | 9.033 |
| 2439000 | 0.2442 | 18.5083 | 216.4865 | 3.2741 | 24.838 | 0.054 | 7.780 | 25.453 |
| 2440000 | 0.9981 | 24.0115 | 176.6260 | 4.8990 | 0.625 | 6.642 | 9.988 | 14.551 |
| 2441000 | 1.7520 | 2.6363 | 136.7655 | 6.5239 | 5.672 | 13.229 | 12.195 | 3.648 |
| 2442000 | 2.5059 | 8.1395 | 96.9050 | 8.1488 | 10.720 | 5.624 | 0.148 | 20.068 |
| 2443000 | 3.2599 | 13.6427 | 57.0445 | 9.7737 | 15.769 | 12.212 | 2.355 | 9.166 |
| 2444000 | 4.0138 | 19.1459 | 17.1840 | 1.3140 | 20.817 | 4.607 | 4.562 | 25.586 |
| 2445000 | 4.7677 | 24.6491 | 323.9436 | 2.9389 | 25.866 | 11.195 | 6.769 | 14.683 |
| 2446000 | 5.5217 | 3.2740 | 284.0830 | 4.5639 | 1.651 | 3.590 | 8.976 | 3.781 |
| 2447000 | 6.2756 | 8.7772 | 244.2225 | 6.1888 | 6.699 | 10.177 | 11.183 | 20.201 |
| 2448000 | 7.0296 | 14.2804 | 204.3620 | 7.8137 | 11.748 | 2.573 | 13.390 | 9.299 |
| 2449000 | 7.7835 | 19.7836 | 164.5014 | 9.4386 | 16.796 | 9.160 | 1.344 | 25.718 |
| 2450000 | 8.5374 | 25.2868 | 124.6409 | 0.9789 | 21.844 | 1.556 | 3.551 | 14.816 |

# TABLE II*b*.

Epochs and Arguments for each Thousandth Day, from 2400000 to 2500000.

For Washington Mean Noon.

| Day of Julian Period. | Arg. 10. | 11. | 12. | 13. | 14. | 15. | 16. | 17. |
|---|---|---|---|---|---|---|---|---|
| | d. | d. | d. | d. | d. | d. | d. | d. |
| 2450000 | 8.5374 | 25.2868 | 124.6409 | 0.9789 | 21.844 | 1.556 | 3.551 | 14.816 |
| 2451000 | 9.2913 | 3.9117 | 84.7804 | 2.6038 | 26.892 | 8.143 | 5.758 | 3.914 |
| 2452000 | 10.0453 | 9.4148 | 44.9198 | 4.2287 | 2.678 | 0.539 | 7.965 | 20.334 |
| 2453000 | 10.7992 | 14.9180 | 5.0593 | 5.8536 | 7.726 | 7.126 | 10.172 | 9.431 |
| 2454000 | 11.5532 | 20.4212 | 311.8189 | 7.4785 | 12.775 | 13.714 | 12.379 | 25.851 |
| 2455000 | 12.3071 | 25.9244 | 271.9583 | 9.1034 | 17.823 | 6.109 | 0.332 | 14.949 |
| 2456000 | 13.0611 | 4.5492 | 232.0978 | 0.6438 | 22.871 | 12.697 | 2.539 | 4.047 |
| 2457000 | 13.8150 | 10.0524 | 192.2372 | 2.2687 | 27.920 | 5.092 | 4.746 | 20.466 |
| 2458000 | 14.5690 | 15.5556 | 152.3767 | 3.8936 | 3.705 | 11.680 | 6.953 | 9.564 |
| 2459000 | 15.3229 | 21.0588 | 112.5161 | 5.5185 | 8.753 | 4.073 | 9.160 | 25.984 |
| 2460000 | 16.0769 | 26.5619 | 72.6556 | 7.1434 | 13.802 | 10.662 | 11.368 | 15.082 |
| 2461000 | 16.8309 | 5.1868 | 32.7950 | 8.7683 | 18.851 | 3.058 | 13.575 | 4.180 |
| 2462000 | 17.5848 | 10.6900 | 339.5545 | 0.3086 | 23.899 | 9.645 | 1.528 | 20.599 |
| 2463000 | 18.3388 | 16.1931 | 299.6940 | 1.9335 | 28.947 | 2.041 | 3.735 | 9.697 |
| 2464000 | 19.0927 | 21.6963 | 259.8334 | 3.5584 | 4.733 | 8.628 | 5.943 | 26.117 |
| 2465000 | 19.8467 | 0.3212 | 219.9729 | 5.1833 | 9.781 | 1.024 | 8.150 | 15.214 |
| 2466000 | 20.6007 | 5.8243 | 180.1123 | 6.8082 | 14.829 | 7.611 | 10.357 | 4.312 |
| 2467000 | 21.3546 | 11.3275 | 140.2517 | 8.4331 | 19.878 | 0.007 | 12.564 | 20.732 |
| 2468000 | 22.1086 | 16.8307 | 100.3911 | 10.0580 | 24.926 | 6.594 | 0.517 | 9.830 |
| 2469000 | 22.8625 | 22.3338 | 60.5306 | 1.5983 | 0.711 | 13.182 | 2.724 | 26.250 |
| 2470000 | 23.6165 | 0.9587 | 20.6699 | 3.2232 | 5.760 | 5.577 | 4.931 | 15.347 |
| 2471000 | 24.3705 | 6.4618 | 327.4295 | 4.8481 | 10.808 | 12.165 | 7.138 | 4.445 |
| 2472000 | 25.1245 | 11.9650 | 287.5689 | 6.4730 | 15.857 | 4.560 | 9.345 | 20.865 |
| 2473000 | 0.2568 | 17.4681 | 247.7083 | 8.0979 | 20.905 | 11.148 | 11.552 | 9.963 |
| 2474000 | 1.0107 | 22.9713 | 207.8477 | 9.7228 | 25.954 | 3.543 | 13.760 | 26.383 |
| 2475000 | 1.7647 | 1.5961 | 167.9871 | 1.2631 | 1.739 | 10.130 | 1.713 | 15.480 |
| 2476000 | 2.5187 | 7.0993 | 128.1265 | 2.8881 | 6.787 | 2.526 | 3.920 | 4.578 |
| 2477000 | 3.2727 | 12.6024 | 88.2659 | 4.5130 | 11.836 | 9.113 | 6.127 | 20.998 |
| 2478000 | 4.0266 | 18.1056 | 48.4053 | 6.1379 | 16.884 | 1.509 | 8.334 | 10.095 |
| 2479000 | 4.7806 | 23.6087 | 8.5447 | 7.7628 | 21.932 | 8.096 | 10.542 | 26.515 |
| 2480000 | 5.5346 | 2.2336 | 315.3042 | 9.3877 | 26.981 | 0.492 | 12.748 | 15.613 |
| 2481000 | 6.2886 | 7.7367 | 275.4436 | 0.9280 | 2.766 | 7.079 | 0.702 | 4.711 |
| 2482000 | 7.0426 | 13.2399 | 235.5830 | 2.5529 | 7.814 | 13.667 | 2.909 | 21.130 |
| 2483000 | 7.7965 | 18.7430 | 195.7223 | 4.1778 | 12.863 | 6.062 | 5.116 | 10.228 |
| 2484000 | 8.5506 | 24.2462 | 155.8617 | 5.8027 | 17.911 | 12.650 | 7.323 | 26.648 |
| 2485000 | 9.3046 | 2.8710 | 116.0011 | 7.4276 | 22.960 | 5.045 | 9.530 | 15.746 |
| 2486000 | 10.0585 | 8.3742 | 76.1405 | 9.0525 | 28.008 | 11.632 | 11.737 | 4.844 |
| 2487000 | 10.8125 | 13.8773 | 36.2799 | 0.5928 | 3.793 | 4.028 | 13.945 | 21.263 |
| 2488000 | 11.5665 | 19.3804 | 343.0394 | 2.2177 | 8.842 | 10.615 | 1.898 | 10.361 |
| 2489000 | 12.3205 | 24.8836 | 303.1787 | 3.8426 | 13.890 | 3.011 | 4.105 | 26.781 |
| 2490000 | 13.0745 | 3.5084 | 263.3181 | 5.4675 | 18.939 | 9.598 | 6.312 | 15.879 |
| 2491000 | 13.8285 | 9.0115 | 223.4575 | 7.0924 | 23.987 | 1.994 | 8.519 | 4.977 |
| 2492000 | 14.5825 | 14.5147 | 183.5968 | 8.7173 | 29.035 | 8.581 | 10.726 | 21.396 |
| 2493000 | 15.3365 | 20.0178 | 143.7362 | 0.2576 | 4.821 | 0.977 | 12.933 | 10.494 |
| 2494000 | 16.0905 | 25.5209 | 103.8755 | 1.8825 | 9.869 | 7.564 | 0.887 | 26.914 |
| 2495000 | 16.8445 | 4.1458 | 64.0149 | 3.5074 | 14.917 | 14.151 | 3.094 | 16.011 |
| 2496000 | 17.5985 | 9.6489 | 24.1542 | 5.1324 | 19.966 | 6.547 | 5.301 | 5.109 |
| 2497000 | 18.3525 | 15.1520 | 330.9137 | 6.7573 | 25.014 | 13.134 | 7.508 | 21.529 |
| 2498000 | 19.1065 | 20.6551 | 291.0530 | 8.3822 | 0.799 | 5.530 | 9.715 | 10.627 |
| 2499000 | 19.8605 | 26.1583 | 251.1924 | 10.0071 | 5.848 | 12.117 | 11.922 | 27.047 |
| 2500000 | 20.6145 | 4.7831 | 211.3316 | 1.5474 | 10.896 | 4.513 | 14.129 | 16.144 |

# TABLE II*b*.

Epochs and Arguments for each Thousandth Day, from 2400000 to 2500000.

For Washington Mean Noon.

| Day of Julian Period. | Arg. **18.** | **19.** | **20.** | **21.** | **22.** | **23.** | **24.** | **25.** | **26.** |
|---|---|---|---|---|---|---|---|---|---|
| | d. | d. | d. | d. | d. | d. | d. | d. | d. |
| 2400000 | 8.137 | 18.503 | 12.791 | 118.93 | 3.342 | 10.320 | 8.124 | 5.633 | 2.449 |
| 2401000 | 1.031 | 22.113 | 10.580 | 65.56 | 7.371 | 11.786 | 12.386 | 3.345 | 0.961 |
| 2402000 | 3.798 | 1.421 | 8.368 | 12.19 | 11.400 | 13.252 | 3.373 | 1.057 | 5.295 |
| 2403000 | 6.564 | 5.031 | 6.156 | 90.49 | 15.430 | 14.718 | 7.636 | 8.137 | 3.807 |
| 2404000 | 9.332 | 8.641 | 3.944 | 37.12 | 19.459 | 16.183 | 11.898 | 5.850 | 2.319 |
| 2405000 | 2.225 | 12.251 | 1.733 | 115.43 | 23.488 | 17.649 | 2.885 | 3.563 | 0.831 |
| 2406000 | 4.993 | 15.861 | 13.838 | 62.06 | 27.518 | 19.115 | 7.148 | 1.275 | 5.165 |
| 2407000 | 7.759 | 19.471 | 11.626 | 8.69 | 31.547 | 20.580 | 11.410 | 8.355 | 3.677 |
| 2408000 | 0.653 | 23.081 | 9.414 | 86.99 | 3.448 | 22.046 | 2.396 | 6.068 | 2.189 |
| 2409000 | 3.420 | 2.389 | 7.202 | 33.62 | 7.478 | 23.512 | 6.659 | 3.780 | 0.700 |
| 2410000 | 6.188 | 5.999 | 4.991 | 111.93 | 11.507 | 1.203 | 10.921 | 1.493 | 5.035 |
| 2411000 | 8.954 | 9.610 | 2.779 | 58.56 | 15.536 | 2.669 | 1.908 | 8.573 | 3.547 |
| 2412000 | 1.848 | 13.220 | 0.567 | 5.19 | 19.566 | 4.135 | 6.171 | 6.285 | 2.059 |
| 2413000 | 4.615 | 16.830 | 12.672 | 83.49 | 23.595 | 5.600 | 10.433 | 3.998 | 0.571 |
| 2414000 | 7.382 | 20.440 | 10.461 | 30.12 | 27.624 | 7.066 | 1.419 | 1.711 | 4.905 |
| 2415000 | 0.276 | 24.050 | 8.249 | 108.42 | 31.654 | 8.532 | 5.682 | 8.790 | 3.417 |
| 2416000 | 3.043 | 3.358 | 6.037 | 55.05 | 3.555 | 9.997 | 9.945 | 6.503 | 1.929 |
| 2417000 | 5.810 | 6.968 | 3.825 | 1.69 | 7.584 | 11.463 | 0.931 | 4.216 | 0.440 |
| 2418000 | 8.577 | 10.578 | 1.613 | 79.99 | 11.614 | 12.928 | 5.194 | 1.928 | 4.775 |
| 2419000 | 1.471 | 14.188 | 13.718 | 26.62 | 15.643 | 14.394 | 9.456 | 9.008 | 3.287 |
| 2420000 | 4.238 | 17.798 | 11.507 | 104.93 | 19.672 | 15.860 | 0.442 | 6.721 | 1.799 |
| 2421000 | 7.004 | 21.408 | 9.295 | 51.56 | 23.702 | 17.326 | 4.705 | 4.434 | 0.311 |
| 2422000 | 9.771 | 0.716 | 7.083 | 129.86 | 27.731 | 18.792 | 8.968 | 2.146 | 4.645 |
| 2423000 | 2.666 | 4.326 | 4.871 | 76.49 | 31.760 | 20.258 | 13.230 | 9.226 | 3.157 |
| 2424000 | 5.433 | 7.936 | 2.660 | 23.12 | 3.662 | 21.723 | 4.217 | 6.938 | 1.669 |
| 2425000 | 8.199 | 11.547 | 0.448 | 101.43 | 7.691 | 23.189 | 8.479 | 4.651 | 0.181 |
| 2426000 | 1.093 | 15.157 | 12.553 | 48.06 | 11.720 | 0.880 | 12.741 | 2.364 | 4.515 |
| 2427000 | 3.860 | 18.767 | 10.342 | 126.36 | 15.750 | 2.345 | 3.728 | 0.077 | 3.027 |
| 2428000 | 6.627 | 22.377 | 8.130 | 72.99 | 19.779 | 3.811 | 7.991 | 7.156 | 1.539 |
| 2429000 | 9.394 | 1.685 | 5.918 | 19.63 | 23.808 | 5.277 | 12.253 | 4.869 | 5.874 |
| 2430000 | 2.288 | 5.295 | 3.706 | 97.93 | 27.838 | 6.743 | 3.240 | 2.582 | 4.385 |
| 2431000 | 5.055 | 8.905 | 1.494 | 44.56 | 31.867 | 8.209 | 7.503 | 0.294 | 2.897 |
| 2432000 | 7.822 | 12.516 | 13.599 | 122.86 | 3.769 | 9.675 | 11.765 | 7.374 | 1.409 |
| 2433000 | 0.716 | 16.126 | 11.388 | 69.49 | 7.798 | 11.141 | 2.752 | 5.087 | 5.744 |
| 2434000 | 3.483 | 19.736 | 9.176 | 16.12 | 11.827 | 12.606 | 7.014 | 2.799 | 4.256 |
| 2435000 | 6.250 | 23.346 | 6.964 | 94.43 | 15.857 | 14.072 | 11.276 | 0.512 | 2.767 |
| 2436000 | 9.017 | 2.654 | 4.753 | 41.06 | 19.886 | 15.538 | 2.263 | 7.592 | 1.279 |
| 2437000 | 1.911 | 6.264 | 2.541 | 119.36 | 23.915 | 17.003 | 6.526 | 5.304 | 5.614 |
| 2438000 | 4.678 | 9.874 | 0.329 | 65.99 | 27.945 | 18.469 | 10.788 | 3.017 | 4.126 |
| 2439000 | 7.444 | 13.485 | 12.434 | 12.62 | 31.974 | 19.935 | 1.775 | 0.730 | 2.638 |
| 2440000 | 0.339 | 17.095 | 10.223 | 90.93 | 3.875 | 21.401 | 6.038 | 7.810 | 1.149 |
| 2441000 | 3.106 | 20.705 | 8.011 | 37.56 | 7.905 | 22.867 | 10.300 | 5.523 | 5.484 |
| 2442000 | 5.873 | 24.315 | 5.799 | 115.86 | 11.934 | 0.558 | 1.286 | 3.235 | 3.996 |
| 2443000 | 8.639 | 3.623 | 3.587 | 62.49 | 15.963 | 2.023 | 5.549 | 0.948 | 2.508 |
| 2444000 | 1.534 | 7.233 | 1.375 | 9.13 | 19.993 | 3.489 | 9.812 | 8.027 | 1.019 |
| 2445000 | 4.301 | 10.844 | 13.481 | 87.43 | 24.022 | 4.955 | 0.798 | 5.740 | 5.354 |
| 2446000 | 7.067 | 14.454 | 11.269 | 34.06 | 28.051 | 6.420 | 5.061 | 3.453 | 3.866 |
| 2447000 | 9.834 | 18.064 | 9.057 | 112.36 | 32.081 | 7.886 | 9.323 | 1.165 | 2.378 |
| 2448000 | 2.728 | 21.674 | 6.846 | 59.00 | 3.982 | 9.351 | 0.310 | 8.245 | 0.890 |
| 2449000 | 5.495 | 0.982 | 4.634 | 5.63 | 8.011 | 10.817 | 4.572 | 5.958 | 5.224 |
| 2450000 | 8.262 | 4.592 | 2.422 | 83.93 | 12.041 | 12.283 | 8.835 | 3.671 | 3.736 |

# TABLE II*b*.

Epochs and Arguments for each Thousandth Day, from 2400000 to 2500000.

For Washington Mean Noon.

| Day of Julian Period. | ARG. **18.** | **19.** | **20.** | **21.** | **22.** | **23.** | **24.** | **25.** | **26.** |
|---|---|---|---|---|---|---|---|---|---|
| | d | d. | d. | d. | d. | d. | d. | d. | d. |
| 2450000 | 8.262 | 4.592 | 2.422 | 83.93 | 12.041 | 12.283 | 8.835 | 3.671 | 3.736 |
| 2451000 | 1.157 | 8.203 | 0.210 | 30.56 | 16.070 | 13.749 | 13.098 | 1.383 | 2.248 |
| 2452000 | 3.924 | 11.813 | 12.316 | 108.86 | 20.100 | 15.215 | 4.084 | 8.463 | 0.760 |
| 2453000 | 6.690 | 15.423 | 10.104 | 55.50 | 24.129 | 16.681 | 8.347 | 6.176 | 5.094 |
| 2454000 | 9.457 | 19.033 | 7.892 | 2.13 | 28.158 | 18.146 | 12.609 | 3.888 | 3.606 |
| 2455000 | 2.352 | 22.643 | 5.680 | 80.43 | 0.060 | 19.612 | 3.596 | 1.601 | 2.118 |
| 2456000 | 5.119 | 1.951 | 3.469 | 27.06 | 4.089 | 21.078 | 7.859 | 8.681 | 0.630 |
| 2457000 | 7.885 | 5.562 | 1.257 | 105.37 | 8.118 | 22.543 | 12.121 | 6.393 | 4.964 |
| 2458000 | 0.780 | 9.172 | 13.362 | 52.00 | 12.148 | 0.234 | 3.107 | 4.106 | 3.476 |
| 2459000 | 3.547 | 12.782 | 11.150 | 130.30 | 16.177 | 1.700 | 7.370 | 1.814 | 1.988 |
| 2460000 | 6.313 | 16.393 | 8.939 | 76.93 | 20.207 | 3.166 | 11.633 | 8.899 | 0.500 |
| 2461000 | 9.080 | 20.003 | 6.727 | 23.56 | 24.236 | 4.632 | 2.620 | 6.611 | 4.834 |
| 2462000 | 1.974 | 23.613 | 4.516 | 101.87 | 28.265 | 6.098 | 6.882 | 4.324 | 3.346 |
| 2463000 | 4.741 | 2.921 | 2.304 | 48.50 | 0.167 | 7.564 | 11.145 | 2.037 | 1.858 |
| 2464000 | 7.508 | 6.532 | 0.092 | 126.80 | 4.196 | 9.029 | 2.131 | 9.117 | 0.370 |
| 2465000 | 0.402 | 10.142 | 12.197 | 73.43 | 8.225 | 10.495 | 6.394 | 6.829 | 4.704 |
| 2466000 | 3.169 | 13.752 | 9.986 | 20.07 | 12.255 | 11.961 | 10.656 | 4.542 | 3.216 |
| 2467000 | 5.936 | 17.363 | 7.774 | 98.37 | 16.284 | 13.426 | 1.643 | 2.255 | 1.728 |
| 2468000 | 8.703 | 20.973 | 5.562 | 45.00 | 20.314 | 14.892 | 5.906 | 9.334 | 0.240 |
| 2469000 | 1.597 | 0.281 | 3.351 | 123.30 | 24.343 | 16.358 | 10.169 | 7.047 | 4.575 |
| 2470000 | 4.364 | 3.891 | 1.139 | 69.94 | 28.372 | 17.824 | 1.155 | 4.760 | 3.087 |
| 2471000 | 7.131 | 7.501 | 13.244 | 16.57 | 0.273 | 19.290 | 5.418 | 2.473 | 1.599 |
| 2472000 | 0.025 | 11.112 | 11.033 | 94.87 | 4.303 | 20.756 | 9.680 | 0.185 | 0.110 |
| 2473000 | 2.792 | 14.722 | 8.821 | 41.50 | 8.332 | 22.221 | 0.667 | 7.265 | 4.445 |
| 2474000 | 5.559 | 18.332 | 6.609 | 119.81 | 12.362 | 23.687 | 4.929 | 4.978 | 2.957 |
| 2475000 | 8.326 | 21.942 | 4.398 | 66.44 | 16.391 | 1.378 | 9.192 | 2.690 | 1.469 |
| 2476000 | 1.220 | 1.251 | 2.186 | 13.07 | 20.420 | 2.844 | 0.178 | 0.403 | 5.803 |
| 2477000 | 3.987 | 4.861 | 14.291 | 91.37 | 24.450 | 4.309 | 4.441 | 7.483 | 4.315 |
| 2478000 | 6.754 | 8.471 | 12.079 | 38.00 | 28.479 | 5.775 | 8.704 | 5.196 | 2.827 |
| 2479000 | 9.521 | 12.082 | 9.868 | 116.31 | 0.380 | 7.241 | 12.966 | 2.908 | 1.339 |
| 2480000 | 2.415 | 15.692 | 7.656 | 62.94 | 4.410 | 8.707 | 3.953 | 0.621 | 5.673 |
| 2481000 | 5.182 | 19.302 | 5.444 | 9.57 | 8.439 | 10.173 | 8.216 | 7.701 | 4.185 |
| 2482000 | 7.949 | 22.913 | 3.233 | 87.88 | 12.469 | 11.639 | 12.478 | 5.413 | 2.697 |
| 2483000 | 0.843 | 2.221 | 1.021 | 34.51 | 16.498 | 13.105 | 3.465 | 3.126 | 1.209 |
| 2484000 | 3.610 | 5.832 | 13.126 | 112.81 | 20.527 | 14.570 | 7.728 | 0.839 | 5.544 |
| 2485000 | 6.377 | 9.442 | 10.915 | 59.44 | 24.557 | 16.036 | 11.990 | 7.919 | 4.056 |
| 2486000 | 9.144 | 13.052 | 8.703 | 6.08 | 28.586 | 17.502 | 2.977 | 5.631 | 2.567 |
| 2487000 | 2.038 | 16.663 | 6.492 | 84.38 | 0.487 | 18.967 | 7.239 | 3.344 | 1.079 |
| 2488000 | 4.805 | 20.273 | 4.280 | 31.01 | 4.517 | 20.433 | 11.502 | 1.057 | 5.414 |
| 2489000 | 7.572 | 23.883 | 2.068 | 109.31 | 8.546 | 21.899 | 2.488 | 8.136 | 3.926 |
| 2490000 | 0.466 | 3.191 | 14.173 | 55.95 | 12.575 | 23.365 | 6.751 | 5.849 | 2.438 |
| 2491000 | 3.233 | 6.801 | 11.962 | 2.58 | 16.605 | 1.056 | 11.014 | 3.562 | 0.951 |
| 2492000 | 6.000 | 10.412 | 9.750 | 80.88 | 20.635 | 2.522 | 2.000 | 1.275 | 5.284 |
| 2493000 | 8.767 | 14.022 | 7.538 | 27.52 | 24.664 | 3.988 | 6.263 | 8.354 | 3.796 |
| 2494000 | 1.661 | 17.633 | 5.327 | 105.82 | 28.693 | 5.453 | 10.526 | 6.067 | 2.308 |
| 2495000 | 4.428 | 21.243 | 3.115 | 52.45 | 0.594 | 6.919 | 1.512 | 3.780 | 0.820 |
| 2496000 | 7.195 | 0.551 | 0.903 | 130.75 | 4.624 | 8.385 | 5.775 | 1.493 | 5.154 |
| 2497000 | 0.089 | 4.162 | 13.009 | 77.39 | 8.653 | 9.850 | 10.038 | 8.572 | 3.666 |
| 2498000 | 2.856 | 7.772 | 10.797 | 24.02 | 12.683 | 11.316 | 1.024 | 6.285 | 2.178 |
| 2499000 | 5.623 | 11.382 | 8.586 | 102.32 | 16.712 | 12.782 | 5.287 | 3.997 | 0.690 |
| 2500000 | 8.390 | 14.993 | 6.374 | 48.96 | 20.741 | 14.248 | 9.550 | 1.710 | 5.024 |

# TABLE IIb.

Epochs and Arguments for each Thousandth Day, from 2400000 to 2500000.

For Washington Mean Noon.

| Day of Julian Period. | Arg. 27. | 28. | 29. | 30. | 31. | 32. | 33. | 34. | 35. |
|---|---|---|---|---|---|---|---|---|---|
| | d. | d. | d. | d. | d. | d. | d. | d. | d. |
| 2400000 | 15.66 | 19.352 | 4.605 | 5.551 | 11.37 | 7.36 | 11.24 | 5.99 | 1.56 |
| 2401000 | 8.43 | 17.780 | 21.696 | 9.942 | 0.61 | 9.55 | 5.27 | 3.56 | 19.93 |
| 2402000 | 1.20 | 16.207 | 6.023 | 3.961 | 5.18 | 11.74 | 31.75 | 1.13 | 14.36 |
| 2403000 | 19.80 | 14.635 | 23.114 | 8.352 | 9.74 | 13.93 | 25.78 | 25.79 | 8.78 |
| 2404000 | 12.57 | 13.062 | 7.441 | 2.371 | 14.31 | 16.12 | 19.81 | 23.36 | 3.21 |
| 2405000 | 5.34 | 11.490 | 24.532 | 6.762 | 3.55 | 1.68 | 13.85 | 20.93 | 21.57 |
| 2406000 | 23.94 | 9.918 | 8.859 | 0.781 | 8.11 | 3.87 | 7.88 | 18.50 | 16.00 |
| 2407000 | 16.71 | 8.345 | 25.950 | 5.172 | 12.68 | 6.06 | 1.91 | 16.07 | 10.43 |
| 2408000 | 9.48 | 6.773 | 10.277 | 9.563 | 1.92 | 8.25 | 28.39 | 13.64 | 4.85 |
| 2409000 | 2.25 | 5.200 | 27.368 | 3.582 | 6.49 | 10.45 | 22.42 | 11.21 | 23.22 |
| 2410000 | 20.85 | 3.628 | 11.695 | 7.973 | 11.05 | 12.64 | 16.46 | 8.78 | 17.65 |
| 2411000 | 13.62 | 2.056 | 28.786 | 1.992 | 0.30 | 14.83 | 10.49 | 6.35 | 12.08 |
| 2412000 | 6.39 | 0.483 | 13.114 | 6.382 | 4.86 | 0.39 | 4.52 | 3.92 | 6.50 |
| 2413000 | 24.99 | 37.433 | 30.205 | 0.402 | 9.42 | 2.58 | 31.00 | 1.49 | 0.93 |
| 2414000 | 17.76 | 35.860 | 14.532 | 4.793 | 13.99 | 4.77 | 25.04 | 26.15 | 19.30 |
| 2415000 | 10.53 | 34.288 | 31.623 | 9.183 | 3.23 | 6.96 | 19.06 | 23.72 | 13.72 |
| 2416000 | 3.30 | 32.716 | 15.950 | 3.203 | 7.80 | 9.15 | 13.10 | 21.29 | 8.15 |
| 2417000 | 21.90 | 31.143 | 0.277 | 7.594 | 12.37 | 11.34 | 7.13 | 18.86 | 2.58 |
| 2418000 | 14.67 | 29.571 | 17.368 | 1.613 | 1.61 | 13.52 | 1.16 | 16.43 | 20.94 |
| 2419000 | 7.44 | 27.998 | 1.695 | 6.004 | 6.17 | 15.72 | 27.65 | 14.00 | 15.37 |
| 2420000 | 0.21 | 26.426 | 18.786 | 0.023 | 10.73 | 1.28 | 21.68 | 11.57 | 9.80 |
| 2421000 | 18.81 | 24.854 | 3.113 | 4.414 | 15.30 | 3.47 | 15.71 | 9.14 | 4.22 |
| 2422000 | 11.58 | 23.281 | 20.204 | 8.804 | 4.54 | 5.66 | 9.74 | 6.71 | 22.59 |
| 2423000 | 4.35 | 21.709 | 4.531 | 2.824 | 9.11 | 7.85 | 3.77 | 4.28 | 17.02 |
| 2424000 | 22.95 | 20.136 | 21.622 | 7.215 | 13.68 | 10.04 | 30.26 | 1.85 | 11.45 |
| 2425000 | 15.72 | 18.564 | 5.951 | 1.234 | 2.92 | 12.23 | 24.29 | 26.51 | 5.87 |
| 2426000 | 8.49 | 17.992 | 23.040 | 5.625 | 7.48 | 14.42 | 18.32 | 24.08 | 0.30 |
| 2427000 | 1.26 | 15.419 | 7.367 | 10.015 | 12.05 | 16.61 | 12.35 | 21.65 | 18.67 |
| 2428000 | 19.86 | 13 847 | 24.458 | 4.035 | 1.29 | 2.17 | 6.38 | 19.22 | 13.09 |
| 2429000 | 12.63 | 12.274 | 8.785 | 8.425 | 5.85 | 4.36 | 0.42 | 16.79 | 7.52 |
| 2430000 | 5.40 | 10.702 | 25.876 | 2.445 | 10.42 | 6.55 | 26.90 | 14.36 | 1.95 |
| 2431000 | 24.00 | 9.130 | 10.203 | 6.835 | 14.99 | 8.74 | 20.93 | 11.93 | 20.31 |
| 2432000 | 16.77 | 7.557 | 27.294 | 0.855 | 4.23 | 10.93 | 14.96 | 9.50 | 14.74 |
| 2433000 | 9.54 | 5.985 | 11.621 | 5.246 | 8.79 | 13.12 | 9.00 | 7.07 | 9.17 |
| 2434000 | 2.31 | 4.412 | 28.712 | 9.636 | 13.36 | 15.31 | 3.03 | 4.64 | 3.59 |
| 2435000 | 20.91 | 2.840 | 13.040 | 3.656 | 2.60 | 0.87 | 29.51 | 2.21 | 21.96 |
| 2436000 | 13.68 | 1.268 | 30.131 | 8.047 | 7.16 | 3.06 | 23.54 | 26.87 | 16.39 |
| 2437000 | 6.45 | 38.217 | 14.458 | 2.066 | 11.73 | 5.25 | 17.58 | 24.44 | 10.81 |
| 2438000 | 25.05 | 36.645 | 31.549 | 6.456 | 0.98 | 7.44 | 11.61 | 22.01 | 5.24 |
| 2439000 | 17.82 | 35.072 | 15.876 | 0.476 | 5.54 | 9.63 | 5.64 | 19.58 | 23.61 |
| 2440000 | 10.59 | 33.500 | 0.203 | 4.866 | 10.10 | 11.82 | 32.12 | 17.15 | 18.04 |
| 2441000 | 3.36 | 31.928 | 17.294 | 9.257 | 14.67 | 14.01 | 26.15 | 14.72 | 12.46 |
| 2442000 | 21.96 | 30.355 | 1.621 | 3.277 | 3.91 | 16.20 | 20.19 | 12.29 | 6.89 |
| 2443000 | 14.73 | 28.783 | 18.712 | 7.667 | 8.47 | 1.76 | 14.22 | 9.86 | 1.31 |
| 2444000 | 7.50 | 27.210 | 3.039 | 1.687 | 13.04 | 3.95 | 8.25 | 7.43 | 19.68 |
| 2445000 | 0.27 | 25.638 | 20.131 | 6.077 | 2.29 | 6.14 | 2.28 | 5.00 | 14.11 |
| 2446000 | 18.87 | 24 066 | 4.458 | 0.097 | 6.85 | 8.33 | 28.77 | 2.57 | 8.53 |
| 2447000 | 11.64 | 22.493 | 21.549 | 4.488 | 11.41 | 10.52 | 22.80 | 0.14 | 2.96 |
| 2448000 | 4.42 | 20.921 | 5.876 | 8.878 | 0.66 | 12.71 | 16.83 | 24.80 | 21.33 |
| 2449000 | 23.02 | 19.348 | 22.967 | 2.897 | 5.22 | 14.90 | 10.86 | 22.37 | 15.76 |
| 2450000 | 15.79 | 17.776 | 7.294 | 7.288 | 9.78 | 0.46 | 4.89 | 19.94 | 10.18 |

# TABLE IIb.

Epochs and Arguments for each Thousandth Day, from 2400000 to 2500000

For Washington Mean Noon.

| Day of Julian Period. | Arg. 27. | 28. | 29. | 30. | 31. | 32. | 33. | 34. | 35. |
|---|---|---|---|---|---|---|---|---|---|
| | d. | d. | d. | d. | d. | d. | d. | d. | d. |
| 2450000 | 15.79 | 17.776 | 7.294 | 7.288 | 9.78 | 0.46 | 4.89 | 19.94 | 10.18 |
| 2451000 | 8.56 | 16.204 | 24.385 | 1.308 | 14.35 | 2.65 | 31.38 | 17.51 | 4.61 |
| 2452000 | 1.33 | 14.631 | 8.712 | 5.698 | 3.60 | 4.84 | 25.41 | 15.08 | 22.98 |
| 2453000 | 19.93 | 13.059 | 25.803 | 10.089 | 8.16 | 7.03 | 19.44 | 12.65 | 17.41 |
| 2454000 | 12.70 | 11.486 | 10.130 | 4.108 | 12.73 | 9.23 | 13.47 | 10.22 | 11.83 |
| 2455000 | 5.47 | 9.914 | 27.222 | 8.499 | 1.97 | 11.42 | 7.50 | 7.79 | 6.26 |
| 2456000 | 24.07 | 8.342 | 11.549 | 2.518 | 6.53 | 13.61 | 1.54 | 5.36 | 0.68 |
| 2457000 | 16.84 | 6.769 | 28.640 | 6.909 | 11.09 | 15.80 | 28.02 | 2.93 | 19.05 |
| 2458000 | 9.61 | 5.197 | 12.967 | 0.929 | 0.34 | 1.36 | 22.05 | 0.50 | 13.48 |
| 2459000 | 2.38 | 3.624 | 30.058 | 5.319 | 4.91 | 3.55 | 16.08 | 25.16 | 7.91 |
| 2460000 | 20.98 | 2.052 | 14.385 | 9.710 | 9.47 | 5.74 | 10.11 | 22.73 | 2.33 |
| 2461000 | 13.75 | 0.480 | 31.476 | 3.729 | 14.04 | 7.93 | 4.15 | 20.30 | 20.70 |
| 2462000 | 6.52 | 37.429 | 15.804 | 8.120 | 3.28 | 10.12 | 30.63 | 17.87 | 15.13 |
| 2463000 | 25.12 | 35.857 | 0.131 | 2.139 | 7.84 | 12.31 | 24.66 | 15.44 | 9.55 |
| 2464000 | 17.89 | 34.284 | 17.222 | 6.530 | 12.41 | 14.50 | 18.69 | 13.01 | 3.98 |
| 2465000 | 10.66 | 32.712 | 1.549 | 0.550 | 1.65 | 0.06 | 12.73 | 10.58 | 22.35 |
| 2466000 | 3.43 | 31.139 | 18.640 | 4.940 | 6.22 | 2.25 | 6.76 | 8.15 | 16.78 |
| 2467000 | 22.03 | 29.566 | 2.967 | 9.331 | 10.78 | 4.44 | 0.79 | 5.71 | 11.20 |
| 2468000 | 14.80 | 27.994 | 20.059 | 3.350 | 15.35 | 6.63 | 27.27 | 3.28 | 5.63 |
| 2469000 | 7.57 | 26.421 | 4.386 | 7.741 | 4.59 | 8.82 | 21.30 | 0.85 | 0.05 |
| 2470000 | 0.34 | 24.849 | 21.477 | 1.760 | 9.15 | 11.01 | 15.34 | 25.51 | 18.42 |
| 2471000 | 18.94 | 23.277 | 5.804 | 6.151 | 13.70 | 13.20 | 9.37 | 23.08 | 12.85 |
| 2472000 | 11.71 | 21.704 | 22.895 | 0.170 | 2.96 | 15.39 | 3.40 | 20.65 | 7.27 |
| 2473000 | 4.48 | 20.132 | 7.222 | 4.561 | 7.53 | 0.95 | 29.88 | 18.22 | 1.70 |
| 2474000 | 23.08 | 18.559 | 24.314 | 8.952 | 12.09 | 3.14 | 23.92 | 15.79 | 20.07 |
| 2475000 | 15.85 | 16.987 | 8.640 | 2.971 | 1.34 | 5.33 | 17.95 | 13.36 | 14.50 |
| 2476000 | 8.62 | 15.415 | 25.732 | 7.361 | 5.90 | 7.52 | 11.98 | 10.93 | 8.92 |
| 2477000 | 1.39 | 13.842 | 10.059 | 1.381 | 10.46 | 9.71 | 6.01 | 8.50 | 3.35 |
| 2478000 | 19.99 | 12.270 | 27.150 | 5.772 | 15.03 | 11.90 | 0.04 | 6.07 | 21.71 |
| 2479000 | 12.76 | 10.697 | 11.477 | 10.163 | 4.27 | 14.09 | 26.53 | 3.64 | 16.14 |
| 2480000 | 5.54 | 9.125 | 28.569 | 4.182 | 8.84 | 16.28 | 20.56 | 1.21 | 10.57 |
| 2481000 | 24.13 | 7.553 | 12.896 | 8.572 | 13.40 | 1.84 | 14.59 | 25.87 | 5.00 |
| 2482000 | 16.90 | 5.980 | 29.987 | 2.592 | 2.65 | 4.03 | 8.62 | 23.44 | 23.36 |
| 2483000 | 9.68 | 4.408 | 14.314 | 6.983 | 7.21 | 6.22 | 2.66 | 21.01 | 17.79 |
| 2484000 | 2.45 | 2.835 | 31.405 | 1.002 | 11.77 | 8.41 | 29.14 | 18.58 | 12.22 |
| 2485000 | 21.04 | 1.263 | 15.733 | 5.393 | 1.02 | 10.60 | 23.17 | 16.15 | 6.64 |
| 2486000 | 13.82 | 38.212 | 0.059 | 9.783 | 5.58 | 12.79 | 17.20 | 13.72 | 1.07 |
| 2487000 | 6.59 | 36.639 | 17.151 | 3.803 | 10.15 | 14.98 | 11.23 | 11.29 | 19.44 |
| 2488000 | 25.18 | 35.067 | 1.478 | 8.194 | 14.71 | 0.54 | 5.27 | 8.86 | 13.87 |
| 2489000 | 17.96 | 33.494 | 18.569 | 2.213 | 3.96 | 2.73 | 31.75 | 6.43 | 8.29 |
| 2490000 | 10.73 | 31.922 | 2.896 | 6.603 | 8.52 | 4.92 | 25.78 | 4.00 | 2.72 |
| 2491000 | 3.50 | 30.350 | 19.988 | 0.623 | 13.09 | 7.11 | 19.81 | 1.57 | 21.09 |
| 2492000 | 22.10 | 28.777 | 4.315 | 5.014 | 2.33 | 9.30 | 13.85 | 26.23 | 15.51 |
| 2493000 | 14.87 | 27.205 | 21.406 | 9.404 | 6.89 | 11.49 | 7.88 | 23.80 | 9.94 |
| 2494000 | 7.64 | 25.632 | 5.733 | 3.423 | 11.46 | 13.68 | 1.91 | 21.37 | 4.37 |
| 2495000 | 0.41 | 24.060 | 22.825 | 7.814 | 0.70 | 15.87 | 28.39 | 18.94 | 22.73 |
| 2496000 | 19.01 | 22.488 | 7.152 | 1.834 | 5.27 | 1.43 | 22.42 | 16.51 | 17.16 |
| 2497000 | 11.78 | 20.915 | 24.243 | 6.224 | 9.83 | 3.62 | 16.46 | 14.08 | 11.59 |
| 2498000 | 4.55 | 19.343 | 8.570 | 0.244 | 14.40 | 5.81 | 10.49 | 11.65 | 6.01 |
| 2499000 | 23.15 | 17.770 | 25.661 | 4.634 | 3.64 | 8.00 | 4.52 | 9.22 | 0.44 |
| 2500000 | 15.92 | 16.198 | 9.988 | 9.025 | 8.20 | 10.19 | 31.00 | 6.79 | 18.81 |

# TABLE IIb.

Epochs and Arguments for each Thousandth Day, from 2400000 to 2500000.

For Washington Mean Noon.

| Day of Julian Period. | Arg. 36. | 37. | 38. | 39. | 40. | 41. | 42. | 43. | 44. |
|---|---|---|---|---|---|---|---|---|---|
| | d. | d. | d. | d. | d. | d. | d. | d. | d. |
| 2400000 | 6.02 | 19.5 | 5.92 | 32.3 | 1.19 | 17.30 | 4.35 | 3.07 | 22.3 |
| 2401000 | 4.55 | 3.6 | 10.12 | 32.5 | 2.48 | 13.83 | 9.85 | 14.51 | 19.7 |
| 2402000 | 3.07 | 25.4 | 14.31 | 32.7 | 3.77 | 10.36 | 5.21 | 11.39 | 17.1 |
| 2403000 | 1.60 | 9.5 | 18.51 | 32.9 | 5.07 | 6.89 | 0.57 | 8.28 | 14.5 |
| 2404000 | 0.13 | 31.2 | 3.91 | 33.2 | 6.36 | 3.42 | 6.07 | 5.16 | 11.9 |
| 2405000 | 12.38 | 15.4 | 8.11 | 33.4 | 7.65 | 17.87 | 1.43 | 2.05 | 9.3 |
| 2406000 | 10.90 | 37.1 | 12.30 | 33.6 | 8.94 | 14.40 | 6.93 | 13.49 | 6.7 |
| 2407000 | 9.43 | 21.2 | 16.50 | 33.9 | 10.23 | 10.93 | 2.29 | 10.37 | 4.2 |
| 2408000 | 7.95 | 5.3 | 1.90 | 34.1 | 11.53 | 7.46 | 7.79 | 7.25 | 1.6 |
| 2409000 | 6.48 | 27.1 | 6.10 | 34.3 | 12.82 | 3.99 | 3.16 | 4.14 | 21.8 |
| 2410000 | 5.01 | 11.2 | 10.29 | 0.0 | 14.11 | 0.52 | 8.65 | 1.03 | 19.2 |
| 2411000 | 3.53 | 32.9 | 14.49 | 0.2 | 15.40 | 14.97 | 4.02 | 12.46 | 16.6 |
| 2412000 | 2.06 | 17.0 | 18.68 | 0.4 | 16.69 | 11.50 | 9.52 | 9.34 | 14.0 |
| 2413000 | 0.59 | 1.2 | 4.09 | 0.6 | 17.99 | 8.03 | 4.88 | 6.23 | 11.4 |
| 2414000 | 12.84 | 22.9 | 8.28 | 0.9 | 0.44 | 4.56 | 0.24 | 3.12 | 8.8 |
| 2415000 | 11.36 | 7.0 | 12.48 | 1.1 | 1.73 | 1.09 | 5.74 | 0.00 | 6.2 |
| 2416000 | 9.89 | 28.8 | 16.67 | 1.3 | 3.02 | 15.54 | 1.10 | 11.43 | 3.6 |
| 2417000 | 8.41 | 12.9 | 2.07 | 1.6 | 4.31 | 12.07 | 6.60 | 8.32 | 1.0 |
| 2418000 | 6.94 | 34.6 | 6.27 | 1.8 | 5.61 | 8.60 | 1.96 | 5.21 | 21.2 |
| 2419000 | 5.47 | 18.7 | 10.46 | 2.0 | 6.90 | 5.13 | 7.46 | 2.10 | 18.6 |
| 2420000 | 3.99 | 2.8 | 14.66 | 2.2 | 8.19 | 1.66 | 2.82 | 13.54 | 16.1 |
| 2421000 | 2.52 | 24.6 | 0.06 | 2.4 | 9.48 | 16.11 | 8.32 | 10.41 | 13.5 |
| 2422000 | 1.05 | 8.7 | 4.26 | 2.6 | 10.77 | 12.64 | 3.69 | 7.30 | 10.9 |
| 2423000 | 13.30 | 30.4 | 8.45 | 2.8 | 12.06 | 9.17 | 9.18 | 4.19 | 8.3 |
| 2424000 | 11.82 | 14.6 | 12.65 | 3.1 | 13.35 | 5.70 | 4.55 | 1.08 | 5.7 |
| 2425000 | 10.35 | 36.3 | 16.84 | 3.3 | 14.65 | 2.23 | 10.05 | 12.50 | 3.1 |
| 2426000 | 8.87 | 20.4 | 2.25 | 3.5 | 15.94 | 16.68 | 5.41 | 9.39 | 0.5 |
| 2427000 | 7.40 | 4.5 | 6.44 | 3.8 | 17.23 | 13.21 | 0.77 | 6.28 | 20.7 |
| 2428000 | 5.93 | 26.3 | 10.64 | 4.0 | 18.52 | 9.74 | 6.27 | 3.17 | 18.1 |
| 2429000 | 4.46 | 10.4 | 14.83 | 4.2 | 0.97 | 6.27 | 1.63 | 0.06 | 15.5 |
| 2430000 | 2.98 | 32.1 | 0.24 | 4.4 | 2.26 | 2.80 | 7.13 | 11.48 | 12.9 |
| 2431000 | 1.51 | 16.3 | 4.44 | 4.6 | 3.55 | 17.25 | 2.49 | 8.37 | 10.3 |
| 2432000 | 0.04 | 0.4 | 8.63 | 4.8 | 4.84 | 13.77 | 7.99 | 5.26 | 7.8 |
| 2433000 | 12.28 | 22.1 | 12.82 | 5.0 | 6.14 | 10.30 | 3.35 | 2.15 | 5.2 |
| 2434000 | 10.81 | 6.2 | 17.02 | 5.2 | 7.43 | 6.83 | 8.85 | 13.58 | 2.6 |
| 2435000 | 9.33 | 28.0 | 2.42 | 5.5 | 8.72 | 3.36 | 4.22 | 10.46 | 0.0 |
| 2436000 | 7.86 | 12.1 | 6.62 | 5.7 | 10.01 | 17.81 | 9.71 | 7.35 | 20.2 |
| 2437000 | 6.39 | 33.8 | 10.81 | 5.9 | 11.30 | 14.34 | 5.08 | 4.24 | 17.6 |
| 2438000 | 4.92 | 18.0 | 15.01 | 6.1 | 12.60 | 10.87 | 0.44 | 1.13 | 15.0 |
| 2439000 | 3.44 | 2.1 | 0.41 | 6.3 | 13.89 | 7.40 | 5.94 | 12.55 | 12.4 |
| 2440000 | 1.97 | 23.8 | 4.60 | 6.5 | 15.18 | 3.93 | 1.30 | 9.44 | 9.8 |
| 2441000 | 0.50 | 7.9 | 8.80 | 6.7 | 16.47 | 0.46 | 6.80 | 6.33 | 7.2 |
| 2442000 | 12.74 | 29.7 | 12.99 | 6.9 | 17.76 | 14.91 | 2.16 | 3.22 | 4.6 |
| 2443000 | 11.27 | 13.8 | 17.19 | 7.1 | 0.22 | 11.44 | 7.66 | 0.11 | 2.1 |
| 2444000 | 9.79 | 35.5 | 2.59 | 7.4 | 1.51 | 7.97 | 3.02 | 11.53 | 22.3 |
| 2445000 | 8.32 | 19.6 | 6.79 | 7.6 | 2.80 | 4.50 | 8.52 | 8.42 | 19.7 |
| 2446000 | 6.85 | 3.8 | 10.98 | 7.8 | 4.09 | 1.03 | 3.88 | 5.31 | 17.1 |
| 2447000 | 5.38 | 25.5 | 15.18 | 8.1 | 5.38 | 15.48 | 9.38 | 2.20 | 14.5 |
| 2448000 | 3.90 | 9.6 | 0.58 | 8.3 | 6.68 | 12.01 | 4.75 | 13.63 | 11.9 |
| 2449000 | 2.43 | 31.3 | 4.78 | 8.5 | 7.97 | 8.54 | 0.10 | 10.51 | 9.3 |
| 2550000 | 0.96 | 15.5 | 8.97 | 8.7 | 9.26 | 5.07 | 5.61 | 7.40 | 6.7 |

# TABLE II*b*.

Epochs and Arguments for each Thousandth Day, from 2400000 to 2500000.

For Washington Mean Noon.

| Day of Julian Period. | Arg. 36. | 37. | 38. | 39. | 40. | 41. | 42. | 43. | 44. |
|---|---|---|---|---|---|---|---|---|---|
| | d. | d. | d. | d. | d. | d. | d. | d. | d. |
| 2450000 | 0.96 | 15.5 | 8.97 | 8.7 | 9.26 | 5.07 | 5.61 | 7.40 | 6.7 |
| 2451000 | 13.20 | 37.2 | 13.17 | 8.9 | 10.55 | 1.60 | 0.96 | 4.29 | 4.1 |
| 2452000 | 11.73 | 21.3 | 17.36 | 9.1 | 11.84 | 16.05 | 6.47 | 1.17 | 1.5 |
| 2453000 | 10.26 | 5.4 | 2.77 | 9.3 | 13.14 | 12.58 | 1.83 | 12.60 | 21.7 |
| 2454000 | 8.78 | 27.2 | 6.96 | 9.6 | 14.43 | 9.11 | 7.33 | 9.49 | 19.1 |
| 2455000 | 7.31 | 11.3 | 11.16 | 9.8 | 15.72 | 5.64 | 2.69 | 6.38 | 16.6 |
| 2456000 | 5.84 | 33.0 | 15.35 | 10.0 | 17.01 | 2.17 | 8.19 | 3.26 | 14.0 |
| 2457000 | 4.36 | 17.2 | 0.76 | 10.3 | 18.30 | 16.62 | 3.55 | 0.16 | 11.4 |
| 2458000 | 2.89 | 1.3 | 4.95 | 10.5 | 0.76 | 13.15 | 9.05 | 11.58 | 8.8 |
| 2459000 | 1.42 | 23.0 | 9.15 | 10.7 | 2.05 | 9.68 | 4.42 | 8.47 | 6.2 |
| 2460000 | 13.66 | 7.1 | 13.34 | 10.9 | 3.34 | 6.21 | 9.91 | 5.36 | 3.6 |
| 2461000 | 12.19 | 28.9 | 17.53 | 11.1 | 4.63 | 2.74 | 5.28 | 2.24 | 1.0 |
| 2462000 | 10.72 | 13.0 | 2.94 | 11.3 | 5.92 | 17.19 | 0.64 | 13.68 | 21.2 |
| 2463000 | 9.24 | 34.7 | 7.13 | 11.5 | 7.22 | 13.72 | 6.14 | 10.56 | 18.6 |
| 2464000 | 7.77 | 18.8 | 11.33 | 11.7 | 8.51 | 10.25 | 1.50 | 7.45 | 16.0 |
| 2465000 | 6.30 | 3.0 | 15.52 | 12.0 | 9.80 | 6.78 | 6.99 | 4.33 | 13.4 |
| 2466000 | 4.82 | 24.7 | 0.93 | 12.2 | 11.09 | 3.31 | 2.36 | 1.22 | 10.8 |
| 2467000 | 3.35 | 8.8 | 5.12 | 12.5 | 12.38 | 17.76 | 7.86 | 12.65 | 8.3 |
| 2468000 | 1.88 | 30.6 | 9.32 | 12.7 | 13.68 | 14.29 | 3.22 | 9.54 | 5.7 |
| 2469000 | 0.40 | 14.7 | 13.51 | 12.9 | 14.97 | 10.82 | 8.72 | 6.43 | 3.1 |
| 2470000 | 12.65 | 36.4 | 17.71 | 13.1 | 16.26 | 7.35 | 4.08 | 3.31 | 0.5 |
| 2471000 | 11.18 | 20.5 | 3.11 | 13.3 | 17.55 | 3.88 | 9.58 | 0.21 | 20.7 |
| 2472000 | 9.70 | 4.6 | 7.31 | 13.5 | 0.00 | 0.41 | 4.95 | 11.63 | 18.1 |
| 2473000 | 8.23 | 26.4 | 11.50 | 13.7 | 1.30 | 14.85 | 0.30 | 8.52 | 15.5 |
| 2474000 | 6.76 | 10.5 | 15.70 | 13.9 | 2.59 | 11.38 | 5.81 | 5.40 | 12.9 |
| 2475000 | 5.28 | 32.2 | 1.10 | 14.2 | 3.88 | 7.91 | 1.17 | 2.29 | 10.3 |
| 2476000 | 3.81 | 16.4 | 5.30 | 14.4 | 5.17 | 4.44 | 6.67 | 13.73 | 7.7 |
| 2477000 | 2.34 | 0.5 | 9.49 | 14.6 | 6.46 | 0.97 | 2.03 | 10.61 | 5.1 |
| 2478000 | 0.87 | 22.2 | 13.69 | 14.8 | 7.76 | 15.42 | 7.52 | 7.49 | 2.6 |
| 2479000 | 13.11 | 6.3 | 17.88 | 15.0 | 9.05 | 11.95 | 2.89 | 4.38 | 0.0 |
| 2480000 | 11.64 | 28.1 | 3.29 | 15.2 | 10.34 | 8.48 | 8.39 | 1.27 | 20.2 |
| 2481000 | 10.16 | 12.2 | 7.48 | 15.4 | 11.63 | 5.01 | 3.75 | 12.70 | 17.6 |
| 2482000 | 8.69 | 33.9 | 11.68 | 15.6 | 12.92 | 1.54 | 9.25 | 9.59 | 15.0 |
| 2483000 | 7.22 | 18.1 | 15.87 | 15.8 | 14.21 | 15.99 | 4.62 | 6.47 | 12.4 |
| 2484000 | 5.74 | 2.2 | 1.28 | 16.1 | 15.50 | 12.52 | 10.11 | 3.36 | 9.8 |
| 2485000 | 4.27 | 23.9 | 5.47 | 16.3 | 16.80 | 9.05 | 5.48 | 0.26 | 7.2 |
| 2486000 | 2.80 | 8.0 | 9.67 | 16.5 | 18.09 | 5.58 | 0.83 | 11.68 | 4.6 |
| 2487000 | 1.33 | 29.8 | 13.86 | 16.8 | 0.54 | 2.11 | 6.34 | 8.56 | 2.0 |
| 2488000 | 13.57 | 13.9 | 18.06 | 17.0 | 1.83 | 16.56 | 1.70 | 5.45 | 22.2 |
| 2489000 | 12.10 | 35.6 | 3.46 | 17.2 | 3.12 | 13.09 | 7.19 | 2.34 | 19.6 |
| 2490000 | 10.62 | 19.7 | 7.66 | 17.4 | 4.41 | 9.62 | 2.56 | 13.78 | 17.0 |
| 2491000 | 9.15 | 3.9 | 11.85 | 17.6 | 5.70 | 6.15 | 8.06 | 10.66 | 14.5 |
| 2492000 | 7.68 | 25.6 | 16.05 | 17.8 | 6.99 | 2.68 | 3.42 | 7.54 | 11.9 |
| 2493000 | 6.21 | 9.7 | 1.45 | 18.0 | 8.29 | 17.13 | 8.92 | 4.43 | 9.3 |
| 2494000 | 4.73 | 31.5 | 5.65 | 18.3 | 9.58 | 13.66 | 4.28 | 1.32 | 6.7 |
| 2495000 | 3.26 | 15.6 | 9.84 | 18.5 | 10.87 | 10.19 | 9.78 | 12.75 | 4.1 |
| 2496000 | 1.79 | 37.3 | 14.04 | 18.7 | 12.16 | 6.72 | 5.15 | 9.63 | 1.5 |
| 2497000 | 0.31 | 21.4 | 18.23 | 19.0 | 13.45 | 3.25 | 0.50 | 6.52 | 21.7 |
| 2498000 | 12.56 | 5.6 | 3.63 | 19.2 | 14.75 | 17.70 | 6.01 | 3.41 | 19.1 |
| 2499000 | 11.09 | 27.3 | 7.83 | 19.4 | 16.04 | 14.23 | 1.37 | 0.31 | 16.5 |
| 2500000 | 9.61 | 11.4 | 12.03 | 19.6 | 17.33 | 10.76 | 6.86 | 11.73 | 13.9 |

# TABLE II*b*.

Epochs and Arguments for each Thousandth Day, from 2400000 to 2500000.

For Washington Mean Noon.

| Day of Julian Period. | Arg. 45. | 46. | 47. | 48. | 49. | 50. | 51. | 52. | 53. |
|---|---|---|---|---|---|---|---|---|---|
| | d. | d. | d. | d. | d. | d. | d. | d. | d. |
| 2400000 | 6.36 | 14.4 | 10.53 | 12.67 | 5.6 | 21.5 | 15.85 | 8.80 | 68.76 |
| 2401000 | 9.26 | 27.9 | 7.12 | 24.84 | 10.1 | 20.1 | 13.92 | 24.77 | 10.91 |
| 2402000 | 12.16 | 12.5 | 3.71 | 7.08 | 1.9 | 18.6 | 11.99 | 15.52 | 70.59 |
| 2403000 | 15.06 | 26.0 | 0.30 | 19.25 | 6.4 | 17.2 | 10.06 | 6.26 | 12.74 |
| 2404000 | 1.05 | 10.6 | 11.02 | 1.49 | 10.8 | 15.7 | 8.13 | 22.24 | 72.42 |
| 2405000 | 3.95 | 24.1 | 7.61 | 13.66 | 2.6 | 14.3 | 6.20 | 12.99 | 14.57 |
| 2406000 | 6.85 | 8.6 | 4.20 | 25.83 | 7.1 | 12.9 | 4.27 | 3.73 | 74.25 |
| 2407000 | 9.75 | 22.2 | 0.78 | 8.07 | 11.7 | 11.4 | 2.34 | 19.71 | 16.40 |
| 2408000 | 12.65 | 6.7 | 11.50 | 20.24 | 3.4 | 10.0 | 0.41 | 10.45 | 76.08 |
| 2409000 | 15.54 | 20.3 | 8.09 | 2.48 | 7.9 | 8.5 | 16.69 | 1.20 | 18.23 |
| 2410000 | 1.54 | 4.8 | 4.68 | 14.65 | 12.5 | 7.1 | 14.76 | 17.17 | 77.91 |
| 2411000 | 4.44 | 18.3 | 1.27 | 26.83 | 4.2 | 5.7 | 12.83 | 7.92 | 20.06 |
| 2412000 | 7.34 | 2.9 | 11.99 | 9.07 | 8.7 | 4.2 | 10.90 | 23.89 | 79.74 |
| 2413000 | 10.24 | 16.4 | 8.58 | 21.24 | 0.4 | 2.8 | 8.97 | 14.64 | 21.89 |
| 2414000 | 13.13 | 1.0 | 5.17 | 3.48 | 4.9 | 1.3 | 7.04 | 5.38 | 81.57 |
| 2415000 | 16.03 | 14.5 | 1.76 | 15.65 | 9.4 | 24.9 | 5.10 | 21.36 | 23.72 |
| 2416000 | 2.03 | 28.1 | 12.48 | 27.82 | 1.2 | 23.5 | 3.17 | 12.11 | 83.40 |
| 2417000 | 4.93 | 12.6 | 9.07 | 10.06 | 5.7 | 22.0 | 1.24 | 2.85 | 25 55 |
| 2418000 | 7.83 | 26.1 | 5.66 | 22.23 | 10.1 | 20.6 | 17.52 | 18.83 | 85.23 |
| 2419000 | 10.72 | 10.7 | 2.24 | 4.47 | 1.9 | 19.1 | 15.59 | 9.57 | 27.38 |
| 2420000 | 13.62 | 24.2 | 12.96 | 16.64 | 6.5 | 17.7 | 13.67 | 0.32 | 87.06 |
| 2421000 | 16.52 | 8.8 | 9.55 | 28.81 | 10.9 | 16.3 | 11.74 | 16.29 | 29.21 |
| 2422000 | 2.52 | 22.3 | 6.14 | 11.05 | 2.7 | 14.8 | 9.81 | 7.04 | 88.89 |
| 2423000 | 5.42 | 6.9 | 2.73 | 23.22 | 7.2 | 13.4 | 7.88 | 23.01 | 31.04 |
| 2424000 | 8.31 | 20.4 | 13.45 | 5.46 | 11.8 | 11.9 | 5.95 | 13.76 | 90.72 |
| 2425000 | 11.21 | 4.9 | 10.04 | 17.64 | 3.5 | 10.5 | 4.02 | 4.51 | 32.87 |
| 2426000 | 14.11 | 18.5 | 6.63 | 29.81 | 8.0 | 9.1 | 2.09 | 20.48 | 92.55 |
| 2427000 | 0.11 | 3.0 | 3.22 | 12.05 | 12.5 | 7.6 | 0.16 | 11.23 | 34.70 |
| 2428000 | 3.01 | 16.6 | 13.94 | 24.22 | 4.2 | 6.2 | 16.44 | 1.97 | 94.38 |
| 2429000 | 5.91 | 1.1 | 10.53 | 6.46 | 8.7 | 4.7 | 14.52 | 17.95 | 36.53 |
| 2430000 | 8.80 | 14.6 | 7.12 | 18.63 | 0.5 | 3.3 | 12.59 | 8.69 | 96.21 |
| 2431000 | 11.70 | 28.2 | 3.70 | 0.87 | 5.0 | 1.9 | 10.66 | 24.67 | 38.36 |
| 2432000 | 14.60 | 12.7 | 0.29 | 13.04 | 9.5 | 0.5 | 8.73 | 15.42 | 98.04 |
| 2433000 | 0.60 | 26.3 | 11.01 | 25.21 | 1.3 | 24.0 | 6.80 | 6.16 | 40.19 |
| 2434000 | 3.49 | 10.8 | 7.60 | 7.45 | 5.8 | 22.6 | 4.87 | 22.14 | 99.87 |
| 2435000 | 6.39 | 24.4 | 4.19 | 19.62 | 10.2 | 21.1 | 2.93 | 12.88 | 32.02 |
| 2436000 | 9.29 | 8.9 | 0.78 | 1.86 | 2.0 | 19.7 | 1.00 | 3.63 | 91.70 |
| 2437000 | 12.19 | 22.4 | 11.50 | 14.03 | 6.5 | 18.3 | 17.28 | 19.60 | 33.85 |
| 2438000 | 15.09 | 7.0 | 8.09 | 26.21 | 11.0 | 16.8 | 15.35 | 10.35 | 93.53 |
| 2439000 | 1.08 | 20.5 | 4.68 | 8.44 | 2.8 | 15.4 | 13.43 | 1.09 | 35.68 |
| 2440000 | 3.98 | 5.1 | 1.27 | 20.62 | 7.3 | 14.0 | 11.50 | 17.07 | 105.36 |
| 2441000 | 6.88 | 18.6 | 11.99 | 2.86 | 11.8 | 12.6 | 9.57 | 7.82 | 47.51 |
| 2442000 | 9.78 | 3.2 | 8.58 | 15.03 | 3.5 | 11.1 | 7.64 | 23.79 | 107.19 |
| 2443000 | 12.67 | 16.7 | 5.16 | 27.20 | 8.1 | 9.7 | 5.71 | 14.54 | 49.34 |
| 2444000 | 15.57 | 1.2 | 1.75 | 9.44 | 12.6 | 8.2 | 3.78 | 5.28 | 109.02 |
| 2445000 | 1.57 | 14.8 | 12.47 | 21.61 | 4.3 | 6.8 | 1.84 | 21.26 | 51.17 |
| 2446000 | 4.47 | 28.3 | 9.06 | 3.85 | 8.8 | 5.4 | 18.12 | 12.00 | 110.85 |
| 2447000 | 7.37 | 12.9 | 5.65 | 16.02 | 0.6 | 3.9 | 16.19 | 2.75 | 53.00 |
| 2448000 | 10.26 | 26.4 | 2.24 | 28.19 | 5.1 | 2.5 | 14.27 | 18.73 | 112.68 |
| 2449000 | 13.16 | 11.0 | 12.96 | 10.43 | 9.6 | 1.0 | 12.34 | 9.47 | 54.83 |
| 2450000 | 16.06 | 24.5 | 9.55 | 22.60 | 1.3 | 24.6 | 10.41 | 0.22 | 114.51 |

# TABLE II*b*.

Epochs and Arguments for each Thousandth Day, from 2400000 to 2500000.

For Washington Mean Noon.

| Day of Julian Period. | Arg. 45. | 46. | 47. | 48. | 49. | 50. | 51. | 52. | 53. |
|---|---|---|---|---|---|---|---|---|---|
| | d. | d. | d. | d. | d. | d. | d. | d. | d. |
| 2450000 | 16.06 | 24.5 | 9.55 | 22.60 | 1.3 | 24.6 | 10.41 | 0.22 | 114.51 |
| 2451000 | 2.06 | 9.0 | 6.14 | 4.84 | 5.8 | 23.2 | 8.48 | 16.19 | 56.66 |
| 2452000 | 4.96 | 22.6 | 2.73 | 17.02 | 10.3 | 21.7 | 6.55 | 6.94 | 116.34 |
| 2453000 | 7.85 | 7.1 | 13.45 | 29.19 | 2.1 | 20.3 | 4.62 | 22.91 | 58.49 |
| 2454000 | 10.75 | 20.7 | 10.04 | 11.43 | 6.6 | 18.8 | 2.69 | 13.66 | 0.63 |
| 2455000 | 13.65 | 5.2 | 6.63 | 23.60 | 11.0 | 17.4 | 0.75 | 4.40 | 60.32 |
| 2456000 | 16.55 | 18.7 | 3.22 | 5.84 | 2.8 | 16.0 | 17.03 | 20.38 | 2.46 |
| 2457000 | 2.55 | 3.3 | 13.93 | 18.01 | 7.4 | 14.5 | 15.11 | 11.13 | 62.15 |
| 2458000 | 5.44 | 16.8 | 10.52 | 0.25 | 11.9 | 13.1 | 13.18 | 1.87 | 4.29 |
| 2459000 | 8.34 | 1.4 | 7.11 | 12.42 | 3.6 | 11.6 | 11.25 | 17.85 | 63.98 |
| 2460000 | 11.24 | 14.9 | 3.70 | 24.59 | 8.1 | 10.2 | 9.32 | 8.59 | 6.12 |
| 2461000 | 14.14 | 28.5 | 0.29 | 6.83 | 12.7 | 8.8 | 7.39 | 24.57 | 65.81 |
| 2462000 | 0.14 | 13.0 | 11.01 | 19.00 | 4.4 | 7.4 | 5.46 | 15.31 | 7.95 |
| 2463000 | 3.03 | 26.5 | 7.60 | 1.24 | 8.9 | 5.9 | 3.53 | 6.06 | 67.64 |
| 2464000 | 5.93 | 11.1 | 4.19 | 13.41 | 0.6 | 4.5 | 1.60 | 22.04 | 9.78 |
| 2465000 | 8.83 | 24.6 | 0.78 | 25.59 | 5.1 | 3.0 | 17.87 | 12.78 | 69.47 |
| 2466000 | 11.73 | 9.2 | 11.50 | 7.83 | 9.6 | 1.6 | 15.94 | 3.53 | 11.61 |
| 2467000 | 14.63 | 22.7 | 8.09 | 20.00 | 1.4 | 0.2 | 14.02 | 19.50 | 71.30 |
| 2468000 | 0.62 | 7.3 | 4.68 | 2.24 | 5.9 | 23.7 | 12.09 | 10.25 | 13.44 |
| 2469000 | 3.52 | 20.8 | 1.26 | 14.41 | 10.3 | 22.3 | 10.16 | 0.99 | 73.13 |
| 2470000 | 6.42 | 5.3 | 11.98 | 26.58 | 2.2 | 20.9 | 8.23 | 16.97 | 15.27 |
| 2471000 | 9.32 | 18.9 | 8.57 | 8.82 | 6.7 | 19.5 | 6.30 | 7.71 | 74.96 |
| 2472000 | 12.21 | 3.4 | 5.16 | 20.99 | 11.1 | 18.0 | 4.37 | 23.69 | 17.10 |
| 2473000 | 15.11 | 17.0 | 1.75 | 3.23 | 2.9 | 16.6 | 2.44 | 14.43 | 76.79 |
| 2474000 | 1.11 | 1.5 | 12.47 | 15.40 | 7.4 | 15.1 | 0.51 | 5.18 | 18.93 |
| 2475000 | 4.01 | 15.0 | 9.06 | 27.57 | 12.0 | 13.7 | 16.78 | 21.16 | 78.62 |
| 2476000 | 6.91 | 28.6 | 5.65 | 9.81 | 3.7 | 12.3 | 14.86 | 11.90 | 20.76 |
| 2477000 | 9.80 | 13.1 | 2.24 | 21.99 | 8.2 | 10.8 | 12.93 | 2.65 | 80.45 |
| 2478000 | 12.70 | 26.7 | 12.96 | 4.22 | 12.7 | 9.4 | 11.00 | 18.62 | 22.59 |
| 2479000 | 15.60 | 11.2 | 9.55 | 16.40 | 4.4 | 7.9 | 9.07 | 9.37 | 82.28 |
| 2480000 | 1.60 | 24.8 | 6.14 | 28.57 | 8.9 | 6.5 | 7.14 | 0.11 | 24.42 |
| 2481000 | 4.50 | 9.3 | 2.73 | 10.81 | 0.7 | 5.1 | 5.21 | 16.09 | 84.11 |
| 2482000 | 7.39 | 22.8 | 13.44 | 22.98 | 5.2 | 3.6 | 3.28 | 6.83 | 26.25 |
| 2483000 | 10.29 | 7.4 | 10.03 | 5.22 | 9.7 | 2.2 | 1.35 | 22.81 | 85.94 |
| 2484000 | 13.19 | 20.9 | 6.62 | 17.39 | 1.4 | 0.7 | 17.63 | 13.56 | 28.08 |
| 2485000 | 16.09 | 5.5 | 3.21 | 29.56 | 6.0 | 24.3 | 15.69 | 4.30 | 87.77 |
| 2486000 | 2.09 | 19.0 | 13.93 | 11.80 | 10.4 | 22.9 | 13.77 | 20.28 | 29.91 |
| 2487000 | 4.98 | 3.6 | 10.52 | 23.97 | 2.2 | 21.4 | 11.84 | 11.02 | 89.60 |
| 2488000 | 7.88 | 17.1 | 7.11 | 6.21 | 6.7 | 20.0 | 9.91 | 1.77 | 31.74 |
| 2489000 | 10.78 | 1.6 | 3.70 | 18.39 | 11.3 | 18.5 | 7.98 | 17.75 | 91.43 |
| 2490000 | 13.68 | 15.2 | 0.29 | 0.62 | 3.0 | 17.1 | 6.05 | 8.49 | 33.57 |
| 2491000 | 16.58 | 28.7 | 11.01 | 12.80 | 7.5 | 15.7 | 4.12 | 24.46 | 93.26 |
| 2492000 | 2.57 | 13.3 | 7.60 | 24.97 | 12.0 | 14.3 | 2.19 | 15.21 | 35.41 |
| 2493000 | 5.47 | 26.8 | 4.19 | 7.21 | 3.7 | 12.8 | 0.26 | 5.96 | 95.09 |
| 2494000 | 8.37 | 11.3 | 0.77 | 19.38 | 8.3 | 11.4 | 16.54 | 21.93 | 37.24 |
| 2495000 | 11.27 | 24.9 | 11.49 | 1.62 | 0.0 | 9.9 | 14.61 | 12.68 | 96.92 |
| 2496000 | 14.17 | 9.4 | 8.08 | 13.79 | 4.5 | 8.5 | 12.68 | 3.42 | 39.07 |
| 2497000 | 0.16 | 23.0 | 4.67 | 25.96 | 9.0 | 7.1 | 10.75 | 19.40 | 98.75 |
| 2498000 | 3.06 | 7.5 | 1.26 | 8.20 | 0.8 | 5.6 | 8.82 | 10.14 | 40.90 |
| 2499000 | 5.96 | 21.1 | 11.98 | 20.37 | 5.3 | 4.2 | 6.89 | 0.89 | 100.58 |
| 2500000 | 8.86 | 5.6 | 8.57 | 2.61 | 9.8 | 2.8 | 4.96 | 16.86 | 42.73 |

# TABLE IIb.

Epochs and Arguments for each Thousandth Day, from 2400000 to 2500000.

For Washington Mean Noon.

| Day of Julian Period. | ARG. 54. | 55. | 56. | 57. | 58. | 59 | 60. | 61. | 62. |
|---|---|---|---|---|---|---|---|---|---|
| | d. | d. | d. | d. | d. | d. | d | d. | d. |
| 2400000 | 4.73 | 3.34 | 7.21 | 8.03 | 3.77 | 11.57 | 15.63 | 3.71 | 8.20 |
| 2401000 | 10.11 | 2.35 | 10.29 | 5.78 | 13.02 | 37.46 | 11.16 | 10.46 | 11.70 |
| 2402000 | 0.43 | 1.35 | 0.24 | 3.52 | 7.04 | 24.41 | 6.68 | 3.61 | 0.76 |
| 2403000 | 5.82 | 0.36 | 3.31 | 1.26 | 1.05 | 11.34 | 2.20 | 10.36 | 4.26 |
| 2404000 | 11.21 | 19.00 | 6.38 | 15.99 | 10.31 | 37.24 | 20.05 | 3.51 | 7.76 |
| 2405000 | 1.52 | 18.00 | 9.45 | 13.74 | 4.32 | 24.18 | 15.57 | 10.27 | 11.27 |
| 2406000 | 6.91 | 17.00 | 12.53 | 11.48 | 13.57 | 11.12 | 11.09 | 3.41 | 0.33 |
| 2407000 | 12.30 | 16.02 | 2.48 | 9.22 | 7.59 | 37.01 | 6.62 | 10.17 | 3.83 |
| 2408000 | 2.62 | 15.03 | 5.55 | 6.97 | 1.61 | 23.96 | 2.14 | 3.31 | 7.33 |
| 2409000 | 8.00 | 14.03 | 8.62 | 4.71 | 10.86 | 10.89 | 19.98 | 10.07 | 10.83 |
| 2410000 | 13.39 | 13.04 | 11.70 | 2.45 | 4.87 | 36.79 | 15.51 | 3.22 | 14.33 |
| 2411000 | 3.71 | 12.05 | 1.65 | 0.19 | 14.13 | 23.73 | 11.03 | 9.97 | 3.40 |
| 2412000 | 9.10 | 11.06 | 4.72 | 14.93 | 8.14 | 10.67 | 6.55 | 3.12 | 6.90 |
| 2413000 | 14.48 | 10.06 | 7.79 | 12.67 | 2.16 | 36.56 | 2.08 | 9.87 | 10.40 |
| 2414000 | 4.80 | 9.07 | 10.87 | 10.41 | 11.41 | 23.50 | 19.92 | 3.02 | 13.90 |
| 2415000 | 10.19 | 8.08 | 0.82 | 8.15 | 5.43 | 10.44 | 15.44 | 9.78 | 2.96 |
| 2416000 | 0.51 | 7.09 | 3.89 | 5.90 | 14.68 | 36.34 | 10.96 | 2.92 | 6.46 |
| 2417000 | 5.89 | 6.10 | 6.96 | 3.64 | 8.70 | 23.28 | 6.49 | 9.68 | 9.96 |
| 2418000 | 11.28 | 5.10 | 10.04 | 1.38 | 2.71 | 10.22 | 2.01 | 2.83 | 13.47 |
| 2419000 | 1.60 | 4.11 | 13.11 | 16.11 | 11.97 | 36.11 | 19.86 | 9.58 | 2.53 |
| 2420000 | 6.99 | 3.12 | 3.06 | 13.86 | 5.98 | 23.05 | 15.38 | 2.73 | 6.03 |
| 2421000 | 12.37 | 2.13 | 6.13 | 11.60 | 15.23 | 9.99 | 10.90 | 9.48 | 9.53 |
| 2422000 | 2.69 | 1.14 | 9.20 | 9.34 | 9.25 | 35.89 | 6.43 | 2.63 | 13.03 |
| 2423000 | 8.08 | 0.14 | 12.28 | 7.09 | 3.26 | 22.83 | 1.95 | 9.38 | 2.09 |
| 2424000 | 13.47 | 18.78 | 2.23 | 4.83 | 12.52 | 9.76 | 19.79 | 2.53 | 5.59 |
| 2425000 | 3.78 | 17.79 | 5.30 | 2.57 | 6.53 | 35.66 | 15.32 | 9.28 | 9.10 |
| 2426000 | 9.17 | 16.80 | 8.37 | 0.31 | 0.55 | 22.60 | 10.84 | 2.43 | 12.60 |
| 2427000 | 14.56 | 15.81 | 11.45 | 15.04 | 9.80 | 9.54 | 6.36 | 9.19 | 1.66 |
| 2428000 | 4.88 | 14.81 | 1.40 | 12.79 | 3.82 | 35.44 | 1.88 | 2.33 | 5.16 |
| 2429000 | 10.26 | 13.82 | 4.47 | 10.53 | 13.07 | 22.38 | 19.73 | 9.09 | 8.66 |
| 2430000 | 0.58 | 12.83 | 7.54 | 8.27 | 7.09 | 9.31 | 15.25 | 2.24 | 12.16 |
| 2431000 | 5.97 | 11.84 | 10.62 | 6.02 | 1.10 | 35.21 | 10.77 | 8.99 | 1.23 |
| 2432000 | 11.36 | 10.85 | 0.57 | 3.76 | 10.36 | 22.15 | 6.30 | 2.14 | 4.73 |
| 2433000 | 1.67 | 9.85 | 3.64 | 1.50 | 4.37 | 9.09 | 1.82 | 8.89 | 8.23 |
| 2434000 | 7.06 | 8.86 | 6.71 | 16.23 | 13.62 | 34.98 | 19.66 | 2.04 | 11.73 |
| 2435000 | 12.45 | 7.87 | 9.78 | 13.98 | 7.64 | 21.92 | 15.19 | 8.79 | 0.79 |
| 2436000 | 2.77 | 6.88 | 12.86 | 11.72 | 1.65 | 8.86 | 10.71 | 1.94 | 4.29 |
| 2437000 | 8.15 | 5.89 | 2.81 | 9.46 | 10.91 | 34.76 | 6.23 | 8.70 | 7.79 |
| 2438000 | 13.54 | 4.89 | 5.88 | 7.21 | 4.92 | 21.70 | 1.76 | 1.84 | 11.30 |
| 2439000 | 3.86 | 3.90 | 8.95 | 4.95 | 14.18 | 8.64 | 19.60 | 8.60 | 0.36 |
| 2440000 | 9.25 | 2.90 | 12.03 | 2.69 | 8.19 | 34.53 | 15.12 | 1.74 | 3.86 |
| 2441000 | 14.63 | 1.91 | 1.98 | 0.43 | 2.21 | 21.47 | 10.65 | 8.50 | 7.36 |
| 2442000 | 4.95 | 0.91 | 5.05 | 15.17 | 11.46 | 8.41 | 6.17 | 1.65 | 10.86 |
| 2443000 | 10.34 | 19.56 | 8.12 | 12.91 | 5.48 | 34.31 | 1.69 | 8.40 | 14.36 |
| 2444000 | 0.66 | 18.57 | 11.20 | 10.65 | 14.73 | 21.25 | 19.54 | 1.55 | 3.43 |
| 2445000 | 6.04 | 17.57 | 1.15 | 8.39 | 8.75 | 8.18 | 15.06 | 8.30 | 6.93 |
| 2446000 | 11.43 | 16.58 | 4.22 | 6.14 | 2.76 | 34.08 | 10.58 | 1.45 | 10.43 |
| 2447000 | 1.75 | 15.59 | 7.29 | 3.88 | 12.02 | 21.02 | 6.11 | 8.20 | 13.93 |
| 2448000 | 7.14 | 14.60 | 10.37 | 1.62 | 6.03 | 7.96 | 1.63 | 1.35 | 2.99 |
| 2449000 | 12.52 | 13.60 | 0.32 | 16.35 | 0.05 | 33.86 | 19.47 | 8.10 | 6.49 |
| 2450000 | 2.84 | 12.61 | 3.39 | 14.10 | 9.30 | 20.79 | 15.00 | 1.25 | 9.99 |

# TABLE IIb.

Epochs and Arguments for each Thousandth Day, from 2400000 to 2500000.

For Washington Mean Noon.

| Day of Julian Period. | Arg. 54. | 55. | 56. | 57. | 58. | 59. | 60. | 61. | 62. |
|---|---|---|---|---|---|---|---|---|---|
| | d. | d. | d. | d. | d. | d. | d. | d. | d. |
| 2450000 | 2.84 | 12.61 | 3.39 | 14.10 | 9.30 | 20.79 | 15.00 | 1.25 | 9.99 |
| 2451000 | 8.23 | 11.62 | 6.46 | 11.84 | 3.31 | 7.73 | 10.52 | 8.01 | 13.50 |
| 2452000 | 13.62 | 10.63 | 9.53 | 9.58 | 12.57 | 33.63 | 6.04 | 1.16 | 2.56 |
| 2453000 | 3.93 | 9.63 | 12.61 | 7.33 | 6.58 | 20.57 | 1.57 | 7.91 | 6.06 |
| 2454000 | 9.32 | 8.64 | 2.56 | 5.07 | 0.60 | 7.51 | 19.41 | 1.06 | 9.56 |
| 2455000 | 14.71 | 7.65 | 5.63 | 2.81 | 9.85 | 33.41 | 14.93 | 7.81 | 13.06 |
| 2456000 | 5.03 | 6.66 | 8.70 | 0.55 | 3.87 | 20.34 | 10.46 | 0.96 | 2.12 |
| 2457000 | 10.41 | 5.67 | 11.78 | 15.29 | 13.12 | 7.28 | 5.98 | 7.71 | 5.62 |
| 2458000 | 0.73 | 4.67 | 1.73 | 13.03 | 7.14 | 33.18 | 1.50 | 0.86 | 9.13 |
| 2459000 | 6.12 | 3.68 | 4.80 | 10.77 | 1.15 | 20.12 | 19.35 | 7.61 | 12.63 |
| 2460000 | 11.51 | 2.69 | 7.87 | 8.52 | 10.41 | 7.05 | 14.87 | 0.76 | 1.69 |
| 2461000 | 1.83 | 1.69 | 10.95 | 6.26 | 4.42 | 32.95 | 10.39 | 7.52 | 5.19 |
| 2462000 | 7.21 | 0.71 | 0.90 | 4.00 | 13.67 | 19.89 | 5.92 | 0.67 | 8.69 |
| 2463000 | 12.60 | 19.34 | 3.97 | 1.74 | 7.69 | 6.83 | 1.44 | 7.42 | 12.19 |
| 2464000 | 2.92 | 18.35 | 7.04 | 16.48 | 1.70 | 32.73 | 19.28 | 0.57 | 1.26 |
| 2465000 | 8.31 | 17.36 | 10.11 | 14.22 | 10.96 | 19.67 | 14.81 | 7.32 | 4.76 |
| 2466000 | 13.69 | 16.37 | 0.07 | 11.96 | 4.97 | 6.60 | 10.33 | 0.47 | 8.26 |
| 2467000 | 4.01 | 15.38 | 3.14 | 9.70 | 14.23 | 32.50 | 5.85 | 7.22 | 11.76 |
| 2468000 | 9.40 | 14.38 | 6.21 | 7.45 | 8.24 | 19.44 | 1.38 | 0.37 | 0.82 |
| 2469000 | 14.78 | 13.39 | 9.28 | 5.19 | 2.26 | 6.38 | 19.22 | 7.13 | 4.32 |
| 2470000 | 5.10 | 12.40 | 12.36 | 2.93 | 11.51 | 32.28 | 14.74 | 0.26 | 7.82 |
| 2471000 | 10.49 | 11.41 | 2.31 | 0.67 | 5.53 | 19.21 | 10.27 | 7.03 | 11.33 |
| 2472000 | 0.81 | 10.42 | 5.38 | 15.41 | 14.78 | 6.15 | 5.79 | 0.17 | 0.39 |
| 2473000 | 6.20 | 9.42 | 8.45 | 13.15 | 8.80 | 32.05 | 1.31 | 6.93 | 3.89 |
| 2474000 | 11.58 | 8.43 | 11.53 | 10.89 | 2.81 | 18.99 | 19.16 | 0.08 | 7.39 |
| 2475000 | 1.90 | 7.44 | 1.48 | 8.64 | 12.06 | 5.93 | 14.68 | 6.83 | 10.89 |
| 2476000 | 7.29 | 6.45 | 4.55 | 6.38 | 6.08 | 31.83 | 10.20 | 13.59 | 14.39 |
| 2477000 | 12.67 | 5.46 | 7.62 | 4.12 | 0.09 | 18.76 | 5.72 | 6.73 | 3.46 |
| 2478000 | 2.99 | 4.46 | 10.70 | 1.86 | 9.35 | 5.70 | 1.25 | 13.49 | 6.96 |
| 2479000 | 8.38 | 3.47 | 0.65 | 16.60 | 3.36 | 31.60 | 19.09 | 6.63 | 10.46 |
| 2480000 | 13.77 | 2.48 | 3.72 | 14.34 | 12.62 | 18.54 | 14.62 | 13.39 | 13.96 |
| 2481000 | 4.09 | 1.49 | 6.79 | 12.08 | 6.64 | 5.47 | 10.14 | 6.54 | 3.02 |
| 2482000 | 9.47 | 0.49 | 9.86 | 9.83 | 0.65 | 31.37 | 5.66 | 13.29 | 6.52 |
| 2483000 | 14.86 | 19.13 | 12.94 | 7.57 | 9.90 | 18.31 | 1.18 | 6.44 | 10.02 |
| 2484000 | 5.18 | 18.14 | 2.89 | 5.31 | 3.92 | 5.25 | 19.03 | 13.20 | 13.53 |
| 2485000 | 10.57 | 17.14 | 5.96 | 3.05 | 13.17 | 31.15 | 14.55 | 6.34 | 2.59 |
| 2486000 | 0.88 | 16.15 | 9.03 | 0.79 | 7.19 | 18.08 | 10.07 | 13.10 | 6.09 |
| 2487000 | 6.28 | 15.16 | 12.11 | 15.53 | 1.20 | 5.02 | 5.60 | 6.24 | 9.59 |
| 2488000 | 11.66 | 14.17 | 2.05 | 13.27 | 10.46 | 30.92 | 1.12 | 13.00 | 13.09 |
| 2489000 | 1.97 | 13.17 | 5.13 | 11.01 | 4.47 | 17.86 | 18.96 | 6.14 | 2.15 |
| 2490000 | 7.36 | 12.18 | 8.20 | 8.76 | 13.72 | 4.79 | 14.49 | 12.90 | 5.65 |
| 2491000 | 12.75 | 11.19 | 11.28 | 6.50 | 7.74 | 30.70 | 10.01 | 6.04 | 9.16 |
| 2492000 | 3.07 | 10.20 | 1.23 | 4.24 | 1.75 | 17.63 | 5.53 | 12.80 | 12.66 |
| 2493000 | 8.46 | 9.20 | 4.30 | 1.98 | 11.01 | 4.57 | 1.06 | 5.95 | 1.72 |
| 2494000 | 13.84 | 8.21 | 7.37 | 16.72 | 5.02 | 30.47 | 18.90 | 12.70 | 5.22 |
| 2495000 | 4.16 | 7.22 | 10.45 | 14.46 | 14.28 | 17.41 | 14.42 | 5.85 | 8.72 |
| 2496000 | 9.55 | 6.23 | 0.40 | 12.20 | 8.29 | 4.34 | 9.95 | 12.61 | 12.22 |
| 2497000 | 14.93 | 5.24 | 3.47 | 9.95 | 2.31 | 30.24 | 5.47 | 5.75 | 1.29 |
| 2498000 | 5.25 | 4.24 | 6.54 | 7.69 | 11.56 | 17.18 | 0.99 | 12.51 | 4.79 |
| 2499000 | 10.64 | 3.25 | 9.61 | 5.43 | 5.58 | 4.12 | 18.84 | 5.65 | 8.29 |
| 2500000 | 0.96 | 2.26 | 12.69 | 3.18 | 14.83 | 30.02 | 14.37 | 12.41 | 11.79 |

# TABLE II*b*.

Epochs and Arguments for each Thousandth Day, from 2400000 to 2500000.

For Washington Mean Noon.

| Day of Julian Period. | Arg. **63.** | **64.** | **65.** | **66.** | **67.** | **68.** | **69.** | **70.** | **71.** |
|---|---|---|---|---|---|---|---|---|---|
| | d. | d. | d. | d. | d. | d. | d. | d. | d. |
| 2400000 | 7.84 | 25.59 | 3.13 | 7.8 | 7.66 | 3.65 | 121.5 | 307.1 | 272.0 |
| 2401000 | 12.61 | 17.81 | 4.51 | 11.1 | 19.70 | 7.65 | 177.7 | 317.7 | 104.2 |
| 2402000 | 3.73 | 10.03 | 5.89 | 14.4 | 4.30 | 11.65 | 234.0 | 328.3 | 520.3 |
| 2403000 | 8.49 | 2.25 | 7.26 | 17.8 | 16.34 | 15.65 | 290.2 | 09.2 | 352.4 |
| 2404000 | 13.26 | 30.46 | 8.64 | 21.1 | 0.94 | 19.65 | 346.4 | 19.8 | 184.6 |
| 2405000 | 4.38 | 22.68 | 10.02 | 24.4 | 12.98 | 23.65 | 402.6 | 30.5 | 16.8 |
| 2406000 | 9.15 | 14.91 | 11.41 | 27.7 | 25.02 | 27.65 | 458.8 | 41.1 | 432.8 |
| 2407000 | 0.28 | 7.13 | 12.79 | 31.0 | 9.61 | 3.98 | 43.1 | 51.7 | 265.0 |
| 2408000 | 5.04 | 35.34 | 14.16 | 34.4 | 21.65 | 7.98 | 99.3 | 62.4 | 97.2 |
| 2409000 | 9.80 | 27.56 | 1.06 | 2.1 | 6.25 | 11.98 | 155.5 | 73.0 | 513.2 |
| 2410000 | 0.93 | 19.78 | 2.44 | 5.4 | 18.29 | 15.98 | 211.8 | 83.6 | 345.4 |
| 2411000 | 5.69 | 12.00 | 3.82 | 8.7 | 2.89 | 19.98 | 268.0 | 94.2 | 177.5 |
| 2412000 | 10.45 | 4.22 | 5.20 | 12.0 | 14.93 | 23.98 | 324.2 | 104.8 | 9.7 |
| 2413000 | 1.58 | 32.43 | 6.58 | 15.3 | 26.98 | 0.31 | 380.4 | 115.5 | 425.8 |
| 2414000 | 6.34 | 24.66 | 7.96 | 18.6 | 11.57 | 4.31 | 436.6 | 126.1 | 257.9 |
| 2415000 | 11.11 | 16.88 | 9.33 | 22.0 | 23.61 | 8.31 | 21.0 | 136.7 | 90.1 |
| 2416000 | 2.23 | 9.10 | 10.71 | 25.3 | 8.20 | 12.31 | 77.2 | 147.3 | 506.1 |
| 2417000 | 7.00 | 1.32 | 12.10 | 28.6 | 20.24 | 16.31 | 133.4 | 157.9 | 338.3 |
| 2418000 | 11.76 | 29.53 | 13.48 | 31.9 | 4.84 | 20.31 | 189.6 | 168.6 | 170.5 |
| 2419000 | 2.89 | 21.75 | 0.38 | 35.2 | 16.88 | 24.31 | 245.8 | 179.2 | 2.6 |
| 2420000 | 7.65 | 13.97 | 1.76 | 2.9 | 1.48 | 0.64 | 302.0 | 189.8 | 418.7 |
| 2421000 | 12.42 | 6.19 | 3.14 | 6.2 | 13.52 | 4.64 | 358.3 | 200.4 | 250.9 |
| 2422000 | 3.54 | 34.40 | 4.52 | 9.5 | 25.57 | 8.64 | 414.5 | 211.0 | 83.0 |
| 2423000 | 8.30 | 26.63 | 5.89 | 12.9 | 10.16 | 12.64 | 470.7 | 221.7 | 499.1 |
| 2424000 | 13.07 | 18.85 | 7.27 | 16.2 | 22.20 | 16.64 | 55.0 | 232.3 | 331.3 |
| 2425000 | 4.19 | 11.07 | 8.65 | 19.5 | 6.80 | 20.64 | 111.2 | 243.0 | 163.4 |
| 2426000 | 8.95 | 3.29 | 10.03 | 22.8 | 18.84 | 24.64 | 167.5 | 253.6 | 579.5 |
| 2427000 | 0.08 | 31.50 | 11.42 | 26.1 | 3.43 | 0.96 | 223.7 | 264.2 | 411.6 |
| 2428000 | 4.85 | 23.72 | 12.79 | 29.5 | 15.47 | 4.96 | 279.9 | 274.9 | 243.8 |
| 2429000 | 9.61 | 15.94 | 14.17 | 32.8 | 0.07 | 8.96 | 336.1 | 285.5 | 76.0 |
| 2430000 | 0.74 | 8.16 | 1.07 | 0.5 | 12.11 | 12.97 | 392.3 | 296.1 | 492.0 |
| 2431000 | 5.50 | 0.38 | 2.45 | 3.8 | 24.15 | 16.97 | 448.5 | 306.7 | 324.2 |
| 2432000 | 10.26 | 28.60 | 3.83 | 7.1 | 8.75 | 20.96 | 32.8 | 317.3 | 156.4 |
| 2433000 | 1.39 | 20.82 | 5.21 | 10.5 | 20.79 | 24.96 | 89.1 | 328.0 | 572.4 |
| 2434000 | 6.15 | 13.04 | 6.59 | 13.8 | 5.39 | 1.29 | 145.3 | 8.8 | 404.6 |
| 2435000 | 10.92 | 5.26 | 7.96 | 17.1 | 17.43 | 5.29 | 201.5 | 19.5 | 236.8 |
| 2436000 | 2.04 | 33.47 | 9.34 | 20.4 | 2.02 | 9.29 | 257.7 | 30.1 | 68.9 |
| 2437000 | 6.80 | 25.69 | 10.72 | 23.7 | 14.06 | 13.29 | 313.9 | 40.7 | 485.0 |
| 2438000 | 11.57 | 17.91 | 12.11 | 27.1 | 26.11 | 17.29 | 370.2 | 51.4 | 317.1 |
| 2439000 | 2.69 | 10.13 | 13.49 | 30.4 | 10.70 | 21.29 | 426.4 | 62.0 | 149.3 |
| 2440000 | 7.46 | 2.36 | 0.39 | 33.7 | 22.74 | 25.29 | 10.7 | 72.6 | 565.4 |
| 2441000 | 12.23 | 30.57 | 1.77 | 1.4 | 7.34 | 1.62 | 66.9 | 83.2 | 397.5 |
| 2442000 | 3.35 | 22.79 | 3.15 | 4.7 | 19.38 | 5.62 | 123.1 | 93.8 | 229.7 |
| 2443000 | 8.11 | 15.01 | 4.53 | 8.1 | 3.98 | 9.62 | 179.3 | 104.5 | 61.9 |
| 2444000 | 12.88 | 7.23 | 5.91 | 11.4 | 16.02 | 13.62 | 235.6 | 115.1 | 477.9 |
| 2445000 | 4.00 | 35.44 | 7.28 | 14.7 | 0.62 | 17.62 | 291.8 | 125.8 | 310.1 |
| 2446000 | 8.76 | 27.66 | 8.66 | 18.0 | 12.66 | 21.62 | 348.0 | 136.4 | 142.3 |
| 2447000 | 13.53 | 19.88 | 10.04 | 21.3 | 24.70 | 25.62 | 404.2 | 147.0 | 558.3 |
| 2448000 | 4.65 | 12.11 | 11.43 | 24.7 | 9.29 | 1.95 | 460.4 | 157.7 | 390.5 |
| 2449000 | 9.42 | 4.33 | 12.81 | 28.0 | 21.33 | 5.95 | 44.7 | 168.3 | 222.6 |
| 2450000 | 0.54 | 32.54 | 14.19 | 31.3 | 5.94 | 9.95 | 100.9 | 178.9 | 54.8 |

# TABLE II*b*.

Epochs and Arguments for each Thousandth Day, from 2400000 to 2500000.

For Washington Mean Noon.

| Day of Julian Period. | Arg. 63. | 64. | 65. | 66. | 67. | 68. | 69. | 70. | 71. |
|---|---|---|---|---|---|---|---|---|---|
| | d. | d. | d. | d. | d. | d. | d. | d. | d. |
| 2450000 | 0.54 | 32.54 | 14.19 | 31.3 | 5.94 | 9.95 | 100.9 | 178.9 | 54.8 |
| 2451000 | 5.31 | 24.76 | 1.09 | 34.6 | 17.97 | 13.95 | 157.2 | 189.5 | 470.9 |
| 2452000 | 10.07 | 16.98 | 2.47 | 2.3 | 2.57 | 17.95 | 213.4 | 200.1 | 303.0 |
| 2453000 | 1.20 | 9.20 | 3.84 | 5.6 | 14.61 | 21.95 | 269.6 | 210.8 | 135.2 |
| 2454000 | 5.96 | 1.42 | 5.22 | 8.9 | 26.66 | 25.95 | 325.8 | 221.4 | 551.3 |
| 2455000 | 10.73 | 29.64 | 6.60 | 12.3 | 11.25 | 2.28 | 382.0 | 232.1 | 383.4 |
| 2456000 | 1.85 | 21.86 | 7.98 | 15.6 | 23.29 | 6.28 | 438.3 | 242.7 | 215.6 |
| 2457000 | 6.61 | 14.08 | 9.36 | 18.9 | 7.88 | 10.28 | 22.6 | 253.3 | 47.7 |
| 2458000 | 11.38 | 6.30 | 10.73 | 22.2 | 19.92 | 14.28 | 78.8 | 264.0 | 463.8 |
| 2459000 | 2.50 | 34.51 | 12.12 | 25.5 | 4.52 | 18.28 | 135.0 | 274.6 | 296.0 |
| 2460000 | 7.26 | 26.73 | 13.50 | 28.8 | 16.56 | 22.28 | 191.2 | 285.2 | 128.1 |
| 2461000 | 12.03 | 18.96 | 0.40 | 32.1 | 1.16 | 26.28 | 247.4 | 295.8 | 544.2 |
| 2462000 | 3.16 | 11.18 | 1.78 | 35.4 | 13.20 | 2.61 | 303.7 | 306.4 | 376.4 |
| 2463000 | 7.92 | 3.40 | 3.16 | 3.2 | 25.25 | 6.61 | 359.9 | 317.1 | 208.5 |
| 2464000 | 12.69 | 31.61 | 4.54 | 6.5 | 9.84 | 10.61 | 416.1 | 327.7 | 40.7 |
| 2465000 | 3.81 | 23.83 | 5.91 | 9.8 | 21.88 | 14.61 | 0.4 | 8.6 | 456.8 |
| 2466000 | 8.57 | 16.05 | 7.29 | 13.1 | 6.47 | 18.61 | 56.6 | 19.2 | 288.9 |
| 2467000 | 13.34 | 8.27 | 8.67 | 16.4 | 18.51 | 22.61 | 112.8 | 29.8 | 121.1 |
| 2468000 | 4.46 | 0.49 | 10.05 | 19.8 | 3.11 | 26.61 | 169.1 | 40.5 | 537.2 |
| 2469000 | 9.22 | 28.71 | 11.44 | 23.1 | 15.15 | 2.94 | 225.3 | 51.1 | 369.3 |
| 2470000 | 0.35 | 20.93 | 12.82 | 26.4 | 27.20 | 6.94 | 281.5 | 61.7 | 201.5 |
| 2471000 | 5.11 | 13.15 | 14.20 | 29.7 | 11.79 | 10.94 | 337.7 | 72.3 | 33.6 |
| 2472000 | 9.88 | 5.37 | 1.10 | 33.0 | 23.84 | 14.94 | 393.9 | 82.9 | 449.7 |
| 2473000 | 1.01 | 33.58 | 2.47 | 0.8 | 8.43 | 18.94 | 450.1 | 93.6 | 281.9 |
| 2474000 | 5.77 | 25.80 | 3.85 | 4.1 | 20.47 | 22.94 | 34.5 | 104.2 | 114.0 |
| 2475000 | 10.53 | 18.03 | 5.23 | 7.4 | 5.07 | 26.94 | 90.7 | 114.9 | 530.1 |
| 2476000 | 1.66 | 10.25 | 6.61 | 10.7 | 17.11 | 3.26 | 146.9 | 125.5 | 362.3 |
| 2477000 | 6.42 | 2.47 | 7.99 | 14.0 | 1.71 | 7.26 | 203.1 | 136.1 | 194.4 |
| 2478000 | 11.19 | 30.68 | 9.36 | 17.4 | 13.75 | 11.27 | 259.3 | 146.8 | 26.6 |
| 2479000 | 2.31 | 22.90 | 10.74 | 20.7 | 25.80 | 15.27 | 315.6 | 157.4 | 442.7 |
| 2480000 | 7.07 | 15.12 | 12.13 | 24.0 | 10.39 | 19.27 | 371.8 | 168.0 | 274.8 |
| 2481000 | 11.84 | 7.34 | 13.51 | 27.3 | 22.43 | 23.27 | 428.0 | 178.6 | 107.0 |
| 2482000 | 2.96 | 35.55 | 0.41 | 30.6 | 7.02 | 27.27 | 12.3 | 189.2 | 523.1 |
| 2483000 | 7.73 | 27.78 | 1.79 | 34.0 | 19.06 | 3.59 | 68.5 | 199.9 | 355.2 |
| 2484000 | 12.49 | 20.00 | 3.17 | 1.7 | 3.66 | 7.59 | 124.7 | 210.5 | 187.4 |
| 2485000 | 3.62 | 12.22 | 4.54 | 5.0 | 15.70 | 11.61 | 181.0 | 221.1 | 19.5 |
| 2486000 | 8.38 | 4.44 | 5.92 | 8.3 | 0.30 | 15.61 | 237.2 | 231.7 | 435.6 |
| 2487000 | 13.15 | 32.65 | 7.30 | 11.6 | 12.34 | 19.60 | 293.4 | 242.3 | 267.8 |
| 2488000 | 4.27 | 24.87 | 8.68 | 15.0 | 24.39 | 23.59 | 349.6 | 253.0 | 99.9 |
| 2489000 | 9.03 | 17.09 | 10.06 | 18.3 | 8.98 | 27.59 | 405.8 | 263.6 | 516.0 |
| 2490000 | 0.16 | 9.31 | 11.45 | 21.6 | 21.02 | 3.92 | 462.0 | 274.2 | 348.2 |
| 2491000 | 4.92 | 1.54 | 12.83 | 24.9 | 5.61 | 7.92 | 46.4 | 284.8 | 180.3 |
| 2492000 | 9.68 | 29.75 | 14.21 | 28.2 | 17.66 | 11.93 | 102.6 | 295.4 | 12.5 |
| 2493000 | 0.81 | 21.97 | 1.11 | 31.5 | 2.25 | 15.93 | 158.8 | 306.1 | 428.6 |
| 2494000 | 5.58 | 14.19 | 2.49 | 34.8 | 14.29 | 19.93 | 215.0 | 316.7 | 260.7 |
| 2495000 | 10.34 | 6.41 | 3.86 | 2.6 | 26.34 | 23.93 | 271.2 | 327.4 | 92.9 |
| 2496000 | 1.47 | 34.62 | 5.24 | 5.9 | 10.93 | 0.25 | 327.5 | 8.2 | 508.9 |
| 2497000 | 6.23 | 26.85 | 6.62 | 9.2 | 22.97 | 4.25 | 383.7 | 18.8 | 341.1 |
| 2498000 | 11.00 | 19.07 | 8.00 | 12.5 | 7.57 | 8.25 | 439.9 | 29.5 | 173.3 |
| 2499000 | 2.12 | 11.29 | 9.38 | 15.8 | 19.61 | 12.26 | 24.2 | 40.1 | 5.4 |
| 2500000 | 6.88 | 3.51 | 10.76 | 19.1 | 4.21 | 16.26 | 80.4 | 50.7 | 421.5 |

# TABLE II*b*.

Epochs and Arguments for each Thousandth Day, from 2400000 to 2500000.

For Washington Mean Noon.

| Day of Julian Period. | ARG. 72. | 73. | 74. | 75. | 76. | 78. | 79. | 80. | 81. |
|---|---|---|---|---|---|---|---|---|---|
| | d. | d. | d. | d. | d | d. | d. | d. | d. |
| 2400000 | 382.9 | 1322.1 | 2813 | 69562 | 7287 | 71.425 | 419.9 | 192.6 | 65.60 |
| 2401000 | 186.2 | 131.8 | 581 | 70562 | 8287 | 130.418 | 104.8 | 253.4 | 71.96 |
| 2402000 | 388.5 | 1131.8 | 1581 | 71562 | 9287 | 1.209 | 228.1 | 1.2 | 78.32 |
| 2403000 | 191.8 | 2131.8 | 2581 | 72562 | 10287 | 60.202 | 351.3 | 62.1 | 84.69 |
| 2404000 | 394.1 | 941.5 | 348 | 73562 | 11286 | 119.194 | 36.3 | 122.9 | 91.05 |
| 2405000 | 197.4 | 1941.5 | 1348 | 74562 | 12286 | 178.187 | 159.5 | 183.7 | 97.41 |
| 2406000 | 0.8 | 751.2 | 2348 | 75562 | 13286 | 48.978 | 282.8 | 244.5 | 103.78 |
| 2407000 | 203.0 | 1751.2 | 115 | 76562 | 14286 | 107.971 | 406.1 | 305.4 | 110.14 |
| 2408000 | 6.3 | 560.8 | 1115 | 77562 | 15285 | 166.963 | 91.0 | 53.2 | 116.51 |
| 2409000 | 208.6 | 1560.8 | 2115 | 78562 | 16285 | 37.754 | 214.3 | 114.0 | 122.87 |
| 2410000 | 11.9 | 370.5 | 3115 | 79562 | 17285 | 96.747 | 337.6 | 174.8 | 5.03 |
| 2411000 | 214.1 | 1370.5 | 882 | 80562 | 18285 | 155.740 | 22.5 | 235.7 | 11.39 |
| 2412000 | 17.5 | 180.1 | 1882 | 81562 | 19285 | 26.531 | 145.8 | 296.5 | 17.75 |
| 2413000 | 219.7 | 1180.1 | 2882 | 82562 | 20284 | 85.524 | 269.1 | 44.3 | 24.12 |
| 2414000 | 23.1 | 2180.1 | 649 | 83562 | 21284 | 144.516 | 392.3 | 105.1 | 30.49 |
| 2415000 | 225.3 | 989.8 | 1649 | 84562 | 22284 | 15.308 | 77.3 | 166.0 | 36.85 |
| 2416000 | 28.6 | 1989.8 | 2649 | 809 | 23284 | 74.300 | 200.5 | 226.8 | 43.21 |
| 2417000 | 230.9 | 799.4 | 416 | 1809 | 24283 | 133.293 | 323.8 | 287.6 | 49.58 |
| 2418000 | 34.2 | 1799.4 | 1416 | 2809 | 25283 | 4.084 | 8.7 | 35.4 | 55.94 |
| 2419000 | 236.5 | 609.1 | 2416 | 3809 | 26283 | 63.077 | 132.0 | 96.3 | 62.31 |
| 2420000 | 39.8 | 1609.1 | 183 | 4809 | 27283 | 122.069 | 255.3 | 157.1 | 68.67 |
| 2421000 | 242.0 | 418.8 | 1183 | 5809 | 28283 | 181.062 | 378.6 | 217.9 | 75.03 |
| 2422000 | 45.4 | 1418.8 | 2183 | 6809 | 29283 | 51.853 | 63.5 | 278.7 | 81.39 |
| 2423000 | 247.6 | 228.4 | 3183 | 7809 | 30282 | 110.846 | 186.8 | 26.5 | 87.76 |
| 2424000 | 51.0 | 1228.4 | 951 | 8809 | 31282 | 169.839 | 310.0 | 87.4 | 94.12 |
| 2425000 | 253.2 | 38.1 | 1951 | 9809 | 32282 | 40.630 | 433.3 | 148.2 | 100.48 |
| 2426000 | 56.5 | 1038.1 | 2951 | 10809 | 33281 | 99.623 | 118.3 | 209.0 | 106.85 |
| 2427000 | 258.8 | 2038.1 | 718 | 11809 | 34281 | 158.615 | 241.5 | 269.9 | 113.21 |
| 2428000 | 62.1 | 847.7 | 1718 | 12809 | 35280 | 29.407 | 364.8 | 17.7 | 119.58 |
| 2429000 | 264.4 | 1847.7 | 2718 | 13809 | 36280 | 88.399 | 49.7 | 78.5 | 1.74 |
| 2430000 | 67.7 | 657.4 | 485 | 14809 | 37280 | 147.392 | 173.0 | 139.3 | 8.10 |
| 2431000 | 269.9 | 1657.4 | 1485 | 15809 | 38280 | 18.183 | 296.3 | 200.2 | 14.46 |
| 2432000 | 73.3 | 467.1 | 2485 | 16809 | 39279 | 77.176 | 419.6 | 261.0 | 20.82 |
| 2433000 | 275.5 | 1467.1 | 252 | 17809 | 40279 | 136.169 | 104.5 | 8.8 | 27.19 |
| 2434000 | 78.9 | 276.7 | 1252 | 18809 | 41278 | 6.960 | 227.8 | 69.6 | 33.55 |
| 2435000 | 281.1 | 1276.7 | 2252 | 19809 | 42278 | 65.953 | 351.0 | 130.5 | 39.91 |
| 2436000 | 84.4 | 86.4 | 19 | 20809 | 43278 | 124.946 | 36.0 | 191.3 | 46.28 |
| 2437000 | 286.7 | 1086.4 | 1019 | 21809 | 44277 | 183.939 | 159.2 | 252.1 | 52.64 |
| 2438000 | 90.0 | 2086.4 | 2019 | 22809 | 45277 | 54.730 | 282.5 | 312.9 | 59.01 |
| 2439000 | 292.2 | 896.0 | 3019 | 23809 | 46276 | 113.723 | 405.8 | 60.7 | 65.37 |
| 2440000 | 95.6 | 1896.0 | 786 | 24809 | 47276 | 172.716 | 90.7 | 121.6 | 71.73 |
| 2441000 | 297.8 | 705.7 | 1786 | 25809 | 48276 | 43.507 | 214.0 | 182.4 | 78.09 |
| 2442000 | 101.2 | 1705.7 | 2786 | 26809 | 49275 | 102.500 | 337.3 | 243.2 | 84.45 |
| 2443000 | 303.4 | 515.3 | 554 | 27809 | 50275 | 161.493 | 22.2 | 304.1 | 90.82 |
| 2444000 | 106.8 | 1515.3 | 1554 | 28809 | 51274 | 32.284 | 145.5 | 51.9 | 97.18 |
| 2445000 | 309.0 | 325.0 | 2554 | 29809 | 52274 | 91.277 | 268.8 | 112.7 | 103.54 |
| 2446000 | 112.3 | 1325.0 | 321 | 30809 | 53274 | 150.270 | 392.0 | 173.5 | 109.91 |
| 2447000 | 314.6 | 134.7 | 1321 | 31809 | 54273 | 21.061 | 77.0 | 234.4 | 116.27 |
| 2448000 | 117.9 | 1134.7 | 2321 | 32809 | 55273 | 80.054 | 200.2 | 295.2 | 122.64 |
| 2449000 | 320.1 | 2134.6 | 88 | 33809 | 56272 | 139.047 | 323.5 | 43.0 | 4.80 |
| 2450000 | 123.5 | 944.3 | 1088 | 34809 | 57272 | 9.838 | 8.4 | 103.8 | 11.16 |

# TABLE IIb.

Epochs and Arguments for each Thousandth Day, from 2400000 to 2500000.

For Washington Mean Noon.

| Day of Julian Period. | Arg. 72. | 73. | 74. | 75. | 76. | 78. | 79. | 80. | 81. |
|---|---|---|---|---|---|---|---|---|---|
| | d. | d. | d. | d. | d. | d. | d. | d. | d. |
| 2450000 | 123.5 | 944.3 | 1088 | 34809 | 57272 | 9.838 | 8.4 | 103.8 | 11.16 |
| 2451000 | 325.7 | 1944.3 | 2088 | 35809 | 58272 | 68.831 | 131.7 | 164.6 | 17.52 |
| 2452000 | 129.1 | 753.9 | 3088 | 36809 | 59271 | 127.824 | 255.0 | 225.5 | 23.89 |
| 2453000 | 331.3 | 1753.9 | 855 | 37809 | 60271 | 186.817 | 378.3 | 286.3 | 30.25 |
| 2454000 | 134.7 | 563.6 | 1855 | 38809 | 61270 | 57.609 | 63.2 | 34.1 | 36.62 |
| 2455000 | 336.9 | 1563.6 | 2855 | 39809 | 62270 | 116.601 | 186.5 | 94.9 | 42.98 |
| 2456000 | 140.2 | 373.2 | 622 | 40809 | 63270 | 175.594 | 309.8 | 155.8 | 49.34 |
| 2457000 | 342.5 | 1373.2 | 1622 | 41809 | 64269 | 46.386 | 433.0 | 216.6 | 55.71 |
| 2458000 | 145.8 | 182.9 | 2622 | 42809 | 65269 | 105.379 | 118.0 | 277.4 | 62.07 |
| 2459000 | 348.0 | 1182.9 | 389 | 43809 | 66268 | 164.372 | 241.2 | 25.2 | 68.44 |
| 2460000 | 151.4 | 2182.9 | 1389 | 44809 | 67268 | 35.163 | 364.5 | 86.0 | 74.80 |
| 2461000 | 353.6 | 992.5 | 2389 | 45809 | 68268 | 94.156 | 49.4 | 146.9 | 81.16 |
| 2462000 | 157.0 | 1992.5 | 157 | 46809 | 69267 | 153.149 | 172.7 | 207.7 | 87.52 |
| 2463000 | 359.2 | 802.2 | 1157 | 47809 | 70267 | 23.941 | 296.0 | 268.5 | 93.89 |
| 2464000 | 162.5 | 1802.2 | 2157 | 48809 | 71266 | 82.934 | 419.3 | 16.3 | 100.25 |
| 2465000 | 364.8 | 611.8 | 3157 | 49809 | 72266 | 141.927 | 104.2 | 77.2 | 106.61 |
| 2466000 | 168.1 | 1611.8 | 924 | 50809 | 73265 | 12.718 | 227.5 | 138.0 | 112.98 |
| 2467000 | 370.4 | 421.5 | 1924 | 51809 | 74264 | 71.711 | 350.8 | 198.8 | 119.34 |
| 2468000 | 173.7 | 1421.5 | 2924 | 52809 | 75264 | 130.704 | 35.7 | 259.7 | 1.51 |
| 2469000 | 375.9 | 231.1 | 691 | 53809 | 76263 | 1.496 | 159.0 | 7.5 | 7.87 |
| 2470000 | 179.3 | 1231.1 | 1691 | 54809 | 77263 | 60.489 | 282.2 | 68.3 | 14.23 |
| 2471000 | 381.5 | 40.8 | 2691 | 55809 | 78262 | 119.482 | 405.5 | 129.1 | 20.59 |
| 2472000 | 184.9 | 1040.8 | 458 | 56809 | 79262 | 178.475 | 90.4 | 189.9 | 26.95 |
| 2473000 | 387.1 | 2040.8 | 1458 | 57809 | 80261 | 49.267 | 213.7 | 250.8 | 33.32 |
| 2474000 | 190.4 | 850.4 | 2458 | 58809 | 81261 | 108.260 | 337.0 | 311.6 | 39.68 |
| 2475000 | 392.7 | 1850.4 | 225 | 59809 | 82260 | 167.253 | 21.9 | 59.4 | 46.04 |
| 2476000 | 196.0 | 660.1 | 1225 | 60809 | 83259 | 38.044 | 145.2 | 120.2 | 52.41 |
| 2477000 | 398.3 | 1660.1 | 2225 | 61809 | 84259 | 97.037 | 268.5 | 181.1 | 58.77 |
| 2478000 | 201.6 | 469.7 | 3225 | 62809 | 85258 | 156.030 | 391.8 | 241.9 | 65.14 |
| 2479000 | 5.0 | 1469.7 | 992 | 63809 | 86258 | 26.822 | 76.7 | 302.7 | 71.50 |
| 2480000 | 207.2 | 279.4 | 1992 | 64809 | 87257 | 85.815 | 200.0 | 50.5 | 77.86 |
| 2481000 | 10.5 | 1279.4 | 2992 | 65809 | 88256 | 144.808 | 323.2 | 111.3 | 84.22 |
| 2482000 | 212.8 | 89.0 | 759 | 66809 | 89256 | 15.600 | 8.2 | 172.2 | 90.58 |
| 2483000 | 16.1 | 1089.0 | 1759 | 67809 | 90255 | 74.593 | 131.4 | 233.0 | 96.95 |
| 2484000 | 218.3 | 2089.0 | 2759 | 68809 | 91255 | 133.586 | 254.7 | 293.8 | 103.31 |
| 2485000 | 21.7 | 898.6 | 527 | 69809 | 92254 | 4.378 | 378.1 | 41.6 | 109.67 |
| 2486000 | 223.9 | 1898.6 | 1527 | 70809 | 93253 | 63.371 | 62.8 | 102.5 | 116.04 |
| 2487000 | 27.3 | 708.3 | 2527 | 71809 | 94253 | 122.364 | 186.2 | 163.3 | 122.40 |
| 2488000 | 229.5 | 1708.3 | 294 | 72809 | 95252 | 181.357 | 309.5 | 224.1 | 4.57 |
| 2489000 | 32.9 | 517.9 | 1294 | 73809 | 762 | 52.149 | 432.8 | 284.9 | 10.93 |
| 2490000 | 235.1 | 1517.9 | 2294 | 74809 | 1761 | 111.142 | 117.7 | 32.7 | 17.29 |
| 2491000 | 38.4 | 327.6 | 61 | 75809 | 2760 | 170.135 | 241.0 | 93.6 | 23.65 |
| 2492000 | 240.7 | 1327.6 | 1061 | 76809 | 3759 | 40.927 | 364.2 | 154.4 | 30.02 |
| 2493000 | 44.0 | 137.2 | 2061 | 77809 | 4759 | 99.920 | 49.2 | 215.2 | 36.38 |
| 2494000 | 246.2 | 1137.2 | 3061 | 78809 | 5758 | 158.913 | 172.4 | 276.1 | 42.75 |
| 2495000 | 49.6 | 2137.2 | 828 | 79808 | 6758 | 29.705 | 295.7 | 23.9 | 49.11 |
| 2496000 | 251.8 | 946.9 | 1828 | 80808 | 7757 | 88.698 | 419.0 | 84.7 | 55.47 |
| 2497000 | 55.2 | 1946.8 | 2828 | 81808 | 8756 | 147.691 | 103.9 | 145.5 | 61.84 |
| 2498000 | 257.4 | 756.5 | 595 | 82808 | 9756 | 18.483 | 227.2 | 206.4 | 68.20 |
| 2499000 | 60.7 | 1756.5 | 1595 | 83808 | 10755 | 77.476 | 350.5 | 267.2 | 74.57 |
| 2500000 | 263.0 | 566.1 | 2595 | 55 | 11754 | 136.470 | 35.4 | 15.0 | 80.93 |

# TABLE IIb.

Epochs and Arguments for each Thousandth Day, from 2400000 to 2500000.

For Washington Mean Noon.

| Day of Julian Period. | Arg. 82. | 83. | 84. | 85. | 86. | 87. | 88. | 89. | 90. |
|---|---|---|---|---|---|---|---|---|---|
| | d. | d. | d. | d. | d. | d. | d. | d. | d. |
| 2400000 | 11.655 | 5.56 | 5.63 | 3.09 | 6.02 | 4.84 | 7.28 | 8.47 | 0.0 |
| 2401000 | 0.801 | 25.27 | 10.17 | 15.27 | 10.67 | 10.27 | 9.96 | 4.23 | 31.6 |
| 2402000 | 4.812 | 5.77 | 14.72 | 3.94 | 15.31 | 1.48 | 12.64 | 0.00 | 30.9 |
| 2403000 | 8.823 | 25.48 | 0.12 | 16.13 | 19.95 | 6.91 | 0.66 | 15.08 | 30.2 |
| 2404000 | 12.834 | 5.98 | 4.66 | 4.80 | 24.59 | 12.33 | 3.34 | 10.85 | 29.5 |
| 2405000 | 1.980 | 25.69 | 9.20 | 16.99 | 29.24 | 3.55 | 6.03 | 6.62 | 28.8 |
| 2406000 | 5.991 | 6.18 | 13.74 | 5.65 | 33.88 | 8.98 | 8.71 | 2.39 | 28.1 |
| 2407000 | 10.003 | 25.89 | 18.29 | 17.84 | 0.24 | 0.20 | 11.39 | 17.47 | 27.4 |
| 2408000 | 14.014 | 6.39 | 3.69 | 6.51 | 4.89 | 5.62 | 14.07 | 13.23 | 26.7 |
| 2409000 | 3.160 | 26.10 | 8.23 | 18.70 | 9.53 | 11.05 | 2.09 | 9.00 | 26.0 |
| 2410000 | 7.171 | 6.60 | 12.77 | 7.37 | 14.17 | 2.26 | 4.77 | 4.77 | 25.3 |
| 2411000 | 11.182 | 26.30 | 17.31 | 19.55 | 18.81 | 7.69 | 7.46 | 0.54 | 24.6 |
| 2412000 | 0.328 | 6.80 | 2.71 | 8.22 | 23.46 | 13.11 | 10.14 | 15.62 | 23.9 |
| 2413000 | 4.339 | 26.51 | 7.26 | 20.41 | 28.10 | 4.33 | 12.82 | 11.39 | 23.2 |
| 2414000 | 8.351 | 7.01 | 11.80 | 9.08 | 32.74 | 9.76 | 0.84 | 7.16 | 22.5 |
| 2415000 | 12.362 | 26.72 | 16.34 | 21.27 | 37.39 | 0.98 | 3.52 | 2.92 | 21.8 |
| 2416000 | 1.508 | 7.22 | 1.74 | 9.93 | 3.75 | 6.40 | 6.21 | 18.01 | 21.0 |
| 2417000 | 5.519 | 26.93 | 6.28 | 22.12 | 8.39 | 11.83 | 8.89 | 13.77 | 20.3 |
| 2418000 | 9.530 | 7.42 | 10.83 | 10.79 | 13.03 | 3.04 | 11.57 | 9.54 | 19.6 |
| 2419000 | 13.542 | 27.13 | 15.37 | 22.98 | 17.68 | 8.47 | 14.25 | 5.31 | 18.9 |
| 2420000 | 2.687 | 7.63 | 0.77 | 11.65 | 22.32 | 13.90 | 2.27 | 1.08 | 18.2 |
| 2421000 | 6.698 | 27.34 | 5.31 | 0.32 | 26.96 | 5.12 | 4.95 | 16.16 | 17.5 |
| 2422000 | 10.710 | 7.84 | 9.86 | 12.50 | 31.61 | 10.54 | 7.64 | 11.93 | 16.8 |
| 2423000 | 14.721 | 27.54 | 14.40 | 1.17 | 36.25 | 1.76 | 10.32 | 7.69 | 16.1 |
| 2424000 | 3.867 | 8.04 | 18.94 | 13.36 | 2.61 | 7.18 | 13.00 | 3.46 | 15.4 |
| 2425000 | 7.878 | 27.75 | 4.34 | 2.03 | 7.25 | 12.61 | 1.02 | 18.54 | 14.7 |
| 2426000 | 11.889 | 8.25 | 8.88 | 14.22 | 11.90 | 3.83 | 3.70 | 14.31 | 14.0 |
| 2427000 | 1.035 | 27.96 | 13.43 | 2.88 | 16.54 | 9.25 | 6.39 | 10.08 | 13.3 |
| 2428000 | 5.046 | 8.46 | 17.97 | 15.07 | 21.18 | 0.47 | 9.07 | 5.85 | 12.6 |
| 2429000 | 9.058 | 28.17 | 3.37 | 3.74 | 25.83 | 5.90 | 11.75 | 1.62 | 11.9 |
| 2430000 | 13.069 | 8.66 | 7.91 | 15.93 | 30.47 | 11.32 | 14.43 | 16.70 | 11.2 |
| 2431000 | 2.215 | 28.37 | 12.45 | 4.60 | 35.11 | 2.54 | 2.45 | 12.46 | 10.5 |
| 2432000 | 6.226 | 8.87 | 17.00 | 16.78 | 1.47 | 7.96 | 5.13 | 8.23 | 9.8 |
| 2433000 | 10.237 | 28.58 | 2.40 | 5.45 | 6.12 | 13.39 | 7.82 | 4.00 | 9.1 |
| 2434000 | 14.248 | 9.08 | 6.94 | 17.64 | 10.76 | 4.61 | 10.50 | 19.08 | 8.4 |
| 2435000 | 3.394 | 28.79 | 11.48 | 6.31 | 15.40 | 10.03 | 13.18 | 14.85 | 7.7 |
| 2436000 | 7.405 | 9.28 | 16.02 | 18.50 | 20.05 | 1.25 | 1.20 | 10.62 | 7.0 |
| 2437000 | 11.417 | 28.99 | 1.42 | 7.16 | 24.69 | 6.68 | 3.88 | 6.38 | 6.3 |
| 2438000 | 0.562 | 9.49 | 5.97 | 19.35 | 29.33 | 12.10 | 6.56 | 2.15 | 5.6 |
| 2439000 | 4.574 | 29.20 | 10.51 | 8.02 | 33.97 | 3.32 | 9.25 | 17.23 | 4.9 |
| 2440000 | 8.585 | 9.70 | 15.05 | 20.21 | 0.33 | 8.74 | 11.93 | 13.00 | 4.2 |
| 2441000 | 12.596 | 29.40 | 0.45 | 8.88 | 4.98 | 14.17 | 14.62 | 8.77 | 3.5 |
| 2442000 | 1.742 | 9.90 | 4.99 | 21.07 | 9.62 | 5.39 | 2.63 | 4.54 | 2.8 |
| 2443000 | 5.753 | 29.61 | 9.54 | 9.73 | 14.26 | 10.82 | 5.32 | 0.31 | 2.1 |
| 2444000 | 9.765 | 10.11 | 14.08 | 21.92 | 18.91 | 2.03 | 8.00 | 15.39 | 1.4 |
| 2445000 | 13.776 | 29.82 | 18.62 | 10.59 | 23.55 | 7.46 | 10.68 | 11.15 | 0.7 |
| 2446000 | 2.922 | 10.32 | 4.02 | 22.78 | 28.19 | 12.88 | 13.36 | 6.92 | 32.2 |
| 2447000 | 6.933 | 30.03 | 8.56 | 11.45 | 32.84 | 4.10 | 1.38 | 2.69 | 31.5 |
| 2448000 | 10.944 | 10.52 | 13.11 | 0.11 | 37.48 | 9.52 | 4.06 | 17.77 | 30.8 |
| 2449000 | 0.090 | 30.23 | 17.65 | 12.30 | 3.84 | 0.74 | 6.75 | 13.54 | 30.1 |
| 2450000 | 4.101 | 10.73 | 3.05 | 0.97 | 8.48 | 6.17 | 9.43 | 9.31 | 29.4 |

# TABLE IIb.

Epochs and Arguments for each Thousandth Day, from 2400000 to 2500000.

For Washington Mean Noon.

| Day of Julian Period. | Arg. 82. | 83. | 84. | 85. | 86. | 87. | 88. | 89. | 90. |
|---|---|---|---|---|---|---|---|---|---|
| | d. | d. | d. | d. | d. | d. | d. | d. | d. |
| 2450000 | 4.101 | 10.73 | 3.05 | 0.97 | 8.48 | 6.17 | 9.43 | 9.31 | 29.4 |
| 2451000 | 8.113 | 30.44 | 7.59 | 13.16 | 13.13 | 11.59 | 12.11 | 5.08 | 28.7 |
| 2452000 | 12.124 | 10.94 | 12.14 | 1.83 | 17.77 | 2.81 | 0.13 | 0.84 | 28.0 |
| 2453000 | 1.269 | 30.64 | 16.68 | 14.01 | 22.41 | 8.24 | 2.81 | 15.92 | 27.3 |
| 2454000 | 5.281 | 11.14 | 2.08 | 2.68 | 27.05 | 13.66 | 5.50 | 11.69 | 26.6 |
| 2455000 | 9.293 | 30.85 | 6.62 | 14.87 | 31.70 | 4.88 | 8.18 | 7.46 | 25.9 |
| 2456000 | 13.304 | 11.35 | 11.16 | 3.54 | 36.34 | 10.30 | 10.86 | 3.23 | 25.2 |
| 2457000 | 2.450 | 31.06 | 15.71 | 15.72 | 2.70 | 1.52 | 13.54 | 18.31 | 24.5 |
| 2458000 | 6.461 | 11.56 | 1.11 | 4.39 | 7.34 | 6.95 | 1.56 | 14.08 | 23.8 |
| 2459000 | 10.472 | 31.27 | 5.65 | 16.58 | 11.99 | 12.37 | 4.24 | 9.85 | 23.1 |
| 2460000 | 14.483 | 11.76 | 10.19 | 5.25 | 16.63 | 3.59 | 6.93 | 5.61 | 22.4 |
| 2461000 | 3.629 | 31.47 | 14.73 | 17.44 | 21.27 | 9.01 | 9.61 | 1.38 | 21.7 |
| 2462000 | 7.641 | 11.97 | 0.13 | 6.11 | 25.92 | 0.23 | 12.29 | 16.46 | 21.0 |
| 2463000 | 11.652 | 31.68 | 4.68 | 18.30 | 30.56 | 5.66 | 0.31 | 12.23 | 20.3 |
| 2464000 | 0.798 | 12.18 | 9.22 | 6.96 | 35.20 | 11.08 | 2.99 | 8.00 | 19.6 |
| 2465000 | 4.809 | 31.89 | 13.76 | 19.15 | 1.56 | 2.30 | 5.68 | 3.77 | 18.9 |
| 2466000 | 8.820 | 12.38 | 18.30 | 7.82 | 6.21 | 7.73 | 8.36 | 18.85 | 18.1 |
| 2467000 | 12.832 | 32.09 | 3.70 | 20.01 | 10.85 | 13.15 | 11.04 | 14.62 | 17.4 |
| 2468000 | 1.977 | 12.59 | 8.25 | 8.68 | 15.49 | 4.37 | 13.73 | 10.38 | 16.7 |
| 2469000 | 5.989 | 32.30 | 12.79 | 20.86 | 20.13 | 9.80 | 1.74 | 6.15 | 16.0 |
| 2470000 | 10.000 | 12.80 | 17.33 | 9.53 | 24.78 | 1.01 | 4.42 | 1.92 | 15.3 |
| 2471000 | 14.011 | 32.50 | 2.73 | 21.72 | 29.42 | 6.44 | 7.11 | 17.00 | 14.6 |
| 2472000 | 3.157 | 13.00 | 7.27 | 10.39 | 34.06 | 11.86 | 9.79 | 12.77 | 13.9 |
| 2473000 | 7.169 | 32.71 | 11.82 | 22.58 | 0.42 | 3.08 | 12.47 | 8.54 | 13.2 |
| 2474000 | 11.180 | 13.21 | 16.36 | 11.24 | 5.07 | 8.51 | 0.49 | 4.31 | 12.5 |
| 2475000 | 0.326 | 32.92 | 1.76 | 23.43 | 9.71 | 13.93 | 3.17 | 0.07 | 11.8 |
| 2476000 | 4.337 | 13.42 | 6.30 | 12.10 | 14.35 | 5.15 | 5.86 | 15.15 | 11.1 |
| 2477000 | 8.348 | 33.13 | 10.84 | 0.77 | 19.00 | 10.58 | 8.54 | 10.92 | 10.4 |
| 2478000 | 12.360 | 13.62 | 15.39 | 12.96 | 23.64 | 1.80 | 11.22 | 6.69 | 9.7 |
| 2479000 | 1.506 | 33.33 | 0.79 | 1.62 | 28.28 | 7.22 | 13.91 | 2.46 | 9.0 |
| 2480000 | 5.517 | 13.83 | 5.33 | 13.81 | 32.93 | 12.65 | 1.92 | 17.54 | 8.3 |
| 2481000 | 9.528 | 33.54 | 9.87 | 2.48 | 37.57 | 3.86 | 4.60 | 13.31 | 7.6 |
| 2482000 | 13.540 | 14.04 | 14.42 | 14.67 | 3.93 | 9.29 | 7.29 | 9.08 | 6.9 |
| 2483000 | 2.685 | 33.75 | 18.96 | 3.34 | 8.57 | 14.71 | 9.97 | 4.84 | 6.2 |
| 2484000 | 6.697 | 14.24 | 4.36 | 15.53 | 13.21 | 5.93 | 12.65 | 0.61 | 5.5 |
| 2485000 | 10.708 | 33.95 | 8.90 | 4.19 | 17.86 | 11.36 | 0.67 | 15.69 | 4.8 |
| 2486000 | 14.719 | 14.45 | 13.44 | 16.38 | 22.50 | 2.58 | 3.35 | 11.46 | 4.0 |
| 2487000 | 3.865 | 34.16 | 17.99 | 5.05 | 27.14 | 8.00 | 6.04 | 7.23 | 3.3 |
| 2488000 | 7.877 | 14.66 | 3.39 | 17.24 | 31.79 | 13.43 | 8.72 | 3.00 | 2.6 |
| 2489000 | 11.888 | 34.37 | 7.93 | 5.91 | 36.43 | 4.65 | 11.40 | 18.08 | 1.9 |
| 2490000 | 1.034 | 14.86 | 12.47 | 18.09 | 2.79 | 10.07 | 14.09 | 13.85 | 1.2 |
| 2491000 | 5.045 | 34.57 | 17.01 | 6.76 | 7.43 | 1.29 | 2.10 | 9.61 | 0.5 |
| 2492000 | 9.056 | 15.07 | 2.41 | 18.95 | 12.08 | 6.71 | 4.79 | 5.38 | 32.1 |
| 2493000 | 13.068 | 34.78 | 6.96 | 7.62 | 16.72 | 12.14 | 7.47 | 1.15 | 31.4 |
| 2494000 | 2.214 | 15.28 | 11.50 | 19.81 | 21.36 | 3.36 | 10.15 | 16.23 | 30.7 |
| 2495000 | 6.225 | 34.99 | 16.04 | 8.47 | 26.00 | 8.78 | 12.83 | 12.00 | 30.0 |
| 2496000 | 10.236 | 15.48 | 1.44 | 20.66 | 30.65 | 0.00 | 0.85 | 7.77 | 29.3 |
| 2497000 | 14.247 | 35.19 | 5.98 | 9.33 | 35.29 | 5.43 | 3.53 | 3.53 | 28.6 |
| 2498000 | 3.393 | 15.69 | 10.53 | 21.52 | 1.65 | 10.85 | 6.22 | 18.62 | 27.9 |
| 2499000 | 7.405 | 35.40 | 15.07 | 10.19 | 6.29 | 2.07 | 8.90 | 14.38 | 27.2 |
| 2500000 | 11.416 | 15.90 | 0.47 | 22.37 | 10.94 | 7.49 | 11.58 | 10.15 | 26.5 |

# TABLE IIIa.

Change of Mean Longitude, and Longitude of the Node for any Interval of Time less than 1000 Days.

| Days. | u′ | | $\frac{1}{100}$ u′ | | $\frac{1}{10000}$ u′ | (y-u′) | | $\frac{1}{100}$ (y-u′) |
|---|---|---|---|---|---|---|---|---|
| | ° | ″ | ° | ″ | ″ | ° | ″ | ″ |
| 0 | 0 | 0.00 | 0 | 0.00 | 0.00 | 0 | 0.0 | 0.0 |
| 10 | 131 | 2750.28 | 1 | 1143.50 | 47.44 | 0 | 1906.3 | 19.1 |
| 20 | 263 | 1900.56 | 2 | 2287.01 | 94.87 | 1 | 212.7 | 38.1 |
| 30 | 35 | 1050.84 | 3 | 3430.51 | 142.31 | 1 | 2119.0 | 57.2 |
| 40 | 167 | 201.12 | 5 | 974.01 | 189.74 | 2 | 425.3 | 76.3 |
| 50 | 298 | 2951.40 | 6 | 2117.51 | 237.18 | 2 | 2331.7 | 95.3 |
| 60 | 70 | 2101.69 | 7 | 3261.02 | 284.61 | 3 | 638.0 | 114.4 |
| 70 | 202 | 1251.97 | 9 | 804.52 | 332.05 | 3 | 2544.3 | 133.4 |
| 80 | 334 | 402.25 | 10 | 1948.02 | 379.48 | 4 | 850.7 | 152.5 |
| 90 | 105 | 3152.53 | 11 | 3091.53 | 426.92 | 4 | 2757.0 | 171.6 |
| 100 | 237 | 2302.81 | 13 | 635.03 | 474.35 | 5 | 1063.4 | 190.6 |
| 110 | 9 | 1453.09 | 14 | 1778.53 | 521.79 | 5 | 2969.7 | 209.7 |
| 120 | 141 | 603.37 | 15 | 2922.03 | 569.22 | 6 | 1276.1 | 228.8 |
| 130 | 272 | 3353.65 | 17 | 465.54 | 616.66 | 6 | 3182.4 | 247.8 |
| 140 | 44 | 2503.93 | 18 | 1609.04 | 664.09 | 7 | 1488.7 | 266.9 |
| 150 | 176 | 1654.21 | 19 | 2752.54 | 711.53 | 7 | 3395.1 | 286.0 |
| 160 | 308 | 804.50 | 21 | 296.04 | 758.96 | 8 | 1701.4 | 305.0 |
| 170 | 79 | 3554.78 | 22 | 1439.55 | 806.40 | 9 | 7.7 | 324.1 |
| 180 | 211 | 2705.06 | 23 | 2583.05 | 853.83 | 9 | 1914.1 | 343.1 |
| 190 | 343 | 1855.34 | 25 | 126.55 | 901.27 | 10 | 220.4 | 362.2 |
| 200 | 115 | 1005.62 | 26 | 1270.06 | 948.70 | 10 | 2126.7 | 381.3 |
| 210 | 247 | 155.90 | 27 | 2413.56 | 996.14 | 11 | 433.1 | 400.3 |
| 220 | 18 | 2906.18 | 28 | 3557.06 | 1043.57 | 11 | 2339.4 | 419.4 |
| 230 | 150 | 2056.46 | 30 | 1100.56 | 1091.01 | 12 | 645.7 | 438.5 |
| 240 | 282 | 1206.74 | 31 | 2244.07 | 1138.44 | 12 | 2552.1 | 457.5 |
| 250 | 54 | 357.02 | 32 | 3387.57 | 1185.88 | 13 | 858.4 | 476.6 |
| 260 | 185 | 3107.30 | 34 | 931.07 | 1233.31 | 13 | 2764.7 | 495.6 |
| 270 | 317 | 2257.59 | 35 | 2074.58 | 1280.75 | 14 | 1071.1 | 514.7 |
| 280 | 89 | 1407.87 | 36 | 3218.08 | 1328.18 | 14 | 2977.4 | 533.8 |
| 290 | 221 | 558.15 | 38 | 761.58 | 1375.62 | 15 | 1283.7 | 552.8 |
| 300 | 352 | 3308.43 | 39 | 1905.08 | 1423.05 | 15 | 3190.1 | 571.9 |
| 310 | 124 | 2458.71 | 40 | 3048.59 | 1470.49 | 16 | 1496.4 | 591.0 |
| 320 | 256 | 1608.99 | 42 | 592.09 | 1517.92 | 16 | 3402.7 | 610.0 |
| 330 | 28 | 759.27 | 43 | 1735.59 | 1565.36 | 17 | 1709.1 | 629.1 |
| 340 | 159 | 3509.55 | 44 | 2879.10 | 1612.79 | 18 | 15.4 | 648.2 |
| 350 | 291 | 2659.83 | 46 | 422.60 | 1660.23 | 18 | 1921.7 | 667.2 |
| 360 | 63 | 1810.11 | 47 | 1566.10 | 1707.66 | 19 | 228.1 | 686.3 |
| 370 | 195 | 960.39 | 48 | 2709.60 | 1755.10 | 19 | 2134.5 | 705.3 |
| 380 | 327 | 110.67 | 50 | 253.11 | 1802.53 | 20 | 440.7 | 724.4 |
| 390 | 98 | 2860.95 | 51 | 1396.61 | 1849.97 | 20 | 2347.1 | 743.5 |
| 400 | 230 | 2011.24 | 52 | 2540.11 | 1897.40 | 21 | 653.5 | 762.5 |
| 410 | 2 | 1161.52 | 54 | 83.62 | 1944.84 | 21 | 2559.7 | 781.6 |
| 420 | 134 | 311.80 | 55 | 1227.12 | 1992.27 | 22 | 866.1 | 800.7 |
| 430 | 265 | 3062.08 | 56 | 2370.62 | 2039.71 | 22 | 2772.5 | 819.7 |
| 440 | 37 | 2212.36 | 57 | 3514.12 | 2087.14 | 23 | 1078.7 | 838.8 |
| 450 | 169 | 1362.64 | 59 | 1057.63 | 2134.58 | 23 | 2985.1 | 857.9 |
| 460 | 301 | 512.92 | 60 | 2201.13 | 2182.01 | 24 | 1291.5 | 876.9 |
| 470 | 72 | 3263.20 | 61 | 3344.63 | 2229.45 | 24 | 3197.7 | 896.0 |
| 480 | 204 | 2413.48 | 63 | 888.13 | 2276.88 | 25 | 1504.1 | 915.0 |
| 490 | 336 | 1563.76 | 64 | 2031.64 | 2324.32 | 25 | 3410.5 | 934.1 |
| 500 | 108 | 714.04 | 65 | 3175.14 | 2371.75 | 26 | 1716.8 | 953.2 |

# TABLE IIIa.

Change of Mean Longitude, and Longitude of the Node for any Interval of Time less than 1000

| Days. | u′ | $\frac{1}{100}$ u′ | $\frac{1}{10000}$ u′ | (y-u′) | $\frac{1}{100}$ (y-u′) |
|---|---|---|---|---|---|
| 500 | 108° 714.04″ | 65° 3175.14″ | 2371.75″ | 26° 1716.8″ | 953.2″ |
| 510 | 239 3464.33 | 67 718.64 | 2419.19 | 27 23.2 | 972.2 |
| 520 | 11 2614.61 | 68 1862.15 | 2466.62 | 27 1929.5 | 991.3 |
| 530 | 143 1764.89 | 69 3005.65 | 2514.06 | 28 235.8 | 1010.4 |
| 540 | 275 915.17 | 71 549.15 | 2561.49 | 28 2142.2 | 1029.4 |
| 550 | 47 65.45 | 72 1692.65 | 2608.93 | 29 448.6 | 1048.5 |
| 560 | 178 2815.73 | 73 2836.16 | 2656.36 | 29 2354.9 | 1067.5 |
| 570 | 310 1966.01 | 75 379.66 | 2703.80 | 30 661.2 | 1086.6 |
| 580 | 82 1116.29 | 76 1523.16 | 2751.23 | 30 2567.6 | 1105.7 |
| 590 | 214 266.57 | 77 2666.67 | 2798.67 | 31 873.9 | 1124.7 |
| 600 | 345 3016.85 | 79 210.17 | 2846.10 | 31 2780.2 | 1143.8 |
| 610 | 117 2167.13 | 80 1353.67 | 2893.54 | 32 1086.6 | 1162.9 |
| 620 | 249 1317.42 | 81 2497.17 | 2940.97 | 32 2993.0 | 1181.9 |
| 630 | 21 467.70 | 83 40.68 | 2988.41 | 33 1299.3 | 1201.0 |
| 640 | 152 3217.98 | 84 1184.18 | 3035.84 | 33 3205.6 | 1220.1 |
| 650 | 284 2368.26 | 85 2327.68 | 3083.28 | 34 1512.0 | 1239.1 |
| 660 | 56 1518.54 | 86 3471.19 | 3130.71 | 34 3418.3 | 1258.2 |
| 670 | 188 668.82 | 88 1014.69 | 3178.15 | 35 1724.6 | 1277.3 |
| 680 | 319 3419.10 | 89 2158.19 | 3225.58 | 36 31.0 | 1296.3 |
| 690 | 91 2569.38 | 90 3301.69 | 3273.02 | 36 1937.3 | 1315.4 |
| 700 | 223 1719.66 | 92 845.20 | 3320.45 | 37 243.6 | 1334.4 |
| 710 | 355 869.94 | 93 1988.70 | 3367.89 | 37 2150.0 | 1353.5 |
| 720 | 127 20.22 | 94 3132.20 | 3415.32 | 38 456.3 | 1372.6 |
| 730 | 258 2770.51 | 96 675.71 | 3462.76 | 38 2362.7 | 1391.6 |
| 740 | 30 1920.79 | 97 1819.21 | 3510.19 | 39 669.0 | 1410.7 |
| 750 | 162 1071.07 | 98 2962.71 | 3557.63 | 39 2575.3 | 1429.8 |
| 760 | 294 221.35 | 100 506.21 | 3605.06 | 40 881.7 | 1448.8 |
| 770 | 65 2971.63 | 101 1649.72 | 3652.50 | 40 2788.0 | 1467.9 |
| 780 | 197 2121.91 | 102 2793.22 | 3699.93 | 41 1094.3 | 1486.9 |
| 790 | 329 1272.19 | 104 336.72 | 3747.37 | 41 3000.6 | 1506.0 |
| 800 | 101 422.47 | 105 1480.22 | 3794.80 | 42 1306.9 | 1525.1 |
| 810 | 232 3172.75 | 106 2623.73 | 3842.24 | 42 3213.2 | 1544.1 |
| 820 | 4 2323.03 | 108 167.23 | 3889.67 | 43 1519.6 | 1563.2 |
| 830 | 136 1473.31 | 109 1310.73 | 3937.11 | 43 3425.9 | 1582.3 |
| 840 | 268 623.59 | 110 2454.24 | 3984.54 | 44 1732.2 | 1601.3 |
| 850 | 39 3373.88 | 111 3597.74 | 4031.98 | 45 38.6 | 1620.4 |
| 860 | 171 2524.16 | 113 1141.24 | 4079.41 | 45 1944.9 | 1639.4 |
| 870 | 303 1674.44 | 114 2284.74 | 4126.85 | 46 251.3 | 1658.5 |
| 880 | 75 824.72 | 115 3428.25 | 4174.28 | 46 2157.6 | 1677.6 |
| 890 | 206 3575.00 | 117 971.75 | 4221.72 | 47 463.9 | 1696.6 |
| 900 | 338 2725.28 | 118 2115.25 | 4269.15 | 47 2370.3 | 1715.7 |
| 910 | 110 1875.56 | 119 3258.76 | 4316.59 | 48 676.6 | 1734.8 |
| 920 | 242 1025.84 | 121 802.26 | 4364.02 | 48 2582.9 | 1753.8 |
| 930 | 14 176.12 | 122 1945.76 | 4411.46 | 49 889.3 | 1772.9 |
| 940 | 145 2926.40 | 123 3089.26 | 4458.89 | 49 2795.7 | 1792.0 |
| 950 | 277 2076.68 | 125 632.77 | 4506.33 | 50 1102.0 | 1811.0 |
| 960 | 49 1226.97 | 126 1776.27 | 4553.76 | 50 3008.3 | 1830.1 |
| 970 | 181 377.25 | 127 2919.77 | 4601.20 | 51 1314.7 | 1849.1 |
| 980 | 312 3127.53 | 129 463.28 | 4648.63 | 51 3221.0 | 1868.2 |
| 990 | 84 2277.81 | 130 1606.78 | 4696.07 | 52 1527.3 | 1887.3 |
| 1000 | 216 1428.09 | 131 2750.28 | 4743.50 | 52 3433.7 | 1906.3 |

# TABLE III*b*.

Multiples of Periods of the Arguments.

| No. of Periods. | Arg. 1. | 2. | 3. | 4. | 5. | 6. |
|---|---|---|---|---|---|---|
| 1 | 27.554552446 | 31.81193574 | 29.53058800 | 365.259687 | 411.785170 | 34.846892 |
| 2 | 55.109104892 | 63.62387147 | 59.06117599 | 730.519373 | 823.570341 | 69.693784 |
| 3 | 82.663657338 | 95.43580721 | 88.59176399 | 1095.779060 | 1235.355511 | 104.540676 |
| 4 | 110.218209784 | 127.24774294 | 118.12235199 | 1461.038747 | 1647.140681 | 139.387568 |
| 5 | 137.772762230 | 159.05967868 | 147.65293999 | 1826.298433 | 2058.925852 | 174.234460 |
| 6 | 165.327314676 | 190.87161442 | 177.18352798 | 2191.558120 | 2470.711022 | 209.081352 |
| 7 | 192.881867122 | 222.68355015 | 206.71411598 | 2556.817807 | 2882.496192 | 243.928244 |
| 8 | 220.436419568 | 254.49548589 | 236.24470398 | 2922.077493 | 3294.281362 | 278.775136 |
| 9 | 247.990972014 | 286.30742162 | 265.77529197 | 3287.337180 | 3706.066533 | 313.622028 |
| 10 | 275.545524460 | 318.11935736 | 295.30587997 | 3652.596867 | 4117.851703 | 348.468920 |

| No. of Periods. | Arg. 7. | 8. | 9. | 10. | 11. | 12. | 13. |
|---|---|---|---|---|---|---|---|
| 1 | 9.613718 | 15.387312 | 29.802826 | 25.621696 | 26.878290 | 346.620112 | 10.084597 |
| 2 | 19.227436 | 30.774624 | 59.605651 | 51.243393 | 53.756580 | 693.240224 | 20.169194 |
| 3 | 28.841154 | 46.161937 | 89.408477 | 76.865089 | 80.634870 | 1039.860336 | 30.253791 |
| 4 | 38.454872 | 61.549249 | 119.211302 | 102.486786 | 107.513160 | 1386.480448 | 40.338387 |
| 5 | 48.068590 | 76.936561 | 149.014128 | 128.108482 | 134.391450 | 1733.100559 | 50.422984 |
| 6 | 57.682308 | 92.323873 | 178.816953 | 153.730179 | 161.269740 | 2079.720671 | 60.507581 |
| 7 | 67.296026 | 107.711186 | 208.619779 | 179.351875 | 188.148029 | 2426.340783 | 70.592178 |
| 8 | 76.909744 | 123.098498 | 238.422604 | 204.973572 | 215.026319 | 2772.960895 | 80.676775 |
| 9 | 86.523462 | 138.485810 | 268.225430 | 230.595268 | 241.904609 | 3119.581007 | 90.761372 |
| 10 | 96.137180 | 153.873122 | 298.028255 | 256.216964 | 268.782899 | 3466.201119 | 100.845968 |

| No. of Periods. | Arg. 14. | 15. | 16. | 17. | 18. | 19. | 20. |
|---|---|---|---|---|---|---|---|
| 1 | 29.26328 | 14.19161 | 14.25418 | 27.32168 | 9.87359 | 24.30220 | 14.31731 |
| 2 | 58.52656 | 28.38322 | 28.50837 | 54.64336 | 19.74719 | 48.60439 | 28.63463 |
| 3 | 87.78984 | 42.57483 | 42.76255 | 81.96504 | 29.62078 | 72.90659 | 42.95194 |
| 4 | 117.05312 | 56.76644 | 57.01674 | 109.28672 | 39.49437 | 97.20878 | 57.26925 |
| 5 | 146.31640 | 70.95805 | 71.27092 | 136.60840 | 49.36797 | 121.51098 | 71.58656 |
| 6 | 175.57967 | 85.14967 | 85.52511 | 163.93008 | 59.24156 | 145.81317 | 85.90388 |
| 7 | 204.84295 | 99.34128 | 99.77929 | 191.25176 | 69.11515 | 170.11537 | 100.22119 |
| 8 | 234.10623 | 113.53289 | 114.03348 | 218.57344 | 78.98875 | 194.41757 | 114.53850 |
| 9 | 263.36951 | 127.72450 | 128.28766 | 245.89511 | 88.86234 | 218.71976 | 128.85581 |
| 10 | 292.63279 | 141.91611 | 142.54185 | 273.21679 | 98.73593 | 243.02196 | 143.17313 |

| No. of Periods. | Arg. 21. | 22. | 23. | 24. | 25. | 26. | 27. |
|---|---|---|---|---|---|---|---|
| 1 | 131.6711 | 32.12809 | 23.77463 | 13.27650 | 9.36717 | 5.82261 | 25.8264 |
| 2 | 263.3422 | 64.25617 | 47.54925 | 26.55300 | 18.73434 | 11.64521 | 51.6528 |
| 3 | 395.0134 | 96.38426 | 71.32388 | 39.82949 | 28.10152 | 17.46782 | 77.4791 |
| 4 | 526.6845 | 128.51234 | 95.09851 | 53.10599 | 37.46869 | 23.29042 | 103.3055 |
| 5 | 658.3556 | 160.64043 | 118.87313 | 66.38249 | 46.83586 | 29.11303 | 129.1319 |
| 6 | 790.0267 | 192.76852 | 142.64776 | 79.65899 | 56.20303 | 34.93563 | 154.9583 |
| 7 | 921.6979 | 224.89660 | 166.42238 | 92.93549 | 65.57020 | 40.75824 | 180.7847 |
| 8 | 1053.3690 | 257.02469 | 190.19701 | 106.21199 | 74.93738 | 46.58084 | 206.6111 |
| 9 | 1185.0401 | 289.15277 | 213.97164 | 119.48848 | 84.30455 | 52.40345 | 232.4374 |
| 10 | 1316.7112 | 321.28086 | 237.74626 | 132.76498 | 93.67172 | 58.22606 | 258.2638 |

# TABLE IIIb.

Multiples of Periods of the Arguments.

| No. of Periods. | Arg. 28. | 29. | 30. | 31. | 32. | 33. | 34. |
|---|---|---|---|---|---|---|---|
| 1 | 38.52201 | 32.76364 | 10.37093 | 15.3144 | 16.6302 | 32.4506 | 27.0927 |
| 2 | 77.04403 | 65.52728 | 20.74186 | 30.6288 | 33.2603 | 64.9012 | 54.1854 |
| 3 | 115.56604 | 98.29092 | 31.11280 | 45.9433 | 49.8905 | 97.3517 | 81.2781 |
| 4 | 154.08805 | 131.05456 | 41.48373 | 61.2577 | 66.5206 | 129.8023 | 108.3708 |
| 5 | 192.61007 | 163.81821 | 51.85467 | 76.5721 | 83.1508 | 162.2529 | 135.4636 |
| 6 | 231.13208 | 196.58185 | 62.22559 | 91.8865 | 99.7810 | 194.7035 | 162.5563 |
| 7 | 269.65409 | 229.34549 | 72.59652 | 107.2009 | 116.4111 | 227.1541 | 189.6490 |
| 8 | 308.17610 | 262.10913 | 82.96746 | 122.5153 | 133.0413 | 259.6047 | 216.7417 |
| 9 | 346.69812 | 294.87277 | 93.33839 | 137.8298 | 149.6715 | 292.0552 | 243.8344 |
| 10 | 385.22013 | 327.63641 | 103.70932 | 153.1442 | 166.3016 | 324.5058 | 270.9271 |

| No. of Periods. | Arg. 35. | 36. | 37. | 38. | 39. | 40. | 41. | 42. |
|---|---|---|---|---|---|---|---|---|
| 1 | 23.9422 | 13.7188 | 37.625 | 9.3944 | 34.475 | 18.8435 | 17.9191 | 10.1479 |
| 2 | 47.8845 | 27.4376 | 75.251 | 18.7888 | 68.951 | 37.6871 | 35.8382 | 20.2958 |
| 3 | 71.8267 | 41.1564 | 112.876 | 28.1832 | 103.426 | 56.5306 | 53.7573 | 30.4437 |
| 4 | 95.7689 | 54.8752 | 150.501 | 37.5776 | 137.901 | 75.3742 | 71.6764 | 40.5916 |
| 5 | 119.7112 | 68.5941 | 188.127 | 46.9720 | 172.376 | 94.2177 | 89.5955 | 50.7395 |
| 6 | 143.6534 | 82.3129 | 225.752 | 56.3664 | 206.852 | 113.0613 | 107.5146 | 60.8874 |
| 7 | 167.5956 | 96.0317 | 263.377 | 65.7607 | 241.327 | 131.9048 | 125.4337 | 71.0354 |
| 8 | 191.5379 | 109.7505 | 301.003 | 75.1551 | 275.802 | 150.7483 | 143.3528 | 81.1833 |
| 9 | 215.4801 | 123.4693 | 338.628 | 84.5495 | 310.278 | 169.5919 | 161.2720 | 91.3312 |
| 10 | 239.4223 | 137.1881 | 376.253 | 93.9439 | 344.753 | 188.4354 | 179.1911 | 101.4791 |

| No. of Periods. | Arg. 43. | 44. | 45. | 46. | 47. | 48. | 49. | 50. |
|---|---|---|---|---|---|---|---|---|
| 1 | 14.5379 | 22.786 | 16.9000 | 29.013 | 14.1326 | 29.9342 | 12.763 | 25.036 |
| 2 | 29.0757 | 45.572 | 33.8001 | 58.027 | 28.2651 | 59.8683 | 25.525 | 50.072 |
| 3 | 43.6136 | 68.358 | 50.7001 | 87.040 | 42.3977 | 89.8025 | 38.288 | 75.108 |
| 4 | 58.1514 | 91.145 | 67.6001 | 116.053 | 56.5302 | 119.7367 | 51.051 | 100.144 |
| 5 | 72.6893 | 113.931 | 84.5002 | 145.066 | 70.6628 | 149.6709 | 63.814 | 125.180 |
| 6 | 87.2271 | 136.717 | 101.4002 | 174.080 | 84.7953 | 179.6050 | 76.576 | 150.216 |
| 7 | 101.7650 | 159.503 | 118.3002 | 203.093 | 98.9279 | 209.5392 | 89.339 | 175.252 |
| 8 | 116.3028 | 182.289 | 135.2003 | 232.106 | 113.0604 | 239.4734 | 102.102 | 200.288 |
| 9 | 130.8407 | 205.075 | 152.1003 | 261.120 | 127.1930 | 269.4075 | 114.864 | 225.324 |
| 10 | 145.3785 | 227.861 | 169.0004 | 290.133 | 141.3256 | 299.3417 | 127.627 | 250.360 |

| No. of Periods. | Arg. 51. | 52. | 53. | 54. | 55. | 56. | 57. | 58. |
|---|---|---|---|---|---|---|---|---|
| 1 | 18.2169 | 25.2314 | 117.5394 | 15.070 | 19.6273 | 13.1175 | 16.9874 | 15.2422 |
| 2 | 36.4338 | 50.4627 | 235.0788 | 30.140 | 39.2546 | 26.2350 | 33.9748 | 30.4844 |
| 3 | 54.6508 | 75.6941 | 352.6183 | 45.210 | 58.8819 | 39.3524 | 50.9622 | 45.7266 |
| 4 | 72.8677 | 100.9255 | 470.1577 | 60.280 | 78.5092 | 52.4699 | 67.9496 | 60.9689 |
| 5 | 91.0846 | 126.1569 | 587.6971 | 75.349 | 98.1365 | 65.5874 | 84.9370 | 76.2111 |
| 6 | 109.3015 | 151.3882 | 705.2365 | 90.419 | 117.7638 | 78.7049 | 101.9244 | 91.4533 |
| 7 | 127.5184 | 176.6196 | 822.7760 | 105.489 | 137.3911 | 91.8223 | 118.9118 | 106.6955 |
| 8 | 145.7354 | 201.8510 | 940.3154 | 120.559 | 157.0184 | 104.9398 | 135.8993 | 121.9377 |
| 9 | 163.9523 | 227.0824 | 1057.8548 | 135.629 | 176.6457 | 118.0573 | 152.8867 | 137.1799 |
| 10 | 182.1692 | 252.3137 | 1175.3942 | 150.699 | 196.2730 | 131.1748 | 169.8741 | 152.4222 |

# TABLE III*b*.

Multiples of Periods of the Arguments.

| No. of Periods. | Arg. 59. | 60. | 61. | 62. | 63. | 64. | 65. |
|---|---|---|---|---|---|---|---|
| 1 | 38.9640 | 22.3217 | 13.6061 | 14.4420 | 13.6334 | 35.9921 | 14.4728 |
| 2 | 77.9279 | 44.6434 | 27.2122 | 28.8840 | 27.2668 | 71.9842 | 28.9455 |
| 3 | 116.8919 | 66.9651 | 40.8183 | 43.3260 | 40.9002 | 107.9764 | 43.4183 |
| 4 | 155.8559 | 89.2869 | 54.4244 | 57.7680 | 54.5336 | 143.9685 | 57.8911 |
| 5 | 194.8198 | 111.6086 | 68.0306 | 72.2100 | 68.1670 | 179.9606 | 72.3639 |
| 6 | 233.7838 | 133.9303 | 81.6367 | 86.6520 | 81.8004 | 215.9527 | 86.8366 |
| 7 | 272.7478 | 156.2520 | 95.2428 | 101.0940 | 95.4338 | 251.9448 | 101.3094 |
| 8 | 311.7118 | 178.5737 | 108.8489 | 115.5360 | 109.0672 | 287.9370 | 115.7822 |
| 9 | 350.6757 | 200.8954 | 122.4550 | 129.9780 | 122.7006 | 323.9291 | 130.2549 |
| 10 | 389.6397 | 223.2171 | 136.0611 | 144.4200 | 136.3340 | 359.9212 | 144.7277 |

| No. of Periods. | Arg. 66. | 67. | 68. | 69. | 70. | 71. | 72. | 73. |
|---|---|---|---|---|---|---|---|---|
| 1 | 35.596 | 27.4433 | 27.6667 | 471.893 | 329.791 | 583.921 | 398.884 | 2190.331 |
| 2 | 71.192 | 54.8866 | 55.3334 | 943.787 | 659.581 | 1167.843 | 797.768 | 4380.661 |
| 3 | 106.787 | 82.3300 | 83.0001 | 1415.680 | 989.372 | 1751.764 | 1196.652 | 6570.992 |
| 4 | 142.383 | 109.7733 | 110.6668 | 1887.573 | 1319.162 | 2335.685 | 1595.536 | 8761.322 |
| 5 | 177.979 | 137.2166 | 138.3334 | 2359.466 | 1648.953 | 2919.606 | 1994.421 | 10951.653 |
| 6 | 213.575 | 164.6599 | 166.0001 | 2831.360 | 1978.743 | 3503.528 | 2393.305 | 13141.984 |
| 7 | 249.171 | 192.1033 | 193.6668 | 3303.253 | 2308.534 | 4087.449 | 2792.189 | 15332.314 |
| 8 | 284.767 | 219.5466 | 221.3335 | 3775.146 | 2638.324 | 4671.370 | 3191.073 | 17522.645 |
| 9 | 320.362 | 246.9899 | 249.0002 | 4247.039 | 2968.115 | 5255.291 | 3589.957 | 19712.975 |
| 10 | 355.958 | 274.4332 | 276.6669 | 4718.933 | 3297.906 | 5839.213 | 3988.841 | 21903.306 |

| No. of Periods. | Arg. 74. | 75. | 76. | 78. | 79. | 80. | 81. | 82. |
|---|---|---|---|---|---|---|---|---|
| 1 | 3232.82 | 84753 | 95490 | 188.20151 | 438.361 | 313.055 | 124.2046 | 14.86550 |
| 2 | 6465.64 | 169506 | 190980 | 376.40303 | 876.722 | 626.109 | 248.4092 | 29.73101 |
| 3 | 9698.46 | 254260 | 286470 | 564.60454 | 1315.082 | 939.164 | 372.6138 | 44.59651 |
| 4 | 12931.28 | 339013 | 381960 | 752.80605 | 1753.443 | 1252.219 | 496.8184 | 59.46202 |
| 5 | 16164.10 | 423766 | 477450 | 941.00757 | 2191.804 | 1565.273 | 621.0230 | 74.32752 |
| 6 | 19396.92 | 508519 | 572940 | 1129.20908 | 2630.165 | 1878.328 | 745.2276 | 89.19303 |
| 7 | 22629.74 | 593273 | 668430 | 1317.41059 | 3068.525 | 2191.383 | 869.4322 | 104.05853 |
| 8 | 25862.56 | 678026 | 763920 | 1505.61211 | 3506.886 | 2504.437 | 993.6368 | 118.92403 |
| 9 | 29095.38 | 762779 | 859409 | 1693.81362 | 3945.247 | 2817.492 | 1117.8414 | 133.78954 |
| 10 | 32328.20 | 847532 | 954899 | 1882.01513 | 4383.608 | 3130.547 | 1242.0460 | 148.65504 |

| No. of Periods. | Arg. 83. | 84. | 85. | 86. | 87. | 88. | 89. | 90. |
|---|---|---|---|---|---|---|---|---|
| 1 | 39.2116 | 19.1434 | 23.5193 | 38.2830 | 14.2082 | 14.6664 | 19.3122 | 32.281 |
| 2 | 78.4233 | 38.2868 | 47.0387 | 76.5659 | 28.4164 | 29.3329 | 38.6243 | 64.562 |
| 3 | 117.6349 | 57.4302 | 70.5580 | 114.8489 | 42.6246 | 43.9993 | 57.9365 | 96.842 |
| 4 | 156.8465 | 76.5736 | 94.0774 | 153.1318 | 56.8328 | 58.6657 | 77.2486 | 129.123 |
| 5 | 196.0582 | 95.7170 | 117.5967 | 191.4148 | 71.0410 | 73.3321 | 96.5608 | 161.404 |
| 6 | 235.2698 | 114.8604 | 141.1160 | 229.6977 | 85.2492 | 87.9986 | 115.8729 | 193.685 |
| 7 | 274.4815 | 134.0039 | 164.6354 | 267.9807 | 99.4574 | 102.6650 | 135.1851 | 225.965 |
| 8 | 313.6931 | 153.1473 | 188.1547 | 306.2636 | 113.6656 | 117.3314 | 154.4972 | 258.246 |
| 9 | 352.9047 | 172.2907 | 211.6741 | 344.5466 | 127.8739 | 131.9978 | 173.8094 | 290.527 |
| 10 | 392.1164 | 191.4341 | 235.1934 | 382.8295 | 142.0821 | 146.6643 | 193.1215 | 322.808 |

# TABLE IV.

Constants of Epochs and Arguments for every Hundred Thousandth Day to 2300000.

| Day. | u | | Log. (-u′) | Log. (-u″) | (y-u) | | Log. (y-u′) | Log. (y-u″) |
|---|---|---|---|---|---|---|---|---|
| | ° | ″ | | | ° | ″ | | |
| 0 | 140 | 306.18 | 8.544661 | 91.41942 | 342 | 1071.9 | 8.396885 | 91.2329 |
| 100000 | 178 | 2905.81 | 8.529434 | 91.40094 | 238 | 1261.1 | 8.381369 | 91.2144 |
| 200000 | 217 | 2028.29 | 8.513363 | 91.38163 | 134 | 1362.1 | 8.365011 | 91.1951 |
| 300000 | 256 | 1274.81 | 8.496369 | 91.36143 | 30 | 1373.7 | 8.347734 | 91.1749 |
| 400000 | 295 | 647.57 | 8.478365 | 91.34024 | 286 | 1294.2 | 8.329452 | 91.1537 |
| 500000 | 334 | 148.78 | 8.459252 | 91.31796 | 182 | 1122.4 | 8.310064 | 91.1314 |
| 600000 | 12 | 3380.62 | 8.438911 | 91.29448 | 78 | 856.8 | 8.289452 | 91.1080 |
| 700000 | 51 | 3145.30 | 8.417204 | 91.26966 | 334 | 495.9 | 8.267479 | 91.0831 |
| 800000 | 90 | 3045.02 | 8.393970 | 91.24333 | 230 | 38.3 | 8.243981 | 91.0568 |
| 900000 | 129 | 3081.98 | 8.369015 | 91.21530 | 125 | 3082.6 | 8.218766 | 91.0288 |
| 1000000 | 168 | 3258.37 | 8.342103 | 91.18534 | 21 | 2427.3 | 8.191598 | 90.9988 |
| 1100000 | 207 | 3576.40 | 8.312949 | 91.15315 | 277 | 1671.1 | 8.162190 | 90.9666 |
| 1200000 | 247 | 438.26 | 8.281195 | 91.11839 | 173 | 812.4 | 8.130188 | 90.9319 |
| 1300000 | 286 | 1046.15 | 8.246395 | 91.08060 | 68 | 3450.0 | 8.095141 | 90.8941 |
| 1400000 | 325 | 1802.27 | 8.207971 | 91.03921 | 324 | 2382.2 | 8.056474 | 90.8527 |
| 1500000 | 4 | 2708.83 | 8.165161 | 90.99346 | 220 | 1207.8 | 8.013424 | 90.8069 |
| 1600000 | 44 | 168.01 | 8.116937 | 90.94230 | 115 | 3525.2 | 7.964963 | 90.7558 |
| 1700000 | 83 | 1382.02 | 8.061854 | 90.88431 | 11 | 2133.0 | 7.909646 | 90.6978 |
| 1800000 | 122 | 2753.06 | 7.997796 | 90.81736 | 267 | 629.9 | 7.845357 | 90.6308 |
| 1900000 | 162 | 683.32 | 7.921485 | 90.73818 | 162 | 2614.3 | 7.768818 | 90.5516 |
| 2000000 | 201 | 2375.01 | 7.827426 | 90.64127 | 58 | 884.9 | 7.674534 | 90.4547 |
| 2100000 | 241 | 630.32 | 7.705321 | 90.51633 | 313 | 2640.2 | 7.552206 | 90.3298 |
| 2200000 | 280 | 2651.46 | 7.532432 | 90.34024 | 209 | 678.7 | 7.378709 | 90.1537 |
| 2300000 | 320 | 1240.62 | 7.233809 | 90.03921 | 104 | 2199.2 | 7.080258 | 89.8526 |

| Day. | Arg. 1. | Log. 1′. | Log. 1″. | Arg. 2. | Log. 2′. | Log. 2″. |
|---|---|---|---|---|---|---|
| 0 | 5.3268824 | −94.480661 | −87.4274 | 17.176849 | +94.28132 | +87.2570 |
| 100000 | 9.5618459 | 94.465942 | 87.4089 | 0.643873 | 94.26692 | 87.2385 |
| 200000 | 13.8069578 | 94.450440 | 87.3896 | 15.916224 | 94.25166 | 87.2192 |
| 300000 | 18.0624409 | 94.433995 | 87.3694 | 31.181815 | 94.23547 | 87.1990 |
| 400000 | 22.3285183 | 94.416533 | 87.3482 | 14.628562 | 94.21824 | 87.1778 |
| 500000 | 26.6054129 | 94.397950 | 87.3260 | 29.880187 | 94.19992 | 87.1556 |
| 600000 | 3.3387953 | 94.378134 | 87.3025 | 13.312665 | 94.18034 | 87.1321 |
| 700000 | 7.6379932 | 94.356947 | 87.2776 | 28.549716 | 94.15938 | 87.1072 |
| 800000 | 11.9486771 | 94.334218 | 87.2513 | 11.967321 | 94.13689 | 87.0809 |
| 900000 | 16.2710701 | 94.309762 | 87.2233 | 27.189199 | 94.11266 | 87.0529 |
| 1000000 | 20.6053951 | 94.283344 | 87.1933 | 10.591328 | 94.08647 | 87.0229 |
| 1100000 | 24.9518750 | 94.254673 | 87.1611 | 25.797429 | 94.05802 | 86.9907 |
| 1200000 | 1.7561803 | 94.223400 | 87.1264 | 9.183481 | 94.02696 | 86.9560 |
| 1300000 | 6.1276389 | 94.189070 | 87.0886 | 24.373204 | 93.99290 | 86.9182 |
| 1400000 | 10.5119214 | 94.151109 | 87.0472 | 7.742576 | 93.95509 | 86.8768 |
| 1500000 | 14.9092506 | 94.108758 | 87.0014 | 22.915317 | 93.91295 | 86.8310 |
| 1600000 | 19.3198495 | 94.060984 | 86.9503 | 6.267407 | 93.86538 | 86.7799 |
| 1700000 | 23.7439410 | 94.006345 | 86.8923 | 21.422565 | 93.81094 | 86.7219 |
| 1800000 | 0.6271958 | 93.942725 | 86.8254 | 4.756769 | 93.74674 | 86.6550 |
| 1900000 | 5.0789415 | 93.866846 | 86.7462 | 19.893742 | 93.67183 | 86.5758 |
| 2000000 | 9.5448488 | 93.773213 | 86.6493 | 3.209459 | 93.57781 | 86.4789 |
| 2100000 | 14.0251406 | 93.651526 | 86.5243 | 18.327643 | 93.45689 | 86.3539 |
| 2200000 | 18.5200399 | 93.478663 | 86.3482 | 1.624271 | 93.28421 | 86.1778 |
| 2300000 | 23.0297695 | −93.180837 | −86.0472 | 16.723064 | +92.98656 | +85.8768 |

# TABLE IV.

Constants of Epochs and Arguments for every Hundred Thousandth Day to 2300000.

| Day. | Arg. **3**. | Log. **3**′. | Log. **3**″. | Arg. **4**. | Arg. **5**. | Log. **5**′. | Log. **5**″. |
|---|---|---|---|---|---|---|---|
| 0 | 10.8269904 | −93.84505 | −86.7744 | 121.4011 | 340.4155 | −95.54931 | −88.501 |
| 100000 | 20.1879472 | 93.83025 | 86.7559 | 40.2469 | 273.1718 | 95.53469 | 88.483 |
| 200000 | 0.0206869 | 93.81459 | 86.7366 | 324.3525 | 206.0468 | 95.51921 | 88.463 |
| 300000 | 9.3864354 | 93.79800 | 86.7164 | 243.1983 | 139.0429 | 95.50279 | 88.443 |
| 400000 | 18.7546540 | 93.78039 | 86.6952 | 162.0442 | 72.1629 | 95.48537 | 88.422 |
| 500000 | 28.1253925 | 93.76167 | 86.6730 | 80.8900 | 5.4095 | 95.46683 | 88.400 |
| 600000 | 7.9681123 | 93.74171 | 86.6495 | 364.9956 | 350.5703 | 95.44703 | 88.376 |
| 700000 | 17.3440390 | 93.72039 | 86.6246 | 283.8414 | 284.0778 | 95.42588 | 88.351 |
| 800000 | 26.7226343 | 93.69753 | 86.5983 | 202.6873 | 217.7198 | 95.40318 | 88.325 |
| 900000 | 6.5733596 | 93.67294 | 86.5703 | 121.5331 | 151.4988 | 95.37875 | 88.297 |
| 1000000 | 15.9574407 | 93.64640 | 86.5403 | 40.3790 | 85.4175 | 95.35236 | 88.267 |
| 1100000 | 25.3443389 | 93.61760 | 86.5081 | 324.4845 | 19.4786 | 95.32370 | 88.235 |
| 1200000 | 5.2035160 | 93.58620 | 86.4734 | 243.3304 | 365.4699 | 95.29245 | 88.200 |
| 1300000 | 14.5961974 | 93.55175 | 86.4356 | 162.1762 | 299.8237 | 95.25814 | 88.162 |
| 1400000 | 23.9918448 | 93.51367 | 86.3942 | 81.0221 | 234.3277 | 95.22020 | 88.121 |
| 1500000 | 3.8599197 | 93.47120 | 86.3484 | 365.1276 | 168.9847 | 95.17784 | 88.075 |
| 1600000 | 13.2616477 | 93.42330 | 86.2973 | 283.9735 | 103.7972 | 95.13007 | 88.024 |
| 1700000 | 22.6664904 | 93.36855 | 86.2393 | 202.8193 | 38.7679 | 95.07544 | 87.966 |
| 1800000 | 2.5439093 | 93.30482 | 86.1724 | 121.6652 | 385.6847 | 95.01177 | 87.899 |
| 1900000 | 11.9551300 | 93.22882 | 86.0932 | 40.5110 | 320.9798 | 94.93584 | 87.820 |
| 2000000 | 21.3696141 | 93.13508 | 85.9963 | 324.6166 | 256.4410 | 94.84212 | 87.723 |
| 2100000 | 1.2568232 | 93.01329 | 85.8713 | 243.4624 | 192.0710 | 94.72109 | 87.598 |
| 2200000 | 10.6779828 | 92.84032 | 85.6952 | 162.3083 | 127.8724 | 94.54826 | 87.422 |
| 2300000 | 20.1025546 | −92.54238 | −85.3942 | 81.1541 | 63.8478 | −94.25046 | −87.121 |

| Day. | Arg. **6**. | Log. **6**′. | Log. **6**″. | Arg. **7**. | Log. **7**′. | Log. **7**″. | Arg. **8**. | Log. **8**′. | Log. **8**″. |
|---|---|---|---|---|---|---|---|---|---|
| 0 | 7.2514 | +94.3374 | +87.597 | 8.9079 | −94.1786 | −87.121 | 6.1678 | −93.8625 | −86.792 |
| 100000 | 31.7296 | 94.3228 | 87.579 | 6.8667 | 94.1640 | 87.103 | 3.9547 | 93.8478 | 86.774 |
| 200000 | 21.3537 | 94.3074 | 87.559 | 4.8305 | 94.1483 | 87.083 | 1.7440 | 93.8322 | 86.754 |
| 300000 | 10.9704 | 94.2910 | 87.539 | 2.7996 | 94.1319 | 87.063 | 14.9232 | 93.8155 | 86.734 |
| 400000 | 0.5795 | 94.2737 | 87.518 | 0.7740 | 94.1143 | 87.042 | 12.7176 | 93.7980 | 86.713 |
| 500000 | 25.0277 | 94.2553 | 87.496 | 8.3675 | 94.0956 | 87.020 | 10.5146 | 93.7793 | 86.691 |
| 600000 | 14.6213 | 94.2355 | 87.472 | 6.3528 | 94.0757 | 86.996 | 8.3143 | 93.7594 | 86.667 |
| 700000 | 4.2067 | 94.2144 | 87.447 | 4.3438 | 94.0544 | 86.971 | 6.1168 | 93.7381 | 86.642 |
| 800000 | 28.6308 | 94.1918 | 87.421 | 2.3405 | 94.0318 | 86.945 | 3.9220 | 93.7152 | 86.616 |
| 900000 | 18.1996 | 94.1674 | 87.393 | 0.3430 | 94.0071 | 86.917 | 1.7300 | 93.6907 | 86.588 |
| 1000000 | 7.7598 | 94.1412 | 87.363 | 7.9653 | 93.9807 | 86.887 | 14.9283 | 93.6641 | 86.558 |
| 1100000 | 32.1583 | 94.1126 | 87.331 | 5.9799 | 93.9525 | 86.855 | 12.7421 | 93.6354 | 86.526 |
| 1200000 | 21.7009 | 94.0813 | 87.296 | 4.0006 | 93.9216 | 86.820 | 10.5590 | 93.6040 | 86.491 |
| 1300000 | 11.2345 | 94.0470 | 87.258 | 2.0277 | 93.8872 | 86.782 | 8.3788 | 93.5695 | 86.453 |
| 1400000 | 0.7588 | 94.0092 | 87.217 | 9.6749 | 93.8492 | 86.741 | 6.2018 | 93.5315 | 86.412 |
| 1500000 | 25.1207 | 93.9670 | 87.171 | 7.7149 | 93.8067 | 86.695 | 4.0279 | 93.4890 | 86.366 |
| 1600000 | 14.6262 | 93.9193 | 87.120 | 5.7616 | 93.7590 | 86.644 | 1.8572 | 93.4412 | 86.315 |
| 1700000 | 4.1219 | 93.8647 | 87.062 | 3.8149 | 93.7013 | 86.586 | 15.0770 | 93.3864 | 86.257 |
| 1800000 | 28.4546 | 93.8011 | 86.995 | 1.8751 | 93.6407 | 86.519 | 12.9129 | 93.3227 | 86.190 |
| 1900000 | 17.9305 | 93.7254 | 86.916 | 9.5560 | 93.5648 | 86.440 | 10.7521 | 93.2467 | 86.111 |
| 2000000 | 7.3961 | 93.6318 | 86.819 | 7.6302 | 93.4711 | 86.343 | 8.5946 | 93.1530 | 86.014 |
| 2100000 | 31.6982 | 93.5102 | 86.694 | 5.7116 | 93.3494 | 86.218 | 6.4407 | 93.0313 | 85.889 |
| 2200000 | 21.1429 | 93.3375 | 86.518 | 3.8003 | 93.1764 | 86.042 | 4.2902 | 92.8583 | 85.713 |
| 2300000 | 10.5769 | +93.0397 | +86.217 | 1.8964 | −92.8786 | −85.741 | 2.1433 | −92.5604 | −85.412 |

# TABLE IV.

Constants of Epochs and Arguments for every Hundred Thousandth Day to 2300000.

| Day. | Arg. 9. | Log. 9′. | Log. 9″. | Arg. 10. | Log. 10′. | Log. 10″. | Arg. 11. | Log. 11′. | Log. 11″. |
|---|---|---|---|---|---|---|---|---|---|
| 0 | 25.6590 | −94.5146 | −87.461 | 13.4695 | −94.4492 | −87.396 | 13.0788 | +94.4033 | +87.348 |
| 100000 | 7.0583 | 94.5001 | 87.443 | 11.7147 | 94.4345 | 87.378 | 26.0864 | 94.3886 | 87.330 |
| 200000 | 18.2714 | 94.4846 | 87.423 | 9.9693 | 94.4190 | 87.358 | 12.2071 | 94.3732 | 87.310 |
| 300000 | 29.4957 | 94.4680 | 87.403 | 8.2335 | 94.4025 | 87.338 | 25.1975 | 94.3567 | 87.290 |
| 400000 | 10.9287 | 94.4506 | 87.382 | 6.5076 | 94.3850 | 87.317 | 11.3007 | 94.3393 | 87.269 |
| 500000 | 22.1762 | 94.4320 | 87.360 | 4.7917 | 94.3664 | 87.295 | 24.2732 | 94.3206 | 87.247 |
| 600000 | 3.6328 | 94.4123 | 87.336 | 3.0862 | 94.3467 | 87.271 | 10.3581 | 94.3009 | 87.223 |
| 700000 | 14.9044 | 94.3911 | 87.311 | 1.3911 | 94.3254 | 87.246 | 23.3119 | 94.2797 | 87.198 |
| 800000 | 26.1885 | 94.3683 | 87.285 | 25.3284 | 94.3027 | 87.220 | 9.3778 | 94.2569 | 87.172 |
| 900000 | 7.6823 | 94.3438 | 87.257 | 23.6548 | 94.2784 | 87.192 | 22.3122 | 94.2324 | 87.144 |
| 1000000 | 18.9920 | 94.3175 | 87.227 | 21.9924 | 94.2519 | 87.162 | 8.3583 | 94.2061 | 87.114 |
| 1100000 | 0.5119 | 94.2887 | 87.195 | 20.3413 | 94.2232 | 87.130 | 21.2726 | 94.1772 | 87.082 |
| 1200000 | 11.8481 | 94.2575 | 87.160 | 18.7017 | 94.1919 | 87.095 | 7.2982 | 94.1457 | 87.047 |
| 1300000 | 23.1979 | 94.2230 | 87.122 | 17.0738 | 94.1575 | 87.057 | 20.1915 | 94.1114 | 87.009 |
| 1400000 | 4.7587 | 94.1853 | 87.081 | 15.4579 | 94.1200 | 87.016 | 6.1959 | 94.0734 | 86.968 |
| 1500000 | 16.1365 | 94.1428 | 87.035 | 13.8541 | 94.0772 | 86.970 | 19.0676 | 94.0311 | 86.922 |
| 1600000 | 27.5286 | 94.0950 | 86.984 | 12.2626 | 94.0295 | 86.919 | 5.0499 | 93.9833 | 86.871 |
| 1700000 | 9.1325 | 94.0405 | 86.926 | 10.6837 | 93.9748 | 86.861 | 17.8993 | 93.9286 | 86.813 |
| 1800000 | 20.5541 | 93.9768 | 86.859 | 9.1175 | 93.9112 | 86.794 | 3.8589 | 93.8649 | 86.746 |
| 1900000 | 2.1879 | 93.9009 | 86.780 | 7.5643 | 93.8354 | 86.715 | 16.6851 | 93.7892 | 86.667 |
| 2000000 | 13.6398 | 93.8073 | 86.683 | 6.0243 | 93.7417 | 86.618 | 2.6212 | 93.6954 | 86.570 |
| 2100000 | 25.1073 | 93.6855 | 86.558 | 4.4976 | 93.6199 | 86.493 | 15.4235 | 93.5737 | 86.445 |
| 2200000 | 6.7878 | 93.5127 | 86.382 | 2.9846 | 93.4471 | 86.317 | 1.3354 | 93.4009 | 86.269 |
| 2300000 | 18.2872 | −93.2149 | −86.081 | 1.4853 | −93.1492 | −86.016 | 14.1131 | +93.1030 | +85.968 |

| Day. | Arg. 12. | Log. 12′. | Log. 12″. | Arg. 13. | Log. 13′. | Arg. 14. | Log. 14′. | Arg. 15. | Log. 15′. |
|---|---|---|---|---|---|---|---|---|---|
| 0 | 337.3723 | +94.7409 | +87.655 | 2.7557 | +93.279 | 25.527 | +94.346 | 0.927 | −93.906 |
| 100000 | 164.6955 | 94.7259 | 87.637 | 3.9081 | 93.261 | 3.816 | 94.328 | 6.772 | 93.887 |
| 200000 | 338.6200 | 94.7101 | 87.617 | 5.0600 | 93.241 | 11.363 | 94.308 | 12.618 | 93.865 |
| 300000 | 165.9052 | 94.6934 | 87.597 | 6.2114 | 93.221 | 18.904 | 94.288 | 4.276 | 93.848 |
| 400000 | 339.7910 | 94.6757 | 87.576 | 7.3623 | 93.200 | 26.438 | 94.267 | 10.128 | 93.827 |
| 500000 | 167.0368 | 94.6568 | 87.554 | 8.5127 | 93.178 | 4.703 | 94.245 | 1.790 | 93.805 |
| 600000 | 340.8823 | 94.6368 | 87.530 | 9.6625 | 93.154 | 12.224 | 94.221 | 7.646 | 93.781 |
| 700000 | 168.0871 | 94.6153 | 87.505 | 0.7273 | 93.129 | 19.738 | 94.196 | 13.505 | 93.756 |
| 800000 | 341.8909 | 94.5924 | 87.479 | 1.8760 | 93.103 | 27.246 | 94.170 | 5.175 | 93.729 |
| 900000 | 169.0532 | 94.5677 | 87.451 | 3.0242 | 93.075 | 5.483 | 94.142 | 11.039 | 93.702 |
| 1000000 | 342.8138 | 94.5410 | 87.421 | 4.1718 | 93.045 | 12.977 | 94.112 | 2.714 | 93.672 |
| 1100000 | 169.9321 | 94.5122 | 87.389 | 5.3188 | 93.013 | 20.463 | 94.080 | 8.583 | 93.640 |
| 1200000 | 343.6479 | 94.4806 | 87.354 | 6.4652 | 92.978 | 27.942 | 94.045 | 0.263 | 93.605 |
| 1300000 | 170.7207 | 94.4461 | 87.316 | 7.6110 | 92.940 | 6.149 | 94.007 | 6.138 | 93.567 |
| 1400000 | 344.3903 | 94.4079 | 87.275 | 8.7561 | 92.899 | 13.613 | 93.966 | 12.016 | 93.526 |
| 1500000 | 171.4161 | 94.3653 | 87.229 | 9.9006 | 92.853 | 21.068 | 93.920 | 3.704 | 93.480 |
| 1600000 | 345.0379 | 94.3173 | 87.178 | 0.9598 | 92.802 | 28.515 | 93.869 | 9.588 | 93.429 |
| 1700000 | 172.0151 | 94.2625 | 87.120 | 2.1030 | 92.744 | 6.691 | 93.811 | 1.283 | 93.372 |
| 1800000 | 345.5877 | 94.1987 | 87.053 | 3.2454 | 92.677 | 14.122 | 93.744 | 7.172 | 93.304 |
| 1900000 | 172.5149 | 94.1225 | 86.974 | 4.3871 | 92.598 | 21.545 | 93.665 | 13.064 | 93.225 |
| 2000000 | 346.0367 | 94.0287 | 86.877 | 5.5281 | 92.501 | 28.959 | 93.568 | 4.768 | 93.128 |
| 2100000 | 172.9123 | 93.9069 | 86.752 | 6.6684 | 92.376 | 7.101 | 93.443 | 10.667 | 93.003 |
| 2200000 | 346.3818 | 93.7338 | 86.576 | 7.8079 | 92.200 | 14.498 | 93.267 | 2.378 | 92.827 |
| 2300000 | 173.2044 | +93.4358 | +86.275 | 8.9466 | +91.899 | 21.885 | +92.966 | 8.283 | −92.526 |

# TABLE IV.

Constants of Epochs and Arguments for every Hundred Thousandth Day to 2300000.

| Day. | Arg. **16.** | Log. **16′.** | Arg. **17.** | Log. **17′.** | Arg. **18.** | Log. **18′.** | Arg. **19.** | Log. **19′.** |
|---|---|---|---|---|---|---|---|---|
| 0 | 7.980 | −94.361 | 19.088 | −93.889 | 5.893 | −94.274 | 20.567 | −94.8382 |
| 100000 | 0.435 | 94.343 | 21.679 | 93.871 | 5.989 | 94.256 | 16.366 | 94.8236 |
| 200000 | 7.151 | 94.323 | 24.273 | 93.851 | 6.090 | 94.236 | 12.188 | 94.8080 |
| 300000 | 13.873 | 94.303 | 26.869 | 93.831 | 6.197 | 94.216 | 8.033 | 94.7916 |
| 400000 | 6.348 | 94.282 | 2.145 | 93.810 | 6.308 | 94.195 | 3.902 | 94.7742 |
| 500000 | 13.084 | 94.260 | 4.745 | 93.788 | 6.426 | 94.173 | 24.097 | 94.7556 |
| 600000 | 5.572 | 94.236 | 7.348 | 93.764 | 6.549 | 94.149 | 20.016 | 94.7358 |
| 700000 | 12.322 | 94.211 | 9.953 | 93.739 | 6.678 | 94.124 | 15.960 | 94.7146 |
| 800000 | 4.825 | 94.185 | 12.560 | 93.713 | 6.814 | 94.098 | 11.930 | 94.6919 |
| 900000 | 11.589 | 94.157 | 15.170 | 93.685 | 6.955 | 94.070 | 7.926 | 94.6675 |
| 1000000 | 4.107 | 94.127 | 17.782 | 93.655 | 7.102 | 94.040 | 3.949 | 94.6412 |
| 1100000 | 10.887 | 94.095 | 20.397 | 93.623 | 7.256 | 94.008 | 0.000 | 94.6123 |
| 1200000 | 3.420 | 94.060 | 23.014 | 93.588 | 7.415 | 93.973 | 20.381 | 94.5811 |
| 1300000 | 10.215 | 94.022 | 25.634 | 93.550 | 7.582 | 93.935 | 16.489 | 94.5467 |
| 1400000 | 2.764 | 93.981 | 0.935 | 93.509 | 7.755 | 93.894 | 12.625 | 94.[illegible]089 |
| 1500000 | 9.575 | 93.935 | 3.560 | 93.463 | 7.935 | 93.848 | 8.791 | 94.4665 |
| 1600000 | 2.141 | 93.884 | 6.189 | 93.412 | 8.121 | 93.797 | 4.987 | 94.4188 |
| 1700000 | 8.969 | 93.826 | 8.820 | 93.354 | 8.315 | 93.739 | 1.213 | 94.3642 |
| 1800000 | 1.552 | 93.759 | 11.454 | 93.287 | 8.516 | 93.672 | 21.773 | 94.3007 |
| 1900000 | 8.398 | 93.680 | 14.091 | 93.208 | 8.723 | 93.593 | 18.062 | 94.2243 |
| 2000000 | 0.998 | 93.583 | 16.731 | 93.111 | 8.938 | 93.496 | 14.384 | 94.1309 |
| 2100000 | 7.862 | 93.458 | 19.374 | 92.986 | 9.161 | 93.371 | 10.738 | 94.0094 |
| 2200000 | 0.480 | 93.282 | 22.020 | 92.810 | 9.391 | 93.195 | 7.125 | 93.8365 |
| 2300000 | 7.363 | −92.981 | 24.669 | −92.509 | 9.628 | −92.894 | 3.545 | −93.5387 |

| Day. | Arg. **20.** | Log. **20′.** | Arg. **21.** | Log. **21′.** | Arg. **22.** | Log. **22′.** | Arg. **23.** | Log. **23′.** |
|---|---|---|---|---|---|---|---|---|
| 0 | 0.771 | −94.580 | 129.77 | −95.438 | 1.111 | −93.961 | 3.326 | −94.352 |
| 100000 | 8.353 | 94.562 | 57.51 | 95.420 | 18.432 | 93.943 | 7.067 | 94.334 |
| 200000 | 1.628 | 94.542 | 117.00 | 95.400 | 3.628 | 93.923 | 10.814 | 94.314 |
| 300000 | 9.232 | 94.522 | 44.90 | 95.380 | 20.955 | 93.903 | 14.567 | 94.294 |
| 400000 | 2.529 | 94.501 | 104.55 | 95.359 | 6.157 | 93.882 | 18.327 | 94.273 |
| 500000 | 10.155 | 94.479 | 32.61 | 95.337 | 23.489 | 93.860 | 22.093 | 94.251 |
| 600000 | 3.475 | 94.455 | 92.42 | 95.313 | 8.696 | 93.836 | 2.092 | 94.227 |
| 700000 | 11.124 | 94.430 | 20.64 | 95.288 | 26.035 | 93.811 | 5.872 | 94.202 |
| 800000 | 4.467 | 94.404 | 80.62 | 95.262 | 11.248 | 93.785 | 9.659 | 94.176 |
| 900000 | 12.140 | 94.376 | 9.02 | 95.234 | 28.592 | 93.757 | 13.454 | 94.148 |
| 1000000 | 5.508 | 94.346 | 69.18 | 95.204 | 13.811 | 93.727 | 17.255 | 94.118 |
| 1100000 | 13.207 | 94.314 | 129.42 | 95.172 | 31.162 | 93.695 | 21.064 | 94.086 |
| 1200000 | 6.600 | 94.279 | 58.09 | 95.137 | 16.387 | 93.660 | 1.106 | 94.051 |
| 1300000 | 0.007 | 94.241 | 118.53 | 95.099 | 1.616 | 93.622 | 4.931 | 94.013 |
| 1400000 | 7.745 | 94.200 | 47.39 | 95.058 | 18.976 | 93.581 | 8.763 | 93.972 |
| 1500000 | 1.178 | 94.154 | 108.02 | 95.012 | 4.212 | 93.535 | 12.603 | 93.926 |
| 1600000 | 8.943 | 94.103 | 37.08 | 94.961 | 21.579 | 93.484 | 16.452 | 93.875 |
| 1700000 | 2.405 | 94.045 | 97.91 | 94.903 | 6.821 | 93.426 | 20.308 | 93.817 |
| 1800000 | 10.198 | 93.978 | 27.17 | 94.836 | 24.194 | 93.359 | 0.399 | 93.750 |
| 1900000 | 3.688 | 93.899 | 88.20 | 94.757 | 9.444 | 93.280 | 4.273 | 93.671 |
| 2000000 | 11.511 | 93.802 | 17.67 | 94.660 | 26.824 | 93.183 | 8.155 | 93.574 |
| 2100000 | 5.031 | 93.677 | 78.93 | 94.535 | 12.081 | 93.058 | 12.046 | 93.449 |
| 2200000 | 12.883 | 93.501 | 8.61 | 94.359 | 29.469 | 92.882 | 15.947 | 93.273 |
| 2300000 | 6.434 | −93.200 | 70.09 | −94.058 | 14.733 | −92.581 | 19.856 | −92.972 |

# TABLE IV.

Constants of Epochs and Arguments for every Hundred Thousandth Day to 2300000.

| Day. | Arg. 24. | Log. 24'. | Arg. 25. | Log. 25'. | Arg. 26. | Log. 26'. | Arg. 27. | Log. 27'. |
|---|---|---|---|---|---|---|---|---|
| 0 | 9.555 | −94.547 | 2.427 | −94.248 | 3.825 | −94.156 | 0.44 | −94.788 |
| 100000 | 10.685 | 94.529 | 7.724 | 94.230 | 0.459 | 94.138 | 0.20 | 94.770 |
| 200000 | 11.825 | 94.509 | 3.660 | 94.210 | 2.919 | 94.118 | 25.80 | 94.750 |
| 300000 | 12.975 | 94.489 | 8.967 | 94.190 | 5.384 | 94.098 | 25.59 | 94.730 |
| 400000 | 0.859 | 94.468 | 4.913 | 94.169 | 2.030 | 94.077 | 25.40 | 94.709 |
| 500000 | 2.030 | 94.446 | 0.863 | 94.147 | 4.502 | 94.055 | 25.23 | 94.687 |
| 600000 | 3.211 | 94.422 | 6.186 | 94.123 | 1.157 | 94.031 | 25.08 | 94.663 |
| 700000 | 4.404 | 94.397 | 2.148 | 94.098 | 3.638 | 94.006 | 24.94 | 94.638 |
| 800000 | 5.607 | 94.371 | 7.482 | 94.072 | 0.302 | 93.980 | 24.82 | 94.612 |
| 900000 | 6.822 | 94.343 | 3.454 | 94.044 | 2.792 | 93.952 | 24.72 | 94.584 |
| 1000000 | 8.049 | 94.313 | 8.800 | 94.014 | 5.287 | 93.922 | 24.65 | 94.554 |
| 1100000 | 9.287 | 94.281 | 4.784 | 93.982 | 1.965 | 93.890 | 24.59 | 94.522 |
| 1200000 | 10.538 | 94.246 | 0.774 | 93.947 | 4.469 | 93.855 | 24.55 | 94.487 |
| 1300000 | 11.800 | 94.208 | 6.138 | 93.909 | 1.156 | 93.817 | 24.53 | 94.449 |
| 1400000 | 13.075 | 94.167 | 2.140 | 93.868 | 3.671 | 93.776 | 24.54 | 94.408 |
| 1500000 | 1.086 | 94.121 | 7.516 | 93.822 | 0.368 | 93.730 | 24.56 | 94.362 |
| 1600000 | 2.386 | 94.070 | 3.532 | 93.771 | 2.893 | 93.679 | 24.61 | 94.311 |
| 1700000 | 3.700 | 94.012 | 8.921 | 93.713 | 5.423 | 93.621 | 24.68 | 94.253 |
| 1800000 | 5.026 | 93.945 | 4.949 | 93.646 | 2.136 | 93.554 | 24.77 | 94.186 |
| 1900000 | 6.367 | 93.866 | 0.984 | 93.567 | 4.677 | 93.475 | 24.89 | 94.107 |
| 2000000 | 7.720 | 93.769 | 6.394 | 93.470 | 1.401 | 93.378 | 25.03 | 94.010 |
| 2100000 | 9.088 | 93.644 | 2.443 | 93.345 | 3.954 | 93.253 | 25.19 | 93.885 |
| 2200000 | 10.470 | 93.468 | 7.866 | 93.169 | 0.689 | 93.077 | 25.38 | 93.709 |
| 2300000 | 11.866 | −93.167 | 3.929 | −92.868 | 3.253 | −92.776 | 25.59 | −93.408 |

| Day. | Arg. 28. | Log. 28'. | Arg. 29. | Log. 29'. | Arg. 30. | Log. 30'. | Arg. 31. | Log. 31'. |
|---|---|---|---|---|---|---|---|---|
| 0 | 33.941 | −94.465 | 8.071 | −94.748 | 9.741 | +93.294 | 13.80 | +93.857 |
| 100000 | 31.030 | 94.447 | 12.988 | 94.730 | 2.861 | 93.276 | 10.70 | 93.839 |
| 200000 | 28.110 | 94.427 | 17.920 | 94.710 | 6.351 | 93.256 | 7.61 | 93.819 |
| 300000 | 25.182 | 94.407 | 22.869 | 94.690 | 9.841 | 93.236 | 4.51 | 93.799 |
| 400000 | 22.246 | 94.386 | 27.833 | 94.669 | 2.959 | 93.215 | 1.41 | 93.778 |
| 500000 | 19.301 | 94.364 | 0.051 | 94.647 | 6.447 | 93.193 | 13.62 | 93.756 |
| 600000 | 16.348 | 94.340 | 5.049 | 94.623 | 9.935 | 93.169 | 10.51 | 93.732 |
| 700000 | 13.385 | 94.315 | 10.064 | 94.598 | 3.051 | 93.144 | 7.40 | 93.707 |
| 800000 | 10.413 | 94.289 | 15.097 | 94.572 | 6.537 | 93.118 | 4.28 | 93.681 |
| 900000 | 7.432 | 94.261 | 20.148 | 94.544 | 10.023 | 93.090 | 1.17 | 93.653 |
| 1000000 | 4.442 | 94.231 | 25.217 | 94.514 | 3.138 | 93.060 | 13.36 | 93.623 |
| 1100000 | 1.442 | 94.199 | 30.304 | 94.482 | 6.622 | 93.028 | 10.24 | 93.591 |
| 1200000 | 36.954 | 94.164 | 2.647 | 94.447 | 10.106 | 92.993 | 7.11 | 93.556 |
| 1300000 | 33.934 | 94.126 | 7.773 | 94.409 | 3.218 | 92.955 | 3.98 | 93.518 |
| 1400000 | 30.904 | 94.085 | 12.919 | 94.368 | 6.700 | 92.914 | 0.85 | 93.477 |
| 1500000 | 27.863 | 94.039 | 18.084 | 94.322 | 10.182 | 92.868 | 13.03 | 93.431 |
| 1600000 | 24.812 | 93.988 | 23.270 | 94.271 | 3.292 | 92.817 | 9.90 | 93.380 |
| 1700000 | 21.750 | 93.930 | 28.476 | 94.213 | 6.772 | 92.759 | 6.75 | 93.322 |
| 1800000 | 18.677 | 93.863 | 0.940 | 94.146 | 10.252 | 92.692 | 3.61 | 93.255 |
| 1900000 | 15.593 | 93.784 | 6.189 | 94.067 | 3.360 | 92.613 | 0.46 | 93.176 |
| 2000000 | 12.498 | 93.687 | 11.459 | 93.970 | 6.838 | 92.516 | 12.63 | 93.079 |
| 2100000 | 9.391 | 93.562 | 16.751 | 93.845 | 10.315 | 92.391 | 9.48 | 92.954 |
| 2200000 | 6.272 | 93.386 | 22.066 | 93.669 | 3.420 | 92.215 | 6.32 | 92.778 |
| 2300000 | 3.142 | −93.085 | 27.403 | −93.368 | 6.896 | +91.914 | 3.16 | +92.477 |

# TABLE IV.

Constants of Epochs and Arguments for every Hundred Thousandth Day to 2300000.

| Day. | Arg. 32. | Log. 32′. | Arg. 33. | Log. 33′. | Arg. 34. | Log. 34′. | Arg. 35. | Log. 35′. |
|---|---|---|---|---|---|---|---|---|
| 0 | 12.55 | +94.405 | 17.07 | −94.635 | 5.54 | +94.314 | 20.52 | −94.501 |
| 100000 | 15.58 | 94.387 | 4.04 | 94.617 | 6.52 | 94.296 | 13.56 | 94.483 |
| 200000 | 1.97 | 94.367 | 23.47 | 94.597 | 7.49 | 94.276 | 6.61 | 94.463 |
| 300000 | 4.99 | 94.347 | 10.46 | 94.577 | 8.45 | 94.256 | 23.62 | 94.443 |
| 400000 | 7.99 | 94.326 | 29.91 | 94.556 | 9.41 | 94.235 | 16.69 | 94.422 |
| 500000 | 11.00 | 94.304 | 16.92 | 94.534 | 10.37 | 94.213 | 9.76 | 94.400 |
| 600000 | 13.99 | 94.280 | 3.95 | 94.510 | 11.31 | 94.189 | 2.85 | 94.376 |
| 700000 | 0.35 | 94.255 | 23.43 | 94.485 | 12.25 | 94.164 | 19.89 | 94.351 |
| 800000 | 3.33 | 94.229 | 10.48 | 94.459 | 13.18 | 94.138 | 13.00 | 94.325 |
| 900000 | 6.31 | 94.201 | 30.00 | 94.431 | 14.11 | 94.110 | 6.12 | 94.297 |
| 1000000 | 9.27 | 94.171 | 17.08 | 94.401 | 15.03 | 94.080 | 23.19 | 94.267 |
| 1100000 | 12.23 | 94.139 | 4.17 | 94.369 | 15.94 | 94.048 | 16.33 | 94.235 |
| 1200000 | 15.18 | 94.104 | 23.72 | 94.334 | 16.84 | 94.013 | 9.48 | 94.200 |
| 1300000 | 1.49 | 94.066 | 10.84 | 94.296 | 17.74 | 93.975 | 2.64 | 94.162 |
| 1400000 | 4.43 | 94.025 | 30.43 | 94.255 | 18.63 | 93.934 | 19.75 | 94.121 |
| 1500000 | 7.35 | 93.979 | 17.58 | 94.209 | 19.51 | 93.888 | 12.93 | 94.075 |
| 1600000 | 10.27 | 93.928 | 4.74 | 94.158 | 20.38 | 93.837 | 6.13 | 94.024 |
| 1700000 | 13.18 | 93.870 | 24.37 | 94.100 | 21.25 | 93.779 | 23.27 | 93.966 |
| 1800000 | 16.08 | 93.803 | 11.57 | 94.033 | 22.11 | 93.712 | 16.49 | 93.899 |
| 1900000 | 2.33 | 93.724 | 31.23 | 93.954 | 22.96 | 93.633 | 9.72 | 93.820 |
| 2000000 | 5.21 | 93.627 | 18.46 | 93.857 | 23.80 | 93.536 | 2.96 | 93.723 |
| 2100000 | 8.08 | 93.502 | 5.71 | 93.732 | 24.64 | 93.411 | 20.16 | 93.598 |
| 2200000 | 10.94 | 93.326 | 25.42 | 93.556 | 25.46 | 93.235 | 13.43 | 93.422 |
| 2300000 | 13.79 | +93.025 | 12.70 | −93.255 | 26.28 | +92.934 | 6.71 | −93.121 |

| Day. | Arg. 36. | Log. 36′. | Arg. 37. | Log. 37′. | Arg. 38. | Log. 38′. | Arg. 39. | Log. 39′. |
|---|---|---|---|---|---|---|---|---|
| 0 | 12.32 | −94.237 | 34.1 | +95.024 | 8.25 | −94.580 | 23.7 | −94.79 |
| 100000 | 2.01 | 94.219 | 26.8 | 95.006 | 14.02 | 94.562 | 11.6 | 94.77 |
| 200000 | 5.41 | 94.199 | 19.4 | 94.986 | 1.02 | 94.542 | 33.8 | 94.75 |
| 300000 | 8.83 | 94.179 | 12.0 | 94.966 | 6.81 | 94.522 | 21.6 | 94.73 |
| 400000 | 12.25 | 94.158 | 4.6 | 94.945 | 12.62 | 94.501 | 9.3 | 94.71 |
| 500000 | 1.96 | 94.136 | 34.7 | 94.923 | 18.44 | 94.479 | 31.5 | 94.69 |
| 600000 | 5.39 | 94.112 | 27.3 | 94.899 | 5.48 | 94.455 | 19.2 | 94.66 |
| 700000 | 8.84 | 94.087 | 19.8 | 94.874 | 11.32 | 94.430 | 6.9 | 94.64 |
| 800000 | 12.29 | 94.061 | 12.2 | 94.848 | 17.18 | 94.404 | 29.0 | 94.61 |
| 900000 | 2.03 | 94.033 | 4.7 | 94.820 | 4.26 | 94.376 | 16.6 | 94.58 |
| 1000000 | 5.49 | 94.003 | 34.7 | 94.790 | 10.14 | 94.346 | 4.2 | 94.55 |
| 1100000 | 8.96 | 93.971 | 27.1 | 94.758 | 16.03 | 94.314 | 26.2 | 94.52 |
| 1200000 | 12.45 | 93.936 | 19.4 | 94.723 | 3.15 | 94.279 | 13.7 | 94.49 |
| 1300000 | 2.22 | 93.898 | 11.7 | 94.685 | 9.07 | 94.241 | 1.3 | 94.45 |
| 1400000 | 5.71 | 93.857 | 4.0 | 94.644 | 15.01 | 94.200 | 23.2 | 94.41 |
| 1500000 | 9.22 | 93.811 | 33.9 | 94.598 | 2.17 | 94.154 | 10.7 | 94.36 |
| 1600000 | 12.73 | 93.760 | 26.1 | 94.547 | 8.13 | 94.103 | 32.6 | 94.31 |
| 1700000 | 2.54 | 93.702 | 18.3 | 94.489 | 14.11 | 94.045 | 20.0 | 94.25 |
| 1800000 | 6.07 | 93.635 | 10.4 | 94.422 | 1.31 | 93.978 | 7.3 | 94.19 |
| 1900000 | 9.61 | 93.556 | 2.5 | 94.343 | 7.32 | 93.899 | 29.2 | 94.11 |
| 2000000 | 13.16 | 93.459 | 32.2 | 94.246 | 13.34 | 93.802 | 16.5 | 94.01 |
| 2100000 | 2.99 | 93.334 | 24.2 | 94.121 | 0.59 | 93.677 | 3.8 | 93.89 |
| 2200000 | 6.56 | 93.158 | 16.2 | 93.945 | 6.64 | 93.501 | 25.5 | 93.71 |
| 2300000 | 10.13 | −92.857 | 8.1 | +93.644 | 12.71 | −93.200 | 12.8 | −93.41 |

# TABLE IV.

Constants of Epochs and Arguments for every Hundred Thousandth Day to 2300000.

| Day. | Arg. **40.** | Log. **40′.** | Arg. **41.** | Log. **41′.** | Arg. **42.** | Log. **42′.** | Arg. **43.** | Log. **43′.** |
|---|---|---|---|---|---|---|---|---|
| 0 | 3.48 | +94.63 | 9.23 | +94.61 | 2.57 | −94.28 | 13.05 | −94.37 |
| 100000 | 1.13 | 94.61 | 3.02 | 94.59 | 4.93 | 94.26 | 6.96 | 94.35 |
| 200000 | 17.62 | 94.59 | 14.71 | 94.57 | 7.29 | 94.24 | 0.88 | 94.33 |
| 300000 | 15.25 | 94.57 | 8.48 | 94.55 | 9.66 | 94.22 | 9.35 | 94.31 |
| 400000 | 12.86 | 94.55 | 2.23 | 94.53 | 1.88 | 94.20 | 3.28 | 94.29 |
| 500000 | 10.47 | 94.53 | 13.89 | 94.51 | 4.26 | 94.18 | 11.76 | 94.27 |
| 600000 | 8.06 | 94.51 | 7.62 | 94.49 | 6.65 | 94.16 | 5.71 | 94.25 |
| 700000 | 5.64 | 94.48 | 1.34 | 94.46 | 9.04 | 94.13 | 14.20 | 94.22 |
| 800000 | 3.21 | 94.45 | 12.97 | 94.43 | 1.29 | 94.10 | 8.17 | 94.19 |
| 900000 | 0.77 | 94.43 | 6.66 | 94.41 | 3.69 | 94.08 | 2.14 | 94.17 |
| 1000000 | 17.15 | 94.40 | 0.34 | 94.38 | 6.10 | 94.05 | 10.66 | 94.14 |
| 1100000 | 14.68 | 94.36 | 11.93 | 94.34 | 8.52 | 94.01 | 4.65 | 94.10 |
| 1200000 | 12.19 | 94.33 | 5.59 | 94.31 | 0.80 | 93.98 | 13.18 | 94.07 |
| 1300000 | 9.69 | 94.29 | 17.15 | 94.27 | 3.23 | 93.94 | 7.19 | 94.03 |
| 1400000 | 7.18 | 94.25 | 10.78 | 94.23 | 5.66 | 93.90 | 1.20 | 93.99 |
| 1500000 | 4.65 | 94.20 | 4.39 | 94.18 | 8.11 | 93.85 | 9.77 | 93.94 |
| 1600000 | 2.10 | 94.15 | 15.91 | 94.13 | 0.41 | 93.80 | 3.80 | 93.89 |
| 1700000 | 18.38 | 94.10 | 9.50 | 94.08 | 2.87 | 93.75 | 12.38 | 93.84 |
| 1800000 | 15.81 | 94.03 | 3.07 | 94.01 | 5.34 | 93.68 | 6.43 | 93.77 |
| 1900000 | 13.22 | 93.95 | 14.54 | 93.93 | 7.81 | 93.60 | 0.49 | 93.69 |
| 2000000 | 10.61 | 93.85 | 8.08 | 93.83 | 0.15 | 93.50 | 9.09 | 93.59 |
| 2100000 | 7.98 | 93.73 | 1.61 | 93.71 | 2.63 | 93.38 | 3.17 | 93.47 |
| 2200000 | 5.34 | 93.55 | 13.03 | 93.53 | 5.13 | 93.20 | 11.80 | 93.29 |
| 2300000 | 2.68 | +93.25 | 6.53 | +93.23 | 7.64 | −92.90 | 5.89 | −93.99 |

| Day. | Arg. **44.** | Arg. **45.** | Arg. **46.** | Arg. **47.** | Arg. **48.** | Log. **48′.** | Arg. **49.** | Arg. **50.** |
|---|---|---|---|---|---|---|---|---|
| 0 | 4.8 | 8.93 | 3.6 | 4.93 | 6.86 | −94.66 | 5.5 | 19.8 |
| 100000 | 18.5 | 11.33 | 24.1 | 2.95 | 26.36 | 94.64 | 9.4 | 1.3 |
| 200000 | 9.4 | 13.74 | 15.7 | 0.97 | 15.95 | 94.62 | 0.5 | 7.9 |
| 300000 | 0.3 | 16.15 | 7.2 | 13.12 | 5.54 | 94.60 | 4.4 | 14.5 |
| 400000 | 14.1 | 1.67 | 27.7 | 11.13 | 25.09 | 94.58 | 8.3 | 21.1 |
| 500000 | 5.1 | 4.09 | 19.2 | 9.15 | 14.71 | 94.56 | 12.3 | 2.6 |
| 600000 | 18.9 | 6.51 | 10.7 | 7.17 | 4.35 | 94.54 | 3.5 | 9.2 |
| 700000 | 10.0 | 8.93 | 2.2 | 5.20 | 23.93 | 94.51 | 7.4 | 15.7 |
| 800000 | 1.1 | 11.36 | 22.6 | 3.22 | 13.59 | 94.48 | 11.4 | 22.3 |
| 900000 | 15.1 | 13.79 | 14.1 | 1.24 | 3.27 | 94.46 | 2.6 | 3.8 |
| 1000000 | 6.2 | 16.22 | 5.5 | 13.40 | 22.89 | 94.43 | 6.6 | 10.3 |
| 1100000 | 20.2 | 1.76 | 25.9 | 11.43 | 12.60 | 94.39 | 10.6 | 16.8 |
| 1200000 | 11.5 | 4.20 | 17.3 | 9.45 | 2.32 | 94.36 | 1.9 | 23.3 |
| 1300000 | 2.7 | 6.64 | 8.7 | 7.48 | 21.99 | 94.33 | 5.9 | 4.7 |
| 1400000 | 16.8 | 9.09 | 0.1 | 5.52 | 11.74 | 94.28 | 10.0 | 11.2 |
| 1500000 | 8.2 | 11.54 | 20.4 | 3.54 | 1.51 | 94.23 | 1.2 | 17.6 |
| 1600000 | 22.3 | 14.00 | 11.8 | 1.57 | 21.23 | 94.18 | 5.3 | 24.0 |
| 1700000 | 13.7 | 16.46 | 3.1 | 13.74 | 11.03 | 94.13 | 9.4 | 5.4 |
| 1800000 | 5.2 | 2.02 | 23.4 | 11.77 | 0.85 | 94.06 | 0.7 | 11.8 |
| 1900000 | 19.4 | 4.49 | 14.7 | 9.81 | 20.62 | 93.98 | 4.8 | 18.2 |
| 2000000 | 10.9 | 6.96 | 6.0 | 7.84 | 10.47 | 93.88 | 8.9 | 24.6 |
| 2100000 | 2.4 | 9.44 | 26.3 | 5.88 | 0.34 | 93.76 | 0.3 | 6.0 |
| 2200000 | 16.8 | 11.92 | 17.5 | 3.92 | 20.17 | 93.58 | 4.4 | 12.3 |
| 2300000 | 8.4 | 14.41 | 8.8 | 1.96 | 10.07 | −93.28 | 8.6 | 18.7 |

# TABLE IV.

Constants of Epochs and Arguments for every Hundred Thousandth Day to 2300000.

| Day. | Arg. **51.** | Log. **51′.** | Arg. **52.** | Arg. **53.** | Log. **53′.** | Arg. **54.** | Arg. **55.** | Arg. **56.** |
|---|---|---|---|---|---|---|---|---|
| 0 | 7.90 | −94.13 | 7.92 | 32.88 | +94.650 | 1.05 | 5.90 | 0.11 |
| 100000 | 15.10 | 94.11 | 16.01 | 7.18 | 94.632 | 12.27 | 4.85 | 5.56 |
| 200000 | 4.10 | 94.09 | 24.10 | 99.01 | 94.612 | 8.42 | 3.79 | 11.01 |
| 300000 | 11.32 | 94.07 | 6.96 | 73.29 | 94.592 | 4.58 | 2.74 | 3.35 |
| 400000 | 0.33 | 94.05 | 15.05 | 47.56 | 94.571 | 0.74 | 1.68 | 8.80 |
| 500000 | 7.56 | 94.03 | 23.14 | 21.82 | 94.549 | 11.97 | 0.62 | 1.13 |
| 600000 | 14.79 | 94.01 | 5.99 | 113.60 | 94.525 | 8.14 | 19.19 | 6.59 |
| 700000 | 3.81 | 93.98 | 14.08 | 87.82 | 94.500 | 4.31 | 18.13 | 12.05 |
| 800000 | 11.05 | 93.95 | 22.16 | 62.04 | 94.474 | 0.48 | 17.07 | 4.38 |
| 900000 | 18.29 | 93.93 | 5.02 | 36.24 | 94.446 | 11.72 | 16.01 | 9.84 |
| 1000000 | 7.32 | 93.90 | 13.10 | 10.43 | 94.416 | 7.90 | 14.95 | 2.18 |
| 1100000 | 14.58 | 93.86 | 21.18 | 102.14 | 94.384 | 4.09 | 13.89 | 7.64 |
| 1200000 | 3.62 | 93.83 | 4.03 | 76.30 | 94.349 | 0.27 | 12.82 | 13.10 |
| 1300000 | 10.88 | 93.79 | 12.11 | 50.44 | 94.311 | 11.53 | 11.76 | 5.45 |
| 1400000 | 18.15 | 93.75 | 20.19 | 24.57 | 94.270 | 7.73 | 10.69 | 10.91 |
| 1500000 | 7.20 | 93.70 | 3.04 | 116.22 | 94.224 | 3.93 | 9.63 | 3.25 |
| 1600000 | 14.48 | 93.65 | 11.11 | 90.31 | 94.173 | 0.13 | 8.56 | 8.72 |
| 1700000 | 3.54 | 93.60 | 19.19 | 64.39 | 94.115 | 11.40 | 7.49 | 1.07 |
| 1800000 | 10.83 | 93.53 | 2.03 | 38.45 | 94.048 | 7.61 | 6.43 | 6.53 |
| 1900000 | 18.12 | 93.45 | 10.11 | 12.50 | 93.969 | 3.82 | 5.36 | 12.00 |
| 2000000 | 7.20 | 93.35 | 18.18 | 104.07 | 93.872 | 0.04 | 4.29 | 4.35 |
| 2100000 | 14.50 | 93.23 | 1.02 | 78.08 | 93.747 | 11.32 | 3.22 | 9.82 |
| 2200000 | 3.58 | 93.05 | 9.09 | 52.07 | 93.571 | 7.55 | 2.15 | 2.17 |
| 2300000 | 10.90 | −92.75 | 17.16 | 26.04 | +93.270 | 3.77 | 1.07 | 7.65 |

| Day. | Arg. **57.** | Arg. **58.** | Arg. **59.** | Arg. **60.** | Arg. **61.** | Arg. **62.** | Arg. **63.** | Arg. **64.** |
|---|---|---|---|---|---|---|---|---|
| 0 | 0.44 | 6.20 | 23.11 | 10.63 | 9.27 | 1.09 | 10.05 | 32.84 |
| 100000 | 12.37 | 2.23 | 2.72 | 9.17 | 4.33 | 4.63 | 9.04 | 10.25 |
| 200000 | 7.31 | 13.48 | 21.29 | 7.72 | 13.01 | 8.17 | 8.03 | 23.68 |
| 300000 | 2.27 | 9.49 | 0.89 | 6.28 | 8.07 | 11.72 | 7.02 | 1.12 |
| 400000 | 14.21 | 5.49 | 19.45 | 4.84 | 3.14 | 0.82 | 6.01 | 14.58 |
| 500000 | 9.18 | 1.49 | 38.00 | 3.41 | 11.82 | 4.37 | 5.01 | 28.05 |
| 600000 | 4.15 | 12.72 | 17.59 | 1.99 | 6.89 | 7.92 | 4.01 | 5.55 |
| 700000 | 16.11 | 8.69 | 36.14 | 0.57 | 1.96 | 11.47 | 3.01 | 19.06 |
| 800000 | 11.10 | 4.66 | 15.72 | 21.49 | 10.64 | 0.58 | 2.01 | 32.59 |
| 900000 | 6.09 | 0.63 | 34.26 | 20.09 | 5.72 | 4.14 | 1.01 | 10.15 |
| 1000000 | 1.10 | 11.82 | 13.83 | 18.69 | 0.79 | 7.70 | 0.02 | 23.72 |
| 1100000 | 13.09 | 7.77 | 32.36 | 17.31 | 9.48 | 11.26 | 12.66 | 1.31 |
| 1200000 | 8.11 | 3.71 | 11.92 | 15.93 | 4.55 | 0.38 | 11.68 | 14.92 |
| 1300000 | 3.14 | 14.88 | 30.43 | 14.56 | 13.24 | 3.95 | 10.69 | 28.55 |
| 1400000 | 15.16 | 10.80 | 9.98 | 13.19 | 8.32 | 7.52 | 9.71 | 6.21 |
| 1500000 | 10.20 | 6.71 | 28.49 | 11.84 | 3.40 | 11.09 | 8.73 | 19.88 |
| 1600000 | 5.26 | 2.61 | 8.03 | 10.49 | 12.09 | 0.22 | 7.75 | 33.58 |
| 1700000 | 0.32 | 13.75 | 26.53 | 9.15 | 7.17 | 3.79 | 6.77 | 11.30 |
| 1800000 | 12.37 | 9.64 | 6.06 | 7.82 | 2.26 | 7.37 | 5.80 | 25.04 |
| 1900000 | 7.46 | 5.51 | 24.55 | 6.49 | 10.95 | 10.95 | 4.83 | 2.81 |
| 2000000 | 2.55 | 1.38 | 4.06 | 5.18 | 6.04 | 0.09 | 3.86 | 16.60 |
| 2100000 | 14.64 | 12.48 | 22.54 | 3.87 | 1.12 | 3.67 | 2.89 | 30.41 |
| 2200000 | 9.75 | 8.33 | 2.04 | 2.57 | 9.82 | 7.26 | 1.92 | 8.26 |
| 2300000 | 4.87 | 4.17 | 20.51 | 1.28 | 4.91 | 10.85 | 0.96 | 22.11 |

# TABLE IV.

Constants of Epochs and Arguments for every Hundred Thousandth Day to 2300000.

| Day. | Arg. **65.** | Arg. **66.** | Arg. **67.** | Log. **67′.** | Arg. **68.** | Log. **68′.** | Arg. **69.** | Log. **69′.** |
|---|---|---|---|---|---|---|---|---|
| 0 | 6.08 | 15.4 | 3.97 | −94.483 | 6.58 | −94.630 | 151.6 | −95.993 |
| 100000 | 13.62 | 26.5 | 0.26 | 94.465 | 18.84 | 94.612 | 102.3 | 95.975 |
| 200000 | 6.69 | 2.0 | 24.01 | 94.445 | 3.43 | 94.592 | 53.3 | 95.955 |
| 300000 | 14.24 | 13.2 | 20.32 | 94.425 | 15.71 | 94.572 | 4.6 | 95.935 |
| 400000 | 7.32 | 24.3 | 16.63 | 94.404 | 0.33 | 94.551 | 428.0 | 95.914 |
| 500000 | 0.41 | 35.5 | 12.97 | 94.382 | 12.63 | 94.529 | 379.8 | 95.892 |
| 600000 | 7.97 | 11.0 | 9.30 | 94.358 | 24.94 | 94.505 | 332.0 | 95.868 |
| 700000 | 1.06 | 22.2 | 5.65 | 94.333 | 9.60 | 94.480 | 284.4 | 95.843 |
| 800000 | 8.63 | 33.4 | 2.00 | 94.307 | 21.94 | 94.454 | 237.2 | 95.817 |
| 900000 | 1.73 | 9.0 | 25.81 | 94.279 | 6.62 | 94.426 | 190.2 | 95.789 |
| 1000000 | 9.30 | 20.2 | 22.19 | 94.249 | 18.99 | 94.396 | 143.6 | 95.759 |
| 1100000 | 2.41 | 31.4 | 18.57 | 94.217 | 3.70 | 94.364 | 97.3 | 95.727 |
| 1200000 | 10.00 | 7.0 | 14.96 | 94.182 | 16.09 | 94.329 | 51.4 | 95.692 |
| 1300000 | 3.11 | 18.2 | 11.37 | 94.144 | 0.83 | 94.291 | 5.8 | 95.654 |
| 1400000 | 10.70 | 29.5 | 7.78 | 94.103 | 13.25 | 94.250 | 432.4 | 95.613 |
| 1500000 | 3.83 | 5.1 | 4.21 | 94.057 | 25.69 | 94.204 | 387.5 | 95.567 |
| 1600000 | 11.43 | 16.4 | 0.65 | 94.006 | 10.47 | 94.153 | 342.9 | 95.516 |
| 1700000 | 4.56 | 27.6 | 24.54 | 93.948 | 22.94 | 94.095 | 298.7 | 95.458 |
| 1800000 | 12.16 | 3.3 | 21.00 | 93.881 | 7.75 | 94.028 | 254.9 | 95.391 |
| 1900000 | 5.30 | 14.6 | 17.47 | 93.802 | 20.25 | 93.949 | 211.4 | 95.312 |
| 2000000 | 12.92 | 25.9 | 13.95 | 93.705 | 5.10 | 93.852 | 168.4 | 95.215 |
| 2100000 | 6.06 | 1.6 | 10.44 | 93.580 | 17.63 | 93.727 | 125.7 | 95.090 |
| 2200000 | 13.69 | 12.9 | 6.95 | 93.404 | 2.52 | 93.551 | 83.4 | 94.914 |
| 2300000 | 6.84 | 24.3 | 3.47 | −93.103 | 15.08 | −93.250 | 41.5 | −94.613 |

| Day. | Arg. **70.** | Log. **70′.** | Arg. **71.** | Arg. **72.** | Arg. **73.** | Log. **73′.** | Arg. **74.** | Log. **74′.** |
|---|---|---|---|---|---|---|---|---|
| 0 | 228.4 | −95.096 | 500.3 | 85.6 | 320.3 | +96.432 | 1633 | +96.526 |
| 100000 | 300.9 | 95.078 | 65.8 | 364.6 | 1777.3 | 96.414 | 1443 | 96.508 |
| 200000 | 43.5 | 95.058 | 215.3 | 244.7 | 1043.1 | 96.394 | 1252 | 96.488 |
| 300000 | 116.2 | 95.038 | 364.7 | 124.8 | 308.2 | 96.374 | 1060 | 96.468 |
| 400000 | 188.8 | 95.017 | 514.2 | 4.9 | 1762.9 | 96.353 | 866 | 96.447 |
| 500000 | 261.4 | 94.995 | 79.8 | 283.8 | 1026.3 | 96.331 | 672 | 96.425 |
| 600000 | 4.3 | 94.971 | 229.2 | 163.9 | 289.0 | 96.307 | 477 | 96.401 |
| 700000 | 77.0 | 94.946 | 378.7 | 44.0 | 1741.2 | 96.282 | 281 | 96.376 |
| 800000 | 149.7 | 94.920 | 528.1 | 323.0 | 1002.1 | 96.256 | 84 | 96.350 |
| 900000 | 222.5 | 94.892 | 93.7 | 203.1 | 262.2 | 96.228 | 3119 | 96.322 |
| 1000000 | 295.3 | 94.862 | 243.2 | 83.2 | 1711.8 | 96.198 | 2919 | 96.292 |
| 1100000 | 38.4 | 94.830 | 392.6 | 362.2 | 970.1 | 96.166 | 2719 | 96.260 |
| 1200000 | 111.3 | 94.795 | 542.1 | 242.2 | 227.5 | 96.131 | 2517 | 96.225 |
| 1300000 | 184.2 | 94.757 | 107.6 | 122.3 | 1674.3 | 96.093 | 2314 | 96.187 |
| 1400000 | 257.2 | 94.716 | 257.1 | 2.4 | 929.8 | 96.052 | 2110 | 96.146 |
| 1500000 | 0.4 | 94.670 | 406.6 | 281.4 | 184.3 | 96.006 | 1905 | 96.100 |
| 1600000 | 73.4 | 94.619 | 556.0 | 161.5 | 1628.2 | 95.955 | 1698 | 96.049 |
| 1700000 | 146.5 | 94.561 | 121.0 | 41.6 | 880.8 | 95.897 | 1491 | 95.991 |
| 1800000 | 219.7 | 94.494 | 271.0 | 320.6 | 132.3 | 95.830 | 1282 | 95.924 |
| 1900000 | 292.9 | 94.415 | 420.5 | 200.7 | 1573.2 | 95.751 | 1071 | 95.845 |
| 2000000 | 36.3 | 94.318 | 570.0 | 80.7 | 822.6 | 95.654 | 860 | 95.748 |
| 2100000 | 109.6 | 94.193 | 135.5 | 359.7 | 71.0 | 95.529 | 647 | 95.623 |
| 2200000 | 183.0 | 94.017 | 285.0 | 239.8 | 1508.7 | 95.353 | 433 | 95.447 |
| 2300000 | 256.3 | −93.716 | 434.5 | 119.9 | 754.9 | +95.052 | 217 | +95.146 |

# TABLE IV.

Constants of Epochs and Arguments for every Hundred Thousandth Day to 2300000.

| Day. | Arg. **75.** | Arg. **76.** | Arg. **78.** | Log. **78′.** | Arg. **79.** | Arg. **80.** | Arg. **81.** | Log. **81′.** |
|---|---|---|---|---|---|---|---|---|
| 0 | 57844 | 69646 | 150.567 | −95.206 | 81.9 | 149.2 | 16.37 | −95.025 |
| 100000 | 73091 | 75172 | 26.076 | 95.188 | 131.3 | 288.0 | 30.83 | 95.007 |
| 200000 | 3584 | 80662 | 89.831 | 95.168 | 180.7 | 113.6 | 45.32 | 94.987 |
| 300000 | 18831 | 86117 | 153.631 | 95.148 | 230.4 | 252.1 | 59.83 | 94.967 |
| 400000 | 34078 | 91534 | 29.276 | 95.127 | 280.2 | 77.4 | 74.38 | 94.946 |
| 500000 | 49325 | 1424 | 93.169 | 95.105 | 330.2 | 215.7 | 88.96 | 94.924 |
| 600000 | 64571 | 6766 | 157.111 | 95.081 | 380.3 | 40.8 | 103.57 | 94.900 |
| 700000 | 79818 | 12069 | 32.899 | 95.056 | 430.6 | 178.9 | 118.21 | 94.875 |
| 800000 | 10312 | 17332 | 96.940 | 95.030 | 42.8 | 3.7 | 8.67 | 94.849 |
| 900000 | 25558 | 22554 | 161.031 | 95.002 | 93.4 | 141.5 | 23.38 | 94.821 |
| 1000000 | 40805 | 27735 | 36.973 | 94.972 | 144.3 | 279.2 | 38.12 | 94.791 |
| 1100000 | 56052 | 32874 | 101.170 | 94.940 | 195.3 | 103.6 | 52.89 | 94.759 |
| 1200000 | 71299 | 37969 | 165.420 | 94.905 | 246.5 | 241.0 | 67.70 | 94.724 |
| 1300000 | 1792 | 43021 | 41.525 | 94.867 | 297.9 | 65.2 | 82.55 | 94.686 |
| 1400000 | 17039 | 48029 | 105.886 | 94.826 | 349.5 | 202.3 | 97.43 | 94.645 |
| 1500000 | 32286 | 52991 | 170.305 | 94.780 | 401.3 | 26.2 | 112.35 | 94.599 |
| 1600000 | 47532 | 57908 | 46.580 | 94.729 | 15.0 | 163.0 | 3.10 | 94.547 |
| 1700000 | 62779 | 62777 | 111.116 | 94.671 | 67.1 | 299.7 | 18.09 | 94.490 |
| 1800000 | 78026 | 67599 | 175.712 | 94.604 | 119.5 | 123.2 | 33.13 | 94.423 |
| 1900000 | 8519 | 72373 | 52.167 | 94.525 | 172.1 | 259.6 | 48.20 | 94.344 |
| 2000000 | 23766 | 77098 | 116.887 | 94.428 | 225.0 | 82.7 | 63.32 | 94.247 |
| 2100000 | 39013 | 81773 | 181.669 | 94.303 | 278.0 | 218.8 | 78.48 | 94.122 |
| 2200000 | 54260 | 86397 | 58.313 | 94.127 | 331.2 | 41.7 | 93.68 | 93.946 |
| 2300000 | 69506 | 90969 | 123.224 | −93.826 | 384.7 | 177.4 | 108.92 | −93.645 |

| Day. | Arg. **82.** | Arg. **83.** | Arg. **84.** | Arg. **85.** | Arg. **86.** | Arg. **87.** | Arg. **88.** | Arg. **89.** | Arg. **90.** |
|---|---|---|---|---|---|---|---|---|---|
| 0 | 8.720 | 28.58 | 9.80 | 6.63 | 28.32 | 8.97 | 12.82 | 1.48 | 12.4 |
| 100000 | 8.256 | 38.75 | 4.57 | 2.47 | 33.75 | 11.51 | 2.55 | 2.92 | 6.4 |
| 200000 | 7.801 | 9.72 | 18.50 | 21.82 | 0.87 | 14.05 | 6.95 | 4.37 | 0.5 |
| 300000 | 7.353 | 19.91 | 13.28 | 17.65 | 6.26 | 2.38 | 11.34 | 5.82 | 26.8 |
| 400000 | 6.913 | 30.10 | 8.06 | 13.48 | 11.64 | 4.93 | 1.06 | 7.29 | 20.9 |
| 500000 | 6.480 | 1.08 | 2.85 | 9.31 | 16.99 | 7.48 | 5.45 | 8.76 | 14.9 |
| 600000 | 6.056 | 11.29 | 16.78 | 5.13 | 22.33 | 10.04 | 9.83 | 10.24 | 9.0 |
| 700000 | 5.641 | 21.50 | 11.57 | 0.95 | 27.65 | 12 60 | 14.21 | 11.73 | 3.0 |
| 800000 | 5.233 | 31.71 | 6.37 | 20.28 | 32.95 | 0.95 | 3.91 | 13.23 | 29.4 |
| 900000 | 4.835 | 2.72 | 1.16 | 16.10 | 38.24 | 3.52 | 8.28 | 14.74 | 23.5 |
| 1000000 | 4.445 | 12.95 | 15.11 | 11.91 | 5.21 | 6.09 | 12.65 | 16.25 | 17.6 |
| 1100000 | 4.064 | 23.18 | 9.91 | 7.71 | 10.45 | 8.67 | 2.34 | 17.78 | 11.7 |
| 1200000 | 3.692 | 33.42 | 4.71 | 3.52 | 15.67 | 11.25 | 6.70 | 0.01 | 5.8 |
| 1300000 | 3.330 | 4.46 | 18.66 | 22.84 | 20.87 | 13.84 | 11.05 | 1.55 | 32.2 |
| 1400000 | 2.977 | 14.71 | 13.47 | 18.64 | 26.05 | 2.22 | 0.73 | 3.11 | 26.3 |
| 1500000 | 2.633 | 24.97 | 8.28 | 14.44 | 31.21 | 4.82 | 5.08 | 4.68 | 20.4 |
| 1600000 | 2 300 | 35.24 | 3.10 | 10.23 | 36.34 | 7.42 | 9.42 | 6.26 | 14.5 |
| 1700000 | 1.976 | 6.30 | 17.06 | 6.02 | 3.17 | 10.02 | 13.75 | 7.85 | 8.6 |
| 1800000 | 1.662 | 16.58 | 11.88 | 1.81 | 8.26 | 12.63 | 3.42 | 9.45 | 2.8 |
| 1900000 | 1.359 | 26.87 | 6.70 | 21.12 | 13.32 | 1.04 | 7.75 | 11.07 | 29.2 |
| 2000000 | 1.065 | 37.17 | 1.53 | 16.90 | 18.36 | 3.66 | 12.07 | 12.69 | 23.4 |
| 2100000 | 0.783 | 8.26 | 15.50 | 12.67 | 23.38 | 6.29 | 1.73 | 14.33 | 17.5 |
| 2200000 | 0.511 | 18.57 | 10.33 | 8.45 | 28.37 | 8.93 | 6.05 | 15.98 | 11.7 |
| 2300000 | 0.250 | 28.89 | 5.16 | 4.23 | 33.34 | 11.56 | 10.36 | 17.64 | 5.8 |

# TABLE Va.

ARGUMENT 75.

| Days. | ARG. 1. | | 2. | | 3. | | 6. | 7. | 8. | 9. | 10. | 11. | 13. | Days. |
|---|---|---|---|---|---|---|---|---|---|---|---|---|---|---|
| | Correction of Arguments | | | | | | | | | | | | | |
| d. | 0.000 | Diff. | 0.00 | Diff. | 0.00 | Diff. | 0.00 | 0.00 | 0.00 | 0.00 | 0.00 | 0.00 | 0.00 | d. |
| 0 | 0834 | 186 | 0119 | 21 | 0084 | 20 | 01 | 01 | 01 | 00 | 01 | 01 | 00 | 100000 |
| 1000 | 0648 | 160 | 0098 | 18 | 0064 | 17 | 01 | 01 | 01 | 00 | 01 | 01 | 00 | 99000 |
| 2000 | 0488 | 135 | 0080 | 16 | 0047 | 15 | 01 | 01 | 01 | 00 | 01 | 01 | 00 | 98000 |
| 3000 | 0353 | 109 | 0064 | 13 | 0032 | 12 | 00 | 00 | 00 | 00 | 00 | 00 | 00 | 97000 |
| 4000 | 0244 | 83 | 0051 | 10 | 0020 | 9 | 00 | 00 | 00 | 00 | 00 | 00 | 00 | 96000 |
| 5000 | 0161 | 56 | 0041 | 7 | 0011 | 6 | 00 | 00 | 00 | 00 | 00 | 00 | 00 | 95000 |
| 6000 | 0105 | 30 | 0034 | 4 | 0005 | 3 | 00 | 00 | 00 | 00 | 00 | 00 | 00 | 94000 |
| 7000 | 0075 | 4 | 0030 | 0 | 0002 | 0 | 00 | 00 | 00 | 00 | 00 | 00 | 00 | 93000 |
| 8000 | 0071 | 22 | 0030 | 3 | 0002 | 2 | 00 | 00 | 00 | 00 | 00 | 00 | 00 | 92000 |
| 9000 | 0093 | 48 | 0033 | 6 | 0004 | 5 | 00 | 00 | 00 | 00 | 00 | 00 | 00 | 91000 |
| 10000 | 0141 | 77 | 0039 | 9 | 0009 | 8 | 00 | 00 | 00 | 00 | 00 | 00 | 00 | 90000 |
| 11000 | 0218 | 103 | 0048 | 12 | 0017 | 11 | 00 | 00 | 00 | 00 | 00 | 00 | 00 | 89000 |
| 12000 | 0321 | 129 | 0060 | 15 | 0028 | 14 | 00 | 00 | 00 | 00 | 00 | 00 | 00 | 88000 |
| 13000 | 0450 | 155 | 0075 | 18 | 0042 | 17 | 01 | 00 | 01 | 00 | 01 | 01 | 00 | 87000 |
| 14000 | 0605 | 181 | 0093 | 21 | 0059 | 19 | 01 | 00 | 01 | 00 | 01 | 01 | 00 | 86000 |
| 15000 | 0786 | 202 | 0114 | 23 | 0078 | 21 | 01 | 00 | 01 | 00 | 01 | 01 | 00 | 85000 |
| 16000 | 0988 | 223 | 0137 | 26 | 0099 | 23 | 01 | 00 | 01 | 01 | 01 | 01 | 00 | 84000 |
| 17000 | 1211 | 244 | 0163 | 28 | 0122 | 26 | 01 | 00 | 01 | 01 | 01 | 01 | 00 | 83000 |
| 18000 | 1455 | 265 | 0191 | 30 | 0148 | 29 | 02 | 01 | 01 | 01 | 01 | 02 | 01 | 82000 |
| 19000 | 1720 | 282 | 0221 | 33 | 0177 | 32 | 02 | 01 | 01 | 02 | 02 | 02 | 01 | 81000 |
| 20000 | 2002 | 298 | 0254 | 35 | 0209 | 33 | 02 | 01 | 01 | 02 | 02 | 02 | 01 | 80000 |
| 21000 | 2300 | 313 | 0289 | 36 | 0242 | 34 | 02 | 01 | 01 | 02 | 02 | 02 | 01 | 79000 |
| 22000 | 2613 | 326 | 0325 | 38 | 0276 | 35 | 03 | 01 | 01 | 03 | 03 | 03 | 01 | 78000 |
| 23000 | 2939 | 337 | 0363 | 39 | 0311 | 35 | 03 | 01 | 02 | 03 | 03 | 03 | 01 | 77000 |
| 24000 | 3276 | 348 | 0402 | 39 | 0346 | 36 | 03 | 01 | 02 | 04 | 03 | 03 | 01 | 76000 |
| 25000 | 3624 | 355 | 0441 | 40 | 0382 | 37 | 04 | 01 | 02 | 04 | 04 | 04 | 01 | 75000 |
| 26000 | 3979 | 360 | 0481 | 41 | 0419 | 38 | 04 | 01 | 02 | 04 | 04 | 04 | 01 | 74000 |
| 27000 | 4339 | 363 | 0522 | 42 | 0457 | 39 | 05 | 01 | 02 | 04 | 04 | 04 | 02 | 73000 |
| 28000 | 4702 | 365 | 0564 | 43 | 0496 | 40 | 05 | 02 | 03 | 05 | 05 | 05 | 02 | 72000 |
| 29000 | 5067 | 367 | 0607 | 43 | 0536 | 40 | 06 | 02 | 03 | 05 | 05 | 05 | 02 | 71000 |
| 30000 | 5434 | 365 | 0650 | 42 | 0576 | 39 | 07 | 02 | 03 | 05 | 05 | 05 | 02 | 70000 |
| 31000 | 5799 | 360 | 0692 | 41 | 0615 | 39 | 07 | 02 | 03 | 05 | 06 | 06 | 02 | 69000 |
| 32000 | 6159 | 352 | 0733 | 40 | 0654 | 38 | 08 | 02 | 03 | 06 | 06 | 06 | 02 | 68000 |
| 33000 | 6511 | 343 | 0773 | 40 | 0692 | 37 | 08 | 02 | 04 | 06 | 06 | 06 | 02 | 67000 |
| 34000 | 6854 | 333 | 0813 | 39 | 0729 | 35 | 09 | 02 | 04 | 07 | 07 | 07 | 03 | 66000 |
| 35000 | 7187 | 321 | 0852 | 38 | 0764 | 34 | 09 | 02 | 04 | 07 | 07 | 07 | 03 | 65000 |
| 36000 | 7508 | 307 | 0890 | 36 | 0798 | 32 | 09 | 02 | 04 | 07 | 07 | 07 | 03 | 64000 |
| 37000 | 7815 | 291 | 0926 | 34 | 0830 | 31 | 10 | 02 | 04 | 08 | 07 | 07 | 03 | 63000 |
| 38000 | 8106 | 274 | 0960 | 31 | 0861 | 30 | 10 | 03 | 05 | 08 | 08 | 08 | 03 | 62000 |
| 39000 | 8380 | 257 | 0991 | 29 | 0891 | 29 | 11 | 03 | 05 | 09 | 08 | 08 | 03 | 61000 |
| 40000 | 8637 | 238 | 1020 | 27 | 0920 | 27 | 11 | 03 | 05 | 09 | 08 | 08 | 03 | 60000 |
| 41000 | 8875 | 217 | 1047 | 24 | 0947 | 24 | 11 | 03 | 05 | 09 | 08 | 08 | 03 | 59000 |
| 42000 | 9092 | 194 | 1071 | 22 | 0971 | 21 | 11 | 03 | 05 | 09 | 08 | 08 | 03 | 58000 |
| 43000 | 9286 | 170 | 1093 | 20 | 0992 | 17 | 12 | 03 | 06 | 09 | 09 | 09 | 04 | 57000 |
| 44000 | 9456 | 144 | 1113 | 18 | 1009 | 14 | 12 | 04 | 06 | 10 | 09 | 09 | 04 | 56000 |
| 45000 | 9600 | 118 | 1131 | 15 | 1023 | 12 | 12 | 04 | 06 | 10 | 09 | 09 | 04 | 55000 |
| 46000 | 9718 | 93 | 1146 | 11 | 1035 | 9 | 12 | 04 | 06 | 10 | 09 | 09 | 04 | 54000 |
| 47000 | 9811 | 67 | 1157 | 7 | 1044 | 7 | 12 | 04 | 06 | 10 | 09 | 09 | 04 | 53000 |
| 48000 | 9878 | 41 | 1164 | 4 | 1051 | 5 | 12 | 04 | 06 | 10 | 10 | 10 | 04 | 52000 |
| 49000 | 9919 | 14 | 1168 | 1 | 1056 | 3 | 12 | 04 | 06 | 10 | 10 | 10 | 04 | 51000 |
| 50000 | 9933 | | 1169 | | 1059 | | 12 | 04 | 06 | 10 | 10 | 10 | 04 | 50000 |

# TABLE V*b*.

ARGUMENT 76.

| | | | | | Correction of Arguments | | | | | | | | | |
|---|---|---|---|---|---|---|---|---|---|---|---|---|---|---|
| Days. | ARG. **1.** | | **2.** | | **3.** | | **6.** | **7.** | **8.** | **9.** | **10.** | **11.** | **13.** | Days. |
| d. | 0.00 | Diff. | 0.00 | Diff. | 0.00 | Diff. | 0.00 | 0.00 | 0.00 | 0.00 | 0.00 | 0.00 | 0.00 | d. |
| 0 | 07832 | 41 | 0145 | 5 | 0067 | 5 | 00 | 07 | 06 | 01 | 00 | 01 | 08 | 100000 |
| 1000 | 07791 | 16 | 0140 | 2 | 0062 | 2 | 00 | 07 | 06 | 01 | 00 | 01 | 08 | 99000 |
| 2000 | 07775 | 8 | 0138 | 1 | 0060 | 1 | 00 | 07 | 06 | 01 | 00 | 01 | 08 | 98000 |
| 3000 | 07783 | 33 | 0139 | 4 | 0061 | 3 | 00 | 07 | 06 | 01 | 00 | 01 | 08 | 97000 |
| 4000 | 07816 | 58 | 0143 | 6 | 0064 | 6 | 00 | 07 | 06 | 01 | 00 | 01 | 08 | 96000 |
| 5000 | 07874 | 82 | 0149 | 9 | 0070 | 9 | 00 | 07 | 06 | 01 | 00 | 01 | 08 | 95000 |
| 6000 | 07956 | 105 | 0158 | 12 | 0079 | 11 | 00 | 07 | 06 | 01 | 00 | 01 | 08 | 94000 |
| 7000 | 08061 | 127 | 0170 | 15 | 0090 | 14 | 00 | 07 | 06 | 01 | 00 | 01 | 08 | 93000 |
| 8000 | 08188 | 149 | 0185 | 18 | 0104 | 16 | 01 | 07 | 06 | 02 | 00 | 01 | 08 | 92000 |
| 9000 | 08337 | 171 | 0203 | 21 | 0120 | 19 | 01 | 07 | 06 | 02 | 00 | 01 | 08 | 91000 |
| 10000 | 08508 | 194 | 0224 | 23 | 0139 | 21 | 01 | 07 | 06 | 02 | 00 | 01 | 08 | 90000 |
| 11000 | 08702 | 216 | 0247 | 25 | 0160 | 24 | 01 | 07 | 06 | 02 | 00 | 01 | 08 | 89000 |
| 12000 | 08918 | 239 | 0272 | 27 | 0184 | 26 | 01 | 07 | 06 | 02 | 00 | 01 | 08 | 88000 |
| 13000 | 09157 | 261 | 0299 | 30 | 0210 | 28 | 02 | 08 | 07 | 03 | 01 | 02 | 09 | 87000 |
| 14000 | 09418 | 281 | 0329 | 32 | 0238 | 29 | 02 | 08 | 07 | 03 | 01 | 02 | 09 | 86000 |
| 15000 | 09699 | 298 | 0361 | 34 | 0267 | 31 | 02 | 08 | 07 | 03 | 01 | 02 | 09 | 85000 |
| 16000 | 09997 | 312 | 0395 | 35 | 0298 | 33 | 02 | 08 | 07 | 03 | 01 | 02 | 09 | 84000 |
| 17000 | 10309 | 322 | 0430 | 37 | 0331 | 35 | 02 | 08 | 07 | 04 | 02 | 03 | 09 | 83000 |
| 18000 | 10631 | 332 | 0467 | 39 | 0366 | 36 | 03 | 08 | 08 | 04 | 02 | 03 | 09 | 82000 |
| 19000 | 10963 | 340 | 0506 | 40 | 0402 | 37 | 03 | 08 | 08 | 05 | 02 | 03 | 09 | 81000 |
| 20000 | 11303 | 351 | 0546 | 41 | 0439 | 38 | 04 | 08 | 08 | 05 | 03 | 04 | 09 | 80000 |
| 21000 | 11654 | 362 | 0587 | 42 | 0477 | 39 | 04 | 08 | 08 | 05 | 03 | 04 | 09 | 79000 |
| 22000 | 12016 | 272 | 0629 | 43 | 0516 | 40 | 05 | 08 | 08 | 06 | 03 | 04 | 10 | 78000 |
| 23000 | 12388 | 381 | 0672 | 44 | 0556 | 41 | 05 | 09 | 09 | 06 | 04 | 05 | 10 | 77000 |
| 24000 | 12769 | 391 | 0716 | 44 | 0597 | 41 | 06 | 09 | 09 | 07 | 04 | 05 | 10 | 76000 |
| 25000 | 13160 | 390 | 0760 | 44 | 0638 | 41 | 06 | 09 | 09 | 07 | 04 | 05 | 10 | 75000 |
| 26000 | 13550 | 388 | 0804 | 44 | 0679 | 41 | 07 | 09 | 09 | 07 | 04 | 05 | 10 | 74000 |
| 27000 | 13938 | 382 | 0848 | 44 | 0720 | 41 | 07 | 09 | 09 | 08 | 05 | 06 | 10 | 73000 |
| 28000 | 14320 | 374 | 0892 | 44 | 0761 | 41 | 08 | 10 | 10 | 08 | 05 | 06 | 10 | 72000 |
| 29000 | 14694 | 366 | 0936 | 44 | 0802 | 40 | 08 | 10 | 10 | 09 | 06 | 07 | 11 | 71000 |
| 30000 | 15060 | 360 | 0980 | 43 | 0842 | 39 | 09 | 10 | 10 | 09 | 06 | 07 | 11 | 70000 |
| 31000 | 15420 | 355 | 1023 | 42 | 0881 | 38 | 09 | 10 | 10 | 09 | 06 | 07 | 11 | 69000 |
| 32000 | 15775 | 349 | 1065 | 40 | 0919 | 37 | 10 | 10 | 10 | 09 | 07 | 08 | 11 | 68000 |
| 33000 | 16124 | 343 | 1105 | 39 | 0956 | 36 | 10 | 10 | 11 | 10 | 07 | 08 | 11 | 67000 |
| 34000 | 16467 | 336 | 1144 | 37 | 0992 | 36 | 11 | 10 | 11 | 10 | 07 | 08 | 11 | 66000 |
| 35000 | 16803 | 321 | 1181 | 36 | 1028 | 34 | 11 | 10 | 11 | 10 | 08 | 09 | 11 | 65000 |
| 36000 | 17124 | 302 | 1217 | 34 | 1062 | 32 | 11 | 10 | 11 | 10 | 08 | 09 | 11 | 64000 |
| 37000 | 17426 | 281 | 1251 | 32 | 1094 | 30 | 12 | 10 | 11 | 11 | 08 | 09 | 11 | 63000 |
| 38000 | 17707 | 259 | 1283 | 30 | 1124 | 28 | 12 | 11 | 12 | 11 | 09 | 10 | 12 | 62000 |
| 39000 | 17966 | 236 | 1313 | 29 | 1152 | 26 | 13 | 11 | 12 | 11 | 09 | 10 | 12 | 61000 |
| 40000 | 18202 | 218 | 1342 | 27 | 1178 | 24 | 13 | 11 | 12 | 12 | 09 | 10 | 12 | 60000 |
| 41000 | 18420 | 200 | 1369 | 24 | 1202 | 22 | 13 | 11 | 12 | 12 | 09 | 10 | 12 | 59000 |
| 42000 | 18620 | 182 | 1393 | 21 | 1224 | 20 | 13 | 11 | 12 | 12 | 09 | 10 | 12 | 58000 |
| 43000 | 18802 | 162 | 1414 | 18 | 1244 | 17 | 14 | 11 | 12 | 13 | 10 | 11 | 12 | 57000 |
| 44000 | 18964 | 142 | 1432 | 15 | 1261 | 15 | 14 | 11 | 12 | 13 | 10 | 11 | 12 | 56000 |
| 45000 | 19106 | 117 | 1447 | 12 | 1276 | 12 | 14 | 11 | 12 | 13 | 10 | 11 | 12 | 55000 |
| 46000 | 19223 | 88 | 1459 | 10 | 1288 | 9 | 14 | 11 | 12 | 13 | 10 | 11 | 12 | 54000 |
| 47000 | 19311 | 60 | 1469 | 7 | 1297 | 6 | 14 | 11 | 12 | 13 | 10 | 11 | 12 | 53000 |
| 48000 | 19371 | 35 | 1476 | 5 | 1303 | 4 | 14 | 11 | 12 | 13 | 10 | 11 | 12 | 52000 |
| 49000 | 19406 | 10 | 1481 | 2 | 1307 | 1 | 14 | 11 | 12 | 13 | 10 | 11 | 12 | 51000 |
| 50000 | 19416 | | 1483 | | 1308 | | 14 | 11 | 12 | 13 | 10 | 11 | 12 | 50000 |

# LONGITUDE TABLES.

---

EQUATIONS.

**TABLES VI.-LXXXII.**

SECOND AND FOURTH DIFFERENCES

FOR A QUARTER OF A DAY.

**TABLES VI''.-XXXV''., VI.$^{IV}$-XXI.$^{IV}$**

# TABLE VI. ARGUMENT 1.

Equation $= 22655''.226 + 22639''.2 \sin. x + 769''.5 \sin. 2x + 36''.7 \sin. 3x + 2''.0 \sin. 4x + 0''.1 \sin. 5x.$

Period, 27.55455245 days.

| Days. | 0 | | 1 | | 2 | | 3 | | 4 | |
|---|---|---|---|---|---|---|---|---|---|---|
| Decimals of a Day. | Equation. | Log. Dif. | Equation. | Log. Dif. | Equation. | Log. Dif. | Equation. | Log. Dif. | Equation. | Log. Dif. |
| .00 | 60″.87 | −0.5682 | 274″.44 | +0.9117 | 1684″.78 | +1.3038 | 4268″.29 | +1.4981 | 7924″.37 | +1.6172 |
| .01 | 57.17 | 0.5539 | 282.60 | 0.9180 | 1704.91 | 1.3065 | 4299.78 | 1.4995 | 7965.79 | 1.6182 |
| .02 | 53.59 | 0.5403 | 290.88 | 0.9243 | 1725.16 | 1.3090 | 4331.37 | 1.5011 | 8007.31 | 1.6192 |
| .03 | 50.12 | 0.5250 | 299.28 | 0.9304 | 1745.53 | 1.3113 | 4363.07 | 1.5025 | 8048.92 | 1.6201 |
| .04 | 46.77 | 0.5092 | 307.80 | 0.9365 | 1766.01 | 1.3139 | 4394.88 | 1.5041 | 8090.62 | 1.6209 |
| .05 | 43.54 | 0.4942 | 316.44 | 0.9425 | 1786.61 | 1.3164 | 4426.80 | 1.5055 | 8132.40 | 1.6219 |
| .06 | 40.42 | 0.4771 | 325.20 | 0.9484 | 1807.33 | 1.3187 | 4458.83 | 1.5069 | 8174.27 | 1.6228 |
| .07 | 37.42 | 0.4594 | 334.08 | 0.9542 | 1828.16 | 1.3212 | 4490.96 | 1.5084 | 8216.23 | 1.6237 |
| .08 | 34.54 | 0.4425 | 343 08 | 0.9600 | 1849.11 | 1.3236 | 4523.20 | 1.5099 | 8258.28 | 1.6247 |
| .09 | 31.77 | 0.4232 | 352.20 | 0.9657 | 1870.18 | 1.3261 | 4555.55 | 1.5112 | 8300.42 | 1.6256 |
| .10 | 29.12 | 0.4048 | 361.44 | 0.9713 | 1891.37 | 1.3284 | 4588.00 | 1.5127 | 8342.65 | 1.6264 |
| .11 | 26.58 | 0.3838 | 370.80 | 0.9768 | 1912.67 | 1.3308 | 4620.56 | 1.5140 | 8384.96 | 1.6274 |
| .12 | 24.16 | 0.3617 | 380.28 | 0.9827 | 1934.09 | 1.3332 | 4653.22 | 1.5154 | 8427.36 | 1.6283 |
| .13 | 21.86 | 0.3385 | 389.89 | 0.9881 | 1955.63 | 1.3357 | 4685.99 | 1.5170 | 8469.85 | 1.6291 |
| .14 | 19.68 | 0.3160 | 399.62 | 0.9930 | 1977.29 | 1.3379 | 4718.87 | 1.5183 | 8512.42 | 1.6300 |
| .15 | 17.61 | 0.2900 | 409.46 | 0.9983 | 1999.06 | 1.3403 | 4751.85 | 1.5197 | 8555.08 | 1.6309 |
| .16 | 15.66 | 0.2625 | 419.42 | 1.0033 | 2020.95 | 1.3426 | 4784.94 | 1.5210 | 8597.83 | 1.6318 |
| .17 | 13.83 | 0.2355 | 429.50 | 1.0090 | 2042.96 | 1.3450 | 4818.13 | 1.5224 | 8640.67 | 1.6327 |
| .18 | 12.11 | 0.2041 | 439.71 | 1.0140 | 2065.09 | 1.3472 | 4851.43 | 1.5238 | 8683.59 | 1.6335 |
| .19 | 10.51 | 0.1703 | 450.04 | 1.0191 | 2087.33 | 1.3495 | 4884.84 | 1.5251 | 8726.59 | 1.6344 |
| .20 | 9.03 | 0.1335 | 460.49 | 1.0237 | 2109.69 | 1.3516 | 4918.35 | 1.5266 | 8769.68 | 1.6353 |
| .21 | 7.67 | 0.0969 | 471.05 | 1.0286 | 2132.16 | 1.3539 | 4951.97 | 1.5278 | 8812.86 | 1.6361 |
| .22 | 6.42 | 0.0531 | 481.73 | 1.0338 | 2154.75 | 1.3562 | 4985.69 | 1.5292 | 8856.12 | 1.6370 |
| .23 | 5.29 | 0.0043 | 492.54 | 1.0386 | 2177.46 | 1.3583 | 5019.51 | 1.5306 | 8899.47 | 1.6378 |
| .24 | 4.28 | 9.9542 | 503.47 | 1.0433 | 2200.28 | 1.3606 | 5053.44 | 1.5319 | 8942.90 | 1.6386 |
| .25 | 3.38 | 9.8921 | 514.52 | 1.0479 | 2223.22 | 1.3628 | 5087.47 | 1.5333 | 8986.41 | 1.6395 |
| .26 | 2.60 | 9.8195 | 525.69 | 1.0526 | 2246.28 | 1.3649 | 5121.61 | 1.5345 | 9030.01 | 1.6403 |
| .27 | 1.94 | 9.7324 | 536.98 | 1.0569 | 2269.45 | 1.3672 | 5155.85 | 1.5358 | 9073.69 | 1.6412 |
| .28 | 1.40 | 9.6232 | 548.38 | 1.0618 | 2292.74 | 1.3692 | 5190.19 | 1.5372 | 9117.46 | 1.6420 |
| .29 | 0.98 | 9.4914 | 559.91 | 1.0664 | 2316.14 | 1.3715 | 5224.64 | 1.5384 | 9161.31 | 1.6428 |
| .30 | 0.67 | 9.2788 | 571.56 | 1.0708 | 2339.66 | 1.3736 | 5259.19 | 1.5399 | 9205.24 | 1.6437 |
| .31 | 0.48 | −8.8451 | 583.33 | 1.0749 | 2363.30 | 1.3756 | 5293.85 | 1.5411 | 9249.26 | 1.6444 |
| .32 | 0.41 | +8.6990 | 595.22 | 1.0795 | 2387.05 | 1.3779 | 5328.61 | 1.5424 | 9293.36 | 1.6452 |
| .33 | 0.46 | 9.2041 | 607.23 | 1.0838 | 2410.92 | 1.3799 | 5363.47 | 1.5437 | 9337.54 | 1.6460 |
| .34 | 0.62 | 9.4472 | 619.36 | 1.0881 | 2434.90 | 1.3820 | 5398.44 | 1.5450 | 9381.80 | 1.6468 |
| .35 | 0.90 | 9.6021 | 631.61 | 1.0923 | 2459.00 | 1.3842 | 5433.51 | 1.5462 | 9426.14 | 1.6476 |
| .36 | 1 30 | 9.7160 | 643.98 | 1.0965 | 2483.22 | 1.3861 | 5468.68 | 1.5474 | 9470.56 | 1.6484 |
| .37 | 1.82 | 9.8062 | 656.47 | 1.1007 | 2507.55 | 1.3881 | 5503.95 | 1.5487 | 9515.06 | 1.6493 |
| .38 | 2.46 | 9.8751 | 669.08 | 1.1052 | 2531.99 | 1.3903 | 5539.32 | 1.5500 | 9559.65 | 1.6500 |
| .39 | 3.21 | 9.9395 | 681.82 | 1.1089 | 2556.55 | 1.3923 | 5574.80 | 1.5512 | 9604.32 | 1.6508 |
| .40 | 4.08 | 9.9956 | 694.67 | 1.1130 | 2581.23 | 1.3943 | 5610.38 | 1.5524 | 9649.07 | 1.6515 |
| .41 | 5.07 | 0.0453 | 707.64 | 1.1168 | 2606.02 | 1.3962 | 5646.06 | 1.5537 | 9693.89 | 1.6522 |
| .42 | 6.18 | 0.0899 | 720.73 | 1.1209 | 2630.92 | 1.3982 | 5681.84 | 1.5549 | 9738.79 | 1.6530 |
| .43 | 7.41 | 0.1303 | 733.94 | 1.1249 | 2655.94 | 1.4004 | 5717.72 | 1.5561 | 9783.77 | 1.6539 |
| .44 | 8.76 | 0.1644 | 747.27 | 1.1287 | 2681.08 | 1.4023 | 5753.70 | 1.5574 | 6828.84 | 1.6547 |
| .45 | 10.22 | 0.1987 | 760.72 | 1.1326 | 2706.33 | 1.4041 | 5789.79 | 1.5586 | 9873.99 | 1.6553 |
| .46 | 11.80 | 0.2304 | 774.29 | 1.1367 | 2731.69 | 1.4062 | 5825.98 | 1.5597 | 9919.21 | 1.6560 |
| .47 | 13.50 | 0.2601 | 787.99 | 1.1405 | 2757.17 | 1.4080 | 5862.26 | 1.5610 | 9964.50 | 1.6568 |
| .48 | 15.32 | 0.2878 | 801.81 | 1.1440 | 2782.76 | 1.4101 | 5898.65 | 1.5622 | 10009.87 | 1.6577 |
| .49 | 17.26 | 0.3139 | 815.74 | 1.1476 | 2808.47 | 1.4119 | 5935.14 | 1.5634 | 10055.33 | 1.6584 |
| .50 | 19.32 | +0.3385 | 829.79 | +1.1513 | 2834.29 | +1.4138 | 5971.73 | +1.5646 | 10100.87 | +1.6591 |

# TABLE VI. ARGUMENT 1.

Equation $= 22655''.226 + 22639''.2 \sin. x + 769''.5 \sin. 2x + 36''.7 \sin. 3x + 2''.0 \sin. 4x + 0''.1 \sin. 5x.$

Period, 27.55455245 days.

| Days. | 0 | | 1 | | 2 | | 3 | | 4 | |
|---|---|---|---|---|---|---|---|---|---|---|
| Decimals of a Day. | Equation. | Log. Dif. | Equation. | Log. Dif. | Equation. | Log. Dif. | Equation. | Log. Dif. | Equation. | Log. Dif. |
| .50 | 19.32″ | +0.3385 | 829.79″ | +1.1513 | 2834.29″ | +1.4138 | 5971.73″ | +1.5646 | 10100.87″ | +1.6591 |
| .51 | 21.50 | 0.3617 | 843.96 | 1.1550 | 2860.22 | 1.4158 | 6008.42 | 1.5656 | 10146.48 | 1.6598 |
| .52 | 23.80 | 0.3820 | 858.25 | 1.1587 | 2886.27 | 1.4176 | 6045.20 | 1.5668 | 10192.17 | 1.6606 |
| .53 | 26.21 | 0.4031 | 872.66 | 1.1626 | 2912.43 | 1.4194 | 6082.08 | 1.5681 | 10237.94 | 1.6614 |
| .54 | 28.74 | 0.4232 | 887.20 | 1.1662 | 2938.70 | 1.4215 | 6119.07 | 1.5692 | 10283.79 | 1.6620 |
| .55 | 31.39 | 0.4425 | 901.86 | 1.1694 | 2965.09 | 1.4232 | 6156.16 | 1.5703 | 10329.71 | 1.6627 |
| .56 | 34.16 | 0.4609 | 916.63 | 1.1730 | 2991.59 | 1.4252 | 6193.34 | 1.5714 | 10375.70 | 1.6634 |
| .57 | 37.05 | 0.4786 | 931.52 | 1.1764 | 3018.21 | 1.4268 | 6230.62 | 1.5726 | 10421.77 | 1.6642 |
| .58 | 40.06 | 0.4955 | 946.53 | 1.1801 | 3044.93 | 1.4288 | 6268.00 | 1.5738 | 10467.92 | 1.6649 |
| .59 | 43.19 | 0.5119 | 961.67 | 1.1833 | 3071.77 | 1.4306 | 6305.48 | 1.5750 | 10514.15 | 1.6658 |
| .60 | 46.44 | 0.5276 | 976.92 | 1.1867 | 3098.72 | 1.4325 | 6343.06 | 1.5760 | 10560.46 | 1.6663 |
| .61 | 49.81 | 0.5416 | 992.29 | 1.1900 | 3125.79 | 1.4343 | 6380.73 | 1.5771 | 10606.84 | 1.6670 |
| .62 | 53.29 | 0.5563 | 1007.78 | 1.1934 | 3152.97 | 1.4360 | 6418.50 | 1.5782 | 10653.29 | 1.6676 |
| .63 | 56.89 | 0.5705 | 1023.39 | 1.1967 | 3180.26 | 1.4378 | 6456.37 | 1.5794 | 10699.81 | 1.6684 |
| .64 | 60.61 | 0.5855 | 1039.12 | 1.2000 | 3207.66 | 1.4396 | 6494.34 | 1.5806 | 10746.41 | 1.6691 |
| .65 | 64.46 | 0.5988 | 1054.97 | 1.2034 | 3235.18 | 1.4414 | 6532.41 | 1.5817 | 10793.09 | 1.6698 |
| .66 | 68.43 | 0.6107 | 1070.94 | 1.2065 | 3262.81 | 1.4433 | 6570.58 | 1.5826 | 10839.84 | 1.6704 |
| .67 | 72.51 | 0.6232 | 1087.03 | 1.2095 | 3290.56 | 1.4449 | 6608.83 | 1.5838 | 10886.66 | 1.6711 |
| .68 | 76.71 | 0.6355 | 1103.23 | 1.2130 | 3318.42 | 1.4467 | 6647.18 | 1.5849 | 10933.55 | 1.6718 |
| .69 | 81.03 | 0.6474 | 1119.56 | 1.2161 | 3346.39 | 1.4484 | 6685.63 | 1.5861 | 10980.52 | 1.6725 |
| .70 | 85.47 | 0.6599 | 1136.01 | 1.2191 | 3374.47 | 1.4501 | 6724.13 | 1.5872 | 11027.56 | 1.6731 |
| .71 | 90.04 | 0.6702 | 1152.57 | 1.2225 | 3402.66 | 1.4518 | 6762.83 | 1.5882 | 11074.67 | 1.6737 |
| .72 | 94.72 | 0.6812 | 1169.26 | 1.2256 | 3430.96 | 1.4535 | 6801.57 | 1.5892 | 11121.85 | 1.6745 |
| .73 | 99.52 | 0.6920 | 1186.07 | 1.2284 | 3459.37 | 1.4553 | 6840.40 | 1.5903 | 11169.11 | 1.6752 |
| .74 | 104.44 | 0.7024 | 1202.99 | 1.2314 | 3487.90 | 1.4570 | 6879.33 | 1.5914 | 11216.44 | 1.6758 |
| .75 | 109.48 | 0.7426 | 1220.03 | 1.2347 | 3516.54 | 1.4587 | 6918.36 | 1.5924 | 11263.84 | 1.6764 |
| .76 | 114.64 | 0.7226 | 1237.20 | 1.2375 | 3545.29 | 1.4602 | 6957.48 | 1.5935 | 11311.31 | 1.6771 |
| .77 | 119.92 | 0.7316 | 1254.48 | 1.2405 | 3574.14 | 1.4620 | 6996.70 | 1.5945 | 11358.85 | 1.6776 |
| .78 | 125.31 | 0.7419 | 1271.88 | 1.2437 | 3603.11 | 1.4637 | 7036.01 | 1.5955 | 11406.45 | 1.6783 |
| .79 | 130.83 | 0.7513 | 1289.41 | 1.2465 | 3632.20 | 1.4652 | 7075.41 | 1.5966 | 11454.13 | 1.6790 |
| .80 | 136.47 | 0.7597 | 1307.05 | 1.2495 | 3661.39 | 1.4669 | 7114.91 | 1.5977 | 11501.88 | 1.6796 |
| .81 | 142.22 | 0.7694 | 1324.81 | 1.2521 | 3690.69 | 1.4684 | 7154.51 | 1.5987 | 11549.70 | 1.6802 |
| .82 | 148.10 | 0.7782 | 1342.68 | 1.2553 | 3720.10 | 1.4701 | 7194.20 | 1.5997 | 11597.59 | 1.6808 |
| .83 | 154.10 | 0.7868 | 1360.68 | 1.2582 | 3749.62 | 1.4719 | 7233.98 | 1.6007 | 11645.54 | 1.6814 |
| .84 | 160.22 | 0.7945 | 1378.80 | 1.2610 | 3779.26 | 1.4735 | 7273.85 | 1.6017 | 11693.56 | 1.6820 |
| .85 | 166.45 | 0.8035 | 1397.04 | 1.2637 | 3809.01 | 1.4749 | 7313.82 | 1.6027 | 11741.65 | 1.6828 |
| .86 | 172.81 | 0.8116 | 1415.39 | 1.2664 | 3838.86 | 1.4766 | 7353.88 | 1.6037 | 11789.82 | 1.6833 |
| .87 | 179.29 | 0.8195 | 1433.86 | 1.2693 | 3868.82 | 1.4781 | 7394.03 | 1.6047 | 11838.05 | 1.6838 |
| .88 | 185.89 | 0.8274 | 1452.45 | 1.2720 | 3898.89 | 1.4799 | 7434.27 | 1.6057 | 11886.34 | 1.6844 |
| .89 | 192.61 | 0.8351 | 1471.16 | 1.2749 | 3929.08 | 1.4814 | 7474.61 | 1.6067 | 11934.70 | 1.6851 |
| .90 | 199.45 | 0.8420 | 1489.99 | 1.2777 | 3959.38 | 1.4829 | 7515.04 | 1.6077 | 11983.13 | 1.6857 |
| .91 | 206.40 | 0.8500 | 1508.94 | 1.2801 | 3989.78 | 1.4844 | 7555.56 | 1.6086 | 12031.63 | 1.6862 |
| .92 | 213.48 | 0.8573 | 1528.00 | 1.2828 | 4020.29 | 1.4860 | 7596.17 | 1.6097 | 12080.19 | 1.6869 |
| .93 | 220.68 | 0.8645 | 1547.18 | 1.2858 | 4050.91 | 1.4875 | 7636.88 | 1.6107 | 12128.82 | 1.6875 |
| .94 | 228.00 | 0.8716 | 1566.49 | 1.2882 | 4081.64 | 1.4892 | 7677.68 | 1.6116 | 12177.52 | 1.6880 |
| .95 | 235.44 | 0.8785 | 1585.91 | 1.2909 | 4112.48 | 1.4907 | 7718.57 | 1.6126 | 12226.28 | 1.6887 |
| .96 | 243.00 | 0.8854 | 1605.45 | 1.2936 | 4143.43 | 1.4921 | 7759.55 | 1.6135 | 12275.11 | 1.6892 |
| .97 | 250.68 | 0.8921 | 1625.11 | 1.2961 | 4174.48 | 1.4936 | 7800.62 | 1.6145 | 12324.00 | 1.6897 |
| .98 | 258.48 | 0.8987 | 1644.88 | 1.2987 | 4205.64 | 1.4952 | 7841.78 | 1.6154 | 12372.95 | 1.6904 |
| .99 | 266.40 | 0.9053 | 1664.77 | 1.3012 | 4236.91 | 1.4966 | 7883.03 | 1.6164 | 12421.97 | 1.6910 |
| 1.00 | 274.44 | +0.9117 | 1684.78 | +1.3038 | 4268.29 | +1.4981 | 7924.37 | +1.6172 | 12471.06 | +1.6915 |

# TABLE VI. ARGUMENT 1.

$$\text{Equation} = 22655''.226 + 22639''.2 \sin. x + 769''.5 \sin. 2x + 36''.7 \sin. 3x + 2''.0 \sin. 4x + 0''.1 \sin. 5x.$$

Period, 27.55455245 days.

| Days | 5 | | 6 | | 7 | | 8 | | 9 | |
|---|---|---|---|---|---|---|---|---|---|---|
| Decimals of a Day. | Equation. | Log. Dif. | Equation. | Log. Dif. | Equation. | Log. Dif. | Equation. | Log. Dif. | Equation. | Log. Dif. |
| .00 | 12471″.06 | +1.6915 | 17650″.56 | +1.7321 | 23146″.27 | +1.7434 | 28610″.81 | +1.7267 | 33699″.84 | +1.6804 |
| .01 | 12520.21 | 1.6921 | 17704.52 | 1.7323 | 23201.66 | 1.7433 | 28664.11 | 1.7264 | 33747.75 | 1.6797 |
| .02 | 12569.42 | 1.6927 | 17758.51 | 1.7325 | 23257.04 | 1.7433 | 28717.37 | 1.7262 | 33795.58 | 1.6791 |
| .03 | 12618.70 | 1.6932 | 17812.52 | 1.7328 | 23312.42 | 1.7433 | 28770.60 | 1.7258 | 33843.35 | 1.6785 |
| .04 | 12668.04 | 1.6937 | 17866.57 | 1.7331 | 23367.80 | 1.7432 | 28823.79 | 1.7255 | 33891.05 | 1.6779 |
| .05 | 12717.44 | 1.6942 | 17920.66 | 1.7333 | 23423.17 | 1.7432 | 28876.94 | 1.7251 | 33938.68 | 1.6772 |
| .06 | 12766.90 | 1.6949 | 17974.77 | 1.7335 | 23478.54 | 1.7432 | 28930.04 | 1.7249 | 33986.24 | 1.6766 |
| .07 | 12816.43 | 1.6954 | 18028.90 | 1.7338 | 23533.90 | 1.7431 | 28983.11 | 1.7245 | 34033.73 | 1.6760 |
| .08 | 12866.02 | 1.6959 | 18083.07 | 1.7340 | 23589.25 | 1.7431 | 29036.14 | 1.7242 | 34081.15 | 1.6753 |
| .09 | 12915.67 | 1.6966 | 18137.27 | 1.7342 | 23644.60 | 1.7431 | 29089.13 | 1.7239 | 34128.49 | 1.6745 |
| .10 | 12965.39 | 1.6970 | 18191.50 | 1.7345 | 23699.95 | 1.7430 | 29142.08 | 1.7235 | 34175.76 | 1.6739 |
| .11 | 13015.16 | 1.6975 | 18245.76 | 1.7346 | 23755.29 | 1.7430 | 29194.98 | 1.7231 | 34222.96 | 1.6733 |
| .12 | 13064.99 | 1.6980 | 18300.04 | 1.7349 | 23810.62 | 1.7429 | 29247.84 | 1.7228 | 34270.09 | 1 6726 |
| .13 | 13114.88 | 1.6986 | 18354.35 | 1.7351 | 23865.94 | 1.7428 | 29300.66 | 1.7225 | 34317.15 | 1.6720 |
| .14 | 13164.84 | 1.6991 | 18408.69 | 1.7354 | 23921.25 | 1.7428 | 29353.44 | 1.7221 | 34364.14 | 1.6713 |
| .15 | 13214.85 | 1.6996 | 18463.06 | 1.7355 | 23976.56 | 1.7427 | 29406.18 | 1.7217 | 34411.05 | 1.6706 |
| .16 | 13264.92 | 1.7001 | 18517.45 | 1.7358 | 24031.86 | 1.7426 | 29458.87 | 1.7214 | 34457.89 | 1.6700 |
| .17 | 13315.05 | 1.7006 | 18571.87 | 1.7360 | 24087.15 | 1.7425 | 29511.52 | 1.7211 | 34504.66 | 1.6692 |
| .18 | 13365.24 | 1.7010 | 18626.32 | 1.7362 | 24142.43 | 1.7425 | 29564.13 | 1.7208 | 34551.35 | 1.6686 |
| .19 | 13415.48 | 1.7017 | 18680.79 | 1.7363 | 24197.70 | 1.7424 | 29616.70 | 1.7204 | 34597.97 | 1.6679 |
| .20 | 13465.79 | 1.7021 | 18735.28 | 1.7366 | 24252.96 | 1.7423 | 29669.22 | 1.7199 | 34644.51 | 1.6672 |
| .21 | 13516.15 | 1.7026 | 18789.80 | 1.7368 | 24308.21 | 1.7422 | 29721.69 | 1.7195 | 34690.98 | 1.6665 |
| .22 | 13566.57 | 1.7031 | 18844.35 | 1.7370 | 24363.45 | 1.7421 | 29774.12 | 1.7192 | 34737.38 | 1.6658 |
| .23 | 13617.05 | 1.7036 | 18898.92 | 1.7372 | 24418.68 | 1.7421 | 29826.51 | 1.7188 | 34783.70 | 1.6651 |
| .24 | 13667.58 | 1.7041 | 18953.52 | 1.7374 | 24473.89 | 1.7420 | 29878.85 | 1.7185 | 34829.95 | 1.6644 |
| .25 | 13718.17 | 1.7046 | 19008.14 | 1.7375 | 24529.10 | 1.7419 | 29931.15 | 1.7181 | 34876.12 | 1.6636 |
| .26 | 13768.82 | 1.7050 | 19062.78 | 1.7377 | 24584.30 | 1.7418 | 29983.40 | 1.7177 | 34922.21 | 1.6630 |
| .27 | 13819.52 | 1.7055 | 19117.44 | 1.7379 | 24639.48 | 1.7417 | 30035.60 | 1.7172 | 34968.23 | 1.6622 |
| .28 | 13870.28 | 1.7060 | 19172.13 | 1.7381 | 24694.65 | 1.7416 | 30087.75 | 1.7169 | 35014.17 | 1.6616 |
| .29 | 13921.09 | 1.7065 | 19226.84 | 1.7382 | 24749.80 | 1.7416 | 30139.86 | 1.7166 | 35060.04 | 1.6608 |
| .30 | 13971.96 | 1.7069 | 19281.57 | 1.7384 | 24804.95 | 1.7414 | 30191.93 | 1.7161 | 35105.83 | 1.6600 |
| .31 | 14022.88 | 1.7074 | 19336.32 | 1.7386 | 24860.08 | 1.7413 | 30243.94 | 1.7158 | 35151.54 | 1.6593 |
| .32 | 14073.86 | 1.7079 | 19391.09 | 1.7388 | 24915.19 | 1.7412 | 30295.91 | 1.7153 | 35197.17 | 1.6586 |
| .33 | 14124.89 | 1.7084 | 19445.89 | 1.7390 | 24970.29 | 1.7410 | 30347.82 | 1.7149 | 35242.73 | 1.6579 |
| .34 | 14175.98 | 1.7087 | 19500.71 | 1.7390 | 25025.38 | 1.7409 | 30399.69 | 1.7145 | 35288.21 | 1.6572 |
| .35 | 14227.12 | 1.7092 | 19555.54 | 1.7392 | 25080.45 | 1.7408 | 30451.51 | 1.7140 | 35333.62 | 1.6563 |
| .36 | 14278.31 | 1.7096 | 19610.39 | 1.7394 | 25135.50 | 1.7407 | 30503.28 | 1.7137 | 35378.94 | 1.6555 |
| .37 | 14329.55 | 1.7101 | 19665.27 | 1.7396 | 25190.54 | 1.7406 | 30555.00 | 1.7132 | 35424.18 | 1.6549 |
| .38 | 14380.85 | 1.7105 | 19720.17 | 1.7397 | 25245.56 | 1.7405 | 30606.67 | 1.7128 | 35469.35 | 1.6541 |
| .39 | 14432.20 | 1.7111 | 19775.08 | 1.7398 | 25300.57 | 1.7404 | 30658.29 | 1.7124 | 35514.44 | 1.6533 |
| .40 | 14483.61 | 1.7114 | 19830.01 | 1.7400 | 25355.57 | 1.7402 | 30709.86 | 1.7120 | 35559.45 | 1.6524 |
| .41 | 14535.06 | 1.7118 | 19884.96 | 1.7402 | 25410.54 | 1.7400 | 30761.38 | 1.7116 | 35604.37 | 1.6518 |
| .42 | 14586.56 | 1.7123 | 19939.93 | 1.7402 | 25465.49 | 1.7398 | 30812.85 | 1.7112 | 35649.22 | 1.6510 |
| .43 | 14638.12 | 1.7127 | 19994.91 | 1.7405 | 25520.42 | 1.7398 | 30864.27 | 1.7107 | 35693.99 | 1.6502 |
| .44 | 14689.73 | 1.7131 | 20049.92 | 1.7405 | 25575.34 | 1.7396 | 30915.64 | 1.7102 | 35738.68 | 1 6494 |
| .45 | 14741.39 | 1.7135 | 20104.94 | 1.7406 | 25630.24 | 1.7394 | 30966.95 | 1.7098 | 35783.29 | 1.6486 |
| .46 | 14793.09 | 1.7140 | 20159.97 | 1.7408 | 25685.12 | 1.7393 | 31018.21 | 1.7094 | 35827.81 | 1.6479 |
| .47 | 14844.85 | 1.7143 | 20215.02 | 1.7409 | 25739.98 | 1.7391 | 31069.42 | 1.7088 | 35872.26 | 1.6470 |
| .48 | 14896.65 | 1.7148 | 20270.09 | 1.7410 | 25794.82 | 1.7390 | 31120.57 | 1.7084 | 35916.62 | 1.6462 |
| .49 | 14948.51 | 1.7153 | 20325.17 | 1.7412 | 25849.64 | 1.7388 | 31171.67 | 1.7080 | 35960.90 | 1.6454 |
| .50 | 15000.42 | +1.7156 | 20380.27 | +1.7413 | 25904.44 | +1.7386 | 31222.72 | +1.7075 | 36005.10 | +1.6446 |

# TABLE VI. ARGUMENT 1.

Equation $= 22655''.226 + 22639''.2 \sin. x + 769''.5 \sin. 2x + 36''.7 \sin. 3x + 2''.0 \sin. 4x + 0''.1 \sin. 5x$.

Period, 27.55455245 days.

| Days. | 5 | | 6 | | 7 | | 8 | | 9 | |
|---|---|---|---|---|---|---|---|---|---|---|
| Decimals of a Day. | Equation. | Log. Dif. | Equation. | Log. Dif. | Equation. | Log. Dif. | Equation. | Log. Dif. | Equation. | Log. Dif. |
| .50 | 15000″.42 | +1.7156 | 20380″.27 | +1.7413 | 25904″.44 | +1.7386 | 31222″.72 | +1.7075 | 36005″.10 | +1.6448 |
| .51 | 15052.37 | 1.7160 | 20435.38 | 1.7413 | 25959.22 | 1.7385 | 31273.71 | 1.7070 | 36049.22 | 1.6439 |
| .52 | 15104.37 | 1.7164 | 20490.50 | 1.7415 | 26013.98 | 1.7383 | 31324.65 | 1.7066 | 36093.26 | 1.6430 |
| .53 | 15156.42 | 1.7167 | 20545.64 | 1.7416 | 26068.72 | 1.7382 | 31375.53 | 1.7062 | 36137.21 | 1.6422 |
| .54 | 15208.51 | 1.7171 | 20600.79 | 1.7417 | 26123.44 | 1.7379 | 31426.36 | 1.7057 | 36181.08 | 1.6414 |
| .55 | 15260.65 | 1.7176 | 20655.96 | 1.7418 | 26178.13 | 1.7378 | 31477.14 | 1.7052 | 36224.87 | 1.6405 |
| .56 | 15312.84 | 1.7180 | 20711.14 | 1.7419 | 26232.80 | 1.7376 | 31527.86 | 1.7047 | 36268.57 | 1.6397 |
| .57 | 15365.08 | 1.7184 | 20766.33 | 1.7419 | 26287.45 | 1.7374 | 31578.52 | 1.7042 | 36312.19 | 1.6389 |
| .58 | 15417.36 | 1.7187 | 20821.53 | 1.7420 | 26342.07 | 1.7372 | 31629.12 | 1.7037 | 36355.73 | 1.6380 |
| .59 | 15469.69 | 1.7191 | 20876.74 | 1.7421 | 26396.67 | 1.7370 | 31679.67 | 1.7032 | 36399.18 | 1.6372 |
| .60 | 15522.06 | 1.7195 | 20931.96 | 1.7422 | 26451.25 | 1.7368 | 31730.16 | 1.7027 | 36442.55 | 1.6363 |
| .61 | 15574.48 | 1.7198 | 20987.19 | 1.7423 | 26505.80 | 1.7366 | 31780.60 | 1.7023 | 36485.83 | 1.6355 |
| .62 | 15626.94 | 1.7203 | 21042.44 | 1.7425 | 26560.33 | 1.7364 | 31830.98 | 1.7018 | 36529.03 | 1.6346 |
| .63 | 15679.45 | 1.7206 | 21097.71 | 1.7425 | 26614.83 | 1.7362 | 31881.30 | 1.7012 | 36572.14 | 1.6338 |
| .64 | 15732.00 | 1.7210 | 21152.98 | 1.7425 | 26669.31 | 1.7360 | 31931.56 | 1.7007 | 36615.17 | 1.6329 |
| .65 | 15784.60 | 1.7213 | 21208.26 | 1.7425 | 26723.76 | 1.7358 | 31981.76 | 1.7002 | 36658.11 | 1.6320 |
| .66 | 15837.24 | 1.7217 | 21263.54 | 1.7427 | 26778.19 | 1.7356 | 32031.91 | 1.6998 | 36700.97 | 1.6311 |
| .67 | 15889.92 | 1.7220 | 21318.84 | 1.7427 | 26832.59 | 1.7354 | 32082.00 | 1.6992 | 36743.74 | 1.6302 |
| .68 | 15942.65 | 1.7224 | 21374.14 | 1.7428 | 26886.96 | 1.7352 | 32132.03 | 1.6987 | 36786.42 | 1.6294 |
| .69 | 15995.42 | 1.7227 | 21429.45 | 1.7429 | 26941.31 | 1.7350 | 32181.99 | 1.6981 | 36829.02 | 1.6285 |
| .70 | 16048.23 | 1.7230 | 21484.77 | 1.7429 | 26995.63 | 1.7347 | 32231.89 | 1.6976 | 36871.53 | 1.6276 |
| .71 | 16101.08 | 1.7233 | 21540.10 | 1.7430 | 27049.92 | 1.7345 | 32281.74 | 1.6972 | 36913.95 | 1.6267 |
| .72 | 16153.97 | 1.7238 | 21595.44 | 1.7430 | 27104.18 | 1.7343 | 32331.53 | 1.6967 | 36956.29 | 1.6258 |
| .73 | 16206.91 | 1.7241 | 21650.78 | 1.7431 | 27158.42 | 1.7341 | 32381.26 | 1.6961 | 36998.54 | 1.6249 |
| .74 | 16259.89 | 1.7245 | 21706.13 | 1.7431 | 27212.63 | 1.7339 | 32430.93 | 1.6955 | 37040.70 | 1.6240 |
| .75 | 16312.91 | 1.7248 | 21761.48 | 1.7432 | 27266.81 | 1.7336 | 32480.53 | 1.6950 | 37082.78 | 1.6231 |
| .76 | 16365.97 | 1.7250 | 21816.84 | 1.7432 | 27320.96 | 1.7334 | 32530.07 | 1.6943 | 37124.77 | 1.6222 |
| .77 | 16419.06 | 1.7254 | 21872.20 | 1.7432 | 27375.08 | 1.7330 | 32579.54 | 1.6939 | 37166.67 | 1.6213 |
| .78 | 16472.20 | 1.7257 | 21927.57 | 1.7433 | 27429.16 | 1.7329 | 32628.96 | 1.6933 | 37208.48 | 1.6203 |
| .79 | 16525.38 | 1.7261 | 21982.95 | 1.7433 | 27483.22 | 1.7326 | 32678.32 | 1.6928 | 37250.20 | 1.6194 |
| .80 | 16578.60 | 1.7263 | 22038.33 | 1.7433 | 27537.25 | 1.7324 | 32727.61 | 1.6923 | 37291.83 | 1.6184 |
| .81 | 16631.85 | 1.7266 | 22093.71 | 1.7434 | 27591.25 | 1.7321 | 32776.84 | 1.6917 | 37333.37 | 1.6175 |
| .82 | 16685.14 | 1.7269 | 22149.10 | 1.7434 | 27645.21 | 1.7318 | 32826.01 | 1.6911 | 37374.82 | 1.6166 |
| .83 | 16738.47 | 1.7273 | 22204.49 | 1.7434 | 27699.14 | 1.7316 | 32875.11 | 1.6906 | 37416.18 | 1.6157 |
| .84 | 16791.84 | 1.7275 | 22259.88 | 1.7435 | 27753.04 | 1.7314 | 32924.15 | 1.6899 | 37457.46 | 1.6147 |
| .85 | 16845.24 | 1.7279 | 22315.28 | 1.7435 | 27806.91 | 1.7311 | 32973.12 | 1.6894 | 37498.65 | 1.6137 |
| .86 | 16898.68 | 1.7282 | 22370.68 | 1.7435 | 27860.75 | 1.7308 | 33022.03 | 1.6888 | 37539.74 | 1.6128 |
| .87 | 16952.16 | 1.7285 | 22426.08 | 1.7435 | 27914.55 | 1.7306 | 33070.88 | 1.6882 | 37580.74 | 1.6118 |
| .88 | 17005.68 | 1.7288 | 22481.48 | 1.7435 | 27968.32 | 1.7303 | 33119.66 | 1.6876 | 37621.65 | 1.6109 |
| .89 | 17059.23 | 1.7290 | 22536.88 | 1.7435 | 28022.06 | 1.7300 | 33168.37 | 1.6870 | 37662.47 | 1.6099 |
| .90 | 17112.81 | 1.7294 | 22592.28 | 1.7436 | 28075.76 | 1.7298 | 33217.02 | 1.6864 | 37703.20 | 1.6089 |
| .91 | 17166.43 | 1.7297 | 22647.69 | 1.7435 | 28129.43 | 1.7294 | 33265.60 | 1.6859 | 37743.84 | 1.6080 |
| .92 | 17220.09 | 1.7299 | 22703.09 | 1.7436 | 28183.06 | 1.7291 | 33314.12 | 1.6852 | 37784.39 | 1.6069 |
| .93 | 17273.78 | 1.7302 | 22758.50 | 1.7435 | 28236.65 | 1.7289 | 33362.57 | 1.6847 | 37824.84 | 1.6061 |
| .94 | 17327.51 | 1.7305 | 22813.90 | 1.7435 | 28290.21 | 1.7286 | 33410.96 | 1.6841 | 37865.21 | 1.6050 |
| .95 | 17381.27 | 1.7307 | 22869.30 | 1.7435 | 28343.74 | 1.7282 | 33459.28 | 1.6834 | 37905.48 | 1.6040 |
| .96 | 17435.06 | 1.7310 | 22924.70 | 1.7435 | 28397.23 | 1.7279 | 33507.52 | 1.6828 | 37945.66 | 1.6031 |
| .97 | 17488.89 | 1.7313 | 22980.10 | 1.7434 | 28450.68 | 1.7276 | 33555.70 | 1.6822 | 37985.75 | 1.6020 |
| .98 | 17542.75 | 1.7315 | 23035.49 | 1.7434 | 28504.09 | 1.7273 | 33603.81 | 1.6816 | 38025.74 | 1.6010 |
| .99 | 17596.64 | 1.7318 | 23090.88 | 1.7434 | 28557.47 | 1.7270 | 33651.86 | 1.6811 | 38065.64 | 1.6000 |
| 1.00 | 17650.56 | +1.7322 | 23146.27 | +1.7434 | 28610.81 | +1.7267 | 33699.84 | +1.6804 | 38105.45 | +1.5989 |

# TABLE VI. ARGUMENT 1.

Equation $= 22655''.226 + 22639''.2 \sin. x + 769''.5 \sin. 2x + 36''.7 \sin. 3x + 2''.0 \sin. 4x + 0''.1 \sin. 5x.$

Period, 27.55455245 days.

| Days. | 10 | | 11 | | 12 | | 13 | | 14 | |
|---|---|---|---|---|---|---|---|---|---|---|
| Decimals of a Day. | Equation. | Log. Dif. | Equation. | Log. Dif. | Equation. | Log. Dif. | Equation. | Log. Dif. | Equation. | Log. Dif. |
| .00 | 38105″.45 | +1.5988 | 41582″.33 | +1.4689 | 43962″.88 | +1.2531 | 45160″.73 | +0.7716 | 45164″.90 | −0.7679 |
| .01 | 38145.16 | 1.5979 | 41611.77 | 1.4673 | 43980.79 | 1.2502 | 45166.64 | 0.7627 | 45159.04 | 0.7760 |
| .02 | 38184.78 | 1.5968 | 41641.10 | 1.4657 | 43998.58 | 1.2475 | 45172.43 | 0.7536 | 45153.07 | 0.7839 |
| .03 | 38224.30 | 1.5958 | 41670.32 | 1.4640 | 44016.26 | 1.2442 | 45178.10 | 0.7443 | 45146.99 | 0.7917 |
| .04 | 38263.73 | 1.5949 | 41699.43 | 1.4625 | 44033.81 | 1.2412 | 45183.65 | 0.7348 | 45140.80 | 0.8000 |
| .05 | 38303.07 | 1.5937 | 41728.44 | 1.4608 | 44051.24 | 1.2385 | 45189.08 | 0.7259 | 45134.49 | 0.8082 |
| .06 | 38342.31 | 1.5927 | 41757.33 | 1.4590 | 44068.56 | 1.2355 | 45194.40 | 0.7152 | 45128.06 | 0.8156 |
| .07 | 38381.46 | 1.5916 | 41786.10 | 1.4575 | 44085.76 | 1.2322 | 45199.59 | 0.7050 | 45121.52 | 0.8228 |
| .08 | 38420.51 | 1.5906 | 41814.77 | 1.4557 | 44102.83 | 1.2295 | 45204.66 | 0.6946 | 45114.87 | 0.8306 |
| .09 | 38459.47 | 1.5895 | 41843.33 | 1.4539 | 44119.79 | 1.2263 | 45209.61 | 0.6839 | 45108.10 | 0.8376 |
| .10 | 38498.33 | 1.5884 | 41871.77 | 1.4523 | 44136.63 | 1.2232 | 45214.44 | 0.6739 | 45101.22 | 0.8445 |
| .11 | 38537.09 | 1.5874 | 41900.10 | 1.4507 | 44153.35 | 1.2201 | 45219.16 | 0.6618 | 45094.23 | 0.8519 |
| .12 | 38575.76 | 1.5864 | 41928.33 | 1.4489 | 44169.95 | 1.2169 | 45223.75 | 0.6503 | 45087.12 | 0.8585 |
| .13 | 38614.34 | 1.5852 | 41956.44 | 1.4470 | 44186.43 | 1.2138 | 45228.22 | 0.6385 | 45079.90 | 0.8651 |
| .14 | 38652.82 | 1.5841 | 41984.43 | 1.4454 | 44202.79 | 1.2106 | 45232.57 | 0.6274 | 45072.57 | 0.8722 |
| .15 | 38691.20 | 1.5830 | 42012.32 | 1.4436 | 44219.03 | 1.2076 | 45236.81 | 0.6149 | 45065.12 | 0.8785 |
| .16 | 38729.48 | 1.5819 | 42040.09 | 1.4418 | 44235.16 | 1.2041 | 45240.93 | 0.6010 | 45057.56 | 0.8848 |
| .17 | 38767.67 | 1.5808 | 42067.75 | 1.4401 | 44251.16 | 1.2009 | 45244.92 | 0.5888 | 45049.89 | 0.8915 |
| .18 | 38805.76 | 1.5798 | 42095.30 | 1.4384 | 44267.04 | 1.1976 | 45248.80 | 0.5752 | 45042.10 | 0.8976 |
| .19 | 38843.76 | 1.5786 | 42122.74 | 1.4365 | 44282.80 | 1.1945 | 45252.56 | 0.5611 | 45034.20 | 0.9036 |
| .20 | 38881.66 | 1.5775 | 42150.06 | 1.4348 | 44298.45 | 1.1909 | 45256.20 | 0.5465 | 45026.19 | 0.9096 |
| .21 | 38919.46 | 1.5763 | 42177.27 | 1.4330 | 44313.97 | 1.1875 | 45259.72 | 0.5315 | 45018.07 | 0.9159 |
| .22 | 38957.16 | 1.5752 | 42204.37 | 1.4313 | 44329.37 | 1.1840 | 45263.12 | 0.5159 | 45009.83 | 0.9217 |
| .23 | 38994.76 | 1.5741 | 42231.36 | 1.4292 | 44344.65 | 1.1810 | 45266.40 | 0.4997 | 45001.48 | 0.9274 |
| .24 | 39032.27 | 1.5730 | 42258.23 | 1.4275 | 44359.82 | 1.1775 | 45269.56 | 0.4829 | 44993.02 | 0.9335 |
| .25 | 39069.68 | 1.5718 | 42284.99 | 1.4257 | 44374.87 | 1.1740 | 45272.60 | 0.4654 | 44984.44 | 0.9390 |
| .26 | 39106.99 | 1.5706 | 42311.64 | 1.4237 | 44389.80 | 1.1703 | 45275.52 | 0.4472 | 44975.75 | 0.9445 |
| .27 | 39144.20 | 1.5695 | 42338.17 | 1.4219 | 44404.60 | 1.1668 | 45278.32 | 0.4298 | 44966.95 | 0.9499 |
| .28 | 39181.31 | 1.5683 | 42364.59 | 1.4200 | 44419.28 | 1.1632 | 45281.01 | 0.4099 | 44958.04 | 0.9552 |
| .29 | 39218.32 | 1.5672 | 42390.89 | 1.4181 | 44433.84 | 1.1599 | 45283.58 | 0.3874 | 44949.02 | 0.9609 |
| .30 | 39255.24 | 1.5659 | 42417.08 | 1.4163 | 44448.29 | 1.1562 | 45286.02 | 0.3674 | 44939.88 | 0.9661 |
| .31 | 39292.05 | 1.5648 | 42443.16 | 1.4145 | 44462.62 | 1.1526 | 45288.35 | 0.3444 | 44930.63 | 0.9713 |
| .32 | 39328.76 | 1.5637 | 42469.13 | 1.4125 | 44476.83 | 1.1486 | 45290.56 | 0.3201 | 44921.27 | 0.9763 |
| .33 | 39365.38 | 1.5624 | 42494.98 | 1.4106 | 44490.91 | 1.1449 | 45292.65 | 0.2945 | 44911.80 | 0.9814 |
| .34 | 39401.89 | 1.5613 | 42520.72 | 1.4085 | 44504.87 | 1.1415 | 45294.62 | 0.2672 | 44902.22 | 0.9863 |
| .35 | 39438.31 | 1.5600 | 42546.34 | 1.4067 | 44518.72 | 1.1377 | 45296.47 | 0.2405 | 44892.53 | 0.9917 |
| .36 | 39474.62 | 1.5588 | 42571.85 | 1.4046 | 44532.45 | 1.1338 | 45298.21 | 0.2068 | 44882.72 | 0.9961 |
| .37 | 39510.83 | 1.5576 | 42597.24 | 1.4028 | 44546.06 | 1.1297 | 45299.82 | 0.1761 | 44872.81 | 1.0013 |
| .38 | 39546.94 | 1.5564 | 42622.52 | 1.4009 | 44559.54 | 1.1258 | 45301.32 | 0.1399 | 44862.78 | 1.0060 |
| .39 | 39582.95 | 1.5552 | 42647.69 | 1.3988 | 44572.90 | 1.1222 | 45302.70 | 0.1004 | 44852.64 | 1.0107 |
| .40 | 39618.86 | 1.5540 | 42672.74 | 1.3967 | 44586.15 | 1.1179 | 45303.96 | 0.0569 | 44842.39 | 1.0154 |
| .41 | 39654.67 | 1.5528 | 42697.67 | 1.3949 | 44599.27 | 1.1142 | 45305.10 | 0.0086 | 44832.03 | 1.0199 |
| .42 | 39690.38 | 1.5515 | 42722.49 | 1.3929 | 44612.28 | 1.1099 | 45306.12 | 9.9590 | 44821.56 | 1.0245 |
| .43 | 39725.99 | 1.5502 | 42747.20 | 1.3908 | 44625.16 | 1.1059 | 45307.03 | 9.8921 | 44810.98 | 1.0290 |
| .44 | 39761.49 | 1.5490 | 42771.79 | 1.3888 | 44637.92 | 1.1021 | 45307.81 | 9.8261 | 44800.29 | 1.0334 |
| .45 | 39796.89 | 1.5478 | 42796.27 | 1.3867 | 44650.57 | 1.0976 | 45308.48 | 9.7404 | 44789.49 | 1.0382 |
| .46 | 39832.19 | 1.5465 | 42820.63 | 1.3845 | 44663.09 | 1.0934 | 45309.03 | 9.6335 | 44778.57 | 1.0422 |
| .47 | 39867.39 | 1.5452 | 42844.87 | 1.3825 | 44675.49 | 1.0895 | 45309.46 | 9.5051 | 44767.55 | 1.0464 |
| .48 | 39902.48 | 1.5439 | 42869.00 | 1.3806 | 44687.78 | 1.0849 | 45309.78 | 9.2788 | 44756.42 | 1.0507 |
| .49 | 39937.47 | 1.5426 | 42893.02 | 1.3784 | 44699.94 | 1.0806 | 45309.97 | 8.9031 | 44745.18 | 1.0554 |
| .50 | 39972.36 | +1.5414 | 42916.92 | +1.3762 | 44711.98 | +1.0763 | 45310.05 | +8.6021 | 44733.82 | −1.0592 |

# TABLE VI. ARGUMENT 1.

Equation = 22655″.226 + 22639″.2 sin. $x$ + 769″.5 sin. $2x$ + 36″.7 sin. $3x$ + 2″.0 sin. $4x$ + 0″.1 sin. $5x$.

Period, 27.55455245 days.

| Days. | 10 | | 11 | | 12 | | 13 | | 14 | |
|---|---|---|---|---|---|---|---|---|---|---|
| Decimals of a Day. | Equation. | Log. Dif. | Equation. | Log. Dif. | Equation. | Log. Dif. | Equation. | Log. Dif. | Equation. | Log. Dif. |
| .50 | 39972″.36 | +1.5414 | 42916″.92 | +1.3762 | 44711″.98 | +1.0763 | 45310″.05 | +8.6021 | 44733″.82 | −1.0592 |
| .51 | 40007.15 | 1.5402 | 42940.70 | 1.3742 | 44723.90 | 1.0723 | 45310.01 | −9.2041 | 44722.36 | 1.0633 |
| .52 | 40041.84 | 1.5388 | 42964.37 | 1.3720 | 44735.71 | 1.0675 | 45309.85 | 9.4314 | 44710.79 | 1.0675 |
| .53 | 40076.42 | 1.5376 | 42987.92 | 1.3699 | 44747.39 | 1.0630 | 45309.58 | 9.6021 | 44699.11 | 1.0716 |
| .54 | 40110.90 | 1.5362 | 43011.36 | 1.3678 | 44758.95 | 1.0584 | 45309.18 | 9.7076 | 44687.32 | 1.0755 |
| .55 | 40145.27 | 1.5349 | 43034.68 | 1.3655 | 44770.39 | 1.0539 | 45308.67 | 9.7993 | 44675.42 | 1.0795 |
| .56 | 40179.54 | 1.5336 | 43057.88 | 1.3634 | 44781.71 | 1.0492 | 45308.04 | 9.8692 | 44663.41 | 1.0835 |
| .57 | 40213.70 | 1.5323 | 43080.97 | 1.3612 | 44792.91 | 1.0445 | 45307.30 | 9.9345 | 44651.29 | 1.0874 |
| .58 | 40247.76 | 1.5310 | 43103.94 | 1.3591 | 44803.99 | 1.0399 | 45306.44 | 9.9912 | 44639.06 | 1.0913 |
| .59 | 40281.72 | 1.5297 | 43126.80 | 1.3568 | 44814.95 | 1.0351 | 45305.46 | 0.0414 | 44626.72 | 1.0948 |
| .60 | 40315.58 | 1.5282 | 43149.54 | 1.3545 | 44825.79 | 1.0302 | 45304.36 | 0.0864 | 44614.28 | 1.0990 |
| .61 | 40349.33 | 1.5268 | 43172.16 | 1.3522 | 44836.51 | 1.0253 | 45303.14 | 0.1239 | 44601.72 | 1.1025 |
| .62 | 40382.97 | 1.5255 | 43194.66 | 1.3500 | 44847.11 | 1.0203 | 45301.81 | 0.1614 | 44589.06 | 1.1066 |
| .63 | 40416.51 | 1.5241 | 43217.05 | 1.3479 | 44857.59 | 1.0149 | 45300.36 | 0.1959 | 44576.28 | 1.1100 |
| .64 | 40449.94 | 1.5228 | 43239.33 | 1.3456 | 44867.94 | 1.0103 | 45298.79 | 0.2279 | 44563.40 | 1.1133 |
| .65 | 40483.27 | 1.5214 | 43261.49 | 1.3430 | 44878.18 | 1.0051 | 45297.10 | 0.2553 | 44550.42 | 1.1173 |
| .66 | 40516.49 | 1.5201 | 43283.52 | 1.3408 | 44888.30 | 0.9996 | 45295.30 | 0.2833 | 44537.32 | 1.1206 |
| .67 | 40549.61 | 1.5186 | 43305.44 | 1.3387 | 44898.29 | 0.9948 | 45293.38 | 0.3096 | 44524.12 | 1.1245 |
| .68 | 40582.62 | 1.5173 | 43327.25 | 1.3363 | 44908.17 | 0.9890 | 45291.34 | 0.3324 | 44510.80 | 1.1277 |
| .69 | 40615.53 | 1.5159 | 43348.94 | 1.3338 | 44917.92 | 0.9841 | 45289.19 | 0.3560 | 44497.38 | 1.1309 |
| .70 | 40648.33 | 1.5145 | 43370.51 | 1.3314 | 44927.56 | 0.9786 | 45286.92 | 0.3766 | 44483.86 | 1.1348 |
| .71 | 40681.03 | 1.5131 | 43391.96 | 1.3292 | 44937.08 | 0.9727 | 45284.54 | 0.3979 | 44470.22 | 1.1380 |
| .72 | 40713.62 | 1.5116 | 43413.30 | 1.3267 | 44946.47 | 0.9675 | 45282.04 | 0.4183 | 44456.48 | 1.1415 |
| .73 | 40746.10 | 1.5101 | 43434.52 | 1.3243 | 44955.75 | 0.9614 | 45279.42 | 0.4378 | 44442.63 | 1.1449 |
| .74 | 40778.47 | 1.5088 | 43455.62 | 1.3220 | 44964.90 | 0.9562 | 45276.68 | 0.4548 | 44428.67 | 1.1479 |
| .75 | 40810.74 | 1.5073 | 43476.61 | 1.3196 | 44973.94 | 0.9499 | 45273.83 | 0.4728 | 44414.61 | 1.1513 |
| .76 | 40842.90 | 1.5058 | 43497.48 | 1.3171 | 44982.85 | 0.9445 | 45270.86 | 0.4886 | 44400.44 | 1.1547 |
| .77 | 40874.95 | 1.5045 | 43518.23 | 1.3145 | 44991.65 | 0.9380 | 45267.78 | 0.5051 | 44386.16 | 1.1580 |
| .78 | 40906.90 | 1.5030 | 43538.86 | 1.3120 | 45000.32 | 0.9325 | 45264.58 | 0.5211 | 44371.77 | 1.1611 |
| .79 | 40938.74 | 1.5015 | 43559.37 | 1.3096 | 45008.88 | 0.9258 | 45261.26 | 0.5353 | 44357.28 | 1.1644 |
| .80 | 40970.47 | 1.5001 | 43579.77 | 1.3071 | 45017.31 | 0.9196 | 45257.83 | 0.5502 | 44342.68 | 1.1676 |
| .81 | 41002.10 | 1.4984 | 43600.05 | 1.3045 | 45025.62 | 0.9133 | 45254.28 | 0.5647 | 44327.97 | 1.1706 |
| .82 | 41033.61 | 1.4970 | 43620.21 | 1.3018 | 45033.81 | 0.9069 | 45250.61 | 0.5775 | 44313.16 | 1.1738 |
| .83 | 41065.02 | 1.4955 | 43640.25 | 1.2993 | 45041.88 | 0.9009 | 45246.83 | 0.5899 | 44298.24 | 1.1767 |
| .84 | 41096.32 | 1.4940 | 43660.17 | 1.2969 | 45049.84 | 0.8938 | 45242.94 | 0.6042 | 44283.22 | 1.1798 |
| .85 | 41127.51 | 1.4925 | 43679.98 | 1.2943 | 45057.67 | 0.8871 | 45238.92 | 0.6160 | 44268.09 | 1.1826 |
| .86 | 41158.59 | 1.4911 | 43699.67 | 1.2916 | 45065.38 | 0.8802 | 45234.79 | 0.6274 | 44252.86 | 1.1858 |
| .87 | 41189.57 | 1.4896 | 43719.24 | 1.2889 | 45072.97 | 0.8733 | 45230.55 | 0.6395 | 44237.52 | 1.1889 |
| .88 | 41220.44 | 1.4880 | 43738.69 | 1.2863 | 45080.44 | 0.8663 | 45226.19 | 0.6503 | 44222.07 | 1.1920 |
| .89 | 41251.20 | 1.4864 | 43758.02 | 1.2837 | 45087.79 | 0.8591 | 45221.72 | 0.6618 | 44206.52 | 1.1948 |
| .90 | 41281.85 | 1.4849 | 43777.24 | 1.2810 | 45095.02 | 0.8525 | 45217.13 | 0.6730 | 44190.86 | 1.1976 |
| .91 | 41312.39 | 1.4833 | 43796.34 | 1.2784 | 45102.14 | 0.8451 | 45212.42 | 0.6830 | 44175.10 | 1.2007 |
| .92 | 41342.82 | 1.4817 | 43815.32 | 1.2756 | 45109.14 | 0.8370 | 45207.60 | 0.6937 | 44159.23 | 1.2034 |
| .93 | 41373.14 | 1.4801 | 43834.18 | 1.2727 | 45116.01 | 0.8287 | 45202.66 | 0.7033 | 44143.26 | 1.2062 |
| .94 | 41403.35 | 1.4787 | 43852.92 | 1.2700 | 45122.75 | 0.8215 | 45197.61 | 0.7126 | 44127.18 | 1.2089 |
| .95 | 41433.46 | 1.4770 | 43871.54 | 1.2674 | 45129.38 | 0.8136 | 45192.45 | 0.7226 | 44111.00 | 1.2119 |
| .96 | 41463.45 | 1.4754 | 43890.05 | 1.2644 | 45135.89 | 0.8055 | 45187.17 | 0.7324 | 44094.71 | 1.2146 |
| .97 | 41493.33 | 1.4740 | 43908.43 | 1.2617 | 45142.28 | 0.7973 | 45181.77 | 0.7412 | 44078.32 | 1.2175 |
| .98 | 41523.11 | 1.4722 | 43926.70 | 1.2589 | 45148.55 | 0.7889 | 45176.26 | 0.7497 | 44061.82 | 1.2201 |
| .99 | 41552.77 | 1.4707 | 43944.85 | 1.2560 | 45154.70 | 0.7803 | 45170.64 | 0.7589 | 44045.22 | 1.2227 |
| 1.00 | 41582.33 | +1.4689 | 43962.88 | +1.2531 | 45160.73 | +0.7716 | 45164.90 | −0.7679 | 44028.52 | −1.2256 |

# TABLE VI. ARGUMENT 1.

Equation $= 22655''.226 + 22639''.2 \text{ sin. } x + 769''.5 \text{ sin. } 2x + 36''.7 \text{ sin. } 3x + 2''.0 \text{ sin. } 4x + 0''.1 \text{ sin. } 5x.$

Period, 27.55455245 days.

| Days. | 15 | | 16 | | 17 | | 18 | | 19 | |
|---|---|---|---|---|---|---|---|---|---|---|
| Decimals of a Day. | Equation. | Log. Dif. | Equation. | Log. Dif. | Equation. | Log. Dif. | Equation. | Log. Dif. | Equation. | Log. Dif. |
| .00 | 44028.52″ | −1.2256 | 41855.39″ | −1.4235 | 38787.01″ | −1.5398 | 34991.50″ | −1.6129 | 30654.69″ | −1.6575 |
| .01 | 44011.71 | 1.2282 | 41828.87 | 1.4251 | 38752.35 | 1.5406 | 34950.49 | 1.6135 | 30609.25 | 1.6579 |
| .02 | 43994.80 | 1.2309 | 41802.26 | 1.4264 | 38717.63 | 1.5416 | 34909.42 | 1.6140 | 30563.77 | 1.6581 |
| .03 | 43977.78 | 1.2335 | 41775.57 | 1.4278 | 38682.83 | 1.5425 | 34868.30 | 1.6145 | 30518.26 | 1.6585 |
| .04 | 43960.66 | 1.2360 | 41748.79 | 1.4292 | 38647.96 | 1.5433 | 34827.13 | 1.6151 | 30472.71 | 1.6588 |
| .05 | 43943.44 | 1.2385 | 41721.92 | 1.4308 | 38613.02 | 1.5443 | 34785.91 | 1.6157 | 30427.13 | 1.6591 |
| .06 | 43926.12 | 1.2412 | 41694.96 | 1.4322 | 38578.00 | 1.5452 | 34744.63 | 1.6163 | 30381.52 | 1.6594 |
| .07 | 43908.69 | 1.2437 | 41667.91 | 1.4336 | 38542.91 | 1.5459 | 34703.30 | 1.6168 | 30335.88 | 1.6598 |
| .08 | 43891.16 | 1.2462 | 41640.77 | 1.4351 | 38507.76 | 1.5469 | 34661.91 | 1.6174 | 30290.20 | 1.6600 |
| .09 | 43873.53 | 1.2490 | 41613.54 | 1.4364 | 38472.53 | 1.5478 | 34620.48 | 1.6179 | 30244.49 | 1.6603 |
| .10 | 43855.79 | 1.2514 | 41586.23 | 1.4378 | 38437.23 | 1.5488 | 34578.99 | 1.6184 | 30198.75 | 1.6607 |
| .11 | 43837.95 | 1.2541 | 41558.83 | 1.4393 | 38401.85 | 1.5495 | 34537.45 | 1.6189 | 30152.97 | 1.6610 |
| .12 | 43820.00 | 1.2565 | 41531.33 | 1.4406 | 38366.41 | 1.5503 | 34495.86 | 1.6196 | 30107.16 | 1.6613 |
| .13 | 43801.95 | 1.2589 | 41503.75 | 1.4418 | 38330.90 | 1.5512 | 34454.21 | 1.6201 | 30061.32 | 1.6616 |
| .14 | 43783.80 | 1.2613 | 41476.09 | 1.4433 | 38295.32 | 1.5521 | 34412.51 | 1.6206 | 30015.45 | 1.6618 |
| .15 | 43765.55 | 1.2637 | 41448.34 | 1.4446 | 38259.66 | 1.5531 | 34370.76 | 1.6212 | 29969.55 | 1.6621 |
| .16 | 43747.20 | 1.2660 | 41420.50 | 1.4461 | 38223.93 | 1.5538 | 34328.96 | 1.6217 | 29923.62 | 1.6625 |
| .17 | 43728.75 | 1.2686 | 41392.57 | 1.4474 | 38188.14 | 1.5548 | 34287.11 | 1.6222 | 29877.65 | 1.6628 |
| .18 | 43710.19 | 1.2709 | 41364.56 | 1.4487 | 38152.27 | 1.5555 | 34245.21 | 1.6227 | 29831.65 | 1.6631 |
| .19 | 43691.53 | 1.2732 | 41336.46 | 1.4501 | 38116.34 | 1.5563 | 34203.26 | 1.6232 | 29785.62 | 1.6634 |
| .20 | 43672.77 | 1.2756 | 41308.27 | 1.4514 | 38080.34 | 1.5571 | 34161.26 | 1.6238 | 29739.56 | 1.6637 |
| .21 | 43653.91 | 1.2779 | 41279.99 | 1.4527 | 38044.27 | 1.5581 | 34119.20 | 1.6243 | 29693.47 | 1.6639 |
| .22 | 43634.95 | 1.2801 | 41251.63 | 1.4541 | 38008.12 | 1.5588 | 34077.10 | 1.6248 | 29647.35 | 1.6642 |
| .23 | 43615.89 | 1.2823 | 41223.18 | 1.4553 | 37971.91 | 1.5595 | 34034.95 | 1.6253 | 29601.20 | 1.6645 |
| .24 | 43596.73 | 1.2849 | 41194.65 | 1.4567 | 37935.64 | 1.5605 | 33992.75 | 1.6259 | 29555.02 | 1.6647 |
| .25 | 43577.46 | 1.2872 | 41166.03 | 1.4581 | 37899.29 | 1.5613 | 33950.49 | 1.6263 | 29508.81 | 1.6650 |
| .26 | 43558.09 | 1.2894 | 41137.32 | 1.4593 | 37862.87 | 1.5622 | 33908.19 | 1.6268 | 29462.57 | 1.6653 |
| .27 | 43538.62 | 1.2913 | 41108.53 | 1.4605 | 37826.38 | 1.5629 | 33865.84 | 1.6274 | 29416.30 | 1.6656 |
| .28 | 43519.06 | 1.2939 | 41079.66 | 1.4618 | 37789.83 | 1.5637 | 33823.44 | 1.6279 | 29370.00 | 1.6658 |
| .29 | 43499.39 | 1.2961 | 41050.70 | 1.4631 | 37753.21 | 1.5645 | 33780.99 | 1.6284 | 29323.68 | 1.6661 |
| .30 | 43479.62 | 1.2980 | 41021.65 | 1.4643 | 37716.53 | 1.5654 | 33738.49 | 1.6289 | 29277.33 | 1.6664 |
| .31 | 43459.76 | 1.3004 | 40992.52 | 1.4657 | 37679.77 | 1.5660 | 33695.94 | 1.6293 | 29230.94 | 1.6666 |
| .32 | 43439.79 | 1.3025 | 40963.30 | 1.4669 | 37642.95 | 1.5669 | 33653.35 | 1.6299 | 29184.53 | 1.6669 |
| .33 | 43419.72 | 1.3047 | 40934.00 | 1.4682 | 37606.06 | 1.5677 | 33610.71 | 1.6303 | 29138.09 | 1.6672 |
| .34 | 43399.55 | 1.3067 | 40904.61 | 1.4693 | 37569.10 | 1.5684 | 33568.02 | 1.6308 | 29091.62 | 1.6675 |
| .35 | 43379.29 | 1.3090 | 40875.14 | 1.4706 | 37532.08 | 1.5692 | 33525.28 | 1.6312 | 29045.12 | 1.6677 |
| .36 | 43358.92 | 1.3111 | 40845.59 | 1.4719 | 37494.99 | 1.5701 | 33482.50 | 1.6318 | 28998.60 | 1.6680 |
| .37 | 43338.45 | 1.3131 | 40815.95 | 1.4731 | 37457.83 | 1.5707 | 33439.66 | 1.6321 | 28952.05 | 1.6682 |
| .38 | 43317.89 | 1.3152 | 40786.23 | 1.4742 | 37420.61 | 1.5715 | 33396.79 | 1.6328 | 28905.47 | 1.6684 |
| .39 | 43297.23 | 1.3173 | 40756.43 | 1.4756 | 37383.32 | 1.5723 | 33353.86 | 1.6332 | 28858.87 | 1.6687 |
| .40 | 43276.47 | 1.3196 | 40726.54 | 1.4767 | 37345.97 | 1.5731 | 33310.89 | 1.6337 | 28812.24 | 1.6689 |
| .41 | 43255.60 | 1.3214 | 40696.57 | 1.4780 | 37308.55 | 1.5739 | 33267.87 | 1.6342 | 28765.59 | 1.6691 |
| .42 | 43234.64 | 1.3232 | 40666.51 | 1.4792 | 37271.06 | 1.5746 | 33224.80 | 1.6346 | 28718.91 | 1.6694 |
| .43 | 43213.59 | 1.3255 | 40636.37 | 1.4803 | 37233.51 | 1.5754 | 33181.69 | 1.6351 | 28672.20 | 1.6697 |
| .44 | 43192.43 | 1.3273 | 40606.15 | 1.4814 | 37195.89 | 1.5761 | 33138.53 | 1.6355 | 28625.46 | 1.6699 |
| .45 | 43171.18 | 1.3296 | 40575.85 | 1.4827 | 37158.21 | 1.5768 | 33095.33 | 1.6360 | 28578.70 | 1.6700 |
| .46 | 43149.82 | 1.3314 | 40545.46 | 1.4838 | 37120.47 | 1.5775 | 33052.08 | 1.6364 | 28531.92 | 1.6703 |
| .47 | 43128.37 | 1.3332 | 40515.00 | 1.4850 | 37082.67 | 1.5783 | 33008.79 | 1.6369 | 28485.11 | 1.6706 |
| .48 | 43106.83 | 1.3355 | 40484.45 | 1.4861 | 37044.80 | 1.5791 | 32965.45 | 1.6373 | 28438.27 | 1.6708 |
| .49 | 43085.18 | 1.3373 | 40453.82 | 1.4872 | 37006.86 | 1.5798 | 32922.07 | 1.6378 | 28391.41 | 1.6709 |
| .50 | 43063.44 | −1.3393 | 40423.11 | −1.4886 | 36968.86 | −1.5806 | 32878.64 | −1.6382 | 28344.53 | −1.6713 |

# TABLE VI. ARGUMENT 1.

Equation = $22655''.223 + 22639''.2 \text{ sin. } x + 769''.5 \text{ sin. } 2x + 36''.7 \text{ sin. } 3x + 2''.0 \text{ sin. } 4x + 0''.1 \text{ sin. } 5x$.

Period, 27.55455245 days.

| Days. | 15 | | 16 | | 17 | | 18 | | 19 | |
|---|---|---|---|---|---|---|---|---|---|---|
| Decimals of a Day. | Equation. | Log. Dif. | Equation. | Log. Dif. | Equation. | Log. Dif. | Equation. | Log. Dif. | Equation. | Log. Dif. |
| .50 | 43063.44″ | −1.3393 | 40423.11″ | −1.4886 | 36968.86″ | −1.5806 | 32878.64″ | −1.6382 | 28344.53″ | −1.6713 |
| .51 | 43041.60 | 1.3412 | 40392.31 | 1.4897 | 36930.79 | 1.5812 | 32835.17 | 1.6387 | 28297.62 | 1.6715 |
| .52 | 43019.66 | 1.3430 | 40361.43 | 1.4909 | 36892.66 | 1.5819 | 32791.65 | 1.6391 | 28250.69 | 1.6718 |
| .53 | 42997.63 | 1.3450 | 403[illegible]0.47 | 1.4920 | 36854.47 | 1.5827 | 32748.09 | 1.6396 | 28203.73 | 1.6719 |
| .54 | 42975.50 | 1.3470 | 40299.43 | 1.4931 | 36816.22 | 1.5834 | 32704.48 | 1.6400 | 28156.75 | 1.6721 |
| .55 | 42953.27 | 1.3487 | 40268.31 | 1.4942 | 36777.90 | 1.5841 | 32660.83 | 1.6404 | 28109.75 | 1.6724 |
| .56 | 42930.95 | 1.3506 | 40237.11 | 1.4953 | 36739.52 | 1.5848 | 32617.14 | 1.6408 | 28062.72 | 1.6725 |
| .57 | 42908.53 | 1.3526 | 40205.83 | 1.4963 | 36701.08 | 1.5856 | 32573.41 | 1.6413 | 28015.67 | 1.6727 |
| .58 | 42886.01 | 1.3543 | 40174.47 | 1.4975 | 36662.57 | 1.5863 | 32529.63 | 1.6417 | 27968.60 | 1.6729 |
| .59 | 42863.40 | 1.3560 | 40143.03 | 1.4985 | 36624.00 | 1.5869 | 32485.81 | 1.6421 | 27921.51 | 1.6732 |
| .60 | 42840.70 | 1.3581 | 40111.51 | 1.4997 | 36585.37 | 1.5876 | 32441.95 | 1.6426 | 27874.39 | 1.6734 |
| .61 | 42817.89 | 1.3598 | 40079.91 | 1.5008 | 36546.68 | 1.5883 | 32398.04 | 1.6430 | 27827.25 | 1.6735 |
| .62 | 42794.99 | 1.3615 | 40048.23 | 1.5019 | 36507.93 | 1.5889 | 32354.09 | 1.6434 | 27780.09 | 1.6738 |
| .63 | 42772.00 | 1.3634 | 40016.47 | 1.5030 | 36469.12 | 1.5897 | 32310.10 | 1.6438 | 27732.90 | 1.6740 |
| .64 | 42748.91 | 1.3653 | 39984.63 | 1.5041 | 36430.24 | 1.5904 | 32266.07 | 1.6442 | 27685.69 | 1.6742 |
| .65 | 42725.72 | 1.3670 | 39952.71 | 1.5051 | 36391.30 | 1.5911 | 32221.99 | 1.6446 | 27638.46 | 1.6744 |
| .66 | 42702.44 | 1.3689 | 39920.71 | 1.5062 | 36352.30 | 1.5918 | 32177.88 | 1.6450 | 27591.21 | 1.6745 |
| .67 | 42679.06 | 1.3705 | 39888.63 | 1.5073 | 36313.24 | 1.5924 | 32133.72 | 1.6454 | 27543.94 | 1.6747 |
| .68 | 42655.59 | 1.3722 | 39856.47 | 1.5083 | 36274.12 | 1.5931 | 32089.52 | 1.6458 | 27496.65 | 1.6750 |
| .69 | 42632.03 | 1.3740 | 39824.24 | 1.5093 | 36234.94 | 1.5937 | 32045.28 | 1.6462 | 27449.34 | 1.6752 |
| .70 | 42608.37 | 1.3758 | 39791.93 | 1.5104 | 36195.70 | 1.5944 | 32001.00 | 1.6466 | 27402.01 | 1.6754 |
| .71 | 42584.61 | 1.3775 | 39759.54 | 1.5114 | 36156.40 | 1.5951 | 31956.68 | 1.6470 | 27354.65 | 1.6756 |
| .72 | 42560.76 | 1.3791 | 39727.07 | 1.5126 | 36117.04 | 1.5956 | 31912.32 | 1.6474 | 27307.27 | 1.6757 |
| .73 | 42536.82 | 1.3807 | 39694.52 | 1.5135 | 36077.63 | 1.5964 | 31867.92 | 1.6478 | 27259.88 | 1.6759 |
| .74 | 42512.79 | 1.3825 | 39661.90 | 1.5145 | 36038.15 | 1.5970 | 31823.48 | 1.6482 | 27212.47 | 1.6761 |
| .75 | 42488.66 | 1.3843 | 39629.20 | 1.5156 | 35998.61 | 1.5976 | 31779.00 | 1.6486 | 27165.04 | 1.6763 |
| .76 | 42464.43 | 1.3860 | 39596.42 | 1.5167 | 35959.02 | 1.5984 | 31734.48 | 1.6490 | 27117.58 | 1.6764 |
| .77 | 42440.11 | 1.3876 | 39563.56 | 1.5176 | 35919.36 | 1.5990 | 31689.92 | 1.6493 | 27070.11 | 1.6766 |
| .78 | 42415.70 | 1.3892 | 39530.63 | 1.5186 | 35879.64 | 1.5996 | 31645.32 | 1.6497 | 27022.62 | 1.6768 |
| .79 | 42391.20 | 1.3908 | 39497.62 | 1.5197 | 35839.87 | 1.6002 | 31600.68 | 1.6500 | 26975.11 | 1.6770 |
| .80 | 42366.61 | 1.3925 | 39464.53 | 1.5206 | 35800.04 | 1.6009 | 31556.01 | 1.6504 | 26927.58 | 1.6771 |
| .81 | 42341.92 | 1.3943 | 39431.37 | 1.5216 | 35760.15 | 1.6015 | 31511.30 | 1.6508 | 26880.04 | 1.6773 |
| .82 | 42317.13 | 1.3957 | 39398.13 | 1.5225 | 35720.20 | 1.6021 | 31466.55 | 1.6512 | 26832.47 | 1.6775 |
| .83 | 42292.26 | 1.3974 | 39364.82 | 1.5236 | 35680.20 | 1.6027 | 31421.76 | 1.6516 | 26784.89 | 1.6776 |
| .84 | 42267.29 | 1.3989 | 39331.43 | 1.5246 | 35640.14 | 1.6033 | 31376.93 | 1.6520 | 26737.29 | 1.6777 |
| .85 | 42242.23 | 1.4006 | 39297.96 | 1.5255 | 35600.02 | 1.6040 | 31332.06 | 1.6522 | 26689.68 | 1.6780 |
| .86 | 42217.08 | 1.4021 | 39264.42 | 1.5264 | 35559.84 | 1.6045 | 31287.16 | 1.6526 | 26642.04 | 1.6781 |
| .87 | 42191.84 | 1.4037 | 39230.81 | 1.5275 | 35519.61 | 1.6052 | 31242.22 | 1.6530 | 26594.39 | 1.6782 |
| .88 | 42166.51 | 1.4053 | 39197.12 | 1.5285 | 35479.32 | 1.6057 | 31197.24 | 1.6534 | 26546.72 | 1.6783 |
| .89 | 42141.08 | 1.4068 | 39163.35 | 1.5294 | 35438.98 | 1.6064 | 31152.22 | 1.6537 | 26499.04 | 1.6785 |
| .90 | 42115.56 | 1.4084 | 39129.51 | 1.5305 | 35398.58 | 1.6070 | 31107.17 | 1.6541 | 26451.34 | 1.6787 |
| .91 | 42089.95 | 1.4099 | 39095.59 | 1.5314 | 35358.12 | 1.6077 | 31062.08 | 1.6544 | 26403.62 | 1.6789 |
| .92 | 42064.25 | 1.4114 | 39061.60 | 1.5324 | 35317.60 | 1.6083 | 31016.96 | 1.6548 | 26355.88 | 1.6790 |
| .93 | 42038.46 | 1.4130 | 39027.53 | 1.5333 | 35277.03 | 1.6087 | 30971.80 | 1.6551 | 26308.13 | 1.6791 |
| .94 | 42012.58 | 1.4145 | 38993.39 | 1.5341 | 35236.41 | 1.6094 | 30926.60 | 1.6554 | 26260.37 | 1.6792 |
| .95 | 41986.61 | 1.4160 | 38959.18 | 1.5351 | 35195.73 | 1.6100 | 30881.37 | 1.6558 | 26212.59 | 1.6794 |
| .96 | 41960.55 | 1.4176 | 38924.89 | 1.5361 | 35154.99 | 1.6106 | 30836.10 | 1.6561 | 26164.79 | 1.6795 |
| .97 | 41934.39 | 1.4191 | 38890.53 | 1.5370 | 35114.20 | 1.6112 | 30790.80 | 1.6565 | 26116.98 | 1.6796 |
| .98 | 41908.14 | 1.4205 | 38856.09 | 1.5379 | 35073.35 | 1.6117 | 30745.46 | 1.6568 | 26069.16 | 1.6798 |
| .99 | 41881.81 | 1.4219 | 38821.59 | 1.5388 | 35032.45 | 1.6122 | 30700.09 | 1.6571 | 26021.32 | 1.6799 |
| 1.00 | 41855.39 | −1.4235 | 38787.01 | −1.5398 | 34991.50 | −1.6129 | 30654.69 | −1.6575 | 25973.47 | −1.6800 |

# TABLE VI. ARGUMENT 1.

Equation $= 22655''.226 + 22639''.2 \sin. x + 769''.5 \sin. 2x + 36''.7 \sin. 3x + 2''.0 \sin. 4x + 0''.1 \sin. 5x.$

Period, 27.55455245 days.

| Days. | 20 | | 21 | | 22 | | 23 | | 24 | |
|---|---|---|---|---|---|---|---|---|---|---|
| Decimals of a Day. | Equation. | Log. Dif. | Equation. | Log. Dif. | Equation. | Log. Dif. | Equation. | Log. Dif. | Equation. | Log. Dif. |
| .00 | 25973″.47 | −1.6800 | 21150″.89 | −1.6834 | 16392″.29 | −1.6682 | 11901″.99 | −1.6321 | 7879″.71 | −1.5705 |
| .01 | 25925.60 | 1.6801 | 21102.64 | 1.6834 | 16345.72 | 1.6679 | 11859.12 | 1.6316 | 7842.51 | 1.5698 |
| .02 | 25877.72 | 1.6803 | 21054.40 | 1.6833 | 16299.18 | 1.6675 | 11816.30 | 1.6312 | 7805.37 | 1.5690 |
| .03 | 25829.82 | 1.6804 | 21006.17 | 1.6832 | 16252.67 | 1.6673 | 11773.53 | 1.6307 | 7768.30 | 1.5682 |
| .04 | 25781.91 | 1.6805 | 20957.95 | 1.6832 | 16206.18 | 1.6671 | 11730.80 | 1.6301 | 7731.30 | 1.5676 |
| .05 | 25733.99 | 1.6806 | 20909.73 | 1.6832 | 16159.72 | 1.6669 | 11688.13 | 1.6297 | 7694.36 | 1.5666 |
| .06 | 25686.06 | 1.6807 | 20861.51 | 1.6830 | 16113.28 | 1.6666 | 11645.50 | 1.6292 | 7657.49 | 1.5659 |
| .07 | 25638.11 | 1.6808 | 20813.31 | 1.6829 | 16066.87 | 1.6663 | 11602.92 | 1.6287 | 7620.68 | 1.5652 |
| .08 | 25590.15 | 1.6810 | 20765.12 | 1.6828 | 16020.49 | 1.6660 | 11560.39 | 1.6283 | 7583.94 | 1.5643 |
| .09 | 25542.18 | 1.6812 | 20716.94 | 1.6828 | 15974.15 | 1.6658 | 11517.90 | 1.6277 | 7547.27 | 1.5635 |
| .10 | 25494.19 | 1.6813 | 20668.76 | 1.6827 | 15927.83 | 1.6654 | 11475.47 | 1.6271 | 7510.67 | 1.5627 |
| .11 | 25446.19 | 1.6813 | 20620.59 | 1.6826 | 15881.54 | 1.6652 | 11433.09 | 1.6266 | 7474.14 | 1.5619 |
| .12 | 25398.19 | 1.6814 | 20572.43 | 1.6825 | 15835.28 | 1.6650 | 11390.76 | 1.6261 | 7437.67 | 1.5611 |
| .13 | 25350.17 | 1.6815 | 20524.28 | 1.6825 | 15789.04 | 1.6646 | 11348.48 | 1.6257 | 7401.27 | 1.5602 |
| .14 | 25302.14 | 1.6815 | 20476.14 | 1.6825 | 15742.84 | 1.6644 | 11306.24 | 1.6252 | 7364.95 | 1.5594 |
| .15 | 25254.09 | 1.6816 | 20428.00 | 1.6824 | 15696.67 | 1.6641 | 11264.05 | 1.6247 | 7328.69 | 1.5586 |
| .16 | 25206.04 | 1.6817 | 20379.87 | 1.6823 | 15650.53 | 1.6638 | 11221.91 | 1.6241 | 7292.50 | 1.5579 |
| .17 | 25157.97 | 1.6818 | 20331.75 | 1.6821 | 15604.42 | 1.6635 | 11179.82 | 1.6235 | 7256.37 | 1.5570 |
| .18 | 25109.90 | 1.6819 | 20283.65 | 1.6820 | 15558.34 | 1.6633 | 11137.79 | 1.6231 | 7220.31 | 1.5561 |
| .19 | 25061.81 | 1.6820 | 20235.56 | 1.6819 | 15512.29 | 1.6630 | 11095.80 | 1.6226 | 7184.33 | 1.5552 |
| .20 | 25013.71 | 1.6822 | 20187.48 | 1.6819 | 15466.27 | 1.6627 | 11053.86 | 1.6221 | 7148.42 | 1.5545 |
| .21 | 24965.60 | 1.6822 | 20139.40 | 1.6817 | 15420.28 | 1.6624 | 11011.97 | 1.6216 | 7112.57 | 1.5537 |
| .22 | 24917.48 | 1.6823 | 20091.34 | 1.6816 | 15374.32 | 1.6620 | 10970.13 | 1.6210 | 7076.79 | 1.5528 |
| .23 | 24869.36 | 1.6823 | 20043.29 | 1.6816 | 15328.40 | 1.6618 | 10928.34 | 1.6204 | 7041.08 | 1.5518 |
| .24 | 24821.22 | 1.6824 | 19995.25 | 1.6815 | 15282.51 | 1.6615 | 10886.61 | 1.6199 | 7005.45 | 1.5509 |
| .25 | 24773.07 | 1.6825 | 19947.22 | 1.6814 | 15236.65 | 1.6612 | 10844.93 | 1.6194 | 6969.89 | 1.5502 |
| .26 | 24724.92 | 1.6825 | 19899.20 | 1.6813 | 15190.82 | 1.6609 | 10803.30 | 1.6188 | 6934.39 | 1.5492 |
| .27 | 24676.75 | 1.6826 | 19851.19 | 1.6812 | 15145.02 | 1.6606 | 10761.72 | 1.6183 | 6898.97 | 1.5484 |
| .28 | 24628.58 | 1.6827 | 19803.19 | 1.6811 | 15099.25 | 1.6602 | 10720.19 | 1.6178 | 6863.62 | 1.5475 |
| .29 | 24580.40 | 1.6828 | 19755.21 | 1.6810 | 15053.52 | 1.6599 | 10678.71 | 1.6173 | 6828 34 | 1.5466 |
| .30 | 24532.21 | 1.6829 | 19707.24 | 1.6809 | 15007.82 | 1.6597 | 10637.28 | 1.6167 | 6793.13 | 1.5458 |
| .31 | 24484.02 | 1.6830 | 19659.28 | 1.6807 | 14962.15 | 1.6593 | 10595.91 | 1.6162 | 6757.99 | 1.5450 |
| .32 | 24435.81 | 1.6831 | 19611.34 | 1.6806 | 14916.52 | 1.6591 | 10554.59 | 1.6155 | 6722.92 | 1.5441 |
| .33 | 24387.60 | 1.6832 | 19563.41 | 1.6805 | 14870.91 | 1.6587 | 10513.33 | 1.6150 | 6687.92 | 1.5431 |
| .34 | 24339.38 | 1.6833 | 19515.49 | 1.6803 | 14825.34 | 1.6583 | 10472.12 | 1.6144 | 6653.00 | 1.5422 |
| .35 | 24291.15 | 1.6833 | 19467.59 | 1.6802 | 14779.81 | 1.6580 | 10430.96 | 1.6139 | 6618.15 | 1.5413 |
| .36 | 24242.92 | 1.6834 | 19419.70 | 1.6801 | 14734.31 | 1.6578 | 10389.85 | 1.6133 | 6583.37 | 1.5404 |
| .37 | 24194.68 | 1.6835 | 19371.82 | 1.6801 | 14688.84 | 1.6575 | 10348.80 | 1.6127 | 6548.66 | 1.5395 |
| .38 | 24146.43 | 1.6835 | 19323.95 | 1.6799 | 14643.40 | 1.6570 | 10307.81 | 1.6121 | 6514.03 | 1.5386 |
| .39 | 24098.18 | 1.6836 | 19276.10 | 1.6797 | 14598.01 | 1.6568 | 10266.87 | 1.6117 | 6479.47 | 1.5377 |
| .40 | 24049.92 | 1.6836 | 19228.27 | 1.6796 | 14552.64 | 1.6564 | 10225.98 | 1.6110 | 6444.98 | 1.5367 |
| .41 | 24001.65 | 1.6836 | 19180.45 | 1.6795 | 14507.31 | 1.6560 | 10185.15 | 1.6105 | 6410.57 | 1.5358 |
| .42 | 23953.38 | 1.6837 | 19132.64 | 1.6793 | 14462.02 | 1.6557 | 10144.37 | 1.6098 | 6376.23 | 1.5348 |
| .43 | 23905.10 | 1.6837 | 19084.85 | 1.6791 | 14416.76 | 1.6553 | 10103.65 | 1.6093 | 6341.97 | 1.5339 |
| .44 | 23856.82 | 1.6838 | 19037.08 | 1.6790 | 14371.54 | 1.6551 | 10062.98 | 1.6086 | 6307.78 | 1.5331 |
| .45 | 23808.53 | 1.6838 | 18989.32 | 1.6789 | 14326.35 | 1.6547 | 10022.37 | 1.6080 | 6273.66 | 1.5321 |
| .46 | 23760.24 | 1.6839 | 18941.57 | 1.6788 | 14281.20 | 1.6543 | 9981.82 | 1.6075 | 6239.61 | 1.5311 |
| .47 | 23711.94 | 1.6839 | 18893.84 | 1.6786 | 14236.08 | 1.6540 | 9941.32 | 1.6068 | 6205.64 | 1.5302 |
| .48 | 23663.64 | 1.6840 | 18846.13 | 1.6784 | 14191.00 | 1.6536 | 9900.88 | 1.6063 | 6171.74 | 1.5292 |
| .49 | 23615.34 | 1.6840 | 18798.44 | 1.6783 | 14145.96 | 1.6532 | 9860.49 | 1.6056 | 6137.92 | 1.5281 |
| .50 | 23567.03 | −1.6841 | 18750.76 | −1.6781 | 14100.96 | −1.6529 | 9820.16 | −1.6051 | 6104.18 | −1.5271 |

# TABLE VI. ARGUMENT 1.

Equation $= 22655''.226 + 22639''.2 \sin. x + 769''.5 \sin. 2x + 36''.7 \sin. 3x + 2''.0 \sin. 4x + 0''.1 \sin. 5x.$

Period, 27.55455245 days.

| Days. | 20 | | 21 | | 22 | | 23 | | 24 | |
|---|---|---|---|---|---|---|---|---|---|---|
| Decimals of a Day | Equation. | Log. Dif. | Equation. | Log. Dif. | Equation. | Log. Dif. | Equation. | Log. Dif. | Equation. | Log. Dif. |
| .50 | 23567.03 | −1.6841 | 18750.76 | −1.6781 | 14100.96 | −1.6529 | 9820.16 | −1.6051 | 6104.18 | −1.5271 |
| .51 | 23518.71 | 1.6841 | 18703.10 | 1.6781 | 14055.99 | 1.6525 | 9779.88 | 1.6043 | 6070.52 | 1.5263 |
| .52 | 23470.40 | 1.6841 | 18655.45 | 1.6779 | 14011.06 | 1.6522 | 9739.67 | 1.6037 | 6036.92 | 1.5254 |
| .53 | 23422.08 | 1.6842 | 18607.82 | 1.6777 | 13966.17 | 1.6519 | 9699.51 | 1.6031 | 6003.39 | 1.5244 |
| .54 | 23373.75 | 1.6842 | 18560.21 | 1.6775 | 13921.31 | 1.6515 | 9659.41 | 1.6026 | 5969.94 | 1.5233 |
| .55 | 23325.43 | 1.6842 | 18512.62 | 1.6774 | 13876.49 | 1.6511 | 9619.36 | 1.6020 | 5936.57 | 1.5223 |
| .56 | 23277.10 | 1.6842 | 18465.04 | 1.6772 | 13831.71 | 1.6507 | 9579.37 | 1.6013 | 5903.28 | 1.5214 |
| .57 | 23228.76 | 1.6842 | 18417.48 | 1.6771 | 13786.97 | 1.6504 | 9539.44 | 1.6007 | 5870.06 | 1.5203 |
| .58 | 23180.43 | 1.6843 | 18369.94 | 1.6769 | 13742.26 | 1.6499 | 9499.57 | 1.6000 | 5836.92 | 1.5194 |
| .59 | 23132.09 | 1.6843 | 18322.42 | 1.6767 | 13697.60 | 1.6495 | 9459.76 | 1.5995 | 5803.85 | 1.5184 |
| .60 | 23083.75 | 1.6843 | 18274.92 | 1.6765 | 13652.98 | 1.6493 | 9420.00 | 1.5988 | 5770.86 | 1.5173 |
| .61 | 23035.41 | 1.6843 | 18227.43 | 1.6764 | 13608.39 | 1.6489 | 9380.30 | 1.5981 | 5737.95 | 1.5164 |
| .62 | 22987.07 | 1.6843 | 18179.96 | 1.6762 | 13563.84 | 1.6485 | 9340.66 | 1.5975 | 5705.11 | 1.5153 |
| .63 | 22938.73 | 1.6843 | 18132.52 | 1.6761 | 13519.33 | 1.6481 | 9301.08 | 1.5968 | 5672.35 | 1.5143 |
| .64 | 22890.38 | 1.6843 | 18085.09 | 1.6759 | 13474.86 | 1.6476 | 9261.56 | 1.5962 | 5639.67 | 1.5132 |
| .65 | 22842.04 | 1.6843 | 18037.68 | 1.6757 | 13430.44 | 1.6473 | 9222.10 | 1.5955 | 5607.07 | 1.5122 |
| .66 | 22793.69 | 1.6843 | 17990.29 | 1.6754 | 13386.05 | 1.6469 | 9182.70 | 1.5949 | 5574.55 | 1.5112 |
| .67 | 22745.34 | 1.6843 | 17942.93 | 1.6754 | 13341.70 | 1.6465 | 9143.35 | 1.5943 | 5542.10 | 1.5101 |
| .68 | 22696.99 | 1.6843 | 17895.58 | 1.6752 | 13297.39 | 1.6461 | 9104.06 | 1.5935 | 5509.73 | 1.5091 |
| .69 | 22648.64 | 1.6843 | 17848.25 | 1.6750 | 13253.12 | 1.6457 | 9064.84 | 1.5929 | 5477.44 | 1.5080 |
| .70 | 22600.30 | 1.6843 | 17800.94 | 1.6747 | 13208.89 | 1.6452 | 9025.68 | 1.5923 | 5445.23 | 1.5070 |
| .71 | 22551.95 | 1.6843 | 17753.66 | 1.6745 | 13164.71 | 1.6448 | 8986.57 | 1.5916 | 5413.09 | 1.5059 |
| .72 | 22503.60 | 1.6843 | 17706.39 | 1.6743 | 13120.57 | 1.6444 | 8947.52 | 1.5909 | 5381.03 | 1.5049 |
| .73 | 22455.26 | 1.6843 | 17659.15 | 1.6742 | 13076.47 | 1.6441 | 8908.53 | 1.5901 | 5349.05 | 1.5038 |
| .74 | 22406.91 | 1.6843 | 17611.92 | 1.6739 | 13032.41 | 1.6437 | 8869.61 | 1.5893 | 5317.15 | 1.5025 |
| .75 | 22358.57 | 1.6843 | 17564.72 | 1.6737 | 12988.39 | 1.6433 | 8830.77 | 1.5887 | 5285.34 | 1.5017 |
| .76 | 22310.22 | 1.6843 | 17517.54 | 1.6736 | 12944.41 | 1.6429 | 8791.98 | 1.5882 | 5253.60 | 1.5005 |
| .77 | 22261.88 | 1.6843 | 17470.38 | 1.6733 | 12900.47 | 1.6424 | 8753.24 | 1.5875 | 5221.94 | 1.4994 |
| .78 | 22213.54 | 1.6843 | 17423.25 | 1.6732 | 12856.58 | 1.6420 | 8714.56 | 1.5867 | 5190.36 | 1.4983 |
| .79 | 22165.20 | 1.6843 | 17376.13 | 1.6729 | 12812.73 | 1.6416 | 8675.95 | 1.5860 | 5158.86 | 1.4973 |
| .80 | 22116.86 | 1.6843 | 17329.04 | 1.6726 | 12768.92 | 1.6412 | 8637.40 | 1.5853 | 5127.44 | 1.4961 |
| .81 | 22068.52 | 1.6842 | 17281.98 | 1.6726 | 12725.15 | 1.6407 | 8598.91 | 1.5846 | 5096.10 | 1.4950 |
| .82 | 22020.19 | 1.6842 | 17234.93 | 1.6723 | 12681.43 | 1.6403 | 8560.48 | 1.5839 | 5064.84 | 1.4939 |
| .83 | 21971.86 | 1.6842 | 17187.91 | 1.6721 | 12637.75 | 1.6399 | 8522.12 | 1.5832 | 5033.66 | 1.4926 |
| .84 | 21923.53 | 1.6841 | 17140.91 | 1.6719 | 12594.11 | 1.6394 | 8483.82 | 1.5826 | 5002.57 | 1.4917 |
| .85 | 21875.21 | 1.6841 | 17093.94 | 1.6717 | 12550.52 | 1.6390 | 8445.58 | 1.5817 | 4971.55 | 1.4906 |
| .86 | 21826.89 | 1.6841 | 17046.99 | 1.6715 | 12506.97 | 1.6386 | 8407.41 | 1.5810 | 4940.61 | 1.4895 |
| .87 | 21778.57 | 1.6840 | 17000.06 | 1.6712 | 12463.46 | 1.6381 | 8369.30 | 1.5804 | 4909.75 | 1.4881 |
| .88 | 21730.27 | 1.6840 | 16953.16 | 1.6709 | 12420.00 | 1.6376 | 8331.25 | 1.5795 | 4878.98 | 1.4870 |
| .89 | 21681.97 | 1.6840 | 16906.28 | 1.6707 | 12376.59 | 1.6372 | 8293.27 | 1.5788 | 4848.29 | 1.4857 |
| .90 | 21633.66 | 1.6839 | 16859.43 | 1.6705 | 12333.22 | 1.6368 | 8255.35 | 1.5782 | 4817.69 | 1.4847 |
| .91 | 21585.36 | 1.6839 | 16812.60 | 1.6703 | 12289.89 | 1.6364 | 8217.49 | 1.5773 | 4787.16 | 1.4836 |
| .92 | 21537.06 | 1.6839 | 16765.79 | 1.6700 | 12246.60 | 1.6359 | 8179.70 | 1.5765 | 4756.71 | 1.4823 |
| .93 | 21488.77 | 1.6838 | 16719.01 | 1.6698 | 12203.36 | 1.6354 | 8141.98 | 1.5759 | 4726.35 | 1.4811 |
| .94 | 21440.49 | 1.6838 | 16672.26 | 1.6695 | 12160.17 | 1.6349 | 8104.32 | 1.5752 | 4696.07 | 1.4800 |
| .95 | 21392.21 | 1.6837 | 16625.54 | 1.6693 | 12117.03 | 1.6345 | 8066.72 | 1.5743 | 4665.87 | 1.4787 |
| .96 | 21343.93 | 1.6837 | 16578.84 | 1.6691 | 12073.93 | 1.6341 | 8029.19 | 1.5737 | 4635.76 | 1.4775 |
| .97 | 21295.66 | 1.6836 | 16532.16 | 1.6689 | 12030.87 | 1.6335 | 7991.72 | 1.5729 | 4605.73 | 1.4764 |
| .98 | 21247.40 | 1.6835 | 16485.51 | 1.6686 | 11987.87 | 1.6331 | 7954.32 | 1.5721 | 4575.78 | 1.4752 |
| .99 | 21199.14 | 1.6834 | 16438.89 | 1.6684 | 11944.91 | 1.6327 | 7916.98 | 1.5713 | 4545.91 | 1.4741 |
| 1.00 | 21150.89 | −1.6834 | 16392.29 | −1.6682 | 11901.99 | −1.6321 | 7879.71 | −1.5705 | 4516.12 | −1.4728 |

# TABLE VI. ARGUMENT 1.

Equation $= 22655''.226 + 22639''.2 \sin. x + 769''.5 \sin. 2x + 36''.7 \sin. 3x + 2''.0 \sin. 4x + 0''.1 \sin. 5x.$

Period, 27.55455245 days.

| Days. | 25 | | 26 | | 27 | |
|---|---|---|---|---|---|---|
| Decimals of a Day. | Equation. | Log. Dif. | Equation. | Log. Dif. | Equation. | Log. Dif. |
| .00 | 4516.12 | −1.4728 | 1986.96 | −1.3126 | 444.93 | −0.9996 |
| .01 | 4486.42 | 1.4716 | 1966.42 | 1.3104 | 434.94 | 0.9948 |
| .02 | 4456.80 | 1.4702 | 1945.98 | 1.3083 | 425.06 | 0.9903 |
| .03 | 4427.27 | 1.4690 | 1925.64 | 1.3062 | 415.28 | 0.9854 |
| .04 | 4397.82 | 1.4678 | 1905.40 | 1.3038 | 405.61 | 0.9800 |
| .05 | 4368.46 | 1.4666 | 1885.27 | 1.3018 | 396.06 | 0.9750 |
| .06 | 4339.18 | 1.4652 | 1865.23 | 1.2998 | 386.62 | 0.9699 |
| .07 | 4309.99 | 1.4640 | 1845.29 | 1.2976 | 377.29 | 0.9647 |
| .08 | 4280.88 | 1.4627 | 1825.45 | 1.2954 | 368.07 | 0.9590 |
| .09 | 4251.86 | 1.4615 | 1805.71 | 1.2932 | 358.97 | 0.9542 |
| .10 | 4222.92 | 1.4602 | 1786.07 | 1.2909 | 349.97 | 0.9484 |
| .11 | 4194.07 | 1.4590 | 1766.53 | 1.2887 | 341.09 | 0.9430 |
| .12 | 4165.30 | 1.4576 | 1747.09 | 1.2865 | 332.32 | 0.9370 |
| .13 | 4136.62 | 1.4562 | 1727.75 | 1.2842 | 323.67 | 0.9320 |
| .14 | 4108.03 | 1.4549 | 1708.51 | 1.2819 | 315.12 | 0.9258 |
| .15 | 4079.52 | 1.4536 | 1689.37 | 1.2797 | 306.69 | 0.9201 |
| .16 | 4051.10 | 1.4524 | 1670.33 | 1.2772 | 298.37 | 0.9138 |
| .17 | 4022.76 | 1.4510 | 1651.40 | 1.2749 | 290.17 | 0.9085 |
| .18 | 3994.51 | 1.4498 | 1632.57 | 1.2725 | 282.07 | 0.9020 |
| .19 | 3966.34 | 1.4484 | 1613.84 | 1.2702 | 274.09 | 0.8960 |
| .20 | 3938.26 | 1.4470 | 1595.21 | 1.2679 | 266.22 | 0.8899 |
| .21 | 3910.27 | 1.4456 | 1576.68 | 1.2655 | 258.46 | 0.8831 |
| .22 | 3882.36 | 1.4444 | 1558.25 | 1.2630 | 250.82 | 0.8768 |
| .23 | 3854.54 | 1.4428 | 1539.93 | 1.2606 | 243.29 | 0.8698 |
| .24 | 3826.82 | 1.4415 | 1521.71 | 1.2582 | 235.88 | 0.8639 |
| .25 | 3799.18 | 1.4402 | 1503.59 | 1.2558 | 228.57 | 0.8567 |
| .26 | 3771.62 | 1.4389 | 1485.57 | 1.2534 | 221.38 | 0.8494 |
| .27 | 3744.15 | 1.4373 | 1467.65 | 1.2506 | 214.31 | 0.8426 |
| .28 | 3716.78 | 1.4360 | 1449.84 | 1.2482 | 207.35 | 0.8357 |
| .29 | 3689.49 | 1.4346 | 1432.13 | 1.2457 | 200.50 | 0.8287 |
| .30 | 3662.29 | 1.4332 | 1414.52 | 1.2430 | 193.76 | 0.8209 |
| .31 | 3635.18 | 1.4319 | 1397.02 | 1.2405 | 187.14 | 0.8136 |
| .32 | 3608.15 | 1.4305 | 1379.62 | 1.2380 | 180.63 | 0.8055 |
| .33 | 3581.21 | 1.4289 | 1362.32 | 1.2355 | 174.24 | 0.7980 |
| .34 | 3554.36 | 1.4273 | 1345.12 | 1.2327 | 167.96 | 0.7903 |
| .35 | 3527.61 | 1.4260 | 1328.03 | 1.2302 | 161.79 | 0.7818 |
| .36 | 3500.94 | 1.4245 | 1311.04 | 1.2273 | 155.74 | 0.7738 |
| .37 | 3474.36 | 1.4231 | 1294.16 | 1.2248 | 149.80 | 0.7649 |
| .38 | 3447.87 | 1.4216 | 1277.38 | 1.2222 | 143.98 | 0.7566 |
| .39 | 3421.47 | 1.4202 | 1260.70 | 1.2193 | 138.27 | 0.7474 |
| .40 | 3395.16 | 1.4185 | 1244.13 | 1.2166 | 132.68 | 0.7388 |
| .41 | 3368.94 | 1.4171 | 1227.66 | 1.2138 | 127.20 | 0.7292 |
| .42 | 3342.81 | 1.4157 | 1211.30 | 1.2111 | 121.84 | 0.7202 |
| .43 | 3316.77 | 1.4142 | 1195.04 | 1.2081 | 116.59 | 0.7110 |
| .44 | 3290.82 | 1.4125 | 1178.89 | 1.2054 | 111.45 | 0.7007 |
| .45 | 3264.97 | 1.4111 | 1162.84 | 1.2028 | 106.43 | 0.6902 |
| .46 | 3239.20 | 1.4095 | 1146.89 | 1.1998 | 101.53 | 0.6803 |
| .47 | 3213.52 | 1.4079 | 1131.05 | 1.1967 | 96.74 | 0.6702 |
| .48 | 3187.94 | 1.4063 | 1115.32 | 1.1939 | 92.06 | 0.6590 |
| .49 | 3162.45 | 1.4048 | 1099.69 | 1.1909 | 87.50 | 0.6474 |
| .50 | 3137.05 | −1.4033 | 1084.17 | −1.1881 | 83.06 | −0.6355 |

# TABLE VI. ARGUMENT 1.

Equation = 22655″.226 + 22639″.2 sin. $x$ + 769″.5 sin. $2x$ + 36″.7 sin. $3x$ + 2″.0 sin. $4x$ + 0″.1 sin. $5x$.

Period, 27.55455245 days.

| Days. | 25 | | 26 | | 27 | |
|---|---|---|---|---|---|---|
| Decimals of a Day. | Equation. | Log. Dif. | Equation. | Log. Dif. | Equation. | Log. Dif. |
| .50 | 3137.05″ | −1.4033 | 1084.17″ | −1.1881 | 83.06″ | −0.6355 |
| .51 | 3111.74 | 1.4017 | 1068.75 | 1.1850 | 78.74 | 0.6243 |
| .52 | 3086.52 | 1.4002 | 1053.44 | 1.1821 | 74.53 | 0.6128 |
| .53 | 3061.39 | 1.3984 | 1038.23 | 1.1790 | 70.43 | 0.5999 |
| .54 | 3036.36 | 1.3969 | 1023.13 | 1.1759 | 66.45 | 0.5877 |
| .55 | 3011.42 | 1.3954 | 1008.14 | 1.1730 | 62.58 | 0.5740 |
| .56 | 2986.57 | 1.3938 | 993.25 | 1.1697 | 58.83 | 0.5599 |
| .57 | 2961.81 | 1.3920 | 978.47 | 1.1668 | 55.20 | 0.5465 |
| .58 | 2937.15 | 1.3904 | 963.79 | 1.1635 | 51.68 | 0.5315 |
| .59 | 2912.58 | 1.3888 | 949.22 | 1.1602 | 48.28 | 0.5159 |
| .60 | 2888.10 | 1.3872 | 934.76 | 1.1568 | 45.00 | 0.5011 |
| .61 | 2863.71 | 1.3854 | 920.41 | 1.1538 | 41.83 | 0.4843 |
| .62 | 2839.42 | 1.3838 | 906.16 | 1.1507 | 38.78 | 0.4683 |
| .63 | 2815.22 | 1.3820 | 892.01 | 1.1473 | 35.84 | 0.4502 |
| .64 | 2791.12 | 1.3804 | 877.97 | 1.1436 | 33.02 | 0.4314 |
| .65 | 2767.11 | 1.3788 | 864.05 | 1.1405 | 30.32 | 0.4133 |
| .66 | 2743.19 | 1.3770 | 850.23 | 1.1373 | 27.73 | 0.3927 |
| .67 | 2719.37 | 1.3753 | 836.51 | 1.1335 | 25.26 | 0.3711 |
| .68 | 2695.64 | 1.3735 | 822.91 | 1.1303 | 22.91 | 0.3502 |
| .69 | 2672.01 | 1.3718 | 809.41 | 1.1268 | 20.67 | 0.3263 |
| .70 | 2648.47 | 1.3701 | 796.02 | 1.1232 | 18.55 | 0.3032 |
| .71 | 2625.02 | 1.3683 | 782.74 | 1.1199 | 16.54 | 0.2765 |
| .72 | 2601.67 | 1.3666 | 769.56 | 1.1162 | 14.65 | 0.2480 |
| .73 | 2578.41 | 1.3647 | 756.49 | 1.1127 | 12.88 | 0.2175 |
| .74 | 2555.25 | 1.3630 | 743.53 | 1.1089 | 11.23 | 0.1847 |
| .75 | 2532.18 | 1.3612 | 730.68 | 1.1052 | 9.70 | 0.1523 |
| .76 | 2509.21 | 1.3593 | 717.94 | 1.1014 | 8.28 | 0.1139 |
| .77 | 2486.34 | 1.3575 | 705.31 | 1.0976 | 6.98 | 0.0719 |
| .78 | 2463.56 | 1.3556 | 692.79 | 1.0941 | 5.80 | 0.0294 |
| .79 | 2440.88 | 1.3537 | 680.37 | 1.0902 | 4.73 | 9.9777 |
| .80 | 2418.30 | 1.3519 | 668.06 | 1.0864 | 3.78 | 9.9191 |
| .81 | 2395.81 | 1.3502 | 655.86 | 1.0824 | 2.95 | 9.8573 |
| .82 | 2373.41 | 1.3483 | 643.77 | 1.0785 | 2.23 | 9.7782 |
| .83 | 2351.11 | 1.3464 | 631.79 | 1.0745 | 1.63 | 9.6812 |
| .84 | 2328.91 | 1.3444 | 619.92 | 1.0705 | 1.15 | 9.5563 |
| .85 | 2306.81 | 1.3426 | 608.16 | 1.0664 | 0.79 | 9.3802 |
| .86 | 2284.80 | 1.3406 | 596.51 | 1.0626 | 0.55 | 9.1139 |
| .87 | 2262.89 | 1.3387 | 584.96 | 1.0580 | 0.42 | −8.0000 |
| .88 | 2241.08 | 1.3367 | 573.53 | 1.0539 | 0.41 | +9.0414 |
| .89 | 2219.37 | 1.3349 | 562.21 | 1.0496 | 0.52 | 9.3617 |
| .90 | 2197.75 | 1.3328 | 551.00 | 1.0457 | 0.75 | 9.5441 |
| .91 | 2176.23 | 1.3308 | 539.89 | 1.0411 | 1.10 | 9.6721 |
| .92 | 2154.81 | 1.3290 | 528.90 | 1.0367 | 1.57 | 9.7634 |
| .93 | 2133.48 | 1.3269 | 518.02 | 1.0323 | 2.15 | 9.8451 |
| .94 | 2112.25 | 1.3249 | 507.25 | 1.0282 | 2.85 | 9.9138 |
| .95 | 2091.12 | 1.3228 | 496.58 | 1.0233 | 3.67 | 9.9731 |
| .96 | 2070.09 | 1.3207 | 486.03 | 1.0187 | 4.61 | 0.0253 |
| .97 | 2049.16 | 1.3187 | 475.59 | 1.0140 | 5.67 | 0.0682 |
| .98 | 2028.33 | 1.3166 | 465.26 | 1.0094 | 6.84 | 0.1106 |
| .99 | 2007.60 | 1.3147 | 455.04 | 1.0047 | 8.13 | 0.1492 |
| 1.00 | 1986.96 | −1.3126 | 444.93 | −0.9996 | 9.54 | +0.1818 |

# TABLE VII. ARGUMENT 2.

Equation $= 4587''.400 + 4586''.9 \sin. (2t - x) + 31''.2 \sin. (4t - 2x)$.

Period, 31.81193574 days.

| Days. | 0 | | 1 | | 2 | | 3 | | 4 | |
|---|---|---|---|---|---|---|---|---|---|---|
| Decimals of a Day. | Equation. | Dif. | Equation. | Dif. | Equation. | Dif. | Equation. | Dif. | Equation. | Dif. |
| .00 | ″2.45 | −.28 | ″62.81 | +1.51 | ″300.36 | +3.25 | ″707.06 | +4.88 | ″1267.93 | +6.32 |
| .01 | 2.17 | .27 | 64.32 | 1.52 | 303.61 | 3.27 | 711.94 | 4.89 | 1274.25 | 6.33 |
| .02 | 1.90 | .25 | 65.84 | 1.54 | 306.88 | 3.28 | 716.83 | 4.91 | 1280.58 | 6.35 |
| .03 | 1.65 | .23 | 67.38 | 1.56 | 310.16 | 3.30 | 721.74 | 4.92 | 1286.93 | 6.36 |
| .04 | 1.42 | .21 | 68.94 | 1.58 | 313.46 | 3.32 | 726.66 | 4.94 | 1293.29 | 6.37 |
| .05 | 1.21 | .19 | 70.52 | 1.59 | 316.78 | 3.33 | 731.60 | 4.95 | 1299.66 | 6.38 |
| .06 | 1.02 | .17 | 72.11 | 1.62 | 320.11 | 3.35 | 736.55 | 4.97 | 1306.04 | 6.40 |
| .07 | 0.85 | .16 | 73.73 | 1.63 | 323.46 | 3.37 | 741.52 | 4.98 | 1312.44 | 6.42 |
| .08 | 0.69 | .14 | 75.36 | 1.65 | 326.83 | 3.38 | 746.50 | 5.00 | 1318.86 | 6.42 |
| .09 | 0.55 | .12 | 77.01 | 1.66 | 330.21 | 3.40 | 751.50 | 5.02 | 1325.28 | 6.44 |
| .10 | 0.43 | .10 | 78.67 | 1.68 | 333.61 | 3.42 | 756.52 | 5.03 | 1331.72 | 6.45 |
| .11 | 0.33 | .09 | 80.35 | 1.70 | 337.03 | 3.44 | 761.55 | 5.05 | 1338.17 | 6.46 |
| .12 | 0.24 | .07 | 82.05 | 1.72 | 340.47 | 3.45 | 766.60 | 5.06 | 1344.63 | 6.48 |
| .13 | 0.17 | .05 | 83.77 | 1.74 | 343.92 | 3.47 | 771.66 | 5.07 | 1351.11 | 6.49 |
| .14 | 0.12 | .03 | 85.51 | 1.75 | 347.39 | 3.48 | 776.73 | 5.10 | 1357.60 | 6.50 |
| .15 | 0.09 | −.01 | 87.26 | 1.78 | 350.87 | 3.51 | 781.83 | 5.10 | 1364.10 | 6.52 |
| .16 | 0.08 | .00 | 89.04 | 1.79 | 354.38 | 3.51 | 786.93 | 5.12 | 1370.62 | 6.53 |
| .17 | 0.08 | +.02 | 90.83 | 1.80 | 357.89 | 3.54 | 792.05 | 5.14 | 1377.15 | 6.55 |
| .18 | 0.10 | .04 | 92.63 | 1.83 | 361.43 | 3.55 | 797.19 | 5.15 | 1383.70 | 6.55 |
| .19 | 0.14 | .06 | 94.46 | 1.84 | 364.98 | 3.57 | 802.34 | 5.16 | 1390.25 | 6.56 |
| .20 | 0.20 | .07 | 96.30 | 1.86 | 368.55 | 3.58 | 807.50 | 5.19 | 1396.81 | 6.59 |
| .21 | 0.27 | .09 | 98.16 | 1.88 | 372.13 | 3.61 | 812.69 | 5.19 | 1403.40 | 6.59 |
| .22 | 0.36 | .12 | 100.04 | 1.90 | 375.74 | 3.62 | 817.88 | 5.21 | 1409.99 | 6.61 |
| .23 | 0.48 | .13 | 101.94 | 1.91 | 379.36 | 3.64 | 823.09 | 5.23 | 1416.60 | 6.61 |
| .24 | 0.61 | .14 | 103.85 | 1.93 | 383.00 | 3.65 | 828.32 | 5.24 | 1423.21 | 6.63 |
| .25 | 0.75 | .17 | 105.78 | 1.95 | 386.65 | 3.67 | 833.56 | 5.26 | 1429.84 | 6.65 |
| .26 | 0.92 | .18 | 107.73 | 1.97 | 390.32 | 3.69 | 838.82 | 5.27 | 1436.49 | 6.66 |
| .27 | 1.10 | .20 | 109.70 | 1.98 | 394.01 | 3.70 | 844.09 | 5.29 | 1443.15 | 6.67 |
| .28 | 1.30 | .22 | 111.68 | 2.00 | 397.71 | 3.72 | 849.38 | 5.30 | 1449.82 | 6.69 |
| .29 | 1.52 | .24 | 113.68 | 2.02 | 401.43 | 3.73 | 854.68 | 5.32 | 1456.51 | 6.69 |
| .30 | 1.76 | .25 | 115.70 | 2.04 | 405.16 | 3.76 | 860.00 | 5.33 | 1463.20 | 6.70 |
| .31 | 2.01 | .27 | 117.74 | 2.05 | 408.92 | 3.77 | 865.33 | 5.34 | 1469.90 | 6.72 |
| .32 | 2.28 | .30 | 119.79 | 2.07 | 412.69 | 3.78 | 870.67 | 5.36 | 1476.62 | 6.74 |
| .33 | 2.58 | .30 | 121.86 | 2.09 | 416.47 | 3.80 | 876.03 | 5.38 | 1483.36 | 6.74 |
| .34 | 2.88 | .33 | 123.95 | 2.11 | 420.27 | 3.82 | 881.41 | 5.39 | 1490.10 | 6.76 |
| .35 | 3.21 | .34 | 126.06 | 2.12 | 424.09 | 3.84 | 886.80 | 5.41 | 1496.86 | 6.77 |
| .36 | 3.55 | .36 | 128.18 | 2.14 | 427.93 | 3.85 | 892.21 | 5.42 | 1503.63 | 6.78 |
| .37 | 3.91 | .39 | 130.32 | 2.16 | 431.78 | 3.87 | 897.63 | 5.43 | 1510.41 | 6.79 |
| .38 | 4.30 | .39 | 132.48 | 2.18 | 435.65 | 3.88 | 903.06 | 5.45 | 1517.20 | 6.81 |
| .39 | 4.69 | .42 | 134.66 | 2.20 | 439.53 | 3.90 | 908.51 | 5.47 | 1524.01 | 6.81 |
| .40 | 5.11 | .43 | 136.86 | 2.21 | 443.43 | 3.92 | 913.98 | 5.47 | 1530.82 | 6.83 |
| .41 | 5.54 | .46 | 139.07 | 2.23 | 447.35 | 3.93 | 919.45 | 5.50 | 1537.65 | 6.85 |
| .42 | 6.00 | .47 | 141.30 | 2.25 | 451.28 | 3.95 | 924.95 | 5.51 | 1544.50 | 6.85 |
| .43 | 6.47 | .48 | 143.55 | 2.26 | 455.23 | 3.97 | 930.46 | 5.52 | 1551.35 | 6.87 |
| .44 | 6.95 | .51 | 145.81 | 2.29 | 459.20 | 3.98 | 935.98 | 5.54 | 1558.22 | 6.88 |
| .45 | 7.46 | .52 | 148.10 | 2.30 | 463.18 | 4.00 | 941.52 | 5.55 | 1565.10 | 6.90 |
| .46 | 7.98 | .54 | 150.40 | 2.32 | 467.18 | 4.02 | 947.07 | 5.57 | 1572.00 | 6.90 |
| .47 | 8.52 | .56 | 152.72 | 2.33 | 471.20 | 4.03 | 952.64 | 5.58 | 1578.90 | 6.92 |
| .48 | 9.08 | .58 | 155.05 | 2.35 | 475.23 | 4.05 | 958.22 | 5.60 | 1585.82 | 6.93 |
| .49 | 9.66 | .60 | 157.40 | 2.37 | 479.28 | 4.07 | 963.82 | 5.61 | 1592.75 | 6.93 |
| .50 | 10.26 | +.61 | 159.77 | +2.39 | 483.35 | +4.08 | 969.43 | +5.62 | 1599.68 | +6.96 |

# TABLE VII. ARGUMENT 2.

Equation $= 4587''.400 + 4586''.9 \text{ sin. } (2t - x) + 31''.2 \text{ sin. } (4t - 2x)$.

Period, 31.81193574 days.

| Days. | 0 | | 1 | | 2 | | 3 | | 4 | |
|---|---|---|---|---|---|---|---|---|---|---|
| Decimals of a Day. | Equation. | Dif. | Equation. | Dif. | Equation. | Dif. | Equation. | Dif. | Equation. | Dif. |
| .50 | 10″.26 | + .61 | 159″.77 | +2.39 | 483″.35 | +4.08 | 969″.43 | +5.62 | 1599″.68 | +6.96 |
| .51 | 10.87 | .63 | 162.16 | 2.41 | 487.43 | 4.10 | 975.05 | 5.64 | 1606.64 | 6.96 |
| .52 | 11.50 | .65 | 164.57 | 2.42 | 491.53 | 4.11 | 980.69 | 5.65 | 1613.60 | 6.98 |
| .53 | 12.15 | .67 | 166.99 | 2.44 | 495.64 | 4.13 | 986.34 | 5.67 | 1620.58 | 6.98 |
| .54 | 12.82 | .68 | 169.43 | 2.46 | 499.77 | 4.15 | 992.01 | 5.68 | 1627.56 | 7.00 |
| .55 | 13.50 | .70 | 171.89 | 2.47 | 503.92 | 4.16 | 997.69 | 5.70 | 1634.56 | 7.02 |
| .56 | 14.20 | .72 | 174.36 | 2.49 | 508.08 | 4.18 | 1003.39 | 5.71 | 1641.58 | 7.02 |
| .57 | 14.92 | .74 | 176.85 | 2.51 | 512.26 | 4.19 | 1009.10 | 5.73 | 1648.60 | 7.04 |
| .58 | 15.66 | .76 | 179.36 | 2.53 | 516.45 | 4.21 | 1014.83 | 5.74 | 1655.64 | 7.04 |
| .59 | 16.42 | .77 | 181.89 | 2.54 | 520.66 | 4.23 | 1020.57 | 5.75 | 1662.68 | 7.06 |
| .60 | 17.19 | .79 | 184.43 | 2.57 | 524.89 | 4.25 | 1026.32 | 5.77 | 1669.74 | 7.07 |
| .61 | 17.98 | .81 | 187.00 | 2.57 | 529.14 | 4.26 | 1032.09 | 5.78 | 1676.81 | 7.09 |
| .62 | 18.79 | .83 | 189.57 | 2.60 | 533.40 | 4.27 | 1037.87 | 5.80 | 1683.90 | 7.09 |
| .63 | 19.62 | .85 | 192.17 | 2.62 | 537.67 | 4.30 | 1043.67 | 5.81 | 1690.99 | 7.11 |
| .64 | 20.47 | .86 | 194.79 | 2.63 | 541.97 | 4.31 | 1049.48 | 5.83 | 1698.10 | 7.12 |
| .65 | 21.33 | .88 | 197.42 | 2.65 | 546.28 | 4.32 | 1055.31 | 5.84 | 1705.22 | 7.13 |
| .66 | 22.21 | .90 | 200.07 | 2.66 | 550.60 | 4.34 | 1061.15 | 5.85 | 1712.35 | 7.14 |
| .67 | 23.11 | .92 | 202.73 | 2.68 | 554.94 | 4.36 | 1067.00 | 5.87 | 1719.49 | 7.15 |
| .68 | 24.03 | .93 | 205.41 | 2.71 | 559.30 | 4.37 | 1072.87 | 5.88 | 1726.64 | 7.17 |
| .69 | 24.96 | .96 | 208.12 | 2.71 | 563.67 | 4.38 | 1078.75 | 5.89 | 1733.81 | 7.17 |
| .70 | 25.92 | .97 | 210.83 | 2.74 | 568.05 | 4.41 | 1084.64 | 5.91 | 1740.98 | 7.19 |
| .71 | 26.89 | .99 | 213.57 | 2.75 | 572.46 | 4.42 | 1090.55 | 5.93 | 1748.17 | 7.20 |
| .72 | 27.88 | 1.00 | 216.32 | 2.77 | 576.88 | 4.44 | 1096.48 | 5.93 | 1755.37 | 7.21 |
| .73 | 28.88 | 1.03 | 219.09 | 2.78 | 581.32 | 4.45 | 1102.41 | 5.96 | 1762.58 | 7.22 |
| .74 | 29.91 | 1.04 | 221.87 | 2.81 | 585.77 | 4.47 | 1108.37 | 5.96 | 1769.80 | 7.23 |
| .75 | 30.95 | 1.06 | 224.68 | 2.82 | 590.24 | 4.48 | 1114.33 | 5.98 | 1777.03 | 7.25 |
| .76 | 32.01 | 1.08 | 227.50 | 2.84 | 594.72 | 4.50 | 1120.31 | 6.00 | 1784.28 | 7.25 |
| .77 | 33.09 | 1·10 | 230.34 | 2.85 | 599.22 | 4.52 | 1126.31 | 6.00 | 1791.53 | 7.27 |
| .78 | 34.19 | 1.11 | 233.19 | 2.88 | 603.74 | 4.53 | 1132.31 | 6.02 | 1798.80 | 7.28 |
| .79 | 35.30 | 1.13 | 236.07 | 2.89 | 608.27 | 4.54 | 1138.33 | 6.03 | 1806.08 | 7.28 |
| .80 | 36.43 | 1.15 | 238.96 | 2.91 | 612.81 | 4.57 | 1144.36 | 6.05 | 1813.36 | 7.31 |
| .81 | 37.58 | 1.17 | 241.87 | 2.92 | 617.38 | 4.58 | 1150.41 | 6.07 | 1820.67 | 7.31 |
| .82 | 38.75 | 1.19 | 244.79 | 2.94 | 621.96 | 4.59 | 1156.48 | 6.07 | 1827.98 | 7.32 |
| .83 | 39.94 | 1.20 | 247.73 | 2.96 | 626.55 | 4.61 | 1162.55 | 6.09 | 1835.30 | 7.33 |
| .84 | 41.14 | 1.22 | 250.69 | 2.98 | 631.16 | 4.63 | 1168.64 | 6.11 | 1842.63 | 7.35 |
| .85 | 42.36 | 1.24 | 253.67 | 2.99 | 635.79 | 4.64 | 1174.75 | 6.12 | 1849.98 | 7.35 |
| .86 | 43.60 | 1.26 | 256.66 | 3.01 | 640.43 | 4.66 | 1180.87 | 6.13 | 1857.33 | 7.37 |
| .87 | 44.86 | 1.27 | 259.67 | 3.03 | 645.09 | 4.67 | 1187.00 | 6.14 | 1864.70 | 7.38 |
| .88 | 46.13 | 1.29 | 262.70 | 3.04 | 649.76 | 4.69 | 1193.14 | 6.16 | 1872.08 | 7.38 |
| .89 | 47.42 | 1.31 | 265.74 | 3.07 | 654.45 | 4.71 | 1199.30 | 6.17 | 1879.46 | 7.40 |
| .90 | 48.73 | 1.33 | 268.81 | 3.07 | 659.16 | 4.72 | 1205.47 | 6.18 | 1886.86 | 7.41 |
| .91 | 50.06 | 1.34 | 271.88 | 3.10 | 663.88 | 4.73 | 1211.65 | 6.20 | 1894.27 | 7.43 |
| .92 | 51.40 | 1.37 | 274.98 | 3.11 | 668.61 | 4.75 | 1217.85 | 6.22 | 1901.70 | 7.43 |
| .93 | 52.77 | 1.38 | 278.09 | 3.13 | 673.36 | 4.78 | 1224.07 | 6.22 | 1909.13 | 7.44 |
| .94 | 54.15 | 1.40 | 281.22 | 3.15 | 678.14 | 4.78 | 1230.29 | 6.24 | 1916.57 | 7.46 |
| .95 | 55.55 | 1.42 | 284.37 | 3.16 | 682.92 | 4.80 | 1236.53 | 6.25 | 1924.03 | 7.46 |
| .96 | 56.97 | 1.44 | 287.53 | 3.19 | 687.72 | 4.81 | 1242.78 | 6.27 | 1931.49 | 7.47 |
| .97 | 58.41 | 1.44 | 290.72 | 3.19 | 692.53 | 4.83 | 1249.05 | 6.28 | 1938.96 | 7.49 |
| .98 | 59.85 | 1.47 | 293.91 | 3.22 | 697.36 | 4.85 | 1255.33 | 6.29 | 1946.45 | 7.50 |
| .99 | 61.32 | +1.49 | 297.13 | +3.23 | 702.21 | +4.85 | 1261.62 | +6.31 | 1953.95 | +7.50 |
| 1.00 | 62.81 | | 300.36 | | 707.06 | | 1267.93 | | 1961.45 | |

# TABLE VII. ARGUMENT 2.

Equation $= 4587''.400 + 4586''.9 \sin. (2t - x) + 31''.2 \sin. (4t - 2x)$.

Period, 31.81193574 days.

| Days. | 5 | | 6 | | 7 | | 8 | | 9 | |
|---|---|---|---|---|---|---|---|---|---|---|
| Decimals of a Day. | Equation. | Dif. | Equation. | Dif. | Equation. | Dif. | Equation. | Dif. | Equation. | Dif. |
| .00 | 1961″.45 | +7.52 | 2760″.43 | +8.42 | 3633″.06 | +8.98 | 4544″.23 | +9.19 | 5457″.15 | +9.01 |
| .01 | 1968.97 | 7.53 | 2768.85 | 8.43 | 3642.04 | 8.99 | 4553.42 | 9.18 | 5466.16 | 9.01 |
| .02 | 1976.50 | 7.54 | 2777.28 | 8.43 | 3651.03 | 8.99 | 4562.60 | 9.18 | 5475.17 | 9.01 |
| .03 | 1984.04 | 7.55 | 2785.71 | 8.44 | 3660.02 | 8.99 | 4571.78 | 9.18 | 5484.18 | 9.00 |
| .04 | 1991.59 | 7.55 | 2794.15 | 8.45 | 3669.01 | 8.99 | 4580.96 | 9.18 | 5493.18 | 9.00 |
| .05 | 1999.14 | 7.57 | 2802.60 | 8.45 | 3678.00 | 9.00 | 4590.14 | 9.19 | 5502.18 | 8.99 |
| .06 | 2006.71 | 7.58 | 2811.05 | 8.47 | 3687.00 | 9.01 | 4599.33 | 9.18 | 5511.17 | 8.99 |
| .07 | 2014.29 | 7.59 | 2819.52 | 8.46 | 3696.01 | 9.00 | 4608.51 | 9.18 | 5520.16 | 8.99 |
| .08 | 2021.88 | 7.61 | 2827.98 | 8.48 | 3705.01 | 9.01 | 4617.69 | 9.19 | 5529.15 | 8.98 |
| .09 | 2029.49 | 7.61 | 2836.46 | 8.48 | 3714.02 | 9.02 | 4626.88 | 9.18 | 5538.13 | 8.98 |
| .10 | 2037.10 | 7.62 | 2844.94 | 8.49 | 3723.04 | 9.02 | 4636.06 | 9.18 | 5547.11 | 8.98 |
| .11 | 2044.72 | 7.63 | 2853.43 | 8.50 | 3732.06 | 9.02 | 4645.24 | 9.18 | 5556.09 | 8.97 |
| .12 | 2052.35 | 7.64 | 2861.93 | 8.50 | 3741.08 | 9.02 | 4654.42 | 9.19 | 5565.06 | 8.96 |
| .13 | 2059.99 | 7.66 | 2870.43 | 8.51 | 3750.10 | 9.03 | 4663.61 | 9.18 | 5574.02 | 8.97 |
| .14 | 2067.65 | 7.66 | 2878.94 | 8.52 | 3759.13 | 9.03 | 4672.79 | 9.18 | 5582.99 | 8.96 |
| .15 | 2075.31 | 7.67 | 2887.46 | 8.53 | 3768.16 | 9.04 | 4681.97 | 9.18 | 5591.95 | 8.95 |
| .16 | 2082.98 | 7.68 | 2895.99 | 8.53 | 3777.20 | 9.04 | 4691.15 | 9.18 | 5600.90 | 8.95 |
| .17 | 2090.66 | 7.69 | 2904.52 | 8.54 | 3786.24 | 9.04 | 4700.33 | 9.18 | 5609.85 | 8.95 |
| .18 | 2098.35 | 7.71 | 2913.06 | 8.54 | 3795.28 | 9.04 | 4709.51 | 9.18 | 5618.80 | 8.94 |
| .19 | 2106.06 | 7.71 | 2921.60 | 8.55 | 3804.32 | 9.05 | 4718.69 | 9.17 | 5627.74 | 8.94 |
| .20 | 2113.77 | 7.72 | 2930.15 | 8.56 | 3813.37 | 9.05 | 4727.86 | 9.18 | 5636.68 | 8.93 |
| .21 | 2121.49 | 7.73 | 2938.71 | 8.57 | 3822.42 | 9.06 | 4737.04 | 9.18 | 5645.61 | 8.93 |
| .22 | 2129.22 | 7.75 | 2947.28 | 8.57 | 3831.48 | 9.05 | 4746.22 | 9.18 | 5654.54 | 8.93 |
| .23 | 2136.97 | 7.75 | 2955.85 | 8.58 | 3840.53 | 9.06 | 4755.40 | 9.17 | 5663.47 | 8.92 |
| .24 | 2144.72 | 7.76 | 2964.43 | 8.59 | 3849.59 | 9.07 | 4764.57 | 9.18 | 5672.39 | 8.92 |
| .25 | 2152.48 | 7.78 | 2973.02 | 8.59 | 3858.66 | 9.06 | 4773.75 | 9.17 | 5681.31 | 8.91 |
| .26 | 2160.26 | 7.78 | 2981.61 | 8.60 | 3867.72 | 9.07 | 4782.92 | 9.18 | 5690.22 | 8.91 |
| .27 | 2168.04 | 7.79 | 2990.21 | 8.60 | 3876.79 | 9.07 | 4792.10 | 9.17 | 5699.13 | 8.90 |
| .28 | 2175.83 | 7.80 | 2998.81 | 8.61 | 3885.86 | 9.08 | 4801.27 | 9.17 | 5708.03 | 8.90 |
| .29 | 2183.63 | 7.81 | 3007.42 | 8.62 | 3894.94 | 9.08 | 4810.44 | 9.17 | 5716.93 | 8.90 |
| .30 | 2191.44 | 7.82 | 3016.04 | 8.62 | 3904.02 | 9.08 | 4819.61 | 9.17 | 5725.83 | 8.89 |
| .31 | 2199.26 | 7.83 | 3024.66 | 8.63 | 3913.10 | 9.08 | 4828.78 | 9.17 | 5734.72 | 8.88 |
| .32 | 2207.09 | 7.84 | 3033.29 | 8.64 | 3922.18 | 9.09 | 4837.95 | 9.17 | 5743.60 | 8.88 |
| .33 | 2214.93 | 7.85 | 3041.93 | 8.64 | 3931.27 | 9.08 | 4847.12 | 9.17 | 5752.48 | 8.88 |
| .34 | 2222.78 | 7.86 | 3050.57 | 8.65 | 3940.35 | 9.10 | 4856.29 | 9.16 | 5761.36 | 8.87 |
| .35 | 2230.64 | 7.87 | 3059.22 | 8.65 | 3949.45 | 9.09 | 4865.45 | 9.17 | 5770.23 | 8.87 |
| .36 | 2238.51 | 7.88 | 3067.87 | 8.67 | 3958.54 | 9.10 | 4874.62 | 9.16 | 5779.10 | 8.86 |
| .37 | 2246.39 | 7.89 | 3076.54 | 8.66 | 3967.64 | 9.10 | 4883.78 | 9.17 | 5787.96 | 8.85 |
| .38 | 2254.28 | 7.89 | 3085.20 | 8.68 | 3976.74 | 9.10 | 4892.95 | 9.16 | 5796.81 | 8.85 |
| .39 | 2262.17 | 7.91 | 3093.88 | 8.67 | 3985.84 | 9.10 | 4902.11 | 9.16 | 5805.66 | 8.85 |
| .40 | 2270.08 | 7.92 | 3102.55 | 8.69 | 3994.94 | 9.11 | 4911.27 | 9.16 | 5814.51 | 8.84 |
| .41 | 2278.00 | 7.92 | 3111.24 | 8.69 | 4004.05 | 9.10 | 4920.43 | 9.16 | 5823.35 | 8.84 |
| .42 | 2285.92 | 7.94 | 3119.93 | 8.70 | 4013.15 | 9.11 | 4929.59 | 9.15 | 5832.19 | 8.83 |
| .43 | 2293.86 | 7.94 | 3128.63 | 8.70 | 4022.26 | 9.12 | 4938.74 | 9.16 | 5841.02 | 8.82 |
| .44 | 2301.80 | 7.96 | 3137.33 | 8.71 | 4031.38 | 9.11 | 4947.90 | 9.15 | 5849.84 | 8.83 |
| .45 | 2309.76 | 7.96 | 3146.04 | 8.72 | 4040.49 | 9.12 | 4957.05 | 9.15 | 5858.67 | 8.81 |
| .46 | 2317.72 | 7.97 | 3154.76 | 8.72 | 4049.61 | 9.12 | 4966.20 | 9.15 | 5867.48 | 8.81 |
| .47 | 2325.69 | 7.98 | 3163.48 | 8.73 | 4058.73 | 9.12 | 4975.35 | 9.15 | 5876.29 | 8.81 |
| .48 | 2333.67 | 7.99 | 3172.21 | 8.73 | 4067.85 | 9.13 | 4984.50 | 9.15 | 5885.10 | 8.80 |
| .49 | 2341.66 | 8.00 | 3180.94 | 8.73 | 4076.98 | 9.12 | 4993.65 | 9.14 | 5893.90 | 8.79 |
| .50 | 2349.66 | +8.00 | 3189.67 | +8.75 | 4086.10 | +9.13 | 5002.79 | +9.15 | 5902.69 | +8.79 |

# TABLE VII. ARGUMENT 2.

Equation $= 4587''.400 + 4586''.9 \sin. (2t - x) + 31''.2 \sin. (4t - 2x)$.

Period, 31.81193574 days.

| Days. | 5 | | 6 | | 7 | | 8 | | 9 | |
|---|---|---|---|---|---|---|---|---|---|---|
| Decimals of a Day. | Equation. | Dif. | Equation. | Dif. | Equation. | Dif. | Equation. | Dif. | Equation. | Dif. |
| .50 | 2349.66 | +8.00 | 3189.67 | +8.75 | 4086.10 | +9.13 | 5002.79 | +9.15 | 5902.69 | +8.79 |
| .51 | 2357.66 | 8.02 | 3198.42 | 8.75 | 4095.23 | 9.13 | 5011.94 | 9.14 | 5911.48 | 8.79 |
| .52 | 2365.68 | 8.03 | 3207.17 | 8.76 | 4104.36 | 9.14 | 5021.08 | 9.14 | 5920.27 | 8.78 |
| .53 | 2373.71 | 8.03 | 3215.93 | 8.75 | 4113.50 | 9.13 | 5030.22 | 9.14 | 5929.05 | 8.77 |
| .54 | 2381.74 | 8.04 | 3224.68 | 8.77 | 4122.63 | 9.14 | 5039.36 | 9.14 | 5937.82 | 8.77 |
| .55 | 2389.78 | 8.05 | 3233.45 | 8.77 | 4131.77 | 9.13 | 5048.50 | 9.13 | 5946.59 | 8.77 |
| .56 | 2397.83 | 8.07 | 3242.22 | 8.78 | 4140.90 | 9.14 | 5057.63 | 9.14 | 5955.36 | 8.75 |
| .57 | 2405.90 | 8.07 | 3251.00 | 8.78 | 4150.04 | 9.14 | 5066.77 | 9.13 | 5964.11 | 8.76 |
| .58 | 2413.97 | 8.08 | 3259.78 | 8.79 | 4159.18 | 9.15 | 5075.90 | 9.13 | 5972.87 | 8.75 |
| .59 | 2422.05 | 8.08 | 3268.57 | 8.79 | 4168.33 | 9.14 | 5085.03 | 9.12 | 5981.62 | 8.73 |
| .60 | 2430.13 | 8.10 | 3277.36 | 8.80 | 4177.47 | 9.15 | 5094.15 | 9.13 | 5990.35 | 8.73 |
| .61 | 2438.23 | 8.11 | 3286.16 | 8.80 | 4186.62 | 9.15 | 5103.28 | 9.12 | 5999.08 | 8.73 |
| .62 | 2446.34 | 8.11 | 3294.96 | 8.81 | 4195.77 | 9.15 | 5112.40 | 9.12 | 6007.81 | 8.73 |
| .63 | 2454.45 | 8.12 | 3303.77 | 8.82 | 4204.92 | 9.15 | 5121.52 | 9.12 | 6016.54 | 8.72 |
| .64 | 2462.57 | 8.13 | 3312.59 | 8.81 | 4214.07 | 9.15 | 5130.64 | 9.12 | 6025.26 | 8.71 |
| .65 | 2470.70 | 8.14 | 3321.40 | 8.83 | 4223.22 | 9.16 | 5139.76 | 9.11 | 6033.97 | 8.70 |
| .66 | 2478.84 | 8.15 | 3330.23 | 8.83 | 4232.38 | 9.15 | 5148.87 | 9.12 | 6042.67 | 8.71 |
| .67 | 2486.99 | 8.16 | 3339.06 | 8.83 | 4241.53 | 9.16 | 5157.99 | 9.10 | 6051.38 | 8.69 |
| .68 | 2495.15 | 8.17 | 3347.89 | 8.84 | 4250.69 | 9.16 | 5167.09 | 9.10 | 6060.07 | 8.69 |
| .69 | 2503.32 | 8.16 | 3356.73 | 8.85 | 4259.85 | 9.15 | 5176.19 | 9.11 | 6068.76 | 8.67 |
| .70 | 2511.48 | 8.18 | 3365.58 | 8.85 | 4269.00 | 9.17 | 5185.30 | 9.10 | 6077.43 | 8.68 |
| .71 | 2519.66 | 8.20 | 3374.43 | 8.85 | 4278.17 | 9.16 | 5194.40 | 9.11 | 6086.11 | 8.67 |
| .72 | 2527.86 | 8.20 | 3383.28 | 8.86 | 4287.33 | 9.16 | 5203.51 | 9.09 | 6094.78 | 8.66 |
| .73 | 2536.06 | 8.20 | 3392.14 | 8.87 | 4296.49 | 9.18 | 5212.60 | 9.10 | 6103.44 | 8.66 |
| .74 | 2544.26 | 8.22 | 3401.01 | 8.87 | 4305.67 | 9.15 | 5221.70 | 9.09 | 6112.10 | 8.65 |
| .75 | 2552.48 | 8.22 | 3409.88 | 8.87 | 4314.82 | 9.17 | 5230.79 | 9.09 | 6120.75 | 8.65 |
| .76 | 2560.70 | 8.23 | 3418.75 | 8.88 | 4323.99 | 9.17 | 5239.88 | 9.09 | 6129.40 | 8.64 |
| .77 | 2568.93 | 8.24 | 3427.63 | 8.88 | 4333.16 | 9.17 | 5248.97 | 9.08 | 6138.04 | 8.63 |
| .78 | 2577.17 | 8.25 | 3436.51 | 8.89 | 4342.33 | 9.17 | 5258.05 | 9.08 | 6146.67 | 8.63 |
| .79 | 2585.42 | 8.25 | 3445.40 | 8.89 | 4351.50 | 9.17 | 5267.13 | 9.08 | 6155.30 | 8.62 |
| .80 | 2593.67 | 8.27 | 3454.29 | 8.90 | 4360.67 | 9.17 | 5276.21 | 9.08 | 6163.92 | 8.61 |
| .81 | 2601.94 | 8.27 | 3463.19 | 8.90 | 4369.84 | 9.18 | 5285.29 | 9.07 | 6172.53 | 8.60 |
| .82 | 2610.21 | 8.28 | 3472.09 | 8.91 | 4379.02 | 9.17 | 5294.36 | 9.07 | 6181.13 | 8.61 |
| .83 | 2618.49 | 8.29 | 3481.00 | 8.91 | 4388.19 | 9.17 | 5303.43 | 9.07 | 6189.74 | 8.59 |
| .84 | 2626.78 | 8.29 | 3489.91 | 8.91 | 4397.36 | 9.18 | 5312.50 | 9.07 | 6198.33 | 8.59 |
| .85 | 2635.07 | 8.31 | 3498.82 | 8.92 | 4406.54 | 9.17 | 5321.57 | 9.05 | 6206.92 | 8.58 |
| .86 | 2643.38 | 8.31 | 3507.74 | 8.92 | 4415.71 | 9.18 | 5330.62 | 9.06 | 6215.50 | 8.57 |
| .87 | 2651.69 | 8.32 | 3516.66 | 8.93 | 4424.89 | 9.18 | 5339.68 | 9.06 | 6224.07 | 8.57 |
| .88 | 2660.01 | 8.32 | 3525.59 | 8.94 | 4434.07 | 9.17 | 5348.74 | 9.05 | 6232.64 | 8.57 |
| .89 | 2668.33 | 8.34 | 3534.53 | 8.93 | 4443.24 | 9.18 | 5357.79 | 9.05 | 6241.21 | 8.55 |
| .90 | 2676.67 | 8.34 | 3543.46 | 8.94 | 4452.42 | 9.18 | 5366.84 | 9.04 | 6249.76 | 8.55 |
| .91 | 2685.01 | 8.35 | 3552.40 | 8.95 | 4461.60 | 9.18 | 5375.88 | 9.05 | 6258.31 | 8.54 |
| .92 | 2693.36 | 8.36 | 3561.35 | 8.95 | 4470.78 | 9.18 | 5384.93 | 9.04 | 6266.85 | 8.53 |
| .93 | 2701.72 | 8.37 | 3570.30 | 8.95 | 4479.96 | 9.18 | 5393.97 | 9.03 | 6275.38 | 8.53 |
| .94 | 2710.09 | 8.37 | 3579.25 | 8.96 | 4489.14 | 9.19 | 5403.00 | 9.04 | 6283.91 | 8.52 |
| .95 | 2718.46 | 8.38 | 3588.21 | 8.96 | 4498.33 | 9.18 | 5412.04 | 9.03 | 6292.43 | 8.52 |
| .96 | 2726.84 | 8.39 | 3597.17 | 8.97 | 4507.51 | 9.18 | 5421.07 | 9.02 | 6300.95 | 8.50 |
| .97 | 2735.23 | 8.39 | 3606.14 | 8.97 | 4516.69 | 9.18 | 5430.09 | 9.03 | 6309.45 | 8.50 |
| .98 | 2743.62 | 8.41 | 3615.11 | 8.97 | 4525.87 | 9.18 | 5439.12 | 9.02 | 6317.95 | 8.50 |
| .99 | 2752.03 | +8.40 | 3624.08 | +8.98 | 4535.05 | +9.18 | 5448.14 | +9.01 | 6326.45 | +8.48 |
| 1.00 | 2760.43 | | 3633.06 | | 4544.23 | | 5457.15 | | 6334.93 | |

# TABLE VII. ARGUMENT 2.

Equation $= 4587''.400 + 4586''.9 \sin. (2t - x) + 31''.2 \sin. (4t - 2x)$.

Period, 31.81193574 days.

| Days. | 10 | | 11 | | 12 | | 13 | | 14 | |
|---|---|---|---|---|---|---|---|---|---|---|
| Decimals of a Day. | Equation. | Dif. | Equation. | Dif. | Equation. | Dif. | Equation. | Dif. | Equation. | Dif. |
| .00 | 6334.93 | +8.48 | 7142.25 | +7.61 | 7846.93 | +6.43 | 8421.28 | +5.00 | 8843.22 | +3.39 |
| .01 | 6343.41 | 8.47 | 7149.86 | 7.60 | 7853.36 | 6.42 | 8426.28 | 4.99 | 8846.61 | 3.37 |
| .02 | 6351.88 | 8.46 | 7157.46 | 7.58 | 7859.78 | 6.41 | 8431.27 | 4.98 | 8849.98 | 3.36 |
| .03 | 6360.34 | 8.46 | 7165.04 | 7.57 | 7866.19 | 6.39 | 8436.25 | 4.95 | 8853.34 | 3.35 |
| .04 | 6368.80 | 8.45 | 7172.61 | 7.57 | 7872.58 | 6.38 | 8441.20 | 4.94 | 8856.69 | 3.32 |
| .05 | 6377.25 | 8.44 | 7180.18 | 7.55 | 7878.96 | 6.36 | 8446.14 | 4.93 | 8860.01 | 3.31 |
| .06 | 6385.69 | 8.43 | 7187.73 | 7.54 | 7885.32 | 6.35 | 8451.07 | 4.91 | 8863.32 | 3.29 |
| .07 | 6394.12 | 8.43 | 7195.27 | 7.53 | 7891.67 | 6.34 | 8455.98 | 4.90 | 8866.61 | 3.27 |
| .08 | 6402.55 | 8.43 | 7202.80 | 7.52 | 7898.01 | 6.32 | 8460.88 | 4.89 | 8869.88 | 3.26 |
| .09 | 6410.98 | 8.41 | 7210.32 | 7.52 | 7904.33 | 6.31 | 8465.77 | 4.87 | 8873.14 | 3.23 |
| .10 | 6419.39 | 8.41 | 7217.84 | 7.50 | 7910.64 | 6.30 | 8470.64 | 4.85 | 8876.37 | 3.22 |
| .11 | 6427.80 | 8.40 | 7225.34 | 7.49 | 7916.94 | 6.29 | 8475.49 | 4.84 | 8879.59 | 3.31 |
| .12 | 6436.20 | 8.39 | 7232.83 | 7.48 | 7923.23 | 6.27 | 8480.33 | 4.82 | 8882.80 | 3.19 |
| .13 | 6444.59 | 8.38 | 7240.31 | 7.46 | 7929.50 | 6.26 | 8485.15 | 4.80 | 8885.99 | 3.17 |
| .14 | 6452.97 | 8.38 | 7247.77 | 7.46 | 7935.76 | 6.24 | 8489.95 | 4.79 | 8889.16 | 3.15 |
| .15 | 6461.35 | 8.37 | 7255.23 | 7.45 | 7942.00 | 6.23 | 8494.74 | 4.78 | 8892.31 | 3.14 |
| .16 | 6469.72 | 8.36 | 7262.68 | 7.43 | 7948.23 | 6.22 | 8499.52 | 4.76 | 8895.45 | 3.12 |
| .17 | 6478.08 | 8.35 | 7270.11 | 7.43 | 7954.45 | 6.20 | 8504.28 | 4.74 | 8898.57 | 3.10 |
| .18 | 6486.43 | 8.35 | 7277.54 | 7.41 | 7960.65 | 6.19 | 8509.02 | 4.73 | 8901.67 | 3.09 |
| .19 | 6494.78 | 8.34 | 7284.95 | 7.41 | 7966.84 | 6.18 | 8513.75 | 4.71 | 8904.76 | 3.07 |
| .20 | 6503.12 | 8.33 | 7292.36 | 7.39 | 7973.02 | 6.17 | 8518.46 | 4.69 | 8907.83 | 3.05 |
| .21 | 6511.45 | 8.32 | 7299.75 | 7.39 | 7979.19 | 6.15 | 8523.15 | 4.68 | 8910.88 | 3.03 |
| .22 | 6519.77 | 8.31 | 7307.14 | 7.37 | 7985.34 | 6.13 | 8527.83 | 4.67 | 8913.91 | 3.02 |
| .23 | 6528.08 | 8.31 | 7314.51 | 7.36 | 7991.47 | 6.12 | 8532.50 | 4.65 | 8916.93 | 3.00 |
| .24 | 6536.39 | 8.30 | 7321.87 | 7.35 | 7997.59 | 6.11 | 8537.15 | 4.63 | 8919.93 | 2.98 |
| .25 | 6544.69 | 8.29 | 7329.22 | 7.33 | 8003.70 | 6.10 | 8541.78 | 4.62 | 8922.91 | 2.97 |
| .26 | 6552.98 | 8.28 | 7336.55 | 7.33 | 8009.80 | 6.08 | 8546.40 | 4.60 | 8925.88 | 2.95 |
| .27 | 6561.26 | 8.27 | 7343.88 | 7.31 | 8015.88 | 6.07 | 8551.00 | 4.58 | 8928.83 | 2.93 |
| .28 | 6569.53 | 8.27 | 7351.19 | 7.31 | 8021.95 | 6.05 | 8555.58 | 4.57 | 8931.76 | 2.91 |
| .29 | 6577.80 | 8.26 | 7358.50 | 7.30 | 8028.00 | 6.04 | 8560.15 | 4.55 | 8934.67 | 2.90 |
| .30 | 6586.06 | 8.25 | 7365.80 | 7.28 | 8034.04 | 6.03 | 8564.70 | 4.54 | 8937.57 | 2.88 |
| .31 | 6594.31 | 8.25 | 7373.08 | 7.27 | 8040.07 | 6.01 | 8569.24 | 4.52 | 8940.45 | 2.86 |
| .32 | 6602.56 | 8.23 | 7380.35 | 7.26 | 8046.08 | 6.00 | 8573.76 | 4.51 | 8943.31 | 2.85 |
| .33 | 6610.79 | 8.23 | 7387.61 | 7.24 | 8052.08 | 5.99 | 8578.27 | 4.49 | 8946.16 | 2.83 |
| .34 | 6619.02 | 8.21 | 7394.85 | 7.24 | 8058.07 | 5.97 | 8582.76 | 4.48 | 8948.99 | 2.81 |
| .35 | 6627.23 | 8.21 | 7402.09 | 7.23 | 8064.04 | 5.96 | 8587.24 | 4.46 | 8951.80 | 2.79 |
| .36 | 6635.44 | 8.20 | 7409.32 | 7.21 | 8070.00 | 5.94 | 8591.70 | 4.44 | 8954.59 | 2.78 |
| .37 | 6643.64 | 8.20 | 7416.53 | 7.20 | 8075.94 | 5.93 | 8596.14 | 4.43 | 8957.37 | 2.76 |
| .38 | 6651.84 | 8.18 | 7423.73 | 7.20 | 8081.87 | 5.91 | 8600.57 | 4.41 | 8960.13 | 2.74 |
| .39 | 6660.02 | 8.18 | 7430.93 | 7.18 | 8087.78 | 5.90 | 8604.98 | 4.39 | 8962.87 | 2.72 |
| .40 | 6668.20 | 8.17 | 7438.11 | 7.17 | 8093.68 | 5.89 | 8609.37 | 4.38 | 8965.59 | 2.71 |
| .41 | 6676.37 | 8.16 | 7445.28 | 7.15 | 8099.57 | 5.87 | 8613.75 | 4.36 | 8968.30 | 2.69 |
| .42 | 6684.53 | 8.15 | 7452.43 | 7.15 | 8105.44 | 5.86 | 8618.11 | 4.35 | 8970.99 | 2.67 |
| .43 | 6692.68 | 8.14 | 7459.58 | 7.13 | 8111.30 | 5.85 | 8622.46 | 4.33 | 8973.66 | 2.66 |
| .44 | 6700.82 | 8.14 | 7466.71 | 7.13 | 8117.15 | 5.83 | 8626.79 | 4.31 | 8976.32 | 2.64 |
| .45 | 6708.96 | 8.12 | 7473.84 | 7.11 | 8122.98 | 5.82 | 8631.10 | 4.30 | 8978.96 | 2.62 |
| .46 | 6717.08 | 8.12 | 7480.95 | 7.09 | 8128.80 | 5.80 | 8635.40 | 4.28 | 8981.58 | 2.60 |
| .47 | 6725.20 | 8.11 | 7488.04 | 7.09 | 8134.60 | 5.79 | 8639.68 | 4.27 | 8984.18 | 2.59 |
| .48 | 6733.31 | 8.10 | 7495.13 | 7.08 | 8140.39 | 5.77 | 8643.95 | 4.25 | 8986.77 | 2.57 |
| .49 | 6741.41 | 8.09 | 7502.21 | 7.06 | 8146.16 | 5.76 | 8648.20 | 4.24 | 8989.34 | 2.55 |
| .50 | 6749.50 | +8.08 | 7509.27 | +7.06 | 8151.92 | +5.75 | 8652.44 | +4.22 | 8991.89 | +2.53 |

# TABLE VII. ARGUMENT 2.

Equation $= 4587''.400 + 4586''.9 \text{ sin. } (2t - x) + 31''.2 \text{ sin. } (4t - 2x)$.

Period, 31.81193574 days.

| Days. | 10 | | 11 | | 12 | | 13 | | 14 | |
|---|---|---|---|---|---|---|---|---|---|---|
| Decimals of a Day. | Equation. | Dif. | Equation. | Dif. | Equation. | Dif. | Equation. | Dif. | Equation. | Dif. |
| .50 | 6749.50″ | +8.08 | 7509.27″ | +7.06 | 8151.92″ | +5.75 | 8652.44″ | +4.22 | 8991.89″ | +2.53 |
| .51 | 6757.58 | 8.07 | 7516.33 | 7.04 | 8157.67 | 5.73 | 8656.66 | 4.20 | 8994.42 | 2.52 |
| .52 | 6765 65 | 8.06 | 7523.37 | 7.03 | 8163.40 | 5.71 | 8660.86 | 4.18 | 8996.94 | 2.50 |
| .53 | 6773.71 | 8.06 | 7530.40 | 7.01 | 8169.11 | 5.70 | 8665.04 | 4.17 | 8999.44 | 2.48 |
| .54 | 6781.77 | 8.05 | 7537.41 | 7.01 | 8174.81 | 5.69 | 8669.21 | 4.15 | 9001.92 | 2.47 |
| .55 | 6789.82 | 8.04 | 7544.42 | 6.99 | 8180.50 | 5.68 | 8673.36 | 4.14 | 9004.39 | 2.44 |
| .56 | 6797.86 | 8.03 | 7551.41 | 6.98 | 8186.18 | 5.66 | 8677.50 | 4.12 | 9006.83 | 2.43 |
| .57 | 6805.89 | 8.02 | 7558.39 | 6.97 | 8191.84 | 5.64 | 8681.62 | 4.10 | 9009.26 | 2.41 |
| .58 | 6813.91 | 8.01 | 7565.36 | 6.96 | 8197.48 | 5.63 | 8685.72 | 4.09 | 9011.67 | 2.40 |
| .59 | 6821.92 | 8.01 | 7572.32 | 6.95 | 8203.11 | 5.62 | 8689.81 | 4.07 | 9014.07 | 2.37 |
| .60 | 6829.93 | 7.99 | 7579.27 | 6.93 | 8208.73 | 5.60 | 8693.88 | 4.06 | 9016.44 | 2.36 |
| .61 | 6837.92 | 7.98 | 7586.20 | 6.92 | 8214.33 | 5.59 | 8697.94 | 4.04 | 9018.80 | 2.35 |
| .62 | 6845.90 | 7.98 | 7593.12 | 6.91 | 8219.92 | 5.57 | 8701.98 | 4.02 | 9021.15 | 2.32 |
| .63 | 6853.88 | 7.96 | 7600.03 | 6.90 | 8225.49 | 5.56 | 8706.00 | 4.01 | 9023.47 | 2.31 |
| .64 | 6861.84 | 7.96 | 7606.93 | 6.89 | 8231.05 | 5.54 | 8710.01 | 3.99 | 9025.78 | 2.29 |
| .65 | 6869.80 | 7.95 | 7613.82 | 6.86 | 8236.59 | 5.53 | 8714.00 | 3.97 | 9028.07 | 2.27 |
| .66 | 6877.75 | 7.93 | 7620.68 | 6.86 | 8242.12 | 5.52 | 8717.97 | 3.96 | 9030.34 | 2.26 |
| .67 | 6885.68 | 7.93 | 7627.54 | 6.85 | 8247.64 | 5.50 | 8721.93 | 3.94 | 9032.60 | 2.23 |
| .68 | 6893.61 | 7.92 | 7634.39 | 6.84 | 8253.14 | 5.48 | 8725.87 | 3.92 | 9034.83 | 2.22 |
| .69 | 6901.53 | 7.92 | 7641.23 | 6.83 | 8258.62 | 5.47 | 8729.79 | 3.91 | 9037.05 | 2.21 |
| .70 | 6909.45 | 7.90 | 7648.06 | 6.81 | 8264.09 | 5.46 | 8733.70 | 3.89 | 9039.26 | 2.18 |
| .71 | 6917.35 | 7.89 | 7654.87 | 6.80 | 8269.55 | 5.44 | 8737.59 | 3.88 | 9041.44 | 2.17 |
| .72 | 6925.24 | 7.88 | 7661.67 | 6.78 | 8274.99 | 5.43 | 8741.47 | 3.86 | 9043.61 | 2.15 |
| .73 | 6933.12 | 7.87 | 7668.45 | 6.78 | 8280.42 | 5.41 | 8745.33 | 3.84 | 9045.76 | 2.13 |
| .74 | 6940.99 | 7.86 | 7675.23 | 6.76 | 8285.83 | 5.39 | 8749.17 | 3.82 | 9047.89 | 2.11 |
| .75 | 6948.85 | 7.86 | 7681.99 | 6.75 | 8291.22 | 5.38 | 8752.99 | 3.81 | 9050.00 | 2.10 |
| .76 | 6956.71 | 7.84 | 7688.74 | 6.73 | 8296.60 | 5.37 | 8756.80 | 3.80 | 9052.10 | 2.08 |
| .77 | 6964.55 | 7.83 | 7695.47 | 6.73 | 8301.97 | 5.35 | 8760.60 | 3.77 | 9054.18 | 2.06 |
| .78 | 6972.38 | 7.83 | 7702.20 | 6.71 | 8307.32 | 5.34 | 8764.37 | 3.76 | 9056.24 | 2.05 |
| .79 | 6980.21 | 7.82 | 7708.91 | 6.70 | 8312.66 | 5.32 | 8768.13 | 3.74 | 9058.29 | 2.02 |
| .80 | 6988.03 | 7.80 | 7715.61 | 6.69 | 8317.98 | 5.31 | 8771.87 | 3.73 | 9060.31 | 2.01 |
| .81 | 6995.83 | 7.80 | 7722.30 | 6.68 | 8323.29 | 5.29 | 8775.60 | 3.71 | 9062.32 | 1.99 |
| .82 | 7003.63 | 7.78 | 7728.98 | 6.66 | 8328.58 | 5.28 | 8779.31 | 3.69 | 9064.31 | 1.97 |
| .83 | 7011.41 | 7.78 | 7735.64 | 6.65 | 8333.86 | 5.26 | 8783.00 | 3.68 | 9066.28 | 1.96 |
| .84 | 7019.19 | 7.76 | 7742.29 | 6.63 | 8339.12 | 5.25 | 8786.68 | 3.66 | 9068.24 | 1.94 |
| .85 | 7026.95 | 7.76 | 7748.92 | 6.63 | 8344.37 | 5.24 | 8790.34 | 3.64 | 9070.18 | 1.92 |
| .86 | 7034.71 | 7.75 | 7755.55 | 6.61 | 8349.61 | 5.21 | 8793.98 | 3.62 | 9072.10 | 1.90 |
| .87 | 7042.46 | 7.73 | 7762.16 | 6.59 | 8354.82 | 5.20 | 8797.60 | 3.61 | 9074.00 | 1.89 |
| .88 | 7050.19 | 7.73 | 7768.75 | 6.59 | 8360.02 | 5.19 | 8801.21 | 3.60 | 9075.89 | 1.87 |
| .89 | 7057.92 | 7.72 | 7775.34 | 6.58 | 8365.21 | 5.17 | 8804.81 | 3.57 | 9077.76 | 1.85 |
| .90 | 7065.64 | 7.71 | 7781.92 | 6.56 | 8370.38 | 5.16 | 8808.38 | 3.56 | 9079.61 | 1.83 |
| .91 | 7073.35 | 7.69 | 7788.48 | 6.54 | 8375.54 | 5.15 | 8811.94 | 3.55 | 9081.44 | 1.81 |
| .92 | 7081.04 | 7.69 | 7795.02 | 6.54 | 8380.69 | 5.13 | 8815.49 | 3.52 | 9083.25 | 1.80 |
| .93 | 7088.73 | 7.68 | 7801.56 | 6.52 | 8385.82 | 5.10 | 8819.01 | 3.51 | 9085.05 | 1.78 |
| .94 | 7096.41 | 7.66 | 7808.08 | 6.51 | 8390.92 | 5.10 | 8822.52 | 3.49 | 9086.83 | 1.76 |
| .95 | 7104.07 | 7.66 | 7814.59 | 6.49 | 8396.02 | 5.08 | 8826.01 | 3.48 | 9088.59 | 1.74 |
| .96 | 7111.73 | 7.64 | 7821.08 | 6.48 | 8401.10 | 5.07 | 8829.49 | 3.46 | 9090.33 | 1.73 |
| .97 | 7119.37 | 7.64 | 7827.56 | 6.48 | 8406.17 | 5.05 | 8832.95 | 3.44 | 9092.06 | 1.71 |
| .98 | 7127.01 | 7.63 | 7834.04 | 6.45 | 8411.22 | 5.04 | 8836.39 | 3.42 | 9093.77 | 1.69 |
| .99 | 7134.64 | +7.61 | 7840.49 | +6.44 | 8416.26 | +5.02 | 8839.81 | +3.41 | 9095.46 | +1.67 |
| 1.00 | 7142.25 | | 7846.93 | | 8421.28 | | 8843.22 | | 9097.13 | |

# TABLE VII. ARGUMENT 2.

Equation = 4587″.400 + 4586″.9 sin. $(2t - x)$ + 31″.2 sin. $(4t - 2x)$.

Period, 31.81193574 days.

| Days. | 15 | | 16 | | 17 | | 18 | | 19 | |
|---|---|---|---|---|---|---|---|---|---|---|
| Decimals of a Day. | Equation. | Dif. | Equation. | Dif. | Equation. | Dif. | Equation. | Dif. | Equation. | Dif. |
| .00 | 9097.13 | +1.65 | 9174.30 | − .13 | 9073.11 | −1.90 | 8798.89 | −3.58 | 8363.46 | −5.11 |
| .01 | 9098.78 | 1.64 | 9174.17 | .15 | 9071.21 | 1.91 | 8795.31 | 3.60 | 8358.35 | 5.13 |
| .02 | 9100.42 | 1.62 | 9174.02 | .17 | 9069.30 | 1.94 | 8791.71 | 3.61 | 8353.22 | 5.14 |
| .03 | 9102.04 | 1.60 | 9173.85 | .19 | 9067.36 | 1.95 | 8788.10 | 3.63 | 8348.08 | 5.16 |
| .04 | 9103.64 | 1.59 | 9173.66 | .20 | 9065.41 | 1.97 | 8784.47 | 3.65 | 8342.92 | 5.17 |
| .05 | 9105.23 | 1.57 | 9173.46 | .22 | 9063.44 | 1.99 | 8780.82 | 3.66 | 8337.75 | 5.18 |
| .06 | 9106.80 | 1.55 | 9173.24 | .24 | 9061.45 | 2.00 | 8777.16 | 3.68 | 8332.57 | 5.20 |
| .07 | 9108.35 | 1.53 | 9173.00 | .26 | 9059.45 | 2.03 | 8773.48 | 3.69 | 8327.37 | 5.21 |
| .08 | 9109.88 | 1.51 | 9172.74 | .27 | 9057.42 | 2.04 | 8769.79 | 3.71 | 8322.16 | 5.23 |
| .09 | 9111.39 | 1.49 | 9172.47 | .30 | 9055.38 | 2.05 | 8766.08 | 3.72 | 8316.93 | 5.24 |
| .10 | 9112.88 | 1.48 | 9172.17 | .31 | 9053.33 | 2.07 | 8762.36 | 3.75 | 8311.69 | 5.26 |
| .11 | 9114.36 | 1.46 | 9171.86 | .33 | 9051.26 | 2.09 | 8758.61 | 3.76 | 8306.43 | 5.27 |
| .12 | 9115.82 | 1.44 | 9171.53 | .34 | 9049.17 | 2.11 | 8754.85 | 3.77 | 8301.16 | 5.28 |
| .13 | 9117.26 | 1.42 | 9171.19 | .37 | 9047.06 | 2.13 | 8751.08 | 3.79 | 8295.88 | 5.30 |
| .14 | 9118.68 | 1.41 | 9170.82 | .38 | 9044.93 | 2.14 | 8747.29 | 3.81 | 8290.58 | 5.31 |
| .15 | 9120.09 | 1.39 | 9170.44 | .40 | 9042.79 | 2.16 | 8743.48 | 3.82 | 8285.27 | 5.33 |
| .16 | 9121.48 | 1.37 | 9170.04 | .42 | 9040.63 | 2.18 | 8739.66 | 3.84 | 8279.94 | 5.34 |
| .17 | 9122.85 | 1.35 | 9169.62 | .44 | 9038.45 | 2.19 | 8735.82 | 3.85 | 8274.60 | 5.35 |
| .18 | 9124.20 | 1.34 | 9169.18 | .45 | 9036.26 | 2.21 | 8731.97 | 3.87 | 8269.25 | 5.37 |
| .19 | 9125.54 | 1.31 | 9168.73 | .47 | 9034.05 | 2.22 | 8728.10 | 3.88 | 8263.88 | 5.38 |
| .20 | 9126.85 | 1.30 | 9168.26 | .49 | 9031.83 | 2.25 | 8724.22 | 3.90 | 8258.50 | 5.40 |
| .21 | 9128.15 | 1.29 | 9167.77 | .51 | 9029.58 | 2.26 | 8720.32 | 3.92 | 8253.10 | 5.41 |
| .22 | 9129.44 | 1.26 | 9167.26 | .52 | 9027.32 | 2.28 | 8716.40 | 3.94 | 8247.69 | 5.42 |
| .23 | 9130.70 | 1.25 | 9166.74 | .55 | 9025.04 | 2.30 | 8712.46 | 3.95 | 8242.27 | 5.44 |
| .24 | 9131.95 | 1.22 | 9166.19 | .56 | 9022.74 | 2.31 | 8708.51 | 3.96 | 8236.83 | 5.45 |
| .25 | 9133.17 | 1.21 | 9165.63 | .58 | 9020.43 | 2.33 | 8704.55 | 3.98 | 8231.38 | 5.47 |
| .26 | 9134.38 | 1.20 | 9165.05 | .59 | 9018.10 | 2.35 | 8700.57 | 4.00 | 8225.91 | 5.48 |
| .27 | 9135.58 | 1.17 | 9164.46 | .62 | 9015.75 | 2.37 | 8696.57 | 4.01 | 8220.43 | 5.50 |
| .28 | 9136.75 | 1.16 | 9163.84 | .63 | 9013.38 | 2.38 | 8692.56 | 4.03 | 8214.93 | 5.50 |
| .29 | 9137.91 | 1.14 | 9163.21 | .65 | 9011.00 | 2.40 | 8688.53 | 4.04 | 8209.43 | 5.52 |
| .30 | 9139.05 | 1.12 | 9162.56 | .67 | 9008.60 | 2.42 | 8684.49 | 4.06 | 8203.91 | 5.54 |
| .31 | 9140.17 | 1.10 | 9161.89 | .68 | 9006.18 | 2.43 | 8680.43 | 4.08 | 8198.37 | 5.55 |
| .32 | 9141.27 | 1.09 | 9161.21 | .70 | 9003.75 | 2.45 | 8676.35 | 4.09 | 8192.82 | 5.56 |
| .33 | 9142.36 | 1.06 | 9160.51 | .73 | 9001.30 | 2.47 | 8672.26 | 4.10 | 8187.26 | 5.57 |
| .34 | 9143.42 | 1.05 | 9159.78 | .74 | 8998.83 | 2.48 | 8668.16 | 4.12 | 8181.69 | 5.59 |
| .35 | 9144.47 | 1.04 | 9159.04 | .75 | 8996.35 | 2.50 | 8664.04 | 4.14 | 8176.10 | 5.61 |
| .36 | 9145.51 | 1.01 | 9158.29 | .78 | 8993.85 | 2.52 | 8659.90 | 4.15 | 8170.49 | 5.62 |
| .37 | 9146.52 | 1.00 | 9157.51 | .79 | 8991.33 | 2.54 | 8655.75 | 4.17 | 8164.87 | 5.63 |
| .38 | 9147.52 | .98 | 9156.72 | .81 | 8988.79 | 2.55 | 8651.58 | 4.19 | 8159.24 | 5.64 |
| .39 | 9148.50 | .96 | 9155.91 | .82 | 8986.24 | 2.57 | 8647.39 | 4.20 | 8153.60 | 5.66 |
| .40 | 9149.46 | .94 | 9155.09 | .85 | 8983.67 | 2.59 | 8643.19 | 4.21 | 8147.94 | 5.67 |
| .41 | 9150.40 | .92 | 9154.24 | .86 | 8981.08 | 2.60 | 8638.98 | 4.23 | 8142.27 | 5.68 |
| .42 | 9151.32 | .91 | 9153.38 | .88 | 8978.48 | 2.62 | 8634.75 | 4.24 | 8136.59 | 5.70 |
| .43 | 9152.23 | .89 | 9152.50 | .90 | 8975.86 | 2.64 | 8630.51 | 4.26 | 8130.89 | 5.71 |
| .44 | 9153.12 | .87 | 9151.60 | .92 | 8973.22 | 2.66 | 8626.25 | 4.28 | 8125.18 | 5.73 |
| .45 | 9153.99 | .85 | 9150.68 | .94 | 8970.56 | 2.67 | 8621.97 | 4.29 | 8119.45 | 5.74 |
| .46 | 9154.84 | .84 | 9149.74 | .95 | 8967.89 | 2.69 | 8617.68 | 4.31 | 8113.71 | 5.75 |
| .47 | 9155.68 | .81 | 9148.79 | .97 | 8965.20 | 2.70 | 8613.37 | 4.33 | 8107.96 | 5.77 |
| .48 | 9156.49 | .80 | 9147.82 | .99 | 8962.50 | 2.72 | 8609.04 | 4.34 | 8102.19 | 5.78 |
| .49 | 9157.29 | .78 | 9146.83 | 1.00 | 8959.78 | 2.74 | 8604.70 | 4.35 | 8096.41 | 5.79 |
| .50 | 9158.07 | + .77 | 9145.83 | −1.02 | 8957.04 | −2.76 | 8600.35 | −4.37 | 8090.62 | −5.80 |

# TABLE VII. ARGUMENT 2.

Equation $= 4587''.400 + 4586''.9 \sin. (2t - x) + 31''.2 \sin. (4t - 2x)$.

Period, 31.81193574 days.

| Days. | 15 | | 16 | | 17 | | 18 | | 19 | |
|---|---|---|---|---|---|---|---|---|---|---|
| Decimals of a Day. | Equation. | Dif. | Equation. | Dif. | Equation. | Dif. | Equation. | Dif. | Equation. | Dif. |
| .50 | 9158.07 | + .77 | 9145.83 | −1.02 | 8957.04 | −2.76 | 8600.35 | −4.37 | 8090.62 | −5.80 |
| .51 | 9158.84 | .74 | 9144.81 | 1.04 | 8954.28 | 2.77 | 8595.98 | 4.38 | 8084.82 | 5.82 |
| .52 | 9159.58 | .73 | 9143.77 | 1.06 | 8951.51 | 2.79 | 8591.60 | 4.40 | 8079.00 | 5.83 |
| .53 | 9160.31 | .71 | 9142.71 | 1.08 | 8948.72 | 2.80 | 8587.20 | 4.42 | 8073.17 | 5.85 |
| .54 | 9161.02 | .69 | 9141.63 | 1.10 | 8945.92 | 2.83 | 8582.78 | 4.43 | 8067.32 | 5.86 |
| .55 | 9161.71 | .68 | 9140.53 | 1.11 | 8943.09 | 2.84 | 8578.35 | 4.45 | 8061.46 | 5.87 |
| .56 | 9162.39 | .65 | 9139.42 | 1.12 | 8940.25 | 2.85 | 8573.90 | 4.46 | 8055.59 | 5.88 |
| .57 | 9163.04 | .64 | 9138.30 | 1.15 | 8937.40 | 2.88 | 8569.44 | 4.47 | 8049.71 | 5.90 |
| .58 | 9163.68 | .62 | 9137.15 | 1.16 | 8934.52 | 2.89 | 8564.97 | 4.49 | 8043.81 | 5.91 |
| .59 | 9164.30 | .60 | 9135.99 | 1.19 | 8931.63 | 2.90 | 8560.48 | 4.51 | 8037.90 | 5.93 |
| .60 | 9164.90 | .59 | 9134.80 | 1.20 | 8928.73 | 2.92 | 8555.97 | 4.52 | 8031.97 | 5.93 |
| .61 | 9165.49 | .56 | 9133.60 | 1.22 | 8925.81 | 2.94 | 8551.45 | 4.54 | 8026.04 | 5.95 |
| .62 | 9166.05 | .55 | 9132.38 | 1.23 | 8922.87 | 2.96 | 8546.91 | 4.55 | 8020.09 | 5.97 |
| .63 | 9166.60 | .53 | 9131.15 | 1.25 | 8919.91 | 2.98 | 8542.36 | 4.57 | 8014.12 | 5.97 |
| .64 | 9167.13 | .51 | 9129.90 | 1.27 | 8916.93 | 2.99 | 8537.79 | 4.58 | 8008.15 | 5.99 |
| .65 | 9167.64 | .50 | 9128.63 | 1.29 | 8913.94 | 3.00 | 8533.21 | 4.60 | 8002.16 | 6.00 |
| .66 | 9168.14 | .48 | 9127.34 | 1.31 | 8910.94 | 3.03 | 8528.61 | 4.62 | 7996.16 | 6.02 |
| .67 | 9168.62 | .46 | 9126.03 | 1.32 | 8907.91 | 3.04 | 8523.99 | 4.63 | 7990.14 | 6.03 |
| .68 | 9169.08 | .44 | 9124.71 | 1.34 | 8904.87 | 3.05 | 8519.36 | 4.64 | 7984.11 | 6.04 |
| .69 | 9169.52 | .42 | 9123.37 | 1.36 | 8901.82 | 3.07 | 8514.72 | 4.65 | 7978.07 | 6.05 |
| .70 | 9169.94 | .40 | 9122.01 | 1.37 | 8898.75 | 3.09 | 8510.07 | 4.67 | 7972.02 | 6.07 |
| .71 | 9170.34 | .39 | 9120.64 | 1.40 | 8895.66 | 3.11 | 8505.40 | 4.69 | 7965.95 | 6.08 |
| .72 | 9170.73 | .37 | 9119.24 | 1.41 | 8892.55 | 3.12 | 8500.71 | 4.70 | 7959.87 | 6.09 |
| .73 | 9171.10 | .35 | 9117.83 | 1.43 | 8889.43 | 3.14 | 8496.01 | 4.72 | 7953.78 | 6.11 |
| .74 | 9171.45 | .33 | 9116.40 | 1.44 | 8886.29 | 3.16 | 8491.29 | 4.73 | 7947.67 | 6.12 |
| .75 | 9171.78 | .32 | 9114.96 | 1.47 | 8883.13 | 3.17 | 8486.56 | 4.74 | 7941.55 | 6.13 |
| .76 | 9172.10 | .30 | 9113.49 | 1.48 | 8879.96 | 3.19 | 8481.82 | 4.77 | 7935.42 | 6.14 |
| .77 | 9172.40 | .28 | 9112.01 | 1.50 | 8876.77 | 3.21 | 8477.05 | 4.78 | 7929.28 | 6.16 |
| .78 | 9172.68 | .26 | 9110.51 | 1.52 | 8873.56 | 3.22 | 8472.27 | 4.79 | 7923.12 | 6.17 |
| .79 | 9172.94 | .24 | 9108.99 | 1.53 | 8870.34 | 3.24 | 8467.48 | 4.80 | 7916.95 | 6.18 |
| .80 | 9173.18 | .23 | 9107.46 | 1.55 | 8867.10 | 3.25 | 8462.68 | 4.82 | 7910.77 | 6.19 |
| .81 | 9173.41 | .21 | 9105.91 | 1.57 | 8863.85 | 3.27 | 8457.86 | 4.84 | 7904.58 | 6.21 |
| .82 | 9173.62 | .19 | 9104.34 | 1.58 | 8860.58 | 3.29 | 8453.02 | 4.85 | 7898.37 | 6.22 |
| .83 | 9173.81 | .17 | 9102.76 | 1.61 | 8857.29 | 3.31 | 8448.17 | 4.87 | 7892.15 | 6.23 |
| .84 | 9173.98 | .15 | 9101.15 | 1.62 | 8853.98 | 3.32 | 8443.30 | 4.88 | 7885.92 | 6.24 |
| .85 | 9174.13 | .14 | 9099.53 | 1.64 | 8850.66 | 3.33 | 8438.42 | 4.89 | 7879.68 | 6.26 |
| .86 | 9174.27 | .12 | 9097.89 | 1.66 | 8847.33 | 3.36 | 8433.53 | 4.91 | 7873.42 | 6.27 |
| .87 | 9174.39 | .10 | 9096.23 | 1.67 | 8843.97 | 3.37 | 8428.62 | 4.93 | 7867.15 | 6.28 |
| .88 | 9174.49 | .08 | 9094.56 | 1.69 | 8840.60 | 3.38 | 8423.69 | 4.94 | 7860.87 | 6.29 |
| .89 | 9174.57 | .07 | 9092.87 | 1.71 | 8837.22 | 3.40 | 8418.75 | 4.95 | 7854.58 | 6.31 |
| .90 | 9174.64 | .05 | 9091.16 | 1.73 | 8833.82 | 3.42 | 8413.80 | 4.97 | 7848.27 | 6.32 |
| .91 | 9174.69 | .03 | 9089.43 | 1.74 | 8830.40 | 3.44 | 8408.83 | 4.99 | 7841.95 | 6.33 |
| .92 | 9174.72 | + .01 | 9087.69 | 1.76 | 8826.96 | 3.45 | 8403.84 | 5.00 | 7835.62 | 6.34 |
| .93 | 9174.73 | − .01 | 9085.93 | 1.78 | 8823.51 | 3.47 | 8398.84 | 5.01 | 7829.28 | 6.35 |
| .94 | 9174.72 | .03 | 9084.15 | 1.80 | 8820.04 | 3.48 | 8393.83 | 5.02 | 7822.93 | 6.37 |
| .95 | 9174.69 | .04 | 9082.35 | 1.81 | 8816.56 | 3.50 | 8388.81 | 5.04 | 7816.56 | 6.38 |
| .96 | 9174 65 | .06 | 9080.54 | 1.83 | 8813.06 | 3.52 | 8383.77 | 5.06 | 7810.18 | 6.39 |
| .97 | 9174.59 | .08 | 9078.71 | 1.85 | 8809.54 | 3.53 | 8378.71 | 5.07 | 7803.79 | 6.40 |
| .98 | 9174.51 | .10 | 9076.86 | 1.87 | 8806.01 | 3.55 | 8373.64 | 5.08 | 7797.39 | 6.42 |
| .99 | 9174.41 | − .11 | 9074.99 | −1.88 | 8802.46 | −3.57 | 8368.56 | −5.10 | 7790.97 | −6.43 |
| 1.00 | 9174.30 | | 9073.11 | | 8798.89 | | 8363.46 | | 7784.54 | |

# TABLE VII. ARGUMENT 2.

Equation $= 4587''.400 + 4586''.9 \sin. (2t - x) + 31''.2 \sin. (4t - 2x)$.

Period, 31.81193574 days.

| Days. | 20 | | 21 | | 22 | | 23 | | 24 | |
|---|---|---|---|---|---|---|---|---|---|---|
| Decimals of a Day. | Equation. | Dif. | Equation. | Dif. | Equation. | Dif. | Equation. | Dif. | Equation. | Dif. |
| .00 | 7784″.54 | −6.45 | 7084″.88 | −7.51 | 6291″.42 | −8.30 | 5434″.21 | −8.79 | 4545″.39 | −8.94 |
| .01 | 7778.09 | 6.45 | 7077.37 | 7.53 | 6283.12 | 8.32 | 5425.42 | 8.79 | 4536.45 | 8.93 |
| .02 | 7771.64 | 6.46 | 7069.84 | 7.54 | 6274.80 | 8.32 | 5416.63 | 8.79 | 4527.52 | 8.94 |
| .03 | 7765.18 | 6.48 | 7062.30 | 7.54 | 6266.48 | 8.33 | 5407.84 | 8.80 | 4518.58 | 8.93 |
| .04 | 7758.70 | 6.49 | 7054.76 | 7.56 | 6258.15 | 8.33 | 5399.04 | 8.80 | 4509.65 | 8.94 |
| .05 | 7752.21 | 6.50 | 7047.20 | 7.56 | 6249.82 | 8.34 | 5390.24 | 8.80 | 4500.71 | 8.93 |
| .06 | 7745.71 | 6.51 | 7039.64 | 7.58 | 6241.48 | 8.35 | 5381.44 | 8.80 | 4491.78 | 8.94 |
| .07 | 7739.20 | 6.53 | 7032.06 | 7.58 | 6233.13 | 8.35 | 5372.64 | 8.81 | 4482.84 | 8.93 |
| .08 | 7732.67 | 6.53 | 7024.48 | 7.59 | 6224.78 | 8.36 | 5363.83 | 8.81 | 4473.91 | 8.93 |
| .09 | 7726.14 | 6.55 | 7016.89 | 7.60 | 6216.42 | 8.37 | 5355.02 | 8.81 | 4464.98 | 8.94 |
| .10 | 7719.59 | 6.56 | 7009.29 | 7.62 | 6208.05 | 8.37 | 5346.21 | 8.82 | 4456.04 | 8.93 |
| .11 | 7713.03 | 6.57 | 7001.67 | 7.62 | 6199.68 | 8.37 | 5337.39 | 8.82 | 4447.11 | 8.93 |
| .12 | 7706.46 | 6.59 | 6994.05 | 7.62 | 6191.31 | 8.39 | 5328.57 | 8.82 | 4438.18 | 8.93 |
| .13 | 7699.87 | 6.59 | 6986.43 | 7.64 | 6182.92 | 8.39 | 5319.75 | 8.83 | 4429.25 | 8.93 |
| .14 | 7693.28 | 6.61 | 6978.79 | 7.65 | 6174.53 | 8.39 | 5310.92 | 8.83 | 4420.32 | 8.93 |
| .15 | 7686.67 | 6.62 | 6971.14 | 7.65 | 6166.14 | 8.40 | 5302.09 | 8.82 | 4411.39 | 8.93 |
| .16 | 7680.05 | 6.63 | 6963.49 | 7.67 | 6157.74 | 8.41 | 5293.27 | 8.84 | 4402.46 | 8.93 |
| .17 | 7673.42 | 6.64 | 6955.82 | 7.67 | 6149.33 | 8.41 | 5284.43 | 8.83 | 4393.53 | 8.93 |
| .18 | 7666.78 | 6.66 | 6948.15 | 7.68 | 6140.92 | 8.42 | 5275.60 | 8.84 | 4384.60 | 8.93 |
| .19 | 7660.12 | 6.66 | 6940.47 | 7.69 | 6132.50 | 8.42 | 5266.76 | 8.84 | 4375.67 | 8.92 |
| .20 | 7653.46 | 6.68 | 6932.78 | 7.71 | 6124.08 | 8.43 | 5257.92 | 8.84 | 4366.75 | 8.93 |
| .21 | 7646.78 | 6.69 | 6925.07 | 7.70 | 6115.65 | 8.44 | 5249.08 | 8.85 | 4357.82 | 8.93 |
| .22 | 7640.09 | 6.70 | 6917.37 | 7.72 | 6107.21 | 8.44 | 5240.23 | 8.85 | 4348.89 | 8.92 |
| .23 | 7633.39 | 6.71 | 6909.65 | 7.73 | 6098.77 | 8.44 | 5231.38 | 8.85 | 4339.97 | 8.92 |
| .24 | 7626.68 | 6.73 | 6901.92 | 7.73 | 6090.33 | 8.46 | 5222.53 | 8.85 | 4331.05 | 8.92 |
| .25 | 7619.95 | 6.73 | 6894.19 | 7.75 | 6081.87 | 8.46 | 5213.68 | 8.85 | 4322.13 | 8.92 |
| .26 | 7613.22 | 6.75 | 6886.44 | 7.75 | 6073.41 | 8.46 | 5204.83 | 8.86 | 4313.21 | 8.92 |
| .27 | 7606.47 | 6.75 | 6878.69 | 7.76 | 6064.95 | 8.47 | 5195.97 | 8.86 | 4304.29 | 8.92 |
| .28 | 7599.72 | 6.78 | 6870.93 | 7.77 | 6056.48 | 8.48 | 5187.11 | 8.86 | 4295.37 | 8.92 |
| .29 | 7592.94 | 6.78 | 6863.16 | 7.78 | 6048.00 | 8.48 | 5178.25 | 8.87 | 4286.45 | 8.92 |
| .30 | 7586.16 | 6.79 | 6855.38 | 7.79 | 6039.52 | 8.48 | 5169.38 | 8.86 | 4277.53 | 8.92 |
| .31 | 7579.37 | 6.80 | 6847.59 | 7.79 | 6031.04 | 8.49 | 5160.52 | 8.87 | 4268.61 | 8.91 |
| .32 | 7572.57 | 6.82 | 6839.80 | 7.81 | 6022.55 | 8.50 | 5151.65 | 8.87 | 4259.70 | 8.91 |
| .33 | 7565.75 | 6.82 | 6831.99 | 7.81 | 6014.05 | 8.50 | 5142.78 | 8.87 | 4250.79 | 8.91 |
| .34 | 7558.93 | 6.84 | 6824.18 | 7.82 | 6005.55 | 8.51 | 5133.91 | 8.88 | 4241.88 | 8.91 |
| .35 | 7552.09 | 6.85 | 6816.36 | 7.83 | 5997.04 | 8.51 | 5125.03 | 8.88 | 4232.97 | 8.91 |
| .36 | 7545.24 | 6.86 | 6808.53 | 7.83 | 5988.53 | 8.52 | 5116.15 | 8.87 | 4224.06 | 8.91 |
| .37 | 7538.38 | 6.87 | 6800.70 | 7.85 | 5980.01 | 8.52 | 5107.28 | 8.89 | 4215.15 | 8.91 |
| .38 | 7531.51 | 6.88 | 6792.85 | 7.85 | 5971.49 | 8.53 | 5098.39 | 8.88 | 4206.24 | 8.90 |
| .39 | 7524.63 | 6.89 | 6785.00 | 7.87 | 5962.96 | 8.54 | 5089.51 | 8.88 | 4197.34 | 8.91 |
| .40 | 7517.74 | 6.91 | 6777.13 | 7.87 | 5954.42 | 8.53 | 5080.63 | 8.89 | 4188.43 | 8.90 |
| .41 | 7510.83 | 6.91 | 6769.26 | 7.88 | 5945.89 | 8.55 | 5071.74 | 8.89 | 4179.53 | 8.90 |
| .42 | 7503.92 | 6.93 | 6761.38 | 7.88 | 5937.34 | 8.55 | 5062.85 | 8.89 | 4170.63 | 8.90 |
| .43 | 7496.99 | 6.93 | 6753.50 | 7.90 | 5928.79 | 8.55 | 5053.96 | 8.89 | 4161.73 | 8.90 |
| .44 | 7490.06 | 6.95 | 6745.60 | 7.90 | 5920.24 | 8.56 | 5045.07 | 8.89 | 4152.83 | 8.90 |
| .45 | 7483.11 | 6.96 | 6737.70 | 7.92 | 5911.68 | 8.56 | 5036.18 | 8.90 | 4143.93 | 8.89 |
| .46 | 7476.15 | 6.97 | 6729.78 | 7.91 | 5903.12 | 8.57 | 5027.28 | 8.89 | 4135.04 | 8.89 |
| .47 | 7469.18 | 6.98 | 6721.87 | 7.93 | 5894.55 | 8.57 | 5018.39 | 8.90 | 4126.15 | 8.89 |
| .48 | 7462.20 | 6.99 | 6713.94 | 7.93 | 5885.98 | 8.58 | 5009.49 | 8.90 | 4117.26 | 8.89 |
| .49 | 7455.21 | 7.01 | 6706.01 | 7.95 | 5877.40 | 8.59 | 5000.59 | 8.90 | 4108.37 | 8.89 |
| .50 | 7448.20 | −7.01 | 6698.06 | −7.95 | 5868.81 | −8.58 | 4991.69 | −8.90 | 4099.48 | −8.88 |

# TABLE VII. ARGUMENT 2.

Equation $= 4587''.400 + 4586''.9 \sin. (2t - x) + 31''.2 \sin. (4t - 2x)$.

Period, 31.81193574 days.

| Days. | 20 | | 21 | | 22 | | 23 | | 24 | |
|---|---|---|---|---|---|---|---|---|---|---|
| Decimals of a Day. | Equation. | Dif. | Equation. | Dif. | Equation. | Dif. | Equation. | Dif. | Equation. | Dif. |
| .50 | 7448.20″ | −7.01 | 6698.06″ | −7.95 | 5868.81″ | −8.58 | 4991.69″ | −8.90 | 4099.48″ | −8.88 |
| .51 | 7441.19 | 7.02 | 6690.11 | 7.96 | 5860.23 | 8.60 | 4982.79 | 8.91 | 4090.60 | 8.89 |
| .52 | 7434.17 | 7.04 | 6682.15 | 7.96 | 5851.63 | 8.59 | 4973.88 | 8.91 | 4081.71 | 8.88 |
| .53 | 7427.13 | 7.04 | 6674.19 | 7.98 | 5843.04 | 8.61 | 4964.97 | 8.90 | 4072.83 | 8.88 |
| .54 | 7420.09 | 7.06 | 6666.21 | 7.98 | 5834.43 | 8.60 | 4956.07 | 8.91 | 4063.95 | 8.88 |
| .55 | 7413.03 | 7.06 | 6658.23 | 7.99 | 5825.83 | 8.61 | 4947.16 | 8.91 | 4055.07 | 8.87 |
| .56 | 7405.97 | 7.08 | 6650.24 | 8.00 | 5817.22 | 8.62 | 4938.25 | 8.91 | 4046.20 | 8.87 |
| .57 | 7398.89 | 7.09 | 6642.24 | 8.01 | 5808.60 | 8.62 | 4929.34 | 8.92 | 4037.33 | 8.88 |
| .58 | 7391.80 | 7.10 | 6634.23 | 8.01 | 5799.98 | 8.63 | 4920.42 | 8.91 | 4028.45 | 8.87 |
| .59 | 7384.70 | 7.11 | 6626.22 | 8.02 | 5791.35 | 8.63 | 4911.51 | 8.91 | 4019.58 | 8.87 |
| .60 | 7377.59 | 7.12 | 6618.20 | 8.03 | 5782.72 | 8.63 | 4902.60 | 8.92 | 4010.71 | 8.86 |
| .61 | 7370.47 | 7.13 | 6610.17 | 8.03 | 5774.09 | 8.64 | 4893.68 | 8.92 | 4001.85 | 8.86 |
| .62 | 7363.34 | 7.14 | 6602.14 | 8.04 | 5765.45 | 8.64 | 4884.76 | 8.91 | 3992.99 | 8.86 |
| .63 | 7356.20 | 7.15 | 6594.10 | 8.06 | 5756.81 | 8.65 | 4875.85 | 8.92 | 3984.13 | 8.86 |
| .64 | 7349.05 | 7.16 | 6586.04 | 8.06 | 5748.16 | 8.65 | 4866.93 | 8.92 | 3975.27 | 8.86 |
| .65 | 7341.89 | 7.17 | 6577.98 | 8.07 | 5739.51 | 8.66 | 4858.01 | 8.93 | 3966.41 | 8.85 |
| .66 | 7334.72 | 7.18 | 6569.91 | 8.07 | 5730.85 | 8.66 | 4849.08 | 8.92 | 3957.56 | 8.85 |
| .67 | 7327.54 | 7.20 | 6561.84 | 8.08 | 5722.19 | 8.66 | 4840.16 | 8.92 | 3948.71 | 8.85 |
| .68 | 7320.34 | 7.20 | 6553.76 | 8.09 | 5713.53 | 8.67 | 4831.24 | 8.92 | 3939.86 | 8.85 |
| .69 | 7313.14 | 7.21 | 6545.67 | 8.10 | 5704.86 | 8.67 | 4822.32 | 8.93 | 3931.01 | 8.85 |
| .70 | 7305.93 | 7.23 | 6537.57 | 8.10 | 5696.19 | 8.68 | 4813.39 | 8.93 | 3922.16 | 8.84 |
| .71 | 7298.70 | 7.23 | 6529.47 | 8.11 | 5687.51 | 8.68 | 4804.46 | 8.92 | 3913.32 | 8.84 |
| .72 | 7291.47 | 7.25 | 6521.36 | 8.12 | 5678.83 | 8.69 | 4795.54 | 8.93 | 3904.48 | 8.84 |
| .73 | 7284.22 | 7.25 | 6513.24 | 8.12 | 5670.14 | 8.69 | 4786.61 | 8.93 | 3895.64 | 8.83 |
| .74 | 7276.97 | 7.26 | 6505.12 | 8.14 | 5661.45 | 8.69 | 4777.68 | 8.93 | 3886.81 | 8.83 |
| .75 | 7269.71 | 7.28 | 6496.98 | 8.14 | 5652.76 | 8.70 | 4768.75 | 8.93 | 3877.98 | 8.83 |
| .76 | 7262.43 | 7.28 | 6488.84 | 8.14 | 5644.06 | 8.70 | 4759.82 | 8.93 | 3869.15 | 8.83 |
| .77 | 7255.15 | 7.30 | 6480.70 | 8.16 | 5635.36 | 8.70 | 4750.89 | 8.93 | 3860.32 | 8.82 |
| .78 | 7247.85 | 7.31 | 6472.54 | 8.16 | 5626.66 | 8.71 | 4741.96 | 8.93 | 3851.50 | 8.82 |
| .79 | 7240.54 | 7.32 | 6464.38 | 8.16 | 5617.95 | 8.72 | 4733.03 | 8.93 | 3842.68 | 8.82 |
| .80 | 7233.22 | 7.32 | 6456.22 | 8.18 | 5609.23 | 8.72 | 4724.10 | 8.94 | 3833.86 | 8.82 |
| .81 | 7225.90 | 7.33 | 6448.04 | 8.18 | 5600.51 | 8.72 | 4715.16 | 8.93 | 3825.04 | 8.81 |
| .82 | 7218.57 | 7.35 | 6439.86 | 8.19 | 5591.79 | 8.72 | 4706.23 | 8.93 | 3816.23 | 8.81 |
| .83 | 7211.22 | 7.35 | 6431.67 | 8.20 | 5583.07 | 8.73 | 4697.30 | 8.94 | 3807.42 | 8.81 |
| .84 | 7203.87 | 7.36 | 6423.47 | 8.20 | 5574.34 | 8.73 | 4688.36 | 8.93 | 3798.61 | 8.80 |
| .85 | 7196.51 | 7.38 | 6415.27 | 8.21 | 5565.61 | 8.74 | 4679.43 | 8.94 | 3789.81 | 8.80 |
| .86 | 7189.13 | 7.38 | 6407.06 | 8.22 | 5556.87 | 8.74 | 4670.49 | 8.93 | 3781.01 | 8.80 |
| .87 | 7181.75 | 7.39 | 6398.84 | 8.22 | 5548.13 | 8.74 | 4661.56 | 8.94 | 3772.21 | 8.79 |
| .88 | 7174.36 | 7.40 | 6390.62 | 8.23 | 5539.39 | 8.75 | 4652.62 | 8.93 | 3763.42 | 8.79 |
| .89 | 7166.96 | 7.42 | 6382.39 | 8.24 | 5530.64 | 8.75 | 4643.69 | 8.94 | 3754.63 | 8.79 |
| .90 | 7159.54 | 7.42 | 6374.15 | 8.24 | 5521.89 | 8.75 | 4634.75 | 8.93 | 3745.84 | 8.79 |
| .91 | 7152.12 | 7.43 | 6365.91 | 8.25 | 5513.14 | 8.76 | 4625.82 | 8.94 | 3737.05 | 8.78 |
| .92 | 7144.69 | 7.44 | 6357.66 | 8.26 | 5504.38 | 8.76 | 4616.88 | 8.94 | 3728.27 | 8.78 |
| .93 | 7137.25 | 7.45 | 6349.40 | 8.26 | 5495.62 | 8.76 | 4607.94 | 8.93 | 3719.49 | 8.77 |
| .94 | 7129.80 | 7.46 | 6341.14 | 8.27 | 5486.86 | 8.77 | 4500.01 | 8.94 | 3710.72 | 8.77 |
| .95 | 7122.34 | 7.48 | 6332.87 | 8.28 | 5478.09 | 8.77 | 4590.07 | 8.94 | 3701.95 | 8.77 |
| .96 | 7114.86 | 7.48 | 6324.59 | 8.28 | 5469.32 | 8.77 | 4581.13 | 8.93 | 3693.18 | 8.77 |
| .97 | 7107.38 | 7.49 | 6316.31 | 8.29 | 5460.55 | 8.78 | 4572.20 | 8.94 | 3684.41 | 8.76 |
| .98 | 7099.89 | 7.50 | 6308.02 | 8.29 | 5451.77 | 8.78 | 4563.26 | 8.93 | 3675.65 | 8.76 |
| .99 | 7092.39 | −7.51 | 6299.73 | −8.31 | 5442.99 | −8.78 | 4554.33 | −8.94 | 3666.89 | −8.75 |
| 1.00 | 7084.88 | | 6291.42 | | 5434.21 | | 4545.39 | | 3658.14 | |

# TABLE VII. ARGUMENT 2.

Equation $= 4587''.400 + 4586''.9 \sin. (2t - x) + 31''.2 \sin. (4t - 2x)$.

Period, 31.81193574 days.

| Days. | 25 | | 26 | | 27 | | 28 | | 29 | |
|---|---|---|---|---|---|---|---|---|---|---|
| Decimals of a Day | Equation. | Dif. | Equation. | Dif. | Equation. | Dif. | Equation. | Dif. | Equation. | Dif. |
| .00 | 3658″.14 | −8.76 | 2805″.57 | −8.24 | 2019″.69 | −7.42 | 1330″.30 | −6.31 | 763″.97 | −4.96 |
| .01 | 3649.38 | 8.75 | 2797.33 | 8.23 | 2012.27 | 7.41 | 1323.99 | 6.30 | 759.01 | 4.95 |
| .02 | 3640.63 | 8.74 | 2789.10 | 8.23 | 2004.86 | 7.40 | 1317.69 | 6.29 | 754.06 | 4.93 |
| .03 | 3631.89 | 8.74 | 2780.87 | 8.22 | 1997.46 | 7.39 | 1311.40 | 6.28 | 749.13 | 4.92 |
| .04 | 3623.15 | 8.74 | 2772.65 | 8.21 | 1990.07 | 7.38 | 1305.12 | 6.26 | 744.21 | 4.91 |
| .05 | 3614.41 | 8.73 | 2764.44 | 8.21 | 1982.69 | 7.36 | 1298.86 | 6.25 | 739.30 | 4.89 |
| .06 | 3605.68 | 8.73 | 2756.23 | 8.20 | 1975.33 | 7.36 | 1292.61 | 6.24 | 734.41 | 4.87 |
| .07 | 3596.95 | 8.73 | 2748.03 | 8.19 | 1967.97 | 7.35 | 1286.37 | 6.23 | 729.54 | 4.86 |
| .08 | 3588.22 | 8.72 | 2739.84 | 8.19 | 1960.62 | 7.35 | 1280.14 | 6.21 | 724.68 | 4.85 |
| .09 | 3579.50 | 8.72 | 2731.65 | 8.18 | 1953.27 | 7.33 | 1273.93 | 6.20 | 719.83 | 4.82 |
| .10 | 3570.78 | 8.72 | 2723.47 | 8.17 | 1945.94 | 7.32 | 1267.73 | 6.19 | 715.01 | 4.82 |
| .11 | 3562.06 | 8.71 | 2715.30 | 8.17 | 1938.62 | 7.31 | 1261.54 | 6.18 | 710.19 | 4.80 |
| .12 | 3553.35 | 8.71 | 2707.13 | 8.16 | 1931.31 | 7.30 | 1255.36 | 6.16 | 705.39 | 4.79 |
| .13 | 3544.64 | 8.70 | 2698.97 | 8.15 | 1924.01 | 7.29 | 1249.20 | 6.15 | 700.60 | 4.77 |
| .14 | 3535.94 | 8.70 | 2690.82 | 8.14 | 1916.72 | 7.28 | 1243.05 | 6.14 | 695.83 | 4.76 |
| .15 | 3527.24 | 8.69 | 2682.68 | 8.14 | 1909.44 | 7.27 | 1236.91 | 6.13 | 691.07 | 4.73 |
| .16 | 3518.55 | 8.69 | 2674.54 | 8.12 | 1902.17 | 7.26 | 1230.78 | 6.11 | 686.34 | 4.73 |
| .17 | 3509.86 | 8.69 | 2666.42 | 8.13 | 1894.91 | 7.25 | 1224.67 | 6.10 | 681.61 | 4.71 |
| .18 | 3501.17 | 8.69 | 2658.29 | 8.11 | 1887.66 | 7.24 | 1218.57 | 6.09 | 676.90 | 4.70 |
| .19 | 3492.48 | 8.68 | 2650.18 | 8.11 | 1880.42 | 7.23 | 1212.48 | 6.07 | 672.20 | 4.68 |
| .20 | 3483.80 | 8.67 | 2642.07 | 8.10 | 1873.19 | 7.22 | 1206.41 | 6.06 | 667.52 | 4.67 |
| .21 | 3475.13 | 8.68 | 2633.97 | 8.09 | 1865.97 | 7.21 | 1200.35 | 6.05 | 662.85 | 4.65 |
| .22 | 3466.45 | 8.66 | 2625.88 | 8.09 | 1858.76 | 7.20 | 1194.30 | 6.04 | 658.20 | 4.63 |
| .23 | 3457.79 | 8.67 | 2617.79 | 8.08 | 1851.56 | 7.18 | 1188.26 | 6.02 | 653.57 | 4.63 |
| .24 | 3449.12 | 8.65 | 2609.71 | 8.07 | 1844.38 | 7.18 | 1182.24 | 6.01 | 648.94 | 4.60 |
| .25 | 3440.47 | 8.66 | 2601.64 | 8.06 | 1837.20 | 7.17 | 1176.23 | 6.00 | 644.34 | 4.59 |
| .26 | 3431.81 | 8.65 | 2593.58 | 8.06 | 1830.03 | 7.16 | 1170.23 | 5.98 | 639.75 | 4.58 |
| .27 | 3423.16 | 8.64 | 2585.52 | 8.05 | 1822.87 | 7.15 | 1164.25 | 5.97 | 635.17 | 4.56 |
| .28 | 3414.52 | 8.64 | 2577.47 | 8.04 | 1815.72 | 7.13 | 1158.28 | 5.96 | 630.61 | 4.55 |
| .29 | 3405.88 | 8.64 | 2569.43 | 8.03 | 1808.59 | 7.13 | 1152.32 | 5.95 | 626.06 | 4.53 |
| .30 | 3397.24 | 8.63 | 2561.40 | 8.03 | 1801.46 | 7.11 | 1146.37 | 5.93 | 621.53 | 4.51 |
| .31 | 3388.61 | 8.63 | 2553.37 | 8.01 | 1794.35 | 7.11 | 1140.44 | 5.90 | 617.02 | 4.51 |
| .32 | 3379.98 | 8.63 | 2545.36 | 8.01 | 1787.24 | 7.09 | 1134.54 | 5.92 | 612.51 | 4.48 |
| .33 | 3371.35 | 8.62 | 2537.35 | 8.01 | 1780.15 | 7.09 | 1128.62 | 5.89 | 608.03 | 4.48 |
| .34 | 3362.73 | 8.61 | 2529.34 | 7.99 | 1773.06 | 7.07 | 1122.73 | 5.88 | 603.55 | 4.45 |
| .35 | 3354.12 | 8.61 | 2521.35 | 7.99 | 1765.99 | 7.06 | 1116.85 | 5.87 | 599.10 | 4.44 |
| .36 | 3345.51 | 8.60 | 2513.36 | 7.98 | 1758.93 | 7.06 | 1110.98 | 5.85 | 594.66 | 4.42 |
| .37 | 3336.91 | 8.60 | 2505.38 | 7.97 | 1751.87 | 7.04 | 1105.13 | 5.84 | 590.24 | 4.41 |
| .38 | 3328.31 | 8.60 | 2497.41 | 7.96 | 1744.83 | 7.03 | 1099.29 | 5.83 | 585.83 | 4.39 |
| .39 | 3319.71 | 8.59 | 2489.45 | 7.96 | 1737.80 | 7.02 | 1093.46 | 5.81 | 581.44 | 4.38 |
| .40 | 3311.12 | 8.59 | 2481.49 | 7.95 | 1730.78 | 7.01 | 1087.65 | 5.80 | 577.06 | 4.37 |
| .41 | 3302.53 | 8.58 | 2473.54 | 7.94 | 1723.77 | 6.99 | 1081.85 | 5.79 | 572.69 | 4.34 |
| .42 | 3293.95 | 8.57 | 2465.60 | 7.93 | 1716.78 | 6.99 | 1076.06 | 5.77 | 568.35 | 4.34 |
| .43 | 3285.38 | 8.57 | 2457.67 | 7.93 | 1709.79 | 6.98 | 1070.29 | 5.76 | 564.01 | 4.31 |
| .44 | 3276.81 | 8.57 | 2449.74 | 7.91 | 1702.81 | 6.96 | 1064.53 | 5.75 | 559.70 | 4.30 |
| .45 | 3268.24 | 8.56 | 2441.83 | 7.91 | 1695.85 | 6.96 | 1058.78 | 5.73 | 555.40 | 4.29 |
| .46 | 3259.68 | 8.56 | 2433.92 | 7.92 | 1688.89 | 6.94 | 1053.05 | 5.72 | 551.11 | 4.27 |
| .47 | 3251.12 | 8.55 | 2426.02 | 7.89 | 1681.95 | 6.93 | 1047.33 | 5.71 | 546.84 | 4.26 |
| .48 | 3242.57 | 8.55 | 2418.13 | 7.89 | 1675.02 | 6.92 | 1041.62 | 5.69 | 542.58 | 4.24 |
| .49 | 3234.02 | 8.54 | 2410.24 | 7.87 | 1668.10 | 6.91 | 1035.93 | 5.68 | 538.34 | 4.22 |
| .50 | 3225.48 | −8.54 | 2402.37 | −7.87 | 1661.19 | −6.90 | 1030.25 | −5.67 | 534.12 | −4.21 |

# TABLE VII. ARGUMENT 2.

Equation $= 4587''.400 + 4586''.9 \sin. (2t - x) + 31''.2 \sin. (4t - 2x)$.

Period, 31.81193574 days.

| Days. | 25 | | 26 | | 27 | | 28 | | 29 | |
|---|---|---|---|---|---|---|---|---|---|---|
| Decimals of a Day. | Equation. | Dif. | Equation. | Dif. | Equation. | Dif. | Equation. | Dif. | Equation. | Dif. |
| .50 | 3225.48 | −8.54 | 2402.37 | −7.87 | 1661.19 | −6.90 | 1030.25 | −5.67 | 534.12 | −4.21 |
| .51 | 3216.94 | 8.53 | 2394.50 | 7.86 | 1654.29 | 6.89 | 1024.58 | 5.65 | 529.91 | 4.19 |
| .52 | 3208.41 | 8.53 | 2386.64 | 7.85 | 1647.40 | 6.88 | 1018.93 | 5.64 | 525.72 | 4.18 |
| .53 | 3199.88 | 8.52 | 2378.79 | 7.84 | 1640.52 | 6.86 | 1013.29 | 5.63 | 521.54 | 4.16 |
| .54 | 3191.36 | 8.51 | 2370.95 | 7.83 | 1633.66 | 6.86 | 1007.66 | 5.61 | 517.38 | 4.15 |
| .55 | 3182.85 | 8.50 | 2363.12 | 7.83 | 1626.80 | 6.84 | 1002.05 | 5.59 | 513.23 | 4.13 |
| .56 | 3174.35 | 8.52 | 2355.29 | 7.82 | 1619.96 | 6.84 | 996.46 | 5.59 | 509.10 | 4.11 |
| .57 | 3165.83 | 8.50 | 2347.47 | 7.80 | 1613.12 | 6.82 | 990.87 | 5.57 | 504.99 | 4.11 |
| .58 | 3157.33 | 8.49 | 2339.67 | 7.80 | 1606.30 | 6.81 | 985.30 | 5.56 | 500.88 | 4.08 |
| .59 | 3148.84 | 8.49 | 2331.87 | 7.80 | 1599.49 | 6.80 | 979.74 | 5.54 | 496.80 | 4.07 |
| .60 | 3140.35 | 8.49 | 2324.07 | 7.78 | 1592.69 | 6.78 | 974.20 | 5.53 | 492.73 | 4.05 |
| .61 | 3131.86 | 8.47 | 2316.29 | 7.78 | 1585.91 | 6.78 | 968.67 | 5.52 | 488.68 | 4.04 |
| .62 | 3123.39 | 8.48 | 2308.51 | 7.76 | 1579.13 | 6.76 | 963.15 | 5.50 | 484.64 | 4.02 |
| .63 | 3114.91 | 8.46 | 2300.75 | 7.76 | 1572.37 | 6.76 | 957.65 | 5.49 | 480.62 | 4.01 |
| .64 | 3106.45 | 8.46 | 2292.99 | 7.75 | 1565.61 | 6.74 | 952.16 | 5.47 | 476.61 | 3.98 |
| .65 | 3097.99 | 8.46 | 2285.24 | 7.74 | 1558.87 | 6.73 | 946.69 | 5.46 | 472.63 | 3.98 |
| .66 | 3089.53 | 8.45 | 2277.50 | 7.73 | 1552.14 | 6.72 | 941.23 | 5.45 | 468.65 | 3.96 |
| .67 | 3081.08 | 8.45 | 2269.77 | 7.72 | 1545.42 | 6.71 | 935.78 | 5.43 | 464.69 | 3.94 |
| .68 | 3072.63 | 8.44 | 2262.05 | 7.72 | 1538.71 | 6.69 | 930.35 | 5.42 | 460.75 | 3.93 |
| .69 | 3064.19 | 8.43 | 2254.33 | 7.70 | 1532.02 | 6.69 | 924.93 | 5.40 | 456.82 | 3.91 |
| .70 | 3055.76 | 8.43 | 2246.63 | 7.70 | 1525.33 | 6.67 | 919.53 | 5.39 | 452.91 | 3.89 |
| .71 | 3047.33 | 8.42 | 2238.93 | 7.69 | 1518.66 | 6.66 | 914.14 | 5.39 | 449.02 | 3.88 |
| .72 | 3038.91 | 8.42 | 2231.24 | 7.68 | 1512.00 | 6.65 | 908.75 | 5.35 | 445.14 | 3.87 |
| .73 | 3030.49 | 8.41 | 2223.56 | 7.67 | 1505.35 | 6.64 | 903.40 | 5.35 | 441.27 | 3.84 |
| .74 | 3022.08 | 8.40 | 2215.89 | 7.66 | 1498.71 | 6.62 | 898.05 | 5.34 | 437.43 | 3.83 |
| .75 | 3013.68 | 8.40 | 2208.23 | 7.65 | 1492.09 | 6.62 | 892.71 | 5.32 | 433.60 | 3.82 |
| .76 | 3005.28 | 8.39 | 2200.58 | 7.64 | 1485.47 | 6.60 | 887.39 | 5.31 | 429.78 | 3.80 |
| .77 | 2996.89 | 8.38 | 2192.94 | 7.64 | 1478.87 | 6.59 | 882.08 | 5.29 | 425.98 | 3.78 |
| .78 | 2988.51 | 8.38 | 2185.30 | 7.62 | 1472.28 | 6.58 | 876.79 | 5.28 | 422.20 | 3.77 |
| .79 | 2980.13 | 8.38 | 2177.68 | 7.62 | 1465.70 | 6.57 | 871.51 | 5.26 | 418.43 | 3.75 |
| .80 | 2971.75 | 8.37 | 2170.06 | 7.60 | 1459.13 | 6.56 | 866.25 | 5.25 | 414.68 | 3.74 |
| .81 | 2963.38 | 8.36 | 2162.46 | 7.60 | 1452.57 | 6.54 | 861.00 | 5.24 | 410.94 | 3.72 |
| .82 | 2955.02 | 8.36 | 2154.86 | 7.59 | 1446.03 | 6.53 | 855.76 | 5.22 | 407.22 | 3.70 |
| .83 | 2946.66 | 8.35 | 2147.27 | 7.58 | 1439.50 | 6.52 | 850.54 | 5.20 | 403.52 | 3.69 |
| .84 | 2938.31 | 8.34 | 2139.69 | 7.57 | 1432.98 | 6.51 | 845.34 | 5.20 | 399.83 | 3.67 |
| .85 | 2929.97 | 8.34 | 2132.12 | 7.56 | 1426.47 | 6.49 | 840.14 | 5.18 | 396.16 | 3.65 |
| .86 | 2921.63 | 8.33 | 2124.56 | 7.55 | 1419.98 | 6.49 | 834.96 | 5.16 | 392.51 | 3.64 |
| .87 | 2913.30 | 8.33 | 2117.01 | 7.55 | 1413.49 | 6.47 | 829.80 | 5.15 | 388.87 | 3.62 |
| .88 | 2904.97 | 8.32 | 2109.46 | 7.53 | 1407.02 | 6.46 | 824.65 | 5.14 | 385.25 | 3.61 |
| .89 | 2896.65 | 8.31 | 2101.93 | 7.52 | 1400.56 | 6.45 | 819.51 | 5.12 | 381.64 | 3.59 |
| .90 | 2888.34 | 8.31 | 2094.41 | 7.52 | 1394.11 | 6.43 | 814.39 | 5.11 | 378.05 | 3.58 |
| .91 | 2880.03 | 8.30 | 2086.89 | 7.50 | 1387.68 | 6.43 | 809.28 | 5.09 | 374.47 | 3.56 |
| .92 | 2871.73 | 8.29 | 2079.39 | 7.50 | 1381.25 | 6.41 | 804.19 | 5.08 | 370.91 | 3.54 |
| .93 | 2863.44 | 8.29 | 2071.89 | 7.48 | 1374.84 | 6.40 | 799.11 | 5.06 | 367.37 | 3.53 |
| .94 | 2855.15 | 8.28 | 2064.41 | 7.48 | 1368.44 | 6.38 | 794.05 | 5.05 | 363.84 | 3.51 |
| .95 | 2846.87 | 8.27 | 2056.93 | 7.47 | 1362.06 | 6.38 | 789.00 | 5.04 | 360.33 | 3.49 |
| .96 | 2838.60 | 8.27 | 2049.46 | 7.45 | 1355.68 | 6.36 | 783.96 | 5.02 | 356.84 | 3.48 |
| .97 | 2830.33 | 8.26 | 2042.01 | 7.45 | 1349.32 | 6.35 | 778.94 | 5.00 | 353.36 | 3.46 |
| .98 | 2822.07 | 8.25 | 2034.56 | 7.44 | 1342.97 | 6.34 | 773.94 | 4.99 | 349.90 | 3.44 |
| .99 | 2813.82 | −8.25 | 2027.12 | −7.43 | 1336.63 | −6.33 | 768.95 | −4.98 | 346.46 | −3.43 |
| 1.00 | 2805.57 | | 2019.69 | | 1330.30 | | 763.97 | | 343.03 | |

# TABLE VII. ARGUMENT 2.

Equation = $4587''.400 + 4586''.9 \sin. (2t - x) + 31''.2 \sin. (4t - 2x)$.

Period, 31.81193574 days.

| Days. | 30 | | 31 | |
|---|---|---|---|---|
| Decimals of a Day. | Equation. | Difference. | Equation. | Difference. |
| | ″ | | ″ | |
| .00 | 343.03 | −3.41 | 84.67 | −1.72 |
| .01 | 339.62 | 3.40 | 82.95 | 1.70 |
| .02 | 336.22 | 3.38 | 81.25 | 1.69 |
| .03 | 332.84 | 3.36 | 79.56 | 1.66 |
| .04 | 329.48 | 3.35 | 77.90 | 1.66 |
| .05 | 326.13 | 3.33 | 76.24 | 1.63 |
| .06 | 322.80 | 3.31 | 74.61 | 1.61 |
| .07 | 319.49 | 3.30 | 73.00 | 1.60 |
| .08 | 316.19 | 3.28 | 71.40 | 1.58 |
| .09 | 312.91 | 3.27 | 69.82 | 1.56 |
| .10 | 309.64 | 3.25 | 68.26 | 1.54 |
| .11 | 306.39 | 3.23 | 66.72 | 1.53 |
| .12 | 303.16 | 3.22 | 65.19 | 1.51 |
| .13 | 299.94 | 3.19 | 63.68 | 1.49 |
| .14 | 296.75 | 3.19 | 62.19 | 1.48 |
| .15 | 293.56 | 3.16 | 60.71 | 1.45 |
| .16 | 290.40 | 3.15 | 59.26 | 1.44 |
| .17 | 287.25 | 3.14 | 57.82 | 1.42 |
| .18 | 284.11 | 3.11 | 56.40 | 1.41 |
| .19 | 281.00 | 3.10 | 54.99 | 1.38 |
| .20 | 277.90 | 3.08 | 53.61 | 1.37 |
| .21 | 274.82 | 3.07 | 52.24 | 1.35 |
| .22 | 271.75 | 3.05 | 50.89 | 1.34 |
| .23 | 268.70 | 3.03 | 49.55 | 1.31 |
| .24 | 265.67 | 3.02 | 48.24 | 1.30 |
| .25 | 262.65 | 3.00 | 46.94 | 1.28 |
| .26 | 259.65 | 2.98 | 45.66 | 1.27 |
| .27 | 256.67 | 2.97 | 44.39 | 1.24 |
| .28 | 253.70 | 2.95 | 43.15 | 1.23 |
| .29 | 250.75 | 2.93 | 41.92 | 1.21 |
| .30 | 247.82 | 2.92 | 40.71 | 1.19 |
| .31 | 244.90 | 2.90 | 39.52 | 1.18 |
| .32 | 242.00 | 2.88 | 38.34 | 1.15 |
| .33 | 239.12 | 2.87 | 37.19 | 1.14 |
| .34 | 236.25 | 2.85 | 36.05 | 1.13 |
| .35 | 233.40 | 2.83 | 34.92 | 1.10 |
| .36 | 230.57 | 2.82 | 33.82 | 1.09 |
| .37 | 227.75 | 2.80 | 32.73 | 1.07 |
| .38 | 224.95 | 2.78 | 31.66 | 1.05 |
| .39 | 222.17 | 2.77 | 30.61 | 1.03 |
| .40 | 219.40 | 2.74 | 29.58 | 1.02 |
| .41 | 216.66 | 2.74 | 28.56 | 1.00 |
| .42 | 213.92 | 2.71 | 27.56 | .98 |
| .43 | 211.21 | 2.70 | 26.58 | .96 |
| .44 | 208.51 | 2.68 | 25.62 | .94 |
| .45 | 205.83 | 2.65 | 24.68 | .93 |
| .46 | 203.18 | 2.64 | 23.75 | .91 |
| .47 | 200.54 | 2.63 | 22.84 | .89 |
| .48 | 197.91 | 2.62 | 21.95 | .88 |
| .49 | 195.29 | 2.62 | 21.07 | .85 |
| .50 | 192.67 | −2.58 | 20.22 | − .84 |

# TABLE VII. ARGUMENT 2.

Equation = $4587''.400 + 4586''.9 \sin. (2t - x) + 31''.2 \sin. (4t - 2x)$.

Period, 31.81193574 days.

| Days. | 30 | | 31 | |
|---|---|---|---|---|
| Decimals of a Day. | Equation. | Difference. | Equation. | Difference. |
| .50 | 192″.67 | −2.58 | 20″.22 | −.84 |
| .51 | 190.09 | 2.56 | 19.38 | .82 |
| .52 | 187.53 | 2.54 | 18.56 | .80 |
| .53 | 184.99 | 2.53 | 17.76 | .79 |
| .54 | 182.46 | 2.51 | 16.97 | .77 |
| .55 | 179.95 | 2.50 | 16.20 | .75 |
| .56 | 177.45 | 2.48 | 15.45 | .73 |
| .57 | 174.97 | 2.46 | 14.72 | .71 |
| .58 | 172.51 | 2.44 | 14.01 | .70 |
| .59 | 170.07 | 2.42 | 13.31 | .67 |
| .60 | 167.65 | 2.41 | 12.64 | .67 |
| .61 | 165.24 | 2.40 | 11.97 | .64 |
| .62 | 162.84 | 2.37 | 11.33 | .62 |
| .63 | 160.47 | 2.36 | 10.71 | .61 |
| .64 | 158.11 | 2.34 | 10.10 | .59 |
| .65 | 155.77 | 2.33 | 9.51 | .57 |
| .66 | 153.44 | 2.31 | 8.94 | .56 |
| .67 | 151.13 | 2.29 | 8.38 | .53 |
| .68 | 148.84 | 2.27 | 7.85 | .52 |
| .69 | 146.57 | 2.25 | 7.33 | .50 |
| .70 | 144.32 | 2.25 | 6.83 | .48 |
| .71 | 142.07 | 2.22 | 6.35 | .47 |
| .72 | 139.85 | 2.20 | 5.88 | .44 |
| .73 | 137.65 | 2.19 | 5.44 | .43 |
| .74 | 135.46 | 2.17 | 5.01 | .41 |
| .75 | 133.29 | 2.15 | 4.60 | .40 |
| .76 | 131.14 | 2.14 | 4.20 | .37 |
| .77 | 129.00 | 2.12 | 3.83 | .36 |
| .78 | 126.88 | 2.10 | 3.47 | .34 |
| .79 | 124.78 | 2.08 | 3.13 | .32 |
| .80 | 122.70 | 2.06 | 2.81 | .30 |
| .81 | 120.64 | 2.05 | 2.51 | .29 |
| .82 | 118.59 | 2.04 | 2.22 | .27 |
| .83 | 116.55 | 2.01 | 1.95 | .25 |
| .84 | 114.54 | 2.00 | 1.70 | .23 |
| .85 | 112.54 | 1.98 | 1.47 | .21 |
| .86 | 110.56 | 1.96 | 1.26 | .20 |
| .87 | 108.60 | 1.94 | 1.06 | .18 |
| .88 | 106.66 | 1.93 | .88 | .16 |
| .89 | 104.73 | 1.91 | .72 | .14 |
| .90 | 102.82 | 1.89 | .58 | .12 |
| .91 | 100.93 | 1.88 | .46 | .11 |
| .92 | 99.05 | 1.86 | .35 | .09 |
| .93 | 97.19 | 1.84 | .26 | .08 |
| .94 | 95.35 | 1.82 | .18 | .05 |
| .95 | 93.53 | 1.81 | .13 | .03 |
| .96 | 91.72 | 1.79 | .10 | −.02 |
| .97 | 89.93 | 1.77 | .08 | .00 |
| .98 | 88.16 | 1.76 | .08 | +.02 |
| .99 | 86.40 | −1.73 | .10 | +.03 |
| 1.00 | 84.67 | | .13 | |

# TABLE VIII. ARGUMENT 3.

Equation $= 2457''.02 - 122''.1 \sin. t + 2371''.0 \sin. 2t + 0''.9 \sin. 3t + 14''.4 \sin. 4t.$

Period, 29.530587997 days.

| Days. | 0 | | 1 | | 2 | | 3 | | 4 | | 5 | |
|---|---|---|---|---|---|---|---|---|---|---|---|---|
| Decimals of a Day. | Equation. | Diff. | Equation. | Diff. | Equation. | Diff. | Equation. | Diff. | Equation. | Diff. | Equation. | Diff. |
| .00 | 2211″.80 | 10.42 | 3243″.69 | 9.91 | 4133″.61 | 7.61 | 4723″.41 | 3.98 | 4913″.02 | 0.28 | 4676″.85 | 4.41 |
| .01 | 2222.22 | 10.42 | 3253.60 | 9 89 | 4141.22 | 7.58 | 4727.39 | 3.94 | 4912.74 | 0.32 | 4672.44 | 4.44 |
| .02 | 2232.64 | 10.42 | 3263 49 | 9.87 | 4148.80 | 7.55 | 4731.33 | 3.91 | 4912.42 | 0.36 | 4668.00 | 4.48 |
| .03 | 2243.06 | 10.43 | 3273.36 | 9.85 | 4156.35 | 7.51 | 4735.24 | 3.86 | 4912.06 | 0.40 | 4663.52 | 4.52 |
| .04 | 2253.49 | 10.43 | 3283.21 | 9.84 | 4163.86 | 7.48 | 4739.10 | 3.82 | 4911.66 | 0.45 | 4659.00 | 4.55 |
| .05 | 2263.92 | 10.44 | 3293.05 | 9.83 | 4171.34 | 7.45 | 4742.92 | 3.78 | 4911.21 | 0.49 | 4654.45 | 4.59 |
| .06 | 2274.36 | 10.44 | 3302.88 | 9.81 | 4178.79 | 7.42 | 4746.70 | 3.74 | 4910.72 | 0.54 | 4649.86 | 4.63 |
| .07 | 2284.80 | 10.44 | 3312.69 | 9.80 | 4186.21 | 7.39 | 4750.44 | 3.70 | 4910.18 | 0.58 | 4645.23 | 4.67 |
| .08 | 2295.24 | 10.45 | 3322.49 | 9.78 | 4193.60 | 7.36 | 4754.14 | 3.66 | 4909.60 | 0.62 | 4640.56 | 4.70 |
| .09 | 2305.69 | 10.44 | 3332.27 | 9.76 | 4200.96 | 7.33 | 4757.80 | 3.62 | 4908.98 | 0.66 | 4635.86 | 4.74 |
| .10 | 2316.13 | 10.45 | 3342.03 | 9.74 | 4208.29 | 7.30 | 4761.42 | 3.57 | 4908.32 | 0.71 | 4631.12 | 4.78 |
| .11 | 2326.58 | 10.45 | 3351.77 | 9.73 | 4215.59 | 7.26 | 4764.99 | 3.52 | 4907.61 | 0.75 | 4626.34 | 4.82 |
| .12 | 2337.03 | 10.46 | 3361.50 | 9.71 | 4222.85 | 7.23 | 4768.51 | 3.49 | 4906.86 | 0.79 | 4621.52 | 4.85 |
| .13 | 2347.49 | 10.46 | 3371.21 | 9.70 | 4230.08 | 7.19 | 4772.00 | 3.45 | 4906.07 | 0.84 | 4616.67 | 4.89 |
| .14 | 2357.95 | 10.45 | 3380.91 | 9.68 | 4237.27 | 7.16 | 4775.45 | 3.41 | 4905.23 | 0.88 | 4611.78 | 4.93 |
| .15 | 2368.40 | 10.46 | 3390.59 | 9.66 | 4244.43 | 7.13 | 4778.86 | 3.37 | 4904.35 | 0.92 | 4606.85 | 4.97 |
| .16 | 2378.86 | 10.47 | 3400.25 | 9.65 | 4251.56 | 7.11 | 4782.23 | 3.32 | 4903.43 | 0.96 | 4601.88 | 5.00 |
| .17 | 2389.33 | 10.46 | 3409.90 | 9.63 | 4258.67 | 7.06 | 4785.55 | 3.29 | 4902.47 | 1.01 | 4596.88 | 5.04 |
| .18 | 2399.79 | 10.46 | 3419.53 | 9.61 | 4265.73 | 7.04 | 4788.84 | 3.24 | 4901.46 | 1.05 | 4591.84 | 5.07 |
| .19 | 2410.25 | 10.46 | 3429.14 | 9.59 | 4272.77 | 7.00 | 4792.08 | 3.20 | 4900.41 | 1.10 | 4586.77 | 5.11 |
| .20 | 2420.71 | 10.46 | 3438.73 | 9.57 | 4279.77 | 6.97 | 4795.28 | 3.16 | 4899.31 | 1.13 | 4581.66 | 5.15 |
| .21 | 2431.17 | 10.47 | 3448.30 | 9.56 | 4286.74 | 6.93 | 4798.44 | 3.12 | 4898.18 | 1.18 | 4576.51 | 5.19 |
| .22 | 2441.64 | 10.47 | 3457.86 | 9.54 | 4293.67 | 6 91 | 4801.56 | 3.07 | 4897.00 | 1.23 | 4571.32 | 5.22 |
| .23 | 2452.11 | 10.47 | 3467.40 | 9.52 | 4300.58 | 6.87 | 4804.63 | 3.03 | 4895.77 | 1.26 | 4566.10 | 5.25 |
| .24 | 2462.58 | 10.46 | 3476.92 | 9.50 | 4307.45 | 6.84 | 4807.66 | 2.99 | 4894.51 | 1.32 | 4560.85 | 5.30 |
| .25 | 2473.04 | 10.47 | 3486.42 | 9.48 | 4314.29 | 6.80 | 4810.65 | 2.95 | 4893.19 | 1.35 | 4555.55 | 5.33 |
| .26 | 2483.51 | 10.47 | 3495.90 | 9.46 | 4321.09 | 6.77 | 4813.60 | 2.91 | 4891.84 | 1.39 | 4550.22 | 5.36 |
| .27 | 2493.98 | 10.46 | 3505.36 | 9.44 | 4327.86 | 6.73 | 4816.51 | 2.86 | 4890.45 | 1.43 | 4544.86 | 5.40 |
| .28 | 2504.44 | 10.46 | 3514.80 | 9.43 | 4334.59 | 6.70 | 4819.37 | 2.82 | 4889.02 | 1.48 | 4539.46 | 5.43 |
| .29 | 2514.90 | 10.46 | 3524.23 | 9.40 | 4341.29 | 6.67 | 4822.19 | 2.79 | 4887.54 | 1.52 | 4534.03 | 5.47 |
| .30 | 2525.36 | 10.46 | 3533.63 | 9.39 | 4347.96 | 6.63 | 4824.98 | 2.74 | 4886.02 | 1.56 | 4528.56 | 5.51 |
| .31 | 2535.82 | 10.46 | 3543.02 | 9.37 | 4354.59 | 6.60 | 4827.72 | 2.69 | 4884.46 | 1 61 | 4523.05 | 5.54 |
| .32 | 2546.28 | 10.46 | 3552.39 | 9.34 | 4361.19 | 6.56 | 4830.41 | 2.65 | 4882.85 | 1.65 | 4517.51 | 5.57 |
| .33 | 2556.74 | 10.46 | 3561.73 | 9.32 | 4367.75 | 6.52 | 4833.06 | 2.62 | 4881.20 | 1.69 | 4511.94 | 5.61 |
| .34 | 2567.20 | 10.45 | 3571.05 | 9.31 | 4374.27 | 6.49 | 4835.68 | 2.57 | 4879.51 | 1.73 | 4506.33 | 5.65 |
| .35 | 2577.65 | 10.45 | 3580.36 | 9.28 | 4380.76 | 6.46 | 4838.25 | 2.52 | 4877.78 | 1.77 | 4500.68 | 5.68 |
| .36 | 2588.10 | 10.45 | 3589.64 | 9.26 | 4387.22 | 6.43 | 4840.77 | 2.48 | 4876.01 | 1.82 | 4495.00 | 5.72 |
| .37 | 2598.55 | 10.45 | 3598.90 | 9.24 | 4393.65 | 6.39 | 4843.25 | 2.44 | 4874.19 | 1.86 | 4489.28 | 5.74 |
| .38 | 2609.00 | 10.44 | 3608.14 | 9.22 | 4400.04 | 6.35 | 4845.69 | 2.40 | 4872.33 | 1.90 | 4483.54 | 5.79 |
| .39 | 2619.44 | 10.44 | 3617.36 | 9.20 | 4406.39 | 6.32 | 4848.09 | 2.36 | 4870.43 | 1.94 | 4477.75 | 5.82 |
| .40 | 2629.88 | 10.44 | 3626.56 | 9.18 | 4412.71 | 6.28 | 4850.45 | 2.31 | 4868.49 | 1.98 | 4471.93 | 5.85 |
| .41 | 2640.32 | 10.43 | 3635.74 | 9.16 | 4418.99 | 6.25 | 4852.76 | 2.27 | 4866.51 | 2.03 | 4466.08 | 5.89 |
| .42 | 2650.75 | 10.43 | 3644 90 | 9.14 | 4425.24 | 6.21 | 4855.03 | 2.23 | 4864.48 | 2.07 | 4460.19 | 5.92 |
| .43 | 2661.18 | 10.43 | 3654.04 | 9.11 | 4431.45 | 6.18 | 4857.26 | 2.19 | 4862.41 | 2.11 | 4454.27 | 5.95 |
| .44 | 2671.61 | 10.43 | 3663.15 | 9.09 | 4437.63 | 6.14 | 4859.45 | 2.14 | 4860.30 | 2.15 | 4448.32 | 5.99 |
| .45 | 2682.04 | 10.42 | 3672.24 | 9.07 | 4443.77 | 6.10 | 4861.59 | 2.10 | 4858.15 | 2.20 | 4442.33 | 6.02 |
| .46 | 2692.46 | 10.41 | 3681.31 | 9.05 | 4449.87 | 6.07 | 4863.69 | 2.06 | 4855.95 | 2.24 | 4436.31 | 6.06 |
| .47 | 2702.87 | 10.41 | 3690.36 | 9.03 | 4455.94 | 6.03 | 4865.75 | 2.01 | 4853.71 | 2.27 | 4430.25 | 6.09 |
| .48 | 2713.28 | 10.40 | 3699.39 | 9.00 | 4461.97 | 5.99 | 4867.76 | 1 97 | 4851.44 | 2.32 | 4424.16 | 6.13 |
| .49 | 2723.68 | 10.40 | 3708.39 | 8.97 | 4467.96 | 5.95 | 4869.73 | 1.92 | 4849.12 | 2.37 | 4418.03 | 6.16 |
| .50 | 2734.08 | 10.40 | 3717.36 | 8.95 | 4473.91 | 5.93 | 4871.65 | 1.89 | 4846.75 | 2.41 | 4411.87 | 6.19 |

# TABLE VIII. ARGUMENT 3.

Equation $= 2457''.02 - 122''.1 \sin. t + 2371''.0 \sin. 2t + 0''.9 \sin. 3t + 14''.4 \sin. 4t.$

Period, 29.530587997 days.

| Days. | 0 | | 1 | | 2 | | 3 | | 4 | | 5 | |
|---|---|---|---|---|---|---|---|---|---|---|---|---|
| Decimals of a Day. | Equation. | Diff. | Equation. | Diff. | Equation. | Diff. | Equation. | Diff. | Equation. | Diff. | Equation. | Diff. |
| .50 | 2734.08 | 10.40 | 3717.36 | 8.95 | 4473.91 | 5.93 | 4871.65 | 1.89 | 4846.75 | 2.41 | 4411.87 | 6.19 |
| .51 | 2744.48 | 10.39 | 3726.31 | 8.93 | 4479.84 | 5.88 | 4873.54 | 1.84 | 4844.34 | 2.44 | 4405.68 | 6.22 |
| .52 | 2754.87 | 10.39 | 3735.24 | 8.91 | 4485.72 | 5.85 | 4875.38 | 1.80 | 4841.90 | 2.49 | 4399.46 | 6.26 |
| .53 | 2765.26 | 10.38 | 3744.15 | 8.89 | 4491.57 | 5.81 | 4877.18 | 1.76 | 4839.41 | 2.53 | 4393.20 | 6.28 |
| .54 | 2775.64 | 10.37 | 3753.04 | 8.86 | 4497.38 | 5.78 | 4878.94 | 1.71 | 4836.88 | 2.57 | 4386.92 | 6.32 |
| .55 | 2786.01 | 10.37 | 3761.90 | 8.84 | 4503.16 | 5.74 | 4880.65 | 1.67 | 4834.31 | 2.61 | 4380.60 | 6.35 |
| .56 | 2796.38 | 10.37 | 3770.74 | 8.81 | 4508.90 | 5.70 | 4882.32 | 1.63 | 4831.70 | 2.65 | 4374.25 | 6.39 |
| .57 | 2806.75 | 10.35 | 3779.55 | 8.79 | 4514.60 | 5.67 | 4883.95 | 1.59 | 4829.05 | 2.70 | 4367.86 | 6.42 |
| .58 | 2817.10 | 10.35 | 3788.34 | 8.77 | 4520.27 | 5.62 | 4885.54 | 1.54 | 4826.35 | 2.73 | 4361.44 | 6.45 |
| .59 | 2827.45 | 10.34 | 3797.11 | 8.74 | 4525.89 | 5.59 | 4887.08 | 1.50 | 4823.62 | 2.77 | 4354.99 | 6.48 |
| .60 | 2837.79 | 10.33 | 3805.85 | 8.71 | 4531.48 | 5.56 | 4888.58 | 1.45 | 4820.85 | 2.82 | 4348.51 | 6.51 |
| .61 | 2848.12 | 10.33 | 3814.56 | 8.68 | 4537.04 | 5.50 | 4890.03 | 1.41 | 4818.03 | 2.86 | 4342.00 | 6.55 |
| .62 | 2858.45 | 10.32 | 3823.24 | 8.67 | 4542.54 | 5.48 | 4891.44 | 1.37 | 4815.17 | 2.90 | 4335.45 | 6.58 |
| .63 | 2868.77 | 10.31 | 3831.91 | 8.64 | 4548.02 | 5.44 | 4892.81 | 1.33 | 4812.27 | 2.93 | 4328.87 | 6.61 |
| .64 | 2879.08 | 10.30 | 3840.55 | 8.62 | 4553.46 | 5.40 | 4894.14 | 1.28 | 4809.34 | 2.98 | 4322.26 | 6.64 |
| .65 | 2889.38 | 10.30 | 3849.17 | 8.59 | 4558.86 | 5.36 | 4895.42 | 1.23 | 4806.36 | 3.03 | 4315.62 | 6.67 |
| .66 | 2899.68 | 10.29 | 3857.76 | 8.57 | 4564.22 | 5.33 | 4896.65 | 1.20 | 4803.33 | 3.07 | 4308.95 | 6.71 |
| .67 | 2909.97 | 10.28 | 3866.33 | 8.54 | 4569.55 | 5.29 | 4897.85 | 1.15 | 4800.26 | 3.10 | 4302.24 | 6.73 |
| .68 | 2920.25 | 10.28 | 3874.87 | 8.51 | 4574.84 | 5.25 | 4899.00 | 1.11 | 4797.16 | 3.14 | 4295.51 | 6.76 |
| .69 | 2930.53 | 10.26 | 3883.38 | 8.49 | 4580.09 | 5.21 | 4900.11 | 1.07 | 4794.02 | 3.18 | 4288.75 | 6.80 |
| .70 | 2940.79 | 10.25 | 3891.87 | 8.46 | 4585.30 | 5.17 | 4901.18 | 1.02 | 4790.84 | 3.23 | 4281.95 | 6.83 |
| .71 | 2951.04 | 10.25 | 3900.33 | 8.43 | 4590.47 | 5.13 | 4902.20 | 0.98 | 4787.61 | 3.26 | 4275.12 | 6.86 |
| .72 | 2961.29 | 10.24 | 3908.76 | 8.41 | 4595.60 | 5.10 | 4903.18 | 0.94 | 4784.35 | 3.30 | 4268.26 | 6.89 |
| .73 | 2971.53 | 10.22 | 3917.17 | 8.38 | 4600.70 | 5.06 | 4904.12 | 0.89 | 4781.05 | 3.35 | 4261.37 | 6.92 |
| .74 | 2981.75 | 10.21 | 3925.55 | 8.35 | 4605.76 | 5.01 | 4905.01 | 0.85 | 4777.70 | 3.38 | 4254.45 | 6.96 |
| .75 | 2991.96 | 10.20 | 3933.90 | 8.33 | 4610.77 | 4.98 | 4905.86 | 0.81 | 4774.32 | 3.43 | 4247.49 | 6.98 |
| .76 | 3002.16 | 10.19 | 3942.23 | 8.30 | 4615.75 | 4.94 | 4906.67 | 0.76 | 4770.89 | 3.46 | 4240.51 | 7.01 |
| .77 | 3012.35 | 10.18 | 3950.53 | 8.27 | 4620.69 | 4.90 | 4907.43 | 0.72 | 4767.43 | 3.51 | 4233.50 | 7.04 |
| .78 | 3022.53 | 10.17 | 3958.80 | 8.25 | 4625.59 | 4.86 | 4908.15 | 0.68 | 4763.92 | 3.54 | 4226.46 | 7.07 |
| .79 | 3032.70 | 10.16 | 3967.05 | 8.22 | 4630.45 | 4.83 | 4908.83 | 0.64 | 4760.38 | 3.58 | 4219.39 | 7.09 |
| .80 | 3042.86 | 10.16 | 3975.27 | 8.19 | 4635.28 | 4.79 | 4909.47 | 0.59 | 4756.80 | 3.63 | 4212.30 | 7.13 |
| .81 | 3053.02 | 10.15 | 3983.46 | 8.16 | 4640.07 | 4.74 | 4910.06 | 0.54 | 4753.17 | 3.66 | 4205.17 | 7.16 |
| .82 | 3063.17 | 10.14 | 3991.62 | 8.13 | 4644.81 | 4.71 | 4910.60 | 0.50 | 4749.51 | 3.71 | 4198.01 | 7.19 |
| .83 | 3073.31 | 10.13 | 3999.75 | 8.11 | 4649.52 | 4.66 | 4911.10 | 0.46 | 4745.80 | 3.75 | 4190.82 | 7.22 |
| .84 | 3083.44 | 10.12 | 4007.86 | 8.08 | 4654.18 | 4.63 | 4911.56 | 0.41 | 4742.05 | 3.78 | 4183.60 | 7.24 |
| .85 | 3093.56 | 10.10 | 4015.94 | 8.04 | 4658.81 | 4.59 | 4911.97 | 0.37 | 4738.27 | 3.82 | 4176.36 | 7.27 |
| .86 | 3103.66 | 10.09 | 4023.98 | 8.02 | 4663.40 | 4.54 | 4912.34 | 0.34 | 4734.45 | 3.86 | 4169.09 | 7.30 |
| .87 | 3113.75 | 10.07 | 4032.00 | 7.99 | 4667.94 | 4.51 | 4912.68 | 0.29 | 4730.59 | 3.90 | 4161.79 | 7.33 |
| .88 | 3123.82 | 10.06 | 4039.99 | 7.97 | 4672.45 | 4.46 | 4912.97 | 0.24 | 4726.69 | 3.94 | 4154.46 | 7.36 |
| .89 | 3133.88 | 10.05 | 4047.96 | 7.93 | 4676.91 | 4.43 | 4913.21 | 0.20 | 4722.75 | 3.98 | 4147.10 | 7.39 |
| .90 | 3143.93 | 10.03 | 4055.89 | 7.91 | 4681.34 | 4.39 | 4913.41 | 0.15 | 4718.77 | 4.02 | 4139.71 | 7.42 |
| .91 | 3153.96 | 10.03 | 4063.80 | 7.88 | 4685.73 | 4.35 | 4913.56 | 0.12 | 4714.75 | 4.06 | 4132.29 | 7.44 |
| .92 | 3163.99 | 10.01 | 4071.68 | 7.85 | 4690.08 | 4.31 | 4913.68 | 0.07 | 4710.69 | 4.09 | 4124.85 | 7.47 |
| .93 | 3174.00 | 10.00 | 4079.53 | 7.81 | 4694.39 | 4.26 | 4913.75 | 0.03 | 4706.60 | 4.13 | 4117.38 | 7.50 |
| .94 | 3184.00 | 9.99 | 4087.34 | 7.79 | 4698.65 | 4.23 | 4913.78 | 0.02 | 4702.47 | 4.17 | 4109.88 | 7.52 |
| .95 | 3193.99 | 9.97 | 4095.13 | 7.76 | 4702.88 | 4.19 | 4913.76 | 0.06 | 4698.30 | 4.21 | 4102.36 | 7.56 |
| .96 | 3203.96 | 9.96 | 4102.89 | 7.73 | 4707.07 | 4.15 | 4913.70 | 0.10 | 4694.09 | 4.26 | 4094.80 | 7.58 |
| .97 | 3213.92 | 9.94 | 4110.62 | 7.70 | 4711.22 | 4.10 | 4913.60 | 0.15 | 4689.83 | 4.29 | 4087.22 | 7.60 |
| .98 | 3223.86 | 9.92 | 4118.32 | 7.66 | 4715.32 | 4.07 | 4913.45 | 0.19 | 4685.54 | 4.32 | 4079.62 | 7.65 |
| .99 | 3233.78 | 9.91 | 4125.98 | 7.63 | 4719.39 | 4.02 | 4913.26 | 0.24 | 4681.22 | 4.37 | 4071.97 | 7.67 |
| 1.00 | 3243.69 | 9.91 | 4133.61 | 7.61 | 4723.41 | 3.98 | 4913.02 | 0.28 | 4676.85 | 4.41 | 4064.30 | 7.69 |

# TABLE VIII. ARGUMENT 3.

Equation $= 2457''.02 - 122''.1 \sin. t + 2371''.0 \sin. 2t + 0''.9 \sin. 3t + 14''.4 \sin. 4t.$

Period, 29.530587997 days.

| Days. | 6 | | 7 | | 8 | | 9 | | 10 | | 11 | |
|---|---|---|---|---|---|---|---|---|---|---|---|---|
| Decimals of a Day. | Equation. | Diff. | Equation. | Diff. | Equation. | Diff. | Equation. | Diff. | Equation. | Diff. | Equation. | Diff. |
| .00 | 4064″.30 | 7.69 | 3187″.42 | 9.62 | 2199″.82 | 9.86 | 1271″.82 | 8.41 | 563″.98 | 5.50 | 201″.50 | 1.59 |
| .01 | 4056.61 | 7.71 | 3177.80 | 9.62 | 2189.96 | 9.85 | 1263.41 | 8.39 | 558.48 | 5.47 | 199.91 | 1.56 |
| .02 | 4048.90 | 7.75 | 3168.18 | 9.63 | 2180.11 | 9.85 | 1255.02 | 8.37 | 553.01 | 5.43 | 198.35 | 1.51 |
| .03 | 4041.15 | 7.77 | 3158.55 | 9.64 | 2170.26 | 9.84 | 1246.65 | 8.35 | 547.58 | 5.40 | 196.84 | 1.47 |
| .04 | 4033.38 | 7.79 | 3148.91 | 9.65 | 2160.42 | 9.83 | 1238.30 | 8.32 | 542.18 | 5.36 | 195.37 | 1.43 |
| .05 | 4025.59 | 7.82 | 3139.26 | 9.66 | 2150.59 | 9.83 | 1229.98 | 8.30 | 536.82 | 5.32 | 193.94 | 1.38 |
| .06 | 4017.77 | 7.85 | 3129.60 | 9.67 | 2140.76 | 9.82 | 1221.68 | 8.28 | 531.50 | 5.29 | 192.56 | 1.35 |
| .07 | 4009.92 | 7.88 | 3119.93 | 9.68 | 2130.94 | 9.81 | 1213.40 | 8.25 | 526.21 | 5.25 | 191.21 | 1.30 |
| .08 | 4002.04 | 7.90 | 3110.25 | 9.69 | 2121.13 | 9.80 | 1205.15 | 8.23 | 520.96 | 5.22 | 189.91 | 1.26 |
| .09 | 3994.14 | 7.92 | 3100.56 | 9.70 | 2111.33 | 9.80 | 1196.92 | 8.21 | 515.74 | 5.18 | 188.65 | 1.21 |
| .10 | 3986.22 | 7.95 | 3090.86 | 9.71 | 2101.53 | 9.79 | 1188.71 | 8.18 | 510.56 | 5.15 | 187.44 | 1.18 |
| .11 | 3978.27 | 7.97 | 3081.15 | 9.72 | 2091.74 | 9.78 | 1180.53 | 8.16 | 505.41 | 5.11 | 186.26 | 1.13 |
| .12 | 3970.30 | 8.00 | 3071.43 | 9.72 | 2081.96 | 9.78 | 1172.37 | 8.14 | 500.30 | 5.07 | 185.13 | 1.09 |
| .13 | 3962.30 | 8.03 | 3061.71 | 9.74 | 2072.18 | 9.76 | 1164.23 | 8.11 | 495.23 | 5.04 | 184.04 | 1.05 |
| .14 | 3954.27 | 8.05 | 3051.97 | 9.75 | 2062.42 | 9.76 | 1156.12 | 8.09 | 490.19 | 5.00 | 182.99 | 1.00 |
| .15 | 3946.22 | 8.07 | 3042.22 | 9.75 | 2052.66 | 9.75 | 1148.03 | 8.06 | 485.19 | 4.97 | 181.99 | 0.95 |
| .16 | 3938.15 | 8.10 | 3032.47 | 9.76 | 2042.91 | 9.74 | 1139.97 | 8.04 | 480.22 | 4.92 | 181.04 | 0.92 |
| .17 | 3930.05 | 8.13 | 3022.71 | 9.77 | 2033.17 | 9.73 | 1131.93 | 8.01 | 475.30 | 4.89 | 180.12 | 0.88 |
| .18 | 3921.92 | 8.14 | 3012.94 | 9.78 | 2023.44 | 9.72 | 1123.92 | 7.99 | 470.41 | 4.86 | 179.24 | 0.84 |
| .19 | 3913.78 | 8.17 | 3003.16 | 9.79 | 2013.72 | 9.71 | 1115.93 | 7.96 | 465.55 | 4.82 | 178.40 | 0.79 |
| .20 | 3905.61 | 8.20 | 2993.37 | 9.80 | 2004.01 | 9.71 | 1107.97 | 7.94 | 460.73 | 4.78 | 177.61 | 0.75 |
| .21 | 3897.41 | 8.22 | 2983.57 | 9.80 | 1994.30 | 9.69 | 1100.03 | 7.91 | 455.95 | 4.74 | 176.86 | 0.71 |
| .22 | 3889.19 | 8.24 | 2973.77 | 9.81 | 1984.61 | 9.68 | 1092.12 | 7.89 | 451.21 | 4.71 | 176.15 | 0.67 |
| .23 | 3880.95 | 8.27 | 2963.96 | 9.82 | 1974.93 | 9.68 | 1084.23 | 7.86 | 446.50 | 4.67 | 175.48 | 0.62 |
| .24 | 3872.68 | 8.29 | 2954.14 | 9.82 | 1965.25 | 9.66 | 1076.37 | 7.83 | 441.83 | 4.62 | 174.86 | 0.58 |
| .25 | 3864.39 | 8.31 | 2944.32 | 9.83 | 1955.59 | 9.65 | 1068.54 | 7.80 | 437.22 | 4.59 | 174.28 | 0.54 |
| .26 | 3856.08 | 8.34 | 2934.49 | 9.84 | 1945.94 | 9.65 | 1060.74 | 7.80 | 432.62 | 4.56 | 173.74 | 0.50 |
| .27 | 3847.74 | 8.36 | 2924.65 | 9.85 | 1936.29 | 9.63 | 1052.94 | 7.75 | 428.06 | 4.52 | 173.24 | 0.45 |
| .28 | 3839.38 | 8.38 | 2914.80 | 9.85 | 1926.66 | 9.62 | 1045.19 | 7.74 | 423.54 | 4.48 | 172.79 | 0.42 |
| .29 | 3831.00 | 8.40 | 2904.95 | 9.85 | 1917.04 | 9.61 | 1037.45 | 7.70 | 419.06 | 4.45 | 172.37 | 0.36 |
| .30 | 3822.60 | 8.43 | 2895.10 | 9.87 | 1907.43 | 9.60 | 1029.75 | 7.68 | 414.61 | 4.40 | 172.01 | 0.33 |
| .31 | 3814.17 | 8.45 | 2885.23 | 9.87 | 1897.83 | 9.58 | 1022.07 | 7.65 | 410.21 | 4.37 | 171.68 | 0.28 |
| .32 | 3805.72 | 8.47 | 2875.36 | 9.87 | 1888.25 | 9.58 | 1014.42 | 7.62 | 405.84 | 4.33 | 171.40 | 0.24 |
| .33 | 3797.25 | 8.50 | 2865.49 | 9.88 | 1878.67 | 9.56 | 1006.80 | 7.60 | 401.51 | 4.30 | 171.16 | 0.20 |
| .34 | 3788.75 | 8.51 | 2855.61 | 9.89 | 1869.11 | 9.56 | 999.20 | 7.57 | 397.21 | 4.25 | 170.96 | 0.15 |
| .35 | 3780.24 | 8.53 | 2845.72 | 9.89 | 1859.55 | 9.54 | 991.63 | 7.54 | 392.96 | 4.22 | 170.81 | 0.12 |
| .36 | 3771.71 | 8.56 | 2835.83 | 9.90 | 1850.01 | 9.53 | 984.09 | 7.52 | 388.74 | 4.18 | 170.69 | 0.07 |
| .37 | 3763.15 | 8.58 | 2825.93 | 9.90 | 1840.48 | 9.51 | 976.57 | 7.49 | 384.56 | 4.14 | 170.62 | 0.03 |
| .38 | 3754.57 | 8.60 | 2816.03 | 9.91 | 1831.97 | 9.50 | 969.08 | 7.46 | 380.42 | 4.10 | 170.59 | 0.02 |
| .39 | 3745.97 | 8.62 | 2806.12 | 9.91 | 1821.47 | 9.49 | 961.62 | 7.43 | 376.32 | 4.06 | 170.61 | 0.05 |
| .40 | 3737.35 | 8.65 | 2796.21 | 9.92 | 1811.98 | 9.48 | 954.19 | 7.40 | 372.26 | 4.02 | 170.66 | 0.10 |
| .41 | 3728.70 | 8.66 | 2786.29 | 9.92 | 1802.50 | 9.47 | 946.79 | 7.38 | 368.24 | 3.99 | 170.76 | 0.14 |
| .42 | 3720.04 | 8.68 | 2776.37 | 9.92 | 1793.03 | 9.45 | 939.41 | 7.35 | 364.25 | 3.95 | 170.90 | 0.19 |
| .43 | 3711.36 | 8.70 | 2766.45 | 9.93 | 1783.58 | 9.44 | 932.06 | 7.32 | 360.30 | 3.90 | 171.09 | 0.23 |
| .44 | 3702.66 | 8.73 | 2756.52 | 9.93 | 1774.14 | 9.43 | 924.74 | 7.29 | 356.40 | 3.87 | 171.32 | 0.27 |
| .45 | 3693.93 | 8.75 | 2746.59 | 9.93 | 1764.71 | 9.41 | 917.45 | 7.26 | 352.53 | 3.83 | 171.59 | 0.31 |
| .46 | 3685.18 | 8.77 | 2736.66 | 9.94 | 1755.30 | 9.40 | 910.19 | 7.23 | 348.70 | 3.80 | 171.90 | 0.35 |
| .47 | 3676.41 | 8.78 | 2726.72 | 9.94 | 1745.90 | 9.38 | 902.96 | 7.21 | 344.90 | 3.75 | 172.25 | 0.40 |
| .48 | 3667.63 | 8.81 | 2716.78 | 9.94 | 1736.52 | 9.36 | 895.75 | 7.17 | 341.15 | 3.70 | 172.65 | 0.45 |
| .49 | 3658.82 | 8.83 | 2706.84 | 9.95 | 1727.16 | 9.35 | 888.58 | 7.14 | 337.45 | 3.67 | 173.10 | 0.49 |
| .50 | 3649.99 | 8.84 | 2696.89 | 9.95 | 1717.81 | 9.35 | 881.44 | 7.12 | 333.78 | 3.64 | 173.59 | 0.52 |

# TABLE VIII. ARGUMENT 3.

Equation = 2457″.02 — 122″.1 sin. $t$ + 2371″.0 sin. $2t$ + 0″.9 sin. $3t$ + 14″.4 sin. $4t$.

Period, 29.530587997 days.

| Days. | 6 | | 7 | | 8 | | 9 | | 10 | | 11 | |
|---|---|---|---|---|---|---|---|---|---|---|---|---|
| Decimals of a Day. | Equation. | Diff. | Equation. | Diff. | Equation. | Diff. | Equation. | Diff. | Equation. | Diff. | Equation. | Diff. |
| .50 | 3649.99″ | 8.84 | 2696.89″ | 9.95 | 1717.81″ | 9.35 | 881.44″ | 7.12 | 333.78″ | 3.64 | 173.59″ | 0.52 |
| .51 | 3641.15 | 8.87 | 2686.94 | 9.95 | 1708.46 | 9.32 | 874.32 | 7.09 | 330.14 | 3.59 | 174.11 | 0.57 |
| .52 | 3632.28 | 8.88 | 2676.99 | 9.96 | 1699.14 | 9.31 | 867.23 | 7.05 | 326.55 | 3.56 | 174.68 | 0.61 |
| .53 | 3623.40 | 8.90 | 2667.03 | 9.95 | 1689.83 | 9.30 | 860.18 | 7.03 | 322.99 | 3.51 | 175.29 | 0.65 |
| .54 | 3614.50 | 8.92 | 2657.08 | 9.96 | 1680.53 | 9.28 | 853.15 | 7.00 | 319.48 | 3.48 | 175.94 | 0.70 |
| .55 | 3605.58 | 8.94 | 2647.12 | 9.96 | 1671.25 | 9.27 | 846.15 | 6.97 | 316.00 | 3.44 | 176.64 | 0.74 |
| .56 | 3596.64 | 8.96 | 2637.16 | 9.96 | 1661.98 | 9.25 | 839.18 | 6.94 | 312.56 | 3.40 | 177.38 | 0.78 |
| .57 | 3587.68 | 8.97 | 2627.20 | 9.96 | 1652.73 | 9.23 | 832.24 | 6.91 | 309.16 | 3.35 | 178.16 | 0.82 |
| .58 | 3578.71 | 8.99 | 2617.24 | 9.97 | 1643.50 | 9.22 | 825.33 | 6.88 | 305.81 | 3.32 | 178.98 | 0.86 |
| .59 | 3569.72 | 9.01 | 2607.27 | 9.96 | 1634.28 | 9.21 | 818.45 | 6.85 | 302.49 | 3.28 | 179.84 | 0.92 |
| .60 | 3560.71 | 9.03 | 2597.31 | 9.97 | 1625.07 | 9.18 | 811.60 | 6.81 | 299.21 | 3.24 | 180.76 | 0.95 |
| .61 | 3551.68 | 9.05 | 2587.34 | 9.96 | 1615.89 | 9.17 | 804.79 | 6.79 | 295.97 | 3.20 | 181.71 | 0.99 |
| .62 | 3542.63 | 9.06 | 2577.38 | 9.97 | 1606.72 | 9.16 | 798.00 | 6.76 | 292.77 | 3.15 | 182.70 | 1.04 |
| .63 | 3533.57 | 9.08 | 2567.41 | 9.97 | 1597.56 | 9.14 | 791.24 | 6.72 | 289.62 | 3.12 | 183.74 | 1.08 |
| .64 | 3524.49 | 9.10 | 2557.44 | 9.97 | 1588.42 | 9.12 | 784.52 | 6.70 | 286.50 | 3.08 | 184.82 | 1.12 |
| .65 | 3515.39 | 9.12 | 2547.47 | 9.96 | 1579.30 | 9.10 | 777.82 | 6.66 | 283.42 | 3.03 | 185.94 | 1.17 |
| .66 | 3506.27 | 9.13 | 2537.51 | 9.97 | 1570.20 | 9.09 | 771.16 | 6.63 | 280.39 | 2.99 | 187.11 | 1.21 |
| .67 | 3497.14 | 9.15 | 2527.54 | 9.97 | 1561.11 | 9.07 | 764.53 | 6.60 | 277.40 | 2.96 | 188.32 | 1.25 |
| .68 | 3487.99 | 9.16 | 2517.57 | 9.97 | 1552.04 | 9.06 | 757.93 | 6.57 | 274.44 | 2.92 | 189.57 | 1.29 |
| .69 | 3478.83 | 9.18 | 2507.60 | 9.96 | 1542.98 | 9.03 | 751.36 | 6.54 | 271.52 | 2.87 | 190.86 | 1.33 |
| .70 | 3469.65 | 9.20 | 2497.64 | 9.97 | 1533.95 | 9.02 | 744.82 | 6.50 | 268.65 | 2.84 | 192.19 | 1.38 |
| .71 | 3460.45 | 9.21 | 2487.67 | 9.96 | 1524.93 | 9.00 | 738.32 | 6.48 | 265.81 | 2.78 | 193.57 | 1.42 |
| .72 | 3451.24 | 9.23 | 2477.71 | 9.97 | 1515.93 | 8.98 | 731.84 | 6.44 | 263.03 | 2.76 | 194.99 | 1.46 |
| .73 | 3442.01 | 9.25 | 2467.74 | 9.96 | 1506.95 | 8.97 | 725.40 | 6.41 | 260.27 | 2.71 | 196.45 | 1.50 |
| .74 | 3432.76 | 9.26 | 2457.78 | 9.96 | 1497.98 | 8.94 | 718.99 | 6.38 | 257.56 | 2.68 | 197.95 | 1.55 |
| .75 | 3423.50 | 9.28 | 2447.82 | 9.96 | 1489.04 | 8.93 | 712.61 | 6.35 | 254.88 | 2.63 | 199.50 | 1.58 |
| .76 | 3414.22 | 9.29 | 2437.86 | 9.95 | 1480.11 | 8.91 | 706.26 | 6.31 | 252.25 | 2.58 | 201.08 | 1.63 |
| .77 | 3404.93 | 9.31 | 2427.91 | 9.96 | 1471.20 | 8.89 | 699.95 | 6.27 | 249.67 | 2.54 | 202.71 | 1.69 |
| .78 | 3395.62 | 9.32 | 2417.95 | 9.95 | 1462.31 | 8.87 | 693.68 | 6.24 | 247.13 | 2.52 | 204.40 | 1.70 |
| .79 | 3386.30 | 9.33 | 2408.00 | 9.95 | 1453.44 | 8.85 | 687.44 | 6.22 | 244.61 | 2.47 | 206.10 | 1.75 |
| .80 | 3376.97 | 9.35 | 2398.05 | 9.95 | 1444.59 | 8.83 | 681.22 | 6.18 | 242.14 | 2.43 | 207.85 | 1.80 |
| .81 | 3367.62 | 9.37 | 2388.10 | 9.95 | 1435.76 | 8.81 | 675.04 | 6.15 | 239.71 | 2.37 | 209.65 | 1.84 |
| .82 | 3358.25 | 9.38 | 2378.15 | 9.94 | 1426.95 | 8.80 | 668.89 | 6.12 | 237.34 | 2.34 | 211.49 | 1.89 |
| .83 | 3348.87 | 9.39 | 2368.21 | 9.93 | 1418.15 | 8.77 | 662.77 | 6.08 | 235.00 | 2.31 | 213.38 | 1.93 |
| .84 | 3339.48 | 9.41 | 2358.28 | 9.94 | 1409.38 | 8.75 | 656.69 | 6.05 | 232.69 | 2.26 | 215.31 | 1.97 |
| .85 | 3330.07 | 9.42 | 2348.34 | 9.93 | 1400.63 | 8.74 | 650.64 | 6.02 | 230.43 | 2.22 | 217.28 | 2.00 |
| .86 | 3320.65 | 9.43 | 2338.41 | 9.93 | 1391.89 | 8.71 | 644.62 | 5.98 | 228.21 | 2.18 | 219.28 | 2.05 |
| .87 | 3311.22 | 9.45 | 2328.48 | 9.92 | 1383.18 | 8.69 | 638.64 | 5.95 | 226.03 | 2.13 | 221.33 | 2.10 |
| .88 | 3301.77 | 9.46 | 2318.56 | 9.92 | 1374.49 | 8.67 | 632.69 | 5.91 | 223.90 | 2.10 | 223.43 | 2.13 |
| .89 | 3292.31 | 9.47 | 2308.64 | 9.92 | 1365.82 | 8.65 | 626.78 | 5.88 | 221.80 | 2.05 | 225.56 | 2.18 |
| .90 | 3282.84 | 9.49 | 2298.72 | 9.91 | 1357.17 | 8.64 | 620.90 | 5.85 | 219.75 | 2.02 | 227.74 | 2.21 |
| .91 | 3273.35 | 9.50 | 2288.81 | 9.91 | 1348.53 | 8.61 | 615.05 | 5.82 | 217.73 | 1.97 | 229.95 | 2.26 |
| .92 | 3263.85 | 9.51 | 2278.90 | 9.90 | 1339.92 | 8.58 | 609.23 | 5.77 | 215.76 | 1.93 | 232.21 | 2.30 |
| .93 | 3254.34 | 9.52 | 2269.00 | 9.90 | 1331.34 | 8.57 | 603.46 | 5.75 | 213.83 | 1.88 | 234.51 | 2.34 |
| .94 | 3244.82 | 9.54 | 2259.10 | 9.89 | 1322.77 | 8.55 | 597.71 | 5.71 | 211.95 | 1.85 | 236.85 | 2.39 |
| .95 | 3235.28 | 9.55 | 2249.21 | 9.89 | 1314.22 | 8.52 | 592.00 | 5.68 | 210.10 | 1.81 | 239.24 | 2.42 |
| .96 | 3225.73 | 9.56 | 2239.32 | 9.88 | 1305.70 | 8.51 | 586.32 | 5.64 | 208.29 | 1.76 | 241.66 | 2.47 |
| .97 | 3216.17 | 9.57 | 2229.44 | 9.88 | 1297.19 | 8.48 | 580.68 | 5.60 | 206.53 | 1.72 | 244.13 | 2.51 |
| .98 | 3206.60 | 9.58 | 2219.56 | 9.87 | 1288.71 | 8.46 | 575.08 | 5.57 | 204.81 | 1.68 | 246.64 | 2.55 |
| .99 | 3197.02 | 9.60 | 2209.69 | 9.87 | 1280.25 | 8.43 | 569.51 | 5.53 | 203.13 | 1.63 | 249.19 | 2.60 |
| 1.00 | 3187.42 | 9.62 | 2199.82 | 9.86 | 1271.82 | 8.41 | 563.98 | 5.50 | 201.50 | 1.59 | 251.79 | 2.63 |

# TABLE VIII. ARGUMENT 3.

Equation = 2457″.02 — 122″.1 sin. $t$ + 2371″.0 sin. $2t$ + 0″.9 sin. $3t$ + 14″.4 sin. $4t$.

Period, 29.530587997 days.

| Days. | 12 | | 13 | | 14 | | 15 | | 16 | | 17 | |
|---|---|---|---|---|---|---|---|---|---|---|---|---|
| Decimals of a Day. | Equation. | Diff. | Equation. | Diff. | Equation. | Diff. | Equation. | Diff. | Equation. | Diff. | Equation. | Diff. |
| .00 | 251″.79 | 2.63 | 709″.32 | 6.41 | 1492″.67 | 9.03 | 2457″.02 | 9.96 | 3421″.36 | 9.02 | 4204″.72 | 6.39 |
| .01 | 254.42 | 2.67 | 715.73 | 6.45 | 1501.70 | 9.05 | 2466.98 | 9.95 | 3430.38 | 9.00 | 4211.11 | 6.34 |
| .02 | 257.09 | 2.72 | 722.18 | 6.48 | 1510.75 | 9.06 | 2476.93 | 9.96 | 3439.38 | 8.97 | 4217.45 | 6.32 |
| .03 | 259.81 | 2.75 | 728.66 | 6.52 | 1519.81 | 9.09 | 2486.89 | 9.95 | 3448.35 | 8.96 | 4223.77 | 6.28 |
| .04 | 262.56 | 2.80 | 735.18 | 6.54 | 1528.90 | 9.10 | 2496.84 | 9.96 | 3457.31 | 8.93 | 4230.05 | 6.25 |
| .05 | 265.36 | 2.84 | 741.72 | 6.58 | 1538.00 | 9.12 | 2506.80 | 9.95 | 3466.24 | 8.92 | 4236.30 | 6.22 |
| .06 | 268.20 | 2.88 | 748.30 | 6.62 | 1547.12 | 9.13 | 2516.75 | 9.95 | 3475.16 | 8.91 | 4242.52 | 6.18 |
| .07 | 271.08 | 2.92 | 754.92 | 6.64 | 1556.25 | 9.16 | 2526.70 | 9.96 | 3484.07 | 8.86 | 4248.70 | 6.15 |
| .08 | 274.00 | 2.96 | 761.56 | 6.68 | 1565.41 | 9.17 | 2536.66 | 9.95 | 3492.93 | 8.86 | 4254.85 | 6.11 |
| .09 | 276.96 | 3.01 | 768.24 | 6.70 | 1574.58 | 9.18 | 2546.61 | 9.94 | 3501.79 | 8.85 | 4260.96 | 6.08 |
| .10 | 279.97 | 3.05 | 774.94 | 6.74 | 1583.76 | 9.21 | 2556.55 | 9.95 | 3510.64 | 8.81 | 4267.04 | 6.04 |
| .11 | 283.02 | 3.09 | 781.68 | 6.78 | 1592.97 | 9.23 | 2566.50 | 9.95 | 3319.45 | 8.80 | 4273.08 | 6.01 |
| .12 | 286.11 | 3.12 | 788.46 | 6.81 | 1602.20 | 9.24 | 2576.45 | 9.95 | 3528.25 | 8.78 | 4279.09 | 5.98 |
| .13 | 289.23 | 3.17 | 795.27 | 6.83 | 1611.44 | 9.25 | 2586.40 | 9.94 | 3537.03 | 8.75 | 4285.07 | 5.94 |
| .14 | 292.40 | 3.21 | 802.10 | 6 87 | 1620.69 | 9.27 | 2596.34 | 9.93 | 3545.78 | 8.74 | 4291.01 | 5.91 |
| .15 | 295.61 | 3.25 | 808.97 | 6.90 | 1629.96 | 9.28 | 2606.27 | 9.94 | 3554.52 | 8.71 | 4296.92 | 5.88 |
| .16 | 298.86 | 3.28 | 815.87 | 6.93 | 1639.24 | 9.31 | 2616.21 | 9.93 | 3563.23 | 8.70 | 4302.80 | 5.84 |
| .17 | 302.14 | 3.33 | 822.80 | 6.96 | 1648.55 | 9.31 | 2626.14 | 9.93 | 3571.93 | 8.67 | 4308.64 | 5.80 |
| .18 | 305.47 | 3.37 | 829.76 | 6.99 | 1657.86 | 9.33 | 2636.07 | 9.93 | 3580.60 | 8.65 | 4314.44 | 5.76 |
| .19 | 308.84 | 3.41 | 836.75 | 7.02 | 1667.19 | 9.35 | 2646.00 | 9.92 | 3589.25 | 8.64 | 4320.20 | 5.73 |
| .20 | 312.25 | 3.46 | 843.77 | 7.05 | 1676.54 | 9.36 | 2655.92 | 9.91 | 3597.89 | 8.61 | 4325.93 | 5.70 |
| .21 | 315.71 | 3.49 | 850.82 | 7.08 | 1685.90 | 9.38 | 2665.83 | 9.92 | 3606.50 | 8.58 | 4331.63 | 5.66 |
| .22 | 319.20 | 3.53 | 857.90 | 7.12 | 1695.28 | 9.39 | 2675.75 | 9.91 | 3615.08 | 8.57 | 4337.29 | 5.63 |
| .23 | 322.73 | 3.57 | 865.02 | 7.14 | 1704.67 | 9.41 | 2685.66 | 9.90 | 3623.65 | 8.53 | 4342.92 | 5.58 |
| .24 | 326.30 | 3.62 | 872.16 | 7.18 | 1714.08 | 9.42 | 2695.56 | 9.91 | 3632.18 | 8.53 | 4348.50 | 5.56 |
| .25 | 329.92 | 3.65 | 879.34 | 7.21 | 1723.50 | 9.44 | 2705.47 | 9.90 | 3640.71 | 8.49 | 4354.06 | 5.52 |
| .26 | 333.57 | 3.69 | 886.55 | 7.23 | 1732.94 | 9.45 | 2715.37 | 9.89 | 3649.20 | 8.48 | 4359.58 | 5.48 |
| .27 | 337.26 | 3.73 | 893.78 | 7.26 | 1742.39 | 9.46 | 2725.26 | 9.89 | 3657.68 | 8.45 | 4365.06 | 5.44 |
| .28 | 340.99 | 3.77 | 901.04 | 7.30 | 1751.85 | 9.47 | 2735.15 | 9.88 | 3666.13 | 8.43 | 4370.50 | 5.41 |
| .29 | 344.76 | 3.81 | 908.34 | 7.32 | 1761.32 | 9.49 | 2745.03 | 9.87 | 3674.56 | 8.41 | 4375.91 | 5.37 |
| .30 | 348.57 | 3.85 | 915.66 | 7.35 | 1770.81 | 9.50 | 2754.90 | 9.87 | 3682.97 | 8.38 | 4381.28 | 5.34 |
| .31 | 352.42 | 3.89 | 923.01 | 7.38 | 1780.31 | 9.52 | 2764.77 | 9.86 | 3691.35 | 8.36 | 4386.62 | 5.30 |
| .32 | 356.31 | 3.93 | 930.39 | 7.41 | 1789.83 | 9.52 | 2774.63 | 9.86 | 3699.71 | 8.33 | 4391.92 | 5.27 |
| .33 | 360.24 | 3.97 | 937.80 | 7.44 | 1799.35 | 9.54 | 2784.49 | 9.85 | 3708.04 | 8.31 | 4397.19 | 5 23 |
| .34 | 364.21 | 4.01 | 945.24 | 7.46 | 1808.89 | 9.56 | 2794.34 | 9.84 | 3716.35 | 8.29 | 4402.42 | 5.19 |
| .35 | 368.22 | 4.06 | 952.70 | 7.50 | 1818.45 | 9.57 | 2804.18 | 9.84 | 3724.64 | 8.26 | 4407.61 | 5.15 |
| .36 | 372.28 | 4.09 | 960.20 | 7.53 | 1828.02 | 9.58 | 2814.02 | 9.83 | 3732.90 | 8.24 | 4412.76 | 5.12 |
| .37 | 376.37 | 4.12 | 967.73 | 7.56 | 1837.60 | 9.58 | 2823.85 | 9.83 | 3741.14 | 8.21 | 4417.88 | 5.08 |
| .38 | 380.49 | 4.17 | 975.29 | 7.58 | 1847.18 | 9.60 | 2833.68 | 9.82 | 3749.35 | 8.19 | 4422.96 | 5.04 |
| .39 | 384.66 | 4.20 | 982.87 | 7.61 | 1856.78 | 9.61 | 2843.50 | 9.81 | 3757.54 | 8.17 | 4428.00 | 5.01 |
| .40 | 388.86 | 4.24 | 990.48 | 7.63 | 1866.39 | 9.62 | 2853.31 | 9.80 | 3765.71 | 8.14 | 4433.01 | 4.97 |
| .41 | 393.10 | 4.28 | 998.11 | 7.67 | 1876.01 | 9.64 | 2863.11 | 9.79 | 3773.85 | 8.11 | 4437.98 | 4.93 |
| .42 | 397.38 | 4.32 | 1005.78 | 7.69 | 1885.65 | 9.64 | 2872.90 | 9.79 | 3781.96 | 8.09 | 4442.91 | 4.89 |
| .43 | 401.70 | 4.36 | 1013.47 | 7.72 | 1895.29 | 9.65 | 2882.69 | 9.77 | 3790.05 | 8.06 | 4447.80 | 4.85 |
| .44 | 406.06 | 4.40 | 1021.19 | 7.75 | 1904.94 | 9.67 | 2892.46 | 9.77 | 3798.11 | 8.04 | 4452.65 | 4.82 |
| .45 | 410.46 | 4.44 | 1028.94 | 7.77 | 1914.61 | 9.67 | 2902.23 | 9.76 | 3806.15 | 8.01 | 4457.47 | 4.78 |
| .46 | 414.90 | 4.47 | 1036.71 | 7.80 | 1924.28 | 9.69 | 2911.99 | 9.75 | 3814.16 | 7.99 | 4462.25 | 4.74 |
| .47 | 419.37 | 4.52 | 1044.51 | 7.83 | 1933.97 | 9.70 | 2921.74 | 9.74 | 3822.15 | 7.96 | 4466.99 | 4.71 |
| .48 | 423.89 | 4.56 | 1052.34 | 7.85 | 1943.67 | 9.71 | 2931.48 | 9.74 | 3830.11 | 7.93 | 4471.70 | 4.66 |
| .49 | 428.45 | 4.59 | 1060.19 | 7.89 | 1953.38 | 9.71 | 2941.22 | 9.73 | 3838.04 | 7.92 | 4476.36 | 4.64 |
| .50 | 433.04 | 4.63 | 1068.08 | 7.91 | 1963.09 | 9.73 | 2950.95 | 9.71 | 3845.96 | 7.88 | 4481.00 | 4.59 |

# TABLE VIII. ARGUMENT 3.

Equation $= 2457''.02 - 122''.1 \sin. t + 2371''.0 \sin. 2t + 0''.9 \sin. 3t + 14''.4 \sin. 4t.$

Period, 29.530587997 days.

| Days. | 12 | | 13 | | 14 | | 15 | | 16 | | 17 | |
|---|---|---|---|---|---|---|---|---|---|---|---|---|
| Decimals of a Day. | Equation. | Diff. | Equation. | Diff. | Equation. | Diff. | Equation. | Diff. | Equation. | Diff. | Equation. | Diff. |
| .50 | 433.04 | 4.63 | 1068.08 | 7.91 | 1963.09 | 9.73 | 2950.95 | 9.71 | 3845.96 | 7.88 | 4481.00 | 4.59 |
| .51 | 437.67 | 4.66 | 1075.99 | 7.94 | 1972.82 | 9.73 | 2960.66 | 9.71 | 3853.84 | 7.85 | 4485.59 | 4.56 |
| .52 | 442.33 | 4.71 | 1083.93 | 7.96 | 1982.55 | 9.74 | 2970.37 | 9.69 | 3861.69 | 7.83 | 4490.15 | 4.51 |
| .53 | 447.04 | 4.74 | 1091.89 | 7.98 | 1992.29 | 9.76 | 2980.06 | 9.69 | 3869.52 | 7.80 | 4494.66 | 4.47 |
| .54 | 451.78 | 4.78 | 1099.87 | 8.01 | 2002.05 | 9.76 | 2989.75 | 9.67 | 3877.33 | 7.77 | 4499.13 | 4.44 |
| .55 | 456.56 | 4.82 | 1107.88 | 8.04 | 2011.81 | 9.76 | 2999.42 | 9.67 | 3885.10 | 7.74 | 4503.57 | 4.40 |
| .56 | 461.38 | 4.85 | 1115.92 | 8.06 | 2021.57 | 9.78 | 3009.09 | 9.65 | 3892.84 | 7.72 | 4507.97 | 4.36 |
| .57 | 466.23 | 4.89 | 1123.98 | 8.09 | 2031.35 | 9.78 | 3018.74 | 9.65 | 3900.56 | 7.69 | 4512.33 | 4.32 |
| .58 | 471.12 | 4.93 | 1132.07 | 8.12 | 2041.13 | 9.80 | 3028.39 | 9.63 | 3908.25 | 7.67 | 4516.65 | 4.28 |
| .59 | 476.05 | 4.97 | 1140.19 | 8.14 | 2050.93 | 9.80 | 3038.02 | 9.62 | 3915.92 | 7.63 | 4520.93 | 4.24 |
| .60 | 481.02 | 5.01 | 1148.33 | 8.16 | 2060.73 | 9.81 | 3047.64 | 9.61 | 3923.55 | 7.61 | 4525.17 | 4.21 |
| .61 | 486.03 | 5.04 | 1156.49 | 8.19 | 2070.54 | 9.82 | 3057.25 | 9.60 | 3931.16 | 7.59 | 4529.38 | 4.17 |
| .62 | 491.07 | 5.08 | 1164.68 | 8.22 | 2080.36 | 9.82 | 3066.85 | 9.60 | 3938.75 | 7.56 | 4533.55 | 4.13 |
| .63 | 496.15 | 5.10 | 1172.90 | 8.23 | 2090.18 | 9.83 | 3076.45 | 9.58 | 3946.31 | 7.52 | 4537.68 | 4.08 |
| .64 | 501.25 | 5.17 | 1181.13 | 8.26 | 2100.01 | 9.84 | 3086.03 | 9.56 | 3953.83 | 7.50 | 4541.76 | 4.05 |
| .65 | 506.42 | 5.20 | 1189.39 | 8.29 | 2109.85 | 9.84 | 3095.59 | 9.55 | 3961.33 | 7.47 | 4545.81 | 4.01 |
| .66 | 511.62 | 5.23 | 1197.68 | 8.31 | 2119.69 | 9.85 | 3105.14 | 9.54 | 3968.80 | 7.43 | 4549.82 | 3.97 |
| .67 | 516.85 | 5.26 | 1205.99 | 8.33 | 2129.54 | 9.86 | 3114.68 | 9.53 | 3976.23 | 7.41 | 4553.79 | 3.93 |
| .68 | 522.11 | 5.30 | 1214.32 | 8.36 | 2139.40 | 9.86 | 3124.21 | 9.51 | 3983.64 | 7.38 | 4557.72 | 3.89 |
| .69 | 527.45 | 5.32 | 1222.68 | 8.39 | 2149.26 | 9.87 | 3133.72 | 9.50 | 3991.02 | 7.35 | 4561.61 | 3.85 |
| .70 | 532.77 | 5.35 | 1231.07 | 8.41 | 2159.13 | 9.87 | 3143.22 | 9.49 | 3998.37 | 7.33 | 4565.46 | 3.81 |
| .71 | 538.12 | 5.41 | 1239.48 | 8.42 | 2169.00 | 9.88 | 3152.71 | 9.47 | 4005.70 | 7.29 | 4569.27 | 3.77 |
| .72 | 543.53 | 5.44 | 1247.90 | 8.46 | 2178.88 | 9.89 | 3162.18 | 9.46 | 4012.99 | 7.26 | 4573.04 | 3.73 |
| .73 | 548.97 | 5.49 | 1256.36 | 8.47 | 2188.77 | 9.90 | 3171.64 | 9.45 | 4020.25 | 7.23 | 4576.77 | 3.69 |
| .74 | 554.46 | 5.51 | 1264.83 | 8.50 | 2198.67 | 9.90 | 3181.09 | 9.44 | 4027.48 | 7.21 | 4580.46 | 3.66 |
| .75 | 559.97 | 5.56 | 1273.33 | 8.52 | 2208.57 | 9.90 | 3190.53 | 9.43 | 4034.69 | 7.18 | 4584.12 | 3.61 |
| .76 | 565.53 | 5.59 | 1281.85 | 8.54 | 2218.47 | 9.90 | 3199.96 | 9.40 | 4041.87 | 7.14 | 4587.73 | 3.57 |
| .77 | 571.12 | 5.62 | 1290.39 | 8.56 | 2228.37 | 9.91 | 3209.36 | 9.39 | 4049.01 | 7.12 | 4591.30 | 3.54 |
| .78 | 576.74 | 5.66 | 1298.95 | 8.59 | 2238.28 | 9.91 | 3218.75 | 9.38 | 4056.13 | 7.08 | 4594.84 | 3.49 |
| .79 | 582.40 | 5.70 | 1307.54 | 8.61 | 2248.19 | 9.92 | 3228.13 | 9.36 | 4063.21 | 7.05 | 4598.33 | 3.45 |
| .80 | 588.10 | 5.73 | 1316.15 | 8.63 | 2258.11 | 9.92 | 3237.49 | 9.35 | 4070.26 | 7.02 | 4601.78 | 3.41 |
| .81 | 593.83 | 5.77 | 1324.78 | 8.65 | 2268.03 | 9.93 | 3246.84 | 9.33 | 4077.28 | 6.99 | 4605.19 | 3.37 |
| .82 | 599.60 | 5.80 | 1333.43 | 8.68 | 2277.96 | 9.93 | 3256.17 | 9.32 | 4084.27 | 6.96 | 4608.56 | 3.33 |
| .83 | 605.40 | 5.84 | 1342.11 | 8.69 | 2287.89 | 9.93 | 3265.49 | 9.30 | 4091.23 | 6.93 | 4611.89 | 3.29 |
| .84 | 611.24 | 5.87 | 1350.80 | 8.71 | 2297.82 | 9.93 | 3274.79 | 9.28 | 4098.16 | 6.90 | 4615.18 | 3.25 |
| .85 | 617.11 | 5.91 | 1359.51 | 8.74 | 2307.75 | 9.94 | 3284.07 | 9.27 | 4105.06 | 6.87 | 4618.43 | 3.20 |
| .86 | 623.02 | 5.94 | 1368.25 | 8.76 | 2317.69 | 9.95 | 3293.34 | 9.26 | 4111.93 | 6.84 | 4621.63 | 3.17 |
| .87 | 628.96 | 5.98 | 1377.01 | 8.77 | 2327.64 | 9.94 | 3302.60 | 9.24 | 4118.77 | 6.81 | 4624.80 | 3.14 |
| .88 | 634.94 | 6.01 | 1385.78 | 8.81 | 2337.58 | 9.94 | 3311.84 | 9.22 | 4125.58 | 6.77 | 4627.94 | 3.08 |
| .89 | 640.95 | 6.04 | 1394.57 | 8.82 | 2347.52 | 9.95 | 3321.06 | 9.21 | 4132.35 | 6.74 | 4631.02 | 3.05 |
| .90 | 646.99 | 6.08 | 1403.41 | 8.83 | 2357.47 | 9.95 | 3330.27 | 9.19 | 4139.09 | 6.71 | 4634.07 | 3.00 |
| .91 | 653.07 | 6.12 | 1412.24 | 8.86 | 2367.42 | 9.95 | 3339.46 | 9.17 | 4145.80 | 6.67 | 4637.07 | 2.96 |
| .92 | 659.19 | 6.14 | 1421.10 | 8.88 | 2377.37 | 9.95 | 3348.63 | 9.15 | 4152.47 | 6.65 | 4640.03 | 2.92 |
| .93 | 665.33 | 6.19 | 1429.98 | 8.90 | 2387.32 | 9.95 | 3357.78 | 9.14 | 4159.12 | 6.61 | 4642.95 | 2.88 |
| .94 | 671.52 | 6.21 | 1438.88 | 8.91 | 2397.27 | 9.96 | 3366.92 | 9.11 | 4165.73 | 6.58 | 4645.83 | 2.84 |
| .95 | 677.73 | 6.25 | 1447.79 | 8.94 | 2407.23 | 9.95 | 3376.03 | 9.10 | 4172.31 | 6.55 | 4648.67 | 2.80 |
| .96 | 683.98 | 6.28 | 1456.73 | 8.95 | 2417.18 | 9.96 | 3385.13 | 9.09 | 4178.86 | 6.51 | 4651.47 | 2.75 |
| .97 | 690.26 | 6.32 | 1465.68 | 8.98 | 2427.14 | 9.96 | 3394.22 | 9.07 | 4185.37 | 6.48 | 4654.22 | 2.72 |
| .98 | 696.58 | 6.35 | 1474.66 | 8.99 | 2437.10 | 9.96 | 3403.29 | 9.04 | 4191.85 | 6.45 | 4656.94 | 2.67 |
| .99 | 702.93 | 6.39 | 1483.65 | 9.02 | 2447.06 | 9.96 | 3412.33 | 9.03 | 4198.30 | 6.42 | 4659.61 | 2.64 |
| 1.00 | 709.32 | 6.41 | 1492.67 | 9.03 | 2457.02 | 9.96 | 3421.36 | 9.02 | 4204.72 | 6.39 | 4662.25 | 2.59 |

# TABLE VIII. ARGUMENT 3.

Equation $= 2457''.02 - 122''.1 \sin. t + 2371''.0 \sin. 2t + 0''.9 \sin. 3t + 14''.4 \sin. 4t.$

Period, 29.530587997 days.

| Days. | 18 | | 19 | | 20 | | 21 | | 22 | | 23 | |
|---|---|---|---|---|---|---|---|---|---|---|---|---|
| Decimals of a Day. | Equation. | Diff. | Equation. | Diff. | Equation. | Diff. | Equation. | Diff. | Equation. | Diff. | Equation. | Diff. |
| .00 | 4662.25 | 2.59 | 4712.54 | 1.64 | 4350.06 | 5.53 | 3642.21 | 8.43 | 2714.21 | 9.86 | 1726.64 | 9.60 |
| .01 | 4664.84 | 2.53 | 4710.90 | 1.68 | 4344.53 | 5.58 | 3633.78 | 8.46 | 2704.35 | 9.87 | 1717.04 | 9.58 |
| .02 | 4667.39 | 2.51 | 4709.22 | 1.72 | 4338.95 | 5.60 | 3625.32 | 8.48 | 2694.48 | 9.88 | 1707.46 | 9.57 |
| .03 | 4669.90 | 2.47 | 4707.50 | 1.76 | 4333.35 | 5.65 | 3616.84 | 8.51 | 2684.60 | 9.88 | 1697.89 | 9.56 |
| .04 | 4672.37 | 2.42 | 4705.74 | 1.81 | 4327.70 | 5.67 | 3608.33 | 8.52 | 2674.72 | 9.89 | 1688.33 | 9.55 |
| .05 | 4674.79 | 2.39 | 4703.93 | 1.85 | 4322.03 | 5.71 | 3599.81 | 8.55 | 2664.83 | 9.89 | 1678.78 | 9.54 |
| .06 | 4677.18 | 2.34 | 4702.08 | 1.88 | 4316.32 | 5.75 | 3591.26 | 8.57 | 2654.94 | 9.90 | 1669.24 | 9.53 |
| .07 | 4679.52 | 2.30 | 4700.20 | 1.93 | 4310.57 | 5.77 | 3582.69 | 8.58 | 2645.04 | 9.91 | 1659.71 | 9.51 |
| .08 | 4681.82 | 2.26 | 4698.27 | 1.98 | 4304.80 | 5.82 | 3574.11 | 8.61 | 2635.14 | 9.91 | 1650.20 | 9.50 |
| .09 | 4684.08 | 2.21 | 4696.29 | 2.01 | 4298.98 | 5.85 | 3565.50 | 8.63 | 2625.23 | 9.91 | 1640.70 | 9.48 |
| .10 | 4686.29 | 2.18 | 4694.28 | 2.05 | 4293.13 | 5.88 | 3556.87 | 8.66 | 2615.32 | 9.92 | 1631.22 | 9.48 |
| .11 | 4688.47 | 2.13 | 4692.23 | 2.10 | 4287.25 | 5.91 | 3548.21 | 8.67 | 2605.40 | 9.92 | 1621.74 | 9.46 |
| .12 | 4690.60 | 2.10 | 4690.13 | 2.14 | 4281.34 | 5.95 | 3539.54 | 8.69 | 2595.48 | 9.92 | 1612.28 | 9.45 |
| .13 | 4692.70 | 2.05 | 4687.99 | 2.17 | 4275.39 | 5.99 | 3530.85 | 8.72 | 2585.56 | 9.93 | 1602.83 | 9.43 |
| .14 | 4694.75 | 2.01 | 4685.82 | 2.22 | 4269.40 | 6.01 | 3522.13 | 8.73 | 2575.63 | 9.93 | 1593.40 | 9.42 |
| .15 | 4696.76 | 1.97 | 4683.60 | 2.25 | 4263.39 | 6.05 | 3513.40 | 8.75 | 2565.70 | 9.93 | 1583.98 | 9.41 |
| .16 | 4698.73 | 1.93 | 4681.35 | 2.31 | 4257.34 | 6.08 | 3504.65 | 8.78 | 2555.77 | 9.94 | 1574.57 | 9.39 |
| .17 | 4700.66 | 1.88 | 4679.04 | 2.34 | 4251.26 | 6.12 | 3495.87 | 8.79 | 2545.83 | 9.95 | 1565.18 | 9.38 |
| .18 | 4702.54 | 1.84 | 4676.70 | 2.38 | 4245.14 | 6.15 | 3487.08 | 8.81 | 2535.88 | 9.94 | 1555.80 | 9.37 |
| .19 | 4704.38 | 1.80 | 4674.32 | 2.43 | 4238.99 | 6.18 | 3478.27 | 8.83 | 2525.94 | 9.94 | 1546.43 | 9.35 |
| .20 | 4706.18 | 1.75 | 4671.89 | 2.47 | 4232.81 | 6.22 | 3469.44 | 8.86 | 2516.00 | 9.96 | 1537.08 | 9.33 |
| .21 | 4707.93 | 1.72 | 4669.42 | 2.50 | 4226.59 | 6.24 | 3460.58 | 8.87 | 2506.04 | 9.95 | 1527.75 | 9.33 |
| .22 | 4709.65 | 1.67 | 4666.92 | 2.55 | 4220.35 | 6.28 | 3451.71 | 8.89 | 2496.09 | 9.95 | 1518.42 | 9.30 |
| .23 | 4711.32 | 1.63 | 4664.37 | 2.59 | 4214.07 | 6.32 | 3442.82 | 8.90 | 2486.14 | 9.96 | 1509.12 | 9.29 |
| .24 | 4712.95 | 1.59 | 4661.78 | 2.63 | 4207.75 | 6.33 | 3433.92 | 8.93 | 2476.18 | 9.96 | 1499.83 | 9.28 |
| .25 | 4714.54 | 1.54 | 4659.15 | 2.67 | 4201.42 | 6.38 | 3424.99 | 8.95 | 2466.22 | 9.96 | 1490.55 | 9.26 |
| .26 | 4716.08 | 1.50 | 4656.48 | 2.72 | 4195.04 | 6.41 | 3416.04 | 8.96 | 2456.26 | 9.96 | 1481.29 | 9.25 |
| .27 | 4717.58 | 1.46 | 4653.76 | 2.75 | 4188.63 | 6.44 | 3407.08 | 8.98 | 2446.30 | 9.96 | 1472.04 | 9.23 |
| .28 | 4719.04 | 1.42 | 4651.01 | 2.79 | 4182.19 | 6.48 | 3398.10 | 9.00 | 2436.34 | 9.97 | 1462.81 | 9.21 |
| .29 | 4720.46 | 1.38 | 4648.22 | 2.84 | 4175.71 | 6.50 | 3389.10 | 9.02 | 2426.37 | 9.96 | 1453.60 | 9.20 |
| .30 | 4721.84 | 1.33 | 4645.38 | 2.87 | 4169.21 | 6.54 | 3380.08 | 9.03 | 2416.41 | 9.97 | 1444.40 | 9.18 |
| .31 | 4723.17 | 1.29 | 4642.51 | 2.92 | 4162.67 | 6.57 | 3371.05 | 9.06 | 2406.44 | 9.97 | 1435.22 | 9.16 |
| .32 | 4724.46 | 1.26 | 4639.59 | 2.95 | 4156.10 | 6.60 | 3361.99 | 9.07 | 2396.47 | 9.97 | 1426.06 | 9.15 |
| .33 | 4725.72 | 1.21 | 4636.64 | 2.99 | 4149.50 | 6.63 | 3352.92 | 9.09 | 2386.50 | 9.96 | 1416.91 | 9.13 |
| .34 | 4726.93 | 1.16 | 4633.65 | 3.02 | 4142.87 | 6.66 | 3343.83 | 9.10 | 2376.54 | 9.97 | 1407.78 | 9.12 |
| .35 | 4728.09 | 1.12 | 4630.63 | 3.10 | 4136.21 | 6.70 | 3334.73 | 9.12 | 2366.57 | 9.97 | 1398.66 | 9.10 |
| .36 | 4729.21 | 1.08 | 4627.53 | 3.12 | 4129.51 | 6.72 | 3325.61 | 9.14 | 2356.60 | 9.97 | 1389.56 | 9.08 |
| .37 | 4730.29 | 1.04 | 4624.41 | 3.16 | 4122.79 | 6.76 | 3316.47 | 9.16 | 2346.63 | 9.97 | 1380.48 | 9.06 |
| .38 | 4731.33 | 0.99 | 4621.25 | 3.19 | 4116.03 | 6.79 | 3307.31 | 9.17 | 2336.66 | 9.96 | 1371.42 | 9.05 |
| .39 | 4732.32 | 0.95 | 4618.06 | 3.24 | 4109.24 | 6.81 | 3298.14 | 9.18 | 2326.70 | 9.97 | 1362.37 | 9.03 |
| .40 | 4733.27 | 0.91 | 4614.82 | 3.28 | 4102.43 | 6.85 | 3288.96 | 9.21 | 2316.73 | 9.97 | 1353.34 | 9.01 |
| .41 | 4734.18 | 0.87 | 4611.54 | 3.32 | 4095.58 | 6.88 | 3279.75 | 9.22 | 2306.76 | 9.96 | 1344.33 | 8.99 |
| .42 | 4735.05 | 0.82 | 4608.22 | 3.35 | 4088.70 | 6.91 | 3270.53 | 9.23 | 2296.80 | 9.96 | 1335.34 | 8.98 |
| .43 | 4735.87 | 0.78 | 4604.87 | 3.40 | 4081.79 | 6.94 | 3261.30 | 9.25 | 2286.84 | 9.96 | 1326.36 | 8.95 |
| .44 | 4736.65 | 0.74 | 4601.47 | 3.44 | 4074.85 | 6.97 | 3252.05 | 9.27 | 2276.88 | 9.96 | 1317.41 | 8.94 |
| .45 | 4737.39 | 0.70 | 4598.03 | 3.47 | 4067.88 | 7.00 | 3242.78 | 9.28 | 2266.92 | 9.96 | 1308.47 | 8.92 |
| .46 | 4738.09 | 0.65 | 4594.56 | 3.52 | 4060.88 | 7.03 | 3233.50 | 9.30 | 2256.96 | 9.96 | 1299.55 | 8.90 |
| .47 | 4738.74 | 0.61 | 4591.04 | 3.56 | 4053.85 | 7.06 | 3224.20 | 9.31 | 2247.00 | 9.95 | 1290.65 | 8.88 |
| .48 | 4739.35 | 0.57 | 4587.48 | 3.59 | 4046.79 | 7.08 | 3214.89 | 9.32 | 2237.05 | 9.95 | 1281.77 | 8.87 |
| .49 | 4739.92 | 0.54 | 4583.89 | 3.63 | 4039.71 | 7.11 | 3205.57 | 9.34 | 2227.10 | 9.95 | 1272.90 | 8.85 |
| .50 | 4740.46 | 0.47 | 4580.26 | 3.67 | 4032.60 | 7.15 | 3196.23 | 9.35 | 2217.15 | 9.95 | 1264.05 | 8.82 |

# TABLE VIII. ARGUMENT 3.

Equation = 2457″.02 — 122″.1 sin. $t$ + 2371″.0 sin. $2t$ + 0″.9 sin. $3t$ + 14″.4 sin. $4t$.

Period, 29.530587997 days.

| Days. | 18 | | 19 | | 20 | | 21 | | 22 | | 23 | |
|---|---|---|---|---|---|---|---|---|---|---|---|---|
| Decimals of a Day. | Equation. | Diff. | Equation. | Diff. | Equation. | Diff. | Equation. | Diff. | Equation. | Diff. | Equation. | Diff. |
| .50 | 4740″.46 | 0.47 | 4580″.26 | 3.67 | 4032″.60 | 7.15 | 3196″.23 | 9.35 | 2217″.15 | 9.95 | 1264″.05 | 8.82 |
| .51 | 4740 93 | 0.45 | 4576.59 | 3.71 | 4025.45 | 7.17 | 3186.88 | 9.37 | 2207.20 | 9.94 | 1255.23 | 8.81 |
| .52 | 4741.38 | 0.40 | 4572.88 | 3.75 | 4018.28 | 7.21 | 3177.51 | 9.39 | 2197.26 | 9.94 | 1246.42 | 8.79 |
| .53 | 4741.78 | 0.35 | 4569.13 | 3.80 | 4011.07 | 7.23 | 3168.12 | 9.40 | 2187.32 | 9.94 | 1237.63 | 8.77 |
| .54 | 4742.13 | 0.32 | 4565.33 | 3.83 | 4003.84 | 7.26 | 3158.72 | 9.41 | 2177.38 | 9.93 | 1228.86 | 8.75 |
| .55 | 4742.45 | 0.27 | 4561.50 | 3.86 | 3996.58 | 7.29 | 3149.31 | 9.42 | 2167.45 | 9.93 | 1220.11 | 8.72 |
| .56 | 4742.72 | 0.21 | 4557.64 | 3.91 | 3989.29 | 7.32 | 3139.89 | 9.43 | 2157.52 | 9.93 | 1211.39 | 8.70 |
| .57 | 4742.93 | 0.20 | 4553.73 | 3.95 | 3981.97 | 7.35 | 3130.46 | 9.46 | 2147.59 | 9.93 | 1202.69 | 8.68 |
| .58 | 4743.13 | 0.14 | 4549.78 | 3.98 | 3974.62 | 7.38 | 3121.00 | 9.47 | 2137.66 | 9.91 | 1194.01 | 8.66 |
| .59 | 4743.27 | 0.10 | 4545.80 | 4.03 | 3967.24 | 7.40 | 3111.53 | 9.48 | 2127.75 | 9.92 | 1185.35 | 8.65 |
| .60 | 4743.37 | 0.05 | 4541.77 | 4.06 | 3959.84 | 7.43 | 3102.05 | 9.49 | 2117.83 | 9.91 | 1176.70 | 8.62 |
| .61 | 4743.42 | 0.02 | 4537.71 | 4.10 | 3952.41 | 7.46 | 3092.56 | 9.50 | 2107.92 | 9.91 | 1168.08 | 8.60 |
| .62 | 4743.44 | 0.03 | 4533.61 | 4.14 | 3944.95 | 7.49 | 3083.06 | 9.52 | 2098.01 | 9.90 | 1159.48 | 8.58 |
| .63 | 4743.41 | 0.07 | 4529.47 | 4.18 | 3937.46 | 7.52 | 3073.54 | 9.52 | 2088.11 | 9.90 | 1150.90 | 8.56 |
| .64 | 4743.34 | 0.12 | 4525.29 | 4.22 | 3929.94 | 7.54 | 3064.02 | 9.54 | 2078.21 | 9.89 | 1142.34 | 8.53 |
| .65 | 4743.22 | 0.14 | 4521.07 | 4.26 | 3922.40 | 7.57 | 3054.48 | 9.56 | 2068.32 | 9.89 | 1133.81 | 8 52 |
| .66 | 4743.08 | 0.20 | 4516.81 | 4.29 | 3914.83 | 7.60 | 3044.92 | 9.56 | 2058.43 | 9.88 | 1125.29 | 8.49 |
| .67 | 4742.88 | 0.24 | 4512.52 | 4.33 | 3907.23 | 7.62 | 3035.36 | 9.58 | 2048.55 | 9.87 | 1116.80 | 8 47 |
| .68 | 4742.64 | 0.29 | 4508.19 | 4.37 | 3899.61 | 7.65 | 3025.78 | 9.59 | 2038.68 | 9.87 | 1108.33 | 8.45 |
| .69 | 4742.35 | 0.32 | 4503.82 | 4.40 | 3891.96 | 7.68 | 3016.19 | 9.59 | 2028.81 | 9.86 | 1099.88 | 8.43 |
| .70 | 4742.03 | 0.37 | 4499.42 | 4.45 | 3884.28 | 7.70 | 3006.60 | 9.61 | 2018.95 | 9.86 | 1091.45 | 8.40 |
| .71 | 4741.66 | 0.42 | 4494.97 | 4.48 | 3876.58 | 7.73 | 2996.99 | 9.62 | 2009.09 | 9.85 | 1083.05 | 8.39 |
| .72 | 4741.24 | 0.45 | 4490.49 | 4.52 | 3868.85 | 7.76 | 2987.37 | 9.64 | 1999.24 | 9.85 | 1074.66 | 8.35 |
| .73 | 4740.79 | 0.50 | 4485.97 | 4.55 | 3861.09 | 7.78 | 2977.73 | 9.64 | 1989.39 | 9.84 | 1066.31 | 8.34 |
| .74 | 4740.29 | 0.54 | 4481.42 | 4.59 | 3853.31 | 7.81 | 2968.09 | 9.65 | 1979.55 | 9.83 | 1057.97 | 8.31 |
| .75 | 4739.75 | 0.58 | 4476.83 | 4.63 | 3845.50 | 7.84 | 2958.44 | 9.66 | 1969.72 | 9.82 | 1049.66 | 8.29 |
| .76 | 4739.17 | 0.62 | 4472.20 | 4.67 | 3837.66 | 7.86 | 2948.78 | 9.68 | 1959.90 | 9.82 | 1041.37 | 8.27 |
| .77 | 4738.55 | 0.67 | 4467.53 | 4.71 | 3829.80 | 7.89 | 2939.10 | 9.68 | 1950.08 | 9.81 | 1033.10 | 8.24 |
| .78 | 4737.88 | 0.71 | 4462.82 | 4.74 | 3821.91 | 7.91 | 2929.42 | 9.70 | 1940.27 | 9.81 | 1024 86 | 8.22 |
| .79 | 4737.17 | 0.75 | 4458.08 | 4.78 | 3814.00 | 7.94 | 2919.72 | 9.70 | 1930.46 | 9.79 | 1016.64 | 8.20 |
| .80 | 4736.42 | 0.79 | 4453.30 | 4.82 | 3806.06 | 7.96 | 2910.02 | 9.71 | 1920.67 | 9.79 | 1008.44 | 8.17 |
| .81 | 4735.63 | 0.84 | 4448.48 | 4.86 | 3798.10 | 7.99 | 2900.31 | 9.72 | 1910.88 | 9.78 | 1000.27 | 8.15 |
| .82 | 4734.79 | 0.85 | 4443.62 | 4.89 | 3790.11 | 8.01 | 2890.59 | 9.73 | 1901.10 | 9.77 | 992.12 | 8.12 |
| .83 | 4733.94 | 0.94 | 4438.73 | 4.92 | 3782.10 | 8.04 | 2880.86 | 9.74 | 1891.33 | 9.76 | 984.00 | 8.10 |
| .84 | 4733.00 | 0.96 | 4433.81 | 4.97 | 3774.06 | 8.06 | 2871.12 | 9.75 | 1881.57 | 9.75 | 975.90 | 8.07 |
| .85 | 4732.04 | 1.00 | 4428.84 | 5.00 | 3766.00 | 8.09 | 2861.37 | 9.76 | 1871.82 | 9.75 | 967.83 | 8.05 |
| .86 | 4731.04 | 1.05 | 4423.84 | 5.04 | 3757.91 | 8.11 | 2851.61 | 9.76 | 1862.07 | 9.74 | 959.78 | 8.03 |
| .87 | 4729.99 | 1.09 | 4418.80 | 5.07 | 3749.80 | 8.14 | 2841.85 | 9.78 | 1852.33 | 9.72 | 951.75 | 8.00 |
| .88 | 4728.90 | 1.13 | 4413.73 | 5.11 | 3741.66 | 8.15 | 2832.07 | 9.78 | 1842.61 | 9.72 | 943.75 | 7.97 |
| .89 | 4727.77 | 1.18 | 4408.62 | 5.14 | 3733.51 | 8.19 | 2822.29 | 9.79 | 1832.89 | 9.71 | 935.78 | 7.95 |
| .90 | 4726.59 | 1.22 | 4403.48 | 5.19 | 3725.32 | 8 20 | 2812.50 | 9.80 | 1823.18 | 9.70 | 927.83 | 7.93 |
| .91 | 4725.37 | 1.25 | 4398.29 | 5.21 | 3717.12 | 8.24 | 2802.70 | 9.80 | 1813.48 | 9.69 | 919.90 | 7.90 |
| .92 | 4724.12 | 1.31 | 4393.08 | 5.26 | 3708.88 | 8.25 | 2792.90 | 9.82 | 1803.79 | 9.68 | 912.00 | 7.87 |
| .93 | 4722.81 | 1.34 | 4387.82 | 5.29 | 3700.63 | 8.28 | 2783.08 | 9.82 | 1794.11 | 9.67 | 904.13 | 7.85 |
| .94 | 4721.47 | 1.39 | 4382.53 | 5.32 | 3692.35 | 8.30 | 2773.26 | 9.82 | 1784.44 | 9.66 | 896.28 | 7.82 |
| .95 | 4720.08 | 1.42 | 4377.21 | 5.36 | 3684.05 | 8.32 | 2763.44 | 9.84 | 1774 78 | 9.65 | 888.46 | 7.79 |
| .96 | 4718.66 | 1.47 | 4371.85 | 5.40 | 3675.73 | 8.35 | 2753.60 | 9.84 | 1765.13 | 9.64 | 880.67 | 7.77 |
| .97 | 4717.19 | 1.52 | 4366.45 | 5.43 | 3667.38 | 8.37 | 2743.76 | 9.84 | 1755.49 | 9.63 | 872.90 | 7.74 |
| .98 | 4715.67 | 1.55 | 4361.02 | 5.47 | 3659.01 | 8.39 | 2733.92 | 9.86 | 1745.86 | 9.61 | 865.16 | 7.72 |
| .99 | 4714.12 | 1.58 | 4355.55 | 5.49 | 3650.62 | 8.41 | 2724.06 | 9.85 | 1736.25 | 9.61 | 857.44 | 7.70 |
| 1.00 | 4712.54 | 1.64 | 4350.06 | 5.53 | 3642.21 | 8.43 | 2714.21 | 9.86 | 1726.64 | 9.60 | 849.74 | 7.66 |

# TABLE VIII. ARGUMENT 3.

Equation $= 2457''.02 - 122''.1 \sin. t + 2371''.0 \sin. 2t + 0''.9 \sin. 3t + 14''.4 \sin. 4t.$

Period, 29.530587997 days.

| Days. | 24 | | 25 | | 26 | | 27 | | 28 | | 29 | |
|---|---|---|---|---|---|---|---|---|---|---|---|---|
| Decimals of a Day. | Equation. | Diff. | Equation. | Diff. | Equation. | Diff. | Equation. | Diff. | Equation. | Diff. | Equation. | Diff. |
| .00 | 849″.74 | 7.66 | 237″.19 | 4.36 | 1″.02 | .23 | 190″.64 | 4.02 | 780″.43 | 7.64 | 1670″.35 | 9.91 |
| .01 | 842.08 | 7.64 | 232.83 | 4.33 | 0.79 | .19 | 194.66 | 4.07 | 788.07 | 7.66 | 1680.26 | 9.93 |
| .02 | 834.44 | 7.61 | 228.50 | 4.29 | 0.60 | .15 | 198.73 | 4.10 | 795.73 | 7.70 | 1690.19 | 9.95 |
| .03 | 826.83 | 7.58 | 224.21 | 4.24 | 0.45 | .10 | 202.83 | 4.15 | 803.43 | 7.73 | 1700.14 | 9.95 |
| .04 | 819.25 | 7.55 | 219.97 | 4.21 | 0.35 | .06 | 206.98 | 4.19 | 811.16 | 7.76 | 1710.09 | 9.98 |
| .05 | 811.70 | 7.53 | 215.76 | 4.18 | 0.29 | .00 | 211.17 | 4.23 | 818.92 | 7.78 | 1720.07 | 9.98 |
| .06 | 804.17 | 7.50 | 211.58 | 4.13 | 0.29 | .01 | 215.40 | 4.26 | 826.70 | 7.82 | 1730.05 | 10.00 |
| .07 | 796.67 | 7.47 | 207.45 | 4.10 | 0.30 | .07 | 219.66 | 4.31 | 834.52 | 7.85 | 1740.05 | 10.01 |
| .08 | 789.20 | 7.44 | 203.35 | 4.05 | 0.37 | .12 | 223.97 | 4.35 | 842.37 | 7.88 | 1750.06 | 10.03 |
| .09 | 781.76 | 7.42 | 199.30 | 4.02 | 0.49 | .15 | 228.32 | 4.39 | 850.25 | 7.91 | 1760.09 | 10.04 |
| .10 | 774.34 | 7.39 | 195.28 | 3.98 | 0.64 | .20 | 232.71 | 4.43 | 858.16 | 7.94 | 1770.13 | 10.05 |
| .11 | 766.95 | 7.36 | 191.30 | 3.94 | 0.84 | .25 | 237.14 | 4.46 | 866.10 | 7.97 | 1780.18 | 10.06 |
| .12 | 759.59 | 7.33 | 187.36 | 3.90 | 1.09 | .28 | 241.60 | 4.51 | 874.05 | 7.99 | 1790.24 | 10.07 |
| .13 | 752.26 | 7.30 | 183.46 | 3.86 | 1.37 | .33 | 246.11 | 4.55 | 882.04 | 8.02 | 1800.31 | 10.08 |
| .14 | 744.96 | 7.28 | 179.60 | 3.82 | 1.70 | .38 | 250.66 | 4.58 | 890.06 | 8.05 | 1810.39 | 10.10 |
| .15 | 737.68 | 7.24 | 175.78 | 3.79 | 2.08 | .41 | 255.24 | 4.63 | 898.11 | 8 08 | 1820.49 | 10.11 |
| .16 | 730.44 | 7.21 | 171.99 | 3.74 | 2.49 | .45 | 259.87 | 4.67 | 906.19 | 8.11 | 1830.60 | 10.12 |
| .17 | 723.23 | 7.19 | 168.25 | 3.71 | 2.94 | .51 | 264.54 | 4.71 | 914.30 | 8.14 | 1840.72 | 10.14 |
| .18 | 716.04 | 7.16 | 164.54 | 3.66 | 3.45 | .55 | 269.25 | 4.74 | 922.44 | 8.16 | 1850.86 | 10.14 |
| .19 | 708.88 | 7.13 | 160.88 | 3.62 | 4.00 | .59 | 273.99 | 4.79 | 930.60 | 8.19 | 1861.00 | 10.16 |
| .20 | 701.75 | 7.10 | 157.26 | 3.59 | 4.59 | .63 | 278.78 | 4.82 | 938.79 | 8.22 | 1871.16 | 10.16 |
| .21 | 694.65 | 7.06 | 153.67 | 3.54 | 5.22 | .68 | 283 60 | 4.87 | 947.01 | 8.25 | 1881.32 | 10.18 |
| .22 | 687.59 | 7.04 | 150.13 | 3 51 | 5.90 | .72 | 288.47 | 4.90 | 955.26 | 8.27 | 1891.50 | 10.19 |
| .23 | 680.55 | 7.01 | 146.62 | 3.46 | 6.62 | .76 | 293.37 | 4.94 | 963.53 | 8.30 | 1901.69 | 10.20 |
| .24 | 673.54 | 6.99 | 143.16 | 3.43 | 7.38 | .81 | 298.31 | 4.97 | 971.83 | 8.32 | 1911.89 | 10.20 |
| .25 | 666.55 | 6.95 | 139.73 | 3.38 | 8.19 | .85 | 303.28 | 5.02 | 980.15 | 8.35 | 1922.09 | 10.21 |
| .26 | 659.60 | 6.92 | 136.35 | 3.35 | 9.04 | .89 | 308.30 | 5.05 | 988.50 | 8.38 | 1932.30 | 10.22 |
| .27 | 652.68 | 6.89 | 133.00 | 3.30 | 9.93 | .94 | 313.35 | 5.10 | 996.88 | 8.41 | 1942.52 | 10.24 |
| .28 | 645.79 | 6.86 | 129.70 | 3.27 | 10.87 | .98 | 318.45 | 5.13 | 1005.29 | 8.44 | 1952.76 | 10.25 |
| .29 | 638.93 | 6.82 | 126.43 | 3.22 | 11.85 | 1.02 | 323.58 | 5.17 | 1013.73 | 8.46 | 1963.01 | 10.25 |
| .30 | 632.11 | 6.80 | 123.21 | 3.18 | 12.87 | 1.07 | 328.75 | 5.21 | 1022.19 | 8.48 | 1973.26 | 10.27 |
| .31 | 625.31 | 6.77 | 120.03 | 3.14 | 13.94 | 1.11 | 333.96 | 5.25 | 1030.67 | 8.52 | 1983.53 | 10.27 |
| .32 | 618.54 | 6.73 | 116.89 | 3.11 | 15.05 | 1.14 | 339.21 | 5.29 | 1039.19 | 8.54 | 1993.80 | 10.28 |
| .33 | 611.81 | 6.71 | 113.78 | 3.06 | 16.19 | 1.20 | 344.50 | 5.33 | 1047.73 | 8.56 | 2004.08 | 10.29 |
| .34 | 605.10 | 6.67 | 110.72 | 3.03 | 17.39 | 1.24 | 349.83 | 5.36 | 1056.29 | 8.59 | 2014.37 | 10.30 |
| .35 | 598.43 | 6.64 | 107.69 | 2.97 | 18.63 | 1.28 | 355.19 | 5.40 | 1064.88 | 8.62 | 2024.67 | 10.30 |
| .36 | 591.79 | 6.61 | 104.72 | 2.94 | 19.91 | 1.33 | 360.59 | 5.43 | 1073.50 | 8.64 | 2034.97 | 10.32 |
| .37 | 585.18 | 6.58 | 101.78 | 2.90 | 21.24 | 1.36 | 366.02 | 5.48 | 1082.14 | 8.66 | 2045.28 | 10.32 |
| .38 | 578.60 | 6.54 | 98.88 | 2.86 | 22.60 | 1.42 | 371.50 | 5.52 | 1090.80 | 8.69 | 2055.60 | 10.33 |
| .39 | 572.06 | 6.52 | 96.02 | 2.81 | 24.02 | 1.45 | 377.02 | 5.55 | 1099.49 | 8.72 | 2065.93 | 10.33 |
| .40 | 565.54 | 6.48 | 93.21 | 2.78 | 25.47 | 1.50 | 382.57 | 5.59 | 1108.21 | 8.74 | 2076.26 | 10.34 |
| .41 | 559.06 | 6.45 | 90.43 | 2.73 | 26.97 | 1.54 | 388.16 | 5.63 | 1116.95 | 8.76 | 2086.60 | 10.35 |
| .42 | 552.61 | 6.42 | 87.70 | 2.70 | 28.51 | 1.59 | 393.79 | 5.66 | 1125.71 | 8.79 | 2096.95 | 10.36 |
| .43 | 546.19 | 6.38 | 85.00 | 2.65 | 30.10 | 1.62 | 399.45 | 5.70 | 1134.50 | 8.82 | 2107.31 | 10.36 |
| .44 | 539.81 | 6.36 | 82.35 | 2.61 | 31.72 | 1.68 | 405.15 | 5.74 | 1143.32 | 8.83 | 2117.67 | 10.37 |
| .45 | 533.45 | 6.32 | 79.74 | 2.57 | 33.40 | 1.71 | 410.89 | 5.78 | 1152.15 | 8.87 | 2128.04 | 10.37 |
| .46 | 527.13 | 6.29 | 77.17 | 2.53 | 35.11 | 1.76 | 416.67 | 5.81 | 1161.02 | 8.88 | 2138.41 | 10.38 |
| .47 | 520.84 | 6.25 | 74.64 | 2.48 | 36.87 | 1.80 | 422.48 | 5.85 | 1169.90 | 8.91 | 2148.79 | 10.39 |
| .48 | 514.59 | 6.22 | 72.16 | 2.45 | 38.67 | 1.84 | 428.33 | 5.89 | 1178.81 | 8.93 | 2159.18 | 10.39 |
| .49 | 508.37 | 6.20 | 69.71 | 2.41 | 40.51 | 1.88 | 434.22 | 5.91 | 1187.74 | 8.95 | 2169.57 | 10.39 |
| .50 | 502.17 | 6.16 | 67.30 | 2.36 | 42.39 | 1.93 | 440.13 | 5.96 | 1196.69 | 8.98 | 2179.96 | 10.40 |

# TABLE VIII. ARGUMENT 3.

Equation $= 2457''.02 - 122''.1 \sin. t + 2371''.0 \sin. 2t + 0''.9 \sin. 3t + 14''.4 \sin. 4t.$

Period, 29.530587997 days.

| Days. | 24 | | 25 | | 26 | | 27 | | 28 | | 29 | |
|---|---|---|---|---|---|---|---|---|---|---|---|---|
| Decimals of a Day. | Equation. | Diff. | Equation. | Diff. | Equation. | Diff. | Equation. | Diff. | Equation. | Diff. | Equation. | Diff. |
| .50 | 502.17″ | 6.16 | 67.30″ | 2.36 | 42.39″ | 1.93 | 440.13″ | 5.96 | 1196.69″ | 8.98 | 2179.96″ | 10.40 |
| .51 | 496.01 | 6.12 | 64.94 | 2.32 | 44.32 | 1.97 | 446.09 | 5.99 | 1205.67 | 9.00 | 2190.36 | 10.41 |
| .52 | 489.89 | 6.09 | 62.62 | 2.28 | 46.29 | 2.01 | 452.08 | 6.03 | 1214.67 | 9.03 | 2200.77 | 10.41 |
| .53 | 483.80 | 6.06 | 60.34 | 2.24 | 48.30 | 2.06 | 458.11 | 6.07 | 1223.70 | 9.04 | 2211.18 | 10.41 |
| .54 | 477.74 | 6.02 | 58.10 | 2.19 | 50.36 | 2.10 | 464.18 | 6.11 | 1232.74 | 9.07 | 2221.59 | 10.42 |
| .55 | 471.72 | 5.99 | 55.91 | 2.16 | 52.46 | 2.14 | 470.29 | 6.14 | 1241.81 | 9.09 | 2232.01 | 10.43 |
| .56 | 465.73 | 5.95 | 53.75 | 2.11 | 54.60 | 2.19 | 476.43 | 6.17 | 1250.90 | 9.12 | 2242.44 | 10.43 |
| .57 | 459.78 | 5.92 | 51.64 | 2.07 | 56.79 | 2.23 | 482.60 | 6.21 | 1260.02 | 9.13 | 2252.87 | 10.43 |
| .58 | 453.86 | 5.89 | 49.57 | 2.02 | 59.02 | 2.27 | 488.81 | 6.25 | 1269.15 | 9.16 | 2263.30 | 10.44 |
| .59 | 447.97 | 5.85 | 47.55 | 1.99 | 61.29 | 2.32 | 495.06 | 6.28 | 1278.31 | 9.18 | 2273.74 | 10.43 |
| .60 | 442.12 | 5.82 | 45.56 | 1.94 | 63.61 | 2.35 | 501.34 | 6.31 | 1287.49 | 9.20 | 2284.17 | 10.44 |
| .61 | 436.30 | 5.79 | 43.62 | 1.90 | 65.96 | 2.39 | 507.65 | 6.36 | 1296.69 | 9.21 | 2294.61 | 10.44 |
| .62 | 430.51 | 5.75 | 41.72 | 1.86 | 68.35 | 2.44 | 514.01 | 6.39 | 1305.90 | 9.24 | 2305.05 | 10.45 |
| .63 | 424.76 | 5.71 | 39.86 | 1.82 | 70.79 | 2.49 | 520.40 | 6.42 | 1315.14 | 9.27 | 2315.50 | 10.45 |
| .64 | 419.05 | 5.68 | 38.04 | 1.77 | 73.28 | 2.52 | 526.82 | 6.47 | 1324.41 | 9.28 | 2325.95 | 10.45 |
| .65 | 413.37 | 5.65 | 36.27 | 1.73 | 75.80 | 2.57 | 533.29 | 6.48 | 1333.69 | 9.31 | 2336.40 | 10.46 |
| .66 | 407.72 | 5.61 | 34.54 | 1.69 | 78.37 | 2.61 | 539.77 | 6.53 | 1343.00 | 9.32 | 2346.86 | 10.45 |
| .67 | 402.11 | 5.57 | 32.85 | 1.65 | 80.98 | 2.66 | 546.30 | 6.56 | 1352.32 | 9.35 | 2357.31 | 10.46 |
| .68 | 396.54 | 5.54 | 31.20 | 1.60 | 83.64 | 2.69 | 552.86 | 6.60 | 1361.67 | 9.36 | 2367.77 | 10.46 |
| .69 | 391.00 | 5.51 | 29.60 | 1.57 | 86.33 | 2.74 | 559.46 | 6.63 | 1371.03 | 9.39 | 2378.23 | 10.46 |
| .70 | 385.49 | 5.47 | 28.03 | 1.52 | 89.07 | 2.79 | 566.09 | 6.67 | 1380.42 | 9.40 | 2388.69 | 10.46 |
| .71 | 380.02 | 5.43 | 26.51 | 1.47 | 91.86 | 2.82 | 572.76 | 6.70 | 1389.82 | 9.43 | 2399.15 | 10.46 |
| .72 | 374.59 | 5.40 | 25.04 | 1.44 | 94.68 | 2.86 | 579.46 | 6.73 | 1399.25 | 9.44 | 2409.61 | 10.47 |
| .73 | 369.19 | 5.36 | 23.60 | 1.39 | 97.54 | 2.91 | 586.19 | 6.77 | 1408.69 | 9.47 | 2420.08 | 10.47 |
| .74 | 363.83 | 5.34 | 22.21 | 1.36 | 100.45 | 2.94 | 592.96 | 6.80 | 1418.16 | 9.48 | 2430.55 | 10.46 |
| .75 | 358 49 | 5.29 | 20.85 | 1.31 | 103.39 | 2.99 | 599.76 | 6.84 | 1427.64 | 9.49 | 2411.01 | 10.47 |
| .76 | 353.20 | 5.26 | 19.54 | 1.26 | 106.38 | 3.04 | 606.60 | 6.87 | 1437.13 | 9.52 | 2451.48 | 10.47 |
| .77 | 347.94 | 5.22 | 18.28 | 1.22 | 109.42 | 3.07 | 613.47 | 6.90 | 1446.65 | 9.54 | 2461.95 | 10.46 |
| .78 | 342.72 | 5.18 | 17.06 | 1.18 | 112.49 | 3.12 | 620.37 | 6.94 | 1456.19 | 9.56 | 2472.41 | 10.47 |
| .79 | 337.54 | 5.15 | 15.88 | 1.14 | 115.61 | 3.16 | 627.31 | 6.97 | 1465.75 | 9.57 | 2482.88 | 10.46 |
| .80 | 332.39 | 5.11 | 14.74 | 1.09 | 118.77 | 3.20 | 634.28 | 7.00 | 1475.32 | 9.59 | 2493.33 | 10.47 |
| .81 | 327.28 | 5.07 | 13.65 | 1.05 | 121.97 | 3.24 | 641.28 | 7.04 | 1484.91 | 9.61 | 2503.80 | 10.46 |
| .82 | 322.21 | 5.04 | 12.60 | 1.01 | 125.21 | 3.29 | 648.32 | 7.06 | 1494.52 | 9.63 | 2514.26 | 10.47 |
| .83 | 317.17 | 5.00 | 11.59 | .97 | 128.50 | 3.32 | 655.38 | 7.10 | 1504.15 | 9.65 | 2524.73 | 10.46 |
| .84 | 312.17 | 4.97 | 10.62 | .92 | 131.82 | 3.37 | 662.48 | 7.13 | 1513.80 | 9.66 | 2535.19 | 10.46 |
| .85 | 307.20 | 4.93 | 9.70 | .88 | 135.19 | 3.41 | 669.61 | 7.17 | 1523.46 | 9.68 | 2545.65 | 10.46 |
| .86 | 302.27 | 4.89 | 8.82 | .83 | 138.60 | 3.44 | 676.78 | 7.19 | 1533.14 | 9.69 | 2556.11 | 10.46 |
| .87 | 297.38 | 4.85 | 7.99 | .80 | 142.04 | 3.49 | 683.97 | 7.23 | 1542.83 | 9.71 | 2566.57 | 10.45 |
| .88 | 292.53 | 4.82 | 7.19 | .75 | 145.53 | 3.54 | 691.20 | 7.27 | 1552.54 | 9.74 | 2577.02 | 10.46 |
| .89 | 287.71 | 4.78 | 6.44 | .71 | 149.07 | 3.57 | 698.47 | 7.29 | 1562.28 | 9.74 | 2587.48 | 10.45 |
| .90 | 282.93 | 4.74 | 5.73 | .66 | 152.64 | 3.62 | 705.76 | 7.33 | 1572.02 | 9.77 | 2597.93 | 10.44 |
| .91 | 278.19 | 4.70 | 5.07 | .62 | 156.26 | 3.65 | 713.09 | 7.36 | 1581.79 | 9.78 | 2608.37 | 10.44 |
| .92 | 273.49 | 4.67 | 4.45 | .58 | 159.91 | 3.70 | 720.45 | 7.39 | 1591.57 | 9.79 | 2618.81 | 10.44 |
| .93 | 268.82 | 4.63 | 3.87 | .53 | 163.61 | 3.74 | 727.84 | 7.42 | 1601.36 | 9.81 | 2629.25 | 10.44 |
| .94 | 204.19 | 4.59 | 3.34 | .50 | 167.35 | 3.78 | 735.26 | 7.45 | 1611.17 | 9.82 | 2639.69 | 10.44 |
| .95 | 259.60 | 4.56 | 2.84 | .45 | 171.13 | 3.82 | 742.71 | 7.48 | 1620.99 | 9.85 | 2650.13 | 10.43 |
| .96 | 255.04 | 4.51 | 2.39 | .40 | 174.95 | 3.87 | 750.19 | 7.52 | 1630.84 | 9.86 | 2660.56 | 10.43 |
| .97 | 250.53 | 4.48 | 1.99 | .36 | 178.82 | 3.90 | 757.71 | 7.55 | 1640.70 | 9.87 | 2670.99 | 10.42 |
| .98 | 246.05 | 4.44 | 1.63 | .32 | 182.72 | 3.94 | 765.26 | 7.57 | 1650.57 | 9.88 | 2681.41 | 10.42 |
| .99 | 241.61 | 4.42 | 1.31 | .29 | 186.66 | 3.98 | 772.83 | 7.60 | 1660.45 | 9.90 | 2691.83 | 10.42 |
| 1.00 | 237.19 | 4.36 | 1.02 | .23 | 190.64 | 4.02 | 780.43 | 7.64 | 1670.35 | 9.91 | 2702.25 | 10.42 |

# TABLE IX. ARGUMENT 4.

Equation = 670″.500 — 670″.3 sin. $z$ — 7″.9 sin. $2z$.

Period, 365.259687 days.

| Days. | 0 | | 10 | | 20 | | 30 | | 40 | |
|---|---|---|---|---|---|---|---|---|---|---|
| Days. | Equation. | Difference. | Equation. | Difference. | Equation. | Difference. | Equation. | Difference. | Equation. | Difference. |
| d 0.0 | 1340.68″ | +.04 | 1334.19″ | —.16 | 1307.89″ | —.37 | 1262.33″ | —.55 | 1198.72″ | —.73 |
| 0.1 | 1340.72 | .03 | 1334.03 | .17 | 1307.52 | .36 | 1261.78 | .55 | 1197.99 | .72 |
| 0.2 | 1340.75 | .03 | 1333.86 | .17 | 1307.16 | .37 | 1261.23 | .55 | 1197.27 | .72 |
| 0.3 | 1340.78 | .03 | 1333.69 | .17 | 1306.79 | .36 | 1260.68 | .56 | 1196.55 | .73 |
| 0.4 | 1340.81 | .02 | 1333.52 | .17 | 1306.43 | .37 | 1260.12 | .55 | 1195.82 | .73 |
| 0.5 | 1340.83 | .03 | 1333.35 | .18 | 1306.06 | .37 | 1259.57 | .56 | 1195.09 | .73 |
| 0.6 | 1340.86 | .02 | 1333.17 | .18 | 1305.69 | .38 | 1259.01 | .56 | 1194.36 | .73 |
| 0.7 | 1340.88 | .02 | 1332.99 | .18 | 1305.31 | .37 | 1258.45 | .56 | 1193.63 | .73 |
| 0.8 | 1340.90 | .02 | 1332.81 | .18 | 1304.94 | .38 | 1257.89 | .57 | 1192.90 | .74 |
| 0.9 | 1340.92 | .01 | 1332.63 | .18 | 1304.56 | .38 | 1257.32 | .56 | 1192.16 | .74 |
| 1.0 | 1340.93 | .02 | 1332.45 | .19 | 1304.18 | .38 | 1256.76 | .57 | 1191.42 | .73 |
| 1.1 | 1340.95 | .01 | 1332.26 | .18 | 1303.80 | .38 | 1256.19 | .57 | 1190.69 | .74 |
| 1.2 | 1340.96 | .01 | 1332.08 | .19 | 1303.42 | .39 | 1255.62 | .57 | 1189.95 | .74 |
| 1.3 | 1340.97 | .01 | 1331.89 | .19 | 1303.03 | .38 | 1255.05 | .57 | 1189.21 | .75 |
| 1.4 | 1340.98 | .00 | 1331.70 | .19 | 1302.65 | .39 | 1254.48 | .58 | 1188.46 | .74 |
| 1.5 | 1340.98 | .00 | 1331.51 | .20 | 1302.26 | .39 | 1253.90 | .57 | 1187.72 | .75 |
| 1.6 | 1340.98 | +.01 | 1331.31 | .20 | 1301.87 | .40 | 1253.33 | .58 | 1186.97 | .74 |
| 1.7 | 1340.99 | .00 | 1331.11 | .20 | 1301.47 | .39 | 1252.75 | .58 | 1186.23 | .75 |
| 1.8 | 1340.99 | —.01 | 1330.91 | .20 | 1301.08 | .40 | 1252.17 | .58 | 1185.48 | .75 |
| 1.9 | 1340.98 | .00 | 1330.71 | .21 | 1300.68 | .40 | 1251.59 | .59 | 1184.73 | .75 |
| 2.0 | 1340.98 | .01 | 1330.50 | .20 | 1300.28 | .40 | 1251.00 | .58 | 1183.98 | .76 |
| 2.1 | 1340.97 | .00 | 1330.30 | .20 | 1299.88 | .40 | 1250.42 | .59 | 1183.22 | .76 |
| 2.2 | 1340.97 | .01 | 1330.10 | .21 | 1299.48 | .40 | 1249.83 | .59 | 1182.46 | .75 |
| 2.3 | 1340.96 | .01 | 1329.89 | .21 | 1299.08 | .41 | 1249.24 | .59 | 1181.71 | .76 |
| 2.4 | 1340.95 | .02 | 1329.68 | .22 | 1298.67 | .41 | 1248.65 | .59 | 1180.95 | .76 |
| 2.5 | 1340.93 | .01 | 1329.46 | .21 | 1298.26 | .41 | 1248.06 | .59 | 1180.19 | .76 |
| 2.6 | 1340 92 | .02 | 1329.25 | .22 | 1297.85 | .41 | 1247.47 | .60 | 1179.43 | .77 |
| 2.7 | 1340.90 | .02 | 1329.03 | .22 | 1297.44 | .41 | 1246.87 | .60 | 1178.66 | .76 |
| 2.8 | 1340.88 | .03 | 1328.81 | .22 | 1297.03 | .42 | 1246.27 | .60 | 1177.90 | .77 |
| 2.9 | 1340.85 | .02 | 1328.59 | .22 | 1296.61 | .41 | 1245.67 | .60 | 1177.13 | .77 |
| 3.0 | 1340.83 | .03 | 1328.37 | .23 | 1296.20 | .42 | 1245.07 | .60 | 1176.36 | .77 |
| 3.1 | 1340.80 | .03 | 1328.14 | .22 | 1295.78 | .42 | 1244.47 | .61 | 1175.59 | .77 |
| 3.2 | 1340.77 | .03 | 1327.92 | .23 | 1295.36 | .42 | 1243.86 | .60 | 1174.82 | .77 |
| 3.3 | 1340.74 | .03 | 1327.69 | .23 | 1294.94 | .43 | 1243.26 | .61 | 1174.05 | .78 |
| 3.4 | 1340.71 | .03 | 1327.46 | .24 | 1294.51 | .43 | 1242.65 | .61 | 1173.27 | .77 |
| 3.5 | 1340.68 | .04 | 1327.22 | .23 | 1294.08 | .43 | 1242.04 | .61 | 1172.50 | .78 |
| 3.6 | 1340.64 | .04 | 1326.99 | .24 | 1293.65 | .43 | 1241.43 | .62 | 1171.72 | .78 |
| 3.7 | 1340.60 | .04 | 1326.75 | .24 | 1293.22 | .43 | 1240.81 | .61 | 1170.94 | .78 |
| 3.8 | 1340.56 | .04 | 1326.51 | .24 | 1292.79 | .43 | 1240.20 | .62 | 1170.16 | .78 |
| 3.9 | 1340.52 | .04 | 1326.27 | .24 | 1292.36 | .44 | 1239.58 | .62 | 1169.38 | .79 |
| 4.0 | 1340.48 | .05 | 1326.03 | .24 | 1291.92 | .44 | 1238.96 | .62 | 1168.59 | .78 |
| 4.1 | 1340.43 | .05 | 1325.79 | .25 | 1291.48 | .44 | 1238.34 | .62 | 1167.81 | .79 |
| 4.2 | 1340.38 | .05 | 1325.54 | .25 | 1291.04 | .44 | 1237.72 | .62 | 1167.02 | .79 |
| 4.3 | 1340.33 | .05 | 1325.29 | .25 | 1290.60 | .44 | 1237.10 | .63 | 1166.23 | .79 |
| 4.4 | 1340.28 | .05 | 1325.04 | .25 | 1290.16 | .45 | 1236.47 | .63 | 1165.44 | .79 |
| 4 5 | 1340.23 | .06 | 1324.79 | .26 | 1289.71 | .45 | 1235.84 | .63 | 1164.65 | .79 |
| 4.6 | 1340.17 | .06 | 1324.53 | .25 | 1289.26 | .45 | 1235.21 | .63 | 1163.86 | .80 |
| 4.7 | 1340.11 | .06 | 1324.28 | .26 | 1288.81 | .45 | 1234.58 | .63 | 1163.06 | .79 |
| 4.8 | 1340.05 | .06 | 1324.02 | .26 | 1288.36 | .45 | 1233.95 | .63 | 1162.27 | .80 |
| 4.9 | 1339.99 | .06 | 1323.76 | .27 | 1287.91 | .46 | 1233.32 | .64 | 1161.47 | .80 |
| 5.0 | 1339.93 | —.07 | 1323.49 | —.26 | 1287.45 | —.45 | 1232.68 | —.64 | 1160.67 | —.80 |

# TABLE IX. ARGUMENT 4.

Equation $= 670''.500 - 670''.3 \text{ sin. } z - 7''.9 \text{ sin. } 2z.$

Period, 365.259687 days.

| Days. | 0 | | 10 | | 20 | | 30 | | 40 | |
|---|---|---|---|---|---|---|---|---|---|---|
| Days. | Equation. | Difference. | Equation. | Difference. | Equation. | Difference. | Equation. | Difference. | Equation. | Difference. |
| d. | ″ | | ″ | | ″ | | ″ | | ″ | |
| 5.0 | 1339.93 | −.07 | 1323.49 | −.26 | 1287.45 | −.45 | 1232.68 | −.64 | 1160.67 | −.80 |
| 5.1 | 1339,86 | .07 | 1323.23 | .27 | 1287.00 | .46 | 1232.04 | .64 | 1159.87 | .80 |
| 5.2 | 1339.79 | .07 | 1322.96 | .26 | 1286.54 | .46 | 1231.40 | .64 | 1159.07 | .81 |
| 5.3 | 1339.72 | .07 | 1322.70 | .27 | 1286.08 | .47 | 1230.76 | .64 | 1158.26 | .80 |
| 5.4 | 1339.65 | .07 | 1322.43 | .28 | 1285.61 | .46 | 1230.12 | .64 | 1157.46 | .81 |
| 5.5 | 1339.58 | .08 | 1322.15 | .27 | 1285.15 | .47 | 1229.48 | .65 | 1156.65 | .81 |
| 5.6 | 1339 50 | .07 | 1321.88 | .27 | 1284.68 | .47 | 1228.83 | .65 | 1155.84 | .80 |
| 5.7 | 1339.43 | .08 | 1321.61 | .28 | 1284.21 | .47 | 1228.18 | .65 | 1155.04 | .82 |
| 5.8 | 1339.35 | .09 | 1321.33 | .28 | 1283.74 | .47 | 1227.53 | .65 | 1154.22 | .81 |
| 5.9 | 1339.26 | .08 | 1321.05 | .29 | 1283.27 | .47 | 1226.88 | .65 | 1153.41 | .81 |
| 6.0 | 1339.18 | .09 | 1320.76 | .28 | 1282.80 | .48 | 1226.23 | .66 | 1152.60 | .82 |
| 6.1 | 1339.09 | .08 | 1320.48 | .29 | 1282.32 | .47 | 1225.57 | .65 | 1151.78 | .81 |
| 6.2 | 1339.01 | .09 | 1320.19 | .28 | 1281.85 | .48 | 1224.92 | .66 | 1150.97 | .82 |
| 6.3 | 1338.92 | .10 | 1319.91 | .29 | 1281.37 | .48 | 1224.26 | .66 | 1150.15 | .82 |
| 6.4 | 1338.82 | .09 | 1319.62 | .30 | 1280.89 | .49 | 1223.60 | .66 | 1149.33 | .82 |
| 6.5 | 1338.73 | .10 | 1319.32 | .29 | 1280.40 | .48 | 1222.94 | .67 | 1148.51 | .83 |
| 6.6 | 1338.63 | .09 | 1319.03 | .30 | 1279.92 | .49 | 1222.27 | .66 | 1147.68 | .82 |
| 6.7 | 1338.54 | .10 | 1318.73 | .29 | 1279.43 | .49 | 1221.61 | .67 | 1146.86 | .83 |
| 6.8 | 1338.44 | .10 | 1318.44 | .30 | 1278.94 | .49 | 1220.94 | .67 | 1146.03 | .83 |
| 6.9 | 1338.34 | .11 | 1318.14 | .30 | 1278.45 | .49 | 1220.27 | .67 | 1145.20 | .82 |
| 7.0 | 1338.23 | .10 | 1317.84 | .31 | 1277.96 | .49 | 1219.60 | .67 | 1144.38 | .84 |
| 7.1 | 1338.13 | .11 | 1317.53 | .30 | 1277.47 | .50 | 1218.93 | ,67 | 1143.54 | .83 |
| 7.2 | 1338.02 | .11 | 1317.23 | .31 | 1276.97 | .50 | 1218.26 | .68 | 1142.71 | .83 |
| 7.3 | 1337.91 | .11 | 1316.92 | .31 | 1276.47 | .50 | 1217.58 | .68 | 1141.88 | .84 |
| 7.4 | 1337.80 | .12 | 1316.61 | .31 | 1275.97 | .50 | 1216.90 | .68 | 1141.04 | .83 |
| 7.5 | 1337.68 | .11 | 1316.30 | .32 | 1275.47 | .50 | 1216.22 | .68 | 1140.21 | .84 |
| 7.6 | 1337.57 | .12 | 1315.98 | .31 | 1274.97 | .51 | 1215.54 | .68 | 1139.37 | .84 |
| 7.7 | 1337.45 | .12 | 1315.67 | .32 | 1274.46 | .51 | 1214.86 | .68 | 1138.53 | .84 |
| 7.8 | 1337.33 | .12 | 1315.35 | .32 | 1273.95 | .51 | 1214.18 | .69 | 1137.69 | .84 |
| 7.9 | 1337.21 | .13 | 1315.03 | .32 | 1273.44 | .51 | 1213.49 | .68 | 1136.85 | .85 |
| 8.0 | 1337.08 | .12 | 1314.71 | .32 | 1272.93 | .51 | 1212.81 | .69 | 1136.00 | .84 |
| 8.1 | 1336.96 | .13 | 1314.39 | .33 | 1272.42 | .51 | 1212.12 | .69 | 1135.16 | .85 |
| 8.2 | 1336.83 | .13 | 1314.06 | .32 | 1271.91 | .52 | 1211.43 | .70 | 1134.31 | .85 |
| 8.3 | 1336.70 | .13 | 1313.74 | .33 | 1271.39 | .52 | 1210.73 | .69 | 1133.46 | .84 |
| 8.4 | 1336.57 | .13 | 1313.41 | .33 | 1270.87 | .52 | 1210.04 | .70 | 1132.62 | .86 |
| 8.5 | 1336.44 | .14 | 1313.08 | .34 | 1270.35 | .52 | 1209.34 | .69 | 1131.76 | .85 |
| 8.6 | 1336.30 | .14 | 1312.74 | .33 | 1269.83 | .52 | 1208.65 | .70 | 1130.91 | .85 |
| 8.7 | 1336.16 | .14 | 1312.41 | .34 | 1269.31 | .53 | 1207.95 | .70 | 1130.06 | .86 |
| 8.8 | 1336.02 | .14 | 1312.07 | .33 | 1268.78 | .53 | 1207.25 | .71 | 1129.20 | .85 |
| 8.9 | 1335.88 | .15 | 1311.74 | .34 | 1268.25 | .53 | 1206.54 | .70 | 1128.35 | .86 |
| 9.0 | 1335.73 | .14 | 1311.40 | .35 | 1267.72 | .53 | 1205.84 | .70 | 1127.49 | .86 |
| 9.1 | 1335.59 | .15 | 1311.05 | .34 | 1267.19 | .53 | 1205.14 | .71 | 1126.63 | .86 |
| 9.2 | 1335.44 | .14 | 1310.71 | .35 | 1266.66 | .54 | 1204.43 | .71 | 1125.77 | .86 |
| 9.3 | 1335.30 | .16 | 1310.36 | .34 | 1266.12 | .53 | 1203.72 | .71 | 1124.91 | .87 |
| 9.4 | 1335.14 | .15 | 1310.02 | .35 | 1265.59 | .54 | 1203.01 | .71 | 1124.04 | .86 |
| 9.5 | 1334.99 | .16 | 1309.67 | .36 | 1265.05 | .54 | 1202.30 | .71 | 1123.18 | .87 |
| 9.6 | 1334.83 | .16 | 1309.31 | .35 | 1264.51 | .54 | 1201.59 | .72 | 1122.31 | .87 |
| 9.7 | 1334.67 | .15 | 1308.96 | .36 | 1263.97 | .55 | 1200.87 | .72 | 1121.44 | .87 |
| 9.8 | 1334.52 | .16 | 1308.60 | .36 | 1263.42 | .54 | 1200.15 | .71 | 1120.57 | .87 |
| 9.9 | 1334.36 | −.17 | 1308.24 | −.35 | 1262.88 | −.55 | 1199.44 | −.72 | 1119.70 | −.87 |
| 10.0 | 1334.19 | | 1307.89 | | 1262.33 | | 1198.72 | | 1118.83 | |

# TABLE IX. ARGUMENT 4.

Equation = 670″.500 — 670″.3 sin. $z$ — 7″.9 sin. 2$z$.

Period, 365.259687 days.

| Days. | 50 | | 60 | | 70 | | 80 | | 90 | |
|---|---|---|---|---|---|---|---|---|---|---|
| Days. | Equation. | Difference. | Equation. | Difference. | Equation. | Difference. | Equation. | Difference. | Equation. | Difference. |
| d. | ″ | | ″ | | ″ | | ″ | | ″ | |
| 0.0 | 1118.83 | −.87 | 1025.03 | −1.00 | 920.14 | −1.09 | 807.42 | −1.16 | 690.38 | −1.18 |
| 0.1 | 1117.96 | .88 | 1024.03 | 1.00 | 919.05 | 1.10 | 806.26 | 1.15 | 689.20 | 1.18 |
| 0.2 | 1117.08 | .87 | 1023.03 | 1.00 | 917.95 | 1.09 | 805.11 | 1.16 | 688.02 | 1.18 |
| 0.3 | 1116.21 | .88 | 1022.03 | 1.01 | 916.86 | 1.10 | 803.95 | 1.15 | 686.84 | 1.18 |
| 0.4 | 1115.33 | .88 | 1021.02 | 1.00 | 915.76 | 1.10 | 802.80 | 1.16 | 685.66 | 1.18 |
| 0.5 | 1114.45 | .89 | 1020.02 | 1.01 | 914.66 | 1.09 | 801.64 | 1.16 | 684.48 | 1.18 |
| 0.6 | 1113.56 | .87 | 1019.01 | 1.00 | 913.57 | 1.10 | 800.48 | 1.15 | 683.30 | 1.17 |
| 0.7 | 1112.69 | .89 | 1018.01 | 1.01 | 912.47 | 1.10 | 799.33 | 1.16 | 682.13 | 1.18 |
| 0.8 | 1111.80 | .88 | 1017.00 | 1.01 | 911.37 | 1.10 | 798.17 | 1.16 | 680.95 | 1.19 |
| 0.9 | 1110.92 | .89 | 1015.99 | 1.00 | 910.27 | 1.10 | 797.01 | 1.16 | 679.76 | 1.18 |
| 1.0 | 1110.03 | .88 | 1014.99 | 1.01 | 909.17 | 1.11 | 795.85 | 1.16 | 678.58 | 1.17 |
| 1.1 | 1109.15 | .89 | 1013.98 | 1.02 | 908.06 | 1.10 | 794.69 | 1.16 | 677.41 | 1.18 |
| 1.2 | 1108.26 | .89 | 1012.96 | 1.01 | 906.96 | 1.10 | 793.53 | 1.16 | 676.23 | 1.19 |
| 1.3 | 1107.37 | .89 | 1011.95 | 1.01 | 905.86 | 1.11 | 792.37 | 1.16 | 675.04 | 1.18 |
| 1.4 | 1106.48 | .90 | 1010.94 | 1.01 | 904.75 | 1.10 | 791.21 | 1.16 | 673.86 | 1.18 |
| 1.5 | 1105.58 | .89 | 1009.93 | 1.02 | 903.65 | 1.11 | 790.05 | 1.16 | 672.68 | 1.18 |
| 1.6 | 1104.69 | .90 | 1008.91 | 1.02 | 902.54 | 1.10 | 788.89 | 1.16 | 671.50 | 1.18 |
| 1.7 | 1103.79 | .89 | 1007.89 | 1.01 | 901.44 | 1.11 | 787.73 | 1.16 | 670.32 | 1.18 |
| 1.8 | 1102.90 | .90 | 1006.88 | 1.02 | 900.33 | 1.11 | 786.57 | 1.17 | 669.14 | 1.18 |
| 1.9 | 1102.00 | .90 | 1005.86 | 1.02 | 899.22 | 1.11 | 785.40 | 1.16 | 667.96 | 1.18 |
| 2.0 | 1101.10 | .90 | 1004.84 | 1.02 | 898.11 | 1.10 | 784.24 | 1.16 | 666.78 | 1.18 |
| 2.1 | 1100.20 | .90 | 1003.82 | 1.03 | 897.01 | 1.11 | 783.08 | 1.16 | 665.60 | 1.18 |
| 2.2 | 1099.30 | .91 | 1002.79 | 1.02 | 895.90 | 1.12 | 781.92 | 1.17 | 664.42 | 1.18 |
| 2.3 | 1098.39 | .90 | 1001.77 | 1.02 | 894.78 | 1.11 | 780.75 | 1.16 | 663.24 | 1.18 |
| 2.4 | 1097.49 | .91 | 1000.75 | 1.03 | 893.67 | 1.11 | 779.59 | 1.17 | 662.06 | 1.18 |
| 2.5 | 1096.58 | .91 | 999.72 | 1.02 | 892.56 | 1.11 | 778.42 | 1.16 | 660.88 | 1.18 |
| 2.6 | 1095.67 | .91 | 998.70 | 1.03 | 891.45 | 1.11 | 777.26 | 1.17 | 659.70 | 1.18 |
| 2.7 | 1094.76 | .91 | 997.67 | 1.03 | 890.34 | 1.12 | 776.09 | 1.16 | 658.52 | 1.18 |
| 2.8 | 1093.85 | .91 | 996.64 | 1.03 | 889.22 | 1.11 | 774.93 | 1.17 | 657.34 | 1.18 |
| 2.9 | 1092.94 | .91 | 995.61 | 1.03 | 888.11 | 1.12 | 773.76 | 1.16 | 656.16 | 1.18 |
| 3.0 | 1092.03 | .91 | 994.58 | 1.03 | 886.99 | 1.11 | 772.60 | 1.17 | 654.98 | 1.18 |
| 3.1 | 1091.12 | .92 | 993.55 | 1.03 | 885.88 | 1.12 | 771.43 | 1.17 | 653.80 | 1.18 |
| 3.2 | 1090.20 | .92 | 992.52 | 1.03 | 884.76 | 1.12 | 770.26 | 1.16 | 652.62 | 1.18 |
| 3.3 | 1089.28 | .91 | 991.49 | 1.04 | 883.64 | 1.11 | 769.10 | 1.17 | 651.44 | 1.18 |
| 3.4 | 1088.37 | .92 | 990.45 | 1.03 | 882.53 | 1.12 | 767.93 | 1.17 | 650.26 | 1.18 |
| 3.5 | 1087.45 | .92 | 989.42 | 1.04 | 881.41 | 1.12 | 766.76 | 1.17 | 649.08 | 1.18 |
| 3.6 | 1086.53 | .93 | 988.38 | 1.03 | 880.29 | 1.12 | 765.59 | 1.17 | 647.90 | 1.18 |
| 3.7 | 1085.60 | .92 | 987.35 | 1.04 | 879.17 | 1.12 | 764.42 | 1.16 | 646.72 | 1.18 |
| 3.8 | 1084.68 | .92 | 986.31 | 1.04 | 878.05 | 1.13 | 763.26 | 1.17 | 645.54 | 1.18 |
| 3.9 | 1083.76 | .93 | 985.27 | 1.04 | 876.92 | 1.12 | 762.09 | 1.17 | 644.36 | 1.17 |
| 4.0 | 1082.83 | .93 | 984.23 | 1.04 | 875.80 | 1.12 | 760.92 | 1.17 | 643.19 | 1.18 |
| 4.1 | 1081.90 | .92 | 983.19 | 1.04 | 874.68 | 1.12 | 759.75 | 1.17 | 642.01 | 1.18 |
| 4.2 | 1080.98 | .93 | 982.15 | 1.05 | 873.56 | 1.13 | 758.58 | 1.17 | 640.83 | 1.18 |
| 4.3 | 1080.05 | .94 | 981.10 | 1.04 | 872.43 | 1.12 | 757.41 | 1.17 | 639.65 | 1.18 |
| 4.4 | 1079.11 | .93 | 980.06 | 1.05 | 871.31 | 1.13 | 756.24 | 1.17 | 638.47 | 1.18 |
| 4.5 | 1078.18 | .93 | 979.01 | 1.04 | 870.18 | 1.12 | 755.07 | 1.17 | 637.29 | 1.18 |
| 4.6 | 1077.25 | .94 | 977.97 | 1.05 | 869.06 | 1.13 | 753.90 | 1.17 | 636.11 | 1.18 |
| 4.7 | 1076.31 | .93 | 976.92 | 1.05 | 867.93 | 1.13 | 752.73 | 1.17 | 634.93 | 1.18 |
| 4.8 | 1075.38 | .94 | 975.87 | 1.05 | 866.80 | 1.13 | 751.56 | 1.18 | 633.75 | 1.17 |
| 4.9 | 1074.44 | .94 | 974.82 | 1.05 | 865.67 | 1.12 | 750.38 | 1.17 | 632.58 | 1.18 |
| 5.0 | 1073.50 | −.94 | 973.77 | −1.05 | 864.55 | −1.13 | 749.21 | −1.17 | 631.40 | −1.18 |

# TABLE IX. ARGUMENT 4.

Equation = 670″.500 — 670″.3 sin. $z$ — 7″.9 sin. $2z$.

Period, 365.259687 days.

| Days. | 50 | | 60 | | 70 | | 80 | | 90 | |
|---|---|---|---|---|---|---|---|---|---|---|
| Days. | Equation. | Difference. | Equation. | Difference. | Equation. | Difference. | Equation. | Difference. | Equation. | Difference. |
| d. | ″ | | ″ | | ″ | | ″ | | ″ | |
| 5.0 | 1073.50 | — .94 | 973.77 | −1.05 | 864.55 | −1.13 | 749.21 | −1.17 | 631.40 | −1.18 |
| 5.1 | 1072.56 | .94 | 972.72 | 1.05 | 863.42 | 1.13 | 748.04 | 1.17 | 630.22 | 1.18 |
| 5.2 | 1071.62 | .94 | 971.67 | 1.05 | 862.29 | 1.13 | 746.87 | 1.17 | 629.04 | 1.18 |
| 5.3 | 1070.68 | .94 | 970.62 | 1.06 | 861.16 | 1.13 | 745.70 | 1.18 | 627.86 | 1.18 |
| 5.4 | 1069.74 | .95 | 969.56 | 1.05 | 860.03 | 1.14 | 744.52 | 1.17 | 626.68 | 1.17 |
| 5.5 | 1068.79 | .95 | 968.51 | 1.06 | 858.89 | 1.13 | 743.35 | 1.17 | 625.51 | 1.18 |
| 5.6 | 1067.84 | .94 | 967.45 | 1.05 | 857.76 | 1.13 | 742.18 | 1.18 | 624.33 | 1.18 |
| 5.7 | 1066.90 | .95 | 966.40 | 1.06 | 856.63 | 1.13 | 741.00 | 1.17 | 623.15 | 1.17 |
| 5.8 | 1065.95 | .95 | 965.34 | 1.06 | 855.50 | 1.14 | 739.83 | 1.17 | 621.98 | 1.18 |
| 5.9 | 1065.00 | .95 | 964.28 | 1.05 | 854.36 | 1.13 | 738.66 | 1.18 | 620.80 | 1.18 |
| 6.0 | 1064.05 | .95 | 963.23 | 1.06 | 853.23 | 1.14 | 737.48 | 1.17 | 619.62 | 1.17 |
| 6.1 | 1063.10 | .96 | 962.17 | 1.06 | 852.09 | 1.13 | 736.31 | 1.18 | 618.45 | 1.18 |
| 6.2 | 1062.14 | .95 | 961.11 | 1.07 | 850.96 | 1.14 | 735.13 | 1.17 | 617.27 | 1.18 |
| 6.3 | 1061.19 | .96 | 960.04 | 1.06 | 849.82 | 1.14 | 733.96 | 1.18 | 616.09 | 1.17 |
| 6.4 | 1060.23 | .95 | 958.98 | 1.06 | 848.68 | 1.13 | 732.78 | 1.17 | 614.92 | 1.18 |
| 6.5 | 1059.28 | .96 | 957.92 | 1.07 | 847.55 | 1.14 | 731.61 | 1.18 | 613.74 | 1.17 |
| 6.6 | 1058.32 | .96 | 956.85 | 1.07 | 846.41 | 1.14 | 730.43 | 1.17 | 612.57 | 1.18 |
| 6.7 | 1057.36 | .96 | 955.78 | 1.06 | 845.27 | 1.14 | 729.26 | 1.18 | 611.39 | 1.18 |
| 6.8 | 1056.40 | .97 | 954.72 | 1.07 | 844.13 | 1.14 | 728.08 | 1.17 | 610.21 | 1.17 |
| 6.9 | 1055.43 | .96 | 953.65 | 1.07 | 842.99 | 1.14 | 726.91 | 1.18 | 609.04 | 1.18 |
| 7.0 | 1054.47 | .96 | 952.58 | 1.06 | 841.85 | 1.14 | 725.73 | 1.17 | 607.86 | 1.17 |
| 7.1 | 1053.51 | .97 | 951.52 | 1.07 | 840.71 | 1.14 | 724.56 | 1.18 | 606.69 | 1.18 |
| 7.2 | 1052.54 | .97 | 950.45 | 1.08 | 839.57 | 1.14 | 723.38 | 1.18 | 605.51 | 1.17 |
| 7.3 | 1051.57 | .97 | 949.37 | 1.07 | 838.43 | 1.14 | 722.20 | 1.18 | 604.34 | 1.17 |
| 7.4 | 1050.60 | .96 | 948.30 | 1.07 | 837.29 | 1.14 | 721.02 | 1.17 | 603.17 | 1.18 |
| 7.5 | 1049.64 | .97 | 947.23 | 1.07 | 836.15 | 1.15 | 719.85 | 1.18 | 601.99 | 1.17 |
| 7.6 | 1048.67 | .98 | 946.16 | 1.08 | 835.00 | 1.14 | 718.67 | 1.18 | 600.82 | 1.18 |
| 7.7 | 1047.69 | .97 | 945.08 | 1.07 | 833.86 | 1.15 | 717.49 | 1.17 | 599.64 | 1.17 |
| 7.8 | 1046.72 | .97 | 944.01 | 1.08 | 832.71 | 1.14 | 716.32 | 1.18 | 598.47 | 1.17 |
| 7.9 | 1045.75 | .98 | 942.93 | 1.07 | 831.57 | 1.14 | 715.14 | 1.18 | 597.30 | 1.17 |
| 8.0 | 1044.77 | .98 | 941.86 | 1.08 | 830.43 | 1.15 | 713.96 | 1.18 | 596.13 | 1.18 |
| 8.1 | 1043.79 | .97 | 940.78 | 1.08 | 829.28 | 1.14 | 712.78 | 1.18 | 594.95 | 1.17 |
| 8.2 | 1042.82 | .98 | 939.70 | 1.08 | 828.14 | 1.15 | 711.60 | 1.17 | 593.78 | 1.17 |
| 8.3 | 1041.84 | .98 | 938.62 | 1.08 | 826.99 | 1.15 | 710.43 | 1.18 | 592.61 | 1.17 |
| 8.4 | 1040.86 | .98 | 937.54 | 1.08 | 825.84 | 1.15 | 709.25 | 1.18 | 591.44 | 1.18 |
| 8.5 | 1039.88 | .98 | 936.46 | 1.08 | 824.69 | 1.15 | 708.07 | 1.18 | 590.26 | 1.17 |
| 8.6 | 1038.90 | .99 | 935.38 | 1.09 | 823.54 | 1.15 | 706.89 | 1.18 | 589.09 | 1.17 |
| 8.7 | 1037.91 | .99 | 934.29 | 1.08 | 822.39 | 1.14 | 705.71 | 1.18 | 587.92 | 1.17 |
| 8.8 | 1036.92 | .98 | 933.21 | 1.09 | 821.25 | 1.15 | 704.53 | 1.17 | 586.75 | 1.17 |
| 8.9 | 1035.94 | .99 | 932.12 | 1.08 | 820.10 | 1.15 | 703.36 | 1.18 | 585.58 | 1.17 |
| 9.0 | 1034.95 | .98 | 931.04 | 1.09 | 818.95 | 1.16 | 702.18 | 1.18 | 584.41 | 1.17 |
| 9.1 | 1033.97 | .99 | 929.95 | 1.08 | 817.79 | 1.15 | 701.00 | 1.18 | 583.24 | 1.17 |
| 9.2 | 1032 98 | .99 | 928.87 | 1.09 | 816.64 | 1.15 | 699.82 | 1.18 | 582.07 | 1.17 |
| 9.3 | 1031.99 | .99 | 927.78 | 1.09 | 815.49 | 1.15 | 698.64 | 1.18 | 580.90 | 1.17 |
| 9.4 | 1031.00 | .99 | 926.69 | 1.09 | 814.34 | 1.15 | 697.46 | 1.18 | 579.73 | 1.17 |
| 9.5 | 1030.01 | 1.00 | 925.60 | 1.09 | 813.19 | 1.16 | 696.28 | 1.18 | 578.56 | 1.17 |
| 9.6 | 1029.01 | .99 | 924.51 | 1.09 | 812.03 | 1.15 | 695.10 | 1.18 | 577.39 | 1.17 |
| 9.7 | 1028.02 | 1.00 | 923.42 | 1.09 | 810.88 | 1.15 | 693.92 | 1.18 | 576.22 | 1.16 |
| 9.8 | 1027.02 | 1.00 | 922.33 | 1.10 | 809.73 | 1.16 | 692.74 | 1.18 | 575.06 | 1.17 |
| 9.9 | 1026.02 | — .99 | 921.23 | −1.09 | 808.57 | −1.15 | 691.56 | −1.18 | 573.89 | −1.17 |
| 10.0 | 1025.03 | | 920.14 | | 807.42 | | 690.38 | | 572.72 | |

# TABLE IX. ARGUMENT 4.

Equation $= 670''.500 - 670''.3 \sin. z - 7''.9 \sin. 2z$.

Period, 365.259687 days.

| Days. | 100 | | 110 | | 120 | | 130 | | 140 | |
|---|---|---|---|---|---|---|---|---|---|---|
| Days. | Equation. | Difference. | Equation. | Difference. | Equation. | Difference. | Equation. | Difference. | Equation. | Difference. |
| d. 0.0 | ″ 572.72 | −1.16 | ″ 458.14 | −1.12 | ″ 350.24 | −1.04 | ″ 252.36 | −.92 | ″ 167.49 | −.77 |
| 0.1 | 571.56 | 1.17 | 457.02 | 1.11 | 349.20 | 1.03 | 251.44 | .91 | 166.72 | .77 |
| 0.2 | 570.39 | 1.17 | 455.91 | 1.12 | 348.17 | 1.03 | 250.53 | .92 | 165.95 | .77 |
| 0.3 | 569.22 | 1.17 | 454.79 | 1.12 | 347.14 | 1.03 | 249.61 | .91 | 165.18 | .77 |
| 0.4 | 568.05 | 1.16 | 453.67 | 1.11 | 346.11 | 1.03 | 248.70 | .92 | 164.41 | .77 |
| 0.5 | 566.89 | 1.17 | 452.56 | 1.12 | 345.08 | 1.03 | 247.78 | .91 | 163.64 | .77 |
| 0.6 | 565.72 | 1.16 | 451.44 | 1.11 | 344.05 | 1.03 | 246.87 | .91 | 162.87 | .76 |
| 0.7 | 564.56 | 1.17 | 450.33 | 1.11 | 343.02 | 1.03 | 245.96 | .91 | 162.11 | .76 |
| 0.8 | 563.39 | 1.16 | 449.22 | 1.12 | 341.99 | 1.02 | 245.05 | .90 | 161.35 | .76 |
| 0.9 | 562.23 | 1.17 | 448.10 | 1.11 | 340.97 | 1.02 | 244.15 | .91 | 160.59 | .77 |
| 1.0 | 561.06 | 1.16 | 446.99 | 1.11 | 339.95 | 1.03 | 243.24 | .90 | 159.82 | .75 |
| 1.1 | 559.90 | 1.16 | 445.88 | 1.11 | 338.92 | 1.02 | 242.34 | .91 | 159.07 | .76 |
| 1.2 | 558.74 | 1.17 | 444.77 | 1.11 | 337.90 | 1.02 | 241.43 | .90 | 158.31 | .75 |
| 1.3 | 557.57 | 1.16 | 443.66 | 1.11 | 336.88 | 1.02 | 240.53 | .90 | 157.56 | .76 |
| 1.4 | 556.41 | 1.16 | 442.55 | 1.11 | 335.86 | 1.02 | 239.63 | .90 | 156.80 | .75 |
| 1.5 | 555.25 | 1.16 | 441.44 | 1.10 | 334.84 | 1.02 | 238.73 | .90 | 156.05 | .75 |
| 1.6 | 554.09 | 1.17 | 440.34 | 1.11 | 333.82 | 1.02 | 237.83 | .89 | 155.30 | .75 |
| 1.7 | 552.92 | 1.16 | 439.23 | 1.11 | 332.80 | 1.01 | 236.94 | .90 | 154.55 | .75 |
| 1.8 | 551.76 | 1.16 | 438.12 | 1.10 | 331.79 | 1.02 | 236.04 | .89 | 153.80 | .74 |
| 1.9 | 550.60 | 1.16 | 437.02 | 1.11 | 330.77 | 1.01 | 235.15 | .89 | 153.06 | .75 |
| 2.0 | 549.44 | 1.16 | 435.91 | 1.10 | 329.76 | 1.02 | 234.26 | .89 | 152.31 | .74 |
| 2.1 | 548.28 | 1.16 | 434.81 | 1.10 | 328.74 | 1.01 | 233.37 | .89 | 151.57 | .74 |
| 2.2 | 547.12 | 1.16 | 433.71 | 1.10 | 327.73 | 1.01 | 232.48 | .89 | 150.83 | .74 |
| 2.3 | 545.96 | 1.16 | 432.61 | 1.11 | 326.72 | 1.01 | 231.59 | .89 | 150.09 | .74 |
| 2.4 | 544.80 | 1.16 | 431.50 | 1.10 | 325.71 | 1.01 | 230.70 | .88 | 149.35 | .73 |
| 2.5 | 543.64 | 1.15 | 430.40 | 1.10 | 324.70 | 1.01 | 229.82 | .89 | 148.62 | .74 |
| 2.6 | 542.49 | 1.16 | 429.30 | 1.10 | 323.69 | 1.00 | 228.93 | .88 | 147.88 | .73 |
| 2.7 | 541.33 | 1.16 | 428.20 | 1.09 | 322.69 | 1.01 | 228.05 | .88 | 147.15 | .73 |
| 2.8 | 540.17 | 1.16 | 427.11 | 1.10 | 321.68 | 1.00 | 227.17 | .88 | 146.42 | .73 |
| 2.9 | 539.01 | 1.15 | 426.01 | 1.10 | 320.68 | 1.00 | 226.29 | .88 | 145.69 | .73 |
| 3.0 | 537.86 | 1.16 | 424.91 | 1.10 | 319.68 | 1.01 | 225.41 | .88 | 144.96 | .72 |
| 3.1 | 536.70 | 1.15 | 423.81 | 1.09 | 318.67 | 1.00 | 224.53 | .87 | 144.24 | .73 |
| 3.2 | 535.55 | 1.16 | 422.72 | 1.10 | 317.67 | 1.00 | 223.66 | .88 | 143.51 | .72 |
| 3.3 | 534.39 | 1.15 | 421.62 | 1.09 | 316.67 | 1.00 | 222.78 | .87 | 142.79 | .72 |
| 3.4 | 533.24 | 1.16 | 420.53 | 1.09 | 315.67 | .99 | 221.91 | .87 | 142.07 | .72 |
| 3.5 | 532.08 | 1.15 | 419.44 | 1.10 | 314.68 | 1.00 | 221.04 | .87 | 141.35 | .72 |
| 3.6 | 530.93 | 1.16 | 418.34 | 1.09 | 313.68 | 1.00 | 220.17 | .87 | 140.63 | .72 |
| 3.7 | 529.77 | 1.15 | 417.25 | 1.09 | 312.68 | .99 | 219.30 | .87 | 139.91 | .71 |
| 3.8 | 528.62 | 1.15 | 416.16 | 1.09 | 311.69 | .99 | 218.43 | .87 | 139.20 | .71 |
| 3.9 | 527.47 | 1.15 | 415.07 | 1.09 | 310.70 | .99 | 217.56 | .86 | 138.49 | .72 |
| 4.0 | 526.32 | 1.16 | 413.98 | 1.08 | 309.71 | 1.00 | 216.70 | .86 | 137.77 | .71 |
| 4.1 | 525.16 | 1.15 | 412.90 | 1.09 | 308.71 | .99 | 215.84 | .87 | 137.06 | .70 |
| 4.2 | 524.01 | 1.15 | 411.81 | 1.09 | 307.72 | .98 | 214.97 | .86 | 136.36 | .71 |
| 4.3 | 522.86 | 1.15 | 410.72 | 1.08 | 306.74 | .99 | 214.11 | .85 | 135.65 | .70 |
| 4.4 | 521.71 | 1.15 | 409.64 | 1.09 | 305.75 | .99 | 213.26 | .86 | 134.95 | .71 |
| 4.5 | 520.56 | 1.15 | 408.55 | 1.08 | 304.76 | .98 | 212.40 | .86 | 134.24 | .70 |
| 4.6 | 519.41 | 1.15 | 407.47 | 1.09 | 303.78 | .99 | 211.54 | .85 | 133.54 | .70 |
| 4.7 | 518.26 | 1.15 | 406.38 | 1.08 | 302.79 | .98 | 210.69 | .86 | 132.84 | .70 |
| 4.8 | 517.11 | 1.14 | 405.30 | 1.08 | 301.81 | .98 | 209.83 | .85 | 132.14 | .69 |
| 4.9 | 515.97 | 1.15 | 404.22 | 1.08 | 300.83 | .98 | 208.98 | .85 | 131.45 | .70 |
| 5.0 | 514.82 | −1.15 | 403.14 | −1.08 | 299.85 | −.98 | 208.13 | −.85 | 130.75 | −.69 |

# TABLE IX. ARGUMENT 4.

Equation = 670″.500 — 670″.3 sin. $z$ — 7″.9 sin. $2z$.

Period, 365.259687 days.

| Days. | 100 | | 110 | | 120 | | 130 | | 140 | |
|---|---|---|---|---|---|---|---|---|---|---|
| Days. | Equation. | Difference. | Equation. | Difference. | Equation. | Difference. | Equation. | Difference. | Equation. | Difference. |
| d. | ″ | | ″ | | ″ | | ″ | | ″ | |
| 5.0 | 514.82 | −1.15 | 403.14 | −1.08 | 299.85 | −.98 | 208.13 | −.85 | 130.75 | −.69 |
| 5.1 | 513.67 | 1.15 | 402.06 | 1.08 | 298.87 | .98 | 207.28 | .85 | 130.06 | .69 |
| 5.2 | 512.52 | 1.14 | 400.98 | 1.08 | 297.89 | .98 | 206.43 | .84 | 129.37 | .69 |
| 5.3 | 511.38 | 1.15 | 399.90 | 1.08 | 296.91 | .97 | 205.59 | .85 | 128.68 | .69 |
| 5.4 | 510.23 | 1.14 | 398.82 | 1.07 | 295.94 | .98 | 204.74 | .84 | 127.99 | .69 |
| 5.5 | 509.09 | 1.15 | 397.75 | 1.08 | 294.96 | .97 | 203.90 | .84 | 127.30 | .68 |
| 5.6 | 507.94 | 1.14 | 396.67 | 1.07 | 293.99 | .98 | 203.06 | .84 | 126.62 | .69 |
| 5.7 | 506.80 | 1.15 | 395.60 | 1.08 | 293.01 | .97 | 202.22 | .84 | 125.93 | .68 |
| 5.8 | 505.65 | 1.14 | 394.52 | 1.07 | 292.04 | .97 | 201.38 | .84 | 125.25 | .68 |
| 5.9 | 504.51 | 1.14 | 393.45 | 1.07 | 291.07 | .96 | 200.54 | .83 | 124.57 | .68 |
| 6.0 | 503.37 | 1.14 | 392.38 | 1.08 | 290.11 | .97 | 199.71 | .84 | 123.89 | .67 |
| 6.1 | 502.23 | 1.14 | 391.30 | 1.07 | 289.14 | .97 | 198.87 | .83 | 123.22 | .68 |
| 6.2 | 501.09 | 1.15 | 390.23 | 1.07 | 288.17 | .96 | 198.04 | .83 | 122.54 | .67 |
| 6.3 | 499.94 | 1.13 | 389.16 | 1.07 | 287.21 | .97 | 197.21 | .83 | 121.87 | .67 |
| 6.4 | 498.81 | 1.15 | 388.09 | 1.06 | 286.24 | .96 | 196.38 | .83 | 121.20 | .67 |
| 6.5 | 497.66 | 1.13 | 387.03 | 1.07 | 285.28 | .96 | 195.55 | .83 | 120.53 | .67 |
| 6.6 | 496.53 | 1.14 | 385.96 | 1.07 | 284.32 | .96 | 194.72 | .83 | 119.86 | .66 |
| 6.7 | 495.39 | 1.14 | 384.89 | 1.06 | 283.36 | .96 | 193.89 | .82 | 119.20 | .67 |
| 6.8 | 494.25 | 1.14 | 383.83 | 1.07 | 282.40 | .96 | 193.07 | .82 | 118.53 | .66 |
| 6.9 | 493.11 | 1.14 | 382.76 | 1.06 | 281.44 | .96 | 192.25 | .82 | 117.87 | .66 |
| 7.0 | 491.97 | 1.13 | 381.70 | 1.06 | 280.48 | .95 | 191.43 | .82 | 117.21 | .66 |
| 7.1 | 490.84 | 1.14 | 380.64 | 1.06 | 279.53 | .96 | 190.61 | .82 | 116.55 | .66 |
| 7.2 | 489.70 | 1.13 | 379.58 | 1.06 | 278.57 | .95 | 189.79 | .82 | 115.89 | .66 |
| 7.3 | 488.57 | 1.14 | 378.52 | 1.06 | 277.62 | .95 | 188.97 | .81 | 115.23 | .65 |
| 7.4 | 487.43 | 1.13 | 377.46 | 1.06 | 276.67 | .95 | 188.16 | .82 | 114.58 | .66 |
| 7.5 | 486.30 | 1.14 | 376.40 | 1.06 | 275.72 | .95 | 187.34 | .81 | 113.92 | .65 |
| 7.6 | 485.16 | 1.13 | 375.34 | 1.06 | 274.77 | .95 | 186.53 | .81 | 113.27 | .65 |
| 7.7 | 484.03 | 1.13 | 374.28 | 1.05 | 273.82 | .95 | 185.72 | .81 | 112.62 | .64 |
| 7.8 | 482.90 | 1.13 | 373.23 | 1.06 | 272.87 | .94 | 184.91 | .81 | 111.98 | .65 |
| 7.9 | 481.77 | 1.13 | 372.17 | 1.05 | 271.93 | .95 | 184.10 | .80 | 111.33 | .64 |
| 8.0 | 480.64 | 1.14 | 371.12 | 1.05 | 270.98 | .94 | 183.30 | .81 | 110.69 | .65 |
| 8.1 | 479.50 | 1.12 | 370.07 | 1.06 | 270.04 | .94 | 182.49 | .80 | 110.04 | .64 |
| 8.2 | 478.38 | 1.13 | 369.01 | 1.05 | 269.10 | .94 | 181.69 | .80 | 109.40 | .64 |
| 8.3 | 477.25 | 1.13 | 367.96 | 1.05 | 268.16 | .94 | 180.89 | .80 | 108.76 | .63 |
| 8.4 | 476.12 | 1.13 | 366.91 | 1.05 | 267.22 | .94 | 180.09 | .80 | 108.13 | .64 |
| 8.5 | 474.99 | 1.13 | 365.86 | 1.05 | 266.28 | .94 | 179.29 | .80 | 107.49 | .63 |
| 8.6 | 473.86 | 1.13 | 364.81 | 1.04 | 265.34 | .93 | 178.49 | .89 | 106.86 | .63 |
| 8.7 | 472.73 | 1.12 | 363.77 | 1.05 | 264.41 | .94 | 177.70 | .80 | 106.23 | .63 |
| 8.8 | 471.61 | 1.13 | 362.72 | 1.05 | 263.47 | .93 | 176.90 | .79 | 105.60 | .63 |
| 8.9 | 470.48 | 1.12 | 361.67 | 1.04 | 262.54 | .93 | 176.11 | .79 | 104.97 | .63 |
| 9.0 | 469.36 | 1.13 | 360.63 | 1.05 | 261.61 | .93 | 175.32 | .79 | 104.34 | .62 |
| 9.1 | 468.23 | 1.12 | 359.58 | 1.04 | 260.68 | .93 | 174.53 | .79 | 103.72 | .63 |
| 9.2 | 467.11 | 1.13 | 358.54 | 1.04 | 259.75 | .93 | 173.74 | .78 | 103.09 | .62 |
| 9.3 | 465.98 | 1.12 | 357.50 | 1.04 | 258.82 | .93 | 172.96 | .79 | 102.47 | .62 |
| 9.4 | 464.86 | 1.12 | 356.46 | 1.04 | 257.89 | .92 | 172.17 | .78 | 101.85 | .62 |
| 9.5 | 463.74 | 1.12 | 355.42 | 1.04 | 256.97 | .93 | 171.39 | .78 | 101.23 | .61 |
| 9.6 | 462.62 | 1.12 | 354.38 | 1.04 | 256.04 | .92 | 170.61 | .78 | 100.62 | .62 |
| 9.7 | 461.50 | 1.12 | 353.34 | 1.04 | 255.12 | .92 | 169.83 | .78 | 100.00 | .61 |
| 9.8 | 460.38 | 1.12 | 352.30 | 1.03 | 254.20 | .92 | 169.05 | .78 | 99.39 | .61 |
| 9.9 | 459.26 | −1.12 | 351.27 | −1.03 | 253.28 | −.92 | 168.27 | −.78 | 98.78 | −.61 |
| 10.0 | 458.14 | | 350.24 | | 252.36 | | 167.49 | | 98.17 | |

# TABLE IX. ARGUMENT 4.

Equation = 670″.500 — 670″.3 sin. $z$ — 7″.9 sin. $2z$.

Period, 365.259687 days.

| Days. | 150 | | 160 | | 170 | | 180 | | 190 | |
|---|---|---|---|---|---|---|---|---|---|---|
| Days. | Equation. | Difference. | Equation. | Difference. | Equation. | Difference. | Equation. | Difference. | Equation. | Difference. |
| d. 0.0 | 98″.17 | —.61 | 46″.36 | —.42 | 13″.47 | —.23 | 0″.28 | —.03 | 6″.94 | +.16 |
| 0.1 | 97.56 | .61 | 45.94 | .42 | 13.24 | .22 | 0.25 | .03 | 7.10 | .17 |
| 0.2 | 96.95 | .60 | 45.52 | .42 | 13.02 | .23 | 0.22 | .03 | 7.27 | .17 |
| 0.3 | 96.35 | .60 | 45.10 | .42 | 12.79 | .23 | 0.19 | .02 | 7.44 | .17 |
| 0.4 | 95.75 | .60 | 44.68 | .42 | 12.56 | .22 | 0.17 | .03 | 7.61 | .18 |
| 0.5 | 95.15 | .60 | 44.26 | .41 | 12.34 | .22 | 0.14 | .02 | 7.79 | .17 |
| 0.6 | 94.55 | .60 | 43.85 | .42 | 12.12 | .22 | 0.12 | .02 | 7.96 | .18 |
| 0.7 | 93.95 | .59 | 43.43 | .41 | 11.90 | .21 | 0.10 | .02 | 8.14 | .18 |
| 0.8 | 93.36 | .60 | 43.02 | .41 | 11.69 | .22 | 0.08 | .02 | 8.32 | .18 |
| 0.9 | 92.76 | .59 | 42.61 | .41 | 11.47 | .21 | 0.06 | .01 | 8.50 | .18 |
| 1.0 | 92.17 | .59 | 42.20 | .40 | 11.26 | .21 | 0.05 | .01 | 8.68 | .19 |
| 1.1 | 91.58 | .59 | 41.80 | .40 | 11.05 | .21 | 0.04 | .01 | 8.87 | .19 |
| 1.2 | 90.99 | .58 | 41.40 | .40 | 10.84 | .20 | 0.03 | .01 | 9.06 | .18 |
| 1.3 | 90.41 | .59 | 41.00 | .40 | 10.64 | .21 | 0.02 | .00 | 9.24 | .20 |
| 1.4 | 89.82 | .58 | 40.60 | .40 | 10.43 | .20 | 0.02 | —.01 | 9.44 | .19 |
| 1.5 | 89.24 | .58 | 40.20 | .40 | 10.23 | .20 | 0.01 | .00 | 9.63 | .19 |
| 1.6 | 88.66 | .58 | 39.80 | .39 | 10.03 | .20 | 0.01 | .00 | 9.82 | .20 |
| 1.7 | 88.08 | .58 | 39.41 | .39 | 9.83 | .20 | 0.01 | .00 | 10.02 | .20 |
| 1.8 | 87.50 | .58 | 39.02 | .39 | 9.63 | .19 | 0.01 | +.01 | 10.22 | .20 |
| 1.9 | 86.92 | .57 | 38.63 | .39 | 9.44 | .20 | 0.02 | .01 | 10.42 | .20 |
| 2.0 | 86.35 | .57 | 38.24 | .39 | 9.24 | .19 | 0.03 | .01 | 10.62 | .21 |
| 2.1 | 85.78 | .57 | 37.85 | .38 | 9.05 | .19 | 0.04 | .01 | 10.83 | .21 |
| 2.2 | 85.21 | .57 | 37.47 | .38 | 8.86 | .18 | 0.05 | .01 | 11.04 | .20 |
| 2.3 | 84.64 | .56 | 37.09 | .38 | 8.68 | .19 | 0.06 | .01 | 11.24 | .22 |
| 2.4 | 84.08 | .57 | 36.71 | .38 | 8.49 | .18 | 0.07 | .02 | 11.46 | .21 |
| 2.5 | 83.51 | .56 | 36.33 | .38 | 8.31 | .18 | 0.09 | .01 | 11.67 | .21 |
| 2.6 | 82.95 | .56 | 35.95 | .37 | 8.13 | .18 | 0.10 | .02 | 11.88 | .22 |
| 2.7 | 82.39 | .56 | 35.58 | .38 | 7.95 | .17 | 0.12 | .03 | 12.10 | .22 |
| 2.8 | 81.83 | .56 | 35.20 | .37 | 7.78 | .18 | 0.15 | .02 | 12.32 | .22 |
| 2.9 | 81.27 | .56 | 34.83 | .37 | 7.60 | .17 | 0.17 | .03 | 12.54 | .22 |
| 3.0 | 80.71 | .55 | 34.46 | .36 | 7.43 | .17 | 0.20 | .03 | 12.76 | .22 |
| 3.1 | 80.16 | .55 | 34.10 | .37 | 7.26 | .17 | 0.23 | .03 | 12.98 | .23 |
| 3.2 | 79.61 | .55 | 33.73 | .36 | 7.09 | .17 | 0.26 | .03 | 13.21 | .23 |
| 3.3 | 79.06 | .55 | 33.37 | .36 | 6.92 | .16 | 0.29 | .03 | 13.44 | .23 |
| 3.4 | 78.51 | .55 | 33.01 | .36 | 6.76 | .17 | 0.32 | .04 | 13.67 | .23 |
| 3.5 | 77.96 | .55 | 32.65 | .36 | 6.59 | .16 | 0.36 | .04 | 13.90 | .23 |
| 3.6 | 77.41 | .54 | 32.29 | .35 | 6.43 | .16 | 0.40 | .04 | 14.13 | .24 |
| 3.7 | 76.87 | .54 | 31.94 | .36 | 6.27 | .15 | 0.44 | .04 | 14.37 | .23 |
| 3.8 | 76.33 | .54 | 31.58 | .35 | 6.12 | .16 | 0.48 | .04 | 14.60 | .24 |
| 3.9 | 75.79 | .54 | 31.23 | .35 | 5.96 | .15 | 0.52 | .05 | 14.84 | .24 |
| 4.0 | 75.25 | .54 | 30.88 | .35 | 5.81 | .15 | 0.57 | .05 | 15.08 | .25 |
| 4.1 | 74.71 | .53 | 30.53 | .34 | 5.66 | .15 | 0.62 | .05 | 15.33 | .24 |
| 4.2 | 74.18 | .53 | 30.19 | .35 | 5.51 | .15 | 0.67 | .05 | 15.57 | .25 |
| 4.3 | 73.65 | .53 | 29.84 | .34 | 5.36 | .14 | 0.72 | .05 | 15.82 | .25 |
| 4.4 | 73.12 | .53 | 29.50 | .34 | 5.22 | .15 | 0.77 | .06 | 16.07 | .25 |
| 4.5 | 72.59 | .53 | 29.16 | .34 | 5.07 | .14 | 0.83 | .06 | 16.32 | .25 |
| 4.6 | 72.06 | .52 | 28.82 | .33 | 4.93 | .14 | 0.89 | .06 | 16.57 | .26 |
| 4.7 | 71.54 | .53 | 28.49 | .34 | 4.79 | .13 | 0.95 | .06 | 16.83 | .25 |
| 4.8 | 71.01 | .52 | 28.15 | .33 | 4.66 | .14 | 1.01 | .06 | 17.08 | .26 |
| 4.9 | 70.49 | .52 | 27.82 | .33 | 4.52 | .13 | 1.07 | .07 | 17.34 | .26 |
| 5.0 | 69.97 | —.52 | 27.49 | —.33 | 4.39 | —.13 | 1.14 | +.07 | 17.60 | +.26 |

# TABLE IX. ARGUMENT 4.

Equation = 670″.500 — 670″.3 sin. $z$ — 7″.9 sin. $2z$.

Period, 365.259687 days.

| Days. | 150 | | 160 | | 170 | | 180 | | 190 | |
|---|---|---|---|---|---|---|---|---|---|---|
| Days. | Equation. | Difference. | Equation. | Difference. | Equation. | Difference. | Equation. | Difference. | Equation. | Difference. |
| d. 5.0 | 69″.97 | −.52 | 27″.49 | −.33 | 4″.39 | −.13 | 1″.14 | +.07 | 17″.60 | +.26 |
| 5.1 | 69.45 | .51 | 27.16 | .33 | 4.26 | .13 | 1.21 | .07 | 17.86 | .27 |
| 5.2 | 68.94 | .52 | 26.83 | .32 | 4.13 | .13 | 1.28 | .07 | 18.13 | .26 |
| 5.3 | 68.42 | .51 | 26.51 | .32 | 4.00 | .12 | 1.35 | .07 | 18.39 | .27 |
| 5.4 | 67.91 | .51 | 26.19 | .32 | 3.88 | .13 | 1.42 | .08 | 18.66 | .27 |
| 5.5 | 67.40 | .51 | 25.87 | .32 | 3.75 | .12 | 1.50 | .08 | 18.93 | .27 |
| 5.6 | 66.89 | .50 | 25.55 | .32 | 3.63 | .12 | 1.58 | .08 | 19.20 | .28 |
| 5.7 | 66.39 | .51 | 25.23 | .31 | 3.51 | .11 | 1.66 | .08 | 19.48 | .27 |
| 5.8 | 65.88 | .50 | 24.92 | .31 | 3.40 | .12 | 1.74 | .08 | 19.75 | .28 |
| 5.9 | 65.38 | .50 | 24.61 | .31 | 3.28 | .11 | 1.82 | .09 | 20.03 | .28 |
| 6.0 | 64.88 | .50 | 24.30 | .31 | 3.17 | .11 | 1.91 | .08 | 20.31 | .28 |
| 6.1 | 64.38 | .50 | 23.99 | .31 | 3.06 | .11 | 1.99 | .09 | 20.59 | .28 |
| 6.2 | 63.88 | .49 | 23.68 | .31 | 2.95 | .11 | 2.08 | .10 | 20.87 | .29 |
| 6.3 | 63.39 | .50 | 23.37 | .30 | 2.84 | .10 | 2.18 | .09 | 21.16 | .28 |
| 6.4 | 62.89 | .49 | 23.07 | .30 | 2.74 | .11 | 2.27 | .09 | 21.44 | .29 |
| 6.5 | 62.40 | .49 | 22.77 | .30 | 2.63 | .10 | 2.36 | .10 | 21.73 | .29 |
| 6.6 | 61.91 | .49 | 22.47 | .29 | 2.53 | .10 | 2.46 | .10 | 22.02 | .30 |
| 6.7 | 61.42 | .48 | 22.18 | .30 | 2.43 | .09 | 2.56 | .10 | 22.32 | .29 |
| 6.8 | 60.94 | .49 | 21.88 | .29 | 2.34 | .10 | 2.66 | .10 | 22.61 | .30 |
| 6.9 | 60.45 | .48 | 21.59 | .29 | 2.24 | .09 | 2.76 | .11 | 22.91 | .29 |
| 7.0 | 59.97 | .48 | 21.30 | .29 | 2.15 | .09 | 2.87 | .11 | 23.20 | .30 |
| 7.1 | 59.49 | .48 | 21.01 | .29 | 2.06 | .09 | 2.98 | .11 | 23.50 | .31 |
| 7.2 | 59.01 | .48 | 20.72 | .28 | 1.97 | .09 | 3.09 | .11 | 23.81 | .30 |
| 7.3 | 58.53 | .47 | 20.44 | .29 | 1.88 | .08 | 3.20 | .11 | 24.11 | .31 |
| 7.4 | 58.06 | .48 | 20.15 | .28 | 1.80 | .09 | 3.31 | .12 | 24.42 | .30 |
| 7.5 | 57.58 | .47 | 19.87 | .28 | 1.71 | .08 | 3.43 | .11 | 24.72 | .31 |
| 7.6 | 57.11 | .47 | 19.59 | .28 | 1.63 | .08 | 3.54 | .12 | 25.03 | .31 |
| 7.7 | 56.64 | .46 | 19.31 | .27 | 1.55 | .08 | 3.66 | .12 | 25.34 | .32 |
| 7.8 | 56.18 | .47 | 19.04 | .28 | 1.47 | .07 | 3.78 | .12 | 25.66 | .31 |
| 7.9 | 55.71 | .46 | 18.76 | .27 | 1.40 | .07 | 3.90 | .13 | 25.97 | .32 |
| 8.0 | 55.25 | .47 | 18.49 | .27 | 1.33 | .08 | 4.03 | .13 | 26.29 | .32 |
| 8.1 | 54.78 | .46 | 18.22 | .27 | 1.25 | .06 | 4.16 | .13 | 26.61 | .32 |
| 8.2 | 54.32 | .45 | 17.95 | .26 | 1.19 | .07 | 4.29 | .13 | 26.93 | .32 |
| 8.3 | 53.87 | .46 | 17.69 | .27 | 1.12 | .07 | 4.42 | .13 | 27.25 | .33 |
| 8.4 | 53.41 | .46 | 17.42 | .26 | 1.05 | .06 | 4.55 | .13 | 27.58 | .32 |
| 8.5 | 52.95 | .45 | 17.16 | .26 | 0.99 | .06 | 4.68 | .14 | 27.90 | .33 |
| 8.6 | 52.50 | .45 | 16.90 | .25 | 0.93 | .06 | 4.82 | .14 | 28.23 | .33 |
| 8.7 | 52.05 | .45 | 16.65 | .26 | 0.87 | .06 | 4.96 | .14 | 28.56 | .33 |
| 8.8 | 51.60 | .45 | 16.39 | .25 | 0.81 | .05 | 5.10 | .14 | 28.89 | .34 |
| 8.9 | 51.15 | .44 | 16.14 | .26 | 0.76 | .06 | 5.24 | .15 | 29.23 | .33 |
| 9.0 | 50.71 | .44 | 15.88 | .25 | 0.70 | .05 | 5.39 | .14 | 29.56 | .34 |
| 9.1 | 50.27 | .44 | 15.63 | .24 | 0.65 | .05 | 5.53 | .15 | 29.90 | .34 |
| 9.2 | 49.83 | .44 | 15.39 | .25 | 0.60 | .05 | 5.68 | .15 | 30.24 | .34 |
| 9.3 | 49.39 | .44 | 15.14 | .24 | 0.55 | .04 | 5.83 | .15 | 30.58 | .34 |
| 9.4 | 48.95 | .44 | 14.90 | .25 | 0.51 | .04 | 5.98 | .16 | 30.92 | .34 |
| 9.5 | 48.51 | .43 | 14.65 | .24 | 0.47 | .05 | 6.14 | .15 | 31.26 | .35 |
| 9.6 | 48.08 | .43 | 14.41 | .23 | 0.42 | .04 | 6.29 | .16 | 31.61 | .35 |
| 9.7 | 47.65 | .43 | 14.18 | .24 | 0.38 | .03 | 6.45 | .16 | 31.96 | .35 |
| 9.8 | 47.22 | .43 | 13.94 | .23 | 0.35 | .04 | 6.61 | .16 | 32.31 | .35 |
| 9.9 | 46.79 | −.43 | 13.71 | −.24 | 0.31 | −.03 | 6.77 | +.17 | 32.66 | +.36 |
| 10.0 | 46.36 | | 13.47 | | 0.28 | | 6.94 | | 33.02 | |

# TABLE IX. ARGUMENT 4.

Equation = 670″.500 — 670″.3 sin. $z$ — 7″.9 sin. $2z$.

Period, 365.259687 days.

| Days. | 200 | | 210 | | 220 | | 230 | | 240 | |
|---|---|---|---|---|---|---|---|---|---|---|
| Days. | Equation. | Difference. | Equation. | Difference. | Equation. | Difference. | Equation. | Difference. | Equation. | Difference. |
| d. | ″ | | ″ | | ″ | | ″ | | ″ | |
| 0.0 | 33.02 | +.35 | 77.53 | +.54 | 139.00 | +.69 | 215.49 | +.83 | 304.72 | + .95 |
| 0.1 | 33.37 | .36 | 78.07 | .53 | 139.69 | .70 | 216.32 | .84 | 305.67 | .95 |
| 0.2 | 33.73 | .36 | 78.60 | .54 | 140.39 | .70 | 217.16 | .83 | 306.62 | .95 |
| 0.3 | 34.09 | .36 | 79.14 | .54 | 141.09 | .69 | 217.99 | .84 | 307.57 | .95 |
| 0.4 | 34.45 | .37 | 79.68 | .54 | 141.78 | .70 | 218.83 | .84 | 308.52 | .95 |
| 0.5 | 34.82 | .36 | 80.22 | .55 | 142.48 | .71 | 219.67 | .84 | 309.47 | .95 |
| 0.6 | 35.18 | .37 | 80.77 | .55 | 143.19 | .70 | 220.51 | .84 | 310.42 | .96 |
| 0.7 | 35.55 | .37 | 81.32 | .54 | 143.89 | .70 | 221.35 | .84 | 311.38 | .95 |
| 0.8 | 35.92 | .37 | 81.86 | .55 | 144.59 | .71 | 222.19 | .85 | 312.33 | .96 |
| 0.9 | 36.29 | .37 | 82.41 | .54 | 145.30 | .71 | 223.04 | .84 | 313.29 | .96 |
| 1.0 | 36.66 | .38 | 82.95 | .55 | 146.01 | .70 | 223.88 | .85 | 314.25 | .95 |
| 1.1 | 37.04 | .37 | 83.50 | .55 | 146.71 | .72 | 224.73 | .84 | 315.20 | .96 |
| 1.2 | 37.41 | .38 | 84.05 | .55 | 147.43 | .71 | 225.57 | .85 | 316.16 | .96 |
| 1.3 | 37.79 | .38 | 84.60 | .56 | 148.14 | .71 | 226.42 | .85 | 317.12 | .96 |
| 1.4 | 38.17 | .38 | 85.16 | .56 | 148.85 | .72 | 227.27 | .85 | 318.08 | .97 |
| 1.5 | 38.55 | .39 | 85.72 | .56 | 149.57 | .71 | 228.12 | .85 | 319.05 | .96 |
| 1.6 | 38.94 | .38 | 86.28 | .56 | 150.28 | .72 | 228.97 | .86 | 320.01 | .96 |
| 1.7 | 39.32 | .39 | 86.84 | .56 | 151.00 | .72 | 229.83 | .85 | 320.97 | .97 |
| 1.8 | 39.71 | .39 | 87.40 | .56 | 151.72 | .72 | 230.68 | .86 | 321.94 | .96 |
| 1.9 | 40.10 | .39 | 87.96 | .57 | 152.44 | .72 | 231.54 | .86 | 322.90 | .97 |
| 2.0 | 40.49 | .39 | 88.53 | .56 | 153.16 | .73 | 232.40 | .85 | 323.87 | .96 |
| 2.1 | 40.88 | .40 | 89.09 | .57 | 153.89 | .72 | 233.25 | .86 | 324.83 | .98 |
| 2.2 | 41.28 | .39 | 89.66 | .57 | 154.61 | .73 | 234.11 | .86 | 325.81 | .97 |
| 2.3 | 41.67 | .40 | 90.23 | .58 | 155.34 | .73 | 234.97 | .87 | 326.78 | .97 |
| 2.4 | 42.07 | .40 | 90.81 | .57 | 156.07 | .73 | 235.84 | .86 | 327.75 | .97 |
| 2.5 | 42.47 | .40 | 91.38 | .58 | 156.80 | .73 | 236.70 | .86 | 328.72 | .97 |
| 2.6 | 42.87 | .41 | 91.96 | .57 | 157.53 | .73 | 237.56 | .87 | 329.69 | .98 |
| 2.7 | 43.28 | .40 | 92.53 | .58 | 158.26 | .73 | 238.43 | .87 | 330.67 | .97 |
| 2.8 | 43.68 | .41 | 93.11 | .58 | 158.99 | .74 | 239.30 | .86 | 331.64 | .98 |
| 2.9 | 44.09 | .41 | 93.69 | .58 | 159.73 | .74 | 240.16 | .87 | 332.62 | .97 |
| 3.0 | 44.50 | .41 | 94.27 | .59 | 160.47 | .73 | 241.03 | .87 | 333.59 | .98 |
| 3.1 | 44.91 | .41 | 94.86 | .58 | 161.20 | .74 | 241.90 | .88 | 334.57 | .98 |
| 3.2 | 45.32 | .41 | 95.44 | .59 | 161.94 | .74 | 242.78 | .87 | 335.55 | .98 |
| 3.3 | 45.73 | .42 | 96.03 | .59 | 162.68 | .75 | 243.65 | .87 | 336.53 | .98 |
| 3.4 | 46.15 | .42 | 96.62 | .59 | 163.43 | .74 | 244.52 | .88 | 337.51 | .98 |
| 3.5 | 46.57 | .42 | 97.21 | .59 | 164.17 | .75 | 245.40 | .87 | 338.49 | .98 |
| 3.6 | 46.99 | .42 | 97.80 | .60 | 164.92 | .74 | 246.27 | .88 | 339.47 | .98 |
| 3.7 | 47.41 | .42 | 98.40 | .59 | 165.66 | .75 | 247.15 | .88 | 340.45 | .99 |
| 3.8 | 47.83 | .43 | 98.99 | .60 | 166.41 | .75 | 248.03 | .88 | 341.44 | .98 |
| 3.9 | 48.26 | .43 | 99.59 | .60 | 167.16 | .75 | 248.91 | .88 | 342.42 | .99 |
| 4.0 | 48.69 | .42 | 100.19 | .60 | 167.91 | .75 | 249.79 | .88 | 343.41 | .98 |
| 4.1 | 49.11 | .44 | 100.79 | .60 | 168.66 | .76 | 250.67 | .89 | 344.39 | .99 |
| 4.2 | 49.55 | .43 | 101.39 | .60 | 169.42 | .75 | 251.56 | .88 | 345.38 | .99 |
| 4.3 | 49.98 | .43 | 101.99 | .61 | 170.17 | .76 | 252.44 | .89 | 346.37 | .99 |
| 4.4 | 50.41 | .44 | 102.60 | .60 | 170.93 | .76 | 253.33 | .88 | 347.36 | .99 |
| 4.5 | 50.85 | .44 | 103.20 | .61 | 171.69 | .76 | 254.21 | .89 | 348.35 | .99 |
| 4.6 | 51.29 | .44 | 103.81 | .61 | 172.45 | .76 | 255.10 | .89 | 349.34 | .99 |
| 4.7 | 51.73 | .44 | 104.42 | .61 | 173.21 | .76 | 255.99 | .89 | 350.33 | .99 |
| 4.8 | 52.17 | .44 | 105.03 | .61 | 173.97 | .77 | 256.88 | .89 | 351.32 | 1.00 |
| 4.9 | 52.61 | .44 | 105.64 | .62 | 174.74 | .76 | 257.77 | .90 | 352.32 | .99 |
| 5.0 | 53.05 | +.45 | 106.26 | +.61 | 175.50 | +.77 | 258.67 | +.89 | 353.31 | +1.00 |

# TABLE IX. ARGUMENT 4.

Equation $= 670''.500 - 670''.3 \sin. z - 7''.9 \sin. 2z$.

Period, 365.259687 days.

| Days. | 200 | | 210 | | 220 | | 230 | | 240 | |
|---|---|---|---|---|---|---|---|---|---|---|
| Days. | Equation. | Difference. | Equation. | Difference. | Equation. | Difference. | Equation. | Difference. | Equation. | Difference. |
| d. | " | | " | | " | | " | | " | |
| 5.0 | 53.05 | +.45 | 106.26 | +.61 | 175.50 | +.77 | 258.67 | +.89 | 353.31 | +1.00 |
| 5.1 | 53.50 | .45 | 106.87 | .62 | 176.27 | .77 | 259.56 | .90 | 354.31 | 1.00 |
| 5.2 | 53.95 | .45 | 107.49 | .62 | 177.04 | .77 | 260.46 | .89 | 355.31 | .99 |
| 5.3 | 54.40 | .45 | 108.11 | .62 | 177.81 | .77 | 261.35 | .90 | 356.30 | 1.00 |
| 5.4 | 54.85 | .46 | 108.73 | .63 | 178.58 | .77 | 262.25 | .90 | 357.30 | 1.00 |
| 5.5 | 55.31 | .45 | 109.36 | .63 | 179.35 | .77 | 263.15 | .90 | 358.30 | 1.00 |
| 5.6 | 55.76 | .46 | 109.99 | .62 | 180.12 | .78 | 264.05 | .90 | 359.30 | 1.00 |
| 5.7 | 56.22 | .46 | 110.61 | .62 | 180.90 | .77 | 264.95 | .90 | 360.30 | 1.00 |
| 5.8 | 56.68 | .46 | 111.23 | .63 | 181.67 | .78 | 265.85 | .90 | 361.30 | 1.00 |
| 5.9 | 57.14 | .46 | 111.86 | .63 | 182.45 | .78 | 266.75 | .91 | 362.30 | 1.01 |
| 6.0 | 57.60 | .46 | 112.49 | .64 | 183.23 | .78 | 267.66 | .90 | 363.31 | 1.00 |
| 6.1 | 58.06 | .47 | 113.13 | .63 | 184.01 | .78 | 268.56 | .91 | 364.31 | 1.01 |
| 6.2 | 58.53 | .47 | 113.76 | .63 | 184.79 | .78 | 269.47 | .91 | 365.32 | 1.00 |
| 6.3 | 59.00 | .47 | 114.39 | .64 | 185.57 | .79 | 270.38 | .91 | 366.32 | 1.01 |
| 6.4 | 59.47 | .47 | 115.03 | .64 | 186.36 | .78 | 271.29 | .91 | 367.33 | 1.01 |
| 6.5 | 59.94 | .47 | 115.67 | .64 | 187.14 | .79 | 272.20 | .91 | 368.34 | 1.00 |
| 6.6 | 60.41 | .48 | 116.31 | .64 | 187.93 | .79 | 273.11 | .91 | 369.34 | 1.01 |
| 6.7 | 60.89 | .47 | 116.95 | .65 | 188.72 | .79 | 274.02 | .91 | 370.35 | 1.01 |
| 6.8 | 61.36 | .48 | 117.60 | .64 | 189.51 | .79 | 274.93 | .92 | 371.36 | 1.01 |
| 6.9 | 61.84 | .48 | 118.24 | .65 | 190.30 | .79 | 275.85 | .91 | 372.37 | 1.02 |
| 7.0 | 62.32 | .49 | 118.89 | .64 | 191.09 | .80 | 276.76 | .92 | 373.39 | 1.01 |
| 7.1 | 62.81 | .48 | 119.53 | .65 | 191.89 | .79 | 277.68 | .92 | 374.40 | 1.01 |
| 7.2 | 63.29 | .49 | 120.18 | .66 | 192.68 | .80 | 278.60 | .91 | 375.41 | 1.02 |
| 7.3 | 63.78 | .48 | 120.84 | .65 | 193.48 | .80 | 279.51 | .92 | 376.43 | 1.01 |
| 7.4 | 64.26 | .49 | 121.49 | .65 | 194.28 | .80 | 280.43 | .93 | 377.44 | 1.02 |
| 7.5 | 64.75 | .49 | 122.14 | .66 | 195.08 | .80 | 281.36 | .92 | 378.46 | 1.01 |
| 7.6 | 65.24 | .49 | 122.80 | .66 | 195.88 | .80 | 282.28 | .92 | 379.47 | 1.02 |
| 7.7 | 65.73 | .50 | 123.46 | .66 | 196.68 | .80 | 283.20 | .92 | 380.49 | 1.02 |
| 7.8 | 66.23 | .49 | 124.12 | .66 | 197.48 | .81 | 284.12 | .93 | 381.51 | 1.02 |
| 7.9 | 66.72 | .50 | 124.78 | .66 | 198.29 | .80 | 285.05 | .92 | 382.53 | 1.02 |
| 8.0 | 67.22 | .50 | 125.44 | .66 | 199.09 | .81 | 285.97 | .93 | 383.55 | 1.02 |
| 8.1 | 67.72 | .50 | 126.10 | .67 | 199.90 | .81 | 286.90 | .93 | 384.57 | 1.02 |
| 8.2 | 68.22 | .50 | 126.77 | .66 | 200.71 | .81 | 287.83 | .93 | 385.59 | 1.02 |
| 8.3 | 68.72 | .51 | 127.43 | .67 | 201.52 | .81 | 288.76 | .93 | 386.61 | 1.02 |
| 8.4 | 69.23 | .51 | 128.10 | .67 | 202.33 | .81 | 289.69 | .93 | 387.63 | 1.03 |
| 8.5 | 69.74 | .50 | 128.77 | .67 | 203.14 | .82 | 290.62 | .93 | 388.66 | 1.02 |
| 8.6 | 70.24 | .51 | 129.44 | .68 | 203.96 | .81 | 291.55 | .94 | 389.68 | 1.03 |
| 8.7 | 70.75 | .52 | 130.12 | .67 | 204.77 | .82 | 292.49 | .93 | 390.71 | 1.02 |
| 8.8 | 71.27 | .51 | 130.79 | .67 | 205.59 | .82 | 293.42 | .94 | 391.73 | 1.03 |
| 8.9 | 71.78 | .51 | 131.46 | .68 | 206.41 | .82 | 294.36 | .93 | 392.76 | 1.03 |
| 9.0 | 72.29 | .52 | 132.14 | .68 | 207.23 | .82 | 295.29 | .94 | 393.79 | 1.03 |
| 9.1 | 72.81 | .52 | 132.82 | .68 | 208.05 | .82 | 296.23 | .94 | 394.82 | 1.02 |
| 9.2 | 73.33 | .52 | 133.50 | .68 | 208.87 | .82 | 297.17 | .94 | 395.84 | 1.03 |
| 9.3 | 73.85 | .52 | 134.18 | .69 | 209.69 | .83 | 298.11 | .94 | 396.87 | 1.04 |
| 9.4 | 74.37 | .52 | 134.87 | .68 | 210.52 | .82 | 299.05 | .94 | 397.91 | 1.03 |
| 9.5 | 74.89 | .53 | 135.55 | .69 | 211.34 | .83 | 299.99 | .95 | 398.94 | 1.03 |
| 9.6 | 75.42 | .52 | 136.24 | .69 | 212.17 | .83 | 300.94 | .94 | 399.97 | 1.03 |
| 9.7 | 75.94 | .53 | 136.93 | .69 | 213.00 | .83 | 301.88 | .95 | 401.00 | 1.04 |
| 9.8 | 76.47 | .53 | 137.62 | .69 | 213.83 | .83 | 302.83 | .94 | 402.04 | 1.03 |
| 9.9 | 77.00 | +.53 | 138.31 | +.69 | 214.66 | +.83 | 303.77 | +.95 | 403.07 | +1.04 |
| 10.0 | 77.53 | | 139.00 | | 215.49 | | 304.72 | | 404.11 | |

# TABLE IX. ARGUMENT 4.

Equation $= 670''.500 - 670''.3 \sin. z - 7''.9 \sin. 2z$.

Period, 365.259687 days.

| Days. | 250 | | 260 | | 270 | | 280 | | 290 | |
|---|---|---|---|---|---|---|---|---|---|---|
| Days. | Equation. | Difference. | Equation. | Difference. | Equation. | Difference. | Equation. | Difference. | Equation. | Difference. |
| d. | ″ | | ″ | | ″ | | ″ | | ″ | |
| 0.0 | 404.11 | +1.03 | 510.84 | +1.10 | 621.96 | +1.12 | 734.41 | +1.12 | 845.11 | +1.09 |
| 0.1 | 405.14 | 1.04 | 511.94 | 1.09 | 623.08 | 1.13 | 735.53 | 1.12 | 846.20 | 1.09 |
| 0.2 | 406.18 | 1.03 | 513.03 | 1.10 | 624.21 | 1.12 | 736.65 | 1.12 | 847.29 | 1.08 |
| 0.3 | 407.21 | 1.04 | 514.13 | 1.09 | 625.33 | 1.13 | 737.77 | 1.12 | 848.37 | 1.09 |
| 0.4 | 408.25 | 1.04 | 515.22 | 1.10 | 626.46 | 1.12 | 738.89 | 1.12 | 849.46 | 1.08 |
| 0.5 | 409.29 | 1.04 | 516.32 | 1.10 | 627.58 | 1.12 | 740.01 | 1.12 | 850.54 | 1.09 |
| 0.6 | 410.33 | 1.04 | 517.42 | 1.09 | 628.70 | 1.13 | 741.13 | 1.12 | 851.63 | 1.08 |
| 0.7 | 411.37 | 1.04 | 518.51 | 1.10 | 629.83 | 1.12 | 742.25 | 1.12 | 852.71 | 1.09 |
| 0.8 | 412.41 | 1.04 | 519.61 | 1.10 | 630.95 | 1.13 | 743.37 | 1.12 | 853.80 | 1.08 |
| 0.9 | 413.45 | 1.05 | 520.71 | 1.09 | 632.08 | 1.12 | 744.49 | 1.12 | 854.88 | 1.09 |
| 1.0 | 414.50 | 1.04 | 521.80 | 1.10 | 633.20 | 1.12 | 745.61 | 1.12 | 855.97 | 1.08 |
| 1.1 | 415.54 | 1.04 | 522.90 | 1.10 | 634.32 | 1.13 | 746.73 | 1.12 | 857.05 | 1.08 |
| 1.2 | 416.58 | 1.05 | 524.00 | 1.10 | 635.45 | 1.12 | 747.85 | 1.12 | 858.13 | 1.08 |
| 1.3 | 417.63 | 1.04 | 525.10 | 1.10 | 636.57 | 1.13 | 748.97 | 1.11 | 859.21 | 1.08 |
| 1.4 | 418.67 | 1.05 | 526.20 | 1.10 | 637.70 | 1.12 | 750.08 | 1.12 | 860.29 | 1.08 |
| 1.5 | 419.72 | 1.04 | 527.30 | 1.10 | 638.82 | 1.12 | 751.20 | 1.12 | 861.37 | 1.08 |
| 1.6 | 420.76 | 1.05 | 528.40 | 1.10 | 639.94 | 1.13 | 752.32 | 1.12 | 862.45 | 1.08 |
| 1.7 | 421.81 | 1.05 | 529.50 | 1.11 | 641.07 | 1.12 | 753.44 | 1.12 | 863.53 | 1.08 |
| 1.8 | 422.86 | 1.05 | 530.61 | 1.10 | 642.19 | 1.13 | 754.56 | 1.11 | 864.61 | 1.08 |
| 1.9 | 423.91 | 1.05 | 531.71 | 1.10 | 643.32 | 1.12 | 755.67 | 1.12 | 865.69 | 1.08 |
| 2.0 | 424.96 | 1.05 | 532.81 | 1.10 | 644.44 | 1.13 | 756.79 | 1.12 | 866.77 | 1.08 |
| 2.1 | 426.01 | 1.05 | 533.91 | 1.11 | 645.57 | 1.12 | 757.91 | 1.11 | 867.85 | 1.07 |
| 2.2 | 427.06 | 1.05 | 535.02 | 1.10 | 646.69 | 1.13 | 759.02 | 1.12 | 868.92 | 1.08 |
| 2.3 | 428.11 | 1.05 | 536.12 | 1.10 | 647.82 | 1.12 | 760.14 | 1.11 | 870.00 | 1.08 |
| 2.4 | 429.16 | 1.05 | 537.22 | 1.11 | 648.94 | 1.13 | 761.25 | 1.12 | 871.08 | 1.07 |
| 2.5 | 430.21 | 1.06 | 538.33 | 1.10 | 650.07 | 1.12 | 762.37 | 1.12 | 872.15 | 1.08 |
| 2.6 | 431.27 | 1.05 | 539.43 | 1.11 | 651.19 | 1.13 | 763.49 | 1.11 | 873.23 | 1.07 |
| 2.7 | 432.32 | 1.06 | 540.54 | 1.10 | 652.32 | 1.13 | 764.60 | 1.12 | 874.30 | 1.07 |
| 2.8 | 433.38 | 1.05 | 541.64 | 1.11 | 653.45 | 1.12 | 765.72 | 1.11 | 875.37 | 1.08 |
| 2.9 | 434.43 | 1.06 | 542.75 | 1.10 | 654.57 | 1.13 | 766.83 | 1.11 | 876.45 | 1.07 |
| 3.0 | 435.49 | 1.05 | 543.85 | 1.11 | 655.70 | 1.12 | 767.94 | 1.12 | 877.52 | 1.07 |
| 3.1 | 436.54 | 1.06 | 544.96 | 1.11 | 656.82 | 1.13 | 769.06 | 1.11 | 878.59 | 1.07 |
| 3.2 | 437.60 | 1.06 | 546.07 | 1.10 | 657.95 | 1.12 | 770.17 | 1.12 | 879.66 | 1.07 |
| 3.3 | 438.66 | 1.06 | 547.17 | 1.11 | 659.07 | 1.13 | 771.29 | 1.11 | 880.73 | 1.07 |
| 3.4 | 439.72 | 1.06 | 548.28 | 1.11 | 660.20 | 1.13 | 772.40 | 1.11 | 881.80 | 1.07 |
| 3.5 | 440.78 | 1.06 | 549.39 | 1.11 | 661.33 | 1.12 | 773.51 | 1.12 | 882.87 | 1.07 |
| 3.6 | 441.84 | 1.06 | 550.50 | 1.10 | 662.45 | 1.13 | 774.63 | 1.11 | 883.94 | 1.07 |
| 3.7 | 442.90 | 1.06 | 551.60 | 1.11 | 663.58 | 1.12 | 775.74 | 1.11 | 885.01 | 1.07 |
| 3.8 | 443.96 | 1.06 | 552.71 | 1.11 | 664.70 | 1.13 | 776.85 | 1.11 | 886.08 | 1.07 |
| 3.9 | 445.02 | 1.06 | 553.82 | 1.11 | 665.83 | 1.12 | 777.96 | 1.11 | 887.15 | 1.06 |
| 4.0 | 446.08 | 1.06 | 554.93 | 1.11 | 666.95 | 1.13 | 779.07 | 1.11 | 888.21 | 1.07 |
| 4.1 | 447.14 | 1.07 | 556.04 | 1.11 | 668.08 | 1.13 | 780.18 | 1.12 | 889.28 | 1.07 |
| 4.2 | 448.21 | 1.06 | 557.15 | 1.11 | 669.21 | 1.12 | 781.30 | 1.11 | 890.35 | 1.06 |
| 4.3 | 449.27 | 1.07 | 558.26 | 1.11 | 670.33 | 1.13 | 782.41 | 1.11 | 891.41 | 1.06 |
| 4.4 | 450.34 | 1.06 | 559.37 | 1.11 | 671.46 | 1.12 | 783.52 | 1.11 | 892.47 | 1.07 |
| 4.5 | 451.40 | 1.07 | 560.48 | 1.11 | 672.58 | 1.13 | 784.63 | 1.11 | 893.54 | 1.06 |
| 4.6 | 452.47 | 1.06 | 561.59 | 1.12 | 673.71 | 1.13 | 785.74 | 1.11 | 894.60 | 1.06 |
| 4.7 | 453.53 | 1.07 | 562.71 | 1.11 | 674.84 | 1.12 | 786.85 | 1.11 | 895.66 | 1.07 |
| 4.8 | 454.60 | 1.07 | 563.82 | 1.11 | 675.96 | 1.13 | 787.96 | 1.10 | 896.73 | 1.06 |
| 4.9 | 455.67 | 1.07 | 564.93 | 1.11 | 677.09 | 1.12 | 789.06 | 1.11 | 897.79 | 1.06 |
| 5.0 | 456.74 | +1.06 | 566.04 | +1.11 | 678.21 | +1.13 | 790.17 | +1.11 | 898.85 | +1.06 |

# TABLE IX. ARGUMENT 4.

Equation = 670″.500 — 670″.3 sin. $z$ — 7″.9 sin. 2$z$.

Period, 365.259687 days.

| Days. | 250 | | 260 | | 270 | | 280 | | 290 | |
|---|---|---|---|---|---|---|---|---|---|---|
| Days. | Equation. | Difference. | Equation. | Difference. | Equation. | Difference. | Equation. | Difference. | Equation. | Difference. |
| d. | ″ | | ″ | | ″ | | ″ | | ″ | |
| 5.0 | 456.74 | +1.06 | 566.04 | +1.11 | 678.21 | +1.13 | 790.17 | +1.11 | 898.85 | +1.06 |
| 5.1 | 457.80 | 1.07 | 567.15 | 1.12 | 679.34 | 1.12 | 791.28 | 1.11 | 899.91 | 1.06 |
| 5.2 | 458.87 | 1.07 | 568.27 | 1.11 | 680.46 | 1.13 | 792.39 | 1.11 | 900.97 | 1.06 |
| 5.3 | 459.94 | 1.08 | 569.38 | 1.11 | 681.59 | 1.13 | 793.50 | 1.10 | 902.03 | 1.05 |
| 5.4 | 461.02 | 1.07 | 570.49 | 1.12 | 682.72 | 1.12 | 794.60 | 1.11 | 903.08 | 1.06 |
| 5.5 | 462.09 | 1.07 | 571.61 | 1.11 | 683.84 | 1.13 | 795.71 | 1.11 | 904.14 | 1.06 |
| 5.6 | 463.16 | 1.07 | 572.72 | 1.12 | 684.97 | 1.12 | 796.82 | 1.10 | 905.20 | 1.05 |
| 5.7 | 464.23 | 1.07 | 573.84 | 1.11 | 686.09 | 1.13 | 797.92 | 1.11 | 906.25 | 1.06 |
| 5.8 | 465.30 | 1.08 | 574.95 | 1.12 | 687.22 | 1.12 | 799.03 | 1.10 | 907.31 | 1.05 |
| 5.9 | 466.38 | 1.07 | 576.07 | 1.11 | 688.34 | 1.11 | 800.13 | 1.11 | 908.36 | 1.06 |
| 6.0 | 467.45 | 1.07 | 577.18 | 1.11 | 689.45 | 1.14 | 801.24 | 1.10 | 909.42 | 1.05 |
| 6.1 | 468.52 | 1.08 | 578.29 | 1.12 | 690.59 | 1.13 | 802.34 | 1.11 | 910.47 | 1.05 |
| 6.2 | 469.60 | 1.08 | 579.41 | 1.12 | 691.72 | 1.12 | 803.45 | 1.10 | 911.52 | 1.06 |
| 6.3 | 470.68 | 1.07 | 580.53 | 1.11 | 692.84 | 1.13 | 804.55 | 1.10 | 912.58 | 1.05 |
| 6.4 | 471.75 | 1.08 | 581.64 | 1.12 | 693.97 | 1.12 | 805.65 | 1.11 | 913.63 | 1.05 |
| 6.5 | 472.83 | 1.08 | 582.76 | 1.12 | 695.09 | 1.13 | 806.76 | 1.10 | 914.68 | 1.05 |
| 6.6 | 473.91 | 1.07 | 583.88 | 1.11 | 696.22 | 1.13 | 807.86 | 1.10 | 915.73 | 1.05 |
| 6.7 | 474.98 | 1.08 | 584.99 | 1.12 | 697.35 | 1.12 | 808.96 | 1.10 | 916.78 | 1.05 |
| 6.8 | 476.06 | 1.08 | 586.11 | 1.12 | 698.47 | 1.13 | 810.06 | 1.11 | 917.83 | 1.04 |
| 6.9 | 477.14 | 1.08 | 587.23 | 1.12 | 699.60 | 1.12 | 811.17 | 1.10 | 918.87 | 1.05 |
| 7.0 | 478.22 | 1.08 | 588.35 | 1.11 | 700.72 | 1.12 | 812.27 | 1.10 | 919.92 | 1.05 |
| 7.1 | 479.30 | 1.08 | 589.46 | 1.12 | 701.84 | 1.13 | 813.37 | 1.10 | 920.97 | 1.04 |
| 7.2 | 480.38 | 1.08 | 590.58 | 1.12 | 702.97 | 1.12 | 814.47 | 1.10 | 922.01 | 1.05 |
| 7.3 | 481.46 | 1.09 | 591.70 | 1.12 | 704.09 | 1.13 | 815.57 | 1.10 | 923.06 | 1.04 |
| 7.4 | 482.55 | 1.08 | 592.82 | 1.12 | 705.22 | 1.12 | 816.67 | 1.10 | 924.10 | 1.05 |
| 7.5 | 483.63 | 1.08 | 593.94 | 1.11 | 706.34 | 1.13 | 817.77 | 1.10 | 925.15 | 1.04 |
| 7.6 | 484.71 | 1.08 | 595.05 | 1.12 | 707.47 | 1.12 | 818.87 | 1.09 | 926.19 | 1.04 |
| 7.7 | 485.79 | 1.09 | 596.17 | 1.12 | 708.59 | 1.12 | 819.96 | 1.10 | 927.23 | 1.05 |
| 7.8 | 486.88 | 1.08 | 597.29 | 1.12 | 709.71 | 1.13 | 821.06 | 1.10 | 928.28 | 1.04 |
| 7.9 | 487.96 | 1.09 | 598.41 | 1.12 | 710.84 | 1.12 | 822.16 | 1.10 | 929.32 | 1.04 |
| 8.0 | 489.05 | 1.08 | 599.53 | 1.12 | 711.96 | 1.13 | 823.26 | 1.09 | 930.36 | 1.04 |
| 8.1 | 490.13 | 1.09 | 600.65 | 1.12 | 713.09 | 1.12 | 824.35 | 1.10 | 931.40 | 1.04 |
| 8.2 | 491.22 | 1.08 | 601.77 | 1.12 | 714.21 | 1.12 | 825.45 | 1.10 | 932.44 | 1.04 |
| 8.3 | 492.30 | 1.09 | 602.89 | 1.12 | 715.33 | 1.13 | 826.55 | 1.09 | 933.48 | 1.03 |
| 8.4 | 493.39 | 1.09 | 604.01 | 1.12 | 716.46 | 1.12 | 827.64 | 1.10 | 934.51 | 1.04 |
| 8.5 | 494.48 | 1.08 | 605.13 | 1.12 | 717.58 | 1.12 | 828.74 | 1.09 | 935.55 | 1.04 |
| 8.6 | 495.56 | 1.09 | 606.25 | 1.12 | 718.70 | 1.13 | 829.83 | 1.10 | 936.59 | 1.03 |
| 8.7 | 496.65 | 1.09 | 607.37 | 1.13 | 719.83 | 1.12 | 830.93 | 1.09 | 937.62 | 1.04 |
| 8.8 | 497.74 | 1.09 | 608.50 | 1.12 | 720.95 | 1.12 | 832.02 | 1.09 | 938.66 | 1.03 |
| 8.9 | 498.83 | 1.09 | 609.62 | 1.12 | 722.07 | 1.12 | 833.11 | 1.10 | 939.69 | 1.03 |
| 9.0 | 499.92 | 1.09 | 610.74 | 1.12 | 723.19 | 1.13 | 834.21 | 1.09 | 940.72 | 1.04 |
| 9.1 | 501.01 | 1.09 | 611.86 | 1.12 | 724.32 | 1.12 | 835.30 | 1.09 | 941.76 | 1.03 |
| 9.2 | 502.10 | 1.09 | 612.98 | 1.12 | 725.44 | 1.12 | 836.39 | 1.09 | 942.79 | 1.03 |
| 9.3 | 503.19 | 1.09 | 614.10 | 1.13 | 726.56 | 1.12 | 837.48 | 1.09 | 943.82 | 1.03 |
| 9.4 | 504.28 | 1.09 | 615.23 | 1.12 | 727.68 | 1.12 | 838.57 | 1.09 | 944.85 | 1.03 |
| 9.5 | 505.37 | 1.10 | 616.35 | 1.12 | 728.80 | 1.13 | 839.66 | 1.09 | 945.88 | 1.03 |
| 9.6 | 506.47 | 1.09 | 617.47 | 1.12 | 729.93 | 1.12 | 840.75 | 1.09 | 946.91 | 1.02 |
| 9.7 | 507.56 | 1.09 | 618.59 | 1.13 | 731.05 | 1.12 | 841.84 | 1.09 | 947.93 | 1.03 |
| 9.8 | 508.65 | 1.10 | 619.72 | 1.12 | 732.17 | 1.12 | 842.93 | 1.09 | 948.96 | 1.03 |
| 9.9 | 509.75 | +1.09 | 620.84 | +1.12 | 733.29 | +1.12 | 844.02 | +1.09 | 949.99 | +1.02 |
| 10.0 | 510.84 | | 621.96 | | 734.41 | | 845.11 | | 951.01 | |

# TABLE IX. ARGUMENT 4.

Equation = 670″.500 — 670″.3 sin. $z$ — 7″.9 sin. $2z$.

Period, 365.259687 days.

| Days. | 300 | | 310 | | 320 | | 330 | | 340 | |
|---|---|---|---|---|---|---|---|---|---|---|
| Days. | Equation. | Difference. | Equation. | Difference. | Equation. | Difference. | Equation. | Difference. | Equation. | Difference. |
| d. 0.0 | ″ 951.01 | +1.03 | ″ 1049.17 | +.93 | ″ 1136.80 | +.81 | ″ 1211.36 | +.67 | ″ 1270.60 | +.51 |
| 0.1 | 952.04 | 1.02 | 1050.10 | .93 | 1137.61 | .81 | 1212.03 | .67 | 1271.11 | .51 |
| 0.2 | 953.06 | 1.02 | 1051.03 | .93 | 1138.42 | .82 | 1212.70 | .67 | 1271.62 | .50 |
| 0.3 | 954.08 | 1.03 | 1051.96 | .93 | 1139.24 | .81 | 1213.37 | .67 | 1272.12 | .51 |
| 0.4 | 955.11 | 1.02 | 1052.89 | .93 | 1140.05 | .80 | 1214.04 | .66 | 1272.63 | .50 |
| 0.5 | 956.13 | 1.02 | 1053.82 | .93 | 1140.85 | .81 | 1214.70 | .67 | 1273.13 | .50 |
| 0.6 | 957.15 | 1.02 | 1054.75 | .93 | 1141.66 | .81 | 1215.37 | .66 | 1273.63 | .50 |
| 0.7 | 958.17 | 1.02 | 1055.68 | .92 | 1142.47 | .80 | 1216.03 | .66 | 1274.13 | .49 |
| 0.8 | 959.19 | 1.02 | 1056.60 | .92 | 1143.27 | .81 | 1216.69 | .66 | 1274.62 | .50 |
| 0.9 | 960.21 | 1.01 | 1057.52 | .93 | 1144.08 | .80 | 1217.35 | .66 | 1275.12 | .49 |
| 1.0 | 961.22 | 1.02 | 1058.45 | .92 | 1144.88 | .80 | 1218.01 | .65 | 1275.61 | .49 |
| 1.1 | 962.24 | 1.02 | 1059.37 | .92 | 1145.68 | .80 | 1218.66 | .66 | 1276.10 | .49 |
| 1.2 | 963.26 | 1.01 | 1060.29 | .92 | 1146.48 | .80 | 1219.32 | .65 | 1276.59 | .49 |
| 1.3 | 964.27 | 1.01 | 1061.21 | .92 | 1147.28 | .80 | 1219.97 | .65 | 1277.08 | .49 |
| 1.4 | 965.28 | 1.02 | 1062.13 | .92 | 1148.08 | .79 | 1220.62 | .65 | 1277.57 | .48 |
| 1.5 | 966.30 | 1.01 | 1063.05 | .91 | 1148.87 | .80 | 1221.27 | .65 | 1278.05 | .48 |
| 1.6 | 967.31 | 1.01 | 1063.96 | .92 | 1149.67 | .79 | 1221.92 | .65 | 1278.53 | .48 |
| 1.7 | 968.32 | 1.01 | 1064.88 | .91 | 1150.46 | .79 | 1222.57 | .64 | 1279.01 | .48 |
| 1.8 | 969.33 | 1.01 | 1065.79 | .92 | 1151.25 | .79 | 1223.21 | .65 | 1279.49 | .48 |
| 1.9 | 970.34 | 1.01 | 1066.71 | .91 | 1152.04 | .79 | 1223.86 | .64 | 1279.97 | .47 |
| 2.0 | 971.35 | 1.01 | 1067.62 | .91 | 1152.83 | .79 | 1224.50 | .64 | 1280.44 | .48 |
| 2.1 | 972.36 | 1.01 | 1068.53 | .91 | 1153.62 | .79 | 1225.14 | .64 | 1280.92 | .47 |
| 2.2 | 973.37 | 1.01 | 1069.44 | .91 | 1154.41 | .78 | 1225.78 | .63 | 1281.39 | .47 |
| 2.3 | 974.38 | 1.00 | 1070.35 | .91 | 1155.19 | .78 | 1226.41 | .64 | 1281.86 | .47 |
| 2.4 | 975.38 | 1.01 | 1071.26 | .91 | 1155.97 | .79 | 1227.05 | .63 | 1282.33 | .47 |
| 2.5 | 976.39 | 1.00 | 1072.17 | .90 | 1156.76 | .78 | 1227.68 | .64 | 1282.80 | .46 |
| 2.6 | 977.39 | 1.01 | 1073.07 | .91 | 1157.54 | .78 | 1228.32 | .63 | 1283.26 | .46 |
| 2.7 | 978.40 | 1.00 | 1073.98 | .90 | 1158.32 | .78 | 1228.95 | .63 | 1283.72 | .46 |
| 2.8 | 979.40 | 1.00 | 1074.88 | .90 | 1159.10 | .77 | 1229.58 | .63 | 1284.18 | .46 |
| 2.9 | 980.40 | 1.00 | 1075.78 | .90 | 1159.87 | .78 | 1230.21 | .62 | 1284.64 | .46 |
| 3.0 | 981.40 | 1.00 | 1076.68 | .90 | 1160.65 | .77 | 1230.83 | .63 | 1285.10 | .46 |
| 3.1 | 982.40 | 1.00 | 1077.58 | .90 | 1161.42 | .77 | 1231.46 | .62 | 1285.56 | .45 |
| 3.2 | 983.40 | 1.00 | 1078.48 | .90 | 1162.19 | .78 | 1232.08 | .62 | 1286.01 | .45 |
| 3.3 | 984.40 | 1.00 | 1079.38 | .90 | 1162.97 | .77 | 1232.70 | .62 | 1286.46 | .45 |
| 3.4 | 985.40 | .99 | 1080.28 | .89 | 1163.74 | .76 | 1233.32 | .62 | 1286.91 | .45 |
| 3.5 | 986.39 | 1.00 | 1081.17 | .90 | 1164.50 | .77 | 1233.94 | .62 | 1287.36 | .45 |
| 3.6 | 987.39 | .99 | 1082.07 | .89 | 1165.27 | .77 | 1234.56 | .61 | 1287.81 | .45 |
| 3.7 | 988.38 | 1.00 | 1082.96 | .89 | 1166.04 | .76 | 1235.17 | .61 | 1288.26 | .44 |
| 3.8 | 989.38 | .99 | 1083.85 | .89 | 1166.80 | .76 | 1235.78 | .62 | 1288.70 | .44 |
| 3.9 | 990.37 | .99 | 1084.74 | .89 | 1167.56 | .77 | 1236.40 | .61 | 1289.14 | .44 |
| 4.0 | 991.36 | .99 | 1085.63 | .89 | 1168.33 | .76 | 1237.01 | .61 | 1289.58 | .44 |
| 4.1 | 992.35 | .99 | 1086.52 | .89 | 1169.09 | .75 | 1237.62 | .60 | 1290.02 | .44 |
| 4.2 | 993.34 | .99 | 1087.41 | .88 | 1169.84 | .76 | 1238.22 | .61 | 1290.46 | .43 |
| 4.3 | 994.33 | .99 | 1088.29 | .89 | 1170.60 | .76 | 1238.83 | .60 | 1290.89 | .44 |
| 4.4 | 995.32 | .99 | 1089.18 | .88 | 1171.36 | .75 | 1239.43 | .60 | 1291.33 | .43 |
| 4.5 | 996.31 | .99 | 1090.06 | .88 | 1172.11 | .75 | 1240.03 | .60 | 1291.76 | .43 |
| 4.6 | 997.30 | .98 | 1090.94 | .89 | 1172.86 | .75 | 1240.63 | .60 | 1292.19 | .42 |
| 4.7 | 998.28 | .99 | 1091.83 | .88 | 1173.61 | .75 | 1241.23 | .60 | 1292.61 | .43 |
| 4.8 | 999.27 | .98 | 1092.71 | .88 | 1174.36 | .75 | 1241.83 | .60 | 1293.04 | .42 |
| 4.9 | 1000.25 | .99 | 1093.59 | .87 | 1175.11 | .75 | 1242.43 | .59 | 1293.46 | .43 |
| 5.0 | 1001.24 | + .98 | 1094.46 | +.88 | 1175.86 | +.75 | 1243.02 | +.59 | 1293.89 | +.42 |

# TABLE IX. ARGUMENT 4.

Equation = 670″.500 — 670″.3 sin. $z$ — 7″.9 sin. 2$z$.

Period, 365.259687 days.

| Days. | 300 | | 310 | | 320 | | 330 | | 340 | |
|---|---|---|---|---|---|---|---|---|---|---|
| Days. | Equation. | Difference. | Equation. | Difference. | Equation. | Difference. | Equation. | Difference. | Equation. | Difference. |
| d. | ″ | | ″ | | ″ | | ″ | | ″ | |
| 5.0 | 1001.24 | +.98 | 1094.46 | +.88 | 1175.86 | +.75 | 1243.02 | +.59 | 1293.89 | +.42 |
| 5.1 | 1002.22 | .98 | 1095.34 | .88 | 1176.61 | .74 | 1243.61 | .59 | 1294.31 | .41 |
| 5.2 | 1003.20 | .98 | 1096.22 | .87 | 1177.35 | .74 | 1244.20 | .59 | 1294.72 | .42 |
| 5.3 | 1004.18 | .98 | 1097.09 | .87 | 1178.09 | .74 | 1244.79 | .59 | 1295.14 | .42 |
| 5.4 | 1005.16 | .98 | 1097.96 | .88 | 1178.83 | .74 | 1245.38 | .59 | 1295.56 | .41 |
| 5.5 | 1006.14 | .97 | 1098.84 | .87 | 1179.57 | .74 | 1245.97 | .58 | 1295.97 | .41 |
| 5.6 | 1007.11 | .98 | 1099.71 | .87 | 1180.31 | .74 | 1246.55 | .58 | 1296.38 | .41 |
| 5.7 | 1008.09 | .98 | 1100.58 | .87 | 1181.05 | .74 | 1247.13 | .58 | 1296.79 | .41 |
| 5.8 | 1009.07 | .97 | 1101.45 | .86 | 1181.79 | .73 | 1247.71 | .58 | 1297.20 | .40 |
| 5.9 | 1010.04 | .98 | 1102.31 | .87 | 1182.52 | .73 | 1248.29 | .58 | 1297.60 | .41 |
| 6.0 | 1011.02 | .97 | 1103.18 | .86 | 1183.25 | .73 | 1248.87 | .58 | 1298.01 | .40 |
| 6.1 | 1011.99 | .97 | 1104.04 | .87 | 1183.98 | .73 | 1249.45 | .57 | 1298.41 | .40 |
| 6.2 | 1012.96 | .97 | 1104.91 | .86 | 1184.71 | .73 | 1250.02 | .57 | 1298.81 | .40 |
| 6.3 | 1013.93 | .97 | 1105.77 | .86 | 1185.44 | .73 | 1250.59 | .58 | 1299.21 | .40 |
| 6.4 | 1014.90 | .97 | 1106.63 | .86 | 1186.17 | .73 | 1251.17 | .56 | 1299.61 | .39 |
| 6.5 | 1015.87 | .97 | 1107.49 | .86 | 1186.90 | .72 | 1251.73 | .57 | 1300.00 | .39 |
| 6.6 | 1016.84 | .97 | 1108.35 | .86 | 1187.62 | .72 | 1252.30 | .57 | 1300.39 | .39 |
| 6.7 | 1017.81 | .96 | 1109.21 | .85 | 1188.34 | .72 | 1252.87 | .56 | 1300.78 | .39 |
| 6.8 | 1018.77 | .97 | 1110.06 | .86 | 1189.06 | .72 | 1253.43 | .57 | 1301.17 | .39 |
| 6.9 | 1019.74 | .96 | 1110.92 | .85 | 1189.78 | .72 | 1254.00 | .56 | 1301.56 | .39 |
| 7.0 | 1020.70 | .97 | 1111.77 | .85 | 1190.50 | .72 | 1254.56 | .56 | 1301.95 | .38 |
| 7.1 | 1021.67 | .96 | 1112.62 | .85 | 1191.22 | .71 | 1255.12 | .55 | 1302.33 | .38 |
| 7.2 | 1022.63 | .96 | 1113.47 | .85 | 1191.93 | .72 | 1255.67 | .56 | 1302.71 | .39 |
| 7.3 | 1023.59 | .96 | 1114.32 | .85 | 1192.65 | .71 | 1256.23 | .55 | 1303.10 | .37 |
| 7.4 | 1024.55 | .96 | 1115.17 | .85 | 1193.36 | .71 | 1256.78 | .56 | 1303.47 | .38 |
| 7.5 | 1025.51 | .96 | 1116.02 | .85 | 1194.07 | .71 | 1257.34 | .55 | 1303.85 | .38 |
| 7.6 | 1026.47 | .96 | 1116.87 | .84 | 1194.78 | .71 | 1257.89 | .55 | 1304.23 | .37 |
| 7.7 | 1027.43 | .95 | 1117.71 | .85 | 1195.49 | .70 | 1258.44 | .54 | 1304.60 | .37 |
| 7.8 | 1028.38 | .96 | 1118.56 | .84 | 1196.19 | .71 | 1258.98 | .55 | 1304.97 | .37 |
| 7.9 | 1029.34 | .95 | 1119.40 | .84 | 1196.90 | .70 | 1259.53 | .55 | 1305.34 | .37 |
| 8.0 | 1030.29 | .96 | 1120.24 | .84 | 1197.60 | .71 | 1260.08 | .54 | 1305.71 | .36 |
| 8.1 | 1031.25 | .95 | 1121.08 | .84 | 1198.31 | .70 | 1260.62 | .54 | 1306.07 | .37 |
| 8.2 | 1032.20 | .95 | 1121.92 | .84 | 1199.01 | .69 | 1261.16 | .54 | 1306.44 | .36 |
| 8.3 | 1033.15 | .95 | 1122.76 | .83 | 1199.70 | .70 | 1261.70 | .54 | 1306.80 | .36 |
| 8.4 | 1034.10 | .95 | 1123.59 | .84 | 1200.40 | .70 | 1262.24 | .53 | 1307.16 | .36 |
| 8.5 | 1035.05 | .95 | 1124.43 | .83 | 1201.10 | .69 | 1262.77 | .54 | 1307.52 | .35 |
| 8.6 | 1036.00 | .94 | 1125.26 | .84 | 1201.79 | .69 | 1263.31 | .53 | 1307.87 | .36 |
| 8.7 | 1036.94 | .95 | 1126.10 | .83 | 1202.48 | .70 | 1263.84 | .53 | 1308.23 | .35 |
| 8.8 | 1037.89 | .94 | 1126.93 | .83 | 1203.18 | .69 | 1264.37 | .53 | 1308.58 | .35 |
| 8.9 | 1038.83 | .95 | 1127.76 | .82 | 1203.87 | .69 | 1264.90 | .53 | 1308.93 | .35 |
| 9.0 | 1039.78 | .94 | 1128.58 | .83 | 1204.56 | .68 | 1265.43 | .52 | 1309.28 | .35 |
| 9.1 | 1040.72 | .95 | 1129.41 | .83 | 1205.24 | .69 | 1265.95 | .52 | 1309.63 | .34 |
| 9.2 | 1041.67 | .94 | 1130.24 | .82 | 1205.93 | .68 | 1266.47 | .53 | 1309.97 | .35 |
| 9.3 | 1042.61 | .94 | 1131.06 | .82 | 1206.61 | .68 | 1267.00 | .52 | 1310.32 | .34 |
| 9.4 | 1043.55 | .94 | 1131.88 | .83 | 1207.29 | .69 | 1267.52 | .52 | 1310.66 | .34 |
| 9.5 | 1044.49 | .93 | 1132.71 | .82 | 1207.98 | .67 | 1268.04 | .51 | 1311.00 | .34 |
| 9.6 | 1045.42 | .94 | 1133.53 | .82 | 1208.65 | .68 | 1268.55 | .52 | 1311.34 | .33 |
| 9.7 | 1046.36 | .94 | 1134.35 | .81 | 1209.33 | .68 | 1269.07 | .51 | 1311.67 | .34 |
| 9.8 | 1047.30 | .93 | 1135.16 | .82 | 1210.01 | .67 | 1269.58 | .51 | 1312.01 | .33 |
| 9.9 | 1048.23 | +.94 | 1135.98 | +.82 | 1210.68 | +.68 | 1270.09 | +.51 | 1312.34 | +.33 |
| 10.0 | 1049.17 | | 1136.80 | | 1211.36 | | 1270.60 | | 1312.67 | |

# TABLE IX. ARGUMENT 4.

Equation = 670″.500 — 670″.3 sin. $z$ — 7″.9 sin. $2z$.

Period, 365.259687 days.

| Days. | 350 | | 360 | |
|---|---|---|---|---|
| Days. | Equation. | Difference. | Equation. | Difference. |
| d. | ″ | | ″ | |
| 0.0 | 1312.67 | +.33 | 1336.14 | +.13 |
| 0.1 | 1313.00 | .33 | 1336.27 | .14 |
| 0.2 | 1313.33 | .32 | 1336.41 | .13 |
| 0.3 | 1313.65 | .33 | 1336.54 | .13 |
| 0.4 | 1313.98 | .32 | 1336.67 | .13 |
| 0.5 | 1314.30 | .32 | 1336.80 | .13 |
| 0.6 | 1314.62 | .31 | 1336.93 | .12 |
| 0.7 | 1314.93 | .32 | 1337.05 | .13 |
| 0.8 | 1315.25 | .31 | 1337.18 | .12 |
| 0.9 | 1315.56 | .31 | 1337.30 | .12 |
| 1.0 | 1315.87 | .31 | 1337.42 | .12 |
| 1.1 | 1316.18 | .31 | 1337.54 | .11 |
| 1.2 | 1316.49 | .31 | 1337.65 | .12 |
| 1.3 | 1316.80 | .30 | 1337.77 | .11 |
| 1.4 | 1317.10 | .30 | 1337.88 | .11 |
| 1.5 | 1317.40 | .30 | 1337.99 | .11 |
| 1.6 | 1317.70 | .30 | 1338.10 | .10 |
| 1.7 | 1318.00 | .30 | 1338.20 | .11 |
| 1.8 | 1318.30 | .30 | 1338.31 | .10 |
| 1.9 | 1318.60 | .29 | 1338.41 | .10 |
| 2.0 | 1318.89 | .29 | 1338.51 | .10 |
| 2.1 | 1319.18 | .29 | 1338.61 | .09 |
| 2.2 | 1319.47 | .29 | 1338.70 | .10 |
| 2.3 | 1319.76 | .28 | 1338.80 | .09 |
| 2.4 | 1320.04 | .29 | 1338.89 | .09 |
| 2.5 | 1320.33 | .28 | 1338.98 | .09 |
| 2.6 | 1320.61 | .28 | 1339.07 | .08 |
| 2.7 | 1320.89 | .28 | 1339.15 | .09 |
| 2.8 | 1321.17 | .27 | 1339.24 | .08 |
| 2.9 | 1321.44 | .28 | 1339.32 | .08 |
| 3.0 | 1321.72 | .27 | 1339.40 | .07 |
| 3.1 | 1321.99 | .26 | 1339.47 | .08 |
| 3.2 | 1322.25 | .27 | 1339.55 | .08 |
| 3.3 | 1322.52 | .27 | 1339.63 | .07 |
| 3.4 | 1322.79 | .26 | 1339.70 | .07 |
| 3.5 | 1323.05 | .27 | 1339.77 | .07 |
| 3.6 | 1323.32 | .26 | 1339.84 | .06 |
| 3.7 | 1323.58 | .26 | 1339.90 | .07 |
| 3.8 | 1323.84 | .26 | 1339.97 | .06 |
| 3.9 | 1324.10 | .25 | 1340.03 | .06 |
| 4.0 | 1324.35 | .26 | 1340.09 | .06 |
| 4.1 | 1324.61 | .25 | 1340.15 | .06 |
| 4.2 | 1324.86 | .25 | 1340.21 | .05 |
| 4.3 | 1325.11 | .24 | 1340.26 | .06 |
| 4.4 | 1325.35 | .25 | 1340.32 | .05 |
| 4.5 | 1325.60 | .24 | 1340.37 | .05 |
| 4.6 | 1325.84 | .24 | 1340.42 | .04 |
| 4.7 | 1326.08 | .24 | 1340.46 | .05 |
| 4.8 | 1326.32 | .24 | 1340.51 | .04 |
| 4.9 | 1326.56 | .24 | 1340.55 | .04 |
| 5.0 | 1326.80 | +.23 | 1340.59 | +.03 |

# TABLE IX. ARGUMENT 4.

Equation = 670″.500 — 670″.3 sin. $z$ — 7″.9 sin. $2z$.

Period, 365.259687 days.

| Days. | 350 | | 360 | |
|---|---|---|---|---|
| Days. | Equation. | Difference. | Equation. | Difference. |
| d. | ″ | | ″ | |
| 5.0 | 1326.80 | +.23 | 1340.59 | +.03 |
| 5.1 | 1327.03 | .23 | 1340.62 | .04 |
| 5.2 | 1327.26 | .24 | 1340.66 | .04 |
| 5.3 | 1327.50 | .22 | 1340.70 | .03 |
| 5.4 | 1327.72 | .23 | 1340.73 | .03 |
| 5.5 | 1327.95 | .22 | 1340.76 | .03 |
| 5.6 | 1328.17 | .23 | 1340.79 | .03 |
| 5.7 | 1328.40 | .22 | 1340.82 | .02 |
| 5.8 | 1328.62 | .22 | 1340.84 | .03 |
| 5.9 | 1328.84 | .21 | 1340.87 | .02 |
| 6.0 | 1329.05 | .22 | 1340.89 | .02 |
| 6.1 | 1329.27 | .21 | 1340.91 | .01 |
| 6.2 | 1329.48 | .21 | 1340.92 | .02 |
| 6.3 | 1329.69 | .21 | 1340.94 | .01 |
| 6.4 | 1329.90 | .21 | 1340.95 | .01 |
| 6.5 | 1330.11 | .20 | 1340.96 | .01 |
| 6.6 | 1330.31 | .21 | 1340.97 | .01 |
| 6.7 | 1330.52 | .20 | 1340.98 | .00 |
| 6.8 | 1330.72 | .20 | 1340.98 | .00 |
| 6.9 | 1330.92 | .20 | 1340.98 | +.01 |
| 7.0 | 1331.12 | .19 | 1340.99 | .00 |
| 7.1 | 1331.31 | .20 | 1340.99 | —.01 |
| 7.2 | 1331.51 | .19 | 1340.98 | .00 |
| 7.3 | 1331.70 | .19 | 1340.98 | .01 |
| 7.4 | 1331.89 | .18 | 1340.97 | .00 |
| 7.5 | 1332.07 | .19 | 1340.97 | .01 |
| 7.6 | 1332.26 | .18 | 1340.96 | .02 |
| 7.7 | 1332.44 | .19 | 1340.94 | .01 |
| 7.8 | 1332.63 | .18 | 1340.93 | .02 |
| 7.9 | 1332.81 | .17 | 1340.91 | .02 |
| 8.0 | 1332.98 | .18 | 1340.89 | .02 |
| 8.1 | 1333.16 | .17 | 1340.87 | .03 |
| 8.2 | 1333.33 | .18 | 1340.84 | .02 |
| 8.3 | 1333.51 | .17 | 1340.82 | .03 |
| 8.4 | 1333.68 | .17 | 1340.79 | .03 |
| 8.5 | 1333.85 | .16 | 1340.76 | .03 |
| 8.6 | 1334.01 | .17 | 1340.73 | .03 |
| 8.7 | 1334.18 | .16 | 1340.70 | .04 |
| 8.8 | 1334.34 | .16 | 1340.66 | .04 |
| 8.9 | 1334.50 | .16 | 1340.62 | .04 |
| 9.0 | 1334.66 | .16 | 1340.58 | .04 |
| 9.1 | 1334.82 | .15 | 1340.54 | .04 |
| 9.2 | 1334.97 | .15 | 1340.50 | .04 |
| 9.3 | 1335.12 | .15 | 1340.46 | .05 |
| 9.4 | 1335.27 | .15 | 1340.41 | .05 |
| 9.5 | 1335.42 | .15 | 1340.36 | .05 |
| 9.6 | 1335.57 | .15 | 1340.31 | .05 |
| 9.7 | 1335.72 | .14 | 1340.26 | .05 |
| 9.8 | 1335.86 | .14 | 1340.21 | .06 |
| 9.9 | 1336.00 | +.14 | 1340.15 | —.06 |
| 10.0 | 1336.14 | | 1340.09 | |

# TABLE X. ARGUMENT 5.

Equation = 225″.300 + 18″.0 sin. $(x - t)$ — 212″.4 sin. 2 $(x - t)$.

Period, 411.78517 days.

| Days. | 0 | | 10 | | 20 | | 30 | | 40 | | 50 | |
|---|---|---|---|---|---|---|---|---|---|---|---|---|
| Days. | Equation. | Diff. | Equation. | Diff. | Equation. | Diff. | Equation. | Diff. | Equation. | Diff. | Equation. | Diff. |
| d. | ″ | | ″ | | ″ | | ″ | | ″ | | ″ | |
| 0.0 | 15.73 | .24 | 0.73 | .05 | 5.62 | .15 | 29.82 | .33 | 71.00 | .48 | 125.26 | .60 |
| 0.1 | 15.49 | .25 | 0.68 | .05 | 5.77 | .15 | 30.15 | .34 | 71.48 | .49 | 125.86 | .59 |
| 0.2 | 15.24 | .24 | 0.63 | .04 | 5.92 | .15 | 30.49 | .34 | 71.97 | .49 | 126.45 | .59 |
| 0.3 | 15.00 | .24 | 0.59 | .05 | 6.07 | .16 | 30.83 | .33 | 72.46 | .49 | 127.04 | .60 |
| 0.4 | 14.76 | .24 | 0.54 | .04 | 6.23 | .15 | 31.16 | .34 | 72.95 | .49 | 127.64 | .60 |
| 0.5 | 14.52 | .23 | 0.50 | .04 | 6.38 | .16 | 31.50 | .34 | 73.44 | .49 | 128.24 | .59 |
| 0.6 | 14.29 | .24 | 0.46 | .04 | 6.54 | .16 | 31.84 | .35 | 73.93 | .49 | 128.83 | .60 |
| 0.7 | 14.05 | .23 | 0.42 | .03 | 6.70 | .17 | 32.19 | .34 | 74.42 | .50 | 129.43 | .60 |
| 0.8 | 13.82 | .23 | 0.39 | .04 | 6.87 | .16 | 32.53 | .35 | 74.92 | .49 | 130.03 | .60 |
| 0.9 | 13.59 | .23 | 0.35 | .03 | 7.03 | .17 | 32.88 | .35 | 75.41 | .50 | 130.63 | .60 |
| 1.0 | 13.36 | .23 | 0.32 | .03 | 7.20 | .16 | 33.23 | .35 | 75.91 | .50 | 131.23 | .60 |
| 1.1 | 13.13 | .22 | 0.29 | .03 | 7.36 | .17 | 33.58 | .35 | 76.41 | .50 | 131.83 | .60 |
| 1.2 | 12.91 | .23 | 0.26 | .02 | 7.53 | .18 | 33.93 | .35 | 76.91 | .50 | 132.43 | .60 |
| 1.3 | 12.68 | .22 | 0.24 | .03 | 7.71 | .17 | 34.28 | .36 | 77.41 | .50 | 133.03 | .60 |
| 1.4 | 12.46 | .22 | 0.21 | .02 | 7.88 | .18 | 34.64 | .35 | 77.91 | .50 | 133.63 | .60 |
| 1.5 | 12.24 | .21 | 0.19 | .02 | 8.06 | .17 | 34.99 | .26 | 78.41 | .51 | 134.23 | .61 |
| 1.6 | 12.03 | .22 | 0.17 | .02 | 8.23 | .18 | 35.35 | .36 | 78.92 | .51 | 134.84 | .60 |
| 1.7 | 11.81 | .22 | 0.15 | .01 | 8.41 | .19 | 35.71 | .36 | 79.43 | .50 | 135.44 | .61 |
| 1.8 | 11.59 | .21 | 0.14 | .02 | 8.60 | .18 | 36.07 | .37 | 79.93 | .51 | 136.05 | .60 |
| 1.9 | 11.38 | .21 | 0.12 | .01 | 8.78 | .19 | 36.44 | .36 | 80.44 | .51 | 136.65 | .61 |
| 2.0 | 11.17 | .20 | 0.11 | .01 | 8.97 | .18 | 36.80 | .37 | 80.95 | .51 | 137.26 | .61 |
| 2.1 | 10.97 | .21 | 0.10 | .01 | 9.15 | .19 | 37.17 | .37 | 81.46 | .51 | 137.87 | .60 |
| 2.2 | 10.76 | .20 | 0.09 | .00 | 9.34 | .19 | 37.54 | .37 | 81.97 | .52 | 138.47 | .61 |
| 2.3 | 10.56 | .20 | 0.09 | .01 | 9.53 | .20 | 37.91 | .37 | 82.49 | .51 | 139.08 | .61 |
| 2.4 | 10.36 | .20 | 0.08 | .00 | 9.73 | .19 | 38.28 | .37 | 83.00 | .52 | 139.69 | .61 |
| 2.5 | 10.16 | .20 | 0.08 | .00 | 9.92 | .20 | 38.65 | .38 | 83.52 | .51 | 140.30 | .61 |
| 2.6 | 9.96 | .20 | 0.08 | .00 | 10.12 | .20 | 39.03 | .37 | 84.03 | .52 | 140.91 | .61 |
| 2.7 | 9.76 | .19 | 0.08 | .01 | 10.32 | .20 | 39.40 | .38 | 84.55 | .52 | 141.52 | .62 |
| 2.8 | 9.57 | .20 | 0.09 | .00 | 10.52 | .20 | 39.78 | .38 | 85.07 | .52 | 142.14 | .61 |
| 2.9 | 9.37 | .19 | 0.09 | .01 | 10.72 | .20 | 40.16 | .38 | 85.59 | .52 | 142.75 | .61 |
| 3.0 | 9.18 | .19 | 0.10 | .01 | 10.93 | .20 | 40.54 | .38 | 86.11 | .53 | 143.36 | .62 |
| 3.1 | 8.99 | .18 | 0.11 | .01 | 11.13 | .21 | 40.92 | .39 | 86.64 | .52 | 143.98 | .61 |
| 3.2 | 8.81 | .19 | 0.12 | .02 | 11.34 | .21 | 41.31 | .38 | 87.16 | .52 | 144.59 | .62 |
| 3.3 | 8.62 | .18 | 0.14 | .01 | 11.55 | .21 | 41.69 | .39 | 87.68 | .53 | 145.21 | .61 |
| 3.4 | 8.44 | .18 | 0.15 | .02 | 11.76 | .22 | 42.08 | .39 | 88.21 | .53 | 145.82 | .62 |
| 3.5 | 8.26 | .18 | 0.17 | .02 | 11.98 | .21 | 42.47 | .39 | 88.74 | .53 | 146.44 | .62 |
| 3.6 | 8.08 | .18 | 0.19 | .02 | 12.19 | .22 | 42.86 | .39 | 89.27 | .53 | 147.06 | .62 |
| 3.7 | 7.90 | .17 | 0.21 | .03 | 12.41 | .22 | 43.25 | .40 | 89.80 | .53 | 147.68 | .61 |
| 3.8 | 7.73 | .18 | 0.24 | .02 | 12.63 | .22 | 43.65 | .39 | 90.33 | .53 | 148.29 | .62 |
| 3.9 | 7.55 | .17 | 0.26 | .03 | 12.85 | .23 | 44.04 | .40 | 90.86 | .53 | 148.91 | .62 |
| 4.0 | 7.38 | .16 | 0.29 | .03 | 13.08 | .22 | 44.44 | .40 | 91.39 | .54 | 149.53 | .62 |
| 4.1 | 7.22 | .17 | 0.32 | .03 | 13.30 | .23 | 44.84 | .40 | 91.93 | .53 | 150.15 | .62 |
| 4.2 | 7.05 | .17 | 0.35 | .04 | 13.53 | .23 | 45.24 | .40 | 92.46 | .54 | 150.77 | .62 |
| 4.3 | 6.88 | .16 | 0.39 | .03 | 13.76 | .23 | 45.64 | .41 | 93.00 | .54 | 151.39 | .63 |
| 4.4 | 6.72 | .16 | 0.42 | .04 | 13.99 | .23 | 46.05 | .40 | 93.54 | .54 | 152.02 | .62 |
| 4.5 | 6.56 | .16 | 0.46 | .04 | 14.22 | .24 | 46.45 | .41 | 94.08 | .54 | 152.64 | .62 |
| 4.6 | 6.40 | .16 | 0.50 | .04 | 14.46 | .23 | 46.86 | .41 | 94.62 | .54 | 153.26 | .63 |
| 4.7 | 6.24 | .15 | 0.54 | .05 | 14.69 | .24 | 47.27 | .41 | 95.16 | .54 | 153.89 | .62 |
| 4.8 | 6.09 | .16 | 0.59 | .04 | 14.93 | .24 | 47.68 | .41 | 95.70 | .54 | 154.51 | .63 |
| 4.9 | 5.93 | .15 | 0.63 | .05 | 15.17 | .24 | 48.09 | .41 | 96.24 | .55 | 155.14 | .62 |
| 5.0 | 5.78 | .15 | 0.68 | .05 | 15.41 | .25 | 48.50 | .41 | 96.79 | .54 | 155.76 | .63 |

# TABLE X. ARGUMENT 5.

Equation = 225″.300 + 18″.0 sin. $(x - t)$ — 212″.4 sin. 2 $(x - t)$.

Period, 411.78517 days.

| Days. | 0 | | 10 | | 20 | | 30 | | 40 | | 50 | |
|---|---|---|---|---|---|---|---|---|---|---|---|---|
| Days. | Equation. | Diff. | Equation. | Diff. | Equation. | Diff. | Equation. | Diff. | Equation. | Diff. | Equation. | Diff. |
| d. | ″ | | ″ | | ″ | | ″ | | ″ | | ″ | |
| 5.0 | 5.78 | .15 | 0.68 | .05 | 15.41 | .25 | 48.50 | .41 | 96.79 | .54 | 155.76 | .63 |
| 5.1 | 5.63 | .15 | 0.73 | .05 | 15.66 | .24 | 48.91 | .42 | 97.33 | .55 | 156.39 | .62 |
| 5.2 | 5.48 | .14 | 0.78 | .06 | 15.90 | .25 | 49.33 | .42 | 97.88 | .55 | 157.01 | .63 |
| 5.3 | 5.34 | .15 | 0.84 | .05 | 16.15 | .25 | 49.75 | .41 | 98.43 | .55 | 157.64 | .63 |
| 5.4 | 5.19 | .14 | 0.89 | .06 | 16.40 | .25 | 50.16 | .42 | 98.98 | .55 | 158.27 | .62 |
| 5.5 | 5.05 | .14 | 0.95 | .06 | 16.65 | .25 | 50.58 | .43 | 99.53 | .55 | 158.89 | .63 |
| 5.6 | 4.91 | .14 | 1.01 | .06 | 16.90 | .26 | 51.01 | .42 | 100.08 | .55 | 159.52 | .63 |
| 5.7 | 4.77 | .13 | 1.07 | .07 | 17.16 | .26 | 51.43 | .42 | 100.63 | .55 | 160.15 | .63 |
| 5.8 | 4.64 | .14 | 1.14 | .06 | 17.42 | .25 | 51.85 | .43 | 101.18 | .56 | 160.78 | .63 |
| 5.9 | 4.50 | .13 | 1.20 | .07 | 17.67 | .26 | 52.28 | .43 | 101.74 | .55 | 161.41 | .63 |
| 6.0 | 4.37 | .13 | 1.27 | .07 | 17.93 | .27 | 52.71 | .43 | 102.29 | .56 | 162.04 | .63 |
| 6.1 | 4.24 | .12 | 1.34 | .07 | 18.20 | .26 | 53.14 | .43 | 102.85 | .55 | 162.67 | .63 |
| 6.2 | 4.12 | .13 | 1.41 | .08 | 18.46 | .27 | 53.57 | .43 | 103.40 | .56 | 163.30 | .63 |
| 6.3 | 3.99 | .12 | 1.49 | .07 | 18.73 | .27 | 54.00 | .43 | 103.96 | .56 | 163 93 | .63 |
| 6.4 | 3.87 | .13 | 1.56 | .08 | 19.00 | .27 | 54.43 | .44 | 104.52 | .56 | 164.56 | .63 |
| 6.5 | 3.74 | .12 | 1.64 | .08 | 19.27 | .27 | 54.87 | .44 | 105.08 | .56 | 165.19 | .64 |
| 6.6 | 3.62 | .11 | 1.72 | .08 | 19.54 | .27 | 55.31 | .43 | 105.64 | .56 | 165.83 | .63 |
| 6.7 | 3.51 | .12 | 1.80 | .09 | 19.81 | .27 | 55.74 | .44 | 106.20 | .57 | 166.46 | .63 |
| 6.8 | 3.39 | .11 | 1.89 | .08 | 20.08 | .28 | 56.18 | .45 | 106.77 | .56 | 167.09 | .64 |
| 6.9 | 3.28 | .12 | 1.97 | .09 | 20.36 | .28 | 56.63 | .44 | 107.33 | .56 | 167.73 | .63 |
| 7.0 | 3.16 | .11 | 2.06 | .09 | 20.64 | .28 | 57.07 | .44 | 107.89 | .57 | 168.36 | .64 |
| 7.1 | 3.05 | .10 | 2.15 | .10 | 20.92 | .28 | 57.51 | .45 | 108.46 | .57 | 169.00 | .63 |
| 7.2 | 2.95 | .11 | 2.25 | .09 | 21.20 | .29 | 57.96 | .44 | 109.03 | .56 | 169.63 | .64 |
| 7.3 | 2.84 | .10 | 2.34 | .10 | 21.49 | .28 | 58.40 | .45 | 109.59 | .57 | 170.27 | .63 |
| 7.4 | 2.74 | .10 | 2.44 | .09 | 21.77 | .29 | 58.85 | .45 | 110.16 | .57 | 170.90 | .64 |
| 7.5 | 2.64 | .10 | 2.53 | .10 | 22.06 | .29 | 59.30 | .45 | 110.73 | .57 | 171.54 | .64 |
| 7.6 | 2.54 | .10 | 2.63 | .11 | 22.35 | .29 | 59.75 | .45 | 111.30 | .57 | 172.18 | .63 |
| 7.7 | 2.44 | .10 | 2.74 | .10 | 22.64 | .29 | 60.20 | .46 | 111.87 | .58 | 172.81 | .64 |
| 7.8 | 2.34 | .09 | 2.84 | .11 | 22.93 | .30 | 60.66 | .45 | 112.45 | .57 | 173.45 | .64 |
| 7.9 | 2.25 | .10 | 2.95 | .10 | 23.23 | .29 | 61.11 | .46 | 113.02 | .57 | 174.09 | .64 |
| 8.0 | 2.15 | .09 | 3.05 | .11 | 23.52 | .30 | 61.57 | .46 | 113.59 | .58 | 174.73 | .63 |
| 8.1 | 2.06 | .08 | 3.16 | .11 | 23.82 | .30 | 62.03 | .46 | 114.17 | .57 | 175.36 | .64 |
| 8.2 | 1.98 | .09 | 3.27 | .12 | 24.12 | .30 | 62.49 | .46 | 114.74 | .58 | 176.00 | .64 |
| 8.3 | 1.89 | .08 | 3.39 | .11 | 24.42 | .31 | 62.95 | .46 | 115.32 | .58 | 176.64 | .64 |
| 8.4 | 1.81 | .09 | 3.50 | .12 | 24.73 | .30 | 63.41 | .47 | 115.90 | .58 | 177.28 | .64 |
| 8.5 | 1.72 | .08 | 3.62 | .12 | 25.03 | .31 | 63.88 | .46 | 116.48 | .58 | 177.92 | .64 |
| 8.6 | 1.64 | .08 | 3.74 | .12 | 25.34 | .31 | 64.34 | .47 | 117.06 | .58 | 178.56 | .64 |
| 8.7 | 1.56 | .07 | 3.86 | .12 | 25.65 | .31 | 64.81 | .47 | 117.64 | .58 | 179.20 | .64 |
| 8.8 | 1.49 | .08 | 3.98 | .13 | 25.96 | .31 | 65.28 | .47 | 118.22 | .58 | 179.84 | .64 |
| 8.9 | 1.41 | .07 | 4.11 | .13 | 26.27 | .32 | 65.75 | .47 | 118.80 | .58 | 180.48 | .65 |
| 9.0 | 1.34 | .07 | 4.24 | .13 | 26.59 | .31 | 66.22 | .47 | 119.38 | .59 | 181.13 | .64 |
| 9.1 | 1.27 | .07 | 4.37 | .13 | 26.90 | .32 | 66.69 | .47 | 119.97 | .58 | 181.77 | .64 |
| 9.2 | 1.20 | .06 | 4.50 | .13 | 27.22 | .32 | 67.16 | .48 | 120.55 | .59 | 182.41 | .64 |
| 9.3 | 1.14 | .07 | 4.63 | .14 | 27.54 | .32 | 67.64 | .47 | 121.14 | .59 | 183.05 | .64 |
| 9.4 | 1.07 | .06 | 4.77 | .13 | 27.86 | .32 | 68.11 | .48 | 121.73 | .58 | 183.69 | .65 |
| 9.5 | 1.01 | .06 | 4.90 | .14 | 28.18 | .33 | 68.59 | .48 | 122.31 | .59 | 184.34 | .64 |
| 9.6 | 0.95 | .06 | 5.04 | .14 | 28.51 | .32 | 69.07 | .48 | 122.90 | .59 | 184.98 | .64 |
| 9.7 | 0.89 | .05 | 5.18 | .14 | 28.83 | .33 | 69.55 | .48 | 123.49 | .59 | 185.62 | .65 |
| 9.8 | 0.84 | .06 | 5.32 | .15 | 29.16 | .33 | 70.03 | .48 | 124.08 | .59 | 186.27 | .64 |
| 9.9 | 0.78 | .05 | 5.47 | .15 | 29.49 | .33 | 70.51 | .49 | 124.67 | .59 | 186.91 | .64 |
| 10.0 | 0.73 | .05 | 5.62 | .15 | 29.82 | .33 | 71.00 | .48 | 125.26 | .60 | 187.55 | .65 |

# TABLE X. ARGUMENT 5.

Equation $= 225''.300 + 18''.0 \sin. (x - t) - 212''.4 \sin. 2 (x - t)$.

Period, 411.78517 days.

| Days. | 60 | | 70 | | 80 | | 90 | | 100 | | 110 | |
|---|---|---|---|---|---|---|---|---|---|---|---|---|
| Days. | Equation. | Diff. | Equation. | Diff. | Equation. | Diff. | Equation. | Diff. | Equation. | Diff. | Equation. | Diff. |
| d. | " | | " | | " | | " | | " | | " | |
| 0.0 | 187.55 | .65 | 252.09 | .64 | 312.91 | .57 | 364.43 | .45 | 401.95 | .29 | 422.10 | .11 |
| 0.1 | 188.20 | .64 | 252.73 | .63 | 313.48 | .57 | 364.88 | .45 | 402.24 | .29 | 422.21 | .10 |
| 0.2 | 188.84 | .65 | 253.36 | .64 | 314.05 | .57 | 365.33 | .45 | 402.53 | .29 | 422.31 | .10 |
| 0.3 | 189.49 | .64 | 254.00 | .63 | 314.62 | .56 | 365.78 | .45 | 402.82 | .29 | 422.41 | .10 |
| 0.4 | 190.13 | .65 | 254.63 | .64 | 315.18 | .57 | 366.23 | .44 | 403.11 | .28 | 422.51 | .10 |
| 0.5 | 190.78 | .64 | 255.27 | .63 | 315.75 | .57 | 366.67 | .45 | 403.39 | .29 | 422.61 | .10 |
| 0.6 | 191.42 | .65 | 255.90 | .64 | 316.32 | .56 | 367.12 | .44 | 403.68 | .28 | 422.71 | .09 |
| 0.7 | 192.07 | .65 | 256.54 | .63 | 316.88 | .56 | 367.56 | .44 | 403.96 | .28 | 422.80 | .10 |
| 0.8 | 192.72 | .64 | 257.17 | .63 | 317.44 | .56 | 368.00 | .44 | 404.24 | .28 | 422.90 | .09 |
| 0.9 | 193.36 | .65 | 257.80 | .64 | 318.00 | .57 | 368.44 | .44 | 404.52 | .27 | 422.99 | .09 |
| 1.0 | 194.01 | .64 | 258.44 | .63 | 318.57 | .56 | 368.88 | .44 | 404.79 | .28 | 423.08 | .08 |
| 1.1 | 194.65 | .65 | 259.07 | .63 | 319.13 | .55 | 369.32 | .43 | 405.07 | .27 | 423.16 | .09 |
| 1.2 | 195.30 | .65 | 259.70 | .63 | 319.68 | .56 | 369.75 | .44 | 405.34 | .27 | 423.25 | .08 |
| 1.3 | 195.95 | .64 | 260.33 | .63 | 320.24 | .56 | 370.19 | .43 | 405.61 | .27 | 423.33 | .08 |
| 1.4 | 196.59 | .65 | 260.96 | .63 | 320.80 | .56 | 370.62 | .43 | 405.88 | .26 | 423.41 | .08 |
| 1.5 | 197.24 | .65 | 261.59 | .63 | 321.36 | .55 | 371.05 | .43 | 406.14 | .27 | 423.49 | .08 |
| 1.6 | 197.89 | .64 | 262.22 | .63 | 321.91 | .55 | 371.48 | .42 | 406.41 | .26 | 423.57 | .07 |
| 1.7 | 198.53 | .65 | 262 85 | .63 | 322.46 | .56 | 371.90 | .44 | 406.67 | .26 | 423.64 | .08 |
| 1.8 | 199.18 | .65 | 263.48 | .63 | 323.02 | .55 | 372.34 | .42 | 406.93 | .26 | 423.72 | .07 |
| 1.9 | 199.83 | .65 | 264.11 | .63 | 323.57 | .55 | 372.76 | .42 | 407.19 | .26 | 423.79 | .07 |
| 2.0 | 200.48 | .64 | 264.74 | .63 | 324.12 | .55 | 373.18 | .43 | 407.45 | .26 | 423.86 | .07 |
| 2.1 | 201.12 | .65 | 265.37 | .62 | 324.67 | .55 | 373.61 | .42 | 407.71 | .25 | 423.93 | .06 |
| 2.2 | 201.77 | .65 | 265.99 | .63 | 325.22 | .55 | 374.03 | .42 | 407.96 | .26 | 423.99 | .07 |
| 2.3 | 202.42 | .65 | 266.62 | .63 | 325.77 | .55 | 374.45 | .41 | 408.22 | .25 | 424.06 | .06 |
| 2.4 | 203.07 | .64 | 267.25 | .62 | 326.32 | .54 | 374.86 | .42 | 408.47 | .25 | 424.12 | .06 |
| 2.5 | 203.71 | .65 | 267.87 | .63 | 326.86 | .55 | 375.28 | .41 | 408.72 | .24 | 424.18 | .06 |
| 2.6 | 204.36 | .65 | 268.50 | .62 | 327.41 | .54 | 375.69 | .42 | 408.96 | .25 | 424.24 | .05 |
| 2.7 | 205.01 | .65 | 269.12 | .62 | 327.95 | .55 | 376.11 | .41 | 409.21 | .24 | 424.29 | .06 |
| 2.8 | 205.66 | .65 | 269.74 | .63 | 328.50 | .54 | 376.52 | .41 | 409.45 | .25 | 424.35 | .05 |
| 2.9 | 206.31 | .64 | 270.37 | .62 | 329.04 | .54 | 376.93 | .41 | 409.70 | .23 | 424.40 | .05 |
| 3.0 | 206.95 | .65 | 270.99 | .62 | 329.58 | .54 | 377.34 | .41 | 409.93 | .24 | 424.45 | .05 |
| 3.1 | 207.60 | .65 | 271.61 | .62 | 330.12 | .54 | 377.75 | .40 | 410.17 | .24 | 424 50 | .04 |
| 3.2 | 208.25 | .65 | 272.23 | .62 | 330.66 | .53 | 378.15 | .41 | 410.41 | .23 | 424.54 | .05 |
| 3.3 | 208.90 | .64 | 272.85 | .63 | 331.19 | .54 | 378.56 | .40 | 410.64 | .24 | 424.59 | .04 |
| 3.4 | 209.54 | .65 | 273.48 | .62 | 331.73 | .53 | 378.96 | .40 | 410.88 | .23 | 424.63 | .04 |
| 3.5 | 210.19 | .65 | 274.10 | .62 | 332.26 | .54 | 379 36 | .40 | 411.11 | .23 | 424.67 | .04 |
| 3.6 | 210.84 | .65 | 274.72 | .61 | 332.80 | .53 | 379.76 | .40 | 411.34 | .22 | 424.71 | .03 |
| 3.7 | 211.49 | .65 | 275.33 | .62 | 333.33 | .53 | 380.16 | .39 | 411.56 | .23 | 424.74 | .04 |
| 3.8 | 212.14 | .65 | 275.95 | .62 | 333.86 | .53 | 380.55 | .40 | 411.79 | .22 | 424.78 | .03 |
| 3.9 | 212.79 | .65 | 276.57 | .62 | 334.39 | .53 | 380.95 | .39 | 412.01 | .22 | 424.81 | .03 |
| 4.0 | 213 44 | .64 | 277.19 | .61 | 334.92 | .53 | 381.34 | .39 | 412.23 | .22 | 424.84 | .03 |
| 4.1 | 214.08 | .65 | 277.80 | .62 | 335.45 | .53 | 381.73 | .39 | 412.45 | .22 | 424.87 | 03 |
| 4.2 | 214.73 | .65 | 278.42 | .61 | 335.98 | .52 | 382.12 | .39 | 412.67 | .22 | 424.90 | .02 |
| 4.3 | 215.38 | .65 | 279.03 | .62 | 336.50 | .53 | 382.51 | .39 | 412.89 | .21 | 424.92 | .03 |
| 4.4 | 216.03 | .65 | 279.65 | .61 | 337.03 | .52 | 382.90 | .39 | 413.10 | .21 | 424.95 | .02 |
| 4.5 | 216.68 | .64 | 280.26 | .62 | 337.55 | .52 | 383.29 | .38 | 413.31 | .22 | 424.97 | .02 |
| 4.6 | 217.32 | .65 | 280.88 | .61 | 338.07 | .53 | 383.67 | .38 | 413.53 | .20 | 424.99 | .01 |
| 4.7 | 217.97 | .65 | 281.49 | .61 | 338 60 | .52 | 384.05 | .38 | 413.73 | .21 | 425.00 | .02 |
| 4.8 | 218.62 | .65 | 282.10 | .61 | 339.12 | .52 | 384.43 | .38 | 413.94 | .21 | 425.02 | .01 |
| 4.9 | 219.27 | .65 | 282.71 | .61 | 339.64 | .51 | 384.81 | .38 | 414.15 | .20 | 425.03 | .01 |
| 5.0 | 219.92 | .64 | 283.32 | .62 | 340.15 | .52 | 385.19 | .37 | 414.35 | .20 | 425.04 | .01 |

# TABLE X. ARGUMENT 5.

Equation $= 225''.300 + 18''.0 \sin.(x - t) - 212''.4 \sin. 2 (x - t)$.

Period, 411.78517 days.

| Days. | 60 | | 70 | | 80 | | 90 | | 100 | | 110 | |
|---|---|---|---|---|---|---|---|---|---|---|---|---|
| Days. | Equation. | Diff. | Equation. | Diff. | Equation. | Diff. | Equation. | Diff. | Equation. | Diff. | Equation. | Diff. |
| d. | ″ | | ″ | | ″ | | ″ | | ″ | | ′ | |
| 5.0 | 219.92 | .64 | 283.32 | .62 | 340.15 | .52 | 385.19 | .37 | 414.35 | .20 | 425.04 | .01 |
| 5.1 | 220.56 | .65 | 283.94 | .61 | 340.67 | .52 | 385.56 | .38 | 414.55 | .20 | 425.05 | .01 |
| 5.2 | 221.21 | .65 | 284.55 | .60 | 341.19 | .51 | 385.94 | .37 | 414.75 | .20 | 425.06 | .00 |
| 5.3 | 221.86 | .65 | 285.15 | .61 | 341.70 | .51 | 386.31 | .37 | 414.95 | .19 | 425.06 | .01 |
| 5.4 | 222.51 | .65 | 285.76 | .61 | 342.21 | .52 | 386.68 | .37 | 415.14 | .20 | 425.07 | .00 |
| 5.5 | 223.16 | .64 | 286.37 | .61 | 342.73 | .51 | 387.05 | .37 | 415.34 | .19 | 425.07 | .00 |
| 5.6 | 223.80 | .65 | 286.98 | .60 | 343.24 | .50 | 387.42 | .37 | 415 53 | .19 | 425.07 | .00 |
| 5.7 | 224.45 | .65 | 287.58 | .61 | 343.74 | .51 | 387.79 | .36 | 415.72 | .19 | 425.07 | .01 |
| 5.8 | 225.10 | .64 | 288.19 | .61 | 344.25 | .51 | 388.15 | .37 | 415.91 | .18 | 425.06 | .00 |
| 5.9 | 225.74 | .65 | 288.80 | .60 | 344.76 | .50 | 388.52 | .35 | 416.09 | .19 | 425.06 | .01 |
| 6.0 | 226.39 | .65 | 289.40 | .60 | 345.26 | .51 | 388.87 | .36 | 416.28 | .18 | 425.05 | .01 |
| 6.1 | 227.04 | .64 | 290.00 | .60 | 345.77 | .50 | 389.23 | .36 | 416.46 | .18 | 425.04 | .02 |
| 6.2 | 227.68 | .65 | 290.60 | .61 | 346.27 | .50 | 389.59 | .36 | 416.64 | .18 | 425.02 | .01 |
| 6.3 | 228.33 | .65 | 291.21 | .60 | 346.77 | .51 | 389.95 | .35 | 416.82 | .18 | 425 01 | .02 |
| 6.4 | 228.98 | .64 | 291.81 | .60 | 347.28 | .49 | 390.30 | .36 | 417.00 | .17 | 424.99 | .01 |
| 6.5 | 229.62 | .65 | 292.41 | .60 | 347.77 | .50 | 390.66 | .35 | 417.17 | .17 | 424.98 | .02 |
| 6.6 | 230.27 | .64 | 293.01 | .60 | 348.27 | .50 | 391.01 | .35 | 417.34 | .18 | 424.96 | .03 |
| 6.7 | 230.91 | .65 | 293.61 | .60 | 348.77 | .49 | 391.36 | .35 | 417.52 | .16 | 424.93 | .02 |
| 6.8 | 231.56 | .65 | 294.21 | .59 | 349.26 | .50 | 391.71 | .34 | 417.68 | .17 | 424.91 | .03 |
| 6.9 | 232.21 | .64 | 294.80 | .60 | 349.76 | .49 | 392 05 | .35 | 417.85 | .17 | 424.88 | .02 |
| 7.0 | 232.85 | .64 | 295.40 | .59 | 350.25 | .49 | 392.40 | .34 | 418.02 | .16 | 424.86 | .03 |
| 7.1 | 233.49 | .65 | 295.99 | .60 | 350.74 | .49 | 392.74 | .34 | 418.18 | .16 | 424.83 | .04 |
| 7.2 | 234.14 | .64 | 296.59 | .59 | 351.23 | .49 | 393.08 | .34 | 418.34 | .16 | 424.79 | .03 |
| 7.3 | 234.78 | .65 | 297.18 | .60 | 351.72 | .49 | 393.42 | .34 | 418.50 | .16 | 424.76 | .03 |
| 7.4 | 235.43 | .64 | 297.78 | .59 | 352.21 | .49 | 393.76 | .34 | 418.66 | .16 | 424.73 | .04 |
| 7.5 | 236.07 | .65 | 298.37 | .59 | 352.70 | .48 | 394.10 | .33 | 418.82 | .15 | 424.69 | .04 |
| 7.6 | 236.72 | .64 | 298.96 | .59 | 353.18 | .49 | 394.43 | .33 | 418.97 | .15 | 424.65 | .04 |
| 7.7 | 237.36 | .65 | 299.55 | .59 | 353.67 | .48 | 394.76 | .34 | 419.12 | .15 | 424.61 | .04 |
| 7.8 | 238.01 | .64 | 300.14 | .59 | 354.15 | .48 | 395.10 | .33 | 419.27 | .15 | 424.57 | .05 |
| 7.9 | 238.65 | .64 | 300.73 | .59 | 354.63 | .48 | 395.43 | .32 | 419.42 | .15 | 424.52 | .05 |
| 8.0 | 239.29 | .64 | 301.32 | .59 | 355.11 | .48 | 395.75 | .33 | 419.57 | .14 | 424.47 | .05 |
| 8.1 | 239.93 | .65 | 301.91 | .59 | 355.59 | .48 | 396.08 | .32 | 419.71 | .15 | 424.42 | .05 |
| 8.2 | 240.58 | .64 | 302.50 | .58 | 356.07 | .47 | 396.40 | .32 | 419.86 | .14 | 424.37 | .05 |
| 8.3 | 241.22 | .64 | 303.08 | .59 | 356.54 | .48 | 396.72 | .33 | 420.00 | .14 | 424.32 | .06 |
| 8.4 | 241.86 | .64 | 303.67 | .58 | 357.02 | .47 | 397.05 | .32 | 420.14 | .14 | 424.26 | .05 |
| 8.5 | 242.50 | .64 | 304.25 | .59 | 357.49 | .48 | 397.37 | .31 | 420.28 | .13 | 424.21 | .06 |
| 8.6 | 243.14 | .64 | 304.84 | .58 | 357.97 | .47 | 397.68 | .32 | 420.41 | .13 | 424.15 | .06 |
| 8.7 | 243.78 | .65 | 305.42 | .58 | 358.44 | .47 | 398.00 | .31 | 420.54 | .14 | 424.09 | .07 |
| 8.8 | 244.43 | .64 | 306.00 | .58 | 358.91 | .46 | 398.31 | .32 | 420.68 | .12 | 424.02 | .06 |
| 8.9 | 245.07 | .64 | 306.58 | .58 | 359.37 | .47 | 398.63 | .31 | 420.80 | .13 | 423.96 | .07 |
| 9.0 | 245.71 | .64 | 307.16 | .58 | 359.84 | .46 | 398.94 | .31 | 420.93 | .13 | 423.89 | .06 |
| 9.1 | 246.35 | .64 | 307.74 | .58 | 360.30 | .47 | 399.25 | .31 | 421.06 | .12 | 423.83 | .07 |
| 9.2 | 246.99 | .63 | 308.32 | .57 | 360.77 | .46 | 399.56 | .30 | 421.18 | .12 | 423.76 | .08 |
| 9.3 | 247.62 | .64 | 308.89 | .58 | 361.23 | .46 | 399.86 | .31 | 421.30 | .12 | 423.68 | .07 |
| 9.4 | 248.26 | .64 | 309.47 | .58 | 361.69 | .46 | 400.17 | .30 | 421.42 | .12 | 423.61 | .08 |
| 9.5 | 248.90 | .64 | 310.05 | .57 | 362.15 | .46 | 400.47 | .30 | 421.54 | .12 | 423.53 | .07 |
| 9.6 | 249.54 | .64 | 310.62 | .57 | 362.61 | .46 | 400.77 | .30 | 421.66 | .11 | 423 46 | .08 |
| 9.7 | 250.18 | .64 | 311.19 | .58 | 363.07 | .45 | 401.07 | .29 | 421.77 | .11 | 423.38 | .09 |
| 9.8 | 250.82 | .63 | 311.77 | .57 | 363.52 | .46 | 401.36 | .30 | 421.88 | .11 | 423.29 | .09 |
| 9.9 | 251.45 | .64 | 312.34 | .57 | 363.98 | .45 | 401.66 | .29 | 421.99 | .11 | 423.21 | .09 |
| 10.0 | 252.09 | .64 | 312.91 | .57 | 364.43 | .45 | 401.95 | .29 | 422.10 | .11 | 423.12 | .09 |

# TABLE X. ARGUMENT 5.

Equation $= 225''.300 + 18''.0 \sin. (x - t) - 212''.4 \sin. 2 (x - t)$.

Period, 411.78517 days.

| Days. | 120 | | 130 | | 140 | | 150 | | 160 | | 170 | |
|---|---|---|---|---|---|---|---|---|---|---|---|---|
| Days. | Equation. | Diff. | Equation. | Diff. | Equation. | Diff. | Equation. | Diff. | Equation. | Diff. | Equation. | Diff. |
| d. 0.0 | 423.12 | .09 | 405.06 | .27 | 369.74 | .43 | 320.59 | .55 | 262.33 | .61 | 200.53 | .61 |
| 0.1 | 423.03 | .09 | 404.79 | .28 | 369.31 | .43 | 320.04 | .55 | 261.72 | .61 | 199.92 | .62 |
| 0.2 | 422.94 | .09 | 404.51 | .27 | 368.88 | .44 | 319.49 | .55 | 261.11 | .61 | 199.30 | .61 |
| 0.3 | 422.85 | .09 | 404.24 | .28 | 368.44 | .43 | 318.94 | .54 | 260.50 | .61 | 198.69 | .62 |
| 0.4 | 422.76 | .10 | 403.96 | .28 | 368.01 | .44 | 318.40 | .55 | 259.89 | .62 | 198.07 | .61 |
| 0.5 | 422.66 | .09 | 403.68 | .28 | 367.57 | .43 | 317.85 | .56 | 259.27 | .61 | 197.46 | .62 |
| 0.6 | 422.57 | .10 | 403.40 | .28 | 367.14 | .44 | 317.29 | .55 | 258.66 | .61 | 196.84 | .61 |
| 0.7 | 422.47 | .10 | 403.12 | .29 | 366.70 | .44 | 316.74 | .55 | 258.05 | .61 | 196.23 | .62 |
| 0.8 | 422.37 | .11 | 402.83 | .28 | 366.26 | .44 | 316.19 | .55 | 257.44 | .62 | 195.61 | .61 |
| 0.9 | 422.26 | .10 | 402.55 | .29 | 365.82 | .44 | 315.64 | .56 | 256.82 | .61 | 195.00 | .61 |
| 1.0 | 422.16 | .11 | 402.26 | .29 | 365.38 | .45 | 315.08 | .55 | 256.21 | .61 | 194.39 | .62 |
| 1.1 | 422.05 | .11 | 401.97 | .29 | 364.93 | .44 | 314.53 | .56 | 255.60 | .61 | 193.77 | .61 |
| 1.2 | 421.94 | .11 | 401.68 | .29 | 364.49 | .45 | 313.97 | .56 | 254.99 | .62 | 193.16 | .61 |
| 1.3 | 421.83 | .11 | 401.39 | .30 | 364.04 | .45 | 313.41 | .55 | 254.37 | .61 | 192.55 | .61 |
| 1.4 | 421.72 | .12 | 401.09 | .29 | 363.59 | .45 | 312.86 | .56 | 253.76 | .62 | 191.94 | .61 |
| 1.5 | 421.60 | .11 | 400.80 | .30 | 363.14 | .45 | 312.30 | .56 | 253.14 | .61 | 191.33 | .62 |
| 1.6 | 421.49 | .12 | 400.50 | .30 | 362.69 | .45 | 311.74 | .56 | 252.53 | .62 | 190.71 | .61 |
| 1.7 | 421.37 | .12 | 400.20 | .30 | 362.24 | .45 | 311.18 | .56 | 251.91 | .61 | 190.10 | .61 |
| 1.8 | 421.25 | .12 | 399.90 | .31 | 361.79 | .46 | 310.62 | .56 | 251.30 | .62 | 189.49 | .61 |
| 1.9 | 421.13 | .13 | 399.59 | .30 | 361.33 | .45 | 310.06 | .57 | 250.68 | .61 | 188.88 | .61 |
| 2.0 | 421.00 | .12 | 399.29 | .31 | 360.88 | .46 | 309.49 | .56 | 250.07 | .62 | 188.27 | .61 |
| 2.1 | 420.88 | .13 | 398.98 | .31 | 360.42 | .46 | 308.93 | .56 | 249.45 | .62 | 187.66 | .61 |
| 2.2 | 420.75 | .13 | 398.67 | .31 | 359.96 | .46 | 308.37 | .57 | 248.83 | .61 | 187.05 | .61 |
| 2.3 | 420.62 | .13 | 398.36 | .31 | 359.50 | .46 | 307.80 | .56 | 248.22 | .62 | 186.44 | .61 |
| 2.4 | 420.49 | .14 | 398.05 | .31 | 359.04 | .46 | 307.24 | .57 | 247.60 | .62 | 185.83 | .60 |
| 2.5 | 420.35 | .13 | 397.74 | .32 | 358.58 | .46 | 306.67 | .57 | 246.98 | .61 | 185.23 | .61 |
| 2.6 | 420.22 | .14 | 397.42 | .31 | 358.12 | .47 | 306.10 | .57 | 246.37 | .62 | 184.62 | .61 |
| 2.7 | 420.08 | .14 | 397.11 | .32 | 357.65 | .46 | 305.53 | .57 | 245.75 | .62 | 184.01 | .61 |
| 2.8 | 419.94 | .14 | 396.79 | .32 | 357.19 | .47 | 304.96 | .57 | 245.13 | .62 | 183.40 | .60 |
| 2.9 | 419.80 | .14 | 396.47 | .32 | 356.72 | .47 | 304.39 | .57 | 244.51 | .61 | 182.80 | .61 |
| 3.0 | 419.66 | .15 | 396.15 | .32 | 356.25 | .47 | 303.82 | .57 | 243.90 | .62 | 182.19 | .61 |
| 3.1 | 419.51 | .14 | 395.83 | .33 | 355.78 | .47 | 303.25 | .57 | 243.28 | .62 | 181.58 | .60 |
| 3.2 | 419.37 | .15 | 395.50 | .33 | 355.31 | .47 | 302.68 | .57 | 242.66 | .62 | 180.98 | .61 |
| 3.3 | 419.22 | .15 | 395.17 | .32 | 354.84 | .48 | 302.11 | .58 | 242.04 | .62 | 180.37 | .60 |
| 3.4 | 419.07 | .16 | 394.85 | .33 | 354.36 | .47 | 301.53 | .57 | 241.42 | .62 | 179.77 | .61 |
| 3.5 | 418.91 | .15 | 394.52 | .33 | 353.89 | .48 | 300.96 | .58 | 240.80 | .62 | 179.16 | .60 |
| 3.6 | 418.76 | .16 | 394.19 | .34 | 353.41 | .47 | 300.38 | .57 | 240.18 | .61 | 178.56 | .60 |
| 3.7 | 418.60 | .15 | 393.85 | .33 | 352.94 | .48 | 299.81 | .58 | 239.57 | .62 | 177.96 | .61 |
| 3.8 | 418.45 | .16 | 393.52 | .34 | 352.46 | .48 | 299.23 | .58 | 238.95 | .62 | 177.35 | .60 |
| 3.9 | 418.29 | .17 | 393.18 | .34 | 351.98 | .48 | 298.65 | .57 | 238.33 | .62 | 176.75 | .60 |
| 4.0 | 418.12 | .16 | 392.84 | .34 | 351.50 | .49 | 298.08 | .58 | 237.71 | .62 | 176.15 | .60 |
| 4.1 | 417.96 | .17 | 392.50 | .34 | 351.01 | .48 | 297.50 | .58 | 237.09 | .62 | 175.55 | .60 |
| 4.2 | 417.79 | .16 | 392.16 | .34 | 350.53 | .48 | 296.92 | .58 | 236.47 | .62 | 174.95 | .60 |
| 4.3 | 417.63 | .17 | 391.82 | .34 | 350.05 | .49 | 296.34 | .58 | 235.85 | .62 | 174.35 | .60 |
| 4.4 | 417.46 | .17 | 391.48 | .35 | 349.56 | .49 | 295.76 | .58 | 235.23 | .62 | 173.75 | .60 |
| 4.5 | 417.29 | .18 | 391.13 | .35 | 349.07 | .48 | 295.18 | .58 | 234.61 | .62 | 173.15 | .60 |
| 4.6 | 417.11 | .17 | 390.78 | .35 | 348.59 | .49 | 294.60 | .59 | 233.99 | .62 | 172.55 | .60 |
| 4.7 | 416.94 | .18 | 390.43 | .35 | 348.10 | .49 | 294.01 | .58 | 233.37 | .62 | 171.95 | .60 |
| 4.8 | 416.76 | .18 | 390.08 | .35 | 347.61 | .50 | 293.43 | .58 | 232.75 | .62 | 171.35 | .60 |
| 4.9 | 416.58 | .18 | 389.73 | .35 | 347.11 | .49 | 292.85 | .59 | 232.13 | .62 | 170.75 | .59 |
| 5.0 | 416.40 | .18 | 389.38 | .36 | 346.62 | .49 | 292.26 | .58 | 231.51 | .62 | 170.16 | .60 |

# TABLE X. ARGUMENT 5.

Equation $= 225''.300 + 18''.0 \sin. (x - t) - 212''.4 \sin. 2 (x - t)$.

Period, 411.78517 days.

| Days. | 120 | | 130 | | 140 | | 150 | | 160 | | 170 | |
|---|---|---|---|---|---|---|---|---|---|---|---|---|
| Days. | Equation | Diff. | Equation. | Diff. | Equation. | Diff. | Equation. | Diff. | Equation. | Diff. | Equation. | Diff. |
| d. | ″ | | ″ | | ″ | | ″ | | ″ | | ″ | |
| 5.0 | 416.40 | .18 | 389.38 | .36 | 346.62 | .49 | 292.26 | .58 | 231.51 | .62 | 170.16 | .60 |
| 5.1 | 416.22 | .18 | 389.02 | .35 | 346.13 | .50 | 291.68 | .59 | 230.89 | .63 | 169.56 | .59 |
| 5.2 | 416.04 | .19 | 388.67 | .36 | 345.63 | .49 | 291.09 | .59 | 230.26 | .62 | 168.97 | .60 |
| 5.3 | 415.85 | .19 | 388.31 | .36 | 345.14 | .50 | 290.50 | .58 | 229.64 | .62 | 168.37 | .60 |
| 5.4 | 415.66 | .19 | 387.95 | .37 | 344.64 | .50 | 289.92 | .59 | 229.02 | .62 | 167.77 | .59 |
| 5.5 | 415.47 | .19 | 387.58 | .36 | 344.14 | .50 | 289.33 | .59 | 228.40 | .62 | 167.18 | .59 |
| 5.6 | 415.28 | .19 | 387.22 | .36 | 343.64 | .50 | 288.74 | .59 | 227.78 | .62 | 166.59 | .60 |
| 5.7 | 415.09 | .20 | 386.86 | .37 | 343.14 | .50 | 288.15 | .59 | 227.16 | .62 | 165.99 | .59 |
| 5.8 | 414.89 | .19 | 386.49 | .37 | 342.64 | .51 | 287.56 | .59 | 226.54 | .62 | 165.40 | .59 |
| 5.9 | 414.70 | .20 | 386.12 | .37 | 342.13 | .50 | 286.97 | .59 | 225.92 | .62 | 164.81 | .59 |
| 6.0 | 414.50 | .20 | 385.75 | .37 | 341.63 | .51 | 286.38 | .59 | 225.30 | .62 | 164.22 | .59 |
| 6.1 | 414.30 | .21 | 385.38 | .37 | 341.12 | .50 | 285.79 | .59 | 224.68 | .62 | 163.63 | .59 |
| 6.2 | 414.09 | .20 | 385.01 | .38 | 340.62 | .51 | 285.20 | .60 | 224.06 | .62 | 163.04 | .59 |
| 6.3 | 413.89 | .21 | 384.63 | .37 | 340.11 | .51 | 284.60 | .59 | 223.44 | .62 | 162.45 | .59 |
| 6.4 | 413.68 | .20 | 384.26 | .38 | 339.60 | .51 | 284.01 | .59 | 222.82 | .62 | 161.86 | .59 |
| 6.5 | 413.48 | .21 | 383.88 | .38 | 339.09 | .51 | 283.42 | .60 | 222.20 | 62 | 161.27 | 59 |
| 6.6 | 413.27 | .22 | 383.50 | .38 | 338.58 | .51 | 282.82 | .59 | 221.58 | .63 | 160.68 | .58 |
| 6.7 | 413.05 | .21 | 383.12 | .38 | 338.07 | .52 | 282.23 | .60 | 220.95 | .62 | 160.10 | .59 |
| 6.8 | 412.84 | .21 | 382.74 | .38 | 337.55 | .51 | 281.63 | .59 | 220.33 | .62 | 159.51 | .59 |
| 6.9 | 412.63 | .22 | 382.36 | .39 | 337.04 | .52 | 281.04 | .60 | 219.71 | .62 | 158.92 | .58 |
| 7.0 | 412.41 | .22 | 381.97 | .39 | 336.52 | .51 | 280.44 | .60 | 219.09 | .62 | 158.34 | .59 |
| 7.1 | 412.19 | .22 | 381.58 | .38 | 336.01 | .52 | 279.84 | .59 | 218.47 | .62 | 157.75 | .58 |
| 7.2 | 411.97 | .22 | 381.20 | .39 | 335.49 | .52 | 279.25 | .60 | 217.85 | .62 | 157.17 | .58 |
| 7.3 | 411.75 | .23 | 380.81 | .39 | 334.97 | .52 | 278.65 | .60 | 217.23 | .62 | 156.59 | .59 |
| 7.4 | 411.52 | .22 | 380.42 | .40 | 334.45 | .52 | 278.05 | .60 | 216.61 | .62 | 156.00 | .58 |
| 7.5 | 411.30 | .23 | 380.02 | .39 | 333.93 | .52 | 277.45 | .60 | 215.99 | .62 | 155.42 | .58 |
| 7.6 | 411.07 | .23 | 379.63 | .39 | 333.41 | .52 | 276.85 | .60 | 215.37 | .62 | 154.84 | .58 |
| 7.7 | 410.84 | .23 | 379.24 | .40 | 332.89 | .53 | 276.25 | .60 | 214.75 | .62 | 154.26 | .58 |
| 7.8 | 410.61 | .24 | 378.84 | .40 | 332.36 | .52 | 275.65 | .60 | 214.13 | .62 | 153.68 | .58 |
| 7.9 | 410.37 | .23 | 378.44 | .40 | 331.84 | .53 | 275.05 | .60 | 213.51 | .62 | 153.10 | .58 |
| 8.0 | 410.14 | .24 | 378.04 | .40 | 331.31 | .53 | 274.45 | .60 | 212.89 | .62 | 152.52 | .58 |
| 8.1 | 409.90 | .24 | 377.64 | .40 | 330.78 | .52 | 273.85 | .61 | 212.27 | .62 | 151.94 | .57 |
| 8.2 | 409.66 | .24 | 377.24 | .41 | 330.26 | .53 | 273.24 | .60 | 211.65 | .62 | 151.37 | .58 |
| 8.3 | 409.42 | .24 | 376.83 | .40 | 329.73 | .53 | 272.64 | .60 | 211.03 | .62 | 150.79 | .58 |
| 8.4 | 409.18 | .24 | 376.43 | .41 | 329.20 | .53 | 272.04 | .61 | 210.41 | .61 | 150.21 | .57 |
| 8.5 | 408.94 | .25 | 376.02 | .41 | 328.67 | .54 | 271.43 | .60 | 209.80 | .62 | 149.64 | .57 |
| 8.6 | 408.69 | .25 | 375.61 | .41 | 328.13 | .53 | 270.83 | .60 | 209.18 | .62 | 149.07 | .58 |
| 8.7 | 408.44 | .25 | 375.20 | .41 | 327.60 | .53 | 270.23 | .61 | 208.56 | .62 | 148.49 | .57 |
| 8.8 | 408.19 | .25 | 374.79 | .41 | 327.07 | .54 | 269.62 | .61 | 207.94 | .62 | 147.92 | .57 |
| 8.9 | 407.94 | .25 | 374.38 | .42 | 326.53 | .53 | 269.01 | .60 | 207.32 | .62 | 147.35 | .57 |
| 9.0 | 407.69 | .26 | 373.96 | .42 | 326.00 | .54 | 268.41 | .61 | 206.70 | .62 | 146.78 | .58 |
| 9.1 | 407.43 | .25 | 373.54 | .41 | 325.46 | .54 | 267.80 | .60 | 206.08 | .61 | 146.20 | .57 |
| 9.2 | 407.18 | .26 | 373.13 | .42 | 324.92 | .54 | 267.20 | .61 | 205.47 | .62 | 145.63 | .56 |
| 9.3 | 406.92 | .26 | 372.71 | .42 | 324.38 | .54 | 266.59 | .61 | 204.85 | .62 | 145.07 | .57 |
| 9.4 | 406.66 | .26 | 372.29 | .42 | 323.84 | .54 | 265.98 | .61 | 204.23 | .61 | 144.50 | .57 |
| 9.5 | 406.40 | .27 | 371.87 | .43 | 323.30 | .54 | 265.37 | .60 | 203.62 | .62 | 143.93 | .57 |
| 9.6 | 406.13 | .26 | 371.44 | .42 | 322.76 | .54 | 264.77 | .61 | 203.00 | .62 | 143.36 | .56 |
| 9.7 | 405.87 | .27 | 371.02 | .43 | 322.22 | .55 | 264.16 | .61 | 202.38 | .61 | 142.80 | .57 |
| 9.8 | 405.60 | .27 | 370.59 | .42 | 321.67 | .54 | 263.55 | .61 | 201.77 | .62 | 142.23 | .56 |
| 9.9 | 405.33 | .27 | 370.17 | .43 | 321.13 | .54 | 262.94 | .61 | 201.15 | .62 | 141.67 | .56 |
| 10.0 | 405.06 | .27 | 369.74 | .43 | 320.59 | .55 | 262.33 | .61 | 200.53 | .61 | 141.11 | .57 |

# TABLE X. ARGUMENT 5.

Equation $= 225''.300 + 18''.0 \sin. (x - t) - 212''.4 \sin. 2 (x - t)$.

Period, 411.78517 days.

| Days. | 180 | | 190 | | 200 | | 210 | | 220 | | 230 | |
|---|---|---|---|---|---|---|---|---|---|---|---|---|
| Days. | Equation. | Diff. | Equation. | Diff. | Equation. | Diff. | Equation. | Diff. | Equation. | Diff. | Equation. | Diff. |
| d. 0.0 | 141″.11 | .57 | 89″.72 | .46 | 51″.31 | .31 | 29″.60 | .13 | 26″.74 | .07 | 43″.15 | .25 |
| 0.1 | 140.54 | .56 | 89.26 | .45 | 51.00 | .30 | 29.47 | .12 | 26.81 | .07 | 43.40 | .26 |
| 0.2 | 139.98 | .56 | 88.81 | .45 | 50.70 | .30 | 29.35 | .12 | 26.88 | .08 | 43.66 | .27 |
| 0.3 | 139.42 | .56 | 88.36 | .45 | 50.40 | .30 | 29.23 | .12 | 26.96 | .07 | 43.93 | .26 |
| 0.4 | 138.86 | .56 | 87.91 | .45 | 50.10 | .30 | 29.11 | .11 | 27.03 | .08 | 44.19 | .26 |
| 0.5 | 138.30 | .56 | 87.46 | .45 | 49.80 | .29 | 29.00 | .12 | 27.11 | .08 | 44.45 | .27 |
| 0.6 | 137.74 | .56 | 87.01 | .45 | 49.51 | .30 | 28.88 | .11 | 27.19 | .08 | 44.72 | .27 |
| 0.7 | 137.18 | .55 | 86.56 | .45 | 49.21 | .29 | 28.77 | .11 | 27.27 | .08 | 44.99 | .27 |
| 0.8 | 136.63 | .56 | 86.11 | .44 | 48.92 | .29 | 28.66 | .11 | 27.35 | .09 | 45.26 | .27 |
| 0.9 | 136.07 | .55 | 85.67 | .45 | 48.63 | .29 | 28.55 | .11 | 27.44 | .08 | 45.53 | .28 |
| 1.0 | 135.52 | .56 | 85.22 | .44 | 48.34 | .29 | 28.44 | .11 | 27.52 | .09 | 45.81 | .27 |
| 1.1 | 134.96 | .55 | 84.78 | .44 | 48.05 | .29 | 28.33 | .10 | 27.61 | .09 | 46.08 | .28 |
| 1.2 | 134.41 | .55 | 84.34 | .44 | 47.76 | .28 | 28.23 | .10 | 27.70 | .10 | 46.36 | .28 |
| 1.3 | 133.86 | .56 | 83.90 | .44 | 47.48 | .28 | 28.13 | .10 | 27.80 | .09 | 46.64 | .28 |
| 1.4 | 133.30 | .55 | 83.46 | .44 | 47.20 | .28 | 28.03 | .10 | 27.89 | .10 | 46.92 | .28 |
| 1.5 | 132.75 | .55 | 83.02 | .43 | 46.92 | .28 | 27.93 | .09 | 27.99 | .10 | 47.20 | .29 |
| 1.6 | 132.20 | .55 | 82.59 | .44 | 46.64 | .28 | 27.84 | .09 | 28.09 | .10 | 47.49 | .29 |
| 1.7 | 131.65 | .54 | 82.15 | .43 | 46.36 | .28 | 27.75 | .10 | 28.19 | .10 | 47.78 | .28 |
| 1.8 | 131.11 | .55 | 81.72 | .43 | 46.08 | .27 | 27.65 | .09 | 28.29 | .10 | 48.06 | .29 |
| 1.9 | 130.56 | .55 | 81.29 | .43 | 45.81 | .27 | 27.56 | .08 | 28.39 | .11 | 48.35 | .30 |
| 2.0 | 130.01 | .54 | 80.86 | .43 | 45.54 | .27 | 27.48 | .09 | 28.50 | .11 | 48.65 | .29 |
| 2.1 | 129.47 | .54 | 80.43 | .43 | 45.27 | .27 | 27.39 | .09 | 28.61 | .11 | 48.94 | 29 |
| 2.2 | 128.93 | .55 | 80.00 | .42 | 45.00 | .27 | 27.30 | .08 | 28.72 | .11 | 49.23 | .30 |
| 2.3 | 128.38 | .54 | 79.58 | .43 | 44.73 | .26 | 27.22 | .08 | 28.83 | .11 | 49.53 | .30 |
| 2.4 | 127.84 | .54 | 79.15 | .42 | 44.47 | .27 | 27.14 | .08 | 28.94 | .12 | 49.83 | .30 |
| 2.5 | 127.30 | .54 | 78.73 | .42 | 44.20 | .26 | 27.06 | .07 | 29.06 | .12 | 50.13 | .30 |
| 2.6 | 126.76 | .54 | 78.31 | .42 | 43.94 | .26 | 26.99 | .08 | 29.18 | .12 | 50.43 | .30 |
| 2.7 | 126.22 | .54 | 77.89 | .42 | 43.68 | .26 | 26.91 | .07 | 29.30 | .12 | 50.73 | .31 |
| 2.8 | 125.68 | .54 | 77.47 | .42 | 43.42 | .25 | 26.84 | .07 | 29.42 | .12 | 51.04 | .31 |
| 2.9 | 125.14 | .54 | 77.05 | .41 | 43.17 | .26 | 26.77 | .06 | 29.54 | .13 | 51.35 | .31 |
| 3.0 | 124.60 | .53 | 76.64 | .42 | 42.91 | .25 | 26.71 | .07 | 29.67 | .12 | 51.66 | .31 |
| 3.1 | 124.07 | .54 | 76.22 | .41 | 42.66 | .25 | 26.64 | .07 | 29.79 | .13 | 51.97 | .31 |
| 3.2 | 123.53 | .53 | 75.81 | .41 | 42.41 | .25 | 26.57 | .06 | 29.92 | .13 | 52.28 | .32 |
| 3.3 | 123.00 | .54 | 75.40 | .41 | 42.16 | .25 | 26.51 | .06 | 30.05 | .14 | 52.60 | .32 |
| 3.4 | 122.46 | .53 | 74.99 | .41 | 41.91 | .25 | 26.45 | .06 | 30.19 | .13 | 52.92 | .31 |
| 3.5 | 121.93 | .53 | 74.58 | .41 | 41.66 | .24 | 26.39 | .06 | 30.32 | .14 | 53.23 | .32 |
| 3.6 | 121.40 | .53 | 74.17 | .40 | 41.42 | .24 | 26.33 | .05 | 30.46 | .14 | 53.55 | .32 |
| 3.7 | 120.87 | .53 | 73.77 | .41 | 41.18 | .24 | 26.28 | .05 | 30.60 | .14 | 53.87 | .33 |
| 3.8 | 120.34 | .53 | 73.36 | .40 | 40.94 | .24 | 26.23 | .05 | 30.74 | .14 | 54.20 | .32 |
| 3.9 | 119.81 | .52 | 72.96 | .40 | 40.70 | .24 | 26.18 | .05 | 30.88 | .15 | 54.52 | .33 |
| 4.0 | 119.29 | .53 | 72.56 | .40 | 40.46 | .23 | 26.13 | .05 | 31.03 | .15 | 54.85 | .32 |
| 4.1 | 118.76 | .52 | 72.16 | .40 | 40.23 | .24 | 26.08 | .05 | 31.18 | .15 | 55.17 | .33 |
| 4.2 | 118.24 | .53 | 71.76 | .40 | 39.99 | .23 | 26.03 | .04 | 31.33 | .15 | 55.50 | .33 |
| 4.3 | 117.71 | .52 | 71.36 | .39 | 39.76 | .22 | 25.99 | .04 | 31.48 | .15 | 55.83 | .34 |
| 4.4 | 117.19 | .52 | 70.97 | .40 | 39.54 | .24 | 25.95 | .04 | 31.63 | .15 | 56.17 | .33 |
| 4.5 | 116.67 | .52 | 70.57 | .39 | 39.30 | .22 | 25.91 | .04 | 31.78 | .16 | 56.50 | .34 |
| 4.6 | 116.15 | .52 | 70.18 | .39 | 39.08 | .23 | 25.87 | .03 | 31.94 | .16 | 56.84 | .34 |
| 4.7 | 115.63 | .52 | 69.79 | .39 | 38.85 | .22 | 25.84 | .04 | 32.10 | .16 | 57.18 | .34 |
| 4.8 | 115.11 | .52 | 69.40 | .39 | 38.63 | .22 | 25.80 | .03 | 32.26 | .16 | 57.52 | .34 |
| 4.9 | 114.59 | .51 | 69.01 | .38 | 38.41 | .22 | 25.77 | .03 | 32.42 | .16 | 57.86 | .34 |
| 5.0 | 114.08 | .52 | 68.63 | .39 | 38.19 | .22 | 25.74 | .02 | 32.58 | .16 | 58.20 | .35 |

# TABLE X. ARGUMENT 5.

Equation $= 225''.300 + 18''.0 \sin. (x - t) - 212''.4 \sin. 2 (x - t)$.

Period, 411.78517 days.

| Days. | 180 | | 190 | | 200 | | 210 | | 220 | | 230 | |
|---|---|---|---|---|---|---|---|---|---|---|---|---|
| Days. | Equation. | Diff. | Equation. | Diff. | Equation. | Diff. | Equation. | Diff. | Equation. | Diff. | Equation. | Diff. |
| d. | '' | | '' | | '' | | '' | | '' | | '' | |
| 5.0 | 114.08 | .52 | 68.63 | .39 | 38.19 | .22 | 25.74 | .02 | 32.58 | .16 | 58.20 | .35 |
| 5.1 | 113.56 | .51 | 68.24 | .38 | 37.97 | .21 | 25.72 | .03 | 32.74 | .17 | 58.55 | .34 |
| 5.2 | 113.05 | .52 | 67.86 | .38 | 37.76 | .21 | 25.69 | .02 | 32.91 | .17 | 58.89 | .35 |
| 5.3 | 112.53 | .51 | 67.48 | .38 | 37.55 | .22 | 25.67 | .03 | 33.08 | .17 | 59.24 | .35 |
| 5.4 | 112.02 | .51 | 67.10 | .38 | 37.33 | .21 | 25.64 | .02 | 33.25 | .18 | 59.59 | .35 |
| 5.5 | 111.51 | .51 | 66.72 | .38 | 37.12 | .20 | 25.62 | .01 | 33.43 | .17 | 59.94 | .36 |
| 5.6 | 111.00 | .51 | 66.34 | .37 | 36.92 | .21 | 25.61 | .02 | 33.60 | .18 | 60.30 | .35 |
| 5.7 | 110.49 | .51 | 65.97 | .38 | 36.71 | .20 | 25.59 | .01 | 33.78 | .18 | 60.65 | .36 |
| 5.8 | 109.98 | .50 | 65.59 | .37 | 36.51 | .21 | 25.58 | .02 | 33.96 | .18 | 61.01 | .36 |
| 5.9 | 109.48 | .51 | 65.22 | .37 | 36.30 | .20 | 25.56 | .01 | 34.14 | .18 | 61.37 | .36 |
| 6.0 | 108.97 | .50 | 64.85 | .37 | 36.10 | .20 | 25.55 | .01 | 34.32 | .19 | 61.73 | .35 |
| 6.1 | 108.47 | .51 | 64.48 | .37 | 35.90 | .19 | 25.54 | .00 | 34.51 | .18 | 62.08 | .37 |
| 6.2 | 107.96 | .50 | 64.11 | .37 | 35.71 | .20 | 25.54 | .01 | 34.69 | .19 | 62.45 | .36 |
| 6.3 | 107.46 | .50 | 63.74 | .36 | 35.51 | .19 | 25.53 | .00 | 34.88 | .19 | 62.81 | .37 |
| 6.4 | 106.96 | .50 | 63.38 | .37 | 35.32 | .19 | 25.53 | .00 | 35.07 | .19 | 63.18 | .37 |
| 6.5 | 106.46 | .50 | 63.01 | .36 | 35.13 | .19 | 25.53 | .00 | 35.26 | .20 | 63.55 | .37 |
| 6.6 | 105.96 | .50 | 62.65 | .36 | 34.94 | .19 | 25.53 | .01 | 35.46 | .19 | 63.92 | .37 |
| 6.7 | 105.46 | .49 | 62.29 | .36 | 34.75 | .19 | 25.54 | .00 | 35.65 | .20 | 64.29 | .37 |
| 6.8 | 104.97 | .50 | 61.93 | .35 | 34.56 | .18 | 25.54 | .01 | 35.85 | .20 | 64.66 | .38 |
| 6.9 | 104.47 | .49 | 61.58 | .36 | 34.38 | .18 | 25.55 | .01 | 36.05 | .20 | 65.04 | .37 |
| 7.0 | 103.98 | .49 | 61.22 | .35 | 34.20 | .18 | 25.56 | .01 | 36.25 | .20 | 65.41 | .38 |
| 7.1 | 103.49 | .50 | 60.87 | .35 | 34.02 | .18 | 25.57 | .01 | 36.45 | .21 | 65.79 | .38 |
| 7.2 | 102.99 | .49 | 60.52 | .36 | 33.84 | .18 | 25.58 | .02 | 36.66 | .20 | 66.17 | .38 |
| 7.3 | 102.50 | .49 | 60.16 | .34 | 33.66 | .17 | 25.60 | .01 | 36.86 | .21 | 66.55 | .38 |
| 7.4 | 102.01 | .48 | 59.82 | .35 | 33.49 | .18 | 25.61 | .02 | 37.07 | .21 | 66.93 | .38 |
| 7.5 | 101.53 | .49 | 59.47 | .35 | 33.31 | .17 | 25.63 | .02 | 37.28 | .22 | 67.31 | .39 |
| 7.6 | 101.04 | .49 | 59.12 | .34 | 33.14 | .17 | 25.65 | .03 | 37.50 | .21 | 67.70 | .39 |
| 7.7 | 100.55 | .48 | 58.78 | .34 | 32.97 | .16 | 25.68 | .02 | 37.71 | .22 | 68.09 | .39 |
| 7.8 | 100.07 | .49 | 58.44 | .34 | 32.81 | .17 | 25.70 | .03 | 37.93 | .22 | 68.48 | .39 |
| 7.9 | 99.58 | .48 | 58.10 | .35 | 32.64 | .16 | 25.73 | .03 | 38.15 | .22 | 68.87 | .39 |
| 8.0 | 99.10 | .48 | 57.75 | .33 | 32.48 | .17 | 25.76 | .03 | 38.37 | .22 | 69.26 | .39 |
| 8.1 | 98.62 | .48 | 57.42 | .34 | 32.31 | .16 | 25.79 | .03 | 38.59 | .22 | 69.65 | .40 |
| 8.2 | 98.14 | .48 | 57.08 | .33 | 32.15 | .15 | 25.82 | .03 | 38.81 | .23 | 70.05 | .39 |
| 8.3 | 97.66 | .47 | 56.75 | .34 | 32.00 | .16 | 25.85 | .04 | 39.04 | .22 | 70.44 | .40 |
| 8.4 | 97.19 | .48 | 56.41 | .33 | 31.84 | .15 | 25.89 | .04 | 39.26 | .23 | 70.84 | .40 |
| 8.5 | 96.71 | .47 | 56.08 | .33 | 31.69 | .16 | 25.93 | .04 | 39.49 | .23 | 71.24 | .40 |
| 8.6 | 96.24 | .48 | 55.75 | .33 | 31.53 | .15 | 25.97 | .04 | 39.72 | .23 | 71.64 | .40 |
| 8.7 | 95.76 | .47 | 55.42 | .32 | 31.38 | .15 | 26.01 | .05 | 39.95 | .24 | 72.04 | .41 |
| 8.8 | 95.29 | .47 | 55.10 | .33 | 31.23 | .14 | 26.06 | .04 | 40.19 | .24 | 72.45 | .40 |
| 8.9 | 94.82 | .47 | 54.77 | .32 | 31.09 | .15 | 26.10 | .05 | 40.43 | .24 | 72.85 | .41 |
| 9.0 | 94.35 | .47 | 54.45 | .32 | 30.94 | .14 | 26.15 | .05 | 40.67 | .23 | 73.26 | .41 |
| 9.1 | 93.88 | .47 | 54.13 | .32 | 30.80 | .14 | 26.20 | .05 | 40.90 | .25 | 73.67 | .41 |
| 9.2 | 93.41 | .46 | 53.81 | .32 | 30.66 | .14 | 26.25 | .06 | 41.15 | .24 | 74.08 | .41 |
| 9.3 | 92.95 | .47 | 53.49 | .32 | 30.52 | .14 | 26.31 | .05 | 41.39 | .25 | 74.49 | .41 |
| 9.4 | 92.48 | .46 | 53.17 | .31 | 30.38 | .13 | 26.36 | .06 | 41.64 | .24 | 74.90 | .42 |
| 9.5 | 92.02 | .46 | 52.86 | .31 | 30.25 | .14 | 26.42 | .06 | 41.88 | .25 | 75.32 | .42 |
| 9.6 | 91.56 | .46 | 52.55 | .32 | 30.11 | .13 | 26.48 | .06 | 42.13 | .25 | 75.74 | .41 |
| 9.7 | 91.10 | .46 | 52.23 | .31 | 29.98 | .13 | 26.54 | .07 | 42.38 | .26 | 76.15 | .42 |
| 9.8 | 90.64 | .46 | 51.92 | .30 | 29.85 | .13 | 26.61 | .06 | 42.64 | .25 | 76.57 | .42 |
| 9.9 | 90.18 | .46 | 51.62 | .31 | 29.72 | .12 | 26.67 | .07 | 42.89 | .26 | 76.99 | .43 |
| 10.0 | 89.72 | .46 | 51.31 | .31 | 29.60 | .13 | 26.74 | .07 | 43.15 | .25 | 77.42 | .42 |

# TABLE X. ARGUMENT 5.

Equation $= 225''.300 + 18''.0 \sin. (x - t) - 212''.4 \sin. 2 (x - t)$.

Period, 411.78517 days.

| Days. | 240 | | 250 | | 260 | | 270 | | 280 | | 290 | |
|---|---|---|---|---|---|---|---|---|---|---|---|---|
| Days. | Equation. | Diff. | Equation. | Diff. | Equation. | Diff. | Equation. | Diff. | Equation. | Diff. | Equation. | Diff. |
| d. | ″ | | ″ | | ″ | | ″ | | ″ | | ″ | |
| 0.0 | 77.42 | .42 | 126.48 | .55 | 185.86 | .63 | 250.12 | .65 | 313.34 | .61 | 369.65 | .51 |
| 0.1 | 77.84 | .42 | 127.03 | .55 | 186.49 | .63 | 250.77 | .65 | 313.95 | .60 | 370.16 | .51 |
| 0.2 | 78.26 | .43 | 127.58 | .55 | 187.12 | .63 | 251.42 | .64 | 314.55 | .61 | 370.67 | .50 |
| 0.3 | 78.69 | .43 | 128.13 | .56 | 187.75 | .63 | 252.06 | .65 | 315.16 | .60 | 371.17 | .51 |
| 0.4 | 79.12 | .43 | 128.69 | .55 | 188.38 | .63 | 252.71 | .65 | 315.76 | .61 | 371.68 | .50 |
| 0.5 | 79.55 | .43 | 129.24 | .56 | 189.01 | .63 | 253.36 | .65 | 316.37 | .60 | 372.18 | .51 |
| 0.6 | 79.98 | .43 | 129.80 | .56 | 189.64 | .63 | 254.01 | .64 | 316.97 | .60 | 372.69 | .50 |
| 0.7 | 80.41 | .44 | 130.36 | .55 | 190.27 | .63 | 254.65 | .65 | 317.57 | .60 | 373.19 | .50 |
| 0.8 | 80.85 | .43 | 130.91 | .56 | 190.90 | .63 | 255.30 | .65 | 318.17 | .60 | 373.69 | .50 |
| 0.9 | 81.28 | .44 | 131.47 | .56 | 191.53 | .63 | 255.95 | .64 | 318.77 | .60 | 374.19 | .50 |
| 1.0 | 81.72 | .44 | 132.03 | .57 | 192.16 | .63 | 256.59 | .65 | 319.37 | .60 | 374.69 | .50 |
| 1.1 | 82.16 | .44 | 132.60 | .56 | 192.79 | .64 | 257.24 | .64 | 319.97 | .60 | 375.19 | .49 |
| 1.2 | 82.60 | .44 | 133.16 | .56 | 193.43 | .63 | 257.88 | .65 | 320.57 | .60 | 375.68 | .50 |
| 1.3 | 83.04 | .44 | 133.72 | .56 | 194.06 | .64 | 258.53 | .64 | 321.17 | .60 | 376.18 | .49 |
| 1.4 | 83.48 | .45 | 134.28 | .57 | 194.70 | .63 | 259.17 | .65 | 321.77 | .59 | 376.67 | .49 |
| 1.5 | 83.93 | .44 | 134.85 | .57 | 195.33 | .64 | 259.82 | .64 | 322.36 | .60 | 377.16 | .49 |
| 1.6 | 84.37 | .45 | 135.42 | .56 | 195.97 | .63 | 260.46 | .65 | 322.96 | .59 | 377.65 | .49 |
| 1.7 | 84.82 | .45 | 135.98 | .57 | 196.60 | .64 | 261.11 | .64 | 323.55 | .60 | 378.14 | .49 |
| 1.8 | 85.27 | .45 | 136.55 | .57 | 197.24 | .63 | 261.75 | .65 | 324.15 | .59 | 378.63 | .49 |
| 1.9 | 85.72 | .45 | 137.12 | .57 | 197.87 | .64 | 262.40 | .64 | 324.74 | .59 | 379.12 | .48 |
| 2.0 | 86.17 | .45 | 137.69 | .57 | 198.51 | .64 | 263.04 | .65 | 325.33 | .60 | 379.60 | .48 |
| 2.1 | 86.62 | .46 | 138.26 | .57 | 199.15 | .63 | 263.69 | .64 | 325.93 | .59 | 380.08 | .49 |
| 2.2 | 87.08 | .45 | 138.83 | .57 | 199.78 | .64 | 264.33 | .65 | 326.52 | .59 | 380.57 | .48 |
| 2.3 | 87.53 | .46 | 139.40 | .58 | 200.42 | .64 | 264.98 | .64 | 327.11 | .59 | 381.05 | .48 |
| 2.4 | 87.99 | .46 | 139.98 | .57 | 201.06 | .64 | 265.62 | .64 | 327.70 | .58 | 381.53 | .48 |
| 2.5 | 88.45 | .46 | 140.55 | .58 | 201.70 | .64 | 266.26 | .64 | 328.28 | .59 | 382.01 | .48 |
| 2.6 | 88.91 | .46 | 141.13 | .57 | 202.34 | .63 | 266.90 | .65 | 328.87 | .59 | 382.49 | .47 |
| 2.7 | 89.37 | .46 | 141.70 | .58 | 202.97 | .64 | 267.55 | .64 | 329.46 | .59 | 382.96 | .48 |
| 2.8 | 89.83 | .46 | 142.28 | .58 | 203.61 | .64 | 268.19 | .64 | 330.05 | .58 | 383.44 | .47 |
| 2.9 | 90.29 | .47 | 142.86 | .58 | 204.25 | .64 | 268.83 | .64 | 330.63 | .58 | 383.91 | .47 |
| 3.0 | 90.76 | .47 | 143.44 | .58 | 204.89 | .64 | 269.47 | .65 | 331.21 | .59 | 384.38 | .47 |
| 3.1 | 91.23 | .46 | 144.02 | .58 | 205.53 | .64 | 270.12 | .64 | 331.80 | .58 | 384.85 | .47 |
| 3.2 | 91.69 | .47 | 144.60 | .58 | 206.17 | .64 | 270.76 | .64 | 332.38 | .58 | 385.32 | .47 |
| 3.3 | 92.16 | .47 | 145.18 | .58 | 206.81 | .65 | 271.40 | .64 | 332.96 | .58 | 385.79 | .47 |
| 3.4 | 92.63 | .48 | 145.76 | .59 | 207.46 | .64 | 272.04 | .64 | 333.54 | .58 | 386.26 | .46 |
| 3.5 | 93.11 | .47 | 146.35 | .58 | 208.10 | .64 | 272.68 | .64 | 334.12 | .58 | 386.72 | .47 |
| 3.6 | 93.58 | .47 | 146.93 | .59 | 208.74 | .64 | 273.32 | .64 | 334.70 | .58 | 387.19 | .46 |
| 3.7 | 94.05 | .48 | 147.52 | .58 | 209.38 | .64 | 273.96 | .64 | 335.28 | .58 | 387.65 | .46 |
| 3.8 | 94.53 | .48 | 148.10 | .59 | 210.02 | .65 | 274.60 | .63 | 335.86 | .57 | 388.11 | .46 |
| 3.9 | 95.01 | .48 | 148.69 | .59 | 210.67 | .64 | 275.23 | .64 | 336.43 | .57 | 388.57 | .46 |
| 4.0 | 95.49 | .48 | 149.28 | .59 | 211.31 | .64 | 275.87 | .64 | 337.00 | .58 | 389.03 | .45 |
| 4.1 | 95.97 | .48 | 149.87 | .59 | 211.95 | .64 | 276.51 | .64 | 337.58 | .57 | 389.48 | .46 |
| 4.2 | 96.45 | .48 | 150.46 | .59 | 212.59 | .65 | 277.15 | .64 | 338.15 | .58 | 389.94 | .45 |
| 4.3 | 96.93 | .48 | 151.05 | .59 | 213.24 | .64 | 277.79 | .63 | 338.73 | .57 | 390.39 | .46 |
| 4.4 | 97.41 | .49 | 151.64 | .59 | 213.88 | .65 | 278.42 | .64 | 339.30 | .57 | 390.85 | .45 |
| 4.5 | 97.90 | .49 | 152.23 | .59 | 214.53 | .64 | 279.06 | .64 | 339.87 | .57 | 391.30 | .45 |
| 4.6 | 98.39 | .49 | 152.82 | .60 | 215.17 | .64 | 279.70 | .63 | 340.44 | .57 | 391.75 | .45 |
| 4.7 | 98.88 | .48 | 153.42 | .59 | 215.81 | .65 | 280.33 | .64 | 341.01 | .56 | 392.20 | .44 |
| 4.8 | 99.36 | .50 | 154.01 | .59 | 216.46 | .64 | 280.97 | .63 | 341.57 | .57 | 392.64 | .45 |
| 4.9 | 99.86 | .49 | 154.60 | .60 | 217.10 | .65 | 281.60 | .64 | 342.14 | .56 | 393.09 | .44 |
| 5.0 | 100.35 | .49 | 155.20 | .60 | 217.75 | .64 | 282.24 | .63 | 342.70 | .57 | 393.53 | .44 |

# TABLE X. ARGUMENT 5.

Equation $= 225''.300 + 18''.0 \sin. (x - t) - 212''.4 \sin. 2 (x - t)$.

Period, 411.78517 days.

| Days. | 240 | | 250 | | 260 | | 270 | | 280 | | 290 | |
|---|---|---|---|---|---|---|---|---|---|---|---|---|
| Days. | Equation. | Diff. | Equation. | Diff. | Equation. | Diff. | Equation. | Diff. | Equation. | Diff. | Equation. | Diff. |
| d. | " | | " | | " | | " | | " | | " | |
| 5.0 | 100.35 | .49 | 155.20 | .60 | 217.75 | .64 | 282.24 | .63 | 342.70 | .57 | 393.53 | .44 |
| 5.1 | 100.84 | .50 | 155.80 | .59 | 218.39 | .65 | 282.87 | .64 | 343.27 | .56 | 393.97 | .44 |
| 5.2 | 101.34 | .49 | 156.39 | .60 | 219.04 | .64 | 283.51 | .63 | 343.83 | .57 | 394.41 | .44 |
| 5.3 | 101.83 | .50 | 156.99 | .60 | 219.68 | .65 | 284.14 | .63 | 344.40 | .56 | 394.85 | .44 |
| 5.4 | 102.33 | .50 | 157.59 | .60 | 220.33 | .65 | 284.77 | .64 | 344.96 | .56 | 395.29 | .44 |
| 5.5 | 102.83 | .50 | 158.19 | .60 | 220.98 | .64 | 285.41 | .63 | 345.52 | .56 | 395.73 | .43 |
| 5.6 | 103.33 | .50 | 158.79 | .60 | 221.62 | .65 | 286.04 | .63 | 346.08 | .56 | 396.16 | .44 |
| 5.7 | 103.83 | .50 | 159.39 | .60 | 222.27 | .64 | 286.67 | .63 | 346.64 | .56 | 396.60 | .43 |
| 5.8 | 104.33 | .50 | 159.99 | .61 | 222.91 | .65 | 287.30 | .63 | 347.20 | .55 | 397.03 | .43 |
| 5.9 | 104.83 | .50 | 160.60 | .60 | 223.56 | .65 | 287.93 | .63 | 347.75 | .56 | 397.46 | .43 |
| 6.0 | 105.33 | .51 | 161.20 | .60 | 224.21 | .64 | 288.56 | .63 | 348.31 | .55 | 397.89 | .43 |
| 6.1 | 105.84 | .51 | 161.80 | .61 | 224.85 | .65 | 289.19 | .63 | 348.86 | .56 | 398.32 | .42 |
| 6.2 | 106.35 | .50 | 162.41 | .60 | 225.50 | .65 | 289.82 | .63 | 349.42 | .55 | 398.74 | .43 |
| 6.3 | 106.85 | .51 | 163.01 | .61 | 226.15 | .65 | 290.45 | .63 | 349.97 | .55 | 399.17 | .42 |
| 6.4 | 107.36 | .51 | 163.62 | .61 | 226.80 | .64 | 291.08 | .63 | 350.52 | .55 | 399.59 | .42 |
| 6.5 | 107.87 | .52 | 164.23 | .61 | 227.44 | .65 | 291.71 | .62 | 351.07 | .55 | 400.01 | .42 |
| 6.6 | 108.39 | .51 | 164.84 | .60 | 228.09 | .65 | 292.33 | .63 | 351.62 | .55 | 400.43 | .42 |
| 6.7 | 108.90 | .51 | 165.44 | .61 | 228.74 | .65 | 292.96 | .63 | 352.17 | .55 | 400.85 | .42 |
| 6.8 | 109.41 | .52 | 166.05 | .61 | 229.39 | .64 | 293.59 | .62 | 352.72 | .55 | 401.27 | .42 |
| 6.9 | 109.93 | .52 | 166.66 | .61 | 230.03 | .65 | 294.21 | .63 | 353.27 | .54 | 401.69 | .41 |
| 7.0 | 110.45 | .51 | 167.27 | .61 | 230.68 | .65 | 294.84 | .62 | 353.81 | .54 | 402.10 | .41 |
| 7.1 | 110.96 | .52 | 167.88 | .62 | 231.33 | .65 | 295.46 | .63 | 354.35 | .55 | 402.51 | .41 |
| 7.2 | 111.48 | .52 | 168.50 | .61 | 231.98 | .65 | 296.09 | .62 | 354.90 | .54 | 402.92 | .41 |
| 7.3 | 112.00 | .52 | 169.11 | .61 | 232.63 | .64 | 296.71 | .62 | 355.44 | .54 | 403.33 | .40 |
| 7.4 | 112.52 | .53 | 169.72 | .62 | 233.27 | .65 | 297.33 | .63 | 355.98 | .54 | 403.73 | .42 |
| 7.5 | 113.05 | .52 | 170.34 | .61 | 233.92 | .65 | 297.96 | .62 | 356.52 | .54 | 404.15 | .40 |
| 7.6 | 113.57 | .53 | 170.95 | .61 | 234.57 | .65 | 298.58 | .62 | 357.06 | .54 | 404.55 | .41 |
| 7.7 | 114.10 | .52 | 171.56 | .62 | 235.22 | .65 | 299.20 | .63 | 357.60 | .53 | 404.96 | .40 |
| 7.8 | 114.62 | .53 | 172.18 | .62 | 235.87 | .65 | 299.83 | .62 | 358.13 | .54 | 405.36 | .40 |
| 7.9 | 115.15 | .53 | 172.80 | .61 | 236.52 | .64 | 300.45 | .62 | 358.67 | .53 | 405.76 | .40 |
| 8.0 | 115.68 | .53 | 173.41 | .62 | 237.16 | .65 | 301.07 | .62 | 359.20 | .54 | 406.16 | .39 |
| 8.1 | 116.21 | .53 | 174.03 | .62 | 237.81 | .65 | 301.69 | .61 | 359.74 | .53 | 406.55 | .40 |
| 8.2 | 116.74 | .53 | 174.65 | .61 | 238.46 | .65 | 302.30 | .62 | 360.27 | .53 | 406.95 | .39 |
| 8.3 | 117.27 | .53 | 175.26 | .62 | 239.11 | .65 | 302.92 | .62 | 360.80 | .53 | 407.34 | .40 |
| 8.4 | 117.80 | .54 | 175.88 | .62 | 239.76 | .65 | 303.54 | .62 | 361.33 | .53 | 407.74 | .39 |
| 8.5 | 118.34 | .53 | 176.50 | .62 | 240.41 | .64 | 304.16 | .62 | 361.86 | .53 | 408.13 | .39 |
| 8.6 | 118.87 | .54 | 177.12 | .62 | 241.05 | .65 | 304.78 | .61 | 362.39 | .52 | 408.52 | .38 |
| 8.7 | 119.41 | .53 | 177.74 | .62 | 241.70 | .65 | 305.39 | .62 | 362.91 | .53 | 408.90 | .39 |
| 8.8 | 119.94 | .54 | 178.36 | .63 | 242.35 | .65 | 306.01 | .61 | 363.44 | .52 | 409.29 | .38 |
| 8.9 | 120.48 | .54 | 178.99 | .62 | 243.00 | .65 | 306.62 | .62 | 363.96 | .52 | 409.67 | .39 |
| 9.0 | 121.02 | .54 | 179.61 | .62 | 243.65 | .64 | 307.24 | .61 | 364.48 | .53 | 410.06 | .38 |
| 9.1 | 121.56 | .54 | 180.23 | .62 | 244.29 | .65 | 307.85 | .61 | 365.01 | .52 | 410.44 | .38 |
| 9.2 | 122.10 | .55 | 180.85 | .63 | 244.94 | .65 | 308.46 | .61 | 365.53 | .52 | 410.82 | .38 |
| 9.3 | 122.65 | .54 | 181.48 | .62 | 245.59 | .65 | 309.07 | .62 | 366.05 | .52 | 411.20 | .37 |
| 9.4 | 123.19 | .55 | 182.10 | .63 | 246.24 | .65 | 309.69 | .61 | 366.57 | .51 | 411.57 | .38 |
| 9.5 | 123.74 | .54 | 182.73 | .62 | 246.89 | .64 | 310.30 | .61 | 367.08 | .52 | 411.95 | .37 |
| 9.6 | 124.28 | .55 | 183.35 | .63 | 247.53 | .65 | 310.91 | .61 | 367.60 | .51 | 412.32 | .37 |
| 9.7 | 124.83 | .55 | 183.98 | .63 | 248.18 | .65 | 311.52 | .60 | 368.11 | .52 | 412.69 | .37 |
| 9.8 | 125.38 | .55 | 184.61 | .62 | 248.83 | .65 | 312.12 | .61 | 368.63 | .51 | 413.06 | .37 |
| 9.9 | 125.93 | .55 | 185.23 | .63 | 249.48 | .64 | 312.73 | .61 | 369.14 | .51 | 413.43 | .36 |
| 10.0 | 126.48 | .55 | 185.86 | .63 | 250.12 | .65 | 313.34 | .61 | 369.65 | .51 | 413.79 | .37 |

# TABLE X. ARGUMENT 5.

Equation $= 225''.300 + 18''.0 \sin.(x - t) - 212''.4 \sin. 2(x - t)$.

Period, 411.78517 days.

| Days. | 300 | | 310 | | 320 | | 330 | | 340 | | 350 | |
|---|---|---|---|---|---|---|---|---|---|---|---|---|
| Days. | Equation. | Diff. | Equation. | Diff. | Equation. | Diff. | Equation. | Diff. | Equation. | Diff. | Equation. | Diff. |
| d. | ″ | | ″ | | ″ | | ″ | | ″ | | ″ | |
| 0.0 | 413.79 | .37 | 441.63 | .19 | 450.49 | .01 | 439.42 | .20 | 409.31 | .39 | 362.78 | .53 |
| 0.1 | 414.16 | .36 | 441.82 | .18 | 450.48 | .02 | 439.22 | .22 | 408.92 | .39 | 362.25 | .54 |
| 0.2 | 414.52 | .37 | 442.00 | .19 | 450.46 | .01 | 439.00 | .21 | 408.53 | .39 | 361.71 | .54 |
| 0.3 | 414.89 | .36 | 442.19 | .18 | 450.45 | .02 | 438.79 | .22 | 408.14 | .40 | 361.17 | .54 |
| 0.4 | 415.25 | .35 | 442.37 | .17 | 450.43 | .02 | 438.57 | .21 | 407.74 | .39 | 360.63 | .54 |
| 0.5 | 415.60 | .36 | 442.54 | .18 | 450.41 | .02 | 438.36 | .22 | 407.35 | .40 | 360.09 | .54 |
| 0.6 | 415.96 | .36 | 442.72 | .17 | 450.39 | .03 | 438.14 | .23 | 406.95 | .40 | 359.55 | .54 |
| 0.7 | 416.32 | .35 | 442.89 | .17 | 450.36 | .02 | 437.91 | .22 | 406.55 | .40 | 359.01 | .55 |
| 0.8 | 416.67 | .35 | 443.06 | .16 | 450.34 | .03 | 437.69 | .22 | 406.15 | .40 | 358.46 | .54 |
| 0.9 | 417.02 | .35 | 443.22 | .16 | 450.31 | .03 | 437.47 | .23 | 405.75 | .41 | 357.92 | .55 |
| 1.0 | 417.37 | .35 | 443.38 | .17 | 450.28 | .03 | 437.24 | .23 | 405.34 | .40 | 357.37 | .55 |
| 1.1 | 417.72 | .35 | 443.55 | .18 | 450.25 | .04 | 437.01 | .23 | 404.94 | .42 | 356.82 | .55 |
| 1.2 | 418.07 | .34 | 443.73 | .17 | 450.21 | .03 | 436.78 | .23 | 404.52 | .40 | 356.27 | .55 |
| 1.3 | 418.41 | .34 | 443.90 | .16 | 450.18 | .04 | 436.55 | .24 | 404.12 | .41 | 355.72 | .55 |
| 1.4 | 418.75 | .35 | 444.06 | .16 | 450.14 | .04 | 436.31 | .23 | 403.71 | .42 | 355.17 | .55 |
| 1.5 | 419.10 | .34 | 444.22 | .15 | 450.10 | .04 | 436.08 | .24 | 403.29 | .41 | 354.62 | .55 |
| 1.6 | 419.44 | .33 | 444.37 | .16 | 450.06 | .05 | 435.84 | .24 | 402.88 | .42 | 354.07 | .56 |
| 1.7 | 419.77 | .34 | 444.53 | .15 | 450.01 | .04 | 435.60 | .24 | 402.46 | .41 | 353.51 | .55 |
| 1.8 | 420.11 | .33 | 444.68 | .15 | 449.97 | .05 | 435.36 | .25 | 402.05 | .42 | 352.96 | .56 |
| 1.9 | 420.44 | .34 | 444.83 | .15 | 449.92 | .05 | 435.11 | .24 | 401.63 | .42 | 352.40 | .56 |
| 2.0 | 420.78 | .33 | 444.98 | .15 | 449.87 | .05 | 434.87 | .25 | 401.21 | .42 | 351.84 | .56 |
| 2.1 | 421.11 | .33 | 445.13 | .14 | 449.82 | .06 | 434.62 | .25 | 400.79 | .43 | 351.28 | .56 |
| 2.2 | 421.44 | .33 | 445.27 | .15 | 449.76 | .05 | 434.37 | .25 | 400.36 | .42 | 350.72 | .56 |
| 2.3 | 421.77 | .32 | 445.42 | .14 | 449.71 | .07 | 434.12 | .26 | 399.94 | .43 | 350.16 | .56 |
| 2.4 | 422.09 | .33 | 445.56 | .14 | 449.64 | .05 | 433.86 | .25 | 399.51 | .43 | 349.60 | .56 |
| 2.5 | 422.42 | .32 | 445.70 | .13 | 449.59 | .06 | 433.61 | .26 | 399.08 | .43 | 349.04 | .57 |
| 2.6 | 422.74 | .32 | 445.83 | .14 | 449.53 | .07 | 433.35 | .26 | 398.65 | .43 | 348.47 | .57 |
| 2.7 | 423.06 | .32 | 445.97 | .13 | 449.46 | .06 | 433.09 | .26 | 398.22 | .43 | 347.90 | .56 |
| 2.8 | 423.38 | .32 | 446.10 | .13 | 449.40 | .07 | 432.83 | .26 | 397.79 | .44 | 347.34 | .57 |
| 2.9 | 423.70 | .31 | 446.23 | .13 | 449.33 | .06 | 432.57 | .27 | 397.35 | .43 | 346.77 | .57 |
| 3.0 | 424.01 | .32 | 446.36 | .13 | 449.26 | .07 | 432.30 | .26 | 396.92 | .44 | 346.20 | .56 |
| 3.1 | 424.33 | .31 | 446.49 | .13 | 449.19 | .08 | 432.04 | .27 | 396.48 | .44 | 345.64 | .58 |
| 3.2 | 424.64 | .31 | 446.62 | .12 | 449.11 | .07 | 431.77 | .27 | 396.04 | .44 | 345.06 | .57 |
| 3.3 | 424.95 | .31 | 446.74 | .12 | 449.04 | .08 | 431.50 | .27 | 395.60 | .44 | 344.49 | .58 |
| 3.4 | 425.26 | .31 | 446.86 | .12 | 448.96 | .08 | 431.23 | .28 | 395.16 | .45 | 343.91 | .57 |
| 3.5 | 425.57 | .30 | 446.98 | .12 | 448.88 | .09 | 430.95 | .27 | 394.71 | .44 | 343.34 | .58 |
| 3.6 | 425.87 | .30 | 447.10 | .11 | 448.79 | .08 | 430.68 | .28 | 394.27 | .45 | 342.76 | .57 |
| 3.7 | 426.17 | .31 | 447.21 | .12 | 448.71 | .09 | 430.40 | .28 | 393.82 | .45 | 342.19 | .58 |
| 3.8 | 426.48 | .30 | 447.33 | .11 | 448.62 | .08 | 430.12 | .28 | 393.37 | .45 | 341.61 | .58 |
| 3.9 | 426.78 | .29 | 447.44 | .11 | 448.54 | .09 | 429.84 | .28 | 392.92 | .45 | 341.03 | .58 |
| 4.0 | 427.07 | .30 | 447.55 | .10 | 448.45 | .10 | 429.56 | .29 | 392.47 | .45 | 340.45 | .58 |
| 4.1 | 427.37 | .30 | 447.65 | .11 | 448.35 | .09 | 429.27 | .28 | 392.02 | .46 | 339.87 | .58 |
| 4.2 | 427.67 | .29 | 447.76 | .10 | 448.26 | .10 | 428.99 | .29 | 391.56 | .45 | 339.29 | .59 |
| 4.3 | 427.96 | .29 | 447.86 | .11 | 448.16 | .10 | 428.70 | .29 | 391.11 | .46 | 338.70 | .58 |
| 4.4 | 428.25 | .29 | 447.97 | .10 | 448.06 | .10 | 428.41 | .30 | 390.65 | .46 | 338.12 | .59 |
| 4.5 | 428.54 | .29 | 448.07 | .09 | 447.96 | .10 | 428.11 | .29 | 390.19 | .46 | 337.53 | .58 |
| 4.6 | 428.83 | .28 | 448.16 | .10 | 447.86 | .10 | 427.82 | .30 | 389.73 | .46 | 336.95 | .59 |
| 4.7 | 429.11 | .29 | 448.26 | .09 | 447.76 | .11 | 427.52 | .29 | 389.27 | .47 | 336.36 | .59 |
| 4.8 | 429.40 | .28 | 448.35 | .10 | 447.65 | .11 | 427.23 | .30 | 388.80 | .46 | 335.77 | .59 |
| 4.9 | 429.68 | .28 | 448.45 | .09 | 447.54 | .11 | 426.93 | .31 | 388.34 | .47 | 335.18 | .59 |
| 5.0 | 429.96 | .28 | 448.54 | .09 | 447.43 | .11 | 426.62 | .30 | 387.87 | .47 | 334.59 | .58 |

# TABLE X. ARGUMENT 5.

Equation = 225″.300 + 18″.0 sin. $(x - t)$ — 212″.4 sin. 2 $(x - t)$.

Period, 411.78517 days.

| Days. | 300 | | 310 | | 320 | | 330 | | 340 | | 350 | |
|---|---|---|---|---|---|---|---|---|---|---|---|---|
| Days. | Equation. | Diff. | Equation. | Diff. | Equation. | Diff. | Equation. | Diff. | Equation. | Diff. | Equation. | Diff. |
| d. | ″ | | ″ | | ″ | | ″ | | ″ | | ″ | |
| 5.0 | 429.96 | .28 | 448.54 | .09 | 447.43 | .11 | 426.62 | .30 | 387.87 | .47 | 334.59 | .58 |
| 5.1 | 430.24 | .28 | 448.63 | .08 | 447.32 | .11 | 426.32 | .30 | 387.40 | .46 | 334.01 | .60 |
| 5.2 | 430.52 | .27 | 448.71 | .09 | 447.21 | .12 | 426.02 | .31 | 386.94 | .48 | 333.41 | .59 |
| 5.3 | 430.79 | .27 | 448.80 | .08 | 447.09 | .12 | 425.71 | .31 | 386.46 | .47 | 332.82 | .59 |
| 5.4 | 431.06 | .27 | 448.88 | .08 | 446.97 | .12 | 425.40 | .31 | 385.99 | .47 | 332.23 | .60 |
| 5.5 | 431.33 | .27 | 448.96 | .07 | 446.85 | .12 | 425.09 | .31 | 385.52 | .48 | 331.63 | .59 |
| 5.6 | 431.60 | .27 | 449.03 | .08 | 446.73 | .12 | 424.78 | .32 | 385.04 | .47 | 331.04 | .60 |
| 5.7 | 431.87 | .27 | 449.11 | .07 | 446.61 | .13 | 424.46 | .31 | 384.57 | .48 | 330.44 | .60 |
| 5.8 | 432.14 | .26 | 449.18 | .08 | 446.48 | .13 | 424.15 | .32 | 384.09 | .48 | 329.84 | .60 |
| 5.9 | 432.40 | .26 | 449.26 | .07 | 446.35 | .13 | 423.83 | .32 | 383.61 | .48 | 329.24 | .60 |
| 6.0 | 432.66 | .26 | 449.33 | .07 | 446.22 | .12 | 423.51 | .32 | 383.13 | .48 | 328.64 | .60 |
| 6.1 | 432.92 | .26 | 449.40 | .06 | 446.10 | .14 | 423.19 | .32 | 382.65 | .49 | 328.04 | .60 |
| 6.2 | 433.18 | .26 | 449.46 | .07 | 445.96 | .13 | 422.87 | .33 | 382.16 | .48 | 327.44 | .60 |
| 6.3 | 433.44 | .26 | 449.53 | .06 | 445.83 | .14 | 422.54 | .32 | 381.68 | .49 | 326.84 | .61 |
| 6.4 | 433.70 | .25 | 449.59 | .06 | 445.69 | .14 | 422.22 | .33 | 381.19 | .49 | 326.23 | .60 |
| 6.5 | 433.95 | .25 | 449.65 | .06 | 445.55 | .14 | 421.89 | .33 | 380.70 | .49 | 325.63 | .60 |
| 6.6 | 434.20 | .25 | 449.71 | .05 | 445.41 | .15 | 421.56 | .33 | 380.21 | .49 | 325.03 | .61 |
| 6.7 | 434.45 | .25 | 449.76 | .06 | 445.26 | .14 | 421.23 | .34 | 379.72 | .49 | 324.42 | .61 |
| 6.8 | 434.70 | .24 | 449.82 | .05 | 445.12 | .15 | 420.89 | .33 | 379.23 | .49 | 323.81 | .61 |
| 6.9 | 434.94 | .25 | 449.87 | .05 | 444.97 | .15 | 420.56 | .34 | 378.74 | .49 | 323.20 | .60 |
| 7.0 | 435.19 | .24 | 449.92 | .05 | 444.82 | .15 | 420.22 | .34 | 378.25 | .50 | 322.60 | .61 |
| 7.1 | 435.43 | .24 | 449.97 | .04 | 444.67 | .16 | 419.88 | .34 | 377.75 | .50 | 321.99 | .61 |
| 7.2 | 435.67 | .24 | 450.01 | .05 | 444.51 | .15 | 419.54 | .34 | 377.25 | .50 | 321.38 | .62 |
| 7.3 | 435.91 | .23 | 450.06 | .04 | 444.36 | .16 | 419.20 | .34 | 376.75 | .50 | 320.76 | .61 |
| 7.4 | 436.14 | .24 | 450.10 | .04 | 444.20 | .16 | 418.86 | .35 | 376.25 | .50 | 320.15 | .61 |
| 7.5 | 436.38 | .23 | 450.14 | .04 | 444.04 | .16 | 418.51 | .35 | 375.75 | .50 | 319.54 | .61 |
| 7.6 | 436.61 | .23 | 450.18 | .03 | 443.88 | .16 | 418.16 | .35 | 375.25 | .51 | 318.93 | .62 |
| 7.7 | 436.84 | .23 | 450.21 | .04 | 443.72 | .17 | 417.81 | .35 | 374.74 | .50 | 318.31 | .62 |
| 7.8 | 437.07 | .23 | 450.25 | .03 | 443.55 | .17 | 417.46 | .35 | 374.24 | .51 | 317.69 | .61 |
| 7.9 | 437.30 | .22 | 450.28 | .03 | 443.38 | .17 | 417.11 | .35 | 373.73 | .51 | 317.08 | .62 |
| 8.0 | 447.52 | .23 | 450.31 | .03 | 443.21 | .16 | 416.76 | .36 | 373.22 | .51 | 316.46 | .62 |
| 8.1 | 437.75 | .22 | 450.34 | .02 | 443.05 | .18 | 416.40 | .36 | 372.71 | .51 | 315.84 | .62 |
| 8.2 | 437.97 | .22 | 450.36 | .03 | 442.87 | .17 | 416.04 | .36 | 372.20 | .51 | 315.22 | .61 |
| 8.3 | 438.19 | .22 | 450.39 | .02 | 442.70 | .18 | 415.68 | .36 | 371.69 | .52 | 314.61 | .63 |
| 8.4 | 438.41 | .21 | 450.41 | .02 | 442.52 | .18 | 415.32 | .36 | 371.17 | .51 | 313.98 | .62 |
| 8.5 | 438.62 | .22 | 450.43 | .02 | 442.34 | .18 | 414.96 | .37 | 370.66 | .52 | 313.36 | .62 |
| 8.6 | 438.84 | .21 | 450.45 | .01 | 442.16 | .18 | 414.59 | .36 | 370.14 | .52 | 312.74 | .62 |
| 8.7 | 439.05 | .21 | 450.46 | .02 | 441.98 | .19 | 414.23 | .37 | 369.62 | .52 | 312.12 | .63 |
| 8.8 | 439.26 | .21 | 450.48 | .01 | 441.79 | .18 | 413.86 | .37 | 369.10 | .52 | 311.49 | .62 |
| 8.9 | 439.47 | .20 | 450.49 | .01 | 441.61 | .19 | 413.49 | .37 | 368.58 | .52 | 310.87 | .63 |
| 9.0 | 439.67 | .21 | 450.50 | .01 | 441.42 | .19 | 413.12 | .38 | 368.06 | .52 | 310.24 | .62 |
| 9.1 | 439.88 | .20 | 450.51 | .00 | 441.23 | .20 | 412.74 | .37 | 367.54 | .52 | 309.62 | .63 |
| 9.2 | 440.08 | .20 | 450.51 | .01 | 441.03 | .19 | 412.37 | .38 | 367.02 | .53 | 308.99 | .62 |
| 9.3 | 440.28 | .20 | 450.52 | .00 | 440.84 | .20 | 411.99 | .37 | 366.49 | .53 | 308.37 | .63 |
| 9.4 | 440.48 | .20 | 450.52 | .00 | 440.64 | .20 | 411.62 | .38 | 365.96 | .52 | 307.74 | .63 |
| 9.5 | 440.68 | .19 | 450.52 | .00 | 440.44 | .20 | 411.24 | .39 | 365.44 | .53 | 307.11 | .63 |
| 9.6 | 440.87 | .20 | 450.52 | .01 | 440.24 | .20 | 410.85 | .38 | 364.91 | .53 | 306.48 | .63 |
| 9.7 | 441.07 | .19 | 450.51 | .00 | 440.04 | .20 | 410.47 | .38 | 364.38 | .53 | 305.85 | .63 |
| 9.8 | 441.26 | .19 | 450.51 | .01 | 439.84 | .21 | 410.09 | .39 | 363.85 | .54 | 305.22 | .64 |
| 9.9 | 441.45 | .18 | 450.50 | .01 | 439.63 | .21 | 409.70 | .39 | 363.31 | .53 | 304.58 | .63 |
| 10.0 | 441.63 | .19 | 450.49 | .01 | 439.42 | .20 | 409.31 | .39 | 362.78 | .53 | 303.95 | .63 |

# TABLE X. ARGUMENT 5.

Equation $= 225''.300 + 18''.0 \sin. (x - t) - 212''.4 \sin. 2 (x - t)$.

Period, 411.78517 days.

| Days. | 360 | | 370 | | 380 | | 390 | | 400 | | 410 | | 420 | |
|---|---|---|---|---|---|---|---|---|---|---|---|---|---|---|
| Days. | Equation. | Diff. | Equation. | Diff. | Equation. | Diff. | Equation. | Diff. | Equation. | Diff. | Equation. | Diff. | Equation. | Diff. |
| d. | " | | " | | " | | " | | " | | " | | " | |
| 0.0 | 303.95 | .63 | 238.08 | .68 | 171.06 | .66 | 108.90 | .58 | 57.16 | .45 | 20.44 | .28 | 1.97 | .09 |
| 0.1 | 303.32 | .63 | 237.40 | .67 | 170.40 | .65 | 108.32 | .57 | 56.71 | .45 | 20.16 | .28 | 1.88 | .08 |
| 0.2 | 302.69 | .64 | 236.73 | .68 | 169.75 | .66 | 107.75 | .57 | 56.26 | .44 | 19.88 | .27 | 1.80 | .09 |
| 0.3 | 302.05 | .64 | 236.05 | .67 | 169.09 | .65 | 107.18 | .57 | 55.82 | .45 | 19.61 | .28 | 1.71 | .08 |
| 0.4 | 301.41 | .63 | 235.38 | .68 | 168.44 | .65 | 106.61 | .58 | 55.37 | .44 | 19.33 | .27 | 1.63 | .08 |
| 0.5 | 300.78 | .64 | 234.70 | .67 | 167.79 | .66 | 106.03 | .58 | 54.93 | .44 | 19.06 | .27 | 1.55 | .07 |
| 0.6 | 300.14 | .64 | 234.03 | .68 | 167.13 | .65 | 105.45 | .57 | 54.49 | .44 | 18.79 | .27 | 1.48 | .08 |
| 0.7 | 299.50 | .63 | 233.35 | .67 | 166.48 | .65 | 104.88 | .56 | 54.05 | .44 | 18.52 | .26 | 1.40 | .07 |
| 0.8 | 298.87 | .64 | 232.68 | .68 | 165.83 | .65 | 104.32 | .57 | 53.61 | .43 | 18.26 | .27 | 1.33 | .07 |
| 0.9 | 298.23 | .64 | 232.00 | .67 | 165.18 | .65 | 103.75 | .57 | 53.18 | .44 | 17.99 | .26 | 1.26 | .07 |
| 1.0 | 297.59 | .64 | 231.33 | .68 | 164.53 | .65 | 103.18 | .57 | 52.74 | .43 | 17.73 | .26 | 1.19 | .06 |
| 1.1 | 296.95 | .64 | 230.65 | .67 | 163.88 | .65 | 102.61 | .56 | 52.31 | .43 | 17.47 | .26 | 1.13 | .07 |
| 1.2 | 296.31 | .64 | 229.98 | .68 | 163.23 | .65 | 102.05 | .57 | 51.88 | .43 | 17.21 | .26 | 1.06 | .06 |
| 1.3 | 295.67 | .65 | 229.30 | .67 | 162.58 | .65 | 101.48 | .56 | 51.45 | .42 | 16.95 | .25 | 1.00 | .06 |
| 1.4 | 295.02 | .64 | 228.63 | .68 | 161.93 | .65 | 100.92 | .56 | 51.03 | .43 | 16.70 | .26 | 0.94 | .06 |
| 1.5 | 294.38 | .64 | 227.95 | .67 | 161.28 | .65 | 100.36 | .57 | 50.60 | .42 | 16.44 | .25 | 0.88 | .05 |
| 1.6 | 293.74 | .65 | 227.28 | .68 | 160.63 | .64 | 99.79 | .56 | 50.18 | .43 | 16.19 | .25 | 0.83 | .06 |
| 1.7 | 293.09 | .64 | 226.60 | .68 | 159.99 | .65 | 99.23 | .55 | 49.75 | .42 | 15.94 | .25 | 0.77 | .05 |
| 1.8 | 292.45 | .65 | 225.92 | .67 | 159.34 | .64 | 98.68 | .56 | 49.33 | .42 | 15.69 | .24 | 0.72 | .05 |
| 1.9 | 291.80 | .64 | 225.25 | .68 | 158.70 | .65 | 98.12 | .56 | 48.91 | .42 | 15.45 | .25 | 0.67 | .05 |
| 2.0 | 291.16 | .65 | 224.57 | .67 | 158.05 | .64 | 97.56 | .55 | 48.49 | .42 | 15.20 | .24 | 0.62 | .04 |
| 2.1 | 290.51 | .65 | 223.90 | .68 | 157.41 | .65 | 97.01 | .56 | 48.07 | .41 | 14.96 | .24 | 0.58 | .05 |
| 2.2 | 289.86 | .64 | 223.22 | .67 | 156.76 | .64 | 96.45 | .55 | 47.66 | .41 | 14.72 | .24 | 0.53 | .04 |
| 2.3 | 289.22 | .65 | 222.55 | .68 | 156.12 | .64 | 95.90 | .55 | 47.25 | .42 | 14.48 | .23 | 0.49 | .04 |
| 2.4 | 288.57 | .65 | 221.87 | .68 | 155.48 | .65 | 95.35 | .56 | 46.83 | .41 | 14.25 | .23 | 0.45 | .04 |
| 2.5 | 287.92 | .65 | 221.19 | .67 | 154.83 | .64 | 94.79 | .55 | 46.42 | .41 | 14.02 | .23 | 0.41 | .03 |
| 2.6 | 287.27 | .65 | 220.52 | .68 | 154.19 | .64 | 94.24 | .54 | 46.01 | .41 | 13.79 | .23 | 0.38 | .04 |
| 2.7 | 286.62 | .65 | 219.84 | .67 | 153.55 | .63 | 93.70 | .55 | 45.60 | .40 | 13.56 | .23 | 0.34 | .02 |
| 2.8 | 285.97 | .65 | 219.17 | .68 | 152.92 | .64 | 93.15 | .55 | 45.20 | .41 | 13.33 | .23 | 0.32 | .03 |
| 2.9 | 285.32 | .65 | 218.49 | .67 | 152.28 | .64 | 92.60 | .54 | 44.79 | .40 | 13.10 | .22 | 0.29 | .03 |
| 3.0 | 284.67 | .65 | 217.82 | .68 | 151.64 | .63 | 92.06 | .55 | 44.39 | .40 | 12.88 | .23 | 0.26 | .02 |
| 3.1 | 284.02 | .65 | 217.14 | .67 | 151.01 | .64 | 91.51 | .54 | 43.99 | .40 | 12.65 | .22 | 0.24 | .03 |
| 3.2 | 283.37 | .66 | 216.47 | .68 | 150.37 | .64 | 90.97 | .54 | 43.59 | .40 | 12.43 | .22 | 0.21 | .02 |
| 3.3 | 282.71 | .65 | 215.79 | .67 | 149.73 | .64 | 90.43 | .54 | 43.19 | .40 | 12.21 | .21 | 0.19 | .02 |
| 3.4 | 282.06 | .66 | 215.12 | .67 | 149.09 | .63 | 89.89 | .54 | 42.79 | .39 | 12.00 | .22 | 0.17 | .02 |
| 3.5 | 281.40 | .65 | 214.45 | .68 | 148.46 | .64 | 89.35 | .54 | 42.40 | .39 | 11.78 | .22 | 0.15 | .01 |
| 3.6 | 280.75 | .66 | 213.77 | .68 | 147.82 | .63 | 88.81 | .53 | 42.01 | .39 | 11.56 | .21 | 0.14 | .02 |
| 3.7 | 280.09 | .65 | 213.09 | .67 | 147.19 | .63 | 88.28 | .54 | 41.62 | .39 | 11.35 | .21 | 0.12 | .01 |
| 3.8 | 279.44 | .66 | 212.42 | .67 | 146.56 | .64 | 87.74 | .53 | 41.23 | .39 | 11.14 | .20 | 0.11 | .01 |
| 3.9 | 278.78 | .65 | 211.75 | .68 | 145.92 | .63 | 87.21 | .54 | 40.84 | .39 | 10.94 | .21 | 0.10 | .01 |
| 4.0 | 278.13 | .66 | 211.07 | .67 | 145.29 | .63 | 86.67 | .53 | 40.45 | .38 | 10.73 | .20 | 0.09 | .00 |
| 4.1 | 277.47 | .66 | 210.40 | .68 | 144.66 | .63 | 86.14 | .53 | 40.07 | .39 | 10.53 | .20 | 0.09 | .01 |
| 4.2 | 276.81 | .66 | 209.72 | .67 | 144.03 | .63 | 85.61 | .53 | 39.68 | .38 | 10.33 | .20 | 0.08 | .00 |
| 4.3 | 276.15 | .65 | 209.05 | .67 | 143.40 | .63 | 85.08 | .53 | 39.30 | .38 | 10.13 | .20 | 0.08 | .00 |
| 4.4 | 275.50 | .66 | 208.38 | .68 | 142.77 | .63 | 84.55 | .53 | 38.92 | .38 | 9.93 | .20 | 0.08 | .00 |
| 4.5 | 274.84 | .66 | 207.70 | .67 | 142.14 | .62 | 84.02 | .52 | 38.54 | .37 | 9.73 | .19 | 0.08 | .01 |
| 4.6 | 274.18 | .66 | 207.03 | .68 | 141.52 | .63 | 83.50 | .52 | 38.17 | .38 | 9.54 | .20 | 0.09 | .00 |
| 4.7 | 273.52 | .66 | 206.35 | .67 | 140.89 | .63 | 82.98 | .52 | 37.79 | .37 | 9.34 | .19 | 0.09 | .01 |
| 4.8 | 272.86 | .66 | 205.68 | .67 | 140.26 | .62 | 82.46 | .53 | 37.42 | .37 | 9.15 | .19 | 0.10 | .01 |
| 4.9 | 272.20 | .66 | 205.01 | .67 | 139.64 | .63 | 81.93 | .52 | 37.05 | .37 | 8.96 | .18 | 0.11 | .01 |
| 5.0 | 271.54 | .66 | 204.34 | .68 | 139.01 | .62 | 81.41 | .51 | 36.68 | .36 | 8.78 | .19 | 0.12 | .02 |

# TABLE X. ARGUMENT 5.

Equation $= 225''.300 + 18''.0 \sin. (x - t) - 212''.4 \sin. 2 (x - t)$.

Period, 411.78517 days.

| Days. | 360 | | 370 | | 380 | | 390 | | 400 | | 410 | | 420 | |
|---|---|---|---|---|---|---|---|---|---|---|---|---|---|---|
| Days. | Equation. | Diff. | Equation. | Diff. | Equation | Diff. | Equation. | Diff. | Equation. | Diff. | Equation. | Diff. | Equation. | Diff. |
| d. | " | | " | | " | | " | | " | | " | | " | |
| 5.0 | 271.54 | .66 | 204.34 | .68 | 139.01 | .62 | 81.41 | .51 | 36.68 | .36 | 8.78 | .19 | 0.12 | .02 |
| 5.1 | 270.88 | .67 | 203.66 | .67 | 138.39 | .62 | 80.90 | .52 | 36.32 | .37 | 8.59 | .18 | 0.14 | .01 |
| 5.2 | 270.21 | .66 | 202.99 | .67 | 137.77 | .62 | 80.38 | .52 | 35.95 | .36 | 8.41 | .18 | 0.15 | .02 |
| 5.3 | 269.55 | .66 | 202.32 | .67 | 137.15 | .63 | 79.86 | .51 | 35.59 | .36 | 8.23 | .18 | 0.17 | .02 |
| 5.4 | 268.89 | .66 | 201.65 | .68 | 136.52 | .62 | 79.35 | .52 | 35.23 | .36 | 8.05 | .18 | 0.19 | .02 |
| 5.5 | 268.23 | .67 | 200.97 | .67 | 135.90 | .62 | 78.83 | .51 | 34.87 | .36 | 7.87 | .17 | 0.21 | .03 |
| 5.6 | 267.56 | .66 | 200.30 | .67 | 135.28 | .62 | 78.32 | .51 | 34.51 | .36 | 7.70 | .18 | 0.24 | .02 |
| 5.7 | 266.90 | .67 | 199.63 | .67 | 134.66 | .61 | 77.81 | .51 | 34.15 | .36 | 7.52 | .17 | 0.26 | .03 |
| 5.8 | 266.23 | .66 | 198.96 | .67 | 134.05 | .62 | 77.30 | .51 | 33.79 | .35 | 7.35 | .16 | 0.29 | .03 |
| 5.9 | 265.57 | .67 | 198.29 | .67 | 133.43 | .62 | 76.79 | .51 | 33.44 | .35 | 7.19 | .16 | 0.32 | .04 |
| 6.0 | 264.90 | .66 | 197.62 | .67 | 132.81 | .61 | 76.28 | .50 | 33.09 | .35 | 7.03 | .17 | 0.36 | .04 |
| 6.1 | 264.24 | .67 | 196.95 | .67 | 132.20 | .62 | 75.78 | .51 | 32.74 | .35 | 6.86 | .16 | 0.40 | .03 |
| 6.2 | 263.57 | .67 | 196.28 | .67 | 131.58 | .61 | 75.27 | .50 | 32.39 | .35 | 6.70 | .16 | 0.43 | .04 |
| 6.3 | 262.90 | .66 | 195.61 | .67 | 130.97 | .61 | 74.77 | .50 | 32.04 | .35 | 6.54 | .16 | 0.47 | .04 |
| 6.4 | 262.24 | .67 | 194.94 | .67 | 130.36 | .62 | 74.27 | .50 | 31.69 | .34 | 6.38 | .16 | 0.51 | .04 |
| 6.5 | 261.57 | .67 | 194.27 | .67 | 129.74 | .61 | 73.77 | .50 | 31.35 | .34 | 6.22 | .15 | 0.55 | .05 |
| 6.6 | 260.90 | .66 | 193.60 | .67 | 129.13 | .61 | 73.27 | .49 | 31.01 | .34 | 6.07 | .16 | 0.60 | .04 |
| 6.7 | 260.24 | .67 | 192.93 | .67 | 128.52 | .61 | 72.78 | .50 | 30.67 | .34 | 5.91 | .15 | 0.64 | .05 |
| 6.8 | 259.57 | .67 | 192.26 | .66 | 127.91 | .61 | 72.28 | .49 | 30.33 | .34 | 5.76 | .15 | 0.69 | .05 |
| 6.9 | 258.90 | .66 | 191.60 | .67 | 127.30 | .60 | 71.79 | .49 | 29.99 | .33 | 5.61 | .15 | 0.74 | .05 |
| 7.0 | 258.24 | .67 | 190.93 | .67 | 126.70 | .61 | 71.30 | .50 | 29.66 | .34 | 5.46 | .14 | 0.79 | .06 |
| 7.1 | 257.57 | .67 | 190.26 | .66 | 126.09 | .61 | 70.80 | .49 | 29.32 | .33 | 5.32 | .15 | 0.85 | .05 |
| 7.2 | 256.90 | .67 | 189.60 | .67 | 125.48 | .60 | 70.31 | .49 | 28.99 | .33 | 5.17 | .14 | 0.90 | .06 |
| 7.3 | 256.23 | .67 | 188.93 | .67 | 124.88 | .61 | 69.82 | .48 | 28.66 | .33 | 5.03 | .14 | 0.96 | .06 |
| 7.4 | 255.56 | .67 | 188.26 | .67 | 124.27 | .60 | 69.34 | .49 | 28.33 | .32 | 4.89 | .14 | 1.02 | .06 |
| 7.5 | 254.89 | .67 | 187.59 | .66 | 123.67 | .60 | 68.85 | .48 | 28.01 | .33 | 4.75 | .13 | 1.08 | .07 |
| 7.6 | 254.22 | .67 | 186.93 | .67 | 123.07 | .60 | 68.37 | .49 | 27.68 | .32 | 4.62 | .14 | 1.15 | .06 |
| 7.7 | 253.55 | .67 | 186.26 | .66 | 122.47 | .60 | 67.88 | .48 | 27.36 | .32 | 4.48 | .13 | 1.21 | .07 |
| 7.8 | 252.88 | .67 | 185.60 | .67 | 121.87 | .60 | 67.40 | .48 | 27.04 | .32 | 4.35 | .13 | 1.28 | .07 |
| 7.9 | 252.21 | .67 | 184.93 | .67 | 121.27 | .60 | 66.92 | .48 | 26.72 | .32 | 4.22 | .12 | 1.35 | .07 |
| 8.0 | 251.54 | .67 | 184.26 | .66 | 120.67 | .60 | 66.44 | .48 | 26.40 | .31 | 4.10 | .13 | 1.42 | .08 |
| 8.1 | 250.87 | .67 | 183.60 | .66 | 120.07 | .60 | 65.96 | .47 | 26.09 | .32 | 3.97 | .12 | 1.50 | .07 |
| 8.2 | 250.20 | .67 | 182.94 | .67 | 119.47 | .60 | 65.49 | .48 | 25.77 | .31 | 3.85 | .13 | 1.57 | .08 |
| 8.3 | 249.53 | .68 | 182.27 | .66 | 118.87 | .60 | 65.01 | .47 | 25.46 | .31 | 3.72 | .12 | 1.65 | .08 |
| 8.4 | 248.85 | .67 | 181.61 | .66 | 118.28 | .59 | 64.54 | .48 | 25.15 | .31 | 3.60 | .11 | 1.73 | .08 |
| 8.5 | 248.18 | .67 | 180.95 | .66 | 117.69 | .59 | 64.06 | .47 | 24.84 | .30 | 3.49 | .12 | 1.81 | .09 |
| 8.6 | 247.51 | .67 | 180.29 | .67 | 117.10 | .60 | 63.59 | .46 | 24.54 | .30 | 3.37 | .11 | 1.90 | .08 |
| 8.7 | 246.84 | .68 | 179.62 | .66 | 116.50 | .59 | 63.13 | .47 | 24.24 | .30 | 3.26 | .12 | 1.98 | .09 |
| 8.8 | 246.16 | .67 | 178.96 | .66 | 115.91 | .59 | 62.66 | .47 | 23.94 | .31 | 3.14 | .11 | 2.07 | .09 |
| 8.9 | 245.49 | .67 | 178.30 | .66 | 115.32 | .58 | 62.19 | .46 | 23.63 | .30 | 3.03 | .10 | 2.16 | .10 |
| 9.0 | 244.82 | .67 | 177.64 | .66 | 114.74 | .59 | 61.73 | .47 | 23.33 | .29 | 2.93 | .10 | 2.26 | .09 |
| 9.1 | 244.15 | .68 | 176.98 | .66 | 114.15 | .59 | 61.26 | .46 | 23.04 | .30 | 2.83 | .10 | 2.35 | .10 |
| 9.2 | 243.47 | .67 | 176.32 | .66 | 113.56 | .59 | 60.80 | .46 | 22.74 | .29 | 2.73 | .10 | 2.45 | .09 |
| 9.3 | 242.80 | .68 | 175.66 | .66 | 112.97 | .58 | 60.34 | .46 | 22.45 | .30 | 2.63 | .10 | 2.54 | .10 |
| 9.4 | 242.12 | .67 | 175.00 | .65 | 112.39 | .58 | 59.88 | .46 | 22.15 | .29 | 2.53 | .10 | 2.64 | .11 |
| 9.5 | 241.45 | .67 | 174.35 | .66 | 111.81 | .59 | 59.42 | .45 | 21.86 | .29 | 2.43 | .10 | 2.75 | .10 |
| 9.6 | 240.78 | .68 | 173.69 | .66 | 111.22 | .58 | 58.97 | .46 | 21.57 | .28 | 2.33 | .09 | 2.85 | .11 |
| 9.7 | 240.10 | .67 | 173.03 | .66 | 110.64 | .58 | 58.51 | .45 | 21.29 | .29 | 2.24 | .10 | 2.96 | .10 |
| 9.8 | 239.43 | .68 | 172.37 | .65 | 110.06 | .58 | 58.06 | .45 | 21.00 | .28 | 2.14 | .09 | 3.06 | .11 |
| 9.9 | 238.75 | .67 | 171.72 | .66 | 109.48 | .58 | 57.61 | .45 | 20.72 | .28 | 2.05 | .08 | 3.17 | .11 |
| 10.0 | 238.08 | .68 | 171.06 | .66 | 108.90 | .58 | 57.16 | .45 | 20.44 | .28 | 1.97 | .09 | 3.28 | .12 |

# TABLE XI. ARGUMENT 6.

Equation $= 206''.9\ [1 + \sin.\ (2t - z - x)]$.

Period, 34.846892 days.

| Days. | 0 | | 1 | | 2 | | 3 | | 4 | | 5 | | Days. |
|---|---|---|---|---|---|---|---|---|---|---|---|---|---|
| Decimals of a Day. | Equation. | Diff. | Equation. | Diff. | Equation. | Diff. | Equation. | Diff. | Equation. | Diff. | Equation. | Diff. | Decimals of a Day. |
| .00 | 1.12 | .04 | 0.61 | .03 | 6.77 | .10 | 19.45 | .16 | 38.18 | .22 | 62.40 | .27 | 1.00 |
| .01 | 1.08 | .04 | 0.64 | .03 | 6.87 | .09 | 19.61 | .16 | 38.40 | .21 | 62.67 | .26 | .99 |
| .02 | 1.04 | .04 | 0.67 | .03 | 6.96 | .10 | 19.77 | .16 | 38.61 | .22 | 62.93 | .27 | .98 |
| .03 | 1.00 | .04 | 0.70 | .03 | 7.06 | .09 | 19.93 | .16 | 38.83 | .22 | 63.20 | .27 | .97 |
| .04 | 0.96 | .04 | 0.73 | .03 | 7.15 | .10 | 20.09 | .16 | 39.05 | .22 | 63.47 | .27 | .96 |
| .05 | 0.92 | .04 | 0.76 | .03 | 7.25 | .10 | 20.25 | .16 | 39.27 | .22 | 63.74 | .27 | .95 |
| .06 | 0.88 | .03 | 0.79 | .04 | 7.35 | .10 | 20.41 | .16 | 39.49 | .22 | 64.01 | .27 | .94 |
| .07 | 0.85 | .03 | 0.83 | .03 | 7.45 | .10 | 20.57 | .16 | 39.71 | .22 | 64.28 | .27 | .93 |
| .08 | 0.82 | .03 | 0.86 | .03 | 7.55 | .10 | 20.73 | .16 | 39.93 | .22 | 64.55 | .27 | .92 |
| .09 | 0.79 | .03 | 0.89 | .04 | 7.65 | .10 | 20.89 | .16 | 40.15 | .22 | 64.82 | .27 | .91 |
| .10 | 0.76 | .03 | 0.93 | .03 | 7.75 | .10 | 21.05 | .16 | 40.37 | .22 | 65.09 | .27 | .90 |
| .11 | 0.73 | .03 | 0.96 | .04 | 7.85 | .10 | 21.21 | .16 | 40.59 | .22 | 65.36 | .27 | .89 |
| .12 | 0.70 | .03 | 1.00 | .03 | 7.95 | .10 | 21.37 | .17 | 40.81 | .23 | 65.63 | .27 | .88 |
| .13 | 0.67 | .03 | 1.03 | .04 | 8.05 | .11 | 21.54 | .16 | 41.04 | .22 | 65.90 | .28 | .87 |
| .14 | 0.64 | .03 | 1.07 | .04 | 8.16 | .10 | 21.70 | .16 | 41.26 | .22 | 66.18 | .27 | .86 |
| .15 | 0.61 | .03 | 1.11 | .04 | 8.26 | .11 | 21.86 | .17 | 41.48 | .23 | 66.45 | .27 | .85 |
| .16 | 0.58 | .03 | 1.15 | .04 | 8.37 | .10 | 22.03 | .17 | 41.71 | .22 | 66.72 | .28 | .84 |
| .17 | 0.55 | .03 | 1.19 | .04 | 8.47 | .11 | 22.20 | .17 | 41.93 | .23 | 67.00 | .27 | .83 |
| .18 | 0.52 | .02 | 1.23 | .04 | 8.58 | .11 | 22.37 | .17 | 42.16 | .22 | 67.27 | .28 | .82 |
| .19 | 0.50 | .03 | 1.27 | .04 | 8.69 | .11 | 22.54 | .17 | 42.38 | .23 | 67.55 | .28 | .81 |
| .20 | 0.47 | .02 | 1.31 | .04 | 8.80 | .11 | 22.71 | .17 | 42.61 | .23 | 67.83 | .27 | .80 |
| .21 | 0.45 | .03 | 1.35 | .04 | 8.91 | .11 | 22.88 | .17 | 42.84 | .22 | 68.10 | .28 | .79 |
| .22 | 0.42 | .02 | 1.39 | .04 | 9.02 | .11 | 23.05 | .17 | 43.06 | .23 | 68.38 | .28 | .78 |
| .23 | 0.40 | .03 | 1.43 | .05 | 9.13 | .11 | 23.22 | .17 | 43.29 | .23 | 68.66 | .27 | .77 |
| .24 | 0.37 | .02 | 1.48 | .04 | 9.24 | .11 | 23.39 | .17 | 43.52 | .23 | 68.93 | .28 | .76 |
| .25 | 0.35 | .02 | 1.52 | .05 | 9.35 | .11 | 23.56 | .18 | 43.75 | .23 | 69.21 | .28 | .75 |
| .26 | 0.33 | .02 | 1.57 | .04 | 9.46 | .11 | 23.74 | .17 | 43.98 | .23 | 69.49 | .28 | .74 |
| .27 | 0.31 | .02 | 1.61 | .05 | 9.57 | .12 | 23.91 | .18 | 44.21 | .23 | 69.77 | .28 | .73 |
| .28 | 0.29 | .02 | 1.66 | .05 | 9.69 | .11 | 24.09 | .17 | 44.44 | .23 | 70.05 | .28 | .72 |
| .29 | 0.27 | .02 | 1.71 | .05 | 9.80 | .11 | 24.26 | .18 | 44.67 | .23 | 70.33 | .28 | .71 |
| .30 | 0.25 | .02 | 1.76 | .05 | 9.91 | .12 | 24.44 | .18 | 44.90 | .23 | 70.61 | .28 | .70 |
| .31 | 0.23 | .02 | 1.81 | .05 | 10.03 | .11 | 24.62 | .17 | 45.13 | .24 | 70.89 | .28 | .69 |
| .32 | 0.21 | .02 | 1.86 | .05 | 10.14 | .12 | 24.79 | .18 | 45.37 | .23 | 71.17 | .28 | .68 |
| .33 | 0.19 | .01 | 1.91 | .05 | 10.26 | .11 | 24.97 | .18 | 45.60 | .24 | 71.45 | .28 | .67 |
| .34 | 0.18 | .02 | 1.96 | .05 | 10.37 | .12 | 25.15 | .18 | 45.84 | .23 | 71.73 | .29 | .66 |
| .35 | 0.16 | .01 | 2.01 | .06 | 10.49 | .12 | 25.33 | .18 | 46.07 | .24 | 72.02 | .28 | .65 |
| .36 | 0.15 | .02 | 2.07 | .05 | 10.61 | .11 | 25.51 | .18 | 46.31 | .23 | 72.30 | .28 | .64 |
| .37 | 0.13 | .01 | 2.12 | .05 | 10.72 | .12 | 25.69 | .18 | 46.54 | .24 | 72.58 | .29 | .63 |
| .38 | 0.12 | .01 | 2.17 | .06 | 10.84 | .12 | 25.87 | .18 | 46.78 | .23 | 72.87 | .28 | .62 |
| .39 | 0.11 | .01 | 2.23 | .05 | 10.96 | .12 | 26.05 | .18 | 47.01 | .24 | 73.15 | .29 | .61 |
| .40 | 0.10 | .01 | 2.28 | .06 | 11.08 | .12 | 26.23 | .18 | 47.25 | .24 | 73.44 | .29 | .60 |
| .41 | 0.09 | .01 | 2.34 | .05 | 11.20 | .12 | 26.41 | .18 | 47.49 | .24 | 73.73 | .28 | .59 |
| .42 | 0.08 | .01 | 2.39 | .06 | 11.32 | .12 | 26.59 | .19 | 47.73 | .24 | 74.01 | .29 | .58 |
| .43 | 0.07 | .01 | 2.45 | .06 | 11.44 | .12 | 26.78 | .18 | 47.97 | .24 | 74.30 | .29 | .57 |
| .44 | 0.06 | .01 | 2.51 | .05 | 11.56 | .12 | 26.96 | .19 | 48.21 | .24 | 74.59 | .28 | .56 |
| .45 | 0.05 | .01 | 2.56 | .06 | 11.68 | .13 | 27.15 | .18 | 48.45 | .24 | 74.87 | .29 | .55 |
| .46 | 0.04 | .01 | 2.62 | .06 | 11.81 | .12 | 27.33 | .19 | 48.69 | .24 | 75.16 | .29 | .54 |
| .47 | 0.03 | .00 | 2.68 | .06 | 11.93 | .13 | 27.52 | .19 | 48.93 | .24 | 75.45 | .29 | .53 |
| .48 | 0.03 | .01 | 2.74 | .06 | 12.06 | .12 | 27.71 | .19 | 49.17 | .24 | 75.74 | .29 | .52 |
| .49 | 0.02 | .00 | 2.80 | .06 | 12.18 | .13 | 27.90 | .19 | 49.41 | .24 | 76.03 | .29 | .51 |
| .50 | 0.02 | .01 | 2.86 | .06 | 12.31 | .13 | 28.09 | .19 | 49.65 | .24 | 76.32 | .29 | .50 |
| Days. | 35 | | 34 | | 33 | | 32 | | 31 | | 30 | | Days. |

# TABLE XI. ARGUMENT 6.

Equation $= 206''.9\ [1 + \sin.\ (2t - z - x)]$.

Period, 34.846892 days.

| Days. | 0 | | 1 | | 2 | | 3 | | 4 | | 5 | | Days. |
|---|---|---|---|---|---|---|---|---|---|---|---|---|---|
| Decimals of a Day. | Equation. | Diff. | Equation. | Diff. | Equation. | Diff. | Equation. | Diff. | Equation. | Diff. | Equation. | Diff. | Decimals of a Day. |
| .50 | $0''.02$ | .01 | $2''.86$ | .06 | $12''.31$ | .13 | $28''.09$ | .19 | $49''.65$ | .24 | $76''.32$ | .29 | .50 |
| .51 | 0.01 | .00 | 2.92 | .06 | 12.44 | .13 | 28.28 | .19 | 49.89 | .24 | 76.61 | .29 | .49 |
| .52 | 0.01 | .00 | 2.98 | .06 | 12.57 | .13 | 28.47 | .19 | 50.13 | .25 | 76.90 | .29 | .48 |
| .53 | 0.01 | .01 | 3.04 | .07 | 12.70 | .13 | 28.66 | .19 | 50.38 | .24 | 77.19 | .29 | .47 |
| .54 | 0.00 | .00 | 3.11 | .06 | 12.83 | .13 | 28.85 | .19 | 50.62 | .25 | 77.48 | .29 | .46 |
| .55 | 0.00 | .00 | 3.17 | .07 | 12.96 | .13 | 29.04 | .19 | 50.87 | .24 | 77.77 | .30 | .45 |
| .56 | 0.00 | .00 | 3.24 | .06 | 13.09 | .13 | 29.23 | .19 | 51.11 | .25 | 78.07 | .29 | .44 |
| .57 | 0.00 | .00 | 3.30 | .07 | 13.22 | .13 | 29.42 | .19 | 51.36 | .24 | 78.36 | .29 | .43 |
| .58 | 0.00 | .00 | 3.37 | .07 | 13.35 | .13 | 29.61 | .20 | 51.60 | .25 | 78.65 | .30 | .42 |
| .59 | 0.00 | .00 | 3.44 | .07 | 13.48 | .13 | 29.81 | .19 | 51.85 | .25 | 78.95 | .29 | .41 |
| .60 | 0.00 | .00 | 3.51 | .07 | 13.61 | .14 | 30.00 | .19 | 52.10 | .25 | 79.24 | .29 | .40 |
| .61 | 0.00 | .00 | 3.58 | .07 | 13.75 | .13 | 30.19 | .19 | 52.35 | .25 | 79.53 | .30 | .39 |
| .62 | 0.00 | .01 | 3.65 | .07 | 13.88 | .14 | 30.38 | .20 | 52.60 | .25 | 79.83 | .29 | .38 |
| .63 | 0.01 | .00 | 3.72 | .07 | 14.02 | .13 | 30.58 | .19 | 52.85 | .25 | 80.12 | .29 | .37 |
| .64 | 0.01 | .00 | 3.79 | .07 | 14.15 | .14 | 30.77 | .20 | 53.10 | .25 | 80.41 | .30 | .36 |
| .65 | 0.01 | .01 | 3.86 | .07 | 14.29 | .14 | 30.97 | .19 | 53.35 | .25 | 80.71 | .29 | .35 |
| .66 | 0.02 | .00 | 3.93 | .08 | 14.43 | .13 | 31.16 | .20 | 53.60 | .25 | 81.00 | .30 | .34 |
| .67 | 0.02 | .01 | 4.01 | .07 | 14.56 | .14 | 31.36 | .20 | 53.85 | .25 | 81.30 | .29 | .33 |
| .68 | 0.03 | .01 | 4.08 | .07 | 14.70 | .14 | 31.56 | .20 | 54.10 | .25 | 81.59 | .30 | .32 |
| .69 | 0.04 | .01 | 4.15 | .08 | 14.84 | .14 | 31.76 | .20 | 54.35 | .25 | 81.89 | .30 | .31 |
| .70 | 0.05 | .01 | 4.23 | .08 | 14.98 | .14 | 31.96 | .20 | 54.60 | .25 | 82.19 | .30 | .30 |
| .71 | 0.06 | .01 | 4.31 | .07 | 15.12 | .14 | 32.16 | .20 | 54.85 | .25 | 82.49 | .29 | .29 |
| .72 | 0.07 | .01 | 4.38 | .08 | 15.26 | .14 | 32.36 | .20 | 55.10 | .26 | 82.78 | .30 | .28 |
| .73 | 0.08 | .01 | 4.46 | .07 | 15.40 | .14 | 32.56 | .20 | 55.36 | .25 | 83.08 | .30 | .27 |
| .74 | 0.09 | .01 | 4.53 | .08 | 15.54 | .15 | 32.76 | .20 | 55.61 | .26 | 83.38 | .30 | .26 |
| .75 | 0.10 | .01 | 4.61 | .08 | 15.69 | .14 | 32.96 | .20 | 55.87 | .25 | 83.68 | .30 | .25 |
| .76 | 0.11 | .01 | 4.69 | .08 | 15.83 | .15 | 33.16 | .21 | 56.12 | .26 | 83.98 | .30 | .24 |
| .77 | 0.12 | .02 | 4.77 | .08 | 15.98 | .14 | 33.37 | .20 | 56.38 | .25 | 84.28 | .30 | .23 |
| .78 | 0.14 | .01 | 4.85 | .08 | 16.12 | .15 | 33.57 | .20 | 56.63 | .26 | 84.58 | .30 | .22 |
| .79 | 0.15 | .02 | 4.93 | .08 | 16.27 | .15 | 33.77 | .21 | 56.89 | .26 | 84.88 | .30 | .21 |
| .80 | 0.17 | .01 | 5.01 | .08 | 16.42 | .15 | 33.98 | .20 | 57.15 | .26 | 85.18 | .30 | .20 |
| .81 | 0.18 | .02 | 5.09 | .08 | 16.57 | .14 | 34.18 | .21 | 57.41 | .26 | 85.48 | .30 | .19 |
| .82 | 0.20 | .01 | 5.17 | .08 | 16.71 | .15 | 34.39 | .21 | 57.67 | .26 | 85.78 | .30 | .18 |
| .83 | 0.21 | .02 | 5.25 | .08 | 16.86 | .15 | 34.60 | .20 | 57.93 | .26 | 86.08 | .31 | .17 |
| .84 | 0.23 | .02 | 5.33 | .09 | 17.01 | .15 | 34.80 | .21 | 58.19 | .26 | 86.39 | .30 | .16 |
| .85 | 0.25 | .02 | 5.42 | .08 | 17.16 | .15 | 35.01 | .21 | 58.45 | .26 | 86.69 | .30 | .15 |
| .86 | 0.27 | .02 | 5.50 | .09 | 17.31 | .15 | 35.22 | .20 | 58.71 | .26 | 86.99 | .31 | .14 |
| .87 | 0.29 | .02 | 5.59 | .09 | 17.46 | .15 | 35.42 | .21 | 58.97 | .26 | 87.30 | .30 | .13 |
| .88 | 0.31 | .02 | 5.68 | .09 | 17.61 | .15 | 35.63 | .21 | 59.23 | .26 | 87.60 | .31 | .12 |
| .89 | 0.33 | .02 | 5.77 | .09 | 17.76 | .15 | 35.84 | .21 | 59.49 | .26 | 87.91 | .31 | .11 |
| .90 | 0.35 | .02 | 5.86 | .09 | 17.91 | .15 | 36.05 | .21 | 59.75 | .26 | 88.22 | .31 | .10 |
| .91 | 0.37 | .02 | 5.95 | .09 | 18.06 | .15 | 36.26 | .21 | 60.01 | .26 | 88.53 | .30 | .09 |
| .92 | 0.39 | .02 | 6.04 | .09 | 18.21 | .15 | 36.47 | .21 | 60.27 | .27 | 88.83 | .31 | .08 |
| .93 | 0.41 | .03 | 6.13 | .09 | 18.36 | .15 | 36.68 | .21 | 60.54 | .26 | 89.14 | .31 | .07 |
| .94 | 0.44 | .02 | 6.22 | .09 | 18.51 | .16 | 36.89 | .22 | 60.80 | .27 | 89.45 | .31 | .06 |
| .95 | 0.46 | .03 | 6.31 | .09 | 18.67 | .15 | 37.11 | .21 | 61.07 | .26 | 89.76 | .30 | .05 |
| .96 | 0.49 | .03 | 6.40 | .09 | 18.82 | .16 | 37.32 | .21 | 61.33 | .27 | 90.06 | .31 | .04 |
| .97 | 0.52 | .03 | 6.49 | .09 | 18.98 | .15 | 37.53 | .22 | 61.60 | .26 | 90.37 | .31 | .03 |
| .98 | 0.55 | .03 | 6.58 | .10 | 19.13 | .16 | 37.75 | .21 | 61.86 | .27 | 90.68 | .31 | .02 |
| .99 | 0.58 | .03 | 6.68 | .09 | 19.29 | .16 | 37.96 | .22 | 62.13 | .27 | 90.99 | .31 | .01 |
| 1.00 | 0.61 | .03 | 6.77 | .10 | 19.45 | .16 | 38.18 | .22 | 62.40 | .27 | 91.30 | .31 | .00 |
| Days. | 35 | | 34 | | 33 | | 32 | | 31 | | 30 | | Days. |

# TABLE XI. ARGUMENT 6.

Equation $= 206''.9\ [1 + \sin.\ (2t - z - x)]$.

Period, 34.846892 days.

| Days. | 6 | | 7 | | 8 | | 9 | | 10 | | 11 | | Days. |
|---|---|---|---|---|---|---|---|---|---|---|---|---|---|
| Decimals of a Day. | Equation. | Diff. | Equation. | Diff. | Equation. | Diff. | Equation. | Diff. | Equation. | Diff. | Equation. | Diff. | Decimals of a Day. |
| .00 | 91.30″ | .31 | 123.94″ | .34 | 159.28″ | .36 | 196.14″ | .37 | 233.37″ | .37 | 269.75″ | .36 | 1.00 |
| .01 | 91.61 | .31 | 124.28 | .34 | 159.64 | .36 | 196.51 | .37 | 233.74 | .37 | 270.11 | .36 | .99 |
| .02 | 91.92 | .31 | 124.62 | .34 | 160.00 | .37 | 196.88 | .38 | 234.11 | .37 | 270.47 | .35 | .98 |
| .03 | 92.23 | .31 | 124.96 | .35 | 160.37 | .36 | 197.26 | .37 | 234.48 | .37 | 270.82 | .36 | .97 |
| .04 | 92.54 | .31 | 125.31 | .34 | 160.73 | .36 | 197.63 | .37 | 234.85 | .37 | 271.18 | .35 | .96 |
| .05 | 92.85 | .31 | 125.65 | .34 | 161.09 | .37 | 198.00 | .38 | 235.22 | .37 | 271.53 | .36 | .95 |
| .06 | 93.16 | .31 | 125.99 | .35 | 161.46 | .36 | 198.38 | .37 | 235.59 | .37 | 271.89 | .35 | .94 |
| .07 | 93.47 | .32 | 126.34 | .34 | 161.82 | .36 | 198.75 | .37 | 235.96 | .37 | 272.24 | .35 | .93 |
| .08 | 93.79 | .31 | 126.68 | .34 | 162.18 | .37 | 199.12 | .38 | 236.33 | .37 | 272.59 | .35 | .92 |
| .09 | 94.10 | .31 | 127.02 | .35 | 162.55 | .36 | 199.50 | .37 | 236.70 | .37 | 272.94 | .35 | .91 |
| .10 | 94.41 | .31 | 127.37 | .34 | 162.91 | .36 | 199.87 | .37 | 237.07 | .37 | 273.29 | .35 | .90 |
| .11 | 94.72 | .32 | 127.71 | .35 | 163.27 | .37 | 200.24 | .37 | 237.44 | .37 | 273.64 | .36 | .89 |
| .12 | 95.04 | .31 | 128.06 | .34 | 163.64 | .36 | 200.61 | .38 | 237.81 | .37 | 274.00 | .35 | .88 |
| .13 | 95.35 | .31 | 128.40 | .35 | 164.00 | .36 | 200.99 | .37 | 238.18 | .37 | 274.35 | .35 | .87 |
| .14 | 95.66 | .32 | 128.75 | .35 | 164.36 | .37 | 201.36 | .37 | 238.55 | .37 | 274.70 | .35 | .86 |
| .15 | 95.98 | .31 | 129.10 | .34 | 164.73 | .36 | 201.73 | .38 | 238.92 | .37 | 275.05 | .35 | .85 |
| .16 | 96.29 | .32 | 129.44 | .35 | 165.09 | .37 | 202.11 | .37 | 239.29 | .36 | 275.40 | .35 | .84 |
| .17 | 96.61 | .31 | 129.79 | .35 | 165.46 | .36 | 202.48 | .37 | 239.65 | .37 | 275.75 | .36 | .83 |
| .18 | 96.92 | .32 | 130.14 | .34 | 165.82 | .37 | 202.85 | .38 | 240.02 | .37 | 276.11 | .35 | .82 |
| .19 | 97.24 | .32 | 130.48 | .35 | 166.19 | .37 | 203.23 | .37 | 240.39 | .37 | 276.46 | .35 | .81 |
| .20 | 97.56 | .32 | 130.83 | .35 | 166.56 | .36 | 203.60 | .37 | 240.76 | .37 | 276.81 | .35 | .80 |
| .21 | 97.88 | .31 | 131.18 | .34 | 166.92 | .37 | 203.97 | .37 | 241.13 | .36 | 277.16 | .35 | .79 |
| .22 | 98.19 | .32 | 131.52 | .35 | 167.29 | .37 | 204.34 | .38 | 241.49 | .37 | 277.51 | .35 | .78 |
| .23 | 98.51 | .32 | 131.87 | .35 | 167.66 | .36 | 204.72 | 37 | 241.86 | .37 | 277.86 | .35 | .77 |
| .24 | 98.83 | .32 | 132.22 | .34 | 168.02 | .37 | 205.09 | .37 | 242.23 | .37 | 278.21 | .35 | .76 |
| .25 | 99.15 | .31 | 132.56 | .35 | 168.39 | .37 | 205.46 | .38 | 242.60 | .37 | 278.56 | .35 | .75 |
| .26 | 99.46 | .32 | 132.91 | .35 | 168.76 | .36 | 205.84 | .37 | 242.97 | .36 | 278.91 | .35 | .74 |
| .27 | 99.78 | .32 | 133.26 | .35 | 169.12 | .37 | 206.21 | .37 | 243.33 | .37 | 279.26 | .35 | .73 |
| .28 | 100.10 | .32 | 133.61 | .35 | 169.49 | .37 | 206.58 | .38 | 243.70 | .37 | 279.61 | .35 | .72 |
| .29 | 100.42 | .32 | 133.96 | .35 | 169.86 | .36 | 206.96 | .37 | 244.07 | .36 | 279.96 | .35 | .71 |
| .30 | 100.74 | .32 | 134.31 | .35 | 170.22 | .37 | 207.33 | .37 | 244.43 | .37 | 280.31 | .35 | .70 |
| .31 | 101.06 | .32 | 134.66 | .35 | 170.59 | .37 | 207.70 | .37 | 244.80 | .37 | 280.66 | .35 | .69 |
| .32 | 101.38 | .32 | 135.01 | .35 | 170.96 | .36 | 208.07 | .38 | 245.17 | .36 | 281.01 | .35 | .68 |
| .33 | 101.70 | .32 | 135.36 | .35 | 171.32 | .37 | 208.45 | .37 | 245.53 | .37 | 281.36 | .35 | .67 |
| .34 | 102.02 | .32 | 135.71 | .35 | 171.69 | .37 | 208.82 | .37 | 245.90 | .36 | 281.71 | .34 | .66 |
| .35 | 102.34 | .33 | 136.06 | .35 | 172.06 | .37 | 209.19 | .38 | 246.26 | .37 | 282.05 | .35 | .65 |
| .36 | 102.67 | .32 | 136.41 | .35 | 172.43 | .36 | 209.57 | .37 | 246.63 | .36 | 282.40 | .35 | .64 |
| .37 | 102.99 | .32 | 136.76 | .35 | 172.79 | .37 | 209.94 | .37 | 246.99 | .37 | 282.75 | .35 | .63 |
| .38 | 103.31 | .33 | 137.11 | .35 | 173.16 | .37 | 210.31 | .38 | 247.36 | .36 | 283.10 | .34 | .62 |
| .39 | 103.64 | .32 | 137.46 | .35 | 173.53 | .37 | 210.69 | .37 | 247.72 | .37 | 283.44 | .35 | .61 |
| .40 | 103.96 | .32 | 137.81 | .35 | 173.90 | .37 | 211.06 | .37 | 248.09 | .36 | 283.79 | .35 | .60 |
| .41 | 104.28 | .33 | 138.16 | .35 | 174.27 | .37 | 211.43 | .38 | 248.45 | .37 | 284.14 | .34 | .59 |
| .42 | 104.61 | .32 | 138.51 | .35 | 174.64 | .36 | 211.81 | .37 | 248.82 | .36 | 284.48 | .35 | .58 |
| .43 | 104.93 | .33 | 138.86 | .35 | 175.00 | .37 | 212.18 | .37 | 249.18 | .37 | 284.83 | .35 | .57 |
| .44 | 105.26 | .32 | 139.21 | .36 | 175.37 | .37 | 212.55 | .38 | 249.55 | .36 | 285.18 | .34 | .56 |
| .45 | 105.58 | .33 | 139.57 | .35 | 175.74 | .37 | 212.93 | .37 | 249.91 | .37 | 285.52 | .35 | .55 |
| .46 | 105.91 | .33 | 139.92 | .35 | 176.11 | .37 | 213.30 | .37 | 250.28 | .36 | 285.87 | .34 | .54 |
| .47 | 106.24 | .32 | 140.27 | .35 | 176.48 | .37 | 213.67 | .38 | 250.64 | .37 | 286.21 | .35 | .53 |
| .48 | 106.56 | .33 | 140.62 | .36 | 176.85 | .37 | 214.05 | .37 | 251.01 | .36 | 286.56 | .34 | .52 |
| .49 | 106.89 | .33 | 140.98 | .35 | 177.22 | .37 | 214.42 | .37 | 251.37 | .37 | 286.90 | .34 | .51 |
| .50 | 107.22 | .32 | 141.33 | .35 | 177.59 | .37 | 214.79 | .37 | 251.74 | .36 | 287.24 | .34 | .50 |
| Days. | 29 | | 28 | | 27 | | 26 | | 25 | | 24 | | Days. |

# TABLE XI. ARGUMENT 6.

Equation $= 206''.9\ [1 + \sin.\ (2t - z - x)]$.

Period, 34.846892 days.

| Days. | 6 | | 7 | | 8 | | 9 | | 10 | | 11 | Days. |
|---|---|---|---|---|---|---|---|---|---|---|---|---|
| Decimals of a Day | Equation. | Diff. | Equation. | Diff. | Equation. | Diff. | Equation. | Diff. | Equation. | Diff. | Equation. | Diff. | Decimals of a Day |
| .50 | 107.22″ | .32 | 141.33″ | .35 | 177.59″ | .37 | 214.79″ | .37 | 251.74″ | .36 | 287.24″ | .34 | .50 |
| .51 | 107.54 | .33 | 141.68 | .36 | 177.96 | .37 | 215.16 | .38 | 252.10 | .37 | 287.58 | .35 | .49 |
| .52 | 107.87 | .33 | 142.04 | .35 | 178.33 | .37 | 215.54 | .37 | 252.47 | .36 | 287.93 | .34 | .48 |
| .53 | 108.20 | .32 | 142.39 | .35 | 178.70 | .37 | 215.91 | .37 | 252.83 | .36 | 288.27 | .34 | .47 |
| .54 | 108.52 | .33 | 142.74 | .36 | 179.07 | .37 | 216.28 | .38 | 253.19 | .37 | 288.61 | .34 | .46 |
| .55 | 108.85 | .33 | 143.10 | .35 | 179.44 | .37 | 216.66 | .37 | 253.56 | .36 | 288.95 | .34 | .45 |
| .56 | 109.18 | .33 | 143.45 | .36 | 179.81 | .37 | 217.03 | .37 | 253.92 | .36 | 289.29 | .35 | .44 |
| .57 | 109.51 | .33 | 143.81 | .35 | 180.18 | .37 | 217.40 | .38 | 254.28 | .36 | 289.64 | .34 | .43 |
| .58 | 109.84 | .33 | 144.16 | .36 | 180.55 | .37 | 217.78 | .37 | 254.64 | .37 | 289.98 | .34 | .42 |
| .59 | 110.17 | .33 | 144.52 | .36 | 180.92 | .37 | 218.15 | .37 | 255.01 | .36 | 290.32 | .34 | .41 |
| .60 | 110.50 | .33 | 144.88 | .35 | 181.29 | .37 | 218.52 | .37 | 255.37 | .36 | 290.66 | .34 | .40 |
| .61 | 110.83 | .33 | 145.23 | .36 | 181.66 | .37 | 218.89 | .38 | 255.73 | .37 | 291.00 | .34 | .39 |
| .62 | 111.16 | .33 | 145.59 | .36 | 182.03 | .37 | 219.27 | .37 | 256.10 | .36 | 291.34 | .34 | .38 |
| .63 | 111.49 | .33 | 145.95 | .35 | 182.40 | .37 | 219.64 | .37 | 256.46 | .36 | 291.68 | .34 | .37 |
| .64 | 111.82 | .33 | 146.30 | .36 | 182.77 | .37 | 220.01 | .37 | 256.82 | .36 | 292.02 | .34 | .36 |
| .65 | 112.15 | .33 | 146.66 | .36 | 183.14 | .37 | 220.38 | .37 | 257.18 | .37 | 292.36 | .34 | .35 |
| .66 | 112.48 | .34 | 147.02 | .35 | 183.51 | .37 | 220.75 | .38 | 257.55 | .36 | 292.70 | .34 | .34 |
| .67 | 112.82 | .33 | 147.37 | .36 | 183.88 | .37 | 221.13 | .37 | 257.91 | .36 | 293.04 | .34 | .33 |
| .68 | 113.15 | .33 | 147.73 | .36 | 184.25 | .37 | 221.50 | .37 | 258.27 | .36 | 293.38 | .34 | .32 |
| .69 | 113.48 | .33 | 148.09 | .36 | 184.62 | .37 | 221.87 | .37 | 258.63 | .36 | 293.72 | .34 | .31 |
| .70 | 113.81 | .34 | 148.45 | .36 | 184.99 | .37 | 222.24 | .37 | 258.99 | .36 | 294.06 | .34 | .30 |
| .71 | 114.15 | .33 | 148.81 | .35 | 185.36 | .37 | 222.61 | .38 | 259.35 | .36 | 294.40 | .34 | .29 |
| .72 | 114.48 | .33 | 149.16 | .36 | 185.73 | .37 | 222.99 | .37 | 259.71 | .36 | 294.74 | .33 | .28 |
| .73 | 114.81 | .34 | 149.52 | .36 | 186.10 | .37 | 223.36 | .37 | 260.07 | .36 | 295.07 | .34 | .27 |
| .74 | 115.15 | .33 | 149.88 | .36 | 186.47 | .37 | 223.73 | .37 | 260.43 | .36 | 295.41 | .34 | .26 |
| .75 | 115.48 | .34 | 150.24 | .36 | 186.84 | .38 | 224.10 | .37 | 260.79 | .36 | 295.75 | .34 | .25 |
| .76 | 115.82 | .33 | 150.60 | .36 | 187.22 | .37 | 224.47 | .38 | 261.15 | .36 | 296.09 | .33 | .24 |
| .77 | 116.15 | .34 | 150.96 | .36 | 187.59 | .37 | 224.85 | .37 | 261.51 | .36 | 296.42 | .34 | .23 |
| .78 | 116.49 | .33 | 151.32 | .36 | 187.96 | .37 | 225.22 | .37 | 261.87 | .36 | 296.76 | .34 | .22 |
| .79 | 116.82 | .34 | 151.68 | .36 | 188.33 | .37 | 225.59 | .37 | 262.23 | .36 | 297.10 | .33 | .21 |
| .80 | 117.16 | .34 | 152.04 | .36 | 188.70 | .37 | 225.96 | .37 | 262.59 | .36 | 297.43 | .34 | .20 |
| .81 | 117.50 | .33 | 152.40 | .36 | 189.07 | .37 | 226.33 | .37 | 262.95 | .36 | 297.77 | .34 | .19 |
| .82 | 117.83 | .34 | 152.76 | .36 | 189.44 | .38 | 226.70 | .37 | 263.31 | .36 | 298.11 | .33 | .18 |
| .83 | 118.17 | .34 | 153.12 | .36 | 189.82 | .37 | 227.07 | .38 | 263.67 | .36 | 298.44 | .34 | .17 |
| .84 | 118.51 | .34 | 153.48 | .36 | 190.19 | .37 | 227.45 | .37 | 264.03 | .36 | 298.78 | .33 | .16 |
| .85 | 118.85 | .33 | 153.84 | .36 | 190.56 | .37 | 227.82 | .37 | 264.39 | .36 | 299.11 | .34 | .15 |
| .86 | 119.18 | .34 | 154.20 | .37 | 190.93 | .37 | 228.19 | .37 | 264.75 | .35 | 299.45 | .33 | .14 |
| .87 | 119.52 | .34 | 154.57 | .36 | 191.30 | .38 | 228.56 | .37 | 265.10 | .36 | 299.78 | .33 | .13 |
| .88 | 119.86 | .34 | 154.93 | .36 | 191.68 | .37 | 228.93 | .37 | 265.46 | .36 | 300.11 | .33 | .12 |
| .89 | 120.20 | .34 | 155.29 | .36 | 192.05 | .37 | 229.30 | .37 | 265.82 | .36 | 300.44 | .33 | .11 |
| .90 | 120.54 | .34 | 155.65 | .36 | 192.42 | .37 | 229.67 | .37 | 266.18 | .36 | 300.77 | .33 | .10 |
| .91 | 120.88 | .34 | 156.01 | .37 | 192.79 | .37 | 230.04 | .37 | 266.54 | .35 | 301.10 | .33 | .09 |
| .92 | 121.22 | .34 | 156.38 | .36 | 193.16 | .38 | 230.41 | .37 | 266.89 | .36 | 301.43 | .34 | .08 |
| .93 | 121.56 | .34 | 156.74 | .36 | 193.54 | .37 | 230.78 | .37 | 267.25 | .36 | 301.77 | .33 | .07 |
| .94 | 121.90 | .34 | 157.10 | .36 | 193.91 | .37 | 231.15 | .37 | 267.61 | .36 | 302.10 | .33 | .06 |
| .95 | 122.24 | .34 | 157.46 | .37 | 194.28 | .37 | 231.52 | .37 | 267.97 | .36 | 302.43 | .33 | .05 |
| .96 | 122.58 | .34 | 157.83 | .36 | 194.65 | .37 | 231.89 | .37 | 268.33 | .35 | 302.76 | .33 | .04 |
| .97 | 122.92 | .34 | 158.19 | .36 | 195.02 | .38 | 232.26 | .37 | 268.68 | .36 | 303.09 | .33 | .03 |
| .98 | 123.26 | .34 | 158.55 | .37 | 195.40 | .37 | 232.63 | .37 | 269.04 | .36 | 303.42 | .33 | .02 |
| .99 | 123.60 | .34 | 158.92 | .36 | 195.77 | .37 | 233.00 | .37 | 269.40 | .35 | 303.75 | .33 | .01 |
| 1.00 | 123.94 | .34 | 159.28 | .36 | 196.14 | .37 | 233.37 | .37 | 269.75 | .36 | 304.08 | .33 | .00 |
| Days. | 29 | | 28 | | 27 | | 26 | | 25 | | 24 | | Days. |

# TABLE XI. ARGUMENT 6.

Equation $= 206''.9\ [1 + \sin.\ (2t - z - x)]$.

Period, 34.846892 days.

| Days. | 12 | | 13 | | 14 | | 15 | | 16 | | 17 | Days. |
|---|---|---|---|---|---|---|---|---|---|---|---|---|
| Decimals of a Day | Equation. | Diff. | Equation. | Diff. | Equation. | Diff. | Equation. | Diff. | Equation. | Diff. | Equation. | Diff. | Decimals of a Day. |
| .00 | 304.08″ | .33 | 335.25″ | .29 | 362.27″ | .25 | 384.25″ | .19 | 400.49″ | .13 | 410.45″ | .07 | 1.00 |
| .01 | 304.41 | .33 | 335.54 | .29 | 362.52 | .25 | 384.44 | .19 | 400.62 | .13 | 410.52 | .07 | .99 |
| .02 | 304.74 | .33 | 335.83 | .30 | 362.77 | .24 | 384.63 | .19 | 400.75 | .13 | 410.59 | .06 | .98 |
| .03 | 305.07 | .33 | 336.13 | .29 | 363.01 | .25 | 384.82 | .19 | 400.88 | .13 | 410.65 | .07 | .97 |
| .04 | 305.40 | .32 | 336.42 | .29 | 363.26 | .24 | 385.01 | .19 | 401.01 | .13 | 410.72 | .06 | .96 |
| .05 | 305.72 | .33 | 336.71 | .29 | 363.50 | .25 | 385.20 | .19 | 401.14 | .13 | 410.78 | .06 | .95 |
| .06 | 306.05 | .33 | 337.00 | .29 | 363.75 | .24 | 385.39 | .19 | 401.27 | .13 | 410.84 | .06 | .94 |
| .07 | 306.38 | .33 | 337.29 | .29 | 363.99 | .24 | 385.58 | .19 | 401.40 | .13 | 410.90 | .06 | .93 |
| .08 | 306.71 | .32 | 337.58 | .29 | 364.23 | .24 | 385.77 | .19 | 401.53 | .12 | 410.96 | .06 | .92 |
| .09 | 307.03 | .33 | 337.87 | .29 | 364.47 | .24 | 385.96 | .19 | 401.65 | .13 | 411.02 | .06 | .91 |
| .10 | 307.36 | .33 | 338.16 | .29 | 364.71 | .24 | 386.15 | .19 | 401.78 | .13 | 411.08 | .06 | .90 |
| .11 | 307.69 | .32 | 338.45 | .29 | 364.95 | .24 | 386.34 | .19 | 401.91 | .12 | 411.14 | .06 | .89 |
| .12 | 308.01 | .33 | 338.74 | .29 | 365.19 | .24 | 386.53 | .18 | 402.03 | .12 | 411.20 | .06 | .88 |
| .13 | 308.34 | .33 | 339.03 | .29 | 365.43 | .24 | 386.71 | .19 | 402.15 | .13 | 411.26 | .06 | .87 |
| .14 | 308.67 | .32 | 339.32 | .28 | 365.67 | .24 | 386.90 | .18 | 402.28 | .12 | 411.32 | .06 | .86 |
| .15 | 308.99 | .32 | 339.60 | .29 | 365.91 | .24 | 387.08 | .19 | 402.40 | .12 | 411.38 | .06 | .85 |
| .16 | 309.31 | .33 | 339.89 | .29 | 366.15 | .23 | 387.27 | .18 | 402.52 | .12 | 411.44 | .05 | .84 |
| .17 | 309.64 | .32 | 340.18 | .28 | 366.38 | .24 | 387.45 | .18 | 402.64 | .12 | 411.49 | .06 | .83 |
| .18 | 309.96 | .32 | 340.46 | .29 | 366.62 | .24 | 387.63 | .18 | 402.76 | .12 | 411.55 | .05 | .82 |
| .19 | 310.28 | .32 | 340.75 | .28 | 366.86 | .24 | 387.81 | .18 | 402.88 | .12 | 411.60 | .05 | .81 |
| .20 | 310.60 | .32 | 341.03 | .28 | 367.10 | .24 | 387.99 | .18 | 403.00 | .12 | 411.65 | .05 | .80 |
| .21 | 310.92 | .33 | 341.31 | .29 | 367.34 | .23 | 388.17 | .18 | 403.12 | .12 | 411.70 | .05 | .79 |
| .22 | 311.25 | .32 | 341.60 | .28 | 367.57 | .24 | 388.35 | .18 | 403.24 | .12 | 411.75 | .05 | .78 |
| .23 | 311.57 | .32 | 341.88 | .28 | 367.81 | .24 | 388.53 | .18 | 403.36 | .12 | 411.80 | .05 | .77 |
| .24 | 311.89 | .32 | 342.16 | .29 | 368.05 | .23 | 388.71 | .18 | 403.48 | .12 | 411.85 | .05 | .76 |
| .25 | 312.21 | .32 | 342.45 | .28 | 368.28 | .24 | 388.89 | .17 | 403.60 | .11 | 411.90 | .05 | .75 |
| .26 | 312.53 | .32 | 342.73 | .28 | 368.52 | .23 | 389.06 | .18 | 403.71 | .12 | 411.95 | .05 | .74 |
| .27 | 312.85 | .33 | 343.01 | .28 | 368.75 | .23 | 389.24 | .17 | 403.83 | .11 | 412.00 | .05 | .73 |
| .28 | 313.18 | .32 | 343.29 | .28 | 368.98 | .23 | 389.41 | .18 | 403.94 | .11 | 412.05 | .05 | .72 |
| .29 | 313.50 | .32 | 343.57 | .28 | 369.21 | .23 | 389.59 | .17 | 404.05 | .11 | 412.10 | .05 | .71 |
| .30 | 313.82 | .32 | 343.85 | .28 | 369.44 | .23 | 389.76 | .17 | 404.16 | .11 | 412.15 | .05 | .70 |
| .31 | 314.14 | .32 | 344.13 | .28 | 369.67 | .23 | 389.93 | .18 | 404.27 | .11 | 412.20 | .05 | .69 |
| .32 | 314.46 | .32 | 344.41 | .28 | 369.90 | .23 | 390.11 | .17 | 404.38 | .11 | 412.25 | .04 | .68 |
| .33 | 314.78 | .32 | 344.69 | .27 | 370.13 | .23 | 390.28 | .17 | 404.49 | .11 | 412.29 | .05 | .67 |
| .34 | 315.10 | .31 | 344.96 | .28 | 370.36 | .23 | 390.45 | .17 | 404.60 | .11 | 412.34 | .04 | .66 |
| .35 | 315.41 | .32 | 345.24 | .28 | 370.59 | .22 | 390.62 | .17 | 404.71 | .11 | 412.38 | .05 | .65 |
| .36 | 315.73 | .32 | 345.52 | .27 | 370.81 | .23 | 390.79 | .17 | 404.82 | .11 | 412.43 | .04 | .64 |
| .37 | 316.05 | .32 | 345.79 | .28 | 371.04 | .23 | 390.96 | .17 | 404.93 | .11 | 412.47 | .04 | .63 |
| .38 | 316.37 | .31 | 346.07 | .28 | 371.27 | .22 | 391.13 | .17 | 405.04 | .11 | 412.51 | .04 | .62 |
| .39 | 316.68 | .32 | 346.35 | .27 | 371.49 | .23 | 391.30 | .17 | 405.15 | .11 | 412.55 | .04 | .61 |
| .40 | 317.00 | .32 | 346.62 | .28 | 371.72 | .23 | 391.47 | .17 | 405.26 | .11 | 412.59 | .04 | .60 |
| .41 | 317.32 | .32 | 346.90 | .27 | 371.95 | .22 | 391.64 | .17 | 405.37 | .10 | 412.63 | .04 | .59 |
| .42 | 317.64 | .31 | 347.17 | .28 | 372.17 | .22 | 391.81 | .17 | 405.47 | .11 | 412.67 | .04 | .58 |
| .43 | 317.95 | .32 | 347.45 | .27 | 372.39 | .23 | 391.98 | .16 | 405.58 | .10 | 412.71 | .04 | .57 |
| .44 | 318.27 | .31 | 347.72 | .27 | 372.62 | .22 | 392.14 | .17 | 405.68 | .11 | 412.75 | .04 | .56 |
| .45 | 318.58 | .32 | 347.99 | .28 | 372.84 | .22 | 392.31 | .17 | 405.79 | .10 | 412.79 | .03 | .55 |
| .46 | 318.90 | .31 | 348.27 | .27 | 373.06 | .23 | 392.48 | .16 | 405.89 | .10 | 412.82 | .04 | .54 |
| .47 | 319.21 | .31 | 348.54 | .27 | 373.29 | .22 | 392.64 | .17 | 405.99 | .10 | 412.86 | .03 | .53 |
| .48 | 319.52 | .31 | 348.81 | .27 | 373.51 | .22 | 392.81 | .16 | 406.09 | .10 | 412.89 | .04 | .52 |
| .49 | 319.83 | .31 | 349.08 | .27 | 373.73 | .22 | 392.97 | .16 | 406.19 | .10 | 412.93 | .03 | .51 |
| .50 | 320.14 | .31 | 349.35 | .27 | 373.95 | .22 | 393.13 | .16 | 406.29 | .10 | 412.96 | .03 | .50 |
| Days. | 23 | | 22 | | 21 | | 20 | | 19 | | 18 | | Days. |

# TABLE XI. ARGUMENT 6.

Equation $= 206''.9\ [1 + \sin.\ (2t - z - x)]$.

Period, 34.846892 days.

| Days. | 12 | | 13 | | 14 | | 15 | | 16 | | 17 | | Days. |
|---|---|---|---|---|---|---|---|---|---|---|---|---|---|
| Decimals of a Day | Equation. | Diff. | Equation. | Diff. | Equation. | Diff. | Equation. | Diff. | Equation. | Diff. | Equation. | Diff. | Decimals of a Day. |
| .50 | 320.14 | .31 | 349.35 | .27 | 373.95 | .22 | 393.13 | .16 | 406.29 | .10 | 412.96 | .03 | .50 |
| .51 | 320.45 | .31 | 349.62 | .27 | 374.17 | .22 | 393.29 | .16 | 406.39 | .10 | 412.99 | .03 | .49 |
| .52 | 320.76 | .31 | 349.89 | .27 | 374.39 | .22 | 393.45 | .16 | 406.49 | .10 | 413.02 | .03 | .48 |
| .53 | 321.07 | .31 | 350.16 | .27 | 374.61 | .22 | 393.61 | .16 | 406.59 | .10 | 413.05 | .03 | .47 |
| .54 | 321.38 | .31 | 350.43 | .27 | 374.83 | .22 | 393.77 | .16 | 406.69 | .10 | 413.08 | .03 | .46 |
| .55 | 321.69 | .31 | 350.70 | .27 | 375.05 | .21 | 393.93 | .16 | 406.79 | .09 | 413.11 | .03 | .45 |
| .56 | 322.00 | .31 | 350.97 | .26 | 375.26 | .22 | 394.09 | .16 | 406.88 | .10 | 413.14 | .03 | .44 |
| .57 | 322.31 | .31 | 351.23 | .27 | 375.48 | .22 | 394.25 | .16 | 406.98 | .09 | 413.17 | .03 | .43 |
| .58 | 322.62 | .31 | 351.50 | .27 | 375.70 | .21 | 394.41 | .16 | 407.07 | .09 | 413.20 | .03 | .42 |
| .59 | 322.93 | .31 | 351.77 | .27 | 375.91 | .22 | 394.57 | .16 | 407.16 | .09 | 413.23 | .03 | .41 |
| .60 | 323.24 | .31 | 352.04 | .27 | 376.13 | .21 | 394.73 | .16 | 407.25 | .09 | 413.26 | .03 | .40 |
| .61 | 323.55 | .31 | 352.31 | .26 | 376.34 | .22 | 394.89 | .15 | 407.34 | .09 | 413.29 | .03 | .39 |
| .62 | 323.86 | .31 | 352.57 | .27 | 376.56 | .21 | 395.04 | .16 | 407.43 | .09 | 413.32 | .02 | .38 |
| .63 | 324.17 | .30 | 352.84 | .27 | 376.77 | .21 | 395.20 | .15 | 407.52 | .09 | 413.34 | .03 | .37 |
| .64 | 324.47 | .31 | 353.11 | .26 | 376.98 | .22 | 395.35 | .16 | 407.61 | .09 | 413.37 | .02 | .36 |
| .65 | 324.78 | .31 | 353.37 | .27 | 377.20 | .21 | 395.51 | .15 | 407.70 | .09 | 413.39 | .02 | .35 |
| .66 | 325.09 | .30 | 353.64 | .26 | 377.41 | .21 | 395.66 | .15 | 407.79 | .09 | 413.41 | .02 | .34 |
| .67 | 325.39 | .31 | 353.90 | .26 | 377.62 | .21 | 395.81 | .15 | 407.88 | .09 | 413.43 | .02 | .33 |
| .68 | 325.70 | .31 | 354.16 | .26 | 377.83 | .21 | 395.96 | .15 | 407.97 | .08 | 413.45 | .02 | .32 |
| .69 | 326.01 | .30 | 354.42 | .26 | 378.04 | .21 | 396.11 | .15 | 408.05 | .09 | 413.47 | .02 | .31 |
| .70 | 326.31 | .31 | 354.68 | .26 | 378.25 | .21 | 396.26 | .15 | 408.14 | .08 | 413.49 | .02 | .30 |
| .71 | 326.62 | .30 | 354.94 | .26 | 378.46 | .21 | 396.41 | .15 | 408.22 | .09 | 413.51 | .02 | .29 |
| .72 | 326.92 | .30 | 355.20 | .26 | 378.67 | .21 | 396.56 | .15 | 408.31 | .08 | 413.53 | .02 | .28 |
| .73 | 327.22 | .31 | 355.46 | .26 | 378.88 | .20 | 396.71 | .15 | 408.39 | .09 | 413.55 | .02 | .27 |
| .74 | 327.53 | .30 | 355.72 | .25 | 379.08 | .21 | 396.86 | .15 | 408.48 | .08 | 413.57 | .02 | .26 |
| .75 | 327.83 | .30 | 355.97 | .26 | 379.29 | .21 | 397.01 | .14 | 408.56 | .09 | 413.59 | .01 | .25 |
| .76 | 328.13 | .30 | 356.23 | .26 | 379.50 | .20 | 397.15 | .15 | 408.65 | .08 | 413.60 | .02 | .24 |
| .77 | 328.43 | .30 | 356.49 | .26 | 379.70 | .21 | 397.30 | .14 | 408.73 | .08 | 413.62 | .01 | .23 |
| .78 | 328.73 | .30 | 356.75 | .25 | 379.91 | .20 | 397.44 | .15 | 408.81 | .08 | 413.63 | .01 | .22 |
| .79 | 329.03 | .30 | 357.00 | .26 | 380.11 | .20 | 397.59 | .14 | 408.89 | .08 | 413.64 | .01 | .21 |
| .80 | 329.33 | .30 | 357.26 | .26 | 380.31 | .20 | 397.73 | .14 | 408.97 | .08 | 413.65 | .01 | .20 |
| .81 | 329.63 | .30 | 357.52 | .25 | 380.51 | .20 | 397.87 | .15 | 409.05 | .08 | 413.66 | .01 | .19 |
| .82 | 329.93 | .30 | 357.77 | .25 | 380.71 | .20 | 398.02 | .14 | 409.13 | .08 | 413.67 | .01 | .18 |
| .83 | 330.23 | .30 | 358.02 | .26 | 380.91 | .20 | 398.16 | .14 | 409.21 | .08 | 413.68 | .01 | .17 |
| .84 | 330.53 | .30 | 358.28 | .25 | 381.11 | .20 | 398.30 | .14 | 409.29 | .08 | 413.69 | .01 | .16 |
| .85 | 330.83 | .29 | 358.53 | .25 | 381.31 | .20 | 398.44 | .14 | 409.37 | .07 | 413.70 | .01 | .15 |
| .86 | 331.12 | .30 | 358.78 | .25 | 381.51 | .20 | 398.58 | .14 | 409.44 | .08 | 413.71 | .01 | .14 |
| .87 | 331.42 | .30 | 359.03 | .26 | 381.71 | .20 | 398.72 | .14 | 409.52 | .07 | 413.72 | .01 | .13 |
| .88 | 331.72 | .29 | 359.29 | .25 | 381.91 | .20 | 398.86 | .14 | 409.59 | .08 | 413.73 | .01 | .12 |
| .89 | 332.01 | .30 | 359.54 | .25 | 382.11 | .20 | 399.00 | .14 | 409.67 | .07 | 413.74 | .01 | .11 |
| .90 | 332.31 | .30 | 359.79 | .25 | 382.31 | .20 | 399.14 | .14 | 409.74 | .07 | 413.75 | .01 | .10 |
| .91 | 332.61 | .29 | 360.04 | .25 | 382.51 | .20 | 399.28 | .14 | 409.81 | .08 | 413.76 | .01 | .09 |
| .92 | 332.90 | .30 | 360.29 | .25 | 382.71 | .19 | 399.42 | .14 | 409.89 | .07 | 413.77 | .01 | .08 |
| .93 | 333.20 | .30 | 360.54 | .25 | 382.90 | .20 | 399.56 | .13 | 409.96 | .07 | 413.78 | .01 | .07 |
| .94 | 333.50 | .29 | 360.79 | .24 | 383.10 | .19 | 399.69 | .14 | 410.03 | .07 | 413.79 | .00 | .06 |
| .95 | 333.79 | .30 | 361.03 | .25 | 383.29 | .20 | 399.83 | .13 | 410.10 | .07 | 413.79 | .01 | .05 |
| .96 | 334.09 | .29 | 361.28 | .25 | 383.49 | .19 | 399.96 | .14 | 410.17 | .07 | 413.80 | .00 | .04 |
| .97 | 334.38 | .29 | 361.53 | .25 | 383.68 | .19 | 400.10 | .13 | 410.24 | .07 | 413.80 | .00 | .03 |
| .98 | 334.67 | .29 | 361.78 | .24 | 383.87 | .19 | 400.23 | .13 | 410.31 | .07 | 413.80 | .00 | .02 |
| .99 | 334.96 | .29 | 362.02 | .25 | 384.06 | .19 | 400.36 | .13 | 410.38 | .07 | 413.80 | .00 | .01 |
| 1.00 | 335.25 | .29 | 362.27 | .25 | 384.25 | .19 | 400.49 | .13 | 410.45 | .07 | 413.80 | .00 | .00 |
| Days. | 23 | | 22 | | 21 | | 20 | | 19 | | 18 | | Days. |

# TABLE XII. ARGUMENT 7.

Equation = 192″.1 [1 + sin. (2$t$ + $x$)].

Period, 9.613718 days.

| Days. | 0 | | 1 | | 2 | | 3 | | 4 | | Days. |
|---|---|---|---|---|---|---|---|---|---|---|---|
| Decimals of a Day. | Equation. | Difference. | Equation. | Difference. | Equation. | Difference. | Equation. | Difference. | Equation. | Difference. | Decimals of a Day. |
| .00 | 1″.53 | .15 | 26″.09 | .64 | 119″.09 | 1.16 | 242″.17 | 1.21 | 344″.61 | .76 | 1.00 |
| .01 | 1.38 | .15 | 26.73 | .65 | 120.25 | 1.16 | 243.38 | 1.21 | 345.37 | .75 | .99 |
| .02 | 1.23 | .14 | 27.38 | .65 | 121.41 | 1.17 | 244.59 | 1.21 | 346.12 | .75 | .98 |
| .03 | 1.09 | .13 | 28.03 | .66 | 122.58 | 1.17 | 245.80 | 1.20 | 346.87 | .74 | .97 |
| .04 | 0.96 | .12 | 28.69 | .66 | 123.75 | 1.18 | 247.00 | 1.20 | 347.61 | .73 | .96 |
| .05 | 0.84 | .11 | 29.35 | .67 | 124.93 | 1.18 | 248.20 | 1.20 | 348.34 | .73 | .95 |
| .06 | 0.73 | .11 | 30.02 | .68 | 126.11 | 1.18 | 249.40 | 1.20 | 349.07 | .72 | .94 |
| .07 | 0.62 | .10 | 30.70 | .68 | 127.29 | 1.18 | 250.60 | 1.20 | 349.79 | .71 | .93 |
| .08 | 0.52 | .09 | 31.38 | .69 | 128.47 | 1.19 | 251.80 | 1.19 | 350.50 | .71 | .92 |
| .09 | 0.43 | .08 | 32.07 | .70 | 129.66 | 1.19 | 252.99 | 1.19 | 351.21 | .70 | .91 |
| .10 | 0.35 | .07 | 32.77 | .70 | 130.85 | 1.19 | 254.18 | 1.19 | 351.91 | .69 | .90 |
| .11 | 0.28 | .06 | 33.47 | .71 | 132.04 | 1.19 | 255.37 | 1.18 | 352.60 | .69 | .89 |
| .12 | 0.22 | .06 | 34.18 | .72 | 133.23 | 1.20 | 256.55 | 1.18 | 353.29 | .68 | .88 |
| .13 | 0.16 | .05 | 34.90 | .73 | 134.43 | 1.20 | 257.73 | 1.18 | 353.97 | .67 | .87 |
| .14 | 0.11 | .04 | 35.63 | .73 | 135.63 | 1.20 | 258.91 | 1.17 | 354.64 | .67 | .86 |
| .15 | 0.07 | .03 | 36.36 | .74 | 136.83 | 1.20 | 260.08 | 1.17 | 355.31 | .66 | .85 |
| .16 | 0.04 | .02 | 37.10 | .75 | 138.03 | 1.21 | 261.25 | 1.17 | 355.97 | .65 | .84 |
| .17 | 0.02 | .01 | 37.85 | .75 | 139.24 | 1.21 | 262.42 | 1.17 | 356.62 | .65 | .83 |
| .18 | 0.01 | .01 | 38.60 | .76 | 140.45 | 1.21 | 263.59 | 1.17 | 357.27 | .64 | .82 |
| .19 | 0.00 | .00 | 39.36 | .76 | 141.66 | 1.21 | 264.76 | 1.16 | 357.91 | .63 | .81 |
| .20 | 0.00 | .01 | 40.12 | .77 | 142.87 | 1.21 | 265.92 | 1.16 | 358.54 | .62 | .80 |
| .21 | 0.01 | .02 | 40.89 | .78 | 144.08 | 1.22 | 267.08 | 1.15 | 359.16 | .62 | .79 |
| .22 | 0.03 | .03 | 41.67 | .78 | 145.30 | 1.22 | 268.23 | 1.15 | 359.78 | .61 | .78 |
| .23 | 0.06 | .03 | 42.45 | .79 | 146.52 | 1.22 | 269.38 | 1.15 | 360.39 | .60 | .77 |
| .24 | 0.09 | .04 | 43.24 | .79 | 147.74 | 1.22 | 270.53 | 1.14 | 360.99 | .60 | .76 |
| .25 | 0.13 | .05 | 44.03 | .80 | 148.96 | 1.22 | 271.67 | 1.14 | 361.59 | .59 | .75 |
| .26 | 0.18 | .06 | 44.83 | .81 | 150.18 | 1.23 | 272.81 | 1.14 | 362.18 | .58 | .74 |
| .27 | 0.24 | .07 | 45.64 | .81 | 151.41 | 1.23 | 273.95 | 1.13 | 362.76 | .57 | .73 |
| .28 | 0.31 | .08 | 46.45 | .82 | 152.64 | 1.23 | 275.08 | 1.13 | 363.33 | .56 | .72 |
| .29 | 0.39 | .08 | 47.27 | .83 | 153.87 | 1.23 | 276.21 | 1.13 | 363.89 | .56 | .71 |
| .30 | 0.47 | .09 | 48.10 | .83 | 155.10 | 1.23 | 277.34 | 1.12 | 364.45 | .55 | .70 |
| .31 | 0.56 | .10 | 48.93 | .84 | 156.33 | 1.23 | 278.46 | 1.12 | 365.00 | .54 | .69 |
| .32 | 0.66 | .11 | 49.77 | .85 | 157.56 | 1.24 | 279.58 | 1.12 | 365.54 | .54 | .68 |
| .33 | 0.77 | .12 | 50.62 | .85 | 158.80 | 1.24 | 280.70 | 1.11 | 366.08 | .53 | .67 |
| .34 | 0.89 | .12 | 51.47 | .86 | 160.04 | 1.24 | 281.81 | 1.11 | 366.61 | .52 | .66 |
| .35 | 1.01 | .13 | 52.33 | .87 | 161.28 | 1.24 | 282.92 | 1.10 | 367.13 | .52 | .65 |
| .36 | 1.14 | .14 | 53.20 | .87 | 162.52 | 1.24 | 284.02 | 1.10 | 367.65 | .51 | .64 |
| .37 | 1.28 | .15 | 54.07 | .88 | 163.76 | 1.24 | 285.12 | 1.10 | 368.16 | .50 | .63 |
| .38 | 1.43 | .16 | 54.95 | .88 | 165.00 | 1.25 | 286.22 | 1.09 | 368.66 | .49 | .62 |
| .39 | 1.59 | .16 | 55.83 | .89 | 166.25 | 1.24 | 287.31 | 1.09 | 369.15 | .47 | .61 |
| .40 | 1.75 | .17 | 56.72 | .90 | 167.49 | 1.25 | 288.40 | 1.08 | 369.62 | .48 | .60 |
| .41 | 1.92 | .18 | 57.62 | .90 | 168.74 | 1.24 | 289.48 | 1.08 | 370.10 | .47 | .59 |
| .42 | 2.10 | .19 | 58.52 | .91 | 169.98 | 1.25 | 290.56 | 1.08 | 370.57 | .46 | .58 |
| .43 | 2.29 | .20 | 59.43 | .91 | 171.23 | 1.25 | 291.64 | 1.07 | 371.03 | .45 | .57 |
| .44 | 2.49 | .21 | 60.34 | .91 | 172.48 | 1.25 | 292.71 | 1.07 | 371.48 | .44 | .56 |
| .45 | 2.70 | .21 | 61.25 | .92 | 173.73 | 1.25 | 293.78 | 1.06 | 371.92 | .44 | .55 |
| .46 | 2.91 | .22 | 62.17 | .93 | 174.98 | 1.25 | 294.84 | 1.06 | 372.36 | .43 | .54 |
| .47 | 3.13 | .23 | 63.10 | .93 | 176.23 | 1.25 | 295.90 | 1.05 | 372.79 | .42 | .53 |
| .48 | 3.36 | .24 | 64.03 | .94 | 177.48 | 1.26 | 296.95 | 1.05 | 373.21 | .41 | .52 |
| .49 | 3.60 | .25 | 64.97 | .94 | 178.74 | 1.25 | 298.00 | 1.05 | 373.62 | .41 | .51 |
| .50 | 3.85 | .25 | 65.91 | .95 | 179.99 | 1.25 | 299.05 | 1.04 | 374.03 | .40 | .50 |
| Days. | 9 | | 8 | | 7 | | 6 | | 5 | | Days. |

# TABLE XII. ARGUMENT 7.

Equation $= 192''.1\ [1 + \sin.\ (2t + x)]$.

Period, 9.613718 days.

| Days. | 0 | | 1 | | 2 | | 3 | | 4 | | Days. |
|---|---|---|---|---|---|---|---|---|---|---|---|
| Decimals of a Day. | Equation. | Difference. | Equation. | Difference. | Equation. | Difference. | Equation. | Difference. | Equation. | Difference. | Decimals of a Day. |
| | '' | | '' | | '' | | '' | | '' | | |
| .50 | 3.85 | .25 | 65.91 | .95 | 179.99 | 1.25 | 299.05 | 1.04 | 374.03 | .40 | .50 |
| .51 | 4.10 | .26 | 66.86 | .95 | 181.24 | 1.26 | 300.09 | 1.04 | 374.43 | .39 | .49 |
| .52 | 4.36 | .27 | 67.81 | .96 | 182.50 | 1.25 | 301.13 | 1.03 | 374.82 | .38 | .48 |
| .53 | 4.63 | .28 | 68.77 | .97 | 183.75 | 1.26 | 302.16 | 1.02 | 375.20 | .38 | .47 |
| .54 | 4.91 | .29 | 69.74 | .97 | 185.01 | 1.25 | 303.18 | 1.02 | 375.58 | .37 | .46 |
| .55 | 5.20 | .29 | 70.71 | .98 | 186.26 | 1.25 | 304.20 | 1.02 | 375.95 | .36 | .45 |
| .56 | 5.49 | .30 | 71.69 | .98 | 187.51 | 1.26 | 305.22 | 1.01 | 376.31 | .35 | .44 |
| .57 | 5.79 | .31 | 72.67 | .99 | 188.77 | 1.25 | 306.23 | 1.01 | 376.66 | .35 | .43 |
| .58 | 6.10 | .32 | 73.66 | .99 | 190.02 | 1.26 | 307.24 | 1.00 | 377.01 | .34 | .42 |
| .59 | 6.42 | .33 | 74.65 | .99 | 191.28 | 1.25 | 308.24 | 1.00 | 377.35 | .33 | .41 |
| .60 | 6.75 | .33 | 75.64 | 1.00 | 192.53 | 1.26 | 309.24 | .99 | 377.68 | .32 | .40 |
| .61 | 7.08 | .34 | 76.64 | 1.01 | 193.79 | 1.25 | 310.23 | .99 | 378.00 | .31 | .39 |
| .62 | 7.42 | .35 | 77.65 | 1.01 | 195.04 | 1.26 | 311.22 | .98 | 378.31 | .30 | .38 |
| .63 | 7.77 | .36 | 78.66 | 1.02 | 196.30 | 1.25 | 312.20 | .98 | 378.61 | .30 | .37 |
| .64 | 8.13 | .37 | 79.68 | 1.02 | 197.55 | 1.26 | 313.18 | .97 | 378.91 | .29 | .36 |
| .65 | 8.50 | .37 | 80.70 | 1.03 | 198.81 | 1.25 | 314.15 | .97 | 379.20 | .28 | .35 |
| .66 | 8.87 | .38 | 81.73 | 1.03 | 200.06 | 1.26 | 315.12 | .96 | 379.48 | .27 | .34 |
| .67 | 9.25 | .39 | 82.76 | 1.03 | 201.32 | 1.25 | 316.08 | .96 | 379.75 | .26 | .33 |
| .68 | 9.64 | .40 | 83.79 | 1.04 | 202.57 | 1.26 | 317.04 | .95 | 380.01 | .26 | .32 |
| .69 | 10.04 | .41 | 84.83 | 1.04 | 203.83 | 1.25 | 317.99 | .94 | 380.27 | .25 | .31 |
| .70 | 10.45 | .41 | 85.87 | 1.05 | 205.08 | 1.25 | 318.93 | .94 | 380.52 | .24 | .30 |
| .71 | 10.86 | .42 | 86.92 | 1.05 | 206.33 | 1.25 | 319.87 | .94 | 380.76 | .23 | .29 |
| .72 | 11.28 | .43 | 87.97 | 1.06 | 207.58 | 1.25 | 320.81 | .93 | 380.99 | .22 | .28 |
| .73 | 11.71 | .44 | 89.03 | 1.06 | 208.83 | 1.25 | 321.74 | .92 | 381.21 | .22 | .27 |
| .74 | 12.15 | .44 | 90.09 | 1.06 | 210.08 | 1.25 | 322.66 | .92 | 381.43 | .21 | .26 |
| .75 | 12.59 | .45 | 91.15 | 1.07 | 211.33 | 1.25 | 323.58 | .91 | 381.64 | .20 | .25 |
| .76 | 13.04 | .46 | 92.22 | 1.07 | 212.58 | 1.25 | 324.49 | .91 | 381.84 | .19 | .24 |
| .77 | 13.50 | .47 | 93.29 | 1.08 | 213.83 | 1.25 | 325.40 | .90 | 382.03 | .18 | .23 |
| .78 | 13.97 | .47 | 94.37 | 1.08 | 215.08 | 1.24 | 326.30 | .90 | 382.21 | .18 | .22 |
| .79 | 14.44 | .48 | 95.45 | 1.09 | 216.32 | 1.25 | 327.20 | .89 | 382.39 | .17 | .21 |
| .80 | 14.92 | .49 | 96.54 | 1.09 | 217.57 | 1.24 | 328.09 | .89 | 382.56 | .16 | .20 |
| .81 | 15.41 | .50 | 97.63 | 1.10 | 218.81 | 1.25 | 328.98 | .88 | 382.72 | .15 | .19 |
| .82 | 15.91 | .50 | 98.73 | 1.10 | 220.06 | 1.24 | 329.86 | .87 | 382.87 | .14 | .18 |
| .83 | 16.41 | .51 | 99.83 | 1.10 | 221.30 | 1.24 | 330.73 | .87 | 383.01 | .14 | .17 |
| .84 | 16.92 | .51 | 100.93 | 1.11 | 222.54 | 1.24 | 331.60 | .86 | 383.15 | .13 | .16 |
| .85 | 17.43 | .52 | 102.04 | 1.11 | 223.78 | 1.24 | 332.46 | .85 | 383.28 | .12 | .15 |
| .86 | 17.95 | .53 | 103.15 | 1.12 | 225.02 | 1.24 | 333.31 | .85 | 383.40 | .11 | .14 |
| .87 | 18.48 | .54 | 104.27 | 1.12 | 226.26 | 1.23 | 334.16 | .84 | 383.51 | .10 | .13 |
| .88 | 19.02 | .55 | 105.39 | 1.12 | 227.49 | 1.23 | 335.00 | .84 | 383.61 | .09 | .12 |
| .89 | 19.57 | .56 | 106.51 | 1.13 | 228.72 | 1.23 | 335.84 | .83 | 383.70 | .09 | .11 |
| .90 | 20.13 | .56 | 107.64 | 1.13 | 229.95 | 1.23 | 336.67 | .82 | 383.79 | .08 | .10 |
| .91 | 20.69 | .57 | 108.77 | 1.13 | 231.18 | 1.23 | 337.49 | .82 | 383.87 | .07 | .09 |
| .92 | 21.26 | .58 | 109.90 | 1.14 | 232.41 | 1.23 | 338.31 | .81 | 383.94 | .06 | .08 |
| .93 | 21.84 | .59 | 111.04 | 1.14 | 233.64 | 1.22 | 339.12 | .80 | 384.00 | .05 | .07 |
| .94 | 22.43 | .59 | 112.18 | 1.15 | 234.86 | 1.22 | 339.92 | .80 | 384.05 | .05 | .06 |
| .95 | 23.02 | .60 | 113.33 | 1.15 | 236.08 | 1.22 | 340.72 | .79 | 384.10 | .04 | .05 |
| .96 | 23.62 | .61 | 114.48 | 1.15 | 237.30 | 1.22 | 341.51 | .78 | 384.14 | .03 | .04 |
| .97 | 24.23 | .61 | 115.63 | 1.15 | 238.52 | 1.22 | 342.29 | .78 | 384.17 | .02 | .03 |
| .98 | 24.84 | .62 | 116.78 | 1.15 | 239.74 | 1.22 | 343.07 | .77 | 384.19 | .01 | .02 |
| .99 | 25.46 | .63 | 117.93 | 1.16 | 240.96 | 1.21 | 343.84 | .77 | 384.20 | .00 | .01 |
| 1.00 | 26.09 | .64 | 119.09 | 1.16 | 242.17 | 1.21 | 344.61 | .76 | 384.20 | .00 | .00 |
| Days. | 9 | | 8 | | 7 | | 6 | | 5 | | Days. |

# TABLE XIII. ARGUMENT 8.

Equation = 165″.9 [1 + sin. (2t — z)].

Period, 15.3873122 days.

| Days. | 0 | | 1 | | 2 | | 3 | | 4 | | 5 | | Days. |
|---|---|---|---|---|---|---|---|---|---|---|---|---|---|
| Decimals of a Day. | Equation. | Diff. | Equation. | Diff. | Equation. | Diff. | Equation. | Diff. | Equation. | Diff. | Equation. | Diff. | Decimals of a Day. |
| | ″ | | ″ | | ″ | | ″ | | ″ | | ″ | | |
| .00 | 1.29 | .08 | 6.62 | .19 | 38.12 | .43 | 90.64 | .60 | 155.53 | .67 | 222.13 | .64 | 1.00 |
| .01 | 1.21 | .08 | 6.81 | .19 | 38.55 | .43 | 91.24 | .60 | 156.20 | .68 | 222.77 | .63 | .99 |
| .02 | 1.13 | .08 | 7.00 | .19 | 38.98 | .44 | 91.84 | .61 | 156.88 | .67 | 223.40 | .64 | .98 |
| .03 | 1.05 | .08 | 7.19 | .20 | 39.42 | .44 | 92.45 | .60 | 157.55 | .68 | 224.04 | .63 | .97 |
| .04 | 0.97 | .07 | 7.39 | .20 | 39.86 | .44 | 93.05 | .61 | 158.23 | .68 | 224.67 | .63 | .96 |
| .05 | 0.90 | .07 | 7.59 | .20 | 40.30 | .44 | 93.66 | .61 | 158.91 | .67 | 225.30 | .63 | .95 |
| .06 | 0.83 | .07 | 7.79 | .21 | 40.74 | .45 | 94.27 | .61 | 159.58 | .68 | 225.93 | .63 | .94 |
| .07 | 0.76 | .06 | 8.00 | .21 | 41.19 | .45 | 94.88 | .61 | 160.26 | .68 | 226.56 | .63 | .93 |
| .08 | 0.70 | .06 | 8.21 | .21 | 41.64 | .45 | 95.49 | .62 | 160.94 | .68 | 227.19 | .63 | .92 |
| .09 | 0.64 | .06 | 8.42 | .21 | 42.09 | .45 | 96.11 | .62 | 161.62 | .68 | 227.82 | .63 | .91 |
| .10 | 0.58 | .05 | 8.63 | .22 | 42.54 | .46 | 96.73 | .62 | 162.30 | .68 | 228.45 | .63 | .90 |
| .11 | 0.53 | .05 | 8.85 | .22 | 43.00 | .46 | 97.35 | .62 | 162.98 | .67 | 229.08 | .62 | .89 |
| .12 | 0.48 | .05 | 9.07 | .22 | 43.46 | .46 | 97.97 | .62 | 163.65 | .68 | 229.70 | .63 | .88 |
| .13 | 0.43 | .05 | 9.29 | .22 | 43.92 | .46 | 98.59 | .62 | 164.33 | .68 | 230.33 | .62 | .87 |
| .14 | 0.38 | .05 | 9.51 | .23 | 44.38 | .46 | 99.21 | .62 | 165.01 | .68 | 230.95 | .62 | .86 |
| .15 | 0.33 | .04 | 9.74 | .23 | 44.84 | .46 | 99.83 | .62 | 165.69 | .68 | 231.57 | .62 | .85 |
| .16 | 0.29 | .04 | 9.97 | .23 | 45.30 | .47 | 100.45 | .62 | 166.37 | .68 | 232.19 | .62 | .84 |
| .17 | 0.25 | .04 | 10.20 | .24 | 45.77 | .47 | 101.07 | .62 | 167.05 | .67 | 232.81 | .62 | .83 |
| .18 | 0.21 | .03 | 10.44 | .24 | 46.24 | .47 | 101.69 | .63 | 167.72 | .68 | 233.43 | .62 | .82 |
| .19 | 0.18 | .03 | 10.68 | .24 | 46.71 | .47 | 102.32 | .63 | 168.40 | .68 | 234.05 | .62 | .81 |
| .20 | 0.15 | .03 | 10.92 | .24 | 47.18 | .47 | 102.95 | .63 | 169.08 | .68 | 234.67 | .62 | .80 |
| .21 | 0.12 | .02 | 11.16 | .25 | 47.65 | .48 | 103.58 | .63 | 169.76 | .68 | 235.29 | .62 | .79 |
| .22 | 0.10 | .02 | 11.41 | .25 | 48.13 | .48 | 104.21 | .63 | 170.44 | .67 | 235.91 | .61 | .78 |
| .23 | 0.08 | .02 | 11.66 | .25 | 48.61 | .48 | 104.84 | .63 | 171.11 | .68 | 236.52 | .62 | .77 |
| .24 | 0.06 | .02 | 11.91 | .25 | 49.09 | .48 | 105.47 | .63 | 171.79 | .67 | 237.14 | .61 | .76 |
| .25 | 0.04 | .01 | 12.16 | .26 | 49.57 | .48 | 106.10 | .63 | 172.46 | .68 | 237.75 | .61 | .75 |
| .26 | 0.03 | .01 | 12.42 | .26 | 50.05 | .48 | 106.73 | .63 | 173.14 | .68 | 238.36 | .61 | .74 |
| .27 | 0.02 | .01 | 12.68 | .26 | 50.53 | .49 | 107.36 | .64 | 173.82 | .67 | 238.97 | .61 | .73 |
| .28 | 0.01 | .01 | 12.94 | .26 | 51.02 | .49 | 108.00 | .63 | 174.49 | .68 | 239.58 | .60 | .72 |
| .29 | 0.00 | .00 | 13.20 | .26 | 51.51 | .49 | 108.63 | .64 | 175.17 | .67 | 240.18 | .61 | .71 |
| .30 | 0.00 | .00 | 13.46 | .27 | 52.00 | .49 | 109.27 | .63 | 175.84 | .68 | 240.79 | .60 | .70 |
| .31 | 0.00 | .00 | 13.73 | .27 | 52.49 | .50 | 109.90 | .64 | 176.52 | .68 | 241.39 | .60 | .69 |
| .32 | 0.00 | .00 | 14.00 | .27 | 52.99 | .50 | 110.54 | .64 | 177.20 | .67 | 241.99 | .60 | .68 |
| .33 | 0.00 | .01 | 14.27 | .28 | 53.49 | .50 | 111.18 | .64 | 177.87 | .68 | 242.59 | .60 | .67 |
| .34 | 0.01 | .01 | 14.55 | .28 | 53.99 | .50 | 111.82 | .64 | 178.55 | .67 | 243.19 | .60 | .66 |
| .35 | 0.02 | .01 | 14.83 | .28 | 54.49 | .50 | 112.46 | .64 | 179.22 | .68 | 243.79 | .60 | .65 |
| .36 | 0.03 | .02 | 15.11 | .29 | 54.99 | .51 | 113.10 | .64 | 179.90 | .68 | 244.39 | .59 | .64 |
| .37 | 0.05 | .02 | 15.40 | .29 | 55.50 | .51 | 113.74 | .64 | 180.58 | .67 | 244.98 | .60 | .63 |
| .38 | 0.07 | .02 | 15.69 | .29 | 56.01 | .51 | 114.38 | .65 | 181.25 | .68 | 245.58 | .59 | .62 |
| .39 | 0.09 | .02 | 15.98 | .29 | 56.52 | .51 | 115.03 | .64 | 181.93 | .67 | 246.17 | .59 | .61 |
| .40 | 0.11 | .03 | 16.27 | .30 | 57.03 | .51 | 115.67 | .65 | 182.60 | .67 | 246.76 | .59 | .60 |
| .41 | 0.14 | .03 | 16.57 | .30 | 57.54 | .51 | 116.32 | .64 | 183.27 | .68 | 247.35 | .59 | .59 |
| .42 | 0.17 | .03 | 16.87 | .30 | 58.05 | .51 | 116.96 | .65 | 183.95 | .67 | 247.94 | .59 | .58 |
| .43 | 0.20 | .04 | 17.17 | .30 | 58.56 | .52 | 117.61 | .65 | 184.62 | .67 | 248.53 | .59 | .57 |
| .44 | 0.24 | .04 | 17.47 | .30 | 59.08 | .52 | 118.26 | .65 | 185.29 | .67 | 249.12 | .59 | .56 |
| .45 | 0.28 | .04 | 17.77 | .31 | 59.60 | .52 | 118.91 | .65 | 185.96 | .67 | 249.71 | .58 | .55 |
| .46 | 0.32 | .05 | 18.08 | .31 | 60.12 | .52 | 119.56 | .65 | 186.63 | .68 | 250.29 | .59 | .54 |
| .47 | 0.37 | .05 | 18.39 | .31 | 60.64 | .52 | 120.21 | .66 | 187.31 | .67 | 250.88 | .58 | .53 |
| .48 | 0.42 | .05 | 18.70 | .31 | 61.16 | .53 | 120.87 | .65 | 187.98 | .67 | 251.46 | .58 | .52 |
| .49 | 0.47 | .05 | 19.01 | .32 | 61.69 | .53 | 121.52 | .66 | 188.65 | .67 | 252.04 | .58 | .51 |
| .50 | 0.52 | .06 | 19.33 | .32 | 62.22 | .53 | 122.18 | .65 | 189.32 | .67 | 252.62 | .57 | .50 |
| Days. | 15 | | 14 | | 13 | | 12 | | 11 | | 10 | | Days. |

# TABLE XIII. ARGUMENT 8.

Equation = 165″.9 [1 + sin. (2*t* — *z*)].

Period, 15.3873122 days.

| Days. | 0 | | 1 | | 2 | | 3 | | 4 | | 5 | | Days. |
|---|---|---|---|---|---|---|---|---|---|---|---|---|---|
| Decimals of a Day | Equation. | Diff. | Equation. | Diff. | Equation. | Diff. | Equation. | Diff. | Equation. | Diff. | Equation. | Diff. | Decimals of a Day. |
| .50 | ″ 0.52 | .06 | ″ 19.33 | .32 | ″ 62.22 | .53 | ″ 122.18 | .65 | ″ 189.32 | .67 | ″ 252.62 | .57 | .50 |
| .51 | 0.58 | .06 | 19.65 | .32 | 62.75 | .53 | 122.83 | .65 | 189.99 | .67 | 253.19 | .58 | .49 |
| .52 | 0.64 | .06 | 19.97 | .32 | 63.28 | .53 | 123.48 | .65 | 190.66 | .67 | 253.77 | .57 | .48 |
| .53 | 0.70 | .06 | 20.29 | .32 | 63.81 | .54 | 124.13 | .66 | 191.33 | .67 | 254.34 | .57 | .47 |
| .54 | 0.76 | .06 | 20.61 | .33 | 64.35 | .54 | 124.79 | .66 | 192.00 | .67 | 254.91 | .57 | .46 |
| .55 | 0.82 | .07 | 20.94 | .33 | 64.89 | .54 | 125.45 | .65 | 192.67 | .67 | 255.48 | .57 | .45 |
| .56 | 0.89 | .07 | 21.27 | .33 | 65.43 | .54 | 126.10 | .66 | 193.34 | .66 | 256.05 | .57 | .44 |
| .57 | 0.96 | .07 | 21.60 | .34 | 65.97 | .54 | 126.76 | .66 | 194.00 | .67 | 256.62 | .56 | .43 |
| .58 | 1.03 | .08 | 21.94 | .34 | 66.51 | .54 | 127.42 | .66 | 194.67 | .66 | 257.18 | .57 | .42 |
| .59 | 1.11 | .08 | 22.28 | .34 | 67.05 | .55 | 128.08 | .66 | 195.33 | .67 | 257.75 | .56 | .41 |
| .60 | 1.19 | .08 | 22.62 | .34 | 67.60 | .55 | 128.74 | .66 | 196.00 | .67 | 258.31 | .56 | .40 |
| .61 | 1.27 | .09 | 22.96 | .34 | 68.15 | .55 | 129.40 | .66 | 196.67 | .66 | 258.87 | .56 | .39 |
| .62 | 1.36 | .09 | 23.30 | .35 | 68.70 | .55 | 130.06 | .67 | 197.33 | .67 | 259.43 | .56 | .38 |
| .63 | 1.45 | .09 | 23.65 | .35 | 69.25 | .55 | 130.73 | .66 | 198.00 | .66 | 259.99 | .56 | .37 |
| .64 | 1.54 | .09 | 24.00 | .35 | 69.80 | .55 | 131.39 | .67 | 198.66 | .67 | 260.55 | .56 | .36 |
| .65 | 1.63 | .10 | 24.35 | .35 | 70.35 | .55 | 132.06 | .66 | 199.33 | .66 | 261.11 | .55 | .35 |
| .66 | 1.73 | .10 | 24.70 | .36 | 70.90 | .56 | 132.72 | .67 | 199.99 | .67 | 261.66 | .55 | .34 |
| .67 | 1.83 | .10 | 25.06 | .36 | 71.46 | .56 | 133.39 | .66 | 200.66 | .66 | 262.21 | .55 | .33 |
| .68 | 1.93 | .10 | 25.42 | .36 | 72.02 | .56 | 134.05 | .67 | 201.32 | .66 | 262.76 | .55 | .32 |
| .69 | 2.03 | .11 | 25.78 | .36 | 72.58 | .56 | 134.72 | .67 | 201.98 | .66 | 263.31 | .55 | .31 |
| .70 | 2.14 | .11 | 26.14 | .37 | 73.14 | .56 | 135.39 | .67 | 202.64 | .66 | 263.86 | .54 | .30 |
| .71 | 2.25 | .11 | 26.51 | .37 | 73.70 | .56 | 136.06 | .66 | 203.30 | .66 | 264.40 | .55 | .29 |
| .72 | 2.36 | .12 | 26.88 | .37 | 74.26 | .57 | 136.72 | .67 | 203.96 | .66 | 264.95 | .54 | .28 |
| .73 | 2.48 | .12 | 27.25 | .37 | 74.83 | .57 | 137.39 | .67 | 204.62 | .65 | 265.49 | .54 | .27 |
| .74 | 2.60 | .12 | 27.62 | .38 | 75.40 | .57 | 138.06 | .67 | 205.27 | .66 | 266.03 | .54 | .26 |
| .75 | 2.72 | .13 | 28.00 | .38 | 75.97 | .57 | 138.73 | .67 | 205.93 | .66 | 266.57 | .54 | .25 |
| .76 | 2.85 | .13 | 28.38 | .38 | 76.54 | .57 | 139.40 | .66 | 206.59 | .66 | 267.11 | .53 | .24 |
| .77 | 2.98 | .13 | 28.76 | .38 | 77.11 | .57 | 140.06 | .67 | 207.25 | .65 | 267.64 | .54 | .23 |
| .78 | 3.11 | .13 | 29.14 | .38 | 77.68 | .57 | 140.73 | .67 | 207.90 | .66 | 268.18 | .53 | .22 |
| .79 | 3.24 | .13 | 29.52 | .39 | 78.25 | .58 | 141.40 | .67 | 208.56 | .65 | 268.71 | .53 | .21 |
| .80 | 3.37 | .14 | 29.91 | .39 | 78.83 | .58 | 142.07 | .67 | 209.21 | .65 | 269.24 | .53 | .20 |
| .81 | 3.51 | .14 | 30.30 | .39 | 79.41 | .58 | 142.74 | .67 | 209.86 | .66 | 269.77 | .53 | .19 |
| .82 | 3.65 | .14 | 30.69 | .39 | 79.99 | .58 | 143.41 | .67 | 210.52 | .65 | 270.30 | .52 | .18 |
| .83 | 3.79 | .14 | 31.08 | .40 | 80.57 | .58 | 144.08 | .67 | 211.17 | .65 | 270.82 | .53 | .17 |
| .84 | 3.93 | .15 | 31.48 | .40 | 81.15 | .58 | 144.75 | .67 | 211.82 | .65 | 271.35 | .52 | .16 |
| .85 | 4.08 | .15 | 31.88 | .40 | 81.73 | .58 | 145.42 | .67 | 212.47 | .65 | 271.87 | .52 | .15 |
| .86 | 4.23 | .15 | 32.28 | .40 | 82.31 | .59 | 146.09 | .67 | 213.12 | .65 | 272.39 | .52 | .14 |
| .87 | 4.38 | .16 | 32.68 | .41 | 82.90 | .59 | 146.76 | .67 | 213.77 | .65 | 272.91 | .51 | .13 |
| .88 | 4.54 | .16 | 33.09 | .41 | 83.49 | .59 | 147.43 | .68 | 214.42 | .64 | 273.42 | .52 | .12 |
| .89 | 4.70 | .16 | 33.50 | .41 | 84.08 | .59 | 148.11 | .67 | 215.06 | .65 | 273.94 | .51 | .11 |
| .90 | 4.86 | .17 | 33.91 | .41 | 84.67 | .59 | 148.78 | .67 | 215.71 | .65 | 274.45 | .51 | .10 |
| .91 | 5.03 | .17 | 34.32 | .41 | 85.26 | .59 | 149.45 | .67 | 216.36 | .64 | 274.96 | .51 | .09 |
| .92 | 5.20 | .17 | 34.73 | .42 | 85.85 | .59 | 150.12 | .68 | 217.00 | .65 | 275.47 | .51 | .08 |
| .93 | 5.37 | .17 | 35.15 | .42 | 86.44 | .60 | 150.80 | .67 | 217.65 | .64 | 275.98 | .50 | .07 |
| .94 | 5.54 | .17 | 35.57 | .42 | 87.04 | .60 | 151.47 | .68 | 218.29 | .64 | 276.48 | .51 | .06 |
| .95 | 5.71 | .18 | 35.99 | .42 | 87.64 | .60 | 152.15 | .67 | 218.93 | .64 | 276.99 | .50 | .05 |
| .96 | 5.89 | .18 | 36.41 | .42 | 88.24 | .60 | 152.82 | .68 | 219.57 | .64 | 277.49 | .50 | .04 |
| .97 | 6.07 | .18 | 36.83 | .43 | 88.84 | .60 | 153.50 | .67 | 220.21 | .64 | 277.99 | .50 | .03 |
| .98 | 6.25 | .18 | 37.26 | .43 | 89.44 | .60 | 154.17 | .68 | 220.85 | .64 | 278.49 | .50 | .02 |
| .99 | 6.43 | .19 | 37.69 | .43 | 90.04 | .60 | 154.85 | .68 | 221.49 | .64 | 278.99 | .50 | .01 |
| 1.00 | 6.62 | .19 | 38.12 | .43 | 90.64 | .60 | 155.53 | .67 | 222.13 | .64 | 279.49 | .49 | .00 |
| Days. | 15 | | 14 | | 13 | | 12 | | 11 | | 10 | | Days. |

## TABLE XIII.

(*Continued.*)

Period, 15.3873122 days.

| Days. Decimals of a Day. | 6 Equation. | Diff. | 7 Equation. | Diff. |
|---|---|---|---|---|
| .00 | 279.49″ | .49 | 318.17″ | .27 |
| .01 | 279.98 | .49 | 318.44 | .26 |
| .02 | 280.47 | .49 | 318.70 | .26 |
| .03 | 280.96 | .49 | 318.96 | .26 |
| .04 | 281.45 | .48 | 319.22 | .26 |
| .05 | 281.93 | .48 | 319.48 | .25 |
| .06 | 282.41 | .48 | 319.73 | .25 |
| .07 | 282.89 | .48 | 319.98 | .25 |
| .08 | 283.37 | .48 | 320.23 | .25 |
| .09 | 283.85 | .47 | 320.48 | .24 |
| .10 | 284.32 | .47 | 320.72 | .24 |
| .11 | 284.79 | .47 | 320.96 | .24 |
| .12 | 285.26 | .47 | 321.20 | .24 |
| .13 | 285.73 | .47 | 321.44 | .24 |
| .14 | 286.20 | .47 | 321.68 | .23 |
| .15 | 286.67 | .46 | 321.91 | .23 |
| .16 | 287.13 | .46 | 322.14 | .23 |
| .17 | 287.59 | .46 | 322.37 | .22 |
| .18 | 288.05 | .46 | 322.59 | .22 |
| .19 | 288.51 | .46 | 322.81 | .22 |
| .20 | 288.97 | .45 | 323.03 | .22 |
| .21 | 289.42 | .45 | 323.25 | .21 |
| .22 | 289.87 | .45 | 323.46 | .21 |
| .23 | 290.32 | .45 | 323.67 | .21 |
| .24 | 290.77 | .45 | 323.88 | .20 |
| .25 | 291.22 | .44 | 324.08 | .20 |
| .26 | 291.66 | .44 | 324.28 | .20 |
| .27 | 292.10 | .44 | 324.48 | .20 |
| .28 | 292.54 | .44 | 324.68 | .19 |
| .29 | 292.98 | .43 | 324.87 | .19 |
| .30 | 293.41 | .43 | 325.06 | .19 |
| .31 | 293.84 | .43 | 325.25 | .19 |
| .32 | 294.27 | .43 | 325.44 | .18 |
| .33 | 294.70 | .43 | 325.62 | .18 |
| .34 | 295.13 | .42 | 325.80 | .18 |
| .35 | 295.55 | .42 | 325.98 | .18 |
| .36 | 295.97 | .42 | 326.16 | .17 |
| .37 | 296.39 | .42 | 326.33 | .17 |
| .38 | 296.81 | .41 | 326.50 | .17 |
| .39 | 297.22 | .41 | 326.67 | .16 |
| .40 | 297.63 | .41 | 326.83 | .16 |
| .41 | 298.04 | .41 | 326.99 | .16 |
| .42 | 298.45 | .41 | 327.15 | .16 |
| .43 | 298.86 | .40 | 327.31 | .16 |
| .44 | 299.26 | .40 | 327.47 | .15 |
| .45 | 299.66 | .40 | 327.62 | .15 |
| .46 | 300.06 | .40 | 327.77 | .15 |
| .47 | 300.46 | .40 | 327.92 | .14 |
| .48 | 300.86 | .39 | 328.06 | .14 |
| .49 | 301.25 | .39 | 328.20 | .14 |
| .50 | 301.64 | .39 | 328.34 | .14 |
| Days. | 9 | | 8 | |

## TABLE XIV. ARGUMENT 9.

Equation = 148″.1 [1 + sin. $(x - z)$].

Period, 29.802826 days.

| 0 Equation. | Diff. | 1 Equation. | Diff. | 2 Equation. | Diff. | Days. Decimals of a Day. |
|---|---|---|---|---|---|---|
| 0.04″ | .01 | 2.67″ | .06 | 11.74″ | .12 | 1.00 |
| 0.03 | .01 | 2.73 | .06 | 11.86 | .12 | .99 |
| 0.02 | .00 | 2.79 | .06 | 11.98 | .13 | .98 |
| 0.02 | .01 | 2.85 | .06 | 12.11 | .12 | .97 |
| 0.01 | .00 | 2.91 | .06 | 12.23 | .12 | .96 |
| 0.01 | .00 | 2.97 | .07 | 12.35 | .13 | .95 |
| 0.01 | .01 | 3.04 | .06 | 12.48 | .13 | .94 |
| 0.00 | .00 | 3.10 | .06 | 12.61 | .12 | .93 |
| 0.00 | .00 | 3.16 | .07 | 12.73 | .13 | .92 |
| 0.00 | .00 | 3.23 | .06 | 12.86 | .13 | .91 |
| 0.00 | .00 | 3.29 | .07 | 12.99 | .13 | .90 |
| 0.00 | .00 | 3.36 | .06 | 13.12 | .13 | .89 |
| 0.00 | .00 | 3.42 | .07 | 13.25 | .13 | .88 |
| 0.00 | .00 | 3.49 | .07 | 13.38 | .13 | .87 |
| 0.00 | .01 | 3.56 | .06 | 13.51 | .13 | .86 |
| 0.01 | .00 | 3.62 | .07 | 13.64 | .13 | .85 |
| 0.01 | .00 | 3.69 | .07 | 13.77 | .14 | .84 |
| 0.01 | .01 | 3.76 | .07 | 13.91 | .13 | .83 |
| 0.02 | .00 | 3.83 | .07 | 14.04 | .13 | .82 |
| 0.02 | .01 | 3.90 | .07 | 14.17 | .13 | .81 |
| 0.03 | .01 | 3.97 | .07 | 14.30 | .13 | .80 |
| 0.04 | .01 | 4.04 | .07 | 14.43 | .14 | .79 |
| 0.05 | .01 | 4.11 | .07 | 14.57 | .13 | .78 |
| 0.06 | .01 | 4.18 | .08 | 14.70 | .13 | .77 |
| 0.07 | .01 | 4.26 | .07 | 14.83 | .14 | .76 |
| 0.08 | .01 | 4.33 | .08 | 14.97 | .13 | .75 |
| 0.09 | .01 | 4.41 | .07 | 15.10 | .14 | .74 |
| 0.10 | .01 | 4.48 | .08 | 15.24 | .14 | .73 |
| 0.11 | .01 | 4.56 | .08 | 15.38 | .14 | .72 |
| 0.12 | .01 | 4.64 | .08 | 15.52 | .14 | .71 |
| 0.13 | .01 | 4.72 | .08 | 15.66 | .14 | .70 |
| 0.14 | .02 | 4.80 | .08 | 15.80 | .14 | .69 |
| 0.16 | .01 | 4.88 | .08 | 15.94 | .14 | .68 |
| 0.17 | .02 | 4.96 | .08 | 16.08 | .15 | .67 |
| 0.19 | .02 | 5.04 | .08 | 16.23 | .14 | .66 |
| 0.21 | .01 | 5.12 | .08 | 16.37 | .14 | .65 |
| 0.22 | .02 | 5.20 | .08 | 16.51 | .15 | .64 |
| 0.24 | .02 | 5.28 | .09 | 16.66 | .14 | .63 |
| 0.26 | .01 | 5.37 | .08 | 16.80 | .14 | .62 |
| 0.27 | .02 | 5.45 | .08 | 16.94 | .15 | .61 |
| 0.29 | .02 | 5.53 | .09 | 17.09 | .15 | .60 |
| 0.31 | .02 | 5.62 | .08 | 17.24 | .15 | .59 |
| 0.33 | .02 | 5.70 | .09 | 17.39 | .14 | .58 |
| 0.35 | .02 | 5.79 | .09 | 17.53 | .15 | .57 |
| 0.37 | .03 | 5.88 | .08 | 17.68 | .15 | .56 |
| 0.40 | .02 | 5.96 | .09 | 17.83 | .15 | .55 |
| 0.42 | .02 | 6.05 | .09 | 17.98 | .15 | .54 |
| 0.44 | .03 | 6.14 | .09 | 18.13 | .15 | .53 |
| 0.47 | .02 | 6.23 | .09 | 18.28 | .15 | .52 |
| 0.49 | .03 | 6.32 | .09 | 18.43 | .15 | .51 |
| 0.52 | .03 | 6.41 | .09 | 18.58 | .15 | .50 |
| 29 | | 28 | | 27 | | Days. |

# TABLE XIII.

*(Continued.)*

Period, 15.3873122 days.

| Decimals of a Day. | 6 Equation. | Diff. | 7 Equation. | Diff. |
|---|---|---|---|---|
| .50 | 301″.64 | .39 | 328″.34 | .14 |
| .51 | 302.03 | .39 | 328.48 | .13 |
| .52 | 302.42 | .38 | 328.61 | .13 |
| .53 | 302.80 | .38 | 328.74 | .13 |
| .54 | 303.18 | .38 | 328.87 | .13 |
| .55 | 303.56 | .38 | 329.00 | .12 |
| .56 | 303.94 | .37 | 329.12 | .12 |
| .57 | 304.31 | .37 | 329.24 | .12 |
| .58 | 304.68 | .37 | 329.36 | .12 |
| .59 | 305.05 | .37 | 329.48 | .11 |
| .60 | 305.42 | .37 | 329.59 | .11 |
| .61 | 305.79 | .36 | 329.70 | .11 |
| .62 | 306.15 | .36 | 329.81 | .10 |
| .63 | 306.51 | .36 | 329.91 | .10 |
| .64 | 306.87 | .36 | 330.01 | .10 |
| .65 | 307.23 | .35 | 330.11 | .10 |
| .66 | 307.58 | .35 | 330.21 | .09 |
| .67 | 307.93 | .35 | 330.30 | .09 |
| .68 | 308.28 | .35 | 330.39 | .09 |
| .69 | 308.63 | .34 | 330.48 | .08 |
| .70 | 308.97 | .34 | 330.56 | .08 |
| .71 | 309.31 | .34 | 330.64 | .08 |
| .72 | 309.65 | .34 | 330.72 | .08 |
| .73 | 309.99 | .33 | 330.80 | .07 |
| .74 | 310.32 | .33 | 330.87 | .07 |
| .75 | 310.65 | .33 | 330.94 | .07 |
| .76 | 310.98 | .33 | 331.01 | .06 |
| .77 | 311.31 | .33 | 331.07 | .06 |
| .78 | 311.64 | .32 | 331.13 | .06 |
| .79 | 311.96 | .32 | 331.19 | .06 |
| .80 | 312.28 | .32 | 331.25 | .05 |
| .81 | 312.60 | .31 | 331.30 | .05 |
| .82 | 312.91 | .31 | 331.35 | .05 |
| .83 | 313.22 | .31 | 331.40 | .05 |
| .84 | 313.53 | .31 | 331.45 | .04 |
| .85 | 313.84 | .30 | 331.49 | .04 |
| .86 | 314.14 | .30 | 331.53 | .04 |
| .87 | 314.44 | .30 | 331.57 | .04 |
| .88 | 314.74 | .30 | 331.61 | .03 |
| .89 | 315.04 | .30 | 331.64 | .03 |
| .90 | 315.34 | .29 | 331.67 | .03 |
| .91 | 315.63 | .29 | 331.70 | .02 |
| .92 | 315.92 | .29 | 331.72 | .02 |
| .93 | 316.21 | .29 | 331.74 | .02 |
| .94 | 316.50 | .29 | 331.76 | .01 |
| .95 | 316.79 | .28 | 331.77 | .01 |
| .96 | 317.07 | .28 | 331.78 | .01 |
| .97 | 317.35 | .28 | 331.79 | .01 |
| .98 | 317.63 | .27 | 331.80 | .00 |
| .99 | 317.90 | .27 | 331.80 | .00 |
| 1.00 | 318.17 | .27 | 331.80 | .00 |
| Days. | 9 | | 8 | |

# TABLE XIV. ARGUMENT 9.

Equation = 148″.1 $[1 + \sin.\ (x - z)]$.

Period, 29.802826 days.

| 0 Equation. | Diff. | 1 Equation. | Diff. | 2 Equation. | Diff. | Decimals of a Day. |
|---|---|---|---|---|---|---|
| 0″.52 | .03 | 6″.41 | .09 | 18″.58 | .15 | .50 |
| 0.55 | .03 | 6.50 | .09 | 18.73 | .15 | .49 |
| 0.58 | .03 | 6.59 | .09 | 18.88 | .15 | .48 |
| 0.61 | .03 | 6.68 | .10 | 19.03 | .16 | .47 |
| 0.64 | .03 | 6.78 | .09 | 19.19 | .15 | .46 |
| 0.67 | .03 | 6.87 | .09 | 19.34 | .15 | .45 |
| 0.70 | .03 | 6.96 | .10 | 19.49 | .16 | .44 |
| 0.73 | .03 | 7.06 | .09 | 19.65 | .15 | .43 |
| 0.76 | .03 | 7.15 | .10 | 19.80 | .16 | .42 |
| 0.79 | .03 | 7.25 | .10 | 19.96 | .16 | .41 |
| 0.82 | .03 | 7.35 | .10 | 20.12 | .16 | .40 |
| 0.85 | .04 | 7.45 | .10 | 20.28 | .16 | .39 |
| 0.89 | .03 | 7.55 | .10 | 20.44 | .16 | .38 |
| 0.92 | .04 | 7.65 | .10 | 20.60 | .16 | .37 |
| 0.96 | .04 | 7.75 | .10 | 20.76 | .16 | .36 |
| 1.00 | .03 | 7.85 | .10 | 20.92 | .16 | .35 |
| 1.03 | .04 | 7.95 | .10 | 21.08 | .16 | .34 |
| 1.07 | .04 | 8.05 | .10 | 21.24 | .16 | .33 |
| 1.11 | .04 | 8.15 | .10 | 21.40 | .16 | .32 |
| 1.15 | .04 | 8.25 | .10 | 21.56 | .16 | .31 |
| 1.19 | .04 | 8.35 | .10 | 21.72 | .16 | .30 |
| 1.23 | .04 | 8.45 | .11 | 21.88 | .16 | .29 |
| 1.27 | .04 | 8.56 | .10 | 22.04 | .17 | .28 |
| 1.31 | .04 | 8.66 | .11 | 22.21 | .16 | .27 |
| 1.35 | .05 | 8.77 | .11 | 22.37 | .16 | .26 |
| 1.40 | .04 | 8.88 | .10 | 22.53 | .17 | .25 |
| 1.44 | .04 | 8.98 | .11 | 22.70 | .16 | .24 |
| 1.48 | .05 | 9.09 | .11 | 22.86 | .17 | .23 |
| 1.53 | .04 | 9.20 | .11 | 23.03 | .17 | .22 |
| 1.57 | .05 | 9.31 | .11 | 23.20 | .17 | .21 |
| 1.62 | .05 | 9.42 | .11 | 23.37 | .17 | .20 |
| 1.67 | .04 | 9.53 | .11 | 23.54 | .17 | .19 |
| 1.71 | .05 | 9.64 | .11 | 23.71 | .17 | .18 |
| 1.76 | .05 | 9.75 | .11 | 23.88 | .17 | .17 |
| 1.81 | .05 | 9.86 | .12 | 24.05 | .17 | .16 |
| 1.86 | .05 | 9.98 | .11 | 24.22 | .17 | .15 |
| 1.91 | .05 | 10.09 | .11 | 24.39 | .18 | .14 |
| 1.96 | .05 | 10.20 | .12 | 24.57 | .17 | .13 |
| 2.01 | .05 | 10.32 | .11 | 24.74 | .17 | .12 |
| 2.06 | .05 | 10.43 | .12 | 24.91 | .17 | .11 |
| 2.11 | .05 | 10.55 | .12 | 25.08 | .18 | .10 |
| 2.16 | .05 | 10.67 | .11 | 25.26 | .17 | .09 |
| 2.21 | .06 | 10.78 | .12 | 25.43 | .18 | .08 |
| 2.27 | .05 | 10.90 | .12 | 25.61 | .18 | .07 |
| 2.32 | .06 | 11.02 | .12 | 25.79 | .17 | .06 |
| 2.38 | .05 | 11.14 | .12 | 25.96 | .18 | .05 |
| 2.43 | .06 | 11.26 | .12 | 26.14 | .18 | .04 |
| 2.49 | .06 | 11.38 | .12 | 26.32 | .18 | .03 |
| 2.55 | .06 | 11.50 | .12 | 26.50 | .17 | .02 |
| 2.61 | .06 | 11.62 | .12 | 26.67 | .18 | .01 |
| 2.67 | .06 | 11.74 | .12 | 26.85 | .18 | .00 |
| 29 | | 28 | | 27 | | Days. |

# TABLE XIV. ARGUMENT 9.

Equation = $148''.1\ [1 + \sin.\ (x - z)]$.

Period, 29.802826 days.

| Days. | 3 | | 4 | | 5 | | 6 | | 7 | | 8 | | Days. |
|---|---|---|---|---|---|---|---|---|---|---|---|---|---|
| Decimals of a Day. | Equation. | Diff. | Equation. | Diff. | Equation. | Diff. | Equation. | Diff. | Equation. | Diff. | Equation. | Diff. | Decimals of a Day. |
| .00 | 26.85″ | .18 | 47.33″ | .23 | 72.28″ | .27 | 100.58″ | .29 | 130.99″ | .31 | 162.15″ | .31 | 1.00 |
| .01 | 27.03 | .18 | 47.56 | .23 | 72.55 | .27 | 100.87 | .30 | 131.30 | .31 | 162.46 | .31 | .99 |
| .02 | 27.21 | .18 | 47.79 | .23 | 72.82 | .27 | 101.17 | .30 | 131.61 | .31 | 162.77 | .31 | .98 |
| .03 | 27.39 | .18 | 48.02 | .23 | 73.09 | .27 | 101.47 | .29 | 131.92 | .31 | 163.08 | .31 | .97 |
| .04 | 27.57 | .18 | 48.25 | .23 | 73.36 | .27 | 101.76 | .30 | 132.23 | .31 | 163.39 | .31 | .96 |
| .05 | 27.75 | .19 | 48.48 | .23 | 73.63 | .27 | 102.06 | .30 | 132.54 | .31 | 163.70 | .31 | .95 |
| .06 | 27.94 | .18 | 48.71 | .24 | 73.90 | .27 | 102.36 | .29 | 132.85 | .31 | 164.01 | .31 | .94 |
| .07 | 28.12 | .18 | 48.95 | .23 | 74.17 | .27 | 102.65 | .30 | 133.16 | .31 | 164.32 | .31 | .93 |
| .08 | 28.30 | .19 | 49.18 | .23 | 74.44 | .27 | 102.95 | .30 | 133.47 | .31 | 164.63 | .31 | .92 |
| .09 | 28.49 | .18 | 49.41 | .23 | 74.71 | .27 | 103.25 | .30 | 133.78 | .31 | 164.94 | .31 | .91 |
| .10 | 28.67 | .18 | 49.64 | .23 | 74.98 | .27 | 103.55 | .30 | 134.09 | .31 | 165.25 | .31 | .90 |
| .11 | 28.85 | .19 | 49.87 | .23 | 75.25 | .27 | 103.85 | .29 | 134.40 | .31 | 165.56 | .31 | .89 |
| .12 | 29.04 | .18 | 50.10 | .23 | 75.52 | .27 | 104.14 | .30 | 134.71 | .31 | 165.87 | .31 | .88 |
| .13 | 29.22 | .19 | 50.33 | .24 | 75.79 | .28 | 104.44 | .30 | 135.02 | .31 | 166.18 | .31 | .87 |
| .14 | 29.41 | .19 | 50.57 | .23 | 76.07 | .27 | 104.74 | .30 | 135.33 | .31 | 166.49 | .31 | .86 |
| .15 | 29.60 | .18 | 50.80 | .24 | 76.34 | .27 | 105.04 | .30 | 135.64 | .32 | 166.80 | .31 | .85 |
| .16 | 29.78 | .19 | 51.04 | .24 | 76.61 | .28 | 105.34 | .30 | 135.96 | .31 | 167.11 | .31 | .84 |
| .17 | 29.97 | .19 | 51.28 | .23 | 76.89 | .27 | 105.64 | .30 | 136.27 | .31 | 167.42 | .31 | .83 |
| .18 | 30.16 | .19 | 51.51 | .24 | 77.16 | .28 | 105.94 | .30 | 136.58 | .31 | 167.73 | .31 | .82 |
| .19 | 30.35 | .19 | 51.75 | .24 | 77.44 | .27 | 106.24 | .30 | 136.89 | .31 | 168.04 | .31 | .81 |
| .20 | 30.54 | .19 | 51.99 | .24 | 77.71 | .28 | 106.54 | .30 | 137.20 | .31 | 168.35 | .31 | .80 |
| .21 | 30.73 | .19 | 52.23 | .24 | 77.99 | .27 | 106.84 | .30 | 137.51 | .31 | 168.66 | .31 | .79 |
| .22 | 30.92 | .19 | 52.47 | .24 | 78.26 | .28 | 107.14 | .30 | 137.82 | .31 | 168.97 | .31 | .78 |
| .23 | 31.11 | .20 | 52.71 | .24 | 78.54 | .27 | 107.44 | .30 | 138.13 | .32 | 169.28 | .31 | .77 |
| .24 | 31.31 | .19 | 52.95 | .24 | 78.81 | .28 | 107.74 | .30 | 138.45 | .31 | 169.59 | .31 | .76 |
| .25 | 31.50 | .19 | 53.19 | .24 | 79.09 | .27 | 108.04 | .30 | 138.76 | .31 | 169.90 | .31 | .75 |
| .26 | 31.69 | .20 | 53.43 | .24 | 79.36 | .28 | 108.34 | .30 | 139.07 | .31 | 170.21 | .30 | .74 |
| .27 | 31.89 | .19 | 53.67 | .24 | 79.64 | .27 | 108.64 | .31 | 139.38 | .31 | 170.51 | .31 | .73 |
| .28 | 32.08 | .19 | 53.91 | .24 | 79.91 | .28 | 108.95 | .30 | 139.69 | .32 | 170.82 | .31 | .72 |
| .29 | 32.27 | .20 | 54.15 | .24 | 80.19 | .28 | 109.25 | .30 | 140.01 | .31 | 171.13 | .31 | .71 |
| .30 | 32.47 | .20 | 54.39 | .24 | 80.47 | .28 | 109.55 | .30 | 140.32 | .31 | 171.44 | .31 | .70 |
| .31 | 32.67 | .19 | 54.63 | .24 | 80.75 | .27 | 109.85 | .30 | 140.63 | .31 | 171.75 | .31 | .69 |
| .32 | 32.86 | .20 | 54.87 | .25 | 81.02 | .28 | 110.15 | .30 | 140.94 | .31 | 172.06 | .30 | .68 |
| .33 | 33.06 | .20 | 55.12 | .24 | 81.30 | .28 | 110.45 | .31 | 141.25 | .32 | 172.36 | .31 | .67 |
| .34 | 33.26 | .20 | 55.36 | .25 | 81.58 | .28 | 110.76 | .30 | 141.57 | .31 | 172.67 | .31 | .66 |
| .35 | 33.46 | .19 | 55.61 | .24 | 81.86 | .28 | 111.06 | .30 | 141.88 | .31 | 172.98 | .31 | .65 |
| .36 | 33.65 | .20 | 55.85 | .25 | 82.14 | .28 | 111.36 | .30 | 142.19 | .31 | 173.29 | .31 | .64 |
| .37 | 33.85 | .20 | 56.10 | .24 | 82.42 | .28 | 111.66 | .30 | 142.50 | .31 | 173.60 | .30 | .63 |
| .38 | 34.05 | .20 | 56.34 | .25 | 82.70 | .28 | 111.96 | .31 | 142.81 | .32 | 173.90 | .31 | .62 |
| .39 | 34.25 | .20 | 56.59 | .25 | 82.98 | .28 | 112.27 | .30 | 143.13 | .31 | 174.21 | .31 | .61 |
| .40 | 34.45 | .20 | 56.84 | .25 | 83.26 | .28 | 112.57 | .30 | 143.44 | .31 | 174.52 | .31 | .60 |
| .41 | 34.65 | .20 | 57.09 | .24 | 83.54 | .28 | 112.87 | .31 | 143.75 | .31 | 174.83 | .31 | .59 |
| .42 | 34.85 | .21 | 57.33 | .25 | 83.82 | .28 | 113.18 | .30 | 144.06 | .31 | 175.14 | .30 | .58 |
| .43 | 35.06 | .20 | 57.58 | .25 | 84.10 | .28 | 113.48 | .30 | 144.37 | .32 | 175.44 | .31 | .57 |
| .44 | 35.26 | .20 | 57.83 | .25 | 84.38 | .28 | 113.78 | .31 | 144.69 | .31 | 175.75 | .31 | .56 |
| .45 | 35.46 | .20 | 58.08 | .24 | 84.66 | .29 | 114.09 | .30 | 145.00 | .31 | 176.06 | .30 | .55 |
| .46 | 35.66 | .21 | 58.32 | .25 | 84.95 | .28 | 114.39 | .31 | 145.31 | .31 | 176.36 | .31 | .54 |
| .47 | 35.87 | .20 | 58.57 | .25 | 85.23 | .28 | 114.70 | .30 | 145.62 | .31 | 176.67 | .31 | .53 |
| .48 | 36.07 | .20 | 58.82 | .25 | 85.51 | .29 | 115.00 | .31 | 145.93 | .32 | 176.98 | .30 | .52 |
| .49 | 36.27 | .21 | 59.07 | .25 | 85.80 | .28 | 115.31 | .30 | 146.25 | .31 | 177.28 | .31 | .51 |
| .50 | 36.48 | .21 | 59.32 | .25 | 86.08 | .28 | 115.61 | .31 | 146.56 | .31 | 177.59 | .31 | .50 |
| Days. | 26 | | 25 | | 24 | | 23 | | 22 | | 21 | | Days. |

# TABLE XIV. ARGUMENT 9.

Equation = 148″.1 [1 + sin. $(x - z)$].

Period, 29.802826 days.

| Days. | 3 | | 4 | | 5 | | 6 | | 7 | | 8 | | Days. |
|---|---|---|---|---|---|---|---|---|---|---|---|---|---|
| Decimals of a Day | Equation. | Diff. | Equation. | Diff. | Equation. | Diff. | Equation. | Diff. | Equation. | Diff. | Equation. | Diff. | Decimals of a Day. |
| .50 | 36.48″ | .21 | 59.32″ | .25 | 86.08″ | .28 | 115.61″ | .31 | 146.56″ | .31 | 177.59″ | .31 | .50 |
| .51 | 36.69 | .20 | 59.57 | .25 | 86.36 | .29 | 115.92 | .30 | 146.87 | .31 | 177.90 | .30 | .49 |
| .52 | 36.89 | .21 | 59.82 | .25 | 86.65 | .28 | 116.22 | .31 | 147.18 | .32 | 178.20 | .31 | .48 |
| .53 | 37.10 | .21 | 60.07 | .25 | 86.93 | .29 | 116.53 | .30 | 147.50 | .31 | 178.51 | .30 | .47 |
| .54 | 37.31 | .21 | 60.32 | .25 | 87.22 | .28 | 116.83 | .31 | 147.81 | .31 | 178.81 | .31 | .46 |
| .55 | 37.52 | .20 | 60.57 | .26 | 87.50 | .29 | 117.14 | .30 | 148.12 | .32 | 179.12 | .30 | .45 |
| .56 | 37.72 | .21 | 60.83 | .25 | 87.79 | .28 | 117.44 | .31 | 148.44 | .31 | 179.42 | .31 | .44 |
| .57 | 37.93 | .21 | 61.08 | .25 | 88.07 | .29 | 117.75 | .30 | 148.75 | .31 | 179.73 | .30 | .43 |
| .58 | 38.14 | .21 | 61.33 | .26 | 88.36 | .28 | 118.05 | .31 | 149.06 | .32 | 180.03 | .31 | .42 |
| .59 | 38.35 | .21 | 61.59 | .25 | 88.64 | .29 | 118.36 | .30 | 149.38 | .31 | 180.34 | .30 | .41 |
| .60 | 38.56 | .21 | 61.84 | .25 | 88.93 | .29 | 118.66 | .31 | 149.69 | .31 | 180.64 | .31 | .40 |
| .61 | 38.77 | .21 | 62.09 | .26 | 89.22 | .28 | 118.97 | .30 | 150.00 | .31 | 180.95 | .30 | .39 |
| .62 | 38.98 | .21 | 62.35 | .25 | 89.50 | .29 | 119.27 | .31 | 150.31 | .31 | 181.25 | .31 | .38 |
| .63 | 39.19 | .21 | 62.60 | .25 | 89.79 | .29 | 119.58 | .30 | 150.62 | .32 | 181.56 | .30 | .37 |
| .64 | 39.40 | .22 | 62.85 | .26 | 90.08 | .29 | 119.88 | .31 | 150.94 | .31 | 181.86 | .31 | .36 |
| .65 | 39.62 | .21 | 63.11 | .25 | 90.37 | .28 | 120.19 | .30 | 151.25 | .31 | 182.17 | .30 | .35 |
| .66 | 39.83 | .21 | 63.36 | .26 | 90.65 | .29 | 120.49 | .31 | 151.56 | .31 | 182.47 | .30 | .34 |
| .67 | 40.04 | .21 | 63.62 | .26 | 90.94 | .29 | 120.80 | .30 | 151.87 | .31 | 182.77 | .31 | .33 |
| .68 | 40.25 | .22 | 63.88 | .25 | 91.23 | .29 | 121.10 | .31 | 152.18 | .32 | 183.08 | .30 | .32 |
| .69 | 40.47 | .21 | 64.13 | .26 | 91.52 | .29 | 121.41 | .31 | 152.50 | .31 | 183.38 | .30 | .31 |
| .70 | 40.68 | .21 | 64.39 | .26 | 91.81 | .29 | 121.72 | .30 | 152.81 | .31 | 183.68 | .30 | .30 |
| .71 | 40.89 | .22 | 64.65 | .26 | 92.10 | .29 | 122.03 | .30 | 153.12 | .31 | 183.98 | .30 | .29 |
| .72 | 41.11 | .21 | 64.91 | .25 | 92.39 | .29 | 122.33 | .31 | 153.43 | .31 | 184.28 | .31 | .28 |
| .73 | 41.32 | .22 | 65.16 | .26 | 92.68 | .29 | 122.64 | .31 | 153.74 | .32 | 184.59 | .30 | .27 |
| .74 | 41.54 | .22 | 65.42 | .26 | 92.97 | .29 | 122.95 | .31 | 154.06 | .31 | 184.89 | .30 | .26 |
| .75 | 41.76 | .21 | 65.68 | .26 | 93.26 | .29 | 123.26 | .31 | 154.37 | .31 | 185.19 | .30 | .25 |
| .76 | 41.97 | .22 | 65.94 | .26 | 93.55 | .29 | 123.57 | .30 | 154.68 | .31 | 185.49 | .30 | .24 |
| .77 | 42.19 | .22 | 66.20 | .26 | 93.84 | .29 | 123.87 | .31 | 154.99 | .31 | 185.79 | .31 | .23 |
| .78 | 42.41 | .22 | 66.46 | .26 | 94.13 | .29 | 124.18 | .31 | 155.30 | .32 | 186.10 | .30 | .22 |
| .79 | 42.63 | .22 | 66.72 | .26 | 94.42 | .29 | 124.49 | .31 | 155.62 | .31 | 186.40 | .30 | .21 |
| .80 | 42.85 | .22 | 66.98 | .26 | 94.71 | .29 | 124.80 | .31 | 155.93 | .31 | 186.70 | .30 | .20 |
| .81 | 43.07 | .22 | 67.24 | .26 | 95.00 | .29 | 125.11 | .31 | 156.24 | .31 | 187.00 | .30 | .19 |
| .82 | 43.29 | .22 | 67.50 | .26 | 95.29 | .29 | 125.42 | .31 | 156.55 | .31 | 187.30 | .30 | .18 |
| .83 | 43.51 | .22 | 67.76 | .27 | 95.58 | .29 | 125.73 | .30 | 156.86 | .31 | 187.60 | .30 | .17 |
| .84 | 43.73 | .23 | 68.03 | .26 | 95.87 | .29 | 126.03 | .31 | 157.17 | .32 | 187.90 | .30 | .16 |
| .85 | 43.96 | .22 | 68.29 | .26 | 96.16 | .30 | 126.34 | .31 | 157.49 | .31 | 188.20 | .30 | .15 |
| .86 | 44.18 | .22 | 68.55 | .27 | 96.46 | .29 | 126.65 | .31 | 157.80 | .31 | 188.50 | .30 | .14 |
| .87 | 44.40 | .22 | 68.82 | .26 | 96.75 | .29 | 126.96 | .31 | 158.11 | .31 | 188.80 | .30 | .13 |
| .88 | 44.62 | .23 | 69.08 | .26 | 97.04 | .30 | 127.27 | .31 | 158.42 | .31 | 189.10 | .30 | .12 |
| .89 | 44.85 | .22 | 69.34 | .27 | 97.34 | .29 | 127.58 | .31 | 158.73 | .31 | 189.40 | .30 | .11 |
| .90 | 45.07 | .22 | 69.61 | .27 | 97.63 | .29 | 127.89 | .31 | 159.04 | .31 | 189.70 | .30 | .10 |
| .91 | 45.29 | .22 | 69.88 | .26 | 97.92 | .30 | 128.20 | .31 | 159.35 | .31 | 190.00 | .30 | .09 |
| .92 | 45.51 | .23 | 70.14 | .27 | 98.22 | .29 | 128.51 | .31 | 159.66 | .32 | 190.30 | .30 | .08 |
| .93 | 45.74 | .22 | 70.41 | .27 | 98.51 | .30 | 128.82 | .31 | 159.98 | .31 | 190.60 | .30 | .07 |
| .94 | 45.96 | .23 | 70.68 | .26 | 98.81 | .29 | 129.13 | .31 | 160.29 | .31 | 190.90 | .30 | .06 |
| .95 | 46.19 | .22 | 70.94 | .27 | 99.10 | .30 | 129.44 | .31 | 160.60 | .31 | 191.20 | .29 | .05 |
| .96 | 46.41 | .23 | 71.21 | .27 | 99.40 | .29 | 129.75 | .31 | 160.91 | .31 | 191.49 | .30 | .04 |
| .97 | 46.64 | .23 | 71.48 | .26 | 99.69 | .30 | 130.06 | .31 | 161.22 | .31 | 191.79 | .30 | .03 |
| .98 | 46.87 | .23 | 71.74 | .27 | 99.99 | .29 | 130.37 | .31 | 161.53 | .31 | 192.09 | .30 | .02 |
| .99 | 47.10 | .23 | 72.01 | .27 | 100.28 | .30 | 130.68 | .31 | 161.84 | .31 | 192.39 | .30 | .01 |
| 1.00 | 47.33 | .23 | 72.28 | .27 | 100.58 | .29 | 130.99 | .31 | 162.15 | .31 | 192.69 | .30 | .00 |
| Days. | 26 | | 25 | | 24 | | 23 | | 22 | | 21 | | Days. |

# TABLE XIV ARGUMENT 9.

Equation = 148″.1 [1 + sin. $(x - z)$]

Period, 29.802826 days.

| Days. | 9 | | 10 | | 11 | | 12 | | 13 | | 14 | | Days. |
|---|---|---|---|---|---|---|---|---|---|---|---|---|---|
| Decimals of a Day. | Equation. | Diff. | Equation. | Diff. | Equation. | Diff. | Equation. | Diff. | Equation. | Diff. | Equation. | Diff. | Decimals of a Day. |
| .00 | 192.69″ | .30 | 221.26″ | .27 | 246.59″ | .23 | 267.56″ | .18 | 283.23″ | .13 | 292.92″ | .06 | 1.00 |
| .01 | 192.99 | .29 | 221.53 | .27 | 246.82 | .24 | 267.74 | .19 | 283.36 | .13 | 292.98 | .07 | .99 |
| .02 | 193.28 | .30 | 221.80 | .27 | 247.06 | .23 | 267.93 | .18 | 283.49 | .13 | 293.05 | .06 | .98 |
| .03 | 193.58 | .30 | 222.07 | .27 | 247.29 | .23 | 268.11 | .18 | 283.62 | .12 | 293.11 | .06 | .97 |
| .04 | 193.88 | .29 | 222.34 | .27 | 247.52 | .23 | 268.29 | .18 | 283.74 | .13 | 293.17 | .07 | .96 |
| .05 | 194.17 | .30 | 222.61 | .27 | 247.75 | .23 | 268.47 | .19 | 283.87 | .12 | 293.24 | .06 | .95 |
| .06 | 194.47 | .30 | 222.88 | .27 | 247.98 | .23 | 268.66 | .18 | 283.99 | .13 | 293.30 | .06 | .94 |
| .07 | 194.77 | .29 | 223.15 | .27 | 248.21 | .23 | 268.84 | .18 | 284.12 | .12 | 293.36 | .06 | .93 |
| .08 | 195.06 | .30 | 223.42 | .27 | 248.44 | .23 | 269.02 | .18 | 284.24 | .12 | 293.42 | .06 | .92 |
| .09 | 195.36 | .30 | 223.69 | .27 | 248.67 | .23 | 269.20 | .18 | 284.36 | .12 | 293.48 | .06 | .91 |
| .10 | 195.66 | .30 | 223.96 | .27 | 248.90 | .23 | 269.38 | .18 | 284.48 | .12 | 293.54 | .06 | .90 |
| .11 | 195.96 | .29 | 224.23 | .27 | 249.13 | .23 | 269.56 | .18 | 284.60 | .12 | 293.60 | .06 | .89 |
| .12 | 196.25 | .30 | 224.50 | .26 | 249.36 | .22 | 269.74 | .18 | 284.72 | .12 | 293.66 | .06 | .88 |
| .13 | 196.55 | .29 | 224.76 | .27 | 249.58 | .23 | 269.92 | .17 | 284.84 | .12 | 293.72 | .05 | .87 |
| .14 | 196.84 | .30 | 225.03 | .27 | 249.81 | .23 | 270.09 | .18 | 284.96 | .12 | 293.77 | .06 | .86 |
| .15 | 197.14 | .29 | 225.30 | .26 | 250.04 | .22 | 270.27 | .18 | 285.08 | .12 | 293.83 | .06 | .85 |
| .16 | 197.43 | .30 | 225.56 | .27 | 250.26 | .23 | 270.45 | .17 | 285.20 | .12 | 293.89 | .05 | .84 |
| .17 | 197.73 | .29 | 225.83 | .27 | 250.49 | .22 | 270.62 | .18 | 285.32 | .11 | 293.94 | .06 | .83 |
| .18 | 198.02 | .30 | 226.10 | .26 | 250.71 | .23 | 270.80 | .17 | 285.43 | .12 | 294.00 | .05 | .82 |
| .19 | 198.32 | .29 | 226.36 | .27 | 250.94 | .22 | 270.97 | .17 | 285.55 | .12 | 294.05 | .05 | .81 |
| .20 | 198.61 | .29 | 226.63 | .26 | 251.16 | .22 | 271.14 | .17 | 285.67 | .11 | 294.10 | .05 | .80 |
| .21 | 198.90 | .30 | 226.89 | .27 | 251.38 | .23 | 271.31 | .17 | 285.78 | .12 | 294.15 | .05 | .79 |
| .22 | 199.20 | .29 | 227.16 | .26 | 251.61 | .22 | 271.48 | .18 | 285.90 | .11 | 294.20 | .05 | .78 |
| .23 | 199.49 | .29 | 227.42 | .26 | 251.83 | .22 | 271.66 | .17 | 286.01 | .12 | 294.25 | .05 | .77 |
| .24 | 199.78 | .30 | 227.68 | .27 | 252.05 | .22 | 271.83 | .17 | 286.13 | .11 | 294.30 | .05 | .76 |
| .25 | 200.08 | .29 | 227.95 | .26 | 252.27 | .23 | 272.00 | .17 | 286.24 | .11 | 294.35 | .05 | .75 |
| .26 | 200.37 | .29 | 228.21 | .26 | 252.50 | .22 | 272.17 | .17 | 286.35 | .12 | 294.40 | .05 | .74 |
| .27 | 200.66 | .29 | 228.47 | .27 | 252.72 | .22 | 272.34 | .17 | 286.47 | .11 | 294.45 | .05 | .73 |
| .28 | 200.95 | .29 | 228.74 | .26 | 252.94 | .22 | 272.51 | .17 | 286.58 | .11 | 294.50 | .04 | .72 |
| .29 | 201.24 | .29 | 229.00 | .26 | 253.16 | .22 | 272.68 | .17 | 286.69 | .11 | 294.54 | .05 | .71 |
| .30 | 201.53 | .29 | 229.26 | .26 | 253.38 | .22 | 272.85 | .17 | 286.80 | .11 | 294.59 | .05 | .70 |
| .31 | 201.82 | .29 | 229.52 | .26 | 253.60 | .22 | 273.02 | .17 | 286.91 | .11 | 294.64 | .04 | .69 |
| .32 | 202.11 | .29 | 229.78 | .26 | 253.82 | .22 | 273.19 | .17 | 287.02 | .11 | 294.68 | .05 | .68 |
| .33 | 202.40 | .29 | 230.04 | .26 | 254.04 | .21 | 273.36 | .16 | 287.13 | .10 | 294.73 | .04 | .67 |
| .34 | 202.69 | .29 | 230.30 | .26 | 254.25 | .22 | 273.52 | .17 | 287.23 | .11 | 294.77 | .04 | .66 |
| .35 | 202.98 | .29 | 230.56 | .26 | 254.47 | .22 | 273.69 | .16 | 287.34 | .11 | 294.81 | .05 | .65 |
| .36 | 203.27 | .29 | 230.82 | .26 | 254.69 | .21 | 273.85 | .17 | 287.45 | .10 | 294.86 | .04 | .64 |
| .37 | 203.56 | .29 | 231.08 | .25 | 254.90 | .22 | 274.02 | .16 | 287.55 | .11 | 294.90 | .04 | .63 |
| .38 | 203.85 | .29 | 231.33 | .26 | 255.12 | .21 | 274.18 | .16 | 287.66 | .10 | 294.94 | .04 | .62 |
| .39 | 204.14 | .29 | 231.59 | .26 | 255.33 | .22 | 274.34 | .16 | 287.76 | .10 | 294.98 | .04 | .61 |
| .40 | 204.43 | .29 | 231.85 | .26 | 255.55 | .21 | 274.50 | .16 | 287.86 | .10 | 295.02 | .04 | .60 |
| .41 | 204.72 | .29 | 232.11 | .25 | 255.76 | .21 | 274.66 | .16 | 287.96 | .10 | 295.06 | .04 | .59 |
| .42 | 205.01 | .29 | 232.36 | .26 | 255.97 | .22 | 274.82 | .16 | 288.06 | .10 | 295.10 | .04 | .58 |
| .43 | 205.30 | .28 | 232.62 | .25 | 256.19 | .21 | 274.98 | .16 | 288.16 | .10 | 295.14 | .03 | .57 |
| .44 | 205.58 | .29 | 232.87 | .26 | 256.40 | .21 | 275.14 | .16 | 288.26 | .10 | 295.17 | .04 | .56 |
| .45 | 205.87 | .29 | 233.13 | .25 | 256.61 | .21 | 275.30 | .16 | 288.36 | .10 | 295.21 | .04 | .55 |
| .46 | 206.16 | .29 | 233.38 | .26 | 256.82 | .22 | 275.46 | .16 | 288.46 | .10 | 295.25 | .03 | .54 |
| .47 | 206.45 | .28 | 233.64 | .25 | 257.04 | .21 | 275.62 | .16 | 288.56 | .10 | 295.28 | .04 | .53 |
| .48 | 206.73 | .29 | 233.89 | .26 | 257.25 | .21 | 275.78 | .16 | 288.66 | .10 | 295.32 | .03 | .52 |
| .49 | 207.02 | .29 | 234.15 | .25 | 257.46 | .21 | 275.94 | .16 | 288.76 | .10 | 295.35 | .03 | .51 |
| .50 | 207.31 | .29 | 234.40 | .25 | 257.67 | .21 | 276.10 | .16 | 288.86 | .10 | 295.38 | .03 | .50 |
| Days. | 20 | | 19 | | 18 | | 17 | | 16 | | 15 | | Days. |

# TABLE XIV. ARGUMENT 9.

Equation = 148″.1 [1 + sin. $(x - z)$].

Period, 29.802826 days.

| Days. | 9 | | 10 | | 11 | | 12 | | 13 | | 14 | | Days. |
|---|---|---|---|---|---|---|---|---|---|---|---|---|---|
| Decimals of a Day. | Equation. | Diff. | Equation. | Diff. | Equation. | Diff. | Equation. | Diff. | Equation. | Diff. | Equation. | Diff. | Decimals of a Day. |
| .50 | 207″.31 | .29 | 234″.40 | .25 | 257″.67 | .21 | 276″.10 | .16 | 288″.86 | .10 | 295″.38 | .03 | .50 |
| .51 | 207.60 | .28 | 234.65 | .26 | 257.88 | .21 | 276.26 | .16 | 288.96 | .10 | 295.41 | .03 | .49 |
| .52 | 207.88 | .29 | 234.91 | .25 | 258.09 | .21 | 276.42 | .15 | 289.06 | .09 | 295.44 | .03 | .48 |
| .53 | 208.17 | .28 | 235.16 | .25 | 258.30 | .21 | 276.57 | .16 | 289.15 | .09 | 295.47 | .03 | .47 |
| .54 | 208.45 | .29 | 235.41 | .25 | 258.51 | .20 | 276.73 | .15 | 289.24 | .10 | 295.50 | .03 | .46 |
| .55 | 208.74 | .28 | 235.66 | .26 | 258.71 | .21 | 276.88 | .15 | 289.34 | .09 | 295.53 | .03 | .45 |
| .56 | 209.02 | .29 | 235.92 | .25 | 258.92 | .21 | 277.04 | .15 | 289.43 | .10 | 295.56 | .03 | .44 |
| .57 | 209.31 | .28 | 236.17 | .25 | 259.13 | .21 | 277.19 | .15 | 289.53 | .09 | 295.59 | .03 | .43 |
| .58 | 209.59 | .29 | 236.42 | .25 | 259.34 | .20 | 277.34 | .15 | 289.62 | .09 | 295.62 | .03 | .42 |
| .59 | 209.88 | .28 | 236.67 | .25 | 259.54 | .21 | 277.49 | .15 | 289.71 | .09 | 295.65 | .03 | .41 |
| .60 | 210.16 | .28 | 236.92 | .25 | 259.75 | .21 | 277.64 | .15 | 289.80 | .09 | 295.68 | .03 | .40 |
| .61 | 210.44 | .29 | 237.17 | .25 | 259.96 | .20 | 277.79 | .15 | 289.89 | .09 | 295.71 | .02 | .39 |
| .62 | 210.73 | .28 | 237.42 | .25 | 260.16 | .21 | 277.94 | .15 | 289.98 | .09 | 295.73 | .03 | .38 |
| .63 | 211.01 | .28 | 237.67 | .25 | 260.37 | .20 | 278.09 | .15 | 290.07 | .09 | 295.76 | .02 | .37 |
| .64 | 211.29 | .28 | 237.92 | .24 | 260.57 | .21 | 278.24 | .15 | 290.16 | .09 | 295.78 | .02 | .36 |
| .65 | 211.57 | .29 | 238.16 | .25 | 260.78 | .20 | 278.39 | .15 | 290.25 | .08 | 295.80 | .03 | .35 |
| .66 | 211.86 | .28 | 238.41 | .25 | 260.98 | .20 | 278.54 | .15 | 290.33 | .09 | 295.83 | .02 | .34 |
| .67 | 212.14 | .28 | 238.66 | .25 | 261.18 | .20 | 278.69 | .14 | 290.42 | .09 | 295.85 | .02 | .33 |
| .68 | 212.42 | .28 | 238.91 | .24 | 261.38 | .20 | 278.83 | .15 | 290.51 | .08 | 295.87 | .02 | .32 |
| .69 | 212.70 | .28 | 239.15 | .25 | 261.58 | .20 | 278.98 | .15 | 290.59 | .09 | 295.89 | .02 | .31 |
| .70 | 212.98 | .28 | 239.40 | .25 | 261.78 | .20 | 279.13 | .15 | 290.68 | .08 | 295.91 | .02 | .30 |
| .71 | 213.26 | .28 | 239.65 | .24 | 261.98 | .20 | 279.28 | .14 | 290.76 | .08 | 295.93 | .02 | .29 |
| .72 | 213.54 | .28 | 239.89 | .25 | 262.18 | .20 | 279.42 | .15 | 290.84 | .09 | 295.95 | .02 | .28 |
| .73 | 213.82 | .28 | 240.14 | .25 | 262.38 | .20 | 279.57 | .15 | 290.93 | .08 | 295.97 | .02 | .27 |
| .74 | 214.10 | .28 | 240.39 | .24 | 262.58 | .20 | 279.72 | .14 | 291.01 | .08 | 295.99 | .01 | .26 |
| .75 | 214.38 | .28 | 240.63 | .25 | 262.78 | .19 | 279.86 | .14 | 291.09 | .08 | 296.00 | .02 | .25 |
| .76 | 214.66 | .27 | 240.88 | .24 | 262.97 | .20 | 280.00 | .14 | 291.17 | .08 | 296.02 | .01 | .24 |
| .77 | 214.93 | .28 | 241.12 | .24 | 263.17 | .20 | 280.14 | .14 | 291.25 | .08 | 296.03 | .02 | .23 |
| .78 | 215.21 | .28 | 241.36 | .24 | 263.37 | .19 | 280.28 | .14 | 291.33 | .08 | 296.05 | .01 | .22 |
| .79 | 215.49 | .28 | 241.60 | .24 | 263.56 | .20 | 280.42 | .14 | 291.41 | .08 | 296.06 | .01 | .21 |
| .80 | 215.77 | .28 | 241.84 | .24 | 263.76 | .20 | 280.56 | .14 | 291.49 | .08 | 296.07 | .01 | .20 |
| .81 | 216.05 | .27 | 242.08 | .24 | 263.96 | .19 | 280.70 | .14 | 291.57 | .08 | 296.08 | .01 | .19 |
| .82 | 216.32 | .28 | 242.32 | .24 | 264.15 | .20 | 280.84 | .14 | 291.65 | .07 | 296.09 | .01 | .18 |
| .83 | 216.60 | .28 | 242.56 | .24 | 264.35 | .19 | 280.98 | .14 | 291.72 | .08 | 296.10 | .01 | .17 |
| .84 | 216.88 | .27 | 242.80 | .24 | 264.54 | .19 | 281.12 | .13 | 291.80 | .08 | 296.11 | .01 | .16 |
| .85 | 217.15 | .28 | 243.04 | .24 | 264.73 | .20 | 281.25 | .14 | 291.88 | .07 | 296.12 | .01 | .15 |
| .86 | 217.43 | .27 | 243.28 | .24 | 264.93 | .19 | 281.39 | .13 | 291.95 | .08 | 296.13 | .01 | .14 |
| .87 | 217.70 | .28 | 243.52 | .24 | 265.12 | .19 | 281.52 | .14 | 292.03 | .07 | 296.14 | .00 | .13 |
| .88 | 217.98 | .27 | 243.76 | .24 | 265.31 | .19 | 281.66 | .13 | 292.10 | .07 | 296.14 | .01 | .12 |
| .89 | 218.25 | .28 | 244.00 | .24 | 265.50 | .19 | 281.79 | .13 | 292.17 | .07 | 296.15 | .01 | .11 |
| .90 | 218.53 | .27 | 244.24 | .24 | 265.69 | .19 | 281.92 | .13 | 292.24 | .07 | 296.16 | .00 | .10 |
| .91 | 218.80 | .28 | 244.48 | .24 | 265.88 | .19 | 282.05 | .13 | 292.31 | .07 | 296.16 | .01 | .09 |
| .92 | 219.08 | .27 | 244.72 | .23 | 266.07 | .19 | 282.18 | .14 | 292.38 | .07 | 296.17 | .01 | .08 |
| .93 | 219.35 | .27 | 244.95 | .24 | 266.26 | .19 | 282.32 | .13 | 292.45 | .07 | 296.18 | .00 | .07 |
| .94 | 219.62 | .28 | 245.19 | .23 | 266.45 | .19 | 282.45 | .13 | 292.52 | .07 | 296.18 | .01 | .06 |
| .95 | 219.90 | .27 | 245.42 | .24 | 266.64 | .19 | 282.58 | .13 | 292.59 | .07 | 296.19 | .00 | .05 |
| .96 | 220.17 | .27 | 245.66 | .23 | 266.83 | .18 | 282.71 | .13 | 292.66 | .06 | 296.19 | .01 | .04 |
| .97 | 220.44 | .28 | 245.89 | .24 | 267.01 | .18 | 282.84 | .13 | 292.72 | .07 | 296.20 | .00 | .03 |
| .98 | 220.72 | .27 | 246.13 | .23 | 267.19 | .19 | 282.97 | .13 | 292.79 | .07 | 296.20 | .00 | .02 |
| .99 | 220.99 | .27 | 246.36 | .23 | 267.38 | .18 | 283.10 | .13 | 292.86 | .06 | 296.20 | .00 | .01 |
| 1.00 | 221.26 | .27 | 246.59 | .23 | 267.56 | .18 | 283.23 | .13 | 292.92 | .06 | 296.20 | .00 | .00 |
| Days. | 20 | | 19 | | 18 | | 17 | | 16 | | 15 | | Days. |

# TABLE XV. ARGUMENT 10.

Equation = 110″.0 [1 — sin. $(x+z)$].

Period, 25.621696 days.

| Days. | 0 | | 1 | | 2 | | 3 | | 4 | | 5 | | Days. |
|---|---|---|---|---|---|---|---|---|---|---|---|---|---|
| Decimals of a Day | Equation. | Diff. | Equation. | Diff. | Equation. | Diff. | Equation. | Diff. | Equation. | Diff. | Equation. | Diff. | Decimals of a Day. |
| .00 | 219.88″ | .01 | 217.84″ | .05 | 209.32″ | .12 | 194.88″ | .17 | 175.36″ | .22 | 151.92″ | .25 | 1.00 |
| .01 | 219.89 | .01 | 217.79 | .06 | 209.20 | .11 | 194.71 | .17 | 175.14 | .22 | 151.67 | .25 | .99 |
| .02 | 219.90 | .01 | 217.73 | .05 | 209.09 | .12 | 194.54 | .17 | 174.92 | .22 | 151.42 | .25 | .98 |
| .03 | 219.91 | .01 | 217.68 | .06 | 208.97 | .12 | 194.37 | .17 | 174.70 | .21 | 151.17 | .25 | .97 |
| .04 | 219.92 | .01 | 217.62 | .06 | 208.85 | .12 | 194.20 | .18 | 174.49 | .22 | 150.92 | .25 | .96 |
| .05 | 219.93 | .01 | 217.56 | .05 | 208.73 | .12 | 194.02 | .17 | 174.27 | .22 | 150.67 | .25 | .95 |
| .06 | 219.94 | .01 | 217.51 | .06 | 208.61 | .12 | 193.85 | .18 | 174.05 | .22 | 150.42 | .26 | .94 |
| .07 | 219.95 | .01 | 217.45 | .06 | 208.49 | .12 | 193.67 | .18 | 173.83 | .22 | 150.16 | .25 | .93 |
| .08 | 219.96 | .01 | 217.39 | .06 | 208.37 | .12 | 193.49 | .18 | 173.61 | .22 | 149.91 | .25 | .92 |
| .09 | 219.97 | .01 | 217.33 | .06 | 208.25 | .12 | 193.31 | .18 | 173.39 | .22 | 149.66 | .25 | .91 |
| .10 | 219.98 | .00 | 217.27 | .06 | 208.13 | .12 | 193.13 | .17 | 173.17 | .22 | 149.41 | .25 | .90 |
| .11 | 219.98 | .01 | 217.21 | .06 | 208.01 | .12 | 192.96 | .18 | 172.95 | .22 | 149.16 | .26 | .89 |
| .12 | 219.99 | .00 | 217.15 | .06 | 207.89 | .12 | 192.78 | .18 | 172.73 | .23 | 148.90 | .25 | .88 |
| .13 | 219.99 | .00 | 217.09 | .06 | 207.77 | .12 | 192.60 | .18 | 172.50 | .22 | 148.65 | .25 | .87 |
| .14 | 219.99 | .01 | 217.03 | .07 | 207.65 | .13 | 192.42 | .18 | 172.28 | .22 | 148.40 | .26 | .86 |
| .15 | 220.00 | .00 | 216.96 | .06 | 207.52 | .12 | 192.24 | .18 | 172.06 | .23 | 148.14 | .25 | .85 |
| .16 | 220.00 | .00 | 216.90 | .06 | 207.40 | .13 | 192.06 | .18 | 171.83 | .22 | 147.89 | .25 | .84 |
| .17 | 220.00 | .00 | 216.84 | .07 | 207.27 | .12 | 191.88 | .18 | 171.61 | .22 | 147.64 | .26 | .83 |
| .18 | 220.00 | .00 | 216.77 | .06 | 207.15 | .13 | 191.70 | .18 | 171.39 | .23 | 147.38 | .25 | .82 |
| .19 | 220.00 | .00 | 216.71 | .07 | 207.02 | .13 | 191.52 | .18 | 171.16 | .22 | 147.13 | .25 | .81 |
| .20 | 220.00 | .00 | 216.64 | .07 | 206.89 | .13 | 191.34 | .18 | 170.94 | .22 | 146.88 | .26 | .80 |
| .21 | 220.00 | .00 | 216.57 | .07 | 206.76 | .13 | 191.16 | .18 | 170.72 | .23 | 146.62 | .25 | .79 |
| .22 | 220.00 | .00 | 216.50 | .07 | 206.63 | .13 | 190.98 | .18 | 170.49 | .22 | 146.37 | .25 | .78 |
| .23 | 220.00 | .00 | 216.43 | .07 | 206.50 | .13 | 190.80 | .18 | 170.27 | .23 | 146.12 | .26 | .77 |
| .24 | 220.00 | .01 | 216.36 | .07 | 206.37 | .13 | 190.62 | .19 | 170.04 | .22 | 145.86 | .25 | .76 |
| .25 | 219.99 | .00 | 216.29 | .07 | 206.24 | .13 | 190.43 | .18 | 169.82 | .23 | 145.61 | .25 | .75 |
| .26 | 219.99 | .01 | 216.22 | .07 | 206.11 | .13 | 190.25 | .18 | 169.59 | .23 | 145.36 | .26 | .74 |
| .27 | 219.98 | .00 | 216.15 | .07 | 205.98 | .13 | 190.07 | .19 | 169.36 | .22 | 145.10 | .25 | .73 |
| .28 | 219.98 | .01 | 216.08 | .07 | 205.85 | .13 | 189.88 | .18 | 169.14 | .23 | 144.85 | .26 | .72 |
| .29 | 219.97 | .01 | 216.01 | .07 | 205.72 | .13 | 189.70 | .19 | 168.91 | .23 | 144.59 | .25 | .71 |
| .30 | 219.96 | .01 | 215.94 | .07 | 205.59 | .13 | 189.51 | .18 | 168.68 | .23 | 144.34 | .26 | .70 |
| .31 | 219.95 | .01 | 215.87 | .07 | 205.46 | .13 | 189.33 | .19 | 168.45 | .23 | 144.08 | .25 | .69 |
| .32 | 219.94 | .01 | 215.80 | .08 | 205.33 | .14 | 189.14 | .19 | 168.22 | .23 | 143.83 | .26 | .68 |
| .33 | 219.93 | .01 | 215.72 | .07 | 205.19 | .13 | 188.95 | .18 | 167.99 | .23 | 143.57 | .26 | .67 |
| .34 | 219.92 | .01 | 215.65 | .08 | 205.06 | .14 | 188.77 | .19 | 167.76 | .23 | 143.31 | .25 | .66 |
| .35 | 219.91 | .01 | 215.57 | .07 | 204.92 | .13 | 188.58 | .19 | 167.53 | .23 | 143.06 | .26 | .65 |
| .36 | 219.90 | .01 | 215.50 | .08 | 204.79 | .14 | 188.39 | .19 | 167.30 | .23 | 142.80 | .26 | .64 |
| .37 | 219.89 | .01 | 215.42 | .08 | 204.65 | .14 | 188.20 | .19 | 167.07 | .23 | 142.54 | .25 | .63 |
| .38 | 219.88 | .02 | 215.34 | .08 | 204.51 | .14 | 188.01 | .19 | 166.84 | .23 | 142.29 | .26 | .62 |
| .39 | 219.86 | .01 | 215.26 | .08 | 204.37 | .14 | 187.82 | .19 | 166.61 | .23 | 142.03 | .26 | .61 |
| .40 | 219.85 | .02 | 215.18 | .08 | 204.23 | .14 | 187.63 | .19 | 166.38 | .23 | 141.77 | .26 | .60 |
| .41 | 219.83 | .01 | 215.10 | .08 | 204.09 | .14 | 187.44 | .19 | 166.15 | .23 | 141.51 | .26 | .59 |
| .42 | 219.82 | .02 | 215.02 | .08 | 203.95 | .14 | 187.25 | .19 | 165.92 | .24 | 141.25 | .25 | .58 |
| .43 | 219.80 | .01 | 214.94 | .08 | 203.81 | .14 | 187.06 | .20 | 165.68 | .23 | 141.00 | .26 | .57 |
| .44 | 219.79 | .02 | 214.86 | .08 | 203.67 | .14 | 186.86 | .19 | 165.45 | .23 | 140.74 | .26 | .56 |
| .45 | 219.77 | .01 | 214.78 | .08 | 203.53 | .14 | 186.67 | .19 | 165.22 | .24 | 140.48 | .26 | .55 |
| .46 | 219.76 | .02 | 214.70 | .09 | 203.39 | .15 | 186.48 | .20 | 164.98 | .23 | 140.22 | .26 | .54 |
| .47 | 219.74 | .02 | 214.61 | .08 | 203.24 | .14 | 186.28 | .19 | 164.75 | .23 | 139.96 | .26 | .53 |
| .48 | 219.72 | .02 | 214.53 | .09 | 203.10 | .15 | 186.09 | .20 | 164.52 | .24 | 139.70 | .26 | .52 |
| .49 | 219.70 | .02 | 214.44 | .08 | 202.95 | .14 | 185.89 | .19 | 164.28 | .23 | 139.44 | .26 | .51 |
| .50 | 219.68 | .02 | 214.36 | .09 | 202.81 | .15 | 185.70 | .20 | 164.05 | .24 | 139.18 | .26 | .50 |
| Days. | 25 | | 24 | | 23 | | 22 | | 21 | | 20 | | Days. |

# TABLE XV. ARGUMENT 10.

Equation $= 110''.0\ [1 - \sin.\ (x + z)]$.

Period, 25.621696 days.

| Days. | 0 | | 1 | | 2 | | 3 | | 4 | | 5 | | Days. |
|---|---|---|---|---|---|---|---|---|---|---|---|---|---|
| Decimals of a Day | Equation. | Diff. | Equation. | Diff. | Equation. | Diff. | Equation. | Diff. | Equation. | Diff. | Equation. | Diff. | Decimals of a Day. |
| .50 | 219.68 | .02 | 214.36 | .09 | 202.81 | .15 | 185.70 | .20 | 164.05 | .24 | 139.18 | .26 | .50 |
| .51 | 219.66 | .02 | 214.27 | .08 | 202.66 | .14 | 185.50 | .19 | 163.81 | .23 | 138.92 | .26 | .49 |
| .52 | 219.64 | .02 | 214.19 | .09 | 202.52 | .15 | 185.31 | .20 | 163.58 | .24 | 138.66 | .26 | .48 |
| .53 | 219.62 | .02 | 214.10 | .09 | 202.37 | .14 | 185.11 | .20 | 163.34 | .24 | 138.40 | .26 | .47 |
| .54 | 219.60 | .03 | 214.01 | .08 | 202.23 | .15 | 184.91 | .19 | 163.10 | .23 | 138.14 | .26 | .46 |
| .55 | 219.57 | .02 | 213.93 | .09 | 202.08 | .15 | 184.72 | .20 | 162.87 | .24 | 137.88 | .26 | .45 |
| .56 | 219.55 | .03 | 213.84 | .09 | 201.93 | .15 | 184.52 | .20 | 162.63 | .24 | 137.62 | .26 | .44 |
| .57 | 219.52 | .02 | 213.75 | .09 | 201.78 | .15 | 184.32 | .20 | 162.39 | .23 | 137.36 | .27 | .43 |
| .58 | 219.50 | .03 | 213.66 | .09 | 201.63 | .15 | 184.12 | .20 | 162.16 | .24 | 137.09 | .26 | .42 |
| .59 | 219.47 | .03 | 213.57 | .09 | 201.48 | .15 | 183.92 | .20 | 161.92 | .24 | 136.83 | .26 | .41 |
| .60 | 219.44 | .03 | 213.48 | .09 | 201.33 | .15 | 183.72 | .20 | 161.68 | .24 | 136.57 | .26 | .40 |
| .61 | 219.41 | .03 | 213.39 | .09 | 201.18 | .15 | 183.52 | .20 | 161.44 | .24 | 136.31 | .27 | .39 |
| .62 | 219.38 | .03 | 213.30 | .09 | 201.03 | .15 | 183.32 | .20 | 161.20 | .24 | 136.04 | .26 | .38 |
| .63 | 219.35 | .03 | 213.21 | .09 | 200.88 | .15 | 183.12 | .21 | 160.96 | .24 | 135.78 | .26 | .37 |
| .64 | 219.32 | .03 | 213.12 | .10 | 200.73 | .15 | 182.91 | .20 | 160.72 | .24 | 135.52 | .27 | .36 |
| .65 | 219.29 | .03 | 213.02 | .09 | 200.58 | .16 | 182.71 | .20 | 160.48 | .24 | 135.25 | .26 | .35 |
| .66 | 219.26 | .03 | 212.93 | .10 | 200.42 | .15 | 182.51 | .21 | 160.24 | .24 | 134.99 | .26 | .34 |
| .67 | 219.23 | .03 | 212.83 | .09 | 200.27 | .16 | 182.30 | .20 | 160.00 | .24 | 134.73 | .27 | .33 |
| .68 | 219.20 | .03 | 212.74 | .10 | 200.11 | .15 | 182.10 | .21 | 159.76 | .24 | 134.46 | .26 | .32 |
| .69 | 219.17 | .03 | 212.64 | .10 | 199.96 | .16 | 181.89 | .20 | 159.52 | .24 | 134.20 | .26 | .31 |
| .70 | 219.14 | .04 | 212.54 | .10 | 199.80 | .16 | 181.69 | .21 | 159.28 | .24 | 133.94 | .27 | .30 |
| .71 | 219.10 | .03 | 212.44 | .10 | 199.64 | .15 | 181.48 | .20 | 159.04 | .24 | 133.67 | .26 | .29 |
| .72 | 219.07 | .04 | 212.34 | .10 | 199.49 | .16 | 181.28 | .21 | 158.80 | .24 | 133.41 | .27 | .28 |
| .73 | 219.03 | .03 | 212.24 | .10 | 199.33 | .16 | 181.07 | .21 | 158.56 | .24 | 133.14 | .26 | .27 |
| .74 | 219.00 | .04 | 212.14 | .10 | 199.17 | .15 | 180.86 | .20 | 158.32 | .25 | 132.88 | .27 | .26 |
| .75 | 218.96 | .03 | 212.04 | .10 | 199.02 | .16 | 180.66 | .21 | 158.07 | .24 | 132.61 | .26 | .25 |
| .76 | 218.93 | .04 | 211.94 | .10 | 198.86 | .16 | 180.45 | .21 | 157.83 | .24 | 132.35 | .27 | .24 |
| .77 | 218.89 | .04 | 211.84 | .11 | 198.70 | .16 | 180.24 | .20 | 157.59 | .24 | 132.08 | .26 | .23 |
| .78 | 218.85 | .04 | 211.73 | .10 | 198.54 | .16 | 180.04 | .21 | 157.35 | .25 | 131.82 | .27 | .22 |
| .79 | 218.81 | .04 | 211.63 | .10 | 198.38 | .16 | 179.83 | .21 | 157.10 | .24 | 131.55 | .26 | .21 |
| .80 | 218.77 | .04 | 211.53 | .11 | 198.22 | .16 | 179.62 | .21 | 156.86 | .24 | 131.29 | .27 | .20 |
| .81 | 218.73 | .04 | 211.42 | .10 | 198.06 | .16 | 179.41 | .21 | 156.62 | .25 | 131.02 | .26 | .19 |
| .82 | 218.69 | .04 | 211.32 | .11 | 197.90 | .16 | 179.20 | .21 | 156.37 | .24 | 130.76 | .27 | .18 |
| .83 | 218.65 | .04 | 211.21 | .10 | 197.74 | .16 | 178.99 | .21 | 156.13 | .25 | 130.49 | .26 | .17 |
| .84 | 218.61 | .04 | 211.11 | .11 | 197.58 | .17 | 178.78 | .21 | 155.88 | .24 | 130.23 | .27 | .16 |
| .85 | 218.57 | .05 | 211.00 | .11 | 197.41 | .16 | 178.57 | .21 | 155.64 | .25 | 129.96 | .26 | .15 |
| .86 | 218.52 | .04 | 210.89 | .10 | 197.25 | .17 | 178.36 | .21 | 155.39 | .24 | 129.70 | .27 | .14 |
| .87 | 218.48 | .05 | 210.79 | .11 | 197.08 | .16 | 178.15 | .22 | 155.15 | .25 | 129.43 | .26 | .13 |
| .88 | 218.43 | .04 | 210.68 | .11 | 196.92 | .17 | 177.93 | .21 | 154.90 | .24 | 129.17 | .27 | .12 |
| .89 | 218.39 | .05 | 210.57 | .11 | 196.75 | .17 | 177.72 | .21 | 154.66 | .25 | 128.90 | .26 | .11 |
| .90 | 218.34 | .05 | 210.46 | .11 | 196.58 | .17 | 177.51 | .22 | 154.41 | .25 | 128.64 | .27 | .10 |
| .91 | 218.29 | .05 | 210.35 | .11 | 196.41 | .17 | 177.29 | .21 | 154.16 | .25 | 128.37 | .26 | .09 |
| .92 | 218.24 | .05 | 210.24 | .11 | 196.24 | .17 | 177.08 | .22 | 153.91 | .24 | 128.11 | .27 | .08 |
| .93 | 218.19 | .05 | 210.13 | .11 | 196.07 | .17 | 176.86 | .21 | 153.67 | .25 | 127.84 | .26 | .07 |
| .94 | 218.14 | .05 | 210.02 | .12 | 195.90 | .17 | 176.65 | .22 | 153.42 | .25 | 127.58 | .27 | .06 |
| .95 | 218.09 | .05 | 209.90 | .11 | 195.73 | .17 | 176.43 | .21 | 153.17 | .25 | 127.31 | .27 | .05 |
| .96 | 218.04 | .05 | 209.79 | .12 | 195.56 | .17 | 176.22 | .22 | 152.92 | .25 | 127.04 | .26 | .04 |
| .97 | 217.99 | .05 | 209.67 | .11 | 195.39 | .17 | 176.00 | .21 | 152.67 | .25 | 126.78 | .27 | .03 |
| .98 | 217.94 | .05 | 209.56 | .12 | 195.22 | .17 | 175.79 | .22 | 152.42 | .25 | 126.51 | .27 | .02 |
| .99 | 217.89 | .05 | 209.44 | .12 | 195.05 | .17 | 175.57 | .21 | 152.17 | .25 | 126.24 | .26 | .01 |
| 1.00 | 217.84 | .05 | 209.32 | .12 | 194.88 | .17 | 175.36 | .22 | 151.92 | .25 | 125.98 | .27 | .00 |
| Days. | 25 | | 24 | | 23 | | 22 | | 21 | | 20 | | Days. |

# TABLE XV. ARGUMENT 10.

Equation = 110″.0 [1 — sin. $(x + z)$].

Period, 25.621696 days.

| Days. | 6 | | 7 | | 8 | | 9 | | 10 | | 11 | | 12 | | Days. |
|---|---|---|---|---|---|---|---|---|---|---|---|---|---|---|---|
| Decimals of a Day. | Equation. | Diff. | Equation. | Diff. | Equation. | Diff. | Equation. | Diff. | Equation. | Diff. | Equation. | Diff. | Equation. | Diff. | Decimals of a Day. |
| .00 | 125.98 | .27 | 99.08 | .27 | 72.84 | .25 | 48.81 | .22 | 28.45 | .18 | 12.97 | .13 | 3.29 | .06 | 1.00 |
| .01 | 125.71 | .26 | 98.81 | .27 | 72.59 | .26 | 48.59 | .23 | 28.27 | .18 | 12.84 | .12 | 3.23 | .07 | .99 |
| .02 | 125.45 | .27 | 98.54 | .27 | 72.33 | .25 | 48.36 | .22 | 28.09 | .18 | 12.72 | .12 | 3.16 | .06 | .98 |
| .03 | 125.18 | .27 | 98.27 | .27 | 72.08 | .25 | 48.14 | .22 | 27.91 | .18 | 12.60 | .13 | 3.10 | .07 | .97 |
| .04 | 124.91 | .26 | 98.00 | .26 | 71.83 | .26 | 47.92 | .23 | 27.73 | .17 | 12.47 | .12 | 3.03 | .06 | .96 |
| .05 | 124.65 | .27 | 97.74 | .27 | 71.57 | .25 | 47.69 | .22 | 27.56 | .18 | 12.35 | .12 | 2.97 | .06 | .95 |
| .06 | 124.38 | .27 | 97.47 | .27 | 71.32 | .25 | 47.47 | .22 | 27.38 | .18 | 12.23 | .13 | 2.91 | .06 | .94 |
| .07 | 124.11 | .26 | 97.20 | .27 | 71.07 | .26 | 47.25 | .23 | 27.20 | .18 | 12.10 | .12 | 2.85 | .06 | .93 |
| .08 | 123.85 | .27 | 96.93 | .26 | 70.81 | .25 | 47.02 | .22 | 27.02 | .17 | 11.98 | .12 | 2.79 | .06 | .92 |
| .09 | 123.58 | .27 | 96.67 | .27 | 70.56 | .25 | 46.80 | .22 | 26.85 | .18 | 11.86 | .12 | 2.73 | .06 | .91 |
| .10 | 123.31 | .27 | 96.40 | .27 | 70.31 | .25 | 46.58 | .22 | 26.67 | .18 | 11.74 | .12 | 2.67 | .06 | .90 |
| .11 | 123.04 | .26 | 96.13 | .27 | 70.06 | .25 | 46.36 | .22 | 26.49 | .17 | 11.62 | .12 | 2.61 | .06 | .89 |
| .12 | 122.78 | .27 | 95.86 | .26 | 69.81 | .25 | 46.14 | .22 | 26.32 | .18 | 11.50 | .12 | 2.55 | .06 | .88 |
| .13 | 122.51 | .27 | 95.60 | .27 | 69.56 | .26 | 45.92 | .22 | 26.14 | .18 | 11.38 | .12 | 2.49 | .06 | .87 |
| .14 | 122.24 | .27 | 95.33 | .27 | 69.30 | .25 | 45.70 | .22 | 25.96 | .17 | 11.26 | .12 | 2.43 | .05 | .86 |
| .15 | 121.97 | .27 | 95.06 | .26 | 69.05 | .25 | 45.48 | .22 | 25.79 | .17 | 11.14 | .12 | 2.38 | .06 | .85 |
| .16 | 121.70 | .26 | 94.80 | .27 | 68.80 | .25 | 45.26 | .21 | 25.62 | .18 | 11.02 | .12 | 2.32 | .05 | .84 |
| .17 | 121.44 | .27 | 94.53 | .27 | 68.55 | .25 | 45.05 | .22 | 25.44 | .17 | 10.90 | .11 | 2.27 | .06 | .83 |
| .18 | 121.17 | .27 | 94.26 | .26 | 68.30 | .25 | 44.83 | .22 | 25.27 | .17 | 10.79 | .12 | 2.21 | .05 | .82 |
| .19 | 120.90 | .27 | 94.00 | .27 | 68.05 | .25 | 44.61 | .22 | 25.10 | .17 | 10.67 | .12 | 2.16 | .05 | .81 |
| .20 | 120.63 | .27 | 93.73 | .27 | 67.80 | .25 | 44.39 | .22 | 24.93 | .17 | 10.55 | .12 | 2.11 | .05 | .80 |
| .21 | 120.36 | .27 | 93.46 | .26 | 67.55 | .25 | 44.17 | .21 | 24.76 | .17 | 10.43 | .11 | 2.06 | .05 | .79 |
| .22 | 120.09 | .26 | 93.20 | .27 | 67.30 | .25 | 43.96 | .22 | 24.59 | .17 | 10.32 | .12 | 2.01 | .05 | .78 |
| .23 | 119.83 | .27 | 92.93 | .27 | 67.05 | .24 | 43.74 | .21 | 24.42 | .17 | 10.20 | .11 | 1.96 | .05 | .77 |
| .24 | 119.56 | .27 | 92.66 | .26 | 66.81 | .25 | 43.53 | .22 | 24.25 | .17 | 10.09 | .12 | 1.91 | .05 | .76 |
| .25 | 119.29 | .27 | 92.40 | .27 | 66.56 | .25 | 43.31 | .21 | 24.08 | .17 | 9.97 | .11 | 1.86 | .05 | .75 |
| .26 | 119.02 | .27 | 92.13 | .26 | 66.31 | .25 | 43.10 | .21 | 23.91 | .17 | 9.86 | .11 | 1.81 | .05 | .74 |
| .27 | 118.75 | .27 | 91.87 | .27 | 66.06 | .25 | 42.89 | .22 | 23.74 | .16 | 9.75 | .11 | 1.76 | .05 | .73 |
| .28 | 118.48 | .27 | 91.60 | .26 | 65.81 | .24 | 42.67 | .21 | 23.58 | .17 | 9.64 | .11 | 1.71 | .04 | .72 |
| .29 | 118.21 | .27 | 91.34 | .27 | 65.57 | .25 | 42.46 | .21 | 23.41 | .17 | 9.53 | .11 | 1.67 | .05 | .71 |
| .30 | 117.94 | .27 | 91.07 | .27 | 65.32 | .25 | 42.25 | .21 | 23.24 | .16 | 9.42 | .11 | 1.62 | .04 | .70 |
| .31 | 117.67 | .27 | 90.80 | .26 | 65.07 | .24 | 42.04 | .21 | 23.08 | .17 | 9.31 | .11 | 1.58 | .05 | .69 |
| .32 | 117.40 | .26 | 90.54 | .27 | 64.83 | .25 | 41.83 | .21 | 22.91 | .16 | 9.20 | .11 | 1.53 | .04 | .68 |
| .33 | 117.14 | .27 | 90.27 | .26 | 64.58 | .24 | 41.62 | .21 | 22.75 | .16 | 9.09 | .11 | 1.49 | .05 | .67 |
| .34 | 116.87 | .27 | 90.01 | .27 | 64.34 | .25 | 41.41 | .21 | 22.59 | .17 | 8.98 | .10 | 1.44 | .04 | .66 |
| .35 | 116.60 | .27 | 89.74 | .27 | 64.09 | .24 | 41.20 | .21 | 22.42 | .16 | 8.88 | .11 | 1.40 | .05 | .65 |
| .36 | 116.33 | .27 | 89.47 | .26 | 63.85 | .25 | 40.99 | .21 | 22.26 | .16 | 8.77 | .10 | 1.35 | .04 | .64 |
| .37 | 116.06 | .27 | 89.21 | .27 | 63.60 | .24 | 40.78 | .21 | 22.10 | .17 | 8.67 | .11 | 1.31 | .04 | .63 |
| .38 | 115.79 | .27 | 88.94 | .26 | 63.36 | .25 | 40.57 | .21 | 21.93 | .16 | 8.56 | .10 | 1.27 | .04 | .62 |
| .39 | 115.52 | .27 | 88.68 | .27 | 63.11 | .24 | 40.36 | .21 | 21.77 | .16 | 8.46 | .10 | 1.23 | .04 | .61 |
| .40 | 115.25 | .27 | 88.41 | .26 | 62.87 | .24 | 40.15 | .21 | 21.61 | .16 | 8.36 | .10 | 1.19 | .04 | .60 |
| .41 | 114.98 | .27 | 88.15 | .27 | 62.63 | .25 | 39.94 | .21 | 21.45 | .16 | 8.26 | .10 | 1.15 | .04 | .59 |
| .42 | 114.71 | .27 | 87.88 | .26 | 62.38 | .24 | 39.73 | .21 | 21.29 | .16 | 8.16 | .10 | 1.11 | .04 | .58 |
| .43 | 114.44 | .27 | 87.62 | .27 | 62.14 | .24 | 39.52 | .20 | 21.13 | .16 | 8.06 | .10 | 1.07 | .04 | .57 |
| .44 | 114.17 | .27 | 87.35 | .26 | 61.90 | .24 | 39.32 | .21 | 20.97 | .16 | 7.96 | .10 | 1.03 | .03 | .56 |
| .45 | 113.90 | .27 | 87.09 | .26 | 61.66 | .25 | 39.11 | .21 | 20.81 | .15 | 7.86 | .10 | 1.00 | .04 | .55 |
| .46 | 113.63 | .27 | 86.83 | .27 | 61.41 | .24 | 38.90 | .20 | 20.66 | .16 | 7.76 | .10 | 0.96 | .03 | .54 |
| .47 | 113.36 | .27 | 86.56 | .26 | 61.17 | .24 | 38.70 | .21 | 20.50 | .16 | 7.66 | .10 | 0.93 | .04 | .53 |
| .48 | 113.09 | .27 | 86.30 | .26 | 60.93 | .24 | 38.49 | .20 | 20.34 | .15 | 7.56 | .10 | 0.89 | .03 | .52 |
| .49 | 112.82 | .27 | 86.04 | .27 | 60.69 | .24 | 38.29 | .20 | 20.19 | .16 | 7.46 | .10 | 0.86 | .03 | .51 |
| .50 | 112.55 | .27 | 85.77 | .26 | 60.45 | .24 | 38.09 | .20 | 20.03 | .15 | 7.36 | .10 | 0.83 | .03 | .50 |
| Days. | 19 | | 18 | | 17 | | 16 | | 15 | | 14 | | 13 | | Days. |

# TABLE XV. ARGUMENT 10.

Equation $= 110''.0 \, [1 - \sin. (x + z)]$.

Period, 25.621696 days.

| Days. | 6 | | 7 | | 8 | | 9 | | 10 | | 11 | | 12 | | Days. |
|---|---|---|---|---|---|---|---|---|---|---|---|---|---|---|---|
| Decimals of a Day. | Equation. | Diff. | Equation. | Diff. | Equation. | Diff. | Equation. | Diff. | Equation. | Diff. | Equation. | Diff. | Equation. | Diff. | Decimals of a Day. |
| | ″ | | ″ | | ″ | | ″ | | ″ | | ″ | | ″ | | |
| .50 | 112.55 | .27 | 85.77 | .26 | 60.45 | .24 | 38.09 | .20 | 20.03 | .15 | 7.36 | .10 | 0.83 | .03 | .50 |
| .51 | 112.28 | .27 | 85.51 | .26 | 60.21 | .24 | 37.89 | .21 | 19.88 | .15 | 7.26 | .10 | 0.80 | .03 | .49 |
| .52 | 112.01 | .27 | 85.25 | .27 | 59.97 | .24 | 37.68 | .20 | 19.73 | .16 | 7.16 | .09 | 0.77 | .03 | .48 |
| .53 | 111.74 | .27 | 84.98 | .26 | 59.73 | .24 | 37.48 | .20 | 19.57 | .15 | 7.07 | .10 | 0.74 | .03 | .47 |
| .54 | 111.47 | .27 | 84.72 | .26 | 59.49 | .24 | 37.28 | .20 | 19.42 | .15 | 6.97 | .09 | 0.71 | .03 | .46 |
| .55 | 111.20 | .27 | 84.46 | .26 | 59.25 | .23 | 37.08 | .20 | 19.27 | .16 | 6.88 | .10 | 0.68 | .03 | .45 |
| .56 | 110.93 | .27 | 84.20 | .27 | 59.02 | .24 | 36.88 | .21 | 19.11 | .15 | 6.78 | .09 | 0.65 | .03 | .44 |
| .57 | 110.66 | .27 | 83.93 | .26 | 58.78 | .24 | 36.67 | .20 | 18.96 | .15 | 6.69 | .09 | 0.62 | .03 | .43 |
| .58 | 110.39 | .27 | 83.67 | .26 | 58.54 | .24 | 36.47 | .20 | 18.81 | .15 | 6.60 | .09 | 0.59 | .03 | .42 |
| .59 | 110.12 | .27 | 83.41 | .26 | 58.30 | .24 | 36.27 | .20 | 18.66 | .15 | 6.51 | .09 | 0.56 | .03 | .41 |
| .60 | 109.85 | .27 | 83.15 | .26 | 58.06 | .24 | 36.07 | .20 | 18.51 | .15 | 6.42 | .09 | 0.53 | .03 | .40 |
| .61 | 109.58 | .27 | 82.89 | .26 | 57.82 | .23 | 35.87 | .20 | 18.36 | .15 | 6.33 | .09 | 0.50 | .02 | .39 |
| .62 | 109.31 | .27 | 82.63 | .26 | 57.59 | .24 | 35.67 | .20 | 18.21 | .15 | 6.24 | .09 | 0.48 | .03 | .38 |
| .63 | 109.04 | .27 | 82.37 | .26 | 57.35 | .24 | 35.47 | .20 | 18.06 | .14 | 6.15 | .09 | 0.45 | .02 | .37 |
| .64 | 108.77 | .27 | 82.11 | .26 | 57.11 | .23 | 35.27 | .20 | 17.92 | .15 | 6.06 | .09 | 0.43 | .03 | .36 |
| .65 | 108.50 | .27 | 81.85 | .26 | 56.88 | .24 | 35.07 | .19 | 17.77 | .15 | 5.97 | .09 | 0.40 | .02 | .35 |
| .66 | 108.23 | .27 | 81.59 | .26 | 56.64 | .24 | 34.88 | .20 | 17.62 | .14 | 5.88 | .08 | 0.38 | .02 | .34 |
| .67 | 107.96 | .27 | 81.33 | .26 | 56.40 | .23 | 34.68 | .20 | 17.48 | .15 | 5.80 | .09 | 0.36 | .02 | .33 |
| .68 | 107.69 | .27 | 81.07 | .26 | 56.17 | .24 | 34.48 | .20 | 17.33 | .14 | 5.71 | .08 | 0.34 | .02 | .32 |
| .69 | 107.42 | .27 | 80.81 | .26 | 55.93 | .23 | 34.28 | .19 | 17.19 | .15 | 5.63 | .09 | 0.32 | .02 | .31 |
| .70 | 107.15 | .27 | 80.55 | .26 | 55.70 | .23 | 34.09 | .19 | 17.04 | .14 | 5.54 | .08 | 0.30 | .02 | .30 |
| .71 | 106.88 | .27 | 80.29 | .26 | 55.47 | .24 | 33.90 | .20 | 16.90 | .14 | 5.46 | .08 | 0.28 | .02 | .29 |
| .72 | 106.61 | .27 | 80.03 | .26 | 55.23 | .23 | 33.70 | .19 | 16.76 | .15 | 5.38 | .09 | 0.26 | .02 | .28 |
| .73 | 106.34 | .27 | 79.77 | .26 | 55.00 | .23 | 33.51 | .19 | 16.61 | .14 | 5.29 | .08 | 0.24 | .02 | .27 |
| .74 | 106.07 | .27 | 79.51 | .26 | 54.77 | .24 | 33.32 | .20 | 16.47 | .14 | 5.21 | .08 | 0.22 | .02 | .26 |
| .75 | 105.80 | .26 | 79.25 | .26 | 54.53 | .23 | 33.12 | .19 | 16.33 | .14 | 5.13 | .08 | 0.20 | .01 | .25 |
| .76 | 105.54 | .27 | 78.99 | .25 | 54.30 | .23 | 32.93 | .19 | 16.19 | .15 | 5.05 | .08 | 0.19 | .02 | .24 |
| .77 | 105.27 | .27 | 78.74 | .26 | 54.07 | .24 | 32.74 | .20 | 16.04 | .14 | 4.97 | .08 | 0.17 | .01 | .23 |
| .78 | 105.00 | .27 | 78.48 | .26 | 53.83 | .23 | 32.54 | .19 | 15.90 | .14 | 4.89 | .08 | 0.16 | .02 | .22 |
| .79 | 104.73 | .27 | 78.22 | .26 | 53.60 | .23 | 32.35 | .19 | 15.76 | .14 | 4.81 | .08 | 0.14 | .01 | .21 |
| .80 | 104.46 | .27 | 77.96 | .26 | 53.37 | .23 | 32.16 | .19 | 15.62 | .14 | 4.73 | .08 | 0.13 | .01 | .20 |
| .81 | 104.19 | .27 | 77.70 | .26 | 53.14 | .23 | 31.97 | .19 | 15.48 | .14 | 4.65 | .08 | 0.12 | .01 | .19 |
| .82 | 103.92 | .27 | 77.44 | .25 | 52.91 | .23 | 31.78 | .19 | 15.34 | .13 | 4.57 | .08 | 0.11 | .01 | .18 |
| .83 | 103.65 | .27 | 77.19 | .26 | 52.68 | .23 | 31.59 | .19 | 15.21 | .14 | 4.49 | .07 | 0.10 | .01 | .17 |
| .84 | 103.38 | .27 | 76.93 | .26 | 52.45 | .23 | 31.40 | .18 | 15.07 | .14 | 4.42 | .08 | 0.09 | .01 | .16 |
| .85 | 103.11 | .27 | 76.67 | .25 | 52.22 | .23 | 31.22 | .19 | 14.93 | .13 | 4.34 | .07 | 0.08 | .01 | .15 |
| .86 | 102.84 | .26 | 76.42 | .26 | 51.99 | .23 | 31.03 | .19 | 14.80 | .14 | 4.27 | .08 | 0.07 | .01 | .14 |
| .87 | 102.58 | .27 | 76.16 | .26 | 51.76 | .23 | 30.84 | .19 | 14.66 | .13 | 4.19 | .07 | 0.06 | .01 | .13 |
| .88 | 102.31 | .27 | 75.90 | .25 | 51.53 | .23 | 30.65 | .18 | 14.53 | .14 | 4.12 | .07 | 0.05 | .01 | .12 |
| .89 | 102.04 | .27 | 75.65 | .26 | 51.30 | .23 | 30.47 | .19 | 14.39 | .13 | 4.05 | .07 | 0.04 | .01 | .11 |
| .90 | 101.77 | .27 | 75.39 | .25 | 51.07 | .23 | 30.28 | .18 | 14.26 | .13 | 3.98 | .07 | 0.03 | .01 | .10 |
| .91 | 101.50 | .27 | 75.14 | .26 | 50.84 | .23 | 30.10 | .19 | 14.13 | .13 | 3.91 | .07 | 0.02 | .00 | .09 |
| .92 | 101.23 | .27 | 74.88 | .25 | 50.61 | .22 | 29.91 | .18 | 14.00 | .13 | 3.84 | .07 | 0.02 | .01 | .08 |
| .93 | 100.96 | .27 | 74.63 | .26 | 50.39 | .23 | 29.73 | .18 | 13.87 | .13 | 3.77 | .07 | 0.01 | .00 | .07 |
| .94 | 100.69 | .27 | 74.37 | .25 | 50.16 | .23 | 29.55 | .19 | 13.74 | .13 | 3.70 | .07 | 0.01 | .01 | .06 |
| .95 | 100.42 | .27 | 74.12 | .26 | 49.93 | .22 | 29.36 | .18 | 13.61 | .13 | 3.63 | .07 | 0.00 | .00 | .05 |
| .96 | 100.15 | .26 | 73.86 | .25 | 49.71 | .23 | 29.18 | .18 | 13.48 | .13 | 3.56 | .07 | 0.00 | .00 | .04 |
| .97 | 99.89 | .27 | 73.61 | .26 | 49.48 | .22 | 29.00 | .19 | 13.35 | .13 | 3.49 | .07 | 0.00 | .00 | .03 |
| .98 | 99.62 | .27 | 73.35 | .25 | 49.26 | .23 | 28.81 | .18 | 13.22 | .12 | 3.42 | .06 | 0.00 | .00 | .02 |
| .99 | 99.35 | .27 | 73.10 | .26 | 49.03 | .22 | 28.63 | .18 | 13.10 | .13 | 3.36 | .07 | 0.00 | .00 | .01 |
| 1.00 | 99.08 | .27 | 72.84 | .25 | 48.81 | .22 | 28.45 | .18 | 12.97 | .13 | 3.29 | .06 | 0.00 | .00 | .00 |
| Days. | 19 | | 18 | | 17 | | 16 | | 15 | | 14 | | 13 | | Days. |

# TABLE XVI. ARGUMENT 11.

Equation $= 85''.0\ [1 - \sin.\ (2y - x)]$.

Period, 26.878290 days.

| Days. | 0 | 1 | 2 | 3 | 4 | 5 | 6 | 7 | 8 | 9 | Days. |
|---|---|---|---|---|---|---|---|---|---|---|---|
| Days. | ″ | ″ | ″ | ″ | ″ | ″ | ″ | ″ | ″ | ″ | Days. |
| .00 | 169.30 | 169.56 | 165.24 | 156.55 | 143.97 | 128.18 | 110.07 | 90.57 | 70.76 | 51.74 | 1.00 |
| .01 | 169.32 | 169.54 | 165.17 | 156.44 | 143.83 | 128.01 | 109.88 | 90.37 | 70.56 | 51.56 | .99 |
| .02 | 169.35 | 169.52 | 165.10 | 156.33 | 143.68 | 127.84 | 109.69 | 90.17 | 70.37 | 51.38 | .98 |
| .03 | 169.37 | 169.50 | 165.03 | 156.22 | 143.54 | 127.67 | 109.49 | 89.98 | 70.17 | 51.20 | .97 |
| .04 | 169.40 | 169.48 | 164.96 | 156.11 | 143.39 | 127.50 | 109.30 | 89.78 | 69.98 | 51.02 | .96 |
| .05 | 169.42 | 169.46 | 164.89 | 156.00 | 143.25 | 127.33 | 109.11 | 89.58 | 69.78 | 50.84 | .95 |
| .06 | 169.44 | 169.44 | 164.82 | 155.89 | 143.10 | 127.16 | 108.92 | 89.38 | 69.59 | 50.66 | .94 |
| .07 | 169.46 | 169.41 | 164.76 | 155.78 | 142.96 | 126.99 | 108.73 | 89.18 | 69.39 | 50.48 | .93 |
| .08 | 169.48 | 169.39 | 164.69 | 155.67 | 142.81 | 126.81 | 108.53 | 88.99 | 69.20 | 50.29 | .92 |
| .09 | 169.50 | 169.36 | 164.62 | 155.56 | 142.67 | 126.64 | 108.34 | 88.79 | 69.00 | 50.11 | .91 |
| .10 | 169.52 | 169.33 | 164.55 | 155.45 | 142.52 | 126.47 | 108.15 | 88.59 | 68.81 | 49.93 | .90 |
| .11 | 169.54 | 169.31 | 164.48 | 155.34 | 142.37 | 126.30 | 107.96 | 88.39 | 68.61 | 49.75 | .89 |
| .12 | 169.56 | 169.28 | 164.41 | 155.23 | 142.23 | 126.12 | 107.77 | 88.19 | 68.42 | 49.57 | .88 |
| .13 | 169.58 | 169.26 | 164.34 | 155.11 | 142.08 | 125.95 | 107.58 | 88.00 | 68.22 | 49.38 | .87 |
| .14 | 169.60 | 169.23 | 164.27 | 155.00 | 141.93 | 125.77 | 107.39 | 87.80 | 68.03 | 49.20 | .86 |
| .15 | 169.62 | 169.21 | 164.20 | 154.89 | 141.78 | 125.60 | 107.20 | 87.60 | 67.83 | 49.02 | .85 |
| .16 | 169.64 | 169.18 | 164.13 | 154.78 | 141.63 | 125.43 | 107.01 | 87.40 | 67.64 | 48.84 | .84 |
| .17 | 169.66 | 169.15 | 164.05 | 154.66 | 141.48 | 125.25 | 106.82 | 87.20 | 67.44 | 48.66 | .83 |
| .18 | 169.67 | 169.12 | 163.98 | 154.55 | 141.33 | 125.08 | 106.62 | 87.00 | 67.25 | 48.48 | .82 |
| .19 | 169.69 | 169.09 | 163.90 | 154.43 | 141.18 | 124.90 | 106.43 | 86.80 | 67.05 | 48.30 | .81 |
| .20 | 169.70 | 169.06 | 163.83 | 154.32 | 141.03 | 124.73 | 106.24 | 86.60 | 66.86 | 48.12 | .80 |
| .21 | 169.72 | 169.03 | 163.76 | 154.20 | 140.88 | 124.55 | 106.05 | 86.40 | 66.67 | 47.94 | .79 |
| .22 | 169.73 | 169.00 | 163.68 | 154.09 | 140.73 | 124.38 | 105.86 | 86.20 | 66.48 | 47.76 | .78 |
| .23 | 169.75 | 168.97 | 163.61 | 153.97 | 140.58 | 124.20 | 105.66 | 86.00 | 66.28 | 47.59 | .77 |
| .24 | 169.76 | 168.94 | 163.53 | 153.86 | 140.43 | 124.03 | 105.47 | 85.80 | 66.09 | 47.41 | .76 |
| .25 | 169.78 | 168.91 | 163.46 | 153.74 | 140.28 | 123.85 | 105.28 | 85.60 | 65.90 | 47.23 | .75 |
| .26 | 169.79 | 168.87 | 163.38 | 153.62 | 140.13 | 123.67 | 105.09 | 85.40 | 65.71 | 47.05 | .74 |
| .27 | 169.81 | 168.84 | 163.31 | 153.50 | 139.98 | 123.49 | 104.90 | 85.20 | 65.51 | 46.87 | .73 |
| .28 | 169.82 | 168.80 | 163.23 | 153.39 | 139.82 | 123.32 | 104.70 | 85.01 | 65.32 | 46.70 | .72 |
| .29 | 169.83 | 168.77 | 163.15 | 153.27 | 139.67 | 123.14 | 104.51 | 84.81 | 65.12 | 46.52 | .71 |
| .30 | 169.84 | 168.73 | 163.07 | 153.15 | 139.52 | 122.96 | 104.32 | 84.61 | 64.93 | 46.34 | .70 |
| .31 | 169.85 | 168.70 | 162.99 | 153.03 | 139.37 | 122.78 | 104.13 | 84.41 | 64.74 | 46.16 | .69 |
| .32 | 169.86 | 168.66 | 162.91 | 152.91 | 139.22 | 122.60 | 103.93 | 84.21 | 64.55 | 45.99 | .68 |
| .33 | 169.87 | 168.63 | 162.82 | 152.79 | 139.06 | 122.43 | 103.74 | 84.01 | 64.35 | 45.81 | .67 |
| .34 | 169.88 | 168.59 | 162.74 | 152.67 | 138.91 | 122.25 | 103.54 | 83.82 | 64.16 | 45.64 | .66 |
| .35 | 169.89 | 168.56 | 162.66 | 152.55 | 138.76 | 122.07 | 103.35 | 83.62 | 63.97 | 45.46 | .65 |
| .36 | 169.90 | 168.52 | 162.58 | 152.43 | 138.60 | 121.89 | 103.15 | 83.42 | 63.78 | 45.28 | .64 |
| .37 | 169.91 | 168.48 | 162.50 | 152.31 | 138.45 | 121.71 | 102.96 | 83.22 | 63.59 | 45.11 | .63 |
| .38 | 169.92 | 168.44 | 162.42 | 152.18 | 138.29 | 121.53 | 102.76 | 83.02 | 63.39 | 44.93 | .62 |
| .39 | 169.93 | 168.40 | 162.34 | 152.06 | 138.14 | 121.35 | 102.57 | 82.82 | 63.20 | 44.76 | .61 |
| .40 | 169.94 | 168.36 | 162.26 | 151.94 | 137.99 | 121.17 | 102.37 | 82.62 | 63.01 | 44.58 | .60 |
| .41 | 169.95 | 168.32 | 162.18 | 151.82 | 137.83 | 120.99 | 102.18 | 82.42 | 62.82 | 44.41 | .59 |
| .42 | 169.96 | 168.28 | 162.09 | 151.70 | 137.68 | 120.81 | 101.98 | 82.23 | 62.63 | 44.24 | .58 |
| .43 | 169.97 | 168.24 | 162.01 | 151.57 | 137.52 | 120.63 | 101.79 | 82.03 | 62.44 | 44.07 | .57 |
| .44 | 169.97 | 168.20 | 161.92 | 151.45 | 137.37 | 120.45 | 101.59 | 81.83 | 62.25 | 43.89 | .56 |
| .45 | 169.98 | 168.16 | 161.84 | 151.33 | 137.21 | 120.27 | 101.40 | 81.63 | 62.06 | 43.72 | .55 |
| .46 | 169.98 | 168.12 | 161.75 | 151.20 | 137.05 | 120.09 | 101.20 | 81.43 | 61.87 | 43.55 | .54 |
| .47 | 169.98 | 168.08 | 161.67 | 151.08 | 136.90 | 119.91 | 101.01 | 81.23 | 61.68 | 43.37 | .53 |
| .48 | 169.99 | 168.04 | 161.58 | 150.95 | 136.74 | 119.73 | 100.81 | 81.04 | 61.48 | 43.20 | .52 |
| .49 | 169.99 | 167.99 | 161.50 | 150.83 | 136.59 | 119.54 | 100.62 | 80.84 | 61.29 | 43.02 | .51 |
| .50 | 169.99 | 167.95 | 161.41 | 150.70 | 136.43 | 119.36 | 100.42 | 80.64 | 61.10 | 42.85 | .50 |
| Days. | 27 | 26 | 25 | 24 | 23 | 22 | 21 | 20 | 19 | 18 | Days. |

# TABLE XVI. ARGUMENT 11.

Equation = 85″.0 [1 — sin. (2$y$ — $x$)].

Period, 26.878290 days.

| Days. | 0 | 1 | 2 | 3 | 4 | 5 | 6 | 7 | 8 | 9 | Days. |
|---|---|---|---|---|---|---|---|---|---|---|---|
| Days. | ″ | ″ | ″ | ″ | ″ | ″ | ″ | ″ | ″ | ″ | Days. |
| .50 | 169.99 | 167.95 | 161.41 | 150.70 | 136.43 | 119.36 | 100.42 | 80.64 | 61.10 | 42.85 | .50 |
| .51 | 169.99 | 167.90 | 161.32 | 150.57 | 136.27 | 119.18 | 100.22 | 80.44 | 60.91 | 42.68 | .49 |
| .52 | 170.00 | 167.86 | 161.25 | 150.44 | 136.11 | 119.00 | 100.02 | 80.24 | 60.72 | 42.51 | .48 |
| .53 | 170.00 | 167.81 | 161.16 | 150.32 | 135.96 | 118.81 | 99.83 | 80.05 | 60.53 | 42.33 | .47 |
| .54 | 170.00 | 167.77 | 161.07 | 150.19 | 135.80 | 118.63 | 99.63 | 79.85 | 60.34 | 42.16 | .46 |
| .55 | 170.00 | 167.72 | 160.98 | 150.06 | 135.64 | 118.45 | 99.43 | 79.65 | 60.15 | 41.99 | .45 |
| .56 | 170.00 | 167.68 | 160.89 | 149.93 | 135.48 | 118.27 | 99.24 | 79.45 | 59.96 | 41.82 | .44 |
| .57 | 170.00 | 167.63 | 160.80 | 149.80 | 135.32 | 118.09 | 99.04 | 79.25 | 59.77 | 41.65 | .43 |
| .58 | 170.00 | 167.59 | 160.71 | 149.68 | 135.15 | 117.90 | 98.84 | 79.06 | 59.58 | 41.48 | .42 |
| .59 | 170.00 | 167.54 | 160.61 | 149.55 | 134.99 | 117.72 | 98.65 | 78.86 | 59.39 | 41.31 | .41 |
| .60 | 169.99 | 167.49 | 160.52 | 149.42 | 134.83 | 117.54 | 98.45 | 78.66 | 59.20 | 41.14 | .40 |
| .61 | 169.99 | 167.44 | 160.43 | 149.29 | 134.67 | 117.36 | 98.25 | 78.46 | 59.01 | 40.97 | .39 |
| .62 | 169.99 | 167.39 | 160.34 | 149.16 | 134.51 | 117.17 | 98.06 | 78.26 | 58.83 | 40.80 | .38 |
| .63 | 169.99 | 167.34 | 160.25 | 149.03 | 134.34 | 116.99 | 97.86 | 78.06 | 58.63 | 40.63 | .37 |
| .64 | 169.98 | 167.29 | 160.16 | 148.90 | 134.18 | 116.80 | 97.67 | 77.87 | 58.44 | 40.46 | .36 |
| .65 | 169.98 | 167.24 | 160.07 | 148.77 | 134.02 | 116.62 | 97.47 | 77.67 | 58.25 | 40.29 | .35 |
| .66 | 169.97 | 167.19 | 159.97 | 148.64 | 133.86 | 116.44 | 97.27 | 77.47 | 58.06 | 40.12 | .34 |
| .67 | 169.97 | 167.14 | 159.88 | 148.51 | 133.69 | 116.25 | 97.08 | 77.27 | 57.87 | 39.95 | .33 |
| .68 | 169.96 | 167.09 | 159.78 | 148.37 | 133.53 | 116.07 | 96.88 | 77.07 | 57.69 | 39.79 | .32 |
| .69 | 169.96 | 167.04 | 159.69 | 148.24 | 133.36 | 115.88 | 96.69 | 76.87 | 57.50 | 39.62 | .31 |
| .70 | 169.95 | 166.99 | 159.59 | 148.11 | 133.20 | 115.70 | 96.49 | 76.67 | 57.31 | 39.45 | .30 |
| .71 | 169.94 | 166.94 | 159.49 | 147.98 | 133.04 | 115.51 | 96.29 | 76.47 | 57.12 | 39.28 | .29 |
| .72 | 169.94 | 166.89 | 159.39 | 147.84 | 132.87 | 115.33 | 96.10 | 76.28 | 56.93 | 39.12 | .28 |
| .73 | 169.93 | 166.84 | 159.30 | 147.71 | 132.71 | 115.14 | 95.90 | 76.08 | 56.75 | 38.95 | .27 |
| .74 | 169.92 | 166.79 | 159.20 | 147.57 | 132.54 | 114.96 | 95.71 | 75.88 | 56.56 | 38.79 | .26 |
| .75 | 169.91 | 166.74 | 159.10 | 147.44 | 132.38 | 114.77 | 95.50 | 75.68 | 56.37 | 38.62 | .25 |
| .76 | 169.90 | 166.68 | 159.00 | 147.31 | 132.21 | 114.58 | 95.31 | 75.49 | 56.18 | 38.45 | .24 |
| .77 | 169.89 | 166.63 | 158.90 | 147.17 | 132.05 | 114.40 | 95.12 | 75.29 | 55.99 | 38.29 | .23 |
| .78 | 169.88 | 166.57 | 158.81 | 147.04 | 131.88 | 114.21 | 94.92 | 75.09 | 55.81 | 38.12 | .22 |
| .79 | 169.87 | 166.51 | 158.71 | 146.90 | 131.72 | 114.03 | 94.73 | 74.89 | 55.62 | 37.96 | .21 |
| .80 | 169.86 | 166.46 | 158.61 | 146.77 | 131.55 | 113.84 | 94.53 | 74.70 | 55.43 | 37.79 | .20 |
| .81 | 169.85 | 166.40 | 158.51 | 146.63 | 131.38 | 113.65 | 94.33 | 74.50 | 55.24 | 37.62 | .19 |
| .82 | 169.84 | 166.34 | 158.41 | 146.49 | 131.21 | 113.46 | 94.13 | 74.30 | 55.06 | 37.46 | .18 |
| .83 | 169.83 | 166.28 | 158.31 | 146.36 | 131.05 | 113.28 | 93.94 | 74.11 | 54.87 | 37.29 | .17 |
| .84 | 169.82 | 166.23 | 158.21 | 146.22 | 130.88 | 113.09 | 93.74 | 73.91 | 54.69 | 37.13 | .16 |
| .85 | 169.81 | 166.17 | 158.11 | 146.08 | 130.71 | 112.90 | 93.54 | 73.71 | 54.50 | 36.96 | .15 |
| .86 | 169.80 | 166.11 | 158.01 | 145.94 | 130.54 | 112.71 | 93.34 | 73.51 | 54.32 | 36.80 | .14 |
| .87 | 169.78 | 166.05 | 157.90 | 145.80 | 130.37 | 112.52 | 93.14 | 73.31 | 54.13 | 36.63 | .13 |
| .88 | 169.76 | 165.99 | 157.80 | 145.66 | 130.21 | 112.34 | 92.95 | 73.12 | 53.95 | 36.47 | .12 |
| .89 | 169.75 | 165.93 | 157.69 | 145.52 | 130.04 | 112.15 | 92.75 | 72.92 | 53.76 | 36.30 | .11 |
| .90 | 169.73 | 165.87 | 157.59 | 145.38 | 129.87 | 111.96 | 92.55 | 72.72 | 53.58 | 36.14 | .10 |
| .91 | 169.72 | 165.81 | 157.48 | 145.24 | 129.70 | 111.77 | 92.35 | 72.52 | 53.40 | 35.98 | .09 |
| .92 | 169.70 | 165.75 | 157.38 | 145.10 | 129.53 | 111.58 | 92.15 | 72.33 | 53.21 | 35.82 | .08 |
| .93 | 169.69 | 165.69 | 157.27 | 144.96 | 129.37 | 111.40 | 91.96 | 72.13 | 53.03 | 35.65 | .07 |
| .94 | 169.67 | 165.63 | 157.17 | 144.82 | 129.20 | 111.21 | 91.76 | 71.93 | 52.84 | 35.49 | .06 |
| .95 | 169.66 | 165.57 | 157.06 | 144.68 | 129.03 | 111.02 | 01.56 | 71.74 | 52.66 | 35.33 | .05 |
| .96 | 169.64 | 165.51 | 156.96 | 144.54 | 128.86 | 110.83 | 91.36 | 71.54 | 52.48 | 35.17 | .04 |
| .97 | 169.62 | 165.44 | 156.86 | 144.40 | 128.69 | 110.64 | 91.16 | 71.35 | 52.29 | 35.01 | .03 |
| .98 | 169.60 | 165.37 | 156.75 | 144.25 | 128.52 | 110.45 | 90.97 | 71.15 | 52.11 | 34.84 | .02 |
| .99 | 169.58 | 165.31 | 156.65 | 144.11 | 128.35 | 110.26 | 90.77 | 70.95 | 51.92 | 34.68 | .01 |
| 1.00 | 169.56 | 165.24 | 156.55 | 143.97 | 128.18 | 110.07 | 90.57 | 70.76 | 51.74 | 34.52 | .00 |
| Days. | 27 | 26 | 25 | 24 | 23 | 22 | 21 | 20 | 19 | 18 | Days. |

## TABLE XVI.

(*Continued*).

Period, 26.878290 days.

| Days. | 10 | 11 | 12 | 13 | Days. |
|---|---|---|---|---|---|
| Days. | " | " | " | " | Days. |
| .00 | 34.52 | 20.06 | 9.11 | 2.33 | 1.00 |
| .01 | 34.36 | 19.93 | 9.02 | 2.28 | .99 |
| .02 | 34.20 | 19.81 | 8.93 | 2.24 | .98 |
| .03 | 34.05 | 19.68 | 8.85 | 2.19 | .97 |
| .04 | 33.89 | 19.56 | 8.76 | 2.15 | .96 |
| .05 | 33.73 | 19.43 | 8.67 | 2.10 | .95 |
| .06 | 33.57 | 19.30 | 8.59 | 2.06 | .94 |
| .07 | 33.41 | 19.18 | 8.50 | 2.01 | .93 |
| .08 | 33.26 | 19.05 | 8.42 | 1.97 | .92 |
| .09 | 33.10 | 18.93 | 8.33 | 1.93 | .91 |
| .10 | 32.94 | 18.80 | 8.25 | 1.89 | .90 |
| .11 | 32.78 | 18.68 | 8.17 | 1.85 | .89 |
| .12 | 32.63 | 18.56 | 8.08 | 1.81 | .88 |
| .13 | 32.47 | 18.43 | 8.00 | 1.77 | .87 |
| .14 | 32.32 | 18.31 | 7.91 | 1.73 | .86 |
| .15 | 32.16 | 18.19 | 7.83 | 1.69 | .85 |
| .16 | 32.01 | 18.07 | 7.75 | 1.65 | .84 |
| .17 | 31.85 | 17.95 | 7.67 | 1.60 | .83 |
| .18 | 31.70 | 17.82 | 7.58 | 1.56 | .82 |
| .19 | 31.54 | 17.70 | 7.50 | 1.52 | .81 |
| .20 | 31.39 | 17.58 | 7.42 | 1.48 | .80 |
| .21 | 31.24 | 17.46 | 7.34 | 1.44 | .79 |
| .22 | 31.09 | 17.34 | 7.26 | 1.40 | .78 |
| .23 | 30.93 | 17.22 | 7.18 | 1.37 | .77 |
| .24 | 30.78 | 17.10 | 7.10 | 1.33 | .76 |
| .25 | 30.63 | 16.98 | 7.02 | 1.30 | .75 |
| .26 | 30.48 | 16.86 | 6.94 | 1.26 | .74 |
| .27 | 30.33 | 16.74 | 6.86 | 1.23 | .73 |
| .28 | 30.17 | 16.63 | 6.79 | 1.19 | .72 |
| .29 | 30.02 | 16.51 | 6.71 | 1.16 | .71 |
| .30 | 29.87 | 16.39 | 6.63 | 1.13 | .70 |
| .31 | 29.72 | 16.27 | 6.55 | 1.10 | .69 |
| .32 | 29.57 | 16.15 | 6.48 | 1.06 | .68 |
| .33 | 29.42 | 16.04 | 6.40 | 1.03 | .67 |
| .34 | 29.27 | 15.92 | 6.33 | 1.00 | .66 |
| .35 | 29.12 | 15.80 | 6.25 | 0.97 | .65 |
| .36 | 28.97 | 15.69 | 6.17 | 0.94 | .64 |
| .37 | 28.82 | 15.57 | 6.10 | 0.91 | .63 |
| .38 | 28.67 | 15.46 | 6.02 | 0.88 | .62 |
| .39 | 28.52 | 15.34 | 5.95 | 0.85 | .61 |
| .40 | 28.37 | 15.23 | 5.87 | 0.82 | .60 |
| .41 | 28.22 | 15.12 | 5.80 | 0.79 | .59 |
| .42 | 28.07 | 15.00 | 5.73 | 0.76 | .58 |
| .43 | 27.93 | 14.89 | 5.65 | 0.73 | .57 |
| .44 | 27.78 | 14.77 | 5.58 | 0.71 | .56 |
| .45 | 27.63 | 14.66 | 5.51 | 0.68 | .55 |
| .46 | 27.48 | 14.55 | 5.44 | 0.65 | .54 |
| .47 | 27.34 | 14.44 | 5.37 | 0.63 | .53 |
| .48 | 27.19 | 14.33 | 5.30 | 0.60 | .52 |
| .49 | 27.05 | 14.22 | 5.23 | 0.58 | .51 |
| .50 | 26.90 | 14.11 | 5.16 | 0.56 | .50 |
| Days. | 17 | 16 | 15 | 14 | Days. |

## TABLE XVII. ARG. 12′.

Equation = 58″.7 [1 — sin. (2*y* — 2*t*)].

Period, 173.31006 days.

| Days. | 0 | 10 | 20 | 30 | 40 | Days. |
|---|---|---|---|---|---|---|
| Days. | " | " | " | " | " | Days. |
| 0.0 | 0.41 | 1.71 | 10.38 | 25.33 | 44.63 | 10.0 |
| 0.1 | 0.39 | 1.76 | 10.50 | 25.51 | 44.84 | 9.9 |
| 0.2 | 0.37 | 1.81 | 10.62 | 25.69 | 45.05 | 9.8 |
| 0.3 | 0.35 | 1.87 | 10.74 | 25.86 | 45.25 | 9.7 |
| 0.4 | 0.33 | 1.92 | 10.87 | 26.04 | 45.46 | 9.6 |
| 0.5 | 0.31 | 1.97 | 10.99 | 26.22 | 45.67 | 9.5 |
| 0.6 | 0.29 | 2.03 | 11.12 | 26.40 | 45.88 | 9.4 |
| 0.7 | 0.27 | 2.08 | 11.24 | 26.58 | 46.09 | 9.3 |
| 0.8 | 0.25 | 2.14 | 11.37 | 26.76 | 46.30 | 9.2 |
| 0.9 | 0.23 | 2.19 | 11.49 | 26.94 | 46.51 | 9.1 |
| 1.0 | 0.21 | 2.25 | 11.62 | 27.12 | 46.72 | 9.0 |
| 1.1 | 0.19 | 2.31 | 11.75 | 27.30 | 46.93 | 8.9 |
| 1.2 | 0.17 | 2.37 | 11.87 | 27.48 | 47.14 | 8.8 |
| 1.3 | 0.16 | 2.43 | 12.00 | 27.66 | 47.34 | 8.7 |
| 1.4 | 0.14 | 2.49 | 12.13 | 27.84 | 47.55 | 8.6 |
| 1.5 | 0.13 | 2.55 | 12.26 | 28.02 | 47.76 | 8.5 |
| 1.6 | 0.12 | 2.61 | 12.39 | 28.20 | 47.97 | 8.4 |
| 1.7 | 0.10 | 2.68 | 12.52 | 28.38 | 48.18 | 8.3 |
| 1.8 | 0.09 | 2.74 | 12.65 | 28.56 | 48.38 | 8.2 |
| 1.9 | 0.08 | 2.81 | 12.79 | 28.75 | 48.59 | 8.1 |
| 2.0 | 0.07 | 2.87 | 12.92 | 28.93 | 48.80 | 8.0 |
| 2.1 | 0.06 | 2.94 | 13.06 | 29.11 | 49.01 | 7.9 |
| 2.2 | 0.05 | 3.00 | 13.19 | 29.30 | 49.22 | 7.8 |
| 2.3 | 0.04 | 3.07 | 13.33 | 29.48 | 49.43 | 7.7 |
| 2.4 | 0.03 | 3.14 | 13.46 | 29.67 | 49.64 | 7.6 |
| 2.5 | 0.02 | 3.21 | 13.60 | 29.85 | 49.85 | 7.5 |
| 2.6 | 0.02 | 3.28 | 13.74 | 30.04 | 50.06 | 7.4 |
| 2.7 | 0.01 | 3.35 | 13.87 | 30.22 | 50.27 | 7.3 |
| 2.8 | 0.01 | 3.42 | 14.01 | 30.41 | 50.48 | 7.2 |
| 2.9 | 0.00 | 3.49 | 14.15 | 30.59 | 50.70 | 7.1 |
| 3.0 | 0.00 | 3.56 | 14.29 | 30.78 | 50.91 | 7.0 |
| 3.1 | 0.00 | 3.63 | 14.43 | 30.97 | 51.12 | 6.9 |
| 3.2 | 0.00 | 3.71 | 14.57 | 31.15 | 51.33 | 6.8 |
| 3.3 | 0.00 | 3.78 | 14.71 | 31.34 | 51.54 | 6.7 |
| 3.4 | 0.00 | 3.86 | 14.85 | 31.53 | 51.75 | 6.6 |
| 3.5 | 0.01 | 3.93 | 14.99 | 31.72 | 51.96 | 6.5 |
| 3.6 | 0.01 | 4.01 | 15.13 | 31.91 | 52.17 | 6.4 |
| 3.7 | 0.01 | 4.08 | 15.28 | 32.10 | 52.38 | 6.3 |
| 3.8 | 0.02 | 4.16 | 15.42 | 32.29 | 52.59 | 6.2 |
| 3.9 | 0.02 | 4.24 | 15.57 | 32.48 | 52.81 | 6.1 |
| 4.0 | 0.02 | 4.32 | 15.71 | 32.67 | 53.02 | 6.0 |
| 4.1 | 0.03 | 4.40 | 15.86 | 32.86 | 53.23 | 5.9 |
| 4.2 | 0.04 | 4.48 | 16.00 | 33.05 | 53.44 | 5.8 |
| 4.3 | 0.05 | 4.56 | 16.15 | 33.24 | 53.65 | 5.7 |
| 4.4 | 0.06 | 4.65 | 16.29 | 33.44 | 53.87 | 5.6 |
| 4.5 | 0.07 | 4.73 | 16.44 | 33.63 | 54.08 | 5.5 |
| 4.6 | 0.08 | 4.81 | 16.59 | 33.82 | 54.29 | 5.4 |
| 4.7 | 0.09 | 4.90 | 16.73 | 34.02 | 54.50 | 5.3 |
| 4.8 | 0.10 | 4.98 | 16.88 | 34.21 | 54.71 | 5.2 |
| 4.9 | 0.11 | 5.07 | 17.03 | 34.41 | 54.93 | 5.1 |
| 5.0 | 0.12 | 5.16 | 17.18 | 34.60 | 55.14 | 5.0 |
| Days. | 170 | 160 | 150 | 140 | 130 | Days. |

**Note.** — Arg. 12′ = Arg. 12.

## TABLE XVI.

(*Continued.*)

Period, 26.878290 days.

| Days. | 10 | 11 | 12 | 13 | Days. |
|---|---|---|---|---|---|
| Days. | ″ | ″ | ″ | ″ | Days. |
| .50 | 26.90 | 14.11 | 5.16 | 0.56 | .50 |
| .51 | 26.76 | 14.00 | 5.09 | 0.54 | .49 |
| .52 | 26.61 | 13.89 | 5.02 | 0.52 | .48 |
| .53 | 26.47 | 13.78 | 4.96 | 0.50 | .47 |
| .54 | 26.32 | 13.67 | 4.89 | 0.48 | .46 |
| .55 | 26.18 | 13.56 | 4.82 | 0.46 | .45 |
| .56 | 26.04 | 13.45 | 4.76 | 0.44 | .44 |
| .57 | 25.89 | 13.35 | 4.69 | 0.42 | .43 |
| .58 | 25.75 | 13.24 | 4.63 | 0.40 | .42 |
| .59 | 25.60 | 13.14 | 4.56 | 0.38 | .41 |
| .60 | 25.46 | 13.03 | 4.50 | 0.36 | .40 |
| .61 | 25.32 | 12.93 | 4.44 | 0.34 | .39 |
| .62 | 25.18 | 12.82 | 4.38 | 0.32 | .38 |
| .63 | 25.03 | 12.72 | 4.31 | 0.31 | .37 |
| .64 | 24.89 | 12.61 | 4.25 | 0.29 | .36 |
| .65 | 24.75 | 12.51 | 4.19 | 0.28 | .35 |
| .66 | 24.61 | 12.41 | 4.13 | 0.26 | .34 |
| .67 | 24.47 | 12.30 | 4.07 | 0.25 | .33 |
| .68 | 24.34 | 12.20 | 4.01 | 0.23 | .32 |
| .69 | 24.20 | 12.09 | 3.95 | 0.22 | .31 |
| .70 | 24.06 | 11.99 | 3.89 | 0.21 | .30 |
| .71 | 23.92 | 11.89 | 3.83 | 0.20 | .29 |
| .72 | 23.78 | 11.79 | 3.77 | 0.18 | .28 |
| .73 | 23.65 | 11.69 | 3.72 | 0.17 | .27 |
| .74 | 23.51 | 11.59 | 3.66 | 0.16 | .26 |
| .75 | 23.37 | 11.49 | 3.60 | 0.15 | .25 |
| .76 | 23.23 | 11.39 | 3.54 | 0.14 | .24 |
| .77 | 23.10 | 11.29 | 3.49 | 0.13 | .23 |
| .78 | 22.96 | 11.20 | 3.43 | 0.12 | .22 |
| .79 | 22.83 | 11.10 | 3.38 | 0.11 | .21 |
| .80 | 22.69 | 11.00 | 3.32 | 0.10 | .20 |
| .81 | 22.56 | 10.90 | 3.27 | 0.09 | .19 |
| .82 | 22.42 | 10.80 | 3.21 | 0.08 | .18 |
| .83 | 22.29 | 10.71 | 3.16 | 0.07 | .17 |
| .84 | 22.15 | 10.61 | 3.10 | 0.06 | .16 |
| .85 | 22.02 | 10.51 | 3.05 | 0.05 | .15 |
| .86 | 21.89 | 10.41 | 3.00 | 0.04 | .14 |
| .87 | 21.76 | 10.32 | 2.95 | 0.04 | .13 |
| .88 | 21.62 | 10.22 | 2.90 | 0.03 | .12 |
| .89 | 21.49 | 10.13 | 2.85 | 0.03 | .11 |
| .90 | 21.36 | 10.03 | 2.80 | 0.03 | .10 |
| .91 | 21.23 | 9.94 | 2.75 | 0.02 | .09 |
| .92 | 21.10 | 9.85 | 2.70 | 0.02 | .08 |
| .93 | 20.97 | 9.75 | 2.66 | 0.01 | .07 |
| .94 | 20.84 | 9.66 | 2.61 | 0.01 | .06 |
| .95 | 20.71 | 9.57 | 2.56 | 0.01 | .05 |
| .96 | 20.58 | 9.48 | 2.51 | 0.00 | .04 |
| .97 | 20.45 | 9.39 | 2.47 | 0.00 | .03 |
| .98 | 20.32 | 9.29 | 2.42 | 0.00 | .02 |
| .99 | 20.19 | 9.20 | 2.38 | 0.00 | .01 |
| 1.00 | 20.06 | 9.11 | 2.33 | 0.00 | .00 |
| Days. | 17 | 16 | 15 | 14 | Days. |

## TABLE XVII. ARG. 12′.

Equation = 58″.7 [1 — sin. (2$y$ — 2$t$)].

Period, 173.31006 days.

| Days. | 0 | 10 | 20 | 30 | 40 | Days. |
|---|---|---|---|---|---|---|
| Days. | ″ | ″ | ″ | ″ | ″ | Days. |
| 5.0 | 0.12 | 5.16 | 17.18 | 34.60 | 55.14 | 5.0 |
| 5.1 | 0.13 | 5.25 | 17.33 | 34.80 | 55.35 | 4.9 |
| 5.2 | 0.14 | 5.33 | 17.48 | 34.99 | 55.56 | 4.8 |
| 5.3 | 0.16 | 5.42 | 17.63 | 35.19 | 55.77 | 4.7 |
| 5.4 | 0.17 | 5.51 | 17.79 | 35.38 | 55.99 | 4.6 |
| 5.5 | 0.19 | 5.60 | 17.94 | 35.58 | 56.20 | 4.5 |
| 5.6 | 0.21 | 5.69 | 18.09 | 35.78 | 56.41 | 4.4 |
| 5.7 | 0.23 | 5.79 | 18.25 | 35.97 | 56.63 | 4.3 |
| 5.8 | 0.25 | 5.88 | 18.40 | 36.17 | 56.84 | 4.2 |
| 5.9 | 0.27 | 5.98 | 18.56 | 36.36 | 57.06 | 4.1 |
| 6.0 | 0.29 | 6.07 | 18.71 | 36.56 | 57.27 | 4.0 |
| 6.1 | 0.31 | 6.17 | 18.86 | 36.76 | 57.48 | 3.9 |
| 6.2 | 0.33 | 6.26 | 19.02 | 36.95 | 57.69 | 3.8 |
| 6.3 | 0.35 | 6.36 | 19.17 | 37.15 | 57.91 | 3.7 |
| 6.4 | 0.38 | 6.45 | 19.33 | 37.34 | 58.12 | 3.6 |
| 6.5 | 0.40 | 6.55 | 19.49 | 37.54 | 58.33 | 3.5 |
| 6.6 | 0.42 | 6.65 | 19.65 | 37.74 | 58.54 | 3.4 |
| 6.7 | 0.44 | 6.75 | 19.81 | 37.93 | 58.76 | 3.3 |
| 6.8 | 0.47 | 6.85 | 19.97 | 38.13 | 58.97 | 3.2 |
| 6.9 | 0.49 | 6.95 | 20.13 | 38.33 | 59.19 | 3.1 |
| 7.0 | 0.52 | 7.05 | 20.29 | 38.53 | 59.40 | 3.0 |
| 7.1 | 0.55 | 7.15 | 20.45 | 38.73 | 59.61 | 2.9 |
| 7.2 | 0.58 | 7.26 | 20.61 | 38.93 | 59.82 | 2.8 |
| 7.3 | 0.61 | 7.36 | 20.77 | 39.13 | 60.04 | 2.7 |
| 7.4 | 0.64 | 7.47 | 20.94 | 39.34 | 60.25 | 2.6 |
| 7.5 | 0.67 | 7.57 | 21.10 | 39.54 | 60.46 | 2.5 |
| 7.6 | 0.70 | 7.68 | 21.26 | 39.74 | 60.67 | 2.4 |
| 7.7 | 0.73 | 7.78 | 21.43 | 39.94 | 60.88 | 2.3 |
| 7.8 | 0.77 | 7.89 | 21.59 | 40.14 | 61.10 | 2.2 |
| 7.9 | 0.80 | 7.99 | 21.76 | 40.35 | 61.31 | 2.1 |
| 8.0 | 0.84 | 8.10 | 21.93 | 40.55 | 61.52 | 2.0 |
| 8.1 | 0.88 | 8.21 | 22.10 | 40.75 | 61.73 | 1.9 |
| 8.2 | 0.92 | 8.31 | 22.26 | 40.95 | 61.94 | 1.8 |
| 8.3 | 0.96 | 8.42 | 22.43 | 41.15 | 62.16 | 1.7 |
| 8.4 | 1.00 | 8.53 | 22.60 | 41.36 | 62.37 | 1.6 |
| 8.5 | 1.04 | 8.64 | 22.77 | 41.56 | 62.58 | 1.5 |
| 8.6 | 1.08 | 8.75 | 22.94 | 41.76 | 62.79 | 1.4 |
| 8.7 | 1.12 | 8.86 | 23.10 | 41.97 | 63.00 | 1.3 |
| 8.8 | 1.17 | 8.97 | 23.27 | 42.17 | 63.22 | 1.2 |
| 8.9 | 1.21 | 9.09 | 23.44 | 42.38 | 63.43 | 1.1 |
| 9.0 | 1.25 | 9.20 | 23.61 | 42.58 | 63.64 | 1.0 |
| 9.1 | 1.29 | 9.32 | 23.78 | 42.78 | 63.85 | 0.9 |
| 9.2 | 1.33 | 9.43 | 23.95 | 42.99 | 64.06 | 0.8 |
| 9.3 | 1.38 | 9.55 | 24.12 | 43.19 | 64.28 | 0.7 |
| 9.4 | 1.42 | 9.66 | 24.29 | 43.40 | 64.49 | 0.6 |
| 9.5 | 1.46 | 9.78 | 24.46 | 43.60 | 64.70 | 0.5 |
| 9.6 | 1.51 | 9.90 | 24.63 | 43.81 | 64.91 | 0.4 |
| 9.7 | 1.56 | 10.02 | 24.81 | 44.01 | 65.12 | 0.3 |
| 9.8 | 1.61 | 10.14 | 24.98 | 44.22 | 65.34 | 0.2 |
| 9.9 | 1.66 | 10.26 | 25.16 | 44.42 | 65.55 | 0.1 |
| 10.0 | 1.71 | 10.38 | 25.33 | 44.63 | 65.76 | 0.0 |
| Days. | 170 | 160 | 150 | 140 | 130 | Days. |

NOTE. — Arg. 12′ = Arg. 12.

## TABLE XVII.

(*Continued*).

Period, 173.31006 days.

| Days. | 50 | 60 | 70 | 80 | Days. |
|---|---|---|---|---|---|
| Days. | ″ | ″ | ″ | ″ | Days. |
| 0.0 | 65.76 | 85.98 | 102.63 | 113.58 | 10.0 |
| 0.1 | 65.97 | 86.17 | 102.77 | 113.65 | 9.9 |
| 0.2 | 66.18 | 86.36 | 102.91 | 113.73 | 9.8 |
| 0.3 | 66.39 | 86.55 | 103.05 | 113.80 | 9.7 |
| 0.4 | 66.61 | 86.73 | 103.18 | 113.88 | 9.6 |
| 0.5 | 66.82 | 86.92 | 103.32 | 113.95 | 9.5 |
| 0.6 | 67.03 | 87.11 | 103.46 | 114.02 | 9.4 |
| 0.7 | 67.24 | 87.29 | 103.59 | 114.09 | 9.3 |
| 0.8 | 67.45 | 87.48 | 103.73 | 114.16 | 9.2 |
| 0.9 | 67.66 | 87.66 | 103.86 | 114.23 | 9.1 |
| 1.0 | 67.87 | 87.85 | 104.00 | 114.30 | 9.0 |
| 1.1 | 68.08 | 88.03 | 104.13 | 114.37 | 8.9 |
| 1.2 | 68.29 | 88.22 | 104.27 | 114.43 | 8.8 |
| 1.3 | 68.50 | 88.40 | 104.40 | 114.50 | 8.7 |
| 1.4 | 68.71 | 88.59 | 104.54 | 114.56 | 8.6 |
| 1.5 | 68.92 | 88.77 | 104.67 | 114.63 | 8.5 |
| 1.6 | 69.13 | 88.95 | 104.80 | 114.69 | 8.4 |
| 1.7 | 69.34 | 89.14 | 104.94 | 114.76 | 8.3 |
| 1.8 | 69.55 | 89.32 | 105.07 | 114.82 | 8.2 |
| 1.9 | 69.76 | 89.50 | 105.20 | 114.88 | 8.1 |
| 2.0 | 69.97 | 89.68 | 105.33 | 114.94 | 8.0 |
| 2.1 | 70.18 | 89.86 | 105.46 | 115.00 | 7.9 |
| 2.2 | 70.39 | 90.04 | 105.59 | 115.06 | 7.8 |
| 2.3 | 70.60 | 90.22 | 105.72 | 115.12 | 7.7 |
| 2.4 | 70.80 | 90.39 | 105.84 | 115.17 | 7.6 |
| 2.5 | 71.01 | 90.57 | 105.97 | 115.23 | 7.5 |
| 2.6 | 71.22 | 90.75 | 106.10 | 115.29 | 7.4 |
| 2.7 | 71.43 | 90.92 | 106.22 | 115.34 | 7.3 |
| 2.8 | 71.64 | 91.10 | 106.35 | 115.40 | 7.2 |
| 2.9 | 71.84 | 91.27 | 106.47 | 115.45 | 7.1 |
| 3.0 | 72.05 | 91.45 | 106.60 | 115.51 | 7.0 |
| 3.1 | 72.26 | 91.62 | 106.72 | 115.56 | 6.9 |
| 3.2 | 72.46 | 91.80 | 106.84 | 115.62 | 6.8 |
| 3.3 | 72.67 | 91.97 | 106.96 | 115.67 | 6.7 |
| 3.4 | 72.87 | 92.15 | 107.08 | 115.72 | 6.6 |
| 3.5 | 73.08 | 92.32 | 107.20 | 115.77 | 6.5 |
| 3.6 | 73.29 | 92.49 | 107.32 | 115.82 | 6.4 |
| 3.7 | 73.49 | 92.67 | 107.44 | 115.87 | 6.3 |
| 3.8 | 73.70 | 92.84 | 107.56 | 115.92 | 6.2 |
| 3.9 | 73.90 | 93.01 | 107.67 | 115.96 | 6.1 |
| 4.0 | 74.11 | 93.18 | 107.79 | 116.01 | 6.0 |
| 4.1 | 74.31 | 93.35 | 107.91 | 116.05 | 5.9 |
| 4.2 | 74.52 | 93.53 | 108.02 | 116.10 | 5.8 |
| 4.3 | 74.72 | 93.70 | 108.14 | 116.14 | 5.7 |
| 4.4 | 74.93 | 93.87 | 108.25 | 116.19 | 5.6 |
| 4.5 | 75.13 | 94.04 | 108.37 | 116.23 | 5.5 |
| 4.6 | 75.33 | 94.21 | 108.48 | 116.27 | 5.4 |
| 4.7 | 75.54 | 94.38 | 108.60 | 116.31 | 5.3 |
| 4.8 | 75.74 | 94.55 | 108.71 | 116.35 | 5.2 |
| 4.9 | 75.95 | 94.72 | 108.82 | 116.39 | 5.1 |
| 5.0 | 76.15 | 94.89 | 108.93 | 116.43 | 5.0 |
| Days. | 120 | 110 | 100 | 90 | Days. |

## TABLE XVIII. ARG. 13.

Equation = 38″.0 [1 + sin. (4*t* — *x*)].

Period, 10.084597 days.

| Days. | 0 | 1 | 2 | 3 | 4 | 5 | Days. |
|---|---|---|---|---|---|---|---|
| Days. | ″ | ″ | ″ | ″ | ″ | ″ | Days. |
| .00 | 6.57 | 0.02 | 7.74 | 26.82 | 50.13 | 68.86 | 1.00 |
| .01 | 6.44 | 0.03 | 7.89 | 27.05 | 50.35 | 69.00 | .99 |
| .02 | 6.31 | 0.04 | 8.03 | 27.27 | 50.58 | 69.13 | .98 |
| .03 | 6.18 | 0.05 | 8.18 | 27.50 | 50.80 | 69.27 | .97 |
| .04 | 6.05 | 0.06 | 8.32 | 27.73 | 51.02 | 69.40 | .96 |
| .05 | 5.92 | 0.07 | 8.47 | 27.96 | 51.24 | 69.54 | .95 |
| .06 | 5.79 | 0.09 | 8.62 | 28.19 | 51.46 | 69.67 | .94 |
| .07 | 5.67 | 0.10 | 8.77 | 28.42 | 51.68 | 69.80 | .93 |
| .08 | 5.54 | 0.12 | 8.92 | 28.65 | 51.90 | 69.93 | .92 |
| .09 | 5.42 | 0.13 | 9.08 | 28.88 | 52.12 | 70.05 | .91 |
| .10 | 5.30 | 0.15 | 9.23 | 29.11 | 52.34 | 70.18 | .90 |
| .11 | 5.18 | 0.17 | 9.39 | 29.34 | 52.56 | 70.30 | .89 |
| .12 | 5.06 | 0.20 | 9.54 | 29.57 | 52.78 | 70.43 | .88 |
| .13 | 4.94 | 0.22 | 9.70 | 29.80 | 53.00 | 70.55 | .87 |
| .14 | 4.83 | 0.25 | 9.86 | 30.04 | 53.21 | 70.67 | .86 |
| .15 | 4.71 | 0.27 | 10.02 | 30.27 | 53.43 | 70.79 | .85 |
| .16 | 4.60 | 0.30 | 10.18 | 30.50 | 53.64 | 70.91 | .84 |
| .17 | 4.49 | 0.33 | 10.34 | 30.73 | 53.86 | 71.02 | .83 |
| .18 | 4.38 | 0.36 | 10.50 | 30.96 | 54.07 | 71.14 | .82 |
| .19 | 4.27 | 0.40 | 10.67 | 31.20 | 54.29 | 71.25 | .81 |
| .20 | 4.16 | 0.43 | 10.83 | 31.43 | 54.50 | 71.37 | .80 |
| .21 | 4.06 | 0.47 | 11.00 | 31.66 | 54.71 | 71.48 | .79 |
| .22 | 3.95 | 0.51 | 11.17 | 31.90 | 54.93 | 71.59 | .78 |
| .23 | 3.85 | 0.55 | 11.33 | 32.13 | 55.14 | 71.70 | .77 |
| .24 | 3.74 | 0.59 | 11.50 | 32.37 | 55.35 | 71.81 | .76 |
| .25 | 3.64 | 0.63 | 11.67 | 32.60 | 55.56 | 71.92 | .75 |
| .26 | 3.54 | 0.68 | 11.84 | 32.83 | 55.77 | 72.02 | .74 |
| .27 | 3.44 | 0.72 | 12.01 | 33.07 | 55.98 | 72.13 | .73 |
| .28 | 3.34 | 0.77 | 12.18 | 33.30 | 56.19 | 72.23 | .72 |
| .29 | 3.25 | 0.81 | 12.36 | 33.54 | 56.40 | 72.34 | .71 |
| .30 | 3.15 | 0.86 | 12.53 | 33.77 | 56.61 | 72.44 | .70 |
| .31 | 3.06 | 0.91 | 12.71 | 34.01 | 56.81 | 72.54 | .69 |
| .32 | 2.96 | 0.97 | 12.88 | 34.24 | 57.02 | 72.64 | .68 |
| .33 | 2.87 | 1.02 | 13.06 | 34.48 | 57.22 | 72.74 | .67 |
| .34 | 2.78 | 1.08 | 13.24 | 34.71 | 57.43 | 72.83 | .66 |
| .35 | 2.69 | 1.13 | 13.42 | 34.95 | 57.63 | 72.93 | .65 |
| .36 | 2.61 | 1.19 | 13.60 | 35.19 | 57.83 | 73.02 | .64 |
| .37 | 2.52 | 1.25 | 13.78 | 35.42 | 58.03 | 73.11 | .63 |
| .38 | 2.44 | 1.31 | 13.96 | 35.66 | 58.23 | 73.20 | .62 |
| .39 | 2.35 | 1.37 | 14.15 | 35.89 | 58.43 | 73.29 | .61 |
| .40 | 2.27 | 1.43 | 14.33 | 36.13 | 58.63 | 73.38 | .60 |
| .41 | 2.19 | 1.50 | 14.52 | 36.37 | 58.83 | 73.46 | .59 |
| .42 | 2.11 | 1.56 | 14.70 | 36.61 | 59.03 | 73.55 | .58 |
| .43 | 2.03 | 1.63 | 14.89 | 36.84 | 59.23 | 73.63 | .57 |
| .44 | 1.96 | 1.70 | 15.08 | 37.08 | 59.42 | 73.71 | .56 |
| .45 | 1.88 | 1.77 | 15.27 | 37.32 | 59.62 | 73.79 | .55 |
| .46 | 1.81 | 1.84 | 15.46 | 37.56 | 59.81 | 73.87 | .54 |
| .47 | 1.74 | 1.92 | 15.65 | 37.79 | 60.00 | 73.94 | .53 |
| .48 | 1.67 | 1.99 | 15.84 | 38.03 | 60.20 | 74.02 | .52 |
| .49 | 1.60 | 2.07 | 16.04 | 38.26 | 60.39 | 74.09 | .51 |
| .50 | 1.53 | 2.15 | 16.23 | 38.50 | 60.58 | 74.17 | .50 |
| Days. | 11 | 10 | 9 | 8 | 7 | 6 | Days. |

## TABLE XVII.

(*Continued.*)

Period, 173.31006 days.

| Days. | 50 | 60 | 70 | 80 | Days. |
|---|---|---|---|---|---|
| Days. | ″ | ″ | ″ | ″ | Days. |
| 5.0 | 76.15 | 94.89 | 108.93 | 116.43 | 5.0 |
| 5.1 | 76.35 | 95.06 | 109.04 | 116.47 | 4.9 |
| 5.2 | 76.56 | 95.22 | 109.15 | 116.50 | 4.8 |
| 5.3 | 76.76 | 95.39 | 109.26 | 116.54 | 4.7 |
| 5.4 | 76.96 | 95.55 | 109.36 | 116.57 | 4.6 |
| 5.5 | 77.16 | 95.72 | 109.47 | 116.61 | 4.5 |
| 5.6 | 77.36 | 95.88 | 109.58 | 116.64 | 4.4 |
| 5.7 | 77.57 | 96.05 | 109.68 | 116.68 | 4.3 |
| 5.8 | 77.77 | 96.21 | 109.79 | 116.71 | 4.2 |
| 5.9 | 77.97 | 96.38 | 109.89 | 116.75 | 4.1 |
| 6.0 | 78.17 | 96.54 | 110.00 | 116.78 | 4.0 |
| 6.1 | 78.37 | 96.70 | 110.10 | 116.81 | 3.9 |
| 6.2 | 78.57 | 96.87 | 110.21 | 116.84 | 3.8 |
| 6.3 | 78.77 | 97.03 | 110.31 | 116.87 | 3.7 |
| 6.4 | 78.97 | 97.19 | 110.41 | 116.90 | 3.6 |
| 6.5 | 79.17 | 97.35 | 110.51 | 116.93 | 3.5 |
| 6.6 | 79.37 | 97.51 | 110.61 | 116.95 | 3.4 |
| 6.7 | 79.57 | 97.67 | 110.70 | 116.98 | 3.3 |
| 6.8 | 79.77 | 97.83 | 110.80 | 117.00 | 3.2 |
| 6.9 | 79.96 | 97.99 | 110.90 | 117.02 | 3.1 |
| 7.0 | 80.16 | 98.15 | 111.00 | 117.04 | 3.0 |
| 7.1 | 80.36 | 98.31 | 111.09 | 117.06 | 2.9 |
| 7.2 | 80.56 | 98.46 | 111.19 | 117.08 | 2.8 |
| 7.3 | 80.76 | 98.62 | 111.28 | 117.10 | 2.7 |
| 7.4 | 80.95 | 98.77 | 111.38 | 117.12 | 2.6 |
| 7.5 | 81.15 | 98.93 | 111.47 | 117.14 | 2.5 |
| 7.6 | 81.35 | 99.08 | 111.56 | 117.16 | 2.4 |
| 7.7 | 81.54 | 99.24 | 111.66 | 117.18 | 2.3 |
| 7.8 | 81.74 | 99.39 | 111.75 | 117.20 | 2.2 |
| 7.9 | 81.93 | 99.55 | 111.84 | 117.21 | 2.1 |
| 8.0 | 82.13 | 99.70 | 111.93 | 117.23 | 2.0 |
| 8.1 | 82.32 | 99.85 | 112.02 | 117.25 | 1.9 |
| 8.2 | 82.52 | 100.00 | 112.11 | 117.26 | 1.8 |
| 8.3 | 82.71 | 100.15 | 112.20 | 117.28 | 1.7 |
| 8.4 | 82.91 | 100.30 | 112.28 | 117.29 | 1.6 |
| 8.5 | 83.10 | 100.45 | 112.37 | 117.31 | 1.5 |
| 8.6 | 83.29 | 100.60 | 112.45 | 117.32 | 1.4 |
| 8.7 | 83.48 | 100.75 | 112.54 | 117.33 | 1.3 |
| 8.8 | 83.68 | 100.90 | 112.62 | 117.34 | 1.2 |
| 8.9 | 83.87 | 101.04 | 112.71 | 117.35 | 1.1 |
| 9.0 | 84.06 | 101.19 | 112.79 | 117.36 | 1.0 |
| 9.1 | 84.25 | 101.34 | 112.87 | 117.37 | 0.9 |
| 9.2 | 84.45 | 101.48 | 112.95 | 117.38 | 0.8 |
| 9.3 | 84.64 | 101.63 | 113.03 | 117.38 | 0.7 |
| 9.4 | 84.83 | 101.77 | 113.11 | 117.39 | 0.6 |
| 9.5 | 85.02 | 101.92 | 113.19 | 117.39 | 0.5 |
| 9.6 | 85.21 | 102.06 | 113.27 | 117.40 | 0.4 |
| 9.7 | 85.41 | 102.21 | 113.35 | 117.40 | 0.3 |
| 9.8 | 85.60 | 102.35 | 113.43 | 117.40 | 0.2 |
| 9.9 | 85.79 | 102.49 | 113.50 | 117.40 | 0.1 |
| 10.0 | 85.98 | 102.63 | 113.58 | 117.40 | 0.0 |
| Days. | 120 | 110 | 100 | 90 | Days. |

## TABLE XVIII. ARG. 13.

Equation $= 38''.0\ [1 + \sin.\ (4t - x)]$.

Period, 10.084597 days.

| Days. | 0 | 1 | 2 | 3 | 4 | 5 | Days. |
|---|---|---|---|---|---|---|---|
| Days. | ″ | ″ | ″ | ″ | ″ | ″ | Days. |
| .50 | 1.53 | 2.15 | 16.23 | 38.50 | 60.58 | 74.17 | .50 |
| .51 | 1.47 | 2.23 | 16.43 | 38.74 | 60.77 | 74.24 | .49 |
| .52 | 1.40 | 2.31 | 16.62 | 38.97 | 60.96 | 74.31 | .48 |
| .53 | 1.34 | 2.39 | 16.82 | 39.21 | 61.15 | 74.38 | .47 |
| .54 | 1.28 | 2.48 | 17.02 | 39.44 | 61.33 | 74.45 | .46 |
| .55 | 1.22 | 2.56 | 17.22 | 39.68 | 61.52 | 74.52 | .45 |
| .56 | 1.16 | 2.65 | 17.42 | 39.92 | 61.70 | 74.58 | .44 |
| .57 | 1.11 | 2.73 | 17.62 | 40.15 | 61.89 | 74.65 | .43 |
| .58 | 1.05 | 2.82 | 17.82 | 40.39 | 62.07 | 74.71 | .42 |
| .59 | 1.00 | 2.91 | 18.02 | 40.62 | 62.26 | 74.77 | .41 |
| .60 | 0.94 | 3.00 | 18.22 | 40.86 | 62.44 | 74.83 | .40 |
| .61 | 0.89 | 3.10 | 18.42 | 41.10 | 62.62 | 74.89 | .39 |
| .62 | 0.84 | 3.19 | 18.63 | 41.33 | 62.80 | 74.94 | .38 |
| .63 | 0.79 | 3.29 | 18.83 | 41.57 | 62.98 | 75.00 | .37 |
| .64 | 0.75 | 3.38 | 19.04 | 41.80 | 63.15 | 75.05 | .36 |
| .65 | 0.70 | 3.48 | 19.24 | 42.04 | 63.33 | 75.10 | .35 |
| .66 | 0.66 | 3.58 | 19.45 | 42.28 | 63.50 | 75.15 | .34 |
| .67 | 0.61 | 3.68 | 19.65 | 42.51 | 63.68 | 75.20 | .33 |
| .68 | 0.57 | 3.78 | 19.86 | 42.75 | 63.85 | 75.25 | .32 |
| .69 | 0.53 | 3.89 | 20.07 | 42.98 | 64.03 | 75.29 | .31 |
| .70 | 0.49 | 3.99 | 20.28 | 43.22 | 64.20 | 75.34 | .30 |
| .71 | 0.45 | 4.10 | 20.49 | 43.45 | 64.37 | 75.38 | .29 |
| .72 | 0.42 | 4.20 | 20.70 | 43.69 | 64.54 | 75.42 | .28 |
| .73 | 0.38 | 4.31 | 20.91 | 43.92 | 64.71 | 75.46 | .27 |
| .74 | 0.35 | 4.42 | 21.12 | 44.16 | 64.88 | 75.50 | .26 |
| .75 | 0.32 | 4.53 | 21.33 | 44.39 | 65.05 | 75.54 | .25 |
| .76 | 0.29 | 4.65 | 21.54 | 44.62 | 65.21 | 75.57 | .24 |
| .77 | 0.27 | 4.76 | 21.76 | 44.85 | 65.38 | 75.61 | .23 |
| .78 | 0.24 | 4.88 | 21.97 | 45.09 | 65.54 | 75.64 | .22 |
| .79 | 0.22 | 4.99 | 22.19 | 45.32 | 65.71 | 75.67 | .21 |
| .80 | 0.19 | 5.11 | 22.40 | 45.55 | 65.87 | 75.70 | .20 |
| .81 | 0.17 | 5.23 | 22.62 | 45.78 | 66.03 | 75.73 | .19 |
| .82 | 0.15 | 5.36 | 22.83 | 46.01 | 66.18 | 75.75 | .18 |
| .83 | 0.13 | 5.48 | 23.05 | 46.25 | 66.34 | 75.78 | .17 |
| .84 | 0.11 | 5.61 | 23.26 | 46.48 | 66.49 | 75.80 | .16 |
| .85 | 0.09 | 5.73 | 23.48 | 46.71 | 66.65 | 75.83 | .15 |
| .86 | 0.08 | 5.86 | 23.70 | 46.94 | 66.80 | 75.85 | .14 |
| .87 | 0.06 | 5.98 | 23.92 | 47.17 | 66.96 | 75.87 | .13 |
| .88 | 0.05 | 6.11 | 24.14 | 47.40 | 67.11 | 75.89 | .12 |
| .89 | 0.04 | 6.24 | 24.36 | 47.63 | 67.26 | 75.90 | .11 |
| .90 | 0.03 | 6.37 | 24.58 | 47.86 | 67.41 | 75.92 | .10 |
| .91 | 0.02 | 6.50 | 24.80 | 48.09 | 67.56 | 75.93 | .09 |
| .92 | 0.02 | 6.64 | 25.02 | 48.32 | 67.71 | 75.95 | .08 |
| .93 | 0.01 | 6.77 | 25.24 | 48.55 | 67.86 | 75.96 | .07 |
| .94 | 0.01 | 6.91 | 25.47 | 48.77 | 68.00 | 75.97 | .06 |
| .95 | 0.00 | 7.04 | 25.69 | 49.00 | 68.15 | 75.98 | .05 |
| .96 | 0.00 | 7.18 | 25.92 | 49.23 | 68.29 | 75.99 | .04 |
| .97 | 0.00 | 7.32 | 26.14 | 49.45 | 68.44 | 75.99 | .03 |
| .98 | 0.01 | 7.46 | 26.37 | 49.68 | 68.58 | 76.00 | .02 |
| .99 | 0.01 | 7.60 | 26.59 | 49.90 | 68.72 | 76.00 | .01 |
| 1.00 | 0.02 | 7.74 | 26.82 | 50.13 | 68.86 | 76.00 | .00 |
| Days. | 11 | 10 | 9 | 8 | 7 | 6 | Days. |

# TABLE XIX. ARGUMENT 14.

Equation $= 28''.8\ [1 - \sin.\ (2t + z - x)]$.

Period, 29.263279 days.

| Days. | 0 | 1 | 2 | 3 | 4 | 5 | 6 | 7 | 8 | 9 | Days. |
|---|---|---|---|---|---|---|---|---|---|---|---|
| Days. | $''$ | $''$ | $''$ | $''$ | $''$ | $''$ | $''$ | $''$ | $''$ | $''$ | Days. |
| .00 | 57.50 | 57.33 | 55.86 | 53.13 | 49.27 | 44.50 | 38.99 | 33.02 | 26.85 | 20.77 | 1.00 |
| .01 | 57.51 | 57.32 | 55.84 | 53.10 | 49.23 | 44.45 | 38.93 | 32.96 | 26.79 | 20.71 | .99 |
| .02 | 57.52 | 57.31 | 55.82 | 53.07 | 49.19 | 44.40 | 38.87 | 32.90 | 26.73 | 20.65 | .98 |
| .03 | 57.52 | 57.30 | 55.79 | 53.03 | 49.14 | 44.34 | 38.82 | 32.84 | 26.67 | 20.59 | .97 |
| .04 | 57.53 | 57.30 | 55.77 | 53.00 | 49.10 | 44.29 | 38.76 | 32.78 | 26.60 | 20.53 | .96 |
| .05 | 57.53 | 57.29 | 55.75 | 52.97 | 49.05 | 44.24 | 38.70 | 32.72 | 26.54 | 20.47 | .95 |
| .06 | 57.54 | 57.28 | 55.73 | 52.93 | 49.01 | 44.18 | 38.64 | 32.65 | 26.48 | 20.42 | .94 |
| .07 | 57.54 | 57.27 | 55.71 | 52.90 | 48.96 | 44.13 | 38.59 | 32.59 | 26.41 | 20.36 | .93 |
| .08 | 57.54 | 57.26 | 55.68 | 52.87 | 48.92 | 44.08 | 38.53 | 32.53 | 26.35 | 20.30 | .92 |
| .09 | 57.55 | 57.25 | 55.66 | 52.83 | 48.87 | 44.02 | 38.47 | 32.47 | 26.29 | 20.24 | .91 |
| .10 | 57.55 | 57.24 | 55.64 | 52.80 | 48.83 | 43.97 | 38.41 | 32.41 | 26.23 | 20.18 | .90 |
| .11 | 57.55 | 57.23 | 55.62 | 52.77 | 48.78 | 43.92 | 38.35 | 32.35 | 26.17 | 20.12 | .89 |
| .12 | 57.56 | 57.22 | 55.60 | 52.73 | 48.74 | 43.86 | 38.29 | 32.29 | 26.11 | 20.06 | .88 |
| .13 | 57.56 | 57.21 | 55.57 | 52.70 | 48.69 | 43.81 | 38.23 | 32.23 | 26.05 | 20.00 | .87 |
| .14 | 57.56 | 57.20 | 55.55 | 52.66 | 48.65 | 43.76 | 38.17 | 32.16 | 25.98 | 19.94 | .86 |
| .15 | 57.57 | 57.19 | 55.53 | 52.63 | 48.60 | 43.71 | 38.11 | 32.10 | 25.92 | 19.88 | .85 |
| .16 | 57.57 | 57.18 | 55.50 | 52.59 | 48.56 | 43.65 | 38.06 | 32.04 | 25.86 | 19.83 | .84 |
| .17 | 57.57 | 57.17 | 55.48 | 52.56 | 48.51 | 43.60 | 38.00 | 31.97 | 25.79 | 19.77 | .83 |
| .18 | 57.58 | 57.16 | 55.46 | 52.52 | 48.47 | 43.55 | 37.94 | 31.91 | 25.75 | 19.71 | .82 |
| .19 | 57.58 | 57.15 | 55.43 | 52.49 | 48.42 | 43.49 | 37.88 | 31.85 | 25.67 | 19.65 | .81 |
| .20 | 57.58 | 57.14 | 55.41 | 52.45 | 48.38 | 43.44 | 37.82 | 31.79 | 25.61 | 19.59 | .80 |
| .21 | 57.58 | 57.13 | 55.39 | 52.41 | 48.33 | 43.39 | 37.76 | 31.73 | 25.55 | 19.53 | .79 |
| .22 | 57.58 | 57.12 | 55.36 | 52.38 | 48.29 | 43.34 | 37.70 | 31.67 | 25.49 | 19.47 | .78 |
| .23 | 57.59 | 57.11 | 55.34 | 52.34 | 48.24 | 43.28 | 37.64 | 31.61 | 25.43 | 19.41 | .77 |
| .24 | 57.59 | 57.10 | 55.31 | 52.30 | 48.20 | 43.23 | 37.58 | 31.54 | 25.36 | 19.36 | .76 |
| .25 | 57.59 | 57.09 | 55.29 | 52.27 | 48.15 | 43.18 | 37.52 | 31.48 | 25.30 | 19.30 | .75 |
| .26 | 57.59 | 57.08 | 55.26 | 52.23 | 48.11 | 43.12 | 37.47 | 31.42 | 25.24 | 19.24 | .74 |
| .27 | 57.59 | 57.06 | 55.24 | 52.19 | 48.06 | 43.07 | 37.41 | 31.35 | 25.17 | 19.19 | .73 |
| .28 | 57.59 | 57.05 | 55.21 | 52.16 | 48.02 | 43.02 | 37.35 | 31.29 | 25.11 | 19.13 | .72 |
| .29 | 57.60 | 57.04 | 55.19 | 52.12 | 47.97 | 42.96 | 37.29 | 31.23 | 25.05 | 19.07 | .71 |
| .30 | 57.60 | 57.03 | 55.16 | 52.08 | 47.93 | 42.91 | 37.23 | 31.17 | 24.99 | 19.01 | .70 |
| .31 | 57.60 | 57.02 | 55.14 | 52.04 | 47.88 | 42.86 | 37.17 | 31.11 | 24.93 | 18.95 | .69 |
| .32 | 57.60 | 57.01 | 55.11 | 52.00 | 47.84 | 42.80 | 37.11 | 31.05 | 24.87 | 18.89 | .68 |
| .33 | 57.60 | 56.99 | 55.09 | 51.97 | 47.79 | 42.75 | 37.05 | 30.99 | 24.81 | 18.83 | .67 |
| .34 | 57.60 | 56.98 | 55.06 | 51.93 | 47.75 | 42.70 | 36.99 | 30.93 | 24.74 | 18.78 | .66 |
| .35 | 57.60 | 56.97 | 55.03 | 51.89 | 47.70 | 42.64 | 36.93 | 30.87 | 24.68 | 18.72 | .65 |
| .36 | 57.60 | 56.95 | 55.01 | 51.85 | 47.66 | 42.59 | 36.88 | 30.80 | 24.62 | 18.66 | .64 |
| .37 | 57.60 | 56.94 | 54.98 | 51.81 | 47.61 | 42.53 | 36.82 | 30.74 | 24.55 | 18.61 | .63 |
| .38 | 57.60 | 56.93 | 54.96 | 51.78 | 47.56 | 42.48 | 36.76 | 30.68 | 24.49 | 18.55 | .62 |
| .39 | 57.60 | 56.91 | 54.93 | 51.74 | 47.52 | 42.42 | 36.70 | 30.62 | 24.43 | 18.49 | .61 |
| .40 | 57.60 | 56.90 | 54.90 | 51.70 | 47.47 | 42.37 | 36.64 | 30.56 | 24.37 | 18.43 | .60 |
| .41 | 57.60 | 56.89 | 54.87 | 51.66 | 47.43 | 42.31 | 36.58 | 30.50 | 24.31 | 18.37 | .59 |
| .42 | 57.59 | 56.87 | 54.85 | 51.62 | 47.38 | 42.26 | 36.52 | 30.44 | 24.25 | 18.31 | .58 |
| .43 | 57.59 | 56.86 | 54.82 | 51.59 | 47.33 | 42.20 | 36.46 | 30.38 | 24.19 | 18.26 | .57 |
| .44 | 57.59 | 56.84 | 54.79 | 51.55 | 47.29 | 42.15 | 36.40 | 30.31 | 24.13 | 18.20 | .56 |
| .45 | 57.59 | 56.83 | 54.77 | 51.51 | 47.24 | 42.09 | 36.34 | 30.25 | 24.07 | 18.14 | .55 |
| .46 | 57.59 | 56.81 | 54.74 | 51.47 | 47.19 | 42.04 | 36.28 | 30.19 | 24.00 | 18.09 | .54 |
| .47 | 57.59 | 56.80 | 54.71 | 51.43 | 47.14 | 41.98 | 36.22 | 30.12 | 23.94 | 18.03 | .53 |
| .48 | 57.58 | 56.78 | 54.69 | 51.40 | 47.09 | 41.93 | 36.16 | 30.06 | 23.88 | 17.98 | .52 |
| .49 | 57.58 | 56.77 | 54.66 | 51.36 | 47.04 | 41.87 | 36.10 | 30.00 | 23.82 | 17.92 | .51 |
| .50 | 57.58 | 56.75 | 54.63 | 51.32 | 46.99 | 41.82 | 36.04 | 29.94 | 23.76 | 17.86 | .50 |
| Days. | 29 | 28 | 27 | 26 | 25 | 24 | 23 | 22 | 21 | 20 | Days. |

# TABLE XIX. ARGUMENT 14.

Equation $= 28''.8\ [1 - \sin.\ (2t + z - x)]$.

Period, 29.263279 days.

| Days. | 0 | 1 | 2 | 3 | 4 | 5 | 6 | 7 | 8 | 9 | Days. |
|---|---|---|---|---|---|---|---|---|---|---|---|
| Days. | " | " | " | " | " | " | " | " | " | " | Days. |
| .50 | 57.58 | 56.75 | 54.63 | 51.32 | 46.99 | 41.82 | 36.04 | 29.94 | 23.76 | 17.86 | .50 |
| .51 | 57.58 | 56.74 | 54.60 | 51.28 | 46.94 | 41.76 | 35.98 | 29.88 | 23.70 | 17.80 | .49 |
| .52 | 57.58 | 56.72 | 54.57 | 51.24 | 46.89 | 41.71 | 35.92 | 29.82 | 23.64 | 17.74 | .48 |
| .53 | 57.57 | 56.71 | 54.55 | 51.20 | 46.85 | 41.65 | 35.86 | 29.76 | 23.58 | 17.69 | .47 |
| .54 | 57.57 | 56.69 | 54.52 | 51.17 | 46.80 | 41.60 | 35.80 | 29.69 | 23.52 | 17.63 | .46 |
| .55 | 57.57 | 56.68 | 54.49 | 51.13 | 46.75 | 41.54 | 35.74 | 29.63 | 23.46 | 17.57 | .45 |
| .56 | 57.57 | 56.66 | 54.46 | 51.09 | 46.70 | 41.49 | 35.68 | 29.57 | 23.40 | 17.52 | .44 |
| .57 | 57.57 | 56.65 | 54.44 | 51.05 | 46.65 | 41.43 | 35.62 | 29.50 | 23.34 | 17.46 | .43 |
| .58 | 57.56 | 56.63 | 54.41 | 51.01 | 46.60 | 41.38 | 35.56 | 29.44 | 23.28 | 17.41 | .42 |
| .59 | 57.56 | 56.62 | 54.38 | 50.97 | 46.55 | 41.32 | 35.50 | 29.38 | 23.22 | 17.35 | .41 |
| .60 | 57.56 | 56.60 | 54.35 | 50.93 | 46.50 | 41.26 | 35.44 | 29.32 | 23.16 | 17.29 | .40 |
| .61 | 57.56 | 56.58 | 54.32 | 50.89 | 46.45 | 41.21 | 35.38 | 29.26 | 23.10 | 17.23 | .39 |
| .62 | 57.55 | 56.57 | 54.29 | 50.85 | 46.40 | 41.15 | 35.32 | 29.20 | 23.04 | 17.17 | .38 |
| .63 | 57.55 | 56.55 | 54.27 | 50.81 | 46.36 | 41.10 | 35.26 | 29.14 | 22.98 | 17.12 | .37 |
| .64 | 57.55 | 56.53 | 54.24 | 50.77 | 46.31 | 41.04 | 35.20 | 29.07 | 22.92 | 17.06 | .36 |
| .65 | 57.54 | 56.52 | 54.21 | 50.73 | 46.26 | 40.98 | 35.14 | 29.01 | 22.86 | 17.00 | .35 |
| .66 | 57.54 | 56.50 | 54.18 | 50.69 | 46.21 | 40.93 | 35.08 | 28.95 | 22.80 | 16.95 | .34 |
| .67 | 57.54 | 56.48 | 54.15 | 50.65 | 46.16 | 40.87 | 35.02 | 28.88 | 22.74 | 16.89 | .33 |
| .68 | 57.53 | 56.47 | 54.13 | 50.61 | 46.11 | 40.81 | 34.96 | 28.82 | 22.68 | 16.84 | .32 |
| .69 | 57.53 | 56.45 | 54.10 | 50.57 | 46.06 | 40.76 | 34.90 | 28.76 | 22.62 | 16.78 | .31 |
| .70 | 57.53 | 56.43 | 54.07 | 50.53 | 46.01 | 40.70 | 34.84 | 28.70 | 22.56 | 16.72 | .30 |
| .71 | 57.52 | 56.41 | 54.04 | 50.49 | 45.96 | 40.64 | 34.78 | 28.64 | 22.50 | 16.66 | .29 |
| .72 | 57.52 | 56.39 | 54.01 | 50.45 | 45.91 | 40.59 | 34.72 | 28.58 | 22.44 | 16.61 | .28 |
| .73 | 57.52 | 56.38 | 53.98 | 50.41 | 45.86 | 40.53 | 34.66 | 28.52 | 22.38 | 16.55 | .27 |
| .74 | 57.51 | 56.36 | 53.95 | 50.37 | 45.82 | 40.47 | 34.60 | 28.46 | 22.32 | 16.50 | .26 |
| .75 | 57.51 | 56.34 | 53.92 | 50.33 | 45.77 | 40.42 | 34.54 | 28.40 | 22.26 | 16.44 | .25 |
| .76 | 57.50 | 56.32 | 53.89 | 50.28 | 45.72 | 40.36 | 34.47 | 28.33 | 22.20 | 16.38 | .24 |
| .77 | 57.50 | 56.30 | 53.86 | 50.24 | 45.67 | 40.30 | 34.41 | 28.27 | 22.14 | 16.33 | .23 |
| .78 | 57.49 | 56.29 | 53.83 | 50.20 | 45.62 | 40.25 | 34.35 | 28.21 | 22.08 | 16.27 | .22 |
| .79 | 57.49 | 56.27 | 53.80 | 50.16 | 45.57 | 40.19 | 34.29 | 28.15 | 22.02 | 16.22 | .21 |
| .80 | 57.48 | 56.25 | 53.77 | 50.12 | 45.52 | 40.13 | 34.23 | 28.09 | 21.96 | 16.16 | .20 |
| .81 | 57.47 | 56.23 | 53.74 | 50.08 | 45.47 | 40.07 | 34.17 | 28.03 | 21.90 | 16.10 | .19 |
| .82 | 57.47 | 56.21 | 53.71 | 50.04 | 45.42 | 40.02 | 34.11 | 27.97 | 21.84 | 16.05 | .18 |
| .83 | 57.46 | 56.19 | 53.68 | 50.00 | 45.37 | 39.96 | 34.05 | 27.91 | 21.78 | 15.99 | .17 |
| .84 | 57.46 | 56.18 | 53.65 | 49.95 | 45.32 | 39.90 | 33.99 | 27.84 | 21.72 | 15.94 | .16 |
| .85 | 57.45 | 56.16 | 53.62 | 49.91 | 45.27 | 39.85 | 33.93 | 27.78 | 21.66 | 15.88 | .15 |
| .86 | 57.45 | 56.14 | 53.59 | 49.87 | 45.22 | 39.79 | 33.86 | 27.72 | 21.60 | 15.83 | .14 |
| .87 | 57.44 | 56.12 | 53.55 | 49.83 | 45.17 | 39.73 | 33.80 | 27.65 | 21.54 | 15.77 | .13 |
| .88 | 57.43 | 56.10 | 53.52 | 49.78 | 45.12 | 39.68 | 33.74 | 27.59 | 21.48 | 15.72 | .12 |
| .89 | 57.42 | 56.08 | 53.49 | 49.74 | 45.07 | 39.62 | 33.68 | 27.53 | 21.42 | 15.66 | .11 |
| .90 | 57.41 | 56.06 | 53.46 | 49.70 | 45.02 | 39.56 | 33.62 | 27.47 | 21.36 | 15.61 | .10 |
| .91 | 57.40 | 56.04 | 53.43 | 49.66 | 44.97 | 39.50 | 33.56 | 27.41 | 21.30 | 15.55 | .09 |
| .92 | 57.40 | 56.02 | 53.40 | 49.62 | 44.92 | 39.45 | 33.50 | 27.35 | 21.24 | 15.50 | .08 |
| .93 | 57.39 | 56.00 | 53.36 | 49.57 | 44.86 | 39.39 | 33.44 | 27.29 | 21.18 | 15.44 | .07 |
| .94 | 57.39 | 55.98 | 53.33 | 49.53 | 44.81 | 39.33 | 33.38 | 27.22 | 21.12 | 15.39 | .06 |
| .95 | 57.38 | 55.96 | 53.30 | 49.49 | 44.76 | 39.28 | 33.32 | 27.16 | 21.07 | 15.33 | .05 |
| .96 | 57.37 | 55.94 | 53.26 | 49.44 | 44.71 | 39.22 | 33.26 | 27.10 | 21.01 | 15.28 | .04 |
| .97 | 57.36 | 55.92 | 53.23 | 49.40 | 44.65 | 39.16 | 33.20 | 27.03 | 20.95 | 15.22 | .03 |
| .98 | 57.35 | 55.90 | 53.20 | 49.36 | 44.60 | 39.11 | 33.14 | 26.97 | 20.89 | 15.17 | .02 |
| .99 | 57.34 | 55.88 | 53.16 | 49.31 | 44.55 | 39.05 | 33.08 | 26.91 | 20.83 | 15.11 | .01 |
| 1.00 | 57.33 | 55.86 | 53.13 | 49.27 | 44.50 | 38.99 | 33.02 | 26.85 | 20.77 | 15.06 | .00 |
| Days. | 29 | 28 | 27 | 26 | 25 | 24 | 23 | 22 | 21 | 20 | Days. |

## TABLE XIX.

(*Continued.*)

Period, 29.263279 days.

## TABLE XX. ARG. 15.

Equation = 25″.0 [1 — sin. (2$t$ + $z$)].

Period, 14.1916109 days.

| Days. | 10 | 11 | 12 | 13 | 14 | 0 | 1 | 2 | 3 | Days. |
|---|---|---|---|---|---|---|---|---|---|---|
| Days. | ″ | ″ | ″ | ″ | ″ | ″ | ″ | ″ | ″ | Days. |
| .00 | 15.06 | 9.98 | 5.77 | 2.62 | 0.66 | 48.06 | 49.98 | 47.12 | 39.98 | 1.00 |
| .01 | 15.01 | 9.93 | 5.73 | 2.59 | 0.65 | 48.10 | 49.98 | 47.07 | 39.89 | .99 |
| .02 | 14.95 | 9.89 | 5.69 | 2.57 | 0.64 | 48.15 | 49.97 | 47.01 | 39.80 | .98 |
| .03 | 14.90 | 9.84 | 5.66 | 2.54 | 0.62 | 48.19 | 49.96 | 46.96 | 39.71 | .97 |
| .04 | 14.84 | 9.79 | 5.62 | 2.52 | 0.61 | 48.23 | 49.96 | 46.91 | 39.62 | .96 |
| .05 | 14.79 | 9.75 | 5.58 | 2.49 | 0.60 | 48.27 | 49.95 | 46.86 | 39.53 | .95 |
| .06 | 14.74 | 9.70 | 5.55 | 2.46 | 0.59 | 48.31 | 49.95 | 46.80 | 39.44 | .94 |
| .07 | 14.68 | 9.66 | 5.51 | 2.44 | 0.57 | 48.35 | 49.94 | 46.75 | 39.35 | .93 |
| .08 | 14.63 | 9.61 | 5.48 | 2.41 | 0.56 | 48.39 | 49.93 | 46.69 | 39.26 | .92 |
| .09 | 14.57 | 9.57 | 5.44 | 2.39 | 0.55 | 48.43 | 49.92 | 46.64 | 39.17 | .91 |
| .10 | 14.52 | 9.52 | 5.40 | 2.36 | 0.54 | 48.47 | 49.91 | 46.58 | 39.08 | .90 |
| .11 | 14.47 | 9.47 | 5.36 | 2.34 | 0.53 | 48.51 | 49.90 | 46.52 | 38.99 | .89 |
| .12 | 14.41 | 9.43 | 5.33 | 2.31 | 0.52 | 48.54 | 49.89 | 46.46 | 38.90 | .88 |
| .13 | 14.36 | 9.38 | 5.29 | 2.29 | 0.51 | 48.58 | 49.88 | 46.41 | 38.81 | .87 |
| .14 | 14.31 | 9.34 | 5.25 | 2.26 | 0.50 | 48.61 | 49.87 | 46.35 | 38.71 | .86 |
| .15 | 14.25 | 9.29 | 5.22 | 2.24 | 0.48 | 48.65 | 49.86 | 46.29 | 38.62 | .85 |
| .16 | 14.20 | 9.25 | 5.18 | 2.22 | 0.47 | 48.68 | 49.84 | 46.24 | 38.53 | .84 |
| .17 | 14.15 | 9.21 | 5.15 | 2.19 | 0.46 | 48.71 | 49.83 | 46.18 | 38.44 | .83 |
| .18 | 14.09 | 9.16 | 5.11 | 2.17 | 0.45 | 48.75 | 49.82 | 46.12 | 38.34 | .82 |
| .19 | 14.04 | 9.12 | 5.08 | 2.14 | 0.44 | 48.78 | 49.80 | 46.06 | 38.25 | .81 |
| .20 | 13.99 | 9.07 | 5.04 | 2.12 | 0.43 | 48.82 | 49.79 | 46.00 | 38.16 | .80 |
| .21 | 13.94 | 9.02 | 5.01 | 2.10 | 0.42 | 48.85 | 49.78 | 45.94 | 38.07 | .79 |
| .22 | 13.88 | 8.98 | 4.97 | 2.08 | 0.41 | 48.88 | 49.76 | 45.88 | 37.97 | .78 |
| .23 | 13.83 | 8.93 | 4.94 | 2.05 | 0.40 | 48.92 | 49.74 | 45.82 | 37.88 | .77 |
| .24 | 13.78 | 8.89 | 4.90 | 2.03 | 0.39 | 48.95 | 49.73 | 45.76 | 37.78 | .76 |
| .25 | 13.72 | 8.84 | 4.87 | 2.00 | 0.38 | 48.98 | 49.71 | 45.69 | 37.69 | .75 |
| .26 | 13.67 | 8.80 | 4.83 | 1.98 | 0.37 | 49.01 | 49.69 | 45.63 | 37.59 | .74 |
| .27 | 13.62 | 8.76 | 4.80 | 1.95 | 0.36 | 49.04 | 49.68 | 45.57 | 37.50 | .73 |
| .28 | 13.56 | 8.71 | 4.77 | 1.93 | 0.35 | 49.07 | 49.66 | 45.50 | 37.40 | .72 |
| .29 | 13.51 | 8.67 | 4.73 | 1.91 | 0.34 | 49.10 | 49.64 | 45.44 | 37.31 | .71 |
| .30 | 13.46 | 8.62 | 4.70 | 1.89 | 0.33 | 49.13 | 49.62 | 45.38 | 37.21 | .70 |
| .31 | 13.41 | 8.58 | 4.67 | 1.87 | 0.32 | 49.16 | 49.60 | 45.31 | 37.11 | .69 |
| .32 | 13.36 | 8.53 | 4.64 | 1.85 | 0.31 | 49.19 | 49.58 | 45.25 | 37.01 | .68 |
| .33 | 13.31 | 8.49 | 4.60 | 1.83 | 0.30 | 49.22 | 49.56 | 45.18 | 36.92 | .67 |
| .34 | 13.25 | 8.44 | 4.57 | 1.81 | 0.29 | 49.25 | 49.54 | 45.11 | 36.82 | .66 |
| .35 | 13.20 | 8.40 | 4.53 | 1.78 | 0.28 | 49.27 | 49.51 | 45.05 | 36.72 | .65 |
| .36 | 13.15 | 8.36 | 4.50 | 1.76 | 0.28 | 49.30 | 49.49 | 44.98 | 36.62 | .64 |
| .37 | 13.09 | 8.31 | 4.47 | 1.74 | 0.27 | 49.33 | 49.47 | 44.91 | 36.53 | .63 |
| .38 | 13.04 | 8.27 | 4.43 | 1.72 | 0.26 | 49.35 | 49.45 | 44.85 | 36.43 | .62 |
| .39 | 12.99 | 8.22 | 4.40 | 1.70 | 0.25 | 49.38 | 49.42 | 44.78 | 36.33 | .61 |
| .40 | 12.94 | 8.18 | 4.37 | 1.68 | 0.24 | 49.40 | 49.40 | 44.71 | 36.23 | .60 |
| .41 | 12.89 | 8.14 | 4.34 | 1.66 | 0.23 | 49.42 | 49.37 | 44.64 | 36.13 | .59 |
| .42 | 12.84 | 8.10 | 4.31 | 1.64 | 0.22 | 49.45 | 49.35 | 44.57 | 36.03 | .58 |
| .43 | 12.79 | 8.06 | 4.28 | 1.62 | 0.22 | 49.47 | 49.32 | 44.50 | 35.93 | .57 |
| .44 | 12.73 | 8.01 | 4.24 | 1.60 | 0.21 | 49.49 | 49.29 | 44.43 | 35.83 | .56 |
| .45 | 12.68 | 7.97 | 4.21 | 1.58 | 0.20 | 49.52 | 49.27 | 44.36 | 35.73 | .55 |
| .46 | 12.63 | 7.93 | 4.18 | 1.56 | 0.20 | 49.54 | 49.24 | 44.29 | 35.63 | .54 |
| .47 | 12.57 | 7.88 | 4.14 | 1.54 | 0.19 | 49.56 | 49.21 | 44.22 | 35.53 | .53 |
| .48 | 12.52 | 7.84 | 4.11 | 1.52 | 0.19 | 49.58 | 49.19 | 44.15 | 35.43 | .52 |
| .49 | 12.47 | 7.80 | 4.08 | 1.50 | 0.18 | 49.60 | 49.16 | 44.08 | 35.33 | .51 |
| .50 | 12.42 | 7.76 | 4.05 | 1.48 | 0.17 | 49.62 | 49.13 | 44.01 | 35.23 | .50 |
| Days. | 19 | 18 | 17 | 16 | 15 | 15 | 14 | 13 | 12 | Days. |

# TABLE XIX.

(*Continued.*)

Period, 29.263279 days.

# TABLE XX. ARG. 15.

Equation = 25″.0 [1 — sin. (2*t* + *z*)].

Period, 14.1916109 days.

| Days. | 10 | 11 | 12 | 13 | 14 | 0 | 1 | 2 | 3 | Days. |
|---|---|---|---|---|---|---|---|---|---|---|
| Days | ″ | ″ | ″ | ″ | ″ | ″ | ″ | ″ | ″ | Days. |
| .50 | 12.42 | 7.76 | 4.05 | 1.48 | 0.17 | 49.62 | 49.13 | 44.01 | 35.23 | .50 |
| .51 | 12.37 | 7.72 | 4.02 | 1.46 | 0.16 | 49.64 | 49.10 | 43.94 | 35.13 | .49 |
| .52 | 12.32 | 7.68 | 3.99 | 1.44 | 0.15 | 49.66 | 49.07 | 43.86 | 35.03 | .48 |
| .53 | 12.27 | 7.64 | 3.96 | 1.42 | 0.15 | 49.68 | 49.04 | 43.79 | 34.93 | .47 |
| .54 | 12.22 | 7.60 | 3.93 | 1.40 | 0.14 | 49.70 | 49.01 | 43.72 | 34.82 | .46 |
| .55 | 12.17 | 7.56 | 3.89 | 1.38 | 0.14 | 49.71 | 48.98 | 43.64 | 34.72 | .45 |
| .56 | 12.12 | 7.51 | 3.86 | 1.37 | 0.13 | 49.73 | 48.94 | 43.57 | 34.62 | .44 |
| .57 | 12.07 | 7.47 | 3.83 | 1.35 | 0.13 | 49.74 | 48.91 | 43.50 | 34.52 | .43 |
| .58 | 12.02 | 7.43 | 3.80 | 1.33 | 0.12 | 49.75 | 48.88 | 43.42 | 34.41 | .42 |
| .59 | 11.97 | 7.39 | 3.77 | 1.31 | 0.12 | 49.77 | 48.85 | 43.35 | 34.31 | .41 |
| .60 | 11.92 | 7.35 | 3.74 | 1.29 | 0.11 | 49.78 | 48.82 | 43.28 | 34.21 | .40 |
| .61 | 11.87 | 7.31 | 3.71 | 1.27 | 0.11 | 49.79 | 48.79 | 43.20 | 34.11 | .39 |
| .62 | 11.82 | 7.27 | 3.68 | 1.25 | 0.10 | 49.81 | 48.75 | 43.13 | 34.00 | .38 |
| .63 | 11.77 | 7.23 | 3.65 | 1.24 | 0.10 | 49.82 | 48.72 | 43.05 | 33.90 | .37 |
| .64 | 11.72 | 7.19 | 3.62 | 1.22 | 0.09 | 49.83 | 48.69 | 42.97 | 33.79 | .36 |
| .65 | 11.67 | 7.15 | 3.59 | 1.20 | 0.08 | 49.85 | 48.65 | 42.90 | 33.69 | .35 |
| .66 | 11.63 | 7.10 | 3.56 | 1.19 | 0.08 | 49.86 | 48.61 | 42.82 | 33.59 | .34 |
| .67 | 11.58 | 7.06 | 3.53 | 1.17 | 0.07 | 49.87 | 48.58 | 42.75 | 33.48 | .33 |
| .68 | 11.53 | 7.02 | 3.50 | 1.15 | 0.07 | 49.88 | 48.54 | 42.67 | 33.38 | .32 |
| .69 | 11.48 | 6.98 | 3.47 | 1.13 | 0.06 | 49.89 | 48.50 | 42.59 | 33.27 | .31 |
| .70 | 11.43 | 6.94 | 3.44 | 1.11 | 0.06 | 49.90 | 48.46 | 42.51 | 33.17 | .30 |
| .71 | 11.38 | 6.90 | 3.41 | 1.09 | 0.06 | 49.91 | 48.42 | 42.43 | 33.07 | .29 |
| .72 | 11.33 | 6.86 | 3.38 | 1.08 | 0.05 | 49.92 | 48.38 | 42.35 | 32.96 | .28 |
| .73 | 11.28 | 6.82 | 3.35 | 1.06 | 0.05 | 49.93 | 48.34 | 42.27 | 32.86 | .27 |
| .74 | 11.23 | 6.78 | 3.33 | 1.04 | 0.05 | 49.94 | 48.30 | 42.19 | 32.75 | .26 |
| .75 | 11.18 | 6.74 | 3.30 | 1.03 | 0.04 | 49.94 | 48.26 | 42.11 | 32.65 | .25 |
| .76 | 11.14 | 6.70 | 3.27 | 1.01 | 0.04 | 49.95 | 48.22 | 42.02 | 32.54 | .24 |
| .77 | 11.09 | 6.66 | 3.25 | 1.00 | 0.04 | 49.95 | 48.18 | 41.94 | 32.43 | .23 |
| .78 | 11.04 | 6.62 | 3.22 | 0.98 | 0.03 | 49.96 | 48.14 | 41.86 | 32.33 | .22 |
| .79 | 10.99 | 6.58 | 3.19 | 0.97 | 0.03 | 49.97 | 48.10 | 41.78 | 32.22 | .21 |
| .80 | 10.94 | 6.54 | 3.16 | 0.95 | 0.03 | 49.97 | 48.06 | 41.70 | 32.12 | .20 |
| .81 | 10.89 | 6.50 | 3.13 | 0.93 | 0.03 | 49.97 | 48.02 | 41.62 | 32.01 | .19 |
| .82 | 10.84 | 6.46 | 3.10 | 0.92 | 0.03 | 49.98 | 47.97 | 41.53 | 31.90 | .18 |
| .83 | 10.79 | 6.42 | 3.08 | 0.90 | 0.03 | 49.98 | 47.93 | 41.45 | 31.80 | .17 |
| .84 | 10.74 | 6.38 | 3.05 | 0.89 | 0.02 | 49.98 | 47.88 | 41.36 | 31.69 | .16 |
| .85 | 10.69 | 6.34 | 3.02 | 0.87 | 0.02 | 49.99 | 47.84 | 41.28 | 31.59 | .15 |
| .86 | 10.65 | 6.31 | 3.00 | 0.86 | 0.02 | 49.99 | 47.79 | 41.19 | 31.49 | .14 |
| .87 | 10.60 | 6.27 | 2.97 | 0.85 | 0.02 | 49.99 | 47.75 | 41.10 | 31.38 | .13 |
| .88 | 10.55 | 6.23 | 2.95 | 0.83 | 0.01 | 50.00 | 47.70 | 41.02 | 31.28 | .12 |
| .89 | 10.50 | 6.19 | 2.92 | 0.82 | 0.01 | 50.00 | 47.66 | 40.93 | 31.17 | .11 |
| .90 | 10.45 | 6.15 | 2.89 | 0.80 | 0.01 | 50.00 | 47.61 | 40.85 | 31.06 | .10 |
| .91 | 10.40 | 6.11 | 2.86 | 0.79 | 0.01 | 50.00 | 47.56 | 40.76 | 30.95 | .09 |
| .92 | 10.35 | 6.07 | 2.83 | 0.77 | 0.01 | 50.00 | 47.51 | 40.68 | 30.84 | .08 |
| .93 | 10.31 | 6.03 | 2.81 | 0.76 | 0.00 | 50.00 | 47.46 | 40.59 | 30.73 | .07 |
| .94 | 10.26 | 6.00 | 2.78 | 0.74 | 0.00 | 49.99 | 47.41 | 40.51 | 30.63 | .06 |
| .95 | 10.22 | 5.96 | 2.75 | 0.73 | 0.00 | 49.99 | 47.37 | 40.42 | 30.52 | .05 |
| .96 | 10.17 | 5.92 | 2.73 | 0.72 | 0.00 | 49.99 | 47.32 | 40.33 | 30.41 | .04 |
| .97 | 10.12 | 5.89 | 2.70 | 0.70 | 0.00 | 49.99 | 47.27 | 40.25 | 30.31 | .03 |
| .98 | 10.08 | 5.85 | 2.68 | 0.69 | 0.00 | 49.98 | 47.22 | 40.16 | 30.20 | .02 |
| .99 | 10.03 | 5.81 | 2.65 | 0.67 | 0.00 | 49.98 | 47.17 | 40.07 | 30.09 | .01 |
| 1.00 | 9.98 | 5.77 | 2.62 | 0.66 | 0.00 | 49.98 | 47.12 | 39.98 | 29.98 | .00 |
| Days. | 19 | 18 | 17 | 16 | 15 | 15 | 14 | 13 | 12 | Days. |

## TABLE XX.

(*Continued.*)

Period, 14.1916109 days.

| Days. | 4 | 5 | 6 | 7 | Days. |
|---|---|---|---|---|---|
| Days. | ″ | ″ | ″ | ″ | Days. |
| .00 | 29.98 | 18.99 | 9.17 | 2.41 | 1.00 |
| .01 | 29.87 | 18.88 | 9.09 | 2.36 | .99 |
| .02 | 29.76 | 18.78 | 9.00 | 2.32 | .98 |
| .03 | 29.65 | 18.67 | 8.92 | 2.27 | .97 |
| .04 | 29.54 | 18.56 | 8.83 | 2.23 | .96 |
| .05 | 29.43 | 18.46 | 8.75 | 2.18 | .95 |
| .06 | 29.32 | 18.35 | 8.67 | 2.14 | .94 |
| .07 | 29.21 | 18.24 | 8.58 | 2.10 | .93 |
| .08 | 29.10 | 18.14 | 8.50 | 2.05 | .92 |
| .09 | 28.99 | 18.03 | 8.41 | 2.01 | .91 |
| .10 | 28.88 | 17.92 | 8.33 | 1.96 | .90 |
| .11 | 28.77 | 17.82 | 8.25 | 1.92 | .89 |
| .12 | 28.66 | 17.71 | 8.17 | 1.88 | .88 |
| .13 | 28.55 | 17.61 | 8.09 | 1.84 | .87 |
| .14 | 28.44 | 17.50 | 8.01 | 1.80 | .86 |
| .15 | 28.33 | 17.39 | 7.92 | 1.75 | .85 |
| .16 | 28.22 | 17.29 | 7.84 | 1.71 | .84 |
| .17 | 28.11 | 17.18 | 7.76 | 1.67 | .83 |
| .18 | 28.00 | 17.08 | 7.68 | 1.63 | .82 |
| .19 | 27.89 | 16.97 | 7.60 | 1.59 | .81 |
| .20 | 27.78 | 16.87 | 7.52 | 1.55 | .80 |
| .21 | 27.67 | 16.77 | 7.44 | 1.51 | .79 |
| .22 | 27.56 | 16.66 | 7.36 | 1.48 | .78 |
| .23 | 27.45 | 16.56 | 7.29 | 1.44 | .77 |
| .24 | 27.34 | 16.45 | 7.21 | 1.40 | .76 |
| .25 | 27.23 | 16.35 | 7.13 | 1.37 | .75 |
| .26 | 27.12 | 16.24 | 7.06 | 1.33 | .74 |
| .27 | 27.01 | 16.14 | 6.98 | 1.30 | .73 |
| .28 | 26.90 | 16.04 | 6.91 | 1.26 | .72 |
| .29 | 26.79 | 15.93 | 6.83 | 1.23 | .71 |
| .30 | 26.68 | 15.83 | 6.75 | 1.19 | .70 |
| .31 | 26.57 | 15.73 | 6.68 | 1.16 | .69 |
| .32 | 26.46 | 15.63 | 6.60 | 1.13 | .68 |
| .33 | 26.35 | 15.52 | 6.53 | 1.10 | .67 |
| .34 | 26.24 | 15.42 | 6.45 | 1.07 | .66 |
| .35 | 26.13 | 15.32 | 6.38 | 1.03 | .65 |
| .36 | 26.02 | 15.22 | 6.30 | 1.00 | .64 |
| .37 | 25.91 | 15.11 | 6.23 | 0.97 | .63 |
| .38 | 25.80 | 15.01 | 6.16 | 0.94 | .62 |
| .39 | 25.69 | 14.91 | 6.08 | 0.91 | .61 |
| .40 | 25.58 | 14.81 | 6.01 | 0.88 | .60 |
| .41 | 25.47 | 14.71 | 5.94 | 0.85 | .59 |
| .42 | 25.36 | 14.61 | 5.87 | 0.82 | .58 |
| .43 | 25.25 | 14.51 | 5.80 | 0.80 | .57 |
| .44 | 25.14 | 14.41 | 5.73 | 0.77 | .56 |
| .45 | 25.03 | 14.31 | 5.66 | 0.74 | .55 |
| .46 | 24.92 | 14.21 | 5.59 | 0.72 | .54 |
| .47 | 24.81 | 14.11 | 5.52 | 0.69 | .53 |
| .48 | 24.70 | 14.01 | 5.45 | 0.67 | .52 |
| .49 | 24.59 | 13.91 | 5.38 | 0.64 | .51 |
| .50 | 24.48 | 13.81 | 5.31 | 0.61 | .50 |
| Days. | 11 | 10 | 9 | 8 | Days. |

## TABLE XXI. ARG. 16.

Equation $= 21''. - 8''.2 \sin. (t + x) + 14''.1 \sin. 2 (t + x)$.

Period, 14.2541847 days.

| Days. | 0 | 1 | 2 | 3 | 4 |
|---|---|---|---|---|---|
| Days. | ″ | ″ | ″ | ″ | ″ |
| .00 | 36.71 | 41.06 | 34.34 | 22.23 | 13.49 |
| .01 | 36.82 | 41.04 | 34.23 | 22.11 | 13.45 |
| .02 | 36.92 | 41.02 | 34.12 | 21.99 | 13.40 |
| .03 | 37.02 | 41.00 | 34.01 | 21.88 | 13.36 |
| .04 | 37.11 | 40.98 | 33.90 | 21.76 | 13.31 |
| .05 | 37.21 | 40.96 | 33.79 | 21.64 | 13.27 |
| .06 | 37.30 | 40.94 | 33.68 | 21.53 | 13.23 |
| .07 | 37.40 | 40.91 | 33.57 | 21.41 | 13.19 |
| .08 | 37.49 | 40.89 | 33.46 | 21.29 | 13.15 |
| .09 | 37.58 | 40.86 | 33.34 | 21.18 | 13.11 |
| .10 | 37.67 | 40.84 | 33.23 | 21.07 | 13.07 |
| .11 | 37.76 | 40.81 | 33.12 | 20.95 | 13.04 |
| .12 | 37.85 | 40.78 | 33.01 | 20.84 | 13.00 |
| .13 | 37.94 | 40.75 | 32.89 | 20.73 | 12.97 |
| .14 | 38.02 | 40.72 | 32.78 | 20.61 | 12.93 |
| .15 | 38.11 | 40.69 | 32.66 | 20.50 | 12.90 |
| .16 | 38.19 | 40.65 | 32.55 | 20.39 | 12.87 |
| .17 | 38.28 | 40.62 | 32.43 | 20.28 | 12.84 |
| .18 | 38.36 | 40.58 | 32.31 | 20.17 | 12.81 |
| .19 | 38.44 | 40.55 | 32.19 | 20.06 | 12.78 |
| .20 | 38.52 | 40.51 | 32.07 | 19.95 | 12.75 |
| .21 | 38.60 | 40.47 | 31.95 | 19.84 | 12.73 |
| .22 | 38.68 | 40.43 | 31.83 | 19.73 | 12.70 |
| .23 | 38.75 | 40.39 | 31.71 | 19.62 | 12.68 |
| .24 | 38.83 | 40.35 | 31.59 | 19.52 | 12.65 |
| .25 | 38.90 | 40.30 | 31.47 | 19.41 | 12.63 |
| .26 | 38.98 | 40.26 | 31.35 | 19.30 | 12.61 |
| .27 | 39.05 | 40.21 | 31.23 | 19.19 | 12.59 |
| .28 | 39.12 | 40.17 | 31.11 | 19.08 | 12.57 |
| .29 | 39.19 | 40.12 | 30.99 | 18.98 | 12.55 |
| .30 | 39.26 | 40.07 | 30.87 | 18.88 | 12.53 |
| .31 | 39.32 | 40.02 | 30.75 | 18.78 | 12.51 |
| .32 | 39.39 | 39.97 | 30.63 | 18.68 | 12.50 |
| .33 | 39.45 | 39.92 | 30.51 | 18.58 | 12.48 |
| .34 | 39.51 | 39.86 | 30.39 | 18.48 | 12.47 |
| .35 | 39.57 | 39.81 | 30.27 | 18.38 | 12.45 |
| .36 | 39.63 | 39.75 | 30.15 | 18.28 | 12.44 |
| .37 | 39.69 | 39.70 | 30.02 | 18.18 | 12.43 |
| .38 | 39.75 | 39.64 | 29.90 | 18.08 | 12.42 |
| .39 | 39.81 | 39.58 | 29.78 | 17.98 | 12.41 |
| .40 | 39.87 | 39.52 | 29.65 | 17.88 | 12.40 |
| .41 | 39.92 | 39.46 | 29.53 | 17.78 | 12.39 |
| .42 | 39.97 | 39.40 | 29.41 | 17.69 | 12.39 |
| .43 | 40.02 | 39.34 | 29.29 | 17.59 | 12.38 |
| .44 | 40.07 | 39.27 | 29.17 | 17.50 | 12.38 |
| .45 | 40.12 | 39.21 | 29.04 | 17.40 | 12.38 |
| .46 | 40.17 | 39.14 | 28.92 | 17.31 | 12.37 |
| .47 | 40.22 | 39.08 | 28.80 | 17.22 | 12.37 |
| .48 | 40.27 | 39.01 | 28.67 | 17.12 | 12.37 |
| .49 | 40.31 | 38.94 | 28.54 | 17.03 | 12.37 |
| .50 | 40.36 | 38.87 | 28.42 | 16.94 | 12.37 |

## TABLE XX.

(*Continued.*)

Period, 14.1916109 days.

| Days. | 4 | 5 | 6 | 7 | Days. |
|---|---|---|---|---|---|
| Days. | ″ | ″ | ″ | ″ | Days. |
| .50 | 24.48 | 13.81 | 5.31 | 0.61 | .50 |
| .51 | 24.37 | 13.71 | 5.24 | 0.59 | .49 |
| .52 | 24.26 | 13.61 | 5.18 | 0.57 | .48 |
| .53 | 24.15 | 13.51 | 5.11 | 0.55 | .47 |
| .54 | 24.04 | 13.42 | 5.05 | 0.52 | .46 |
| .55 | 23.93 | 13.32 | 4.98 | 0.50 | .45 |
| .56 | 23.82 | 13.22 | 4.92 | 0.48 | .44 |
| .57 | 23.71 | 13.12 | 4.85 | 0.45 | .43 |
| .58 | 23.60 | 13.03 | 4.78 | 0.43 | .42 |
| .59 | 23.49 | 12.93 | 4.72 | 0.41 | .41 |
| .60 | 23.38 | 12.83 | 4.65 | 0.39 | .40 |
| .61 | 23.27 | 12.73 | 4.59 | 0.37 | .39 |
| .62 | 23.16 | 12.63 | 4.53 | 0.35 | .38 |
| .63 | 23.05 | 12.54 | 4.47 | 0.34 | .37 |
| .64 | 22.94 | 12.44 | 4.40 | 0.32 | .36 |
| .65 | 22.83 | 12.35 | 4.34 | 0.30 | .35 |
| .66 | 22.72 | 12.25 | 4.27 | 0.29 | .34 |
| .67 | 22.61 | 12.16 | 4.21 | 0.27 | .33 |
| .68 | 22.50 | 12.06 | 4.14 | 0.26 | .32 |
| .69 | 22.39 | 11.97 | 4.08 | 0.24 | .31 |
| .70 | 22.28 | 11.87 | 4.02 | 0.22 | .30 |
| .71 | 22.17 | 11.78 | 3.96 | 0.21 | .29 |
| .72 | 22.06 | 11.69 | 3.90 | 0.20 | .28 |
| .73 | 21.95 | 11.59 | 3.85 | 0.19 | .27 |
| .74 | 21.84 | 11.50 | 3.79 | 0.17 | .26 |
| .75 | 21.73 | 11.41 | 3.73 | 0.16 | .25 |
| .76 | 21.62 | 11.31 | 3.67 | 0.15 | .24 |
| .77 | 21.51 | 11.22 | 3.62 | 0.13 | .23 |
| .78 | 21.40 | 11.12 | 3.56 | 0.12 | .22 |
| .79 | 21.29 | 11.03 | 3.50 | 0.11 | .21 |
| .80 | 21.18 | 10.94 | 3.44 | 0.10 | .20 |
| .81 | 21.07 | 10.85 | 3.39 | 0.09 | .19 |
| .82 | 20.96 | 10.76 | 3.33 | 0.08 | .18 |
| .83 | 20.85 | 10.67 | 3.28 | 0.08 | .17 |
| .84 | 20.74 | 10.58 | 3.22 | 0.07 | .16 |
| .85 | 20.63 | 10.49 | 3.17 | 0.06 | .15 |
| .86 | 20.52 | 10.40 | 3.11 | 0.06 | .14 |
| .87 | 20.41 | 10.31 | 3.06 | 0 05 | .13 |
| .88 | 20.30 | 10.22 | 3.01 | 0.05 | .12 |
| .89 | 20.19 | 10.13 | 2.95 | 0.04 | .11 |
| .90 | 20.08 | 10.04 | 2.90 | 0.03 | .10 |
| .91 | 19.97 | 9.95 | 2.85 | 0.03 | .09 |
| .92 | 19.86 | 9.86 | 2.80 | 0.03 | .08 |
| .93 | 19.75 | 9.78 | 2.75 | 0.02 | .07 |
| .94 | 19.64 | 9.69 | 2.70 | 0.02 | .06 |
| .95 | 19.53 | 9.60 | 2.65 | 0.01 | .05 |
| .96 | 19.42 | 9.52 | 2.61 | 0.01 | .04 |
| .97 | 19.32 | 9.43 | 2.56 | 0.01 | .03 |
| .98 | 19.21 | 9.35 | 2.51 | 0.00 | .02 |
| .99 | 19.10 | 9.26 | 2.46 | 0.00 | .01 |
| 1.00 | 18.99 | 9.17 | 2.41 | 0.00 | .00 |
| Days. | 11 | 10 | 9 | 8 | Days. |

## TABLE XXI. ARG. 16.

Equation = 21″. — 8″.2 sin. $(t + x)$ + 14″.1 sin. $2\,(t + x)$.

Period, 14.2541847 days.

| Days. | 0 | 1 | 2 | 3 | 4 |
|---|---|---|---|---|---|
| Days. | ″ | ″ | ″ | ″ | ″ |
| .50 | 40.36 | 38.87 | 28.42 | 16.94 | 12.37 |
| .51 | 40.40 | 38.80 | 28.29 | 16.85 | 12.37 |
| .52 | 40.44 | 38.73 | 28.17 | 16.76 | 12.38 |
| .53 | 40.48 | 38.66 | 28.05 | 16.67 | 12.38 |
| .54 | 40.52 | 38.59 | 27.92 | 16.59 | 12.38 |
| .55 | 40.56 | 38.51 | 27.80 | 16.50 | 12.39 |
| .56 | 40.60 | 38.44 | 27.66 | 16.41 | 12.40 |
| .57 | 40.63 | 38.36 | 27.54 | 16.33 | 12.41 |
| .58 | 40.67 | 38.29 | 27.42 | 16.24 | 12.42 |
| .59 | 40.70 | 38.21 | 27.29 | 16.16 | 12.43 |
| .60 | 40.74 | 38.13 | 27.16 | 16.08 | 12.44 |
| .61 | 40.77 | 38.05 | 27.04 | 16.00 | 12.45 |
| .62 | 40.80 | 37.97 | 26.91 | 15.92 | 12.46 |
| .63 | 40.83 | 37.89 | 26.79 | 15.84 | 12.48 |
| .64 | 40.86 | 37.81 | 26.66 | 15.76 | 12.49 |
| .65 | 40.88 | 37.73 | 26.54 | 15.68 | 12.50 |
| .66 | 40.91 | 37.64 | 26.41 | 15.61 | 12.52 |
| .67 | 40.93 | 37.56 | 26.29 | 15.53 | 12.54 |
| .68 | 40.96 | 37.47 | 26.16 | 15.46 | 12.56 |
| .69 | 40.98 | 37.39 | 26.04 | 15.38 | 12.58 |
| .70 | 41.00 | 37.30 | 25.91 | 15.31 | 12.60 |
| .71 | 41.02 | 37.21 | 25.78 | 15.24 | 12.62 |
| .72 | 41.04 | 37.12 | 25.66 | 15.17 | 12.64 |
| .73 | 41.05 | 37.03 | 25.53 | 15.10 | 12.67 |
| .74 | 41.07 | 36.94 | 25.41 | 15.03 | 12.69 |
| .75 | 41.08 | 36.85 | 25.28 | 14.96 | 12.72 |
| .76 | 41.10 | 36.76 | 25.16 | 14.89 | 12.74 |
| .77 | 41.11 | 36.67 | 25.03 | 14.82 | 12.77 |
| .78 | 41.12 | 36.57 | 24.91 | 14.76 | 12.79 |
| .79 | 41.13 | 36.48 | 24.78 | 14.69 | 12.82 |
| .80 | 41.14 | 36.38 | 24.66 | 14.62 | 12.85 |
| .81 | 41.14 | 36.28 | 24.53 | 14.56 | 12.88 |
| .82 | 41.15 | 36.19 | 24.41 | 14.49 | 12.92 |
| .83 | 41.15 | 36.09 | 24.29 | 14.43 | 12.95 |
| .84 | 41.16 | 35.99 | 24.16 | 14.37 | 12.99 |
| .85 | 41.16 | 35.89 | 24.04 | 14.31 | 13.02 |
| .86 | 41.16 | 35.79 | 23.92 | 14.25 | 13.06 |
| .87 | 41.16 | 35.69 | 23.79 | 14.19 | 13.09 |
| .88 | 41.16 | 35.59 | 23.67 | 14.13 | 13.12 |
| .89 | 41.16 | 35.49 | 23.55 | 14.07 | 13.16 |
| .90 | 41.16 | 35.39 | 23.43 | 14.01 | 13.19 |
| .91 | 41.15 | 35.29 | 23.31 | 13.96 | 13.23 |
| .92 | 41.14 | 35.19 | 23.19 | 13.90 | 13.27 |
| .93 | 41.13 | 35.09 | 23.07 | 13.85 | 13.31 |
| .04 | 41.12 | 34.98 | 22.95 | 13.79 | 13.35 |
| .95 | 41.11 | 34.88 | 22.83 | 13.74 | 13.40 |
| .96 | 41.10 | 34.77 | 22.71 | 13.69 | 13.44 |
| .97 | 41.09 | 34.67 | 22.59 | 13.64 | 13.48 |
| .98 | 41.08 | 34.56 | 22.47 | 13.59 | 13.53 |
| .99 | 41.07 | 34.45 | 22.35 | 13.54 | 13.57 |
| 1.00 | 41.06 | 34.34 | 22.23 | 13.49 | 13.62 |

# TABLE XXI. ARGUMENT 16.

Equation $= 21''. - 8''.2 \sin. (t + x) + 14''.1 \sin. 2 (t + x)$.

Period, 14.2541847 days.

| Days. | 5 | 6 | 7 | 8 | 9 | 10 | 11 | 12 | 13 | 14 |
|---|---|---|---|---|---|---|---|---|---|---|
| Days. | ″ | ″ | ″ | ″ | ″ | ″ | ″ | ″ | ″ | ″ |
| .00 | 13.62 | 21.00 | 28.38 | 28.51 | 19.77 | 7.66 | 0.94 | 5.28 | 18.97 | 33.88 |
| .01 | 13.67 | 21.09 | 28.43 | 28.46 | 19.65 | 7.55 | 0.93 | 5.38 | 19.13 | 34.00 |
| .02 | 13.72 | 21.17 | 28.47 | 28.41 | 19.53 | 7.44 | 0.92 | 5.48 | 19.29 | 34.12 |
| .03 | 13.77 | 21.26 | 28.52 | 28.36 | 19.41 | 7.34 | 0.91 | 5.58 | 19.45 | 34.24 |
| .04 | 13.82 | 21.35 | 28.56 | 28.31 | 19.29 | 7.23 | 0.90 | 5.69 | 19.60 | 34.36 |
| .05 | 13.87 | 21.44 | 28.60 | 28.26 | 19.17 | 7.13 | 0.89 | 5.79 | 19.76 | 34.48 |
| .06 | 13.92 | 21.53 | 28.65 | 28.20 | 19.05 | 7.02 | 0.88 | 5.90 | 19.92 | 34.60 |
| .07 | 13.97 | 21.61 | 28.69 | 28.15 | 18.93 | 6.92 | 0.87 | 6.00 | 20.08 | 34.71 |
| .08 | 14.02 | 21.70 | 28.73 | 28.10 | 18.81 | 6.81 | 0.86 | 6.11 | 20.24 | 34.83 |
| .09 | 14.08 | 21.79 | 28.77 | 28.04 | 18.69 | 6.71 | 0.85 | 6.22 | 20.40 | 34.95 |
| .10 | 14.13 | 21.88 | 28.81 | 27.99 | 18.57 | 6.61 | 0.84 | 6.33 | 20.56 | 35.06 |
| .11 | 14.18 | 21.97 | 28.85 | 27.93 | 18.45 | 6.51 | 0.84 | 6.44 | 20.72 | 35.17 |
| .12 | 14.23 | 22.05 | 28.89 | 27.87 | 18.33 | 6.41 | 0.83 | 6.55 | 20.88 | 35.28 |
| .13 | 14.29 | 22.14 | 28.92 | 27.81 | 18.21 | 6.31 | 0.83 | 6.66 | 21.04 | 35.39 |
| .14 | 14.34 | 22.23 | 28.96 | 27.75 | 18.08 | 6.21 | 0.83 | 6.77 | 21.20 | 35.50 |
| .15 | 14.40 | 22.32 | 28.99 | 27.69 | 17.96 | 6.11 | 0.84 | 6.89 | 21.36 | 35.61 |
| .16 | 14.46 | 22.40 | 29.02 | 27.63 | 17.84 | 6.01 | 0.84 | 7.00 | 21.52 | 35.72 |
| .17 | 14.51 | 22.49 | 29.06 | 27.57 | 17.71 | 5.91 | 0.84 | 7.12 | 21.68 | 35.83 |
| .18 | 14.57 | 22.58 | 29.09 | 27.50 | 17.59 | 5.82 | 0.85 | 7.23 | 21.84 | 35.94 |
| .19 | 14.63 | 22.66 | 29.12 | 27.44 | 17.47 | 5.72 | 0.85 | 7.35 | 22.00 | 36.05 |
| .20 | 14.69 | 22.75 | 29.15 | 27.38 | 17.34 | 5.62 | 0.86 | 7.47 | 22.16 | 36.16 |
| .21 | 14.75 | 22.84 | 29.18 | 27.32 | 17.22 | 5.53 | 0.87 | 7.59 | 22.32 | 36.26 |
| .22 | 14.81 | 22.92 | 29.21 | 27.25 | 17.09 | 5.43 | 0.88 | 7.71 | 22.48 | 36.36 |
| .23 | 14.87 | 23.01 | 29.24 | 27.18 | 16.97 | 5.34 | 0.89 | 7.83 | 22.64 | 36.46 |
| .24 | 14.93 | 23.09 | 29.26 | 27.11 | 16.84 | 5.25 | 0.90 | 7.95 | 22.80 | 36.56 |
| .25 | 14.99 | 23.18 | 29.29 | 27.04 | 16.72 | 5.15 | 0.92 | 8.07 | 22.96 | 36.66 |
| .26 | 15.06 | 23.27 | 29.32 | 26.97 | 16.59 | 5.06 | 0.93 | 8.19 | 23.12 | 36.76 |
| .27 | 15.12 | 23.35 | 29.34 | 26.90 | 16.47 | 4.97 | 0.94 | 8.32 | 23.28 | 36.86 |
| .28 | 15.18 | 23.44 | 29.36 | 26.83 | 16.34 | 4.88 | 0.96 | 8.44 | 23.44 | 36.96 |
| .29 | 15.25 | 23.53 | 29.38 | 26.76 | 16.22 | 4.79 | 0.98 | 8.56 | 23.60 | 37.06 |
| .30 | 15.31 | 23.61 | 29.40 | 26.69 | 16.09 | 4.70 | 1.00 | 8.69 | 23.76 | 37.16 |
| .31 | 15.38 | 23.70 | 29.42 | 26.62 | 15.97 | 4.61 | 1.02 | 8.82 | 23.92 | 37.25 |
| .32 | 15.44 | 23.78 | 29.44 | 26.54 | 15.84 | 4.53 | 1.04 | 8.94 | 24.08 | 37.34 |
| .33 | 15.51 | 23.86 | 29.46 | 26.47 | 15.72 | 4.44 | 1.06 | 9.07 | 24.24 | 37.43 |
| .34 | 15.58 | 23.95 | 29.47 | 26.39 | 15.59 | 4.36 | 1.09 | 9.20 | 24.39 | 37.52 |
| .35 | 15.65 | 24.03 | 29.49 | 26.31 | 15.47 | 4.28 | 1.11 | 9.33 | 24.55 | 37.61 |
| .36 | 15.72 | 24.11 | 29.51 | 26.24 | 15.34 | 4.19 | 1.14 | 9.46 | 24.71 | 37.70 |
| .37 | 15.79 | 24.20 | 29.52 | 26.16 | 15.22 | 4.11 | 1.17 | 9.59 | 24.87 | 37.79 |
| .38 | 15.86 | 24.28 | 29.54 | 26.08 | 15.09 | 4.03 | 1.20 | 9.72 | 25.02 | 37.88 |
| .39 | 15.93 | 24.36 | 29.55 | 26.00 | 14.97 | 3.95 | 1.23 | 9.85 | 25.18 | 37.97 |
| .40 | 16.00 | 24.44 | 29.56 | 25.92 | 14.84 | 3.87 | 1.26 | 9.98 | 25.34 | 38.06 |
| .41 | 16.07 | 24.52 | 29.57 | 25.84 | 14.72 | 3.79 | 1.30 | 10.11 | 25.50 | 38.14 |
| .42 | 16.14 | 24.60 | 29.58 | 25.76 | 14.59 | 3.71 | 1.33 | 10.25 | 25.65 | 38.22 |
| .43 | 16.22 | 24.68 | 29.59 | 25.67 | 14.47 | 3.64 | 1.37 | 10.38 | 25.81 | 38.30 |
| .44 | 16.30 | 24.76 | 29.59 | 25.59 | 14.34 | 3.56 | 1.41 | 10.52 | 25.97 | 38.38 |
| .45 | 16.37 | 24.84 | 29.60 | 25.50 | 14.22 | 3.49 | 1.44 | 10.66 | 26.12 | 38.46 |
| .46 | 16.45 | 24.92 | 29.61 | 25.41 | 14.09 | 3.41 | 1.48 | 10.79 | 26.28 | 38.54 |
| .47 | 16.53 | 25.00 | 29.61 | 25.33 | 13.97 | 3.34 | 1.52 | 10.93 | 26.43 | 38.62 |
| .48 | 16.60 | 25.08 | 29.62 | 25.24 | 13.84 | 3.27 | 1.56 | 11.07 | 26.59 | 38.69 |
| .49 | 16.68 | 25.16 | 29.63 | 25.15 | 13.72 | 3.20 | 1.60 | 11.21 | 26.74 | 38.77 |
| .50 | 16.76 | 25.24 | 29.63 | 25.06 | 13.59 | 3.13 | 1.64 | 11.35 | 26.89 | 38.85 |

# TABLE XXI. ARGUMENT 16.

Equation = 21″. — 8″.2 sin. $(t + x)$ + 14″.1 sin. 2 $(t + x)$.

Period, 14.2541847 days.

| Days. | 5 | 6 | 7 | 8 | 9 | 10 | 11 | 12 | 13 | 14 |
|---|---|---|---|---|---|---|---|---|---|---|
| Days. .50 | 16″.76 | 25″.24 | 29″.63 | 25″.06 | 13″.59 | 3″.13 | 1″.64 | 11″.35 | 26″.89 | 38″.85 |
| .51 | 16.84 | 25.32 | 29.63 | 24.97 | 13.47 | 3.06 | 1.69 | 11.49 | 27.04 | 38.92 |
| .52 | 16.92 | 25.40 | 29.63 | 24.88 | 13.34 | 2.99 | 1.74 | 11.63 | 27.20 | 38.99 |
| .53 | 17.00 | 25.47 | 29.62 | 24.78 | 13.22 | 2.92 | 1.78 | 11.77 | 27.35 | 39.06 |
| .54 | 17.08 | 25.55 | 29.62 | 24.69 | 13.09 | 2.86 | 1.83 | 11.91 | 27.50 | 39.13 |
| .55 | 17.16 | 25.63 | 29.62 | 24.60 | 12.97 | 2.79 | 1.88 | 12.06 | 27.65 | 39.20 |
| .56 | 17.24 | 25.70 | 29.61 | 24.50 | 12.84 | 2.73 | 1.93 | 12.20 | 27.80 | 39.26 |
| .57 | 17.32 | 25.78 | 29.61 | 24.41 | 12.72 | 2.66 | 1.98 | 12.35 | 27.95 | 39.33 |
| .58 | 17.40 | 25.85 | 29.61 | 24.31 | 12.60 | 2.60 | 2.03 | 12.49 | 28.10 | 39.40 |
| .59 | 17.48 | 25.93 | 29.60 | 24.22 | 12.47 | 2.54 | 2.08 | 12.64 | 28.25 | 39.46 |
| .60 | 17.56 | 26.00 | 29.60 | 24.12 | 12.35 | 2.48 | 2.13 | 12.79 | 28.40 | 39.53 |
| .61 | 17.64 | 26.07 | 29.59 | 24.02 | 12.23 | 2.42 | 2.19 | 12.94 | 28.55 | 39.59 |
| .62 | 17.72 | 26.14 | 29.58 | 23.92 | 12.10 | 2.36 | 2.25 | 13.08 | 28.70 | 39.65 |
| .63 | 17.80 | 26.21 | 29.57 | 23.82 | 11.98 | 2.30 | 2.31 | 13.23 | 28.85 | 39.71 |
| .64 | 17.88 | 26.28 | 29.56 | 23.72 | 11.86 | 2.25 | 2.37 | 13.38 | 29.00 | 39.77 |
| .65 | 17.97 | 26.35 | 29.54 | 23.62 | 11.74 | 2.19 | 2.43 | 13.53 | 29.14 | 39.83 |
| .66 | 18.05 | 26.42 | 29.53 | 23.52 | 11.61 | 2.14 | 2.49 | 13.68 | 29.29 | 39.88 |
| .67 | 18.13 | 26.49 | 29.51 | 23.42 | 11.49 | 2.08 | 2.55 | 13.83 | 29.44 | 39.94 |
| .68 | 18.22 | 26.55 | 29.50 | 23.32 | 11.37 | 2.05 | 2.61 | 13.98 | 29.58 | 39.99 |
| .69 | 18.30 | 26.62 | 29.48 | 23.22 | 11.25 | 1.98 | 2.68 | 14.13 | 29.73 | 40.05 |
| .70 | 18.39 | 26.69 | 29.47 | 23.12 | 11.13 | 1.93 | 2.74 | 14.28 | 29.88 | 40.10 |
| .71 | 18.47 | 26.75 | 29.45 | 23.01 | 11.01 | 1.88 | 2.81 | 14.43 | 30.02 | 40.15 |
| .72 | 18.55 | 26.82 | 29.43 | 22.91 | 10.89 | 1.83 | 2.88 | 14.58 | 30.16 | 40.20 |
| .73 | 18.64 | 26.88 | 29.41 | 22.80 | 10.77 | 1.79 | 2.95 | 14.73 | 30.30 | 40.25 |
| .74 | 18.72 | 26.94 | 29.39 | 22.70 | 10.65 | 1.74 | 3.02 | 14.88 | 30.44 | 40.29 |
| .75 | 18.81 | 27.01 | 29.37 | 22.59 | 10.53 | 1.70 | 3.10 | 15.04 | 30.58 | 40.34 |
| .76 | 18.90 | 27.07 | 29.35 | 22.48 | 10.41 | 1.66 | 3.17 | 15.19 | 30.72 | 40.38 |
| .77 | 18.98 | 27.13 | 29.32 | 22.38 | 10.29 | 1.61 | 3.25 | 15.34 | 30.86 | 40.43 |
| .78 | 19.07 | 27.19 | 29.30 | 22.27 | 10.17 | 1.57 | 3.32 | 15.50 | 31.00 | 40.47 |
| .79 | 19.16 | 27.25 | 29.28 | 22.16 | 10.05 | 1.53 | 3.40 | 15.65 | 31.14 | 40.51 |
| .80 | 19.25 | 27.31 | 29.25 | 22.05 | 9.93 | 1.49 | 3.48 | 15.81 | 31.28 | 40.55 |
| .81 | 19.34 | 27.37 | 29.22 | 21.94 | 9.81 | 1.45 | 3.56 | 15.96 | 31.42 | 40.59 |
| .82 | 19.43 | 27.43 | 29.19 | 21.83 | 9.69 | 1.42 | 3.64 | 16.12 | 31.56 | 40.62 |
| .83 | 19.51 | 27.49 | 29.16 | 21.72 | 9.58 | 1.38 | 3.72 | 16.27 | 31.69 | 40.66 |
| .84 | 19.59 | 27.54 | 29.13 | 21.61 | 9.46 | 1.35 | 3.81 | 16.43 | 31.83 | 40.69 |
| .85 | 19.68 | 27.60 | 29.10 | 21.50 | 9.35 | 1.32 | 3.89 | 16.59 | 31.96 | 40.72 |
| .86 | 19.77 | 27.65 | 29.06 | 21.38 | 9.23 | 1.28 | 3.97 | 16.74 | 32.09 | 40.76 |
| .87 | 19.85 | 27.71 | 29.03 | 21.27 | 9.12 | 1.25 | 4.06 | 16.90 | 32.23 | 40.79 |
| .88 | 19.94 | 27.77 | 29.00 | 21.16 | 9.00 | 1.22 | 4.15 | 17.06 | 32.36 | 40.82 |
| .89 | 20.03 | 27.82 | 28.96 | 21.04 | 8.89 | 1.19 | 4.24 | 17.22 | 32.49 | 40.85 |
| .90 | 20.12 | 27.87 | 28.93 | 20.93 | 8.77 | 1.16 | 4.33 | 17.38 | 32.62 | 40.88 |
| .91 | 20.21 | 27.92 | 28.89 | 20.82 | 8.66 | 1.14 | 4.42 | 17.54 | 32.75 | 40.90 |
| .92 | 20.30 | 27.97 | 28.85 | 20.70 | 8.54 | 1.11 | 4.51 | 17.70 | 32.88 | 40.92 |
| .93 | 20.38 | 28.02 | 28.81 | 20.59 | 8.43 | 1.09 | 4.60 | 17.86 | 33.01 | 40.95 |
| .94 | 20.47 | 28.07 | 28.77 | 20.47 | 8.32 | 1.07 | 4.70 | 18.01 | 33.14 | 40.97 |
| .95 | 20.56 | 28.12 | 28.73 | 20.35 | 8.21 | 1.04 | 4.79 | 18.17 | 33.26 | 40.99 |
| .96 | 20.65 | 28.17 | 28.68 | 20.24 | 8.10 | 1.02 | 4.89 | 18.33 | 33.39 | 41.01 |
| .97 | 20.74 | 28.22 | 28.64 | 20.12 | 7.99 | 1.00 | 4.98 | 18.49 | 33.51 | 41.03 |
| .98 | 20.82 | 28.28 | 28.60 | 20.00 | 7.88 | 0.98 | 5.08 | 18.65 | 33.64 | 41.05 |
| .99 | 20.91 | 28.33 | 28.55 | 19.89 | 7.77 | 0.96 | 5.18 | 18.81 | 33.76 | 41.07 |
| 1.00 | 21.00 | 28.38 | 28.51 | 19.77 | 7.66 | 0.94 | 5.28 | 18.97 | 33.88 | 41.08 |

# TABLE XXII. ARGUMENT 17.

Equation $= 17''.2\ [1 + \sin.\ (t + z)]$.

Period, 27.3216794 days.

| Days. | **0** | **1** | **2** | **3** | **4** | **5** | **6** | **7** | **8** | **9** | Days. |
|---|---|---|---|---|---|---|---|---|---|---|---|
| Days. | ″ | ″ | ″ | ″ | ″ | ″ | ″ | ″ | ″ | ″ | Days. |
| .00 | 0.05 | 0.20 | 1.23 | 3.12 | 5.74 | 8.97 | 12.64 | 16.52 | 20.47 | 24.24 | 1.00 |
| .01 | 0.05 | 0.21 | 1.24 | 3.14 | 5.77 | 9.00 | 12.68 | 16.56 | 20.51 | 24.28 | .99 |
| .02 | 0.04 | 0.21 | 1.26 | 3.16 | 5.80 | 9.04 | 12.72 | 16.60 | 20.55 | 24.31 | .98 |
| .03 | 0.04 | 0.22 | 1.27 | 3.19 | 5.83 | 9.07 | 12.76 | 16.64 | 20.59 | 24.35 | .97 |
| .04 | 0.04 | 0.23 | 1.29 | 3.21 | 5.86 | 9.11 | 12.79 | 16.68 | 20.63 | 24.38 | .96 |
| .05 | 0.03 | 0.23 | 1.30 | 3.23 | 5.89 | 9.15 | 12.83 | 16.71 | 20.67 | 24.42 | .95 |
| .06 | 0.03 | 0.24 | 1.32 | 3.26 | 5.92 | 9.18 | 12.87 | 16.75 | 20.70 | 24.46 | .94 |
| .07 | 0.03 | 0.25 | 1.33 | 3.28 | 5.95 | 9.22 | 12.90 | 16.79 | 20.74 | 24.49 | .93 |
| .08 | 0.03 | 0.25 | 1.35 | 3.30 | 5.98 | 9.25 | 12.94 | 16.83 | 20.78 | 24.53 | .92 |
| .09 | 0.02 | 0.26 | 1.36 | 3.33 | 6.01 | 9.29 | 12.98 | 16.87 | 20.82 | 24.56 | .91 |
| .10 | 0.02 | 0.27 | 1.38 | 3.35 | 6.04 | 9.32 | 13.02 | 16.91 | 20.86 | 24.60 | .90 |
| .11 | 0.02 | 0.28 | 1.40 | 3.37 | 6.07 | 9.35 | 13.06 | 16.95 | 20.90 | 24.64 | .89 |
| .12 | 0.02 | 0.28 | 1.41 | 3.39 | 6.10 | 9.39 | 13.10 | 16.99 | 20.94 | 24.67 | .88 |
| .13 | 0.01 | 0.29 | 1.43 | 3.42 | 6.13 | 9.42 | 13.14 | 17.03 | 20.98 | 24.71 | .87 |
| .14 | 0.01 | 0.30 | 1.44 | 3.44 | 6.16 | 9.46 | 13.17 | 17.07 | 21.01 | 24.74 | .86 |
| .15 | 0.01 | 0.30 | 1.46 | 3.47 | 6.19 | 9.50 | 13.21 | 17.10 | 21.05 | 24.78 | .85 |
| .16 | 0.01 | 0.31 | 1.47 | 3.49 | 6.23 | 9.53 | 13.25 | 17.14 | 21.09 | 24.81 | .84 |
| .17 | 0.01 | 0.32 | 1.49 | 3.52 | 6.26 | 9.57 | 13.28 | 17.18 | 21.12 | 24.84 | .83 |
| .18 | 0.00 | 0.32 | 1.51 | 3.54 | 6.29 | 9.60 | 13.32 | 17.22 | 21.16 | 24.88 | .82 |
| .19 | 0.00 | 0.33 | 1.52 | 3.57 | 6.32 | 9.64 | 13.36 | 17.26 | 21.20 | 24.91 | .81 |
| .20 | 0.00 | 0.34 | 1.54 | 3.59 | 6.35 | 9.67 | 13.40 | 17.30 | 21.24 | 24.95 | .80 |
| .21 | 0.00 | 0.35 | 1.56 | 3.61 | 6.38 | 9.71 | 13.44 | 17.34 | 21.28 | 24.99 | .79 |
| .22 | 0.00 | 0.36 | 1.58 | 3.64 | 6.41 | 9.74 | 13.48 | 17.38 | 21.32 | 25.02 | .78 |
| .23 | 0.00 | 0.36 | 1.59 | 3.66 | 6.44 | 9.78 | 13.52 | 17.42 | 21.36 | 25.06 | .77 |
| .24 | 0.00 | 0.37 | 1.61 | 3.69 | 6.47 | 9.81 | 13.55 | 17.46 | 21.39 | 25.09 | .76 |
| .25 | 0.00 | 0.38 | 1.63 | 3.71 | 6.50 | 9.85 | 13.59 | 17.50 | 21.43 | 25.13 | .75 |
| .26 | 0.00 | 0.39 | 1.65 | 3.74 | 6.54 | 9.89 | 13.63 | 17.54 | 21.47 | 25.16 | .74 |
| .27 | 0.00 | 0.40 | 1.67 | 3.76 | 6.57 | 9.92 | 13.66 | 17.58 | 21.50 | 25.19 | .73 |
| .28 | 0.00 | 0.40 | 1.68 | 3.79 | 6.60 | 9.96 | 13.70 | 17.62 | 21.54 | 25.23 | .72 |
| .29 | 0.00 | 0.41 | 1.70 | 3.81 | 6.63 | 9.99 | 13.74 | 17.66 | 21.58 | 25.26 | .71 |
| .30 | 0.00 | 0.42 | 1.72 | 3.84 | 6.66 | 10.03 | 13.78 | 17.70 | 21.62 | 25.30 | .70 |
| .31 | 0.00 | 0.43 | 1.74 | 3.86 | 6.69 | 10.07 | 13.82 | 17.74 | 21.66 | 25.33 | .69 |
| .32 | 0.00 | 0.44 | 1.76 | 3.89 | 6.72 | 10.10 | 13.86 | 17.78 | 21.70 | 25.37 | .68 |
| .33 | 0.00 | 0.45 | 1.77 | 3.91 | 6.75 | 10.14 | 13.90 | 17.82 | 21.73 | 25.40 | .67 |
| .34 | 0.00 | 0.46 | 1.79 | 3.94 | 6.78 | 10.17 | 13.94 | 17.86 | 21.77 | 25.44 | .66 |
| .35 | 0.00 | 0.46 | 1.81 | 3.96 | 6.81 | 10.21 | 13.97 | 17.90 | 21.81 | 25.47 | .65 |
| .36 | 0.00 | 0.47 | 1.83 | 3.99 | 6.85 | 10.25 | 14.01 | 17.94 | 21.85 | 25.50 | .64 |
| .37 | 0.00 | 0.48 | 1.85 | 4.01 | 6.88 | 10.28 | 14.05 | 17.98 | 21.88 | 25.54 | .63 |
| .38 | 0.00 | 0.49 | 1.86 | 4.04 | 6.91 | 10.32 | 14.09 | 18.02 | 21.92 | 25.57 | .62 |
| .39 | 0.00 | 0.50 | 1.88 | 4.06 | 6.94 | 10.35 | 14.13 | 18.06 | 21.96 | 25.61 | .61 |
| .40 | 0.00 | 0.51 | 1.90 | 4.09 | 6.97 | 10.39 | 14.17 | 18.10 | 22.00 | 25.64 | .60 |
| .41 | 0.00 | 0.52 | 1.92 | 4.12 | 7.00 | 10.43 | 14.21 | 18.14 | 22.04 | 25.67 | .59 |
| .42 | 0.00 | 0.53 | 1.94 | 4.14 | 7.03 | 10.47 | 14.25 | 18.18 | 22.08 | 25.71 | .58 |
| .43 | 0.00 | 0.54 | 1.95 | 4.17 | 7.07 | 10.50 | 14.29 | 18.22 | 22.12 | 25.74 | .57 |
| .44 | 0.00 | 0.55 | 1.97 | 4.19 | 7.10 | 10.54 | 14.33 | 18.26 | 22.15 | 25.78 | .56 |
| .45 | 0.00 | 0.56 | 1.99 | 4.22 | 7.13 | 10.57 | 14.36 | 18.30 | 22.19 | 25.81 | .55 |
| .46 | 0.01 | 0.57 | 2.01 | 4.24 | 7.16 | 10.61 | 14.40 | 18.34 | 22.23 | 25.84 | .54 |
| .47 | 0.01 | 0.58 | 2.03 | 4.27 | 7.20 | 10.65 | 14.44 | 18.38 | 22.26 | 25.88 | .53 |
| .48 | 0.01 | 0.59 | 2.04 | 4.29 | 7.23 | 10.68 | 14.48 | 18.42 | 22.30 | 25.91 | .52 |
| .49 | 0.01 | 0.60 | 2.06 | 4.32 | 7.26 | 10.72 | 14.52 | 18.46 | 22.34 | 25.95 | .51 |
| .50 | 0.01 | 0.61 | 2.08 | 4.35 | 7.29 | 10.76 | 14.56 | 18.50 | 22.38 | 25.98 | .50 |
| Days. | **27** | **26** | **25** | **24** | **23** | **22** | **21** | **20** | **19** | **18** | Days. |

# TABLE XXII. ARGUMENT 17.

Equation = 17″.2 [1 + sin. $(t + z)$].

Period, 27.3216794 days.

| Days. | 0 | 1 | 2 | 3 | 4 | 5 | 6 | 7 | 8 | 9 | Days. |
|---|---|---|---|---|---|---|---|---|---|---|---|
| Days. | ″ | ″ | ″ | ″ | ″ | ″ | ″ | ″ | ″ | ″ | Days. |
| .50 | 0.01 | 0.61 | 2.08 | 4.35 | 7.29 | 10.76 | 14.56 | 18.50 | 22.38 | 25.98 | .50 |
| .51 | 0.01 | 0.62 | 2.10 | 4.39 | 7.32 | 10.80 | 14.60 | 18.54 | 22.42 | 26.01 | .49 |
| .52 | 0.01 | 0.63 | 2.12 | 4.40 | 7.35 | 10.84 | 14.64 | 18.58 | 22.46 | 26.05 | .48 |
| .53 | 0.02 | 0.64 | 2.14 | 4.42 | 7.39 | 10.87 | 14.68 | 18.62 | 22.50 | 26.08 | .47 |
| .54 | 0.02 | 0.65 | 2.16 | 4.45 | 7.42 | 10.91 | 14.72 | 18.66 | 22.53 | 26.12 | .46 |
| .55 | 0.02 | 0.66 | 2.17 | 4.48 | 7.45 | 10.94 | 14.75 | 18.70 | 22.57 | 26.15 | .45 |
| .56 | 0.02 | 0.68 | 2.19 | 4.50 | 7.48 | 10.98 | 14.79 | 18.74 | 22.61 | 26.18 | .44 |
| .57 | 0.03 | 0.69 | 2.21 | 4.53 | 7.52 | 11.02 | 14.83 | 18.78 | 22.64 | 26.22 | .43 |
| .58 | 0.03 | 0.70 | 2.23 | 4.55 | 7.55 | 11.05 | 14.87 | 18.82 | 22.68 | 26.25 | .42 |
| .59 | 0.03 | 0.71 | 2.25 | 4.58 | 7.58 | 11.09 | 14.91 | 18.86 | 22.72 | 26.29 | .41 |
| .60 | 0.03 | 0.72 | 2.27 | 4.61 | 7.61 | 11.13 | 14.95 | 18.90 | 22.76 | 26.32 | .40 |
| .61 | 0.03 | 0.73 | 2.29 | 4.64 | 7.64 | 11.17 | 14.99 | 18.94 | 22.80 | 26.35 | .39 |
| .62 | 0.04 | 0.74 | 2.31 | 4.66 | 7.67 | 11.21 | 15.03 | 18.98 | 22.84 | 26.39 | .38 |
| .63 | 0.04 | 0.75 | 2.33 | 4.69 | 7.71 | 11.24 | 15.07 | 19.02 | 22.87 | 26.42 | .37 |
| .64 | 0.04 | 0.77 | 2.35 | 4.72 | 7.74 | 11.28 | 15.11 | 19.06 | 22.91 | 26.46 | .36 |
| .65 | 0.04 | 0.78 | 2.37 | 4.74 | 7.77 | 11.31 | 15.14 | 19.10 | 22.95 | 26.49 | .35 |
| .66 | 0.05 | 0.79 | 2.39 | 4.77 | 7.81 | 11.35 | 15.18 | 19.14 | 22.98 | 26.52 | .34 |
| .67 | 0.05 | 0.80 | 2.41 | 4.80 | 7.84 | 11.39 | 15.22 | 19.18 | 23.02 | 26.56 | .33 |
| .68 | 0.05 | 0.82 | 2.43 | 4.82 | 7.87 | 11.42 | 15.26 | 19.22 | 23.05 | 26.59 | .32 |
| .69 | 0.06 | 0.83 | 2.45 | 4.85 | 7.91 | 11.46 | 15.30 | 19.26 | 23.09 | 26.63 | .31 |
| .70 | 0.06 | 0.84 | 2.47 | 4.88 | 7.94 | 11.50 | 15.34 | 19.30 | 23.13 | 26.66 | .30 |
| .71 | 0.06 | 0.85 | 2.49 | 4.91 | 7.97 | 11.54 | 15.38 | 19.34 | 23.17 | 26.69 | .29 |
| .72 | 0.07 | 0.87 | 2.51 | 4.94 | 8.00 | 11.58 | 15.42 | 19.38 | 23.21 | 26.72 | .28 |
| .73 | 0.07 | 0.88 | 2.53 | 4.96 | 8.04 | 11.61 | 15.46 | 19.42 | 23.24 | 26.76 | .27 |
| .74 | 0.08 | 0.89 | 2.55 | 4.99 | 8.07 | 11.65 | 15.50 | 19.46 | 23.28 | 26.79 | .26 |
| .75 | 0.08 | 0.90 | 2.57 | 5.02 | 8.11 | 11.69 | 15.54 | 19.50 | 23.32 | 26.82 | .25 |
| .76 | 0.08 | 0.91 | 2.59 | 5.05 | 8.14 | 11.73 | 15.58 | 19.53 | 23.35 | 26.86 | .24 |
| .77 | 0.09 | 0.93 | 2.62 | 5.08 | 8.18 | 11.77 | 15.62 | 19.57 | 23.39 | 26.89 | .23 |
| .78 | 0.09 | 0.94 | 2.64 | 5.10 | 8.21 | 11.80 | 15.66 | 19.61 | 23.42 | 26.93 | .22 |
| .79 | 0.10 | 0.95 | 2.66 | 5.13 | 8.25 | 11.84 | 15.70 | 19.65 | 23.46 | 26.96 | .21 |
| .80 | 0.10 | 0.96 | 2.68 | 5.16 | 8.28 | 11.88 | 15.74 | 19.69 | 23.50 | 26.99 | .20 |
| .81 | 0.11 | 0.97 | 2.70 | 5.19 | 8.31 | 11.92 | 15.78 | 19.73 | 23.54 | 27.02 | .19 |
| .82 | 0.11 | 0.99 | 2.72 | 5.22 | 8.35 | 11.96 | 15.82 | 19.77 | 23.58 | 27.05 | .18 |
| .83 | 0.11 | 1.00 | 2.75 | 5.24 | 8.38 | 12.00 | 15.86 | 19.81 | 23.61 | 27.09 | .17 |
| .84 | 0.12 | 1.01 | 2.77 | 5.27 | 8.42 | 12.03 | 15.90 | 19.85 | 23.65 | 27.12 | .16 |
| .85 | 0.12 | 1.03 | 2.79 | 5.30 | 8.45 | 12.07 | 15.93 | 19.89 | 23.69 | 27.15 | .15 |
| .86 | 0.13 | 1.04 | 2.81 | 5.31 | 8.48 | 12.11 | 15.97 | 19.92 | 23.72 | 27.18 | .14 |
| .87 | 0.13 | 1.05 | 2.83 | 5.36 | 8.52 | 12.14 | 16.01 | 19.96 | 23.76 | 27.22 | .13 |
| .88 | 0.13 | 1.07 | 2.86 | 5.38 | 8.55 | 12.18 | 16.05 | 20.00 | 23.79 | 27.25 | .12 |
| .89 | 0.14 | 1.08 | 2.88 | 5.41 | 8.58 | 12.22 | 16.09 | 20.04 | 23.83 | 27.28 | .11 |
| .90 | 0.14 | 1.09 | 2.90 | 5.44 | 8.62 | 12.26 | 16.13 | 20.08 | 23.87 | 27.31 | .10 |
| .91 | 0.15 | 1.10 | 2.92 | 5.47 | 8.65 | 12.30 | 16.17 | 20.12 | 23.91 | 27.34 | .09 |
| .92 | 0.15 | 1.12 | 2.94 | 5.50 | 8.69 | 12.34 | 16.21 | 20.16 | 23.95 | 27.37 | .08 |
| .93 | 0.16 | 1.13 | 2.97 | 5.53 | 8.72 | 12.38 | 16.25 | 20.20 | 23.98 | 27.40 | .07 |
| .94 | 0.16 | 1.15 | 2.99 | 5.56 | 8.76 | 12.41 | 16.29 | 20.24 | 24.02 | 27.43 | .06 |
| .95 | 0.17 | 1.16 | 3.01 | 5.59 | 8.79 | 12.45 | 16.32 | 20.28 | 24.06 | 27.47 | .05 |
| .96 | 0.17 | 1.17 | 3.03 | 5.62 | 8.83 | 12.49 | 16.36 | 20.31 | 24.09 | 27.50 | .04 |
| .97 | 0.18 | 1.19 | 3.05 | 5.65 | 8.86 | 12.52 | 16.40 | 20.35 | 24.13 | 27.53 | .03 |
| .98 | 0.19 | 1.20 | 3.08 | 5.68 | 8.89 | 12.56 | 16.44 | 20.39 | 24.16 | 27.56 | .02 |
| .99 | 0.19 | 1.21 | 3.10 | 5.71 | 8.93 | 12.60 | 16.48 | 20.43 | 24.20 | 27.59 | .01 |
| 1.00 | 0.20 | 1.23 | 3.12 | 5.74 | 8.97 | 12.64 | 16.52 | 20.47 | 24.24 | 27.62 | .00 |
| Days. | 27 | 26 | 25 | 24 | 23 | 22 | 21 | 20 | 19 | 18 | Days. |

## TABLE XXII.

(*Continued.*)

Period, 27.3216794 days.

## TABLE XXIII. ARG. 18.

Equation = 14″.0 [1 + sin. $(2t + x - z)$].

Period, 9.873593 days.

| Days. | 10 | 11 | 12 | 13 | 0 | 1 | 2 | 3 | 4 | Days. |
|---|---|---|---|---|---|---|---|---|---|---|
| Days. | ″ | ″ | ″ | ″ | ″ | ″ | ″ | ″ | ″ | Days. |
| .00 | 27.62 | 30.47 | 32.61 | 33.94 | 0.01 | 2.42 | 9.35 | 18.11 | 25.25 | 1.00 |
| .01 | 27.65 | 30.49 | 32.63 | 33.95 | 0.01 | 2.47 | 9.43 | 18.19 | 25.30 | .99 |
| .02 | 27.68 | 30.52 | 32.65 | 33.96 | 0.01 | 2.52 | 9.52 | 18.28 | 25.35 | .98 |
| .03 | 27.71 | 30.54 | 32.66 | 33.97 | 0.01 | 2.58 | 9.60 | 18.36 | 25.41 | .97 |
| .04 | 27.74 | 30.57 | 32.68 | 33.98 | 0.00 | 2.63 | 9.69 | 18.45 | 25.46 | .96 |
| .05 | 27.78 | 30.59 | 32.70 | 33.99 | 0.00 | 2.68 | 9.77 | 18.53 | 25.51 | .95 |
| .06 | 27.81 | 30.61 | 32.72 | 33.99 | 0.00 | 2.73 | 9.86 | 18.61 | 25.56 | .94 |
| .07 | 27.84 | 30.64 | 32.74 | 34.00 | 0.00 | 2.78 | 9.94 | 18.70 | 25.61 | .93 |
| .08 | 27.87 | 30.66 | 32.75 | 34.01 | 0.00 | 2.84 | 10.03 | 18.78 | 25.66 | .92 |
| .09 | 27.90 | 30.69 | 32.77 | 34.02 | 0.00 | 2.89 | 10.11 | 18.87 | 25.71 | .91 |
| .10 | 27.93 | 30.71 | 32.79 | 34.03 | 0.00 | 2.94 | 10.20 | 18.95 | 25.76 | .90 |
| .11 | 27.96 | 30.73 | 32.81 | 34.04 | 0.00 | 3.00 | 10.29 | 19.03 | 25.81 | .89 |
| .12 | 27.99 | 30.76 | 32.83 | 34.05 | 0.01 | 3.05 | 10.37 | 19.12 | 25.86 | .88 |
| .13 | 28.02 | 30.78 | 32.84 | 34.05 | 0.01 | 3.11 | 10.46 | 19.20 | 25.90 | .87 |
| .14 | 28.05 | 30.81 | 32.86 | 34.06 | 0.02 | 3.16 | 10.54 | 19.29 | 25.95 | .86 |
| .15 | 28.09 | 30.83 | 32.88 | 34.07 | 0.02 | 3.22 | 10.63 | 19.37 | 26.00 | .85 |
| .16 | 28.12 | 30.85 | 32.89 | 34.08 | 0.03 | 3.28 | 10.72 | 19.45 | 26.04 | .84 |
| .17 | 28.15 | 30.88 | 32.91 | 34.09 | 0.03 | 3.34 | 10.80 | 19.53 | 26.09 | .83 |
| .18 | 28.18 | 30.90 | 32.92 | 34.09 | 0.04 | 3.39 | 10.89 | 19.62 | 26.13 | .82 |
| .19 | 28.21 | 30.93 | 32.94 | 34.10 | 0.04 | 3.45 | 10.97 | 19.70 | 26.18 | .81 |
| .20 | 28.24 | 30.95 | 32.96 | 34.11 | 0.05 | 3.51 | 11.06 | 19.78 | 26.22 | .80 |
| .21 | 28.27 | 30.97 | 32.98 | 34.12 | 0.06 | 3.57 | 11.15 | 19.86 | 26.26 | .79 |
| .22 | 28.30 | 31.00 | 32.99 | 34.13 | 0.07 | 3.63 | 11.24 | 19.94 | 26.30 | .78 |
| .23 | 28.33 | 31.02 | 33.01 | 34.13 | 0.08 | 3.69 | 11.32 | 20.02 | 26.35 | .77 |
| .24 | 28.36 | 31.05 | 33.02 | 34.14 | 0.09 | 3.75 | 11.41 | 20.10 | 26.39 | .76 |
| .25 | 28.39 | 31.07 | 33.04 | 34.15 | 0.10 | 3.81 | 11.50 | 20.18 | 26.43 | .75 |
| .26 | 28.42 | 31.09 | 33.05 | 34.15 | 0.11 | 3.87 | 11.59 | 20.26 | 26.47 | .74 |
| .27 | 28.45 | 31.12 | 33.06 | 34.16 | 0.12 | 3.93 | 11.68 | 20.34 | 26.51 | .73 |
| .28 | 28.48 | 31.14 | 33.08 | 34.16 | 0.14 | 4.00 | 11.76 | 20.42 | 26.55 | .72 |
| .29 | 28.51 | 31.17 | 33.09 | 34.17 | 0.15 | 4.06 | 11.85 | 20.50 | 26.59 | .71 |
| .30 | 28.54 | 31.19 | 33.11 | 34.18 | 0.16 | 4.12 | 11.94 | 20.58 | 26.63 | .70 |
| .31 | 28.57 | 31.21 | 33.12 | 34.19 | 0.17 | 4.18 | 12.03 | 20.66 | 26.67 | .69 |
| .32 | 28.60 | 31.23 | 33.14 | 34.19 | 0.19 | 4.25 | 12.12 | 20.74 | 26.71 | .68 |
| .33 | 28.63 | 31.26 | 33.15 | 34.20 | 0.20 | 4.31 | 12.20 | 20.81 | 26.74 | .67 |
| .34 | 28.66 | 31.28 | 33.17 | 34.20 | 0.22 | 4.38 | 12.29 | 20.89 | 26.78 | .66 |
| .35 | 28.69 | 31.30 | 33.18 | 34.21 | 0.23 | 4.44 | 12.38 | 20.97 | 26.82 | .65 |
| .36 | 28.72 | 31.33 | 33.19 | 34.22 | 0.25 | 4.51 | 12.47 | 21.05 | 26.85 | .64 |
| .37 | 28.75 | 31.35 | 33.21 | 34.22 | 0.27 | 4.57 | 12.56 | 21.12 | 26.89 | .63 |
| .38 | 28.78 | 31.38 | 33.22 | 34.23 | 0.28 | 4.64 | 12.65 | 21.20 | 26.92 | .62 |
| .39 | 28.81 | 31.40 | 33.24 | 34.23 | 0.30 | 4.70 | 12.74 | 21.27 | 26.96 | .61 |
| .40 | 28.84 | 31.42 | 33.25 | 34.24 | 0.32 | 4.77 | 12.83 | 21.35 | 26.99 | .60 |
| .41 | 28.87 | 31.44 | 33.26 | 34.24 | 0.34 | 4.84 | 12.92 | 21.42 | 27.02 | .59 |
| .42 | 28.90 | 31.46 | 33.28 | 34.25 | 0.36 | 4.91 | 13.01 | 21.50 | 27.05 | .58 |
| .43 | 28.93 | 31.49 | 33.29 | 34.25 | 0.38 | 4.97 | 13.10 | 21.57 | 27.09 | .57 |
| .44 | 28.96 | 31.51 | 33.31 | 34.26 | 0.40 | 5.04 | 13.19 | 21.65 | 27.12 | .56 |
| .45 | 28.99 | 31.53 | 33.32 | 34.27 | 0.42 | 5.11 | 13.27 | 21.72 | 27.15 | .55 |
| .46 | 29.01 | 31.55 | 33.33 | 34.27 | 0.44 | 5.18 | 13.36 | 21.79 | 27.18 | .54 |
| .47 | 29.04 | 31.58 | 33.35 | 34.28 | 0.47 | 5.25 | 13.45 | 21.87 | 27.21 | .53 |
| .48 | 29.07 | 31.60 | 33.36 | 34.28 | 0.49 | 5.32 | 13.54 | 21.94 | 27.23 | .52 |
| .49 | 29.10 | 31.62 | 33.38 | 34.29 | 0.52 | 5.39 | 13.63 | 22.02 | 27.26 | .51 |
| .50 | 29.13 | 31.64 | 33.39 | 34.29 | 0.54 | 5.46 | 13.72 | 22.09 | 27.29 | .50 |
| Days. | 17 | 16 | 15 | 14 | 9 | 8 | 7 | 6 | 5 | Days. |

## TABLE XXII.

(*Continued.*)

Period, 27.3216794 days.

| Days. | 10 | 11 | 12 | 13 |
|---|---|---|---|---|
| Days. | ″ | ″ | ″ | ″ |
| .50 | 29.13 | 31.64 | 33.39 | 34.29 |
| .51 | 29.16 | 31.66 | 33.40 | 34.29 |
| .52 | 29.19 | 31.68 | 33.41 | 34.30 |
| .53 | 29.21 | 31.70 | 33.43 | 34.30 |
| .54 | 29.24 | 31.72 | 33.44 | 34.31 |
| .55 | 29.27 | 31.75 | 33.46 | 34.31 |
| .56 | 29.30 | 31.77 | 33.47 | 34.31 |
| .57 | 29.32 | 31.79 | 33.48 | 34.32 |
| .58 | 29.35 | 31.81 | 33.50 | 34.32 |
| .59 | 29.38 | 31.83 | 33.51 | 34.33 |
| .60 | 29.41 | 31.85 | 33.52 | 34.33 |
| .61 | 29.44 | 31.87 | 33.53 | 34.33 |
| .62 | 29.47 | 31.89 | 33.54 | 34.33 |
| .63 | 29.49 | 31.91 | 33.56 | 34.34 |
| .64 | 29.52 | 31.93 | 33.57 | 34.34 |
| .65 | 29.55 | 31.95 | 33.58 | 34.35 |
| .66 | 29.57 | 31.97 | 33.59 | 34.35 |
| .67 | 29.60 | 31.99 | 33.60 | 34.35 |
| .68 | 29.62 | 32.01 | 33.62 | 34.36 |
| .69 | 29.65 | 32.03 | 33.63 | 34.36 |
| .70 | 29.68 | 32.05 | 33.64 | 34.36 |
| .71 | 29.71 | 32.07 | 33.65 | 34.36 |
| .72 | 29.74 | 32.09 | 33.66 | 34.36 |
| .73 | 29.76 | 32.11 | 33.67 | 34.37 |
| .74 | 29.79 | 32.13 | 33.68 | 34.37 |
| .75 | 29.82 | 32.15 | 33.70 | 34.38 |
| .76 | 29.84 | 32.16 | 33.71 | 34.38 |
| .77 | 29.87 | 32.18 | 33.72 | 34.38 |
| .78 | 29.89 | 32.20 | 33.73 | 34.39 |
| .79 | 29.92 | 32.22 | 33.74 | 34.39 |
| .80 | 29.95 | 32.24 | 33.75 | 34.39 |
| .81 | 29.98 | 32.26 | 33.76 | 34.39 |
| .82 | 30.00 | 32.28 | 33.77 | 34.39 |
| .83 | 30.03 | 32.30 | 33.78 | 34.39 |
| .84 | 30.05 | 32.32 | 33.79 | 34.39 |
| .85 | 30.08 | 32.34 | 33.80 | 34.39 |
| .86 | 30.11 | 32.35 | 33.81 | 34.40 |
| .87 | 30.13 | 32.37 | 33.82 | 34.40 |
| .88 | 30.16 | 32.39 | 33.83 | 34.40 |
| .89 | 30.18 | 32.41 | 33.84 | 34.40 |
| .90 | 30.21 | 32.43 | 33.85 | 34.40 |
| .91 | 30.24 | 32.45 | 33.86 | 34.40 |
| .92 | 30.26 | 32.47 | 33.87 | 34.40 |
| .93 | 30.29 | 32.48 | 33.88 | 34.40 |
| .94 | 30.31 | 32.50 | 33.89 | 34.40 |
| .95 | 30.34 | 32.52 | 33.90 | 34.40 |
| .96 | 30.37 | 32.54 | 33.90 | 34.40 |
| .97 | 30.39 | 32.55 | 33.91 | 34.40 |
| .98 | 30.42 | 32.57 | 33.92 | 34.40 |
| .99 | 30.44 | 32.59 | 33.93 | 34.40 |
| 1.00 | 30.47 | 32.61 | 33.94 | 34.40 |
| Days. | 17 | 16 | 15 | 14 |

## TABLE XXIII. ARG. 18.

Equation $= 14''.0\ [1 + \sin.\ (2t + x - z)]$.

Period, 9.873593 days.

| 0 | 1 | 2 | 3 | 4 | Days. |
|---|---|---|---|---|---|
| ″ | ″ | ″ | ″ | ″ | Days. |
| 0.54 | 5.46 | 13.72 | 22.09 | 27.29 | .50 |
| 0.57 | 5.53 | 13.81 | 22.16 | 27.32 | .49 |
| 0.59 | 5.60 | 13.90 | 22.23 | 27.34 | .48 |
| 0.62 | 5.68 | 13.99 | 22.31 | 27.37 | .47 |
| 0.64 | 5.75 | 14.08 | 22.38 | 27.39 | .46 |
| 0.67 | 5.82 | 14.16 | 22.45 | 27.42 | .45 |
| 0.70 | 5.89 | 14.25 | 22.52 | 27.44 | .44 |
| 0.73 | 5.96 | 14.34 | 22.59 | 27.47 | .43 |
| 0.75 | 6.04 | 14.43 | 22.66 | 27.49 | .42 |
| 0.78 | 6.11 | 14.52 | 22.73 | 27.52 | .41 |
| 0.81 | 6.18 | 14.61 | 22.80 | 27.54 | .40 |
| 0.84 | 6.25 | 14.70 | 22.87 | 27.56 | .39 |
| 0.87 | 6.33 | 14.79 | 22.94 | 27.58 | .38 |
| 0.90 | 6.40 | 14.88 | 23.01 | 27.61 | .37 |
| 0.93 | 6.48 | 14.97 | 23.08 | 27.63 | .36 |
| 0.96 | 6.55 | 15.06 | 23.15 | 27.65 | .35 |
| 0.99 | 6.63 | 15.14 | 23.22 | 27.67 | .34 |
| 1.03 | 6.70 | 15.23 | 23.28 | 27.69 | .33 |
| 1.06 | 6.78 | 15.32 | 23.35 | 27.70 | .32 |
| 1.10 | 6.85 | 15.41 | 23.41 | 27.72 | .31 |
| 1.13 | 6.93 | 15.50 | 23.48 | 27.74 | .30 |
| 1.17 | 7.01 | 15.59 | 23.54 | 27.76 | .29 |
| 1.20 | 7.09 | 15.68 | 23.61 | 27.77 | .28 |
| 1.24 | 7.16 | 15.77 | 23.67 | 27.79 | .27 |
| 1.27 | 7.24 | 15.86 | 23.74 | 27.80 | .26 |
| 1.31 | 7.32 | 15.95 | 23.80 | 27.82 | .25 |
| 1.35 | 7.40 | 16.04 | 23.86 | 27.83 | .24 |
| 1.39 | 7.48 | 16.13 | 23.92 | 27.85 | .23 |
| 1.43 | 7.55 | 16.21 | 23.99 | 27.86 | .22 |
| 1.47 | 7.63 | 16.30 | 24.05 | 27.88 | .21 |
| 1.51 | 7.71 | 16.39 | 24.11 | 27.89 | .20 |
| 1.55 | 7.79 | 16.48 | 24.17 | 27.90 | .19 |
| 1.59 | 7.87 | 16.57 | 24.23 | 27.91 | .18 |
| 1.64 | 7.95 | 16.65 | 24.29 | 27.92 | .17 |
| 1.68 | 8.03 | 16.74 | 24.35 | 27.93 | .16 |
| 1.72 | 8.11 | 16.83 | 24.41 | 27.94 | .15 |
| 1.76 | 8.19 | 16.92 | 24.47 | 27.95 | .14 |
| 1.81 | 8.27 | 17.00 | 24.53 | 27.96 | .13 |
| 1.85 | 8.36 | 17.09 | 24.58 | 27.96 | .12 |
| 1.90 | 8.44 | 17.17 | 24.64 | 27.97 | .11 |
| 1.94 | 8.52 | 17.26 | 24.70 | 27.98 | .10 |
| 1.99 | 8.60 | 17.35 | 24.76 | 27.98 | .09 |
| 2.03 | 8.68 | 17.43 | 24.81 | 27.99 | .08 |
| 2.08 | 8.77 | 17.52 | 24.87 | 27.99 | .07 |
| 2.12 | 8.85 | 17.60 | 24.92 | 28.00 | .06 |
| 2.17 | 8.93 | 17.69 | 24.98 | 28.00 | .05 |
| 2.22 | 9.01 | 17.77 | 25.03 | 28.00 | .04 |
| 2.27 | 9.10 | 17.86 | 25.09 | 28.00 | .03 |
| 2.32 | 9.18 | 17.94 | 25.14 | 28.00 | .02 |
| 2.37 | 9.27 | 18.03 | 25.20 | 28.00 | .01 |
| 2.42 | 9.35 | 18.11 | 25.25 | 28.00 | .00 |
| 9 | 8 | 7 | 6 | 5 | Days. |

# TABLE XXIV. ARGUMENT 19.

Equation = 12″.8 [1 — sin. (3$x$ — 2$t$)].

Period, 24.302196 days.

| Days. | 0 | 1 | 2 | 3 | 4 | 5 | 6 | 7 | 8 | Days. |
|---|---|---|---|---|---|---|---|---|---|---|
| .00 | 25.29 | 25.59 | 25.03 | 23.67 | 21.59 | 18.91 | 15.83 | 12.55 | 9.29 | 1.00 |
| .01 | 25.30 | 25.59 | 25.02 | 23.65 | 21.56 | 18.88 | 15.80 | 12.52 | 9.26 | .99 |
| .02 | 25.31 | 25.59 | 25.01 | 23.63 | 21.53 | 18.85 | 15.77 | 12.49 | 9.23 | .98 |
| .03 | 25.31 | 25.58 | 25.00 | 23.62 | 21.51 | 18.82 | 15.73 | 12.45 | 9.20 | .97 |
| .04 | 25.32 | 25.58 | 24.99 | 23.60 | 21.48 | 18.79 | 15.70 | 12.42 | 9.16 | .96 |
| .05 | 25.33 | 25.58 | 24.98 | 23.58 | 21.46 | 18.76 | 15.67 | 12.39 | 9.13 | .95 |
| .06 | 25.33 | 25.58 | 24.97 | 23.56 | 21.44 | 18.74 | 15.63 | 12.35 | 9.10 | .94 |
| .07 | 25.34 | 25.58 | 24.96 | 23.54 | 21.41 | 18.71 | 15.60 | 12.32 | 9.06 | .93 |
| .08 | 25.35 | 25.57 | 24.95 | 23.53 | 21.39 | 18.68 | 15.56 | 12.28 | 9.03 | .92 |
| .09 | 25.35 | 25.57 | 24.94 | 23.51 | 21.36 | 18.65 | 15.53 | 12.25 | 9.00 | .91 |
| .10 | 25.36 | 25.57 | 24.93 | 23.49 | 21.34 | 18.62 | 15.50 | 12.22 | 8.97 | .90 |
| .11 | 25.37 | 25.57 | 24.92 | 23.47 | 21.32 | 18.59 | 15.47 | 12.19 | 8.94 | .89 |
| .12 | 25.38 | 25.57 | 24.91 | 23.45 | 21.29 | 18.56 | 15.44 | 12.16 | 8.91 | .88 |
| .13 | 25.38 | 25.56 | 24.90 | 23.44 | 21.27 | 18.53 | 15.41 | 12.12 | 8.88 | .87 |
| .14 | 25.39 | 25.56 | 24.89 | 23.42 | 21.24 | 18.50 | 15.37 | 12.09 | 8.84 | .86 |
| .15 | 25.39 | 25.56 | 24.88 | 23.40 | 21.22 | 18.47 | 15.34 | 12.06 | 8.81 | .85 |
| .16 | 25.40 | 25.55 | 24.86 | 23.38 | 21.20 | 18.44 | 15.31 | 12.02 | 8.78 | .84 |
| .17 | 25.40 | 25.55 | 24.85 | 23.36 | 21.17 | 18.41 | 15.27 | 11.99 | 8.74 | .83 |
| .18 | 25.41 | 25.55 | 24.84 | 23.35 | 21.15 | 18.38 | 15.24 | 11.95 | 8.71 | .82 |
| .19 | 25.41 | 25.54 | 24.83 | 23.33 | 21.12 | 18.35 | 15.21 | 11.92 | 8.68 | .81 |
| .20 | 25.42 | 25.54 | 24.82 | 23.31 | 21.10 | 18.32 | 15.18 | 11.89 | 8.65 | .80 |
| .21 | 25.42 | 25.54 | 24.81 | 23.29 | 21.08 | 18.29 | 15.15 | 11.86 | 8.62 | .79 |
| .22 | 25.43 | 25.54 | 24.80 | 23.27 | 21.05 | 18.26 | 15.12 | 11.82 | 8.59 | .78 |
| .23 | 25.43 | 25.53 | 24.79 | 23.25 | 21.03 | 18.23 | 15.09 | 11.79 | 8.56 | .77 |
| .24 | 25.44 | 25.53 | 24.78 | 23.23 | 21.00 | 18.20 | 15.05 | 11.75 | 8.53 | .76 |
| .25 | 25.44 | 25.53 | 24.77 | 23.21 | 20.98 | 18.17 | 15.02 | 11.72 | 8.50 | .75 |
| .26 | 25.45 | 25.52 | 24.75 | 23.20 | 20.95 | 18.13 | 14.99 | 11.69 | 8.48 | .74 |
| .27 | 25.45 | 25.52 | 24.74 | 23.18 | 20.92 | 18.10 | 14.95 | 11.65 | 8.45 | .73 |
| .28 | 25.46 | 25.52 | 24.73 | 23.16 | 20.90 | 18.07 | 14.92 | 11.62 | 8.40 | .72 |
| .29 | 25.46 | 25.51 | 24.72 | 23.14 | 20.87 | 18.04 | 14.89 | 11.58 | 8.37 | .71 |
| .30 | 25.47 | 25.51 | 24.71 | 23.12 | 20.85 | 18.01 | 14.86 | 11.55 | 8.34 | .70 |
| .31 | 25.47 | 25.51 | 24.70 | 23.10 | 20.82 | 17.98 | 14.83 | 11.52 | 8.31 | .69 |
| .32 | 25.48 | 25.50 | 24.69 | 23.08 | 20.80 | 17.95 | 14.80 | 11.49 | 8.28 | .68 |
| .33 | 25.48 | 25.50 | 24.68 | 23.06 | 20.77 | 17.92 | 14.76 | 11.45 | 8.25 | .67 |
| .34 | 25.49 | 25.49 | 24.66 | 23.04 | 20.75 | 17.89 | 14.73 | 11.42 | 8.22 | .66 |
| .35 | 25.49 | 25.49 | 24.65 | 23.02 | 20.72 | 17.86 | 14.70 | 11.39 | 8.19 | .65 |
| .36 | 25.50 | 25.49 | 24.64 | 23.00 | 20.69 | 17.82 | 14.66 | 11.35 | 8.15 | .64 |
| .37 | 25.50 | 25.48 | 24.63 | 22.98 | 20.67 | 17.79 | 14.63 | 11.32 | 8.12 | .63 |
| .38 | 25.50 | 25.48 | 24.62 | 22.96 | 20.64 | 17.76 | 14.59 | 11.28 | 8.09 | .62 |
| .39 | 25.51 | 25.47 | 24.60 | 22.94 | 20.62 | 17.73 | 14.56 | 11.25 | 8.06 | .61 |
| .40 | 25.51 | 25.47 | 24.59 | 22.92 | 20.59 | 17.70 | 14.53 | 11.22 | 8.03 | .60 |
| .41 | 25.51 | 25.46 | 24.58 | 22.90 | 20.56 | 17.67 | 14.50 | 11.19 | 8.00 | .59 |
| .42 | 25.52 | 25.46 | 24.57 | 22.88 | 20.53 | 17.64 | 14.47 | 11.16 | 7.97 | .58 |
| .43 | 25.52 | 25.45 | 24.55 | 22.86 | 20.51 | 17.61 | 14.43 | 11.12 | 7.94 | .57 |
| .44 | 25.52 | 25.45 | 24.54 | 22.84 | 20.48 | 17.58 | 14.40 | 11.09 | 7.91 | .56 |
| .45 | 25.53 | 25.44 | 24.52 | 22.82 | 20.46 | 17.55 | 14.37 | 11.06 | 7.88 | .55 |
| .46 | 25.53 | 25.44 | 24.51 | 22.79 | 20.43 | 17.52 | 14.33 | 11.02 | 7.85 | .54 |
| .47 | 25.53 | 25.43 | 24.49 | 22.77 | 20.40 | 17.49 | 14.30 | 10.99 | 7.82 | .53 |
| .48 | 25.54 | 25.43 | 24.48 | 22.75 | 20.38 | 17.46 | 14.26 | 10.95 | 7.79 | .52 |
| .49 | 25.54 | 25.42 | 24.46 | 22.73 | 20.35 | 17.43 | 14.23 | 10.92 | 7.76 | .51 |
| .50 | 25.54 | 25.42 | 24.45 | 22.71 | 20.32 | 17.40 | 14.20 | 10.89 | 7.73 | .50 |
| Days. | 25 | 24 | 23 | 22 | 21 | 20 | 19 | 18 | 17 | Days. |

# TABLE XXIV. ARGUMENT 19.

Equation = 12″.8 [1 — sin. $(3x - 2t)$].

Period, 24.302196 days.

| Days. | 0 | 1 | 2 | 3 | 4 | 5 | 6 | 7 | 8 | Days. |
|---|---|---|---|---|---|---|---|---|---|---|
| Days | ″ | ″ | ″ | ″ | ″ | ″ | ″ | ″ | ″ | Days. |
| .50 | 25.54 | 25.42 | 24.45 | 22.71 | 20.32 | 17.40 | 14.20 | 10.89 | 7.73 | .50 |
| .51 | 25.54 | 25.41 | 24.44 | 22.69 | 20.29 | 17.37 | 14.17 | 10.86 | 7.70 | .49 |
| .52 | 25.55 | 25.41 | 24.42 | 22.67 | 20.26 | 17.34 | 14.14 | 10.83 | 7.67 | .48 |
| .53 | 25.55 | 25.40 | 24.41 | 22.65 | 20.24 | 17.31 | 14.10 | 10.80 | 7.64 | .47 |
| .54 | 25.55 | 25.40 | 24.39 | 22.63 | 20.21 | 17.28 | 14.07 | 10.76 | 7.61 | .46 |
| .55 | 25.55 | 25.39 | 24.38 | 22.61 | 20.18 | 17.25 | 14.04 | 10.73 | 7.58 | .45 |
| .56 | 25.56 | 25.39 | 24.37 | 22.58 | 20.15 | 17.21 | 14.00 | 10.70 | 7.55 | .44 |
| .57 | 25.56 | 25.38 | 24.35 | 22.56 | 20.12 | 17.18 | 13.97 | 10.66 | 7.52 | .43 |
| .58 | 25.56 | 25.37 | 24.34 | 22.54 | 20.10 | 17.15 | 13.93 | 10.63 | 7.49 | .42 |
| .59 | 25.56 | 25.37 | 24.32 | 22.52 | 20.07 | 17.12 | 13.90 | 10.60 | 7.46 | .41 |
| .60 | 25.57 | 25.36 | 24.31 | 22.50 | 20.04 | 17.09 | 13.87 | 10.57 | 7.43 | .40 |
| .61 | 25.57 | 25.35 | 24.29 | 22.48 | 20.01 | 17.06 | 13.84 | 10.54 | 7.40 | .39 |
| .62 | 25.57 | 25.35 | 24.28 | 22.46 | 19.98 | 17.03 | 13.81 | 10.51 | 7.37 | .38 |
| .63 | 25.57 | 25.34 | 24.26 | 22.43 | 19.95 | 17.00 | 13.77 | 10.48 | 7.34 | .37 |
| .64 | 25.58 | 25.33 | 24.25 | 22.41 | 19.93 | 16.97 | 13.74 | 10.44 | 7.31 | .36 |
| .65 | 25.58 | 25.33 | 24.23 | 22.39 | 19.90 | 16.94 | 13.71 | 10.41 | 7.28 | .35 |
| .66 | 25.58 | 25.32 | 24.22 | 22.37 | 19.87 | 16.90 | 13.67 | 10.38 | 7.25 | .34 |
| .67 | 25.58 | 25.31 | 24.20 | 22.35 | 19.85 | 16.87 | 13.64 | 10.34 | 7.22 | .33 |
| .68 | 25.59 | 25.31 | 24.19 | 22.32 | 19.82 | 16.84 | 13.60 | 10.31 | 7.19 | .32 |
| .69 | 25.59 | 25.30 | 24.17 | 22.30 | 19.79 | 16.81 | 13.57 | 10.28 | 7.16 | .31 |
| .70 | 25.59 | 25.29 | 24.16 | 22.28 | 19.76 | 16.78 | 13.54 | 10.25 | 7.13 | .30 |
| .71 | 25.59 | 25.28 | 24.14 | 22.26 | 19.73 | 16.75 | 13.51 | 10.22 | 7.10 | .29 |
| .72 | 25.59 | 25.27 | 24.13 | 22.24 | 19.70 | 16.72 | 13.48 | 10.19 | 7.07 | .28 |
| .73 | 25.59 | 25.27 | 24.11 | 22.21 | 19.67 | 16.69 | 13.44 | 10.16 | 7.04 | .27 |
| .74 | 25.60 | 25.26 | 24.10 | 22.19 | 19.65 | 16.66 | 13.41 | 10.12 | 7.01 | .26 |
| .75 | 25.60 | 25.25 | 24.08 | 22.17 | 19.62 | 16.63 | 13.38 | 10.09 | 6.98 | .25 |
| .76 | 25.60 | 25.24 | 24.07 | 22.15 | 19.59 | 16.59 | 13.34 | 10.06 | 6.95 | .24 |
| .77 | 25.60 | 25.23 | 24.05 | 22.13 | 19.57 | 16.56 | 13.31 | 10.02 | 6.92 | .23 |
| .78 | 25.60 | 25.23 | 24.04 | 22.10 | 19.54 | 16.53 | 13.27 | 9.99 | 6.89 | .22 |
| .79 | 25.60 | 25.22 | 24.02 | 22.08 | 19.51 | 16.50 | 13.24 | 9.96 | 6.86 | .21 |
| .80 | 25.60 | 25.21 | 24.01 | 22.06 | 19.48 | 16.47 | 13.21 | 9.93 | 6.83 | .20 |
| .81 | 25.60 | 25.20 | 23.99 | 22.04 | 19.45 | 16.44 | 13.18 | 9.90 | 6.80 | .19 |
| .82 | 25.60 | 25.19 | 23.98 | 22.02 | 19.42 | 16.41 | 13.15 | 9.87 | 6.77 | .18 |
| .83 | 25.60 | 25.18 | 23.96 | 21.99 | 19.39 | 16.38 | 13.11 | 9.84 | 6.74 | .17 |
| .84 | 25.60 | 25.18 | 23.95 | 21.97 | 19.37 | 16.34 | 13.08 | 9.80 | 6.71 | .16 |
| .85 | 25.60 | 25.17 | 23.93 | 21.95 | 19.34 | 16.31 | 13.05 | 9.77 | 6.68 | .15 |
| .86 | 25.60 | 25.16 | 23.92 | 21.92 | 19.31 | 16.28 | 13.01 | 9.74 | 6.66 | .14 |
| .87 | 25.60 | 25.15 | 23.90 | 21.90 | 19.29 | 16.24 | 12.98 | 9.70 | 6.63 | .13 |
| .88 | 25.60 | 25.14 | 23.88 | 21.88 | 19.26 | 16.21 | 12.94 | 9.67 | 6.60 | .12 |
| .89 | 25.60 | 25.13 | 23.87 | 21.85 | 19.23 | 16.18 | 12.91 | 9.64 | 6.57 | .11 |
| .90 | 25.60 | 25.12 | 23.85 | 21.83 | 19.20 | 16.15 | 12.88 | 9.61 | 6.54 | .10 |
| .91 | 25.60 | 25.11 | 23.83 | 21.81 | 19.17 | 16.12 | 12.85 | 9.58 | 6.51 | .09 |
| .92 | 25.60 | 25.10 | 23.82 | 21.79 | 19.14 | 16.09 | 12.82 | 9.55 | 6.48 | .08 |
| .93 | 25.60 | 25.10 | 23.80 | 21.76 | 19.11 | 16.06 | 12.78 | 9.52 | 6.45 | .07 |
| .94 | 25.60 | 25.09 | 23.78 | 21.74 | 19.08 | 16.02 | 12.75 | 9.48 | 6.42 | .06 |
| .95 | 25.60 | 25.08 | 23.76 | 21.72 | 19.05 | 15.99 | 12.72 | 9.45 | 6.39 | .05 |
| .96 | 25.60 | 25.07 | 23.74 | 21.69 | 19.03 | 15.96 | 12.68 | 9.42 | 6.37 | .04 |
| .97 | 25.59 | 25.06 | 23.73 | 21.67 | 19.00 | 15.92 | 12.65 | 9.38 | 6.34 | .03 |
| .98 | 25.59 | 25.05 | 23.71 | 21.65 | 18.97 | 15.89 | 12.61 | 9.35 | 6.31 | .02 |
| .99 | 25.59 | 25.04 | 23.69 | 21.62 | 18.94 | 15.86 | 12.58 | 9.32 | 6.28 | .01 |
| 1.00 | 25.59 | 25.03 | 23.67 | 21.59 | 18.91 | 15.83 | 12.55 | 9.29 | 6.25 | .00 |
| Days. | 25 | 24 | 23 | 22 | 21 | 20 | 19 | 18 | 17 | Days. |

## TABLE XXIV.

(*Continued.*)

Period, 24.302196 days.

| Days. | 9 | 10 | 11 | 12 |
|---|---|---|---|---|
| Days | ″ | ″ | ″ | ″ |
| .00 | 6.25 | 3.66 | 1.67 | 0.43 |
| .01 | 6.22 | 3.64 | 1.65 | 0.42 |
| .02 | 6.19 | 3.62 | 1.64 | 0.41 |
| .03 | 6.16 | 3.59 | 1.62 | 0.40 |
| .04 | 6.14 | 3.57 | 1.61 | 0.40 |
| .05 | 6.11 | 3.54 | 1.59 | 0.39 |
| .06 | 6.08 | 3.52 | 1.57 | 0.38 |
| .07 | 6.06 | 3.50 | 1.56 | 0.38 |
| .08 | 6.03 | 3.47 | 1.54 | 0.37 |
| .09 | 6.00 | 3.45 | 1.53 | 0.36 |
| .10 | 5.97 | 3.43 | 1.51 | 0.35 |
| .11 | 5.94 | 3.41 | 1.49 | 0.34 |
| .12 | 5.91 | 3.39 | 1.48 | 0.33 |
| .13 | 5.88 | 3.37 | 1.46 | 0.32 |
| .14 | 5.86 | 3.34 | 1.45 | 0.32 |
| .15 | 5.83 | 3.32 | 1.43 | 0.31 |
| .16 | 5.80 | 3.30 | 1.42 | 0.30 |
| .17 | 5.78 | 3.27 | 1.41 | 0.30 |
| .18 | 5.75 | 3.25 | 1.39 | 0.29 |
| .19 | 5.72 | 3.23 | 1.38 | 0.28 |
| .20 | 5.69 | 3.21 | 1.36 | 0.27 |
| .21 | 5.66 | 3.19 | 1.35 | 0.26 |
| .22 | 5.63 | 3.17 | 1.33 | 0.26 |
| .23 | 5.61 | 3.15 | 1.32 | 0.25 |
| .24 | 5.58 | 3.12 | 1.30 | 0.25 |
| .25 | 5.55 | 3.10 | 1.29 | 0.24 |
| .26 | 5.53 | 3.08 | 1.28 | 0.23 |
| .27 | 5.50 | 3.05 | 1.26 | 0.23 |
| .28 | 5.48 | 3.03 | 1.25 | 0.22 |
| .29 | 5.45 | 3.01 | 1.23 | 0.22 |
| .30 | 5.42 | 2.99 | 1.22 | 0.21 |
| .31 | 5.39 | 2.97 | 1.21 | 0.20 |
| .32 | 5.36 | 2.95 | 1.19 | 0.20 |
| .33 | 5.34 | 2.93 | 1.18 | 0.19 |
| .34 | 5.31 | 2.91 | 1.16 | 0.19 |
| .35 | 5.28 | 2.88 | 1.15 | 0.18 |
| .36 | 5.26 | 2.86 | 1.14 | 0.18 |
| .37 | 5.23 | 2.84 | 1.12 | 0.18 |
| .38 | 5.21 | 2.82 | 1.11 | 0.17 |
| .39 | 5.18 | 2.80 | 1.09 | 0.17 |
| .40 | 5.15 | 2.78 | 1.08 | 0.16 |
| .41 | 5.12 | 2.76 | 1.07 | 0.15 |
| .42 | 5.10 | 2.74 | 1.05 | 0.15 |
| .43 | 5.07 | 2.72 | 1.04 | 0.14 |
| .44 | 5.05 | 2.70 | 1.03 | 0.14 |
| .45 | 5.02 | 2.68 | 1.01 | 0.13 |
| .46 | 4.99 | 2.66 | 1.00 | 0.13 |
| .47 | 4.97 | 2.64 | 0.99 | 0.13 |
| .48 | 4.94 | 2.62 | 0.97 | 0.12 |
| .49 | 4.92 | 2.60 | 0.96 | 0.12 |
| .50 | 4.89 | 2.58 | 0.95 | 0.11 |
| Days. | 16 | 15 | 14 | 13 |

## TABLE XXV. ARG. 20.

Equation $= 9''.6\ [1 + \sin.\ (2x - z)]$.

Period, 14.317313 days.

| 0 | 1 | 2 | 3 | 4 | Days. |
|---|---|---|---|---|---|
| ″ | ″ | ″ | ″ | ″ | Days. |
| 0.65 | 0.02 | 1.21 | 4.00 | 7.84 | 1.00 |
| 0.64 | 0.02 | 1.23 | 4.03 | 7.88 | .99 |
| 0.62 | 0.03 | 1.25 | 4.07 | 7.92 | .98 |
| 0.61 | 0.03 | 1.27 | 4.10 | 7.96 | .97 |
| 0.59 | 0.04 | 1.30 | 4.14 | 8.01 | .96 |
| 0.58 | 0.04 | 1.32 | 4.17 | 8.05 | .95 |
| 0.57 | 0.04 | 1.34 | 4.21 | 8.09 | .94 |
| 0.55 | 0.05 | 1.37 | 4.25 | 8.14 | .93 |
| 0.54 | 0.05 | 1.39 | 4.28 | 8.18 | .92 |
| 0.52 | 0.06 | 1.41 | 4.32 | 8.22 | .91 |
| 0.51 | 0.06 | 1.43 | 4.35 | 8.26 | .90 |
| 0.50 | 0.07 | 1.45 | 4.39 | 8.30 | .89 |
| 0.48 | 0.07 | 1.47 | 4.42 | 8.34 | .88 |
| 0.47 | 0.08 | 1.50 | 4.46 | 8.38 | .87 |
| 0.45 | 0.08 | 1.52 | 4.49 | 8.43 | .86 |
| 0.44 | 0.08 | 1.54 | 4.53 | 8.47 | .85 |
| 0.43 | 0.09 | 1.57 | 4.57 | 8.51 | .84 |
| 0.42 | 0.09 | 1.59 | 4.60 | 8.56 | .83 |
| 0.40 | 0.10 | 1.62 | 4.64 | 8.60 | .82 |
| 0.39 | 0.11 | 1.64 | 4.67 | 8.64 | .81 |
| 0.38 | 0.12 | 1.66 | 4.71 | 8.68 | .80 |
| 0.37 | 0.13 | 1.68 | 4.75 | 8.72 | .79 |
| 0.36 | 0.14 | 1.71 | 4.78 | 8.76 | .78 |
| 0.35 | 0.14 | 1.73 | 4.82 | 8.80 | .77 |
| 0.34 | 0.15 | 1.76 | 4.85 | 8.85 | .76 |
| 0.32 | 0.16 | 1.78 | 4.89 | 8.89 | .75 |
| 0.31 | 0.17 | 1.81 | 4.93 | 8.93 | .74 |
| 0.30 | 0.17 | 1.84 | 4.96 | 8.98 | .73 |
| 0.29 | 0.18 | 1.86 | 5.00 | 9.02 | .72 |
| 0.28 | 0.19 | 1.89 | 5.03 | 9.06 | .71 |
| 0.27 | 0.20 | 1.91 | 5.07 | 9.10 | .70 |
| 0.26 | 0.21 | 1.94 | 5.11 | 9.14 | .69 |
| 0.25 | 0.22 | 1.96 | 5.15 | 9.18 | .68 |
| 0.24 | 0.23 | 1.99 | 5.18 | 9.22 | .67 |
| 0.23 | 0.24 | 2.01 | 5.22 | 9.27 | .66 |
| 0.22 | 0.24 | 2.04 | 5.25 | 9.31 | .65 |
| 0.22 | 0.25 | 2.07 | 5.29 | 9.35 | .64 |
| 0.21 | 0.26 | 2.09 | 5.33 | 9.40 | .63 |
| 0.20 | 0.27 | 2.12 | 5.36 | 9.44 | .62 |
| 0.19 | 0.28 | 2.14 | 5.40 | 9.48 | .61 |
| 0.18 | 0.29 | 2.17 | 5.44 | 9.52 | .60 |
| 0.17 | 0.30 | 2.20 | 5.48 | 9.56 | .59 |
| 0.16 | 0.31 | 2.22 | 5.52 | 9.60 | .58 |
| 0.16 | 0.32 | 2.25 | 5.55 | 9.64 | .57 |
| 0.15 | 0.33 | 2.27 | 5.59 | 9.69 | .56 |
| 0.14 | 0.34 | 2.29 | 5.63 | 9.73 | .55 |
| 0.13 | 0.36 | 2.32 | 5.67 | 9.77 | .54 |
| 0.13 | 0.37 | 2.34 | 5.70 | 9.81 | .53 |
| 0.12 | 0.38 | 2.37 | 5.74 | 9.86 | .52 |
| 0.12 | 0.39 | 2.41 | 5.78 | 9.90 | .51 |
| 0.11 | 0.40 | 2.44 | 5.82 | 9.94 | .50 |
| 15 | 14 | 13 | 12 | 11 | Days. |

## TABLE XXIV.

*(Continued.)*

Period, 24.302196 days.

| Days. | 9 | 10 | 11 | 12 |
|---|---|---|---|---|
| Days | ″ | ″ | ″ | ″ |
| .50 | 4.89 | 2.58 | 0.95 | 0.11 |
| .51 | 4.86 | 2.56 | 0.94 | 0.11 |
| .52 | 4.84 | 2.54 | 0.93 | 0.10 |
| .53 | 4.81 | 2.52 | 0.92 | 0.10 |
| .54 | 4.79 | 2.50 | 0.90 | 0.09 |
| .55 | 4.76 | 2.48 | 0.89 | 0.09 |
| .56 | 4.73 | 2.47 | 0.88 | 0.09 |
| .57 | 4.71 | 2.45 | 0.86 | 0.08 |
| .58 | 4.68 | 2.43 | 0.85 | 0.08 |
| .59 | 4.66 | 2.41 | 0.84 | 0.07 |
| .60 | 4.63 | 2.39 | 0.83 | 0.07 |
| .61 | 4.60 | 2.37 | 0.82 | 0.07 |
| .62 | 4.58 | 2.35 | 0.81 | 0.07 |
| .63 | 4.55 | 2.33 | 0.80 | 0.06 |
| .64 | 4.53 | 2.31 | 0.79 | 0.06 |
| .65 | 4.50 | 2.29 | 0.77 | 0.06 |
| .66 | 4.48 | 2.28 | 0.76 | 0.05 |
| .67 | 4.46 | 2.26 | 0.75 | 0.05 |
| .68 | 4.43 | 2.24 | 0.74 | 0.04 |
| .69 | 4.41 | 2.22 | 0.73 | 0.04 |
| .70 | 4.38 | 2.20 | 0.72 | 0.04 |
| .71 | 4.35 | 2.18 | 0.71 | 0.04 |
| .72 | 4.33 | 2.16 | 0.70 | 0.04 |
| .73 | 4.30 | 2.14 | 0.69 | 0.03 |
| .74 | 4.28 | 2.13 | 0.68 | 0.03 |
| .75 | 4.25 | 2.11 | 0.67 | 0.03 |
| .76 | 4.23 | 2.09 | 0.66 | 0.02 |
| .77 | 4.21 | 2.08 | 0.65 | 0.02 |
| .78 | 4.18 | 2.06 | 0.64 | 0.01 |
| .79 | 4.16 | 2.04 | 0.63 | 0.01 |
| .80 | 4.13 | 2.02 | 0.62 | 0.01 |
| .81 | 4.11 | 2.00 | 0.61 | 0.01 |
| .82 | 4.08 | 1.98 | 0.60 | 0.01 |
| .83 | 4.06 | 1.96 | 0.59 | 0.01 |
| .84 | 4.03 | 1.95 | 0.58 | 0.01 |
| .85 | 4.01 | 1.93 | 0.57 | 0.01 |
| .86 | 3.99 | 1.91 | 0.56 | 0.00 |
| .87 | 3.96 | 1.90 | 0.55 | 0.00 |
| .88 | 3.94 | 1.88 | 0.54 | 0.00 |
| .89 | 3.91 | 1.86 | 0.53 | 0.00 |
| .90 | 3.89 | 1.84 | 0.52 | 0.00 |
| .91 | 3.87 | 1.82 | 0.51 | 0.00 |
| .92 | 3.85 | 1.80 | 0.50 | 0.00 |
| .93 | 3.82 | 1.79 | 0.49 | 0.00 |
| .94 | 3.80 | 1.77 | 0.48 | 0.00 |
| .95 | 3.77 | 1.75 | 0.47 | 0.00 |
| .96 | 3.75 | 1.74 | 0.47 | 0.00 |
| .97 | 3.73 | 1.72 | 0.46 | 0.00 |
| .98 | 3.70 | 1.71 | 0.45 | 0.00 |
| .99 | 3.68 | 1.69 | 0.44 | 0.00 |
| 1.00 | 3.66 | 1.67 | 0.43 | 0.00 |
| Days. | 16 | 15 | 14 | 13 |

## TABLE XXV. ARG. 20.

Equation $= 9''.6\ [1 + \sin.\ (2x - z)]$.

Period, 14.317313 days.

| 0 | 1 | 2 | 3 | 4 | Days. |
|---|---|---|---|---|---|
| ″ | ″ | ″ | ″ | ″ | Days. |
| 0.11 | 0.40 | 2.44 | 5.82 | 9.94 | .50 |
| 0.11 | 0.41 | 2.47 | 5.86 | 9.98 | .49 |
| 0.10 | 0.42 | 2.50 | 5.90 | 10.02 | .48 |
| 0.10 | 0.44 | 2.53 | 5.94 | 10.06 | .47 |
| 0.09 | 0.45 | 2.55 | 5.98 | 10.11 | .46 |
| 0.08 | 0.46 | 2.58 | 6.01 | 10.15 | .45 |
| 0.08 | 0.48 | 2.61 | 6.05 | 10.19 | .44 |
| 0.07 | 0.49 | 2.63 | 6.09 | 10.24 | .43 |
| 0.07 | 0.51 | 2.66 | 6.13 | 10.28 | .42 |
| 0.06 | 0.52 | 2.69 | 6.17 | 10.32 | .41 |
| 0.06 | 0.53 | 2.72 | 6.21 | 10.36 | .40 |
| 0.06 | 0.54 | 2.75 | 6.25 | 10.40 | .39 |
| 0.05 | 0.56 | 2.78 | 6.29 | 10.44 | .38 |
| 0.05 | 0.57 | 2.81 | 6.33 | 10.48 | .37 |
| 0.04 | 0.59 | 2.84 | 6.37 | 10.52 | .36 |
| 0.04 | 0.60 | 2.87 | 6.41 | 10.57 | .35 |
| 0.04 | 0.62 | 2.90 | 6.45 | 10.61 | .34 |
| 0.03 | 0.64 | 2.93 | 6.49 | 10.65 | .33 |
| 0.03 | 0.65 | 2.96 | 6.53 | 10.69 | .32 |
| 0.02 | 0.67 | 2.99 | 6.57 | 10.73 | .31 |
| 0.02 | 0.68 | 3.02 | 6.61 | 10.77 | .30 |
| 0.02 | 0.70 | 3.05 | 6.65 | 10.81 | .29 |
| 0.02 | 0.71 | 3.08 | 6.69 | 10.85 | .28 |
| 0.01 | 0.73 | 3.11 | 6.73 | 10.89 | .27 |
| 0.01 | 0.74 | 3.14 | 6.77 | 10.94 | .26 |
| 0.01 | 0.76 | 3.17 | 6.81 | 10.98 | .25 |
| 0.01 | 0.78 | 3.21 | 6.85 | 11.02 | .24 |
| 0.00 | 0.79 | 3.24 | 6.89 | 11.07 | .23 |
| 0.00 | 0.81 | 3.27 | 6.93 | 11.11 | .22 |
| 0.00 | 0.82 | 3.30 | 6.97 | 11.15 | .21 |
| 0.00 | 0.84 | 3.33 | 7.01 | 11.19 | .20 |
| 0.00 | 0.86 | 3.36 | 7.05 | 11.23 | .19 |
| 0.00 | 0.88 | 3.39 | 7.09 | 11.27 | .18 |
| 0.00 | 0.89 | 3.43 | 7.13 | 11.31 | .17 |
| 0.00 | 0.91 | 3.46 | 7.17 | 11.36 | .16 |
| 0.00 | 0.92 | 3.49 | 7.21 | 11.40 | .15 |
| 0.00 | 0.94 | 3.53 | 7.26 | 11.44 | .14 |
| 0.00 | 0.96 | 3.56 | 7.30 | 11.49 | .13 |
| 0.00 | 0.97 | 3.60 | 7.34 | 11.53 | .12 |
| 0.00 | 0.99 | 3.63 | 7.38 | 11.57 | .11 |
| 0.00 | 1.01 | 3.66 | 7.42 | 11.61 | .10 |
| 0.00 | 1.03 | 3.69 | 7.46 | 11.65 | .09 |
| 0.00 | 1.05 | 3.73 | 7.50 | 11.69 | .08 |
| 0.00 | 1.07 | 3.76 | 7.54 | 11.73 | .07 |
| 0.01 | 1.09 | 3.80 | 7.59 | 11.78 | .06 |
| 0.01 | 1.11 | 3.83 | 7.63 | 11.82 | .05 |
| 0.01 | 1.13 | 3.86 | 7.67 | 11.86 | .04 |
| 0.01 | 1.15 | 3.90 | 7.71 | 11.91 | .03 |
| 0.02 | 1.17 | 3.93 | 7.76 | 11.95 | .02 |
| 0.02 | 1.19 | 3.97 | 7.80 | 11.99 | .01 |
| 0.02 | 1.21 | 4.00 | 7.84 | 12.03 | .00 |
| 15 | 14 | 13 | 12 | 11 | Days. |

# TABLE XXV.

(*Continued.*)

Period, 14.317313 days

| Days. | 5 | 6 | 7 | Days. |
|---|---|---|---|---|
| Days. | ″ | ″ | ″ | Days. |
| .00 | 12.03 | 15.73 | 18.29 | 1.00 |
| .01 | 12.07 | 15.76 | 18.31 | .99 |
| .02 | 12.11 | 15.79 | 18.33 | .98 |
| .03 | 12.15 | 15.83 | 18.34 | .97 |
| .04 | 12.19 | 15.86 | 18.36 | .96 |
| .05 | 12.24 | 15.89 | 18.38 | .95 |
| .06 | 12.28 | 15.92 | 18.39 | .94 |
| .07 | 12.32 | 15.96 | 18.41 | .93 |
| .08 | 12.36 | 15.99 | 18.42 | .92 |
| .09 | 12.40 | 16.02 | 18.44 | .91 |
| .10 | 12.44 | 16.05 | 18.46 | .90 |
| .11 | 12.48 | 16.08 | 18.48 | .89 |
| .12 | 12.52 | 16.11 | 18.49 | .88 |
| .13 | 12.56 | 16.14 | 18.51 | .87 |
| .14 | 12.60 | 16.17 | 18.52 | .86 |
| .15 | 12.64 | 16.21 | 18.54 | .85 |
| .16 | 12.68 | 16.24 | 18.55 | .84 |
| .17 | 12.72 | 16.27 | 18.56 | .83 |
| .18 | 12.76 | 16.30 | 18.58 | .82 |
| .19 | 12.80 | 16.33 | 18.59 | .81 |
| .20 | 12.84 | 16.36 | 18.61 | .80 |
| .21 | 12.88 | 16.39 | 18.62 | .79 |
| .22 | 12.92 | 16.42 | 18.64 | .78 |
| .23 | 12.96 | 16.45 | 18.65 | .77 |
| .24 | 13.00 | 16.48 | 18.67 | .76 |
| .25 | 13.04 | 16.51 | 18.68 | .75 |
| .26 | 13.07 | 16.53 | 18.69 | .74 |
| .27 | 13.11 | 16.56 | 18.71 | .73 |
| .28 | 13.15 | 16.59 | 18.72 | .72 |
| .29 | 13.19 | 16.62 | 18.74 | .71 |
| .30 | 13.23 | 16.65 | 18.75 | .70 |
| .31 | 13.27 | 16.68 | 18.76 | .69 |
| .32 | 13.31 | 16.71 | 18.77 | .68 |
| .33 | 13.35 | 16.74 | 18.79 | .67 |
| .34 | 13.38 | 16.76 | 18.80 | .66 |
| .35 | 13.42 | 16.79 | 18.81 | .65 |
| .36 | 13.46 | 16.82 | 18.82 | .64 |
| .37 | 13.49 | 16.84 | 18.84 | .63 |
| .38 | 13.53 | 16.87 | 18.85 | .62 |
| .39 | 13.57 | 16.90 | 18.86 | .61 |
| .40 | 13.61 | 16.93 | 18.87 | .60 |
| .41 | 13.65 | 16.96 | 18.88 | .59 |
| .42 | 13.69 | 16.98 | 18.89 | .58 |
| .43 | 13.72 | 17.01 | 18.90 | .57 |
| .44 | 13.76 | 17.03 | 18.91 | .56 |
| .45 | 13.80 | 17.06 | 18.92 | .55 |
| .46 | 13.83 | 17.09 | 18.93 | .54 |
| .47 | 13.87 | 17.11 | 18.94 | .53 |
| .48 | 13.90 | 17.14 | 18.95 | .52 |
| .49 | 13.94 | 17.16 | 18.96 | .51 |
| .50 | 13.98 | 17.19 | 18.97 | .50 |
| Days. | 10 | 9 | 8 | Days. |

# TABLE XXVI. ARG. 21.

Equation $= 9''.2\ [1 - \sin.\ (2x + z - 2t)]$.

Period, 131.671123 days.

| Days. | 0 | 10 | 20 | 30 | 40 | 50 | 60 | Days. |
|---|---|---|---|---|---|---|---|---|
| Days | ″ | ″ | ″ | ″ | ″ | ″ | ″ | Days |
| 0.0 | 18.22 | 18.04 | 15.89 | 12.25 | 7.92 | 3.88 | 1.02 | 10.0 |
| 0.1 | 18.23 | 18.03 | 15.86 | 12.21 | 7.88 | 3.85 | 1.00 | 9.9 |
| 0.2 | 18.24 | 18.02 | 15.83 | 12.17 | 7.83 | 3.81 | 0.98 | 9.8 |
| 0.3 | 18.25 | 18.00 | 15.80 | 12.12 | 7.79 | 3.78 | 0.96 | 9.7 |
| 0.4 | 18.25 | 17.99 | 15.77 | 12.08 | 7.74 | 3.74 | 0.94 | 9.6 |
| 0.5 | 18.26 | 17.98 | 15.74 | 12.04 | 7.70 | 3.71 | 0.92 | 9.5 |
| 0.6 | 18.27 | 17.96 | 15.71 | 12.00 | 7.66 | 3.67 | 0.91 | 9.4 |
| 0.7 | 18.28 | 17.95 | 15.68 | 11.96 | 7.61 | 3.64 | 0.89 | 9.3 |
| 0.8 | 18.28 | 17.94 | 15.65 | 11.91 | 7.57 | 3.60 | 0.87 | 9.2 |
| 0.9 | 18.29 | 17.92 | 15.62 | 11.87 | 7.52 | 3.57 | 0.85 | 9.1 |
| 1.0 | 18.30 | 17.91 | 15.59 | 11.83 | 7.48 | 3.53 | 0.83 | 9.0 |
| 1.1 | 18.30 | 17.89 | 15.56 | 11.79 | 7.44 | 3.50 | 0.81 | 8.9 |
| 1.2 | 18.31 | 17.88 | 15.53 | 11.75 | 7.39 | 3.46 | 0.79 | 8.8 |
| 1.3 | 18.32 | 17.86 | 15.50 | 11.70 | 7.35 | 3.43 | 0.78 | 8.7 |
| 1.4 | 18.32 | 17.85 | 15.46 | 11.66 | 7.31 | 3.39 | 0.76 | 8.6 |
| 1.5 | 18.33 | 17.83 | 15.43 | 11.62 | 7.26 | 3.36 | 0.74 | 8.5 |
| 1.6 | 18.33 | 17.82 | 15.40 | 11.58 | 7.22 | 3.33 | 0.73 | 8.4 |
| 1.7 | 18.34 | 17.80 | 15.37 | 11.54 | 7.18 | 3.29 | 0.71 | 8.3 |
| 1.8 | 18.35 | 17.78 | 15.33 | 11.49 | 7.13 | 3.26 | 0.69 | 8.2 |
| 1.9 | 18.36 | 17.76 | 15.30 | 11.45 | 7.09 | 3.22 | 0.68 | 8.1 |
| 2.0 | 18.36 | 17.77 | 15.27 | 11.41 | 7.05 | 3.19 | 0.66 | 8.0 |
| 2.1 | 18.36 | 17.75 | 15.24 | 11.37 | 7.01 | 3.16 | 0.65 | 7.9 |
| 2.2 | 18.36 | 17.74 | 15.20 | 11.32 | 6.97 | 3.12 | 0.63 | 7.8 |
| 2.3 | 18.37 | 17.72 | 15.17 | 11.28 | 6.92 | 3.09 | 0.62 | 7.7 |
| 2.4 | 18.37 | 17.70 | 15.13 | 11.24 | 6.88 | 3.06 | 0.60 | 7.6 |
| 2.5 | 18.37 | 17.69 | 15.10 | 11.19 | 6.84 | 3.02 | 0.59 | 7.5 |
| 2.6 | 18.38 | 17.67 | 15.07 | 11.15 | 6.80 | 2.99 | 0.57 | 7.4 |
| 2.7 | 18.38 | 17.65 | 15.03 | 11.11 | 6.75 | 2.96 | 0.56 | 7.3 |
| 2.8 | 18.38 | 17.64 | 15.00 | 11.06 | 6.71 | 2.92 | 0.54 | 7.2 |
| 2.9 | 18.39 | 17.62 | 14.96 | 11.02 | 6.67 | 2.89 | 0.53 | 7.1 |
| 3.0 | 18.39 | 17.60 | 14.93 | 10.98 | 6.63 | 2.86 | 0.51 | 7.0 |
| 3.1 | 18.39 | 17.58 | 14.89 | 10.94 | 6.59 | 2.83 | 0.50 | 6.9 |
| 3.2 | 18.39 | 17.56 | 14.86 | 10.89 | 6.55 | 2.80 | 0.48 | 6.8 |
| 3.3 | 18.39 | 17.54 | 14.82 | 10.85 | 6.50 | 2.76 | 0.47 | 6.7 |
| 3.4 | 18.40 | 17.53 | 14.79 | 10.81 | 6.46 | 2.73 | 0.46 | 6.6 |
| 3.5 | 18.40 | 17.51 | 14.75 | 10.76 | 6.42 | 2.70 | 0.44 | 6.5 |
| 3.6 | 18.40 | 17.49 | 14.72 | 10.72 | 6.38 | 2.67 | 0.43 | 6.4 |
| 3.7 | 18.40 | 17.47 | 14.68 | 10.67 | 6.33 | 2.64 | 0.42 | 6.3 |
| 3.8 | 18.40 | 17.45 | 14.65 | 10.63 | 6.29 | 2.61 | 0.40 | 6.2 |
| 3.9 | 18.40 | 17.43 | 14.61 | 10.58 | 6.25 | 2.58 | 0.39 | 6.1 |
| 4.0 | 18.40 | 17.41 | 14.58 | 10.54 | 6.21 | 2.55 | 0.38 | 6.0 |
| 4.1 | 18.40 | 17.39 | 14.54 | 10.49 | 6.17 | 2.52 | 0.37 | 5.9 |
| 4.2 | 18.40 | 17.37 | 14.51 | 10.45 | 6.13 | 2.49 | 0.36 | 5.8 |
| 4.3 | 18.40 | 17.35 | 14.47 | 10.41 | 6.09 | 2.46 | 0.34 | 5.7 |
| 4.4 | 18.40 | 17.33 | 14.44 | 10.36 | 6.04 | 2.43 | 0.33 | 5.6 |
| 4.5 | 18.40 | 17.31 | 14.40 | 10.32 | 6.00 | 2.40 | 0.32 | 5.5 |
| 4.6 | 18.40 | 17.29 | 14.37 | 10.28 | 5.96 | 2.37 | 0.31 | 5.4 |
| 4.7 | 18.40 | 17.26 | 14.33 | 10.23 | 5.92 | 2.35 | 0.30 | 5.3 |
| 4.8 | 18.39 | 17.24 | 14.30 | 10.19 | 5.88 | 2.32 | 0.29 | 5.2 |
| 4.9 | 18.39 | 17.22 | 14.26 | 10.15 | 5.84 | 2.29 | 0.28 | 5.1 |
| 5.0 | 18.39 | 17.20 | 14.22 | 10.11 | 5.80 | 2.26 | 0.27 | 5.0 |
| Days. | 130 | 120 | 110 | 100 | 90 | 80 | 70 | Days. |

## TABLE XXV.

(*Continued.*)

Period, 14.317313 days

| Days. | 5 | 6 | 7 | Days. |
|---|---|---|---|---|
| Days. | ″ | ″ | ″ | Days. |
| .50 | 13.98 | 17.19 | 18.97 | .50 |
| .51 | 14.02 | 17.22 | 18.98 | .49 |
| .52 | 14.06 | 17.24 | 18.99 | .48 |
| .53 | 14.09 | 17.27 | 19.00 | .47 |
| .54 | 14.13 | 17.29 | 19.00 | .46 |
| .55 | 14.17 | 17.32 | 19.01 | .45 |
| .56 | 14.20 | 17.34 | 19.02 | .44 |
| .57 | 14.24 | 17.36 | 19.03 | .43 |
| .58 | 14.27 | 17.39 | 19.03 | .42 |
| .59 | 14.31 | 17.41 | 19.04 | .41 |
| .60 | 14.35 | 17.44 | 19.05 | .40 |
| .61 | 14.39 | 17.46 | 19.06 | .39 |
| .62 | 14.42 | 17.49 | 19.06 | .38 |
| .63 | 14.46 | 17.51 | 19.07 | .37 |
| .64 | 14.49 | 17.54 | 19.07 | .36 |
| .65 | 14.53 | 17.56 | 19.08 | .35 |
| .66 | 14.57 | 17.58 | 19.09 | .34 |
| .67 | 14.60 | 17.61 | 19.09 | .33 |
| .68 | 14.64 | 17.63 | 19.10 | .32 |
| .69 | 14.67 | 17.66 | 19.10 | .31 |
| .70 | 14.71 | 17.68 | 19.11 | .30 |
| .71 | 14.75 | 17.70 | 19.12 | .29 |
| .72 | 14.78 | 17.72 | 19.12 | .28 |
| .73 | 14.82 | 17.75 | 19.13 | .27 |
| .74 | 14.85 | 17.77 | 19.13 | .26 |
| .75 | 14.89 | 17.79 | 19.14 | .25 |
| .76 | 14.92 | 17.81 | 19.14 | .24 |
| .77 | 14.95 | 17.84 | 19.15 | .23 |
| .78 | 14.99 | 17.86 | 19.15 | .22 |
| .79 | 15.02 | 17.88 | 19.16 | .21 |
| .80 | 15.06 | 17.90 | 19.16 | .20 |
| .81 | 15.09 | 17.92 | 19.16 | .19 |
| .82 | 15.13 | 17.94 | 19.17 | .18 |
| .83 | 15.16 | 17.96 | 19.17 | .17 |
| .84 | 15.20 | 17.98 | 19.17 | .16 |
| .85 | 15.23 | 18.00 | 19.18 | .15 |
| .86 | 15.26 | 18.02 | 19.18 | .14 |
| .87 | 15.30 | 18.04 | 19.18 | .13 |
| .88 | 15.33 | 18.06 | 19.19 | .12 |
| .89 | 15.37 | 18.08 | 19.19 | .11 |
| .90 | 15.40 | 18.10 | 19.19 | .10 |
| .91 | 15.43 | 18.12 | 19.19 | .09 |
| .92 | 15.46 | 18.14 | 19.19 | .08 |
| .93 | 15.50 | 18.16 | 19.19 | .07 |
| .94 | 15.53 | 18.18 | 19.20 | .06 |
| .95 | 15.57 | 18.20 | 19.20 | .05 |
| .96 | 15.60 | 18.21 | 19.20 | .04 |
| .97 | 15.63 | 18.23 | 19.20 | .03 |
| .98 | 15.67 | 18.25 | 19.20 | .02 |
| .99 | 15.70 | 18.27 | 19.20 | .01 |
| 1.00 | 15.73 | 18.29 | 19.20 | .00 |
| Days. | 10 | 9 | 8 | Days. |

## TABLE XXVI. ARG. 21.

Equation $= 9''.2\ [1 - \sin.\ (2x + z - 2t)]$.

Period, 131.671123 days.

| Days. | 0 | 10 | 20 | 30 | 40 | 50 | 60 | Days. |
|---|---|---|---|---|---|---|---|---|
| Days. | ″ | ″ | ″ | ″ | ″ | ″ | ″ | Days |
| 5.0 | 18.39 | 17.20 | 14.22 | 10.11 | 5.80 | 2.26 | 0.27 | 5.0 |
| 5.1 | 18.39 | 17.18 | 14.18 | 10.06 | 5.76 | 2.23 | 0.26 | 4.9 |
| 5.2 | 18.39 | 17.15 | 14.15 | 10.02 | 5.72 | 2.20 | 0.25 | 4.8 |
| 5.3 | 18.38 | 17.13 | 14.11 | 9.97 | 5.68 | 2.18 | 0.24 | 4.7 |
| 5.4 | 18.38 | 17.11 | 14.07 | 9.93 | 5.64 | 2.15 | 0.23 | 4.6 |
| 5.5 | 18.38 | 17.08 | 14.04 | 9.88 | 5.60 | 2.12 | 0.22 | 4.5 |
| 5.6 | 18.37 | 17.06 | 14.00 | 9.84 | 5.56 | 2.09 | 0.21 | 4.4 |
| 5.7 | 18.37 | 17.04 | 13.96 | 9.79 | 5.52 | 2.07 | 0.20 | 4.3 |
| 5.8 | 18.37 | 17.01 | 13.93 | 9.75 | 5.48 | 2.04 | 0.19 | 4.2 |
| 5.9 | 18.36 | 16.99 | 13.89 | 9.71 | 5.44 | 2.01 | 0.18 | 4.1 |
| 6.0 | 18.36 | 16.97 | 13.85 | 9.67 | 5.40 | 1.98 | 0.17 | 4.0 |
| 6.1 | 18.36 | 16.95 | 13.81 | 9.62 | 5.36 | 1.95 | 0.16 | 3.9 |
| 6.2 | 18.35 | 16.92 | 13.77 | 9.58 | 5.32 | 1.93 | 0.15 | 3.8 |
| 6.3 | 18.35 | 16.90 | 13.74 | 9.53 | 5.28 | 1.90 | 0.14 | 3.7 |
| 6.4 | 18.35 | 16.87 | 13.70 | 9.49 | 5.24 | 1.87 | 0.14 | 3.6 |
| 6.5 | 18.34 | 16.85 | 13.66 | 9.44 | 5.20 | 1.85 | 0.13 | 3.5 |
| 6.6 | 18.34 | 16.82 | 13.62 | 9.40 | 5.17 | 1.82 | 0.12 | 3.4 |
| 6.7 | 18.33 | 16.80 | 13.58 | 9.36 | 5.13 | 1.79 | 0.11 | 3.3 |
| 6.8 | 18.33 | 16.77 | 13.54 | 9.32 | 5.09 | 1.77 | 0.11 | 3.2 |
| 6.9 | 18.32 | 16.75 | 13.50 | 9.27 | 5.05 | 1.74 | 0.10 | 3.1 |
| 7.0 | 18.32 | 16.72 | 13.46 | 9.23 | 5.01 | 1.71 | 0.09 | 3.0 |
| 7.1 | 18.31 | 16.70 | 13.42 | 9.19 | 4.97 | 1.69 | 0.09 | 2.9 |
| 7.2 | 18.30 | 16.67 | 13.38 | 9.14 | 4.93 | 1.66 | 0.08 | 2.8 |
| 7.3 | 18.30 | 16.65 | 13.34 | 9.10 | 4.89 | 1.64 | 0.08 | 2.7 |
| 7.4 | 18.29 | 16.62 | 13.30 | 9.06 | 4.85 | 1.61 | 0.07 | 2.6 |
| 7.5 | 18.28 | 16.60 | 13.26 | 9.01 | 4.82 | 1.59 | 0.07 | 2.5 |
| 7.6 | 18.28 | 16.57 | 13.22 | 8.97 | 4.78 | 1.56 | 0.06 | 2.4 |
| 7.7 | 18.27 | 16.54 | 13.18 | 8.93 | 4.74 | 1.54 | 0.06 | 2.3 |
| 7.8 | 18.26 | 16.52 | 13.14 | 8.88 | 4.70 | 1.51 | 0.05 | 2.2 |
| 7.9 | 18.26 | 16.49 | 13.10 | 8.84 | 4.66 | 1.49 | 0.05 | 2.1 |
| 8.0 | 18.25 | 16.46 | 13.06 | 8.80 | 4.62 | 1.46 | 0.04 | 2.0 |
| 8.1 | 18.24 | 16.43 | 13.02 | 8.76 | 4.58 | 1.44 | 0.04 | 1.9 |
| 8.2 | 18.23 | 16.41 | 12.98 | 8.71 | 4.54 | 1.41 | 0.03 | 1.8 |
| 8.3 | 18.22 | 16.38 | 12.94 | 8.67 | 4.51 | 1.39 | 0.03 | 1.7 |
| 8.4 | 18.21 | 16.35 | 12.90 | 8.62 | 4.47 | 1.37 | 0.03 | 1.6 |
| 8.5 | 18.20 | 16.32 | 12.86 | 8.58 | 4.43 | 1.34 | 0.02 | 1.5 |
| 8.6 | 18.19 | 16.30 | 12.82 | 8.54 | 4.39 | 1.32 | 0.02 | 1.4 |
| 8.7 | 18.18 | 16.27 | 12.78 | 8.49 | 4.35 | 1.30 | 0.02 | 1.3 |
| 8.8 | 18.17 | 16.24 | 12.74 | 8.45 | 4.32 | 1.27 | 0.02 | 1.2 |
| 8.9 | 18.16 | 16.21 | 12.70 | 8.40 | 4.28 | 1.25 | 0.01 | 1.1 |
| 9.0 | 18.15 | 16.18 | 12.66 | 8.36 | 4.24 | 1.23 | 0.01 | 1.0 |
| 9.1 | 18.14 | 16.15 | 12.62 | 8.31 | 4.20 | 1.21 | 0.01 | 0.9 |
| 9.2 | 18.13 | 16.12 | 12.58 | 8.27 | 4.17 | 1.19 | 0.01 | 0.8 |
| 9.3 | 18.12 | 16.10 | 12.54 | 8.23 | 4.13 | 1.16 | 0.01 | 0.7 |
| 9.4 | 18.11 | 16.07 | 12.50 | 8.18 | 4.09 | 1.14 | 0.00 | 0.6 |
| 9.5 | 18.10 | 16.04 | 12.46 | 8.14 | 4.06 | 1.12 | 0.00 | 0.5 |
| 9.6 | 18.09 | 16.01 | 12.41 | 8.10 | 4.02 | 1.10 | 0.00 | 0.4 |
| 9.7 | 18.07 | 15.98 | 12.37 | 8.05 | 3.99 | 1.08 | 0.00 | 0.3 |
| 9.8 | 18.06 | 15.95 | 12.33 | 8.01 | 3.95 | 1.06 | 0.00 | 0.2 |
| 9.9 | 18.05 | 15.92 | 12.29 | 7.96 | 3.92 | 1.04 | 0.00 | 0.1 |
| 10.0 | 18.04 | 15.89 | 12.25 | 7.92 | 3.88 | 1.02 | 0.00 | 0.0 |
| Days. | 130 | 120 | 110 | 100 | 90 | 80 | 70 | Days. |

# TABLE XXVII. ARGUMENT 22.

Equation $= 8''.1 - 0''.4 \sin. (t - z) + 7''.8 \sin. 2 (t - z)$.

Period, 32.128086 days.

| Days. | 0 | 1 | 2 | 3 | 4 | 5 | 6 | 7 | 8 | 9 |
|---|---|---|---|---|---|---|---|---|---|---|
| Days. | ″ | ″ | ″ | ″ | ″ | ″ | ″ | ″ | ″ | ″ |
| .00 | 0.02 | 0.78 | 2.59 | 5.23 | 8.30 | 11.33 | 13.89 | 15.59 | 16.18 | 15.59 |
| .01 | 0.02 | 0.79 | 2.62 | 5.26 | 8.33 | 11.36 | 13.92 | 15.60 | 16.18 | 15.58 |
| .02 | 0.03 | 0.80 | 2.64 | 5.29 | 8.36 | 11.39 | 13.94 | 15.62 | 16.18 | 15.56 |
| .03 | 0.03 | 0.82 | 2.66 | 5.32 | 8.39 | 11.42 | 13.96 | 15.63 | 16.18 | 15.55 |
| .04 | 0.03 | 0.83 | 2.68 | 5.35 | 8.42 | 11.45 | 13.98 | 15.64 | 16.18 | 15.54 |
| .05 | 0.03 | 0.84 | 2.70 | 5.38 | 8.45 | 11.48 | 14.00 | 15.65 | 16.18 | 15.53 |
| .06 | 0.03 | 0.86 | 2.73 | 5.41 | 8.48 | 11.51 | 14.02 | 15.66 | 16.18 | 15.52 |
| .07 | 0.04 | 0.87 | 2.75 | 5.44 | 8.51 | 11.53 | 14.04 | 15.67 | 16.18 | 15.51 |
| .08 | 0.04 | 0.89 | 2.78 | 5.47 | 8.54 | 11.56 | 14.06 | 15.69 | 16.18 | 15.49 |
| .09 | 0.04 | 0.90 | 2.80 | 5.50 | 8.58 | 11.59 | 14.08 | 15.70 | 16.18 | 15.48 |
| .10 | 0.05 | 0.91 | 2.82 | 5.53 | 8.61 | 11.62 | 14.11 | 15.71 | 16.18 | 15.47 |
| .11 | 0.05 | 0.93 | 2.85 | 5.56 | 8.64 | 11.65 | 14.13 | 15.72 | 16.17 | 15.45 |
| .12 | 0.05 | 0.94 | 2.87 | 5.59 | 8.67 | 11.67 | 14.15 | 15.73 | 16.17 | 15.44 |
| .13 | 0.06 | 0.96 | 2.90 | 5.62 | 8.70 | 11.70 | 14.17 | 15.74 | 16.17 | 15.43 |
| .14 | 0.06 | 0.97 | 2.92 | 5.65 | 8.73 | 11.73 | 14.19 | 15.75 | 16.17 | 15.41 |
| .15 | 0.06 | 0.99 | 2.95 | 5.68 | 8.76 | 11.76 | 14.21 | 15.76 | 16.17 | 15.40 |
| .16 | 0.07 | 1.00 | 2.97 | 5.71 | 8.79 | 11.79 | 14.23 | 15.77 | 16.17 | 15.39 |
| .17 | 0.07 | 1.02 | 3.00 | 5.74 | 8.82 | 11.81 | 14.25 | 15.78 | 16.17 | 15.37 |
| .18 | 0.08 | 1.03 | 3.02 | 5.77 | 8.85 | 11.84 | 14.27 | 15.79 | 16.16 | 15.36 |
| .19 | 0.08 | 1.05 | 3.05 | 5.80 | 8.89 | 11.87 | 14.29 | 15.80 | 16.16 | 15.35 |
| .20 | 0.08 | 1.06 | 3.07 | 5.83 | 8.92 | 11.90 | 14.31 | 15.81 | 16.16 | 15.33 |
| .21 | 0.09 | 1.08 | 3.10 | 5.86 | 8.95 | 11.93 | 14.33 | 15.81 | 16.16 | 15.32 |
| .22 | 0.09 | 1.09 | 3.12 | 5.89 | 8.98 | 11.95 | 14.35 | 15.82 | 16.15 | 15.31 |
| .23 | 0.10 | 1.11 | 3.15 | 5.92 | 9.01 | 11.98 | 14.37 | 15.83 | 16.15 | 15.29 |
| .24 | 0.10 | 1.12 | 3.17 | 5.95 | 9.04 | 12.01 | 14.39 | 15.84 | 16.15 | 15.28 |
| .25 | 0.11 | 1.14 | 3.20 | 5.98 | 9.07 | 12.04 | 14.41 | 15.85 | 16.15 | 15.26 |
| .26 | 0.11 | 1.15 | 3.22 | 6.01 | 9.10 | 12.07 | 14.43 | 15.86 | 16.15 | 15.25 |
| .27 | 0.12 | 1.17 | 3.25 | 6.04 | 9.13 | 12.09 | 14.45 | 15.87 | 16.14 | 15.23 |
| .28 | 0.12 | 1.18 | 3.27 | 6.07 | 9.16 | 12.12 | 14.47 | 15.87 | 16.14 | 15.22 |
| .29 | 0.13 | 1.20 | 3.30 | 6.10 | 9.20 | 12.15 | 14.48 | 15.88 | 16.14 | 15.20 |
| .30 | 0.13 | 1.22 | 3.32 | 6.13 | 9.23 | 12.17 | 14.50 | 15.89 | 16.13 | 15.19 |
| .31 | 0.14 | 1.23 | 3.35 | 6.16 | 9.26 | 12.20 | 14.52 | 15.90 | 16.13 | 15.17 |
| .32 | 0.14 | 1.25 | 3.37 | 6.19 | 9.29 | 12.23 | 14.54 | 15.90 | 16.13 | 15.16 |
| .33 | 0.15 | 1.26 | 3.40 | 6.22 | 9.32 | 12.25 | 14.56 | 15.91 | 16.12 | 15.14 |
| .34 | 0.15 | 1.28 | 3.42 | 6.25 | 9.35 | 12.28 | 14.58 | 15.92 | 16.12 | 15.13 |
| .35 | 0.16 | 1.30 | 3.45 | 6.28 | 9.38 | 12.31 | 14.60 | 15.93 | 16.11 | 15.11 |
| .36 | 0.16 | 1.31 | 3.47 | 6.31 | 9.41 | 12.33 | 14.62 | 15.94 | 16.11 | 15.10 |
| .37 | 0.17 | 1.33 | 3.50 | 6.34 | 9.44 | 12.36 | 14.64 | 15.94 | 16.10 | 15.08 |
| .38 | 0.17 | 1.35 | 3.52 | 6.37 | 9.47 | 12.38 | 14.66 | 15.95 | 16.10 | 15.07 |
| .39 | 0.18 | 1.36 | 3.55 | 6.41 | 9.51 | 12.41 | 14.68 | 15.96 | 16.09 | 15.05 |
| .40 | 0.19 | 1.38 | 3.58 | 6.44 | 9.54 | 12.44 | 14.69 | 15.96 | 16.09 | 15.03 |
| .41 | 0.20 | 1.40 | 3.60 | 6.47 | 9.57 | 12.46 | 14.71 | 15.97 | 16.08 | 15.02 |
| .42 | 0.20 | 1.41 | 3.63 | 6.50 | 9.60 | 12.49 | 14.73 | 15.98 | 16.08 | 15.00 |
| .43 | 0.21 | 1.43 | 3.65 | 6.53 | 9.63 | 12.51 | 14.75 | 15.98 | 16.07 | 14.99 |
| .44 | 0.21 | 1.45 | 3.68 | 6.56 | 9.66 | 12.54 | 14.77 | 15.99 | 16.07 | 14.97 |
| .45 | 0.22 | 1.47 | 3.71 | 6.59 | 9.69 | 12.57 | 14.79 | 16.00 | 16.06 | 14.95 |
| .46 | 0.22 | 1.49 | 3.73 | 6.62 | 9.72 | 12.59 | 14.81 | 16.00 | 16.06 | 14.94 |
| .47 | 0.23 | 1.51 | 3.76 | 6.65 | 9.75 | 12.62 | 14.82 | 16.01 | 16.05 | 14.92 |
| .48 | 0.24 | 1.53 | 3.78 | 6.68 | 9.78 | 12.64 | 14.84 | 16.01 | 16.05 | 14.90 |
| .49 | 0.24 | 1.54 | 3.81 | 6.72 | 9.82 | 12.67 | 14.86 | 16.02 | 16.04 | 14.89 |
| .50 | 0.25 | 1.56 | 3.84 | 6.75 | 9.85 | 12.70 | 14.87 | 16.03 | 16.03 | 14.87 |

# TABLE XXVII. ARGUMENT 22.

Equation $= 8''.1 - 0''.4 \sin. (t - z) + 7''.8 \sin. 2 (t - z)$.

Period, 32.128086 days.

| Days. | 0 | 1 | 2 | 3 | 4 | 5 | 6 | 7 | 8 | 9 |
|---|---|---|---|---|---|---|---|---|---|---|
| Days. | " | " | " | " | " | " | " | " | " | " |
| .50 | 0.25 | 1.56 | 3.84 | 6.75 | 9.85 | 12.70 | 14.87 | 16.03 | 16.03 | 14.87 |
| .51 | 0.26 | 1.58 | 3.86 | 6.78 | 9.88 | 12.72 | 14.89 | 16.03 | 16.03 | 14.85 |
| .52 | 0.26 | 1.60 | 3.89 | 6.81 | 9.91 | 12.75 | 14.91 | 16.04 | 16.02 | 14.84 |
| .53 | 0.27 | 1.62 | 3.91 | 6.84 | 9.94 | 12.77 | 14.92 | 16.04 | 16.02 | 14.82 |
| .54 | 0.28 | 1.64 | 3.94 | 6.87 | 9.97 | 12.80 | 14.94 | 16.05 | 16.01 | 14.80 |
| .55 | 0.29 | 1.66 | 3.97 | 6.90 | 10.00 | 12.82 | 14.96 | 16.05 | 16.00 | 14.78 |
| .56 | 0.30 | 1.68 | 3.99 | 6.93 | 10.03 | 12.85 | 14.97 | 16.06 | 16.00 | 14.76 |
| .57 | 0.31 | 1.70 | 4.02 | 6.96 | 10.06 | 12.87 | 14.99 | 16.06 | 15.99 | 14.75 |
| .58 | 0.32 | 1.71 | 4.05 | 6.99 | 10.09 | 12.90 | 15.00 | 16.07 | 15.98 | 14.73 |
| .59 | 0.32 | 1.73 | 4.07 | 7.03 | 10.12 | 12.92 | 15.02 | 16.07 | 15.98 | 14.71 |
| .60 | 0.33 | 1.75 | 4.10 | 7.06 | 10.15 | 12.95 | 15.04 | 16.08 | 15.97 | 14.69 |
| .61 | 0.34 | 1.77 | 4.13 | 7.09 | 10.18 | 12.97 | 15.05 | 16.08 | 15.96 | 14.67 |
| .62 | 0.35 | 1.79 | 4.15 | 7.12 | 10.21 | 13.00 | 15.07 | 16.09 | 15.96 | 14.66 |
| .63 | 0.36 | 1.81 | 4.18 | 7.15 | 10.24 | 13.02 | 15.08 | 16.09 | 15.95 | 14.64 |
| .64 | 0.37 | 1.83 | 4.21 | 7.18 | 10.27 | 13.05 | 15.10 | 16.10 | 15.94 | 14.62 |
| .65 | 0.38 | 1.85 | 4.24 | 7.21 | 10.30 | 13.07 | 15.11 | 16.10 | 15.93 | 14.60 |
| .66 | 0.39 | 1.87 | 4.26 | 7.24 | 10.33 | 13.10 | 15.13 | 16.11 | 15.92 | 14.58 |
| .67 | 0.40 | 1.89 | 4.29 | 7.27 | 10.36 | 13.12 | 15.14 | 16.11 | 15.91 | 14.56 |
| .68 | 0.41 | 1.91 | 4.32 | 7.30 | 10.39 | 13.15 | 15.16 | 16.12 | 15.91 | 14.54 |
| .69 | 0.42 | 1.93 | 4.35 | 7.34 | 10.42 | 13.17 | 15.17 | 16.12 | 15.90 | 14.53 |
| .70 | 0.43 | 1.95 | 4.38 | 7.37 | 10.45 | 13.20 | 15.19 | 16.12 | 15.89 | 14.51 |
| .71 | 0.44 | 1.97 | 4.40 | 7.40 | 10.48 | 13.22 | 15.20 | 16.13 | 15.88 | 14.49 |
| .72 | 0.45 | 1.99 | 4.43 | 7.43 | 10.51 | 13.25 | 15.22 | 16.13 | 15.88 | 14.47 |
| .73 | 0.46 | 2.01 | 4.46 | 7.46 | 10.54 | 13.27 | 15.23 | 16.13 | 15.87 | 14.45 |
| .74 | 0.47 | 2.03 | 4.49 | 7.49 | 10.57 | 13.30 | 15.25 | 16.14 | 15.86 | 14.43 |
| .75 | 0.48 | 2.05 | 4.52 | 7.52 | 10.60 | 13.32 | 15.26 | 16.14 | 15.85 | 14.41 |
| .76 | 0.49 | 2.07 | 4.54 | 7.55 | 10.63 | 13.35 | 15.28 | 16.14 | 15.84 | 14.39 |
| .77 | 0.50 | 2.09 | 4.57 | 7.58 | 10.66 | 13.37 | 15.29 | 16.15 | 15.83 | 14.37 |
| .78 | 0.51 | 2.12 | 4.60 | 7.61 | 10.69 | 13.40 | 15.31 | 16.15 | 15.82 | 14.36 |
| .79 | 0.53 | 2.14 | 4.63 | 7.65 | 10.72 | 13.42 | 15.32 | 16.15 | 15.81 | 14.34 |
| .80 | 0.54 | 2.16 | 4.66 | 7.68 | 10.75 | 13.44 | 15.33 | 16.16 | 15.80 | 14.32 |
| .81 | 0.55 | 2.18 | 4.68 | 7.71 | 10.78 | 13.47 | 15.34 | 16.16 | 15.79 | 14.30 |
| .82 | 0.56 | 2.20 | 4.71 | 7.74 | 10.81 | 13.49 | 15.36 | 16.16 | 15.78 | 14.28 |
| .83 | 0.57 | 2.22 | 4.74 | 7.77 | 10.84 | 13.52 | 15.38 | 16.17 | 15.77 | 14.26 |
| .84 | 0.58 | 2.24 | 4.77 | 7.80 | 10.87 | 13.54 | 15.39 | 16.17 | 15.76 | 14.24 |
| .85 | 0.59 | 2.26 | 4.80 | 7.83 | 10.90 | 13.56 | 15.40 | 16.17 | 15.75 | 14.22 |
| .86 | 0.61 | 2.29 | 4.83 | 7.86 | 10.93 | 13.59 | 15.42 | 16.17 | 15.74 | 14.20 |
| .87 | 0.62 | 2.31 | 4.86 | 7.89 | 10.96 | 13.61 | 15.43 | 16.18 | 15.73 | 14.18 |
| .88 | 0.63 | 2.33 | 4.88 | 7.93 | 10.98 | 13.63 | 15.44 | 16.18 | 15.72 | 14.16 |
| .89 | 0.64 | 2.35 | 4.91 | 7.96 | 11.01 | 13.65 | 15.46 | 16.18 | 15.71 | 14.14 |
| .90 | 0.65 | 2.37 | 4.94 | 7.99 | 11.04 | 13.67 | 15.47 | 16.18 | 15.70 | 14.11 |
| .91 | 0.67 | 2.40 | 4.97 | 8.02 | 11.07 | 13.70 | 15.48 | 16.18 | 15.69 | 14.09 |
| .92 | 0.68 | 2.42 | 5.00 | 8.05 | 11.10 | 13.72 | 15.50 | 16.18 | 15.68 | 14.07 |
| .93 | 0.69 | 2.44 | 5.03 | 8.08 | 11.13 | 13.74 | 15.51 | 16.18 | 15.67 | 14.05 |
| .94 | 0.70 | 2.46 | 5.06 | 8.11 | 11.16 | 13.76 | 15.52 | 16.18 | 15.66 | 14.03 |
| .95 | 0.71 | 2.48 | 5.09 | 8.14 | 11.19 | 13.78 | 15.53 | 16.18 | 15.65 | 14.01 |
| .96 | 0.72 | 2.51 | 5.12 | 8.17 | 11.22 | 13.81 | 15.54 | 16.18 | 15.64 | 13.99 |
| .97 | 0.74 | 2.53 | 5.15 | 8.20 | 11.25 | 13.83 | 15.56 | 16.18 | 15.63 | 13.97 |
| .98 | 0.75 | 2.55 | 5.17 | 8.23 | 11.27 | 13.85 | 15.57 | 16.18 | 15.61 | 13.94 |
| .99 | 0.76 | 2.57 | 5.20 | 8.27 | 11.30 | 13.87 | 15.58 | 16.18 | 15.60 | 13.92 |
| 1.00 | 0.78 | 2.59 | 5.23 | 8.30 | 11.33 | 13.89 | 15.59 | 16.18 | 15.59 | 13.90 |

# TABLE XXVII. ARGUMENT 22.

Equation = $8''.1 - 0''.4 \sin. (t - z) + 7''.8 \sin. 2 (t - z)$.

Period, 32.128086 days.

| Days. | 10 | 11 | 12 | 13 | 14 | 15 | 16 | 17 | 18 | 19 |
|---|---|---|---|---|---|---|---|---|---|---|
| Days. | ″ | ″ | ″ | ″ | ″ | ″ | ″ | ″ | ″ | ″ |
| .00 | 13.90 | 11.38 | 8.40 | 5.42 | 2.90 | 1.20 | 0.58 | 1.13 | 2.76 | 5.21 |
| .01 | 13.88 | 11.36 | 8.37 | 5.39 | 2.88 | 1.19 | 0.58 | 1.14 | 2.78 | 5.23 |
| .02 | 13.85 | 11.33 | 8.34 | 5.36 | 2.86 | 1.18 | 0.58 | 1.15 | 2.80 | 5.26 |
| .03 | 13.83 | 11.30 | 8.31 | 5.34 | 2.84 | 1.16 | 0.58 | 1.17 | 2.82 | 5.29 |
| .04 | 13.81 | 11.27 | 8.27 | 5.31 | 2.81 | 1.15 | 0.58 | 1.18 | 2.84 | 5.31 |
| .05 | 13.79 | 11.24 | 8.24 | 5.28 | 2.79 | 1.14 | 0.58 | 1.19 | 2.86 | 5.34 |
| .06 | 13.77 | 11.21 | 8.21 | 5.26 | 2.77 | 1.13 | 0.58 | 1.20 | 2.89 | 5.37 |
| .07 | 13.75 | 11.18 | 8.18 | 5.23 | 2.75 | 1.12 | 0.59 | 1.21 | 2.91 | 5.39 |
| .08 | 13.72 | 11.15 | 8.15 | 5.20 | 2.73 | 1.10 | 0.59 | 1.23 | 2.93 | 5.43 |
| .09 | 13.70 | 11.13 | 8.12 | 5.18 | 2.71 | 1.09 | 0.59 | 1.24 | 2.95 | 5.45 |
| .10 | 13.68 | 11.10 | 8.09 | 5.15 | 2.69 | 1.08 | 0.59 | 1.25 | 2.97 | 5.48 |
| .11 | 13.66 | 11.07 | 8.06 | 5.12 | 2.67 | 1.07 | 0.59 | 1.26 | 2.99 | 5.51 |
| .12 | 13.63 | 11.04 | 8.03 | 5.10 | 2.65 | 1.06 | 0.59 | 1.27 | 3.01 | 5.54 |
| .13 | 13.61 | 11.01 | 8.00 | 5.07 | 2.63 | 1.05 | 0.59 | 1.29 | 3.04 | 5.56 |
| .14 | 13.59 | 10.98 | 7.97 | 5.04 | 2.61 | 1.04 | 0.59 | 1.30 | 3.06 | 5.59 |
| .15 | 13.57 | 10.94 | 7.94 | 5.02 | 2.58 | 1.03 | 0.59 | 1.31 | 3.08 | 5.62 |
| .16 | 13.55 | 10.91 | 7.91 | 4.99 | 2.56 | 1.02 | 0.60 | 1.33 | 3.10 | 5.65 |
| .17 | 13.52 | 10.89 | 7.88 | 4.96 | 2.54 | 1.01 | 0.60 | 1.34 | 3.12 | 5.68 |
| .18 | 13.50 | 10.86 | 7.85 | 4.94 | 2.52 | 1.00 | 0.60 | 1.36 | 3.15 | 5.70 |
| .19 | 13.48 | 10.84 | 7.82 | 4.91 | 2.50 | 0.99 | 0.60 | 1.37 | 3.17 | 5.73 |
| .20 | 13.45 | 10.81 | 7.79 | 4.88 | 2.48 | 0.98 | 0.60 | 1.38 | 3.19 | 5.76 |
| .21 | 13.43 | 10.78 | 7.76 | 4.86 | 2.46 | 0.97 | 0.60 | 1.39 | 3.21 | 5.79 |
| .22 | 13.41 | 10.75 | 7.73 | 4.83 | 2.44 | 0.96 | 0.60 | 1.41 | 3.23 | 5.82 |
| .23 | 13.38 | 10.72 | 7.70 | 4.80 | 2.42 | 0.95 | 0.61 | 1.42 | 3.26 | 5.85 |
| .24 | 13.36 | 10.69 | 7.67 | 4.78 | 2.40 | 0.94 | 0.61 | 1.43 | 3.28 | 5.87 |
| .25 | 13.33 | 10.66 | 7.64 | 4.75 | 2.38 | 0.93 | 0.61 | 1.45 | 3.30 | 5.90 |
| .26 | 13.31 | 10.63 | 7.61 | 4.71 | 2.37 | 0.93 | 0.62 | 1.46 | 3.33 | 5.93 |
| .27 | 13.28 | 10.60 | 7.58 | 4.69 | 2.35 | 0.92 | 0.62 | 1.48 | 3.35 | 5.96 |
| .28 | 13.26 | 10.57 | 7.55 | 4.66 | 2.33 | 0.91 | 0.62 | 1.49 | 3.37 | 5.99 |
| .29 | 13.23 | 10.55 | 7.52 | 4.64 | 2.31 | 0.90 | 0.63 | 1.51 | 3.40 | 6.02 |
| .30 | 13.21 | 10.52 | 7.49 | 4.61 | 2.29 | 0.89 | 0.63 | 1.52 | 3.42 | 6.05 |
| .31 | 13.18 | 10.49 | 7.46 | 4.58 | 2.27 | 0.88 | 0.63 | 1.53 | 3.44 | 6.08 |
| .32 | 13.16 | 10.46 | 7.43 | 4.56 | 2.25 | 0.87 | 0.64 | 1.55 | 3.47 | 6.11 |
| .33 | 13.13 | 10.43 | 7.40 | 4.53 | 2.24 | 0.86 | 0.64 | 1.57 | 3.49 | 6.14 |
| .34 | 13.11 | 10.40 | 7.37 | 4.50 | 2.22 | 0.86 | 0.65 | 1.58 | 3.51 | 6.17 |
| .35 | 13.08 | 10.37 | 7.34 | 4.48 | 2.20 | 0.85 | 0.65 | 1.60 | 3.54 | 6.19 |
| .36 | 13.06 | 10.34 | 7.31 | 4.45 | 2.18 | 0.84 | 0.65 | 1.61 | 3.56 | 6.22 |
| .37 | 13.03 | 10.31 | 7.28 | 4.43 | 2.17 | 0.83 | 0.66 | 1.63 | 3.59 | 6.25 |
| .38 | 13.01 | 10.28 | 7.25 | 4.40 | 2.15 | 0.83 | 0.66 | 1.64 | 3.61 | 6.28 |
| .39 | 12.98 | 10.25 | 7.22 | 4.38 | 2.13 | 0.82 | 0.67 | 1.66 | 3.64 | 6.31 |
| .40 | 12.96 | 10.22 | 7.19 | 4.35 | 2.11 | 0.81 | 0.67 | 1.67 | 3.66 | 6.34 |
| .41 | 12.93 | 10.19 | 7.16 | 4.33 | 2.09 | 0.80 | 0.67 | 1.69 | 3.68 | 6.37 |
| .42 | 12.91 | 10.16 | 7.13 | 4.30 | 2.07 | 0.79 | 0.68 | 1.70 | 3.71 | 6.40 |
| .43 | 12.88 | 10.13 | 7.10 | 4.28 | 2.06 | 0.79 | 0.68 | 1.72 | 3.73 | 6.43 |
| .44 | 12.86 | 10.10 | 7.07 | 4.25 | 2.04 | 0.78 | 0.69 | 1.73 | 3.75 | 6.46 |
| .45 | 12.83 | 10.07 | 7.04 | 4.23 | 2.02 | 0.78 | 0.69 | 1.75 | 3.78 | 6.48 |
| .46 | 12.81 | 10.04 | 7.01 | 4.21 | 2.00 | 0.77 | 0.69 | 1.76 | 3.80 | 6.51 |
| .47 | 12.78 | 10.01 | 6.98 | 4.18 | 1.98 | 0.76 | 0.70 | 1.78 | 3.82 | 6.54 |
| .48 | 12.76 | 9.98 | 6.95 | 4.16 | 1.97 | 0.76 | 0.70 | 1.79 | 3.85 | 6.57 |
| .49 | 12.73 | 9.95 | 6.92 | 4.12 | 1.95 | 0.75 | 0.71 | 1.81 | 3.87 | 6.60 |
| .50 | 12.71 | 9.92 | 6.89 | 4.09 | 1.93 | 0.75 | 0.71 | 1.82 | 3.90 | 6.63 |

# TABLE XXVII. ARGUMENT 22.

Equation $= 8''.1 - 0''.4 \sin. (t - z) + 7''.8 \sin. 2 (t - z)$.

Period, 32.128086 days.

| Days. | 10 | 11 | 12 | 13 | 14 | 15 | 16 | 17 | 18 | 19 |
|---|---|---|---|---|---|---|---|---|---|---|
| Days. | ″ | ″ | ″ | ″ | ″ | ″ | ″ | ″ | ″ | ″ |
| .50 | 12.71 | 9.92 | 6.89 | 4.09 | 1.93 | 0.75 | 0.71 | 1.82 | 3.90 | 6.63 |
| .51 | 12.68 | 9.89 | 6.86 | 4.06 | 1.91 | 0.74 | 0.72 | 1.84 | 3.92 | 6.66 |
| .52 | 12.66 | 9.86 | 6.83 | 4.04 | 1.89 | 0.74 | 0.72 | 1.85 | 3.95 | 6.69 |
| .53 | 12.63 | 9.83 | 6.80 | 4.01 | 1.88 | 0.73 | 0.73 | 1.87 | 3.97 | 6.72 |
| .54 | 12.61 | 9.80 | 6.77 | 3.99 | 1.86 | 0.73 | 0.74 | 1.88 | 4.00 | 6.75 |
| .55 | 12.58 | 9.77 | 6.74 | 3.96 | 1.84 | 0.72 | 0.74 | 1.90 | 4.02 | 6.77 |
| .56 | 12.56 | 9.74 | 6.71 | 3.94 | 1.83 | 0.72 | 0.75 | 1.92 | 4.05 | 6.80 |
| .57 | 12.53 | 9.71 | 6.68 | 3.91 | 1.81 | 0.71 | 0.75 | 1.93 | 4.07 | 6.83 |
| .58 | 12.51 | 9.68 | 6.65 | 3.89 | 1.79 | 0.71 | 0.76 | 1.95 | 4.10 | 6.86 |
| .59 | 12.48 | 9.65 | 6.62 | 3.86 | 1.78 | 0.70 | 0.77 | 1.96 | 4.12 | 6.89 |
| .60 | 12.45 | 9.62 | 6.59 | 3.84 | 1.76 | 0.70 | 0.77 | 1.98 | 4.15 | 6.92 |
| .61 | 12.43 | 9.59 | 6.56 | 3.81 | 1.74 | 0.69 | 0.78 | 2.00 | 4.17 | 6.95 |
| .62 | 12.40 | 9.56 | 6.53 | 3.79 | 1.73 | 0.69 | 0.79 | 2.02 | 4.20 | 6.98 |
| .63 | 12.38 | 9.53 | 6.50 | 3.76 | 1.71 | 0.68 | 0.79 | 2.03 | 4.22 | 7.01 |
| .64 | 12.35 | 9.50 | 6.47 | 3.74 | 1.70 | 0.68 | 0.80 | 2.05 | 4.25 | 7.04 |
| .65 | 12.32 | 9.47 | 6.44 | 3.71 | 1.68 | 0.67 | 0.81 | 2.07 | 4.28 | 7.06 |
| .66 | 12.30 | 9.44 | 6.41 | 3.69 | 1.67 | 0.67 | 0.81 | 2.09 | 4.30 | 7.09 |
| .67 | 12.27 | 9.41 | 6.38 | 3.66 | 1.65 | 0.66 | 0.82 | 2.11 | 4.33 | 7.12 |
| .68 | 12.25 | 9.38 | 6.35 | 3.64 | 1.64 | 0.66 | 0.83 | 2.12 | 4.35 | 7.15 |
| .69 | 12.22 | 9.35 | 6.32 | 3.61 | 1.62 | 0.65 | 0.83 | 2.14 | 4.38 | 7.18 |
| .70 | 12.19 | 9.32 | 6.29 | 3.59 | 1.61 | 0.65 | 0.84 | 2.16 | 4.41 | 7.21 |
| .71 | 12.17 | 9.29 | 6.26 | 3.56 | 1.59 | 0.64 | 0.85 | 2.18 | 4.43 | 7.24 |
| .72 | 12.14 | 9.26 | 6.23 | 3.54 | 1.58 | 0.64 | 0.86 | 2.20 | 4.46 | 7.27 |
| .73 | 12.12 | 9.23 | 6.20 | 3.51 | 1.56 | 0.63 | 0.86 | 2.22 | 4.48 | 7.30 |
| .74 | 12.09 | 9.20 | 6.17 | 3.49 | 1.55 | 0.63 | 0.87 | 2.24 | 4.51 | 7.33 |
| .75 | 12.06 | 9.17 | 6.14 | 3.47 | 1.54 | 0.63 | 0.88 | 2.25 | 4.54 | 7.36 |
| .76 | 12.04 | 9.14 | 6.11 | 3.44 | 1.52 | 0.62 | 0.89 | 2.27 | 4.56 | 7.39 |
| .77 | 12.01 | 9.11 | 6.08 | 3.42 | 1.51 | 0.62 | 0.90 | 2.29 | 4.59 | 7.42 |
| .78 | 11.98 | 9.08 | 6.05 | 3.39 | 1.49 | 0.61 | 0.90 | 2.31 | 4.61 | 7.45 |
| .79 | 11.96 | 9.05 | 6.02 | 3.37 | 1.48 | 0.61 | 0.91 | 2.33 | 4.64 | 7.48 |
| .80 | 11.93 | 9.02 | 5.99 | 3.35 | 1.47 | 0.61 | 0.92 | 2.35 | 4.67 | 7.51 |
| .81 | 11.90 | 8.99 | 5.96 | 3.32 | 1.45 | 0.61 | 0.93 | 2.37 | 4.70 | 7.54 |
| .82 | 11.88 | 8.96 | 5.93 | 3.30 | 1.44 | 0.60 | 0.94 | 2.39 | 4.72 | 7.57 |
| .83 | 11.85 | 8.93 | 5.90 | 3.28 | 1.42 | 0.60 | 0.95 | 2.41 | 4.75 | 7.60 |
| .84 | 11.82 | 8.90 | 5.87 | 3.25 | 1.41 | 0.60 | 0.96 | 2.43 | 4.78 | 7.63 |
| .85 | 11.79 | 8.87 | 5.84 | 3.23 | 1.40 | 0.60 | 0.97 | 2.45 | 4.80 | 7.66 |
| .86 | 11.77 | 8.84 | 5.82 | 3.21 | 1.38 | 0.60 | 0.98 | 2.47 | 4.83 | 7.69 |
| .87 | 11.74 | 8.81 | 5.79 | 3.19 | 1.37 | 0.59 | 0.99 | 2.49 | 4.86 | 7.72 |
| .88 | 11.71 | 8.78 | 5.76 | 3.16 | 1.35 | 0.59 | 1.00 | 2.51 | 4.88 | 7.75 |
| .89 | 11.69 | 8.75 | 5.73 | 3.14 | 1.34 | 0.59 | 1.01 | 2.53 | 4.91 | 7.78 |
| .90 | 11.66 | 8.71 | 5.70 | 3.12 | 1.33 | 0.59 | 1.02 | 2.55 | 4.94 | 7.81 |
| .91 | 11.63 | 8.68 | 5.67 | 3.10 | 1.32 | 0.59 | 1.03 | 2.57 | 4.96 | 7.84 |
| .92 | 11.61 | 8.65 | 5.64 | 3.07 | 1.30 | 0.59 | 1.04 | 2.59 | 4.99 | 7.87 |
| .93 | 11.58 | 8.62 | 5.61 | 3.05 | 1.29 | 0.59 | 1.05 | 2.61 | 5.02 | 7.90 |
| .94 | 11.55 | 8.59 | 5.59 | 3.03 | 1.27 | 0.58 | 1.06 | 2.63 | 5.04 | 7.93 |
| .95 | 11.52 | 8.56 | 5.56 | 3.01 | 1.26 | 0.58 | 1.07 | 2.65 | 5.07 | 7.96 |
| .96 | 11.49 | 8.53 | 5.53 | 2.99 | 1.25 | 0.58 | 1.08 | 2.68 | 5.10 | 7.98 |
| .97 | 11.46 | 8.50 | 5.50 | 2.96 | 1.24 | 0.58 | 1.10 | 2.70 | 5.12 | 8.01 |
| .98 | 11.44 | 8.46 | 5.48 | 2.94 | 1.22 | 0.58 | 1.11 | 2.72 | 5.15 | 8.04 |
| .99 | 11.41 | 8.43 | 5.45 | 2.92 | 1.21 | 0.58 | 1.12 | 2.74 | 5.18 | 8.07 |
| 1.00 | 11.38 | 8.40 | 5.42 | 2.90 | 1.20 | 0.58 | 1.13 | 2.76 | 5.21 | 8.10 |

# TABLE XXVII. ARGUMENT 22.

Equation = $8''.1 - 0''.4 \sin. (t - z) + 7''.8 \sin. 2 (t - z)$.

Period, 32.128086 days.

| Days. | 20 | 21 | 22 | 23 | 24 | 25 | 26 | 27 | 28 | 29 |
|---|---|---|---|---|---|---|---|---|---|---|
| Days. | ″ | ″ | ″ | ″ | ″ | ″ | ″ | ″ | ″ | ″ |
| .00 | 8.10 | 10.99 | 13.44 | 15.07 | 15.62 | 15.00 | 13.30 | 10.78 | 7.80 | 4.82 |
| .01 | 8.13 | 11.02 | 13.46 | 15.08 | 15.62 | 14.99 | 13.28 | 10.75 | 7.77 | 4.79 |
| .02 | 8.16 | 11.04 | 13.48 | 15.09 | 15.62 | 14.98 | 13.26 | 10.72 | 7.74 | 4.76 |
| .03 | 8.19 | 11.07 | 13.50 | 15.10 | 15.62 | 14.96 | 13.23 | 10.70 | 7.70 | 4.74 |
| .04 | 8.22 | 11.10 | 13.52 | 15.11 | 15.62 | 14.95 | 13.21 | 10.67 | 7.67 | 4.71 |
| .05 | 8.25 | 11.12 | 13.55 | 15.13 | 15.62 | 14.94 | 13.19 | 10.64 | 7.64 | 4.68 |
| .06 | 8.27 | 11.15 | 13.57 | 15.14 | 15.62 | 14.92 | 13.17 | 10.61 | 7.61 | 4.65 |
| .07 | 8.30 | 11.18 | 13.59 | 15.15 | 15.61 | 14.91 | 13.15 | 10.58 | 7.58 | 4.62 |
| .08 | 8.33 | 11.20 | 13.61 | 15.16 | 15.61 | 14.90 | 13.12 | 10.56 | 7.55 | 4.60 |
| .09 | 8.36 | 11.23 | 13.63 | 15.17 | 15.61 | 14.88 | 13.10 | 10.53 | 7.52 | 4.57 |
| .10 | 8.39 | 11.26 | 13.65 | 15.18 | 15.61 | 14.87 | 13.08 | 10.50 | 7.49 | 4.54 |
| .11 | 8.42 | 11.28 | 13.67 | 15.19 | 15.61 | 14.86 | 13.06 | 10.47 | 7.45 | 4.52 |
| .12 | 8.45 | 11.31 | 13.69 | 15.20 | 15.61 | 14.84 | 13.04 | 10.44 | 7.42 | 4.49 |
| .13 | 8.48 | 11.34 | 13.71 | 15.21 | 15.60 | 14.83 | 13.01 | 10.41 | 7.39 | 4.46 |
| .14 | 8.51 | 11.36 | 13.73 | 15.22 | 15.60 | 14.81 | 12.99 | 10.38 | 7.36 | 4.44 |
| .15 | 8.54 | 11.39 | 13.75 | 15.23 | 15.60 | 14.80 | 12.97 | 10.36 | 7.33 | 4.41 |
| .16 | 8.57 | 11.42 | 13.77 | 15.24 | 15.60 | 14.79 | 12.94 | 10.33 | 7.30 | 4.38 |
| .17 | 8.60 | 11.44 | 13.79 | 15.25 | 15.60 | 14.77 | 12.92 | 10.30 | 7.27 | 4.35 |
| .18 | 8.63 | 11.47 | 13.81 | 15.26 | 15.59 | 14.76 | 12.90 | 10.27 | 7.24 | 4.33 |
| .19 | 8.66 | 11.50 | 13.83 | 15.27 | 15.59 | 14.74 | 12.87 | 10.24 | 7.21 | 4.30 |
| .20 | 8.69 | 11.53 | 13.85 | 15.28 | 15.59 | 14.73 | 12.85 | 10.21 | 7.18 | 4.27 |
| .21 | 8.72 | 11.55 | 13.87 | 15.29 | 15.59 | 14.72 | 12.83 | 10.18 | 7.15 | 4.25 |
| .22 | 8.75 | 11.58 | 13.89 | 15.30 | 15.58 | 14.70 | 12.80 | 10.15 | 7.12 | 4.22 |
| .23 | 8.78 | 11.61 | 13.91 | 15.30 | 15.58 | 14.69 | 12.78 | 10.12 | 7.09 | 4.19 |
| .24 | 8.81 | 11.63 | 13.93 | 15.31 | 15.57 | 14.67 | 12.75 | 10.09 | 7.06 | 4.17 |
| .25 | 8.84 | 11.66 | 13.95 | 15.32 | 15.57 | 14.66 | 12.73 | 10.06 | 7.03 | 4.14 |
| .26 | 8.87 | 11.68 | 13.96 | 15.33 | 15.57 | 14.65 | 12.71 | 10.03 | 7.00 | 4.11 |
| .27 | 8.90 | 11.71 | 13.98 | 15.34 | 15.56 | 14.63 | 12.68 | 10.00 | 6.97 | 4.08 |
| .28 | 8.93 | 11.74 | 14.00 | 15.34 | 15.56 | 14.62 | 12.66 | 9.97 | 6.94 | 4.06 |
| .29 | 8.96 | 11.76 | 14.02 | 15.35 | 15.55 | 14.60 | 12.63 | 9.94 | 6.91 | 4.03 |
| .30 | 8.99 | 11.79 | 14.04 | 15.36 | 15.55 | 14.59 | 12.61 | 9.91 | 6.88 | 4.01 |
| .31 | 9.03 | 11.82 | 14.06 | 15.37 | 15.55 | 14.58 | 12.59 | 9.88 | 6.85 | 3.98 |
| .32 | 9.05 | 11.84 | 14.08 | 15.38 | 15.54 | 14.56 | 12.56 | 9.85 | 6.82 | 3.95 |
| .33 | 9.08 | 11.87 | 14.09 | 15.38 | 15.54 | 14.55 | 12.54 | 9.82 | 6.79 | 3.93 |
| .34 | 9.11 | 11.90 | 14.11 | 15.39 | 15.53 | 14.53 | 12.51 | 9.79 | 6.76 | 3.90 |
| .35 | 9.14 | 11.92 | 14.13 | 15.40 | 15.53 | 14.52 | 12.49 | 9.76 | 6.73 | 3.88 |
| .36 | 9.16 | 11.95 | 14.15 | 15.40 | 15.52 | 14.50 | 12.46 | 9.73 | 6.70 | 3.85 |
| .37 | 9.19 | 11.98 | 14.17 | 15.41 | 15.52 | 14.49 | 12.44 | 9.70 | 6.67 | 3.82 |
| .38 | 9.22 | 12.00 | 14.18 | 15.42 | 15.51 | 14.47 | 12.41 | 9.67 | 6.64 | 3.80 |
| .39 | 9.25 | 12.03 | 14.20 | 15.42 | 15.51 | 14.46 | 12.39 | 9.64 | 6.61 | 3.77 |
| .40 | 9.28 | 12.05 | 14.22 | 15.43 | 15.50 | 14.44 | 12.36 | 9.61 | 6.58 | 3.75 |
| .41 | 9.31 | 12.08 | 14.24 | 15.44 | 15.50 | 14.42 | 12.34 | 9.58 | 6.55 | 3.72 |
| .42 | 9.34 | 12.10 | 14.25 | 15.44 | 15.49 | 14.41 | 12.31 | 9.55 | 6.52 | 3.69 |
| .43 | 9.37 | 12.13 | 14.27 | 15.45 | 15.49 | 14.39 | 12.29 | 9.52 | 6.49 | 3.67 |
| .44 | 9.40 | 12.15 | 14.28 | 15.45 | 15.48 | 14.37 | 12.26 | 9.49 | 6.46 | 3.64 |
| .45 | 9.43 | 12.18 | 14.30 | 15.46 | 15.48 | 14.36 | 12.24 | 9.46 | 6.43 | 3.62 |
| .46 | 9.45 | 12.20 | 14.32 | 15.47 | 15.47 | 14.34 | 12.21 | 9.43 | 6.40 | 3.59 |
| .47 | 9.48 | 12.23 | 14.33 | 15.47 | 15.47 | 14.32 | 12.19 | 9.40 | 6.37 | 3.57 |
| .48 | 9.51 | 12.25 | 14.35 | 15.48 | 15.46 | 14.31 | 12.16 | 9.37 | 6.34 | 3.54 |
| .49 | 9.54 | 12.28 | 14.36 | 15.48 | 15.46 | 14.29 | 12.14 | 9.34 | 6.31 | 3.52 |
| .50 | 9.57 | 12.30 | 14.38 | 15.49 | 15.45 | 14.27 | 12.11 | 9.31 | 6.28 | 3.49 |

# TABLE XXVII. ARGUMENT 22.

Equation $= 8''.1 - 0''.4 \sin. (t - z) + 7''.8 \sin. 2 (t - z)$.

Period, 32.128086 days.

| Days. | 20 | 21 | 22 | 23 | 24 | 25 | 26 | 27 | 28 | 29 |
|---|---|---|---|---|---|---|---|---|---|---|
| Days. | ″ | ″ | ″ | ″ | ″ | ″ | ″ | ″ | ″ | ″ |
| .50 | 9.57 | 12.30 | 14.38 | 15.49 | 15.45 | 14.27 | 12.11 | 9.31 | 6.28 | 3.49 |
| .51 | 9.60 | 12.33 | 14.40 | 15.49 | 15.44 | 14.25 | 12.08 | 9.28 | 6.25 | 3.47 |
| .52 | 9.63 | 12.35 | 14.41 | 15.50 | 15.44 | 14.23 | 12.06 | 9.25 | 6.22 | 3.44 |
| .53 | 9.66 | 12.38 | 14.43 | 15.50 | 15.43 | 14.22 | 12.03 | 9.22 | 6.19 | 3.42 |
| .54 | 9.69 | 12.40 | 14.44 | 15.51 | 15.43 | 14.20 | 12.01 | 9.19 | 6.16 | 3.39 |
| .55 | 9.72 | 12.42 | 14.46 | 15.51 | 15.42 | 14.18 | 11.98 | 9.16 | 6.13 | 3.37 |
| .56 | 9.76 | 12.45 | 14.47 | 15.51 | 15.41 | 14.16 | 11.95 | 9.13 | 6.10 | 3.34 |
| .57 | 9.79 | 12.47 | 14.49 | 15.52 | 15.41 | 14.14 | 11.93 | 9.10 | 6.07 | 3.32 |
| .58 | 9.82 | 12.50 | 14.50 | 15.52 | 15.40 | 14.13 | 11.90 | 9.07 | 6.04 | 3.29 |
| .59 | 9.85 | 12.52 | 14.52 | 15.53 | 15.40 | 14.11 | 11.88 | 9.04 | 6.01 | 3.27 |
| .60 | 9.86 | 12.54 | 14.53 | 15.53 | 15.39 | 14.09 | 11.85 | 9.01 | 5.98 | 3.24 |
| .61 | 9.89 | 12.57 | 14.55 | 15.53 | 15.38 | 14.07 | 11.82 | 8.98 | 5.95 | 3.22 |
| .62 | 9.92 | 12.59 | 14.56 | 15.54 | 15.37 | 14.05 | 11.80 | 8.95 | 5.92 | 3.19 |
| .63 | 9.95 | 12.62 | 14.58 | 15.54 | 15.37 | 14.04 | 11.77 | 8.92 | 5.89 | 3.17 |
| .64 | 9.98 | 12.64 | 14.59 | 15.55 | 15.36 | 14.02 | 11.75 | 8.89 | 5.86 | 3.14 |
| .65 | 10.01 | 12.66 | 14.61 | 15.55 | 15.35 | 14.00 | 11.72 | 8.86 | 5.83 | 3.12 |
| .66 | 10.03 | 12.69 | 14.62 | 15.55 | 15.34 | 13.98 | 11.69 | 8.83 | 5.80 | 3.09 |
| .67 | 10.06 | 12.71 | 14.64 | 15.56 | 15.33 | 13.96 | 11.67 | 8.80 | 5.77 | 3.07 |
| .68 | 10.09 | 12.74 | 14.65 | 15.56 | 15.33 | 13.95 | 11.64 | 8.77 | 5.74 | 3.04 |
| .69 | 10.12 | 12.76 | 14.67 | 15.57 | 15.32 | 13.93 | 11.62 | 8.74 | 5.71 | 3.02 |
| .70 | 10.15 | 12.78 | 14.68 | 15.57 | 15.31 | 13.91 | 11.59 | 8.71 | 5.68 | 2.99 |
| .71 | 10.18 | 12.80 | 14.69 | 15.57 | 15.30 | 13.89 | 11.56 | 8.68 | 5.65 | 2.97 |
| .72 | 10.21 | 12.83 | 14.71 | 15.58 | 15.29 | 13.87 | 11.54 | 8.65 | 5.62 | 2.94 |
| .73 | 10.24 | 12.85 | 14.72 | 15.58 | 15.28 | 13.85 | 11.51 | 8.62 | 5.60 | 2.92 |
| .74 | 10.27 | 12.87 | 14.74 | 15.58 | 15.27 | 13.83 | 11.48 | 8.59 | 5.57 | 2.89 |
| .75 | 10.30 | 12.90 | 14.75 | 15.59 | 15.27 | 13.82 | 11.46 | 8.56 | 5.54 | 2.87 |
| .76 | 10.32 | 12.92 | 14.76 | 15.59 | 15.26 | 13.80 | 11.43 | 8.53 | 5.51 | 2.84 |
| .77 | 10.35 | 12.94 | 14.78 | 15.59 | 15.25 | 13.78 | 11.40 | 8.50 | 5.48 | 2.82 |
| .78 | 10.38 | 12.97 | 14.79 | 15.60 | 15.24 | 13.76 | 11.38 | 8.47 | 5.45 | 2.79 |
| .79 | 10.41 | 12.99 | 14.81 | 15.60 | 15.23 | 13.74 | 11.35 | 8.44 | 5.42 | 2.77 |
| .80 | 10.44 | 13.01 | 14.82 | 15.60 | 15.22 | 13.72 | 11.32 | 8.41 | 5.39 | 2.75 |
| .81 | 10.47 | 13.03 | 14.83 | 15.60 | 15.21 | 13.70 | 11.29 | 8.38 | 5.36 | 2.72 |
| .82 | 10.50 | 13.05 | 14.85 | 15.60 | 15.20 | 13.68 | 11.27 | 8.35 | 5.33 | 2.70 |
| .83 | 10.52 | 13.08 | 14.86 | 15.60 | 15.19 | 13.66 | 11.24 | 8.32 | 5.31 | 2.68 |
| .84 | 10.55 | 13.10 | 14.87 | 15.60 | 15.18 | 13.64 | 11.21 | 8.29 | 5.28 | 2.65 |
| .85 | 10.58 | 13.12 | 14.89 | 15.61 | 15.17 | 13.62 | 11.19 | 8.26 | 5.25 | 2.63 |
| .86 | 10.61 | 13.14 | 14.90 | 15.61 | 15.16 | 13.59 | 11.16 | 8.23 | 5.22 | 2.61 |
| .87 | 10.64 | 13.16 | 14.91 | 15.61 | 15.15 | 13.57 | 11.13 | 8.20 | 5.19 | 2.59 |
| .88 | 10.66 | 13.19 | 14.93 | 15.61 | 15.14 | 13.55 | 11.11 | 8.17 | 5.16 | 2.57 |
| .89 | 10.69 | 13.21 | 14.94 | 15.61 | 15.13 | 13.52 | 11.08 | 8.14 | 5.13 | 2.54 |
| .90 | 10.72 | 13.23 | 14.95 | 15.61 | 15.12 | 13.51 | 11.05 | 8.11 | 5.10 | 2.52 |
| .91 | 10.75 | 13.25 | 14.96 | 15.61 | 15.11 | 13.49 | 11.02 | 8.08 | 5.07 | 2.50 |
| .92 | 10.78 | 13.27 | 14.97 | 15.61 | 15.10 | 13.47 | 11.00 | 8.05 | 5.04 | 2.48 |
| .93 | 10.80 | 13.29 | 14.99 | 15.61 | 15.08 | 13.45 | 10.97 | 8.02 | 5.02 | 2.46 |
| .94 | 10.83 | 13.31 | 15.00 | 15.61 | 15.07 | 13.43 | 10.94 | 7.99 | 4.99 | 2.43 |
| .95 | 10.86 | 13.34 | 15.01 | 15.62 | 15.06 | 13.41 | 10.92 | 7.96 | 4.96 | 2.41 |
| .96 | 10.88 | 13.36 | 15.02 | 15.62 | 15.05 | 13.38 | 10.89 | 7.93 | 4.93 | 2.39 |
| .97 | 10.91 | 13.38 | 15.03 | 15.62 | 15.04 | 13.36 | 10.86 | 7.90 | 4.90 | 2.37 |
| .98 | 10.94 | 13.40 | 15.05 | 15.62 | 15.02 | 13.34 | 10.84 | 7.86 | 4.87 | 2.35 |
| .99 | 10.96 | 13.42 | 15.06 | 15.62 | 15.01 | 13.32 | 10.81 | 7.83 | 4.85 | 2.32 |
| 1.00 | 10.99 | 13.44 | 15.07 | 15.62 | 15.00 | 13.30 | 10.78 | 7.80 | 4.82 | 2.30 |

## TABLE XXVII.

(*Continued.*)

Period, 32.128086 days.

| Days. | 30 | 31 | 32 |
|---|---|---|---|
| Days. | ″ | ″ | ″ |
| .00 | 2.30 | 0.61 | 0.02 |
| .01 | 2.28 | 0.60 | 0.02 |
| .02 | 2.26 | 0.58 | 0.02 |
| .03 | 2.24 | 0.57 | 0.02 |
| .04 | 2.21 | 0.56 | 0.02 |
| .05 | 2.19 | 0.54 | 0.02 |
| .06 | 2.17 | 0.53 | 0.02 |
| .07 | 2.15 | 0.52 | 0.02 |
| .08 | 2.13 | 0.51 | 0.02 |
| .09 | 2.11 | 0.50 | 0.02 |
| .10 | 2.09 | 0.49 | 0.02 |
| .11 | 2.07 | 0.48 | 0.02 |
| .12 | 2.05 | 0.47 | 0.02 |
| .13 | 2.02 | 0.46 | 0.03 |
| .14 | 2.00 | 0.45 | 0.03 |
| .15 | 1.98 | 0.44 | 0.03 |
| .16 | 1.96 | 0.43 | 0.03 |
| .17 | 1.94 | 0.42 | 0.03 |
| .18 | 1.92 | 0.41 | 0.04 |
| .19 | 1.90 | 0.40 | 0.04 |
| .20 | 1.88 | 0.39 | 0.04 |
| .21 | 1.86 | 0.38 | 0.05 |
| .22 | 1.84 | 0.38 | 0.05 |
| .23 | 1.83 | 0.37 | 0.05 |
| .24 | 1.81 | 0.36 | 0.06 |
| .25 | 1.79 | 0.35 | 0.06 |
| .26 | 1.77 | 0.34 | 0.06 |
| .27 | 1.75 | 0.33 | 0.07 |
| .28 | 1.73 | 0.32 | 0.07 |
| .29 | 1.71 | 0.32 | 0.07 |
| .30 | 1.69 | 0.31 | 0.08 |
| .31 | 1.67 | 0.30 | 0.08 |
| .32 | 1.65 | 0.29 | 0.08 |
| .33 | 1.64 | 0.28 | 0.09 |
| .34 | 1.62 | 0.28 | 0.09 |
| .35 | 1.60 | 0.27 | 0.10 |
| .36 | 1.58 | 0.26 | 0.10 |
| .37 | 1.56 | 0.25 | 0.11 |
| .38 | 1.54 | 0.25 | 0.11 |
| .39 | 1.53 | 0.24 | 0.12 |
| .40 | 1.51 | 0.23 | 0.12 |
| .41 | 1.49 | 0.23 | 0.13 |
| .42 | 1.47 | 0.22 | 0.13 |
| .43 | 1.45 | 0.21 | 0.14 |
| .44 | 1.44 | 0.21 | 0.14 |
| .45 | 1.42 | 0.20 | 0.15 |
| .46 | 1.40 | 0.19 | 0.15 |
| .47 | 1.38 | 0.19 | 0.16 |
| .48 | 1.37 | 0.18 | 0.16 |
| .49 | 1.35 | 0.17 | 0.17 |
| .50 | 1.33 | 0.17 | 0.17 |

## TABLE XXVIII. ARG. 23.

Equation = 9″.8 [1 — sin. $(x + 2y - 2t)$].

Period, 23.774626 days.

| Days. | 0 | 1 | 2 | 3 | 4 | 5 | Days. |
|---|---|---|---|---|---|---|---|
| Days. | ″ | ″ | ″ | ″ | ″ | ″ | Days. |
| .00 | 19.59 | 19.33 | 18.40 | 16.88 | 14.87 | 12.49 | 1.00 |
| .01 | 19.59 | 19.32 | 18.39 | 16.86 | 14.85 | 12.46 | .99 |
| .02 | 19.59 | 19.32 | 18.38 | 16.84 | 14.82 | 12.44 | .98 |
| .03 | 19.60 | 19.31 | 18.36 | 16.83 | 14.80 | 12.41 | .97 |
| .04 | 19.60 | 19.31 | 18.35 | 16.81 | 14.77 | 12.39 | .96 |
| .05 | 19.60 | 19.30 | 18.34 | 16.79 | 14.75 | 12.36 | .95 |
| .06 | 19.60 | 19.29 | 18.33 | 16.77 | 14.73 | 12.34 | .94 |
| .07 | 19.60 | 19.29 | 18.32 | 16.75 | 14.71 | 12.31 | .93 |
| .08 | 19.60 | 19.28 | 18.30 | 16.74 | 14.68 | 12.29 | .92 |
| .09 | 19.60 | 19.28 | 18.29 | 16.72 | 14.66 | 12.26 | .91 |
| .10 | 19.60 | 19.27 | 18.28 | 16.70 | 14.64 | 12.24 | .90 |
| .11 | 19.60 | 19.26 | 18.27 | 16.68 | 14.62 | 12.21 | .89 |
| .12 | 19.60 | 19.25 | 18.25 | 16.66 | 14.59 | 12.19 | .88 |
| .13 | 19.60 | 19.25 | 18.24 | 16.65 | 14.57 | 12.16 | .87 |
| .14 | 19.60 | 19.24 | 18.22 | 16.63 | 14.54 | 12.14 | .86 |
| .15 | 19.60 | 19.23 | 18.21 | 16.61 | 14.52 | 12.11 | .85 |
| .16 | 19.60 | 19.22 | 18.20 | 16.59 | 14.50 | 12.09 | .84 |
| .17 | 19.60 | 19.21 | 18.18 | 16.57 | 14.48 | 12.06 | .83 |
| .18 | 19.60 | 19.21 | 18.17 | 16.55 | 14.45 | 12.04 | .82 |
| .19 | 19.60 | 19.20 | 18.15 | 16.53 | 14.43 | 12.01 | .81 |
| .20 | 19.60 | 19.19 | 18.14 | 16.51 | 14.41 | 11.99 | .80 |
| .21 | 19.60 | 19.18 | 18.13 | 16.49 | 14.39 | 11.96 | .79 |
| .22 | 19.60 | 19.17 | 18.11 | 16.47 | 14.36 | 11.94 | .78 |
| .23 | 19.59 | 19.17 | 18.10 | 16.46 | 14.34 | 11.91 | .77 |
| .24 | 19.59 | 19.16 | 18.08 | 16.44 | 14.31 | 11.89 | .76 |
| .25 | 19.59 | 19.15 | 18.07 | 16.42 | 14.29 | 11.86 | .75 |
| .26 | 19.59 | 19.14 | 18.05 | 16.40 | 14.27 | 11.84 | .74 |
| .27 | 19.59 | 19.14 | 18.04 | 16.38 | 14.25 | 11.81 | .73 |
| .28 | 19.59 | 19.13 | 18.02 | 16.37 | 14.22 | 11.79 | .72 |
| .29 | 19.59 | 19.13 | 18.01 | 16.35 | 14.20 | 11.76 | .71 |
| .30 | 19.59 | 19.12 | 17.99 | 16.33 | 14.18 | 11.74 | .70 |
| .31 | 19.59 | 19.11 | 17.98 | 16.31 | 14.16 | 11.71 | .69 |
| .32 | 19.59 | 19.10 | 17.96 | 16.29 | 14.13 | 11.69 | .68 |
| .33 | 19.58 | 19.10 | 17.95 | 16.27 | 14.11 | 11.66 | .67 |
| .34 | 19.58 | 19.09 | 17.93 | 16.25 | 14.08 | 11.64 | .66 |
| .35 | 19.58 | 19.08 | 17.92 | 16.23 | 14.06 | 11.61 | .65 |
| .36 | 19.58 | 19.07 | 17.91 | 16.21 | 14.04 | 11.59 | .64 |
| .37 | 19.58 | 19.06 | 17.89 | 16.19 | 14.02 | 11.56 | .63 |
| .38 | 19.57 | 19.06 | 17.88 | 16.17 | 13.99 | 11.54 | .62 |
| .39 | 19.57 | 19.05 | 17.86 | 16.15 | 13.97 | 11.51 | .61 |
| .40 | 19.57 | 19.04 | 17.85 | 16.13 | 13.95 | 11.49 | .60 |
| .41 | 19.57 | 19.03 | 17.84 | 16.11 | 13.93 | 11.46 | .59 |
| .42 | 19.57 | 19.02 | 17.82 | 16.09 | 13.90 | 11.44 | .58 |
| .43 | 19.56 | 19.02 | 17.81 | 16.07 | 13.88 | 11.41 | .57 |
| .44 | 19.56 | 19.01 | 17.79 | 16.05 | 13.85 | 11.39 | .56 |
| .45 | 19.56 | 19.00 | 17.78 | 16.03 | 13.83 | 11.36 | .55 |
| .46 | 19.56 | 18.99 | 17.76 | 16.01 | 13.81 | 11.33 | .54 |
| .47 | 19.56 | 18.98 | 17.75 | 15.99 | 13.78 | 11.31 | .53 |
| .48 | 19.55 | 18.97 | 17.73 | 15.97 | 13.76 | 11.28 | .52 |
| .49 | 19.55 | 18.96 | 17.72 | 15.95 | 13.73 | 11.26 | .51 |
| .50 | 19.55 | 18.95 | 17.70 | 15.93 | 13.71 | 11.23 | .50 |
| Days. | 23 | 22 | 21 | 20 | 19 | 18 | Days. |

# TABLE XXVII.

*(Continued.)*

Period, 32.128086 days.

| Days. | 30 | 31 | 32 |
|---|---|---|---|
| Days. | ″ | ″ | ″ |
| .50 | 1.33 | 0.17 | 0.17 |
| .51 | 1.32 | 0.16 | 0.18 |
| .52 | 1.30 | 0.15 | 0.19 |
| .53 | 1.28 | 0.15 | 0.19 |
| .54 | 1.27 | 0.14 | 0.20 |
| .55 | 1.25 | 0.13 | 0.20 |
| .56 | 1.23 | 0.13 | 0.21 |
| .57 | 1.21 | 0.12 | 0.22 |
| .58 | 1.20 | 0.12 | 0.22 |
| .59 | 1.18 | 0.11 | 0.23 |
| .60 | 1.17 | 0.11 | 0.24 |
| .61 | 1.15 | 0.10 | 0.24 |
| .62 | 1.13 | 0.10 | 0.25 |
| .63 | 1.12 | 0.09 | 0.26 |
| .64 | 1.10 | 0.09 | 0.26 |
| .65 | 1.09 | 0.08 | 0.27 |
| .66 | 1.07 | 0.08 | 0.28 |
| .67 | 1.06 | 0.08 | 0.29 |
| .68 | 1.04 | 0.07 | 0.30 |
| .69 | 1.03 | 0.07 | 0.30 |
| .70 | 1.01 | 0.07 | 0.31 |
| .71 | 1.00 | 0.06 | 0.32 |
| .72 | 0.98 | 0.06 | 0.33 |
| .73 | 0.97 | 0.06 | 0.34 |
| .74 | 0.95 | 0.05 | 0.34 |
| .75 | 0.94 | 0.05 | 0.35 |
| .76 | 0.92 | 0.05 | 0.36 |
| .77 | 0.91 | 0.05 | 0.37 |
| .78 | 0.89 | 0.04 | 0.38 |
| .79 | 0.88 | 0.04 | 0.39 |
| .80 | 0.87 | 0.04 | 0.40 |
| .81 | 0.85 | 0.04 | 0.41 |
| .82 | 0.84 | 0.04 | 0.42 |
| .83 | 0.83 | 0.03 | 0.43 |
| .84 | 0.81 | 0.03 | 0.44 |
| .85 | 0.80 | 0.03 | 0.45 |
| .86 | 0.79 | 0.03 | 0.46 |
| .87 | 0.77 | 0.03 | 0.47 |
| .88 | 0.76 | 0.03 | 0.48 |
| .89 | 0.75 | 0.03 | 0.49 |
| .90 | 0.73 | 0.03 | 0.50 |
| .91 | 0.72 | 0.02 | 0.51 |
| .92 | 0.71 | 0.02 | 0.53 |
| .93 | 0.70 | 0.02 | 0.54 |
| .94 | 0.68 | 0.02 | 0.55 |
| .95 | 0.67 | 0.02 | 0.56 |
| .96 | 0.66 | 0.02 | 0.57 |
| .97 | 0.65 | 0.02 | 0.58 |
| .98 | 0.63 | 0.02 | 0.59 |
| .99 | 0.62 | 0.02 | 0.61 |
| 1.00 | 0.61 | 0.02 | 0.62 |

# TABLE XXVIII. ARG. 23.

Equation $= 9''.8\ [1 - \sin.\ (x + 2y - 2t)]$.

Period, 23.774626 days.

| Days. | 0 | 1 | 2 | 3 | 4 | 5 | Days. |
|---|---|---|---|---|---|---|---|
| Days. | ″ | ″ | ″ | ″ | ″ | ″ | Days. |
| .50 | 19.55 | 18.95 | 17.70 | 15.93 | 13.71 | 11.23 | .50 |
| .51 | 19.55 | 18.94 | 17.68 | 15.91 | 13.69 | 11.20 | .49 |
| .52 | 19.55 | 18.93 | 17.67 | 15.89 | 13.66 | 11.18 | .48 |
| .53 | 19.54 | 18.92 | 17.65 | 15.87 | 13.64 | 11.15 | .47 |
| .54 | 19.54 | 18.91 | 17.64 | 15.85 | 13.61 | 11.13 | .46 |
| .55 | 19.54 | 18.90 | 17.62 | 15.83 | 13.59 | 11.10 | .45 |
| .56 | 19.54 | 18.89 | 17.60 | 15.81 | 13.57 | 11.08 | .44 |
| .57 | 19.53 | 18.88 | 17.59 | 15.79 | 13.54 | 11.05 | .43 |
| .58 | 19.53 | 18.88 | 17.57 | 15.77 | 13.52 | 11.03 | .42 |
| .59 | 19.52 | 18.87 | 17.56 | 15.75 | 13.49 | 11.00 | .41 |
| .60 | 19.52 | 18.86 | 17.54 | 15.73 | 13.47 | 10.98 | .40 |
| .61 | 19.52 | 18.85 | 17.52 | 15.71 | 13.45 | 10.95 | .39 |
| .62 | 19.51 | 18.84 | 17.51 | 15.69 | 13.42 | 10.93 | .38 |
| .63 | 19.51 | 18.83 | 17.49 | 15.67 | 13.40 | 10.90 | .37 |
| .64 | 19.50 | 18.82 | 17.48 | 15.65 | 13.37 | 10.88 | .36 |
| .65 | 19.50 | 18.81 | 17.46 | 15.63 | 13.35 | 10.85 | .35 |
| .66 | 19.50 | 18.80 | 17.45 | 15.61 | 13.33 | 10.82 | .34 |
| .67 | 19.49 | 18.79 | 17.43 | 15.59 | 13.30 | 10.80 | .33 |
| .68 | 19.49 | 18.78 | 17.42 | 15.56 | 13.28 | 10.77 | .32 |
| .69 | 19.48 | 18.77 | 17.40 | 15.54 | 13.25 | 10.75 | .31 |
| .70 | 19.48 | 18.76 | 17.39 | 15.52 | 13.23 | 10.72 | .30 |
| .71 | 19.47 | 18.75 | 17.37 | 15.50 | 13.21 | 10.69 | .29 |
| .72 | 19.47 | 18.74 | 17.36 | 15.48 | 13.18 | 10.67 | .28 |
| .73 | 19.46 | 18.72 | 17.34 | 15.46 | 13.16 | 10.64 | .27 |
| .74 | 19.46 | 18.71 | 17.33 | 15.44 | 13.13 | 10.62 | .26 |
| .75 | 19.45 | 18.70 | 17.31 | 15.42 | 13.11 | 10.59 | .25 |
| .76 | 19.45 | 18.69 | 17.29 | 15.40 | 13.09 | 10.57 | .24 |
| .77 | 19.44 | 18.68 | 17.27 | 15.38 | 13.06 | 10.54 | .23 |
| .78 | 19.44 | 18.66 | 17.26 | 15.35 | 13.04 | 10.52 | .22 |
| .79 | 19.43 | 18.65 | 17.24 | 15.33 | 13.01 | 10.49 | .21 |
| .80 | 19.43 | 18.64 | 17.22 | 15.31 | 12.99 | 10.47 | .20 |
| .81 | 19.42 | 18.63 | 17.20 | 15.29 | 12.97 | 10.44 | .19 |
| .82 | 19.42 | 18.62 | 17.19 | 15.27 | 12.94 | 10.42 | .18 |
| .83 | 19.41 | 18.61 | 17.17 | 15.24 | 12.92 | 10.39 | .17 |
| .84 | 19.41 | 18.60 | 17.16 | 15.22 | 12.89 | 10.37 | .16 |
| .85 | 19.40 | 18.59 | 17.14 | 15.20 | 12.87 | 10.34 | .15 |
| .86 | 19.40 | 18.58 | 17.12 | 15.18 | 12.84 | 10.31 | .14 |
| .87 | 19.39 | 18.57 | 17.11 | 15.16 | 12.82 | 10.29 | .13 |
| .88 | 19.39 | 18.55 | 17.09 | 15.13 | 12.79 | 10.26 | .12 |
| .89 | 19.38 | 18.54 | 17.08 | 15.11 | 12.77 | 10.24 | .11 |
| .90 | 19.38 | 18.53 | 17.06 | 15.09 | 12.74 | 10.21 | .10 |
| .91 | 19.37 | 18.52 | 17.04 | 15.07 | 12.71 | 10.18 | .09 |
| .92 | 19.37 | 18.50 | 17.02 | 15.05 | 12.69 | 10.16 | .08 |
| .93 | 19.36 | 18.49 | 17.01 | 15.02 | 12.66 | 10.13 | .07 |
| .94 | 19.36 | 18.47 | 16.99 | 15.00 | 12.64 | 10.11 | .06 |
| .95 | 19.35 | 18.46 | 16.97 | 14.98 | 12.61 | 10.08 | .05 |
| .96 | 19.35 | 18.45 | 16.95 | 14.96 | 12.59 | 10.05 | .04 |
| .97 | 19.34 | 18.44 | 16.93 | 14.94 | 12.56 | 10.03 | .03 |
| .98 | 19.34 | 18.42 | 16.92 | 14.91 | 12.54 | 10.00 | .02 |
| .99 | 19.33 | 18.41 | 16.90 | 14.89 | 12.51 | 9.98 | .01 |
| 1.00 | 19.33 | 18.40 | 16.88 | 14.87 | 12.49 | 9.95 | .00 |
| Days. | 23 | 22 | 21 | 20 | 19 | 18 | Days. |

# TABLE XXVIII.

*(Continued.)*

Period, 23.774626 days.

# TABLE XXIX. ARG. 24.

Equation = 7″.3 [1 — sin. $(2x + z)$].

Period, 13.276498 days.

| Days. | 6 | 7 | 8 | 9 | 10 | 11 | 0 | 1 | 2 | Days. |
|---|---|---|---|---|---|---|---|---|---|---|
| .00 | 9.95 | 7.39 | 4.98 | 2.92 | 1.33 | 0.35 | 14.50 | 14.27 | 12.51 | 1.00 |
| .01 | 9.92 | 7.36 | 4.96 | 2.90 | 1.32 | 0.34 | 14.50 | 14.26 | 12.49 | .99 |
| .02 | 9.90 | 7.34 | 4.94 | 2.88 | 1.31 | 0.33 | 14.51 | 14.25 | 12.46 | .98 |
| .03 | 9.87 | 7.31 | 4.91 | 2.87 | 1.29 | 0.33 | 14.52 | 14.24 | 12.44 | .97 |
| .04 | 9.85 | 7.29 | 4.89 | 2.85 | 1.28 | 0.32 | 14.52 | 14.23 | 12.41 | .96 |
| .05 | 9.82 | 7.26 | 4.87 | 2.83 | 1.27 | 0.31 | 14.53 | 14.22 | 12.39 | .95 |
| .06 | 9.79 | 7.23 | 4.85 | 2.81 | 1.26 | 0.30 | 14.53 | 14.20 | 12.36 | .94 |
| .07 | 9.77 | 7.21 | 4.82 | 2.79 | 1.25 | 0.30 | 14.53 | 14.19 | 12.33 | .93 |
| .08 | 9.74 | 7.18 | 4.80 | 2.78 | 1.23 | 0.29 | 14.54 | 14 18 | 12.31 | .92 |
| .09 | 9.72 | 7.16 | 4.77 | 2.76 | 1.22 | 0.29 | 14.54 | 14.17 | 12.28 | .91 |
| .10 | 9.69 | 7.13 | 4.75 | 2.74 | 1.21 | 0.28 | 14.55 | 14.16 | 12.26 | .90 |
| .11 | 9.66 | 7.11 | 4.73 | 2.72 | 1.20 | 0.27 | 14.55 | 14.15 | 12.23 | .89 |
| .12 | 9.64 | 7.08 | 4.71 | 2.70 | 1.19 | 0.27 | 14.56 | 14.14 | 12.21 | .88 |
| .13 | 9.61 | 7.06 | 4.68 | 2.69 | 1.17 | 0.26 | 14.56 | 14.12 | 12.18 | .87 |
| .14 | 9.59 | 7.03 | 4.66 | 2.67 | 1.16 | 0.26 | 14.56 | 14.11 | 12.16 | .86 |
| .15 | 9.56 | 7.01 | 4.64 | 2.65 | 1.15 | 0.25 | 14.57 | 14.10 | 12.13 | .85 |
| .16 | 9.53 | 6.98 | 4.62 | 2.63 | 1.14 | 0.24 | 14.57 | 14.08 | 12.10 | .84 |
| .17 | 9.51 | 6.96 | 4.60 | 2.61 | 1.12 | 0.24 | 14.57 | 14.07 | 12.08 | .83 |
| .18 | 9.48 | 6.93 | 4.57 | 2.60 | 1.11 | 0.23 | 14.58 | 14.05 | 12.05 | .82 |
| .19 | 9.46 | 6.91 | 4.55 | 2.58 | 1.09 | 0.23 | 14.58 | 14.04 | 12.03 | .81 |
| .20 | 9.43 | 6.88 | 4.53 | 2.56 | 1.08 | 0.22 | 14.58 | 14.03 | 12.00 | .80 |
| .21 | 9.40 | 6.86 | 4.51 | 2.54 | 1.07 | 0.21 | 14.58 | 14.02 | 11.97 | .79 |
| .22 | 9.38 | 6.83 | 4.49 | 2.53 | 1.06 | 0.21 | 14.58 | 14.00 | 11.94 | .78 |
| .23 | 9.35 | 6.81 | 4.46 | 2.51 | 1.04 | 0.20 | 14.59 | 13.99 | 11.92 | .77 |
| .24 | 9.33 | 6.78 | 4.44 | 2.50 | 1.03 | 0.20 | 14.59 | 13.97 | 11.89 | .76 |
| .25 | 9.30 | 6.76 | 4.42 | 2.48 | 1.02 | 0.19 | 14.59 | 13.96 | 11.87 | .75 |
| .26 | 9.27 | 6.73 | 4.40 | 2.46 | 1.01 | 0.19 | 14.59 | 13.95 | 11.84 | .74 |
| .27 | 9.25 | 6.71 | 4.38 | 2.45 | 1.00 | 0.18 | 14.60 | 13.93 | 11.81 | .73 |
| .28 | 9.22 | 6.68 | 4.36 | 2.43 | 0.99 | 0.18 | 14.60 | 13.92 | 11.79 | .72 |
| .29 | 9.20 | 6.66 | 4.34 | 2.42 | 0.98 | 0.17 | 14.60 | 13.90 | 11.76 | .71 |
| .30 | 9.17 | 6.63 | 4.32 | 2.40 | 0.97 | 0.17 | 14.60 | 13.89 | 11.73 | .70 |
| .31 | 9.15 | 6.61 | 4.30 | 2.38 | 0.96 | 0.17 | 14.60 | 13.88 | 11.70 | .69 |
| .32 | 9.12 | 6.58 | 4.28 | 2.36 | 0.95 | 0.16 | 14.60 | 13.86 | 11.67 | .68 |
| .33 | 9.10 | 6.56 | 4.25 | 2.35 | 0.93 | 0.16 | 14.60 | 13.85 | 11.65 | .67 |
| .34 | 9.07 | 6.53 | 4.23 | 2.33 | 0.92 | 0.15 | 14.60 | 13.83 | 11.62 | .66 |
| .35 | 9.05 | 6.51 | 4.21 | 2.31 | 0.91 | 0.15 | 14.60 | 13.82 | 11.60 | .65 |
| .36 | 9.02 | 6.49 | 4.19 | 2.29 | 0.90 | 0.15 | 14.60 | 13.80 | 11.57 | .64 |
| .37 | 9.00 | 6.46 | 4.17 | 2.28 | 0.89 | 0.14 | 14.60 | 13.78 | 11.54 | .63 |
| .38 | 8.97 | 6.44 | 4.15 | 2.26 | 0.87 | 0.14 | 14.60 | 13.77 | 11.52 | .62 |
| .39 | 8.95 | 6.41 | 4.13 | 2.25 | 0.86 | 0.13 | 14.60 | 13.75 | 11.49 | .61 |
| .40 | 8.92 | 6.39 | 4.11 | 2.23 | 0.85 | 0.13 | 14.60 | 13.74 | 11.46 | .60 |
| .41 | 8.89 | 6.37 | 4.09 | 2.21 | 0.84 | 0.12 | 14.60 | 13.72 | 11.43 | .59 |
| .42 | 8.87 | 6.34 | 4.07 | 2.20 | 0.83 | 0.12 | 14.60 | 13.70 | 11.40 | .58 |
| .43 | 8.84 | 6.32 | 4.04 | 2.18 | 0.82 | 0.11 | 14.60 | 13.69 | 11.37 | .57 |
| .44 | 8.82 | 6.29 | 4.02 | 2.17 | 0.81 | 0.11 | 14.60 | 13.67 | 11.34 | .56 |
| .45 | 8.79 | 6.27 | 4.00 | 2.15 | 0.80 | 0.10 | 14.60 | 13.66 | 11.32 | .55 |
| .46 | 8.76 | 6.25 | 3.98 | 2.13 | 0.79 | 0.10 | 14.59 | 13.64 | 11.29 | .54 |
| .47 | 8.74 | 6.22 | 3.96 | 2.11 | 0.78 | 0.09 | 14.59 | 13.62 | 11.26 | .53 |
| .48 | 8.71 | 6.20 | 3.94 | 2.10 | 0.77 | 0.09 | 14.59 | 13.61 | 11.23 | .52 |
| .49 | 8.69 | 6.17 | 3.92 | 2.08 | 0.76 | 0.08 | 14.59 | 13.59 | 11.20 | .51 |
| .50 | 8.66 | 6.15 | 3.90 | 2.06 | 0.75 | 0.08 | 14.59 | 13.57 | 11.17 | .50 |
| Days. | 17 | 16 | 15 | 14 | 13 | 12 | 13 | 12 | 11 | Days. |

# TABLE XXVIII.

(*Continued.*)

Period, 23.774626 days.

# TABLE XXIX. ARG. 24.

Equation $= 7''.3\ [1 - \sin.\ (2x + z)]$.

Period, 13.276498 days.

| Days. | 6 | 7 | 8 | 9 | 10 | 11 | 0 | 1 | 2 | Days. |
|---|---|---|---|---|---|---|---|---|---|---|
| Days. | " | " | " | " | " | " | " | " | " | Days. |
| .50 | 8.66 | 6.15 | 3.90 | 2.06 | 0.75 | 0.08 | 14.59 | 13.57 | 11.17 | .50 |
| .51 | 8.63 | 6.13 | 3.88 | 2.04 | 0.74 | 0.08 | 14.59 | 13.55 | 11.14 | .49 |
| .52 | 8.61 | 6.10 | 3.86 | 2.03 | 0.73 | 0.07 | 14.59 | 13.53 | 11.11 | .48 |
| .53 | 8.58 | 6.07 | 3.83 | 2.01 | 0.72 | 0.07 | 14.58 | 13.51 | 11.08 | .47 |
| .54 | 8.56 | 6.05 | 3.81 | 2.00 | 0.71 | 0.06 | 14.58 | 13.49 | 11.05 | .46 |
| .55 | 8.53 | 6.03 | 3.79 | 1.98 | 0.70 | 0.06 | 14.58 | 13.48 | 11.02 | .45 |
| .56 | 8.50 | 6.01 | 3.77 | 1.97 | 0.69 | 0.06 | 14.57 | 13.46 | 10.99 | .44 |
| .57 | 8.48 | 5.98 | 3.75 | 1.95 | 0.68 | 0.06 | 14.57 | 13.44 | 10.96 | .43 |
| .58 | 8.45 | 5.96 | 3.73 | 1.94 | 0.68 | 0.05 | 14.57 | 13.42 | 10.93 | .42 |
| .59 | 8.43 | 5.93 | 3.71 | 1.92 | 0.67 | 0.05 | 14.56 | 13.40 | 10.90 | .41 |
| .60 | 8.40 | 5.91 | 3.69 | 1.91 | 0.66 | 0.05 | 14.56 | 13.38 | 10.87 | .40 |
| .61 | 8.37 | 5.89 | 3.67 | 1.89 | 0.65 | 0.05 | 14.56 | 13.36 | 10.84 | .39 |
| .62 | 8.35 | 5.86 | 3.65 | 1.88 | 0.64 | 0.05 | 14.55 | 13.34 | 10.81 | .38 |
| .63 | 8.32 | 5.84 | 3.63 | 1.86 | 0.64 | 0.04 | 14.55 | 13.32 | 10.78 | .37 |
| .64 | 8.30 | 5.81 | 3.61 | 1.85 | 0.63 | 0.04 | 14.54 | 13.30 | 10.75 | .36 |
| .65 | 8.27 | 5.79 | 3.59 | 1.83 | 0.62 | 0.04 | 14.54 | 13.28 | 10.72 | .35 |
| .66 | 8.24 | 5.77 | 3.57 | 1.82 | 0.61 | 0.04 | 14.53 | 13.26 | 10.69 | .34 |
| .67 | 8.22 | 5.74 | 3.55 | 1.80 | 0.60 | 0.04 | 14.53 | 13.24 | 10.66 | .33 |
| .68 | 8.19 | 5.72 | 3.53 | 1.79 | 0.59 | 0.03 | 14.52 | 13.22 | 10.63 | .32 |
| .69 | 8.17 | 5.69 | 3.51 | 1.77 | 0.58 | 0.03 | 14.52 | 13.20 | 10.60 | .31 |
| .70 | 8.14 | 5.67 | 3.49 | 1.76 | 0.57 | 0.03 | 14.51 | 13.18 | 10.57 | .30 |
| .71 | 8.12 | 5.65 | 3.47 | 1.75 | 0.56 | 0.03 | 14.50 | 13.16 | 10.54 | .29 |
| .72 | 8.09 | 5.63 | 3.45 | 1.73 | 0.55 | 0.03 | 14.50 | 13.14 | 10.51 | .28 |
| .73 | 8.07 | 5.60 | 3.43 | 1.72 | 0.55 | 0.02 | 14.49 | 13.12 | 10.48 | .27 |
| .74 | 8.04 | 5.58 | 3.41 | 1.70 | 0.54 | 0.02 | 14.48 | 13.10 | 10.45 | .26 |
| .75 | 8.02 | 5.56 | 3.39 | 1.69 | 0.53 | 0.02 | 14.48 | 13.08 | 10.42 | .25 |
| .76 | 7.99 | 5.54 | 3.37 | 1.68 | 0.52 | 0.02 | 14.47 | 13.05 | 10.38 | .24 |
| .77 | 7.97 | 5.51 | 3.35 | 1.66 | 0.51 | 0.02 | 14.46 | 13.03 | 10.35 | .23 |
| .78 | 7.94 | 5.49 | 3.33 | 1.65 | 0.51 | 0.01 | 14.46 | 13.01 | 10.32 | .22 |
| .79 | 7.92 | 5.46 | 3.31 | 1.63 | 0.50 | 0.01 | 14.45 | 12.99 | 10.29 | .21 |
| .80 | 7.89 | 5.44 | 3.29 | 1.62 | 0.49 | 0.01 | 14.44 | 12.97 | 10.26 | .20 |
| .81 | 7.87 | 5.42 | 3.27 | 1.60 | 0.48 | 0.01 | 14.43 | 12.95 | 10.23 | .19 |
| .82 | 7.84 | 5.40 | 3.25 | 1.59 | 0.47 | 0.01 | 14.42 | 12.93 | 10.20 | .18 |
| .83 | 7.82 | 5.37 | 3.24 | 1.57 | 0.47 | 0.01 | 14.41 | 12.91 | 10.17 | .17 |
| .84 | 7.79 | 5.35 | 3.22 | 1.56 | 0.46 | 0.00 | 14.41 | 12.88 | 10.13 | .16 |
| .85 | 7.77 | 5.33 | 3.20 | 1.54 | 0.45 | 0.00 | 14.40 | 12.86 | 10.10 | .15 |
| .86 | 7.74 | 5.31 | 3.18 | 1.53 | 0.44 | 0.00 | 14.39 | 12.84 | 10.07 | .14 |
| .87 | 7.72 | 5.28 | 3.16 | 1.51 | 0.44 | 0.00 | 14.39 | 12.81 | 10.03 | .13 |
| .88 | 7.69 | 5.26 | 3.15 | 1.50 | 0.43 | 0.00 | 14.38 | 12.79 | 10.00 | .12 |
| .89 | 7.67 | 5.23 | 3.13 | 1.48 | 0.43 | 0.00 | 14.37 | 12.77 | 9.97 | .11 |
| .90 | 7.64 | 5.21 | 3.11 | 1.47 | 0.42 | 0.00 | 14.36 | 12.75 | 9.94 | .10 |
| .91 | 7.62 | 5.19 | 3.09 | 1.46 | 0.41 | 0.00 | 14.35 | 12.73 | 9.91 | .09 |
| .92 | 7.59 | 5.17 | 3.07 | 1.44 | 0.40 | 0.00 | 14.34 | 12.70 | 9.88 | .08 |
| .93 | 7.57 | 5.14 | 3.05 | 1.43 | 0.40 | 0.00 | 14.33 | 12.68 | 9.84 | .07 |
| .94 | 7.54 | 5.12 | 3.03 | 1.41 | 0.39 | 0.00 | 14.32 | 12.65 | 9.81 | .06 |
| .95 | 7.52 | 5.10 | 3.01 | 1.40 | 0.38 | 0.00 | 14.32 | 12.63 | 9.78 | .05 |
| .96 | 7.49 | 5.08 | 2.99 | 1.39 | 0.37 | 0.00 | 14.31 | 12.61 | 9.74 | .04 |
| .97 | 7.47 | 5.05 | 2.97 | 1.37 | 0.37 | 0.00 | 14.30 | 12.58 | 9.71 | .03 |
| .98 | 7.44 | 5.03 | 2.96 | 1.36 | 0.36 | 0.00 | 14.29 | 12.56 | 9.67 | .02 |
| .99 | 7.42 | 5.00 | 2.94 | 1.34 | 0.36 | 0.00 | 14.28 | 12.53 | 9.64 | .01 |
| 1.00 | 7.39 | 4.98 | 2.92 | 1.33 | 0.35 | 0.00 | 14.27 | 12.51 | 9.61 | .00 |
| Days. | 17 | 16 | 15 | 14 | 13 | 12 | 13 | 12 | 11 | Days. |

## TABLE XXIX.

(*Continued.*)

Period, 13.276498 days.

| Days. | 3 | 4 | 5 | 6 |
|---|---|---|---|---|
| Days. | ″ | ″ | ″ | ″ |
| .00 | 9.61 | 6.20 | 3.03 | 0.80 |
| .01 | 9.58 | 6.17 | 3.00 | 0.78 |
| .02 | 9.55 | 6.13 | 2.97 | 0.77 |
| .03 | 9.51 | 6.10 | 2.95 | 0.75 |
| .04 | 9.48 | 6.06 | 2.92 | 0.74 |
| .05 | 9.45 | 6.03 | 2.89 | 0.72 |
| .06 | 9.41 | 6.00 | 2.87 | 0.71 |
| .07 | 9.38 | 5.96 | 2.84 | 0.69 |
| .08 | 9.34 | 5.93 | 2.82 | 0.68 |
| .09 | 9.31 | 5.89 | 2.79 | 0.66 |
| .10 | 9.28 | 5.86 | 2.76 | 0.65 |
| .11 | 9.25 | 5.83 | 2.73 | 0.64 |
| .12 | 9.22 | 5.79 | 2.70 | 0.62 |
| .13 | 9.18 | 5.76 | 2.68 | 0.61 |
| .14 | 9.15 | 5.72 | 2.65 | 0.59 |
| .15 | 9.12 | 5.69 | 2.62 | 0.57 |
| .16 | 9.08 | 5.66 | 2.60 | 0.56 |
| .17 | 9.05 | 5.62 | 2.57 | 0.54 |
| .18 | 9.01 | 5.59 | 2.55 | 0.53 |
| .19 | 8.98 | 5.55 | 2.52 | 0.52 |
| .20 | 8.95 | 5.52 | 2.49 | 0.51 |
| .21 | 8.92 | 5.49 | 2.46 | 0.50 |
| .22 | 8.88 | 5.46 | 2.44 | 0.49 |
| .23 | 8.85 | 5.42 | 2.41 | 0.47 |
| .24 | 8.81 | 5.39 | 2.39 | 0.46 |
| .25 | 8.78 | 5.35 | 2.36 | 0.45 |
| .26 | 8.75 | 5.32 | 2.33 | 0.44 |
| .27 | 8.71 | 5.29 | 2.31 | 0.42 |
| .28 | 8.68 | 5.25 | 2.28 | 0.41 |
| .29 | 8.64 | 5.22 | 2.26 | 0.40 |
| .30 | 8.61 | 5.19 | 2.23 | 0.39 |
| .31 | 8.58 | 5.16 | 2.21 | 0.38 |
| .32 | 8.54 | 5.13 | 2.18 | 0.37 |
| .33 | 8.51 | 5.09 | 2.16 | 0.36 |
| .34 | 8.47 | 5.06 | 2.13 | 0.35 |
| .35 | 8.44 | 5.02 | 2.11 | 0.34 |
| .36 | 8.41 | 4.99 | 2.09 | 0.33 |
| .37 | 8.37 | 4.96 | 2.06 | 0.32 |
| .38 | 8.34 | 4.92 | 2.04 | 0.31 |
| .39 | 8.30 | 4.89 | 2.01 | 0.30 |
| .40 | 8.27 | 4.86 | 1.99 | 0.29 |
| .41 | 8.24 | 4.83 | 1.97 | 0.28 |
| .42 | 8.20 | 4.80 | 1.95 | 0.27 |
| .43 | 8.17 | 4.76 | 1.92 | 0.26 |
| .44 | 8.13 | 4.73 | 1.90 | 0.25 |
| .45 | 8.10 | 4.69 | 1.87 | 0.24 |
| .46 | 8.07 | 4.66 | 1.85 | 0.24 |
| .47 | 8.03 | 4.63 | 1.82 | 0.23 |
| .48 | 8.00 | 4.59 | 1.80 | 0.22 |
| .49 | 7.96 | 4.56 | 1.78 | 0.21 |
| .50 | 7.93 | 4.53 | 1.76 | 0.20 |
| Days. | 10 | 9 | 8 | 7 |

## TABLE XXX. ARG. 25.

Equation $= 2''.9\ [1 - \sin.\ (2t + z + x)]$.

Period, 9.36717 days.

| 0 | 1 | 2 | 3 | 4 | Days. |
|---|---|---|---|---|---|
| ″ | ″ | ″ | ″ | ″ | Days. |
| 5.73 | 5.50 | 4.14 | 2.24 | 0.63 | 1.00 |
| 5.74 | 5.49 | 4.12 | 2.22 | 0.62 | .99 |
| 5.74 | 5.48 | 4.11 | 2.20 | 0.61 | .98 |
| 5.75 | 5.48 | 4.09 | 2.18 | 0.59 | .97 |
| 5.75 | 5.47 | 4.07 | 2.16 | 0.58 | .96 |
| 5.76 | 5.46 | 4.05 | 2.14 | 0.57 | .95 |
| 5.76 | 5.45 | 4.03 | 2.13 | 0.56 | .94 |
| 5.76 | 5.44 | 4.02 | 2.11 | 0.55 | .93 |
| 5.77 | 5.43 | 4.00 | 2.09 | 0.53 | .92 |
| 5.77 | 5.42 | 3.98 | 2.07 | 0.52 | .91 |
| 5.77 | 5.41 | 3.96 | 2.05 | 0.51 | .90 |
| 5.77 | 5.40 | 3.94 | 2.03 | 0.50 | .89 |
| 5.78 | 5.39 | 3.93 | 2.01 | 0.49 | .88 |
| 5.78 | 5.38 | 3.91 | 1.99 | 0.48 | .87 |
| 5.78 | 5.37 | 3.89 | 1.98 | 0.47 | .86 |
| 5.78 | 5.36 | 3.87 | 1.96 | 0.46 | .85 |
| 5.79 | 5.35 | 3.85 | 1.94 | 0.44 | .84 |
| 5.79 | 5.33 | 3.84 | 1.92 | 0.43 | .83 |
| 5.79 | 5.32 | 3.82 | 1.90 | 0.42 | .82 |
| 5.79 | 5.31 | 3.80 | 1.89 | 0.41 | .81 |
| 5.79 | 5.30 | 3.78 | 1.87 | 0.40 | .80 |
| 5.79 | 5.29 | 3.76 | 1.85 | 0.39 | .79 |
| 5.79 | 5.28 | 3.74 | 1.83 | 0.38 | .78 |
| 5.80 | 5.27 | 3.72 | 1.82 | 0.37 | .77 |
| 5.80 | 5.26 | 3.70 | 1.80 | 0.36 | .76 |
| 5.80 | 5.25 | 3.68 | 1.78 | 0.35 | .75 |
| 5.80 | 5.23 | 3.67 | 1.76 | 0.35 | .74 |
| 5.80 | 5.22 | 3.65 | 1.74 | 0.34 | .73 |
| 5.80 | 5.21 | 3.63 | 1.73 | 0.33 | .72 |
| 5.80 | 5.20 | 3.61 | 1.71 | 0.32 | .71 |
| 5.80 | 5.19 | 3.59 | 1.69 | 0.31 | .70 |
| 5.80 | 5.18 | 3.57 | 1.67 | 0.30 | .69 |
| 5.80 | 5.17 | 3.55 | 1.65 | 0.29 | .68 |
| 5.80 | 5.15 | 3.53 | 1.64 | 0.28 | .67 |
| 5.80 | 5.14 | 3.51 | 1.62 | 0.28 | .66 |
| 5.80 | 5.13 | 3.49 | 1.60 | 0.27 | .65 |
| 5.80 | 5.12 | 3.48 | 1.58 | 0.26 | .64 |
| 5.80 | 5.11 | 3.46 | 1.56 | 0.25 | .63 |
| 5.79 | 5.09 | 3.44 | 1.55 | 0.24 | .62 |
| 5.79 | 5.08 | 3.42 | 1.53 | 0.24 | .61 |
| 5.79 | 5.07 | 3.40 | 1.51 | 0.23 | .60 |
| 5.79 | 5.06 | 3.38 | 1.49 | 0.22 | .59 |
| 5.79 | 5.04 | 3.36 | 1.47 | 0.21 | .58 |
| 5.78 | 5.03 | 3.34 | 1.46 | 0.21 | .57 |
| 5.78 | 5.01 | 3.32 | 1.44 | 0.20 | .56 |
| 5.78 | 5.00 | 3.30 | 1.42 | 0.19 | .55 |
| 5.78 | 4.99 | 3.28 | 1.41 | 0.19 | .54 |
| 5.78 | 4.97 | 3.26 | 1.39 | 0.18 | .53 |
| 5.77 | 4.96 | 3.24 | 1.36 | 0.17 | .52 |
| 5.77 | 4.94 | 3.22 | 1.36 | 0.17 | .51 |
| 5.77 | 4.93 | 3.20 | 1.34 | 0.16 | .50 |
| 9 | 8 | 7 | 6 | 5 | Days. |

# TABLE XXIX.

(*Continued.*)

Period, 13.276498 days.

| Days. | 3 | 4 | 5 | 6 |
|---|---|---|---|---|
| Days | " | " | " | " |
| .50 | 7.93 | 4.53 | 1.76 | 0.20 |
| .51 | 7.90 | 4.50 | 1.74 | 0.19 |
| .52 | 7.86 | 4.47 | 1.72 | 0.18 |
| .53 | 7.83 | 4.44 | 1.70 | 0.18 |
| .54 | 7.79 | 4.40 | 1.67 | 0.17 |
| .55 | 7.76 | 4.37 | 1.65 | 0.16 |
| .56 | 7.73 | 4.34 | 1.63 | 0.16 |
| .57 | 7.69 | 4.30 | 1.60 | 0.15 |
| .58 | 7.66 | 4.27 | 1.58 | 0.14 |
| .59 | 7.62 | 4.24 | 1.56 | 0.14 |
| .60 | 7.59 | 4.21 | 1.54 | 0.13 |
| .61 | 7.56 | 4.18 | 1.52 | 0.12 |
| .62 | 7.52 | 4.15 | 1.50 | 0.12 |
| .63 | 7.49 | 4.12 | 1.48 | 0.11 |
| .64 | 7.45 | 4.09 | 1.46 | 0.11 |
| .65 | 7.42 | 4.06 | 1.44 | 0.10 |
| .66 | 7.38 | 4.03 | 1.42 | 0.09 |
| .67 | 7.34 | 4.00 | 1.40 | 0.09 |
| .68 | 7.31 | 3.97 | 1.38 | 0.08 |
| .69 | 7.27 | 3.94 | 1.36 | 0.08 |
| .70 | 7.24 | 3.91 | 1.34 | 0.07 |
| .71 | 7.21 | 3.88 | 1.32 | 0.07 |
| .72 | 7.17 | 3.85 | 1.30 | 0.06 |
| .73 | 7.14 | 3.82 | 1.28 | 0.06 |
| .74 | 7.10 | 3.79 | 1.26 | 0.05 |
| .75 | 7.07 | 3.76 | 1.24 | 0.05 |
| .76 | 7.03 | 3.73 | 1.23 | 0.05 |
| .77 | 6.99 | 3.70 | 1.21 | 0.04 |
| .78 | 6.96 | 3.67 | 1.19 | 0.04 |
| .79 | 6.92 | 3.64 | 1.17 | 0.03 |
| .80 | 6.89 | 3.61 | 1.15 | 0.03 |
| .81 | 6.86 | 3.58 | 1.13 | 0.03 |
| .82 | 6.82 | 3.55 | 1.11 | 0.02 |
| .83 | 6 79 | 3.52 | 1.09 | 0.02 |
| .84 | 6.75 | 3.49 | 1.08 | 0.02 |
| .85 | 6.72 | 3.46 | 1.06 | 0.02 |
| .86 | 6.68 | 3.43 | 1.04 | 0.01 |
| .87 | 6.64 | 3.40 | 1.03 | 0.01 |
| .88 | 6.61 | 3.37 | 1.01 | 0.01 |
| .89 | 6.57 | 3.34 | 0.99 | 0.01 |
| .90 | 6.54 | 3.31 | 0.97 | 0.01 |
| .91 | 6.51 | 3.28 | 0.95 | 0.01 |
| .92 | 6.47 | 3.25 | 0.93 | 0.01 |
| .93 | 6.44 | 3.22 | 0.92 | 0.00 |
| .94 | 6.40 | 3.20 | 0.90 | 0.00 |
| .95 | 6.37 | 3.17 | 0.88 | 0.00 |
| .96 | 6.34 | 3.14 | 0.87 | 0.00 |
| .97 | 6.30 | 3.12 | 0.85 | 0.00 |
| .98 | 6.27 | 3.09 | 0.83 | 0.00 |
| .99 | 6.23 | 3.06 | 0.82 | 0.00 |
| 1.00 | 6.20 | 3.03 | 0.80 | 0.00 |
| Days. | 10 | 9 | 8 | 7 |

# TABLE XXX. ARG. 25.

Equation $= 2''.9\ [1 - \sin.\ (2t + z + x)]$.

Period, 9.36717 days.

| 0 | 1 | 2 | 3 | 4 | Days. |
|---|---|---|---|---|---|
| " | " | " | " | " | Days. |
| 5.77 | 4.93 | 3.20 | 1.34 | 0.16 | .50 |
| 5.77 | 4.92 | 3.18 | 1.32 | 0.15 | .49 |
| 5.76 | 4.90 | 3.16 | 1.31 | 0.15 | .48 |
| 5.76 | 4.89 | 3.14 | 1.29 | 0.14 | .47 |
| 5.76 | 4.87 | 3.12 | 1.28 | 0.14 | .46 |
| 5.75 | 4.86 | 3.10 | 1.26 | 0.13 | .45 |
| 5.75 | 4.85 | 3.09 | 1.25 | 0.12 | .44 |
| 5.75 | 4.83 | 3.07 | 1.23 | 0.12 | .43 |
| 5.74 | 4.82 | 3.05 | 1.22 | 0.11 | .42 |
| 5.74 | 4.80 | 3.03 | 1.20 | 0.11 | .41 |
| 5.74 | 4.79 | 3.01 | 1.19 | 0.10 | .40 |
| 5.73 | 4.77 | 2.99 | 1.17 | 0.10 | .39 |
| 5.73 | 4.76 | 2.97 | 1.16 | 0.09 | .38 |
| 5.73 | 4.74 | 2.95 | 1.14 | 0.09 | .37 |
| 5.73 | 4.73 | 2.93 | 1.13 | 0.08 | .36 |
| 5.72 | 4.71 | 2.91 | 1.11 | 0.08 | .35 |
| 5.72 | 4.70 | 2.90 | 1.10 | 0.08 | .34 |
| 5.71 | 4.68 | 2.88 | 1.08 | 0.07 | .33 |
| 5.71 | 4.67 | 2.86 | 1.07 | 0.07 | .32 |
| 5.70 | 4.65 | 2.84 | 1.05 | 0.06 | .31 |
| 5.70 | 4.64 | 2.82 | 1.04 | 0.06 | .30 |
| 5.69 | 4.62 | 2.80 | 1.02 | 0.06 | .29 |
| 5.69 | 4.61 | 2.78 | 1.01 | 0.05 | .28 |
| 5.68 | 4.59 | 2.76 | 0.99 | 0.05 | .27 |
| 5.68 | 4.58 | 2.74 | 0.98 | 0.05 | .26 |
| 5.67 | 4.56 | 2.72 | 0.96 | 0.04 | .25 |
| 5.67 | 4.54 | 2.71 | 0.95 | 0.04 | .24 |
| 5.66 | 4.53 | 2.69 | 0.93 | 0.04 | .23 |
| 5.66 | 4.51 | 2.67 | 0.92 | 0.04 | .22 |
| 5.65 | 4.50 | 2.65 | 0.90 | 0.03 | .21 |
| 5.65 | 4.48 | 2.63 | 0.89 | 0.03 | .20 |
| 5.64 | 4.46 | 2.61 | 0.88 | 0.03 | .19 |
| 5.63 | 4.45 | 2.59 | 0.86 | 0.03 | .18 |
| 5.63 | 4.43 | 2.57 | 0.85 | 0.02 | .17 |
| 5.62 | 4.41 | 2.55 | 0.83 | 0.02 | .16 |
| 5.61 | 4.40 | 2.53 | 0.82 | 0.02 | .15 |
| 5.61 | 4.38 | 2.51 | 0.81 | 0.02 | .14 |
| 5.60 | 4.36 | 2.49 | 0.79 | 0.02 | .13 |
| 5.59 | 4.35 | 2.47 | 0.78 | 0.01 | .12 |
| 5.59 | 4.33 | 2.45 | 0.76 | 0.01 | .11 |
| 5.58 | 4.31 | 2.43 | 0.75 | 0.01 | .10 |
| 5.57 | 4.29 | 2.41 | 0.74 | 0.01 | .09 |
| 5.56 | 4.28 | 2.39 | 0.73 | 0.01 | .08 |
| 5.56 | 4.26 | 2.37 | 0.71 | 0.01 | .07 |
| 5.55 | 4.24 | 2.35 | 0.70 | 0.00 | .06 |
| 5.54 | 4.23 | 2.33 | 0.69 | 0.00 | .05 |
| 5.53 | 4.21 | 2.32 | 0.68 | 0.00 | .04 |
| 5.52 | 4.19 | 2.30 | 0.67 | 0.00 | .03 |
| 5.52 | 4.18 | 2.28 | 0.65 | 0.00 | .02 |
| 5.51 | 4.16 | 2.26 | 0.64 | 0.00 | .01 |
| 5.50 | 4.14 | 2.24 | 0.63 | 0.00 | .00 |
| 9 | 8 | 7 | 6 | 5 | Days. |

# TABLES XXXI-LXXXI.

ARGUMENTS, PERIODS, AND EQUATIONS.

| TABLE. | ARGUMENT. | PERIOD. | EQUATION. |
|---|---|---|---|
| | | Days. | |
| XXXI. | 26 | 5.822606 | $1''.9 + 1''.9 \sin. (4t + x).$ |
| XXXII. | 27 | 25.82638 | $1.6 + 0.8 \sin. (2x - t) - 0''.9 \sin. (4x - 2t).$ |
| XXXIII. | 28 | 38.52204 | $7.5 + 7.5 \sin. (2t - 2z - x).$ |
| XXXIV. | 29 | 32.76364 | $6.3 - 6.3 \sin. (2t + x - 2y).$ |
| XXXV. | 30 | 10.37093 | $3.8 + 3.8 \sin. (4t - x - z).$ |
| XXXVI. | 31 | 15.31442 | $3.0 - 3.0 \sin. (3t - x).$ |
| XXXVII. | 32 | 16.63016 | $3.0 + 3.0 \sin. (4t - 2x - z).$ |
| XXXVIII. | 33 | 32.45058 | $2.1 + 2.1 \sin. (x - 2z).$ |
| XXXIX. | 34 | 27.09271 | $2.0 - 2.0 \sin. (2t + 2z - x).$ |
| XL. | 35 | 23.94223 | $1.2 - 1.2 \sin. (x + 2z).$ |
| XLI. | 36 | 13.71881 | $1.0 + 1.0 \sin. (t + z + x).$ |
| XLII. | 37 | 37.62533 | $0.5 + 0.5 \sin. (4t - 3x).$ |
| XLIII. | 38 | 18.78878 | $0.4 - 0.4 \sin. (t + 2x).$ |
| XLIV. | 39 | 34.47528 | $0.6 - 0.6 \sin. (3t - 2x).$ |
| XLV. | 40 | 18.84354 | $0.4 + 0.4 \sin. (3x - z).$ |
| XLVI. | 41 | 17.91910 | $0.4 - 0.4 \sin. (3x + z).$ |
| XLVII. | 42 | 10.14791 | $0.3 + 0.3 \sin. (2t + x - 2z).$ |
| XLVIII. | 43 | 14.53786 | $0.6 + 0.6 \sin. (2t + 2x - z).$ |
| XLIX. | 44 | 22.78614 | $0.3 - 0.3 \sin. (3x - 2t + z).$ |
| L. | 45 | 16.90004 | $0.2 - 0.2 \sin. (2t + x + 2y).$ |
| LI. | 46 | 29.01328 | $0.4 - 0.4 \sin. (x + z - 2y).$ |
| LII. | 47 | 14.13256 | $1.3 + 1.3 \sin. (2y - z).$ |
| LIII. | 48 | 14.96709 | $0.5 - 0.5 \sin. (2t + 2x - 2y).$ |
| LIV. | 49 | 12.76271 | $0.2 - 0.2 \sin. (2x - 2t + 2y).$ |
| LV. | 50 | 25.03597 | $0.4 - 0.4 \sin. (2y + z - x).$ |
| LVI. | 51 | 18.21692 | $0.2 - 0.2 \sin. (x + 2y).$ |
| LVII. | 52 | 25.23137 | $1.0 + 1.0 \sin. (2y - t).$ |
| LVIII. | 53 | 117.53942 | $2.6 - 2.6 \sin. (2y - 2t + z).$ |
| LIX. | 54 | 15.06989 | $1.2 + 1.2 \sin. (4t - z).$ |
| LX. | 55 | 19.62730 | $0.9 - 0.9 \sin. (4t - x + z).$ |
| LXI. | 56 | 13.11748 | $0.7 - 0.7 \sin. (2y + z).$ |
| LXII. | 57 | 16.98741 | $0.8 + 0.8 \sin. (2t + 3x).$ |
| LXIII. | 58 | 15.24221 | $0.5 - 0.5 \sin. (4t - 2x + z).$ |
| LXIV. | 59 | 38.96397 | $0.6 - 0.6 \sin. (x - 4t + 2y).$ |
| LXV. | 60 | 22.32171 | $0.4 - 0.4 \sin. (x - 2t + 2y + z).$ |
| LXVI. | 61 | 13.60611 | $0.4 + 0.4 \sin. (4y).$ |
| LXVII. | 62 | 14.44200 | $0.3 + 0.3 \sin. (2t + 2y - z).$ |
| LXVIII. | 63 | 13.63340 | $0.3 + 0.3 \sin. (u + y).$ |
| LXIX. | 64 | 35.99212 | $0.3 - 0.3 \sin. (2t + x - 2y - z).$ |
| LXX. | 65 | 14.47277 | $0.2 - 0.2 \sin. (4t + z).$ |
| LXXI. | 66 | 35.59582 | $0.2 - 0.2 \sin. (3t - 2y).$ |
| LXXII. | 67 | 27.44332 | $1.0 - 1.0 \sin. (x + y - u).$ |
| LXXIII. | 68 | 27.66669 | $0.7 + 0.7 \sin. (x - y + u).$ |
| LXXIV. | 69 | 471.89326 | $2.2 - 2.2 \sin. (2x - 2t - z).$ |
| LXXV. | 70 | 329.79056 | $1.5 + 1.5 \sin. (2y - z - 2t).$ |
| LXXVI. | 71 | 583.921 | $1.3 - 1.1 \sin. (♀ - \oplus) + 0''.4 \sin. 2 (♀ - \oplus).$ |
| LXXVII. | 72 | 398.884 | $0.8 + 0.7 \sin. (\oplus - ♃) - 0''.2 \sin. 2 (\oplus - ♃).$ |
| LXXVIII. | 73 | 1095.1653 | $2.0 + 2.0 \sin. (2y - 2x).$ |
| LXXIX. | 74 | 3232.8202 | $0.5 + 0.5 \sin. (t - x + z).$ |
| LXXX. | 75 | 84753.24 | $53.2 + 23.2 \sin. (8g'' - 13z + 315^\circ 30').$ |
| LXXXI. | 76 | 95489.94 | $65.64 + 27.4 \sin. (18g'' - 16z - x + 35^\circ 20'.2).$ |

# TABLE XXXI. ARGUMENT 26.

Equation = 1″.9 [1 + sin. (4*t* + *x*)].

Period, 5.822606 days.

| Days. | 0 | 1 | 2 | Days. | Days. | 0 | 1 | 2 | Days. |
|---|---|---|---|---|---|---|---|---|---|
| Days. | ″ | ″ | ″ | Days. | Days. | ″ | ″ | ″ | Days. |
| .00 | 0.01 | 0.85 | 2.80 | 1.00 | .50 | 0.18 | 1.81 | 3.53 | .50 |
| .01 | 0.01 | 0.87 | 2.82 | .99 | .51 | 0.19 | 1.83 | 3.54 | .49 |
| .02 | 0.01 | 0.89 | 2.84 | .98 | .52 | 0.20 | 1.85 | 3.55 | .48 |
| .03 | 0.01 | 0.91 | 2.85 | .97 | .53 | 0.21 | 1.87 | 3.56 | .47 |
| .04 | 0.01 | 0.92 | 2.87 | .96 | .54 | 0.22 | 1.89 | 3.57 | .46 |
| .05 | 0.01 | 0.94 | 2.89 | .95 | .55 | 0.23 | 1.91 | 3.58 | .45 |
| .06 | 0.00 | 0.96 | 2.90 | .94 | .56 | 0.24 | 1.93 | 3.58 | .44 |
| .07 | 0.00 | 0.97 | 2.92 | .93 | .57 | 0.25 | 1.95 | 3.59 | .43 |
| .08 | 0.00 | 0.99 | 2.93 | .92 | .58 | 0.26 | 1.97 | 3.60 | .42 |
| .09 | 0.00 | 1.01 | 2.95 | .91 | .59 | 0.27 | 1.99 | 3.61 | .41 |
| .10 | 0.00 | 1.03 | 2.97 | .90 | .60 | 0.28 | 2.01 | 3.62 | .40 |
| .11 | 0.00 | 1.05 | 2.99 | .89 | .61 | 0.29 | 2.03 | 3.63 | .39 |
| .12 | 0.00 | 1.07 | 3.00 | .88 | .62 | 0.30 | 2.05 | 3.64 | .38 |
| .13 | 0.00 | 1.09 | 3.02 | .87 | .63 | 0.31 | 2.07 | 3.65 | .37 |
| .14 | 0.00 | 1.11 | 3.03 | .86 | .64 | 0.33 | 2.09 | 3.65 | .36 |
| .15 | 0.00 | 1.12 | 3.05 | .85 | .65 | 0.34 | 2.11 | 3.66 | .35 |
| .16 | 0.01 | 1.14 | 3.07 | .84 | .66 | 0.35 | 2.14 | 3.67 | .34 |
| .17 | 0.01 | 1.16 | 3.08 | .83 | .67 | 0.37 | 2.16 | 3.68 | .33 |
| .18 | 0.01 | 1.18 | 3.10 | .82 | .68 | 0.38 | 2.18 | 3.68 | .32 |
| .19 | 0.01 | 1.20 | 3.11 | .81 | .69 | 0.39 | 2.20 | 3.69 | .31 |
| .20 | 0.01 | 1.22 | 3.13 | .80 | .70 | 0.40 | 2.22 | 3.70 | .30 |
| .21 | 0.01 | 1.24 | 3.15 | .79 | .71 | 0.41 | 2.24 | 3.71 | .29 |
| .22 | 0.01 | 1.26 | 3.16 | .78 | .72 | 0.42 | 2.26 | 3.71 | .28 |
| .23 | 0.02 | 1.28 | 3.18 | .77 | .73 | 0.44 | 2.28 | 3.72 | .27 |
| .24 | 0.02 | 1.30 | 3.19 | .76 | .74 | 0.45 | 2.30 | 3.72 | .26 |
| .25 | 0.02 | 1.31 | 3.21 | .75 | .75 | 0.46 | 2.32 | 3.73 | .25 |
| .26 | 0.03 | 1.33 | 3.22 | .74 | .76 | 0.48 | 2.34 | 3.74 | .24 |
| .27 | 0.03 | 1.35 | 3.23 | .73 | .77 | 0.49 | 2.36 | 3.74 | .23 |
| .28 | 0.04 | 1.37 | 3.25 | .72 | .78 | 0.51 | 2.38 | 3.75 | .22 |
| .29 | 0.04 | 1.39 | 3.26 | .71 | .79 | 0.52 | 2.40 | 3.75 | .21 |
| .30 | 0.04 | 1.41 | 3.28 | .70 | .80 | 0.53 | 2.42 | 3.76 | .20 |
| .31 | 0.05 | 1.43 | 3.29 | .69 | .81 | 0.54 | 2.44 | 3.76 | .19 |
| .32 | 0.05 | 1.45 | 3.31 | .68 | .82 | 0.56 | 2.46 | 3.77 | .18 |
| .33 | 0.06 | 1.47 | 3.32 | .67 | .83 | 0.57 | 2.48 | 3.77 | .17 |
| .34 | 0.06 | 1.49 | 3.34 | .66 | .84 | 0.59 | 2.50 | 3.77 | .16 |
| .35 | 0.07 | 1.51 | 3.35 | .65 | .85 | 0.60 | 2.52 | 3.78 | .15 |
| .36 | 0.08 | 1.53 | 3.36 | .64 | .86 | 0.62 | 2.54 | 3.78 | .14 |
| .37 | 0.08 | 1.55 | 3.38 | .63 | .87 | 0.64 | 2.56 | 3.78 | .13 |
| .38 | 0.09 | 1.57 | 3.39 | .62 | .88 | 0.65 | 2.58 | 3.79 | .12 |
| .39 | 0.09 | 1.59 | 3.41 | .61 | .89 | 0.67 | 2.60 | 3.79 | .11 |
| .40 | 0.10 | 1.61 | 3.42 | .60 | .90 | 0.68 | 2.62 | 3.79 | .10 |
| .41 | 0.11 | 1.63 | 3.43 | .59 | .91 | 0.70 | 2.64 | 3.79 | .09 |
| .42 | 0.12 | 1.65 | 3.44 | .58 | .92 | 0.72 | 2.66 | 3.79 | .08 |
| .43 | 0.13 | 1.67 | 3.45 | .57 | .93 | 0.73 | 2.68 | 3.79 | .07 |
| .44 | 0.13 | 1.69 | 3.46 | .56 | .94 | 0.75 | 2.69 | 3.79 | .06 |
| .45 | 0.14 | 1.71 | 3.48 | .55 | .95 | 0.76 | 2.71 | 3.80 | .05 |
| .46 | 0.15 | 1.73 | 3.49 | .54 | .96 | 0.78 | 2.73 | 3.80 | .04 |
| .47 | 0.15 | 1.75 | 3.50 | .53 | .97 | 0.80 | 2.74 | 3.80 | .03 |
| .48 | 0.16 | 1.77 | 3.51 | .52 | .98 | 0.81 | 2.76 | 3.80 | .02 |
| .49 | 0.17 | 1.79 | 3.52 | .51 | .99 | 0.83 | 2.78 | 3.80 | .01 |
| .50 | 0.18 | 1.81 | 3.53 | .50 | 1.00 | 0.85 | 2.80 | 3.80 | .00 |
| Days. | 5 | 4 | 3 | Days. | Days. | 5 | 4 | 3 | Days. |

# TABLES XXXII - XXXVI.

| Table | XXXII. | | |
|---|---|---|---|
| Argument | **27.** | | |
| Days. | **0** | **10** | **20** |
| Days | ″ | ″ | ″ |
| 0.0 | 1.65 | 1.96 | 2.62 |
| 0.1 | 1.59 | 1.97 | 2.66 |
| 0.2 | 1.52 | 1.98 | 2.70 |
| 0.3 | 1.46 | 1.98 | 2.73 |
| 0.4 | 1.39 | 1.99 | 2.77 |
| 0.5 | 1.33 | 1.99 | 2.80 |
| 0.6 | 1.27 | 1.99 | 2.83 |
| 0.7 | 1.21 | 1.99 | 2.86 |
| 0.8 | 1.15 | 1.99 | 2.89 |
| 0.9 | 1.09 | 1.98 | 2.92 |
| 1.0 | 1.03 | 1.98 | 2.95 |
| 1.1 | 0.97 | 1.97 | 2.97 |
| 1.2 | 0.92 | 1.96 | 3.00 |
| 1.3 | 0.86 | 1.95 | 3.02 |
| 1.4 | 0.81 | 1.93 | 3.04 |
| 1.5 | 0.76 | 1.92 | 3.06 |
| 1.6 | 0.71 | 1.90 | 3.07 |
| 1.7 | 0.66 | 1.89 | 3.08 |
| 1.8 | 0.61 | 1.87 | 3.09 |
| 1.9 | 0.57 | 1.85 | 3.10 |
| 2.0 | 0.52 | 1.83 | 3.11 |
| 2.1 | 0.48 | 1.81 | 3.11 |
| 2.2 | 0.44 | 1.79 | 3.11 |
| 2.3 | 0.40 | 1.77 | 3.10 |
| 2.4 | 0.37 | 1.74 | 3.10 |
| 2.5 | 0.33 | 1.72 | 3.09 |
| 2.6 | 0.30 | 1.70 | 3.08 |
| 2.7 | 0.27 | 1.67 | 3.06 |
| 2.8 | 0.24 | 1.65 | 3.05 |
| 2.9 | 0.22 | 1.62 | 3.03 |
| 3.0 | 0.19 | 1.60 | 3.01 |
| 3.1 | 0.17 | 1.58 | 2.98 |
| 3.2 | 0.15 | 1.55 | 2.96 |
| 3.3 | 0.14 | 1.53 | 2.93 |
| 3.4 | 0.12 | 1.50 | 2.90 |
| 3.5 | 0.11 | 1.48 | 2.87 |
| 3.6 | 0.10 | 1.46 | 2.83 |
| 3.7 | 0.10 | 1.43 | 2.80 |
| 3.8 | 0.09 | 1.41 | 2.76 |
| 3.9 | 0.09 | 1.39 | 2.72 |
| 4.0 | 0.09 | 1.37 | 2.68 |
| 4.1 | 0.10 | 1.35 | 2.63 |
| 4.2 | 0.11 | 1.33 | 2.59 |
| 4.3 | 0.12 | 1.31 | 2.54 |
| 4.4 | 0.13 | 1.30 | 2.49 |
| 4.5 | 0.14 | 1.28 | 2.44 |
| 4.6 | 0.16 | 1.27 | 2.39 |
| 4.7 | 0.18 | 1.25 | 2.34 |
| 4.8 | 0.20 | 1.24 | 2.28 |
| 4.9 | 0.23 | 1.23 | 2.23 |
| 5.0 | 0.25 | 1.22 | 2.17 |

| Table | XXXIII. | | XXXIV. | | XXXV. | XXXVI. | |
|---|---|---|---|---|---|---|---|
| Argument | **28.** | | **29.** | | **30.** | **31.** | |
| Days. | **0** | **10** | **0** | **10** | **0** | **0** | Days. |
| Days. | ″ | ″ | ″ | ″ | ″ | ″ | Days. |
| 0.0 | 0.05 | 7.05 | 1.45 | 4.15 | 7.50 | 4.72 | 10.0 |
| 0.1 | 0.04 | 7.17 | 1.38 | 4.26 | 7.44 | 4.81 | 9.9 |
| 0.2 | 0.03 | 7.29 | 1.30 | 4.38 | 7.37 | 4.91 | 9.8 |
| 0.3 | 0.02 | 7.41 | 1.23 | 4.49 | 7.30 | 5.00 | 9.7 |
| 0.4 | 0.01 | 7.53 | 1.16 | 4.61 | 7.20 | 5.09 | 9.6 |
| 0.5 | 0.01 | 7.65 | 1.09 | 4.72 | 7.08 | 5.18 | 9.5 |
| 0.6 | 0.00 | 7.77 | 1.02 | 4.84 | 6.96 | 5.26 | 9.4 |
| 0.7 | 0.00 | 7.89 | 0.96 | 4.96 | 6.83 | 5.34 | 9.3 |
| 0.8 | 0.00 | 8.02 | 0.89 | 5.07 | 6.68 | 5.42 | 9.2 |
| 0.9 | 0.01 | 8.14 | 0.83 | 5.19 | 6.53 | 5.49 | 9.1 |
| 1.0 | 0.01 | 8.27 | 0.77 | 5.31 | 6.36 | 5.56 | 9.0 |
| 1.1 | 0.02 | 8.39 | 0.71 | 5.43 | 6.18 | 5.62 | 8.9 |
| 1.2 | 0.03 | 8.51 | 0.66 | 5.55 | 6.00 | 5.68 | 8.8 |
| 1.3 | 0.04 | 8.63 | 0.60 | 5.68 | 5.81 | 5.73 | 8.7 |
| 1.4 | 0.05 | 8.76 | 0.55 | 5.80 | 5.61 | 5.78 | 8.6 |
| 1.5 | 0.06 | 8.88 | 0.50 | 5.92 | 5.41 | 5.82 | 8.5 |
| 1.6 | 0.07 | 9.00 | 0.46 | 6.04 | 5.20 | 5.86 | 8.4 |
| 1.7 | 0.09 | 9.12 | 0.41 | 6.16 | 4.98 | 5.89 | 8.3 |
| 1.8 | 0.11 | 9.24 | 0.37 | 6.29 | 4.76 | 5.92 | 8.2 |
| 1.9 | 0.14 | 9.36 | 0.33 | 6.41 | 4.54 | 5.95 | 8.1 |
| 2.0 | 0.16 | 9.47 | 0.29 | 6.53 | 4.31 | 5.97 | 8.0 |
| 2.1 | 0.19 | 9.59 | 0.26 | 6.65 | 4.08 | 5.99 | 7.9 |
| 2.2 | 0.22 | 9.70 | 0.23 | 6.77 | 3.85 | 6.00 | 7.8 |
| 2.3 | 0.25 | 9.82 | 0.20 | 6.89 | 3.62 | 6.00 | 7.7 |
| 2.4 | 0.28 | 9.94 | 0.17 | 7.01 | 3.39 | 6.00 | 7.6 |
| 2.5 | 0.31 | 10.06 | 0.14 | 7.13 | 3.16 | 5.99 | 7.5 |
| 2.6 | 0.34 | 10.17 | 0.12 | 7.25 | 2.93 | 5.98 | 7.4 |
| 2.7 | 0.38 | 10.29 | 0.10 | 7.37 | 2.71 | 5.96 | 7.3 |
| 2.8 | 0.42 | 10.40 | 0.08 | 7.49 | 2.49 | 5.94 | 7.2 |
| 2.9 | 0.47 | 10.52 | 0.06 | 7.61 | 2.28 | 5.92 | 7.1 |
| 3.0 | 0.50 | 10.63 | 0.04 | 7.73 | 2.07 | 5.89 | 7.0 |
| 3.1 | 0.55 | 10.74 | 0.03 | 7.85 | 1.87 | 5.86 | 6.9 |
| 3.2 | 0.60 | 10.85 | 0.02 | 7.97 | 1.68 | 5.82 | 6.8 |
| 3.3 | 0.65 | 10.96 | 0.01 | 8.08 | 1.49 | 5.77 | 6.7 |
| 3.4 | 0.70 | 11.06 | 0.01 | 8.20 | 1.31 | 5.72 | 6.6 |
| 3.5 | 0.75 | 11.17 | 0.00 | 8.31 | 1.14 | 5.67 | 6.5 |
| 3.6 | 0.80 | 11.27 | 0.00 | 8.42 | 0.99 | 5.61 | 6.4 |
| 3.7 | 0.86 | 11.38 | 0.00 | 8.54 | 0.84 | 5.55 | 6.3 |
| 3.8 | 0.92 | 11.48 | 0.01 | 8.65 | 0.70 | 5.48 | 6.2 |
| 3.9 | 0.98 | 11.59 | 0.01 | 8.76 | 0.57 | 5.41 | 6.1 |
| 4.0 | 1.03 | 11.69 | 0.02 | 8.87 | 0.45 | 5.33 | 6.0 |
| 4.1 | 1.09 | 11.79 | 0.03 | 8.98 | 0.35 | 5.25 | 5.9 |
| 4.2 | 1.16 | 11.89 | 0.04 | 9.09 | 0.26 | 5.17 | 5.8 |
| 4.3 | 1.23 | 11.99 | 0.06 | 9.20 | 0.18 | 5.09 | 5.7 |
| 4.4 | 1.30 | 12.08 | 0.07 | 9.30 | 0.12 | 5.00 | 5.6 |
| 4.5 | 1.37 | 12.18 | 0.09 | 9.41 | 0.07 | 4.91 | 5.5 |
| 4.6 | 1.44 | 12.27 | 0.11 | 9.51 | 0.03 | 4.81 | 5.4 |
| 4.7 | 1.51 | 12.37 | 0.13 | 9.61 | 0.01 | 4.71 | 5.3 |
| 4.8 | 1.59 | 12.46 | 0.16 | 9.71 | 0.00 | 4.60 | 5.2 |
| 4.9 | 1.66 | 12.55 | 0.18 | 9.81 | 0.01 | 4.49 | 5.1 |
| 5.0 | 1.74 | 12.64 | 0.21 | 9.91 | 0.03 | 4.38 | 5.0 |
| Days. | **30** | **20** | **30** | **20** | **10** | **10** | Days. |

# TABLES XXXII - XXXVI.

| Table | XXXII. | | |
|---|---|---|---|
| Argument | **27.** | | |
| Days. | **0** | **10** | **20** |
| Days | " | " | " |
| 5.0 | 0.25 | 1.22 | 2.17 |
| 5.1 | 0.28 | 1.22 | 2.11 |
| 5.2 | 0.31 | 1.21 | 2.05 |
| 5.3 | 0.34 | 1.21 | 1.99 |
| 5.4 | 0.37 | 1.21 | 1.93 |
| 5.5 | 0.40 | 1.21 | 1.87 |
| 5.6 | 0.43 | 1.21 | 1.81 |
| 5.7 | 0.47 | 1.22 | 1.74 |
| 5.8 | 0.50 | 1.22 | 1.67 |
| 5.9 | 0.54 | 1.23 | 1.61 |
| 6.0 | 0.58 | 1.24 | 1.55 |
| 6.1 | 0.62 | 1.25 | 1.49 |
| 6.2 | 0.66 | 1.26 | 1.42 |
| 6.3 | 0.70 | 1.28 | 1.36 |
| 6.4 | 0.75 | 1.29 | 1.30 |
| 6.5 | 0.79 | 1.31 | 1.24 |
| 6.6 | 0.83 | 1.33 | 1.18 |
| 6.7 | 0.88 | 1.35 | 1.12 |
| 6.8 | 0.92 | 1.37 | 1.06 |
| 6.9 | 0.97 | 1.40 | 1.00 |
| 7.0 | 1.01 | 1.42 | 0.94 |
| 7.1 | 1.05 | 1.45 | 0.88 |
| 7.2 | 1.10 | 1.48 | 0.83 |
| 7.3 | 1.14 | 1.51 | 0.77 |
| 7.4 | 1.19 | 1.54 | 0.72 |
| 7.5 | 1.23 | 1.57 | 0.67 |
| 7.6 | 1.27 | 1.61 | 0.62 |
| 7.7 | 1.32 | 1.64 | 0.57 |
| 7.8 | 1.36 | 1.68 | 0.53 |
| 7.9 | 1.40 | 1.72 | 0.48 |
| 8.0 | 1.44 | 1.76 | 0.44 |
| 8.1 | 1.48 | 1.80 | 0.40 |
| 8.2 | 1.52 | 1.84 | 0.37 |
| 8.3 | 1.56 | 1.88 | 0.33 |
| 8.4 | 1.59 | 1.93 | 0.30 |
| 8.5 | 1.63 | 1.97 | 0.27 |
| 8.6 | 1.66 | 2.01 | 0.25 |
| 8.7 | 1.69 | 2.06 | 0.22 |
| 8.8 | 1.72 | 2.10 | 0.20 |
| 8.9 | 1.75 | 2.15 | 0.18 |
| 9.0 | 1.78 | 2.19 | 0.16 |
| 9.1 | 1.80 | 2.23 | 0.14 |
| 9.2 | 1.83 | 2.28 | 0.13 |
| 9.3 | 1.85 | 2.32 | 0.12 |
| 9.4 | 1.87 | 2.37 | 0.11 |
| 9.5 | 1.89 | 2.41 | 0.11 |
| 9.6 | 1.91 | 2.45 | 0.10 |
| 9.7 | 1.92 | 2.50 | 0.10 |
| 9.8 | 1.94 | 2.54 | 0.10 |
| 9.9 | 1.95 | 2.58 | 0.10 |
| 10.0 | 1.96 | 2.62 | 0.11 |

| Table | XXXIII. | | XXXIV. | | XXXV. | XXXVI. | |
|---|---|---|---|---|---|---|---|
| Argument | **28.** | | **29.** | | **30.** | **31.** | |
| Days. | **0** | **10** | **0** | **10** | **0** | **0** | Days. |
| Days. | " | " | " | " | " | " | Days. |
| 5.0 | 1.74 | 12.64 | 0.21 | 9.91 | 0.03 | 4.38 | 5.0 |
| 5.1 | 1.82 | 12.73 | 0.24 | 10.01 | 0.06 | 4.27 | 4.9 |
| 5.2 | 1.90 | 12.82 | 0.27 | 10.10 | 0.11 | 4.16 | 4.8 |
| 5.3 | 1.98 | 12.91 | 0.31 | 10.20 | 0.17 | 4.05 | 4.7 |
| 5.4 | 2.06 | 12.99 | 0.35 | 10.29 | 0.24 | 3.93 | 4.6 |
| 5.5 | 2.14 | 13.07 | 0.39 | 10.38 | 0.32 | 3.81 | 4.5 |
| 5.6 | 2.23 | 13.15 | 0.44 | 10.47 | 0.42 | 3.69 | 4.4 |
| 5.7 | 2.32 | 13.23 | 0.48 | 10.56 | 0.54 | 3.57 | 4.3 |
| 5.8 | 2.41 | 13.31 | 0.53 | 10.65 | 0.66 | 3.45 | 4.2 |
| 5.9 | 2.50 | 13.39 | 0.58 | 10.73 | 0.79 | 3.33 | 4.1 |
| 6.0 | 2.59 | 13.46 | 0.63 | 10.82 | 0.94 | 3.21 | 4.0 |
| 6.1 | 2.68 | 13.54 | 0.67 | 10.90 | 1.10 | 3.09 | 3.9 |
| 6.2 | 2.78 | 13.61 | 0.75 | 10.98 | 1.27 | 2.97 | 3.8 |
| 6.3 | 2.88 | 13.68 | 0.81 | 11.06 | 1.45 | 2.85 | 3.7 |
| 6.4 | 2.98 | 13.75 | 0.87 | 11.14 | 1.63 | 2.72 | 3.6 |
| 6.5 | 3.08 | 13.82 | 0.93 | 11.22 | 1.82 | 2.60 | 3.5 |
| 6.6 | 3.18 | 13.88 | 1.00 | 11.29 | 2.02 | 2.47 | 3.4 |
| 6.7 | 3.28 | 13.94 | 1.07 | 11.36 | 2.23 | 2.35 | 3.3 |
| 6.8 | 3.38 | 14.00 | 1.14 | 11.43 | 2.44 | 2.23 | 3.2 |
| 6.9 | 3.48 | 14.06 | 1.21 | 11.50 | 2.65 | 2.11 | 3.1 |
| 7.0 | 3.59 | 14.12 | 1.28 | 11.57 | 2.87 | 2.00 | 3.0 |
| 7.1 | 3.69 | 14.18 | 1.36 | 11.63 | 3.09 | 1.88 | 2.9 |
| 7.2 | 3.80 | 14.23 | 1.43 | 11.69 | 3.32 | 1.77 | 2.8 |
| 7.3 | 3.90 | 14.28 | 1.51 | 11.75 | 3.55 | 1.66 | 2.7 |
| 7.4 | 4.01 | 14.33 | 1.59 | 11.81 | 3.78 | 1.55 | 2.6 |
| 7.5 | 4.12 | 14.38 | 1.67 | 11.87 | 4.01 | 1.44 | 2.5 |
| 7.6 | 4.23 | 14.43 | 1.75 | 11.92 | 4.24 | 1.34 | 2.4 |
| 7.7 | 4.34 | 14.48 | 1.83 | 11.98 | 4.47 | 1.24 | 2.3 |
| 7.8 | 4.45 | 14.52 | 1.92 | 12.03 | 4.70 | 1.14 | 2.2 |
| 7.9 | 4.56 | 14.56 | 2.00 | 12.08 | 4.92 | 1.04 | 2.1 |
| 8.0 | 4.67 | 14.60 | 2.09 | 12.13 | 5.14 | 0.95 | 2.0 |
| 8.1 | 4.78 | 14.64 | 2.18 | 12.17 | 5.35 | 0.86 | 1.9 |
| 8.2 | 4.90 | 14.67 | 2.27 | 12.21 | 5.56 | 0.78 | 1.8 |
| 8.3 | 5.02 | 14.71 | 2.36 | 12.25 | 5.76 | 0.70 | 1.7 |
| 8.4 | 5.14 | 14.74 | 2.46 | 12.29 | 5.95 | 0.62 | 1.6 |
| 8.5 | 5.26 | 14.77 | 2.55 | 12.33 | 6.13 | 0.55 | 1.5 |
| 8.6 | 5.38 | 14.80 | 2.65 | 12.36 | 6.31 | 0.48 | 1.4 |
| 8.7 | 5.50 | 14.83 | 2.75 | 12.39 | 6.48 | 0.42 | 1.3 |
| 8.8 | 5.62 | 14.85 | 2.85 | 12.42 | 6.63 | 0.36 | 1.2 |
| 8.9 | 5.74 | 14.88 | 2.95 | 12.45 | 6.78 | 0.30 | 1.1 |
| 9.0 | 5.85 | 14.90 | 3.05 | 12.48 | 6.92 | 0.25 | 1.0 |
| 9.1 | 5.97 | 14.92 | 3.16 | 12.50 | 7.05 | 0.20 | 0.9 |
| 9.2 | 6.08 | 14.94 | 3.26 | 12.52 | 7.17 | 0.16 | 0.8 |
| 9.3 | 6.20 | 14.95 | 3.37 | 12.54 | 7.26 | 0.12 | 0.7 |
| 9.4 | 6.32 | 14.96 | 3.48 | 12.55 | 7.35 | 0.09 | 0.6 |
| 9.5 | 6.44 | 14.07 | 3.59 | 12.57 | 7.43 | 0.06 | 0.5 |
| 9.6 | 6.56 | 14.98 | 3.70 | 12.58 | 7.49 | 0.04 | 0.4 |
| 9.7 | 6.68 | 14.99 | 3.81 | 12.59 | 7.54 | 0.02 | 0.3 |
| 9.8 | 6.81 | 14.99 | 3.92 | 12.59 | 7.57 | 0.01 | 0.2 |
| 9.9 | 6.93 | 15.00 | 4.04 | 12.60 | 7.59 | 0.00 | 0.1 |
| 10.0 | 7.05 | 15.00 | 4.15 | 12.60 | 7.60 | 0.00 | 0.0 |
| Days. | **30** | **20** | **30** | **20** | **10** | **10** | Days. |

# TABLES XXXVII.-XLII.

| Tables | XXXVII. | XXXVIII. | | XXXIX. | | XL. | | XLI. | XLII. | | |
|---|---|---|---|---|---|---|---|---|---|---|---|
| Arguments | **32.** | **33.** | | **34.** | | **35.** | | **36.** | **37.** | | |
| Days. | **0** | **0** | **10** | **0** | **10** | **0** | **10** | **0** | **0** | **10** | Days. |
| Days. | ″ | ″ | ″ | ″ | ″ | ″ | ″ | ″ | ″ | ″ | Days. |
| 0.0 | 0.58 | 0.54 | 1.35 | 2.15 | 3.36 | 0.58 | 2.24 | 0.86 | 0.01 | 0.45 | 10.0 |
| 0.1 | 0.52 | 0.52 | 1.39 | 2.20 | 3.33 | 0.61 | 2.22 | 0.82 | 0.01 | 0.46 | 9.9 |
| 0.2 | 0.46 | 0.48 | 1.43 | 2.24 | 3.29 | 0.64 | 2.21 | 0.77 | 0.01 | 0.47 | 9.8 |
| 0.3 | 0.40 | 0.46 | 1.47 | 2.29 | 3.25 | 0.67 | 2.19 | 0.73 | 0.01 | 0.47 | 9.7 |
| 0.4 | 0.35 | 0.43 | 1.51 | 2.33 | 3.22 | 0.70 | 2.17 | 0.69 | 0.01 | 0.48 | 9.6 |
| 0.5 | 0.30 | 0.41 | 1.55 | 2.38 | 3.18 | 0.73 | 2.15 | 0.65 | 0.00 | 0.49 | 9.5 |
| 0.6 | 0.25 | 0.39 | 1.59 | 2.42 | 3.15 | 0.76 | 2.13 | 0.61 | 0.00 | 0.50 | 9.4 |
| 0.7 | 0.21 | 0.36 | 1.63 | 2.47 | 3.11 | 0.79 | 2.11 | 0.57 | 0.00 | 0.51 | 9.3 |
| 0.8 | 0.17 | 0.34 | 1.67 | 2.51 | 3.07 | 0.82 | 2.09 | 0.53 | 0.00 | 0.51 | 9.2 |
| 0.9 | 0.13 | 0.32 | 1.71 | 2.56 | 3.03 | 0.85 | 2.07 | 0.49 | 0.00 | 0.52 | 9.1 |
| 1.0 | 0.10 | 0.30 | 1.75 | 2.60 | 2.99 | 0.88 | 2.05 | 0.45 | 0.00 | 0.53 | 9.0 |
| 1.1 | 0.07 | 0.28 | 1.79 | 2.65 | 2.95 | 0.91 | 2.03 | 0.41 | 0.00 | 0.54 | 8.9 |
| 1.2 | 0.05 | 0.26 | 1.83 | 2.69 | 2.91 | 0.94 | 2.01 | 0.37 | 0.00 | 0.55 | 8.8 |
| 1.3 | 0.03 | 0.24 | 1.87 | 2.74 | 2.87 | 0.97 | 1.99 | 0.33 | 0.00 | 0.56 | 8.7 |
| 1.4 | 0.02 | 0.22 | 1.91 | 2.78 | 2.82 | 1.00 | 1.96 | 0.30 | 0.00 | 0.57 | 8.6 |
| 1.5 | 0.01 | 0.20 | 1.95 | 2.82 | 2.78 | 1.03 | 1.94 | 0.27 | 0.00 | 0.58 | 8.5 |
| 1.6 | 0.00 | 0.18 | 1.99 | 2.86 | 2.74 | 1.06 | 1.91 | 0.24 | 0.00 | 0.58 | 8.4 |
| 1.7 | 0.00 | 0.16 | 2.03 | 2.90 | 2.69 | 1.09 | 1.89 | 0.20 | 0.00 | 0.59 | 8.3 |
| 1.8 | 0.00 | 0.15 | 2.07 | 2.94 | 2.65 | 1.12 | 1.86 | 0.18 | 0.00 | 0.60 | 8.2 |
| 1.9 | 0.01 | 0.13 | 2.11 | 2.98 | 2.60 | 1.16 | 1.84 | 0.16 | 0.00 | 0.61 | 8.1 |
| 2.0 | 0.02 | 0.12 | 2.15 | 3.02 | 2.56 | 1.19 | 1.81 | 0.13 | 0.00 | 0.62 | 8.0 |
| 2.1 | 0.04 | 0.11 | 2.19 | 3.06 | 2.51 | 1.22 | 1.78 | 0.11 | 0.00 | 0.63 | 7.9 |
| 2.2 | 0.06 | 0.09 | 2.23 | 3.10 | 2.47 | 1.26 | 1.75 | 0.09 | 0.00 | 0.64 | 7.8 |
| 2.3 | 0.08 | 0.08 | 2.27 | 3.14 | 2.42 | 1.29 | 1.72 | 0.07 | 0,00 | 0.64 | 7.7 |
| 2.4 | 0.11 | 0.07 | 2.31 | 3.17 | 2.38 | 1.32 | 1.69 | 0.06 | 0.01 | 0.65 | 7.6 |
| 2.5 | 0.14 | 0.06 | 2.35 | 3.21 | 2.33 | 1.35 | 1.66 | 0.04 | 0.01 | 0.66 | 7.5 |
| 2.6 | 0.18 | 0.05 | 2.39 | 3.25 | 2.28 | 1.38 | 1.63 | 0.03 | 0.01 | 0.67 | 7.4 |
| 2.7 | 0.22 | 0.04 | 2.43 | 3.29 | 2.24 | 1.41 | 1.60 | 0.02 | 0.01 | 0.68 | 7.3 |
| 2.8 | 0.27 | 0.03 | 2.47 | 3.32 | 2.19 | 1.44 | 1.57 | 0.01 | 0.02 | 0.68 | 7.2 |
| 2.9 | 0.32 | 0.03 | 2.51 | 3.36 | 2.15 | 1.47 | 1.54 | 0.01 | 0.02 | 0.69 | 7.1 |
| 3.0 | 0.37 | 0.02 | 2.55 | 3.39 | 2.10 | 1.50 | 1.51 | 0.00 | 0.02 | 0.70 | 7.0 |
| 3.1 | 0.42 | 0.02 | 2.59 | 3.42 | 2.05 | 1.53 | 1.48 | 0.00 | 0.02 | 0.71 | 6.9 |
| 3.2 | 0.48 | 0.01 | 2.63 | 3.46 | 2.01 | 1.56 | 1.45 | 0.00 | 0.03 | 0.72 | 6.8 |
| 3.3 | 0.54 | 0.01 | 2.67 | 3.49 | 1.96 | 1.59 | 1.42 | 0.00 | 0.03 | 0.72 | 6.7 |
| 3.4 | 0.61 | 0.00 | 2.71 | 3.52 | 1.92 | 1.62 | 1.39 | 0.01 | 0.03 | 0.73 | 6.6 |
| 3.5 | 0.68 | 0.00 | 2.75 | 3.55 | 1.87 | 1.65 | 1.36 | 0.02 | 0.03 | 0.74 | 6.5 |
| 3.6 | 0.75 | 0.00 | 2.79 | 3.58 | 1.82 | 1.68 | 1.33 | 0.03 | 0.04 | 0.74 | 6.4 |
| 3.7 | 0.83 | 0.00 | 2.83 | 3.61 | 1.78 | 1.71 | 1.30 | 0.04 | 0.04 | 0.75 | 6.3 |
| 3.8 | 0.91 | 0.00 | 2.87 | 3.64 | 1.73 | 1.74 | 1.27 | 0.05 | 0.04 | 0.76 | 6.2 |
| 3.9 | 0.98 | 0.00 | 2.90 | 3.66 | 1.69 | 1.76 | 1.23 | 0.06 | 0.05 | 0.76 | 6.1 |
| 4.0 | 1.08 | 0.00 | 2.94 | 3.69 | 1.64 | 1.79 | 1.20 | 0.08 | 0.05 | 0.77 | 6.0 |
| 4.1 | 1.17 | 0.00 | 2.98 | 3.71 | 1.60 | 1.82 | 1.17 | 0.10 | 0.05 | 0.78 | 5.9 |
| 4.2 | 1.26 | 0.00 | 3.01 | 3.74 | 1.55 | 1.84 | 1.13 | 0.12 | 0.06 | 0.78 | 5.8 |
| 4.3 | 1.35 | 0.01 | 3.05 | 3.76 | 1.51 | 1.87 | 1.10 | 0.14 | 0.06 | 0.79 | 5.7 |
| 4.4 | 1.45 | 0.01 | 3.08 | 3.78 | 1.46 | 1.89 | 1.07 | 0.17 | 0.07 | 0.79 | 5.6 |
| 4.5 | 1.55 | 0.02 | 3.12 | 3.80 | 1.42 | 1.92 | 1.04 | 0.19 | 0.07 | 0.80 | 5.5 |
| 4.6 | 1.65 | 0.02 | 3.16 | 3.82 | 1.38 | 1.94 | 1.01 | 0.22 | 0.08 | 0.81 | 5.4 |
| 4.7 | 1.75 | 0.03 | 3.19 | 3.84 | 1.33 | 1.97 | 0.98 | 0.25 | 0.08 | 0.81 | 5.3 |
| 4.8 | 1.85 | 0.03 | 3.23 | 3.86 | 1.29 | 1.99 | 0.95 | 0.28 | 0.09 | 0.82 | 5.2 |
| 4.9 | 1.95 | 0.04 | 3.26 | 3.87 | 1.24 | 2.02 | 0.92 | 0.31 | 0.09 | 0.82 | 5.1 |
| 5.0 | 2.06 | 0.05 | 3.29 | 3.89 | 1.20 | 2.04 | 0.89 | 0.34 | 0.10 | 0.83 | 5.0 |
| Days. | **10** | **30** | **20** | **30** | **20** | **30** | **20** | **10** | **30** | **20** | Days. |

# TABLES XXXVII.-XLII.

| Tables | XXXVII. | XXXVIII. | | XXXIX. | | XL. | | XLI. | XLII. | | |
|---|---|---|---|---|---|---|---|---|---|---|---|
| Arguments | **32.** | **33.** | | **34.** | | **35.** | | **36.** | **37.** | | |
| Days. | **0** | **0** | **10** | **0** | **10** | **0** | **10** | **0** | **0** | **10** | Days. |
| Days. | " | " | " | " | " | " | " | " | " | " | Days. |
| 5.0 | 2.06 | 0.05 | 3.29 | 3.89 | 1.20 | 2.04 | 0.89 | 0.34 | 0.10 | 0.83 | 5.0 |
| 5.1 | 2.17 | 0.06 | 3.32 | 3.90 | 1.16 | 2.06 | 0.86 | 0.37 | 0.11 | 0.84 | 4.9 |
| 5.2 | 2.28 | 0.07 | 3.36 | 3.92 | 1.11 | 2.08 | 0.83 | 0.41 | 0.11 | 0.84 | 4.8 |
| 5.3 | 2.39 | 0.08 | 3.39 | 3.93 | 1.07 | 2.10 | 0.80 | 0.45 | 0.12 | 0.85 | 4.7 |
| 5.4 | 2.50 | 0.10 | 3.42 | 3.94 | 1.03 | 2.12 | 0.78 | 0.49 | 0.12 | 0.85 | 4.6 |
| 5.5 | 2.61 | 0.11 | 3.45 | 3.95 | 0.99 | 2.14 | 0.75 | 0.53 | 0.13 | 0.86 | 4.5 |
| 5.6 | 2.73 | 0.12 | 3.48 | 3.96 | 0.95 | 2.16 | 0.72 | 0.57 | 0.14 | 0.87 | 4.4 |
| 5.7 | 2.84 | 0.14 | 3.51 | 3.97 | 0.91 | 2.18 | 0.69 | 0.61 | 0.14 | 0.87 | 4.3 |
| 5.8 | 2.96 | 0.15 | 3.54 | 3.98 | 0.87 | 2.20 | 0.67 | 0.65 | 0.15 | 0.88 | 4.2 |
| 5.9 | 3.07 | 0.16 | 3.57 | 3.98 | 0.84 | 2.21 | 0.64 | 0.69 | 0.15 | 0.88 | 4.1 |
| 6.0 | 3.19 | 0.18 | 3.60 | 3.99 | 0.80 | 2.23 | 0.61 | 0.74 | 0.16 | 0.89 | 4.0 |
| 6.1 | 3.30 | 0.20 | 3.63 | 3.99 | 0.76 | 2.24 | 0.58 | 0.78 | 0.17 | 0.89 | 3.9 |
| 6.2 | 3.41 | 0.22 | 3.66 | 4.00 | 0.72 | 2.26 | 0.56 | 0.83 | 0.17 | 0.90 | 3.8 |
| 6.3 | 3.52 | 0.24 | 3.68 | 4.00 | 0.69 | 2.27 | 0.53 | 0.87 | 0.18 | 0.90 | 3.7 |
| 6.4 | 3.63 | 0.26 | 3.71 | 4.00 | 0.65 | 2.29 | 0.51 | 0.92 | 0.18 | 0.91 | 3.6 |
| 6.5 | 3.74 | 0.28 | 3.73 | 4.00 | 0.62 | 2.30 | 0.48 | 0.96 | 0.19 | 0.91 | 3.5 |
| 6.6 | 3.85 | 0.30 | 3.76 | 4.00 | 0.59 | 2.31 | 0.46 | 1.01 | 0.20 | 0.92 | 3.4 |
| 6.7 | 3.96 | 0.32 | 3.78 | 4.00 | 0.55 | 2.33 | 0.43 | 1.06 | 0.20 | 0.92 | 3.3 |
| 6.8 | 4.06 | 0.35 | 3.81 | 3.99 | 0.52 | 2.34 | 0.41 | 1.11 | 0.21 | 0.93 | 3.2 |
| 6.9 | 4.17 | 0.37 | 3.83 | 3.99 | 0.49 | 2.35 | 0.38 | 1.16 | 0.21 | 0.93 | 3.1 |
| 7.0 | 4.27 | 0.40 | 3.85 | 3.98 | 0.46 | 2.36 | 0.36 | 1.20 | 0.22 | 0.94 | 3.0 |
| 7.1 | 4.37 | 0.42 | 3.87 | 3.97 | 0.43 | 2.37 | 0.34 | 1.25 | 0.23 | 0.94 | 2.9 |
| 7.2 | 4.47 | 0.45 | 3.89 | 3.97 | 0.40 | 2.37 | 0.31 | 1.29 | 0.23 | 0.95 | 2.8 |
| 7.3 | 4.57 | 0.47 | 3.91 | 3.96 | 0.37 | 2.38 | 0.29 | 1.33 | 0.24 | 0.95 | 2.7 |
| 7.4 | 4.67 | 0.50 | 3.93 | 3.95 | 0.35 | 2.38 | 0.27 | 1.37 | 0.25 | 0.95 | 2.6 |
| 7.5 | 4.76 | 0.53 | 3.95 | 3.94 | 0.32 | 2.39 | 0.25 | 1.41 | 0.25 | 0.96 | 2.5 |
| 7.6 | 4.85 | 0.56 | 3.97 | 3.93 | 0.30 | 2.39 | 0.23 | 1.45 | 0.26 | 0.96 | 2.4 |
| 7.7 | 4.94 | 0.58 | 3.99 | 3.92 | 0.27 | 2.40 | 0.21 | 1.49 | 0.27 | 0.96 | 2.3 |
| 7.8 | 5.02 | 0.61 | 4.01 | 3.90 | 0.25 | 2.40 | 0.19 | 1.53 | 0.27 | 0.97 | 2.2 |
| 7.9 | 5.10 | 0.64 | 4.02 | 3.89 | 0.23 | 2.40 | 0.18 | 1.57 | 0.28 | 0.97 | 2.1 |
| 8.0 | 5.18 | 0.67 | 4.04 | 3.87 | 0.21 | 2.40 | 0.16 | 1.61 | 0.29 | 0.97 | 2.0 |
| 8.1 | 5.26 | 0.70 | 4.06 | 3.85 | 0.19 | 2.40 | 0.15 | 1.65 | 0.30 | 0.97 | 1.9 |
| 8.2 | 5.33 | 0.73 | 4.07 | 3.84 | 0.17 | 2.40 | 0.13 | 1.68 | 0.31 | 0.98 | 1.8 |
| 8.3 | 5.40 | 0.76 | 4.09 | 3.82 | 0.15 | 2.40 | 0.12 | 1.71 | 0.31 | 0.98 | 1.7 |
| 8.4 | 5.47 | 0.79 | 4.10 | 3.80 | 0.14 | 2.39 | 0.10 | 1.74 | 0.32 | 0.98 | 1.6 |
| 8.5 | 5.53 | 0.82 | 4.11 | 3.78 | 0.12 | 2.39 | 0.09 | 1.77 | 0.33 | 0.98 | 1.5 |
| 8.6 | 5.59 | 0.85 | 4.12 | 3.76 | 0.10 | 2.38 | 0.08 | 1.80 | 0.34 | 0.98 | 1.4 |
| 8.7 | 5.65 | 0.88 | 4.13 | 3.73 | 0.09 | 2.38 | 0.07 | 1.83 | 0.35 | 0.99 | 1.3 |
| 8.8 | 5.70 | 0.91 | 4.14 | 3.71 | 0.07 | 2.37 | 0.06 | 1.85 | 0.35 | 0.99 | 1.2 |
| 8.9 | 5.75 | 0.95 | 4.15 | 3.69 | 0.06 | 2.37 | 0.05 | 1.87 | 0.36 | 0.99 | 1.1 |
| 9.0 | 5.79 | 0.98 | 4.16 | 3.66 | 0.05 | 2.36 | 0.04 | 1.89 | 0.37 | 0.99 | 1.0 |
| 9.1 | 5.83 | 1.01 | 4.17 | 3.64 | 0.04 | 2.35 | 0.03 | 1.91 | 0.38 | 0.99 | 0.9 |
| 9.2 | 5.86 | 1.05 | 4.18 | 3.61 | 0.03 | 2.34 | 0.03 | 1.93 | 0.39 | 0.99 | 0.8 |
| 9.3 | 5.89 | 1.08 | 4.18 | 3.58 | 0.02 | 2.33 | 0.02 | 1.95 | 0.39 | 0.99 | 0.7 |
| 9.4 | 5.92 | 1.12 | 4.19 | 3.55 | 0.02 | 2.32 | 0.02 | 1.96 | 0.40 | 1.00 | 0.6 |
| 9.5 | 5.94 | 1.16 | 4.19 | 3.52 | 0.01 | 2.31 | 0.01 | 1.97 | 0.41 | 1.00 | 0.5 |
| 9.6 | 5.96 | 1.20 | 4.19 | 3.49 | 0.01 | 2.30 | 0.01 | 1.98 | 0.42 | 1.00 | 0.4 |
| 9.7 | 5.98 | 1.23 | 4.20 | 3.46 | 0.00 | 2.28 | 0.01 | 1.99 | 0.43 | 1.00 | 0.3 |
| 9.8 | 5.99 | 1.27 | 4.20 | 3.43 | 0.00 | 2.27 | 0.00 | 1.99 | 0.43 | 1.00 | 0.2 |
| 9.9 | 6.00 | 1.31 | 4.20 | 3.39 | 0.00 | 2.25 | 0.00 | 2.00 | 0.44 | 1.00 | 0.1 |
| 10.0 | 6.00 | 1.35 | 4.20 | 3.36 | 0.00 | 2.24 | 0.00 | 2.00 | 0.45 | 1.00 | 0.0 |
| Days. | **10** | **30** | **20** | **30** | **20** | **30** | **20** | **10** | **30** | **20** | Days. |

# TABLES XLIII.-L.

| Tables | XLIII. | XLIV. | | XLV. | XLVI. | XLVII. | XLVIII. | XLIX. | | L. | |
|---|---|---|---|---|---|---|---|---|---|---|---|
| Arguments | **38.** | **39.** | | **40.** | **41.** | **42.** | **43.** | **44.** | | **45.** | |
| Days. | **0** | **0** | **10** | **0** | **0** | **0** | **0** | **0** | **10** | **0** | Days. |
| Days. | | | | | | | | | | | Days. |
| 0.0 | ″0.03 | ″1.12 | ″0.75 | ″0.77 | ″0.10 | ″0.60 | ″0.17 | ″0.09 | ″0.58 | ″0.17 | 10.0 |
| 0.1 | 0.02 | 1.13 | 0.74 | 0.78 | 0.08 | 0.60 | 0.21 | 0.10 | 0.58 | 0.19 | 9.9 |
| 0.2 | 0.01 | 1.13 | 0.73 | 0.79 | 0.07 | 0.59 | 0.25 | 0.10 | 0.57 | 0.21 | 9.8 |
| 0.3 | 0.01 | 1.14 | 0.71 | 0.80 | 0.05 | 0.59 | 0.30 | 0.11 | 0.57 | 0.24 | 9.7 |
| 0.4 | 0.00 | 1.15 | 0.70 | 0.80 | 0.04 | 0.58 | 0.35 | 0.11 | 0.56 | 0.26 | 9.6 |
| 0.5 | 0.00 | 1.15 | 0.69 | 0.80 | 0.03 | 0.58 | 0.40 | 0.12 | 0.56 | 0.28 | 9.5 |
| 0.6 | 0.00 | 1.15 | 0.68 | 0.80 | 0.02 | 0.57 | 0.45 | 0.13 | 0.56 | 0.30 | 9.4 |
| 0.7 | 0.00 | 1.16 | 0.67 | 0.80 | 0.01 | 0.56 | 0.50 | 0.13 | 0.55 | 0.32 | 9.3 |
| 0.8 | 0.00 | 1.16 | 0.66 | 0.79 | 0.01 | 0.55 | 0.55 | 0.14 | 0.55 | 0.34 | 9.2 |
| 0.9 | 0.01 | 1.17 | 0.65 | 0.79 | 0.00 | 0.54 | 0.60 | 0.14 | 0.54 | 0.35 | 9.1 |
| 1.0 | 0.01 | 1.17 | 0.64 | 0.78 | 0.00 | 0.53 | 0.65 | 0.15 | 0.54 | 0.36 | 9.0 |
| 1.1 | 0.02 | 1.17 | 0.63 | 0.77 | 0.00 | 0.52 | 0.70 | 0.16 | 0.53 | 0.37 | 8.9 |
| 1.2 | 0.03 | 1.17 | 0.62 | 0.76 | 0.00 | 0.50 | 0.75 | 0.17 | 0.53 | 0.38 | 8.8 |
| 1.3 | 0.04 | 1.18 | 0.61 | 0.75 | 0.00 | 0.48 | 0.80 | 0.17 | 0.52 | 0.39 | 8.7 |
| 1.4 | 0.05 | 1.18 | 0.60 | 0.74 | 0.01 | 0.47 | 0.85 | 0.18 | 0.52 | 0.40 | 8.6 |
| 1.5 | 0.06 | 1.18 | 0.59 | 0.73 | 0.02 | 0.45 | 0.89 | 0.19 | 0.51 | 0.40 | 8.5 |
| 1.6 | 0.08 | 1.18 | 0.58 | 0.71 | 0.03 | 0.44 | 0.93 | 0.20 | 0.50 | 0.40 | 8.4 |
| 1.7 | 0.10 | 1.18 | 0.57 | 0.69 | 0.04 | 0.42 | 0.97 | 0.21 | 0.50 | 0.40 | 8.3 |
| 1.8 | 0.12 | 1.19 | 0.55 | 0.67 | 0.06 | 0.41 | 1.01 | 0.21 | 0.49 | 0.39 | 8.2 |
| 1.9 | 0.14 | 1.19 | 0.54 | 0.65 | 0.07 | 0.39 | 1.05 | 0.22 | 0.49 | 0.38 | 8.1 |
| 2.0 | 0.16 | 1.19 | 0.53 | 0.63 | 0.09 | 0.37 | 1.08 | 0.23 | 0.48 | 0.37 | 8.0 |
| 2.1 | 0.18 | 1.19 | 0.52 | 0.61 | 0.11 | 0.35 | 1.11 | 0.24 | 0.47 | 0.36 | 7.9 |
| 2.2 | 0.21 | 1.19 | 0.51 | 0.59 | 0.13 | 0.33 | 1.14 | 0.25 | 0.46 | 0.35 | 7.8 |
| 2.3 | 0.23 | 1.20 | 0.50 | 0.57 | 0.15 | 0.31 | 1.16 | 0.25 | 0.46 | 0.33 | 7.7 |
| 2.4 | 0.26 | 1.20 | 0.49 | 0.54 | 0.17 | 0.30 | 1.17 | 0.26 | 0.45 | 0.31 | 7.6 |
| 2.5 | 0.28 | 1.20 | 0.48 | 0.52 | 0.19 | 0.28 | 1.18 | 0.27 | 0.44 | 0.29 | 7.5 |
| 2.6 | 0.31 | 1.20 | 0.47 | 0.49 | 0.22 | 0.27 | 1.19 | 0.28 | 0.43 | 0.27 | 7.4 |
| 2.7 | 0.33 | 1.20 | 0.46 | 0.46 | 0.24 | 0.25 | 1.20 | 0.29 | 0.42 | 0.25 | 7.3 |
| 2.8 | 0.36 | 1.20 | 0.45 | 0.43 | 0.27 | 0.23 | 1.20 | 0.29 | 0.42 | 0.23 | 7.2 |
| 2.9 | 0.38 | 1.20 | 0.44 | 0.40 | 0.29 | 0.21 | 1.20 | 0.30 | 0.41 | 0.21 | 7.1 |
| 3.0 | 0.41 | 1.20 | 0.43 | 0.38 | 0.32 | 0.19 | 1.19 | 0.31 | 0.40 | 0.19 | 7.0 |
| 3.1 | 0.44 | 1.20 | 0.42 | 0.35 | 0.35 | 0.17 | 1.17 | 0.32 | 0.39 | 0.17 | 6.9 |
| 3.2 | 0.47 | 1.20 | 0.41 | 0.33 | 0.38 | 0.15 | 1.15 | 0.33 | 0.38 | 0.14 | 6.8 |
| 3.3 | 0.50 | 1.19 | 0.40 | 0.30 | 0.41 | 0.13 | 1.13 | 0.33 | 0.38 | 0.12 | 6.7 |
| 3.4 | 0.52 | 1.19 | 0.39 | 0.28 | 0.43 | 0.12 | 1.10 | 0.34 | 0.37 | 0.10 | 6.6 |
| 3.5 | 0.55 | 1.19 | 0.38 | 0.25 | 0.46 | 0.10 | 1.07 | 0.35 | 0.36 | 0.08 | 6.5 |
| 3.6 | 0.57 | 1.19 | 0.37 | 0.23 | 0.49 | 0.09 | 1.04 | 0.36 | 0.35 | 0.06 | 6.4 |
| 3.7 | 0.59 | 1.19 | 0.36 | 0.20 | 0.52 | 0.08 | 1.00 | 0.37 | 0.34 | 0.05 | 6.3 |
| 3.8 | 0.61 | 1.18 | 0.35 | 0.18 | 0.54 | 0.07 | 0.96 | 0.37 | 0.34 | 0.04 | 6.2 |
| 3.9 | 0.63 | 1.18 | 0.34 | 0.16 | 0.57 | 0.06 | 0.92 | 0.38 | 0.33 | 0.03 | 6.1 |
| 4.0 | 0.65 | 1.18 | 0.33 | 0.14 | 0.59 | 0.05 | 0.87 | 0.39 | 0.32 | 0.02 | 6.0 |
| 4.1 | 0.67 | 1.18 | 0.32 | 0.12 | 0.62 | 0.04 | 0.82 | 0.40 | 0.31 | 0.01 | 5.9 |
| 4.2 | 0.69 | 1.18 | 0.31 | 0.10 | 0.64 | 0.03 | 0.77 | 0.41 | 0.30 | 0.01 | 5.8 |
| 4.3 | 0.71 | 1.17 | 0.30 | 0.08 | 0.66 | 0.02 | 0.72 | 0.41 | 0.30 | 0.00 | 5.7 |
| 4.4 | 0.73 | 1.17 | 0.29 | 0.07 | 0.68 | 0.02 | 0.67 | 0.42 | 0.29 | 0.00 | 5.6 |
| 4.5 | 0.75 | 1.17 | 0.28 | 0.05 | 0.70 | 0.01 | 0.62 | 0.43 | 0.28 | 0.01 | 5.5 |
| 4.6 | 0.76 | 1.17 | 0.27 | 0.04 | 0.72 | 0.01 | 0.57 | 0.44 | 0.27 | 0.01 | 5.4 |
| 4.7 | 0.77 | 1.16 | 0.26 | 0.03 | 0.74 | 0.00 | 0.52 | 0.45 | 0.26 | 0.02 | 5.3 |
| 4.8 | 0.78 | 1.16 | 0.25 | 0.02 | 0.75 | 0.00 | 0.47 | 0.45 | 0.26 | 0.03 | 5.2 |
| 4.9 | 0.79 | 1.15 | 0.24 | 0.01 | 0.76 | 0.00 | 0.42 | 0.46 | 0.25 | 0.04 | 5.1 |
| 5.0 | 0.79 | 1.15 | 0.23 | 0.01 | 0.77 | 0.00 | 0.37 | 0.47 | 0.24 | 0.05 | 5.0 |
| Days. | **10** | **30** | **20** | **10** | **10** | **10** | **10** | **30** | **20** | **10** | Days. |

# TABLES XLIII. - L.

| Tables | XLIII. | XLIV. | | XLV. | XLVI. | XLVII. | XLVIII. | XLIX. | | L. | |
|---|---|---|---|---|---|---|---|---|---|---|---|
| Arguments | **38.** | **39.** | | **40.** | **41.** | **42.** | **43.** | **44.** | | **45.** | |
| Days. | **0** | **0** | **10** | **0** | **0** | **0** | **0** | **0** | **10** | **0** | Days. |
| Days. 5.0 | 0″.79 | 1″.15 | 0″.23 | 0″.01 | 0″.77 | 0″.00 | 0″.37 | 0″.47 | 0″.24 | 0″.05 | Days. 5.0 |
| 5.1 | 0.80 | 1.15 | 0.22 | 0.00 | 0.78 | 0.00 | 0.32 | 0.48 | 0.23 | 0.06 | 4.9 |
| 5.2 | 0.80 | 1.14 | 0.21 | 0.00 | 0.79 | 0.00 | 0.28 | 0.48 | 0.22 | 0.08 | 4.8 |
| 5.3 | 0.80 | 1.14 | 0.21 | 0.00 | 0.80 | 0.00 | 0.24 | 0.49 | 0.22 | 0.10 | 4.7 |
| 5.4 | 0.80 | 1.13 | 0.20 | 0.00 | 0.80 | 0.01 | 0.20 | 0.49 | 0.21 | 0.12 | 4.6 |
| 5.5 | 0.80 | 1.13 | 0.19 | 0.00 | 0.80 | 0.01 | 0.16 | 0.50 | 0.20 | 0.14 | 4.5 |
| 5.6 | 0.79 | 1.12 | 0.18 | 0.01 | 0.80 | 0.02 | 0.13 | 0.51 | 0.19 | 0.16 | 4.4 |
| 5.7 | 0.79 | 1.12 | 0.17 | 0.02 | 0.80 | 0.03 | 0.10 | 0.51 | 0.18 | 0.18 | 4.3 |
| 5.8 | 0.78 | 1.11 | 0.17 | 0.03 | 0.79 | 0.04 | 0.07 | 0.52 | 0.18 | 0.20 | 4.2 |
| 5.9 | 0.77 | 1.10 | 0.16 | 0.04 | 0.78 | 0.05 | 0.05 | 0.52 | 0.17 | 0.23 | 4.1 |
| 6.0 | 0.76 | 1.10 | 0.15 | 0.05 | 0.77 | 0.06 | 0.03 | 0.53 | 0.16 | 0.25 | 4.0 |
| 6.1 | 0.75 | 1.09 | 0.14 | 0.06 | 0.76 | 0.07 | 0.02 | 0.53 | 0.15 | 0.27 | 3.9 |
| 6.2 | 0.73 | 1.09 | 0.14 | 0.08 | 0.75 | 0.09 | 0.01 | 0.54 | 0.15 | 0.29 | 3.8 |
| 6.3 | 0.72 | 1.08 | 0.13 | 0.09 | 0.74 | 0.10 | 0.00 | 0.54 | 0.14 | 0.31 | 3.7 |
| 6.4 | 0.70 | 1.07 | 0.13 | 0.11 | 0.72 | 0.12 | 0.00 | 0.55 | 0.14 | 0.33 | 3.6 |
| 6.5 | 0.68 | 1.07 | 0.12 | 0.13 | 0.71 | 0.13 | 0.00 | 0.55 | 0.13 | 0.35 | 3.5 |
| 6.6 | 0.66 | 1.06 | 0.12 | 0.15 | 0.69 | 0.15 | 0.01 | 0.55 | 0.12 | 0.36 | 3.4 |
| 6.7 | 0.64 | 1.05 | 0.11 | 0.17 | 0.67 | 0.16 | 0.02 | 0.56 | 0.12 | 0.37 | 3.3 |
| 6.8 | 0.62 | 1.05 | 0.10 | 0.19 | 0.65 | 0.18 | 0.04 | 0.56 | 0.11 | 0.38 | 3.2 |
| 6.9 | 0.60 | 1.04 | 0.09 | 0.21 | 0.63 | 0.19 | 0.06 | 0.57 | 0.11 | 0.39 | 3.1 |
| 7.0 | 0.57 | 1.03 | 0.09 | 0.24 | 0.60 | 0.21 | 0.09 | 0.57 | 0.10 | 0.40 | 3.0 |
| 7.1 | 0.55 | 1.02 | 0.08 | 0.26 | 0.58 | 0.23 | 0.12 | 0.57 | 0.09 | 0.40 | 2.9 |
| 7.2 | 0.52 | 1.01 | 0.07 | 0.29 | 0.55 | 0.25 | 0.15 | 0.58 | 0.09 | 0.40 | 2.8 |
| 7.3 | 0.50 | 1.01 | 0.07 | 0.31 | 0.53 | 0.27 | 0.19 | 0.58 | 0.08 | 0.40 | 2.7 |
| 7.4 | 0.47 | 1.00 | 0.06 | 0.34 | 0.50 | 0.29 | 0.23 | 0.59 | 0.08 | 0.39 | 2.6 |
| 7.5 | 0.44 | 0.99 | 0.06 | 0.36 | 0.47 | 0.31 | 0.27 | 0.59 | 0.07 | 0.38 | 2.5 |
| 7.6 | 0.41 | 0.98 | 0.06 | 0.39 | 0.44 | 0.33 | 0.31 | 0.59 | 0.06 | 0.37 | 2.4 |
| 7.7 | 0.38 | 0.97 | 0.05 | 0.41 | 0.41 | 0.35 | 0.36 | 0.59 | 0.06 | 0.36 | 2.3 |
| 7.8 | 0.36 | 0.97 | 0.05 | 0.44 | 0.39 | 0.37 | 0.41 | 0.60 | 0.05 | 0.35 | 2.2 |
| 7.9 | 0.33 | 0.96 | 0.04 | 0.46 | 0.36 | 0.39 | 0.46 | 0.60 | 0.05 | 0.34 | 2.1 |
| 8.0 | 0.31 | 0.95 | 0.04 | 0.49 | 0.34 | 0.40 | 0.51 | 0.60 | 0.04 | 0.32 | 2.0 |
| 8.1 | 0.28 | 0.94 | 0.04 | 0.52 | 0.31 | 0.42 | 0.56 | 0.60 | 0.04 | 0.30 | 1.9 |
| 8.2 | 0.26 | 0.93 | 0.03 | 0.55 | 0.28 | 0.43 | 0.61 | 0.60 | 0.03 | 0.28 | 1.8 |
| 8.3 | 0.23 | 0.92 | 0.03 | 0.58 | 0.25 | 0.45 | 0.66 | 0.60 | 0.03 | 0.26 | 1.7 |
| 8.4 | 0.21 | 0.91 | 0.02 | 0.60 | 0.23 | 0.46 | 0.71 | 0.60 | 0.02 | 0.24 | 1.6 |
| 8.5 | 0.18 | 0.90 | 0.02 | 0.62 | 0.20 | 0.48 | 0.76 | 0.60 | 0.02 | 0.22 | 1.5 |
| 8.6 | 0.16 | 0.89 | 0.02 | 0.64 | 0.18 | 0.49 | 0.81 | 0.60 | 0.02 | 0.20 | 1.4 |
| 8.7 | 0.14 | 0.88 | 0.02 | 0.66 | 0.15 | 0.51 | 0.86 | 0.60 | 0.02 | 0.18 | 1.3 |
| 8.8 | 0.12 | 0.87 | 0.01 | 0.68 | 0.13 | 0.52 | 0.91 | 0.60 | 0.01 | 0.15 | 1.2 |
| 8.9 | 0.10 | 0.86 | 0.01 | 0.70 | 0.11 | 0.53 | 0.95 | 0.60 | 0.01 | 0.13 | 1.1 |
| 9.0 | 0.09 | 0.85 | 0.01 | 0.71 | 0.09 | 0.54 | 0.99 | 0.60 | 0.01 | 0.11 | 1.0 |
| 9.1 | 0.07 | 0.84 | 0.01 | 0.73 | 0.07 | 0.55 | 1.03 | 0.60 | 0.01 | 0.09 | 0.9 |
| 9.2 | 0.06 | 0.83 | 0.01 | 0.74 | 0.06 | 0.56 | 1.06 | 0.60 | 0.01 | 0.07 | 0.8 |
| 9.3 | 0.04 | 0.82 | 0.00 | 0.75 | 0.05 | 0.57 | 1.09 | 0.59 | 0.00 | 0.05 | 0.7 |
| 9.4 | 0.03 | 0.81 | 0.00 | 0.76 | 0.04 | 0.58 | 1.12 | 0.59 | 0.00 | 0.04 | 0.6 |
| 9.5 | 0.02 | 0.80 | 0.00 | 0.77 | 0.03 | 0.59 | 1.14 | 0.59 | 0.00 | 0.03 | 0.5 |
| 9.6 | 0.01 | 0.79 | 0.00 | 0.78 | 0.02 | 0.59 | 1.16 | 0.59 | 0.00 | 0.02 | 0.4 |
| 9.7 | 0.00 | 0.78 | 0.00 | 0.79 | 0.01 | 0.60 | 1.18 | 0.59 | 0.00 | 0.01 | 0.3 |
| 9.8 | 0.00 | 0.77 | 0.00 | 0.79 | 0.01 | 0.60 | 1.19 | 0.58 | 0.00 | 0.01 | 0.2 |
| 9.9 | 0.00 | 0.76 | 0.00 | 0.80 | 0.00 | 0.60 | 1.20 | 0.58 | 0.00 | 0.00 | 0.1 |
| 10.0 | 0.00 | 0.75 | 0.00 | 0.80 | 0.00 | 0.60 | 1.20 | 0.58 | 0.00 | 0.00 | 0.0 |
| Days. | **10** | **30** | **20** | **10** | **10** | **10** | **10** | **30** | **20** | **10** | Days. |

# TABLES LI.-LVII.

| Tables | LI. | | LII. | LIII. | LIV. | LV. | | LVI. | LVII. | | |
|---|---|---|---|---|---|---|---|---|---|---|---|
| Arguments | **46.** | | **47.** | **48′.** | **49.** | **50.** | | **51.** | **52.** | | |
| Days. | **0** | **10** | **0** | **0** | **0** | **0** | **10** | **0** | **0** | **10** | Days. |
| 0.0 | 0.54″ | 0.61″ | 0.96″ | 0.75″ | 0.16″ | 0.28″ | 0.73″ | 0.03″ | 1.26″ | 0.21″ | 10.0 |
| 0.1 | 0.55 | 0.60 | 0.90 | 0.76 | 0.17 | 0.29 | 0.72 | 0.03 | 1.23 | 0.22 | 9.9 |
| 0.2 | 0.56 | 0.60 | 0.85 | 0.78 | 0.18 | 0.30 | 0.72 | 0.02 | 1.21 | 0.24 | 9.8 |
| 0.3 | 0.56 | 0.59 | 0.79 | 0.79 | 0.19 | 0.31 | 0.71 | 0.02 | 1.18 | 0.25 | 9.7 |
| 0.4 | 0.57 | 0.59 | 0.74 | 0.81 | 0.20 | 0.32 | 0.70 | 0.01 | 1.16 | 0.27 | 9.6 |
| 0.5 | 0.58 | 0.58 | 0.69 | 0.82 | 0.21 | 0.33 | 0.70 | 0.01 | 1.13 | 0.29 | 9.5 |
| 0.6 | 0.59 | 0.57 | 0.64 | 0.83 | 0.22 | 0.34 | 0.69 | 0.01 | 1.11 | 0.31 | 9.4 |
| 0.7 | 0.59 | 0.56 | 0.59 | 0.85 | 0.23 | 0.35 | 0.68 | 0.00 | 1.08 | 0.32 | 9.3 |
| 0.8 | 0.60 | 0.56 | 0.54 | 0.86 | 0.24 | 0.36 | 0.68 | 0.00 | 1.06 | 0.34 | 9.2 |
| 0.9 | 0.60 | 0.55 | 0.50 | 0.88 | 0.25 | 0.37 | 0.67 | 0.00 | 1.03 | 0.36 | 9.1 |
| 1.0 | 0.61 | 0.54 | 0.45 | 0.89 | 0.26 | 0.38 | 0.66 | 0.00 | 1.01 | 0.38 | 9.0 |
| 1.1 | 0.62 | 0.53 | 0.41 | 0.90 | 0.27 | 0.39 | 0.65 | 0.00 | 0.98 | 0.40 | 8.9 |
| 1.2 | 0.63 | 0.52 | 0.37 | 0.91 | 0.28 | 0.40 | 0.64 | 0.01 | 0.96 | 0.42 | 8.8 |
| 1.3 | 0.63 | 0.52 | 0.33 | 0.93 | 0.28 | 0.41 | 0.63 | 0.01 | 0.93 | 0.44 | 8.7 |
| 1.4 | 0.64 | 0.51 | 0.30 | 0.94 | 0.29 | 0.42 | 0.63 | 0.01 | 0.91 | 0.46 | 8.6 |
| 1.5 | 0.65 | 0.50 | 0.26 | 0.95 | 0.30 | 0.43 | 0.62 | 0.02 | 0.88 | 0.48 | 8.5 |
| 1.6 | 0.66 | 0.49 | 0.23 | 0.96 | 0.31 | 0.44 | 0.61 | 0.02 | 0.86 | 0.50 | 8.4 |
| 1.7 | 0.66 | 0.48 | 0.20 | 0.97 | 0.32 | 0.45 | 0.60 | 0.03 | 0.83 | 0.52 | 8.3 |
| 1.8 | 0.67 | 0.48 | 0.17 | 0.97 | 0.32 | 0.46 | 0.59 | 0.03 | 0.81 | 0.54 | 8.2 |
| 1.9 | 0.67 | 0.47 | 0.15 | 0.98 | 0.33 | 0.47 | 0.58 | 0.04 | 0.78 | 0.57 | 8.1 |
| 2.0 | 0.68 | 0.46 | 0.12 | 0.99 | 0.34 | 0.48 | 0.57 | 0.05 | 0.76 | 0.59 | 8.0 |
| 2.1 | 0.69 | 0.45 | 0.10 | 0.99 | 0.35 | 0.49 | 0.56 | 0.06 | 0.73 | 0.61 | 7.9 |
| 2.2 | 0.69 | 0.44 | 0.08 | 0.99 | 0.35 | 0.50 | 0.55 | 0.07 | 0.71 | 0.64 | 7.8 |
| 2.3 | 0.70 | 0.44 | 0.06 | 1.00 | 0.36 | 0.51 | 0.54 | 0.08 | 0.68 | 0.66 | 7.7 |
| 2.4 | 0.70 | 0.43 | 0.05 | 1.00 | 0.36 | 0.52 | 0.53 | 0.09 | 0.66 | 0.69 | 7.6 |
| 2.5 | 0.71 | 0.42 | 0.03 | 1.00 | 0.37 | 0.53 | 0.52 | 0.10 | 0.64 | 0.71 | 7.5 |
| 2.6 | 0.72 | 0.41 | 0.02 | 1.00 | 0.37 | 0.53 | 0.51 | 0.11 | 0.62 | 0.73 | 7.4 |
| 2.7 | 0.72 | 0.40 | 0.01 | 1.00 | 0.38 | 0.54 | 0.50 | 0.13 | 0.59 | 0.76 | 7.3 |
| 2.8 | 0.73 | 0.40 | 0.01 | 0.99 | 0.38 | 0.55 | 0.49 | 0.14 | 0.57 | 0.78 | 7.2 |
| 2.9 | 0.73 | 0.39 | 0.00 | 0.99 | 0.39 | 0.56 | 0.48 | 0.15 | 0.55 | 0.81 | 7.1 |
| 3.0 | 0.74 | 0.38 | 0.00 | 0.99 | 0.39 | 0.57 | 0.47 | 0.16 | 0.53 | 0.83 | 7.0 |
| 3.1 | 0.74 | 0.37 | 0.01 | 0.98 | 0.39 | 0.58 | 0.46 | 0.18 | 0.50 | 0.85 | 6.9 |
| 3.2 | 0.75 | 0.36 | 0.01 | 0.98 | 0.39 | 0.59 | 0.45 | 0.19 | 0.49 | 0.88 | 6.8 |
| 3.3 | 0.75 | 0.36 | 0.02 | 0.97 | 0.40 | 0.59 | 0.44 | 0.21 | 0.47 | 0.90 | 6.7 |
| 3.4 | 0.76 | 0.35 | 0.03 | 0.97 | 0.40 | 0.60 | 0.43 | 0.22 | 0.45 | 0.93 | 6.6 |
| 3.5 | 0.76 | 0.34 | 0.04 | 0.96 | 0.40 | 0.61 | 0.42 | 0.24 | 0.43 | 0.95 | 6.5 |
| 3.6 | 0.76 | 0.33 | 0.06 | 0.95 | 0.40 | 0.62 | 0.41 | 0.26 | 0.41 | 0.98 | 6.4 |
| 3.7 | 0.77 | 0.32 | 0.08 | 0.94 | 0.40 | 0.63 | 0.40 | 0.27 | 0.39 | 1.00 | 6.3 |
| 3.8 | 0.77 | 0.32 | 0.10 | 0.93 | 0.40 | 0.63 | 0.39 | 0.28 | 0.37 | 1.03 | 6.2 |
| 3.9 | 0.78 | 0.31 | 0.12 | 0.92 | 0.40 | 0.64 | 0.38 | 0.29 | 0.35 | 1.05 | 6.1 |
| 4.0 | 0.78 | 0.30 | 0.14 | 0.91 | 0.40 | 0.65 | 0.37 | 0.30 | 0.33 | 1.08 | 6.0 |
| 4.1 | 0.78 | 0.29 | 0.17 | 0.90 | 0.40 | 0.66 | 0.36 | 0.31 | 0.31 | 1.10 | 5.9 |
| 4.2 | 0.78 | 0.28 | 0.20 | 0.88 | 0.39 | 0.66 | 0.35 | 0.32 | 0.29 | 1.13 | 5.8 |
| 4.3 | 0.79 | 0.28 | 0.23 | 0.87 | 0.39 | 0.67 | 0.34 | 0.33 | 0.28 | 1.15 | 5.7 |
| 4.4 | 0.79 | 0.27 | 0.27 | 0.85 | 0.38 | 0.68 | 0.33 | 0.34 | 0.26 | 1.18 | 5.6 |
| 4.5 | 0.79 | 0.26 | 0.30 | 0.84 | 0.38 | 0.68 | 0.32 | 0.35 | 0.25 | 1.20 | 5.5 |
| 4.6 | 0.79 | 0.25 | 0.34 | 0.82 | 0.37 | 0.69 | 0.32 | 0.36 | 0.23 | 1.22 | 5.4 |
| 4.7 | 0.79 | 0.24 | 0.38 | 0.80 | 0.37 | 0.70 | 0.31 | 0.37 | 0.21 | 1.25 | 5.3 |
| 4.8 | 0.80 | 0.24 | 0.42 | 0.79 | 0.36 | 0.70 | 0.30 | 0.38 | 0.20 | 1.27 | 5.2 |
| 4.9 | 0.80 | 0.23 | 0.47 | 0.77 | 0.36 | 0.71 | 0.29 | 0.38 | 0.18 | 1.30 | 5.1 |
| 5.0 | 0.80 | 0.22 | 0.51 | 0.75 | 0.35 | 0.72 | 0.28 | 0.39 | 0.17 | 1.32 | 5.0 |
| Days. | **30** | **20** | **10** | **10** | **10** | **30** | **20** | **10** | **30** | **20** | Days. |

**Note.** — Arg. 48′ = Arg. 48 — 6.26.

# TABLES LI. - LVII.

| Tables | LI. | | LII. | LIII. | LIV. | LV. | | LVI. | LVII. | | |
|---|---|---|---|---|---|---|---|---|---|---|---|
| Arguments | **46.** | | **47.** | **48′.** | **49.** | **50.** | | **51.** | **52.** | | |
| Days. | **0** | **10** | **0** | **0** | **0** | **0** | **10** | **0** | **0** | **10** | Days. |
| Days. 5.0 | ″0.80 | ″0.22 | ″0.51 | ″0.75 | ″0.35 | ″0.72 | ″0.28 | ″0.39 | ″0.17 | ″1.32 | Days. 5.0 |
| 5.1 | 0.80 | 0.21 | 0.56 | 0.73 | 0.34 | 0.72 | 0.27 | 0.39 | 0.16 | 1.34 | 4.9 |
| 5.2 | 0.80 | 0.20 | 0.61 | 0.71 | 0.34 | 0.73 | 0.26 | 0.39 | 0.14 | 1.36 | 4.8 |
| 5.3 | 0.80 | 0.20 | 0.66 | 0.69 | 0.33 | 0.73 | 0.25 | 0.40 | 0.13 | 1.39 | 4.7 |
| 5.4 | 0.80 | 0.19 | 0.71 | 0.67 | 0.33 | 0.74 | 0.24 | 0.40 | 0.12 | 1.41 | 4.6 |
| 5.5 | 0.80 | 0.18 | 0.76 | 0.65 | 0.32 | 0.74 | 0.23 | 0.40 | 0.11 | 1.43 | 4.5 |
| 5.6 | 0.80 | 0.17 | 0.81 | 0.63 | 0.31 | 0.75 | 0.23 | 0.40 | 0.10 | 1.45 | 4.4 |
| 5.7 | 0.80 | 0.16 | 0.86 | 0.61 | 0.30 | 0.75 | 0.22 | 0.39 | 0.09 | 1.47 | 4.3 |
| 5.8 | 0.80 | 0.16 | 0.92 | 0.59 | 0.30 | 0.76 | 0.21 | 0.39 | 0.08 | 1.50 | 4.2 |
| 5.9 | 0.80 | 0.15 | 0.97 | 0.57 | 0.29 | 0.76 | 0.20 | 0.39 | 0.07 | 1.52 | 4.1 |
| 6.0 | 0.80 | 0.14 | 1.03 | 0.55 | 0.28 | 0.77 | 0.19 | 0.38 | 0.06 | 1.54 | 4.0 |
| 6.1 | 0.80 | 0.13 | 1.09 | 0.53 | 0.27 | 0.77 | 0.18 | 0.38 | 0.05 | 1.56 | 3.9 |
| 6.2 | 0.80 | 0.13 | 1.14 | 0.51 | 0.26 | 0.78 | 0.17 | 0.37 | 0.04 | 1.58 | 3.8 |
| 6.3 | 0.79 | 0.12 | 1.20 | 0.49 | 0.25 | 0.78 | 0.17 | 0.36 | 0.03 | 1.60 | 3.7 |
| 6.4 | 0.79 | 0.12 | 1.26 | 0.47 | 0.24 | 0.78 | 0.16 | 0.35 | 0.03 | 1.62 | 3.6 |
| 6.5 | 0.79 | 0.11 | 1.32 | 0.45 | 0.23 | 0.79 | 0.15 | 0.34 | 0.02 | 1.64 | 3.5 |
| 6.6 | 0.79 | 0.10 | 1.38 | 0.43 | 0.22 | 0.79 | 0.14 | 0.33 | 0.02 | 1.66 | 3.4 |
| 6.7 | 0.79 | 0.10 | 1.44 | 0.41 | 0.21 | 0.79 | 0.14 | 0.32 | 0.01 | 1.68 | 3.3 |
| 6.8 | 0.78 | 0.09 | 1.50 | 0.39 | 0.20 | 0.80 | 0.13 | 0.31 | 0.01 | 1.69 | 3.2 |
| 6.9 | 0.78 | 0.09 | 1.55 | 0.37 | 0.19 | 0.80 | 0.12 | 0.30 | 0.01 | 1.71 | 3.1 |
| 7.0 | 0.78 | 0.08 | 1.61 | 0.35 | 0.18 | 0.80 | 0.11 | 0.29 | 0.00 | 1.73 | 3.0 |
| 7.1 | 0.78 | 0.08 | 1.67 | 0.33 | 0.17 | 0.80 | 0.10 | 0.28 | 0.00 | 1.75 | 2.9 |
| 7.2 | 0.77 | 0.07 | 1.72 | 0.31 | 0.16 | 0.80 | 0.10 | 0.27 | 0.00 | 1.76 | 2.8 |
| 7.3 | 0.77 | 0.07 | 1.78 | 0.29 | 0.15 | 0.80 | 0.09 | 0.26 | 0.00 | 1.78 | 2.7 |
| 7.4 | 0.76 | 0.06 | 1.83 | 0.27 | 0.14 | 0.80 | 0.09 | 0.24 | 0.00 | 1.79 | 2.6 |
| 7.5 | 0.76 | 0.06 | 1.88 | 0.25 | 0.13 | 0.80 | 0.08 | 0.22 | 0.00 | 1.81 | 2.5 |
| 7.6 | 0.76 | 0.06 | 1.93 | 0.23 | 0.12 | 0.80 | 0.07 | 0.21 | 0.00 | 1.82 | 2.4 |
| 7.7 | 0.75 | 0.05 | 1.98 | 0.21 | 0.11 | 0.80 | 0.07 | 0.19 | 0.01 | 1.84 | 2.3 |
| 7.8 | 0.75 | 0.05 | 2.03 | 0.20 | 0.11 | 0.80 | 0.06 | 0.18 | 0.01 | 1.85 | 2.2 |
| 7.9 | 0.74 | 0.04 | 2.07 | 0.18 | 0.10 | 0.80 | 0.06 | 0.16 | 0.01 | 1.87 | 2.1 |
| 8.0 | 0.74 | 0.04 | 2.12 | 0.16 | 0.09 | 0.80 | 0.05 | 0.15 | 0.01 | 1.88 | 2.0 |
| 8.1 | 0.73 | 0.04 | 2.16 | 0.15 | 0.08 | 0.80 | 0.05 | 0.14 | 0.02 | 1.89 | 1.9 |
| 8.2 | 0.73 | 0.03 | 2.20 | 0.13 | 0.07 | 0.80 | 0.04 | 0.13 | 0.02 | 1.90 | 1.8 |
| 8.3 | 0.72 | 0.03 | 2.24 | 0.12 | 0.07 | 0.80 | 0.04 | 0.11 | 0.03 | 1.91 | 1.7 |
| 8.4 | 0.72 | 0.02 | 2.28 | 0.10 | 0.06 | 0.79 | 0.03 | 0.10 | 0.03 | 1.92 | 1.6 |
| 8.5 | 0.71 | 0.02 | 2.32 | 0.09 | 0.05 | 0.79 | 0.03 | 0.09 | 0.04 | 1.93 | 1.5 |
| 8.6 | 0.70 | 0.02 | 2.35 | 0.08 | 0.04 | 0.79 | 0.02 | 0.08 | 0.05 | 1.94 | 1.4 |
| 8.7 | 0.70 | 0.02 | 2.38 | 0.07 | 0.04 | 0.79 | 0.02 | 0.07 | 0.05 | 1.95 | 1.3 |
| 8.8 | 0.69 | 0.01 | 2.41 | 0.06 | 0.03 | 0.78 | 0.02 | 0.06 | 0.06 | 1.96 | 1.2 |
| 8.9 | 0.69 | 0.01 | 2.44 | 0.05 | 0.03 | 0.78 | 0.01 | 0.05 | 0.07 | 1.96 | 1.1 |
| 9.0 | 0.68 | 0.01 | 2.47 | 0.04 | 0.02 | 0.78 | 0.01 | 0.04 | 0.08 | 1.97 | 1.0 |
| 9.1 | 0.67 | 0.01 | 2.49 | 0.03 | 0.02 | 0.77 | 0.01 | 0.03 | 0.09 | 1.97 | 0.9 |
| 9.2 | 0.67 | 0.01 | 2.51 | 0.03 | 0.02 | 0.77 | 0.01 | 0.03 | 0.10 | 1.98 | 0.8 |
| 9.3 | 0.66 | 0.00 | 2.53 | 0.02 | 0.01 | 0.76 | 0.01 | 0.02 | 0.11 | 1.98 | 0.7 |
| 9.4 | 0.66 | 0.00 | 2.55 | 0.02 | 0.01 | 0.76 | 0.00 | 0.02 | 0.13 | 1.99 | 0.6 |
| 9.5 | 0.65 | 0.00 | 2.57 | 0.01 | 0.01 | 0.75 | 0.00 | 0.01 | 0.14 | 1.99 | 0.5 |
| 9.6 | 0.64 | 0.00 | 2.58 | 0.01 | 0.01 | 0.75 | 0.00 | 0.01 | 0.15 | 1.99 | 0.4 |
| 9.7 | 0.63 | 0.00 | 2.59 | 0.01 | 0.00 | 0.74 | 0.00 | 0.01 | 0.16 | 2.00 | 0.3 |
| 9.8 | 0.63 | 0.00 | 2.59 | 0.00 | 0.00 | 0.74 | 0.00 | 0.00 | 0.18 | 2.00 | 0.2 |
| 9.9 | 0.62 | 0.00 | 2.60 | 0.00 | 0.00 | 0.73 | 0.00 | 0.00 | 0.19 | 2.00 | 0.1 |
| 10.0 | 0.61 | 0.00 | 2.60 | 0.00 | 0.00 | 0.73 | 0.00 | 0.00 | 0.21 | 2.00 | 0.0 |
| Days. | **30** | **20** | **10** | **10** | **10** | **30** | **20** | **10** | **30** | **20** | Days. |

**Note.—Arg. 48′ = Arg. 48 — 6.26.**

# TABLES LVIII.-LXII.

| Tables | LVIII. | | | | | | LIX. | LX. | LXI. | LXII. | |
|---|---|---|---|---|---|---|---|---|---|---|---|
| Arguments | **53.** | | | | | | **54.** | **55.** | **56.** | **57.** | |
| Days. | **0** | **10** | **20** | **30** | **40** | **50** | **0** | **0** | **0** | **0** | Days. |
| 0.0 | 5″.19 | 4″.92 | 4″.00 | 2″.69 | 1″.35 | 0″.37 | 0″.64 | 0″.01 | 0″.65 | 0″.88 | 10.0 |
| 0.1 | 5.19 | 4.91 | 3.99 | 2.67 | 1.34 | 0.36 | 0.73 | 0.00 | 0.68 | 0.80 | 9.9 |
| 0.2 | 5.19 | 4.91 | 3.98 | 2.66 | 1.33 | 0.36 | 0.83 | 0.00 | 0.71 | 0.71 | 9.8 |
| 0.3 | 5.19 | 4.90 | 3.97 | 2.65 | 1.31 | 0.35 | 0.92 | 0.00 | 0.75 | 0.62 | 9.7 |
| 0.4 | 5.19 | 4.90 | 3.95 | 2.63 | 1.30 | 0.34 | 1.02 | 0.01 | 0.78 | 0.53 | 9.6 |
| 0.5 | 5.19 | 4.89 | 3.94 | 2.62 | 1.29 | 0.34 | 1.12 | 0.02 | 0.81 | 0.45 | 9.5 |
| 0.6 | 5.20 | 4.88 | 3.93 | 2.61 | 1.28 | 0.33 | 1.22 | 0.04 | 0.84 | 0.37 | 9.4 |
| 0.7 | 5.20 | 4.87 | 3.92 | 2.59 | 1.27 | 0.32 | 1.32 | 0.05 | 0.87 | 0.30 | 9.3 |
| 0.8 | 5.20 | 4.87 | 3.91 | 2.58 | 1.25 | 0.32 | 1.42 | 0.07 | 0.91 | 0.23 | 9.2 |
| 0.9 | 5.20 | 4.86 | 3.89 | 2.57 | 1.24 | 0.31 | 1.52 | 0.10 | 0.94 | 0.17 | 9.1 |
| 1.0 | 5.20 | 4.85 | 3.88 | 2.55 | 1.23 | 0.30 | 1.61 | 0.12 | 0.97 | 0.12 | 9.0 |
| 1.1 | 5.20 | 4.84 | 3.87 | 2.54 | 1.22 | 0.30 | 1.70 | 0.15 | 1.00 | 0.08 | 8.9 |
| 1.2 | 5.20 | 4.84 | 3.86 | 2.52 | 1.21 | 0.29 | 1.79 | 0.19 | 1.03 | 0.04 | 8.8 |
| 1.3 | 5.20 | 4.83 | 3.85 | 2.51 | 1.19 | 0.28 | 1.88 | 0.22 | 1.06 | 0.02 | 8.7 |
| 1.4 | 5.20 | 4.83 | 3.83 | 2.50 | 1.18 | 0.28 | 1.96 | 0.26 | 1.09 | 0.01 | 8.6 |
| 1.5 | 5.20 | 4.82 | 3.82 | 2.48 | 1.17 | 0.27 | 2.03 | 0.30 | 1.12 | 0.00 | 8.5 |
| 1.6 | 5.20 | 4.81 | 3.81 | 2.47 | 1.16 | 0.26 | 2.10 | 0.35 | 1.15 | 0.00 | 8.4 |
| 1.7 | 5.20 | 4.80 | 3.80 | 2.45 | 1.15 | 0.26 | 2.16 | 0.39 | 1.17 | 0.01 | 8.3 |
| 1.8 | 5.20 | 4.80 | 3.79 | 2.44 | 1.13 | 0.25 | 2.22 | 0.44 | 1.20 | 0.04 | 8.2 |
| 1.9 | 5.20 | 4.79 | 3.77 | 2.43 | 1.12 | 0.24 | 2.27 | 0.49 | 1.22 | 0.08 | 8.1 |
| 2.0 | 5.20 | 4.78 | 3.76 | 2.41 | 1.11 | 0.24 | 2.31 | 0.54 | 1.24 | 0.12 | 8.0 |
| 2.1 | 5.20 | 4.77 | 3.75 | 2.40 | 1.10 | 0.23 | 2.34 | 0.59 | 1.26 | 0.17 | 7.9 |
| 2.2 | 5.20 | 4.76 | 3.74 | 2.38 | 1.09 | 0.22 | 2.37 | 0.65 | 1.28 | 0.23 | 7.8 |
| 2.3 | 5.20 | 4.76 | 3.72 | 2.37 | 1.08 | 0.22 | 2.39 | 0.70 | 1.30 | 0.29 | 7.7 |
| 2.4 | 5.20 | 4.75 | 3.71 | 2.36 | 1.07 | 0.21 | 2.40 | 0.76 | 1.31 | 0.36 | 7.6 |
| 2.5 | 5.20 | 4.74 | 3.70 | 2.34 | 1.06 | 0.20 | 2.40 | 0.82 | 1.33 | 0.44 | 7.5 |
| 2.6 | 5.19 | 4.73 | 3.68 | 2.33 | 1.04 | 0.20 | 2.39 | 0.88 | 1.34 | 0.52 | 7.4 |
| 2.7 | 5.19 | 4.73 | 3.67 | 2.31 | 1.03 | 0.19 | 2.37 | 0.94 | 1.35 | 0.60 | 7.3 |
| 2.8 | 5.19 | 4.72 | 3.66 | 2.30 | 1.02 | 0.19 | 2.35 | 1.00 | 1.36 | 0.69 | 7.2 |
| 2.9 | 5.19 | 4.71 | 3.64 | 2.29 | 1.01 | 0.18 | 2.32 | 1.06 | 1.37 | 0.78 | 7.1 |
| 3.0 | 5.19 | 4.70 | 3.63 | 2.27 | 1.00 | 0.18 | 2.28 | 1.12 | 1.38 | 0.87 | 7.0 |
| 3.1 | 5.19 | 4.69 | 3.62 | 2.26 | 0.99 | 0.17 | 2.23 | 1.17 | 1.38 | 0.96 | 6.9 |
| 3.2 | 5.19 | 4.68 | 3.60 | 2.24 | 0.98 | 0.17 | 2.18 | 1.23 | 1.39 | 1.04 | 6.8 |
| 3.3 | 5.18 | 4.67 | 3.59 | 2.23 | 0.97 | 0.16 | 2.12 | 1.28 | 1.40 | 1.12 | 6.7 |
| 3.4 | 5.18 | 4.66 | 3.58 | 2.22 | 0.96 | 0.16 | 2.05 | 1.33 | 1.40 | 1.20 | 6.6 |
| 3.5 | 5.18 | 4.65 | 3.56 | 2.20 | 0.95 | 0.15 | 1.98 | 1.38 | 1.39 | 1.28 | 6.5 |
| 3.6 | 5.18 | 4.65 | 3.55 | 2.19 | 0.93 | 0.15 | 1.90 | 1.42 | 1.39 | 1.35 | 6.4 |
| 3.7 | 5.18 | 4.64 | 3.54 | 2.17 | 0.92 | 0.14 | 1.82 | 1.47 | 1.38 | 1.41 | 6.3 |
| 3.8 | 5.17 | 4.63 | 3.52 | 2.16 | 0.91 | 0.14 | 1.73 | 1.51 | 1.38 | 1.46 | 6.2 |
| 3.9 | 5.17 | 4.62 | 3.51 | 2.15 | 0.90 | 0.13 | 1.64 | 1.55 | 1.37 | 1.50 | 6.1 |
| 4.0 | 5.17 | 4.61 | 3.50 | 2.13 | 0.89 | 0.13 | 1.54 | 1.59 | 1.37 | 1.54 | 6.0 |
| 4.1 | 5.17 | 4.60 | 3.48 | 2.12 | 0.88 | 0.12 | 1.45 | 1.63 | 1.36 | 1.57 | 5.9 |
| 4.2 | 5.17 | 4.59 | 3.47 | 2.10 | 0.87 | 0.12 | 1.35 | 1.66 | 1.35 | 1.59 | 5.8 |
| 4.3 | 5.16 | 4.58 | 3.46 | 2.09 | 0.86 | 0.11 | 1.25 | 1.69 | 1.34 | 1.60 | 5.7 |
| 4.4 | 5.16 | 4.57 | 3.44 | 2.08 | 0.85 | 0.11 | 1.15 | 1.72 | 1.32 | 1.60 | 5.6 |
| 4.5 | 5.16 | 4.57 | 3.43 | 2.06 | 0.84 | 0.10 | 1.05 | 1.74 | 1.31 | 1.59 | 5.5 |
| 4.6 | 5.16 | 4.56 | 3.42 | 2.05 | 0.83 | 0.10 | 0.95 | 1.76 | 1.29 | 1.57 | 5.4 |
| 4.7 | 5.16 | 4.55 | 3.40 | 2.03 | 0.82 | 0.10 | 0.85 | 1.77 | 1.27 | 1.54 | 5.3 |
| 4.8 | 5.15 | 4.54 | 3.39 | 2.02 | 0.81 | 0.09 | 0.76 | 1.78 | 1.25 | 1.50 | 5.2 |
| 4.9 | 5.15 | 4.53 | 3.38 | 2.01 | 0.80 | 0.09 | 0.67 | 1.79 | 1.23 | 1.45 | 5.1 |
| 5.0 | 5.15 | 4.52 | 3.37 | 1.99 | 0.79 | 0.09 | 0.58 | 1.80 | 1.21 | 1.39 | 5.0 |
| Days. | **110** | **100** | **90** | **80** | **70** | **60** | **10** | **10** | **10** | **10** | Days. |

# TABLES LVIII. - LXII.

| Tables | LVIII. | | | | | | LIX. | LX. | LXI. | LXII. | |
|---|---|---|---|---|---|---|---|---|---|---|---|
| Arguments | **53.** | | | | | | **54.** | **55.** | **56.** | **57.** | |
| Days. | **0** | **10** | **20** | **30** | **40** | **50** | **0** | **0** | **0** | **0** | Days. |
| Days. | " | " | " | " | " | " | " | " | " | " | Days. |
| 5.0 | 5.15 | 4.52 | 3.37 | 1.99 | 0.79 | 0.09 | 0.58 | 1.80 | 1.21 | 1.39 | 5.0 |
| 5.1 | 5.15 | 4.51 | 3.35 | 1.98 | 0.78 | 0.08 | 0.50 | 1.80 | 1.19 | 1.33 | 4.9 |
| 5.2 | 5.14 | 4.50 | 3.34 | 1.97 | 0.77 | 0.08 | 0.42 | 1.80 | 1.16 | 1.26 | 4.8 |
| 5.3 | 5.14 | 4.49 | 3.33 | 1.95 | 0.76 | 0.08 | 0.35 | 1.79 | 1.14 | 1.18 | 4.7 |
| 5.4 | 5.14 | 4.48 | 3.31 | 1.94 | 0.75 | 0.07 | 0.28 | 1.78 | 1.11 | 1.10 | 4.6 |
| 5.5 | 5.14 | 4.48 | 3.30 | 1.93 | 0.74 | 0.07 | 0.22 | 1.77 | 1.08 | 1.02 | 4.5 |
| 5.6 | 5.13 | 4.47 | 3.29 | 1.91 | 0.73 | 0.07 | 0.17 | 1.75 | 1.05 | 0.94 | 4.4 |
| 5.7 | 5.13 | 4.46 | 3.27 | 1.90 | 0.72 | 0.06 | 0.12 | 1.72 | 1.02 | 0.85 | 4.3 |
| 5.8 | 5.13 | 4.45 | 3.26 | 1.89 | 0.71 | 0.06 | 0.08 | 1.70 | 0.99 | 0.76 | 4.2 |
| 5.9 | 5.12 | 4.44 | 3.24 | 1.87 | 0.70 | 0.06 | 0.05 | 1.67 | 0.96 | 0.67 | 4.1 |
| 6.0 | 5.12 | 4.43 | 3.23 | 1.86 | 0.69 | 0.06 | 0.02 | 1.64 | 0.93 | 0.58 | 4.0 |
| 6.1 | 5.12 | 4.42 | 3.22 | 1.85 | 0.68 | 0.06 | 0.01 | 1.61 | 0.90 | 0.50 | 3.9 |
| 6.2 | 5.11 | 4.41 | 3.20 | 1.83 | 0.67 | 0.05 | 0.00 | 1.57 | 0.87 | 0.42 | 3.8 |
| 6.3 | 5.11 | 4.40 | 3.19 | 1.82 | 0.66 | 0.05 | 0.00 | 1.54 | 0.83 | 0.34 | 3.7 |
| 6.4 | 5.10 | 4.39 | 3.18 | 1.81 | 0.65 | 0.05 | 0.01 | 1.50 | 0.80 | 0.27 | 3.6 |
| 6.5 | 5.10 | 4.38 | 3.16 | 1.79 | 0.64 | 0.05 | 0.03 | 1.46 | 0.77 | 0.21 | 3.5 |
| 6.6 | 5.10 | 4.37 | 3.15 | 1.78 | 0.64 | 0.05 | 0.05 | 1.41 | 0.74 | 0.15 | 3.4 |
| 6.7 | 5.09 | 4.36 | 3.14 | 1.77 | 0.63 | 0.04 | 0.09 | 1.36 | 0.70 | 0.11 | 3.3 |
| 6.8 | 5.09 | 4.35 | 3.12 | 1.75 | 0.62 | 0.04 | 0.13 | 1.31 | 0.67 | 0.07 | 3.2 |
| 6.9 | 5.08 | 4.34 | 3.11 | 1.74 | 0.61 | 0.04 | 0.18 | 1.26 | 0.63 | 0.04 | 3.1 |
| 7.0 | 5.08 | 4.33 | 3.10 | 1.73 | 0.60 | 0.04 | 0.24 | 1.21 | 0.60 | 0.01 | 3.0 |
| 7.1 | 5.08 | 4.32 | 3.08 | 1.72 | 0.59 | 0.04 | 0.30 | 1.15 | 0.57 | 0.00 | 2.9 |
| 7.2 | 5.07 | 4.31 | 3.07 | 1.70 | 0.58 | 0.03 | 0.37 | 1.09 | 0.54 | 0.00 | 2.8 |
| 7.3 | 5.07 | 4.30 | 3.06 | 1.69 | 0.57 | 0.03 | 0.44 | 1.03 | 0.50 | 0.01 | 2.7 |
| 7.4 | 5.06 | 4.29 | 3.04 | 1.68 | 0.57 | 0.03 | 0.52 | 0.97 | 0.47 | 0.03 | 2.6 |
| 7.5 | 5.06 | 4.28 | 3.03 | 1.66 | 0.56 | 0.03 | 0.60 | 0.91 | 0.44 | 0.06 | 2.5 |
| 7.6 | 5.05 | 4.26 | 3.02 | 1.65 | 0.55 | 0.03 | 0.69 | 0.85 | 0.41 | 0.09 | 2.4 |
| 7.7 | 5.05 | 4.25 | 3.00 | 1.64 | 0.54 | 0.03 | 0.78 | 0.80 | 0.38 | 0.14 | 2.3 |
| 7.8 | 5.04 | 4.24 | 2.99 | 1.62 | 0.53 | 0.02 | 0.88 | 0.74 | 0.35 | 0.19 | 2.2 |
| 7.9 | 5.04 | 4.23 | 2.98 | 1.61 | 0.53 | 0.02 | 0.98 | 0.69 | 0.33 | 0.25 | 2.1 |
| 8.0 | 5.03 | 4.22 | 2.96 | 1.60 | 0.52 | 0.02 | 1.08 | 0.64 | 0.30 | 0.32 | 2.0 |
| 8.1 | 5.03 | 4.21 | 2.95 | 1.58 | 0.51 | 0.02 | 1.18 | 0.59 | 0.27 | 0.39 | 1.9 |
| 8.2 | 5.02 | 4.20 | 2.93 | 1.57 | 0.50 | 0.02 | 1.28 | 0.53 | 0.25 | 0.47 | 1.8 |
| 8.3 | 5.02 | 4.19 | 2.92 | 1.56 | 0.50 | 0.02 | 1.38 | 0.48 | 0.22 | 0.55 | 1.7 |
| 8.4 | 5.01 | 4.18 | 2.91 | 1.54 | 0.49 | 0.02 | 1.48 | 0.43 | 0.20 | 0.64 | 1.6 |
| 8.5 | 5.01 | 4.17 | 2.89 | 1.53 | 0.48 | 0.01 | 1.58 | 0.38 | 0.18 | 0.72 | 1.5 |
| 8.6 | 5.00 | 4.15 | 2.88 | 1.52 | 0.47 | 0.01 | 1.67 | 0.34 | 0.16 | 0.81 | 1.4 |
| 8.7 | 5.00 | 4.14 | 2.86 | 1.50 | 0.46 | 0.01 | 1.76 | 0.30 | 0.14 | 0.90 | 1.3 |
| 8.8 | 4.99 | 4.13 | 2.85 | 1.49 | 0.46 | 0.01 | 1.85 | 0.26 | 0.12 | 0.99 | 1.2 |
| 8.9 | 4.99 | 4.12 | 2.84 | 1.48 | 0.45 | 0.01 | 1.93 | 0.22 | 0.10 | 1.08 | 1.1 |
| 9.0 | 4.98 | 4.11 | 2.82 | 1.47 | 0.44 | 0.01 | 2.01 | 0.18 | 0.08 | 1.16 | 1.0 |
| 9.1 | 4.97 | 4.10 | 2.81 | 1.46 | 0.43 | 0.01 | 2.08 | 0.15 | 0.07 | 1.23 | 0.9 |
| 9.2 | 4.97 | 4.09 | 2.80 | 1.45 | 0.42 | 0.01 | 2.14 | 0.12 | 0.05 | 1.30 | 0.8 |
| 9.3 | 4.96 | 4.08 | 2.78 | 1.43 | 0.42 | 0.01 | 2.20 | 0.10 | 0.04 | 1.37 | 0.7 |
| 9.4 | 4.96 | 4.07 | 2.77 | 1.42 | 0.41 | 0.00 | 2.25 | 0.07 | 0.03 | 1.43 | 0.6 |
| 9.5 | 4.95 | 4.06 | 2.76 | 1.41 | 0.40 | 0.00 | 2.29 | 0.05 | 0.02 | 1.48 | 0.5 |
| 9.6 | 4.94 | 4.04 | 2.74 | 1.40 | 0.40 | 0.00 | 2.33 | 0.03 | 0.01 | 1.52 | 0.4 |
| 9.7 | 4.94 | 4.03 | 2.73 | 1.39 | 0.39 | 0.00 | 2.36 | 0.02 | 0.01 | 1.55 | 0.3 |
| 9.8 | 4.93 | 4.02 | 2.72 | 1.37 | 0.38 | 0.00 | 2.38 | 0.01 | 0.00 | 1.58 | 0.2 |
| 9.9 | 4.93 | 4.01 | 2.70 | 1.36 | 0.38 | 0.00 | 2.39 | 0.00 | 0.00 | 1.59 | 0.1 |
| 10.0 | 4.92 | 4.00 | 2.69 | 1.35 | 0.37 | 0.00 | 2.40 | 0.00 | 0.00 | 1.60 | 0.0 |
| Days. | **110** | **100** | **90** | **80** | **70** | **60** | **10** | **10** | **10** | **10** | Days. |

# TABLES LXIII.-LXIX.

| Tables | LXIII. | LXIV. | | LXV. | | LXVI. | LXVII. | LXVIII. | LXIX. | | |
|---|---|---|---|---|---|---|---|---|---|---|---|
| Arguments | **58.** | **59.** | | **60.** | | **61.** | **62.** | **63.** | **64.** | | |
| Days. | **0** | **0** | **10** | **0** | **10** | **0** | **0** | **0** | **0** | **10** | Days. |
| Days. | | | | | | | | | | | Days. |
| 0.0 | ″0.78 | ″1.20 | ″0.62 | ″0.08 | ″0.78 | ″0.01 | ″0.08 | ″0.27 | ″0.58 | ″0.35 | 10.0 |
| 0.1 | 0.79 | 1.20 | 0.61 | 0.09 | 0.77 | 0.02 | 0.10 | 0.26 | 0.58 | 0.35 | 9.9 |
| 0.2 | 0.81 | 1.20 | 0.60 | 0.09 | 0.77 | 0.03 | 0.12 | 0.24 | 0.58 | 0.34 | 9.8 |
| 0.3 | 0.82 | 1.20 | 0.59 | 0.10 | 0.76 | 0.05 | 0.14 | 0.23 | 0.58 | 0.34 | 9.7 |
| 0.4 | 0.84 | 1.20 | 0.58 | 0.11 | 0.76 | 0.07 | 0.16 | 0.21 | 0.58 | 0.33 | 9.6 |
| 0.5 | 0.85 | 1.20 | 0.57 | 0.12 | 0.75 | 0.09 | 0.18 | 0.20 | 0.59 | 0.33 | 9.5 |
| 0.6 | 0.86 | 1.20 | 0.57 | 0.13 | 0.75 | 0.11 | 0.20 | 0.19 | 0.59 | 0.32 | 9.4 |
| 0.7 | 0.88 | 1.20 | 0.56 | 0.13 | 0.74 | 0.13 | 0.23 | 0.17 | 0.59 | 0.32 | 9.3 |
| 0.8 | 0.89 | 1.20 | 0.55 | 0.14 | 0.74 | 0.16 | 0.25 | 0.16 | 0.59 | 0.31 | 9.2 |
| 0.9 | 0.91 | 1.20 | 0.54 | 0.15 | 0.73 | 0.19 | 0.28 | 0.15 | 0.59 | 0.31 | 9.1 |
| 1.0 | 0.92 | 1.20 | 0.53 | 0.16 | 0.73 | 0.22 | 0.31 | 0.14 | 0.59 | 0.30 | 9.0 |
| 1.1 | 0.93 | 1.20 | 0.52 | 0.17 | 0.72 | 0.25 | 0.34 | 0.13 | 0.59 | 0.30 | 8.9 |
| 1.2 | 0.94 | 1.20 | 0.51 | 0.18 | 0.71 | 0.28 | 0.37 | 0.12 | 0.59 | 0.29 | 8.8 |
| 1.3 | 0.95 | 1.19 | 0.50 | 0.19 | 0.71 | 0.32 | 0.39 | 0.11 | 0.59 | 0.29 | 8.7 |
| 1.4 | 0.96 | 1.19 | 0.49 | 0.20 | 0.70 | 0.36 | 0.42 | 0.10 | 0.59 | 0.28 | 8.6 |
| 1.5 | 0.97 | 1.19 | 0.48 | 0.21 | 0.69 | 0.40 | 0.44 | 0.09 | 0.60 | 0.28 | 8.5 |
| 1.6 | 0.97 | 1.19 | 0.47 | 0.22 | 0.68 | 0.44 | 0.46 | 0.08 | 0.60 | 0.27 | 8.4 |
| 1.7 | 0.98 | 1.19 | 0.46 | 0.23 | 0.68 | 0.47 | 0.48 | 0.07 | 0.60 | 0.27 | 8.3 |
| 1.8 | 0.98 | 1.18 | 0.45 | 0.24 | 0.67 | 0.51 | 0.50 | 0.06 | 0.60 | 0.26 | 8.2 |
| 1.9 | 0.99 | 1.18 | 0.44 | 0.25 | 0.66 | 0.55 | 0.51 | 0.05 | 0.60 | 0.26 | 8.1 |
| 2.0 | 0.99 | 1.18 | 0.43 | 0.26 | 0.65 | 0.59 | 0.53 | 0.04 | 0.60 | 0.25 | 8.0 |
| 2.1 | 0.99 | 1.18 | 0.42 | 0.27 | 0.64 | 0.62 | 0.54 | 0.03 | 0.60 | 0.25 | 7.9 |
| 2.2 | 1.00 | 1.17 | 0.41 | 0.28 | 0.63 | 0.65 | 0.55 | 0.03 | 0.60 | 0.24 | 7.8 |
| 2.3 | 1.00 | 1.17 | 0.40 | 0.29 | 0.62 | 0.68 | 0.56 | 0.02 | 0.60 | 0.24 | 7.7 |
| 2.4 | 1.00 | 1.17 | 0.39 | 0.30 | 0.61 | 0.70 | 0.57 | 0.02 | 0.60 | 0.23 | 7.6 |
| 2.5 | 0.99 | 1.16 | 0.38 | 0.31 | 0.60 | 0.72 | 0.58 | 0.01 | 0.60 | 0.23 | 7.5 |
| 2.6 | 0.99 | 1.16 | 0.38 | 0.33 | 0.59 | 0.74 | 0.59 | 0.01 | 0.59 | 0.22 | 7.4 |
| 2.7 | 0.99 | 1.16 | 0.37 | 0.34 | 0.58 | 0.75 | 0.60 | 0.01 | 0.59 | 0.22 | 7.3 |
| 2.8 | 0.98 | 1.15 | 0.36 | 0.35 | 0.57 | 0.77 | 0.59 | 0.00 | 0.59 | 0.21 | 7.2 |
| 2.9 | 0.98 | 1.15 | 0.35 | 0.36 | 0.56 | 0.78 | 0.58 | 0.00 | 0.59 | 0.21 | 7.1 |
| 3.0 | 0.98 | 1.15 | 0.34 | 0.37 | 0.55 | 0.79 | 0.57 | 0.00 | 0.59 | 0.20 | 7.0 |
| 3.1 | 0.97 | 1.14 | 0.33 | 0.38 | 0.54 | 0.80 | 0.56 | 0.00 | 0.59 | 0.20 | 6.9 |
| 3.2 | 0.97 | 1.14 | 0.32 | 0.39 | 0.53 | 0.80 | 0.55 | 0.00 | 0.59 | 0.19 | 6.8 |
| 3.3 | 0.96 | 1.13 | 0.32 | 0.40 | 0.52 | 0.80 | 0.54 | 0.00 | 0.59 | 0.19 | 6.7 |
| 3.4 | 0.96 | 1.13 | 0.31 | 0.41 | 0.51 | 0.79 | 0.53 | 0.00 | 0.59 | 0.18 | 6.6 |
| 3.5 | 0.95 | 1.13 | 0.30 | 0.42 | 0.50 | 0.78 | 0.52 | 0.00 | 0.59 | 0.18 | 6.5 |
| 3.6 | 0.94 | 1.12 | 0.29 | 0.44 | 0.49 | 0.76 | 0.50 | 0.00 | 0.58 | 0.17 | 6.4 |
| 3.7 | 0.93 | 1.12 | 0.28 | 0.45 | 0.48 | 0.75 | 0.49 | 0.01 | 0.58 | 0.17 | 6.3 |
| 3.8 | 0.92 | 1.12 | 0.28 | 0.46 | 0.47 | 0.73 | 0.47 | 0.01 | 0.58 | 0.16 | 6.2 |
| 3.9 | 0.90 | 1.11 | 0.27 | 0.47 | 0.46 | 0.71 | 0.45 | 0.01 | 0.58 | 0.16 | 6.1 |
| 4.0 | 0.89 | 1.11 | 0.26 | 0.48 | 0.45 | 0.69 | 0.43 | 0.02 | 0.58 | 0.15 | 6.0 |
| 4.1 | 0.88 | 1.10 | 0.25 | 0.49 | 0.44 | 0.66 | 0.41 | 0.02 | 0.58 | 0.15 | 5.9 |
| 4.2 | 0.86 | 1.10 | 0.24 | 0.50 | 0.43 | 0.63 | 0.39 | 0.03 | 0.58 | 0.14 | 5.8 |
| 4.3 | 0.85 | 1.09 | 0.24 | 0.51 | 0.42 | 0.60 | 0.36 | 0.03 | 0.57 | 0.14 | 5.7 |
| 4.4 | 0.84 | 1.09 | 0.23 | 0.52 | 0.41 | 0.57 | 0.34 | 0.04 | 0.57 | 0.13 | 5.6 |
| 4.5 | 0.82 | 1.08 | 0.22 | 0.53 | 0.40 | 0.54 | 0.31 | 0.05 | 0.57 | 0.13 | 5.5 |
| 4.6 | 0.80 | 1.07 | 0.21 | 0.55 | 0.38 | 0.50 | 0.28 | 0.06 | 0.57 | 0.12 | 5.4 |
| 4.7 | 0.79 | 1.07 | 0.20 | 0.56 | 0.37 | 0.47 | 0.25 | 0.07 | 0.57 | 0.12 | 5.3 |
| 4.8 | 0.77 | 1.06 | 0.20 | 0.57 | 0.36 | 0.43 | 0.23 | 0.08 | 0.56 | 0.11 | 5.2 |
| 4.9 | 0.75 | 1.06 | 0.19 | 0.58 | 0.35 | 0.39 | 0.21 | 0.09 | 0.56 | 0.11 | 5.1 |
| 5.0 | 0.73 | 1.05 | 0.18 | 0.59 | 0.34 | 0.35 | 0.19 | 0.10 | 0.56 | 0.10 | 5.0 |
| Days. | **10** | **30** | **20** | **30** | **20** | **10** | **10** | **10** | **30** | **20** | Days. |

# TABLES LXIII.-LXIX.

| Tables | LXIII. | LXIV. | | LXV. | | LXVI. | LXVII. | LXVIII. | LXIX. | | |
|---|---|---|---|---|---|---|---|---|---|---|---|
| Arguments | **58.** | **59.** | | **60.** | | **61.** | **62.** | **63.** | **64.** | | |
| Days. | **0** | **0** | **10** | **0** | **10** | **0** | **0** | **0** | **0** | **10** | Days. |
| 5.0 | 0.73 | 1.05 | 0.18 | 0.59 | 0.34 | 0.35 | 0.19 | 0.10 | 0.56 | 0.10 | 5.0 |
| 5.1 | 0.71 | 1.04 | 0.17 | 0.60 | 0.33 | 0.31 | 0.17 | 0.11 | 0.56 | 0.10 | 4.9 |
| 5.2 | 0.69 | 1.04 | 0.17 | 0.61 | 0.32 | 0.28 | 0.15 | 0.12 | 0.56 | 0.09 | 4.8 |
| 5.3 | 0.68 | 1.03 | 0.16 | 0.62 | 0.31 | 0.24 | 0.13 | 0.13 | 0.55 | 0.09 | 4.7 |
| 5.4 | 0.66 | 1.02 | 0.15 | 0.63 | 0.30 | 0.21 | 0.11 | 0.14 | 0.55 | 0.09 | 4.6 |
| 5.5 | 0.64 | 1.02 | 0.15 | 0.64 | 0.29 | 0.18 | 0.09 | 0.15 | 0.55 | 0.08 | 4.5 |
| 5.6 | 0.62 | 1.01 | 0.14 | 0.64 | 0.27 | 0.15 | 0.07 | 0.16 | 0.55 | 0.08 | 4.4 |
| 5.7 | 0.60 | 1.00 | 0.14 | 0.65 | 0.26 | 0.13 | 0.06 | 0.18 | 0.55 | 0.08 | 4.3 |
| 5.8 | 0.58 | 1.00 | 0.13 | 0.66 | 0.25 | 0.10 | 0.04 | 0.19 | 0.54 | 0.07 | 4.2 |
| 5.9 | 0.56 | 0.99 | 0.12 | 0.67 | 0.24 | 0.08 | 0.03 | 0.21 | 0.54 | 0.07 | 4.1 |
| 6.0 | 0.54 | 0.98 | 0.12 | 0.68 | 0.23 | 0.06 | 0.02 | 0.22 | 0.54 | 0.07 | 4.0 |
| 6.1 | 0.52 | 0.97 | 0.11 | 0.69 | 0.22 | 0.04 | 0.01 | 0.23 | 0.54 | 0.07 | 3.9 |
| 6.2 | 0.50 | 0.96 | 0.11 | 0.70 | 0.21 | 0.03 | 0.01 | 0.25 | 0.53 | 0.06 | 3.8 |
| 6.3 | 0.48 | 0.96 | 0.10 | 0.70 | 0.20 | 0.02 | 0.00 | 0.26 | 0.53 | 0.06 | 3.7 |
| 6.4 | 0.46 | 0.95 | 0.10 | 0.71 | 0.19 | 0.01 | 0.00 | 0.28 | 0.53 | 0.06 | 3.6 |
| 6.5 | 0.44 | 0.94 | 0.09 | 0.72 | 0.18 | 0.00 | 0.00 | 0.29 | 0.52 | 0.05 | 3.5 |
| 6.6 | 0.42 | 0.93 | 0.09 | 0.72 | 0.18 | 0.00 | 0.01 | 0.30 | 0.52 | 0.05 | 3.4 |
| 6.7 | 0.40 | 0.92 | 0.08 | 0.73 | 0.17 | 0.01 | 0.01 | 0.32 | 0.52 | 0.05 | 3.3 |
| 6.8 | 0.38 | 0.92 | 0.08 | 0.74 | 0.16 | 0.01 | 0.02 | 0.33 | 0.51 | 0.05 | 3.2 |
| 6.9 | 0.36 | 0.91 | 0.07 | 0.74 | 0.15 | 0.02 | 0.03 | 0.35 | 0.51 | 0.04 | 3.1 |
| 7.0 | 0.34 | 0.90 | 0.07 | 0.75 | 0.14 | 0.03 | 0.04 | 0.36 | 0.50 | 0.04 | 3.0 |
| 7.1 | 0.32 | 0.89 | 0.06 | 0.75 | 0.13 | 0.05 | 0.06 | 0.37 | 0.50 | 0.04 | 2.9 |
| 7.2 | 0.30 | 0.88 | 0.06 | 0.76 | 0.12 | 0.07 | 0.07 | 0.39 | 0.49 | 0.04 | 2.8 |
| 7.3 | 0.28 | 0.87 | 0.05 | 0.76 | 0.12 | 0.09 | 0.09 | 0.40 | 0.49 | 0.03 | 2.7 |
| 7.4 | 0.26 | 0.86 | 0.05 | 0.77 | 0.11 | 0.11 | 0.11 | 0.41 | 0.48 | 0.03 | 2.6 |
| 7.5 | 0.24 | 0.85 | 0.04 | 0.77 | 0.10 | 0.13 | 0.13 | 0.42 | 0.48 | 0.03 | 2.5 |
| 7.6 | 0.22 | 0.85 | 0.04 | 0.78 | 0.09 | 0.16 | 0.15 | 0.43 | 0.47 | 0.03 | 2.4 |
| 7.7 | 0.21 | 0.84 | 0.04 | 0.78 | 0.08 | 0.19 | 0.17 | 0.45 | 0.47 | 0.03 | 2.3 |
| 7.8 | 0.19 | 0.83 | 0.03 | 0.78 | 0.08 | 0.22 | 0.20 | 0.46 | 0.46 | 0.02 | 2.2 |
| 7.9 | 0.18 | 0.82 | 0.03 | 0.79 | 0.07 | 0.25 | 0.22 | 0.47 | 0.46 | 0.02 | 2.1 |
| 8.0 | 0.16 | 0.81 | 0.03 | 0.79 | 0.06 | 0.29 | 0.25 | 0.48 | 0.45 | 0.02 | 2.0 |
| 8.1 | 0.15 | 0.80 | 0.03 | 0.79 | 0.05 | 0.32 | 0.27 | 0.49 | 0.45 | 0.02 | 1.9 |
| 8.2 | 0.13 | 0.79 | 0.02 | 0.79 | 0.05 | 0.36 | 0.30 | 0.50 | 0.44 | 0.02 | 1.8 |
| 8.3 | 0.12 | 0.78 | 0.02 | 0.79 | 0.04 | 0.39 | 0.32 | 0.51 | 0.44 | 0.02 | 1.7 |
| 8.4 | 0.10 | 0.77 | 0.02 | 0.80 | 0.04 | 0.43 | 0.35 | 0.52 | 0.43 | 0.01 | 1.6 |
| 8.5 | 0.09 | 0.76 | 0.02 | 0.80 | 0.04 | 0.47 | 0.38 | 0.53 | 0.43 | 0.01 | 1.5 |
| 8.6 | 0.08 | 0.76 | 0.02 | 0.80 | 0.03 | 0.51 | 0.40 | 0.54 | 0.42 | 0.01 | 1.4 |
| 8.7 | 0.07 | 0.75 | 0.01 | 0.80 | 0.03 | 0.54 | 0.43 | 0.55 | 0.42 | 0.01 | 1.3 |
| 8.8 | 0.06 | 0.74 | 0.01 | 0.80 | 0.03 | 0.58 | 0.45 | 0.56 | 0.41 | 0.01 | 1.2 |
| 8.9 | 0.05 | 0.73 | 0.01 | 0.80 | 0.02 | 0.61 | 0.47 | 0.56 | 0.41 | 0.01 | 1.1 |
| 9.0 | 0.04 | 0.72 | 0.01 | 0.80 | 0.02 | 0.64 | 0.49 | 0.57 | 0.40 | 0.01 | 1.0 |
| 9.1 | 0.03 | 0.71 | 0.01 | 0.80 | 0.02 | 0.67 | 0.51 | 0.57 | 0.40 | 0.01 | 0.9 |
| 9.2 | 0.03 | 0.70 | 0.01 | 0.79 | 0.01 | 0.69 | 0.53 | 0.58 | 0.39 | 0.01 | 0.8 |
| 9.3 | 0.02 | 0.69 | 0.01 | 0.79 | 0.01 | 0.72 | 0.54 | 0.58 | 0.39 | 0.00 | 0.7 |
| 9.4 | 0.02 | 0.68 | 0.00 | 0.79 | 0.01 | 0.74 | 0.56 | 0.59 | 0.38 | 0.00 | 0.6 |
| 9.5 | 0.01 | 0.67 | 0.00 | 0.79 | 0.01 | 0.76 | 0.57 | 0.59 | 0.38 | 0.00 | 0.5 |
| 9.6 | 0.01 | 0.66 | 0.00 | 0.79 | 0.01 | 0.77 | 0.58 | 0.59 | 0.37 | 0.00 | 0.4 |
| 9.7 | 0.01 | 0.65 | 0.00 | 0.78 | 0.00 | 0.78 | 0.59 | 0.59 | 0.37 | 0.00 | 0.3 |
| 9.8 | 0.00 | 0.64 | 0.00 | 0.78 | 0.00 | 0.79 | 0.59 | 0.60 | 0.36 | 0.00 | 0.2 |
| 9.9 | 0.00 | 0.63 | 0.00 | 0.78 | 0.00 | 0.80 | 0.60 | 0.60 | 0.36 | 0.00 | 0.1 |
| 10.0 | 0.00 | 0.62 | 0.00 | 0.78 | 0.00 | 0.80 | 0.60 | 0.60 | 0.35 | 0.00 | 0.0 |
| Days. | **10** | **30** | **20** | **30** | **20** | **10** | **10** | **10** | **30** | **20** | Days. |

# TABLES LXX.-LXXIV.

| Tables | LXX. | LXXI. | | LXXII. | | LXXIII. | | |
|---|---|---|---|---|---|---|---|---|
| Arguments | **65.** | **66.** | | **67.** | | **68.** | | |
| Days. | **0** | **0** | **10** | **0** | **10** | **0** | **10** | Days. |
| Days | ″ | ″ | ″ | ″ | ″ | ″ | ″ | Days. |
| 0.0 | 0.35 | 0.38 | 0.24 | 1.13 | 1.66 | 0.58 | 0.25 | 10.0 |
| 0.1 | 0.34 | 0.38 | 0.23 | 1.15 | 1.64 | 0.56 | 0.26 | 9.9 |
| 0.2 | 0.32 | 0.38 | 0.23 | 1.17 | 1.62 | 0.55 | 0.27 | 9.8 |
| 0.3 | 0.31 | 0.38 | 0.23 | 1.19 | 1.61 | 0.53 | 0.29 | 9.7 |
| 0.4 | 0.29 | 0.38 | 0.22 | 1.22 | 1.59 | 0.52 | 0.30 | 9.6 |
| 0.5 | 0.28 | 0.38 | 0.22 | 1.24 | 1.57 | 0.50 | 0.31 | 9.5 |
| 0.6 | 0.26 | 0.39 | 0.22 | 1.26 | 1.55 | 0.49 | 0.33 | 9.4 |
| 0.7 | 0.24 | 0.39 | 0.21 | 1.28 | 1.53 | 0.47 | 0.34 | 9.3 |
| 0.8 | 0.23 | 0.39 | 0.21 | 1.31 | 1.51 | 0.46 | 0.35 | 9.2 |
| 0.9 | 0.21 | 0.39 | 0.20 | 1.33 | 1.49 | 0.44 | 0.37 | 9.1 |
| 1.0 | 0.19 | 0.39 | 0.20 | 1.35 | 1.47 | 0.43 | 0.38 | 9.0 |
| 1.1 | 0.17 | 0.39 | 0.20 | 1.37 | 1.45 | 0.41 | 0.39 | 8.9 |
| 1.2 | 0.16 | 0.39 | 0.19 | 1.39 | 1.43 | 0.40 | 0.41 | 8.8 |
| 1.3 | 0.14 | 0.39 | 0.19 | 1.41 | 1.41 | 0.38 | 0.42 | 8.7 |
| 1.4 | 0.13 | 0.39 | 0.19 | 1.43 | 1.39 | 0.37 | 0.44 | 8.6 |
| 1.5 | 0.11 | 0.40 | 0.18 | 1.46 | 1.37 | 0.36 | 0.45 | 8.5 |
| 1.6 | 0.10 | 0.40 | 0.18 | 1.48 | 1.34 | 0.34 | 0.47 | 8.4 |
| 1.7 | 0.08 | 0.40 | 0.18 | 1.50 | 1.32 | 0.33 | 0.48 | 8.3 |
| 1.8 | 0.07 | 0.40 | 0.17 | 1.52 | 1.30 | 0.31 | 0.50 | 8.2 |
| 1.9 | 0.05 | 0.40 | 0.17 | 1.54 | 1.28 | 0.30 | 0.51 | 8.1 |
| 2.0 | 0.04 | 0.40 | 0.17 | 1.56 | 1.26 | 0.29 | 0.53 | 8.0 |
| 2.1 | 0.03 | 0.40 | 0.16 | 1.58 | 1.24 | 0.28 | 0.55 | 7.9 |
| 2.2 | 0.03 | 0.40 | 0.16 | 1.59 | 1.22 | 0.26 | 0.56 | 7.8 |
| 2.3 | 0.02 | 0.40 | 0.16 | 1.61 | 1.19 | 0.25 | 0.58 | 7.7 |
| 2.4 | 0.02 | 0.40 | 0.15 | 1.63 | 1.17 | 0.24 | 0.59 | 7.6 |
| 2.5 | 0.01 | 0.40 | 0.15 | 1.64 | 1.15 | 0.23 | 0.61 | 7.5 |
| 2.6 | 0.01 | 0.40 | 0.15 | 1.66 | 1.12 | 0.21 | 0.63 | 7.4 |
| 2.7 | 0.01 | 0.40 | 0.14 | 1.68 | 1.10 | 0.20 | 0.64 | 7.3 |
| 2.8 | 0.00 | 0.40 | 0.14 | 1.69 | 1.08 | 0.19 | 0.66 | 7.2 |
| 2.9 | 0.00 | 0.40 | 0.14 | 1.71 | 1.05 | 0.18 | 0.67 | 7.1 |
| 3.0 | 0.00 | 0.40 | 0.13 | 1.73 | 1.03 | 0.17 | 0.69 | 7.0 |
| 3.1 | 0.01 | 0.40 | 0.13 | 1.75 | 1.01 | 0.16 | 0.70 | 6.9 |
| 3.2 | 0.01 | 0.40 | 0.13 | 1.76 | 0.98 | 0.15 | 0.72 | 6.8 |
| 3.3 | 0.02 | 0.40 | 0.12 | 1.78 | 0.96 | 0.14 | 0.73 | 6.7 |
| 3.4 | 0.03 | 0.40 | 0.12 | 1.79 | 0.94 | 0.13 | 0.75 | 6.6 |
| 3.5 | 0.04 | 0.40 | 0.12 | 1.81 | 0.91 | 0.12 | 0.76 | 6.5 |
| 3.6 | 0.05 | 0.39 | 0.11 | 1.82 | 0.89 | 0.11 | 0.78 | 6.4 |
| 3.7 | 0.06 | 0.39 | 0.11 | 1.83 | 0.87 | 0.11 | 0.79 | 6.3 |
| 3.8 | 0.08 | 0.39 | 0.11 | 1.85 | 0.84 | 0.10 | 0.81 | 6.2 |
| 3.9 | 0.09 | 0.39 | 0.10 | 1.86 | 0.82 | 0.09 | 0.82 | 6.1 |
| 4.0 | 0.10 | 0.39 | 0.10 | 1.87 | 0.80 | 0.08 | 0.84 | 6.0 |
| 4.1 | 0.12 | 0.39 | 0.10 | 1.88 | 0.78 | 0.07 | 0.85 | 5.9 |
| 4.2 | 0.13 | 0.39 | 0.09 | 1.89 | 0.76 | 0.07 | 0.87 | 5.8 |
| 4.3 | 0.15 | 0.39 | 0.09 | 1.90 | 0.74 | 0.06 | 0.88 | 5.7 |
| 4.4 | 0.17 | 0.39 | 0.09 | 1.91 | 0.71 | 0.05 | 0.90 | 5.6 |
| 4.5 | 0.19 | 0.39 | 0.08 | 1.92 | 0.69 | 0.05 | 0.91 | 5.5 |
| 4.6 | 0.21 | 0.38 | 0.08 | 1.93 | 0.67 | 0.04 | 0.93 | 5.4 |
| 4.7 | 0.22 | 0.38 | 0.08 | 1.94 | 0.65 | 0.04 | 0.94 | 5.3 |
| 4.8 | 0.24 | 0.38 | 0.07 | 1.94 | 0.63 | 0.03 | 0.96 | 5.2 |
| 4.9 | 0.25 | 0.38 | 0.07 | 1.95 | 0.61 | 0.03 | 0.97 | 5.1 |
| 5.0 | 0.27 | 0.38 | 0.07 | 1.96 | 0.59 | 0.02 | 0.99 | 5.0 |
| Days. | **10** | **30** | **20** | **30** | **20** | **30** | **20** | Days. |

| LXXIV. | | | | |
|---|---|---|---|---|
| **69.** | | | | |
| Days. | **0** | **100** | **200** | Days. |
| Days. | ″ | ″ | ″ | Days. |
| 0 | 3.65 | 4.15 | 1.68 | 100 |
| 1 | 3.67 | 4.14 | 1.65 | 99 |
| 2 | 3.69 | 4.13 | 1.62 | 98 |
| 3 | 3.71 | 4.11 | 1.60 | 97 |
| 4 | 3.73 | 4.10 | 1.57 | 96 |
| 5 | 3.75 | 4.08 | 1.54 | 95 |
| 6 | 3.77 | 4.07 | 1.51 | 94 |
| 7 | 3.79 | 4.05 | 1.48 | 93 |
| 8 | 3.81 | 4.04 | 1.46 | 92 |
| 9 | 3.83 | 4.02 | 1.43 | 91 |
| 10 | 3.85 | 4.00 | 1.40 | 90 |
| 11 | 3.87 | 3.98 | 1.37 | 89 |
| 12 | 3.89 | 3.97 | 1.34 | 88 |
| 13 | 3.90 | 3.95 | 1.32 | 87 |
| 14 | 3.92 | 3.93 | 1.29 | 86 |
| 15 | 3.94 | 3.91 | 1.26 | 85 |
| 16 | 3.96 | 3.89 | 1.24 | 84 |
| 17 | 3.98 | 3.88 | 1.21 | 83 |
| 18 | 3.99 | 3.86 | 1.18 | 82 |
| 19 | 4.01 | 3.84 | 1.16 | 81 |
| 20 | 4.03 | 3.82 | 1.13 | 80 |
| 21 | 4.05 | 3.80 | 1.11 | 79 |
| 22 | 4.07 | 3.78 | 1.08 | 78 |
| 23 | 4.08 | 3.76 | 1.06 | 77 |
| 24 | 4.10 | 3.74 | 1.03 | 76 |
| 25 | 4.11 | 3.72 | 1.00 | 75 |
| 26 | 4.13 | 3.69 | 0.98 | 74 |
| 27 | 4.14 | 3.67 | 0.95 | 73 |
| 28 | 4.16 | 3.65 | 0.93 | 72 |
| 29 | 4.17 | 3.63 | 0.91 | 71 |
| 30 | 4.18 | 3.61 | 0.89 | 70 |
| 31 | 4.19 | 3.59 | 0.87 | 69 |
| 32 | 4.20 | 3.56 | 0.84 | 68 |
| 33 | 4.22 | 3.54 | 0.82 | 67 |
| 34 | 4.23 | 3.52 | 0.80 | 66 |
| 35 | 4.24 | 3.49 | 0.78 | 65 |
| 36 | 4.25 | 3.47 | 0.76 | 64 |
| 37 | 4.26 | 3.44 | 0.73 | 63 |
| 38 | 4.27 | 3.42 | 0.71 | 62 |
| 39 | 4.28 | 3.39 | 0.69 | 61 |
| 40 | 4.29 | 3.37 | 0.67 | 60 |
| 41 | 4.30 | 3.35 | 0.65 | 59 |
| 42 | 4.31 | 3.32 | 0.63 | 58 |
| 43 | 4.31 | 3.30 | 0.61 | 57 |
| 44 | 4.32 | 3.27 | 0.59 | 56 |
| 45 | 4.33 | 3.25 | 0.57 | 55 |
| 46 | 4.33 | 3.22 | 0.55 | 54 |
| 47 | 4.34 | 3.19 | 0.53 | 53 |
| 48 | 4.35 | 3.17 | 0.51 | 52 |
| 49 | 4.35 | 3.14 | 0.49 | 51 |
| 50 | 4.36 | 3.11 | 0.47 | 50 |
| Days. | **500** | **400** | **300** | Days. |

# TABLES LXX.-LXXIV.

| TABLES | LXX. | LXXI. | | LXXII. | | LXXIII. | | | LXXIV. | | | | |
|---|---|---|---|---|---|---|---|---|---|---|---|---|---|
| ARGUMENTS | **65.** | **66.** | | **67.** | | **68.** | | | **69.** | | | | |
| Days. | **0** | **0** | **10** | **0** | **10** | **0** | **10** | Days. | Days. | **0** | **100** | **200** | Days. |
| Days | " | " | " | " | " | " | " | Days | Days | " | " | " | Days. |
| 5.0 | 0.27 | 0.38 | 0.07 | 1.96 | 0.59 | 0.02 | 0.99 | 5.0 | 50 | 4.36 | 3.11 | 0.47 | 50 |
| 5.1 | 0.28 | 0.38 | 0.07 | 1.96 | 0.57 | 0.02 | 1.00 | 4.9 | 51 | 4.36 | 3.08 | 0.45 | 49 |
| 5.2 | 0.30 | 0.38 | 0.06 | 1.97 | 0.55 | 0.02 | 1.02 | 4.8 | 52 | 4.37 | 3.06 | 0.44 | 48 |
| 5.3 | 0.31 | 0.37 | 0.06 | 1.97 | 0.53 | 0.01 | 1.03 | 4.7 | 53 | 4.37 | 3.03 | 0.42 | 47 |
| 5.4 | 0.33 | 0.37 | 0.06 | 1.98 | 0.51 | 0.01 | 1.05 | 4.6 | 54 | 4.38 | 3.00 | 0.41 | 46 |
| 5.5 | 0.34 | 0.37 | 0.06 | 1.98 | 0.49 | 0.01 | 1.06 | 4.5 | 55 | 4.38 | 2.98 | 0.39 | 45 |
| 5.6 | 0.35 | 0.37 | 0.06 | 1.98 | 0.47 | 0.01 | 1.07 | 4.4 | 56 | 4.39 | 2.95 | 0.38 | 44 |
| 5.7 | 0.36 | 0.37 | 0.05 | 1.99 | 0.45 | 0.00 | 1.09 | 4.3 | 57 | 4.39 | 2.92 | 0.36 | 43 |
| 5.8 | 0.37 | 0.36 | 0.05 | 1.99 | 0.43 | 0.00 | 1.10 | 4.2 | 58 | 4.39 | 2.90 | 0.34 | 42 |
| 5.9 | 0.38 | 0.36 | 0.05 | 2.00 | 0.41 | 0.00 | 1.12 | 4.1 | 59 | 4.40 | 2.87 | 0.33 | 41 |
| 6.0 | 0.39 | 0.36 | 0.05 | 2.00 | 0.39 | 0.00 | 1.13 | 4.0 | 60 | 4.40 | 2.84 | 0.31 | 40 |
| 6.1 | 0.39 | 0.36 | 0.05 | 2.00 | 0.37 | 0.00 | 1.14 | 3.9 | 61 | 4.40 | 2.81 | 0.29 | 39 |
| 6.2 | 0.39 | 0.35 | 0.05 | 2.00 | 0.35 | 0.00 | 1.15 | 3.8 | 62 | 4.40 | 2.78 | 0.28 | 38 |
| 6.3 | 0.40 | 0.35 | 0.04 | 2.00 | 0.34 | 0.00 | 1.17 | 3.7 | 63 | 4.40 | 2.75 | 0.26 | 37 |
| 6.4 | 0.40 | 0.35 | 0.04 | 2.00 | 0.32 | 0.00 | 1.18 | 3.6 | 64 | 4.40 | 2.73 | 0.25 | 36 |
| 6.5 | 0.40 | 0.34 | 0.04 | 2.00 | 0.30 | 0.00 | 1.19 | 3.5 | 65 | 4.40 | 2.70 | 0.23 | 35 |
| 6.6 | 0.39 | 0.34 | 0.04 | 2.00 | 0.29 | 0.00 | 1.20 | 3.4 | 66 | 4.40 | 2.67 | 0.22 | 34 |
| 6.7 | 0.39 | 0.34 | 0.04 | 1.99 | 0.27 | 0.01 | 1.21 | 3.3 | 67 | 4.39 | 2.64 | 0.20 | 33 |
| 6.8 | 0.38 | 0.33 | 0.04 | 1.99 | 0.26 | 0.01 | 1.23 | 3.2 | 68 | 4.39 | 2.61 | 0.19 | 32 |
| 6.9 | 0.38 | 0.33 | 0.03 | 1.99 | 0.24 | 0.01 | 1.24 | 3.1 | 69 | 4.39 | 2.58 | 0.18 | 31 |
| 7.0 | 0.37 | 0.33 | 0.03 | 1.99 | 0.23 | 0.01 | 1.25 | 3.0 | 70 | 4.39 | 2.55 | 0.17 | 30 |
| 7.1 | 0.36 | 0.33 | 0.03 | 1.98 | 0.21 | 0.01 | 1.26 | 2.9 | 71 | 4.38 | 2.52 | 0.16 | 29 |
| 7.2 | 0.35 | 0.32 | 0.03 | 1.98 | 0.20 | 0.02 | 1.27 | 2.8 | 72 | 4.38 | 2.49 | 0.15 | 28 |
| 7.3 | 0.34 | 0.32 | 0.03 | 1.97 | 0.18 | 0.02 | 1.28 | 2.7 | 73 | 4.38 | 2.46 | 0.14 | 27 |
| 7.4 | 0.32 | 0.32 | 0.02 | 1.97 | 0.17 | 0.02 | 1.28 | 2.6 | 74 | 4.37 | 2.43 | 0.13 | 26 |
| 7.5 | 0.31 | 0.31 | 0.02 | 1.96 | 0.16 | 0.03 | 1.29 | 2.5 | 75 | 4.37 | 2.41 | 0.12 | 25 |
| 7.6 | 0.29 | 0.31 | 0.02 | 1.95 | 0.14 | 0.03 | 1.30 | 2.4 | 76 | 4.36 | 2.38 | 0.11 | 24 |
| 7.7 | 0.28 | 0.31 | 0.02 | 1.95 | 0.13 | 0.04 | 1.31 | 2.3 | 77 | 4.36 | 2.35 | 0.11 | 23 |
| 7.8 | 0.26 | 0.30 | 0.02 | 1.94 | 0.12 | 0.04 | 1.32 | 2.2 | 78 | 4.36 | 2.32 | 0.10 | 22 |
| 7.9 | 0.25 | 0.30 | 0.01 | 1.93 | 0.11 | 0.05 | 1.32 | 2.1 | 79 | 4.35 | 2.29 | 0.09 | 21 |
| 8.0 | 0.23 | 0.30 | 0.01 | 1.92 | 0.10 | 0.06 | 1.33 | 2.0 | 80 | 4.35 | 2.26 | 0.08 | 20 |
| 8.1 | 0.21 | 0.30 | 0.01 | 1.91 | 0.09 | 0.07 | 1.34 | 1.9 | 81 | 4.34 | 2.23 | 0.07 | 19 |
| 8.2 | 0.19 | 0.29 | 0.01 | 1.90 | 0.08 | 0.07 | 1.34 | 1.8 | 82 | 4.33 | 2.20 | 0.07 | 18 |
| 8.3 | 0.18 | 0.29 | 0.01 | 1.89 | 0.07 | 0.08 | 1.35 | 1.7 | 83 | 4.33 | 2.17 | 0.06 | 17 |
| 8.4 | 0.16 | 0.29 | 0.01 | 1.88 | 0.07 | 0.09 | 1.35 | 1.6 | 84 | 4.32 | 2.14 | 0.06 | 16 |
| 8.5 | 0.14 | 0.28 | 0.01 | 1.87 | 0.06 | 0.10 | 1.36 | 1.5 | 85 | 4.31 | 2.11 | 0.05 | 15 |
| 8.6 | 0.13 | 0.28 | 0.01 | 1.86 | 0.05 | 0.10 | 1.36 | 1.4 | 86 | 4.30 | 2.09 | 0.04 | 14 |
| 8.7 | 0.11 | 0.28 | 0.00 | 1.84 | 0.05 | 0.11 | 1.37 | 1.3 | 87 | 4.30 | 2.06 | 0.04 | 13 |
| 8.8 | 0.10 | 0.27 | 0.00 | 1.83 | 0.04 | 0.12 | 1.37 | 1.2 | 88 | 4.29 | 2.03 | 0.03 | 12 |
| 8.9 | 0.08 | 0.27 | 0.00 | 1.82 | 0.03 | 0.13 | 1.38 | 1.1 | 89 | 4.28 | 2.00 | 0.03 | 11 |
| 9.0 | 0.07 | 0.27 | 0.00 | 1.81 | 0.03 | 0.14 | 1.38 | 1.0 | 90 | 4.27 | 1.97 | 0.02 | 10 |
| 9.1 | 0.06 | 0.27 | 0.00 | 1.80 | 0.03 | 0.15 | 1.38 | 0.9 | 91 | 4.26 | 1.94 | 0.02 | 09 |
| 9.2 | 0.05 | 0.26 | 0.00 | 1.79 | 0.02 | 0.16 | 1.39 | 0.8 | 92 | 4.25 | 1.91 | 0.02 | 08 |
| 9.3 | 0.04 | 0.26 | 0.00 | 1.77 | 0.02 | 0.17 | 1.39 | 0.7 | 93 | 4.23 | 1.88 | 0.01 | 07 |
| 9.4 | 0.03 | 0.26 | 0.00 | 1.76 | 0.02 | 0.18 | 1.39 | 0.6 | 94 | 4.22 | 1.85 | 0.01 | 06 |
| 9.5 | 0.02 | 0.25 | 0.00 | 1.74 | 0.01 | 0.19 | 1.39 | 0.5 | 95 | 4.21 | 1.82 | 0.01 | 05 |
| 9.6 | 0.02 | 0.25 | 0.00 | 1.73 | 0.01 | 0.21 | 1.39 | 0.4 | 96 | 4.20 | 1.80 | 0.01 | 04 |
| 9.7 | 0.01 | 0.25 | 0.00 | 1.71 | 0.01 | 0.22 | 1.40 | 0.3 | 97 | 4.19 | 1.77 | 0.00 | 03 |
| 9.8 | 0.01 | 0.24 | 0.00 | 1.70 | 0.00 | 0.23 | 1.40 | 0.2 | 98 | 4.17 | 1.74 | 0.00 | 02 |
| 9.9 | 0.00 | 0.24 | 0.00 | 1.68 | 0.00 | 0.24 | 1.40 | 0.1 | 99 | 4.16 | 1.71 | 0.00 | 01 |
| 10.0 | 0.00 | 0.24 | 0.00 | 1.66 | 0.00 | 0.25 | 1.40 | 0.0 | 100 | 4.15 | 1.68 | 0.00 | 00 |
| Days. | **10** | **30** | **20** | **30** | **20** | **30** | **20** | Days. | Days. | **500** | **400** | **300** | Days. |

# TABLES LXXV. LXXVI.

| Tables | LXXV. | LXXVI. |
|---|---|---|
| Arguments | **70.** | **71.** |

**Table LXXV. Argument 70.**

| Days. | **0** | **100** | Days. |
|---|---|---|---|
| Days. | ″ | ″ | Days. |
| 0 | 0.32 | 1.01 | 100 |
| 1 | 0.30 | 1.04 | 99 |
| 2 | 0.28 | 1.07 | 98 |
| 3 | 0.27 | 1.09 | 97 |
| 4 | 0.25 | 1.12 | 96 |
| 5 | 0.24 | 1.15 | 95 |
| 6 | 0.22 | 1.18 | 94 |
| 7 | 0.21 | 1.21 | 93 |
| 8 | 0.19 | 1.23 | 92 |
| 9 | 0.18 | 1.26 | 91 |
| 10 | 0.17 | 1.29 | 90 |
| 11 | 0.16 | 1.32 | 89 |
| 12 | 0.14 | 1.35 | 88 |
| 13 | 0.13 | 1.37 | 87 |
| 14 | 0.12 | 1.40 | 86 |
| 15 | 0.11 | 1.43 | 85 |
| 16 | 0.10 | 1.46 | 84 |
| 17 | 0.09 | 1.49 | 83 |
| 18 | 0.08 | 1.51 | 82 |
| 19 | 0.07 | 1.54 | 81 |
| 20 | 0.06 | 1.57 | 80 |
| 21 | 0.05 | 1.60 | 79 |
| 22 | 0.05 | 1.63 | 78 |
| 23 | 0.04 | 1.65 | 77 |
| 24 | 0.04 | 1.68 | 76 |
| 25 | 0.03 | 1.71 | 75 |
| 26 | 0.03 | 1.74 | 74 |
| 27 | 0.02 | 1.77 | 73 |
| 28 | 0.02 | 1.79 | 72 |
| 29 | 0.01 | 1.82 | 71 |
| 30 | 0.01 | 1.85 | 70 |
| 31 | 0.01 | 1.88 | 69 |
| 32 | 0.00 | 1.91 | 68 |
| 33 | 0.00 | 1.93 | 67 |
| 34 | 0.00 | 1.96 | 66 |
| 35 | 0.00 | 1.99 | 65 |
| 36 | 0.00 | 2.01 | 64 |
| 37 | 0.00 | 2.04 | 63 |
| 38 | 0.01 | 2.07 | 62 |
| 39 | 0.01 | 2.09 | 61 |
| 40 | 0.01 | 2.12 | 60 |
| 41 | 0.02 | 2.15 | 59 |
| 42 | 0.02 | 2.17 | 58 |
| 43 | 0.03 | 2.20 | 57 |
| 44 | 0.03 | 2.22 | 56 |
| 45 | 0.04 | 2.25 | 55 |
| 46 | 0.04 | 2.27 | 54 |
| 47 | 0.05 | 2.30 | 53 |
| 48 | 0.05 | 2.32 | 52 |
| 49 | 0.06 | 2.35 | 51 |
| 50 | 0.06 | 2.37 | 50 |
| Days. | **300** | **200** | Days. |

**Table LXXVI. Argument 71.**

| Days. | **0** | **100** | **200** | **300** | **400** | **500** |
|---|---|---|---|---|---|---|
| Days. | ″ | ″ | ″ | ″ | ″ | ″ |
| 0 | 1.14 | 2.57 | 1.93 | 1.30 | 0.67 | 0.03 |
| 1 | 1.16 | 2.57 | 1.92 | 1.30 | 0.66 | 0.04 |
| 2 | 1.18 | 2.58 | 1.91 | 1.29 | 0.65 | 0.04 |
| 3 | 1.20 | 2.58 | 1.90 | 1.29 | 0.64 | 0.04 |
| 4 | 1.22 | 2.58 | 1.89 | 1.29 | 0.63 | 0.05 |
| 5 | 1.24 | 2.58 | 1.88 | 1.28 | 0.62 | 0.05 |
| 6 | 1.26 | 2.58 | 1.87 | 1.28 | 0.60 | 0.06 |
| 7 | 1.28 | 2.59 | 1.86 | 1.28 | 0.59 | 0.06 |
| 8 | 1.30 | 2.59 | 1.85 | 1.27 | 0.58 | 0.06 |
| 9 | 1.32 | 2.59 | 1.84 | 1.27 | 0.57 | 0.07 |
| 10 | 1.34 | 2.59 | 1.83 | 1.27 | 0.56 | 0.07 |
| 11 | 1.36 | 2.59 | 1.82 | 1.27 | 0.55 | 0.08 |
| 12 | 1.38 | 2.59 | 1.81 | 1.26 | 0.54 | 0.08 |
| 13 | 1.40 | 2.59 | 1.80 | 1.26 | 0.53 | 0.09 |
| 14 | 1.42 | 2.59 | 1.79 | 1.26 | 0.52 | 0.10 |
| 15 | 1.44 | 2.59 | 1.78 | 1.25 | 0.51 | 0.10 |
| 16 | 1.46 | 2.58 | 1.78 | 1.25 | 0.49 | 0.11 |
| 17 | 1.48 | 2.58 | 1.77 | 1.25 | 0.48 | 0.12 |
| 18 | 1.50 | 2.58 | 1.76 | 1.24 | 0.47 | 0.12 |
| 19 | 1.52 | 2.58 | 1.75 | 1.24 | 0.46 | 0.13 |
| 20 | 1.54 | 2.58 | 1.74 | 1.24 | 0.45 | 0.14 |
| 21 | 1.56 | 2.58 | 1.73 | 1.23 | 0.44 | 0.15 |
| 22 | 1.58 | 2.57 | 1.72 | 1.23 | 0.43 | 0.16 |
| 23 | 1.60 | 2.57 | 1.71 | 1.23 | 0.42 | 0.17 |
| 24 | 1.62 | 2.57 | 1.71 | 1.22 | 0.41 | 0.18 |
| 25 | 1.64 | 2.56 | 1.70 | 1.22 | 0.40 | 0.19 |
| 26 | 1.65 | 2.56 | 1.69 | 1.21 | 0.39 | 0.20 |
| 27 | 1.67 | 2.56 | 1.68 | 1.21 | 0.38 | 0.21 |
| 28 | 1.69 | 2.55 | 1.68 | 1.21 | 0.37 | 0.22 |
| 29 | 1.71 | 2.55 | 1.67 | 1.20 | 0.36 | 0.23 |
| 30 | 1.73 | 2.55 | 1.66 | 1.20 | 0.35 | 0.24 |
| 31 | 1.75 | 2.54 | 1.65 | 1.19 | 0.34 | 0.25 |
| 32 | 1.77 | 2.54 | 1.64 | 1.19 | 0.33 | 0.26 |
| 33 | 1.79 | 2.53 | 1.63 | 1.18 | 0.32 | 0.28 |
| 34 | 1.80 | 2.53 | 1.63 | 1.18 | 0.31 | 0.29 |
| 35 | 1.82 | 2.52 | 1.62 | 1.17 | 0.30 | 0.30 |
| 36 | 1.84 | 2.52 | 1.61 | 1.17 | 0.30 | 0.32 |
| 37 | 1.86 | 2.51 | 1.60 | 1.16 | 0.29 | 0.33 |
| 38 | 1.88 | 2.51 | 1.59 | 1.16 | 0.28 | 0.34 |
| 39 | 1.89 | 2.50 | 1.59 | 1.15 | 0.27 | 0.36 |
| 40 | 1.91 | 2.49 | 1.58 | 1.15 | 0.26 | 0.37 |
| 41 | 1.93 | 2.48 | 1.57 | 1.14 | 0.25 | 0.38 |
| 42 | 1.95 | 2.48 | 1.56 | 1.14 | 0.24 | 0.40 |
| 43 | 1.96 | 2.47 | 1.56 | 1.13 | 0.24 | 0.41 |
| 44 | 1.98 | 2.46 | 1.55 | 1.13 | 0.23 | 0.43 |
| 45 | 2.00 | 2.46 | 1.54 | 1.12 | 0.22 | 0.44 |
| 46 | 2.01 | 2.45 | 1.54 | 1.12 | 0.21 | 0.46 |
| 47 | 2.03 | 2.44 | 1.53 | 1.11 | 0.20 | 0.47 |
| 48 | 2.05 | 2.44 | 1.52 | 1.10 | 0.20 | 0.49 |
| 49 | 2.06 | 2.43 | 1.52 | 1.10 | 0.19 | 0.50 |
| 50 | 2.08 | 2.42 | 1.51 | 1.09 | 0.18 | 0.52 |

# TABLES LXXV. LXXVI.

| Tables | LXXV. | LXXVI. |
|---|---|---|
| Arguments | **70.** | **71.** |

**Table LXXV. Argument 70.**

| Days. | **0** | **100** | Days. |
|---|---|---|---|
| Days. | ″ | ″ | Days. |
| 50 | 0.06 | 2.37 | 50 |
| 51 | 0.07 | 2.39 | 49 |
| 52 | 0.08 | 2.41 | 48 |
| 53 | 0.09 | 2.44 | 47 |
| 54 | 0.10 | 2.46 | 46 |
| 55 | 0.11 | 2.48 | 45 |
| 56 | 0.12 | 2.50 | 44 |
| 57 | 0.13 | 2.52 | 43 |
| 58 | 0.15 | 2.54 | 42 |
| 59 | 0.16 | 2.56 | 41 |
| 60 | 0.17 | 2.58 | 40 |
| 61 | 0.18 | 2.60 | 39 |
| 62 | 0.19 | 2.62 | 38 |
| 63 | 0.21 | 2.64 | 37 |
| 64 | 0.22 | 2.65 | 36 |
| 65 | 0.24 | 2.67 | 35 |
| 66 | 0.25 | 2.69 | 34 |
| 67 | 0.27 | 2.71 | 33 |
| 68 | 0.28 | 2.72 | 32 |
| 69 | 0.30 | 2.74 | 31 |
| 70 | 0.32 | 2.76 | 30 |
| 71 | 0.34 | 2.77 | 29 |
| 72 | 0.36 | 2.79 | 28 |
| 73 | 0.38 | 2.80 | 27 |
| 74 | 0.40 | 2.81 | 26 |
| 75 | 0.42 | 2.83 | 25 |
| 76 | 0.44 | 2.84 | 24 |
| 77 | 0.46 | 2.85 | 23 |
| 78 | 0.48 | 2.87 | 22 |
| 79 | 0.50 | 2.88 | 21 |
| 80 | 0.52 | 2.89 | 20 |
| 81 | 0.54 | 2.90 | 19 |
| 82 | 0.56 | 2.91 | 18 |
| 83 | 0.59 | 2.92 | 17 |
| 84 | 0.61 | 2.93 | 16 |
| 85 | 0.63 | 2.93 | 15 |
| 86 | 0.66 | 2.94 | 14 |
| 87 | 0.68 | 2.95 | 13 |
| 88 | 0.70 | 2.96 | 12 |
| 89 | 0.73 | 2.96 | 11 |
| 90 | 0.75 | 2.97 | 10 |
| 91 | 0.77 | 2.97 | 09 |
| 92 | 0.80 | 2.98 | 08 |
| 93 | 0.82 | 2.98 | 07 |
| 94 | 0.85 | 2.98 | 06 |
| 95 | 0.88 | 2.99 | 05 |
| 96 | 0.90 | 2.99 | 04 |
| 97 | 0.93 | 2.99 | 03 |
| 98 | 0.95 | 3.00 | 02 |
| 99 | 0.98 | 3.00 | 01 |
| 100 | 1.01 | 3.00 | 00 |
| Days. | **300** | **200** | Days. |

**Table LXXVI. Argument 71.**

| Days. | **0** | **100** | **200** | **300** | **400** | **500** |
|---|---|---|---|---|---|---|
| Days. | ″ | ″ | ″ | ″ | ″ | |
| 50 | 2.08 | 2.42 | 1.51 | 1.09 | 0.18 | 0.52 |
| 51 | 2.10 | 2.41 | 1.50 | 1.08 | 0.17 | 0.54 |
| 52 | 2.11 | 2.40 | 1.50 | 1.08 | 0.16 | 0.55 |
| 53 | 2.13 | 2.40 | 1.49 | 1.07 | 0.16 | 0.57 |
| 54 | 2.15 | 2.39 | 1.49 | 1.06 | 0.15 | 0.59 |
| 55 | 2.16 | 2.38 | 1.48 | 1.06 | 0.14 | 0.60 |
| 56 | 2.18 | 2.37 | 1.47 | 1.05 | 0.14 | 0.62 |
| 57 | 2.19 | 2.37 | 1.47 | 1.04 | 0.13 | 0.64 |
| 58 | 2.20 | 2.36 | 1.46 | 1.04 | 0.12 | 0.65 |
| 59 | 2.22 | 2.35 | 1.46 | 1.03 | 0.12 | 0.67 |
| 60 | 2.23 | 2.34 | 1.45 | 1.02 | 0.11 | 0.69 |
| 61 | 2.24 | 2.33 | 1.45 | 1.01 | 0.10 | 0.71 |
| 62 | 2.26 | 2.32 | 1.44 | 1.00 | 0.10 | 0.73 |
| 63 | 2.27 | 2.31 | 1.44 | 1.00 | 0.09 | 0.74 |
| 64 | 2.28 | 2.30 | 1.43 | 0.99 | 0.09 | 0.76 |
| 65 | 2.30 | 2.30 | 1.43 | 0.98 | 0.08 | 0.78 |
| 66 | 2.31 | 2.29 | 1.42 | 0.97 | 0.07 | 0.80 |
| 67 | 2.32 | 2.28 | 1.42 | 0.97 | 0.07 | 0.82 |
| 68 | 2.34 | 2.27 | 1.41 | 0.96 | 0.06 | 0.83 |
| 69 | 2.35 | 2.26 | 1.41 | 0.95 | 0.06 | 0.85 |
| 70 | 2.36 | 2.25 | 1.40 | 0.94 | 0.05 | 0.87 |
| 71 | 2.37 | 2.24 | 1.40 | 0.93 | 0.05 | 0.89 |
| 72 | 2.38 | 2.23 | 1.39 | 0.92 | 0.04 | 0.91 |
| 73 | 2.39 | 2.22 | 1.39 | 0.92 | 0.04 | 0.93 |
| 74 | 2.40 | 2.21 | 1.38 | 0.91 | 0.04 | 0.95 |
| 75 | 2.41 | 2.20 | 1.38 | 0.90 | 0.03 | 0.96 |
| 76 | 2.42 | 2.19 | 1.37 | 0.89 | 0.03 | 0.98 |
| 77 | 2.43 | 2.18 | 1.37 | 0.88 | 0.03 | 1.00 |
| 78 | 2.44 | 2.17 | 1.37 | 0.88 | 0.02 | 1.02 |
| 79 | 2.45 | 2.16 | 1.36 | 0.87 | 0.02 | 1.04 |
| 80 | 2.46 | 2.15 | 1.36 | 0.86 | 0.02 | 1.06 |
| 81 | 2.47 | 2.14 | 1.36 | 0.85 | 0.02 | 1.08 |
| 82 | 2.48 | 2.13 | 1.35 | 0.84 | 0.02 | 1.10 |
| 83 | 2.48 | 2.12 | 1.35 | 0.83 | 0.02 | 1.12 |
| 84 | 2.49 | 2.11 | 1.35 | 0.82 | 0.01 | 1.14 |
| 85 | 2.50 | 2.10 | 1.34 | 0.81 | 0.01 | 1.16 |
| 86 | 2.50 | 2.08 | 1.34 | 0.81 | 0.01 | 1.18 |
| 87 | 2.51 | 2.07 | 1.34 | 0.80 | 0.01 | 1.20 |
| 88 | 2.52 | 2.06 | 1.33 | 0.79 | 0.01 | 1.22 |
| 89 | 2.52 | 2.05 | 1.33 | 0.78 | 0.01 | 1.24 |
| 90 | 2.53 | 2.04 | 1.33 | 0.77 | 0.01 | 1.26 |
| 91 | 2.53 | 2.03 | 1.33 | 0.76 | 0.01 | 1.28 |
| 92 | 2.54 | 2.02 | 1.32 | 0.75 | 0.01 | 1.30 |
| 93 | 2.54 | 2.01 | 1.32 | 0.74 | 0.02 | 1.32 |
| 94 | 2.55 | 2.00 | 1.32 | 0.73 | 0.02 | 1.34 |
| 95 | 2.55 | 1.99 | 1.31 | 0.72 | 0.02 | 1.36 |
| 96 | 2.56 | 1.97 | 1.31 | 0.71 | 0.02 | 1.38 |
| 97 | 2.56 | 1.96 | 1.31 | 0.70 | 0.02 | 1.40 |
| 98 | 2.56 | 1.95 | 1.30 | 0.69 | 0.03 | 1.42 |
| 99 | 2.57 | 1.94 | 1.30 | 0.68 | 0.03 | 1.44 |
| 100 | 2.57 | 1.93 | 1.30 | 0.67 | 0.03 | 1.46 |

# TABLES LXXVII.-LXXIX.

| Tables | LXXVII. | LXXVIII. | LXXIX. |
|---|---|---|---|
| Arguments | **72.** | **73'.** | **74.** |

**Table LXXVII. (Argument 72.)**

| Days. | **0** | **100** | **200** | **300** |
|---|---|---|---|---|
| Days. | " | " | " | " |
| 0 | 0.80 | 1.50 | 0.80 | 0.10 |
| 1 | 0.80 | 1.50 | 0.78 | 0.11 |
| 2 | 0.81 | 1.51 | 0.77 | 0.12 |
| 3 | 0.81 | 1.51 | 0.75 | 0.12 |
| 4 | 0.82 | 1.52 | 0.73 | 0.13 |
| 5 | 0.82 | 1.52 | 0.72 | 0.14 |
| 6 | 0.83 | 1.53 | 0.70 | 0.15 |
| 7 | 0.83 | 1.53 | 0.68 | 0.16 |
| 8 | 0.84 | 1.54 | 0.67 | 0.16 |
| 9 | 0.84 | 1.54 | 0.65 | 0.17 |
| 10 | 0.85 | 1.55 | 0.63 | 0.18 |
| 11 | 0.85 | 1.55 | 0.61 | 0.19 |
| 12 | 0.86 | 1.56 | 0.60 | 0.19 |
| 13 | 0.86 | 1.56 | 0.58 | 0.20 |
| 14 | 0.87 | 1.56 | 0.56 | 0.21 |
| 15 | 0.88 | 1.57 | 0.55 | 0.21 |
| 16 | 0.88 | 1.57 | 0.53 | 0.22 |
| 17 | 0.89 | 1.58 | 0.51 | 0.23 |
| 18 | 0.89 | 1.58 | 0.50 | 0.23 |
| 19 | 0.90 | 1.59 | 0.48 | 0.24 |
| 20 | 0.91 | 1.59 | 0.46 | 0.25 |
| 21 | 0.91 | 1.59 | 0.44 | 0.26 |
| 22 | 0.92 | 1.59 | 0.43 | 0.27 |
| 23 | 0.92 | 1.59 | 0.41 | 0.28 |
| 24 | 0.93 | 1.59 | 0.40 | 0.29 |
| 25 | 0.93 | 1.59 | 0.38 | 0.29 |
| 26 | 0.94 | 1.59 | 0.36 | 0.30 |
| 27 | 0.94 | 1.58 | 0.35 | 0.31 |
| 28 | 0.95 | 1.58 | 0.34 | 0.32 |
| 29 | 0.95 | 1.58 | 0.33 | 0.33 |
| 30 | 0.96 | 1.58 | 0.32 | 0.34 |
| 31 | 0.96 | 1.58 | 0.30 | 0.35 |
| 32 | 0.97 | 1.57 | 0.29 | 0.36 |
| 33 | 0.98 | 1.57 | 0.28 | 0.36 |
| 34 | 0.98 | 1.57 | 0.26 | 0.37 |
| 35 | 0.99 | 1.57 | 0.25 | 0.38 |
| 36 | 0.99 | 1.57 | 0.24 | 0.39 |
| 37 | 1.00 | 1.56 | 0.22 | 0.40 |
| 38 | 1.00 | 1.56 | 0.21 | 0.40 |
| 39 | 1.01 | 1.56 | 0.20 | 0.41 |
| 40 | 1.02 | 1.56 | 0.19 | 0.42 |
| 41 | 1.03 | 1.55 | 0.18 | 0.43 |
| 42 | 1.03 | 1.55 | 0.17 | 0.44 |
| 43 | 1.04 | 1.54 | 0.16 | 0.45 |
| 44 | 1.05 | 1.54 | 0.15 | 0.46 |
| 45 | 1.05 | 1.53 | 0.14 | 0.46 |
| 46 | 1.06 | 1.53 | 0.13 | 0.47 |
| 47 | 1.07 | 1.52 | 0.13 | 0.48 |
| 48 | 1.07 | 1.51 | 0.12 | 0.49 |
| 49 | 1.08 | 1.51 | 0.11 | 0.50 |
| 50 | 1.09 | 1.50 | 0.10 | 0.51 |

**Table LXXVIII. (Argument 73'.)**

| Days. | **0** |
|---|---|
| Days. | " |
| 0 | 3.71 |
| 10 | 3.64 |
| 20 | 3.57 |
| 30 | 3.50 |
| 40 | 3.42 |
| 50 | 3.34 |
| 60 | 3.25 |
| 70 | 3.16 |
| 80 | 3.07 |
| 90 | 2.97 |
| 100 | 2.87 |
| 110 | 2.77 |
| 120 | 2.66 |
| 130 | 2.55 |
| 140 | 2.44 |
| 150 | 2.33 |
| 160 | 2.22 |
| 170 | 2.11 |
| 180 | 2.00 |
| 190 | 1.88 |
| 200 | 1.77 |
| 210 | 1.66 |
| 220 | 1.55 |
| 230 | 1.44 |
| 240 | 1.33 |
| 250 | 1.22 |
| 260 | 1.12 |
| 270 | 1.03 |
| 280 | 0.93 |
| 290 | 0.83 |
| 300 | 0.73 |
| 310 | 0.64 |
| 320 | 0.56 |
| 330 | 0.48 |
| 340 | 0.41 |
| 350 | 0.34 |
| 360 | 0.28 |
| 370 | 0.22 |
| 380 | 0.17 |
| 390 | 0.13 |
| 400 | 0.09 |
| 410 | 0.06 |
| 420 | 0.03 |
| 430 | 0.01 |
| 440 | 0.00 |
| 450 | 0.00 |
| 460 | 0.01 |
| 470 | 0.02 |
| 480 | 0.03 |
| 490 | 0.05 |
| 500 | 0.08 |
| Days. | **1000** |

**Table LXXIX. (Argument 74.)**

| **0** | **1000** | Days. |
|---|---|---|
| " | " | Days. |
| 0.13 | 0.32 | 1000 |
| 0.12 | 0.33 | 990 |
| 0.12 | 0.34 | 980 |
| 0.11 | 0.35 | 970 |
| 0.10 | 0.36 | 960 |
| 0.10 | 0.36 | 950 |
| 0.09 | 0.37 | 940 |
| 0.09 | 0.38 | 930 |
| 0.08 | 0.39 | 920 |
| 0.08 | 0.40 | 910 |
| 0.07 | 0.41 | 900 |
| 0.07 | 0.42 | 890 |
| 0.06 | 0.43 | 880 |
| 0.06 | 0.44 | 870 |
| 0.05 | 0.45 | 860 |
| 0.05 | 0.46 | 850 |
| 0.04 | 0.47 | 840 |
| 0.04 | 0.48 | 830 |
| 0.04 | 0.49 | 820 |
| 0.03 | 0.50 | 810 |
| 0.03 | 0.51 | 800 |
| 0.03 | 0.52 | 790 |
| 0.02 | 0.53 | 780 |
| 0.02 | 0.54 | 770 |
| 0.02 | 0.55 | 760 |
| 0.02 | 0.56 | 750 |
| 0.02 | 0.56 | 740 |
| 0.01 | 0.57 | 730 |
| 0.01 | 0.58 | 720 |
| 0.01 | 0.59 | 710 |
| 0.01 | 0.60 | 700 |
| 0.01 | 0.61 | 690 |
| 0.01 | 0.62 | 680 |
| 0.01 | 0.63 | 670 |
| 0.01 | 0.64 | 660 |
| 0.00 | 0.65 | 650 |
| 0.00 | 0.65 | 640 |
| 0.00 | 0.66 | 630 |
| 0.00 | 0.67 | 620 |
| 0.00 | 0.68 | 610 |
| 0.00 | 0.69 | 600 |
| 0.00 | 0.70 | 590 |
| 0.00 | 0.71 | 580 |
| 0.00 | 0.72 | 570 |
| 0.00 | 0.73 | 560 |
| 0.00 | 0.74 | 550 |
| 0.01 | 0.74 | 540 |
| 0.01 | 0.75 | 530 |
| 0.01 | 0.76 | 520 |
| 0.01 | 0.77 | 510 |
| 0.01 | 0.78 | 500 |
| **3000** | **2000** | Days. |

**Note.** — Arg. 73' = Arg. 73 + 173.792.

# TABLES LXXVII. - LXXIX.

| Tables | LXXVII. | LXXVIII. | LXXIX. |
|---|---|---|---|
| Arguments | **72.** | **73′.** | **74.** |

**Table LXXVII.**

| Days. | **0** | **100** | **200** | **300** |
|---|---|---|---|---|
| 50 | 1.09″ | 1.50″ | 0.10″ | 0.51″ |
| 51 | 1.10 | 1.49 | 0.09 | 0.52 |
| 52 | 1.11 | 1.48 | 0.09 | 0.52 |
| 53 | 1.12 | 1.47 | 0.08 | 0.53 |
| 54 | 1.12 | 1.47 | 0.07 | 0.54 |
| 55 | 1.13 | 1.46 | 0.07 | 0.54 |
| 56 | 1.14 | 1.45 | 0.06 | 0.55 |
| 57 | 1.15 | 1.44 | 0.06 | 0.56 |
| 58 | 1.16 | 1.43 | 0.05 | 0.56 |
| 59 | 1.17 | 1.42 | 0.05 | 0.57 |
| 60 | 1.18 | 1.41 | 0.04 | 0.58 |
| 61 | 1.19 | 1.40 | 0.04 | 0.59 |
| 62 | 1.20 | 1.39 | 0.04 | 0.60 |
| 63 | 1.20 | 1.37 | 0.03 | 0.60 |
| 64 | 1.21 | 1.36 | 0.03 | 0.61 |
| 65 | 1.22 | 1.35 | 0.03 | 0.62 |
| 66 | 1.23 | 1.33 | 0.03 | 0.62 |
| 67 | 1.23 | 1.32 | 0.02 | 0.63 |
| 68 | 1.24 | 1.31 | 0.02 | 0.63 |
| 69 | 1.25 | 1.29 | 0.02 | 0.64 |
| 70 | 1.26 | 1.28 | 0.02 | 0.64 |
| 71 | 1.27 | 1.27 | 0.02 | 0.65 |
| 72 | 1.28 | 1.25 | 0.02 | 0.65 |
| 73 | 1.29 | 1.24 | 0.01 | 0.66 |
| 74 | 1.30 | 1.22 | 0.01 | 0.66 |
| 75 | 1.30 | 1.21 | 0.01 | 0.67 |
| 76 | 1.31 | 1.20 | 0.01 | 0.67 |
| 77 | 1.32 | 1.18 | 0.01 | 0.68 |
| 78 | 1.33 | 1.17 | 0.01 | 0.68 |
| 79 | 1.34 | 1.15 | 0.01 | 0.69 |
| 80 | 1.35 | 1.14 | 0.01 | 0.69 |
| 81 | 1.36 | 1.12 | 0.01 | 0.70 |
| 82 | 1.37 | 1.11 | 0.02 | 0.70 |
| 83 | 1.37 | 1.09 | 0.02 | 0.71 |
| 84 | 1.38 | 1.07 | 0.02 | 0.71 |
| 85 | 1.39 | 1.06 | 0.03 | 0.72 |
| 86 | 1.39 | 1.04 | 0.03 | 0.73 |
| 87 | 1.40 | 1.02 | 0.04 | 0.73 |
| 88 | 1.41 | 1.01 | 0.04 | 0.74 |
| 89 | 1.41 | 0.99 | 0.05 | 0.74 |
| 90 | 1.42 | 0.97 | 0.05 | 0.75 |
| 91 | 1.43 | 0.95 | 0.06 | 0.75 |
| 92 | 1.44 | 0.94 | 0.06 | 0.76 |
| 93 | 1.44 | 0.92 | 0.07 | 0.76 |
| 94 | 1.45 | 0.90 | 0.07 | 0.77 |
| 95 | 1.46 | 0.89 | 0.08 | 0.77 |
| 96 | 1.47 | 0.87 | 0.08 | 0.78 |
| 97 | 1.47 | 0.85 | 0.09 | 0.78 |
| 98 | 1.48 | 0.84 | 0.09 | 0.79 |
| 99 | 1.49 | 0.82 | 0.10 | 0.79 |
| 100 | 1.50 | 0.80 | 0.10 | 0.80 |

**Table LXXVIII.**

| Days. | **0** |
|---|---|
| 500 | 0.08″ |
| 510 | 0.12 |
| 520 | 0.16 |
| 530 | 0.21 |
| 540 | 0.26 |
| 550 | 0.31 |
| 560 | 0.37 |
| 570 | 0.44 |
| 580 | 0.51 |
| 590 | 0.59 |
| 600 | 0.68 |
| 610 | 0.77 |
| 620 | 0.86 |
| 630 | 0.96 |
| 640 | 1.06 |
| 650 | 1.16 |
| 660 | 1.26 |
| 670 | 1.37 |
| 680 | 1.48 |
| 690 | 1.59 |
| 700 | 1.70 |
| 710 | 1.81 |
| 720 | 1.92 |
| 730 | 2.04 |
| 740 | 2.15 |
| 750 | 2.27 |
| 760 | 2.38 |
| 770 | 2.49 |
| 780 | 2.60 |
| 790 | 2.71 |
| 800 | 2.82 |
| 810 | 2.92 |
| 820 | 3.02 |
| 830 | 3.11 |
| 840 | 3.21 |
| 850 | 3.30 |
| 860 | 3.38 |
| 870 | 3.46 |
| 880 | 3.54 |
| 890 | 3.61 |
| 900 | 3.68 |
| 910 | 3.74 |
| 920 | 3.79 |
| 930 | 3.84 |
| 940 | 3.88 |
| 950 | 3.92 |
| 960 | 3.95 |
| 970 | 3.97 |
| 980 | 3.98 |
| 990 | 3.99 |
| 1000 | 4.00 |
| Days. | **1000** |

**Table LXXIX.**

| **0** | **1000** | Days. |
|---|---|---|
| 0.01″ | 0.78″ | 500 |
| 0.01 | 0.79 | 490 |
| 0.02 | 0.80 | 480 |
| 0.02 | 0.80 | 470 |
| 0.02 | 0.81 | 460 |
| 0.02 | 0.82 | 450 |
| 0.03 | 0.83 | 440 |
| 0.03 | 0.84 | 430 |
| 0.03 | 0.84 | 420 |
| 0.04 | 0.85 | 410 |
| 0.04 | 0.86 | 400 |
| 0.05 | 0.87 | 390 |
| 0.05 | 0.87 | 380 |
| 0.06 | 0.88 | 370 |
| 0.06 | 0.88 | 360 |
| 0.07 | 0.89 | 350 |
| 0.07 | 0.90 | 340 |
| 0.08 | 0.90 | 330 |
| 0.08 | 0.91 | 320 |
| 0.09 | 0.91 | 310 |
| 0.09 | 0.92 | 300 |
| 0.10 | 0.92 | 290 |
| 0.10 | 0.93 | 280 |
| 0.11 | 0.93 | 270 |
| 0.12 | 0.94 | 260 |
| 0.12 | 0.94 | 250 |
| 0.13 | 0.95 | 240 |
| 0.14 | 0.95 | 230 |
| 0.14 | 0.95 | 220 |
| 0.15 | 0.96 | 210 |
| 0.16 | 0.96 | 200 |
| 0.17 | 0.96 | 190 |
| 0.18 | 0.97 | 180 |
| 0.18 | 0.97 | 170 |
| 0.19 | 0.97 | 160 |
| 0.20 | 0.98 | 150 |
| 0.21 | 0.98 | 140 |
| 0.21 | 0.98 | 130 |
| 0.22 | 0.98 | 120 |
| 0.23 | 0.99 | 110 |
| 0.24 | 0.99 | 100 |
| 0.25 | 0.99 | 90 |
| 0.26 | 0.99 | 80 |
| 0.26 | 0.99 | 70 |
| 0.27 | 0.99 | 60 |
| 0.28 | 1.00 | 50 |
| 0.29 | 1.00 | 40 |
| 0.30 | 1.00 | 30 |
| 0.30 | 1.00 | 20 |
| 0.31 | 1.00 | 10 |
| 0.32 | 1.00 | 0 |
| **3000** | **2000** | Days. |

**Note.** — Arg. 73′ = Arg. 73 + 173.792.

# TABLES LXXX. LXXXI.

| TABLES | LXXX. | | | | | LXXXI. | | | | | |
|---|---|---|---|---|---|---|---|---|---|---|---|
| ARGUMENTS | **75.** | | | | | **76.** | | | | | |
| Days. | **0** | **10000** | **20000** | **30000** | **40000** | **0** | **10000** | **20000** | **30000** | **40000** | Days. |
| 0 | 33.61″ | 30.35″ | 39.10″ | 55.24″ | 70.31″ | 38.56″ | 41.74″ | 54.89″ | 72.56″ | 87.33″ | 10000 |
| 100 | 33.52 | 30.38 | 39.24 | 55.41 | 70.43 | 38.53 | 41.83 | 55.06 | 72.74 | 87.44 | 9900 |
| 200 | 33.43 | 30.41 | 39.37 | 55.58 | 70.54 | 38.51 | 41.92 | 55.22 | 72.91 | 87.55 | 9800 |
| 300 | 33.34 | 30.45 | 39.51 | 55.76 | 70.66 | 38.48 | 42.01 | 55.39 | 73.08 | 87.66 | 9700 |
| 400 | 33.25 | 30.48 | 39.65 | 55.93 | 70.77 | 38.46 | 42.10 | 55.56 | 73.26 | 87.76 | 9600 |
| 500 | 33.16 | 30.52 | 39.79 | 56.10 | 70.88 | 38.44 | 42.19 | 55.73 | 73.43 | 87.87 | 9500 |
| 600 | 33.07 | 30.56 | 39.93 | 56.27 | 70.99 | 38.42 | 42.28 | 55.90 | 73.60 | 87.97 | 9400 |
| 700 | 32.99 | 30.60 | 40.07 | 56.44 | 71.10 | 38.40 | 42.38 | 56.07 | 73.77 | 88.08 | 9300 |
| 800 | 32.90 | 30.64 | 40.21 | 56.61 | 71.21 | 38.38 | 42.47 | 56.24 | 73.94 | 88.18 | 9200 |
| 900 | 32.82 | 30.68 | 40.36 | 56.78 | 71.32 | 38.37 | 42.57 | 56.42 | 74.11 | 88.28 | 9100 |
| 1000 | 32.74 | 30.72 | 40.50 | 56.95 | 71.43 | 38.35 | 42.67 | 56.59 | 74.28 | 88.38 | 9000 |
| 1100 | 32.66 | 30.76 | 40.64 | 57.12 | 71.54 | 38.34 | 42.77 | 56.76 | 74.45 | 88.48 | 8900 |
| 1200 | 32.58 | 30.81 | 40.79 | 57.29 | 71.64 | 38.32 | 42.87 | 56.93 | 74.62 | 88.58 | 8800 |
| 1300 | 32.50 | 30.85 | 40.93 | 57.45 | 71.75 | 38.31 | 42.97 | 57.10 | 74.79 | 88.68 | 8700 |
| 1400 | 32.43 | 30.90 | 41.08 | 57.62 | 71.85 | 38.30 | 43.07 | 57.27 | 74.96 | 88.77 | 8600 |
| 1500 | 32.35 | 30.95 | 41.23 | 57.79 | 71.95 | 38.29 | 43.17 | 57.44 | 75.13 | 88.87 | 8500 |
| 1600 | 32.28 | 31.00 | 41.38 | 57.96 | 72.05 | 38.28 | 43.27 | 57.61 | 75.30 | 88.96 | 8400 |
| 1700 | 32.20 | 31.05 | 41.52 | 58.13 | 72.15 | 38.28 | 43.37 | 57.78 | 75.47 | 89.06 | 8300 |
| 1800 | 32.13 | 31.10 | 41.67 | 58.29 | 72.25 | 38.27 | 43.48 | 57.96 | 75.64 | 89.15 | 8200 |
| 1900 | 32.06 | 31.16 | 41.82 | 58.46 | 72.34 | 38.27 | 43.58 | 58.13 | 75.81 | 89.24 | 8100 |
| 2000 | 31.99 | 31.21 | 41.97 | 58.63 | 72.44 | 38.26 | 43.69 | 58.30 | 75.98 | 89.33 | 8000 |
| 2100 | 31.92 | 31.27 | 42.12 | 58.80 | 72.54 | 38.26 | 43.80 | 58.47 | 76.15 | 89.42 | 7900 |
| 2200 | 31.85 | 31.32 | 42.27 | 58.97 | 72.63 | 38.25 | 43.91 | 58.65 | 76.31 | 89.51 | 7800 |
| 2300 | 31.78 | 31.38 | 42.42 | 59.13 | 72.72 | 38.25 | 44.02 | 58.82 | 76.48 | 89.60 | 7700 |
| 2400 | 31.72 | 31.44 | 42.58 | 59.30 | 72.82 | 38.26 | 44.13 | 59.00 | 76.64 | 89.68 | 7600 |
| 2500 | 31.65 | 31.50 | 42.73 | 59.46 | 72.91 | 38.26 | 44.24 | 59.17 | 76.81 | 89.77 | 7500 |
| 2600 | 31.59 | 31.56 | 42.88 | 59.63 | 73.00 | 38.27 | 44.35 | 59.35 | 76.97 | 89.86 | 7400 |
| 2700 | 31.53 | 31.62 | 43.04 | 59.79 | 73.09 | 38.27 | 44.47 | 59.52 | 77.14 | 89.94 | 7300 |
| 2800 | 31.47 | 31.68 | 43.19 | 59.96 | 73.18 | 38.28 | 44.58 | 59.70 | 77.30 | 90.03 | 7200 |
| 2900 | 31.41 | 31.75 | 43.35 | 60.12 | 73.26 | 38.28 | 44.70 | 59.87 | 77.46 | 90.11 | 7100 |
| 3000 | 31.35 | 31.81 | 43.51 | 60.29 | 73.35 | 38.29 | 44.82 | 60.05 | 77.62 | 90.19 | 7000 |
| 3100 | 31.29 | 31.88 | 43.67 | 60.46 | 73.43 | 38.30 | 44.94 | 60.23 | 77.78 | 90.27 | 6900 |
| 3200 | 31.24 | 31.95 | 43.83 | 60.62 | 73.52 | 38.31 | 45.06 | 60.41 | 77.94 | 90.35 | 6800 |
| 3300 | 31.18 | 32.02 | 43.98 | 60.79 | 73.60 | 38.32 | 45.18 | 60.58 | 78.10 | 90.43 | 6700 |
| 3400 | 31.13 | 32.09 | 44.14 | 60.95 | 73.68 | 38.34 | 45.30 | 60.76 | 78.26 | 90.50 | 6600 |
| 3500 | 31.08 | 32.16 | 44.30 | 61.11 | 73.76 | 38.35 | 45.42 | 60.94 | 78.42 | 90.58 | 6500 |
| 3600 | 31.03 | 32.23 | 44.46 | 61.27 | 73.84 | 38.36 | 45.54 | 61.12 | 78.58 | 90.65 | 6400 |
| 3700 | 30.98 | 32.31 | 44.62 | 61.43 | 73.92 | 38.38 | 45.66 | 61.30 | 78.74 | 90.73 | 6300 |
| 3800 | 30.93 | 32.38 | 44.78 | 61.59 | 73.99 | 38.39 | 45.79 | 61.47 | 78.90 | 90.80 | 6200 |
| 3900 | 30.89 | 32.46 | 44.94 | 61.75 | 74.07 | 38.41 | 45.91 | 61.65 | 79.05 | 90.87 | 6100 |
| 4000 | 30.84 | 32.54 | 45.10 | 61.91 | 74.14 | 38.43 | 46.04 | 61.83 | 79.21 | 90.94 | 6000 |
| 4100 | 30.80 | 32.62 | 45.26 | 62.07 | 74.21 | 38.45 | 46.17 | 62.01 | 79.37 | 91.01 | 5900 |
| 4200 | 30.75 | 32.70 | 45.42 | 62.23 | 74.29 | 38.47 | 46.29 | 62.19 | 79.52 | 91.08 | 5800 |
| 4300 | 30.71 | 32.78 | 45.59 | 62.39 | 74.36 | 38.50 | 46.42 | 62.36 | 79.68 | 91.15 | 5700 |
| 4400 | 30.67 | 32.87 | 45.75 | 62.54 | 74.43 | 38.52 | 46.55 | 62.54 | 79.83 | 91.21 | 5600 |
| 4500 | 30.63 | 32.95 | 45.91 | 62.70 | 74.50 | 38.55 | 46.68 | 62.72 | 79.99 | 91.28 | 5500 |
| 4600 | 30.59 | 33.03 | 46.07 | 62.86 | 74.57 | 38.58 | 46.81 | 62.90 | 80.14 | 91.34 | 5400 |
| 4700 | 30.55 | 33.12 | 46.24 | 63.01 | 74.64 | 38.61 | 46.94 | 63.08 | 80.30 | 91.40 | 5300 |
| 4800 | 30.51 | 33.20 | 46.40 | 63.17 | 74.70 | 38.64 | 47.07 | 63.26 | 80.45 | 91.46 | 5200 |
| 4900 | 30.48 | 33.29 | 46.57 | 63.32 | 74.77 | 38.67 | 47.21 | 63.44 | 80.60 | 91.52 | 5100 |
| 5000 | 30.44 | 33.38 | 46.73 | 63.48 | 74.83 | 38.70 | 47.34 | 63.62 | 80.75 | 91.58 | 5000 |
| Days. | **90000** | **80000** | **70000** | **60000** | **50000** | **90000** | **80000** | **70000** | **60000** | **50000** | Days. |

# TABLES LXXX. LXXXI.

| Tables | LXXX. | LXXXI. |
|---|---|---|
| Arguments | **75.** | **76.** |

| Days. | **0** | **10000** | **20000** | **30000** | **40000** | **0** | **10000** | **20000** | **30000** | **40000** | Days. |
|---|---|---|---|---|---|---|---|---|---|---|---|
| Days. | ″ | ″ | ″ | ″ | ″ | ″ | ″ | ″ | ″ | ″ | Days. |
| 5000 | 30.44 | 33.38 | 46.73 | 63.48 | 74.83 | 38.70 | 47.34 | 63.62 | 80.75 | 91.58 | 5000 |
| 5100 | 30.41 | 33.47 | 46.90 | 63.63 | 74.89 | 38.73 | 47.47 | 63.80 | 80.90 | 91.64 | 4900 |
| 5200 | 30.37 | 33.56 | 47.06 | 63.79 | 74.95 | 38.77 | 47.61 | 63.98 | 81.05 | 91.69 | 4800 |
| 5300 | 30.34 | 33.65 | 47.23 | 63.94 | 75.01 | 38.80 | 47.74 | 64.16 | 81.20 | 91.75 | 4700 |
| 5400 | 30.31 | 33.75 | 47.39 | 64.09 | 75.06 | 38.84 | 47.88 | 64.34 | 81.35 | 91.80 | 4600 |
| 5500 | 30.28 | 33.84 | 47.56 | 64.24 | 75.12 | 38.88 | 48.02 | 64.52 | 81.50 | 91.85 | 4500 |
| 5600 | 30.25 | 33.94 | 47.73 | 64.39 | 75.18 | 38.92 | 48.15 | 64.70 | 81.65 | 91.90 | 4400 |
| 5700 | 30.23 | 34.03 | 47.90 | 64.54 | 75.23 | 38.96 | 48.30 | 64.88 | 81.80 | 91.95 | 4300 |
| 5800 | 30.20 | 34.13 | 48.06 | 64.69 | 75.29 | 39.00 | 48.44 | 65.06 | 81.94 | 92.00 | 4200 |
| 5900 | 30.18 | 34.23 | 48.23 | 64.84 | 75.34 | 39.04 | 48.58 | 65.24 | 82.09 | 92.05 | 4100 |
| 6000 | 30.16 | 34.33 | 48.40 | 64.99 | 75.39 | 39.08 | 48.72 | 65.42 | 82.23 | 92.10 | 4000 |
| 6100 | 30.14 | 34.43 | 48.57 | 65.14 | 75.44 | 39.13 | 48.86 | 65.60 | 82.37 | 92.15 | 3900 |
| 6200 | 30.12 | 34.53 | 48.74 | 65.29 | 75.49 | 39.18 | 49.00 | 65.78 | 82.51 | 92.19 | 3800 |
| 6300 | 30.10 | 34.63 | 48.90 | 65.43 | 75.54 | 39.22 | 49.14 | 65.96 | 82.65 | 92.24 | 3700 |
| 6400 | 30.09 | 34.74 | 49.07 | 65.58 | 75.58 | 39.27 | 49.29 | 66.14 | 82.79 | 92.28 | 3600 |
| 6500 | 30.07 | 34.84 | 49.24 | 65.72 | 75.63 | 39.32 | 49.43 | 66.32 | 82.93 | 92.32 | 3500 |
| 6600 | 30.06 | 34.95 | 49.41 | 65.86 | 75.67 | 39.37 | 49.57 | 66.50 | 83.07 | 92.36 | 3400 |
| 6700 | 30.05 | 35.05 | 49.58 | 66.01 | 75.71 | 39.42 | 49.72 | 66.68 | 83.21 | 92.40 | 3300 |
| 6800 | 30.04 | 35.16 | 49.75 | 66.15 | 75.75 | 39.47 | 49.86 | 66.86 | 83.35 | 92.44 | 3200 |
| 6900 | 30.03 | 35.27 | 49.92 | 66.29 | 75.79 | 39.53 | 50.01 | 67.04 | 83.48 | 92.47 | 3100 |
| 7000 | 30.02 | 35.38 | 50.09 | 66.43 | 75.83 | 39.58 | 50.16 | 67.22 | 83.62 | 92.51 | 3000 |
| 7100 | 30.01 | 35.49 | 50.26 | 66.57 | 75.87 | 39.64 | 50.31 | 67.40 | 83.76 | 92.55 | 2900 |
| 7200 | 30.01 | 35.60 | 50.43 | 66.71 | 75.90 | 39.69 | 50.46 | 67.58 | 83.89 | 92.58 | 2800 |
| 7300 | 30.00 | 35.71 | 50.60 | 66.85 | 75.94 | 39.75 | 50.61 | 67.76 | 84.03 | 92.62 | 2700 |
| 7400 | 30.00 | 35.83 | 50.77 | 66.99 | 75.97 | 39.81 | 50.77 | 67.94 | 84.16 | 92.65 | 2600 |
| 7500 | 30.00 | 35.94 | 50.94 | 67.13 | 76.00 | 39.87 | 50.92 | 68.12 | 84.29 | 92.68 | 2500 |
| 7600 | 30.00 | 36.06 | 51.11 | 67.27 | 76.03 | 39.93 | 51.07 | 68.30 | 84.42 | 92.71 | 2400 |
| 7700 | 30.00 | 36.17 | 51.28 | 67.41 | 76.06 | 39.99 | 51.23 | 68.48 | 84.55 | 92.74 | 2300 |
| 7800 | 30.00 | 36.29 | 51.46 | 67.54 | 76.09 | 40.06 | 51.38 | 68.66 | 84.68 | 92.77 | 2200 |
| 7900 | 30.01 | 36.41 | 51.63 | 67.68 | 76.12 | 40.12 | 51.53 | 68.84 | 84.81 | 92.79 | 2100 |
| 8000 | 30.01 | 36.53 | 51.80 | 67.81 | 76.15 | 40.19 | 51.69 | 69.02 | 84.94 | 92.82 | 2000 |
| 8100 | 30.02 | 36.65 | 51.97 | 67.94 | 76.17 | 40.26 | 51.85 | 69.20 | 85.07 | 92.84 | 1900 |
| 8200 | 30.02 | 36.77 | 52.14 | 68.08 | 76.20 | 40.32 | 52.00 | 69.38 | 85.20 | 92.86 | 1800 |
| 8300 | 30.03 | 36.89 | 52.32 | 68.21 | 76.22 | 40.39 | 52.16 | 69.55 | 85.32 | 92.88 | 1700 |
| 8400 | 30.04 | 37.02 | 52.49 | 68.34 | 76.24 | 40.46 | 52.31 | 69.73 | 85.45 | 92.90 | 1600 |
| 8500 | 30.05 | 37.14 | 52.66 | 68.47 | 76.26 | 40.53 | 52.47 | 69.91 | 85.57 | 92.92 | 1500 |
| 8600 | 30.06 | 37.26 | 52.83 | 68.60 | 76.28 | 40.60 | 52.63 | 70.09 | 85.69 | 92.94 | 1400 |
| 8700 | 30.07 | 37.39 | 53.00 | 68.73 | 76.30 | 40.67 | 52.78 | 70.27 | 85.81 | 92.95 | 1300 |
| 8800 | 30.09 | 37.51 | 53.18 | 68.86 | 76.31 | 40.75 | 52.94 | 70.44 | 85.93 | 92.97 | 1200 |
| 8900 | 30.10 | 37.64 | 53.35 | 68.98 | 76.33 | 40.82 | 53.10 | 70.62 | 86.05 | 92.98 | 1100 |
| 9000 | 30.12 | 37.77 | 53.52 | 69.11 | 76.34 | 40.90 | 53.26 | 70.80 | 86.17 | 92.99 | 1000 |
| 9100 | 30.14 | 37.90 | 53.69 | 69.23 | 76.35 | 40.98 | 53.42 | 70.98 | 86.29 | 93.00 | 900 |
| 9200 | 30.16 | 38.03 | 53.86 | 69.36 | 76.36 | 41.06 | 53.58 | 71.15 | 86.41 | 93.01 | 800 |
| 9300 | 30.18 | 38.16 | 54.04 | 69.48 | 76.37 | 41.14 | 53.74 | 71.33 | 86.53 | 93.02 | 700 |
| 9400 | 30.20 | 38.29 | 54.21 | 69.60 | 76.37 | 41.23 | 53.91 | 71.50 | 86.64 | 93.02 | 600 |
| 9500 | 30.22 | 38.42 | 54.38 | 69.72 | 76.38 | 41.31 | 54.07 | 71.68 | 86.76 | 93.03 | 500 |
| 9600 | 30.24 | 38.55 | 54.55 | 69.84 | 76.38 | 41.39 | 54.23 | 71.86 | 86.88 | 93.03 | 400 |
| 9700 | 30.27 | 38.69 | 54.72 | 69.96 | 76.39 | 41.48 | 54.40 | 72.03 | 86.99 | 93.03 | 300 |
| 9800 | 30.29 | 38.82 | 54.90 | 70.08 | 76.39 | 41.56 | 54.56 | 72.21 | 87.11 | 93.04 | 200 |
| 9900 | 30.32 | 38.96 | 55.07 | 70.19 | 76.40 | 41.65 | 54.73 | 72.38 | 87.22 | 93.04 | 100 |
| 10000 | 30.35 | 39.10 | 55.24 | 70.31 | 76.40 | 41.74 | 54.89 | 72.56 | 87.33 | 93.04 | 0 |
| Days. | **90000** | **80000** | **70000** | **60000** | **50000** | **90000** | **80000** | **70000** | **60000** | **50000** | Days. |

# TABLE LXXXIA.

Argument $y - u$.

Equation $= - 6''.38 \sin (y - u) - 0''.97 \cos (y - u)$

| $y - u$ | 0°+ 180− | 10°+ 190− | 20°+ 200− | 30°+ 210− | 40°+ 220− | 50°+ 230− | 60°+ 240− | 70°+ 250− | 80°+ 260− |
|---|---|---|---|---|---|---|---|---|---|
| ° ″ | ″ | ″ | ″ | ″ | ″ | ″ | ″ | ″ | ″ |
| 0 0 | −0.97 | −2.07 | −3.09 | −4.03 | −4.84 | −5.51 | −6.01 | −6.32 | −6.46 |
| 0 1000 | 1.00 | 2.10 | 3.12 | 4.05 | 4.86 | 5.53 | 6.02 | 6.33 | 6.46 |
| 0 2000 | 1.03 | 2.13 | 3.14 | 4.08 | 4.88 | 5.54 | 6.03 | 6.33 | 6.46 |
| 0 3000 | 1.06 | 2.16 | 3.17 | 4.10 | 4.90 | 5.56 | 6.04 | 6.34 | 6.46 |
| 1 400 | 1.09 | 2.19 | 3.20 | 4.12 | 4.92 | 5.57 | 6.05 | 6.34 | 6.46 |
| 1 1400 | 1.12 | 2.22 | 3.22 | 4.15 | 4.94 | 5.59 | 6.06 | 6.35 | 6.47 |
| 1 2400 | 1.15 | 2.24 | 3.25 | 4.17 | 4.96 | 5.60 | 6.07 | 6.35 | 6.47 |
| 1 3400 | 1.19 | 2.27 | 3.28 | 4.19 | 4.98 | 5.62 | 6.08 | 6.36 | 6.47 |
| 2 800 | 1.22 | 2.30 | 3.30 | 4.22 | 5.00 | 5.63 | 6.09 | 6.36 | 6.47 |
| 2 1800 | 1.25 | 2.33 | 3.33 | 4.24 | 5.02 | 5.65 | 6.10 | 6.37 | 6.47 |
| 2 2800 | 1.28 | 2.36 | 3.36 | 4.26 | 5.04 | 5.66 | 6.11 | 6.37 | 6.47 |
| 3 200 | 1.31 | 2.39 | 3.38 | 4.29 | 5.06 | 5.68 | 6.12 | 6.38 | 6.47 |
| 3 1200 | 1.34 | 2.42 | 3.41 | 4.31 | 5.08 | 5.69 | 6.13 | 6.38 | 6.47 |
| 3 2200 | 1.38 | 2.44 | 3.44 | 4.33 | 5.10 | 5.71 | 6.14 | 6.39 | 6.46 |
| 3 3200 | 1.41 | 2.47 | 3.46 | 4.36 | 5.12 | 5.72 | 6.15 | 6.39 | 6.46 |
| 4 600 | 1.44 | 2.50 | 3.49 | 4.38 | 5.14 | 5.74 | 6.16 | 6.40 | 6.46 |
| 4 1600 | 1.47 | 2.53 | 3.52 | 4.40 | 5.16 | 5.75 | 6.17 | 6.40 | 6.46 |
| 4 2600 | 1.50 | 2.56 | 3.54 | 4.43 | 5.18 | 5.77 | 6.18 | 6.41 | 6.46 |
| 5 0 | 1.53 | 2.59 | 3.57 | 4.45 | 5.20 | 5.78 | 6.19 | 6.41 | 6.46 |
| 5 1000 | 1.56 | 2.62 | 3.60 | 4.47 | 5.22 | 5.79 | 6.20 | 6.41 | 6.46 |
| 5 2000 | 1.59 | 2.65 | 3.62 | 4.49 | 5.24 | 5.81 | 6.20 | 6.42 | 6.45 |
| 5 3000 | 1.62 | 2.67 | 3.65 | 4.52 | 5.25 | 5.82 | 6.21 | 6.42 | 6.45 |
| 6 400 | 1.65 | 2.70 | 3.67 | 4.54 | 5.27 | 5.84 | 6.22 | 6.42 | 6.45 |
| 6 1400 | 1.68 | 2.73 | 3.70 | 4.56 | 5.29 | 5.85 | 6.22 | 6.43 | 6.44 |
| 6 2400 | 1.71 | 2.76 | 3.72 | 4.58 | 5.30 | 5.86 | 6.23 | 6.43 | 6.44 |
| 6 3400 | 1.74 | 2.78 | 3.75 | 4.60 | 5.32 | 5.88 | 6.24 | 6.43 | 6.43 |
| 7 800 | 1.77 | 2.81 | 3.78 | 4.63 | 5.34 | 5.89 | 6.24 | 6.43 | 6.43 |
| 7 1800 | 1.80 | 2.84 | 3.80 | 4.65 | 5.36 | 5.90 | 6.25 | 6.44 | 6.42 |
| 7 2800 | 1.83 | 2.87 | 3.83 | 4.67 | 5.37 | 5.92 | 6.26 | 6.44 | 6.42 |
| 8 200 | 1.86 | 2.89 | 3.85 | 4.69 | 5.39 | 5.93 | 6.27 | 6.44 | 6.41 |
| 8 1200 | 1.89 | 2.92 | 3.88 | 4.71 | 5.41 | 5.95 | 6.27 | 6.44 | 6.41 |
| 8 2200 | 1.92 | 2.95 | 3.90 | 4.74 | 5.42 | 5.96 | 6.28 | 6.44 | 6.40 |
| 8 3200 | 1.95 | 2.98 | 3.93 | 4.76 | 5.44 | 5.97 | 6.29 | 6.45 | 6.40 |
| 9 600 | 1.98 | 3.00 | 3.95 | 4.78 | 5.46 | 5.98 | 6.30 | 6.45 | 6.39 |
| 9 1600 | 2.01 | 3.03 | 3.98 | 4.80 | 5.47 | 5.99 | 6.30 | 6.45 | 6.39 |
| 9 2600 | 2.04 | 3.06 | 4.00 | 4.82 | 5.49 | 6.00 | 6.31 | 6.46 | 6.38 |
| 10 0 | −2.07 | −3.09 | −4.03 | −4.84 | −5.51 | −6.01 | −6.32 | −6.46 | −6.38 |

NOTE. — When $y - u$ exceeds 180° the Sign of the Equation is to be reversed.

# TABLE LXXXIA.

Argument $y-u$.

Equation $= -6''.38 \sin(y-u) - 0''.97 \cos(y-u)$.

| $y-u$ | | 90° + 270 − | 100° + 280 − | 110° + 290 − | 120° + 300 − | 130° + 310 − | 140° + 320 − | 150° + 330 − | 160° + 340 − | 170° + 350 − |
|---|---|---|---|---|---|---|---|---|---|---|
| ° 0 | ″ 0 | ″ −6.38 | ″ −6.12 | ″ −5.66 | ″ −5.04 | ″ −4.26 | ″ −3.36 | ″ −2.35 | ″ −1.27 | ″ −0.15 |
| 0 | 1000 | 6.38 | 6.11 | 5.64 | 5.02 | 4.24 | 3.33 | 2.32 | 1.24 | 0.12 |
| 0 | 2000 | 6.37 | 6.10 | 5.63 | 5.00 | 4.21 | 3.30 | 2.29 | 1.21 | 0.09 |
| 0 | 3000 | 6.37 | 6.08 | 5.61 | 4.98 | 4.19 | 3.28 | 2.26 | 1.18 | 0.06 |
| 1 | 400 | 6.36 | 6.07 | 5.59 | 4.96 | 4.16 | 3.25 | 2.23 | 1.15 | −0.02 |
| 1 | 1400 | 6.36 | 6.06 | 5.58 | 4.94 | 4.14 | 3.22 | 2.20 | 1.11 | +0.01 |
| 1 | 2400 | 6.35 | 6.05 | 5.56 | 4.92 | 4.11 | 3.20 | 2.17 | 1.08 | 0.04 |
| 1 | 3400 | 6.35 | 6.04 | 5.55 | 4.90 | 4.09 | 3.17 | 2.14 | 1.05 | 0.07 |
| 2 | 800 | 6.34 | 6.02 | 5.53 | 4.88 | 4.07 | 3.14 | 2.11 | 1.02 | 0.10 |
| 2 | 1800 | 6.34 | 6.01 | 5.51 | 4.85 | 4.04 | 3.11 | 2.08 | 0.99 | 0.13 |
| 2 | 2800 | 6.33 | 6.00 | 5.50 | 4.83 | 4.02 | 3.09 | 2.06 | 0.96 | 0.16 |
| 3 | 200 | 6.33 | 5.99 | 5.48 | 4.81 | 3.99 | 3.06 | 2.03 | 0.93 | 0.20 |
| 3 | 1200 | 6.32 | 5.98 | 5.47 | 4.79 | 3.97 | 3.03 | 2.00 | 0.90 | 0.23 |
| 3 | 2200 | 6.31 | 5.97 | 5.45 | 4.77 | 3.94 | 3.01 | 1.97 | 0.86 | 0.26 |
| 3 | 3200 | 6.31 | 5.95 | 5.43 | 4.75 | 3.92 | 2.98 | 1.94 | 0.83 | 0.29 |
| 4 | 600 | 6.30 | 5.94 | 5.42 | 4.73 | 3.89 | 2.95 | 1.91 | 0.80 | 0.32 |
| 4 | 1600 | 6.29 | 5.93 | 5.40 | 4.71 | 3.87 | 2.93 | 1.88 | 0.77 | 0.35 |
| 4 | 2600 | 6.29 | 5.92 | 5.39 | 4.69 | 3.84 | 2.90 | 1.85 | 0.74 | 0.38 |
| 5 | 0 | 6.28 | 5.91 | 5.37 | 4.67 | 3.82 | 2.87 | 1.82 | 0.71 | 0.41 |
| 5 | 1000 | 6.27 | 5.90 | 5.35 | 4.65 | 3.79 | 2.84 | 1.79 | 0.68 | 0.44 |
| 5 | 2000 | 6.26 | 5.88 | 5.33 | 4.63 | 3.77 | 2.81 | 1.76 | 0.65 | 0.47 |
| 5 | 3000 | 6.26 | 5.87 | 5.32 | 4.60 | 3.74 | 2.78 | 1.73 | 0.62 | 0.50 |
| 6 | 400 | 6.25 | 5.86 | 5.30 | 4.58 | 3.71 | 2.76 | 1.70 | 0.59 | 0.53 |
| 6 | 1400 | 6.24 | 5.84 | 5.28 | 4.56 | 3.69 | 2.73 | 1.67 | 0.55 | 0.56 |
| 6 | 2400 | 6.23 | 5.83 | 5.26 | 4.54 | 3.66 | 2.70 | 1.64 | 0.52 | 0.60 |
| 6 | 3400 | 6.22 | 5.81 | 5.24 | 4.51 | 3.64 | 2.67 | 1.61 | 0.49 | 0.63 |
| 7 | 800 | 6.21 | 5.80 | 5.23 | 4.49 | 3.61 | 2.64 | 1.58 | 0.46 | 0.66 |
| 7 | 1800 | 6.20 | 5.78 | 5.21 | 4.47 | 3.58 | 2.61 | 1.54 | 0.43 | 0.69 |
| 7 | 2800 | 6.20 | 5.77 | 5.19 | 4.45 | 3.56 | 2.58 | 1.51 | 0.40 | 0.72 |
| 8 | 200 | 6.19 | 5.75 | 5.17 | 4.42 | 3.53 | 2.56 | 1.48 | 0.37 | 0.75 |
| 8 | 1200 | 6.18 | 5.74 | 5.15 | 4.40 | 3.50 | 2.53 | 1.45 | 0.33 | 0.79 |
| 8 | 2200 | 6.17 | 5.73 | 5.14 | 4.38 | 3.48 | 2.50 | 1.42 | 0.30 | 0.82 |
| 8 | 3200 | 6.16 | 5.71 | 5.12 | 4.35 | 3.45 | 2.47 | 1.39 | 0.27 | 0.85 |
| 9 | 000 | 6.15 | 5.70 | 5.10 | 4.33 | 3.43 | 2.44 | 1.36 | 0.24 | 0.88 |
| 9 | 1600 | 6.14 | 5.68 | 5.08 | 4.31 | 3.40 | 2.41 | 1.33 | 0.21 | 0.91 |
| 9 | 2600 | 6.13 | 5.67 | 5.06 | 4.28 | 3.38 | 2.38 | 1.30 | 0.18 | 0.94 |
| 10 | 0 | −6.12 | −5.66 | −5.04 | −4.26 | −3.36 | −2.35 | −1.27 | −0.15 | +0.97 |

NOTE. — When $y-u$ exceeds 180° the Sign of the Equation is to be reversed.

# TABLE LXXXII. ARGUMENT 77.

Equation = — 416″.9 sin. 2*y*.

| *y* | 270° +<br>180 —<br>90 +<br>0 — | 271° +<br>181 —<br>91 +<br>1 — | 272° +<br>182 —<br>92 +<br>2 — | 273° +<br>183 —<br>93 +<br>3 — | 274° +<br>184 —<br>94 +<br>4 — | 275° +<br>185 —<br>95 +<br>5 — | 276° +<br>186 —<br>96 +<br>6 — | 277° +<br>187 —<br>97 +<br>7 — | 278° +<br>188 —<br>98 +<br>8 — | *y* |
|---|---|---|---|---|---|---|---|---|---|---|
| 0″ | 0″.00 | 14″.55 | 29″.08 | 43″.58 | 58″.02 | 72″.39 | 86″.68 | 100″.86 | 114″.91 | 3600″ |
| 100 | 0.40 | 14.95 | 29.48 | 43.98 | 58.42 | 72.79 | 87.07 | 101.25 | 115.30 | 3500 |
| 200 | 0.81 | 15.36 | 29.89 | 44.38 | 58.82 | 73.19 | 87.47 | 101.64 | 115.69 | 3400 |
| 300 | 1.21 | 15.76 | 30.29 | 44.78 | 59.22 | 73.59 | 87.86 | 102.03 | 116.08 | 3300 |
| 400 | 1.62 | 16.16 | 30.69 | 45.18 | 59.62 | 73.99 | 88.26 | 102.42 | 116.47 | 3200 |
| 500 | 2.02 | 16.57 | 31.10 | 45.59 | 60.02 | 74.38 | 88.65 | 102.82 | 116.85 | 3100 |
| 600 | 2.43 | 16.97 | 31.50 | 45.99 | 60.42 | 74.78 | 89.05 | 103.21 | 117.24 | 3000 |
| 700 | 2.83 | 17.37 | 31.90 | 46.39 | 60.82 | 75.18 | 89.44 | 103.60 | 117.63 | 2900 |
| 800 | 3.24 | 17.78 | 32.31 | 46.79 | 61.22 | 75.57 | 89.84 | 103.99 | 118.01 | 2800 |
| 900 | 3.64 | 18.18 | 32.71 | 47.19 | 61.62 | 75.97 | 90.23 | 104.38 | 118.40 | 2700 |
| 1000 | 4.04 | 18.59 | 33.11 | 47.59 | 62.02 | 76.37 | 90.63 | 104.77 | 118.79 | 2600 |
| 1100 | 4.45 | 18.99 | 33.52 | 48.00 | 62.42 | 76.77 | 91.02 | 105.17 | 119.18 | 2500 |
| 1200 | 4.85 | 19.40 | 33.92 | 48.40 | 62.82 | 77.17 | 91.42 | 105.56 | 119.57 | 2400 |
| 1300 | 5.25 | 19.80 | 34.32 | 48.80 | 63.22 | 77.57 | 91.81 | 105.95 | 119.96 | 2300 |
| 1400 | 5.66 | 20.21 | 34.73 | 49.20 | 63.62 | 77.96 | 92.21 | 106.34 | 120.34 | 2200 |
| 1500 | 6.06 | 20.61 | 35.13 | 49.60 | 64.02 | 78.36 | 92.60 | 106.73 | 120.73 | 2100 |
| 1600 | 6.46 | 21.01 | 35.53 | 50.00 | 64.42 | 78.76 | 92.99 | 107.12 | 121.12 | 2000 |
| 1700 | 6.87 | 21.42 | 35.94 | 50.41 | 64.82 | 79.15 | 93.39 | 107.51 | 121.50 | 1900 |
| 1800 | 7.28 | 21.82 | 36.34 | 50.81 | 65.22 | 79.55 | 93.78 | 107.90 | 121.89 | 1800 |
| 1900 | 7.68 | 22.22 | 36.74 | 51.21 | 65.62 | 79.95 | 94.17 | 108.29 | 122.28 | 1700 |
| 2000 | 8.09 | 22.63 | 37.15 | 51.61 | 66.01 | 80.34 | 94.57 | 108.68 | 122.66 | 1600 |
| 2100 | 8.49 | 23.03 | 37.55 | 52.01 | 66.41 | 80.74 | 94.96 | 109.07 | 123.05 | 1500 |
| 2200 | 8.89 | 23.43 | 37.95 | 52.41 | 66.81 | 81.14 | 95.35 | 109.46 | 123.43 | 1400 |
| 2300 | 9.30 | 23.84 | 38.35 | 52.81 | 67.21 | 81.53 | 95.75 | 109.85 | 123.82 | 1300 |
| 2400 | 9.70 | 24.24 | 38.75 | 53.21 | 67.61 | 81.93 | 96.14 | 110.24 | 124.20 | 1200 |
| 2500 | 10.10 | 24.64 | 39.15 | 53.61 | 68.01 | 82.33 | 96.53 | 110.63 | 124.59 | 1100 |
| 2600 | 10.51 | 25.05 | 39.56 | 54.02 | 68.41 | 82.72 | 96.93 | 111.02 | 124.97 | 1000 |
| 2700 | 10.91 | 25.45 | 39.96 | 54.42 | 68.81 | 83.12 | 97.32 | 111.41 | 125.36 | 900 |
| 2800 | 11.32 | 25.85 | 40.36 | 54.82 | 69.21 | 83.51 | 97.71 | 111.80 | 125.75 | 800 |
| 2900 | 11.72 | 26.26 | 40.77 | 55.22 | 69.60 | 83.91 | 98.11 | 112.19 | 126.13 | 700 |
| 3000 | 12.13 | 26.66 | 41.17 | 55.62 | 70.00 | 84.30 | 98.50 | 112.58 | 126.52 | 600 |
| 3100 | 12.53 | 27.06 | 41.57 | 56.02 | 70.40 | 84.70 | 98.89 | 112.97 | 126.90 | 500 |
| 3200 | 12.94 | 27.47 | 41.98 | 56.42 | 70.80 | 85.09 | 99.29 | 113.36 | 127.29 | 400 |
| 3300 | 13.34 | 27.87 | 42.38 | 56.82 | 71.20 | 85.49 | 99.68 | 113.75 | 127.67 | 300 |
| 3400 | 13.74 | 28.27 | 42.78 | 57.22 | 71.60 | 85.89 | 100.07 | 114.14 | 128.06 | 200 |
| 3500 | 14.15 | 28.68 | 43.18 | 57.62 | 71.99 | 86.28 | 100.47 | 114.52 | 128.44 | 100 |
| 3600 | 14.55 | 29.08 | 43.58 | 58.02 | 72.39 | 86.68 | 100.86 | 114.91 | 128.83 | 0 |
| *y* | 89° —<br>179 +<br>269 —<br>359 + | 88° —<br>178 +<br>268 —<br>358 + | 87° —<br>177 +<br>267 —<br>357 + | 86° —<br>176 +<br>266 —<br>356 + | 85° —<br>175 +<br>265 —<br>355 + | 84° —<br>174 +<br>264 —<br>354 + | 83° —<br>173 +<br>263 —<br>353 + | 82° —<br>172 +<br>262 —<br>352 + | 81° —<br>171 +<br>261 —<br>351 + | *y* |

# TABLE LXXXII. ARGUMENT 77.

Equation = — 416″.9 sin. 2ȳ.

| ȳ | 279° +<br>189 —<br>99 +<br>9 — | 280° +<br>190 —<br>100 +<br>10 — | 281° +<br>191 —<br>101 +<br>11 — | 282° +<br>192 —<br>102 +<br>12 — | 283° +<br>193 —<br>103 +<br>13 — | 284° +<br>194 —<br>104 +<br>14 — | 285° +<br>195 —<br>105 +<br>15 — | 286° +<br>196 —<br>106 +<br>16 — | 287° +<br>197 —<br>107 +<br>17 — | ȳ |
|---|---|---|---|---|---|---|---|---|---|---|
| 0″ | 128″.83 | 142″.59 | 156″.17 | 169″.57 | 182″.76 | 195″.72 | 208″.45 | 220″.92 | 233″.13 | 3600″ |
| 100 | 129.21 | 142.97 | 156.55 | 169.94 | 183.12 | 196.08 | 208.80 | 221.26 | 233.46 | 3500 |
| 200 | 129.60 | 143.35 | 156.92 | 170.31 | 183.48 | 196.43 | 209.15 | 221.61 | 233.80 | 3400 |
| 300 | 129.98 | 143.73 | 157.30 | 170.68 | 183.84 | 196.79 | 209.50 | 221.95 | 234.13 | 3300 |
| 400 | 130.36 | 144.11 | 157.67 | 171.05 | 184.20 | 197.15 | 209.85 | 222.29 | 234.46 | 3200 |
| 500 | 130.75 | 144.48 | 158.05 | 171.42 | 184.57 | 197.50 | 210.20 | 222.64 | 234.80 | 3100 |
| 600 | 131.13 | 144.86 | 158.42 | 171.79 | 184.93 | 197.86 | 210.55 | 222.98 | 235.13 | 3000 |
| 700 | 131.51 | 145.24 | 158.79 | 172.16 | 185.29 | 198.22 | 210.90 | 223.32 | 235.46 | 2900 |
| 800 | 131.90 | 145.62 | 159.17 | 172.52 | 185.66 | 198.57 | 211.24 | 223.66 | 235.80 | 2800 |
| 900 | 132.28 | 146.00 | 159.54 | 172.89 | 186.02 | 198.93 | 211.59 | 224.00 | 236.13 | 2700 |
| 1000 | 132.66 | 146.38 | 159.91 | 173.26 | 186.38 | 199.28 | 211.94 | 224.34 | 236.46 | 2600 |
| 1100 | 133.05 | 146.76 | 160.29 | 173.62 | 186.75 | 199.64 | 212.29 | 224.68 | 236.80 | 2500 |
| 1200 | 133.43 | 147.14 | 160.66 | 173.99 | 187.11 | 199.99 | 212.64 | 225.02 | 237.13 | 2400 |
| 1300 | 133.81 | 147.52 | 161.03 | 174.36 | 187.47 | 200.34 | 212.99 | 225.36 | 237.46 | 2300 |
| 1400 | 134.20 | 147.89 | 161.41 | 174.72 | 187.83 | 200.70 | 213.33 | 225.70 | 237.80 | 2200 |
| 1500 | 134.58 | 148.27 | 161.78 | 175.09 | 188.19 | 201.05 | 213.68 | 226.04 | 238.13 | 2100 |
| 1600 | 134.96 | 148.65 | 162.15 | 175.46 | 188.55 | 201.41 | 214.03 | 226.38 | 238.46 | 2000 |
| 1700 | 135.35 | 149.02 | 162.53 | 175.82 | 188.91 | 201.76 | 214.37 | 226.72 | 238.79 | 1900 |
| 1800 | 135.73 | 149.40 | 162.90 | 176.19 | 189.27 | 202.12 | 214.72 | 227.06 | 239.12 | 1800 |
| 1900 | 136.11 | 149.78 | 163.27 | 176.56 | 189.63 | 202.47 | 215.06 | 227.40 | 239.45 | 1700 |
| 2000 | 136.50 | 150.15 | 163.64 | 176.92 | 189.99 | 202.83 | 215.41 | 227.73 | 239.79 | 1600 |
| 2100 | 136.88 | 150.53 | 164.01 | 177.29 | 190.35 | 203.18 | 215.75 | 228.07 | 240.12 | 1500 |
| 2200 | 137.26 | 150.91 | 164.38 | 177.66 | 190.71 | 203.53 | 216.10 | 228.41 | 240.45 | 1400 |
| 2300 | 137.64 | 151.28 | 164.75 | 178.02 | 191.07 | 203.89 | 216.44 | 228.74 | 240.78 | 1300 |
| 2400 | 138.02 | 151.66 | 165.12 | 178.39 | 191.43 | 204.24 | 216.79 | 229.08 | 241.11 | 1200 |
| 2500 | 138.40 | 152.04 | 165.49 | 178.75 | 191.79 | 204.59 | 217.14 | 229.42 | 241.44 | 1100 |
| 2600 | 138.78 | 152.41 | 165.87 | 179.12 | 192.15 | 204.94 | 217.48 | 229.76 | 241.77 | 1000 |
| 2700 | 139.16 | 152.79 | 166.24 | 179.48 | 192.51 | 205.29 | 217.83 | 230.10 | 242.10 | 900 |
| 2800 | 139.54 | 153.17 | 166.61 | 179.84 | 192.87 | 205.64 | 218.17 | 230.44 | 242.43 | 800 |
| 2900 | 139.93 | 153.54 | 166.98 | 180.21 | 193.22 | 206.00 | 218.52 | 230.77 | 242.75 | 700 |
| 3000 | 140.31 | 153.92 | 167.35 | 180.57 | 193.58 | 206.35 | 218.86 | 231.11 | 243.08 | 600 |
| 3100 | 140.69 | 154.30 | 167.72 | 180.94 | 193.94 | 206.70 | 219.20 | 231.45 | 243.41 | 500 |
| 3200 | 141.07 | 154.67 | 168.09 | 181.30 | 194.29 | 207.05 | 219.55 | 231.78 | 243.73 | 400 |
| 3300 | 141.45 | 155.05 | 168.46 | 181.67 | 194.65 | 207.40 | 219.89 | 232.12 | 244.06 | 300 |
| 3400 | 141.83 | 155.42 | 168.83 | 182.03 | 195.01 | 207.75 | 220.23 | 232.46 | 244.39 | 200 |
| 3500 | 142.21 | 155.80 | 169.20 | 182.40 | 195.36 | 208.10 | 220.58 | 232.79 | 244.71 | 100 |
| 3600 | 142.59 | 156.17 | 169.57 | 182.76 | 195.72 | 208.45 | 220.92 | 233.13 | 245.04 | 0 |
| ȳ | 80° —<br>170 +<br>260 —<br>350 + | 79° —<br>169 +<br>259 —<br>349 + | 78° —<br>168 +<br>258 —<br>348 + | 77° —<br>167 +<br>257 —<br>347 + | 76° —<br>166 +<br>256 —<br>346 + | 75° —<br>165 +<br>255 —<br>345 + | 74° —<br>164 +<br>254 —<br>344 + | 73° —<br>163 +<br>253 —<br>343 + | 72° —<br>162 +<br>252 —<br>342 + | ȳ |

# TABLE LXXXII. ARGUMENT 77.

Equation = — 416″.9 sin. 2ȳ.

| ȳ | 288° +<br>198 —<br>108 +<br>18 — | 289° +<br>199 —<br>109 +<br>19 — | 290° +<br>200 —<br>110 +<br>20 — | 291° +<br>201 —<br>111 +<br>21 — | 292° +<br>202 —<br>112 +<br>22 — | 293° +<br>203 —<br>113 +<br>23 — | 294° +<br>204 —<br>114 +<br>24 — | 295° +<br>205 —<br>115 +<br>25 — | 296° +<br>206 —<br>116 +<br>26 — | ȳ |
|---|---|---|---|---|---|---|---|---|---|---|
| 0″ | 245″.04 | 256″.67 | 267″.98 | 278″.96 | 289″.60 | 299″.88 | 309″.82 | 319″.36 | 328″.52 | 3600″ |
| 100 | 245.37 | 256.99 | 268.29 | 279.26 | 289.89 | 300.16 | 310.09 | 319.62 | 328.77 | 3500 |
| 200 | 245.69 | 257.30 | 268.59 | 279.56 | 290.18 | 300.45 | 310.36 | 319.88 | 329.02 | 3400 |
| 300 | 246.02 | 257.62 | 268.90 | 279.86 | 290.47 | 300.73 | 310.63 | 320.14 | 329.27 | 3300 |
| 400 | 246.35 | 257.94 | 269.21 | 280.16 | 290.76 | 301.01 | 310.90 | 320.40 | 329.52 | 3200 |
| 500 | 246.67 | 258.25 | 269.52 | 280.46 | 291.05 | 301.29 | 311.17 | 320.65 | 329.76 | 3100 |
| 600 | 247.00 | 258.57 | 269.83 | 280.76 | 291.34 | 301.57 | 311.44 | 320.91 | 330.01 | 3000 |
| 700 | 247.33 | 258.88 | 270.14 | 281.06 | 291.63 | 301.85 | 311.71 | 321.17 | 330.26 | 2900 |
| 800 | 247.65 | 259.20 | 270.44 | 281.35 | 291.91 | 302.13 | 311.97 | 321.42 | 330.50 | 2800 |
| 900 | 247.98 | 259.52 | 270.75 | 281.65 | 292.20 | 302.41 | 312.24 | 321.68 | 330.75 | 2700 |
| 1000 | 248.31 | 259.84 | 271.06 | 281.95 | 292.49 | 302.69 | 312.51 | 321.94 | 330.99 | 2600 |
| 1100 | 248.63 | 260.15 | 271.37 | 282.24 | 292.77 | 302.96 | 312.77 | 322.19 | 331.24 | 2500 |
| 1200 | 248.96 | 260.47 | 271.68 | 282.54 | 293.06 | 303.24 | 313.04 | 322.45 | 331.48 | 2400 |
| 1300 | 249.28 | 260.79 | 271.99 | 282.84 | 293.35 | 303.52 | 313.31 | 322.71 | 331.73 | 2300 |
| 1400 | 249.61 | 261.10 | 272.29 | 283.13 | 293.64 | 303.79 | 313.57 | 322.96 | 331.97 | 2200 |
| 1500 | 249.93 | 261.42 | 272.60 | 283.43 | 293.93 | 304.07 | 313.84 | 323.22 | 332.22 | 2100 |
| 1600 | 250.25 | 261.73 | 272.90 | 283.73 | 294.22 | 304.35 | 314.11 | 323.47 | 332.46 | 2000 |
| 1700 | 250.58 | 262.05 | 273.21 | 284.02 | 294.50 | 304.62 | 314.37 | 323.73 | 332.71 | 1900 |
| 1800 | 250.90 | 262.36 | 273.51 | 284.32 | 294.79 | 304.90 | 314.64 | 323.98 | 332.95 | 1800 |
| 1900 | 251.22 | 262.67 | 273.81 | 284.61 | 295.08 | 305.17 | 314.90 | 324.24 | 333.19 | 1700 |
| 2000 | 251.54 | 262.99 | 274.12 | 284.91 | 295.36 | 305.45 | 315.17 | 324.49 | 333.44 | 1600 |
| 2100 | 251.86 | 263.30 | 274.42 | 285.20 | 295.65 | 305.72 | 315.43 | 324.75 | 333.68 | 1500 |
| 2200 | 252.18 | 263.61 | 274.72 | 285.50 | 295.93 | 306.00 | 315.69 | 325.00 | 333.92 | 1400 |
| 2300 | 252.51 | 263.93 | 275.03 | 285.79 | 296.22 | 306.27 | 315.96 | 325.26 | 334.16 | 1300 |
| 2400 | 252.83 | 264.24 | 275.33 | 286.09 | 296.50 | 306.55 | 316.22 | 325.51 | 334.40 | 1200 |
| 2500 | 253.15 | 264.55 | 275.63 | 286.38 | 296.78 | 306.82 | 316.48 | 325.76 | 334.64 | 1100 |
| 2600 | 253.47 | 264.87 | 275.94 | 286.68 | 297.07 | 307.10 | 316.75 | 326.01 | 334.89 | 1000 |
| 2700 | 253.79 | 265.18 | 276.24 | 286.97 | 297.35 | 307.37 | 317.01 | 326.26 | 335.13 | 900 |
| 2800 | 254.11 | 265.49 | 276.54 | 287.26 | 297.63 | 307.64 | 317.27 | 326.51 | 335.37 | 800 |
| 2900 | 254.43 | 265.81 | 276.85 | 287.56 | 297.92 | 307.92 | 317.54 | 326.77 | 335.61 | 700 |
| 3000 | 254.75 | 266.12 | 277.15 | 287.85 | 298.20 | 308.19 | 317.80 | 327.02 | 335.85 | 600 |
| 3100 | 255.07 | 266.43 | 277.45 | 288.14 | 298.48 | 308.46 | 318.06 | 327.27 | 336.09 | 500 |
| 3200 | 255.39 | 266.74 | 277.76 | 288.44 | 298.76 | 308.73 | 318.32 | 327.52 | 336.33 | 400 |
| 3300 | 255.71 | 267.05 | 278.06 | 288.73 | 299.04 | 309.00 | 318.58 | 327.77 | 336.57 | 300 |
| 3400 | 256.03 | 267.36 | 278.36 | 289.02 | 299.32 | 309.27 | 318.84 | 328.02 | 336.81 | 200 |
| 3500 | 256.35 | 267.67 | 278.66 | 289.31 | 299.60 | 309.55 | 319.10 | 328.27 | 337.04 | 100 |
| 3600 | 256.67 | 267.98 | 278.96 | 289.60 | 299.88 | 309.82 | 319.36 | 328.52 | 337.28 | 0 |
| ȳ | 71° —<br>161 +<br>251 —<br>341 + | 70° —<br>160 +<br>250 —<br>340 + | 69° —<br>159 +<br>249 —<br>339 + | 68° —<br>158 +<br>248 —<br>338 + | 67° —<br>157 +<br>247 —<br>337 + | 66° —<br>156 +<br>246 —<br>336 + | 65° —<br>155 +<br>245 —<br>335 + | 64° —<br>154 +<br>244 —<br>334 + | 63° —<br>153 +<br>243 —<br>333 + | ȳ |

# TABLE LXXXII. ARGUMENT 77.

Equation = — 416″.9 sin. 2ŷ.

| ŷ | 297° +<br>207 −<br>117 +<br>27 − | 298° +<br>208 −<br>118 +<br>28 − | 299° +<br>209 −<br>119 +<br>29 − | 300° +<br>210 −<br>120 +<br>30 − | 301° +<br>211 −<br>121 +<br>31 − | 302° +<br>212 −<br>122 +<br>32 − | 303° +<br>213 −<br>123 +<br>33 − | 304° +<br>214 −<br>124 +<br>34 − | 305° +<br>215 −<br>125 +<br>35 − | ŷ |
|---|---|---|---|---|---|---|---|---|---|---|
| 0″ | 337″.28 | 345″.62 | 353″.55 | 361″.05 | 368″.09 | 374″.71 | 380″.85 | 386″.54 | 391″.76 | 3600″ |
| 100 | 337.51 | 345.85 | 353.76 | 361.25 | 368.28 | 374.89 | 381.02 | 386.69 | 391.90 | 3500 |
| 200 | 337.75 | 346.07 | 353.98 | 361.45 | 368.47 | 375.06 | 381.18 | 386.84 | 392.03 | 3400 |
| 300 | 337.98 | 346.30 | 354.19 | 361.65 | 368.66 | 375.24 | 381.35 | 386.99 | 392.17 | 3300 |
| 400 | 338.22 | 346.53 | 354.40 | 361.85 | 368.85 | 375.42 | 381.51 | 387.14 | 392.31 | 3200 |
| 500 | 338.45 | 346.75 | 354.62 | 362.05 | 369.04 | 375.59 | 381.68 | 387.29 | 392.44 | 3100 |
| 600 | 338.69 | 346.98 | 354.83 | 362.25 | 369.23 | 375.77 | 381.84 | 387.44 | 392.58 | 3000 |
| 700 | 338.93 | 347.20 | 355.04 | 362.45 | 369.42 | 375.94 | 382.00 | 387.59 | 392.72 | 2900 |
| 800 | 339.16 | 347.43 | 355.26 | 362.65 | 369.60 | 376.12 | 382.16 | 387.74 | 392.85 | 2800 |
| 900 | 339.40 | 347.65 | 355.47 | 362.85 | 369.79 | 376.29 | 382.32 | 387.89 | 392.99 | 2700 |
| 1000 | 339.63 | 347.87 | 355.68 | 363.05 | 369.98 | 376.46 | 382.48 | 388.04 | 393.12 | 2600 |
| 1100 | 339.87 | 348.09 | 355.89 | 363.25 | 370.16 | 376.64 | 382.64 | 388.18 | 393.26 | 2500 |
| 1200 | 340.10 | 348.31 | 356.10 | 363.45 | 370.35 | 376.81 | 382.80 | 388.33 | 393.39 | 2400 |
| 1300 | 340.33 | 348.53 | 356.31 | 363.65 | 370.53 | 376.99 | 382.96 | 388.48 | 393.52 | 2300 |
| 1400 | 340.57 | 348.76 | 356.51 | 363.84 | 370.72 | 377.16 | 383.12 | 388.62 | 393.65 | 2200 |
| 1500 | 340.80 | 348.98 | 356.72 | 364.04 | 370.90 | 377.33 | 383.28 | 388.77 | 393.78 | 2100 |
| 1600 | 341.03 | 349.20 | 356.93 | 364.24 | 371.09 | 377.50 | 383.44 | 388.92 | 393.91 | 2000 |
| 1700 | 341.27 | 349.42 | 357.14 | 364.43 | 371.27 | 377.67 | 383.60 | 389.06 | 394.05 | 1900 |
| 1800 | 341.50 | 349.64 | 357.35 | 364.63 | 371.46 | 377.84 | 383.76 | 389.21 | 394.18 | 1800 |
| 1900 | 341.73 | 349.86 | 357.56 | 364.83 | 371.64 | 378.01 | 383.92 | 389.35 | 394.31 | 1700 |
| 2000 | 341.97 | 350.08 | 357.76 | 365.02 | 371.83 | 378.18 | 384.07 | 389.50 | 394.44 | 1600 |
| 2100 | 342.20 | 350.30 | 357.97 | 365.22 | 372.01 | 378.35 | 384.23 | 389.64 | 394.57 | 1500 |
| 2200 | 342.43 | 350.52 | 358.18 | 365.41 | 372.19 | 378.52 | 384.39 | 389.78 | 394.70 | 1400 |
| 2300 | 342.66 | 350.73 | 358.38 | 365.61 | 372.37 | 378.68 | 384.54 | 389.93 | 394.83 | 1300 |
| 2400 | 342.89 | 350.95 | 358.59 | 365.80 | 372.55 | 378.85 | 384.70 | 390.07 | 394.96 | 1200 |
| 2500 | 343.12 | 351.17 | 358.80 | 365.99 | 372.73 | 379.02 | 384.85 | 390.21 | 395.09 | 1100 |
| 2600 | 343.35 | 351.39 | 359.00 | 366.19 | 372.91 | 379.18 | 385.01 | 390.36 | 395.22 | 1000 |
| 2700 | 343.58 | 351.61 | 359.21 | 366.38 | 373.09 | 379.35 | 385.16 | 390.50 | 395.35 | 900 |
| 2800 | 343.81 | 351.83 | 359.42 | 366.57 | 373.27 | 379.52 | 385.32 | 390.64 | 395.48 | 800 |
| 2900 | 344.03 | 352.04 | 359.62 | 366.76 | 373.45 | 379.69 | 385.47 | 390.78 | 395.61 | 700 |
| 3000 | 344.26 | 352.26 | 359.83 | 366.95 | 373.63 | 379.86 | 385.63 | 390.92 | 395.74 | 600 |
| 3100 | 344.49 | 352.48 | 360.03 | 367.14 | 373.81 | 380.03 | 385.78 | 391.06 | 395.87 | 500 |
| 3200 | 344.71 | 352.69 | 360.24 | 367.33 | 373.99 | 380.19 | 385.94 | 391.20 | 395.99 | 400 |
| 3300 | 344.94 | 352.91 | 360.44 | 367.52 | 374.17 | 380.36 | 386.09 | 391.34 | 396.12 | 300 |
| 3400 | 345.17 | 353.12 | 360.64 | 367.71 | 374.35 | 380.52 | 386.24 | 391.48 | 396.25 | 200 |
| 3500 | 345.39 | 353.34 | 360.85 | 367.90 | 374.53 | 380.69 | 386.39 | 391.62 | 396.37 | 100 |
| 3600 | 345.62 | 353.55 | 361.05 | 368.09 | 374.71 | 380.85 | 386.54 | 391.76 | 396.50 | 0 |
| ŷ | 62° −<br>152 +<br>242 −<br>332 + | 61° −<br>151 +<br>241 −<br>331 + | 60° −<br>150 +<br>240 −<br>330 + | 59° −<br>149 +<br>239 −<br>329 + | 58° −<br>148 +<br>238 −<br>328 + | 57° −<br>147 +<br>237 −<br>327 + | 56° −<br>146 +<br>236 −<br>326 + | 55° −<br>145 +<br>235 −<br>325 + | 54° −<br>144 +<br>234 −<br>324 + | ŷ |

# TABLE LXXXII. ARGUMENT 77.

Equation = $-416''.9 \sin. 2\bar{y}$.

| $\bar{y}$ | 306° + <br> 216 − <br> 126 + <br> 36 − | 307 + <br> 217 − <br> 127 + <br> 37 − | 308 + <br> 218 − <br> 128 + <br> 38 − | 309 + <br> 219 − <br> 129 + <br> 39 − | 310 + <br> 220 − <br> 130 + <br> 40 − | 311 + <br> 221 − <br> 131 + <br> 41 − | 312 + <br> 222 − <br> 132 + <br> 42 − | 313 + <br> 223 − <br> 133 + <br> 43 − | 314 + <br> 224 − <br> 134 + <br> 44 − | $\bar{y}$ |
|---|---|---|---|---|---|---|---|---|---|---|
| 0″ | 396″.50 | 400″.75 | 404″.51 | 407″.78 | 410″.56 | 412″.84 | 414″.61 | 415″.89 | 416″.65 | 3600″ |
| 100 | 396.62 | 400.86 | 404.61 | 407.86 | 410.63 | 412.90 | 414.65 | 415.92 | 416.66 | 3500 |
| 200 | 396.75 | 400.97 | 404.71 | 407.95 | 410.70 | 412.95 | 414.70 | 415.94 | 416.68 | 3400 |
| 300 | 396.87 | 401.08 | 404.81 | 408.03 | 410.77 | 413.01 | 414.74 | 415.97 | 416.69 | 3300 |
| 400 | 396.99 | 401.19 | 404.91 | 408.11 | 410.84 | 413.06 | 414.78 | 416.00 | 416.70 | 3200 |
| 500 | 397.12 | 401.30 | 405.00 | 408.20 | 410.91 | 413.12 | 414.82 | 416.02 | 416.72 | 3100 |
| 600 | 397.24 | 401.41 | 405.10 | 408.28 | 410.98 | 413.17 | 414.86 | 416.05 | 416.73 | 3000 |
| 700 | 397.36 | 401.52 | 405.19 | 408.36 | 411.05 | 413.22 | 414.90 | 416.07 | 416.74 | 2900 |
| 800 | 397.48 | 401.63 | 405.29 | 408.45 | 411.11 | 413.28 | 414.94 | 416.10 | 416.75 | 2800 |
| 900 | 397.60 | 401.74 | 405.38 | 408.53 | 411.18 | 413.33 | 414.98 | 416.12 | 416.76 | 2700 |
| 1000 | 397.72 | 401.85 | 405.47 | 408.61 | 411.25 | 413.38 | 415.02 | 416.14 | 416.77 | 2600 |
| 1100 | 397.85 | 401.95 | 405.57 | 408.69 | 411.31 | 413.43 | 415.05 | 416.17 | 416.78 | 2500 |
| 1200 | 397.97 | 402.06 | 405.66 | 408.77 | 411.38 | 413.48 | 415.09 | 416.19 | 416.79 | 2400 |
| 1300 | 398.09 | 402.16 | 405.75 | 408.85 | 411.44 | 413.54 | 415.13 | 416.21 | 416.80 | 2300 |
| 1400 | 398.21 | 402.27 | 405.85 | 408.93 | 411.51 | 413.59 | 415.16 | 416.24 | 416.80 | 2200 |
| 1500 | 398.33 | 402.37 | 405.94 | 409.01 | 411.57 | 413.64 | 415.20 | 416.26 | 416.81 | 2100 |
| 1600 | 398.45 | 402.48 | 406.03 | 409.09 | 411.63 | 413.69 | 415.24 | 416.28 | 416.82 | 2000 |
| 1700 | 398.56 | 402.58 | 406.12 | 409.16 | 411.70 | 413.74 | 415.27 | 416.30 | 416.82 | 1900 |
| 1800 | 398.68 | 402.69 | 406.21 | 409.24 | 411.76 | 413.79 | 415.31 | 416.32 | 416.83 | 1800 |
| 1900 | 398.80 | 402.79 | 406.30 | 409.32 | 411.82 | 413.84 | 415.34 | 416.34 | 416.84 | 1700 |
| 2000 | 398.91 | 402.90 | 406.39 | 409.39 | 411.89 | 413.88 | 415.38 | 416.37 | 416.84 | 1600 |
| 2100 | 399.03 | 403.00 | 406.48 | 409.47 | 411.95 | 413.93 | 415.41 | 416.39 | 416.85 | 1500 |
| 2200 | 399.15 | 403.10 | 406.57 | 409.54 | 412.01 | 413.98 | 415.44 | 416.41 | 416.86 | 1400 |
| 2300 | 399.26 | 403.21 | 406.66 | 409.62 | 412.08 | 414.02 | 415.48 | 416.43 | 416.86 | 1300 |
| 2400 | 399.38 | 403.31 | 406.75 | 409.69 | 412.14 | 414.07 | 415.51 | 416.45 | 416.87 | 1200 |
| 2500 | 399.50 | 403.41 | 406.84 | 409.77 | 412.20 | 414.12 | 415.54 | 416.47 | 416.87 | 1100 |
| 2600 | 399.61 | 403.52 | 406.93 | 409.84 | 412.26 | 414.16 | 415.58 | 416.48 | 416.88 | 1000 |
| 2700 | 399.73 | 403.62 | 407.02 | 409.92 | 412.32 | 414.21 | 415.61 | 416.50 | 416.88 | 900 |
| 2800 | 399.84 | 403.72 | 407.11 | 409.99 | 412.38 | 414.26 | 415.64 | 416.52 | 416.88 | 800 |
| 2900 | 399.96 | 403.82 | 407.19 | 410.07 | 412.44 | 414.30 | 415.68 | 416.53 | 416.89 | 700 |
| 3000 | 400.07 | 403.92 | 407.28 | 410.14 | 412.50 | 414.35 | 415.71 | 416.55 | 416.89 | 600 |
| 3100 | 400.18 | 404.02 | 407.36 | 410.21 | 412.56 | 414.39 | 415.74 | 416.57 | 416.89 | 500 |
| 3200 | 400.30 | 404.12 | 407.45 | 410.28 | 412.61 | 414.44 | 415.77 | 416.58 | 416.90 | 400 |
| 3300 | 400.41 | 404.22 | 407.53 | 410.35 | 412.67 | 414.48 | 415.80 | 416.60 | 416.90 | 300 |
| 3400 | 400.52 | 404.32 | 407.61 | 410.42 | 412.73 | 414.52 | 415.83 | 416.62 | 416.90 | 200 |
| 3500 | 400.64 | 404.41 | 407.70 | 410.49 | 412.78 | 414.57 | 415.86 | 416.63 | 416.90 | 100 |
| 3600 | 400.75 | 404.51 | 407.78 | 410.56 | 412.84 | 414.61 | 415.89 | 416.65 | 416.90 | 0 |
| $\bar{y}$ | 53° − <br> 143 + <br> 233 − <br> 323 + | 52 − <br> 142 + <br> 232 − <br> 322 + | 51 − <br> 141 + <br> 231 − <br> 321 + | 50 − <br> 140 + <br> 230 − <br> 320 + | 49 − <br> 139 + <br> 229 − <br> 319 + | 48 − <br> 138 + <br> 228 − <br> 318 + | 47 − <br> 137 + <br> 227 − <br> 317 + | 46 − <br> 136 + <br> 226 − <br> 316 + | 45 − <br> 135 + <br> 225 − <br> 315 + | $\bar{y}$ |

# TABLES VI″. - XXI.IV.

ARGUMENTS AND EQUATIONS.

| TABLE. | ARGUMENT. | EQUATION. |
|---|---|---|
| VI″. | 1 | $\overset{''}{7}6.0 - \overset{''}{7}3.563 \text{ sin. } x - 9''.993 \text{ sin. } 2x - 1''.071 \text{ sin. } 3x$ $- 0''.104 \text{ sin. } 4x - 0''.008 \text{ sin. } 5x.$ |
| VII″. | 2 | $11.2 - 11.18 \text{ sin. } (2t - x) - 0''.304 \text{ sin. } (4t - 2x).$ |
| VIII″. | 3 | $31.16 + 0.345 \text{ sin. } t - 20''.808 \text{ sin. } 2t - 0''.023 \text{ sin. } 3t$ $- 0''.65 \text{ sin. } 4t.$ |
| XI″. | 6 | $0.42 - 0.420 \text{ sin. } (2t - z - x).$ |
| XII″. | 7 | $5.12 - 5.117 \text{ sin. } (2t + x).$ |
| XIII″. | 8 | $1.73 - 1.727 \text{ sin. } (2t - z).$ |
| XIV″. | 9 | $0.41 - 0.411 \text{ sin. } (x - z).$ |
| XV″. | 10 | $0.41 + 0.413 \text{ sin. } (x + z).$ |
| XVI″. | 11 | $0.29 + 0.288 \text{ sin. } (2y - x).$ |
| XVIII″. | 13 | $0.92 - 0.920 \text{ sin. } (4t - x).$ |
| XIX″. | 14 | $0.08 + 0.083 \text{ sin. } (2t + z - x).$ |
| XX″. | 15 | $0.31 + 0.306 \text{ sin. } (2t + z).$ |
| XXI″. | 16 | $0.80 - 0.100 \text{ sin. } (2t + 2x).$ |
| XXII″. | 17 | $0.06 - 0.057 \text{ sin. } (t + z).$ |
| XXIII″. | 18 | $0.35 - 0.354 \text{ sin. } (2t + x - z).$ |
| XXIV″. | 19 | $0.05 + 0.054 \text{ sin. } (3x - 2t).$ |
| XXV″. | 20 | $0.11 - 0.115 \text{ sin. } (2x - z).$ |
| XXVII″. | 22 | $0.07 - 0.074 \text{ sin. } (2t - 2z).$ |
| XXIX″. | 24 | $0.10 + 0.102 \text{ sin. } (2x + z).$ |
| XXX″. | 25 | $0.08 + 0.081 \text{ sin. } (2t + z + x).$ |
| XXXI″. | 26 | $0.14 - 0.137 \text{ sin. } (4t + x).$ |
| XXXV″. | 30 | $0.19 - 0.087 \text{ sin. } (4t - x - z).$ |
| VI.IV. | 1 | $0.45 + 0.239 \text{ sin. } x + 0''.130 \text{ sin. } 2x + 0''.031 \text{ sin. } 3x$ $+ 0''.005 \text{ sin. } 4x.$ |
| VII.IV. | 2 | $0.03 + 0.027 \text{ sin. } (2t - x) + 0''.003 \text{ sin. } (4t - 2x).$ |
| VIII.IV. | 3 | $0.31 + 0.303 \text{ sin. } 2t + 0''.006 \text{ sin. } 3t + 0''.029 \text{ sin. } 4t.$ |
| XII.IV. | 7 | $0.14 + 0.136 \text{ sin. } (2t + x).$ |
| XIII.IV. | 8 | $0.02 + 0.018 \text{ sin. } (2t - x).$ |
| XVIII.IV. | 13 | $0.02 + 0.022 \text{ sin. } (4t - x).$ |
| XXI.IV. | 16 | $0.03 + 0.033 \text{ sin. } (2t + 2x).$ |

# TABLE VI″. ARGUMENT 1.

Equation = 76″. — 73″.563 sin. $x$ — 9″.993 sin. $2x$ — 1″.071 sin. $3x$ — 0″.104 sin. $4x$ — 0″.008 sin. $5x$.

Period, 27.55455246 days.

| Days. | 0 | 1 | 2 | 3 | 4 | 5 | 6 | 7 | 8 | 9 |
|---|---|---|---|---|---|---|---|---|---|---|
| Days. .00 | 148″.41 | 151″.14 | 149″.71 | 143″.45 | 132″.05 | 115″.85 | 95″.92 | 74″.04 | 52″.34 | 32″.97 |
| .01 | 148.45 | 151.15 | 149.67 | 143.36 | 131.91 | 115.67 | 95.71 | 73.82 | 52.13 | 32.80 |
| .02 | 148.50 | 151.16 | 149.63 | 143.27 | 131.77 | 115.48 | 95.50 | 73.60 | 51.92 | 32.62 |
| .03 | 148.54 | 151.16 | 149.59 | 143.18 | 131.63 | 115.30 | 95.28 | 73.38 | 51.72 | 32.45 |
| .04 | 148.58 | 151.17 | 149.55 | 143.09 | 131.49 | 115.11 | 95.07 | 73.15 | 51.51 | 32.27 |
| .05 | 148.63 | 151.17 | 149.51 | 143.00 | 131.34 | 114.93 | 94.86 | 72.93 | 51.30 | 32.10 |
| .06 | 148.67 | 151.18 | 149.47 | 142.91 | 131.20 | 114.74 | 94.64 | 72.71 | 51.10 | 31.93 |
| .07 | 148.72 | 151.18 | 149.43 | 142.82 | 131.06 | 114.56 | 94.43 | 72.48 | 50.89 | 31.75 |
| .08 | 148.76 | 151.18 | 149.39 | 142.72 | 130.91 | 114.37 | 94.22 | 72.26 | 50.69 | 31.58 |
| .09 | 148.80 | 151.19 | 149.35 | 142.63 | 130.77 | 114.19 | 94.01 | 72.04 | 50.48 | 31.40 |
| .10 | 148.84 | 151.19 | 149.31 | 142.54 | 130.63 | 114.00 | 93.79 | 71.82 | 50.27 | 31.23 |
| .11 | 148.88 | 151.19 | 149.27 | 142.44 | 130.48 | 113.81 | 93.58 | 71.60 | 50.06 | 31.06 |
| .12 | 148.92 | 151.19 | 149.23 | 142.35 | 130.34 | 113.62 | 93.36 | 71.38 | 49.86 | 30.89 |
| .13 | 148.97 | 151.20 | 149.18 | 142.26 | 130.19 | 113.44 | 93.15 | 71.16 | 49.65 | 30.72 |
| .14 | 149.01 | 151.20 | 149.14 | 142.17 | 130.05 | 113.25 | 92.93 | 70.94 | 49.45 | 30.55 |
| .15 | 149.05 | 151.20 | 149.10 | 142.07 | 129.90 | 113.06 | 92.72 | 70.71 | 49.24 | 30.38 |
| .16 | 149.09 | 151.20 | 149.05 | 141.97 | 129.76 | 112.87 | 92.50 | 70.49 | 49.04 | 30.21 |
| .17 | 149.13 | 151.21 | 149.01 | 141.87 | 129.61 | 112.68 | 92.29 | 70.27 | 48.83 | 30.04 |
| .18 | 149.17 | 151.21 | 148.96 | 141.78 | 129.47 | 112.49 | 92.07 | 70.05 | 48.63 | 29.87 |
| .19 | 149.21 | 151.21 | 148.92 | 141.68 | 129.32 | 112.30 | 91.86 | 69.83 | 48.42 | 29.70 |
| .20 | 149.25 | 151.21 | 148.87 | 141.58 | 129.17 | 112.11 | 91.64 | 69.61 | 48.22 | 29.53 |
| .21 | 149.29 | 151.21 | 148.82 | 141.48 | 129.02 | 111.92 | 91.42 | 69.39 | 48.02 | 29.36 |
| .22 | 149.33 | 151.21 | 148.78 | 141.38 | 128.87 | 111.73 | 91.21 | 69.17 | 47.82 | 29.20 |
| .23 | 149.37 | 151.20 | 148.73 | 141.28 | 128.72 | 111.53 | 90.99 | 68.95 | 47.62 | 29.03 |
| .24 | 149.40 | 151.20 | 148.68 | 141.18 | 128.57 | 111.34 | 90.78 | 68.73 | 47.41 | 28.87 |
| .25 | 149.44 | 151.20 | 148.63 | 141.08 | 128.42 | 111.15 | 90.56 | 68.50 | 47.21 | 28.70 |
| .26 | 149.47 | 151.19 | 148.58 | 140.98 | 128.27 | 110.96 | 90.34 | 68.28 | 47.01 | 28.53 |
| .27 | 149.51 | 151.19 | 148.53 | 140.88 | 128.11 | 110.77 | 90.12 | 68.06 | 46.80 | 28.37 |
| .28 | 149.54 | 151.19 | 148.47 | 140.77 | 127.96 | 110.57 | 89.91 | 67.84 | 46.60 | 28.20 |
| .29 | 149.58 | 151.18 | 148.42 | 140.67 | 127.81 | 110.38 | 89.69 | 67.62 | 46.40 | 28.04 |
| .30 | 149.62 | 151.18 | 148.37 | 140.57 | 127.66 | 110.19 | 89.47 | 67.40 | 46.20 | 27.87 |
| .31 | 149.65 | 151.17 | 148.31 | 140.47 | 127.51 | 109.99 | 89.25 | 67.18 | 46.00 | 27.71 |
| .32 | 149.68 | 151.17 | 148.26 | 140.36 | 127.35 | 109.80 | 89.03 | 66.96 | 45.80 | 27.55 |
| .33 | 149.72 | 151.16 | 148.20 | 140.25 | 127.20 | 109.61 | 88.82 | 66.74 | 45.60 | 27.38 |
| .34 | 149.75 | 151.16 | 148.15 | 140.14 | 127.04 | 109.42 | 88.60 | 66.52 | 45.40 | 27.22 |
| .35 | 149.79 | 151.15 | 148.09 | 140.04 | 126.89 | 109.22 | 88.38 | 66.30 | 45.20 | 27.06 |
| .36 | 149.82 | 151.14 | 148.04 | 139.93 | 126.73 | 109.02 | 88.16 | 66.09 | 45.01 | 26.90 |
| .37 | 149.86 | 151.14 | 147.98 | 139.82 | 126.58 | 108.83 | 87.94 | 65.87 | 44.81 | 26.74 |
| .38 | 149.89 | 151.13 | 147.93 | 139.72 | 126.42 | 108.63 | 87.73 | 65.65 | 44.61 | 26.58 |
| .39 | 149.92 | 151.12 | 147.87 | 139.61 | 126.26 | 108.44 | 87.51 | 65.43 | 44.41 | 26.42 |
| .40 | 149.95 | 151.11 | 147.82 | 139.50 | 126.10 | 108.24 | 87.29 | 65.21 | 44.21 | 26.26 |
| .41 | 149.98 | 151.10 | 147.76 | 139.39 | 125.94 | 108.04 | 87.07 | 64.99 | 44.01 | 26.10 |
| .42 | 150.01 | 151.09 | 147.71 | 139.28 | 125.78 | 107.84 | 86.85 | 64.77 | 43.82 | 25.94 |
| .43 | 150.04 | 151.08 | 147.65 | 139.17 | 125.62 | 107.65 | 86.63 | 64.55 | 43.62 | 25.79 |
| .44 | 150.07 | 151.07 | 147.59 | 139.06 | 125.46 | 107.45 | 86.41 | 64.34 | 43.43 | 25.63 |
| .45 | 150.10 | 151.06 | 147.53 | 138.95 | 125.30 | 107.25 | 86.19 | 64.12 | 43.23 | 25.47 |
| .46 | 150.13 | 151.05 | 147.47 | 138.84 | 125.14 | 107.05 | 85.97 | 63.90 | 43.03 | 25.31 |
| .47 | 150.16 | 151.03 | 147.41 | 138.73 | 124.98 | 106.85 | 85.75 | 63.69 | 42.84 | 25.16 |
| .48 | 150.19 | 151.02 | 147.34 | 138.61 | 124.82 | 106.65 | 85.53 | 63.47 | 42.64 | 25.00 |
| .49 | 150.22 | 151.01 | 147.28 | 138.50 | 124.66 | 106.45 | 85.31 | 63.25 | 42.45 | 24.85 |
| .50 | 150.25 | 151.00 | 147.22 | 138.39 | 124.50 | 106.25 | 85.09 | 63.03 | 42.25 | 24.69 |

# TABLE VI″. ARGUMENT 1.

Equation $= 76''. - 73''.563 \sin. x - 9''.993 \sin. 2x - 1''.071 \sin. 3x - 0''.104 \sin. 4x - 0''.008 \sin. 5x.$

Period, 27.55455246 days.

| Days. | 0 | 1 | 2 | 3 | 4 | 5 | 6 | 7 | 8 | 9 |
|---|---|---|---|---|---|---|---|---|---|---|
| Days. | ″ | ″ | ″ | ″ | ″ | ″ | ″ | ″ | ″ | ″ |
| .50 | 150.25 | 151.00 | 147.22 | 138.39 | 124.50 | 106.25 | 85.09 | 63.03 | 42.25 | 24.69 |
| .51 | 150.28 | 150.98 | 147.16 | 138.27 | 124.34 | 106.05 | 84.87 | 62.81 | 42.06 | 24.54 |
| .52 | 150.30 | 150.97 | 147.09 | 138.16 | 124.17 | 105.85 | 84.65 | 62.59 | 41.86 | 24.38 |
| .53 | 150.33 | 150.95 | 147.03 | 138.04 | 124.01 | 105.65 | 84.43 | 62.38 | 41.67 | 24.23 |
| .54 | 150.35 | 150.94 | 146.96 | 137.93 | 123.84 | 105.45 | 84.21 | 62.16 | 41.47 | 24.07 |
| .55 | 150.38 | 150.92 | 146.90 | 137.81 | 123.68 | 105.25 | 83.99 | 61.94 | 41.28 | 23.92 |
| .56 | 150.40 | 150.91 | 146.83 | 137.69 | 123.51 | 105.05 | 83.77 | 61.73 | 41.09 | 23.77 |
| .57 | 150.43 | 150.89 | 146.77 | 137.57 | 123.35 | 104.85 | 83.55 | 61.51 | 40.90 | 23.62 |
| .58 | 150.45 | 150.87 | 146.70 | 137.46 | 123.18 | 104.64 | 83.33 | 61.30 | 40.70 | 23.47 |
| .59 | 150.48 | 150.85 | 146.64 | 137.34 | 123.02 | 104.44 | 83.11 | 61.08 | 40.51 | 23.32 |
| .60 | 150.50 | 150.83 | 146.57 | 137.22 | 122.85 | 104.24 | 82.89 | 60.86 | 40.32 | 23.17 |
| .61 | 150.52 | 150.81 | 146.50 | 137.10 | 122.68 | 104.04 | 82.67 | 60.64 | 40.13 | 23.02 |
| .62 | 150.54 | 150.79 | 146.43 | 136.98 | 122.51 | 103.83 | 82.45 | 60.43 | 39.94 | 22.87 |
| .63 | 150.57 | 150.77 | 146.37 | 136.86 | 122.35 | 103.63 | 82.23 | 60.21 | 39.75 | 22.73 |
| .64 | 150.59 | 150.75 | 146.30 | 136.74 | 122.18 | 103.42 | 82.01 | 60.00 | 39.56 | 22.58 |
| .65 | 150.62 | 150.73 | 146.23 | 136.62 | 122.01 | 103.22 | 81.79 | 59.78 | 39.37 | 22.43 |
| .66 | 150.64 | 150.71 | 146.16 | 136.50 | 121.84 | 103.02 | 81.57 | 59.56 | 39.18 | 22.28 |
| .67 | 150.66 | 150.68 | 146.09 | 136.37 | 121.67 | 102.81 | 81.35 | 59.35 | 39.00 | 22.13 |
| .68 | 150.68 | 150.66 | 146.01 | 136.25 | 121.50 | 102.61 | 81.12 | 59.13 | 38.81 | 21.99 |
| .69 | 150.70 | 150.64 | 145.94 | 136.12 | 121.33 | 102.40 | 80.90 | 58.92 | 38.62 | 21.84 |
| .70 | 150.72 | 150.62 | 145.87 | 136.00 | 121.16 | 102.20 | 80.68 | 58.70 | 38.43 | 21.69 |
| .71 | 150.74 | 150.60 | 145.79 | 135.88 | 120.99 | 101.99 | 80.46 | 58.49 | 38.24 | 21.55 |
| .72 | 150.76 | 150.58 | 145.72 | 135.75 | 120.82 | 101.78 | 80.24 | 58.27 | 38.06 | 21.40 |
| .73 | 150.78 | 150.55 | 145.64 | 135.63 | 120.64 | 101.58 | 80.02 | 58.06 | 37.87 | 21.26 |
| .74 | 150.80 | 150.53 | 145.57 | 135.50 | 120.47 | 101.38 | 79.80 | 57.84 | 37.69 | 21.11 |
| .75 | 150.81 | 150.50 | 145.49 | 135.38 | 120.30 | 101.17 | 79.58 | 57.63 | 37.50 | 20.97 |
| .76 | 150.83 | 150.47 | 145.41 | 135.25 | 120.13 | 100.96 | 79.36 | 57.42 | 37.31 | 20.83 |
| .77 | 150.85 | 150.45 | 145.34 | 135.12 | 119.95 | 100.75 | 79.14 | 57.20 | 37.13 | 20.69 |
| .78 | 150.86 | 150.42 | 145.26 | 135.00 | 119.78 | 100.55 | 78.91 | 56.99 | 36.94 | 20.55 |
| .79 | 150.88 | 150.40 | 145.19 | 134.87 | 119.60 | 100.34 | 78.69 | 56.77 | 36.76 | 20.41 |
| .80 | 150.90 | 150.37 | 145.11 | 134.74 | 119.43 | 100.13 | 78.47 | 56.56 | 36.57 | 20.27 |
| .81 | 150.91 | 150.34 | 145.03 | 134.61 | 119.25 | 99.92 | 78.25 | 56.35 | 36.39 | 20.13 |
| .82 | 150.93 | 150.31 | 144.95 | 134.48 | 119.08 | 99.71 | 78.03 | 56.14 | 36.21 | 19.99 |
| .83 | 150.94 | 150.28 | 144.88 | 134.35 | 118.90 | 99.51 | 77.80 | 55.92 | 36.02 | 19.86 |
| .84 | 150.95 | 150.25 | 144.80 | 134.22 | 118.73 | 99.30 | 77.58 | 55.71 | 35.84 | 19.72 |
| .85 | 150.97 | 150.22 | 144.72 | 134.09 | 118.55 | 99.09 | 77.36 | 55.50 | 35.66 | 19.58 |
| .86 | 150.98 | 150.19 | 144.64 | 133.96 | 118.37 | 98.88 | 77.14 | 55.29 | 35.48 | 19.44 |
| .87 | 151.00 | 150.15 | 144.56 | 133.82 | 118.19 | 98.67 | 76.92 | 55.08 | 35.30 | 19.30 |
| .88 | 151.01 | 150.12 | 144.47 | 133.69 | 118.02 | 98.46 | 76.69 | 54.86 | 35.11 | 19.17 |
| .89 | 151.02 | 150.09 | 144.39 | 133.55 | 117.84 | 98.25 | 76.47 | 54.65 | 34.93 | 19.03 |
| .90 | 151.04 | 150.06 | 144.31 | 133.42 | 117.66 | 98.04 | 76.25 | 54.44 | 34.75 | 18.89 |
| .91 | 151.05 | 150.03 | 144.23 | 133.28 | 117.48 | 97.83 | 76.03 | 54.23 | 34.57 | 18.76 |
| .92 | 151.06 | 150.00 | 144.14 | 133.15 | 117.30 | 97.62 | 75.81 | 54.02 | 34.39 | 18.62 |
| .93 | 151.07 | 149.96 | 144.06 | 133.01 | 117.12 | 97.40 | 75.59 | 53.81 | 34.21 | 18.49 |
| .94 | 151.08 | 149.93 | 143.97 | 132.88 | 116.94 | 97.19 | 75.37 | 53.60 | 34.04 | 18.35 |
| .95 | 151.09 | 149.89 | 143.89 | 132.74 | 116.76 | 96.98 | 75.15 | 53.39 | 33.86 | 18.22 |
| .96 | 151.10 | 149.86 | 143.80 | 132.60 | 116.58 | 96.77 | 74.93 | 53.18 | 33.68 | 18.09 |
| .97 | 151.11 | 149.82 | 143.71 | 132.46 | 116.40 | 96.56 | 74.71 | 52.97 | 33.51 | 17.96 |
| .98 | 151.12 | 149.79 | 143.63 | 132.33 | 116.21 | 96.34 | 74.48 | 52.76 | 33.33 | 17.82 |
| .99 | 151.13 | 149.75 | 143.54 | 132.19 | 116.03 | 96.13 | 74.26 | 52.55 | 33.15 | 17.69 |
| 1.00 | 151.14 | 149.71 | 143.45 | 132.05 | 115.85 | 95.92 | 74.04 | 52.34 | 32.97 | 17.56 |

# TABLE VI″. ARGUMENT 1.

Equation = 76″. — 73″.563 sin. $x$ — 9″.993 sin. $2x$ — 1″.071 sin. $3x$ — 0″.104 sin. $4x$ — 0″.008 sin. $5x$.

Period, 27.55455246 days.

| Days. | 10 | 11 | 12 | 13 | 14 | 15 | 16 | 17 | 18 |
|---|---|---|---|---|---|---|---|---|---|
| Days. | ″ | ″ | ″ | ″ | ″ | ″ | ″ | ″ | ″ |
| .00 | 17.56 | 7.07 | 1.70 | 1.07 | 4.46 | 11.01 | 19.91 | 30.46 | 42.11 |
| .01 | 17.43 | 6.99 | 1.67 | 1.09 | 4.51 | 11.09 | 20.01 | 30.57 | 42.23 |
| .02 | 17.30 | 6.91 | 1.64 | 1.10 | 4.56 | 11.17 | 20.11 | 30.68 | 42.35 |
| .03 | 17.17 | 6.84 | 1.62 | 1.12 | 4.62 | 11.25 | 20.21 | 30.80 | 42.47 |
| .04 | 17.04 | 6.76 | 1.59 | 1.13 | 4.67 | 11.33 | 20.31 | 30.91 | 42.59 |
| .05 | 16.91 | 6.68 | 1.56 | 1.15 | 4.72 | 11.41 | 20.41 | 31.02 | 42.71 |
| .06 | 16.78 | 6.61 | 1.53 | 1.17 | 4.77 | 11.49 | 20.50 | 31.14 | 42.84 |
| .07 | 16.66 | 6.53 | 1.51 | 1.19 | 4.83 | 11.57 | 20.60 | 31.25 | 42.96 |
| .08 | 16.53 | 6.46 | 1.48 | 1.20 | 4.88 | 11.65 | 20.70 | 31.37 | 43.08 |
| .09 | 16.41 | 6.38 | 1.46 | 1.22 | 4.94 | 11.73 | 20.80 | 31.48 | 43.20 |
| .10 | 16.28 | 6.31 | 1.43 | 1.24 | 4.99 | 11.81 | 20.90 | 31.59 | 43.32 |
| .11 | 16.16 | 6.24 | 1.41 | 1.26 | 5.04 | 11.89 | 21.00 | 31.70 | 43.44 |
| .12 | 16.03 | 6.16 | 1.38 | 1.28 | 5.10 | 11.97 | 21.10 | 31.81 | 43.56 |
| .13 | 15.91 | 6.09 | 1.36 | 1.30 | 5.15 | 12.06 | 21.20 | 31.93 | 43.68 |
| .14 | 15.78 | 6.01 | 1.33 | 1.32 | 5.21 | 12.14 | 21.30 | 32.04 | 43.80 |
| .15 | 15.66 | 5.94 | 1.31 | 1.34 | 5.26 | 12.22 | 21.40 | 32.15 | 43.92 |
| .16 | 15.54 | 5.87 | 1.29 | 1.36 | 5.32 | 12.30 | 21.51 | 32.27 | 44.05 |
| .17 | 15.42 | 5.80 | 1.27 | 1.38 | 5.37 | 12.38 | 21.61 | 32.38 | 44.17 |
| .18 | 15.29 | 5.73 | 1.25 | 1.41 | 5.43 | 12.47 | 21.71 | 32.50 | 44.29 |
| .19 | 15.17 | 5.66 | 1.23 | 1.43 | 5.48 | 12.55 | 21.81 | 32.61 | 44.41 |
| .20 | 15.05 | 5.59 | 1.21 | 1.45 | 5.54 | 12.63 | 21.91 | 32.72 | 44.53 |
| .21 | 14.93 | 5.52 | 1.19 | 1.47 | 5.60 | 12.71 | 22.01 | 32.83 | 44.65 |
| .22 | 14.81 | 5.45 | 1.17 | 1.50 | 5.66 | 12.80 | 22.11 | 32.94 | 44.77 |
| .23 | 14.69 | 5.39 | 1.16 | 1.52 | 5.71 | 12.88 | 22.21 | 33.06 | 44.89 |
| .24 | 14.57 | 5.32 | 1.14 | 1.55 | 5.77 | 12.97 | 22.32 | 33.17 | 45.02 |
| .25 | 14.45 | 5.25 | 1.12 | 1.57 | 5.83 | 13.05 | 22.42 | 33.29 | 45.14 |
| .26 | 14.33 | 5.19 | 1.10 | 1.60 | 5.89 | 13.13 | 22.52 | 33.40 | 45.26 |
| .27 | 14.22 | 5.12 | 1.09 | 1.62 | 5.95 | 13.22 | 22.63 | 33.52 | 45.39 |
| .28 | 14.10 | 5.06 | 1.07 | 1.65 | 6.01 | 13.30 | 22.73 | 33.63 | 45.51 |
| .29 | 13.99 | 4.99 | 1.06 | 1.67 | 6.07 | 13.39 | 22.83 | 33.75 | 45.63 |
| .30 | 13.87 | 4.93 | 1.04 | 1.70 | 6.13 | 13.47 | 22.93 | 33.86 | 45.75 |
| .31 | 13.76 | 4.87 | 1.03 | 1.73 | 6.19 | 13.56 | 23.03 | 33.98 | 45.87 |
| .32 | 13.64 | 4.81 | 1.01 | 1.76 | 6.25 | 13.64 | 23.14 | 34.09 | 45.99 |
| .33 | 13.53 | 4.74 | 1.00 | 1.78 | 6.32 | 13.73 | 23.24 | 34.21 | 46.12 |
| .34 | 13.41 | 4.68 | 0.98 | 1.81 | 6.38 | 13.81 | 23.34 | 34.32 | 46.24 |
| .35 | 13.30 | 4.62 | 0.97 | 1.84 | 6.44 | 13.90 | 23.45 | 34.44 | 46.36 |
| .36 | 13.19 | 4.56 | 0.96 | 1.87 | 6.50 | 13.99 | 23.55 | 34.56 | 46.49 |
| .37 | 13.08 | 4.50 | 0.95 | 1.90 | 6.56 | 14.07 | 23.66 | 34.67 | 46.61 |
| .38 | 12.97 | 4.44 | 0.93 | 1.93 | 6.63 | 14.16 | 23.76 | 34.79 | 46.74 |
| .39 | 12.86 | 4.38 | 0.92 | 1.96 | 6.69 | 14.24 | 23.87 | 34.90 | 46.86 |
| .40 | 12.75 | 4.32 | 0.91 | 1.99 | 6.75 | 14.33 | 23.97 | 35.02 | 46.98 |
| .41 | 12.64 | 4.26 | 0.90 | 2.02 | 6.81 | 14.42 | 24.07 | 35.14 | 47.10 |
| .42 | 12.53 | 4.20 | 0.89 | 2.05 | 6.88 | 14.51 | 24.18 | 35.25 | 47.22 |
| .43 | 12.42 | 4.15 | 0.88 | 2.09 | 6.94 | 14.59 | 24.28 | 35.37 | 47.35 |
| .44 | 12.31 | 4.09 | 0.87 | 2.12 | 7.01 | 14.68 | 24.39 | 35.48 | 47.47 |
| .45 | 12.20 | 4.03 | 0.86 | 2.15 | 7.07 | 14.77 | 24.49 | 35.60 | 47.59 |
| .46 | 12.09 | 3.97 | 0.85 | 2.18 | 7.13 | 14.86 | 24.60 | 35.72 | 47.72 |
| .47 | 11.99 | 3.92 | 0.85 | 2.22 | 7.20 | 14.95 | 24.70 | 35.83 | 47.84 |
| .48 | 11.88 | 3.86 | 0.84 | 2.25 | 7.26 | 15.03 | 24.81 | 35.95 | 47.97 |
| .49 | 11.78 | 3.81 | 0.84 | 2.29 | 7.33 | 15.12 | 24.91 | 36.06 | 48.09 |
| .50 | 11.67 | 3.75 | 0.83 | 2.32 | 7.39 | 15.21 | 25.02 | 36.18 | 48.21 |

# TABLE VI″. ARGUMENT 1.

Equation = 76″. — 73″.563 sin. $x$ — 9″.993 sin. $2x$ — 1″.071 sin. $3x$ — 0″.104 sin. $4x$ — 0″.008 sin. $5x$.

Period, 27.55455246 days.

| Days. | 10 | 11 | 12 | 13 | 14 | 15 | 16 | 17 | 18 |
|---|---|---|---|---|---|---|---|---|---|
| Days. .50 | ″ 11.67 | ″ 3.75 | ″ 0.83 | ″ 2.32 | ″ 7.39 | ″ 15.21 | ″ 25.02 | ″ 36.18 | ″ 48.21 |
| .51 | 11.57 | 3.70 | 0.83 | 2.35 | 7.46 | 15.30 | 25.13 | 36.30 | 48.33 |
| .52 | 11.46 | 3.65 | 0.82 | 2.39 | 7.52 | 15.39 | 25.23 | 36.42 | 48.46 |
| .53 | 11.36 | 3.59 | 0.82 | 2.42 | 7.59 | 15.48 | 25.34 | 36.53 | 48.58 |
| .54 | 11.25 | 3.54 | 0.81 | 2.46 | 7.65 | 15.57 | 25.44 | 36.65 | 48.71 |
| .55 | 11.15 | 3.49 | 0.81 | 2.49 | 7.72 | 15.66 | 25.55 | 36.76 | 48.83 |
| .56 | 11.05 | 3.44 | 0.81 | 2.53 | 7.79 | 15.75 | 25.66 | 36.88 | 48.95 |
| .57 | 10.95 | 3.39 | 0.81 | 2.56 | 7.86 | 15.84 | 25.76 | 37.00 | 49.08 |
| .58 | 10.85 | 3.35 | 0.80 | 2.60 | 7.92 | 15.93 | 25.87 | 37.11 | 49.20 |
| .59 | 10.75 | 3.30 | 0.80 | 2.63 | 7.99 | 16.02 | 25.97 | 37.23 | 49.33 |
| .60 | 10.65 | 3.25 | 0.80 | 2.67 | 8.06 | 16.11 | 26.08 | 37.35 | 49.45 |
| .61 | 10.55 | 3.20 | 0.80 | 2.71 | 8.13 | 16.20 | 26.19 | 37.47 | 49.57 |
| .62 | 10.45 | 3.15 | 0.80 | 2.75 | 8.20 | 16.29 | 26.30 | 37.59 | 49.70 |
| .63 | 10.36 | 3.11 | 0.80 | 2.78 | 8.27 | 16.39 | 26.40 | 37.71 | 49.82 |
| .64 | 10.26 | 3.06 | 0.79 | 2.82 | 8.34 | 16.48 | 26.51 | 37.82 | 49.95 |
| .65 | 10.16 | 3.01 | 0.79 | 2.86 | 8.41 | 16.57 | 26.62 | 37.94 | 50.07 |
| .66 | 10.06 | 2.97 | 0.79 | 2.90 | 8.48 | 16.66 | 26.73 | 38.06 | 50.19 |
| .67 | 9.97 | 2.92 | 0.80 | 2.94 | 8.55 | 16.76 | 26.84 | 38.17 | 50.32 |
| .68 | 9.87 | 2.88 | 0.80 | 2.99 | 8.62 | 16.85 | 26.94 | 38.29 | 50.44 |
| .69 | 9.78 | 2.83 | 0.80 | 3.03 | 8.69 | 16.95 | 27.05 | 38.41 | 50.57 |
| .70 | 9.68 | 2.79 | 0.80 | 3.07 | 8.76 | 17.04 | 27.16 | 38.53 | 50.69 |
| .71 | 9.59 | 2.75 | 0.80 | 3.11 | 8.83 | 17.13 | 27.27 | 38.65 | 50.81 |
| .72 | 9.49 | 2.71 | 0.81 | 3.15 | 8.90 | 17.23 | 27.38 | 38.77 | 50.94 |
| .73 | 9.40 | 2.66 | 0.81 | 3.20 | 8.98 | 17.32 | 27.48 | 38.89 | 51.06 |
| .74 | 9.30 | 2.62 | 0.82 | 3.24 | 9.05 | 17.42 | 27.59 | 39.00 | 51.19 |
| .75 | 9.21 | 2.58 | 0.82 | 3.28 | 9.12 | 17.51 | 27.70 | 39.12 | 51.31 |
| .76 | 9.12 | 2.54 | 0.83 | 3.32 | 9.19 | 17.60 | 27.81 | 39.24 | 51.44 |
| .77 | 9.03 | 2.50 | 0.83 | 3.37 | 9.27 | 17.70 | 27.92 | 39.35 | 51.56 |
| .78 | 8.94 | 2.46 | 0.84 | 3.41 | 9.34 | 17.79 | 28.03 | 39.47 | 51.69 |
| .79 | 8.85 | 2.42 | 0.84 | 3.46 | 9.42 | 17.89 | 28.14 | 39.59 | 51.81 |
| .80 | 8.76 | 2.38 | 0.85 | 3.50 | 9.49 | 17.98 | 28.25 | 39.71 | 51.94 |
| .81 | 8.67 | 2.34 | 0.86 | 3.55 | 9.56 | 18.08 | 28.36 | 39.83 | 52.06 |
| .82 | 8.58 | 2.30 | 0.87 | 3.59 | 9.64 | 18.17 | 28.47 | 39.95 | 52.19 |
| .83 | 8.49 | 2.27 | 0.87 | 3.64 | 9.71 | 18.27 | 28.58 | 40.07 | 52.31 |
| .84 | 8.40 | 2.23 | 0.88 | 3.68 | 9.79 | 18.36 | 28.69 | 40.19 | 52.44 |
| .85 | 8.31 | 2.19 | 0.89 | 3.73 | 9.86 | 18.46 | 28.80 | 40.31 | 52.56 |
| .86 | 8.22 | 2.15 | 0.90 | 3.78 | 9.94 | 18.56 | 28.91 | 40.43 | 52.69 |
| .87 | 8.14 | 2.12 | 0.91 | 3.82 | 10.01 | 18.65 | 29.02 | 40.55 | 52.82 |
| .88 | 8.05 | 2.08 | 0.92 | 3.87 | 10.09 | 18.75 | 29.13 | 40.67 | 52.94 |
| .89 | 7.97 | 2.05 | 0.93 | 3.91 | 10.16 | 18.84 | 29.24 | 40.79 | 53.07 |
| .90 | 7.88 | 2.01 | 0.94 | 3.96 | 10.24 | 18.94 | 29.35 | 40.91 | 53.19 |
| .91 | 7.80 | 1.98 | 0.95 | 4.01 | 10.32 | 19.04 | 29.46 | 41.03 | 53.31 |
| .92 | 7.72 | 1.95 | 0.96 | 4.06 | 10.39 | 19.14 | 29.57 | 41.15 | 53.44 |
| .93 | 7.63 | 1.91 | 0.98 | 4.11 | 10.47 | 19.23 | 29.68 | 41.27 | 53.56 |
| .94 | 7.55 | 1.88 | 0.99 | 4.16 | 10.54 | 19.33 | 29.79 | 41.39 | 53.69 |
| .95 | 7.47 | 1.85 | 1.00 | 4.21 | 10.62 | 19.42 | 29.90 | 41.51 | 53.81 |
| .96 | 7.39 | 1.82 | 1.01 | 4.26 | 10.70 | 19.52 | 30.01 | 41.63 | 53.94 |
| .97 | 7.31 | 1.79 | 1.03 | 4.31 | 10.78 | 19.62 | 30.13 | 41.75 | 54.07 |
| .98 | 7.23 | 1.76 | 1.04 | 4.36 | 10.85 | 19.71 | 30.24 | 41.87 | 54.19 |
| .99 | 7.15 | 1.73 | 1.06 | 4.41 | 10.93 | 19.81 | 30.35 | 41.99 | 54.32 |
| 1.00 | 7.07 | 1.70 | 1.07 | 4.46 | 11.01 | 19.91 | 30.46 | 42.11 | 54.44 |

# TABLE VI″. ARGUMENT 1.

Equation $= 76''. - 73''.563 \sin. x - 9''.993 \sin. 2x - 1''.071 \sin. 3x - 0''.104 \sin. 4x - 0''.008 \sin. 5x.$

Period, 27.55455246 days.

| Days. | 19 | 20 | 21 | 22 | 23 | 24 | 25 | 26 | 27 |
|---|---|---|---|---|---|---|---|---|---|
| Days. | ″ | ″ | ″ | ″ | ″ | ″ | ″ | ″ | ″ |
| .00 | 54.44 | 67.15 | 80.01 | 92.79 | 105.30 | 117.25 | 128.27 | 137.87 | 145.39 |
| .01 | 54.57 | 67.28 | 80.14 | 92.92 | 105.42 | 117.37 | 128.37 | 137.96 | 145.45 |
| .02 | 54.69 | 67.41 | 80.27 | 93.05 | 105.54 | 117.48 | 128.47 | 138.04 | 145.51 |
| .03 | 54.82 | 67.54 | 80.40 | 93.17 | 105.67 | 117.60 | 128.58 | 138.13 | 145.57 |
| .04 | 54.94 | 67.67 | 80.52 | 93.30 | 105.79 | 117.71 | 128.68 | 138.21 | 145.63 |
| .05 | 55.07 | 67.80 | 80.65 | 93.42 | 105.92 | 117.83 | 128.78 | 138.30 | 145.70 |
| .06 | 55.20 | 67.92 | 80.78 | 93.55 | 106.04 | 117.95 | 128.89 | 138.39 | 145.76 |
| .07 | 55.32 | 68.05 | 80.90 | 93.68 | 106.16 | 118.05 | 128.99 | 138.47 | 145.82 |
| .08 | 55.45 | 68.18 | 81.03 | 93.80 | 106.29 | 118.17 | 129.10 | 138.56 | 145.88 |
| .09 | 55.57 | 68.31 | 81.16 | 93.93 | 106.41 | 118.28 | 129.20 | 138.64 | 145.94 |
| .10 | 55.70 | 68.44 | 81.29 | 94.06 | 106.53 | 118.40 | 129.30 | 138.73 | 146.00 |
| .11 | 55.83 | 68.57 | 81.42 | 94.19 | 106.65 | 118.51 | 129.40 | 138.81 | 146.06 |
| .12 | 55.95 | 68.70 | 81.55 | 94.32 | 106.77 | 118.63 | 129.50 | 138.89 | 146.12 |
| .13 | 56.08 | 68.83 | 81.68 | 94.44 | 106.89 | 118.74 | 129.60 | 138.98 | 146.18 |
| .14 | 56.20 | 68.95 | 81.80 | 94.57 | 107.02 | 118.86 | 129.71 | 139.06 | 146.23 |
| .15 | 56.33 | 69.08 | 81.93 | 94.69 | 107.14 | 118.97 | 129.81 | 139.15 | 146.29 |
| .16 | 56.46 | 69.21 | 82.06 | 94.82 | 107.26 | 119.08 | 129.91 | 139.23 | 146.35 |
| .17 | 56.58 | 69.33 | 82.18 | 94.95 | 107.39 | 119.20 | 130.02 | 139.31 | 146.40 |
| .18 | 56.71 | 69.46 | 82.31 | 95.07 | 107.51 | 119.31 | 130.12 | 139.40 | 146.46 |
| .19 | 56.83 | 69.59 | 82.44 | 95.20 | 107.63 | 119.43 | 130.22 | 139.48 | 146.52 |
| .20 | 56.96 | 69.72 | 82.57 | 95.33 | 107.75 | 119.54 | 130.32 | 139.56 | 146.58 |
| .21 | 57.09 | 69.85 | 82.70 | 95.46 | 107.87 | 119.65 | 130.42 | 139.64 | 146.64 |
| .22 | 57.22 | 69.98 | 82.83 | 95.58 | 107.99 | 119.76 | 130.52 | 139.72 | 146.69 |
| .23 | 57.34 | 70.11 | 82.96 | 95.71 | 108.11 | 119.88 | 130.62 | 139.80 | 146.75 |
| .24 | 57.47 | 70.23 | 83.09 | 95.83 | 108.23 | 119.99 | 130.72 | 139.89 | 146.80 |
| .25 | 57.59 | 70.36 | 83.22 | 95.96 | 108.35 | 120.11 | 130.82 | 139.97 | 146 86 |
| .26 | 57.72 | 70.49 | 83.34 | 96.09 | 108.48 | 120.22 | 130.92 | 140.05 | 146.91 |
| .27 | 57.85 | 70.61 | 83.47 | 96.21 | 108.60 | 120.34 | 131.02 | 140.14 | 146.97 |
| .28 | 57.97 | 70.74 | 83.60 | 96.34 | 108.72 | 120.45 | 131.12 | 140.22 | 147.02 |
| .29 | 58.10 | 70.87 | 83.73 | 96.46 | 108.84 | 120.56 | 131.22 | 140.30 | 147.08 |
| .30 | 58.23 | 71.00 | 83.86 | 96.59 | 108.96 | 120.67 | 131.32 | 140.38 | 147.13 |
| .31 | 58.36 | 71.13 | 83.99 | 96.72 | 109.08 | 120.78 | 131.42 | 140.46 | 147.18 |
| .32 | 58.48 | 71.26 | 84.12 | 96.85 | 109.20 | 120.89 | 131 52 | 140.54 | 147.23 |
| .33 | 58.61 | 71.39 | 84.25 | 96.97 | 109.32 | 121.00 | 131.62 | 140.62 | 147.28 |
| .34 | 58.73 | 71.52 | 84.37 | 97.10 | 109.44 | 121.12 | 131.72 | 140.70 | 147.34 |
| .35 | 58.86 | 71.65 | 84.50 | 97.22 | 109.56 | 121.23 | 131.82 | 140.78 | 147.39 |
| .36 | 58.99 | 71.77 | 84.63 | 97.34 | 109.68 | 121.34 | 131.91 | 140.85 | 147.45 |
| .37 | 59.11 | 71.90 | 84.75 | 97.46 | 109.80 | 121.46 | 132.01 | 140.93 | 147.50 |
| .38 | 59.24 | 72.03 | 84.88 | 97.59 | 109.92 | 121.57 | 132.11 | 141.01 | 147.55 |
| .39 | 59.36 | 72.16 | 85.01 | 97.71 | 110.04 | 121.68 | 132.21 | 141.09 | 147.60 |
| .40 | 59.49 | 72.29 | 85.14 | 97.84 | 110.16 | 121.79 | 132.31 | 141.17 | 147.65 |
| .41 | 59.62 | 72.42 | 85.27 | 97.97 | 110.28 | 121.90 | 132.41 | 141.25 | 147.70 |
| .42 | 59.75 | 72.55 | 85.40 | 98.09 | 110.40 | 122.01 | 132.51 | 141.32 | 147.75 |
| .43 | 59.87 | 72.68 | 85.53 | 98.22 | 110.52 | 122.12 | 132.60 | 141.40 | 147.80 |
| .44 | 60.00 | 72.80 | 85.65 | 98.34 | 110.64 | 122.23 | 132.70 | 141.47 | 147.85 |
| .45 | 60.12 | 72.93 | 85.78 | 98.47 | 110.76 | 122.35 | 132.80 | 141.55 | 147.90 |
| .46 | 60.25 | 73.06 | 85.91 | 98.60 | 110.88 | 122.46 | 132.89 | 141.63 | 147.94 |
| .47 | 60.38 | 73.18 | 86.03 | 98.72 | 111.00 | 122.57 | 132.99 | 147.70 | 147.99 |
| .48 | 60.50 | 73.31 | 86.16 | 98.85 | 111.12 | 122.68 | 133.09 | 141.78 | 148.04 |
| .49 | 60.63 | 73.44 | 86.29 | 98.97 | 111.24 | 122.79 | 133.18 | 141.85 | 148.09 |
| .50 | 60.76 | 73.57 | 86.42 | 99.10 | 111.36 | 122.90 | 133.28 | 141.93 | 148.14 |

# TABLE VI″. ARGUMENT 1.

Equation = 76″. — 73″.563 sin. $x$ — 9″.993 sin. $2x$ — 1″.071 sin. $3x$ — 0″.104 sin. $4x$ — 0″.008 sin. $5x$.

Period, 27.55455246 days.

| Days. | 19 | 20 | 21 | 22 | 23 | 24 | 25 | 26 | 27 |
|---|---|---|---|---|---|---|---|---|---|
| Days. | ″ | ″ | ″ | ″ | ″ | ″ | ″ | ″ | ″ |
| .50 | 60.76 | 73.57 | 86.42 | 99.10 | 111.36 | 122.90 | 133.28 | 141.93 | 148.14 |
| .51 | 60.89 | 73.70 | 86.55 | 99.23 | 111.48 | 123.01 | 133.38 | 142.00 | 148.19 |
| .52 | 61.02 | 73.83 | 86.68 | 99.35 | 111.60 | 123.12 | 133.47 | 142.08 | 148.23 |
| .53 | 61.15 | 73.96 | 86.81 | 99.48 | 111.72 | 123.23 | 133.57 | 142.15 | 148.28 |
| .54 | 61.27 | 74.09 | 86.93 | 99.60 | 111.84 | 123.34 | 133.66 | 142.23 | 148.32 |
| .55 | 61.40 | 74.22 | 87.06 | 99.73 | 111.96 | 123.45 | 133.76 | 142.30 | 148.37 |
| .56 | 61.53 | 74.34 | 87.19 | 99.85 | 112.07 | 123.56 | 133.86 | 142.37 | 148.41 |
| .57 | 61.65 | 74.47 | 87.31 | 99.98 | 112.19 | 123.67 | 133.95 | 142.45 | 148.46 |
| .58 | 61.78 | 74.60 | 87.44 | 100.10 | 112.31 | 123.78 | 134.05 | 142.52 | 148.50 |
| .59 | 61.91 | 74.73 | 87.57 | 100.23 | 112.43 | 123.89 | 134.14 | 142.60 | 148.55 |
| .60 | 62.04 | 74.86 | 87.70 | 100.35 | 112.55 | 124.00 | 134.24 | 142.67 | 148.59 |
| .61 | 62.17 | 74.99 | 87.83 | 100.47 | 112.67 | 124.11 | 134.33 | 142.74 | 148.63 |
| .62 | 62.30 | 75.12 | 87.96 | 100.60 | 112.79 | 124.22 | 134.43 | 142.81 | 148.67 |
| .63 | 62.42 | 75.25 | 88.09 | 100.72 | 112.91 | 124.33 | 134.52 | 142.88 | 148.72 |
| .64 | 62.55 | 75.38 | 88.21 | 100.85 | 113.03 | 124.44 | 134.62 | 142.96 | 148.76 |
| .65 | 62.67 | 75.51 | 88.34 | 100.97 | 113.15 | 124.55 | 134.71 | 143.03 | 148.80 |
| .66 | 62.80 | 75.63 | 88.47 | 101.09 | 113.26 | 124.65 | 134.80 | 143.10 | 148.85 |
| .67 | 62.93 | 75.76 | 88.59 | 101.22 | 113.38 | 124.76 | 134.89 | 143.18 | 148.89 |
| .68 | 63.05 | 75.89 | 88.72 | 101.34 | 113.50 | 124.87 | 134.99 | 143.25 | 148.93 |
| .69 | 63.18 | 76.02 | 88.85 | 101.47 | 113.62 | 124.98 | 135.07 | 143.32 | 148.97 |
| .70 | 63.31 | 76.15 | 88.98 | 101.59 | 113.74 | 125.09 | 135.17 | 143.39 | 149.01 |
| .71 | 63.44 | 76.28 | 89.11 | 101.71 | 113.86 | 125.20 | 135.26 | 143.46 | 149.05 |
| .72 | 63.57 | 76.41 | 89.24 | 101.84 | 113.98 | 125.31 | 135.35 | 143.53 | 149.09 |
| .73 | 63.70 | 76.54 | 89.36 | 101.96 | 114.10 | 125.41 | 135.44 | 143.60 | 149.13 |
| .74 | 63.82 | 76.66 | 89.49 | 102.09 | 114.21 | 125.52 | 135.54 | 143.67 | 149.17 |
| .75 | 63.95 | 76.79 | 89.61 | 102.21 | 114.33 | 125.63 | 135.63 | 143.74 | 149.21 |
| .76 | 64.08 | 76.92 | 89.74 | 102.33 | 114.45 | 125.73 | 135.72 | 143.80 | 149.25 |
| .77 | 64.20 | 77.04 | 89.87 | 102.46 | 114.56 | 125.84 | 135.82 | 143.87 | 149.29 |
| .78 | 64.33 | 77.17 | 89.99 | 102.58 | 114.68 | 125.94 | 135.91 | 143.94 | 149.33 |
| .79 | 64.46 | 77.30 | 90.12 | 102.71 | 114.80 | 126.05 | 136.00 | 144.01 | 149.37 |
| .80 | 64.59 | 77.43 | 90.25 | 102.83 | 114.92 | 126.16 | 136.09 | 144.08 | 149.41 |
| .81 | 64.72 | 77.56 | 90.38 | 102.95 | 115.04 | 126.27 | 136.18 | 144.15 | 149.45 |
| .82 | 64.85 | 77.69 | 90.51 | 103.08 | 115.16 | 126.37 | 136.27 | 144.22 | 149.48 |
| .83 | 64.98 | 77.82 | 90.63 | 103.20 | 115.27 | 126.48 | 136.36 | 144.28 | 149.52 |
| .84 | 65.10 | 77.95 | 90.76 | 103.33 | 115.39 | 126.58 | 136.45 | 144.35 | 149.55 |
| .85 | 65.23 | 78.08 | 90.88 | 103.45 | 115.51 | 126.69 | 136.54 | 144.42 | 149.59 |
| .86 | 65.36 | 78.20 | 91.01 | 103.57 | 115.62 | 126.80 | 136.63 | 144.48 | 149.63 |
| .87 | 65.48 | 78.33 | 91.14 | 103.70 | 115.74 | 126.90 | 136.72 | 144.55 | 149.66 |
| .88 | 65.61 | 78.46 | 91.26 | 103.82 | 115.85 | 127.01 | 136.81 | 144.61 | 149.69 |
| .89 | 65.74 | 78.59 | 91.40 | 103.95 | 115.97 | 127.11 | 136.90 | 144.68 | 149.73 |
| .90 | 65.87 | 78.72 | 91.52 | 104.07 | 116.09 | 127.22 | 136.99 | 144.75 | 149.76 |
| .91 | 66.00 | 78.85 | 91.65 | 104.19 | 116.21 | 127.33 | 137.08 | 144.81 | 149.80 |
| .92 | 66.13 | 78.98 | 91.78 | 104.31 | 116.32 | 127.43 | 137.17 | 144.88 | 149.83 |
| .93 | 66.26 | 79.11 | 91.90 | 104.44 | 116.44 | 127.54 | 137.26 | 144.94 | 149.87 |
| .94 | 66.38 | 79.24 | 92.03 | 104.56 | 116.55 | 127.64 | 137.34 | 145.01 | 149.90 |
| .95 | 66.51 | 79.37 | 92.15 | 104.69 | 116.67 | 127.75 | 137.43 | 145.07 | 149.93 |
| .96 | 66.64 | 79.49 | 92.28 | 104.81 | 116.79 | 127.85 | 137.52 | 145.13 | 149.96 |
| .97 | 66.76 | 79.62 | 92.40 | 104.93 | 116.90 | 127.96 | 137.60 | 145.20 | 149.99 |
| .98 | 66.89 | 79.75 | 92.53 | 105.06 | 117.02 | 128.06 | 137.69 | 145.26 | 150.02 |
| .99 | 67.02 | 79.88 | 92.66 | 105.18 | 117.13 | 128.17 | 137.78 | 145.33 | 150.05 |
| 1.00 | 67.15 | 80.01 | 92.79 | 105.30 | 117.25 | 128.27 | 137.87 | 145.39 | 150.08 |

# TABLE VII″. ARGUMENT 2.

Equation $= 11''.2 - 11''.18 \sin. (2t - x) - 0''.304 \sin. (4t - 2x)$.

Period, 31.81193574 days.

| Days. | 0 | 1 | 2 | 3 | 4 | 5 | 6 | 7 | 8 | 9 |
|---|---|---|---|---|---|---|---|---|---|---|
| Days. | ″ | ″ | ″ | ″ | ″ | ″ | ″ | ″ | ″ | ″ |
| .00 | 22.37 | 22.31 | 21.81 | 20.87 | 19.52 | 17.81 | 15.82 | 13.62 | 11.31 | 9.00 |
| .01 | 22.37 | 22.30 | 21.80 | 20.86 | 19.51 | 17.80 | 15.80 | 13.60 | 11.29 | 8.98 |
| .02 | 22.37 | 22.30 | 21.79 | 20.85 | 19.49 | 17.78 | 15.78 | 13.58 | 11.27 | 8.96 |
| .03 | 22.37 | 22.30 | 21.78 | 20.84 | 19.48 | 17.76 | 15.76 | 13 55 | 11.24 | 8.93 |
| .04 | 22.37 | 22.29 | 21.77 | 20.83 | 19.46 | 17.74 | 15.74 | 13.53 | 11.22 | 8.91 |
| .05 | 22.37 | 22.29 | 21.77 | 20.81 | 19.44 | 17.72 | 15.72 | 13.51 | 11.20 | 8.89 |
| .06 | 22.38 | 22.29 | 21.76 | 20.80 | 19.43 | 17.70 | 15.70 | 13.48 | 11.17 | 8.86 |
| .07 | 22.38 | 22.29 | 21.75 | 20.79 | 19.41 | 17.68 | 15.68 | 13.46 | 11.15 | 8.84 |
| .08 | 22.38 | 22.28 | 21.74 | 20.78 | 19.40 | 17.66 | 15.66 | 13.44 | 11.13 | 8.82 |
| .09 | 22.38 | 22.28 | 21.74 | 20.77 | 19.38 | 17.64 | 15.64 | 13.42 | 11.11 | 8.80 |
| .10 | 22.38 | 22.28 | 21.73 | 20.75 | 19.36 | 17.62 | 15.60 | 13.39 | 11.08 | 8.77 |
| .11 | 22.38 | 22.27 | 21.72 | 20.74 | 19.35 | 17.61 | 15.59 | 13.37 | 11.06 | 8.75 |
| .12 | 22.38 | 22.27 | 21.71 | 20.73 | 19.33 | 17.59 | 15.57 | 13.35 | 11.04 | 8.73 |
| .13 | 22.38 | 22.27 | 21.70 | 20.72 | 19.32 | 17.57 | 15.55 | 13.32 | 11.01 | 8.70 |
| .14 | 22.38 | 22.26 | 21.69 | 20.71 | 19.30 | 17.55 | 15.53 | 13.30 | 10.99 | 8.68 |
| .15 | 22.38 | 22.26 | 21.69 | 20.69 | 19.28 | 17.53 | 15.50 | 13.28 | 10.96 | 8.66 |
| .16 | 22.39 | 22.26 | 21.68 | 20.68 | 19.27 | 17.51 | 15.48 | 13.25 | 10.94 | 8.63 |
| .17 | 22.39 | 22.25 | 21.67 | 20.67 | 19.25 | 17.49 | 15.46 | 13.23 | 10.91 | 8.61 |
| .18 | 22.39 | 22.25 | 21.66 | 20.66 | 19.24 | 17.47 | 15.44 | 13.21 | 10.89 | 8.59 |
| .19 | 22.39 | 22.25 | 21.66 | 20.65 | 19.22 | 17.45 | 15.42 | 13.19 | 10.87 | 8.57 |
| .20 | 22.39 | 22.24 | 21.65 | 20.63 | 19.20 | 17.43 | 15.39 | 13.16 | 10.84 | 8.54 |
| .21 | 22.39 | 22.24 | 21.64 | 20.62 | 19.19 | 17.42 | 15.37 | 13.14 | 10.82 | 8.52 |
| .22 | 22.39 | 22.24 | 21.63 | 20.61 | 19.17 | 17.40 | 15.35 | 13.12 | 10.80 | 8.50 |
| .23 | 22.39 | 22.23 | 21.62 | 20.59 | 19.16 | 17.38 | 15.33 | 13.09 | 10.77 | 8.48 |
| .24 | 22.39 | 22.23 | 21.61 | 20.58 | 19.14 | 17.36 | 15.31 | 13.07 | 10.75 | 8.46 |
| .25 | 22.39 | 22.23 | 21.61 | 20.57 | 19.12 | 17.34 | 15.28 | 13.05 | 10.73 | 8.44 |
| .26 | 22.39 | 22.22 | 21.60 | 20.55 | 19.11 | 17.32 | 15.26 | 13.02 | 10.70 | 8.41 |
| .27 | 22.39 | 22.22 | 21.59 | 20.54 | 19.09 | 17.30 | 15.24 | 13.00 | 10.68 | 8.39 |
| .28 | 22.40 | 22.21 | 21.58 | 20.53 | 19.08 | 17.28 | 15.22 | 12.98 | 10.66 | 8.37 |
| .29 | 22.40 | 22.21 | 21.57 | 20.52 | 19.06 | 17.26 | 15.20 | 12.96 | 10.64 | 8.35 |
| .30 | 22.40 | 22.20 | 21.57 | 20.50 | 19.04 | 17.24 | 15.17 | 12.93 | 10.61 | 8.32 |
| .31 | 22.40 | 22.20 | 21.56 | 20.49 | 19.03 | 17.23 | 15.15 | 12.91 | 10.59 | 8.30 |
| .32 | 22.40 | 22.20 | 21.55 | 20.48 | 19.01 | 17.21 | 15.13 | 12.89 | 10.57 | 8.28 |
| .33 | 22.40 | 22.19 | 21.54 | 20.47 | 19.00 | 17.19 | 15.11 | 12.86 | 10.54 | 8.25 |
| .34 | 22.40 | 22.19 | 21.53 | 20.46 | 18.98 | 17.17 | 15.09 | 12.84 | 10.52 | 8.23 |
| .35 | 22.40 | 22.18 | 21.52 | 20.44 | 18.96 | 17.15 | 15.07 | 12.82 | 10.50 | 8.21 |
| .36 | 22.40 | 22.18 | 21.51 | 20.43 | 18.95 | 17.13 | 15.05 | 12.79 | 10.47 | 8.18 |
| .37 | 22.40 | 22.17 | 21.50 | 20.42 | 18.93 | 17.11 | 15.03 | 12.77 | 10.45 | 8.16 |
| .38 | 22.40 | 22.17 | 21.49 | 20.41 | 18.92 | 17.09 | 15.01 | 12.75 | 10.43 | 8.14 |
| .39 | 22.40 | 22.16 | 21.49 | 20.40 | 18.90 | 17.07 | 14.99 | 12.73 | 10.41 | 8.12 |
| .40 | 22.40 | 22.16 | 21.48 | 20.38 | 18.88 | 17.05 | 14.96 | 12.70 | 10.38 | 8.09 |
| .41 | 22.40 | 22.15 | 21.47 | 20.37 | 18.87 | 17.03 | 14.94 | 12.68 | 10.36 | 8.07 |
| .42 | 22.40 | 22.15 | 21.46 | 20.35 | 18.85 | 17.01 | 14.92 | 12.66 | 10.34 | 8.05 |
| .43 | 22.40 | 22.15 | 21.45 | 20.34 | 18.83 | 16.99 | 14.90 | 12.63 | 10.31 | 8.03 |
| .44 | 22.39 | 22.14 | 21.44 | 20.33 | 18.82 | 16.97 | 14.88 | 12.61 | 10.29 | 8.01 |
| .45 | 22.39 | 22.14 | 21.43 | 20.31 | 18.80 | 16.95 | 14.85 | 12.59 | 10.27 | 7.98 |
| .46 | 22.39 | 22.13 | 21.42 | 20.30 | 18.78 | 16.93 | 14.83 | 12.56 | 10.24 | 7.96 |
| .47 | 22.39 | 22.13 | 21.41 | 20.28 | 18.77 | 16.91 | 14.81 | 12.54 | 10.22 | 7.94 |
| .48 | 22.39 | 22.12 | 21.40 | 20.27 | 18.75 | 16.89 | 14.79 | 12.52 | 10.20 | 7.92 |
| .49 | 22.39 | 22.12 | 21.40 | 20.26 | 18.73 | 16.87 | 14.77 | 12.50 | 10.18 | 7.90 |
| .50 | 22.39 | 22.11 | 21.39 | 20.24 | 18.71 | 16.85 | 14.74 | 12.47 | 10.15 | 7.87 |

# TABLE VII″. ARGUMENT 2.

Equation $= 11''.2 - 11''.18 \sin. (2t - x) - 0''.304 \sin. (4t - 2x)$.

Period, 31.81193574 days.

| Days. | 0 | 1 | 2 | 3 | 4 | 5 | 6 | 7 | 8 | 9 |
|---|---|---|---|---|---|---|---|---|---|---|
| Days. | ″ | ″ | ″ | ″ | ″ | ″ | ″ | ″ | ″ | ″ |
| .50 | 22.39 | 22.11 | 21.39 | 20.24 | 18.71 | 16.85 | 14.74 | 12.47 | 10.15 | 7.87 |
| .51 | 22.39 | 22.11 | 21.38 | 20.23 | 18.70 | 16.83 | 14.72 | 12.45 | 10.13 | 7.85 |
| .52 | 22.39 | 22.10 | 21.37 | 20.22 | 18.68 | 16.81 | 14.70 | 12.43 | 10.11 | 7.83 |
| .53 | 22.39 | 22.10 | 21.36 | 20.20 | 18.66 | 16.79 | 14.68 | 12.40 | 10.08 | 7.81 |
| .54 | 22.39 | 22.09 | 21.35 | 20.19 | 18.65 | 16.77 | 14.66 | 12.38 | 10.06 | 7.79 |
| .55 | 22.39 | 22.09 | 21.34 | 20.17 | 18.63 | 16.75 | 14.63 | 12.36 | 10.03 | 7.76 |
| .56 | 22.39 | 22.08 | 21.33 | 20.16 | 18.61 | 16.73 | 14.61 | 12.33 | 10.01 | 7.74 |
| .57 | 22.39 | 22.08 | 21.32 | 20.14 | 18.60 | 16.71 | 14.59 | 12.31 | 9.98 | 7.72 |
| .58 | 22.39 | 22.07 | 21.31 | 20.13 | 18.58 | 16.69 | 14.57 | 12.29 | 9.96 | 7.70 |
| .59 | 22.39 | 22.07 | 21.30 | 20.12 | 18.56 | 16.67 | 14.55 | 12.27 | 9.94 | 7.68 |
| .60 | 22.38 | 22.06 | 21.29 | 20.10 | 18.54 | 16.65 | 14.52 | 12.24 | 9.91 | 7.65 |
| .61 | 22.38 | 22.06 | 21.28 | 20.09 | 18.53 | 16.63 | 14.50 | 12.22 | 9.89 | 7.63 |
| .62 | 22.38 | 22.05 | 21.27 | 20.08 | 18.51 | 16.61 | 14.48 | 12.20 | 9.87 | 7.61 |
| .63 | 22.38 | 22.05 | 21.26 | 20.06 | 18.49 | 16.59 | 14.45 | 12.17 | 9.84 | 7.58 |
| .64 | 22.38 | 22.04 | 21.25 | 20.05 | 18.47 | 16.57 | 14.43 | 12.15 | 9.82 | 7.56 |
| .65 | 22.38 | 22.04 | 21.24 | 20.03 | 18.45 | 16.55 | 14.41 | 12.13 | 9.80 | 7.54 |
| .66 | 22.38 | 22.03 | 21.23 | 20.02 | 18.44 | 16.53 | 14.38 | 12.10 | 9.77 | 7.52 |
| .67 | 22.38 | 22.02 | 21.22 | 20.00 | 18.42 | 16.51 | 14.36 | 12.08 | 9.75 | 7.49 |
| .68 | 22.37 | 22.02 | 21.21 | 19.99 | 18.40 | 16.49 | 14.34 | 12.06 | 9.73 | 7.47 |
| .69 | 22.37 | 22.01 | 21.20 | 19.98 | 18.38 | 16.47 | 14.32 | 12.04 | 9.71 | 7.45 |
| .70 | 22.37 | 22.00 | 21.19 | 19.96 | 18.36 | 16.44 | 14.29 | 12.01 | 9.68 | 7.43 |
| .71 | 22.37 | 22.00 | 21.18 | 19.95 | 18.35 | 16.42 | 14.27 | 11.99 | 9.66 | 7.40 |
| .72 | 22.37 | 21.99 | 21.17 | 19.94 | 18.33 | 16.40 | 14.25 | 11.97 | 9.64 | 7.38 |
| .73 | 22.37 | 21.99 | 21.16 | 19.92 | 18.31 | 16.38 | 14.23 | 11.94 | 9.61 | 7.36 |
| .74 | 22.37 | 21.98 | 21.15 | 19.91 | 18.29 | 16.36 | 14.21 | 11.92 | 9.59 | 7.34 |
| .75 | 22.36 | 21.98 | 21.14 | 19.89 | 18.27 | 16.34 | 14.18 | 11.89 | 9.57 | 7.32 |
| .76 | 22.36 | 21.97 | 21.13 | 19.88 | 18.26 | 16.32 | 14.16 | 11.87 | 9.54 | 7.29 |
| .77 | 22.36 | 21.96 | 21.12 | 19.86 | 18.24 | 16.30 | 14.14 | 11.85 | 9.52 | 7.27 |
| .78 | 22.36 | 21.96 | 21.11 | 19.85 | 18.22 | 16.28 | 14.12 | 11.81 | 9.50 | 7.25 |
| .79 | 22.36 | 21.95 | 21.10 | 19.84 | 18.20 | 16.26 | 14.10 | 11.79 | 9.48 | 7.23 |
| .80 | 22.35 | 21.94 | 21.09 | 19.82 | 18.18 | 16.24 | 14.07 | 11.77 | 9.45 | 7.21 |
| .81 | 22.35 | 21.94 | 21.08 | 19.81 | 18.17 | 16.22 | 14.05 | 11.75 | 9.43 | 7.18 |
| .82 | 22.35 | 21.93 | 21.07 | 19.79 | 18.15 | 16.20 | 14.03 | 11.73 | 9.41 | 7.16 |
| .83 | 22.35 | 21.93 | 21.06 | 19.78 | 18.13 | 16.18 | 14.00 | 11.70 | 9.38 | 7.14 |
| .84 | 22.35 | 21.92 | 21.05 | 19.76 | 18.11 | 16.16 | 13.98 | 11.68 | 9.36 | 7.12 |
| .85 | 22.34 | 21.91 | 21.04 | 19.75 | 18.09 | 16.14 | 13.96 | 11.66 | 9.34 | 7.10 |
| .86 | 22.34 | 21.91 | 21.03 | 19.73 | 18.08 | 16.12 | 13.93 | 11.63 | 9.31 | 7.08 |
| .87 | 22.34 | 21.90 | 21.02 | 19.72 | 18.06 | 16.10 | 13.91 | 11.61 | 9.29 | 7.06 |
| .88 | 22.34 | 21.90 | 21.01 | 19.70 | 18.04 | 16.08 | 13.89 | 11.59 | 9.27 | 7.04 |
| .89 | 22.34 | 21.89 | 21.00 | 19.69 | 18.02 | 16.06 | 13.87 | 11.57 | 9.25 | 7.02 |
| .90 | 22.33 | 21.88 | 20.98 | 19.67 | 18.00 | 16.03 | 13.84 | 11.54 | 9.22 | 7.00 |
| .91 | 22.33 | 21.87 | 20.97 | 19.66 | 17.99 | 16.01 | 13.82 | 11.52 | 9.20 | 6.97 |
| .92 | 22.33 | 21.87 | 20.96 | 19.64 | 17.97 | 15.99 | 13.80 | 11.50 | 9.18 | 6.95 |
| .93 | 22.33 | 21.86 | 20.95 | 19.63 | 17.95 | 15.97 | 13.78 | 11.47 | 9.16 | 6.93 |
| .94 | 22.32 | 21.86 | 20.94 | 19.61 | 17.93 | 15.95 | 13.76 | 11.45 | 9.14 | 6.91 |
| .95 | 22.32 | 21.85 | 20.93 | 19.60 | 17.91 | 15.93 | 13.73 | 11.43 | 9.11 | 6.89 |
| .96 | 22.32 | 21.84 | 20.92 | 19.58 | 17.89 | 15.91 | 13.71 | 11.40 | 9.09 | 6.86 |
| .97 | 22.32 | 21.83 | 20.91 | 19.57 | 17.87 | 15.89 | 13.69 | 11.38 | 9.07 | 6.84 |
| .98 | 22.31 | 21.82 | 20.90 | 19.55 | 17.85 | 15.87 | 13.67 | 11.36 | 9.05 | 6.82 |
| .99 | 22.31 | 21.81 | 20.89 | 19.54 | 17.83 | 15.85 | 13.65 | 11.34 | 9.03 | 6.80 |
| 1.00 | 22.31 | 21.81 | 20.87 | 19.52 | 17.81 | 15.82 | 13.62 | 11.31 | 9.00 | 6.78 |

# TABLE VII″. ARGUMENT 2.

Equation $= 11''.2 - 11''.18 \sin.(2t - x) - 0''.304 \sin.(4t - 2x)$.

Period, 31.81193574 days.

| Days. | 10 | 11 | 12 | 13 | 14 | 15 | 16 | 17 | 18 | 19 | 20 |
|---|---|---|---|---|---|---|---|---|---|---|---|
| Days. | ″ | ″ | ″ | ″ | ″ | ″ | ″ | ″ | ″ | ″ | ″ |
| .00 | 6.78 | 4.76 | 3.03 | 1.64 | 0.66 | 0.12 | 0.02 | 0.35 | 1.10 | 2.21 | 3.63 |
| .01 | 6.75 | 4.74 | 3.01 | 1.62 | 0.66 | 0.11 | 0.02 | 0.35 | 1.10 | 2.22 | 3.64 |
| .02 | 6.73 | 4.72 | 2.99 | 1.61 | 0.65 | 0.11 | 0.02 | 0.36 | 1.11 | 2.23 | 3.66 |
| .03 | 6.71 | 4.70 | 2.98 | 1.60 | 0.64 | 0.11 | 0.02 | 0.36 | 1.12 | 2.25 | 3.67 |
| .04 | 6.69 | 4.68 | 2.96 | 1.59 | 0.64 | 0.10 | 0.02 | 0.37 | 1.13 | 2.26 | 3.69 |
| .05 | 6.67 | 4.66 | 2.95 | 1.58 | 0.63 | 0.10 | 0.03 | 0.37 | 1.14 | 2.27 | 3.71 |
| .06 | 6.65 | 4.64 | 2.93 | 1.56 | 0.62 | 0.10 | 0.03 | 0.38 | 1.15 | 2.28 | 3.72 |
| .07 | 6.63 | 4.62 | 2.91 | 1.55 | 0.62 | 0.09 | 0.03 | 0.39 | 1.16 | 2.30 | 3.73 |
| .08 | 6.61 | 4.60 | 2.90 | 1.54 | 0.61 | 0.09 | 0.03 | 0.39 | 1.17 | 2.31 | 3.75 |
| .09 | 6.59 | 4.58 | 2.88 | 1.53 | 0.60 | 0.09 | 0.03 | 0.40 | 1.18 | 2.32 | 3.77 |
| .10 | 6.57 | 4.57 | 2.87 | 1.52 | 0.59 | 0.09 | 0.03 | 0.41 | 1.19 | 2.34 | 3.79 |
| .11 | 6.54 | 4.55 | 2.85 | 1.50 | 0.59 | 0.08 | 0.04 | 0.41 | 1.20 | 2.35 | 3.80 |
| .12 | 6.52 | 4.53 | 2.84 | 1.49 | 0.58 | 0.08 | 0.04 | 0.42 | 1.21 | 2.36 | 3.82 |
| .13 | 6.50 | 4.51 | 2.82 | 1.48 | 0.57 | 0.08 | 0.04 | 0.42 | 1.22 | 2.37 | 3.83 |
| .14 | 6.48 | 4.49 | 2.81 | 1.47 | 0.57 | 0.07 | 0.04 | 0.43 | 1.23 | 2.39 | 3.85 |
| .15 | 6.46 | 4.48 | 2.79 | 1.46 | 0.56 | 0.07 | 0.04 | 0.43 | 1.24 | 2.40 | 3.87 |
| .16 | 6.44 | 4.46 | 2.78 | 1.45 | 0.55 | 0.07 | 0.05 | 0.44 | 1.25 | 2.41 | 3.88 |
| .17 | 6.42 | 4.44 | 2.76 | 1.44 | 0.55 | 0.06 | 0.05 | 0.45 | 1.26 | 2.43 | 3.90 |
| .18 | 6.40 | 4.42 | 2.75 | 1.43 | 0.54 | 0.06 | 0.05 | 0.45 | 1.27 | 2.44 | 3.91 |
| .19 | 6.38 | 4.40 | 2.73 | 1.42 | 0.53 | 0.06 | 0.05 | 0.46 | 1.28 | 2.45 | 3.93 |
| .20 | 6.36 | 4.39 | 2.72 | 1.41 | 0.52 | 0.06 | 0.05 | 0.47 | 1.29 | 2.47 | 3.95 |
| .21 | 6.33 | 4.37 | 2.70 | 1.40 | 0.52 | 0.05 | 0.06 | 0.47 | 1.30 | 2.48 | 3.96 |
| .22 | 6.31 | 4.35 | 2.69 | 1.39 | 0.51 | 0.05 | 0.06 | 0.48 | 1.31 | 2.49 | 3.98 |
| .23 | 6.29 | 4.33 | 2.67 | 1.38 | 0.50 | 0.05 | 0.06 | 0.48 | 1.32 | 2.50 | 4.00 |
| .24 | 6.27 | 4.31 | 2.66 | 1.37 | 0.50 | 0.05 | 0.06 | 0.49 | 1.33 | 2.52 | 4.01 |
| .25 | 6.25 | 4.30 | 2.64 | 1.36 | 0.49 | 0.05 | 0.06 | 0.50 | 1.34 | 2.54 | 4.03 |
| .26 | 6.23 | 4.28 | 2.63 | 1.35 | 0.48 | 0.04 | 0.07 | 0.50 | 1.35 | 2.55 | 4.05 |
| .27 | 6.21 | 4.26 | 2.61 | 1.34 | 0.48 | 0.04 | 0.07 | 0.51 | 1.36 | 2.56 | 4.06 |
| .28 | 6.19 | 4.24 | 2.59 | 1.33 | 0.47 | 0.04 | 0.07 | 0.51 | 1.37 | 2.57 | 4.08 |
| .29 | 6.17 | 4.22 | 2.58 | 1.32 | 0.46 | 0.04 | 0.07 | 0.52 | 1.38 | 2.58 | 4.10 |
| .30 | 6.15 | 4.21 | 2.57 | 1.31 | 0.45 | 0.04 | 0.07 | 0.53 | 1.39 | 2.60 | 4.12 |
| .31 | 6.13 | 4.19 | 2.55 | 1.29 | 0.44 | 0.04 | 0.08 | 0.53 | 1.40 | 2.61 | 4.13 |
| .32 | 6.11 | 4.17 | 2.54 | 1.28 | 0.43 | 0.04 | 0.08 | 0.54 | 1.41 | 2.62 | 4.15 |
| .33 | 6.09 | 4.15 | 2.52 | 1.27 | 0.43 | 0.04 | 0.08 | 0.55 | 1.42 | 2.64 | 4.16 |
| .34 | 6.07 | 4.13 | 2.51 | 1.26 | 0.42 | 0.04 | 0.08 | 0.55 | 1.43 | 2.65 | 4.18 |
| .35 | 6.05 | 4.12 | 2.49 | 1.25 | 0.41 | 0.03 | 0.09 | 0.56 | 1.44 | 2.66 | 4.20 |
| .36 | 6.03 | 4.10 | 2.48 | 1.24 | 0.41 | 0.03 | 0.09 | 0.57 | 1.45 | 2.68 | 4.21 |
| .37 | 6.01 | 4.08 | 2.47 | 1.23 | 0.40 | 0.03 | 0.09 | 0.57 | 1.46 | 2.69 | 4.23 |
| .38 | 5.99 | 4.06 | 2.45 | 1.22 | 0.40 | 0.03 | 0.10 | 0.58 | 1.47 | 2.71 | 4.24 |
| .39 | 5.97 | 4.04 | 2.44 | 1.21 | 0.39 | 0.03 | 0.10 | 0.59 | 1.48 | 2.72 | 4.26 |
| .40 | 5.95 | 4.03 | 2.43 | 1.20 | 0.39 | 0.03 | 0.10 | 0.60 | 1.50 | 2.74 | 4.28 |
| .41 | 5.92 | 4.01 | 2.41 | 1.19 | 0.38 | 0.03 | 0.11 | 0.60 | 1.51 | 2.75 | 4.29 |
| .42 | 5.90 | 3.99 | 2.40 | 1.18 | 0.38 | 0.03 | 0.11 | 0.61 | 1.52 | 2.77 | 4.31 |
| .43 | 5.88 | 3.97 | 2.38 | 1.17 | 0.37 | 0.03 | 0.11 | 0.62 | 1.53 | 2.78 | 4.32 |
| .44 | 5.86 | 3.95 | 2.37 | 1.16 | 0.37 | 0.02 | 0.11 | 0.63 | 1.54 | 2.79 | 4.34 |
| .45 | 5.84 | 3.94 | 2.36 | 1.15 | 0.36 | 0.02 | 0.12 | 0.64 | 1.55 | 2.81 | 4.36 |
| .46 | 5.82 | 3.92 | 2.34 | 1.14 | 0.36 | 0.02 | 0.12 | 0.64 | 1.56 | 2.82 | 4.37 |
| .47 | 5.80 | 3.90 | 2.33 | 1.13 | 0.35 | 0.02 | 0.12 | 0.65 | 1.57 | 2.84 | 4.39 |
| .48 | 5.78 | 3.88 | 2.31 | 1.12 | 0.35 | 0.02 | 0.13 | 0.66 | 1.58 | 2.85 | 4.41 |
| .49 | 5.76 | 3.86 | 2.30 | 1.11 | 0.34 | 0.02 | 0.13 | 0.67 | 1.59 | 2.86 | 4.43 |
| .50 | 5.74 | 3.85 | 2.29 | 1.10 | 0.34 | 0.01 | 0.13 | 0.68 | 1.61 | 2.88 | 4.45 |

# TABLE VII″. ARGUMENT 2.

Equation $= 11''.2 - 11''.18 \sin. (2t - x) - 0''.304 \sin. (4t - 2x)$.

Period, 31.81193574 days.

| Days. | 10 | 11 | 12 | 13 | 14 | 15 | 16 | 17 | 18 | 19 | 20 |
|---|---|---|---|---|---|---|---|---|---|---|---|
| Days. | ″ | ″ | ″ | ″ | ″ | ″ | ″ | ″ | ″ | ″ | ″ |
| .50 | 5.74 | 3.85 | 2.29 | 1.10 | 0.34 | 0.01 | 0.13 | 0.68 | 1.61 | 2.88 | 4.45 |
| .51 | 5.72 | 3.83 | 2.27 | 1.09 | 0.33 | 0.01 | 0.13 | 0.68 | 1.62 | 2.89 | 4.46 |
| .52 | 5.70 | 3.81 | 2.26 | 1.08 | 0.33 | 0.01 | 0.13 | 0.69 | 1.63 | 2.91 | 4.48 |
| .53 | 5.68 | 3.79 | 2.24 | 1.07 | 0.32 | 0.01 | 0.14 | 0.70 | 1.64 | 2.92 | 4.50 |
| .54 | 5.66 | 3.78 | 2.23 | 1.06 | 0.32 | 0.01 | 0.14 | 0.70 | 1.65 | 2.94 | 4.51 |
| .55 | 5.64 | 3.76 | 2.22 | 1.05 | 0.31 | 0.01 | 0.15 | 0.71 | 1.66 | 2.95 | 4.53 |
| .56 | 5.62 | 3.74 | 2.20 | 1.04 | 0.31 | 0.01 | 0.15 | 0.72 | 1.67 | 2.97 | 4.55 |
| .57 | 5.60 | 3.73 | 2.19 | 1.03 | 0.30 | 0.01 | 0.15 | 0.72 | 1.68 | 2.98 | 4.56 |
| .58 | 5.58 | 3.71 | 2.17 | 1.02 | 0.30 | 0.01 | 0.16 | 0.73 | 1.69 | 3.00 | 4.58 |
| .59 | 5.56 | 3.69 | 2.16 | 1.01 | 0.29 | 0.01 | 0.16 | 0.74 | 1.70 | 3.01 | 4.60 |
| .60 | 5.54 | 3.68 | 2.15 | 1.01 | 0.29 | 0.01 | 0.17 | 0.75 | 1.72 | 3.03 | 4.62 |
| .61 | 5.52 | 3.66 | 2.13 | 1.00 | 0.28 | 0.01 | 0.17 | 0.75 | 1.73 | 3.04 | 4.63 |
| .62 | 5.50 | 3.64 | 2.12 | 0.99 | 0.28 | 0.01 | 0.17 | 0.76 | 1.74 | 3.06 | 4.65 |
| .63 | 5.48 | 3.62 | 2.11 | 0.98 | 0.27 | 0.01 | 0.18 | 0.77 | 1.75 | 3.07 | 4.67 |
| .64 | 5.46 | 3.61 | 2.09 | 0.97 | 0.27 | 0.01 | 0.18 | 0.78 | 1.76 | 3.09 | 4.68 |
| .65 | 5.44 | 3.59 | 2.08 | 0.96 | 0.26 | 0.01 | 0.19 | 0.79 | 1.78 | 3.10 | 4.70 |
| .66 | 5.42 | 3.57 | 2.06 | 0.95 | 0.26 | 0.00 | 0.19 | 0.79 | 1.79 | 3.12 | 4.71 |
| .67 | 5.40 | 3.56 | 2.05 | 0.94 | 0.25 | 0.00 | 0.19 | 0.80 | 1.80 | 3.13 | 4.73 |
| .68 | 5.38 | 3.54 | 2.04 | 0.93 | 0.25 | 0.00 | 0.20 | 0.81 | 1.81 | 3.15 | 4.75 |
| .69 | 5.36 | 3.52 | 2.03 | 0.92 | 0.24 | 0.00 | 0.20 | 0.82 | 1.82 | 3.16 | 4.77 |
| .70 | 5.34 | 3.51 | 2.02 | 0.91 | 0.24 | 0.00 | 0.21 | 0.83 | 1.84 | 3.18 | 4.79 |
| .71 | 5.32 | 3.49 | 2.00 | 0.90 | 0.23 | 0.00 | 0.21 | 0.83 | 1.85 | 3.19 | 4.80 |
| .72 | 5.30 | 3.47 | 1.99 | 0.89 | 0.23 | 0.00 | 0.21 | 0.84 | 1.86 | 3.21 | 4.82 |
| .73 | 5.28 | 3.46 | 1.98 | 0.88 | 0.22 | 0.00 | 0.22 | 0.85 | 1.87 | 3.22 | 4.84 |
| .74 | 5.26 | 3.44 | 1.96 | 0.87 | 0.22 | 0.00 | 0.22 | 0.86 | 1.88 | 3.24 | 4.86 |
| .75 | 5.24 | 3.43 | 1.95 | 0.87 | 0.21 | 0.00 | 0.23 | 0.87 | 1.90 | 3.25 | 4.88 |
| .76 | 5.22 | 3.41 | 1.93 | 0.86 | 0.21 | 0.00 | 0.23 | 0.88 | 1.91 | 3.27 | 4.89 |
| .77 | 5.20 | 3.39 | 1.92 | 0.85 | 0.20 | 0.00 | 0.23 | 0.89 | 1.92 | 3.28 | 4.91 |
| .78 | 5.18 | 3.38 | 1.91 | 0.84 | 0.20 | 0.00 | 0.24 | 0.90 | 1.93 | 3.30 | 4.93 |
| .79 | 5.16 | 3.36 | 1.90 | 0.83 | 0.19 | 0.00 | 0.24 | 0.91 | 1.94 | 3.31 | 4.95 |
| .80 | 5.15 | 3.35 | 1.89 | 0.83 | 0.19 | 0.00 | 0.25 | 0.92 | 1.96 | 3.33 | 4.97 |
| .81 | 5.13 | 3.33 | 1.87 | 0.82 | 0.18 | 0.00 | 0.25 | 0.92 | 1.97 | 3.34 | 4.98 |
| .82 | 5.11 | 3.31 | 1.86 | 0.81 | 0.18 | 0.00 | 0.26 | 0.93 | 1.98 | 3.36 | 5.00 |
| .83 | 5.09 | 3.29 | 1.85 | 0.80 | 0.17 | 0.00 | 0.26 | 0.94 | 1.99 | 3.37 | 5.02 |
| .84 | 5.07 | 3.28 | 1.83 | 0.79 | 0.17 | 0.01 | 0.27 | 0.95 | 2.00 | 3.39 | 5.03 |
| .85 | 5.05 | 3.26 | 1.82 | 0.78 | 0.17 | 0.01 | 0.27 | 0.96 | 2.02 | 3.40 | 5.05 |
| .86 | 5.03 | 3.24 | 1.81 | 0.77 | 0.16 | 0.01 | 0.28 | 0.96 | 2.03 | 3.42 | 5.07 |
| .87 | 5.01 | 3.23 | 1.79 | 0.76 | 0.16 | 0.01 | 0.28 | 0.97 | 2.04 | 3.43 | 5.08 |
| .88 | 4.99 | 3.21 | 1.78 | 0.75 | 0.15 | 0.01 | 0.29 | 0.98 | 2.05 | 3.45 | 5.10 |
| .89 | 4.97 | 3.19 | 1.77 | 0.74 | 0.15 | 0.01 | 0.29 | 0.99 | 2.06 | 3.46 | 5.12 |
| .90 | 4.95 | 3.18 | 1.76 | 0.74 | 0.15 | 0.01 | 0.30 | 1.00 | 2.08 | 3.48 | 5.14 |
| .91 | 4.93 | 3.16 | 1.74 | 0.73 | 0.14 | 0.01 | 0.30 | 1.01 | 2.09 | 3.49 | 5.15 |
| .92 | 4.91 | 3.15 | 1.73 | 0.72 | 0.14 | 0.01 | 0.31 | 1.02 | 2.10 | 3.51 | 5.17 |
| .93 | 4.89 | 3.13 | 1.72 | 0.71 | 0.14 | 0.01 | 0.31 | 1.03 | 2.12 | 3.52 | 5.19 |
| .94 | 4.87 | 3.12 | 1.71 | 0.70 | 0.13 | 0.01 | 0.32 | 1.04 | 2.13 | 3.54 | 5.21 |
| .95 | 4.85 | 3.10 | 1.70 | 0.70 | 0.13 | 0.01 | 0.32 | 1.05 | 2.14 | 3.55 | 5.23 |
| .96 | 4.83 | 3.09 | 1.68 | 0.69 | 0.13 | 0.02 | 0.33 | 1.06 | 2.16 | 3.57 | 5.24 |
| .97 | 4.81 | 3.07 | 1.67 | 0.68 | 0.12 | 0.02 | 0.33 | 1.07 | 2.17 | 3.58 | 5.26 |
| .98 | 4.79 | 3.06 | 1.66 | 0.67 | 0.12 | 0.02 | 0.34 | 1.08 | 2.18 | 3.60 | 5.28 |
| .99 | 4.77 | 3.04 | 1.65 | 0.66 | 0.12 | 0.02 | 0.34 | 1.09 | 2.19 | 3.61 | 5.30 |
| 1.00 | 4.76 | 3.03 | 1.64 | 0.66 | 0.12 | 0.02 | 0.35 | 1.10 | 2.21 | 3.63 | 5.32 |

# TABLE VII″. ARGUMENT 2.

Equation $= 11''.2 - 11''.18 \sin. (2t - x) - 0''.304 \sin. (4t - 2x)$.

Period, 31.81193574 days.

| Days. | 21 | 22 | 23 | 24 | 25 | 26 | 27 | 28 | 29 | 30 | 31 |
|---|---|---|---|---|---|---|---|---|---|---|---|
| Days. .00 | 5″.32 | 7″.21 | 9″.22 | 11″.30 | 13″.37 | 15″.38 | 17″.25 | 18″.91 | 20″.31 | 21″.39 | 22″.10 |
| .01 | 5.33 | 7.22 | 9.24 | 11.32 | 13.39 | 15.40 | 17.27 | 18.93 | 20.33 | 21.40 | 22.11 |
| .02 | 5.35 | 7.24 | 9.26 | 11.34 | 13.41 | 15.42 | 17.29 | 18.94 | 20.34 | 21.41 | 22.11 |
| .03 | 5.37 | 7.26 | 9.28 | 11.36 | 13.43 | 15.44 | 17.30 | 18.96 | 20.35 | 21.42 | 22.12 |
| .04 | 5.39 | 7.28 | 9.30 | 11.38 | 13.45 | 15.46 | 17.32 | 18.97 | 20.36 | 21.43 | 22.12 |
| .05 | 5.41 | 7.30 | 9.32 | 11.40 | 13.47 | 15.48 | 17.34 | 18.98 | 20.37 | 21.44 | 22.13 |
| .06 | 5.42 | 7.32 | 9.34 | 11.42 | 13.49 | 15.50 | 17.36 | 19.00 | 20.39 | 21.45 | 22.13 |
| .07 | 5.44 | 7.34 | 9.36 | 11.44 | 13.51 | 15.52 | 17.37 | 19.01 | 20.40 | 21.46 | 22.13 |
| .08 | 5.46 | 7.36 | 9.38 | 11.46 | 13.53 | 15.54 | 17.39 | 19.03 | 20.41 | 21.47 | 22.14 |
| .09 | 5.48 | 7.38 | 9.40 | 11.48 | 13.55 | 15.56 | 17.41 | 19.04 | 20.42 | 21.48 | 22.14 |
| .10 | 5.50 | 7.40 | 9.43 | 11.51 | 13.58 | 15.57 | 17.42 | 19.05 | 20.43 | 21.48 | 22.14 |
| .11 | 5.51 | 7.42 | 9.45 | 11.53 | 13.60 | 15.59 | 17.44 | 19.07 | 20.45 | 21.49 | 22.15 |
| .12 | 5.53 | 7.44 | 9.47 | 11.55 | 13.62 | 15.61 | 17.46 | 19.09 | 20.46 | 21.50 | 22.15 |
| .13 | 5.55 | 7.46 | 9.49 | 11.57 | 13.64 | 15.63 | 17.48 | 19.10 | 20.47 | 21.51 | 22.16 |
| .14 | 5.57 | 7.48 | 9.51 | 11.59 | 13.66 | 15.65 | 17.50 | 19.12 | 20.48 | 21.52 | 22.16 |
| .15 | 5.59 | 7.50 | 9.53 | 11.61 | 13.68 | 15.67 | 17.51 | 19.13 | 20.49 | 21.52 | 22.17 |
| .16 | 5.60 | 7.52 | 9.55 | 11.63 | 13.70 | 15.69 | 17.53 | 19.15 | 20.51 | 21.53 | 22.17 |
| .17 | 5.62 | 7.54 | 9.57 | 11.65 | 13.72 | 15.71 | 17.55 | 19.17 | 20.52 | 21.54 | 22.17 |
| .18 | 5.64 | 7.56 | 9.59 | 11.67 | 13.74 | 15.73 | 17.57 | 19.18 | 20.53 | 21.55 | 22.18 |
| .19 | 5.66 | 7.58 | 9.61 | 11.69 | 13.76 | 15.75 | 17.59 | 19.20 | 20.54 | 21.56 | 22.18 |
| .20 | 5.68 | 7.60 | 9.63 | 11.71 | 13.78 | 15.77 | 17.60 | 19.21 | 20.55 | 21.56 | 22.19 |
| .21 | 5.69 | 7.62 | 9.65 | 11.73 | 13.80 | 15.79 | 17.62 | 19.23 | 20.57 | 21.57 | 22.19 |
| .22 | 5.71 | 7.64 | 9.67 | 11.75 | 13.82 | 15.81 | 17.64 | 19.24 | 20.58 | 21.58 | 22.20 |
| .23 | 5.73 | 7.66 | 9.69 | 11.77 | 13.84 | 15.83 | 17.66 | 19.26 | 20.59 | 21.59 | 22.20 |
| .24 | 5.75 | 7.68 | 9.71 | 11.79 | 13.86 | 15.85 | 17.67 | 19.27 | 20.60 | 21.60 | 22.20 |
| .25 | 5.77 | 7.70 | 9.73 | 11.81 | 13.88 | 15.87 | 17.69 | 19.29 | 20.61 | 21.60 | 22.21 |
| .26 | 5.79 | 7.72 | 9.75 | 11.83 | 13.90 | 15.89 | 17.71 | 19.30 | 20.63 | 21.61 | 22.21 |
| .27 | 5.81 | 7.74 | 9.77 | 11.85 | 13.92 | 15.91 | 17.72 | 19.32 | 20.64 | 21.62 | 22.22 |
| .28 | 5.83 | 7.76 | 9.79 | 11.87 | 13.94 | 15.93 | 17.74 | 19.33 | 20.65 | 21.63 | 22.22 |
| .29 | 5.85 | 7.78 | 9.81 | 11.89 | 13.96 | 15.95 | 17.76 | 19.35 | 20.66 | 21.64 | 22.22 |
| .30 | 5.87 | 7.80 | 9.84 | 11.92 | 13.99 | 15.96 | 17.77 | 19.36 | 20.67 | 21.64 | 22.23 |
| .31 | 5.88 | 7.82 | 9.86 | 11.94 | 14.01 | 15.98 | 17.79 | 19.38 | 20.69 | 21.65 | 22.23 |
| .32 | 5.90 | 7.84 | 9.88 | 11.96 | 14.03 | 16.00 | 17.81 | 19.39 | 20.70 | 21.66 | 22.23 |
| .33 | 5.92 | 7.86 | 9.90 | 11.98 | 14.05 | 16.02 | 17.83 | 19.41 | 20.71 | 21.67 | 22.24 |
| .34 | 5.94 | 7.88 | 9.92 | 12.00 | 14.07 | 16.04 | 17.84 | 19.42 | 20.72 | 21.68 | 22.24 |
| .35 | 5.96 | 7.90 | 9.94 | 12.02 | 14.09 | 16.06 | 17.86 | 19.43 | 20.73 | 21.68 | 22.24 |
| .36 | 5.97 | 7.92 | 9.96 | 12.04 | 14.11 | 16.08 | 17.88 | 19.45 | 20.75 | 21.69 | 22.25 |
| .37 | 5.99 | 7.94 | 9.98 | 12.06 | 14.13 | 16.10 | 17.89 | 19.47 | 20.76 | 21.70 | 22.25 |
| .38 | 6.01 | 7.96 | 10.00 | 12.08 | 14.15 | 16.12 | 17.91 | 19.48 | 20.77 | 21.71 | 22.25 |
| .39 | 6.03 | 7.98 | 10.02 | 12.10 | 14.17 | 16.14 | 17.93 | 19.49 | 20.78 | 21.72 | 22.25 |
| .40 | 6.05 | 8.00 | 10.05 | 12.13 | 14.19 | 16.15 | 17.94 | 19.50 | 20.79 | 21.72 | 22.26 |
| .41 | 6.06 | 8.02 | 10.07 | 12.15 | 14.21 | 16.17 | 17.96 | 19.52 | 20.81 | 21.73 | 22.26 |
| .42 | 6.08 | 8.04 | 10.09 | 12.17 | 14.23 | 16.19 | 17.98 | 19.53 | 20.82 | 21.74 | 22.26 |
| .43 | 6.10 | 8.06 | 10.11 | 12.19 | 14.25 | 16.21 | 18.00 | 19.55 | 20.83 | 21.75 | 22.27 |
| .44 | 6.12 | 8.08 | 10.13 | 12.21 | 14.27 | 16.23 | 18.01 | 19.56 | 20.84 | 21.75 | 22.27 |
| .45 | 6.14 | 8.10 | 10.15 | 12.23 | 14.29 | 16.24 | 18.03 | 19.58 | 20.85 | 21.76 | 22.28 |
| .46 | 6.16 | 8.12 | 10.17 | 12.25 | 14.31 | 16.26 | 18.05 | 19.59 | 20.86 | 21.77 | 22.28 |
| .47 | 6.18 | 8.14 | 10.19 | 12.27 | 14.33 | 16.28 | 18.06 | 19.61 | 20.87 | 21.77 | 22.28 |
| .48 | 6.20 | 8.16 | 10.21 | 12.29 | 14.35 | 16.30 | 18.08 | 19.62 | 20.88 | 21.78 | 22.29 |
| .49 | 6.22 | 8.18 | 10.23 | 12.31 | 14.37 | 16.32 | 18.10 | 19.64 | 20.89 | 21.79 | 22.29 |
| .50 | 6.24 | 8.20 | 10.25 | 12.34 | 14.39 | 16.33 | 18.11 | 19.65 | 20.90 | 21.79 | 22.30 |

# TABLE VII″. ARGUMENT 2.

Equation = 11″.2 — 11″.18 sin. $(2t - x)$ — 0″.304 sin. $(4t - 2x)$.

Period, 31.81193574 days.

| Days. | 21 | 22 | 23 | 24 | 25 | 26 | 27 | 28 | 29 | 30 | 31 |
|---|---|---|---|---|---|---|---|---|---|---|---|
| Days. | ″ | ″ | ″ | ″ | ″ | ″ | ″ | ″ | ″ | ″ | ″ |
| .50 | 6.24 | 8.20 | 10.25 | 12.34 | 14.39 | 16.33 | 18.11 | 19.65 | 20.90 | 21.79 | 22.30 |
| .51 | 6.25 | 8.22 | 10.27 | 12.36 | 14.41 | 16.35 | 18.13 | 19.67 | 20.91 | 21.80 | 22.30 |
| .52 | 6.27 | 8.24 | 10.29 | 12.38 | 14.43 | 16.37 | 18.15 | 19.68 | 20.92 | 21.81 | 22.30 |
| .53 | 6.29 | 8.26 | 10.31 | 12.40 | 14.45 | 16.39 | 18.16 | 19.70 | 20.93 | 21.81 | 22.30 |
| .54 | 6.31 | 8.28 | 10.33 | 12.42 | 14.47 | 16.41 | 18.18 | 19.71 | 20.94 | 21.82 | 22.30 |
| .55 | 6.33 | 8.30 | 10.35 | 12.44 | 14.49 | 16.43 | 18.19 | 19.72 | 20.95 | 21.83 | 22.31 |
| .56 | 6.35 | 8.32 | 10.37 | 12.46 | 14.51 | 16.45 | 18.21 | 19.74 | 20.96 | 21.83 | 22.31 |
| .57 | 6.37 | 8.34 | 10.39 | 12.48 | 14.53 | 16.47 | 18.23 | 19.75 | 20.97 | 21.84 | 22.31 |
| .58 | 6.39 | 8.36 | 10.41 | 12.50 | 14.55 | 16.49 | 18.24 | 19.77 | 20.98 | 21.85 | 22.31 |
| .59 | 6.41 | 8.38 | 10.43 | 12.52 | 14.57 | 16.51 | 18.26 | 19.78 | 20.99 | 21.86 | 22.31 |
| .60 | 6.43 | 8.40 | 10.46 | 12.55 | 14.59 | 16.52 | 18.27 | 19.79 | 21.00 | 21.86 | 22.32 |
| .61 | 6.44 | 8.42 | 10.48 | 12.57 | 14.61 | 16.54 | 18.29 | 19.81 | 21.01 | 21.87 | 22.32 |
| .62 | 6.46 | 8.44 | 10.50 | 12.59 | 14.63 | 16.56 | 18.31 | 19.82 | 21.02 | 21.88 | 22.32 |
| .63 | 6.48 | 8.46 | 10.52 | 12.61 | 14.65 | 16.58 | 18.33 | 19.83 | 21.03 | 21.88 | 22.33 |
| .64 | 6.50 | 8.48 | 10.54 | 12.63 | 14.67 | 16.60 | 18.34 | 19.85 | 21.04 | 21.89 | 22.33 |
| .65 | 6.52 | 8.50 | 10.56 | 12.65 | 14.69 | 16 61 | 18.36 | 19.86 | 21.05 | 21.90 | 22.33 |
| .66 | 6.54 | 8.52 | 10.58 | 12.67 | 14.71 | 16.63 | 18.37 | 19.87 | 21.06 | 21.90 | 22.34 |
| .67 | 6.56 | 8.54 | 10.60 | 12.69 | 14.73 | 16.65 | 18.39 | 19.89 | 21.07 | 21.91 | 22.34 |
| .68 | 6.58 | 8.56 | 10.62 | 12.71 | 14.75 | 16.67 | 18.40 | 19.90 | 21.08 | 21.92 | 22.34 |
| .69 | 6.60 | 8.58 | 10.64 | 12.73 | 14.77 | 16.69 | 18.42 | 19.91 | 21.09 | 21.93 | 22.34 |
| .70 | 6.62 | 8.61 | 10.67 | 12.76 | 14.79 | 16.70 | 18.44 | 19.92 | 21.10 | 21.93 | 22.35 |
| .71 | 6.64 | 8.63 | 10.69 | 12.78 | 14.81 | 16.72 | 18.46 | 19.94 | 21.11 | 21.94 | 22.35 |
| .72 | 6.66 | 8.65 | 10.71 | 12.80 | 14.83 | 16.74 | 18.48 | 19.95 | 21.12 | 21.95 | 22.35 |
| .73 | 6.68 | 8.67 | 10.73 | 12.82 | 14.85 | 16.76 | 18.49 | 19.96 | 21.13 | 21.95 | 22.35 |
| .74 | 6.70 | 8.69 | 10.75 | 12.84 | 14.87 | 16.78 | 18.51 | 19.98 | 21.14 | 21.96 | 22.35 |
| .75 | 6.72 | 8.71 | 10.77 | 12.86 | 14.89 | 16.80 | 18.52 | 19 99 | 21.15 | 21.96 | 22.36 |
| .76 | 6.74 | 8.73 | 10.79 | 12.88 | 14.91 | 16.82 | 18.54 | 20.01 | 21.16 | 21.97 | 22.36 |
| .77 | 6.76 | 8.75 | 10.81 | 12.90 | 14.93 | 16.84 | 18.56 | 20.02 | 21.17 | 21.98 | 22.36 |
| .78 | 6.78 | 8.77 | 10.83 | 12.92 | 14.95 | 16.86 | 18.57 | 20.03 | 21.18 | 21.98 | 22.36 |
| .79 | 6.80 | 8.79 | 10.85 | 12.94 | 14.97 | 16.88 | 18.59 | 20.04 | 21.19 | 21.99 | 22.36 |
| .80 | 6.82 | 8.81 | 10.88 | 12.96 | 14.99 | 16.89 | 18.60 | 20.05 | 21.20 | 21.99 | 22.36 |
| .81 | 6.83 | 8.83 | 10.90 | 12.98 | 15.01 | 16.91 | 18.62 | 20.07 | 21.21 | 22.00 | 22.37 |
| .82 | 6.85 | 8.85 | 10.92 | 13.00 | 15.03 | 16.93 | 18.64 | 20.08 | 21.22 | 22.00 | 22.37 |
| .83 | 6.87 | 8.87 | 10.94 | 13.02 | 15.05 | 16.95 | 18.65 | 20.09 | 21.23 | 22.01 | 22.37 |
| .84 | 6.89 | 8.89 | 10.96 | 13.04 | 15.07 | 16.97 | 18.67 | 20.11 | 21.24 | 22.01 | 22.37 |
| .85 | 6.91 | 8.91 | 10.98 | 13.06 | 15.09 | 16.98 | 18.68 | 20.12 | 21.25 | 22.02 | 22.38 |
| .86 | 6.93 | 8.93 | 11.00 | 13.08 | 15.11 | 17.00 | 18.70 | 20.13 | 21.26 | 22.02 | 22.38 |
| .87 | 6.95 | 8.95 | 11.02 | 13.10 | 15.13 | 17.02 | 18.72 | 20.15 | 21.27 | 22.03 | 22.38 |
| .88 | 6.97 | 8.97 | 11.04 | 13.12 | 15.15 | 17.04 | 18.73 | 20.16 | 21.28 | 22.03 | 22.38 |
| .89 | 6.99 | 8.99 | 11.06 | 13.14 | 15.17 | 17.06 | 18.75 | 20.17 | 21.29 | 22.04 | 22.38 |
| .90 | 7.01 | 9.01 | 11.09 | 13.17 | 15.18 | 17.07 | 18.76 | 20.18 | 21.30 | 22.04 | 22.38 |
| .91 | 7.03 | 9.03 | 11.11 | 13.19 | 15.20 | 17.09 | 18.78 | 20.20 | 21.31 | 22.05 | 22.38 |
| .92 | 7.05 | 9.05 | 11.13 | 13.21 | 15.22 | 17.11 | 18.79 | 20.21 | 21.32 | 22.05 | 22.38 |
| .93 | 7.07 | 9.07 | 11.15 | 13.23 | 15.24 | 17.13 | 18.81 | 20.22 | 21.33 | 22.06 | 22.38 |
| .94 | 7.00 | 0.00 | 11.17 | 13.25 | 15.26 | 17.15 | 18.82 | 20.24 | 21.34 | 22.06 | 22.38 |
| .95 | 7.11 | 9.11 | 11.19 | 13.27 | 15.28 | 17.16 | 18.84 | 20.25 | 21.35 | 22.07 | 22.39 |
| .96 | 7.13 | 9.13 | 11.21 | 13.29 | 15.30 | 17.18 | 18.85 | 20.26 | 21.36 | 22.08 | 22.39 |
| .97 | 7.15 | 9.15 | 11.23 | 13.31 | 15.32 | 17.20 | 18.87 | 20.28 | 21.37 | 22.08 | 22.39 |
| .98 | 7.17 | 9.17 | 11.25 | 13.33 | 15.34 | 17.22 | 18.88 | 20.29 | 21.38 | 22.09 | 22.39 |
| .99 | 7.19 | 9.19 | 11.27 | 13.35 | 15.36 | 17.24 | 18.90 | 20.30 | 21.39 | 22.10 | 22.39 |
| 1.00 | 7.21 | 9.22 | 11.30 | 13.37 | 15.38 | 17.25 | 18.91 | 20.31 | 21.39 | 22.10 | 22.39 |

# TABLE VIII″. ARGUMENT 3.

Equation $= 31''.16 + 0''.345 \sin. t - 20''.808 \sin. 2t - 0''.023 \sin. 3t - 0''.65 \sin. 4t.$

Period, 29.530588 days.

| Days. | 0 | 1 | 2 | 3 | 4 | 5 | 6 | 7 | 8 | 9 |
|---|---|---|---|---|---|---|---|---|---|---|
| Days. | ″ | ″ | ″ | ″ | ″ | ″ | ″ | ″ | ″ | ″ |
| .00 | 33.97 | 22.14 | 12.11 | 5.78 | 4.18 | 7.33 | 14.43 | 24.16 | 34.93 | 45.10 |
| .01 | 33.85 | 22.03 | 12.03 | 5.74 | 4.19 | 7.38 | 14.52 | 24.27 | 35.04 | 45.19 |
| .02 | 33.73 | 21.92 | 11.94 | 5.70 | 4.20 | 7.44 | 14.61 | 24.37 | 35.15 | 45.28 |
| .03 | 33.62 | 21.80 | 11.86 | 5.66 | 4.20 | 7.49 | 14.69 | 24.48 | 35.25 | 45.38 |
| .04 | 33.50 | 21.69 | 11.77 | 5.62 | 4.21 | 7.55 | 14.78 | 24.58 | 35.36 | 45.47 |
| .05 | 33.38 | 21.58 | 11.69 | 5.58 | 4.22 | 7.60 | 14.87 | 24.69 | 35.47 | 45.56 |
| .06 | 33.26 | 21.47 | 11.61 | 5.54 | 4.23 | 7.66 | 14.96 | 24.80 | 35.58 | 45.65 |
| .07 | 33.14 | 21.36 | 11.53 | 5.51 | 4.24 | 7.71 | 15.05 | 24.90 | 35.68 | 45.74 |
| .08 | 33.02 | 21.24 | 11.45 | 5.47 | 4.26 | 7.77 | 15.13 | 25.01 | 35.79 | 45.83 |
| .09 | 32.90 | 21.13 | 11.37 | 5.44 | 4.27 | 7.82 | 15.22 | 25.11 | 35.89 | 45.92 |
| .10 | 32.78 | 21.02 | 11.29 | 5.40 | 4.28 | 7.88 | 15.31 | 25.22 | 36.00 | 46.01 |
| .11 | 32.66 | 20.91 | 11.21 | 5.36 | 4.30 | 7.94 | 15.40 | 25.33 | 36.11 | 46.10 |
| .12 | 32.54 | 20.80 | 11.13 | 5.33 | 4.31 | 8.00 | 15.49 | 25.43 | 36.21 | 46.19 |
| .13 | 32.42 | 20.69 | 11.05 | 5.29 | 4.33 | 8.05 | 15.58 | 25.54 | 36.32 | 46.28 |
| .14 | 32.30 | 20.58 | 10.97 | 5.26 | 4.34 | 8.11 | 15.67 | 25.64 | 36.42 | 46.37 |
| .15 | 32.18 | 20.47 | 10.89 | 5.22 | 4.36 | 8.17 | 15.76 | 25.75 | 36.53 | 46.46 |
| .16 | 32.06 | 20.36 | 10.81 | 5.19 | 4.38 | 8.23 | 15.85 | 25.86 | 36.64 | 46.55 |
| .17 | 31.94 | 20.25 | 10.73 | 5.16 | 4.39 | 8.29 | 15.94 | 25.96 | 36.74 | 46.64 |
| .18 | 31.82 | 20.14 | 10.66 | 5.12 | 4.41 | 8.35 | 16.04 | 26.07 | 36.85 | 46.73 |
| .19 | 31.70 | 20.03 | 10.58 | 5.09 | 4.42 | 8.41 | 16.13 | 26.17 | 36.95 | 46.82 |
| .20 | 31.58 | 19.92 | 10.50 | 5.06 | 4.44 | 8.47 | 16.22 | 26.28 | 37.06 | 46.91 |
| .21 | 31.46 | 19.81 | 10.42 | 5.03 | 4.46 | 8.53 | 16.31 | 26.39 | 37.17 | 47.00 |
| .22 | 31.34 | 19.70 | 10.35 | 5.00 | 4.48 | 8.59 | 16.40 | 26.50 | 37.27 | 47.09 |
| .23 | 31.22 | 19.60 | 10.27 | 4.98 | 4.50 | 8.66 | 16.50 | 26.60 | 37.38 | 47.17 |
| .24 | 31.10 | 19.49 | 10.20 | 4.95 | 4.52 | 8.72 | 16.59 | 26.71 | 37.48 | 47.26 |
| .25 | 30.98 | 19.38 | 10.12 | 4.92 | 4.54 | 8.78 | 16.68 | 26.82 | 37.59 | 47.35 |
| .26 | 30.86 | 19.27 | 10.05 | 4.89 | 4.56 | 8.84 | 16.77 | 26.93 | 37.70 | 47.44 |
| .27 | 30.74 | 19.16 | 9.98 | 4.86 | 4.58 | 8.90 | 16.87 | 27.04 | 37.80 | 47.52 |
| .28 | 30.62 | 19.06 | 9.90 | 4.84 | 4.60 | 8.97 | 16.96 | 27.14 | 37.91 | 47.61 |
| .29 | 30.50 | 18.95 | 9.83 | 4.81 | 4.62 | 9.03 | 17.06 | 27.25 | 38.01 | 47.69 |
| .30 | 30.38 | 18.84 | 9.76 | 4.78 | 4.64 | 9.09 | 17.15 | 27.36 | 38.12 | 47.78 |
| .31 | 30.26 | 18.73 | 9.69 | 4.76 | 4.66 | 9.16 | 17.24 | 27.47 | 38.22 | 47.86 |
| .32 | 30.14 | 18.63 | 9.62 | 4.73 | 4.69 | 9.22 | 17.34 | 27.58 | 38.33 | 47.95 |
| .33 | 30.01 | 18.52 | 9.54 | 4.71 | 4.71 | 9.29 | 17.43 | 27.68 | 38.43 | 48.03 |
| .34 | 29.89 | 18.42 | 9.47 | 4.68 | 4.74 | 9.35 | 17.53 | 27.79 | 38.54 | 48.12 |
| .35 | 29.77 | 18.31 | 9.40 | 4.66 | 4.76 | 9.42 | 17.62 | 27.90 | 38.64 | 48.20 |
| .36 | 29.65 | 18.21 | 9.33 | 4.64 | 4.79 | 9.49 | 17.72 | 28.01 | 38.74 | 48.28 |
| .37 | 29.53 | 18.10 | 9.26 | 4.62 | 4.82 | 9.56 | 17.81 | 28.12 | 38.85 | 48.37 |
| .38 | 29.41 | 18.00 | 9.19 | 4.59 | 4.84 | 9.62 | 17.91 | 28.22 | 38.95 | 48.45 |
| .39 | 29.29 | 17.89 | 9.12 | 4.57 | 4.87 | 9.69 | 18.00 | 28.33 | 39.06 | 48.54 |
| .40 | 29.17 | 17.79 | 9.05 | 4.55 | 4.90 | 9.75 | 18.10 | 28.44 | 39.16 | 48.62 |
| .41 | 29.05 | 17.69 | 8.98 | 4.53 | 4.93 | 9.83 | 18.20 | 28.55 | 39.26 | 48.70 |
| .42 | 28.93 | 17.59 | 8.92 | 4.51 | 4.96 | 9.90 | 18.29 | 28.66 | 39.37 | 48.78 |
| .43 | 28.81 | 17.48 | 8.85 | 4.49 | 4.98 | 9.96 | 18.39 | 28.76 | 39.47 | 48.87 |
| .44 | 28.69 | 17.38 | 8.79 | 4.47 | 5.01 | 10.03 | 18.48 | 28.87 | 39.58 | 48.95 |
| .45 | 28.57 | 17.28 | 8.72 | 4.45 | 5.04 | 10.10 | 18.58 | 28.98 | 39.68 | 49.03 |
| .46 | 28.45 | 17.18 | 8.65 | 4.43 | 5.07 | 10.17 | 18.68 | 29.09 | 39.78 | 49.11 |
| .47 | 28.33 | 17.08 | 8.59 | 4.41 | 5.10 | 10.24 | 18.77 | 29.20 | 39.88 | 49.19 |
| .48 | 28.21 | 16.97 | 8.52 | 4.40 | 5.13 | 10.31 | 18.87 | 29.30 | 39.99 | 49.28 |
| .49 | 28.09 | 16.87 | 8.46 | 4.38 | 5.16 | 10.38 | 18.96 | 29.41 | 40.09 | 49.36 |
| .50 | 27.97 | 16.77 | 8.39 | 4.36 | 5.19 | 10.45 | 19.06 | 29.52 | 40.19 | 49.44 |

# TABLE VIII″. ARGUMENT 3.

Equation = 31″.16 + 0″.345 sin. $t$ — 20″.808 sin. $2t$ — 0″.023 sin. $3t$ — 0″.65 sin. $4t$.

Period, 29.530588 days.

| Days. | 0 | 1 | 2 | 3 | 4 | 5 | 6 | 7 | 8 | 9 |
|---|---|---|---|---|---|---|---|---|---|---|
| Days. .50 | 27″.97 | 16″.77 | 8″.39 | 4″.36 | 5″.19 | 10″.45 | 19″.06 | 29″.52 | 40″.19 | 49″.44 |
| .51 | 27.85 | 16.67 | 8.33 | 4.35 | 5.22 | 10.52 | 19.16 | 29.63 | 40.29 | 49.52 |
| .52 | 27.73 | 16.57 | 8.27 | 4.33 | 5.26 | 10.59 | 19.26 | 29.74 | 40.39 | 49.60 |
| .53 | 27.62 | 16.46 | 8.20 | 4.32 | 5.29 | 10.67 | 19.36 | 29.84 | 40.50 | 49.67 |
| .54 | 27.50 | 16.36 | 8.14 | 4.30 | 5.33 | 10.74 | 19.46 | 29.95 | 40.60 | 49.75 |
| .55 | 27.38 | 16.26 | 8.08 | 4.29 | 5.36 | 10.81 | 19.56 | 30.06 | 40.70 | 49.83 |
| .56 | 27.26 | 16.16 | 8.02 | 4.28 | 5.39 | 10.89 | 19.66 | 30.17 | 40.80 | 49.91 |
| .57 | 27.14 | 16.06 | 7.96 | 4.27 | 5.43 | 10.96 | 19.76 | 30.28 | 40.90 | 49.99 |
| .58 | 27.03 | 15.97 | 7.90 | 4.25 | 5.46 | 11.04 | 19.85 | 30.38 | 41.01 | 50.06 |
| .59 | 26.91 | 15.87 | 7.84 | 4.24 | 5.50 | 11.11 | 19.95 | 30.49 | 41.11 | 50.14 |
| .60 | 26.79 | 15.77 | 7.78 | 4.23 | 5.53 | 11.19 | 20.05 | 30.60 | 41.21 | 50.22 |
| .61 | 26.67 | 15.67 | 7.72 | 4.22 | 5.57 | 11.27 | 20.15 | 30.71 | 41.31 | 50.30 |
| .62 | 26.55 | 15.57 | 7.66 | 4.21 | 5.61 | 11.34 | 20.25 | 30.82 | 41.41 | 50.37 |
| .63 | 26.44 | 15.48 | 7.61 | 4.20 | 5.65 | 11.42 | 20.35 | 30.93 | 41.51 | 50.45 |
| .64 | 26.32 | 15.38 | 7.55 | 4.19 | 5.69 | 11.49 | 20.45 | 31.04 | 41.61 | 50.52 |
| .65 | 26.20 | 15.28 | 7.49 | 4.18 | 5.73 | 11.57 | 20.55 | 31.15 | 41.71 | 50.60 |
| .66 | 26.08 | 15.18 | 7.43 | 4.17 | 5.77 | 11.65 | 20.65 | 31.26 | 41.81 | 50.67 |
| .67 | 25.96 | 15.09 | 7.38 | 4.16 | 5.81 | 11.73 | 20.75 | 31.37 | 41.91 | 50.75 |
| .68 | 25.85 | 14.99 | 7.32 | 4.16 | 5.85 | 11.80 | 20.86 | 31.47 | 42.01 | 50.82 |
| .69 | 25.73 | 14.90 | 7.27 | 4.15 | 5.89 | 11.88 | 20.96 | 31.58 | 42.11 | 50.90 |
| .70 | 25.61 | 14.80 | 7.21 | 4.14 | 5.93 | 11.96 | 21.06 | 31.69 | 42.21 | 50.97 |
| .71 | 25.49 | 14.71 | 7.16 | 4.13 | 5.97 | 12.04 | 21.16 | 31.80 | 42.31 | 51.04 |
| .72 | 25.37 | 14.61 | 7.10 | 4.13 | 6.01 | 12.12 | 21.26 | 31.91 | 42.41 | 51.12 |
| .73 | 25.26 | 14.52 | 7.05 | 4.12 | 6.05 | 12.19 | 21.37 | 32.02 | 42.50 | 51.19 |
| .74 | 25.14 | 14.42 | 6.99 | 4.12 | 6.09 | 12.27 | 21.47 | 32.13 | 42.60 | 51.27 |
| .75 | 25.02 | 14.33 | 6.94 | 4.11 | 6.13 | 12.35 | 21.57 | 32.23 | 42.70 | 51.34 |
| .76 | 24.90 | 14.24 | 6.89 | 4.11 | 6.17 | 12.43 | 21.67 | 32.34 | 42.80 | 51.41 |
| .77 | 24.79 | 14.15 | 6.84 | 4.11 | 6.22 | 12.51 | 21.77 | 32.45 | 42.90 | 51.48 |
| .78 | 24.67 | 14.05 | 6.79 | 4.10 | 6.26 | 12.59 | 21.88 | 32.55 | 42.99 | 51.56 |
| .79 | 24.56 | 13.96 | 6.74 | 4.10 | 6.31 | 12.67 | 21.98 | 32.66 | 43.09 | 51.63 |
| .80 | 24.44 | 13.87 | 6.69 | 4.10 | 6.35 | 12.75 | 22.08 | 32.77 | 43.19 | 51.70 |
| .81 | 24.32 | 13.78 | 6.64 | 4.10 | 6.40 | 12.83 | 22.18 | 32.88 | 43.29 | 51.77 |
| .82 | 24.21 | 13.69 | 6.59 | 4.10 | 6.44 | 12.91 | 22.28 | 32.99 | 43.38 | 51.84 |
| .83 | 24.09 | 13.60 | 6.54 | 4.10 | 6.49 | 13.00 | 22.39 | 33.09 | 43.48 | 51.90 |
| .84 | 23.98 | 13.51 | 6.49 | 4.10 | 6.53 | 13.08 | 22.49 | 33.20 | 43.57 | 51.97 |
| .85 | 23.86 | 13.42 | 6.44 | 4.10 | 6.58 | 13.16 | 22.59 | 33.31 | 43.67 | 52.04 |
| .86 | 23.74 | 13.33 | 6.39 | 4.10 | 6.63 | 13.24 | 22.69 | 33.42 | 43.77 | 52.11 |
| .87 | 23.63 | 13.24 | 6.35 | 4.11 | 6.68 | 13.32 | 22.80 | 33.53 | 43.86 | 52.18 |
| .88 | 23.51 | 13.15 | 6.30 | 4.11 | 6.72 | 13.41 | 22.90 | 33.63 | 43.96 | 52.24 |
| .89 | 23.40 | 13.06 | 6.26 | 4.12 | 6.77 | 13.49 | 23.01 | 33.74 | 44.05 | 52.31 |
| .90 | 23.28 | 12.97 | 6.21 | 4.12 | 6.82 | 13.57 | 23.11 | 33.85 | 44.15 | 52.38 |
| .91 | 23.17 | 12.88 | 6.17 | 4.12 | 6.87 | 13.66 | 23.22 | 33.96 | 44.25 | 52.45 |
| .92 | 23.05 | 12.80 | 6.12 | 4.13 | 6.92 | 13.74 | 23.32 | 34.07 | 44.34 | 52.51 |
| .93 | 22.94 | 12.71 | 6.08 | 4.13 | 6.97 | 13.83 | 23.43 | 34.17 | 44.44 | 52.58 |
| .94 | 22.82 | 12.63 | 6.03 | 4.14 | 7.02 | 13.91 | 23.53 | 34.28 | 44.53 | 52.64 |
| .95 | 22.71 | 12.54 | 5.99 | 4.14 | 7.07 | 14.00 | 23.64 | 34.39 | 44.63 | 52.71 |
| .96 | 22.60 | 12.45 | 5.95 | 4.15 | 7.12 | 14.09 | 23.74 | 34.50 | 44.72 | 52.77 |
| .97 | 22.48 | 12.37 | 5.91 | 4.16 | 7.17 | 14.17 | 23.85 | 34.61 | 44.82 | 52.84 |
| .98 | 22.37 | 12.28 | 5.86 | 4.16 | 7.23 | 14.26 | 23.95 | 34.71 | 44.91 | 52.90 |
| .99 | 22.25 | 12.20 | 5.82 | 4.17 | 7.28 | 14.34 | 24.06 | 34.82 | 45.01 | 52.97 |
| 1.00 | 22.14 | 12.11 | 5.78 | 4.18 | 7.33 | 14.43 | 24.16 | 34.93 | 45.10 | 53.03 |

# TABLE VIII″. ARGUMENT 3.

Equation $= 31''.16 + 0''.345 \sin. t - 20''.808 \sin. 2t - 0''.023 \sin. 3t - 0''.65 \sin. 4t.$

Period, 29.530588 days.

| Days. | 10 | 11 | 12 | 13 | 14 | 15 | 16 | 17 | 18 | 19 |
|---|---|---|---|---|---|---|---|---|---|---|
| Days. .00 | 53″.03 | 57″.32 | 56″.99 | 51″.84 | 42″.65 | 31″.16 | 19″.67 | 10″.48 | 5″.33 | 5″.00 |
| .01 | 53.09 | 57.34 | 56.96 | 51.77 | 42.54 | 31.04 | 19.56 | 10.41 | 5.30 | 5.02 |
| .02 | 53.15 | 57.36 | 56.93 | 51.69 | 42.44 | 30.92 | 19.45 | 10.34 | 5.28 | 5.04 |
| .03 | 53.22 | 57.38 | 56.91 | 51.62 | 42.33 | 30.80 | 19.35 | 10.26 | 5.25 | 5.07 |
| .04 | 53.28 | 57.40 | 56.88 | 51.54 | 42.23 | 30.68 | 19.24 | 10.19 | 5.23 | 5.09 |
| .05 | 53.34 | 57.42 | 56.85 | 51.47 | 42.12 | 30.56 | 19.13 | 10.12 | 5.20 | 5.11 |
| .06 | 53.40 | 57.44 | 56.82 | 51.39 | 42.01 | 30.44 | 19.03 | 10.05 | 5.18 | 5.13 |
| .07 | 53.46 | 57.46 | 56.79 | 51.31 | 41.90 | 30.32 | 18.92 | 9.98 | 5.15 | 5.16 |
| .08 | 53.53 | 57.47 | 56.75 | 51.24 | 41.79 | 30.21 | 18.82 | 9.90 | 5.13 | 5.18 |
| .09 | 53.59 | 57.49 | 56.72 | 51.16 | 41.68 | 30.09 | 18.71 | 9.83 | 5.10 | 5.21 |
| .10 | 53.65 | 57.51 | 56.69 | 51.08 | 41.57 | 29.97 | 18.61 | 9.76 | 5.08 | 5.23 |
| .11 | 53.71 | 57.52 | 56.66 | 51.00 | 41.46 | 29.85 | 18.51 | 9.69 | 5.06 | 5.26 |
| .12 | 53.77 | 57.54 | 56.62 | 50.92 | 41.35 | 29.73 | 18.40 | 9.62 | 5.04 | 5.28 |
| .13 | 53.82 | 57.55 | 56.59 | 50.85 | 41.24 | 29.62 | 18.30 | 9.56 | 5.01 | 5.31 |
| .14 | 53.88 | 57.57 | 56.55 | 50.77 | 41.13 | 29.50 | 18.19 | 9.49 | 4.99 | 5.33 |
| .15 | 53.94 | 57.58 | 56.52 | 50.69 | 41.02 | 29.38 | 18.09 | 9.42 | 4.97 | 5.36 |
| .16 | 54.00 | 57.59 | 56.48 | 50.61 | 40.91 | 29.26 | 17.99 | 9.35 | 4.95 | 5.39 |
| .17 | 54.05 | 57.61 | 56.45 | 50.53 | 40.80 | 29.14 | 17.89 | 9.29 | 4.93 | 5.42 |
| .18 | 54.11 | 57.62 | 56.41 | 50.44 | 40.69 | 29.02 | 17.78 | 9.22 | 4.91 | 5.45 |
| .19 | 54.16 | 57.64 | 56.38 | 50.36 | 40.58 | 28.90 | 17.68 | 9.16 | 4.89 | 5.48 |
| .20 | 54.22 | 57.65 | 56.34 | 50.28 | 40.47 | 28.78 | 17.58 | 9.09 | 4.87 | 5.51 |
| .21 | 54.28 | 57.66 | 56.30 | 50.20 | 40.36 | 28.66 | 17.48 | 9.02 | 4.85 | 5.54 |
| .22 | 54.33 | 57.67 | 56.26 | 50.12 | 40.25 | 28.54 | 17.38 | 8.96 | 4.83 | 5.57 |
| .23 | 54.39 | 57.68 | 56.23 | 50.03 | 40.13 | 28.43 | 17.27 | 8.89 | 4.82 | 5.60 |
| .24 | 54.44 | 57.69 | 56.19 | 49.95 | 40.02 | 28.31 | 17.17 | 8.83 | 4.80 | 5.63 |
| .25 | 54.50 | 57.70 | 56.15 | 49.87 | 39.91 | 28.19 | 17.07 | 8.76 | 4.78 | 5.66 |
| .26 | 54.55 | 57.71 | 56.11 | 49.79 | 39.80 | 28.07 | 16.97 | 8.70 | 4.77 | 5.69 |
| .27 | 54.60 | 57.71 | 56.07 | 49.70 | 39.69 | 27.95 | 16.87 | 8.64 | 4.75 | 5.73 |
| .28 | 54.66 | 57.72 | 56.02 | 49.62 | 39.57 | 27.84 | 16.77 | 8.57 | 4.74 | 5.76 |
| .29 | 54.71 | 57.72 | 55.98 | 49.53 | 39.46 | 27.72 | 16.67 | 8.51 | 4.72 | 5.80 |
| .30 | 54.76 | 57.73 | 55.94 | 49.45 | 39.35 | 27.60 | 16.57 | 8.45 | 4.71 | 5.83 |
| .31 | 54.81 | 57.74 | 55.90 | 49.36 | 39.24 | 27.48 | 16.47 | 8.39 | 4.70 | 5.87 |
| .32 | 54.86 | 57.74 | 55.85 | 49.28 | 39.12 | 27.37 | 16.37 | 8.33 | 4.69 | 5.90 |
| .33 | 54.91 | 57.75 | 55.81 | 49.19 | 39.01 | 27.25 | 16.28 | 8.28 | 4.68 | 5.94 |
| .34 | 54.96 | 57.75 | 55.76 | 49.11 | 38.89 | 27.14 | 16.18 | 8.22 | 4.67 | 5.97 |
| .35 | 55.01 | 57.76 | 55.72 | 49.02 | 38.78 | 27.02 | 16.08 | 8.16 | 4.66 | 6.01 |
| .36 | 55.06 | 57.76 | 55.67 | 48.93 | 38.67 | 26.90 | 15.98 | 8.10 | 4.65 | 6.05 |
| .37 | 55.11 | 57.77 | 55.63 | 48.84 | 38.55 | 26.78 | 15.89 | 8.04 | 4.64 | 6.09 |
| .38 | 55.16 | 57.77 | 55.58 | 48.75 | 38.44 | 26.67 | 15.79 | 7.99 | 4.63 | 6.12 |
| .39 | 55.21 | 57.78 | 55.54 | 48.66 | 38.32 | 26.55 | 15.70 | 7.93 | 4.62 | 6.16 |
| .40 | 55.26 | 57.78 | 55.49 | 48.57 | 38.21 | 26.43 | 15.60 | 7.87 | 4.61 | 6.20 |
| .41 | 55.31 | 57.78 | 55.44 | 48.48 | 38.10 | 26.31 | 15.50 | 7.81 | 4.60 | 6.24 |
| .42 | 55.35 | 57.78 | 55.39 | 48.39 | 37.98 | 26.19 | 15.41 | 7.76 | 4.60 | 6.28 |
| .43 | 55.40 | 57.78 | 55.35 | 48.30 | 37.87 | 26.08 | 15.31 | 7.70 | 4.59 | 6.32 |
| .44 | 55.44 | 57.78 | 55.30 | 48.21 | 37.75 | 25.96 | 15.22 | 7.65 | 4.59 | 6.36 |
| .45 | 55.49 | 57.78 | 55.25 | 48.12 | 37.64 | 25.84 | 15.12 | 7.59 | 4.58 | 6.40 |
| .46 | 55.53 | 57.78 | 55.20 | 48.03 | 37.52 | 25.72 | 15.03 | 7.54 | 4.57 | 6.44 |
| .47 | 55.58 | 57.78 | 55.15 | 47.94 | 37.41 | 25.61 | 14.94 | 7.49 | 4.57 | 6.48 |
| .48 | 55.62 | 57.77 | 55.09 | 47.85 | 37.29 | 25.49 | 14.84 | 7.43 | 4.56 | 6.53 |
| .49 | 55.67 | 57.77 | 55.04 | 47.76 | 37.18 | 25.38 | 14.75 | 7.38 | 4.56 | 6.57 |
| .50 | 55.71 | 57.77 | 54.99 | 47.67 | 37.06 | 25.26 | 14.66 | 7.33 | 4.55 | 6.61 |

# TABLE VIII″. ARGUMENT 3.

Equation = 31″.16 + 0″.345 sin. $t$ — 20″.808 sin. $2t$ — 0″.023 sin. $3t$ — 0″.65 sin. $4t$.

Period, 29.530588 days.

| Days. | 10 | 11 | 12 | 13 | 14 | 15 | 16 | 17 | 18 | 19 |
|---|---|---|---|---|---|---|---|---|---|---|
| Days. | ″ | ″ | ″ | ″ | ″ | ″ | ″ | ″ | ″ | ″ |
| .50 | 55.71 | 57.77 | 54.99 | 47.67 | 37.06 | 25.26 | 14.66 | 7.33 | 4.55 | 6.61 |
| .51 | 55.75 | 57.77 | 54.94 | 47.58 | 36.94 | 25.14 | 14.57 | 7.28 | 4.55 | 6.65 |
| .52 | 55.79 | 57.76 | 54.89 | 47.48 | 36.82 | 25.03 | 14.48 | 7.23 | 4.55 | 6.70 |
| .53 | 55.84 | 57.76 | 54.83 | 47.39 | 36.71 | 24.91 | 14.38 | 7.17 | 4.54 | 6.74 |
| .54 | 55.88 | 57.75 | 54.78 | 47.29 | 36.60 | 24.80 | 14.29 | 7.12 | 4.54 | 6.79 |
| .55 | 55.92 | 57.75 | 54.73 | 47.20 | 36.48 | 24.68 | 14.20 | 7.07 | 4.54 | 6.83 |
| .56 | 55.96 | 57.74 | 54.67 | 47.10 | 36.36 | 24.57 | 14.11 | 7.02 | 4.54 | 6.88 |
| .57 | 56.00 | 57.73 | 54.62 | 47.01 | 36.24 | 24.45 | 14.02 | 6.97 | 4.54 | 6.92 |
| .58 | 56.04 | 57.73 | 54.56 | 46.91 | 36.13 | 24.34 | 13.93 | 6.93 | 4.54 | 6.97 |
| .59 | 56.08 | 57.72 | 54.51 | 46.82 | 36.01 | 24.22 | 13.84 | 6.88 | 4.54 | 7.01 |
| .60 | 56.12 | 57.71 | 54.45 | 46.72 | 35.89 | 24.11 | 13.75 | 6.83 | 4.54 | 7.06 |
| .61 | 56.16 | 57.70 | 54.39 | 46.62 | 35.77 | 24.00 | 13.66 | 6.78 | 4.54 | 7.11 |
| .62 | 56.20 | 57.69 | 54.33 | 46.53 | 35.65 | 23.88 | 13.57 | 6.74 | 4.55 | 7.16 |
| .63 | 56.23 | 57.68 | 54.28 | 46.43 | 35.54 | 23.77 | 13.48 | 6.69 | 4.55 | 7.21 |
| .64 | 56.27 | 57.67 | 54.22 | 46.34 | 35.42 | 23.65 | 13.39 | 6.65 | 4.56 | 7.26 |
| .65 | 56.31 | 57.66 | 54.16 | 46.24 | 35.30 | 23.54 | 13.30 | 6.60 | 4.56 | 7.31 |
| .66 | 56.35 | 57.65 | 54.10 | 46.14 | 35.18 | 23.43 | 13.21 | 6.56 | 4.57 | 7.36 |
| .67 | 56.38 | 57.64 | 54.04 | 46.04 | 35.06 | 23.31 | 13.13 | 6.51 | 4.57 | 7.41 |
| .68 | 56.42 | 57.63 | 53.99 | 45.95 | 34.95 | 23.20 | 13.04 | 6.47 | 4.58 | 7.46 |
| .69 | 56.45 | 57.62 | 53.93 | 45.85 | 34.83 | 23.08 | 12.96 | 6.42 | 4.58 | 7.51 |
| .70 | 56.49 | 57.61 | 53.87 | 45.75 | 34.71 | 22.97 | 12.87 | 6.38 | 4.59 | 7.56 |
| .71 | 56.52 | 57.60 | 53.81 | 45.65 | 34.59 | 22.86 | 12.79 | 6.34 | 4.60 | 7.61 |
| .72 | 56.56 | 57.58 | 53.75 | 45.55 | 34.48 | 22.75 | 12.70 | 6.30 | 4.60 | 7.66 |
| .73 | 56.59 | 57.57 | 53.69 | 45.45 | 34.36 | 22.63 | 12.62 | 6.26 | 4.61 | 7.72 |
| .74 | 56.63 | 57.55 | 53.63 | 45.35 | 34.25 | 22.52 | 12.53 | 6.22 | 4.61 | 7.77 |
| .75 | 56.66 | 57.54 | 53.57 | 45.25 | 34.13 | 22.41 | 12.45 | 6.18 | 4.62 | 7.82 |
| .76 | 56.69 | 57.52 | 53.50 | 45.15 | 34.01 | 22.30 | 12.37 | 6.14 | 4.63 | 7.87 |
| .77 | 56.72 | 57.50 | 53.44 | 45.05 | 33.89 | 22.19 | 12.29 | 6.10 | 4.64 | 7.93 |
| .78 | 56.75 | 57.49 | 53.37 | 44.94 | 33.78 | 22.07 | 12.20 | 6.06 | 4.65 | 7.98 |
| .79 | 56.78 | 57.47 | 53.31 | 44.84 | 33.66 | 21.96 | 12.12 | 6.02 | 4.66 | 8.04 |
| .80 | 56.81 | 57.45 | 53.24 | 44.74 | 33.54 | 21.85 | 12.04 | 5.98 | 4.67 | 8.10 |
| .81 | 56.84 | 57.43 | 53.17 | 44.64 | 33.42 | 21.74 | 11.96 | 5.94 | 4.68 | 8.16 |
| .82 | 56.87 | 57.41 | 53.10 | 44.54 | 33.30 | 21.63 | 11.88 | 5.91 | 4.70 | 8.21 |
| .83 | 56.90 | 57.39 | 53.04 | 44.43 | 33.18 | 21.52 | 11.79 | 5.87 | 4.71 | 8.27 |
| .84 | 56.93 | 57.37 | 52.97 | 44.33 | 33.06 | 21.41 | 11.71 | 5.84 | 4.73 | 8.32 |
| .85 | 56.96 | 57.35 | 52.90 | 44.23 | 32.94 | 21.30 | 11.63 | 5.80 | 4.74 | 8.38 |
| .86 | 56.99 | 57.33 | 52.83 | 44.13 | 32.82 | 21.19 | 11.55 | 5.77 | 4.75 | 8.44 |
| .87 | 57.01 | 57.31 | 52.76 | 44.02 | 32.70 | 21.08 | 11.47 | 5.73 | 4.77 | 8.50 |
| .88 | 57.04 | 57.29 | 52.70 | 43.92 | 32.59 | 20.97 | 11.39 | 5.70 | 4.78 | 8.55 |
| .89 | 57.06 | 57.27 | 52.63 | 43.81 | 32.47 | 20.86 | 11.31 | 5.66 | 4.80 | 8.61 |
| .90 | 57.09 | 57.25 | 52.56 | 43.71 | 32.35 | 20.75 | 11.23 | 5.63 | 4.81 | 8.67 |
| .91 | 57.11 | 57.23 | 52.49 | 43.61 | 32.23 | 20.64 | 11.15 | 5.60 | 4.83 | 8.73 |
| .92 | 57.14 | 57.20 | 52.42 | 43.50 | 32.11 | 20.53 | 11.08 | 5.57 | 4.85 | 8.79 |
| .93 | 57.16 | 57.18 | 52.35 | 43.40 | 32.00 | 20.43 | 11.00 | 5.53 | 4.86 | 8.86 |
| .94 | 57.19 | 57.15 | 52.28 | 43.29 | 31.88 | 20.32 | 10.93 | 5.50 | 4.88 | 8.92 |
| .95 | 57.21 | 57.13 | 52.21 | 43.19 | 31.76 | 20.21 | 10.85 | 5.47 | 4.90 | 8.98 |
| .96 | 57.23 | 57.10 | 52.14 | 43.08 | 31.64 | 20.10 | 10.78 | 5.44 | 4.92 | 9.04 |
| .97 | 57.25 | 57.07 | 52.06 | 42.97 | 31.52 | 19.99 | 10.70 | 5.41 | 4.94 | 9.10 |
| .98 | 57.28 | 57.05 | 51.99 | 42.87 | 31.40 | 19.89 | 10.63 | 5.39 | 4.96 | 9.17 |
| .99 | 57.30 | 57.02 | 51.91 | 42.76 | 31.28 | 19.78 | 10.55 | 5.36 | 4.98 | 9.23 |
| 1.00 | 57.32 | 56.99 | 51.84 | 42.65 | 31.16 | 19.67 | 10.48 | 5.33 | 5.00 | 9.29 |

# TABLE VIII″. ARGUMENT 3.

Equation $= 31''.16 + 0''.345 \sin. t - 20''.808 \sin. 2t - 0''.023 \sin. 3t - 0''.65 \sin. 4t.$

Period, 29.530588 days.

| Days. | 20 | 21 | 22 | 23 | 24 | 25 | 26 | 27 | 28 | 29 |
|---|---|---|---|---|---|---|---|---|---|---|
| Days. | ″ | ″ | ″ | ″ | ″ | ″ | ″ | ″ | ″ | ″ |
| .00 | 9.29 | 17.23 | 27.39 | 38.16 | 47.89 | 54.99 | 58.14 | 56.54 | 50.21 | 40.18 |
| .01 | 9.35 | 17.32 | 27.50 | 38.26 | 47.98 | 55.04 | 58.15 | 56.50 | 50.12 | 40.07 |
| .02 | 9.42 | 17.42 | 27.61 | 38.37 | 48.06 | 55.09 | 58.16 | 56.46 | 50.04 | 39.95 |
| .03 | 9.48 | 17.51 | 27.71 | 38.47 | 48.15 | 55.15 | 58.16 | 56.41 | 49.95 | 39.84 |
| .04 | 9.55 | 17.61 | 27.82 | 38.58 | 48.23 | 55.20 | 58.17 | 56.37 | 49.87 | 39.72 |
| .05 | 9.61 | 17.70 | 27.93 | 38.68 | 48.32 | 55.25 | 58.18 | 56.33 | 49.78 | 39.61 |
| .06 | 9.68 | 17.79 | 28.04 | 38.79 | 48.40 | 55.30 | 58.18 | 56.29 | 49.69 | 39.50 |
| .07 | 9.74 | 17.89 | 28.14 | 38.89 | 48.49 | 55.35 | 58.19 | 56.24 | 49.60 | 39.38 |
| .08 | 9.81 | 17.98 | 28.25 | 39.00 | 48.57 | 55.40 | 58.19 | 56.20 | 49.52 | 39.27 |
| .09 | 9.87 | 18.08 | 28.35 | 39.10 | 48.66 | 55.45 | 58.20 | 56.15 | 49.43 | 39.15 |
| .10 | 9.94 | 18.17 | 28.46 | 39.21 | 48.74 | 55.50 | 58.20 | 56.11 | 49.34 | 39.04 |
| .11 | 10.01 | 18.27 | 28.57 | 39.31 | 48.82 | 55.55 | 58.20 | 56.06 | 49.25 | 38.92 |
| .12 | 10.08 | 18.36 | 28.68 | 39.42 | 48.91 | 55.60 | 58.21 | 56.02 | 49.16 | 38.81 |
| .13 | 10.14 | 18.46 | 28.78 | 39.52 | 48.99 | 55.64 | 58.21 | 55.97 | 49.08 | 38.69 |
| .14 | 10.21 | 18.55 | 28.89 | 39.63 | 49.08 | 55.69 | 58.22 | 55.93 | 48.99 | 38.58 |
| .15 | 10.28 | 18.65 | 29.00 | 39.73 | 49.16 | 55.74 | 58.22 | 55.88 | 48.90 | 38.46 |
| .16 | 10.35 | 18.75 | 29.11 | 39.83 | 49.24 | 55.79 | 58.22 | 55.83 | 48.81 | 38.34 |
| .17 | 10.42 | 18.84 | 29.22 | 39.93 | 49.32 | 55.83 | 58.22 | 55.78 | 48.72 | 38.23 |
| .18 | 10.49 | 18.94 | 29.33 | 40.04 | 49.41 | 55.88 | 58.22 | 55.73 | 48.63 | 38.11 |
| .19 | 10.56 | 19.03 | 29.44 | 40.14 | 49.49 | 55.92 | 58.22 | 55.68 | 48.54 | 38.00 |
| .20 | 10.63 | 19.13 | 29.55 | 40.24 | 49.57 | 55.97 | 58.22 | 55.63 | 48.45 | 37.88 |
| .21 | 10.70 | 19.23 | 29.66 | 40.34 | 49.65 | 56.01 | 58.22 | 55.58 | 48.36 | 37.76 |
| .22 | 10.77 | 19.33 | 29.77 | 40.44 | 49.73 | 56.06 | 58.22 | 55.53 | 48.27 | 37.65 |
| .23 | 10.84 | 19.42 | 29.87 | 40.55 | 49.81 | 56.10 | 58.21 | 55.48 | 48.17 | 37.53 |
| .24 | 10.91 | 19.52 | 29.98 | 40.65 | 49.89 | 56.15 | 58.21 | 55.43 | 48.08 | 37.42 |
| .25 | 10.98 | 19.62 | 30.09 | 40.75 | 49.97 | 56.19 | 58.21 | 55.38 | 47.99 | 37.30 |
| .26 | 11.05 | 19.72 | 30.20 | 40.85 | 50.05 | 56.23 | 58.20 | 55.33 | 47.89 | 37.18 |
| .27 | 11.13 | 19.82 | 30.31 | 40.95 | 50.13 | 56.27 | 58.20 | 55.27 | 47.80 | 37.06 |
| .28 | 11.20 | 19.91 | 30.41 | 41.06 | 50.20 | 56.32 | 58.19 | 55.22 | 47.70 | 36.95 |
| .29 | 11.28 | 20.01 | 30.52 | 41.16 | 50.28 | 56.36 | 58.19 | 55.16 | 47.61 | 36.83 |
| .30 | 11.35 | 20.11 | 30.63 | 41.26 | 50.36 | 56.40 | 58.18 | 55.11 | 47.52 | 36.71 |
| .31 | 11.42 | 20.21 | 30.74 | 41.36 | 50.44 | 56.44 | 58.17 | 55.05 | 47.42 | 36.59 |
| .32 | 11.50 | 20.31 | 30.85 | 41.46 | 50.52 | 56.48 | 58.16 | 55.00 | 47.33 | 36.47 |
| .33 | 11.57 | 20.41 | 30.95 | 41.57 | 50.59 | 56.52 | 58.16 | 54.94 | 47.23 | 36.36 |
| .34 | 11.65 | 20.51 | 31.06 | 41.67 | 50.67 | 56.56 | 58.15 | 54.89 | 47.14 | 36.24 |
| .35 | 11.72 | 20.61 | 31.17 | 41.77 | 50.75 | 56.60 | 58.14 | 54.83 | 47.04 | 36.12 |
| .36 | 11.80 | 20.71 | 31.28 | 41.87 | 50.83 | 56.64 | 58.13 | 54.77 | 46.94 | 36.00 |
| .37 | 11.87 | 20.81 | 31.39 | 41.97 | 50.90 | 56.68 | 58.12 | 54.71 | 46.84 | 35.88 |
| .38 | 11.95 | 20.91 | 31.50 | 42.07 | 50.98 | 56.71 | 58.11 | 54.66 | 46.75 | 35.77 |
| .39 | 12.02 | 21.01 | 31.61 | 42.17 | 51.05 | 56.75 | 58.10 | 54.60 | 46.65 | 35.65 |
| .40 | 12.10 | 21.11 | 31.72 | 42.27 | 51.13 | 56.79 | 58.09 | 54.54 | 46.55 | 35.53 |
| .41 | 12.18 | 21.21 | 31.83 | 42.37 | 51.20 | 56.82 | 58.08 | 54.48 | 46.45 | 35.41 |
| .42 | 12.26 | 21.31 | 31.93 | 42.47 | 51.28 | 56.86 | 58.07 | 54.42 | 46.35 | 35.29 |
| .43 | 12.33 | 21.42 | 32.04 | 42.56 | 51.35 | 56.89 | 58.05 | 54.36 | 46.26 | 35.18 |
| .44 | 12.41 | 21.52 | 32.15 | 42.66 | 51.43 | 56.93 | 58.04 | 54.30 | 46.16 | 35.06 |
| .45 | 12.49 | 21.62 | 32.26 | 42.76 | 51.50 | 56.96 | 58.03 | 54.24 | 46.06 | 34.94 |
| .46 | 12.57 | 21.72 | 32.37 | 42.86 | 51.57 | 56.99 | 58.02 | 54.18 | 45.96 | 34.82 |
| .47 | 12.65 | 21.82 | 32.48 | 42.96 | 51.64 | 57.02 | 58.00 | 54.12 | 45.86 | 34.70 |
| .48 | 12.72 | 21.93 | 32.58 | 43.05 | 51.72 | 57.06 | 57.99 | 54.05 | 45.76 | 34.58 |
| .49 | 12.80 | 22.03 | 32.69 | 43.15 | 51.79 | 57.09 | 57.97 | 53.99 | 45.66 | 34.46 |
| .50 | 12.88 | 22.13 | 32.80 | 43.25 | 51.86 | 57.13 | 57.96 | 53.93 | 45.55 | 34.34 |

# TABLE VIII″. ARGUMENT 3.

Equation $= 31''.16 + 0''.345 \sin. t - 20''.808 \sin. 2t - 0''.023 \sin. 3t - 0''.65 \sin. 4t$.

Period, 29.530588 days.

| Days. | 20 | 21 | 22 | 23 | 24 | 25 | 26 | 27 | 28 | 29 |
|---|---|---|---|---|---|---|---|---|---|---|
| Days. | ″ | ″ | ″ | ″ | ″ | ″ | ″ | ″ | ″ | ″ |
| .50 | 12.88 | 22.13 | 32.80 | 43.25 | 51.86 | 57.13 | 57.96 | 53.93 | 45.55 | 34.34 |
| .51 | 12.96 | 22.23 | 32.91 | 43.35 | 51.93 | 57.15 | 57.94 | 53.86 | 45.45 | 34.22 |
| .52 | 13.04 | 22.33 | 33.02 | 43.45 | 52.00 | 57.18 | 57.92 | 53.80 | 45.35 | 34.10 |
| .53 | 13.13 | 22.44 | 33.12 | 43.54 | 52.08 | 57.21 | 57.91 | 53.73 | 45.24 | 33.98 |
| .54 | 13.21 | 22.54 | 33.23 | 43.64 | 52.15 | 57.24 | 57.89 | 53.67 | 45.14 | 33.86 |
| .55 | 13.29 | 22.64 | 33.34 | 43.74 | 52.22 | 57.27 | 57.87 | 53.60 | 45.04 | 33.74 |
| .56 | 13.37 | 22.74 | 33.45 | 43.84 | 52.29 | 57.30 | 57.85 | 53.53 | 44.94 | 33.62 |
| .57 | 13.45 | 22.85 | 33.56 | 43.93 | 52.36 | 57.33 | 57.83 | 53.47 | 44.84 | 33.50 |
| .58 | 13.54 | 22.95 | 33.66 | 44.03 | 52.43 | 57.36 | 57.80 | 53.40 | 44.73 | 33.39 |
| .59 | 13.62 | 23.06 | 33.77 | 44.12 | 52.50 | 57.39 | 57.78 | 53.34 | 44.63 | 33.27 |
| .60 | 13.70 | 23.16 | 33.88 | 44.22 | 52.57 | 57.42 | 57.76 | 53.27 | 44.53 | 33.15 |
| .61 | 13.78 | 23.26 | 33.99 | 44.32 | 52.64 | 57.45 | 57.74 | 53.20 | 44.43 | 33.03 |
| .62 | 13.87 | 23.37 | 34.10 | 44.41 | 52.70 | 57.48 | 57.72 | 53.13 | 44.32 | 32.91 |
| .63 | 13.95 | 23.47 | 34.20 | 44.51 | 52.77 | 57.50 | 57.69 | 53.06 | 44.22 | 32.79 |
| .64 | 14.04 | 23.58 | 34.31 | 44.60 | 52.83 | 57.53 | 57.67 | 52.99 | 44.11 | 32.67 |
| .65 | 14.12 | 23.68 | 34.42 | 44.70 | 52.90 | 57.56 | 57.65 | 52.92 | 44.01 | 32.55 |
| .66 | 14.20 | 23.78 | 34.53 | 44.79 | 52.96 | 57.58 | 57.63 | 52.85 | 43.90 | 32.43 |
| .67 | 14.29 | 23.89 | 34.64 | 44.89 | 53.03 | 57.61 | 57.60 | 52.78 | 43.80 | 32.31 |
| .68 | 14.37 | 23.99 | 34.74 | 44.98 | 53.09 | 57.63 | 57.58 | 52.70 | 43.69 | 32.18 |
| .69 | 14.46 | 24.10 | 34.85 | 45.08 | 53.16 | 57.66 | 57.55 | 52.63 | 43.59 | 32.06 |
| .70 | 14.54 | 24.20 | 34.96 | 45.17 | 53.22 | 57.68 | 57.53 | 52.56 | 43.48 | 31.94 |
| .71 | 14.63 | 24.31 | 35.07 | 45.26 | 53.28 | 57.70 | 57.50 | 52.49 | 43.37 | 31.82 |
| .72 | 14.71 | 24.41 | 35.18 | 45.36 | 53.35 | 57.72 | 57.48 | 52.42 | 43.26 | 31.70 |
| .73 | 14.80 | 24.52 | 35.28 | 45.45 | 53.41 | 57.74 | 57.45 | 52.34 | 43.16 | 31.58 |
| .74 | 14.88 | 24.62 | 35.39 | 45.55 | 53.48 | 57.76 | 57.43 | 52.27 | 43.05 | 31.46 |
| .75 | 14.97 | 24.73 | 35.50 | 45.64 | 53.54 | 57.78 | 57.40 | 52.20 | 42.94 | 31.34 |
| .76 | 15.06 | 24.84 | 35.61 | 45.73 | 53.60 | 57.80 | 57.37 | 52.12 | 42.83 | 31.22 |
| .77 | 15.15 | 24.94 | 35.72 | 45.82 | 53.66 | 57.82 | 57.34 | 52.05 | 42.72 | 31.10 |
| .78 | 15.23 | 25.05 | 35.82 | 45.92 | 53.73 | 57.83 | 57.32 | 51.97 | 42.62 | 30.98 |
| .79 | 15.32 | 25.15 | 35.93 | 46.01 | 53.79 | 57.85 | 57.29 | 51.90 | 42.51 | 30.86 |
| .80 | 15.41 | 25.26 | 36.04 | 46.10 | 53.85 | 57.87 | 57.26 | 51.82 | 42.40 | 30.74 |
| .81 | 15.50 | 25.37 | 36.15 | 46.19 | 53.91 | 57.89 | 57.23 | 51.74 | 42.29 | 30.62 |
| .82 | 15.59 | 25.47 | 36.25 | 46.28 | 53.97 | 57.91 | 57.20 | 51.66 | 42.18 | 30.50 |
| .83 | 15.68 | 25.58 | 36.36 | 46.38 | 54.03 | 57.92 | 57.16 | 51.59 | 42.07 | 30.38 |
| .84 | 15.77 | 25.68 | 36.46 | 46.47 | 54.09 | 57.94 | 57.13 | 51.51 | 41.96 | 30.26 |
| .85 | 15.86 | 25.79 | 36.57 | 46.56 | 54.15 | 57.96 | 57.10 | 51.43 | 41.85 | 30.14 |
| .86 | 15.95 | 25.90 | 36.68 | 46.65 | 54.21 | 57.97 | 57.06 | 51.35 | 41.74 | 30.02 |
| .87 | 16.04 | 26.00 | 36.78 | 46.74 | 54.27 | 57.99 | 57.03 | 51.27 | 41.63 | 29.90 |
| .88 | 16.13 | 26.11 | 36.89 | 46.83 | 54.32 | 58.00 | 56.99 | 51.19 | 41.52 | 29.78 |
| .89 | 16.22 | 26.21 | 36.99 | 46.92 | 54.38 | 58.02 | 56.96 | 51.11 | 41.41 | 29.66 |
| .90 | 16.31 | 26.32 | 37.10 | 47.01 | 54.44 | 58.03 | 56.92 | 51.03 | 41.30 | 29.54 |
| .91 | 16.40 | 26.43 | 37.21 | 47.10 | 54.50 | 58.04 | 56.88 | 50.95 | 41.19 | 29.42 |
| .92 | 16.49 | 26.53 | 37.31 | 47.19 | 54.55 | 58.05 | 56.84 | 50.87 | 41.08 | 29.30 |
| .93 | 16.59 | 26.64 | 37.42 | 47.27 | 54.61 | 58.07 | 56.81 | 50.79 | 40.96 | 29.18 |
| .94 | 16.68 | 26.74 | 37.52 | 47.36 | 54.66 | 58.08 | 56.77 | 50.71 | 40.85 | 29.06 |
| .95 | 16.77 | 26.85 | 37.63 | 47.45 | 54.72 | 58.09 | 56.73 | 50.63 | 40.74 | 28.94 |
| .96 | 16.86 | 26.96 | 37.74 | 47.54 | 54.77 | 58.10 | 56.69 | 50.55 | 40.63 | 28.82 |
| .97 | 16.95 | 27.07 | 37.84 | 47.63 | 54.83 | 58.11 | 56.65 | 50.46 | 40.52 | 28.70 |
| .98 | 17.05 | 27.17 | 37.95 | 47.71 | 54.88 | 58.12 | 56.62 | 50.38 | 40.40 | 28.58 |
| .99 | 17.14 | 27.28 | 38.05 | 47.80 | 54.94 | 58.13 | 56.58 | 50.29 | 40.29 | 28.46 |
| 1.00 | 17.23 | 27.39 | 38.16 | 47.89 | 54.99 | 58.14 | 56.54 | 50.21 | 40.18 | 28.34 |

# TABLES XI″. XII″.

Tables XI″. — Arguments 6.

| Days. | 0 | 10 | 20 | 30 |
|---|---|---|---|---|
| 0.0 | 0.84 | 0.35 | 0.02 | 0.65 |
| 0.1 | 0.84 | 0.34 | 0.02 | 0.65 |
| 0.2 | 0.84 | 0.33 | 0.03 | 0.66 |
| 0.3 | 0.84 | 0.33 | 0.03 | 0.66 |
| 0.4 | 0.84 | 0.32 | 0.03 | 0.67 |
| 0.5 | 0.84 | 0.31 | 0.04 | 0.68 |
| 0.6 | 0.84 | 0.30 | 0.04 | 0.68 |
| 0.7 | 0.84 | 0.30 | 0.04 | 0.69 |
| 0.8 | 0.84 | 0.29 | 0.05 | 0.69 |
| 0.9 | 0.84 | 0.28 | 0.05 | 0.70 |
| 1.0 | 0.84 | 0.27 | 0.05 | 0.70 |
| 1.1 | 0.84 | 0.26 | 0.06 | 0.71 |
| 1.2 | 0.84 | 0.25 | 0.06 | 0.71 |
| 1.3 | 0.83 | 0.25 | 0.07 | 0.72 |
| 1.4 | 0.83 | 0.24 | 0.07 | 0.72 |
| 1.5 | 0.83 | 0.23 | 0.07 | 0.73 |
| 1.6 | 0.83 | 0.23 | 0.08 | 0.73 |
| 1.7 | 0.83 | 0.22 | 0.08 | 0.74 |
| 1.8 | 0.82 | 0.21 | 0.08 | 0.74 |
| 1.9 | 0.82 | 0.21 | 0.09 | 0.75 |
| 2.0 | 0.82 | 0.20 | 0.09 | 0.75 |
| 2.1 | 0.82 | 0.19 | 0.10 | 0.76 |
| 2.2 | 0.81 | 0.19 | 0.10 | 0.76 |
| 2.3 | 0.81 | 0.18 | 0.11 | 0.77 |
| 2.4 | 0.81 | 0.18 | 0.11 | 0.77 |
| 2.5 | 0.80 | 0.17 | 0.12 | 0.78 |
| 2.6 | 0.80 | 0.16 | 0.12 | 0.78 |
| 2.7 | 0.80 | 0.16 | 0.13 | 0.78 |
| 2.8 | 0.79 | 0.15 | 0.13 | 0.79 |
| 2.9 | 0.79 | 0.15 | 0.14 | 0.79 |
| 3.0 | 0.79 | 0.14 | 0.14 | 0.79 |
| 3.1 | 0.78 | 0.14 | 0.15 | 0.80 |
| 3.2 | 0.78 | 0.13 | 0.15 | 0.80 |
| 3.3 | 0.77 | 0.13 | 0.16 | 0.80 |
| 3.4 | 0.77 | 0.12 | 0.16 | 0.81 |
| 3.5 | 0.77 | 0.12 | 0.17 | 0.81 |
| 3.6 | 0.76 | 0.11 | 0.18 | 0.81 |
| 3.7 | 0.76 | 0.11 | 0.18 | 0.82 |
| 3.8 | 0.75 | 0.10 | 0.19 | 0.82 |
| 3.9 | 0.75 | 0.10 | 0.20 | 0.82 |
| 4.0 | 0.75 | 0.09 | 0.20 | 0.82 |
| 4.1 | 0.74 | 0.09 | 0.21 | 0.83 |
| 4.2 | 0.74 | 0.08 | 0.21 | 0.83 |
| 4.3 | 0.73 | 0.08 | 0.22 | 0.83 |
| 4.4 | 0.73 | 0.07 | 0.23 | 0.83 |
| 4.5 | 0.72 | 0.07 | 0.23 | 0.83 |
| 4.6 | 0.72 | 0.06 | 0.24 | 0.84 |
| 4.7 | 0.71 | 0.06 | 0.25 | 0.84 |
| 4.8 | 0.71 | 0.06 | 0.26 | 0.84 |
| 4.9 | 0.70 | 0.05 | 0.27 | 0.84 |
| 5.0 | 0.70 | 0.05 | 0.27 | 0.84 |

Tables XII″. — Arguments 7.

| Days. | 0 | 1 | 2 | 3 | 4 | Days. |
|---|---|---|---|---|---|---|
| .00 | 10.19 | 9.55 | 7.06 | 3.79 | 1.06 | 1.00 |
| .01 | 10.19 | 9.53 | 7.03 | 3.76 | 1.04 | .99 |
| .02 | 10.20 | 9.51 | 7.00 | 3.72 | 1.02 | .98 |
| .03 | 10.20 | 9.50 | 6.97 | 3.69 | 1.00 | .97 |
| .04 | 10.21 | 9.48 | 6.94 | 3.65 | 0.98 | .96 |
| .05 | 10.21 | 9.46 | 6.91 | 3.62 | 0.96 | .95 |
| .06 | 10.21 | 9.44 | 6.88 | 3.59 | 0.94 | .94 |
| .07 | 10.21 | 9.42 | 6.85 | 3.56 | 0.92 | .93 |
| .08 | 10.22 | 9.41 | 6.81 | 3.52 | 0.90 | .92 |
| .09 | 10.22 | 9.39 | 6.78 | 3.49 | 0.88 | .91 |
| .10 | 10.22 | 9.37 | 6.75 | 3.46 | 0.86 | .90 |
| .11 | 10.22 | 9.35 | 6.72 | 3.43 | 0.84 | .89 |
| .12 | 10.22 | 9.33 | 6.69 | 3.40 | 0.82 | .88 |
| .13 | 10.23 | 9.31 | 6.65 | 3.36 | 0.81 | .87 |
| .14 | 10.23 | 9.29 | 6.62 | 3.33 | 0.79 | .86 |
| .15 | 10.23 | 9.27 | 6.59 | 3.30 | 0.77 | .85 |
| .16 | 10.23 | 9.25 | 6.56 | 3.27 | 0.75 | .84 |
| .17 | 10.23 | 9.23 | 6.53 | 3.24 | 0.73 | .83 |
| .18 | 10.24 | 9.21 | 6.49 | 3.21 | 0.72 | .82 |
| .19 | 10.24 | 9.19 | 6.46 | 3.18 | 0.70 | .81 |
| .20 | 10.24 | 9.17 | 6.43 | 3.15 | 0.68 | .80 |
| .21 | 10.24 | 9.15 | 6.40 | 3.12 | 0.66 | .79 |
| .22 | 10.24 | 9.13 | 6.37 | 3.09 | 0.65 | .78 |
| .23 | 10.23 | 9.11 | 6.33 | 3.06 | 0.63 | .77 |
| .24 | 10.23 | 9.09 | 6.30 | 3.03 | 0.62 | .76 |
| .25 | 10.23 | 9.07 | 6.27 | 3.00 | 0.60 | .75 |
| .26 | 10.23 | 9.05 | 6.24 | 2.97 | 0.59 | .74 |
| .27 | 10.23 | 9.03 | 6.21 | 2.94 | 0.57 | .73 |
| .28 | 10.22 | 9.00 | 6.17 | 2.91 | 0.56 | .72 |
| .29 | 10.22 | 8.98 | 6.14 | 2.88 | 0.54 | .71 |
| .30 | 10.22 | 8.96 | 6.11 | 2.85 | 0.53 | .70 |
| .31 | 10.22 | 8.94 | 6.08 | 2.82 | 0.52 | .69 |
| .32 | 10.21 | 8.92 | 6.04 | 2.79 | 0.50 | .68 |
| .33 | 10.21 | 8.89 | 6.01 | 2.76 | 0.49 | .67 |
| .34 | 10.21 | 8.87 | 5.97 | 2.73 | 0.47 | .66 |
| .35 | 10.20 | 8.85 | 5.94 | 2.70 | 0.46 | .65 |
| .36 | 10.20 | 8.83 | 5.91 | 2.67 | 0.45 | .64 |
| .37 | 10.20 | 8.80 | 5.88 | 2.64 | 0.43 | .63 |
| .38 | 10.19 | 8.78 | 5.84 | 2.62 | 0.42 | .62 |
| .39 | 10.19 | 8.75 | 5.81 | 2.59 | 0.40 | .61 |
| .40 | 10.19 | 8.73 | 5.78 | 2.56 | 0.39 | .60 |
| .41 | 10.18 | 8.71 | 5.75 | 2.53 | 0.38 | .59 |
| .42 | 10.18 | 8.68 | 5.71 | 2.50 | 0.37 | .58 |
| .43 | 10.17 | 8.66 | 5.68 | 2.47 | 0.35 | .57 |
| .44 | 10.17 | 8.63 | 5.64 | 2.44 | 0.34 | .56 |
| .45 | 10.16 | 8.61 | 5.61 | 2.41 | 0.33 | .55 |
| .46 | 10.15 | 8.58 | 5.58 | 2.38 | 0.32 | .54 |
| .47 | 10.15 | 8.56 | 5.54 | 2.35 | 0.31 | .53 |
| .48 | 10.14 | 8.53 | 5.51 | 2.33 | 0.29 | .52 |
| .49 | 10.14 | 8.51 | 5.47 | 2.30 | 0.28 | .51 |
| .50 | 10.13 | 8.48 | 5.44 | 2.27 | 0.27 | .50 |
| Days. | 9 | 8 | 7 | 6 | 5 | Days. |

# TABLES XI″. XII″.

TABLES XI″. ARGUMENTS 6.

| Days. | 0 | 10 | 20 | 30 |
|---|---|---|---|---|
| 5.0 | ″0.70 | ″0.05 | ″0.27 | ″0.84 |
| 5.1 | 0.69 | 0.05 | 0.28 | 0.84 |
| 5.2 | 0.69 | 0.04 | 0.29 | 0.84 |
| 5.3 | 0.68 | 0.04 | 0.29 | 0.84 |
| 5.4 | 0.68 | 0.04 | 0.30 | 0.84 |
| 5.5 | 0.67 | 0.03 | 0.31 | 0.84 |
| 5.6 | 0.66 | 0.03 | 0.32 | 0.84 |
| 5.7 | 0.66 | 0.03 | 0.32 | 0.84 |
| 5.8 | 0.65 | 0.03 | 0.33 | 0.84 |
| 5.9 | 0.65 | 0.02 | 0.35 | 0.84 |
| 6.0 | 0.64 | 0.02 | 0.36 | 0.84 |
| 6.1 | 0.63 | 0.02 | 0.37 | 0.83 |
| 6.2 | 0.62 | 0.02 | 0.37 | 0.83 |
| 6.3 | 0.62 | 0.01 | 0.38 | 0.83 |
| 6.4 | 0.61 | 0.01 | 0.39 | 0.83 |
| 6.5 | 0.60 | 0.01 | 0.39 | 0.83 |
| 6.6 | 0.59 | 0.01 | 0.40 | 0.82 |
| 6.7 | 0.58 | 0.01 | 0.40 | 0.82 |
| 6.8 | 0.58 | 0.00 | 0.41 | 0.82 |
| 6.9 | 0.57 | 0.00 | 0.42 | 0.82 |
| 7.0 | 0.56 | 0.00 | 0.42 | 0.81 |
| 7.1 | 0.55 | 0.00 | 0.43 | 0.81 |
| 7.2 | 0.54 | 0.00 | 0.43 | 0.81 |
| 7.3 | 0.54 | 0.00 | 0.44 | 0.80 |
| 7.4 | 0.53 | 0.00 | 0.45 | 0.80 |
| 7.5 | 0.52 | 0.00 | 0.45 | 0.80 |
| 7.6 | 0.52 | 0.00 | 0.46 | 0.79 |
| 7.7 | 0.51 | 0.00 | 0.47 | 0.79 |
| 7.8 | 0.50 | 0.00 | 0.48 | 0.79 |
| 7.9 | 0.50 | 0.00 | 0.49 | 0.78 |
| 8.0 | 0.49 | 0.00 | 0.50 | 0.78 |
| 8.1 | 0.48 | 0.00 | 0.50 | 0.77 |
| 8.2 | 0.48 | 0.00 | 0.51 | 0.77 |
| 8.3 | 0.47 | 0.00 | 0.52 | 0.77 |
| 8.4 | 0.46 | 0.00 | 0.52 | 0.76 |
| 8.5 | 0.46 | 0.00 | 0.53 | 0.76 |
| 8.6 | 0.45 | 0.00 | 0.54 | 0.75 |
| 8.7 | 0.44 | 0.00 | 0.54 | 0.75 |
| 8.8 | 0.44 | 0.00 | 0.55 | 0.75 |
| 8.9 | 0.43 | 0.00 | 0.56 | 0.74 |
| 9.0 | 0.42 | 0.00 | 0.57 | 0.74 |
| 9.1 | 0.41 | 0.00 | 0.58 | 0.73 |
| 9.2 | 0.40 | 0.00 | 0.58 | 0.73 |
| 9.3 | 0.40 | 0.01 | 0.59 | 0.72 |
| 9.4 | 0.39 | 0.01 | 0.60 | 0.72 |
| 9.5 | 0.38 | 0.01 | 0.61 | 0.71 |
| 9.6 | 0.38 | 0.01 | 0.61 | 0.71 |
| 9.7 | 0.37 | 0.01 | 0.62 | 0.70 |
| 9.8 | 0.36 | 0.02 | 0.63 | 0.70 |
| 9.9 | 0.36 | 0.02 | 0.64 | 0.69 |
| 10.0 | 0.35 | 0.02 | 0.65 | 0.69 |

TABLES XII″. ARGUMENTS 7.

| Days. | 0 | 1 | 2 | 3 | 4 | Days. |
|---|---|---|---|---|---|---|
| .50 | ″10.13 | ″8.48 | ″5.44 | ″2.27 | ″0.27 | .50 |
| .51 | 10.12 | 8.45 | 5.41 | 2.24 | 0.26 | .49 |
| .52 | 10.11 | 8.43 | 5.37 | 2.21 | 0.25 | .48 |
| .53 | 10.11 | 8.40 | 5.34 | 2.19 | 0.24 | .47 |
| .54 | 10.10 | 8.38 | 5.30 | 2.16 | 0.23 | .46 |
| .55 | 10.09 | 8.35 | 5.27 | 2.13 | 0.22 | .45 |
| .56 | 10.08 | 8.32 | 5.24 | 2.10 | 0.21 | .44 |
| .57 | 10.07 | 8.30 | 5.20 | 2.08 | 0.20 | .43 |
| .58 | 10.07 | 8.27 | 5.17 | 2.05 | 0.20 | .42 |
| .59 | 10.06 | 8.25 | 5.13 | 2.03 | 0.19 | .41 |
| .60 | 10.05 | 8.22 | 5.10 | 2.00 | 0.18 | .40 |
| .61 | 10.04 | 8.19 | 5.07 | 1.97 | 0.17 | .39 |
| .62 | 10.03 | 8.17 | 5.04 | 1.95 | 0.16 | .38 |
| .63 | 10.03 | 8.14 | 5.00 | 1.92 | 0.16 | .37 |
| .64 | 10.02 | 8.12 | 4.97 | 1.90 | 0.15 | .36 |
| .65 | 10.01 | 8.09 | 4.94 | 1.87 | 0.14 | .35 |
| .66 | 10.00 | 8.06 | 4.91 | 1.84 | 0.13 | .34 |
| .67 | 9.99 | 8.03 | 4.87 | 1.82 | 0.12 | .33 |
| .68 | 9.98 | 8.01 | 4.84 | 1.79 | 0.12 | .32 |
| .69 | 9.97 | 7.98 | 4.80 | 1.77 | 0.11 | .31 |
| .70 | 9.96 | 7.95 | 4.77 | 1.74 | 0.10 | .30 |
| .71 | 9.95 | 7.92 | 4.74 | 1.72 | 0.09 | .29 |
| .72 | 9.94 | 7.89 | 4.71 | 1.69 | 0.09 | .28 |
| .73 | 9.92 | 7.87 | 4.67 | 1.67 | 0.08 | .27 |
| .74 | 9.91 | 7.84 | 4.64 | 1.64 | 0.08 | .26 |
| .75 | 9.90 | 7.81 | 4.61 | 1.62 | 0.07 | .25 |
| .76 | 9.89 | 7.78 | 4.58 | 1.60 | 0.07 | .24 |
| .77 | 9.88 | 7.75 | 4.54 | 1.57 | 0.06 | .23 |
| .78 | 9.86 | 7.72 | 4.51 | 1.55 | 0.06 | .22 |
| .79 | 9.85 | 7.69 | 4.47 | 1.52 | 0.05 | .21 |
| .80 | 9.84 | 7.66 | 4.44 | 1.50 | 0.05 | .20 |
| .81 | 9.83 | 7.63 | 4.41 | 1.48 | 0.05 | .19 |
| .82 | 9.81 | 7.60 | 4.38 | 1.45 | 0.05 | .18 |
| .83 | 9.80 | 7.58 | 4.34 | 1.43 | 0.04 | .17 |
| .84 | 9.78 | 7.55 | 4.31 | 1.40 | 0.04 | .16 |
| .85 | 9.77 | 7.52 | 4.28 | 1.38 | 0.04 | .15 |
| .86 | 9.76 | 7.49 | 4.25 | 1.36 | 0.03 | .14 |
| .87 | 9.74 | 7.46 | 4.21 | 1.34 | 0.03 | .13 |
| .88 | 9.73 | 7.43 | 4.18 | 1.31 | 0.03 | .12 |
| .89 | 9.71 | 7.40 | 4.14 | 1.29 | 0.02 | .11 |
| .90 | 9.70 | 7.37 | 4.11 | 1.27 | 0.02 | .10 |
| .91 | 9.69 | 7.34 | 4.08 | 1.25 | 0.02 | .09 |
| .92 | 9.67 | 7.31 | 4.05 | 1.23 | 0.02 | .08 |
| .93 | 9.66 | 7.28 | 4.01 | 1.20 | 0.01 | .07 |
| .94 | 9.64 | 7.25 | 3.98 | 1.18 | 0.01 | .06 |
| .95 | 9.63 | 7.22 | 3.95 | 1.16 | 0.01 | .05 |
| .96 | 9.61 | 7.19 | 3.92 | 1.14 | 0.01 | .04 |
| .97 | 9.60 | 7.16 | 3.89 | 1.12 | 0.01 | .03 |
| .98 | 9.58 | 7.12 | 3.85 | 1.10 | 0.00 | .02 |
| .99 | 9.57 | 7.09 | 3.82 | 1.08 | 0.00 | .01 |
| 1.00 | 9.55 | 7.06 | 3.79 | 1.06 | 0.00 | .00 |
| Days. | 9 | 8 | 7 | 6 | 5 | Days. |

# TABLES XIII″. - XV″.

| Tables | XIII″. | | XIV″. | | | XV″. | | |
|---|---|---|---|---|---|---|---|---|
| Arguments | **8.** | | **9.** | | | **10.** | | |
| Days. | **0** | **10** | **0** | **10** | **20** | **0** | **10** | **20** |
| Days. 0.0 | 3″.44 | 0″.55 | 0″.82 | 0″.21 | 0″.21 | 0″.00 | 0″.72 | 0″.35 |
| 0.1 | 3.45 | 0.60 | 0.82 | 0.20 | 0.22 | 0.00 | 0.73 | 0.34 |
| 0.2 | 3.45 | 0.66 | 0.82 | 0.19 | 0.23 | 0.00 | 0.74 | 0.33 |
| 0.3 | 3.46 | 0.71 | 0.82 | 0.19 | 0.23 | 0.00 | 0.74 | 0.32 |
| 0.4 | 3.46 | 0.77 | 0.82 | 0.18 | 0.24 | 0.00 | 0.75 | 0.31 |
| 0.5 | 3.46 | 0.83 | 0.82 | 0.17 | 0.25 | 0.00 | 0.75 | 0.30 |
| 0.6 | 3.45 | 0.89 | 0.82 | 0.16 | 0.26 | 0.00 | 0.76 | 0.29 |
| 0.7 | 3.44 | 0.95 | 0.82 | 0.16 | 0.27 | 0.00 | 0.76 | 0.28 |
| 0.8 | 3.43 | 1.02 | 0.81 | 0.15 | 0.27 | 0.01 | 0.77 | 0.27 |
| 0.9 | 3.41 | 1.08 | 0.81 | 0.15 | 0.28 | 0.01 | 0.77 | 0.26 |
| 1.0 | 3.39 | 1.15 | 0.81 | 0.14 | 0.29 | 0.01 | 0.77 | 0.25 |
| 1.1 | 3.37 | 1.22 | 0.81 | 0.13 | 0.30 | 0.01 | 0.78 | 0.24 |
| 1.2 | 3.34 | 1.28 | 0.81 | 0.13 | 0.31 | 0.01 | 0.78 | 0.23 |
| 1.3 | 3.31 | 1.35 | 0.80 | 0.12 | 0.31 | 0.02 | 0.79 | 0.23 |
| 1.4 | 3.28 | 1.42 | 0.80 | 0.12 | 0.32 | 0.02 | 0.79 | 0.22 |
| 1.5 | 3.25 | 1.49 | 0.80 | 0.11 | 0.33 | 0.02 | 0.80 | 0.21 |
| 1.6 | 3.21 | 1.56 | 0.80 | 0.10 | 0.34 | 0.02 | 0.80 | 0.20 |
| 1.7 | 3.18 | 1.63 | 0.80 | 0.10 | 0.35 | 0.03 | 0.80 | 0.19 |
| 1.8 | 3.14 | 1.70 | 0.79 | 0.09 | 0.36 | 0.03 | 0.81 | 0.19 |
| 1.9 | 3.10 | 1.77 | 0.79 | 0.09 | 0.37 | 0.04 | 0.81 | 0.18 |
| 2.0 | 3.06 | 1.84 | 0.79 | 0.08 | 0.38 | 0.04 | 0.81 | 0.17 |
| 2.1 | 3.01 | 1.91 | 0.79 | 0.07 | 0.39 | 0.04 | 0.81 | 0.16 |
| 2.2 | 2.96 | 1.98 | 0.79 | 0.07 | 0.40 | 0.05 | 0.81 | 0.15 |
| 2.3 | 2.91 | 2.05 | 0.78 | 0.06 | 0.40 | 0.05 | 0.82 | 0.15 |
| 2.4 | 2.86 | 2.11 | 0.78 | 0.06 | 0.41 | 0.06 | 0.82 | 0.14 |
| 2.5 | 2.81 | 2.18 | 0.78 | 0.05 | 0.42 | 0.06 | 0.82 | 0.13 |
| 2.6 | 2.75 | 2.25 | 0.77 | 0.05 | 0.43 | 0.07 | 0.82 | 0.12 |
| 2.7 | 2.69 | 2.32 | 0.77 | 0.04 | 0.44 | 0.07 | 0.82 | 0.11 |
| 2.8 | 2.63 | 2.38 | 0.76 | 0.04 | 0.44 | 0.08 | 0.82 | 0.11 |
| 2.9 | 2.57 | 2.45 | 0.76 | 0.03 | 0.45 | 0.08 | 0.82 | 0.10 |
| 3.0 | 2.51 | 2.51 | 0.75 | 0.03 | 0.46 | 0.09 | 0.82 | 0.09 |
| 3.1 | 2.45 | 2.57 | 0.74 | 0.03 | 0.47 | 0.10 | 0.82 | 0.08 |
| 3.2 | 2.39 | 2.63 | 0.74 | 0.03 | 0.48 | 0.11 | 0.82 | 0.08 |
| 3.3 | 2.32 | 2.69 | 0.73 | 0.02 | 0.48 | 0.11 | 0.82 | 0.07 |
| 3.4 | 2.25 | 2.75 | 0.73 | 0.02 | 0.49 | 0.12 | 0.82 | 0.07 |
| 3.5 | 2.18 | 2.81 | 0.72 | 0.02 | 0.50 | 0.13 | 0.82 | 0.06 |
| 3.6 | 2.11 | 2.86 | 0.71 | 0.02 | 0.51 | 0.14 | 0.82 | 0.06 |
| 3.7 | 2.05 | 2.91 | 0.71 | 0.02 | 0.52 | 0.15 | 0.82 | 0.05 |
| 3.8 | 1.98 | 2.96 | 0.70 | 0.01 | 0.52 | 0.15 | 0.81 | 0.05 |
| 3.9 | 1.91 | 3.01 | 0.70 | 0.01 | 0.53 | 0.16 | 0.81 | 0.04 |
| 4.0 | 1.84 | 3.06 | 0.69 | 0.01 | 0.54 | 0.17 | 0.81 | 0.04 |
| 4.1 | 1.77 | 3.10 | 0.68 | 0.01 | 0.55 | 0.18 | 0.81 | 0.04 |
| 4.2 | 1.70 | 3.14 | 0.68 | 0.01 | 0.56 | 0.19 | 0.81 | 0.03 |
| 4.3 | 1.63 | 3.18 | 0.67 | 0.00 | 0.56 | 0.19 | 0.80 | 0.03 |
| 4.4 | 1.56 | 3.21 | 0.67 | 0.00 | 0.57 | 0.20 | 0.80 | 0.02 |
| 4.5 | 1.49 | 3.25 | 0.66 | 0.00 | 0.58 | 0.21 | 0.80 | 0.02 |
| 4.6 | 1.42 | 3.28 | 0.65 | 0.00 | 0.59 | 0.22 | 0.80 | 0.02 |
| 4.7 | 1.35 | 3.31 | 0.64 | 0.00 | 0.60 | 0.23 | 0.79 | 0.02 |
| 4.8 | 1.28 | 3.34 | 0.64 | 0.00 | 0.60 | 0.23 | 0.79 | 0.01 |
| 4.9 | 1.22 | 3.37 | 0.63 | 0.00 | 0.61 | 0.24 | 0.78 | 0.01 |
| 5.0 | 1.15 | 3.39 | 0.62 | 0.00 | 0.62 | 0.25 | 0.78 | 0.01 |

# TABLES XIII''. - XV''.

| Tables | XIII''. | | XIV''. | | | XV''. | | |
|---|---|---|---|---|---|---|---|---|
| Arguments | 8. | | 9. | | | 10. | | |
| Days. | 0 | 10 | 0 | 10 | 20 | 0 | 10 | 20 |
| Days. 5.0 | 1.15'' | 3.39'' | 0.62'' | 0.00'' | 0.62'' | 0.25'' | 0.78'' | 0.01'' |
| 5.1 | 1.08 | 3.41 | 0.61 | 0.00 | 0.63 | 0.26 | 0.78 | 0.01 |
| 5.2 | 1.02 | 3.43 | 0.60 | 0.00 | 0.64 | 0.27 | 0.77 | 0.01 |
| 5.3 | 0.95 | 3.44 | 0.60 | 0.00 | 0.64 | 0.28 | 0.77 | 0.00 |
| 5.4 | 0.89 | 3.45 | 0.59 | 0.00 | 0.65 | 0.29 | 0.76 | 0.00 |
| 5.5 | 0.83 | 3.46 | 0.58 | 0.00 | 0.66 | 0.30 | 0.75 | 0.00 |
| 5.6 | 0.77 | 3.46 | 0.57 | 0.00 | 0.67 | 0.31 | 0.74 | 0.00 |
| 5.7 | 0.71 | 3.46 | 0.56 | 0.00 | 0.67 | 0.32 | 0.74 | 0.00 |
| 5.8 | 0.66 | 3.45 | 0.56 | 0.01 | 0.68 | 0.33 | 0.73 | 0.00 |
| 5.9 | 0.60 | 3.45 | 0.55 | 0.01 | 0.68 | 0.34 | 0.73 | 0.00 |
| 6.0 | 0.55 | 3.44 | 0.54 | 0.01 | 0.69 | 0.35 | 0.72 | 0.00 |
| 6.1 | 0.50 | 3.43 | 0.53 | 0.01 | 0.70 | 0.36 | 0.71 | 0.00 |
| 6.2 | 0.45 | 3.41 | 0.52 | 0.01 | 0.70 | 0.37 | 0.70 | 0.00 |
| 6.3 | 0.41 | 3.40 | 0.52 | 0.02 | 0.71 | 0.38 | 0.70 | 0.00 |
| 6.4 | 0.36 | 3.38 | 0.51 | 0.02 | 0.71 | 0.39 | 0.69 | 0.00 |
| 6.5 | 0.32 | 3.36 | 0.50 | 0.02 | 0.72 | 0.40 | 0.68 | 0.00 |
| 6.6 | 0.28 | 3.33 | 0.49 | 0.02 | 0.73 | 0.41 | 0.67 | 0.00 |
| 6.7 | 0.25 | 3.30 | 0.48 | 0.02 | 0.73 | 0.42 | 0.66 | 0.00 |
| 6.8 | 0.21 | 3.27 | 0.48 | 0.03 | 0.74 | 0.43 | 0.66 | 0.01 |
| 6.9 | 0.18 | 3.24 | 0.47 | 0.03 | 0.74 | 0.44 | 0.65 | 0.01 |
| 7.0 | 0.15 | 3.20 | 0.46 | 0.03 | 0.75 | 0.45 | 0.64 | 0.01 |
| 7.1 | 0.12 | 3.17 | 0.45 | 0.03 | 0.75 | 0.46 | 0.63 | 0.01 |
| 7.2 | 0.10 | 3.13 | 0.44 | 0.04 | 0.76 | 0.47 | 0.62 | 0.02 |
| 7.3 | 0.08 | 3.09 | 0.43 | 0.04 | 0.76 | 0.48 | 0.62 | 0.02 |
| 7.4 | 0.06 | 3.05 | 0.42 | 0.05 | 0.77 | 0.49 | 0.61 | 0.03 |
| 7.5 | 0.04 | 3.00 | 0.41 | 0.05 | 0.77 | 0.50 | 0.60 | 0.03 |
| 7.6 | 0.03 | 2.95 | 0.40 | 0.06 | 0.77 | 0.51 | 0.59 | 0.04 |
| 7.7 | 0.02 | 2.90 | 0.39 | 0.06 | 0.78 | 0.52 | 0.58 | 0.04 |
| 7.8 | 0.01 | 2.85 | 0.39 | 0.07 | 0.78 | 0.53 | 0.57 | 0.05 |
| 7.9 | 0.00 | 2.80 | 0.38 | 0.07 | 0.79 | 0.54 | 0.56 | 0.05 |
| 8.0 | 0.00 | 2.74 | 0.37 | 0.08 | 0.79 | 0.55 | 0.55 | 0.06 |
| 8.1 | 0.00 | 2.68 | 0.36 | 0.09 | 0.79 | 0.56 | 0.54 | 0.07 |
| 8.2 | 0.01 | 2.62 | 0.35 | 0.10 | 0.80 | 0.57 | 0.53 | 0.07 |
| 8.3 | 0.02 | 2.56 | 0.35 | 0.10 | 0.80 | 0.58 | 0.52 | 0.08 |
| 8.4 | 0.03 | 2.50 | 0.34 | 0.11 | 0.80 | 0.59 | 0.51 | 0.08 |
| 8.5 | 0.04 | 2.44 | 0.33 | 0.11 | 0.80 | 0.60 | 0.50 | 0.09 |
| 8.6 | 0.06 | 2.37 | 0.32 | 0.12 | 0.80 | 0.61 | 0.49 | 0.10 |
| 8.7 | 0.08 | 2.31 | 0.31 | 0.12 | 0.81 | 0.62 | 0.48 | 0.10 |
| 8.8 | 0.10 | 2.24 | 0.31 | 0.13 | 0.81 | 0.62 | 0.47 | 0.11 |
| 8.9 | 0.12 | 2.17 | 0.30 | 0.13 | 0.81 | 0.63 | 0.46 | 0.11 |
| 9.0 | 0.15 | 2.10 | 0.29 | 0.14 | 0.81 | 0.64 | 0.45 | 0.12 |
| 9.1 | 0.18 | 2.04 | 0.28 | 0.15 | 0.81 | 0.65 | 0.44 | 0.13 |
| 9.2 | 0.21 | 1.97 | 0.27 | 0.15 | 0.81 | 0.66 | 0.43 | 0.14 |
| 9.3 | 0.25 | 1.90 | 0.27 | 0.16 | 0.82 | 0.66 | 0.42 | 0.14 |
| 9.4 | 0.28 | 1.83 | 0.26 | 0.16 | 0.82 | 0.67 | 0.41 | 0.15 |
| 9.5 | 0.32 | 1.76 | 0.25 | 0.17 | 0.82 | 0.68 | 0.40 | 0.16 |
| 9.6 | 0.36 | 1.69 | 0.24 | 0.18 | 0.82 | 0.69 | 0.39 | 0.17 |
| 9.7 | 0.41 | 1.62 | 0.23 | 0.19 | 0.82 | 0.70 | 0.38 | 0.18 |
| 9.8 | 0.45 | 1.55 | 0.23 | 0.19 | 0.82 | 0.70 | 0.37 | 0.19 |
| 9.9 | 0.50 | 1.48 | 0.22 | 0.20 | 0.82 | 0.71 | 0.36 | 0.20 |
| 10.0 | 0.55 | 1.41 | 0.21 | 0.21 | 0.82 | 0.72 | 0.35 | 0.21 |

# TABLES XVI''.-XX''.

| Tables | XVI''. | | | XVIII''. | XIX''. | | | XX''. | |
|---|---|---|---|---|---|---|---|---|---|
| Arguments | **11.** | | | **13.** | **14.** | | | **15.** | |
| Days. | **0** | **10** | **20** | **0** | **0** | **10** | **20** | **0** | **10** |
| Days. 0.0 | ″ 0.00 | ″ 0.46 | ″ 0.34 | ″ 1.68 | ″ 0.00 | ″ 0.12 | ″ 0.14 | ″ 0.03 | ″ 0.50 |
| 0.1 | 0.00 | 0.47 | 0.33 | 1.71 | 0.00 | 0.12 | 0.14 | 0.03 | 0.49 |
| 0.2 | 0.00 | 0.47 | 0.32 | 1.74 | 0.00 | 0.12 | 0.13 | 0.02 | 0.48 |
| 0.3 | 0.00 | 0.48 | 0.32 | 1.76 | 0.00 | 0.12 | 0.13 | 0.02 | 0.47 |
| 0.4 | 0.00 | 0.48 | 0.31 | 1.78 | 0.00 | 0.12 | 0.13 | 0.01 | 0.46 |
| 0.5 | 0.00 | 0.49 | 0.30 | 1.80 | 0.00 | 0.12 | 0.13 | 0.01 | 0.45 |
| 0.6 | 0.00 | 0.49 | 0.29 | 1.81 | 0.00 | 0.13 | 0.13 | 0.01 | 0.44 |
| 0.7 | 0.00 | 0.50 | 0.29 | 1.82 | 0.00 | 0.13 | 0.12 | 0.01 | 0.42 |
| 0.8 | 0.00 | 0.50 | 0.28 | 1.83 | 0.00 | 0.13 | 0.12 | 0.00 | 0.41 |
| 0.9 | 0.00 | 0.51 | 0.28 | 1.84 | 0.00 | 0.13 | 0.12 | 0.00 | 0.39 |
| 1.0 | 0.00 | 0.51 | 0.27 | 1.84 | 0.00 | 0.13 | 0.12 | 0.00 | 0.38 |
| 1.1 | 0.00 | 0.51 | 0.26 | 1.83 | 0.00 | 0.13 | 0.12 | 0.00 | 0.37 |
| 1.2 | 0.00 | 0.52 | 0.26 | 1.83 | 0.00 | 0.14 | 0.12 | 0.00 | 0.36 |
| 1.3 | 0.01 | 0.52 | 0.25 | 1.82 | 0.00 | 0.14 | 0.12 | 0.01 | 0.34 |
| 1.4 | 0.01 | 0.53 | 0.25 | 1.81 | 0.00 | 0.14 | 0.12 | 0.01 | 0.33 |
| 1.5 | 0.01 | 0.53 | 0.24 | 1.79 | 0.00 | 0.14 | 0.12 | 0.01 | 0.32 |
| 1.6 | 0.01 | 0.53 | 0.23 | 1.77 | 0.00 | 0.14 | 0.11 | 0.02 | 0.31 |
| 1.7 | 0.01 | 0.54 | 0.22 | 1.74 | 0.00 | 0.14 | 0.11 | 0.02 | 0.29 |
| 1.8 | 0.02 | 0.54 | 0.22 | 1.71 | 0.00 | 0.15 | 0.11 | 0.03 | 0.28 |
| 1.9 | 0.02 | 0.55 | 0.21 | 1.68 | 0.00 | 0.15 | 0.11 | 0.03 | 0.26 |
| 2.0 | 0.02 | 0.55 | 0.20 | 1.65 | 0.00 | 0.15 | 0.11 | 0.04 | 0.25 |
| 2.1 | 0.02 | 0.55 | 0.19 | 1.61 | 0.00 | 0.15 | 0.11 | 0.05 | 0.24 |
| 2.2 | 0.02 | 0.55 | 0.19 | 1.57 | 0.00 | 0.15 | 0.10 | 0.06 | 0.23 |
| 2.3 | 0.03 | 0.56 | 0.18 | 1.53 | 0.00 | 0.15 | 0.10 | 0.06 | 0.21 |
| 2.4 | 0.03 | 0.56 | 0.18 | 1.49 | 0.00 | 0.15 | 0.10 | 0.07 | 0.20 |
| 2.5 | 0.03 | 0.56 | 0.17 | 1.45 | 0.01 | 0.15 | 0.10 | 0.08 | 0.19 |
| 2.6 | 0.03 | 0.56 | 0.16 | 1.40 | 0.01 | 0.15 | 0.10 | 0.09 | 0.18 |
| 2.7 | 0.04 | 0.56 | 0.16 | 1.35 | 0.01 | 0.15 | 0.10 | 0.10 | 0.17 |
| 2.8 | 0.04 | 0.57 | 0.15 | 1.30 | 0.01 | 0.15 | 0.09 | 0.11 | 0.15 |
| 2.9 | 0.05 | 0.57 | 0.15 | 1.24 | 0.01 | 0.15 | 0.09 | 0.12 | 0.14 |
| 3.0 | 0.05 | 0.57 | 0.14 | 1.19 | 0.01 | 0.15 | 0.09 | 0.13 | 0.13 |
| 3.1 | 0.05 | 0.57 | 0.13 | 1.13 | 0.01 | 0.15 | 0.09 | 0.14 | 0.12 |
| 3.2 | 0.06 | 0.57 | 0.13 | 1.08 | 0.01 | 0.15 | 0.09 | 0.15 | 0.11 |
| 3.3 | 0.06 | 0.58 | 0.12 | 1.02 | 0.01 | 0.15 | 0.08 | 0.16 | 0.10 |
| 3.4 | 0.07 | 0.58 | 0.12 | 0.97 | 0.01 | 0.15 | 0.08 | 0.18 | 0.09 |
| 3.5 | 0.07 | 0.58 | 0.11 | 0.91 | 0.01 | 0.15 | 0.08 | 0.19 | 0.08 |
| 3.6 | 0.07 | 0.58 | 0.11 | 0.85 | 0.02 | 0.15 | 0.08 | 0.20 | 0.07 |
| 3.7 | 0.08 | 0.58 | 0.10 | 0.80 | 0.02 | 0.15 | 0.07 | 0.21 | 0.06 |
| 3.8 | 0.08 | 0.58 | 0.10 | 0.74 | 0.02 | 0.15 | 0.07 | 0.23 | 0.06 |
| 3.9 | 0.09 | 0.58 | 0.09 | 0.69 | 0.02 | 0.15 | 0.07 | 0.24 | 0.05 |
| 4.0 | 0.09 | 0.58 | 0.09 | 0.63 | 0.02 | 0.16 | 0.06 | 0.25 | 0.04 |
| 4.1 | 0.09 | 0.58 | 0.09 | 0.58 | 0.02 | 0.16 | 0.06 | 0.26 | 0.03 |
| 4.2 | 0.10 | 0.58 | 0.08 | 0.52 | 0.02 | 0.16 | 0.06 | 0.28 | 0.03 |
| 4.3 | 0.10 | 0.58 | 0.08 | 0.47 | 0.03 | 0.16 | 0.06 | 0.29 | 0.02 |
| 4.4 | 0.11 | 0.58 | 0.07 | 0.42 | 0.03 | 0.16 | 0.05 | 0.31 | 0.02 |
| 4.5 | 0.11 | 0.58 | 0.07 | 0.37 | 0.03 | 0.16 | 0.05 | 0.32 | 0.01 |
| 4.6 | 0.12 | 0.58 | 0.07 | 0.33 | 0.03 | 0.16 | 0.05 | 0.33 | 0.01 |
| 4.7 | 0.12 | 0.58 | 0.06 | 0.29 | 0.03 | 0.16 | 0.05 | 0.34 | 0.01 |
| 4.8 | 0.13 | 0.57 | 0.06 | 0.25 | 0.03 | 0.16 | 0.04 | 0.36 | 0.00 |
| 4.9 | 0.13 | 0.57 | 0.05 | 0.21 | 0.04 | 0.16 | 0.04 | 0.37 | 0.00 |
| 5.0 | 0.14 | 0.57 | 0.05 | 0.17 | 0.04 | 0.16 | 0.04 | 0.38 | 0.00 |

# TABLES XVI″. - XX″.

| Tables | XVI″. | | | XVIII″. | XIX″. | | | XX″. | |
|---|---|---|---|---|---|---|---|---|---|
| Arguments | **11.** | | | **13.** | **14.** | | | **15.** | |
| Days. | **0** | **10** | **20** | **0** | **0** | **10** | **20** | **0** | **10** |
| Days | ″ | ″ | ″ | ″ | ″ | ″ | ″ | ″ | ″ |
| 5.0 | 0.14 | 0.57 | 0.05 | 0.17 | 0.04 | 0.16 | 0.04 | 0.38 | 0.00 |
| 5.1 | 0.15 | 0.57 | 0.05 | 0.14 | 0.04 | 0.16 | 0.04 | 0.39 | 0.00 |
| 5.2 | 0.15 | 0.57 | 0.04 | 0.11 | 0.04 | 0.16 | 0.04 | 0.41 | 0.00 |
| 5.3 | 0.16 | 0.56 | 0.04 | 0.09 | 0.04 | 0.16 | 0.04 | 0.42 | 0.00 |
| 5.4 | 0.16 | 0.56 | 0.03 | 0.07 | 0.04 | 0.16 | 0.04 | 0.44 | 0.01 |
| 5.5 | 0.17 | 0.56 | 0.03 | 0.05 | 0.05 | 0.16 | 0.04 | 0.45 | 0.01 |
| 5.6 | 0.18 | 0.56 | 0.03 | 0.03 | 0.05 | 0.16 | 0.03 | 0.46 | 0.01 |
| 5.7 | 0.18 | 0.56 | 0.03 | 0.02 | 0.05 | 0.16 | 0.03 | 0.47 | 0.01 |
| 5.8 | 0.19 | 0.55 | 0.02 | 0.01 | 0.05 | 0.16 | 0.03 | 0.48 | 0.02 |
| 5.9 | 0.19 | 0.55 | 0.02 | 0.01 | 0.05 | 0.16 | 0.03 | 0.49 | 0.02 |
| 6.0 | 0.20 | 0.55 | 0.02 | 0.00 | 0.05 | 0.16 | 0.03 | 0.50 | 0.02 |
| 6.1 | 0.21 | 0.55 | 0.02 | 0.01 | 0.05 | 0.16 | 0.03 | 0.51 | 0.03 |
| 6.2 | 0.22 | 0.54 | 0.02 | 0.01 | 0.06 | 0.16 | 0.03 | 0.52 | 0.04 |
| 6.3 | 0.22 | 0.54 | 0.01 | 0.02 | 0.06 | 0.16 | 0.02 | 0.53 | 0.04 |
| 6.4 | 0.23 | 0.53 | 0.01 | 0.03 | 0.06 | 0.16 | 0.02 | 0.54 | 0.05 |
| 6.5 | 0.24 | 0 53 | 0.01 | 0.05 | 0.06 | 0.16 | 0.02 | 0.55 | 0.06 |
| 6.6 | 0.25 | 0.53 | 0.01 | 0.07 | 0.06 | 0.16 | 0.02 | 0.56 | 0.07 |
| 6.7 | 0.25 | 0.52 | 0.01 | 0.09 | 0.06 | 0.16 | 0.02 | 0.57 | 0.08 |
| 6.8 | 0.26 | 0.52 | 0.01 | 0.11 | 0.07 | 0.16 | 0.01 | 0.57 | 0.08 |
| 6.9 | 0.26 | 0.51 | 0.00 | 0.14 | 0.07 | 0.16 | 0.01 | 0.58 | 0.09 |
| 7.0 | 0.27 | 0.51 | 0.00 | 0.17 | 0.07 | 0.16 | 0.01 | 0.59 | 0.10 |
| 7.1 | 0.28 | 0.51 | 0.00 | 0.20 | 0.07 | 0.16 | 0.01 | 0.59 | 0.11 |
| 7.2 | 0.28 | 0.50 | 0.00 | 0.24 | 0.07 | 0.16 | 0.01 | 0.60 | 0.12 |
| 7.3 | 0.29 | 0.50 | 0.00 | 0.28 | 0.07 | 0.16 | 0.01 | 0.60 | 0.13 |
| 7.4 | 0.29 | 0.49 | 0.00 | 0.32 | 0.07 | 0.16 | 0.01 | 0.61 | 0.14 |
| 7.5 | 0.30 | 0.49 | 0.00 | 0.37 | 0.08 | 0.16 | 0.01 | 0.61 | 0.15 |
| 7.6 | 0.31 | 0.48 | 0.00 | 0.42 | 0.08 | 0.16 | 0.01 | 0.61 | 0.16 |
| 7.7 | 0.32 | 0.48 | 0.00 | 0.47 | 0.08 | 0.16 | 0.01 | 0.61 | 0.17 |
| 7.8 | 0.32 | 0.47 | 0.00 | 0.52 | 0.08 | 0.16 | 0.01 | 0.62 | 0.19 |
| 7.9 | 0.33 | 0.47 | 0.00 | 0.58 | 0.08 | 0.16 | 0.01 | 0.62 | 0.20 |
| 8.0 | 0.34 | 0.46 | 0.00 | 0.63 | 0.08 | 0.16 | 0.01 | 0.62 | 0.21 |
| 8.1 | 0.35 | 0.45 | 0.00 | 0.69 | 0.08 | 0.16 | 0.01 | 0.62 | 0.22 |
| 8.2 | 0.35 | 0.45 | 0.00 | 0.74 | 0.09 | 0.16 | 0.01 | 0.62 | 0.24 |
| 8.3 | 0.36 | 0.44 | 0.01 | 0.80 | 0.09 | 0.16 | 0.01 | 0.61 | 0.25 |
| 8.4 | 0.36 | 0.44 | 0.01 | 0.85 | 0.09 | 0.16 | 0.01 | 0.61 | 0.27 |
| 8.5 | 0.37 | 0.43 | 0.01 | 0.91 | 0.09 | 0.16 | 0.00 | 0.61 | 0.28 |
| 8.6 | 0.38 | 0.42 | 0.01 | 0.97 | 0.09 | 0.15 | 0.00 | 0.61 | 0.29 |
| 8.7 | 0.38 | 0.42 | 0.01 | 1.02 | 0.09 | 0.15 | 0.00 | 0.60 | 0.31 |
| 8.8 | 0.39 | 0.41 | 0.02 | 1.08 | 0.10 | 0.15 | 0.00 | 0.60 | 0.32 |
| 8.9 | 0.39 | 0.41 | 0.02 | 1.13 | 0.10 | 0.15 | 0.00 | 0.59 | 0.34 |
| 9.0 | 0.40 | 0.40 | 0.02 | 1.19 | 0.10 | 0.15 | 0.00 | 0.59 | 0.35 |
| 9.1 | 0.41 | 0.39 | 0.02 | 1.24 | 0.10 | 0.15 | 0.00 | 0.58 | 0.36 |
| 9.2 | 0.41 | 0.39 | 0.03 | 1.30 | 0.10 | 0.15 | 0.00 | 0.57 | 0.37 |
| 9.3 | 0.42 | 0.38 | 0.03 | 1.35 | 0.10 | 0.15 | 0.00 | 0.57 | 0.39 |
| 9.4 | 0.42 | 0.38 | 0.03 | 1.40 | 0.11 | 0.15 | 0.00 | 0.56 | 0.40 |
| 9.5 | 0.43 | 0.37 | 0.03 | 1.45 | 0.11 | 0.15 | 0.00 | 0.55 | 0.41 |
| 9.6 | 0.44 | 0.36 | 0.04 | 1.50 | 0.11 | 0.14 | 0.00 | 0.54 | 0.42 |
| 9.7 | 0.44 | 0.36 | 0.04 | 1.54 | 0.11 | 0.14 | 0.00 | 0.53 | 0.43 |
| 9.8 | 0.45 | 0.35 | 0.04 | 1.58 | 0.11 | 0.14 | 0.00 | 0.52 | 0.45 |
| 9.9 | 0.45 | 0.35 | 0.05 | 1.62 | 0.12 | 0.14 | 0.00 | 0.51 | 0.46 |
| 10.0 | 0.46 | 0.34 | 0.05 | 1.65 | 0.12 | 0.14 | 0.00 | 0.50 | 0.47 |

# TABLES XXI″. - XXV″.

| Tables | XXI″. | | XXII″. | | | XXIII″. | XXIV″. | | | XXV.″ | |
|---|---|---|---|---|---|---|---|---|---|---|---|
| Arguments | **16.** | | **17.** | | | **18.** | **19.** | | | **20.** | |
| Days. | **0** | **10** | **0** | **10** | **20** | **0** | **0** | **10** | **20** | **0** | **10** |
| Days. 0.0 | ″ 0.18 | ″ 1.15 | ″ 0.12 | ″ 0.03 | ″ 0.05 | ″ 0.70 | ″ 0.00 | ″ 0.09 | ″ 0.04 | ″ 0.22 | ″ 0.04 |
| 0.1 | 0.14 | 1.20 | 0.12 | 0.03 | 0.05 | 0.70 | 0.00 | 0.09 | 0.04 | 0.22 | 0.04 |
| 0.2 | 0.11 | 1.25 | 0.12 | 0.03 | 0.05 | 0.70 | 0.00 | 0.09 | 0.04 | 0.22 | 0.05 |
| 0.3 | 0.09 | 1.30 | 0.12 | 0.03 | 0.05 | 0.69 | 0.00 | 0.09 | 0.03 | 0.22 | 0.05 |
| 0.4 | 0.07 | 1.34 | 0.12 | 0.03 | 0.05 | 0.69 | 0.00 | 0.09 | 0.03 | 0.22 | 0.06 |
| 0.5 | 0.06 | 1.39 | 0.12 | 0.03 | 0.06 | 0.69 | 0.00 | 0.10 | 0.03 | 0.22 | 0.06 |
| 0.6 | 0.05 | 1.43 | 0.12 | 0.02 | 0.06 | 0.68 | 0.00 | 0.10 | 0.03 | 0.22 | 0.06 |
| 0.7 | 0.04 | 1.46 | 0.12 | 0.02 | 0.06 | 0.67 | 0.00 | 0.10 | 0.03 | 0.22 | 0.07 |
| 0.8 | 0.05 | 1.49 | 0.12 | 0.02 | 0.06 | 0.66 | 0.00 | 0.10 | 0.03 | 0.22 | 0.07 |
| 0.9 | 0.06 | 1.51 | 0.12 | 0.02 | 0.06 | 0.65 | 0.00 | 0.10 | 0.02 | 0.22 | 0.08 |
| 1.0 | 0.07 | 1.53 | 0.12 | 0.02 | 0.06 | 0.64 | 0.00 | 0.10 | 0.02 | 0.22 | 0.08 |
| 1.1 | 0.09 | 1.54 | 0.12 | 0.02 | 0.06 | 0.63 | 0.00 | 0.10 | 0.02 | 0.22 | 0.09 |
| 1.2 | 0.11 | 1.55 | 0.12 | 0.02 | 0.06 | 0.62 | 0.00 | 0.10 | 0.02 | 0.22 | 0.09 |
| 1.3 | 0.14 | 1.56 | 0.12 | 0.02 | 0.07 | 0.60 | 0.00 | 0.10 | 0.02 | 0.22 | 0.10 |
| 1.4 | 0.17 | 1.55 | 0.12 | 0.02 | 0.07 | 0.59 | 0.00 | 0.10 | 0.02 | 0.22 | 0.10 |
| 1.5 | 0.21 | 1.54 | 0.12 | 0.02 | 0.07 | 0.57 | 0.00 | 0.10 | 0.02 | 0.22 | 0.11 |
| 1.6 | 0.25 | 1.53 | 0.11 | 0.01 | 0.07 | 0.55 | 0.00 | 0.10 | 0.01 | 0.22 | 0.11 |
| 1.7 | 0.30 | 1.51 | 0.11 | 0.01 | 0.07 | 0.53 | 0.00 | 0.10 | 0.01 | 0.22 | 0.12 |
| 1.8 | 0.35 | 1.48 | 0.11 | 0.01 | 0.08 | 0.51 | 0.00 | 0.10 | 0.01 | 0.21 | 0.12 |
| 1.9 | 0.40 | 1.45 | 0.11 | 0.01 | 0.08 | 0.49 | 0.00 | 0.10 | 0.01 | 0.21 | 0.13 |
| 2.0 | 0.45 | 1.42 | 0.11 | 0.01 | 0.08 | 0.47 | 0.00 | 0.10 | 0.01 | 0.21 | 0.13 |
| 2.1 | 0.51 | 1.38 | 0.11 | 0.01 | 0.08 | 0.45 | 0.00 | 0.10 | 0.01 | 0.21 | 0.13 |
| 2.2 | 0.56 | 1.33 | 0.11 | 0.01 | 0.08 | 0.43 | 0.00 | 0.10 | 0.01 | 0.21 | 0.14 |
| 2.3 | 0.62 | 1.28 | 0.11 | 0.01 | 0.08 | 0.40 | 0.00 | 0.10 | 0.01 | 0.20 | 0.14 |
| 2.4 | 0.68 | 1.23 | 0.11 | 0.01 | 0.08 | 0.38 | 0.00 | 0.10 | 0.01 | 0.20 | 0.15 |
| 2.5 | 0.74 | 1.18 | 0.11 | 0.01 | 0.09 | 0.36 | 0.00 | 0.10 | 0.00 | 0.20 | 0.15 |
| 2.6 | 0.81 | 1.12 | 0.11 | 0.00 | 0.09 | 0.34 | 0.00 | 0.10 | 0.00 | 0.20 | 0.16 |
| 2.7 | 0.87 | 1.06 | 0.11 | 0.00 | 0.09 | 0.32 | 0.00 | 0.10 | 0.00 | 0.19 | 0.16 |
| 2.8 | 0.93 | 1.00 | 0.11 | 0.00 | 0.09 | 0.29 | 0.00 | 0.10 | 0.00 | 0.19 | 0.17 |
| 2.9 | 0.98 | 0.94 | 0.11 | 0.00 | 0.09 | 0.27 | 0.00 | 0.10 | 0.00 | 0.18 | 0.17 |
| 3.0 | 1.03 | 0.88 | 0.11 | 0.00 | 0.09 | 0.25 | 0.00 | 0.10 | 0.00 | 0.18 | 0.18 |
| 3.1 | 1.08 | 0.82 | 0.11 | 0.00 | 0.09 | 0.23 | 0.00 | 0.10 | 0.00 | 0.17 | 0.18 |
| 3.2 | 1.13 | 0.75 | 0.11 | 0.00 | 0.09 | 0.21 | 0.00 | 0.10 | 0.00 | 0.17 | 0.19 |
| 3.3 | 1.18 | 0.69 | 0.11 | 0.00 | 0.09 | 0.19 | 0.00 | 0.10 | 0.00 | 0.16 | 0.19 |
| 3.4 | 1.22 | 0.62 | 0.11 | 0.00 | 0.09 | 0.17 | 0.00 | 0.10 | 0.00 | 0.16 | 0.20 |
| 3.5 | 1.26 | 0.56 | 0.11 | 0.00 | 0.10 | 0.15 | 0.01 | 0.10 | 0.00 | 0.15 | 0.20 |
| 3.6 | 1.29 | 0.50 | 0.10 | 0.00 | 0.10 | 0.13 | 0.01 | 0.10 | 0.00 | 0.15 | 0.20 |
| 3.7 | 1.32 | 0.44 | 0.10 | 0.00 | 0.10 | 0.11 | 0.01 | 0.10 | 0.00 | 0.14 | 0.20 |
| 3.8 | 1.35 | 0.39 | 0.10 | 0.00 | 0.10 | 0.10 | 0.01 | 0.10 | 0.00 | 0.14 | 0.21 |
| 3.9 | 1.37 | 0.34 | 0.10 | 0.00 | 0.10 | 0.08 | 0.01 | 0.10 | 0.00 | 0.13 | 0.21 |
| 4.0 | 1.39 | 0.29 | 0.10 | 0.00 | 0.10 | 0.07 | 0.01 | 0.10 | 0.00 | 0.13 | 0.21 |
| 4.1 | 1.40 | 0.25 | 0.10 | 0.00 | 0.10 | 0.05 | 0.01 | 0.10 | 0.00 | 0.13 | 0.21 |
| 4.2 | 1.40 | 0.21 | 0.10 | 0.00 | 0.10 | 0.04 | 0.01 | 0.10 | 0.00 | 0.12 | 0.21 |
| 4.3 | 1.41 | 0.17 | 0.10 | 0.00 | 0.10 | 0.03 | 0.01 | 0.10 | 0.00 | 0.12 | 0.22 |
| 4.4 | 1.41 | 0.13 | 0.10 | 0.00 | 0.10 | 0.02 | 0.01 | 0.10 | 0.00 | 0.11 | 0.22 |
| 4.5 | 1.40 | 0.10 | 0.10 | 0.00 | 0.10 | 0.01 | 0.01 | 0.10 | 0.00 | 0.11 | 0.22 |
| 4.6 | 1.39 | 0.08 | 0.09 | 0.00 | 0.11 | 0.01 | 0.02 | 0.10 | 0.00 | 0.10 | 0.22 |
| 4.7 | 1.37 | 0.07 | 0.09 | 0.00 | 0.11 | 0.01 | 0.02 | 0.10 | 0.00 | 0.10 | 0.22 |
| 4.8 | 1.34 | 0.06 | 0.09 | 0.00 | 0.11 | 0.00 | 0.02 | 0.10 | 0.00 | 0.09 | 0.22 |
| 4.9 | 1.31 | 0.05 | 0.09 | 0.00 | 0.11 | 0.00 | 0.02 | 0.10 | 0.00 | 0.09 | 0.22 |
| 5.0 | 1.28 | 0.05 | 0.09 | 0.00 | 0.11 | 0.00 | 0.02 | 0.10 | 0.00 | 0.08 | 0.22 |

# TABLES XXI″. - XXV″.

| Tables | XXI″. | | XXII″. | | | XXIII″. | XXIV″. | | | XXV.″ | |
|---|---|---|---|---|---|---|---|---|---|---|---|
| Arguments | **16.** | | **17.** | | | **18.** | **19.** | | | **20.** | |
| Days. | **0** | **10** | **0** | **10** | **20** | **0** | **0** | **10** | **20** | **0** | **10** |
| Days. | ″ | ″ | ″ | ″ | ″ | ″ | ″ | ″ | ″ | ″ | ″ |
| 5.0 | 1.28 | 0.05 | 0.09 | 0.00 | 0.11 | 0.00 | 0.02 | 0.10 | 0.00 | 0.08 | 0.22 |
| 5.1 | 1.25 | 0.05 | 0.09 | 0.00 | 0.11 | 0.00 | 0.02 | 0.10 | 0.00 | 0.08 | 0.22 |
| 5.2 | 1.21 | 0.06 | 0.09 | 0.00 | 0.11 | 0.00 | 0.03 | 0.10 | 0.00 | 0.07 | 0.22 |
| 5.3 | 1.17 | 0.07 | 0.09 | 0.00 | 0.11 | 0.01 | 0.03 | 0.09 | 0.00 | 0.07 | 0.22 |
| 5.4 | 1.12 | 0.09 | 0.09 | 0.00 | 0.11 | 0.01 | 0.03 | 0.09 | 0.00 | 0.06 | 0.22 |
| 5.5 | 1.07 | 0.12 | 0.08 | 0.01 | 0.11 | 0.01 | 0.03 | 0.09 | 0.00 | 0.06 | 0.22 |
| 5.6 | 1.02 | 0.15 | 0.08 | 0.01 | 0.11 | 0.02 | 0.03 | 0.09 | 0.00 | 0.06 | 0.22 |
| 5.7 | 0.97 | 0.19 | 0.08 | 0.01 | 0.11 | 0.03 | 0.04 | 0.09 | 0.00 | 0.05 | 0.22 |
| 5.8 | 0.91 | 0.23 | 0.08 | 0.01 | 0.11 | 0.04 | 0.04 | 0.09 | 0.00 | 0.05 | 0.22 |
| 5.9 | 0.85 | 0.27 | 0.08 | 0.01 | 0.11 | 0.06 | 0.04 | 0.09 | 0.00 | 0.04 | 0.22 |
| 6.0 | 0.80 | 0.32 | 0.08 | 0.01 | 0.11 | 0.07 | 0.04 | 0.09 | 0.00 | 0.04 | 0.22 |
| 6.1 | 0.75 | 0.37 | 0.08 | 0.01 | 0.11 | 0.08 | 0.04 | 0.09 | 0.00 | 0.04 | 0.22 |
| 6.2 | 0.69 | 0.42 | 0.08 | 0.01 | 0.11 | 0.10 | 0.04 | 0.09 | 0.00 | 0.03 | 0.22 |
| 6.3 | 0.63 | 0.48 | 0.07 | 0.01 | 0.11 | 0.11 | 0.04 | 0.09 | 0.00 | 0.03 | 0.21 |
| 6.4 | 0.58 | 0.53 | 0.07 | 0.01 | 0.11 | 0.13 | 0.04 | 0.08 | 0.00 | 0.02 | 0.21 |
| 6.5 | 0.53 | 0.59 | 0.07 | 0.01 | 0.11 | 0.15 | 0.05 | 0.08 | 0.00 | 0.02 | 0.21 |
| 6.6 | 0.48 | 0.65 | 0.07 | 0.02 | 0.12 | 0.17 | 0.05 | 0.08 | 0.00 | 0.02 | 0.21 |
| 6.7 | 0.44 | 0.71 | 0.07 | 0.02 | 0.12 | 0.19 | 0.05 | 0.08 | 0.00 | 0.02 | 0.20 |
| 6.8 | 0.40 | 0.77 | 0.07 | 0.02 | 0.12 | 0.21 | 0.05 | 0.08 | 0.00 | 0.01 | 0.20 |
| 6.9 | 0.36 | 0.84 | 0.06 | 0.02 | 0.12 | 0.23 | 0.05 | 0.08 | 0.00 | 0.01 | 0.19 |
| 7.0 | 0.32 | 0.90 | 0.06 | 0.02 | 0.12 | 0.25 | 0.05 | 0.08 | 0.00 | 0.01 | 0.19 |
| 7.1 | 0.29 | 0.96 | 0.06 | 0.02 | 0.12 | 0.27 | 0.05 | 0.08 | 0.00 | 0.01 | 0.19 |
| 7.2 | 0.26 | 1.01 | 0.06 | 0.02 | 0.12 | 0.29 | 0.06 | 0.08 | 0.00 | 0.01 | 0.18 |
| 7.3 | 0.23 | 1.05 | 0.06 | 0.02 | 0.12 | 0.32 | 0.06 | 0.08 | 0.00 | 0.00 | 0.18 |
| 7.4 | 0.21 | 1.10 | 0.06 | 0.02 | 0.12 | 0.34 | 0.06 | 0.08 | 0.00 | 0.00 | 0.17 |
| 7.5 | 0.20 | 1.15 | 0.06 | 0.02 | 0.12 | 0.36 | 0.06 | 0.07 | 0.00 | 0.00 | 0.17 |
| 7.6 | 0.19 | 1.20 | 0.05 | 0.03 | 0.12 | 0.38 | 0.06 | 0.07 | 0.00 | 0.00 | 0.16 |
| 7.7 | 0.19 | 1.24 | 0.05 | 0.03 | 0.12 | 0.40 | 0.06 | 0.07 | 0.00 | 0.00 | 0.16 |
| 7.8 | 0.19 | 1.27 | 0.05 | 0.03 | 0.12 | 0.43 | 0.07 | 0.07 | 0.01 | 0.00 | 0.15 |
| 7.9 | 0.20 | 1.30 | 0.05 | 0.03 | 0.12 | 0.45 | 0.07 | 0.07 | 0.01 | 0.00 | 0.15 |
| 8.0 | 0.21 | 1.33 | 0.05 | 0.03 | 0.12 | 0.47 | 0.07 | 0.07 | 0.01 | 0.00 | 0.14 |
| 8.1 | 0.23 | 1.36 | 0.05 | 0.03 | 0.12 | 0.49 | 0.07 | 0.07 | 0.01 | 0.00 | 0.14 |
| 8.2 | 0.25 | 1.38 | 0.05 | 0.03 | 0.12 | 0.51 | 0.07 | 0.07 | 0.01 | 0.00 | 0.13 |
| 8.3 | 0.28 | 1.39 | 0.05 | 0.03 | 0.12 | 0.53 | 0.07 | 0.06 | 0.01 | 0.00 | 0.13 |
| 8.4 | 0.31 | 1.40 | 0.05 | 0.03 | 0.12 | 0.55 | 0.07 | 0.06 | 0.01 | 0.00 | 0.12 |
| 8.5 | 0.34 | 1.40 | 0.05 | 0.03 | 0.12 | 0.57 | 0.07 | 0.06 | 0.01 | 0.00 | 0.12 |
| 8.6 | 0.38 | 1.41 | 0.04 | 0.04 | 0.12 | 0.59 | 0.08 | 0.06 | 0.01 | 0.00 | 0.12 |
| 8.7 | 0.42 | 1.41 | 0.04 | 0.04 | 0.12 | 0.60 | 0.08 | 0.06 | 0.01 | 0.00 | 0.11 |
| 8.8 | 0.47 | 1.40 | 0.04 | 0.04 | 0.11 | 0.62 | 0.08 | 0.05 | 0.02 | 0.01 | 0.11 |
| 8.9 | 0.52 | 1.38 | 0.04 | 0.04 | 0.11 | 0.63 | 0.08 | 0.05 | 0.02 | 0.01 | 0.10 |
| 9.0 | 0.57 | 1.36 | 0.04 | 0.04 | 0.11 | 0.64 | 0.08 | 0.05 | 0.02 | 0.01 | 0.10 |
| 9.1 | 0.62 | 1.33 | 0.04 | 0.04 | 0.11 | 0.65 | 0.08 | 0.05 | 0.02 | 0.01 | 0.09 |
| 9.2 | 0.68 | 1.30 | 0.04 | 0.04 | 0.11 | 0.66 | 0.08 | 0.05 | 0.02 | 0.01 | 0.09 |
| 9.3 | 0.74 | 1.27 | 0.04 | 0.04 | 0.11 | 0.67 | 0.08 | 0.05 | 0.03 | 0.02 | 0.08 |
| 9.4 | 0.80 | 1.23 | 0.04 | 0.04 | 0.11 | 0.68 | 0.08 | 0.05 | 0.03 | 0.02 | 0.08 |
| 9.5 | 0.86 | 1.19 | 0.04 | 0.04 | 0.11 | 0.69 | 0.08 | 0.04 | 0.03 | 0.02 | 0.07 |
| 9.6 | 0.91 | 1.15 | 0.03 | 0.05 | 0.11 | 0.69 | 0.09 | 0.04 | 0.03 | 0.02 | 0.07 |
| 9.7 | 0.97 | 1.10 | 0.03 | 0.05 | 0.11 | 0.69 | 0.09 | 0.04 | 0.03 | 0.03 | 0.06 |
| 9.8 | 1.03 | 1.05 | 0.03 | 0.05 | 0.11 | 0.70 | 0.09 | 0.04 | 0.04 | 0.03 | 0.06 |
| 9.9 | 1.09 | 1.00 | 0.03 | 0.05 | 0.11 | 0.70 | 0.09 | 0.04 | 0.04 | 0.04 | 0.05 |
| 10.0 | 1.15 | 0.95 | 0.03 | 0.05 | 0.11 | 0.70 | 0.09 | 0.04 | 0.04 | 0.04 | 0.05 |

# TABLES XXVII″.-XXXV″.

| Tables | XXVII″. | | | | XXIX″. | | XXX″. | XXXI″. | XXXV″. | |
|---|---|---|---|---|---|---|---|---|---|---|
| Arguments | **22.** | | | | **24.** | | **25.** | **26.** | **30.** | |
| Days. | **0** | **10** | **20** | **30** | **0** | **10** | **0** | **0** | **0** | **10** |
| Days. | | | | | | | | | | |
| 0.0 | 0″.14 | 0″.02 | 0″.07 | 0″.12 | 0″.00 | 0″.11 | 0″.00 | 0″.28 | 0″.11 | 0″.10 |
| 0.1 | 0.14 | 0.02 | 0.07 | 0.12 | 0.00 | 0.11 | 0.00 | 0.28 | 0.11 | 0.10 |
| 0.2 | 0.14 | 0.02 | 0.07 | 0.12 | 0.00 | 0.10 | 0.00 | 0.28 | 0.11 | 0.10 |
| 0.3 | 0.14 | 0.03 | 0.06 | 0.13 | 0.00 | 0.10 | 0.00 | 0.28 | 0.12 | 0.11 |
| 0.4 | 0.14 | 0.03 | 0.06 | 0.13 | 0.00 | 0.09 | 0.00 | 0.27 | 0.12 | 0.11 |
| 0.5 | 0.14 | 0.03 | 0.06 | 0.13 | 0.00 | 0.09 | 0.00 | 0.27 | 0.12 | 0.11 |
| 0.6 | 0.14 | 0.03 | 0.05 | 0.13 | 0.00 | 0.09 | 0.00 | 0.26 | 0.12 | 0.11 |
| 0.7 | 0.14 | 0.03 | 0.05 | 0.13 | 0.00 | 0.08 | 0.00 | 0.25 | 0.13 | 0.11 |
| 0.8 | 0.14 | 0.04 | 0.05 | 0.14 | 0.00 | 0.08 | 0.01 | 0.24 | 0.13 | 0.12 |
| 0.9 | 0.14 | 0.04 | 0.04 | 0.14 | 0.00 | 0.07 | 0.01 | 0.23 | 0.14 | 0.12 |
| 1.0 | 0.14 | 0.04 | 0.04 | 0.14 | 0.00 | 0.07 | 0.01 | 0.21 | 0.14 | 0.12 |
| 1.1 | 0.14 | 0.05 | 0.04 | 0.14 | 0.00 | 0.07 | 0.01 | 0.20 | 0.14 | 0.12 |
| 1.2 | 0.14 | 0.05 | 0.04 | 0.14 | 0.00 | 0.06 | 0.01 | 0.19 | 0.15 | 0.13 |
| 1.3 | 0.13 | 0.05 | 0.03 | 0.14 | 0.01 | 0.06 | 0.02 | 0.18 | 0.15 | 0.13 |
| 1.4 | 0.13 | 0.06 | 0.03 | 0.14 | 0.01 | 0.05 | 0.02 | 0.16 | 0.16 | 0.14 |
| 1.5 | 0.13 | 0.06 | 0.03 | 0.14 | 0.01 | 0.05 | 0.02 | 0.14 | 0.16 | 0.14 |
| 1.6 | 0.13 | 0.06 | 0.03 | 0.14 | 0.01 | 0.05 | 0.03 | 0.13 | 0.16 | 0.14 |
| 1.7 | 0.13 | 0.06 | 0.03 | 0.14 | 0.01 | 0.04 | 0.03 | 0.11 | 0.17 | 0.15 |
| 1.8 | 0.12 | 0.07 | 0.02 | 0.14 | 0.02 | 0.04 | 0.04 | 0.10 | 0.17 | 0.15 |
| 1.9 | 0.12 | 0.07 | 0.02 | 0.14 | 0.02 | 0.03 | 0.04 | 0.09 | 0.18 | 0.16 |
| 2.0 | 0.12 | 0.07 | 0.02 | 0.14 | 0.02 | 0.03 | 0.05 | 0.08 | 0.18 | 0.16 |
| 2.1 | 0.12 | 0.07 | 0.02 | 0.14 | 0.02 | 0.03 | 0.05 | 0.06 | 0.19 | 0.17 |
| 2.2 | 0.12 | 0.07 | 0.02 | 0.14 | 0.03 | 0.02 | 0.06 | 0.05 | 0.19 | 0.17 |
| 2.3 | 0.11 | 0.08 | 0.01 | 0.14 | 0.03 | 0.02 | 0.06 | 0.04 | 0.20 | 0.18 |
| 2.4 | 0.11 | 0.08 | 0.01 | 0.14 | 0.03 | 0.01 | 0.07 | 0.03 | 0.20 | 0.18 |
| 2.5 | 0.11 | 0.08 | 0.01 | 0.14 | 0.04 | 0.01 | 0.07 | 0.02 | 0.21 | 0.19 |
| 2.6 | 0.11 | 0.09 | 0.01 | 0.14 | 0.04 | 0.01 | 0.08 | 0.02 | 0.21 | 0.19 |
| 2.7 | 0.11 | 0.09 | 0.01 | 0.14 | 0.05 | 0.01 | 0.08 | 0.01 | 0.22 | 0.20 |
| 2.8 | 0.10 | 0.09 | 0.00 | 0.14 | 0.05 | 0.00 | 0.09 | 0.01 | 0.22 | 0.20 |
| 2.9 | 0.10 | 0.10 | 0.00 | 0.14 | 0.06 | 0.00 | 0.09 | 0.00 | 0.23 | 0.21 |
| 3.0 | 0.10 | 0.10 | 0.00 | 0.14 | 0.06 | 0.00 | 0.10 | 0.00 | 0.23 | 0.21 |
| 3.1 | 0.10 | 0.10 | 0.00 | 0.14 | 0.07 | 0.00 | 0.10 | 0.00 | 0.23 | 0.21 |
| 3.2 | 0.09 | 0.10 | 0.00 | 0.14 | 0.07 | 0.00 | 0.11 | 0.01 | 0.24 | 0.22 |
| 3.3 | 0.09 | 0.11 | 0.00 | 0.13 | 0.08 | 0.00 | 0.11 | 0.01 | 0.24 | 0.22 |
| 3.4 | 0.09 | 0.11 | 0.00 | 0.13 | 0.08 | 0.00 | 0.12 | 0.02 | 0.25 | 0.23 |
| 3.5 | 0.08 | 0.11 | 0.00 | 0.13 | 0.09 | 0.00 | 0.12 | 0.02 | 0.25 | 0.23 |
| 3.6 | 0.08 | 0.11 | 0.00 | 0.13 | 0.09 | 0.00 | 0.12 | 0.03 | 0.25 | 0.23 |
| 3.7 | 0.08 | 0.11 | 0.00 | 0.13 | 0.10 | 0.00 | 0.13 | 0.04 | 0.26 | 0.24 |
| 3.8 | 0.07 | 0.12 | 0.00 | 0.12 | 0.10 | 0.00 | 0.13 | 0.05 | 0.26 | 0.24 |
| 3.9 | 0.07 | 0.12 | 0.00 | 0.12 | 0.11 | 0.00 | 0.14 | 0.06 | 0.27 | 0.25 |
| 4.0 | 0.07 | 0.12 | 0.00 | 0.12 | 0.11 | 0.00 | 0.14 | 0.08 | 0.27 | 0.25 |
| 4.1 | 0.06 | 0.12 | 0.00 | 0.12 | 0.12 | 0.00 | 0.14 | 0.09 | 0.27 | 0.25 |
| 4.2 | 0.06 | 0.12 | 0.00 | 0.12 | 0.12 | 0.00 | 0.15 | 0.10 | 0.27 | 0.26 |
| 4.3 | 0.06 | 0.13 | 0.00 | 0.11 | 0.13 | 0.00 | 0.15 | 0.11 | 0.28 | 0.26 |
| 4.4 | 0.05 | 0.13 | 0.00 | 0.11 | 0.13 | 0.00 | 0.16 | 0.13 | 0.28 | 0.27 |
| 4.5 | 0.05 | 0.13 | 0.00 | 0.11 | 0.14 | 0.00 | 0.16 | 0.14 | 0.28 | 0.27 |
| 4.6 | 0.05 | 0.13 | 0.00 | 0.11 | 0.14 | 0.01 | 0.16 | 0.16 | 0.28 | 0.27 |
| 4.7 | 0.05 | 0.13 | 0.00 | 0.11 | 0.15 | 0.01 | 0.16 | 0.17 | 0.28 | 0.27 |
| 4.8 | 0.04 | 0.14 | 0.00 | 0.10 | 0.15 | 0.01 | 0.16 | 0.19 | 0.28 | 0.28 |
| 4.9 | 0.04 | 0.14 | 0.00 | 0.10 | 0.16 | 0.01 | 0.16 | 0.20 | 0.28 | 0.28 |
| 5.0 | 0.04 | 0.14 | 0.00 | 0.10 | 0.16 | 0.01 | 0.16 | 0.21 | 0.28 | 0.28 |

# TABLES XXVII″.-XXXV″.

| Tables | XXVII″. | | | | XXIX″. | | XXX″. | XXXI″. | XXXV″. | |
|---|---|---|---|---|---|---|---|---|---|---|
| Arguments | 22. | | | | 24. | | 25. | 26. | 30. | |
| Days. | 0 | 10 | 20 | 30 | 0 | 10 | 0 | 0 | 0 | 10 |
| Days. 5.0 | ″ 0.04 | ″ 0.14 | ″ 0.00 | ″ 0.10 | ″ 0.16 | ″ 0.01 | ″ 0.16 | ″ 0.21 | ″ 0.28 | ″ 0.28 |
| 5.1 | 0.04 | 0.14 | 0.00 | 0.10 | 0.16 | 0.02 | 0.16 | 0.23 | 0.28 | 0.28 |
| 5.2 | 0.04 | 0.14 | 0.00 | 0.10 | 0.17 | 0.02 | 0.16 | 0.24 | 0.28 | 0.28 |
| 5.3 | 0.03 | 0.14 | 0.01 | 0.09 | 0.17 | 0.02 | 0.16 | 0.25 | 0.27 | 0.28 |
| 5.4 | 0.03 | 0.14 | 0.01 | 0.09 | 0.18 | 0.02 | 0.16 | 0.26 | 0.27 | 0.28 |
| 5.5 | 0.03 | 0.14 | 0.01 | 0.09 | 0.18 | 0.03 | 0.16 | 0.27 | 0.27 | 0.28 |
| 5.6 | 0.03 | 0.14 | 0.01 | 0.09 | 0.18 | 0.03 | 0.16 | 0.27 | 0.27 | 0.28 |
| 5.7 | 0.03 | 0.14 | 0.01 | 0.08 | 0.18 | 0.03 | 0.15 | 0.28 | 0.26 | 0.28 |
| 5.8 | 0.02 | 0.14 | 0.02 | 0.08 | 0.19 | 0.04 | 0.15 | 0.28 | 0.26 | 0.27 |
| 5.9 | 0.02 | 0.14 | 0.02 | 0.08 | 0.19 | 0.04 | 0.14 | 0.28 | 0.25 | 0.27 |
| 6.0 | 0.02 | 0.14 | 0.02 | 0.07 | 0.19 | 0.05 | 0.14 | 0.28 | 0.25 | 0.27 |
| 6.1 | 0.02 | 0.14 | 0.02 | 0.07 | 0.19 | 0.05 | 0.14 | 0.28 | 0.25 | 0.27 |
| 6.2 | 0.02 | 0.14 | 0.02 | 0.07 | 0.19 | 0.06 | 0.13 | 0.27 | 0.24 | 0.26 |
| 6.3 | 0.01 | 0.14 | 0.03 | 0.06 | 0.20 | 0.06 | 0.13 | 0.26 | 0.24 | 0.26 |
| 6.4 | 0.01 | 0.14 | 0.03 | 0.06 | 0.20 | 0.07 | 0.12 | 0.25 | 0.23 | 0.25 |
| 6.5 | 0.01 | 0.14 | 0.03 | 0.06 | 0.20 | 0.07 | 0.12 | 0.25 | 0.23 | 0.25 |
| 6.6 | 0.01 | 0.14 | 0.03 | 0.06 | 0.20 | 0.07 | 0.12 | 0.24 | 0.23 | 0.25 |
| 6.7 | 0.01 | 0.14 | 0.03 | 0.05 | 0.20 | 0.08 | 0.11 | 0.23 | 0.22 | 0.24 |
| 6.8 | 0.00 | 0.14 | 0.04 | 0.05 | 0.20 | 0.08 | 0.11 | 0.22 | 0.22 | 0.24 |
| 6.9 | 0.00 | 0.14 | 0.04 | 0.05 | 0.20 | 0.09 | 0.10 | 0.21 | 0.21 | 0.23 |
| 7.0 | 0.00 | 0.14 | 0.04 | 0.04 | 0.20 | 0.10 | 0.10 | 0.19 | 0.21 | 0.23 |
| 7.1 | 0.00 | 0.14 | 0.04 | 0.04 | 0.20 | 0.10 | 0.09 | 0.18 | 0.21 | 0.23 |
| 7.2 | 0.00 | 0.14 | 0.05 | 0.04 | 0.20 | 0.11 | 0.09 | 0.16 | 0.20 | 0.22 |
| 7.3 | 0.00 | 0.13 | 0.05 | 0.03 | 0.20 | 0.11 | 0.08 | 0.14 | 0.20 | 0.22 |
| 7.4 | 0.00 | 0.13 | 0.05 | 0.03 | 0.20 | 0.12 | 0.08 | 0.13 | 0.19 | 0.21 |
| 7.5 | 0.00 | 0.13 | 0.06 | 0.03 | 0.20 | 0.12 | 0.07 | 0.11 | 0.19 | 0.21 |
| 7.6 | 0.00 | 0.13 | 0.06 | 0.03 | 0.20 | 0.12 | 0.07 | 0.10 | 0.18 | 0.20 |
| 7.7 | 0.00 | 0.13 | 0.06 | 0.03 | 0.20 | 0.13 | 0.06 | 0.09 | 0.18 | 0.20 |
| 7.8 | 0.00 | 0.12 | 0.07 | 0.02 | 0.19 | 0.13 | 0.06 | 0.08 | 0.17 | 0.19 |
| 7.9 | 0.00 | 0.12 | 0.07 | 0.02 | 0.19 | 0.14 | 0.05 | 0.06 | 0.17 | 0.19 |
| 8.0 | 0.00 | 0.12 | 0.07 | 0.02 | 0.19 | 0.15 | 0.05 | 0.05 | 0.16 | 0.18 |
| 8.1 | 0.00 | 0.12 | 0.07 | 0.02 | 0.19 | 0.15 | 0.04 | 0.04 | 0.16 | 0.18 |
| 8.2 | 0.00 | 0.12 | 0.07 | 0.02 | 0.19 | 0.16 | 0.04 | 0.03 | 0.15 | 0.17 |
| 8.3 | 0.00 | 0.11 | 0.08 | 0.01 | 0.18 | 0.16 | 0.03 | 0.02 | 0.15 | 0.17 |
| 8.4 | 0.00 | 0.11 | 0.08 | 0.01 | 0.18 | 0.17 | 0.03 | 0.02 | 0.14 | 0.16 |
| 8.5 | 0.00 | 0.11 | 0.08 | 0.01 | 0.18 | 0.17 | 0.02 | 0.01 | 0.14 | 0.16 |
| 8.6 | 0.00 | 0.11 | 0.09 | 0.01 | 0.18 | 0.17 | 0.02 | 0.01 | 0.14 | 0.16 |
| 8.7 | 0.00 | 0.11 | 0.09 | 0.01 | 0.17 | 0.17 | 0.02 | 0.00 | 0.13 | 0.15 |
| 8.8 | 0.00 | 0.10 | 0.09 | 0.00 | 0.17 | 0.18 | 0.01 | 0.00 | 0.13 | 0.15 |
| 8.9 | 0.00 | 0.10 | 0.10 | 0.00 | 0.16 | 0.18 | 0.01 | 0.00 | 0.12 | 0.14 |
| 9.0 | 0.00 | 0.10 | 0.10 | 0.00 | 0.16 | 0.18 | 0.01 | 0.01 | 0.12 | 0.14 |
| 9.1 | 0.00 | 0.10 | 0.10 | 0.00 | 0.16 | 0.18 | 0.01 | 0.01 | 0.12 | 0.14 |
| 9.2 | 0.00 | 0.09 | 0.10 | 0.00 | 0.15 | 0.19 | 0.01 | 0.02 | 0.12 | 0.13 |
| 9.3 | 0.01 | 0.09 | 0.11 | 0.00 | 0.15 | 0.19 | 0.00 | 0.02 | 0.11 | 0.13 |
| 9.4 | 0.01 | 0.09 | 0.11 | 0.00 | 0.14 | 0.19 | 0.00 | 0.03 | 0.11 | 0.12 |
| 9.5 | 0.01 | 0.08 | 0.11 | 0.00 | 0.14 | 0.19 | 0.00 | 0.04 | 0.11 | 0.12 |
| 9.6 | 0.01 | 0.08 | 0.11 | 0.00 | 0.13 | 0.19 | 0.00 | 0.05 | 0.11 | 0.12 |
| 9.7 | 0.01 | 0.08 | 0.11 | 0.00 | 0.13 | 0.20 | 0.00 | 0.06 | 0.11 | 0.12 |
| 9.8 | 0.02 | 0.07 | 0.12 | 0.00 | 0.12 | 0.20 | 0.00 | 0.08 | 0.10 | 0.11 |
| 9.9 | 0.02 | 0.07 | 0.12 | 0.00 | 0.12 | 0.20 | 0.00 | 0.09 | 0.10 | 0.11 |
| 10.0 | 0.02 | 0.07 | 0.12 | 0.00 | 0.11 | 0.20 | 0.00 | 0.10 | 0.10 | 0.11 |

# TABLES VI.^IV. - XII.^IV.

| Tables | VI.^IV. | | | VII.^IV. | | | | VIII.^IV. | | | XII.^IV. |
|---|---|---|---|---|---|---|---|---|---|---|---|
| Arguments | 1. | | | 2. | | | | 3. | | | 7. |
| Days. | 0 | 10 | 20 | 0 | 10 | 20 | 30 | 0 | 10 | 20 | 0 |
| 0.0 | 0.24″ | 0.76″ | 0.46″ | 0.00″ | 0.04″ | 0.05″ | 0.01″ | 0.28″ | 0.08″ | 0.54″ | 0.01″ |
| 0.1 | 0.24 | 0.76 | 0.45 | 0.00 | 0.04 | 0.05 | 0.01 | 0.30 | 0.07 | 0.53 | 0.00 |
| 0.2 | 0.24 | 0.77 | 0.45 | 0.00 | 0.04 | 0.05 | 0.01 | 0.31 | 0.06 | 0.52 | 0.00 |
| 0.3 | 0.23 | 0.77 | 0.45 | 0.00 | 0.04 | 0.05 | 0.01 | 0.32 | 0.06 | 0.52 | 0.00 |
| 0.4 | 0.22 | 0.77 | 0.45 | 0.00 | 0.04 | 0.05 | 0.01 | 0.34 | 0.05 | 0.51 | 0.01 |
| 0.5 | 0.22 | 0.77 | 0.45 | 0.00 | 0.04 | 0.05 | 0.01 | 0.35 | 0.04 | 0.50 | 0.01 |
| 0.6 | 0.21 | 0.77 | 0.45 | 0.00 | 0.05 | 0.05 | 0.00 | 0.37 | 0.03 | 0.49 | 0.01 |
| 0.7 | 0.21 | 0.77 | 0.45 | 0.00 | 0.05 | 0.05 | 0.00 | 0.38 | 0.03 | 0.48 | 0.01 |
| 0.8 | 0.20 | 0.77 | 0.45 | 0.00 | 0.05 | 0.05 | 0.00 | 0.39 | 0.02 | 0.47 | 0.02 |
| 0.9 | 0.19 | 0.77 | 0.45 | 0.00 | 0.05 | 0.05 | 0.00 | 0.41 | 0.02 | 0.46 | 0.02 |
| 1.0 | 0.19 | 0.77 | 0.45 | 0.00 | 0.05 | 0.05 | 0.00 | 0.42 | 0.01 | 0.45 | 0.02 |
| 1.1 | 0.18 | 0.77 | 0.44 | 0.00 | 0.05 | 0.04 | 0.00 | 0.44 | 0.01 | 0.44 | 0.03 |
| 1.2 | 0.18 | 0.77 | 0.44 | 0.00 | 0.05 | 0.04 | 0.00 | 0.45 | 0.01 | 0.43 | 0.03 |
| 1.3 | 0.17 | 0.77 | 0.44 | 0.00 | 0.05 | 0.04 | 0.00 | 0.46 | 0.00 | 0.42 | 0.04 |
| 1.4 | 0.17 | 0.77 | 0.44 | 0.00 | 0.05 | 0.04 | 0.00 | 0.47 | 0.00 | 0.41 | 0.04 |
| 1.5 | 0.16 | 0.77 | 0.44 | 0.00 | 0.05 | 0.04 | 0.00 | 0.49 | 0.00 | 0.40 | 0.05 |
| 1.6 | 0.16 | 0.76 | 0.44 | 0.00 | 0.05 | 0.04 | 0.00 | 0.50 | 0.00 | 0.39 | 0.06 |
| 1.7 | 0.15 | 0.76 | 0.44 | 0.00 | 0.05 | 0.04 | 0.00 | 0.51 | 0.00 | 0.38 | 0.06 |
| 1.8 | 0.15 | 0.76 | 0.44 | 0.00 | 0.05 | 0.04 | 0.00 | 0.52 | 0.00 | 0.36 | 0.07 |
| 1.9 | 0.15 | 0.76 | 0.44 | 0.00 | 0.05 | 0.04 | 0.00 | 0.53 | 0.00 | 0.35 | 0.07 |
| 2.0 | 0.15 | 0.75 | 0.44 | 0.00 | 0.05 | 0.04 | 0.00 | 0.54 | 0.00 | 0.34 | 0.08 |
| 2.1 | 0.14 | 0.75 | 0.43 | 0.00 | 0.05 | 0.04 | 0.00 | 0.55 | 0.00 | 0.33 | 0.09 |
| 2.2 | 0.14 | 0.74 | 0.43 | 0.00 | 0.05 | 0.04 | 0.00 | 0.56 | 0.00 | 0.32 | 0.10 |
| 2.3 | 0.14 | 0.74 | 0.43 | 0.00 | 0.05 | 0.04 | 0.00 | 0.57 | 0.01 | 0.31 | 0.11 |
| 2.4 | 0.14 | 0.73 | 0.43 | 0.00 | 0.05 | 0.04 | 0.00 | 0.57 | 0.01 | 0.30 | 0.12 |
| 2.5 | 0.14 | 0.73 | 0.43 | 0.00 | 0.05 | 0.04 | 0.00 | 0.58 | 0.01 | 0.29 | 0.13 |
| 2.6 | 0.13 | 0.72 | 0.42 | 0.00 | 0.05 | 0.03 | 0.00 | 0.58 | 0.02 | 0.28 | 0.14 |
| 2.7 | 0.13 | 0.72 | 0.42 | 0.00 | 0.05 | 0.03 | 0.00 | 0.59 | 0.03 | 0.27 | 0.15 |
| 2.8 | 0.13 | 0.71 | 0.42 | 0.00 | 0.05 | 0.03 | 0.00 | 0.59 | 0.03 | 0.27 | 0.16 |
| 2.9 | 0.13 | 0.71 | 0.42 | 0.00 | 0.05 | 0.03 | 0.00 | 0.60 | 0.04 | 0.26 | 0.16 |
| 3.0 | 0.13 | 0.70 | 0.42 | 0.00 | 0.05 | 0.03 | 0.00 | 0.60 | 0.05 | 0.25 | 0.17 |
| 3.1 | 0.13 | 0.70 | 0.41 | 0.00 | 0.06 | 0.03 | 0.00 | 0.61 | 0.06 | 0.24 | 0.18 |
| 3.2 | 0.13 | 0.69 | 0.41 | 0.01 | 0.06 | 0.03 | 0.00 | 0.61 | 0.07 | 0.23 | 0.19 |
| 3.3 | 0.13 | 0.69 | 0.41 | 0.01 | 0.06 | 0.03 | 0.00 | 0.61 | 0.08 | 0.21 | 0.19 |
| 3.4 | 0.13 | 0.68 | 0.41 | 0.01 | 0.06 | 0.03 | 0.00 | 0.61 | 0.09 | 0.20 | 0.20 |
| 3.5 | 0.13 | 0.68 | 0.41 | 0.01 | 0.06 | 0.03 | 0.00 | 0.61 | 0.10 | 0.19 | 0.21 |
| 3.6 | 0.14 | 0.67 | 0.40 | 0.01 | 0.06 | 0.03 | 0.00 | 0.61 | 0.11 | 0.18 | 0.22 |
| 3.7 | 0.14 | 0.67 | 0.40 | 0.01 | 0.06 | 0.03 | 0.00 | 0.61 | 0.12 | 0.17 | 0.23 |
| 3.8 | 0.14 | 0.66 | 0.40 | 0.01 | 0.06 | 0.03 | 0.00 | 0.61 | 0.14 | 0.17 | 0.23 |
| 3.9 | 0.14 | 0.65 | 0.40 | 0.01 | 0.06 | 0.03 | 0.00 | 0.61 | 0.15 | 0.16 | 0.24 |
| 4.0 | 0.15 | 0.65 | 0.39 | 0.01 | 0.06 | 0.03 | 0.00 | 0.60 | 0.16 | 0.15 | 0.25 |
| 4.1 | 0.15 | 0.64 | 0.39 | 0.01 | 0.06 | 0.03 | 0.00 | 0.60 | 0.17 | 0.14 | 0.25 |
| 4.2 | 0.16 | 0.64 | 0.38 | 0.01 | 0.06 | 0.03 | 0.00 | 0.60 | 0.19 | 0.13 | 0.26 |
| 4.3 | 0.16 | 0.63 | 0.38 | 0.01 | 0.06 | 0.03 | 0.00 | 0.60 | 0.20 | 0.12 | 0.26 |
| 4.4 | 0.17 | 0.63 | 0.38 | 0.01 | 0.06 | 0.03 | 0.00 | 0.59 | 0.22 | 0.11 | 0.27 |
| 4.5 | 0.18 | 0.62 | 0.38 | 0.01 | 0.06 | 0.03 | 0.00 | 0.59 | 0.23 | 0.10 | 0.27 |
| 4.6 | 0.18 | 0.62 | 0.37 | 0.01 | 0.06 | 0.03 | 0.00 | 0.58 | 0.25 | 0.09 | 0.27 |
| 4.7 | 0.19 | 0.61 | 0.37 | 0.01 | 0.06 | 0.03 | 0.00 | 0.58 | 0.26 | 0.08 | 0.27 |
| 4.8 | 0.20 | 0.61 | 0.37 | 0.01 | 0.06 | 0.03 | 0.00 | 0.57 | 0.28 | 0.08 | 0.28 |
| 4.9 | 0.21 | 0.60 | 0.37 | 0.01 | 0.06 | 0.03 | 0.00 | 0.56 | 0.29 | 0.07 | 0.28 |
| 5.0 | 0.22 | 0.60 | 0.36 | 0.01 | 0.06 | 0.03 | 0.00 | 0.56 | 0.31 | 0.06 | 0.28 |

# TABLES VI.^IV.-XII.^IV.

| Tables | VI.^IV. | | | VII.^IV. | | | | VIII.^IV. | | | XII.^IV. |
|---|---|---|---|---|---|---|---|---|---|---|---|
| Arguments | **1.** | | | **2.** | | | | **3.** | | | **7.** |
| Days. | **0** | **10** | **20** | **0** | **10** | **20** | **30** | **0** | **10** | **20** | **0** |
| Days. 5.0 | ″ 0.22 | ″ 0.60 | ″ 0.36 | ″ 0.01 | ″ 0.06 | ″ 0.03 | ″ 0.00 | ″ 0.56 | ″ 0.31 | ″ 0.06 | ″ 0.28 |
| 5.1 | 0.22 | 0.59 | 0.36 | 0.01 | 0.06 | 0.03 | 0.00 | 0.55 | 0.33 | 0.05 | 0.28 |
| 5.2 | 0.23 | 0.59 | 0.35 | 0.01 | 0.06 | 0.02 | 0.01 | 0.54 | 0.34 | 0.05 | 0.28 |
| 5.3 | 0.24 | 0.58 | 0.35 | 0.01 | 0.06 | 0.02 | 0.01 | 0.53 | 0.36 | 0.04 | 0.27 |
| 5.4 | 0.25 | 0.58 | 0.35 | 0.01 | 0.06 | 0.02 | 0.01 | 0.52 | 0.37 | 0.04 | 0.27 |
| 5.5 | 0.26 | 0.57 | 0.34 | 0.02 | 0.06 | 0.02 | 0.01 | 0.52 | 0.39 | 0.03 | 0.27 |
| 5.6 | 0.28 | 0.57 | 0.34 | 0.02 | 0.06 | 0.02 | 0.01 | 0.51 | 0.40 | 0.03 | 0.27 |
| 5.7 | 0.29 | 0.56 | 0.33 | 0.02 | 0.06 | 0.02 | 0.01 | 0.50 | 0.42 | 0.03 | 0.26 |
| 5.8 | 0.30 | 0.56 | 0.33 | 0.02 | 0.06 | 0.02 | 0.01 | 0.49 | 0.43 | 0.02 | 0.26 |
| 5.9 | 0.31 | 0.56 | 0.33 | 0.02 | 0.06 | 0.02 | 0.01 | 0.48 | 0.45 | 0.02 | 0.25 |
| 6.0 | 0.33 | 0.55 | 0.32 | 0.02 | 0.06 | 0.02 | 0.01 | 0.47 | 0.46 | 0.02 | 0.25 |
| 6.1 | 0.34 | 0.55 | 0.32 | 0.02 | 0.06 | 0.02 | 0.01 | 0.46 | 0.47 | 0.02 | 0.24 |
| 6.2 | 0.36 | 0.54 | 0.31 | 0.02 | 0.06 | 0.02 | 0.01 | 0.45 | 0.48 | 0.02 | 0.23 |
| 6.3 | 0.37 | 0.54 | 0.31 | 0.02 | 0.06 | 0.02 | 0.01 | 0.44 | 0.50 | 0.01 | 0.23 |
| 6.4 | 0.38 | 0.54 | 0.30 | 0.02 | 0.06 | 0.02 | 0.01 | 0.43 | 0.51 | 0.01 | 0.22 |
| 6.5 | 0.40 | 0.53 | 0.30 | 0.02 | 0.06 | 0.02 | 0.01 | 0.43 | 0.52 | 0.01 | 0.21 |
| 6.6 | 0.41 | 0.53 | 0.29 | 0.02 | 0.06 | 0.02 | 0.01 | 0.42 | 0.53 | 0.01 | 0.21 |
| 6.7 | 0.43 | 0.52 | 0.29 | 0.02 | 0.06 | 0.02 | 0.01 | 0.41 | 0.54 | 0.01 | 0.20 |
| 6.8 | 0.44 | 0.52 | 0.28 | 0.02 | 0.06 | 0.02 | 0.01 | 0.40 | 0.55 | 0.02 | 0.20 |
| 6.9 | 0.45 | 0.52 | 0.28 | 0.02 | 0.06 | 0.02 | 0.01 | 0.39 | 0.56 | 0.02 | 0.19 |
| 7.0 | 0.46 | 0.52 | 0.27 | 0.02 | 0.06 | 0.02 | 0.01 | 0.37 | 0.57 | 0.02 | 0.17 |
| 7.1 | 0.48 | 0.51 | 0.27 | 0.02 | 0.06 | 0.02 | 0.01 | 0.36 | 0.58 | 0.02 | 0.16 |
| 7.2 | 0.49 | 0.51 | 0.26 | 0.02 | 0.06 | 0.02 | 0.01 | 0.35 | 0.59 | 0.03 | 0.15 |
| 7.3 | 0.50 | 0.51 | 0.26 | 0.02 | 0.06 | 0.02 | 0.02 | 0.34 | 0.59 | 0.03 | 0.15 |
| 7.4 | 0.51 | 0.51 | 0.25 | 0.02 | 0.06 | 0.02 | 0.02 | 0.34 | 0.60 | 0.04 | 0.14 |
| 7.5 | 0.53 | 0.51 | 0.25 | 0.03 | 0.06 | 0.02 | 0.02 | 0.33 | 0.61 | 0.04 | 0.13 |
| 7.6 | 0.54 | 0.50 | 0.24 | 0.03 | 0.06 | 0.01 | 0.02 | 0.32 | 0.61 | 0.05 | 0.12 |
| 7.7 | 0.56 | 0.50 | 0.24 | 0.03 | 0.06 | 0.01 | 0.02 | 0.31 | 0.61 | 0.06 | 0.11 |
| 7.8 | 0.57 | 0.50 | 0.23 | 0.03 | 0.06 | 0.01 | 0.02 | 0.30 | 0.62 | 0.06 | 0.10 |
| 7.9 | 0.58 | 0.50 | 0.22 | 0.03 | 0.06 | 0.01 | 0.02 | 0.29 | 0.62 | 0.07 | 0.09 |
| 8.0 | 0.59 | 0.49 | 0.22 | 0.03 | 0.06 | 0.01 | 0.02 | 0.28 | 0.62 | 0.08 | 0.08 |
| 8.1 | 0.61 | 0.49 | 0.21 | 0.03 | 0.05 | 0.01 | 0.02 | 0.27 | 0.62 | 0.09 | 0.07 |
| 8.2 | 0.62 | 0.48 | 0.21 | 0.03 | 0.05 | 0.01 | 0.02 | 0.26 | 0.62 | 0.10 | 0.07 |
| 8.3 | 0.63 | 0.48 | 0.20 | 0.03 | 0.05 | 0.01 | 0.02 | 0.24 | 0.62 | 0.11 | 0.06 |
| 8.4 | 0.64 | 0.48 | 0.20 | 0.03 | 0.05 | 0.01 | 0.02 | 0.23 | 0.62 | 0.12 | 0.06 |
| 8.5 | 0.65 | 0.48 | 0.19 | 0.03 | 0.05 | 0.01 | 0.02 | 0.22 | 0.62 | 0.13 | 0.05 |
| 8.6 | 0.66 | 0.47 | 0.19 | 0.04 | 0.05 | 0.01 | 0.02 | 0.21 | 0.62 | 0.14 | 0.04 |
| 8.7 | 0.67 | 0.47 | 0.18 | 0.04 | 0.05 | 0.01 | 0.02 | 0.20 | 0.62 | 0.16 | 0.04 |
| 8.8 | 0.68 | 0.47 | 0.18 | 0.04 | 0.05 | 0.01 | 0.02 | 0.19 | 0.61 | 0.17 | 0.03 |
| 8.9 | 0.69 | 0.47 | 0.17 | 0.04 | 0.05 | 0.01 | 0.02 | 0.18 | 0.61 | 0.19 | 0.03 |
| 9.0 | 0.70 | 0.47 | 0.17 | 0.04 | 0.05 | 0.01 | 0.02 | 0.17 | 0.61 | 0.20 | 0.02 |
| 9.1 | 0.70 | 0.47 | 0.17 | 0.04 | 0.05 | 0.01 | 0.02 | 0.16 | 0.60 | 0.21 | 0.02 |
| 9.2 | 0.71 | 0.47 | 0.16 | 0.04 | 0.05 | 0.01 | 0.02 | 0.15 | 0.59 | 0.23 | 0.02 |
| 9.3 | 0.72 | 0.47 | 0.16 | 0.04 | 0.05 | 0.01 | 0.03 | 0.14 | 0.59 | 0.24 | 0.01 |
| 9.4 | 0.73 | 0.47 | 0.15 | 0.04 | 0.05 | 0.01 | 0.03 | 0.13 | 0.58 | 0.26 | 0.01 |
| 9.5 | 0.73 | 0.47 | 0.15 | 0.04 | 0.05 | 0.01 | 0.03 | 0.12 | 0.57 | 0.27 | 0.01 |
| 9.6 | 0.74 | 0.46 | 0.15 | 0.04 | 0.05 | 0.01 | 0.03 | 0.11 | 0.56 | 0.29 | 0.01 |
| 9.7 | 0.74 | 0.46 | 0.15 | 0.04 | 0.05 | 0.01 | 0.03 | 0.10 | 0.56 | 0.31 | 0.00 |
| 9.8 | 0.75 | 0.46 | 0.14 | 0.04 | 0.05 | 0.01 | 0.03 | 0.10 | 0.55 | 0.32 | 0.00 |
| 9.9 | 0.75 | 0.46 | 0.14 | 0.04 | 0.05 | 0.01 | 0.03 | 0.09 | 0.55 | 0.34 | 0.00 |
| 10.0 | 0.76 | 0.46 | 0.14 | 0.04 | 0.05 | 0.01 | 0.03 | 0.08 | 0.54 | 0.35 | 0.01 |

# TABLES XIII.IV. - XXI.IV.

| Tables | XIII.IV. | | XVIII.IV. | XXI.IV. | | | XIII.IV. | | XVIII.IV. | XXI.IV. | |
|---|---|---|---|---|---|---|---|---|---|---|---|
| Arguments | **8.** | | **13.** | **16.** | | | **8.** | | **13.** | **16.** | |
| Days. | **0** | **10** | **0** | **0** | **10** | Days. | **0** | **10** | **0** | **0** | **10** |
| Days. 0.0 | ″0.00 | ″0.03 | ″0.00 | ″0.06 | ″0.02 | Days. 5.0 | ″0.03 | ″0.00 | ″0.04 | ″0.00 | ″0.06 |
| 0.1 | 0.00 | 0.03 | 0.00 | 0.06 | 0.01 | 5.1 | 0.03 | 0.00 | 0.04 | 0.00 | 0.06 |
| 0.2 | 0.00 | 0.03 | 0.00 | 0.06 | 0.01 | 5.2 | 0.03 | 0.00 | 0.04 | 0.01 | 0.06 |
| 0.3 | 0.00 | 0.03 | 0.00 | 0.06 | 0.01 | 5.3 | 0.03 | 0.00 | 0.04 | 0.01 | 0.06 |
| 0.4 | 0.00 | 0.03 | 0.00 | 0.06 | 0.00 | 5.4 | 0.03 | 0.00 | 0.04 | 0.02 | 0.06 |
| 0.5 | 0.00 | 0.03 | 0.00 | 0.06 | 0.00 | 5.5 | 0.03 | 0.00 | 0.04 | 0.02 | 0.06 |
| 0.6 | 0.00 | 0.03 | 0.00 | 0.06 | 0.00 | 5.6 | 0.03 | 0.00 | 0.04 | 0.02 | 0.06 |
| 0.7 | 0.00 | 0.03 | 0.00 | 0.06 | 0.00 | 5.7 | 0.03 | 0.00 | 0.04 | 0.02 | 0.05 |
| 0.8 | 0.00 | 0.03 | 0.00 | 0.06 | 0.00 | 5.8 | 0.03 | 0.00 | 0.04 | 0.03 | 0.05 |
| 0.9 | 0.00 | 0.03 | 0.00 | 0.06 | 0.00 | 5.9 | 0.03 | 0.00 | 0.04 | 0.03 | 0.05 |
| 1.0 | 0.00 | 0.03 | 0.00 | 0.06 | 0.00 | 6.0 | 0.03 | 0.00 | 0.04 | 0.03 | 0.04 |
| 1.1 | 0.00 | 0.03 | 0.00 | 0.06 | 0.00 | 6.1 | 0.03 | 0.00 | 0.04 | 0.03 | 0.04 |
| 1.2 | 0.00 | 0.03 | 0.00 | 0.06 | 0.00 | 6.2 | 0.03 | 0.00 | 0.04 | 0.03 | 0.04 |
| 1.3 | 0.00 | 0.03 | 0.00 | 0.06 | 0.00 | 6.3 | 0.04 | 0.00 | 0.04 | 0.04 | 0.03 |
| 1.4 | 0.00 | 0.02 | 0.00 | 0.05 | 0.00 | 6.4 | 0.04 | 0.00 | 0.04 | 0.04 | 0.03 |
| 1.5 | 0.00 | 0.02 | 0.00 | 0.05 | 0.00 | 6.5 | 0.04 | 0.00 | 0.04 | 0.04 | 0.03 |
| 1.6 | 0.00 | 0.02 | 0.00 | 0.05 | 0.00 | 6.6 | 0.04 | 0.00 | 0.04 | 0.04 | 0.03 |
| 1.7 | 0.00 | 0.02 | 0.00 | 0.05 | 0.00 | 6.7 | 0.04 | 0.00 | 0.04 | 0.05 | 0.02 |
| 1.8 | 0.00 | 0.02 | 0.00 | 0.04 | 0.00 | 6.8 | 0.04 | 0.00 | 0.04 | 0.05 | 0.02 |
| 1.9 | 0.00 | 0.02 | 0.00 | 0.04 | 0.00 | 6.9 | 0.04 | 0.00 | 0.04 | 0.05 | 0.02 |
| 2.0 | 0.00 | 0.02 | 0.00 | 0.04 | 0.00 | 7.0 | 0.04 | 0.00 | 0.04 | 0.06 | 0.01 |
| 2.1 | 0.01 | 0.02 | 0.00 | 0.04 | 0.00 | 7.1 | 0.04 | 0.01 | 0.04 | 0.06 | 0.01 |
| 2.2 | 0.01 | 0.02 | 0.00 | 0.04 | 0.01 | 7.2 | 0.04 | 0.01 | 0.04 | 0.06 | 0.01 |
| 2.3 | 0.01 | 0.02 | 0.01 | 0.03 | 0.01 | 7.3 | 0.04 | 0.01 | 0.03 | 0.06 | 0.01 |
| 2.4 | 0.01 | 0.02 | 0.01 | 0.03 | 0.01 | 7.4 | 0.04 | 0.01 | 0.03 | 0.06 | 0.00 |
| 2.5 | 0.01 | 0.02 | 0.01 | 0.03 | 0.02 | 7.5 | 0.04 | 0.01 | 0.03 | 0.06 | 0.00 |
| 2.6 | 0.01 | 0.02 | 0.01 | 0.03 | 0.02 | 7.6 | 0.04 | 0.01 | 0.03 | 0.06 | 0.00 |
| 2.7 | 0.01 | 0.02 | 0.01 | 0.02 | 0.02 | 7.7 | 0.04 | 0.01 | 0.03 | 0.06 | 0.00 |
| 2.8 | 0.01 | 0.01 | 0.01 | 0.02 | 0.03 | 7.8 | 0.04 | 0.01 | 0.03 | 0.06 | 0.00 |
| 2.9 | 0.01 | 0.01 | 0.01 | 0.01 | 0.03 | 7.9 | 0.04 | 0.01 | 0.03 | 0.06 | 0.00 |
| 3.0 | 0.01 | 0.01 | 0.01 | 0.01 | 0.03 | 8.0 | 0.04 | 0.01 | 0.03 | 0.06 | 0.00 |
| 3.1 | 0.02 | 0.01 | 0.01 | 0.01 | 0.03 | 8.1 | 0.04 | 0.01 | 0.03 | 0.06 | 0.00 |
| 3.2 | 0.02 | 0.01 | 0.01 | 0.01 | 0.03 | 8.2 | 0.04 | 0.01 | 0.03 | 0.06 | 0.00 |
| 3.3 | 0.02 | 0.01 | 0.02 | 0.00 | 0.04 | 8.3 | 0.04 | 0.01 | 0.02 | 0.06 | 0.00 |
| 3.4 | 0.02 | 0.01 | 0.02 | 0.00 | 0.04 | 8.4 | 0.04 | 0.01 | 0.02 | 0.06 | 0.00 |
| 3.5 | 0.02 | 0.01 | 0.02 | 0.00 | 0.04 | 8.5 | 0.04 | 0.01 | 0.02 | 0.06 | 0.00 |
| 3.6 | 0.02 | 0.01 | 0.02 | 0.00 | 0.04 | 8.6 | 0.04 | 0.02 | 0.02 | 0.06 | 0.00 |
| 3.7 | 0.02 | 0.01 | 0.02 | 0.00 | 0.05 | 8.7 | 0.04 | 0.02 | 0.02 | 0.06 | 0.00 |
| 3.8 | 0.02 | 0.01 | 0.03 | 0.00 | 0.05 | 8.8 | 0.04 | 0.02 | 0.01 | 0.05 | 0.00 |
| 3.9 | 0.02 | 0.01 | 0.03 | 0.00 | 0.05 | 8.9 | 0.04 | 0.02 | 0.01 | 0.05 | 0.00 |
| 4.0 | 0.02 | 0.01 | 0.03 | 0.00 | 0.06 | 9.0 | 0.04 | 0.02 | 0.01 | 0.05 | 0.00 |
| 4.1 | 0.02 | 0.01 | 0.03 | 0.00 | 0.06 | 9.1 | 0.04 | 0.02 | 0.01 | 0.04 | 0.00 |
| 4.2 | 0.02 | 0.01 | 0.03 | 0.00 | 0.06 | 9.2 | 0.04 | 0.02 | 0.01 | 0.04 | 0.00 |
| 4.3 | 0.02 | 0.00 | 0.03 | 0.00 | 0.06 | 9.3 | 0.04 | 0.02 | 0.01 | 0.04 | 0.01 |
| 4.4 | 0.02 | 0.00 | 0.03 | 0.00 | 0.06 | 9.4 | 0.04 | 0.02 | 0.01 | 0.03 | 0.01 |
| 4.5 | 0.02 | 0 00 | 0.03 | 0.00 | 0.06 | 9.5 | 0.04 | 0.02 | 0.01 | 0.03 | 0.01 |
| 4.6 | 0.02 | 0.00 | 0.03 | 0.00 | 0.06 | 9.6 | 0.04 | 0.02 | 0.01 | 0.03 | 0.02 |
| 4.7 | 0.02 | 0.00 | 0.03 | 0.00 | 0.06 | 9.7 | 0.04 | 0.02 | 0.01 | 0.03 | 0.02 |
| 4.8 | 0.03 | 0.00 | 0.04 | 0.00 | 0.06 | 9.8 | 0.03 | 0.02 | 0.00 | 0 02 | 0.02 |
| 4.9 | 0.03 | 0.00 | 0.04 | 0.00 | 0.06 | 9.9 | 0.03 | 0.02 | 0.00 | 0.02 | 0.03 |
| 5.0 | 0.03 | 0.00 | 0.04 | 0.00 | 0.06 | 10.0 | 0.03 | 0.02 | 0.00 | 0.02 | 0.03 |

# LATITUDE TABLES, LXXXIII.-CIX.

ARGUMENTS, PERIODS, AND EQUATIONS.

| TABLE. | ARGUMENT. | PERIOD. | EQUATION. |
|---|---|---|---|
| LXXXIII. | 12′ | 173.31006 | $846''.0 + 527''.5 \sin(2t - 2y)$. |
| LXXXIV. | 73″ | 1095.1653 | $25.7 - 25.7 \sin(2y - 2x)$. |
| LXXXV. | 53 | 117.5394 | $22.1 - 22.1 \sin(2y - 2t + z)$. |
| LXXXVI. | 1 | 27.5546 | $1.3 - 1.3 \sin x$. |
| LXXXVII. | 70 | 329.7906 | $10.3 + 10.3 \sin(2y - 2t - z)$. |
| LXXXVIII. | 4 | 365.2597 | $88.9 + 48.9 \sin z$. |
| LXXXIX. | 4 | 365.2597 | $6.63 - 1.3 \cos z$. |
| XC. | 5′ | 205.8926 | $4.7 + 4.7 \sin 2(x - t)$ |
| XCI. | 5 | 411.7852 | $1.0 - 1.0 \sin(x - t)$. |
| XCII. | 78 | 188.2015 | $15.8 + 15.8 \sin(x + y - 2t)$. |
| XCIII. | 73 | 2190.3306 | $22.2 + 14.4 \sin(y - x)$. |
| XCIV. | 12‴ | 346.6021 | $0.6 - 0.6 \sin(y - t)$. |
| XCV. | 79 | 438.3608 | $0.2 - 0.2 \sin(x - y + z)$. |
| XCVI. | 80 | 313.0547 | $0.1 - 0.1 \sin(y + z - x)$. |
| XCVII. | 81 | 124.2046 | $0.7 + 0.7 \sin(y + z + x - 2t)$. |
| XCVIII. | 82 | 14.8655 | $1.8 + 1.8 \sin(2t - y + x)$. |
| XCIX. | 83 | 39.2116 | $0.7 + 0.7 \sin(2t - y - 2z)$. |
| C. | 84 | 19.1434 | $0.6 - 0.6 \sin(2t + y)$. |
| CI. | 48 | 29.9342 | $0.5 - 0.5 \sin(x + t - y)$. |
| CII. | 85 | 23.5193 | $0.4 + 0.4 \sin(3y - 2t)$. |
| CIII. | 86 | 38.2830 | $0.3 + 0.3 \sin(4t - y - 2x)$. |
| CIV. | 87 | 14.2082 | $0.2 - 0.2 \sin(2t + y + x)$. |
| CV. | 88 | 14.6664 | $0.2 + 0.2 \sin(2t + y - x)$. |
| CVI. | 89 | 19.3122 | $0.2 + 0.2 \sin(2t - y + 2x)$. |
| CVII. | 90 | 32.2808 | $0.2 - 0.2 \sin(2t - y)$. |
| CVIII. | 77 | | $6.2 - 6.18 \sin 3\bar{y}$. |
| CIX. | | | $9.1 + 2.17 \cos \bar{u} - 8''.80 \sin \bar{u}$. |

# TABLE LXXXIII. ARGUMENT 12′.

Equation $= 846''.0 + 527''.5 \sin. (2t - 2y)$.

| Days. | 0 | | 10 | | 20 | | 30 | | Days. |
|---|---|---|---|---|---|---|---|---|---|
| Days. | Equation. | Diff. | Equation. | Diff. | Equation. | Diff. | Equation. | Diff. | Days. |
| d. | ″ | | ″ | | ″ | | ″ | | d. |
| 0.0 | 322.38 | 0.23 | 333.78 | 0.46 | 411.77 | 1.09 | 546.22 | 1.58 | 10.0 |
| 0.1 | 322.15 | 0.22 | 334.24 | 0.47 | 412.86 | 1.09 | 547.80 | 1.58 | 9.9 |
| 0.2 | 321.93 | 0.21 | 334.71 | 0.47 | 413.95 | 1.10 | 549.38 | 1.58 | 9.8 |
| 0.3 | 321.72 | 0.21 | 335.18 | 0.48 | 415.05 | 1.11 | 550.96 | 1.59 | 9.7 |
| 0.4 | 321.51 | 0.20 | 335.66 | 0.49 | 416.16 | 1.11 | 552.55 | 1.59 | 9.6 |
| 0.5 | 321.31 | 0.19 | 336.15 | 0.49 | 417.27 | 1.12 | 554.14 | 1.59 | 9.5 |
| 0.6 | 321.12 | 0.19 | 336.64 | 0.50 | 418.39 | 1.12 | 555.73 | 1.60 | 9.4 |
| 0.7 | 320.93 | 0.18 | 337.14 | 0.51 | 419.51 | 1.13 | 557.33 | 1.60 | 9.3 |
| 0.8 | 320.75 | 0.17 | 337.65 | 0.51 | 420.64 | 1.13 | 558.93 | 1.61 | 9.2 |
| 0.9 | 320.58 | 0.17 | 338.16 | 0.52 | 421.77 | 1.14 | 560.54 | 1.61 | 9.1 |
| 1.0 | 320.41 | 0.16 | 338.68 | 0.53 | 422.91 | 1.14 | 562.15 | 1.61 | 9.0 |
| 1.1 | 320.25 | 0.15 | 339.21 | 0.53 | 424.05 | 1.15 | 563.76 | 1.62 | 8.9 |
| 1.2 | 320.10 | 0.15 | 339.74 | 0.54 | 425.20 | 1.16 | 565.38 | 1.62 | 8.8 |
| 1.3 | 319.95 | 0.14 | 340.28 | 0.55 | 426.36 | 1.16 | 567.00 | 1.62 | 8.7 |
| 1.4 | 319.81 | 0.13 | 340.83 | 0.55 | 427.52 | 1.17 | 568.62 | 1.63 | 8.6 |
| 1.5 | 319.68 | 0.12 | 341.38 | 0.56 | 428.69 | 1.17 | 570.25 | 1.63 | 8.5 |
| 1.6 | 319.56 | 0.12 | 341.94 | 0.57 | 429.86 | 1.18 | 571.88 | 1.64 | 8.4 |
| 1.7 | 319.44 | 0.11 | 342.51 | 0.58 | 431.04 | 1.18 | 573.52 | 1.64 | 8.3 |
| 1.8 | 319.33 | 0.10 | 343.09 | 0.58 | 432.22 | 1.19 | 575.16 | 1.64 | 8.2 |
| 1.9 | 319.23 | 0.10 | 343.67 | 0.59 | 433.41 | 1.20 | 576.80 | 1.65 | 8.1 |
| 2.0 | 319.13 | 0.09 | 344.26 | 0.59 | 434.61 | 1.20 | 578.45 | 1.65 | 8.0 |
| 2.1 | 319.04 | 0.08 | 344.85 | 0.60 | 435.81 | 1.20 | 580.10 | 1.65 | 7.9 |
| 2.2 | 318.96 | 0.08 | 345.45 | 0.61 | 437.01 | 1.21 | 581.75 | 1.66 | 7.8 |
| 2.3 | 318.88 | 0.07 | 346.06 | 0.61 | 438.22 | 1.22 | 583.41 | 1.66 | 7.7 |
| 2.4 | 318.81 | 0.06 | 346.67 | 0.62 | 439.44 | 1.22 | 585.07 | 1.66 | 7.6 |
| 2.5 | 318.75 | 0.06 | 347.29 | 0.63 | 440.66 | 1.23 | 586.73 | 1.67 | 7.5 |
| 2.6 | 318.69 | 0.05 | 347.92 | 0.63 | 441.89 | 1.23 | 588.40 | 1.67 | 7.4 |
| 2.7 | 318.64 | 0.04 | 348.55 | 0.64 | 443.12 | 1.24 | 590.07 | 1.68 | 7.3 |
| 2.8 | 318.60 | 0.03 | 349.19 | 0.65 | 444.36 | 1.24 | 591.75 | 1.68 | 7.2 |
| 2.9 | 318.57 | 0.03 | 349.84 | 0.65 | 445.60 | 1.25 | 593.43 | 1.68 | 7.1 |
| 3.0 | 318.54 | 0.02 | 350.49 | 0.66 | 446.85 | 1.25 | 595.11 | 1.68 | 7.0 |
| 3.1 | 318.52 | 0.01 | 351.15 | 0.67 | 448.10 | 1.26 | 596.79 | 1.69 | 6.9 |
| 3.2 | 318.51 | 0.01 | 351.82 | 0.67 | 449.36 | 1.26 | 598.48 | 1.69 | 6.8 |
| 3.3 | 318.50 | 0.00 | 352.49 | 0.68 | 450.62 | 1.27 | 600.17 | 1.69 | 6.7 |
| 3.4 | 318.50 | 0.01 | 353.17 | 0.68 | 451.89 | 1.27 | 601.86 | 1.70 | 6.6 |
| 3.5 | 318.51 | 0.01 | 353.85 | 0.69 | 453.16 | 1.28 | 603.56 | 1.70 | 6.5 |
| 3.6 | 318.52 | 0.02 | 354.54 | 0.70 | 454.44 | 1.29 | 605.26 | 1.70 | 6.4 |
| 3.7 | 318.54 | 0.03 | 355.24 | 0.70 | 455.73 | 1.29 | 606.96 | 1.71 | 6.3 |
| 3.8 | 318.57 | 0.04 | 355.94 | 0.71 | 457.02 | 1.30 | 608.67 | 1.71 | 6.2 |
| 3.9 | 318.61 | 0.04 | 356.65 | 0.72 | 458.32 | 1.30 | 610.38 | 1.71 | 6.1 |
| 4.0 | 318.65 | 0.05 | 357.37 | 0.72 | 459.62 | 1.31 | 612.09 | 1.72 | 6.0 |
| 4.1 | 318.70 | 0.06 | 358.09 | 0.73 | 460.93 | 1.31 | 613.81 | 1.72 | 5.9 |
| 4.2 | 318.76 | 0.06 | 358.82 | 0.74 | 462.24 | 1.32 | 615.53 | 1.72 | 5.8 |
| 4.3 | 318.82 | 0.07 | 359.56 | 0.74 | 463.56 | 1.32 | 617.25 | 1.72 | 5.7 |
| 4.4 | 318.89 | 0.08 | 360.30 | 0.75 | 464.88 | 1.32 | 618.97 | 1.73 | 5.6 |
| 4.5 | 318.97 | 0.08 | 361.05 | 0.76 | 466.20 | 1.33 | 620.70 | 1.73 | 5.5 |
| 4.6 | 319.05 | 0.09 | 361.81 | 0.76 | 467.53 | 1.33 | 622.43 | 1.73 | 5.4 |
| 4.7 | 319.14 | 0.10 | 362.57 | 0.77 | 468.86 | 1.34 | 624.16 | 1.74 | 5.3 |
| 4.8 | 319.24 | 0.10 | 363.34 | 0.78 | 470.20 | 1.34 | 625.90 | 1.74 | 5.2 |
| 4.9 | 319.34 | 0.11 | 364.12 | 0.78 | 471.54 | 1.35 | 627.64 | 1.74 | 5.1 |
| 5.0 | 319.45 | 0.12 | 364.90 | 0.79 | 472.89 | 1.35 | 629.38 | 1.74 | 5.0 |
| Days. | 170 | | 160 | | 150 | | 140 | | Days. |

NOTE. — Arg. 12′ = Arg. 12.

# TABLE LXXXIII. ARGUMENT 12′.

Equation = 846″.0 + 527″.5 sin. (2t — 2y).

| Days. | 0 | | 10 | | 20 | | 30 | | Days. |
|---|---|---|---|---|---|---|---|---|---|
| Days. | Equation. | Diff. | Equation. | Diff. | Equation. | Diff. | Equation. | Diff. | Days. |
| d. | ″ | | ″ | | ″ | | ″ | | d. |
| 5.0 | 319.45 | 0.12 | 364.90 | 0.79 | 472.89 | 1.35 | 629.38 | 1.74 | 5.0 |
| 5.1 | 319.57 | 0.13 | 365.69 | 0.79 | 474.24 | 1.36 | 631.12 | 1.75 | 4.9 |
| 5.2 | 319.70 | 0.13 | 366.48 | 0.80 | 475.60 | 1.36 | 632.87 | 1.75 | 4.8 |
| 5.3 | 319.83 | 0.14 | 367.28 | 0.80 | 476.96 | 1.37 | 634.62 | 1.75 | 4.7 |
| 5.4 | 319.97 | 0.15 | 368.08 | 0.81 | 478.33 | 1.37 | 636.37 | 1.76 | 4.6 |
| 5.5 | 320.12 | 0.15 | 368.89 | 0.82 | 479.70 | 1.38 | 638.13 | 1.76 | 4.5 |
| 5.6 | 320.27 | 0.16 | 369.71 | 0.82 | 481.08 | 1.38 | 639.89 | 1.76 | 4.4 |
| 5.7 | 320.43 | 0.17 | 370.53 | 0.83 | 482.46 | 1.39 | 641.65 | 1.77 | 4.3 |
| 5.8 | 320.60 | 0.17 | 371.36 | 0.83 | 483.85 | 1.40 | 643.42 | 1.77 | 4.2 |
| 5.9 | 320.77 | 0.18 | 372.19 | 0.84 | 485.25 | 1.40 | 645.19 | 1.77 | 4.1 |
| 6.0 | 320.95 | 0.19 | 373.03 | 0.85 | 486.65 | 1.40 | 646.96 | 1.77 | 4.0 |
| 6.1 | 321.14 | 0.19 | 373.88 | 0.86 | 488.05 | 1.41 | 648.73 | 1.78 | 3.9 |
| 6.2 | 321.33 | 0.20 | 374.74 | 0.87 | 489.46 | 1.41 | 650.51 | 1.78 | 3.8 |
| 6.3 | 321.53 | 0.21 | 375.61 | 0.87 | 490.87 | 1.42 | 652.29 | 1.78 | 3.7 |
| 6.4 | 321.74 | 0.22 | 376.48 | 0.88 | 492.29 | 1.42 | 654.07 | 1.78 | 3.6 |
| 6.5 | 321.96 | 0.22 | 377.36 | 0.88 | 493.71 | 1.43 | 655.85 | 1.79 | 3.5 |
| 6.6 | 322.18 | 0.23 | 378.24 | 0.89 | 495.14 | 1.43 | 657.64 | 1.79 | 3.4 |
| 6.7 | 322.41 | 0.24 | 379.13 | 0.89 | 496.57 | 1.43 | 659.43 | 1.79 | 3.3 |
| 6.8 | 322.65 | 0.24 | 380.02 | 0.90 | 498.00 | 1.44 | 661.22 | 1.79 | 3.2 |
| 6.9 | 322.89 | 0.25 | 380.92 | 0.91 | 499.44 | 1.44 | 663.01 | 1.79 | 3.1 |
| 7.0 | 323.14 | 0.26 | 381.83 | 0.91 | 500.88 | 1.45 | 664.80 | 1.80 | 3.0 |
| 7.1 | 323.40 | 0.26 | 382.74 | 0.92 | 502.33 | 1.45 | 666.60 | 1.80 | 2.9 |
| 7.2 | 323.66 | 0.27 | 383.66 | 0.92 | 503.78 | 1.46 | 668.40 | 1.80 | 2.8 |
| 7.3 | 323.93 | 0.28 | 384.58 | 0.93 | 505.24 | 1.46 | 670.20 | 1.80 | 2.7 |
| 7.4 | 324 21 | 0.28 | 385.51 | 0.94 | 506.70 | 1.47 | 672.00 | 1.81 | 2.6 |
| 7.5 | 324.49 | 0.29 | 386.45 | 0.94 | 508.17 | 1.47 | 673.81 | 1.81 | 2.5 |
| 7.6 | 324.78 | 0.30 | 387.39 | 0.95 | 509.64 | 1.47 | 675.62 | 1.81 | 2.4 |
| 7.7 | 325.08 | 0.30 | 388.34 | 0.95 | 511.11 | 1.48 | 677.43 | 1.81 | 2.3 |
| 7.8 | 325.38 | 0.31 | 389.29 | 0.96 | 512.59 | 1.48 | 679.24 | 1.81 | 2.2 |
| 7.9 | 325.69 | 0.31 | 390.25 | 0.97 | 514.07 | 1.49 | 681.05 | 1.82 | 2.1 |
| 8.0 | 326.00 | 0.32 | 391.22 | 0.97 | 515.56 | 1.49 | 682.87 | 1.82 | 2.0 |
| 8.1 | 326.32 | 0.33 | 392.19 | 0.98 | 517.05 | 1.50 | 684.69 | 1.82 | 1.9 |
| 8.2 | 326.65 | 0.34 | 393.17 | 0.98 | 518.55 | 1.50 | 686.51 | 1.82 | 1.8 |
| 8.3 | 326.99 | 0.34 | 394.15 | 0.99 | 520.05 | 1.51 | 688.33 | 1.83 | 1.7 |
| 8.4 | 327.33 | 0.35 | 395.14 | 1.00 | 521.56 | 1.51 | 690.16 | 1.83 | 1.6 |
| 8.5 | 327.68 | 0.36 | 396.14 | 1.00 | 523.07 | 1.51 | 691.99 | 1.83 | 1.5 |
| 8.6 | 328.04 | 0.37 | 397.14 | 1.01 | 524.58 | 1.52 | 693.82 | 1.83 | 1.4 |
| 8.7 | 328.41 | 0.37 | 398.15 | 1.01 | 526.10 | 1.52 | 695.65 | 1.83 | 1.3 |
| 8.8 | 328.78 | 0.38 | 399.16 | 1.02 | 527.62 | 1.53 | 697.48 | 1.84 | 1.2 |
| 8.9 | 329.16 | 0.39 | 400.18 | 1.02 | 529.15 | 1.53 | 699.32 | 1.84 | 1.1 |
| 9.0 | 329.55 | 0.39 | 401.20 | 1.03 | 530.68 | 1.54 | 701.16 | 1.84 | 1.0 |
| 9.1 | 329.94 | 0.40 | 402.23 | 1.04 | 532.22 | 1.54 | 703 00 | 1.84 | 0.9 |
| 9.2 | 330.34 | 0.41 | 403.27 | 1.04 | 533.76 | 1.54 | 704.84 | 1.84 | 0.8 |
| 9.3 | 330.75 | 0.41 | 404.31 | 1.05 | 535.30 | 1.55 | 706.68 | 1.85 | 0.7 |
| 9.4 | 331.16 | 0.42 | 405.36 | 1 05 | 536.85 | 1.55 | 708.53 | 1.85 | 0.6 |
| 9.5 | 331.58 | 0.43 | 406.41 | 1.06 | 538.40 | 1.56 | 710.38 | 1.85 | 0.5 |
| 9.6 | 332.01 | 0.43 | 407.47 | 1.07 | 539.96 | 1.56 | 712.23 | 1.85 | 0.4 |
| 9.7 | 332.44 | 0.44 | 408.54 | 1.07 | 541.52 | 1.56 | 714.08 | 1.85 | 0.3 |
| 9.8 | 332.88 | 0.45 | 409.61 | 1.08 | 543.08 | 1.57 | 715.93 | 1.85 | 0.2 |
| 9.9 | 333.33 | 0.45 | 410.69 | 1.08 | 544.65 | 1.57 | 717.78 | 1.85 | 0.1 |
| 10.0 | 333.78 | 0.46 | 411.77 | 1.09 | 546.22 | 1.58 | 719.63 | 1.86 | 0.0 |
| Days. | 170 | | 160 | | 150 | | 140 | | Days. |

NOTE. — Arg. 12′ = Arg. 12.

# TABLE LXXXIII. ARGUMENT 12′.

Equation = 846″.0 + 527″.5 sin. (2t — 2y).

| Days. | 40 | | 50 | | 60 | | 70 | | 80 | | Days. |
|---|---|---|---|---|---|---|---|---|---|---|---|
| Days. | Equation. | Diff. | Equation. | Diff. | Equation. | Diff. | Equation. | Diff. | Equation. | Diff. | Days. |
| d. | ″ | | ″ | | ″ | | ″ | | ″ | | d. |
| 0.0 | 719.63 | 1.86 | 909.49 | 1.90 | 1091.07 | 1.69 | 1240.80 | 1.27 | 1339.22 | 0.68 | 10.0 |
| 0.1 | 721.49 | 1.86 | 911.39 | 1.90 | 1092.76 | 1.69 | 1242.07 | 1.26 | 1339.90 | 0.67 | 9.9 |
| 0.2 | 723.35 | 1.86 | 913.29 | 1.90 | 1094.45 | 1.69 | 1243.33 | 1.25 | 1340.57 | 0.66 | 9.8 |
| 0.3 | 725.21 | 1.86 | 915.19 | 1.89 | 1096.14 | 1.68 | 1244.58 | 1.25 | 1341.23 | 0.66 | 9.7 |
| 0.4 | 727.07 | 1.86 | 917.08 | 1.89 | 1097.82 | 1.68 | 1245.83 | 1.24 | 1341.89 | 0.65 | 9.6 |
| 0.5 | 728.93 | 1.87 | 918.97 | 1.89 | 1099.50 | 1.68 | 1247.07 | 1.24 | 1342.54 | 0.64 | 9.5 |
| 0.6 | 730.80 | 1.87 | 920.86 | 1.89 | 1101.18 | 1.67 | 1248.31 | 1.23 | 1343.18 | 0.63 | 9.4 |
| 0.7 | 732.67 | 1.87 | 922.75 | 1.89 | 1102.85 | 1.67 | 1249.54 | 1.23 | 1343.81 | 0.63 | 9.3 |
| 0.8 | 734.54 | 1.87 | 924.64 | 1.89 | 1104.52 | 1.66 | 1250.77 | 1.23 | 1344.44 | 0.62 | 9.2 |
| 0.9 | 736.41 | 1.87 | 926.53 | 1.89 | 1106.18 | 1.66 | 1252.00 | 1.22 | 1345.06 | 0.61 | 9.1 |
| 1.0 | 738.28 | 1.87 | 928.42 | 1.89 | 1107.84 | 1.66 | 1253.22 | 1.21 | 1345.67 | 0.61 | 9.0 |
| 1.1 | 740.15 | 1.88 | 930.31 | 1.89 | 1109.50 | 1.66 | 1254.43 | 1.21 | 1346.28 | 0.60 | 8.9 |
| 1.2 | 742.03 | 1.88 | 932.20 | 1.89 | 1111.16 | 1.65 | 1255.64 | 1.20 | 1346.88 | 0.60 | 8.8 |
| 1.3 | 743.91 | 1.88 | 934.09 | 1.88 | 1112.81 | 1.65 | 1256.84 | 1.20 | 1347.48 | 0.59 | 8.7 |
| 1.4 | 745.79 | 1.88 | 935.97 | 1.88 | 1114.46 | 1.64 | 1258.04 | 1.19 | 1348.07 | 0.58 | 8.6 |
| 1.5 | 747.67 | 1.88 | 937.85 | 1.88 | 1116.10 | 1.64 | 1259.23 | 1.19 | 1348.65 | 0.58 | 8.5 |
| 1.6 | 749.55 | 1.88 | 939.73 | 1.88 | 1117.74 | 1.64 | 1260.42 | 1.18 | 1349.23 | 0.57 | 8.4 |
| 1.7 | 751.43 | 1.88 | 941.61 | 1.88 | 1119.38 | 1.63 | 1261.60 | 1.17 | 1349.80 | 0.56 | 8.3 |
| 1.8 | 753.31 | 1.88 | 943.49 | 1.88 | 1121.01 | 1.63 | 1262.77 | 1.17 | 1350.36 | 0.55 | 8.2 |
| 1.9 | 755.19 | 1.88 | 945.37 | 1.88 | 1122.64 | 1.63 | 1263.94 | 1.16 | 1350.91 | 0.55 | 8.1 |
| 2.0 | 757.07 | 1.89 | 947.25 | 1.88 | 1124.27 | 1.62 | 1265.10 | 1.16 | 1351.46 | 0.54 | 8.0 |
| 2.1 | 758.96 | 1.89 | 949.13 | 1.87 | 1125.89 | 1.62 | 1266.26 | 1.15 | 1352.00 | 0.54 | 7.9 |
| 2.2 | 760.85 | 1.89 | 951.00 | 1.87 | 1127.51 | 1.62 | 1267.41 | 1.15 | 1352.54 | 0.53 | 7.8 |
| 2.3 | 762.74 | 1.89 | 952.87 | 1.87 | 1129.13 | 1.61 | 1268.56 | 1.14 | 1353.07 | 0.52 | 7.7 |
| 2.4 | 764.63 | 1.89 | 954.74 | 1.87 | 1130.74 | 1.61 | 1269.70 | 1.14 | 1353.59 | 0.52 | 7.6 |
| 2.5 | 766.52 | 1.89 | 956.61 | 1.87 | 1132.35 | 1.60 | 1270.84 | 1.13 | 1354.11 | 0.51 | 7.5 |
| 2.6 | 768.41 | 1.89 | 958.48 | 1.87 | 1133.95 | 1.60 | 1271.97 | 1.13 | 1354.62 | 0.51 | 7.4 |
| 2.7 | 770.30 | 1.89 | 960.35 | 1.87 | 1135.55 | 1.60 | 1273.10 | 1.12 | 1355.13 | 0.50 | 7.3 |
| 2.8 | 772.19 | 1.89 | 962.22 | 1.86 | 1137.15 | 1.59 | 1274.22 | 1.11 | 1355.63 | 0.49 | 7.2 |
| 2.9 | 774.08 | 1.90 | 964.08 | 1.86 | 1138.74 | 1.59 | 1275.33 | 1.11 | 1356.12 | 0.49 | 7.1 |
| 3.0 | 775.98 | 1.89 | 965.94 | 1.86 | 1140.33 | 1.58 | 1276.44 | 1.10 | 1356.61 | 0.48 | 7.0 |
| 3.1 | 777.87 | 1.90 | 967.80 | 1.86 | 1141.91 | 1.58 | 1277.54 | 1.10 | 1357.09 | 0.47 | 6.9 |
| 3.2 | 779.77 | 1.90 | 969.66 | 1.86 | 1143.49 | 1.58 | 1278.64 | 1.09 | 1357.56 | 0.46 | 6.8 |
| 3.3 | 781.67 | 1.90 | 971.52 | 1.86 | 1145.07 | 1.57 | 1279.73 | 1.09 | 1358.02 | 0.46 | 6.7 |
| 3.4 | 783.57 | 1.90 | 973.38 | 1.85 | 1146.64 | 1.57 | 1280.82 | 1.08 | 1358.48 | 0.45 | 6.6 |
| 3.5 | 785.47 | 1.90 | 975.23 | 1.85 | 1148.21 | 1.57 | 1281.90 | 1.07 | 1358.93 | 0.44 | 6.5 |
| 3.6 | 787.37 | 1.90 | 977.08 | 1.85 | 1149.78 | 1.56 | 1282.97 | 1.07 | 1359.37 | 0.44 | 6.4 |
| 3.7 | 789.27 | 1.90 | 978.93 | 1.85 | 1151.34 | 1.56 | 1284.04 | 1.06 | 1359.81 | 0.43 | 6.3 |
| 3.8 | 791.17 | 1.90 | 980.78 | 1.85 | 1152.90 | 1.55 | 1285.10 | 1.06 | 1360.24 | 0.42 | 6.2 |
| 3.9 | 793.07 | 1.90 | 982.63 | 1.85 | 1154.45 | 1.55 | 1286.16 | 1.05 | 1360.66 | 0.42 | 6.1 |
| 4.0 | 794.97 | 1.90 | 984.48 | 1.84 | 1156.00 | 1.55 | 1287.21 | 1.05 | 1361.08 | 0.41 | 6.0 |
| 4.1 | 796.87 | 1.90 | 986.32 | 1.84 | 1157.55 | 1.54 | 1288.26 | 1.04 | 1361.49 | 0.40 | 5.9 |
| 4.2 | 798.77 | 1.90 | 988.16 | 1.84 | 1159.09 | 1.54 | 1289.30 | 1.03 | 1361.89 | 0.40 | 5.8 |
| 4.3 | 800.67 | 1.91 | 990.00 | 1.84 | 1160.63 | 1.53 | 1290.33 | 1.03 | 1362.29 | 0.39 | 5.7 |
| 4.4 | 802.58 | 1.91 | 991.84 | 1.84 | 1162.16 | 1.53 | 1291.36 | 1.02 | 1362.68 | 0.38 | 5.6 |
| 4.5 | 804.49 | 1.91 | 993.68 | 1.84 | 1163.69 | 1.52 | 1292.38 | 1.02 | 1363.06 | 0.37 | 5.5 |
| 4.6 | 806.40 | 1.91 | 995.52 | 1.83 | 1165.21 | 1.52 | 1293.40 | 1.01 | 1363.43 | 0.37 | 5.4 |
| 4.7 | 808.31 | 1.91 | 997.35 | 1.83 | 1166.73 | 1.52 | 1294.41 | 1.00 | 1363 80 | 0.36 | 5.3 |
| 4.8 | 810.22 | 1.91 | 999.18 | 1.83 | 1168.25 | 1.51 | 1295.41 | 1.00 | 1364.16 | 0.35 | 5.2 |
| 4.9 | 812.13 | 1.91 | 1001.01 | 1.83 | 1169.76 | 1.51 | 1296.41 | 0.99 | 1364.51 | 0.35 | 5.1 |
| 5.0 | 814.04 | 1.91 | 1002.84 | 1.82 | 1171.27 | 1.50 | 1297.40 | 0.99 | 1364.86 | 0.34 | 5.0 |
| Days. | 130 | | 120 | | 110 | | 100 | | 90 | | Days. |

NOTE. — Arg. 12′ = Arg. 12.

# TABLE LXXXIII. ARGUMENT 12′.

Equation = 846″.0 + 527″.5 sin. (2t — 2y).

| Days. | 40 | | 50 | | 60 | | 70 | | 80 | | Days. |
|---|---|---|---|---|---|---|---|---|---|---|---|
| Days. | Equation. | Diff. | Equation. | Diff. | Equation. | Diff. | Equation. | Diff. | Equation. | Diff. | Days. |
| d. | ″ | | ″ | | ″ | | ″ | | ″ | | d. |
| 5.0 | 814.04 | 1.91 | 1002.84 | 1.82 | 1171.27 | 1.50 | 1297.40 | 0.99 | 1364.86 | 0.34 | 5.0 |
| 5.1 | 815.95 | 1.91 | 1004.66 | 1.82 | 1172.77 | 1.50 | 1298.39 | 0.98 | 1365.20 | 0 33 | 4.9 |
| 5.2 | 817.86 | 1.91 | 1006.48 | 1.82 | 1174.27 | 1.49 | 1299.37 | 0.97 | 1365.53 | 0.33 | 4.8 |
| 5.3 | 819.77 | 1.91 | 1008.30 | 1.82 | 1175.76 | 1.49 | 1300.34 | 0.97 | 1365.86 | 0.32 | 4.7 |
| 5.4 | 821.68 | 1.91 | 1010.12 | 1.82 | 1177.25 | 1.48 | 1301.31 | 0.96 | 1366.18 | 0.31 | 4.6 |
| 5.5 | 823.59 | 1.91 | 1011.94 | 1.82 | 1178.73 | 1.48 | 1302.27 | 0.96 | 1366.49 | 0.31 | 4.5 |
| 5.6 | 825.50 | 1.91 | 1013.76 | 1.81 | 1180.21 | 1.48 | 1303.23 | 0.95 | 1366.80 | 0.30 | 4.4 |
| 5.7 | 827.41 | 1.91 | 1015.57 | 1.81 | 1181.69 | 1.47 | 1304.18 | 0.95 | 1367.10 | 0.29 | 4.3 |
| 5.8 | 829.32 | 1.91 | 1017.38 | 1.81 | 1183.16 | 1.47 | 1305.13 | 0.94 | 1367.39 | 0.29 | 4.2 |
| 5.9 | 831.23 | 1.91 | 1019.19 | 1.81 | 1184.63 | 1.47 | 1306.07 | 0.93 | 1367.68 | 0.28 | 4.1 |
| 6.0 | 833.14 | 1.91 | 1021.00 | 1.80 | 1186.10 | 1.46 | 1307.00 | 0.93 | 1367.96 | 0.27 | 4.0 |
| 6.1 | 835.05 | 1.92 | 1022.80 | 1.80 | 1187.56 | 1.45 | 1307.93 | 0.92 | 1368.23 | 0.27 | 3.9 |
| 6.2 | 836.97 | 1.91 | 1024.60 | 1.80 | 1189.01 | 1.45 | 1308.85 | 0.91 | 1368.50 | 0.26 | 3.8 |
| 6.3 | 838.88 | 1.91 | 1026.40 | 1.80 | 1190.46 | 1.45 | 1309.76 | 0.91 | 1368.76 | 0.25 | 3.7 |
| 6.4 | 840.79 | 1.91 | 1028.20 | 1.79 | 1191.91 | 1.44 | 1310.67 | 0.90 | 1369.01 | 0.25 | 3.6 |
| 6.5 | 842.70 | 1.92 | 1029.99 | 1.79 | 1193.35 | 1.44 | 1311.57 | 0.90 | 1369 26 | 0.24 | 3.5 |
| 6.6 | 844.62 | 1.91 | 1031.78 | 1.79 | 1194.79 | 1.43 | 1312.47 | 0.89 | 1369.50 | 0.23 | 3.4 |
| 6.7 | 846.53 | 1.91 | 1033.57 | 1.79 | 1196.22 | 1.43 | 1313.36 | 0.88 | 1369.73 | 0.22 | 3.3 |
| 6.8 | 848.44 | 1.91 | 1035.36 | 1.78 | 1197.65 | 1.42 | 1314.24 | 0.88 | 1369.95 | 0.22 | 3.2 |
| 6.9 | 850.35 | 1.91 | 1037.14 | 1.78 | 1199.07 | 1.42 | 1315.12 | 0.87 | 1370.17 | 0.21 | 3.1 |
| 7.0 | 852.26 | 1.92 | 1038.92 | 1.78 | 1200.49 | 1.41 | 1315.99 | 0.87 | 1370.38 | 0.20 | 3 0 |
| 7.1 | 854.18 | 1.91 | 1040.70 | 1.78 | 1201.90 | 1.41 | 1316.86 | 0.86 | 1370.58 | 0.20 | 2.9 |
| 7.2 | 856.09 | 1.91 | 1042.48 | 1.77 | 1203.31 | 1.40 | 1317.72 | 0.85 | 1370.78 | 0.19 | 2.8 |
| 7.3 | 858.00 | 1.91 | 1044.25 | 1.77 | 1204.71 | 1.40 | 1318.57 | 0.85 | 1370.97 | 0.18 | 2.7 |
| 7.4 | 859.91 | 1.91 | 1046.02 | 1.77 | 1206.11 | 1.39 | 1319.42 | 0.84 | 1371.15 | 0.18 | 2.6 |
| 7.5 | 861.82 | 1.92 | 1047.79 | 1.77 | 1207.50 | 1.39 | 1320.26 | 0.84 | 1371.33 | 0.17 | 2.5 |
| 7.6 | 863.74 | 1.91 | 1049.56 | 1.76 | 1208.89 | 1.39 | 1321.10 | 0.83 | 1371.50 | 0.16 | 2.4 |
| 7.7 | 865.65 | 1.91 | 1051.32 | 1.76 | 1210.28 | 1.38 | 1321.93 | 0.82 | 1371.66 | 0.16 | 2.3 |
| 7.8 | 867.56 | 1.91 | 1053.08 | 1.76 | 1211.66 | 1.38 | 1322.75 | 0.81 | 1371.82 | 0.15 | 2.2 |
| 7.9 | 869.47 | 1.91 | 1054.84 | 1.75 | 1213.04 | 1.38 | 1323.56 | 0.81 | 1371.97 | 0.14 | 2.1 |
| 8.0 | 871.38 | 1.91 | 1056.59 | 1.75 | 1214.42 | 1.37 | 1324.37 | 0.80 | 1372.11 | 0.14 | 2.0 |
| 8.1 | 873.29 | 1.91 | 1058.34 | 1.75 | 1215.79 | 1.36 | 1325.17 | 0.80 | 1372.25 | 0.13 | 1.9 |
| 8.2 | 875.20 | 1.91 | 1060.09 | 1.75 | 1217.15 | 1.36 | 1325.97 | 0.79 | 1372.38 | 0.12 | 1.8 |
| 8.3 | 877.11 | 1.90 | 1061.84 | 1.74 | 1218.51 | 1.35 | 1326.76 | 0.78 | 1372.50 | 0.11 | 1.7 |
| 8.4 | 879.01 | 1.91 | 1063.58 | 1.74 | 1219.86 | 1.35 | 1327.54 | 0.78 | 1372.61 | 0.11 | 1.6 |
| 8.5 | 880.92 | 1.91 | 1065.32 | 1.74 | 1221.21 | 1.34 | 1328.32 | 0.77 | 1372.72 | 0.10 | 1.5 |
| 8.6 | 882.83 | 1.91 | 1067.06 | 1.73 | 1222.55 | 1.34 | 1329.09 | 0.76 | 1372.82 | 0.09 | 1.4 |
| 8.7 | 884.74 | 1.91 | 1068.79 | 1.73 | 1223.89 | 1.33 | 1329.85 | 0.76 | 1372.91 | 0.09 | 1.3 |
| 8.8 | 886.65 | 1.90 | 1070.52 | 1.73 | 1225.22 | 1.32 | 1330.61 | 0.75 | 1373.00 | 0.08 | 1.2 |
| 8.9 | 888.55 | 1.91 | 1072.25 | 1.73 | 1226.54 | 1.32 | 1331.36 | 0.74 | 1373.08 | 0.07 | 1.1 |
| 9.0 | 890.46 | 1.91 | 1073.98 | 1.72 | 1227.86 | 1.32 | 1332.10 | 0.74 | 1373.15 | 0.07 | 1.0 |
| 9.1 | 892.37 | 1.91 | 1075.70 | 1.72 | 1229.18 | 1.31 | 1332.84 | 0.73 | 1373.22 | 0.06 | 0.9 |
| 9.2 | 894.28 | 1.91 | 1077.42 | 1.72 | 1230.49 | 1.31 | 1333.57 | 0.73 | 1373.28 | 0.05 | 0.8 |
| 9.3 | 896.19 | 1.90 | 1079.14 | 1.71 | 1231.80 | 1.30 | 1334.30 | 0.72 | 1373.33 | 0.05 | 0.7 |
| 9.4 | 898.09 | 1.90 | 1080.85 | 1.71 | 1233.10 | 1.30 | 1335.02 | 0.71 | 1373.38 | 0.04 | 0.6 |
| 9.5 | 899.99 | 1.90 | 1082.56 | 1.71 | 1234.40 | 1.29 | 1335.73 | 0.71 | 1373.42 | 0.03 | 0.5 |
| 9.6 | 901.89 | 1.90 | 1084.27 | 1.70 | 1235.69 | 1.29 | 1336.44 | 0.70 | 1373.45 | 0.02 | 0.4 |
| 9.7 | 903.79 | 1.90 | 1085.97 | 1.70 | 1236.98 | 1.28 | 1337.14 | 0.70 | 1373.47 | 0.02 | 0.3 |
| 9.8 | 905.69 | 1.90 | 1087.67 | 1.70 | 1238.26 | 1.27 | 1337.84 | 0.69 | 1373.49 | 0.01 | 0.2 |
| 9.9 | 907.59 | 1.90 | 1089.37 | 1.70 | 1239.53 | 1.27 | 1338.53 | 0.69 | 1373.50 | 0.00 | 0.1 |
| 10.0 | 909.49 | 1.90 | 1091.07 | 1.69 | 1240.80 | 1.27 | 1339.22 | 0.68 | 1373.50 | 0.00 | 0.0 |
| Days. | 130 | | 120 | | 110 | | 100 | | 90 | | Days. |

Note. — Arg. 12′ = Arg. 12.

# TABLES LXXXIV. LXXXV.

| TABLES | LXXXIV. | LXXXV. |
|---|---|---|
| ARGUMENTS | **73″.** | **53.** |

**Table LXXXIV.**

| Days. | **0** | **100** | **200** | **300** | **400** | **500** | Days. |
|---|---|---|---|---|---|---|---|
| Days. | | | | | | | Days. |
| 0 | 1.15″ | 0.95″ | 8.68″ | 21.85″ | 36.26″ | 47.29″ | 100 |
| 01 | 1.11 | 0.99 | 8.79 | 21.99 | 36.40 | 47.37 | 99 |
| 02 | 1.07 | 1.03 | 8.90 | 22.14 | 36.53 | 47.45 | 98 |
| 03 | 1.03 | 1.07 | 9.01 | 22.28 | 36.67 | 47.53 | 97 |
| 04 | 0.99 | 1.11 | 9.12 | 22.43 | 36.80 | 47.61 | 96 |
| 05 | 0.95 | 1.16 | 9.23 | 22.58 | 36.93 | 47.68 | 95 |
| 06 | 0.91 | 1.20 | 9.34 | 22.72 | 37.06 | 47.76 | 94 |
| 07 | 0.87 | 1.25 | 9.46 | 22.87 | 37.19 | 47.83 | 93 |
| 08 | 0.83 | 1.29 | 9.57 | 23.01 | 37.32 | 47.91 | 92 |
| 09 | 0.79 | 1.34 | 9.69 | 23.16 | 37.45 | 47.98 | 91 |
| 10 | 0.76 | 1.39 | 9.81 | 23.31 | 37.58 | 48.05 | 90 |
| 11 | 0.72 | 1.44 | 9.92 | 23.45 | 37.71 | 48.12 | 89 |
| 12 | 0.69 | 1.49 | 10.04 | 23.60 | 37.84 | 48.19 | 88 |
| 13 | 0.65 | 1.54 | 10.15 | 23.75 | 37.97 | 48.26 | 87 |
| 14 | 0.62 | 1.59 | 10.27 | 23.90 | 38.10 | 48.33 | 86 |
| 15 | 0.59 | 1.64 | 10.39 | 24.05 | 38.23 | 48.40 | 85 |
| 16 | 0.56 | 1.69 | 10.51 | 24.19 | 38.36 | 48.47 | 84 |
| 17 | 0.53 | 1.74 | 10.63 | 24.34 | 38.49 | 48.54 | 83 |
| 18 | 0.50 | 1.80 | 10.75 | 24.48 | 38.62 | 48.61 | 82 |
| 19 | 0.47 | 1.85 | 10.87 | 24.63 | 38.75 | 48.68 | 81 |
| 20 | 0.44 | 1.91 | 10.99 | 24.78 | 38.87 | 48.74 | 80 |
| 21 | 0.41 | 1.97 | 11.11 | 24.92 | 39.00 | 48.81 | 79 |
| 22 | 0.39 | 2.02 | 11.23 | 25.07 | 39.13 | 48.87 | 78 |
| 23 | 0.36 | 2.08 | 11.35 | 25.22 | 39.25 | 48.94 | 77 |
| 24 | 0.34 | 2.14 | 11.47 | 25.37 | 39.38 | 49.00 | 76 |
| 25 | 0.32 | 2.20 | 11.60 | 25.52 | 39.50 | 49.06 | 75 |
| 26 | 0.29 | 2.26 | 11.72 | 25.66 | 39.63 | 49.12 | 74 |
| 27 | 0.27 | 2.32 | 11.84 | 25.81 | 39.75 | 49.18 | 73 |
| 28 | 0.25 | 2.38 | 11.97 | 25.96 | 39.87 | 49.24 | 72 |
| 29 | 0.23 | 2.44 | 12.09 | 26.11 | 39.99 | 49.30 | 71 |
| 30 | 0.21 | 2.50 | 12.22 | 26.26 | 40.11 | 49.35 | 70 |
| 31 | 0.19 | 2.56 | 12.35 | 26.40 | 40.24 | 49.41 | 69 |
| 32 | 0.17 | 2.63 | 12.47 | 26.55 | 40.36 | 49.47 | 68 |
| 33 | 0.16 | 2.69 | 12.60 | 26.70 | 40.48 | 49.52 | 67 |
| 34 | 0.14 | 2.76 | 12.73 | 26.85 | 40.60 | 49.58 | 66 |
| 35 | 0.13 | 2.83 | 12.86 | 27.00 | 40.72 | 49.63 | 65 |
| 36 | 0.11 | 2.90 | 12.98 | 27.14 | 40.84 | 49.69 | 64 |
| 37 | 0.10 | 2.97 | 13.11 | 27.29 | 40.96 | 49.74 | 63 |
| 38 | 0.09 | 3.04 | 13.24 | 27.44 | 41.08 | 49.79 | 62 |
| 39 | 0.08 | 3.11 | 13.37 | 27.58 | 41.20 | 49.84 | 61 |
| 40 | 0.07 | 3.18 | 13.50 | 27.73 | 41.31 | 49.89 | 60 |
| 41 | 0.06 | 3.25 | 13.63 | 27.88 | 41.43 | 49.94 | 59 |
| 42 | 0.05 | 3.32 | 13.76 | 28.03 | 41.55 | 49.99 | 58 |
| 43 | 0.04 | 3.39 | 13.89 | 28.17 | 41.66 | 50.04 | 57 |
| 44 | 0.03 | 3.46 | 14.02 | 28.32 | 41.78 | 50.09 | 56 |
| 45 | 0.02 | 3.54 | 14.15 | 28.47 | 41.89 | 50.13 | 55 |
| 46 | 0.01 | 3.61 | 14.28 | 28.62 | 42.01 | 50.18 | 54 |
| 47 | 0.01 | 3.69 | 14.41 | 28.76 | 42.12 | 50.22 | 53 |
| 48 | 0.01 | 3.76 | 14.55 | 28.91 | 42.24 | 50.27 | 52 |
| 49 | 0.00 | 3.84 | 14.68 | 29.05 | 42.35 | 50.31 | 51 |
| 50 | 0.00 | 3.92 | 14.82 | 29.20 | 42.46 | 50.35 | 50 |
| Days. | **1100** | **1000** | **900** | **800** | **700** | **600** | Days. |

**Table LXXXV.**

| Days. | **0** | **10** | **20** | Days. |
|---|---|---|---|---|
| Days. | | | | Days. |
| 0.0 | 44.15″ | 41.82″ | 33.98″ | 10.0 |
| 0.1 | 44.16 | 41.77 | 33.88 | 9.9 |
| 0.2 | 44.17 | 41.71 | 33.78 | 9.8 |
| 0.3 | 44.17 | 41.66 | 33.68 | 9.7 |
| 0.4 | 44.18 | 41.60 | 33.58 | 9.6 |
| 0.5 | 44.18 | 41.55 | 33.48 | 9.5 |
| 0.6 | 44.18 | 41.49 | 33.38 | 9.4 |
| 0.7 | 44.19 | 41.43 | 33.28 | 9.3 |
| 0.8 | 44.19 | 41.38 | 33.18 | 9.2 |
| 0.9 | 44.19 | 41.32 | 33.08 | 9.1 |
| 1.0 | 44.20 | 41.26 | 32.97 | 9.0 |
| 1.1 | 44.20 | 41.20 | 32.87 | 8.9 |
| 1.2 | 44.20 | 41.14 | 32.76 | 8.8 |
| 1.3 | 44.20 | 41.08 | 32.66 | 8.7 |
| 1.4 | 44.20 | 41.02 | 32.55 | 8.6 |
| 1.5 | 44.20 | 40.96 | 32.45 | 8.5 |
| 1.6 | 44.20 | 40.89 | 32.34 | 8.4 |
| 1.7 | 44.19 | 40.83 | 32.24 | 8.3 |
| 1.8 | 44.19 | 40.77 | 32.13 | 8.2 |
| 1.9 | 44.19 | 40.71 | 32.03 | 8.1 |
| 2.0 | 44.18 | 40.64 | 31.92 | 8.0 |
| 2.1 | 44.18 | 40.58 | 31.82 | 7.9 |
| 2.2 | 44.17 | 40.51 | 31.71 | 7.8 |
| 2.3 | 44.17 | 40.44 | 31.61 | 7.7 |
| 2.4 | 44.16 | 40.38 | 31.50 | 7.6 |
| 2.5 | 44.15 | 40.31 | 31.39 | 7.5 |
| 2.6 | 44.14 | 40.24 | 31.29 | 7.4 |
| 2.7 | 44.13 | 40.18 | 31.18 | 7.3 |
| 2.8 | 44.12 | 40.11 | 31.07 | 7.2 |
| 2.9 | 44.11 | 40.04 | 30.96 | 7.1 |
| 3.0 | 44.10 | 39.97 | 30.85 | 7.0 |
| 3.1 | 44.09 | 39.90 | 30.74 | 6.9 |
| 3.2 | 44.08 | 39.83 | 30.63 | 6.8 |
| 3.3 | 44.06 | 39.76 | 30.52 | 6.7 |
| 3.4 | 44.05 | 39.69 | 30.41 | 6.6 |
| 3.5 | 44.04 | 39.62 | 30.30 | 6.5 |
| 3.6 | 44.02 | 39.54 | 30.19 | 6.4 |
| 3.7 | 44.01 | 39.47 | 30.08 | 6.3 |
| 3.8 | 43.99 | 39.40 | 29.97 | 6.2 |
| 3.9 | 43.98 | 39.33 | 29.86 | 6.1 |
| 4.0 | 43.96 | 39.25 | 29.75 | 6.0 |
| 4.1 | 43.94 | 39.18 | 29.64 | 5.9 |
| 4.2 | 43.92 | 39.10 | 29.53 | 5.8 |
| 4.3 | 43.90 | 39.03 | 29.42 | 5.7 |
| 4.4 | 43.88 | 38.95 | 29.31 | 5.6 |
| 4.5 | 43.86 | 38.87 | 29.20 | 5.5 |
| 4.6 | 43.84 | 38.80 | 29.08 | 5.4 |
| 4.7 | 43.82 | 38.72 | 28.97 | 5.3 |
| 4.8 | 43.80 | 38.64 | 28.86 | 5.2 |
| 4.9 | 43.78 | 38.56 | 28.75 | 5.1 |
| 5.0 | 43.75 | 38.48 | 28.63 | 5.0 |
| Days. | **110** | **100** | **90** | Days. |

**NOTE.** — Arg. 73″ = Arg. 73 + 321.37.

# TABLES LXXXIV. LXXXV.

TABLES LXXXIV. ARGUMENTS 73″.

| Days. | 0 | 100 | 200 | 300 | 400 | 500 | Days. |
|---|---|---|---|---|---|---|---|
| Days. | ″ | ″ | ″ | ″ | ″ | ″ | Days |
| 50 | 0.00 | 3.92 | 14.82 | 29.20 | 42.46 | 50.35 | 50 |
| 51 | 0.00 | 4.00 | 14.95 | 29.35 | 42.57 | 50.39 | 49 |
| 52 | 0.00 | 4.08 | 15.08 | 29.49 | 42.68 | 50.43 | 48 |
| 53 | 0.00 | 4.16 | 15.22 | 29.64 | 42.79 | 50.47 | 47 |
| 54 | 0.00 | 4.24 | 15.35 | 29.78 | 42.90 | 50.51 | 46 |
| 55 | 0.00 | 4.32 | 15.49 | 29.93 | 43.01 | 50.55 | 45 |
| 56 | 0.00 | 4.40 | 15.62 | 30.08 | 43.12 | 50.59 | 44 |
| 57 | 0.00 | 4.48 | 15.76 | 30.22 | 43.23 | 50.63 | 43 |
| 58 | 0.01 | 4.57 | 15.89 | 30.37 | 43.34 | 50.66 | 42 |
| 59 | 0.01 | 4.65 | 16.03 | 30.51 | 43.45 | 50.70 | 41 |
| 60 | 0.02 | 4.74 | 16.17 | 30.65 | 43.55 | 50.73 | 40 |
| 61 | 0.03 | 4.83 | 16.30 | 30.80 | 43.66 | 50.76 | 39 |
| 62 | 0.04 | 4.91 | 16.44 | 30.94 | 43.76 | 50.79 | 38 |
| 63 | 0.05 | 5.00 | 16.58 | 31.09 | 43.87 | 50.82 | 37 |
| 64 | 0.06 | 5.09 | 16.72 | 31.23 | 43.97 | 50.85 | 36 |
| 65 | 0.07 | 5.18 | 16.86 | 31.37 | 44.07 | 50.88 | 35 |
| 66 | 0.08 | 5.27 | 17.00 | 31.52 | 44.18 | 50.91 | 34 |
| 67 | 0.09 | 5.36 | 17.14 | 31.66 | 44.28 | 50.94 | 33 |
| 68 | 0.10 | 5.45 | 17.28 | 31.81 | 44.38 | 50.97 | 32 |
| 69 | 0.11 | 5.54 | 17.42 | 31.95 | 44.48 | 51.00 | 31 |
| 70 | 0.13 | 5.63 | 17.56 | 32.09 | 44.58 | 51.02 | 30 |
| 71 | 0.14 | 5.72 | 17.70 | 32.24 | 44.68 | 51.05 | 29 |
| 72 | 0.16 | 5.81 | 17.84 | 32.38 | 44.78 | 51.07 | 28 |
| 73 | 0.18 | 5.91 | 17.98 | 32.53 | 44.88 | 51.10 | 27 |
| 74 | 0.20 | 6.00 | 18.12 | 32.67 | 44.98 | 51.12 | 26 |
| 75 | 0.22 | 6.10 | 18.26 | 32.81 | 45.07 | 51.14 | 25 |
| 76 | 0.24 | 6.19 | 18.40 | 32.95 | 45.17 | 51.16 | 24 |
| 77 | 0.26 | 6.29 | 18.54 | 33.09 | 45.27 | 51.18 | 23 |
| 78 | 0.28 | 6.38 | 18.68 | 33.23 | 45.36 | 51.20 | 22 |
| 79 | 0.30 | 6.48 | 18.82 | 33.37 | 45.46 | 51.22 | 21 |
| 80 | 0.32 | 6.58 | 18.97 | 33.51 | 45.55 | 51.23 | 20 |
| 81 | 0.34 | 6.68 | 19.11 | 33.65 | 45.65 | 51.25 | 19 |
| 82 | 0.37 | 6.78 | 19.25 | 33.79 | 45.74 | 51.26 | 18 |
| 83 | 0.39 | 6.88 | 19.39 | 33.93 | 45.83 | 51.28 | 17 |
| 84 | 0.42 | 6.98 | 19.53 | 34.07 | 45.92 | 51.29 | 16 |
| 85 | 0.45 | 7.08 | 19.68 | 34.21 | 46.01 | 51.30 | 15 |
| 86 | 0.47 | 7.18 | 19.82 | 34.35 | 46.10 | 51.32 | 14 |
| 87 | 0.50 | 7.28 | 19.96 | 34.49 | 46.19 | 51.33 | 13 |
| 88 | 0.53 | 7.39 | 20.11 | 34.63 | 46.28 | 51.34 | 12 |
| 89 | 0.56 | 7.49 | 20.25 | 34.77 | 46.37 | 51.35 | 11 |
| 90 | 0.59 | 7.60 | 20.40 | 34.90 | 46.45 | 51.36 | 10 |
| 91 | 0.62 | 7.70 | 20.54 | 35.04 | 46.54 | 51.37 | 09 |
| 92 | 0.65 | 7.81 | 20.68 | 35.18 | 46.63 | 51.38 | 08 |
| 93 | 0.69 | 7.91 | 20.83 | 35.31 | 46.71 | 51.38 | 07 |
| 94 | 0.72 | 8.02 | 20.97 | 35.45 | 46.80 | 51.39 | 06 |
| 95 | 0.76 | 8.13 | 21.12 | 35.58 | 46.88 | 51.39 | 05 |
| 96 | 0.79 | 8.24 | 21.26 | 35.72 | 46.97 | 51.39 | 04 |
| 97 | 0.83 | 8.35 | 21.41 | 35.86 | 47.05 | 51.40 | 03 |
| 98 | 0.87 | 8.46 | 21.55 | 35.99 | 47.13 | 51.40 | 02 |
| 99 | 0.91 | 8.57 | 21.70 | 36.13 | 47.21 | 51.40 | 01 |
| 100 | 0.95 | 8.68 | 21.85 | 36.26 | 47.29 | 51.40 | 0 |
| Days. | 1100 | 1000 | 900 | 800 | 700 | 600 | Days. |

TABLES LXXXV. ARGUMENTS 53.

| Days. | 0 | 10 | 20 | Days. |
|---|---|---|---|---|
| Days | ″ | ″ | ″ | Days. |
| 5.0 | 43.75 | 38.48 | 28.63 | 5.0 |
| 5.1 | 43.73 | 38.40 | 28.52 | 4.9 |
| 5.2 | 43.70 | 38.32 | 28.41 | 4.8 |
| 5.3 | 43.68 | 38.24 | 28.30 | 4.7 |
| 5.4 | 43.65 | 38.16 | 28.18 | 4.6 |
| 5.5 | 43.63 | 38.08 | 28.07 | 4.5 |
| 5.6 | 43.60 | 37.99 | 27.96 | 4.4 |
| 5.7 | 43.57 | 37.91 | 27.85 | 4.3 |
| 5.8 | 43.55 | 37.83 | 27.73 | 4.2 |
| 5.9 | 43.52 | 37.75 | 27.62 | 4.1 |
| 6.0 | 43.49 | 37.66 | 27.50 | 4.0 |
| 6.1 | 43.46 | 37.58 | 27.39 | 3.9 |
| 6.2 | 43.43 | 37.49 | 27.27 | 3.8 |
| 6.3 | 43.40 | 37.41 | 27.16 | 3.7 |
| 6.4 | 43.36 | 37.32 | 27.04 | 3.6 |
| 6.5 | 43.33 | 37.24 | 26.93 | 3.5 |
| 6.6 | 43.30 | 37.15 | 26.81 | 3.4 |
| 6.7 | 43.26 | 37.07 | 26.70 | 3.3 |
| 6.8 | 43.23 | 36.98 | 26.58 | 3.2 |
| 6.9 | 43.20 | 36.89 | 26.46 | 3.1 |
| 7.0 | 43.16 | 36.80 | 26.34 | 3.0 |
| 7.1 | 43.13 | 36.71 | 26.23 | 2.9 |
| 7.2 | 43.09 | 36.62 | 26.11 | 2.8 |
| 7.3 | 43.05 | 36.53 | 26.00 | 2.7 |
| 7.4 | 43.01 | 36.44 | 25.88 | 2.6 |
| 7.5 | 42.97 | 36.35 | 25.77 | 2.5 |
| 7.6 | 42.93 | 36.26 | 25.65 | 2.4 |
| 7.7 | 42.89 | 36.17 | 25.53 | 2.3 |
| 7.8 | 42.85 | 36.08 | 25.42 | 2.2 |
| 7.9 | 42.81 | 35.99 | 25.30 | 2.1 |
| 8.0 | 42.77 | 35.90 | 25.18 | 2.0 |
| 8.1 | 42.73 | 35.81 | 25.07 | 1.9 |
| 8.2 | 42.69 | 35.72 | 24.95 | 1.8 |
| 8.3 | 42.65 | 35.62 | 24.83 | 1.7 |
| 8.4 | 42.61 | 35.53 | 24.72 | 1.6 |
| 8.5 | 42.56 | 35.44 | 24.60 | 1.5 |
| 8.6 | 42.52 | 35.35 | 24.48 | 1.4 |
| 8.7 | 42.47 | 35.25 | 24.37 | 1.3 |
| 8.8 | 42.42 | 35.16 | 24.25 | 1.2 |
| 8.9 | 42.37 | 35.06 | 24.13 | 1.1 |
| 9.0 | 42.32 | 34.96 | 24.01 | 1.0 |
| 9.1 | 42.27 | 34.87 | 23.90 | 0.9 |
| 9.2 | 42.22 | 34.77 | 23.78 | 0.8 |
| 9.3 | 42.17 | 34.67 | 23.66 | 0.7 |
| 9.4 | 42.12 | 34.58 | 23.54 | 0.6 |
| 9.5 | 42.07 | 34.48 | 23.43 | 0.5 |
| 9.6 | 42.02 | 34.38 | 23.31 | 0.4 |
| 9.7 | 41.97 | 34.28 | 23.19 | 0.3 |
| 9.8 | 41.92 | 34.18 | 23.07 | 0.2 |
| 9.9 | 41.87 | 34.08 | 22.95 | 0.1 |
| 10.0 | 41.82 | 33.98 | 22.83 | 0.0 |
| Days. | 110 | 100 | 90 | Days. |

NOTE. — Arg. 73″ = Arg. 73 + 321.37.

# TABLES LXXXV.-LXXXVII.

| Tables | LXXXV. | LXXXVI. | LXXXVII. |
|---|---|---|---|
| Arguments | 53. | 1. | 70. |

**Table LXXXV. Argument 53.**

| Days. | 30 | 40 | 50 | Days. |
|---|---|---|---|---|
| 0.0 | 22.83 | 11.47 | 3.08 | 10.0 |
| 0.1 | 22.72 | 11.37 | 3.02 | 9.9 |
| 0.2 | 22.60 | 11.27 | 2.96 | 9.8 |
| 0.3 | 22.48 | 11.16 | 2.90 | 9.7 |
| 0.4 | 22.36 | 11.06 | 2.85 | 9.6 |
| 0.5 | 22.25 | 10.96 | 2.79 | 9.5 |
| 0.6 | 22.13 | 10.85 | 2.73 | 9.4 |
| 0.7 | 22.01 | 10.75 | 2.68 | 9.3 |
| 0.8 | 21.89 | 10.65 | 2.62 | 9.2 |
| 0.9 | 21.77 | 10.55 | 2.56 | 9.1 |
| 1.0 | 21.65 | 10.45 | 2.51 | 9.0 |
| 1.1 | 21.54 | 10.35 | 2.45 | 8.9 |
| 1.2 | 21.42 | 10.25 | 2.40 | 8.8 |
| 1.3 | 21.30 | 10.15 | 2.35 | 8.7 |
| 1.4 | 21.18 | 10.05 | 2.30 | 8.6 |
| 1.5 | 21.07 | 9.96 | 2.24 | 8.5 |
| 1.6 | 20.95 | 9.86 | 2.19 | 8.4 |
| 1.7 | 20.83 | 9.76 | 2.14 | 8.3 |
| 1.8 | 20.71 | 9.66 | 2.09 | 8.2 |
| 1.9 | 20.59 | 9.56 | 2.04 | 8.1 |
| 2.0 | 20.47 | 9.47 | 1.99 | 8.0 |
| 2.1 | 20.36 | 9.37 | 1.94 | 7.9 |
| 2.2 | 20.24 | 9.27 | 1.89 | 7.8 |
| 2.3 | 20.12 | 9.18 | 1.85 | 7.7 |
| 2.4 | 20.00 | 9.08 | 1.80 | 7.6 |
| 2.5 | 19.88 | 8.98 | 1.75 | 7.5 |
| 2.6 | 19.77 | 8.89 | 1.71 | 7.4 |
| 2.7 | 19.65 | 8.79 | 1.66 | 7.3 |
| 2.8 | 19.53 | 8.70 | 1.62 | 7.2 |
| 2.9 | 19.41 | 8.60 | 1.57 | 7.1 |
| 3.0 | 19.29 | 8.51 | 1.53 | 7.0 |
| 3.1 | 19.17 | 8.41 | 1.49 | 6.9 |
| 3.2 | 19.05 | 8.32 | 1.45 | 6.8 |
| 3.3 | 18.94 | 8.23 | 1.41 | 6.7 |
| 3.4 | 18.82 | 8.14 | 1.37 | 6.6 |
| 3.5 | 18.70 | 8.05 | 1.33 | 6.5 |
| 3.6 | 18.58 | 7.96 | 1.29 | 6.4 |
| 3.7 | 18.47 | 7.87 | 1.25 | 6.3 |
| 3.8 | 18.35 | 7.78 | 1.21 | 6.2 |
| 3.9 | 18.23 | 7.69 | 1.17 | 6.1 |
| 4.0 | 18.12 | 7.60 | 1.13 | 6.0 |
| 4.1 | 18.00 | 7.51 | 1.09 | 5.9 |
| 4.2 | 17.89 | 7.42 | 1.05 | 5.8 |
| 4.3 | 17.77 | 7.33 | 1.02 | 5.7 |
| 4.4 | 17.66 | 7.25 | 0.98 | 5.6 |
| 4.5 | 17.54 | 7.16 | 0.95 | 5.5 |
| 4.6 | 17.43 | 7.07 | 0.91 | 5.4 |
| 4.7 | 17.31 | 6.99 | 0.88 | 5.3 |
| 4.8 | 17.20 | 6.90 | 0.84 | 5.2 |
| 4.9 | 17.08 | 6.81 | 0.81 | 5.1 |
| 5.0 | 16.97 | 6.73 | 0.78 | 5.0 |
| Days. | 80 | 70 | 60 | Days. |

**Table LXXXVI. Argument 1.**

| Days. | 0 | 10 | 20 |
|---|---|---|---|
| 0.0 | 2.60 | 0.45 | 1.09 |
| 0.1 | 2.60 | 0.43 | 1.12 |
| 0.2 | 2.60 | 0.41 | 1.15 |
| 0.3 | 2.60 | 0.39 | 1.18 |
| 0.4 | 2.60 | 0.37 | 1.21 |
| 0.5 | 2.60 | 0.35 | 1.24 |
| 0.6 | 2.59 | 0.33 | 1.27 |
| 0.7 | 2.59 | 0.31 | 1.30 |
| 0.8 | 2.58 | 0.29 | 1.33 |
| 0.9 | 2.58 | 0.27 | 1.36 |
| 1.0 | 2.57 | 0.26 | 1.39 |
| 1.1 | 2.56 | 0.24 | 1.42 |
| 1.2 | 2.55 | 0.22 | 1.45 |
| 1.3 | 2.54 | 0.21 | 1.48 |
| 1.4 | 2.54 | 0.19 | 1.51 |
| 1.5 | 2.53 | 0.17 | 1.54 |
| 1.6 | 2.52 | 0.16 | 1.57 |
| 1.7 | 2.51 | 0.14 | 1.60 |
| 1.8 | 2.50 | 0.13 | 1.63 |
| 1.9 | 2.49 | 0.11 | 1.66 |
| 2.0 | 2.47 | 0.10 | 1.69 |
| 2.1 | 2.46 | 0.09 | 1.72 |
| 2.2 | 2.45 | 0.08 | 1.75 |
| 2.3 | 2.43 | 0.07 | 1.77 |
| 2.4 | 2.42 | 0.06 | 1.80 |
| 2.5 | 2.40 | 0.05 | 1.82 |
| 2.6 | 2.39 | 0.04 | 1.85 |
| 2.7 | 2.37 | 0.03 | 1.88 |
| 2.8 | 2.35 | 0.03 | 1.90 |
| 2.9 | 2.33 | 0.02 | 1.93 |
| 3.0 | 2.31 | 0.02 | 1.96 |
| 3.1 | 2.29 | 0.01 | 1.98 |
| 3.2 | 2.27 | 0.01 | 2.01 |
| 3.3 | 2.25 | 0.01 | 2.03 |
| 3.4 | 2.23 | 0.01 | 2.06 |
| 3.5 | 2.21 | 0.00 | 2.08 |
| 3.6 | 2.19 | 0.00 | 2.10 |
| 3.7 | 2.17 | 0.00 | 2.12 |
| 3.8 | 2.14 | 0.00 | 2.14 |
| 3.9 | 2.12 | 0.00 | 2.17 |
| 4.0 | 2.10 | 0.00 | 2.19 |
| 4.1 | 2.08 | 0.00 | 2.21 |
| 4.2 | 2.06 | 0.01 | 2.23 |
| 4.3 | 2.03 | 0.01 | 2.25 |
| 4.4 | 2.01 | 0.01 | 2.27 |
| 4.5 | 1.98 | 0.01 | 2.29 |
| 4.6 | 1.96 | 0.02 | 2.31 |
| 4.7 | 1.93 | 0.02 | 2.33 |
| 4.8 | 1.90 | 0.03 | 2.35 |
| 4.9 | 1.88 | 0.03 | 2.37 |
| 5.0 | 1.85 | 0.04 | 2.39 |

**Table LXXXVII. Argument 70.**

| Days. | 0 | 100 | Days. |
|---|---|---|---|
| 0 | 2.22 | 6.92 | 100 |
| 01 | 2.10 | 7.10 | 99 |
| 02 | 1.98 | 7.29 | 98 |
| 03 | 1.87 | 7.48 | 97 |
| 04 | 1.76 | 7.67 | 96 |
| 05 | 1.65 | 7.86 | 95 |
| 06 | 1.55 | 8.05 | 94 |
| 07 | 1.45 | 8.24 | 93 |
| 08 | 1.35 | 8.43 | 92 |
| 09 | 1.25 | 8.62 | 91 |
| 10 | 1.16 | 8.82 | 90 |
| 11 | 1.07 | 9.01 | 89 |
| 12 | 0.98 | 9.21 | 88 |
| 13 | 0.90 | 9.40 | 87 |
| 14 | 0.82 | 9.60 | 86 |
| 15 | 0.75 | 9.80 | 85 |
| 16 | 0.68 | 9.99 | 84 |
| 17 | 0.61 | 10.19 | 83 |
| 18 | 0.54 | 10.38 | 82 |
| 19 | 0.48 | 10.58 | 81 |
| 20 | 0.42 | 10.78 | 80 |
| 21 | 0.37 | 10.97 | 79 |
| 22 | 0.32 | 11.17 | 78 |
| 23 | 0.27 | 11.37 | 77 |
| 24 | 0.23 | 11.56 | 76 |
| 25 | 0.19 | 11.76 | 75 |
| 26 | 0.15 | 11.96 | 74 |
| 27 | 0.12 | 12.15 | 73 |
| 28 | 0.09 | 12.34 | 72 |
| 29 | 0.07 | 12.53 | 71 |
| 30 | 0.05 | 12.72 | 70 |
| 31 | 0.03 | 12.91 | 69 |
| 32 | 0.02 | 13.10 | 68 |
| 33 | 0.01 | 13.29 | 67 |
| 34 | 0.00 | 13.48 | 66 |
| 35 | 0.00 | 13.66 | 65 |
| 36 | 0.00 | 13.85 | 64 |
| 37 | 0.00 | 14.03 | 63 |
| 38 | 0.01 | 14.21 | 62 |
| 39 | 0.02 | 14.39 | 61 |
| 40 | 0.04 | 14.57 | 60 |
| 41 | 0.06 | 14.75 | 59 |
| 42 | 0.09 | 14.93 | 58 |
| 43 | 0.12 | 15.10 | 57 |
| 44 | 0.15 | 15.27 | 56 |
| 45 | 0.18 | 15.44 | 55 |
| 46 | 0.22 | 15.61 | 54 |
| 47 | 0.26 | 15.78 | 53 |
| 48 | 0.31 | 15.95 | 52 |
| 49 | 0.36 | 16.11 | 51 |
| 50 | 0.41 | 16.27 | 50 |
| Days. | 300 | 200 | Days. |

# TABLES LXXXV.-LXXXVII.

**Table LXXXV.** Argument 53.

| Days. | 30 | 40 | 50 | Days. |
|---|---|---|---|---|
| 5.0 | 16.97 | 6.73 | 0.78 | 5.0 |
| 5.1 | 16.85 | 6.64 | 0.75 | 4.9 |
| 5.2 | 16.74 | 6.56 | 0.72 | 4.8 |
| 5.3 | 16.62 | 6.48 | 0.69 | 4.7 |
| 5.4 | 16.51 | 6.40 | 0.66 | 4.6 |
| 5.5 | 16.39 | 6.31 | 0.64 | 4.5 |
| 5.6 | 16.28 | 6.23 | 0.61 | 4.4 |
| 5.7 | 16.17 | 6.15 | 0.58 | 4.3 |
| 5.8 | 16.05 | 6.07 | 0.55 | 4.2 |
| 5.9 | 15.94 | 5.99 | 0.52 | 4.1 |
| 6.0 | 15.83 | 5.91 | 0.50 | 4.0 |
| 6.1 | 15.71 | 5.83 | 0.47 | 3.9 |
| 6.2 | 15.60 | 5.75 | 0.45 | 3.8 |
| 6.3 | 15.49 | 5.67 | 0.43 | 3.7 |
| 6.4 | 15.37 | 5.59 | 0.41 | 3.6 |
| 6.5 | 15.26 | 5.51 | 0.38 | 3.5 |
| 6.6 | 15.15 | 5.43 | 0.36 | 3.4 |
| 6.7 | 15.03 | 5.35 | 0.34 | 3.3 |
| 6.8 | 14.92 | 5.27 | 0.32 | 3.2 |
| 6.9 | 14.81 | 5.19 | 0.30 | 3.1 |
| 7.0 | 14.70 | 5.12 | 0.28 | 3.0 |
| 7.1 | 14.59 | 5.04 | 0.26 | 2.9 |
| 7.2 | 14.48 | 4.97 | 0.24 | 2.8 |
| 7.3 | 14.37 | 4.90 | 0.23 | 2.7 |
| 7.4 | 14.26 | 4.82 | 0.21 | 2.6 |
| 7.5 | 14.15 | 4.75 | 0.19 | 2.5 |
| 7.6 | 14.04 | 4.68 | 0.18 | 2.4 |
| 7.7 | 13.93 | 4.60 | 0.16 | 2.3 |
| 7.8 | 13.82 | 4.53 | 0.15 | 2.2 |
| 7.9 | 13.71 | 4.46 | 0.14 | 2.1 |
| 8.0 | 13.60 | 4.39 | 0.13 | 2.0 |
| 8.1 | 13.49 | 4.32 | 0.12 | 1.9 |
| 8.2 | 13.38 | 4.25 | 0.11 | 1.8 |
| 8.3 | 13.27 | 4.18 | 0.10 | 1.7 |
| 8.4 | 13.16 | 4.11 | 0.09 | 1.6 |
| 8.5 | 13.05 | 4.05 | 0.08 | 1.5 |
| 8.6 | 12.95 | 3.98 | 0.07 | 1.4 |
| 8.7 | 12.84 | 3.91 | 0.06 | 1.3 |
| 8.8 | 12.73 | 3.84 | 0.05 | 1.2 |
| 8.9 | 12.62 | 3.77 | 0.04 | 1.1 |
| 9.0 | 12.52 | 3.71 | 0.03 | 1.0 |
| 9.1 | 12.41 | 3.64 | 0.03 | 0.9 |
| 9.2 | 12.30 | 3.58 | 0.02 | 0.8 |
| 9.3 | 12.20 | 3.52 | 0.02 | 0.7 |
| 9.4 | 12.09 | 3.45 | 0.02 | 0.6 |
| 9.5 | 11.99 | 3.39 | 0.01 | 0.5 |
| 9.6 | 11.88 | 3.33 | 0.01 | 0.4 |
| 9.7 | 11.78 | 3.26 | 0.01 | 0.3 |
| 9.8 | 11.67 | 3.20 | 0.00 | 0.2 |
| 9.9 | 11.57 | 3.14 | 0.00 | 0.1 |
| 10.0 | 11.47 | 3.08 | 0.00 | 0.0 |
| Days. | 80 | 70 | 60 | Days. |

**Table LXXXVI.** Argument 1.

| Days. | 0 | 10 | 20 |
|---|---|---|---|
| 5.0 | 1.85 | 0.04 | 2.39 |
| 5.1 | 1.82 | 0.05 | 2.40 |
| 5.2 | 1.80 | 0.06 | 2.42 |
| 5.3 | 1.77 | 0.07 | 2.43 |
| 5.4 | 1.75 | 0.08 | 2.45 |
| 5.5 | 1.72 | 0.09 | 2.46 |
| 5.6 | 1.69 | 0.10 | 2.47 |
| 5.7 | 1.66 | 0.11 | 2.49 |
| 5.8 | 1.63 | 0.13 | 2.50 |
| 5.9 | 1.60 | 0.14 | 2.51 |
| 6.0 | 1.57 | 0.16 | 2.52 |
| 6.1 | 1.54 | 0.17 | 2.53 |
| 6.2 | 1.51 | 0.19 | 2.54 |
| 6.3 | 1.48 | 0.21 | 2.54 |
| 6.4 | 1.45 | 0.22 | 2.55 |
| 6.5 | 1.42 | 0.24 | 2.56 |
| 6.6 | 1.39 | 0.26 | 2.57 |
| 6.7 | 1.36 | 0.27 | 2.58 |
| 6.8 | 1.33 | 0.29 | 2.58 |
| 6.9 | 1.30 | 0.31 | 2.59 |
| 7.0 | 1.27 | 0.33 | 2.59 |
| 7.1 | 1.24 | 0.35 | 2.60 |
| 7.2 | 1.21 | 0.37 | 2.60 |
| 7.3 | 1.18 | 0.39 | 2.60 |
| 7.4 | 1.15 | 0.41 | 2.60 |
| 7.5 | 1.12 | 0.43 | 2.60 |
| 7.6 | 1.09 | 0.45 | 2.60 |
| 7.7 | 1.06 | 0.47 | 2.60 |
| 7.8 | 1.04 | 0.50 | 2.60 |
| 7.9 | 1.01 | 0.52 | 2.60 |
| 8.0 | 0.98 | 0.54 | 2.60 |
| 8.1 | 0.95 | 0.57 | 2.60 |
| 8.2 | 0.92 | 0.59 | 2.59 |
| 8.3 | 0.90 | 0.62 | 2.59 |
| 8.4 | 0.87 | 0.64 | 2.58 |
| 8.5 | 0.84 | 0.67 | 2.58 |
| 8.6 | 0.81 | 0.70 | 2.57 |
| 8.7 | 0.78 | 0.73 | 2.56 |
| 8.8 | 0.76 | 0.76 | 2.55 |
| 8.9 | 0.73 | 0.78 | 2.54 |
| 9.0 | 0.70 | 0.81 | 2.54 |
| 9.1 | 0.67 | 0.84 | 2.53 |
| 9.2 | 0.64 | 0.87 | 2.52 |
| 9.3 | 0.62 | 0.90 | 2.51 |
| 9.4 | 0.59 | 0.92 | 2.50 |
| 9.5 | 0.57 | 0.95 | 2.48 |
| 9.6 | 0.54 | 0.98 | 2.47 |
| 9.7 | 0.52 | 1.01 | 2.46 |
| 9.8 | 0.50 | 1.04 | 2.44 |
| 9.9 | 0.47 | 1.06 | 2.43 |
| 10.0 | 0.45 | 1.09 | 2.42 |

**Table LXXXVII.** Argument 70.

| Days. | 0 | 100 | Days. |
|---|---|---|---|
| 50 | 0.41 | 16.27 | 50 |
| 51 | 0.47 | 16.43 | 49 |
| 52 | 0.53 | 16.59 | 48 |
| 53 | 0.59 | 16.74 | 47 |
| 54 | 0.66 | 16.89 | 46 |
| 55 | 0.73 | 17.04 | 45 |
| 56 | 0.80 | 17.19 | 44 |
| 57 | 0.88 | 17.33 | 43 |
| 58 | 0.96 | 17.47 | 42 |
| 59 | 1.05 | 17.61 | 41 |
| 60 | 1.14 | 17.75 | 40 |
| 61 | 1.23 | 17.88 | 39 |
| 62 | 1.33 | 18.01 | 38 |
| 63 | 1.43 | 18.14 | 37 |
| 64 | 1.53 | 18.27 | 36 |
| 65 | 1.63 | 18.39 | 35 |
| 66 | 1.74 | 18.51 | 34 |
| 67 | 1.85 | 18.63 | 33 |
| 68 | 1.96 | 18.75 | 32 |
| 69 | 2.07 | 18.86 | 31 |
| 70 | 2.19 | 18.96 | 30 |
| 71 | 2.31 | 19.07 | 29 |
| 72 | 2.44 | 19.17 | 28 |
| 73 | 2.57 | 19.27 | 27 |
| 74 | 2.70 | 19.36 | 26 |
| 75 | 2.83 | 19.45 | 25 |
| 76 | 2.97 | 19.54 | 24 |
| 77 | 3.11 | 19.62 | 23 |
| 78 | 3.25 | 19.70 | 22 |
| 79 | 3.39 | 19.78 | 21 |
| 80 | 3.54 | 19.86 | 20 |
| 81 | 3.69 | 19.93 | 19 |
| 82 | 3.84 | 20.00 | 18 |
| 83 | 3.99 | 20.06 | 17 |
| 84 | 4.15 | 20.12 | 16 |
| 85 | 4.31 | 20.18 | 15 |
| 86 | 4.47 | 20.23 | 14 |
| 87 | 4.63 | 20.28 | 13 |
| 88 | 4.80 | 20.33 | 12 |
| 89 | 4.97 | 20.37 | 11 |
| 90 | 5.14 | 20.41 | 10 |
| 91 | 5.31 | 20.45 | 09 |
| 92 | 5.48 | 20.48 | 08 |
| 93 | 5.65 | 20.51 | 07 |
| 94 | 5.83 | 20.53 | 06 |
| 95 | 6.01 | 20.55 | 05 |
| 96 | 6.19 | 20.57 | 04 |
| 97 | 6.37 | 20.58 | 03 |
| 98 | 6.55 | 20.59 | 02 |
| 99 | 6.73 | 20.60 | 01 |
| 100 | 6.92 | 20.60 | 00 |
| Days. | 300 | 200 | Days. |

# TABLE LXXXVIII. ARGUMENT 4.

Equation $= 88''.9 + 48''.9 \sin. z.$

| Days. | 0 | 10 | 20 | 30 | 40 | 50 | 60 | 70 | 80 | 90 |
|---|---|---|---|---|---|---|---|---|---|---|
| Days. 0.0 | 40.00 | 40.67 | 42.76 | 46.22 | 50.93 | 56.76 | 63.55 | 71.08 | 79.14 | 87.48 |
| 0.1 | 40.00 | 40.68 | 42.78 | 46.26 | 50.98 | 56.82 | 63.62 | 71.15 | 79.22 | 87.56 |
| 0.2 | 40.00 | 40.70 | 42.81 | 46.30 | 51.03 | 56.88 | 63.69 | 71.23 | 79.30 | 87.64 |
| 0.3 | 40.00 | 40.71 | 42.84 | 46.34 | 51.09 | 56.95 | 63.76 | 71.31 | 79.38 | 87.73 |
| 0.4 | 40.00 | 40.73 | 42.87 | 46.38 | 51.14 | 57.01 | 63.83 | 71.39 | 79.46 | 87.81 |
| 0.5 | 40.00 | 40.74 | 42.90 | 46.42 | 51.19 | 57.07 | 63.91 | 71.47 | 79.55 | 87.89 |
| 0.6 | 40.00 | 40.76 | 42.93 | 46.46 | 51.25 | 57.14 | 63.98 | 71.55 | 79.63 | 87.98 |
| 0.7 | 40.00 | 40.77 | 42.96 | 46.50 | 51.30 | 57.20 | 64.05 | 71.63 | 79.71 | 88.06 |
| 0.8 | 40.00 | 40.79 | 42.99 | 46.54 | 51.36 | 57.27 | 64.12 | 71.71 | 79.79 | 88.15 |
| 0.9 | 40.00 | 40.80 | 43.02 | 46.58 | 51.41 | 57.33 | 64.19 | 71.79 | 79.87 | 88.23 |
| 1.0 | 40.00 | 40.82 | 43.05 | 46.63 | 51.47 | 57.40 | 64.27 | 71.87 | 79.96 | 88.32 |
| 1.1 | 40.00 | 40.83 | 43.08 | 46.67 | 51.52 | 57.46 | 64.34 | 71.94 | 80.04 | 88.40 |
| 1.2 | 40.00 | 40.85 | 43.11 | 46.71 | 51.57 | 57.53 | 64.41 | 72.02 | 80.12 | 88.48 |
| 1.3 | 40.00 | 40.86 | 43.14 | 46.75 | 51.63 | 57.59 | 64.48 | 72.10 | 80.20 | 88.57 |
| 1.4 | 40.00 | 40.88 | 43.17 | 46.80 | 51.68 | 57.66 | 64.56 | 72.18 | 80.29 | 88.65 |
| 1.5 | 40.01 | 40.90 | 43.20 | 46.84 | 51.73 | 57.72 | 64.63 | 72.26 | 80.37 | 88.74 |
| 1.6 | 40.01 | 40.91 | 43.23 | 46.88 | 51.79 | 57.79 | 64.70 | 72.34 | 80.45 | 88.82 |
| 1.7 | 40.01 | 40.93 | 43.26 | 46.93 | 51.84 | 57.85 | 64.78 | 72.42 | 80.54 | 88.90 |
| 1.8 | 40.01 | 40.94 | 43.29 | 46.97 | 51.90 | 57.92 | 64.85 | 72.50 | 80.62 | 88.99 |
| 1.9 | 40.01 | 40.96 | 43.32 | 47.01 | 51.95 | 57.98 | 64.92 | 72.58 | 80.70 | 89.07 |
| 2.0 | 40.02 | 40.98 | 43.35 | 47.06 | 52.01 | 58.05 | 65.00 | 72.66 | 80.79 | 89.16 |
| 2.1 | 40.02 | 40.99 | 43.38 | 47.10 | 52.06 | 58.11 | 65.07 | 72.73 | 80.87 | 89.24 |
| 2.2 | 40.02 | 41.01 | 43.41 | 47.14 | 52.12 | 58.18 | 65.14 | 72.81 | 80.95 | 89.33 |
| 2.3 | 40.02 | 41.03 | 43.44 | 47.19 | 52.17 | 58.24 | 65.22 | 72.89 | 81.03 | 89.41 |
| 2.4 | 40.03 | 41.04 | 43.47 | 47.23 | 52.23 | 58.31 | 65.29 | 72.97 | 81.12 | 89.50 |
| 2.5 | 40.03 | 41.06 | 43.50 | 47.27 | 52.28 | 58.37 | 65.36 | 73.05 | 81.20 | 89.58 |
| 2.6 | 40.03 | 41.08 | 43.53 | 47.32 | 52.34 | 58.44 | 65.44 | 73.13 | 81.28 | 89.67 |
| 2.7 | 40.04 | 41.09 | 43.56 | 47.36 | 52.40 | 58.51 | 65.51 | 73.21 | 81.37 | 89.75 |
| 2.8 | 40.04 | 41.11 | 43.59 | 47.41 | 52.45 | 58.57 | 65.59 | 73.29 | 81.45 | 89.84 |
| 2.9 | 40.04 | 41.13 | 43.62 | 47.45 | 52.51 | 58.64 | 65.66 | 73.37 | 81.53 | 89.92 |
| 3.0 | 40.05 | 41.15 | 43.66 | 47.50 | 52.57 | 58.71 | 65.74 | 73.45 | 81.62 | 90.01 |
| 3.1 | 40.05 | 41.16 | 43.69 | 47.54 | 52.62 | 58.77 | 65.81 | 73.53 | 81.70 | 90.10 |
| 3.2 | 40.06 | 41.18 | 43.72 | 47.59 | 52.68 | 58.84 | 65.88 | 73.61 | 81.78 | 90.18 |
| 3.3 | 40.06 | 41.20 | 43.75 | 47.63 | 52.74 | 58.90 | 65.96 | 73.69 | 81.86 | 90.27 |
| 3.4 | 40.07 | 41.22 | 43.78 | 47.68 | 52.79 | 58.97 | 66.03 | 73.77 | 81.95 | 90.35 |
| 3.5 | 40.07 | 41.24 | 43.82 | 47.72 | 52.85 | 59.04 | 66.10 | 73.85 | 82.03 | 90.43 |
| 3.6 | 40.08 | 41.26 | 43.85 | 47.77 | 52.91 | 59.10 | 66.18 | 73.93 | 82.11 | 90.52 |
| 3.7 | 40.08 | 41.28 | 43.88 | 47.82 | 52.96 | 59.17 | 66.25 | 74.01 | 82.20 | 90.60 |
| 3.8 | 40.09 | 41.30 | 43.91 | 47.86 | 53.02 | 59.24 | 66.33 | 74.09 | 82.28 | 90.69 |
| 3.9 | 40.09 | 41.32 | 43.94 | 47.91 | 53.08 | 59.30 | 66.40 | 74.17 | 82.36 | 90.77 |
| 4.0 | 40.10 | 41.34 | 43.98 | 47.96 | 53.14 | 59.37 | 66.48 | 74.25 | 82.45 | 90.85 |
| 4.1 | 40.10 | 41.36 | 44.01 | 48.00 | 53.19 | 59.44 | 66.55 | 74.33 | 82.53 | 90.94 |
| 4.2 | 40.11 | 41.38 | 44.04 | 48.05 | 53.25 | 59.50 | 66.63 | 74.41 | 82.61 | 91.02 |
| 4.3 | 40.11 | 41.40 | 44.08 | 48.09 | 53.31 | 59.57 | 66.70 | 74.49 | 82.70 | 91.11 |
| 4.4 | 40.12 | 41.42 | 44.11 | 48.14 | 53.37 | 59.64 | 66.78 | 74.57 | 82.78 | 91.19 |
| 4.5 | 40.12 | 41.44 | 44.14 | 48.18 | 53.43 | 59.71 | 66.85 | 74.65 | 82.86 | 91.28 |
| 4.6 | 40.13 | 41.46 | 44.18 | 48.23 | 53.48 | 59.77 | 66.93 | 74.73 | 82.95 | 91.36 |
| 4.7 | 40.14 | 41.48 | 44.21 | 48.28 | 53.54 | 59.84 | 67.00 | 74.81 | 83.03 | 91.44 |
| 4.8 | 40.14 | 41.50 | 44.25 | 48.32 | 53.60 | 59.91 | 67.08 | 74.89 | 83.12 | 91.53 |
| 4.9 | 40.15 | 41.52 | 44.28 | 48.37 | 53.66 | 59.98 | 67.15 | 74.97 | 83.20 | 91.61 |
| 5.0 | 40.16 | 41.54 | 44.32 | 48.42 | 53.72 | 60.05 | 67.23 | 75.06 | 83.29 | 91.69 |

# TABLE LXXXVIII. ARGUMENT 4.

Equation $= 88''.9 + 48''.9 \sin. z.$

| Days. | 0 | 10 | 20 | 30 | 40 | 50 | 60 | 70 | 80 | 90 |
|---|---|---|---|---|---|---|---|---|---|---|
| Days. | " | " | " | " | " | " | " | " | " | " |
| 5.0 | 40.16 | 41.54 | 44.32 | 48.42 | 53.72 | 60.05 | 67.23 | 75.06 | 83.29 | 91.69 |
| 5.1 | 40.16 | 41.56 | 44.35 | 48.46 | 53.77 | 60.11 | 67.30 | 75.14 | 83.37 | 91.78 |
| 5.2 | 40.17 | 41.58 | 44.39 | 48.51 | 53.83 | 60.18 | 67.38 | 75.22 | 83.45 | 91.86 |
| 5.3 | 40.18 | 41.60 | 44.42 | 48.56 | 53.89 | 60.25 | 67.45 | 75.30 | 83.54 | 91.95 |
| 5.4 | 40.18 | 41.62 | 44.46 | 48.61 | 53.95 | 60.32 | 67.53 | 75.38 | 83.62 | 92.03 |
| 5.5 | 40.19 | 41.65 | 44.49 | 48.66 | 54.01 | 60.39 | 67.61 | 75.46 | 83.70 | 92.11 |
| 5.6 | 40.20 | 41.67 | 44.53 | 48.70 | 54.07 | 60.45 | 67.68 | 75.54 | 83.79 | 92.20 |
| 5.7 | 40.20 | 41.69 | 44.57 | 48.75 | 54.13 | 60.52 | 67.76 | 75.62 | 83.87 | 92.28 |
| 5.8 | 40.21 | 41.71 | 44.60 | 48.80 | 54.19 | 60.59 | 67.83 | 75.70 | 83.96 | 92.37 |
| 5.9 | 40.22 | 41.73 | 44.64 | 48.85 | 54.25 | 60.66 | 67.91 | 75.78 | 84.04 | 92.45 |
| 6.0 | 40.23 | 41.76 | 44.68 | 48.90 | 54.31 | 60.73 | 67.99 | 75.87 | 84.13 | 92.53 |
| 6.1 | 40.23 | 41.78 | 44.71 | 48.94 | 54.37 | 60.79 | 68.06 | 75.95 | 84.21 | 92.62 |
| 6.2 | 40.24 | 41.80 | 44.75 | 48.99 | 54.43 | 60.86 | 68.14 | 76.03 | 84.29 | 92.70 |
| 6.3 | 40.25 | 41.82 | 44.78 | 49.04 | 54.49 | 60.93 | 68.21 | 76.11 | 84.37 | 92.78 |
| 6.4 | 40.26 | 41.85 | 44.82 | 49.09 | 54.55 | 61.00 | 68.29 | 76.19 | 84.46 | 92.87 |
| 6.5 | 40.27 | 41.87 | 44.85 | 49.14 | 54.61 | 61.07 | 68.37 | 76.27 | 84.54 | 92.95 |
| 6.6 | 40.28 | 41.89 | 44.89 | 49.19 | 54.67 | 61.14 | 68.44 | 76.35 | 84.62 | 93.03 |
| 6.7 | 40.29 | 41.92 | 44.93 | 49.24 | 54.73 | 61.21 | 68.52 | 76.43 | 84.71 | 93.12 |
| 6.8 | 40.30 | 41.94 | 44.96 | 49.29 | 54.79 | 61.28 | 68.59 | 76.51 | 84.79 | 93.20 |
| 6.9 | 40.31 | 41.96 | 45.00 | 49.34 | 54.85 | 61.35 | 68.67 | 76.59 | 84.87 | 93.28 |
| 7.0 | 40.32 | 41.99 | 45.04 | 49.39 | 54.91 | 61.42 | 68.75 | 76.68 | 84.96 | 93.36 |
| 7.1 | 40.33 | 42.01 | 45.07 | 49.44 | 54.97 | 61.49 | 68.82 | 76.76 | 85.04 | 93.45 |
| 7.2 | 40.34 | 42.03 | 45.11 | 49.49 | 55.03 | 61.56 | 68.90 | 76.84 | 85.12 | 93.53 |
| 7.3 | 40.35 | 42.06 | 45.15 | 49.54 | 55.09 | 61.63 | 68.98 | 76.92 | 85.21 | 93.62 |
| 7.4 | 40.36 | 42.08 | 45.19 | 49.59 | 55.15 | 61.70 | 69.05 | 77.00 | 85.29 | 93.70 |
| 7.5 | 40.37 | 42.10 | 45.23 | 49.64 | 55.21 | 61.77 | 69.13 | 77.08 | 85.37 | 93.79 |
| 7.6 | 40.38 | 42.13 | 45.26 | 49.69 | 55.27 | 61.84 | 69.21 | 77.16 | 85.46 | 93.87 |
| 7.7 | 40.39 | 42.15 | 45.30 | 49.74 | 55.33 | 61.91 | 69.28 | 77.24 | 85.54 | 93.95 |
| 7.8 | 40.40 | 42.18 | 45.34 | 49.79 | 55.39 | 61.98 | 69.36 | 77.32 | 85.63 | 94.04 |
| 7.9 | 40.41 | 42.20 | 45.38 | 49.84 | 55.45 | 62.05 | 69.44 | 77.40 | 85.71 | 94.12 |
| 8.0 | 40.42 | 42.23 | 45.42 | 49.89 | 55.52 | 62.12 | 69.52 | 77.49 | 85.80 | 94.20 |
| 8.1 | 40.43 | 42.25 | 45.45 | 49.94 | 55.58 | 62.19 | 69.59 | 77.57 | 85.88 | 94.29 |
| 8.2 | 40.44 | 42.28 | 45.49 | 49.99 | 55.64 | 62.26 | 69.67 | 77.65 | 85.96 | 94.37 |
| 8.3 | 40.45 | 42.30 | 45.53 | 50.04 | 55.70 | 62.33 | 69.75 | 77.73 | 86.05 | 94.46 |
| 8.4 | 40.46 | 42.33 | 45.57 | 50.09 | 55.76 | 62.40 | 69.83 | 77.81 | 86.13 | 94.54 |
| 8.5 | 40.48 | 42.35 | 45.61 | 50.14 | 55.83 | 62.47 | 69.91 | 77.90 | 86.21 | 94.63 |
| 8.6 | 40.49 | 42.38 | 45.65 | 50.19 | 55.89 | 62.54 | 69.98 | 77.98 | 86.30 | 94.71 |
| 8.7 | 40.50 | 42.41 | 45.69 | 50.24 | 55.95 | 62.61 | 70.06 | 78.06 | 86.38 | 94.79 |
| 8.8 | 40.51 | 42.43 | 45.73 | 50.29 | 56.01 | 62.68 | 70.14 | 78.14 | 86.47 | 94.88 |
| 8.9 | 40.52 | 42.46 | 45.77 | 50.34 | 56.07 | 62.75 | 70.22 | 78.22 | 86.55 | 94.96 |
| 9.0 | 40 54 | 42.49 | 45.81 | 50.40 | 56.14 | 62.83 | 70.30 | 78.31 | 86.64 | 95.04 |
| 9.1 | 40.55 | 42.51 | 45.85 | 50.45 | 56.20 | 62.90 | 70.37 | 78.39 | 86.72 | 95.13 |
| 9.2 | 40.56 | 42.54 | 45.89 | 50.50 | 56.26 | 62.97 | 70.45 | 78.47 | 86.80 | 95.21 |
| 9.3 | 40.58 | 42.57 | 45.93 | 50.55 | 56.32 | 63.04 | 70.53 | 78.55 | 86.80 | 95.29 |
| 9.4 | 40.59 | 42.59 | 45.97 | 50.61 | 56.38 | 63.11 | 70.61 | 78.64 | 86.97 | 95.38 |
| 9.5 | 40.60 | 42.62 | 46.01 | 50.66 | 56.45 | 63.19 | 70.69 | 78.72 | 87.05 | 95.46 |
| 9.6 | 40.62 | 42.65 | 46.05 | 50.71 | 56.51 | 63 26 | 70.76 | 78.80 | 87.14 | 95.54 |
| 9.7 | 40.63 | 42.67 | 46.09 | 50.77 | 56.57 | 63.33 | 70.84 | 78.89 | 87.22 | 95.63 |
| 9.8 | 40.64 | 42.70 | 46.13 | 50.82 | 56.63 | 63.40 | 70.92 | 78.97 | 87.31 | 95.71 |
| 9.9 | 40.65 | 42.73 | 46.17 | 50.87 | 56.69 | 63.47 | 71.00 | 79.05 | 87.39 | 95.79 |
| 10.0 | 40.67 | 42.76 | 46.22 | 50.93 | 56.76 | 63.55 | 71.08 | 79.14 | 87.48 | 95.87 |

# TABLE LXXXVIII. ARGUMENT 4.

Equation $= 88''.9 + 48''.9 \sin. z.$

| Days. | 100 | 110 | 120 | 130 | 140 | 150 | 160 | 170 | 180 |
|---|---|---|---|---|---|---|---|---|---|
| Days. | ″ | ″ | ″ | ″ | ″ | ″ | ″ | ″ | ″ |
| 0.0 | 95.87 | 104.05 | 111.79 | 118.85 | 125.02 | 130.13 | 134.02 | 136.58 | 137.73 |
| 0.1 | 95.96 | 104.13 | 111.87 | 118.92 | 125.08 | 130.18 | 134.06 | 136.60 | 137.74 |
| 0.2 | 96.04 | 104.21 | 111.94 | 118.99 | 125.14 | 130.22 | 134.09 | 136.62 | 137.74 |
| 0.3 | 96.12 | 104.29 | 112.02 | 119.05 | 125.19 | 130.27 | 134.12 | 136.64 | 137.75 |
| 0.4 | 96.21 | 104.37 | 112.09 | 119.12 | 125.25 | 130.31 | 134.15 | 136.66 | 137.75 |
| 0.5 | 96.29 | 104.45 | 112.17 | 119.19 | 125.31 | 130.36 | 134.18 | 136.67 | 137.75 |
| 0.6 | 96.37 | 104.53 | 112.24 | 119.25 | 125.36 | 130.40 | 134.22 | 136.69 | 137.76 |
| 0.7 | 96.46 | 104.61 | 112.31 | 119.32 | 125.42 | 130.45 | 134.25 | 136.71 | 137.76 |
| 0.8 | 96.54 | 104.69 | 112.39 | 119.38 | 125.47 | 130.49 | 134.28 | 136.73 | 137.76 |
| 0.9 | 96.62 | 104.77 | 112.46 | 119.45 | 125.53 | 130.54 | 134.31 | 136.75 | 137.76 |
| 1.0 | 96.70 | 104.85 | 112.53 | 119.51 | 125.58 | 130.58 | 134.34 | 136.76 | 137.77 |
| 1.1 | 96.79 | 104.93 | 112.61 | 119.58 | 125.64 | 130.63 | 134.37 | 136.78 | 137.77 |
| 1.2 | 96.87 | 105.01 | 112.68 | 119.64 | 125.69 | 130.67 | 134.40 | 136.80 | 137.77 |
| 1.3 | 96.95 | 105.09 | 112.75 | 119.71 | 125.75 | 130.71 | 134.43 | 136.82 | 137.77 |
| 1.4 | 97.04 | 105.17 | 112.83 | 119.77 | 125.80 | 130.76 | 134.46 | 136.83 | 137.77 |
| 1.5 | 97.12 | 105.25 | 112.90 | 119.84 | 125.86 | 130.80 | 134.49 | 136.85 | 137.78 |
| 1.6 | 97.20 | 105.33 | 112.97 | 119.90 | 125.91 | 130.84 | 134.52 | 136.87 | 137.78 |
| 1.7 | 97.29 | 105.41 | 113.05 | 119.97 | 125.97 | 130.89 | 134.55 | 136.88 | 137.78 |
| 1.8 | 97.37 | 105.49 | 113.12 | 120.03 | 126.02 | 130.93 | 134.58 | 136.90 | 137.78 |
| 1.9 | 97.45 | 105.57 | 113.19 | 120.10 | 126.08 | 130.97 | 134.61 | 136.92 | 137.78 |
| 2.0 | 97.53 | 105.64 | 113.26 | 120.16 | 126.13 | 131.01 | 134.64 | 136.93 | 137.79 |
| 2.1 | 97.62 | 105.72 | 113.34 | 120.23 | 126.19 | 131.06 | 134.67 | 136.95 | 137.79 |
| 2.2 | 97.70 | 105.80 | 113.41 | 120.29 | 126.24 | 131.10 | 134.70 | 136.96 | 137.79 |
| 2.3 | 97.78 | 105.88 | 113.48 | 120.36 | 126.30 | 131.14 | 134.73 | 136.98 | 137.79 |
| 2.4 | 97.87 | 105.96 | 113.56 | 120.42 | 126.35 | 131.18 | 134.76 | 136.99 | 137.79 |
| 2.5 | 97.95 | 106.04 | 113.63 | 120.49 | 126.41 | 131.22 | 134.79 | 137.01 | 137.80 |
| 2.6 | 98.03 | 106.12 | 113.70 | 120.55 | 126.46 | 131.27 | 134.82 | 137.02 | 137.80 |
| 2.7 | 98.12 | 106.20 | 113.78 | 120.62 | 126.51 | 131.31 | 134.85 | 137.04 | 137.80 |
| 2.8 | 98.20 | 106.28 | 113.85 | 120.68 | 126.57 | 131.35 | 134.88 | 137.05 | 137.80 |
| 2.9 | 98.28 | 106.36 | 113.92 | 120.74 | 126.62 | 131.39 | 134.91 | 137.07 | 137.80 |
| 3.0 | 98.36 | 106.43 | 113.99 | 120.80 | 126.67 | 131.43 | 134.93 | 137.08 | 137.80 |
| 3.1 | 98.45 | 106.51 | 114.07 | 120.87 | 126.73 | 131.48 | 134.96 | 137.10 | 137.80 |
| 3.2 | 98.53 | 106.59 | 114.14 | 120.93 | 126.78 | 131.52 | 134.99 | 137.11 | 137.80 |
| 3.3 | 98.61 | 106.67 | 114.21 | 120.99 | 126.83 | 131.56 | 135.02 | 137.12 | 137.80 |
| 3.4 | 98.69 | 106.75 | 114.28 | 121.06 | 126.89 | 131.60 | 135.05 | 137.14 | 137.80 |
| 3.5 | 98.77 | 106.82 | 114.35 | 121.12 | 126.94 | 131.64 | 135.07 | 137.15 | 137.80 |
| 3.6 | 98.86 | 106.90 | 114.43 | 121.18 | 126.99 | 131.68 | 135.10 | 137.16 | 137.79 |
| 3.7 | 98.94 | 106.98 | 114.50 | 121.25 | 127.05 | 131.72 | 135.13 | 137.18 | 137.79 |
| 3.8 | 99.02 | 107.06 | 114.57 | 121.31 | 127.10 | 131.76 | 135.16 | 137.19 | 137.79 |
| 3.9 | 99.10 | 107.14 | 114.64 | 121.37 | 127.15 | 131.80 | 135.19 | 137.20 | 137.79 |
| 4.0 | 99.18 | 107.21 | 114.71 | 121.43 | 127.20 | 131.84 | 135.21 | 137.21 | 137.79 |
| 4.1 | 99.27 | 107.29 | 114.79 | 121.50 | 127.26 | 131.88 | 135.24 | 137.23 | 137.78 |
| 4.2 | 99.35 | 107.37 | 114.86 | 121.56 | 127.31 | 131.92 | 135.27 | 137.24 | 137.78 |
| 4.3 | 99.43 | 107.45 | 114.93 | 121.62 | 127.36 | 131.96 | 135.29 | 137.25 | 137.78 |
| 4.4 | 99.51 | 107.53 | 115.00 | 121.69 | 127.41 | 132.00 | 135.32 | 137.27 | 137.78 |
| 4.5 | 99.59 | 107.60 | 115.07 | 121.75 | 127.46 | 132.04 | 135.35 | 137.28 | 137.78 |
| 4.6 | 99.68 | 107.68 | 115.14 | 121.81 | 127.52 | 132.08 | 135.37 | 137.29 | 137.77 |
| 4.7 | 99.76 | 107.76 | 115.21 | 121.88 | 127.57 | 132.12 | 135.40 | 137.31 | 137.77 |
| 4.8 | 99.84 | 107.84 | 115.28 | 121.94 | 127.62 | 132.16 | 135.42 | 137.32 | 137.77 |
| 4.9 | 99.92 | 107.92 | 115.35 | 122.00 | 127.67 | 132.20 | 135.45 | 137.33 | 137.77 |
| 5.0 | 100.00 | 107.99 | 115.42 | 122.06 | 127.72 | 132.24 | 135.47 | 137.34 | 137.77 |

# TABLE LXXXVIII. ARGUMENT 4.

Equation = 88″.9 + 48″.9 sin. *z*.

| Days. | 100 | 110 | 120 | 130 | 140 | 150 | 160 | 170 | 180 |
|---|---|---|---|---|---|---|---|---|---|
| Days. 5.0 | 100″.00 | 107″.99 | 115″.42 | 122″.06 | 127″.72 | 132″.24 | 135″.47 | 137″.34 | 137″.77 |
| 5.1 | 100.09 | 108.07 | 115.49 | 122.13 | 127.78 | 132.28 | 135.50 | 137.36 | 137.76 |
| 5.2 | 100.17 | 108.15 | 115.56 | 122.19 | 127.83 | 132.32 | 135.52 | 137.37 | 137.76 |
| 5.3 | 100.25 | 108.23 | 115.63 | 122.25 | 127.88 | 132.36 | 135.55 | 137.38 | 137.76 |
| 5.4 | 100.33 | 108.30 | 115.70 | 122.31 | 127.93 | 132.40 | 135.57 | 137.39 | 137.76 |
| 5.5 | 100.41 | 108.38 | 115.77 | 122.37 | 127.98 | 132.43 | 135.60 | 137.40 | 137.75 |
| 5.6 | 100.50 | 108.46 | 115.84 | 122.43 | 128.03 | 132.47 | 135.62 | 137.41 | 137.75 |
| 5.7 | 100.58 | 108.53 | 115.91 | 122.49 | 128.08 | 132.51 | 135.65 | 137.42 | 137.75 |
| 5.8 | 100.66 | 108.61 | 115.98 | 122.55 | 128.13 | 132.55 | 135.67 | 137.43 | 137.74 |
| 5.9 | 100.74 | 108.69 | 116.05 | 122.61 | 128.18 | 132.59 | 135.70 | 137.44 | 137.74 |
| 6.0 | 100.82 | 108.76 | 116.12 | 122.67 | 128.23 | 132.62 | 135.72 | 137.45 | 137.73 |
| 6.1 | 100.91 | 108.84 | 116.19 | 122.73 | 128.28 | 132.66 | 135.75 | 137.46 | 137.72 |
| 6.2 | 100.99 | 108.92 | 116.26 | 122.79 | 128.33 | 132.70 | 135.77 | 137.47 | 137.72 |
| 6.3 | 101.07 | 109.00 | 116.33 | 122.85 | 128.38 | 132.74 | 135.80 | 137.48 | 137.71 |
| 6.4 | 101.15 | 109.07 | 116.40 | 122.91 | 128.43 | 132.77 | 135.82 | 137.49 | 137.71 |
| 6.5 | 101.23 | 109.15 | 116.47 | 122.97 | 128.48 | 132.81 | 135.85 | 137.50 | 137.70 |
| 6.6 | 101.31 | 109.23 | 116.54 | 123.03 | 128.53 | 132.85 | 135.87 | 137.51 | 137.70 |
| 6.7 | 101.39 | 109.30 | 116.61 | 123.09 | 128.58 | 132.88 | 135.89 | 137.52 | 137.69 |
| 6.8 | 101.47 | 109.38 | 116.68 | 123.15 | 128.63 | 132.92 | 135.92 | 137.53 | 137.69 |
| 6.9 | 101.55 | 109.46 | 116.75 | 123.21 | 128.68 | 132.96 | 135.94 | 137.54 | 137.68 |
| 7.0 | 101.63 | 109.53 | 116.81 | 123.27 | 128.72 | 132.99 | 135.96 | 137.54 | 137.68 |
| 7.1 | 101.72 | 109.61 | 116.88 | 123.33 | 128.77 | 133.03 | 135.99 | 137.55 | 137.67 |
| 7.2 | 101.80 | 109.69 | 116.95 | 123.39 | 128.82 | 133.07 | 136.01 | 137.56 | 137.67 |
| 7.3 | 101.88 | 109.76 | 117.02 | 123.45 | 128.87 | 133.10 | 136.03 | 137.57 | 137.66 |
| 7.4 | 101.96 | 109.84 | 117.09 | 123.51 | 128.92 | 133.14 | 136.05 | 137.58 | 137.65 |
| 7.5 | 102.04 | 109.92 | 117.16 | 123.57 | 128.96 | 133.18 | 136.07 | 137.58 | 137.65 |
| 7.6 | 102.12 | 109.99 | 117.23 | 123.63 | 129.01 | 133.21 | 136.10 | 137.59 | 137.64 |
| 7.7 | 102.20 | 110.07 | 117.30 | 123.69 | 129.06 | 133.25 | 136.12 | 137.60 | 137.64 |
| 7.8 | 102.28 | 110.14 | 117.37 | 123.75 | 129.11 | 133.28 | 136.14 | 137.61 | 137.63 |
| 7.9 | 102.36 | 110.22 | 117.44 | 123.81 | 129.16 | 133.32 | 136.16 | 137.62 | 137.63 |
| 8.0 | 102.44 | 110.29 | 117.50 | 123.87 | 129.21 | 133.35 | 136.18 | 137.62 | 137.62 |
| 8.1 | 102.53 | 110.37 | 117.57 | 123.93 | 129.25 | 133.39 | 136.21 | 137.63 | 137.62 |
| 8.2 | 102.61 | 110.44 | 117.64 | 123.99 | 129.30 | 133.42 | 136.23 | 137.63 | 137.61 |
| 8.3 | 102.69 | 110.52 | 117.71 | 124.05 | 129.35 | 133.46 | 136.25 | 137.64 | 137.60 |
| 8.4 | 102.77 | 110.59 | 117.78 | 124.11 | 129.39 | 133.49 | 136.27 | 137.64 | 137.59 |
| 8.5 | 102.85 | 110.67 | 117.84 | 124.16 | 129.44 | 133.53 | 136.29 | 137.65 | 137.58 |
| 8.6 | 102.93 | 110.74 | 117.91 | 124.22 | 129.49 | 133.56 | 136.31 | 137.65 | 137.58 |
| 8.7 | 103.01 | 110.82 | 117.98 | 124.28 | 129.53 | 133.59 | 136.33 | 137.66 | 137.57 |
| 8.8 | 103.09 | 110.89 | 118.05 | 124.34 | 129.58 | 133.63 | 136.35 | 137.67 | 137.56 |
| 8.9 | 103.17 | 110.97 | 118.12 | 124.40 | 129.63 | 133.66 | 136.37 | 137.67 | 137.55 |
| 9.0 | 103.25 | 111.04 | 118.18 | 124.45 | 129.67 | 133.69 | 136.39 | 137.68 | 137.54 |
| 9.1 | 103.33 | 111.12 | 118.25 | 124.51 | 129.72 | 133.73 | 136.41 | 137.68 | 137.54 |
| 9.2 | 103.41 | 111.19 | 118.32 | 124.57 | 129.77 | 133.76 | 136.43 | 137.69 | 137.53 |
| 9.3 | 103.49 | 111.27 | 118.39 | 124.63 | 129.81 | 133.79 | 136.45 | 137.69 | 137.52 |
| 9.4 | 103.57 | 111.34 | 118.45 | 124.68 | 129.86 | 133.83 | 136.47 | 137.70 | 137.51 |
| 9.5 | 103.65 | 111.42 | 118.52 | 124.74 | 129.91 | 133.86 | 136.49 | 137.70 | 137.50 |
| 9.6 | 103.73 | 111.49 | 118.59 | 124.80 | 129.95 | 133.89 | 136.51 | 137.71 | 137.49 |
| 9.7 | 103.81 | 111.57 | 118.65 | 124.85 | 130.00 | 133.93 | 136.53 | 137.71 | 137.48 |
| 9.8 | 103.89 | 111.64 | 118.72 | 124.91 | 130.04 | 133.96 | 136.55 | 137.72 | 137.47 |
| 9.9 | 103.97 | 111.72 | 118.79 | 124.97 | 130.09 | 133.99 | 136.57 | 137.72 | 137.46 |
| 10.0 | 104.05 | 111.79 | 118.85 | 125.02 | 130.13 | 134.02 | 136.58 | 137.73 | 137.45 |

# TABLE LXXXVIII. ARGUMENT 4.

Equation $= 88''.9 + 48''.9$ sin. $z$.

| Days. | 190 | 200 | 210 | 220 | 230 | 240 | 250 | 260 | 270 |
|---|---|---|---|---|---|---|---|---|---|
| 0.0 | 137.45 | 135.72 | 132.62 | 128.23 | 122.67 | 116.12 | 108.76 | 100.82 | 92.53 |
| 0.1 | 137.44 | 135.70 | 132.59 | 128.18 | 122.61 | 116.05 | 108.69 | 100.74 | 92.45 |
| 0.2 | 137.43 | 135.67 | 132.55 | 128.13 | 122.55 | 115.98 | 108.61 | 100.66 | 92.37 |
| 0.3 | 137.42 | 135.65 | 132.51 | 128.08 | 122.49 | 115.91 | 108.53 | 100.58 | 92.28 |
| 0.4 | 137.41 | 135.62 | 132.47 | 128.03 | 122.43 | 115.84 | 108.46 | 100.50 | 92.20 |
| 0.5 | 137.40 | 135.60 | 132.43 | 127.98 | 122.37 | 115.77 | 108.38 | 100.41 | 92.11 |
| 0.6 | 137.39 | 135.57 | 132.40 | 127.93 | 122.31 | 115.70 | 108.30 | 100.33 | 92.03 |
| 0.7 | 137.38 | 135.55 | 132.36 | 127.88 | 122.25 | 115.63 | 108.23 | 100.25 | 91.95 |
| 0.8 | 137.37 | 135.52 | 132.32 | 127.83 | 122.19 | 115.56 | 108.15 | 100.17 | 91.86 |
| 0.9 | 137.36 | 135.50 | 132.28 | 127.78 | 122.13 | 115.49 | 108.07 | 100.09 | 91.78 |
| 1.0 | 137.34 | 135.47 | 132.24 | 127.72 | 122.06 | 115.42 | 107.99 | 100.00 | 91.69 |
| 1.1 | 137.33 | 135.45 | 132.20 | 127.67 | 122.00 | 115.35 | 107.92 | 99.92 | 91.61 |
| 1.2 | 137.32 | 135.42 | 132.16 | 127.62 | 121.94 | 115.28 | 107.84 | 99.84 | 91.53 |
| 1.3 | 137.31 | 135.40 | 132.12 | 127.57 | 121.88 | 115.21 | 107.76 | 99.76 | 91.44 |
| 1.4 | 137.29 | 135.37 | 132.08 | 127.52 | 121.81 | 115.14 | 107.68 | 99.68 | 91.36 |
| 1.5 | 137.28 | 135.35 | 132.04 | 127.46 | 121.75 | 115.07 | 107.60 | 99.59 | 91.28 |
| 1.6 | 137.27 | 135.32 | 132.00 | 127.41 | 121.69 | 115.00 | 107.53 | 99.51 | 91.19 |
| 1.7 | 137.25 | 135.29 | 131.96 | 127.36 | 121.62 | 114.93 | 107.45 | 99.43 | 91.11 |
| 1.8 | 137.24 | 135.27 | 131.92 | 127.31 | 121.56 | 114.86 | 107.37 | 99.35 | 91.02 |
| 1.9 | 137.23 | 135.24 | 131.88 | 127.26 | 121.50 | 114.79 | 107.29 | 99.27 | 90.94 |
| 2.0 | 137.21 | 135.21 | 131.84 | 127.20 | 121.43 | 114.71 | 107.21 | 99.18 | 90.85 |
| 2.1 | 137.20 | 135.19 | 131.80 | 127.15 | 121.37 | 114.64 | 107.14 | 99.10 | 90.77 |
| 2.2 | 137.19 | 135.16 | 131.76 | 127.10 | 121.31 | 114.57 | 107.06 | 99.02 | 90.69 |
| 2.3 | 137.18 | 135.13 | 131.72 | 127.05 | 121.25 | 114.50 | 106.98 | 98.94 | 90.60 |
| 2.4 | 137.16 | 135.10 | 131.68 | 126.99 | 121.18 | 114.43 | 106.90 | 98.86 | 90.52 |
| 2.5 | 137.15 | 135.07 | 131.64 | 126.94 | 121.12 | 114.35 | 106.82 | 98.77 | 90.43 |
| 2.6 | 137.14 | 135.05 | 131.60 | 126.89 | 121.06 | 114.28 | 106.75 | 98.69 | 90.35 |
| 2.7 | 137.12 | 135.02 | 131.56 | 126.83 | 120.99 | 114.21 | 106.67 | 98.61 | 90.27 |
| 2.8 | 137.11 | 134.99 | 131.52 | 126.78 | 120.93 | 114.14 | 106.59 | 98.53 | 90.18 |
| 2.9 | 137.10 | 134.96 | 131.48 | 126.73 | 120.87 | 114.07 | 106.51 | 98.45 | 90.10 |
| 3.0 | 137.08 | 134.93 | 131.43 | 126.67 | 120.80 | 113.99 | 106.43 | 98.36 | 90.01 |
| 3.1 | 137.07 | 134.91 | 131.39 | 126.62 | 120.74 | 113.92 | 106.36 | 98.28 | 89.92 |
| 3.2 | 137.05 | 134.88 | 131.35 | 126.57 | 120.68 | 113.85 | 106.28 | 98.20 | 89.84 |
| 3.3 | 137.04 | 134.85 | 131.31 | 126.51 | 120.62 | 113.78 | 106.20 | 98.12 | 89.75 |
| 3.4 | 137.02 | 134.82 | 131.27 | 126.46 | 120.55 | 113.70 | 106.12 | 98.03 | 89.67 |
| 3.5 | 137.01 | 134.79 | 131.22 | 126.41 | 120.49 | 113.63 | 106.04 | 97.95 | 89.58 |
| 3.6 | 136.99 | 134.76 | 131.18 | 126.35 | 120.42 | 113.56 | 105.96 | 97.87 | 89.50 |
| 3.7 | 136.98 | 134.73 | 131.14 | 126.30 | 120.36 | 113.48 | 105.88 | 97.78 | 89.41 |
| 3.8 | 136.96 | 134.70 | 131.10 | 126.24 | 120.29 | 113.41 | 105.80 | 97.70 | 89.33 |
| 3.9 | 136.95 | 134.67 | 131.06 | 126.19 | 120.23 | 113.34 | 105.72 | 97.62 | 89.24 |
| 4.0 | 136.93 | 134.64 | 131.01 | 126.13 | 120.16 | 113.26 | 105.64 | 97.53 | 89.16 |
| 4.1 | 136.92 | 134.61 | 130.97 | 126.08 | 120.10 | 113.19 | 105.57 | 97.45 | 89.07 |
| 4.2 | 136.90 | 134.58 | 130.93 | 126.02 | 120.03 | 113.12 | 105.49 | 97.37 | 88.99 |
| 4.3 | 136.88 | 134.55 | 130.89 | 125.97 | 119.97 | 113.05 | 105.41 | 97.29 | 88.90 |
| 4.4 | 136.87 | 134.52 | 130.84 | 125.91 | 119.90 | 112.97 | 105.33 | 97.20 | 88.82 |
| 4.5 | 136.85 | 134.49 | 130.80 | 125.86 | 119.84 | 112.90 | 105.25 | 97.12 | 88.74 |
| 4.6 | 136.83 | 134.46 | 130.76 | 125.80 | 119.77 | 112.83 | 105.17 | 97.04 | 88.65 |
| 4.7 | 136.82 | 134.43 | 130.71 | 125.75 | 119.71 | 112.75 | 105.09 | 96.95 | 88.57 |
| 4.8 | 136.80 | 134.40 | 130.67 | 125.69 | 119.64 | 112.68 | 105.01 | 96.87 | 88.48 |
| 4.9 | 136.78 | 134.37 | 130.63 | 125.64 | 119.58 | 112.61 | 104.93 | 96.79 | 88.40 |
| 5.0 | 136.76 | 134.34 | 130.58 | 125.58 | 119.51 | 112.53 | 104.85 | 96.70 | 88.32 |

# TABLE LXXXVIII. ARGUMENT 4.

Equation $= 88''.9 + 48''.9 \sin. z.$

| Days. | 190 | 200 | 210 | 220 | 230 | 240 | 250 | 260 | 270 |
|---|---|---|---|---|---|---|---|---|---|
| Days. 5.0 | 136″.76 | 134″.34 | 130″.58 | 125″.58 | 119″.51 | 112″.53 | 104″.85 | 96″.70 | 88″.32 |
| 5.1 | 136.75 | 134.31 | 130.54 | 125.53 | 119.45 | 112.46 | 104.77 | 96.62 | 88.23 |
| 5.2 | 136.73 | 134.28 | 130.49 | 125.47 | 119.38 | 112.39 | 104.69 | 96.54 | 88.15 |
| 5.3 | 136.71 | 134.25 | 130.45 | 125.42 | 119.32 | 112.31 | 104.61 | 96.46 | 88.06 |
| 5.4 | 136.69 | 134.22 | 130.40 | 125.36 | 119.25 | 112.24 | 104.53 | 96.37 | 87.98 |
| 5.5 | 136.67 | 134.18 | 130.36 | 125.31 | 119.19 | 112.17 | 104.45 | 96.29 | 87.89 |
| 5.6 | 136.66 | 134.15 | 130.31 | 125.25 | 119.12 | 112.09 | 104.37 | 96.21 | 87.81 |
| 5.7 | 136.64 | 134.12 | 130.27 | 125.19 | 119.05 | 112.02 | 104.29 | 96.12 | 87.73 |
| 5.8 | 136.62 | 134.09 | 130.22 | 125.14 | 118.99 | 111.94 | 104.21 | 96.04 | 87.64 |
| 5.9 | 136.60 | 134.06 | 130.18 | 125.08 | 118.92 | 111.87 | 104.13 | 95.96 | 87.56 |
| 6.0 | 136.58 | 134.02 | 130.13 | 125.02 | 118.85 | 111.79 | 104.05 | 95.87 | 87.48 |
| 6.1 | 136.57 | 133.99 | 130.09 | 124.97 | 118.79 | 111.72 | 103.97 | 95.79 | 87.39 |
| 6.2 | 136.55 | 133.96 | 130.04 | 124.91 | 118.72 | 111.64 | 103.89 | 95.71 | 87.31 |
| 6.3 | 136.53 | 133.93 | 130.00 | 124.85 | 118.65 | 111.57 | 103.81 | 95.63 | 87.22 |
| 6.4 | 136.51 | 133.89 | 129.95 | 124.80 | 118.59 | 111.49 | 103.73 | 95.54 | 87.14 |
| 6.5 | 136.49 | 133.86 | 129.91 | 124.74 | 118.52 | 111.42 | 103.65 | 95.46 | 87.05 |
| 6.6 | 136.47 | 133.83 | 129.86 | 124.68 | 118.45 | 111.34 | 103.57 | 95.38 | 86.97 |
| 6.7 | 136.45 | 133.79 | 129.81 | 124.63 | 118.39 | 111.27 | 103.49 | 95.29 | 86.89 |
| 6.8 | 136.43 | 133.76 | 129.77 | 124.57 | 118.32 | 111.19 | 103.41 | 95.21 | 86.80 |
| 6.9 | 136.41 | 133.73 | 129.72 | 124.51 | 118.25 | 111.12 | 103.33 | 95.13 | 86.72 |
| 7.0 | 136.39 | 133.69 | 129.67 | 124.45 | 118.18 | 111.04 | 103.25 | 95.04 | 86.64 |
| 7.1 | 136.37 | 133.66 | 129.63 | 124.40 | 118.12 | 110.97 | 103.17 | 94.96 | 86.55 |
| 7.2 | 136.35 | 133.63 | 129.58 | 124.34 | 118.05 | 110.89 | 103.09 | 94.88 | 86.47 |
| 7.3 | 136.33 | 133.59 | 129.53 | 124.28 | 117.98 | 110.82 | 103.01 | 94.79 | 86.38 |
| 7.4 | 136.31 | 133.56 | 129.49 | 124.22 | 117.91 | 110.74 | 102.93 | 94.71 | 86.30 |
| 7.5 | 136.29 | 133.53 | 129.44 | 124.16 | 117.84 | 110.67 | 102.85 | 94.63 | 86.21 |
| 7.6 | 136.27 | 133.49 | 129.39 | 124.11 | 117.78 | 110.59 | 102.77 | 94.54 | 86.13 |
| 7.7 | 136.25 | 133.46 | 129.35 | 124.05 | 117.71 | 110.52 | 102.69 | 94.46 | 86.05 |
| 7.8 | 136.23 | 133.42 | 129.30 | 123.99 | 117.64 | 110.44 | 102.61 | 94.37 | 85.96 |
| 7.9 | 136.21 | 133.39 | 129.25 | 123.93 | 117.57 | 110.37 | 102.53 | 94.29 | 85.88 |
| 8.0 | 136.18 | 133.35 | 129.20 | 123.87 | 117.50 | 110.29 | 102.44 | 94.20 | 85.80 |
| 8.1 | 136.16 | 133.32 | 129.16 | 123.81 | 117.44 | 110.22 | 102.36 | 94.12 | 85.71 |
| 8.2 | 136.14 | 133.28 | 129.11 | 123.75 | 117.37 | 110.14 | 102.28 | 94.04 | 85.63 |
| 8.3 | 136.12 | 133.25 | 129.06 | 123.69 | 117.30 | 110.07 | 102.20 | 93.95 | 85.54 |
| 8.4 | 136.10 | 133.21 | 129.01 | 123.63 | 117.23 | 109.99 | 102.12 | 93.87 | 85.46 |
| 8.5 | 136.07 | 133.18 | 128.96 | 123.57 | 117.16 | 109.92 | 102.04 | 93.79 | 85.37 |
| 8.6 | 136.05 | 133.14 | 128.92 | 123.51 | 117.09 | 109.84 | 101.96 | 93.70 | 85.29 |
| 8.7 | 136.03 | 133.10 | 128.87 | 123.45 | 117.02 | 109.76 | 101.88 | 93.62 | 85.21 |
| 8.8 | 136.01 | 133.07 | 128.82 | 123.39 | 116.95 | 109.69 | 101.80 | 93.53 | 85.12 |
| 8.9 | 135.99 | 133.03 | 128.77 | 123.33 | 116.88 | 109.61 | 101.72 | 93.45 | 85.04 |
| 9.0 | 135.96 | 132.99 | 128.72 | 123.27 | 116.81 | 109.53 | 101.63 | 93.36 | 84.96 |
| 9.1 | 135.94 | 132.96 | 128.68 | 123.21 | 116.75 | 109.46 | 101.55 | 93.28 | 84.87 |
| 9.2 | 135.92 | 132.92 | 128.63 | 123.15 | 116.68 | 109.38 | 101.47 | 93.20 | 84.79 |
| 9.3 | 135.89 | 132.88 | 128.58 | 123.09 | 116.61 | 109.30 | 101.39 | 93.12 | 84.71 |
| 9.4 | 135.87 | 132.85 | 128.53 | 123.03 | 116.54 | 109.23 | 101.31 | 93.03 | 84.62 |
| 9.5 | 135.85 | 132.81 | 128.48 | 122.97 | 116.47 | 109.15 | 101.23 | 92.95 | 84.54 |
| 9.6 | 135.82 | 132.77 | 128.43 | 122.91 | 116.40 | 109.07 | 101.15 | 92.87 | 84.46 |
| 9.7 | 135.80 | 132.74 | 128.38 | 122.85 | 116.33 | 109.00 | 101.07 | 92.78 | 84.37 |
| 9.8 | 135.77 | 132.70 | 128.33 | 122.79 | 116.26 | 108.92 | 100.99 | 92.70 | 84.29 |
| 9.9 | 135.75 | 132.66 | 128.28 | 122.73 | 116.19 | 108.84 | 100.91 | 92.62 | 84.21 |
| 10.0 | 135.72 | 132.62 | 128.23 | 122.67 | 116.12 | 108.76 | 100.82 | 92.53 | 84.13 |

# TABLE LXXXVIII. ARGUMENT 4.

Equation = 88″.9 + 48″.9 sin z.

| Days. | 280 | 290 | 300 | 310 | 320 | 330 | 340 | 350 | 360 |
|---|---|---|---|---|---|---|---|---|---|
| Days. | ″ | ″ | ″ | ″ | ″ | ″ | ″ | ″ | ″ |
| 0.0 | 84.13 | 75.87 | 67.99 | 60.73 | 54.31 | 48.90 | 44.68 | 41.76 | 40.23 |
| 0.1 | 84.04 | 75.78 | 67.91 | 60.66 | 54.25 | 48.85 | 44.64 | 41.73 | 40.22 |
| 0.2 | 83.96 | 75.70 | 67.83 | 60.59 | 54.19 | 48.80 | 44.60 | 41.71 | 40.21 |
| 0.3 | 83.87 | 75.62 | 67.76 | 60.52 | 54.13 | 48.75 | 44.57 | 41.69 | 40.20 |
| 0.4 | 83.79 | 75.54 | 67.68 | 60.45 | 54.07 | 48.70 | 44.53 | 41.67 | 40.20 |
| 0.5 | 83.70 | 75.46 | 67.61 | 60.39 | 54.01 | 48.66 | 44.49 | 41.65 | 40.19 |
| 0.6 | 83.62 | 75.38 | 67.53 | 60.32 | 53.95 | 48.61 | 44.46 | 41.62 | 40.18 |
| 0.7 | 83.54 | 75.30 | 67.45 | 60.25 | 53.89 | 48.56 | 44.42 | 41.60 | 40.18 |
| 0.8 | 83.45 | 75.22 | 67.38 | 60.18 | 53.83 | 48.51 | 44.39 | 41.58 | 40.17 |
| 0.9 | 83.37 | 75.14 | 67.30 | 60.11 | 53.77 | 48.46 | 44.35 | 41.56 | 40.16 |
| 1.0 | 83.29 | 75.06 | 67.23 | 60.05 | 53.72 | 48.42 | 44.32 | 41.54 | 40.16 |
| 1.1 | 83.20 | 74.97 | 67.15 | 59.98 | 53.66 | 48.37 | 44.28 | 41.52 | 40.15 |
| 1.2 | 83.12 | 74.89 | 67.08 | 59.91 | 53.60 | 48.32 | 44.25 | 41.50 | 40.14 |
| 1.3 | 83.03 | 74.81 | 67.00 | 59.84 | 53.54 | 48.28 | 44.21 | 41.48 | 40.14 |
| 1.4 | 82.95 | 74.73 | 66.93 | 59.77 | 53.48 | 48.23 | 44.18 | 41.46 | 40.13 |
| 1.5 | 82.86 | 74.65 | 66.85 | 59.71 | 53.43 | 48.18 | 44.14 | 41.44 | 40.12 |
| 1.6 | 82.78 | 74.57 | 66.78 | 59.64 | 53.37 | 48.14 | 44.11 | 41.42 | 40.12 |
| 1.7 | 82.70 | 74.49 | 66.70 | 59.57 | 53.31 | 48.09 | 44.08 | 41.40 | 40.11 |
| 1.8 | 82.61 | 74.41 | 66.63 | 59.50 | 53.25 | 48.05 | 44.04 | 41.38 | 40.11 |
| 1.9 | 82.53 | 74.33 | 66.55 | 59.44 | 53.19 | 48.00 | 44.01 | 41.36 | 40.10 |
| 2.0 | 82.45 | 74.25 | 66.48 | 59.37 | 53.14 | 47.96 | 43.98 | 41.34 | 40.10 |
| 2.1 | 82.36 | 74.17 | 66.40 | 59.30 | 53.08 | 47.91 | 43.94 | 41.32 | 40.09 |
| 2.2 | 82.28 | 74.09 | 66.33 | 59.24 | 53.02 | 47.86 | 43.91 | 41.30 | 40.09 |
| 2.3 | 82.20 | 74.01 | 66.25 | 59.17 | 52.96 | 47.82 | 43.88 | 41.28 | 40.08 |
| 2.4 | 82.11 | 73.93 | 66.18 | 59.10 | 52.91 | 47.77 | 43.85 | 41.26 | 40.08 |
| 2.5 | 82.03 | 73.85 | 66.10 | 59.04 | 52.85 | 47.72 | 43.82 | 41.24 | 40.07 |
| 2.6 | 81.95 | 73.77 | 66.03 | 58.97 | 52.79 | 47.68 | 43.78 | 41.22 | 40.07 |
| 2.7 | 81.86 | 73.69 | 65.96 | 58.90 | 52.74 | 47.63 | 43.75 | 41.20 | 40.06 |
| 2.8 | 81.78 | 73.61 | 65.88 | 58.84 | 52.68 | 47.59 | 43.72 | 41.18 | 40.06 |
| 2.9 | 81.70 | 73.53 | 65.81 | 58.77 | 52.62 | 47.54 | 43.69 | 41.16 | 40.05 |
| 3.0 | 81.62 | 73.45 | 65.74 | 58.71 | 52.57 | 47.50 | 43.66 | 41.15 | 40.05 |
| 3.1 | 81.53 | 73.37 | 65.66 | 58.64 | 52.51 | 47.45 | 43.62 | 41.13 | 40.04 |
| 3.2 | 81.45 | 73.29 | 65.59 | 58.57 | 52.45 | 47.41 | 43.59 | 41.11 | 40.04 |
| 3.3 | 81.37 | 73.21 | 65.51 | 58.51 | 52.40 | 47.36 | 43.56 | 41.09 | 40.04 |
| 3.4 | 81.28 | 73.13 | 65.44 | 58.44 | 52.34 | 47.32 | 43.53 | 41.08 | 40.03 |
| 3.5 | 81.20 | 73.05 | 65.36 | 58.37 | 52.28 | 47.27 | 43.50 | 41.06 | 40.03 |
| 3.6 | 81.12 | 72.97 | 65.29 | 58.31 | 52.23 | 47.23 | 43.47 | 41.04 | 40.03 |
| 3.7 | 81.03 | 72.89 | 65.22 | 58.24 | 52.17 | 47.19 | 43.44 | 41.03 | 40.02 |
| 3.8 | 80.95 | 72.81 | 65.14 | 58.18 | 52.12 | 47.14 | 43.41 | 41.01 | 40.02 |
| 3.9 | 80.87 | 72.73 | 65.07 | 58.11 | 52.06 | 47.10 | 43.38 | 40.99 | 40.02 |
| 4.0 | 80.79 | 72.66 | 65.00 | 58.05 | 52.01 | 47.06 | 43.35 | 40.98 | 40.02 |
| 4.1 | 80.70 | 72.58 | 64.92 | 57.98 | 51.95 | 47.01 | 43.32 | 40.96 | 40.01 |
| 4.2 | 80.62 | 72.50 | 64.85 | 57.92 | 51.90 | 46.97 | 43.29 | 40.94 | 40.01 |
| 4.3 | 80.54 | 72.42 | 64.78 | 57.85 | 51.84 | 46.93 | 43.26 | 40.93 | 40.01 |
| 4.4 | 80.45 | 72.34 | 64.70 | 57.79 | 51.79 | 46.88 | 43.23 | 40.91 | 40.01 |
| 4.5 | 80.37 | 72.26 | 64.63 | 57.72 | 51.73 | 46.84 | 43.20 | 40.90 | 40.01 |
| 4.6 | 80.29 | 72.18 | 64.56 | 57.66 | 51.68 | 46.80 | 43.17 | 40.88 | 40.00 |
| 4.7 | 80.20 | 72.10 | 64.48 | 57.59 | 51.63 | 46.75 | 43.14 | 40.86 | 40.00 |
| 4.8 | 80.12 | 72.02 | 64.41 | 57.53 | 51.57 | 46.71 | 43.11 | 40.85 | 40.00 |
| 4.9 | 80.04 | 71.94 | 64.34 | 57.46 | 51.52 | 46.67 | 43.08 | 40.83 | 40.00 |
| 5.0 | 79.96 | 71.87 | 64.27 | 57.40 | 51.47 | 46.63 | 43.05 | 40.82 | 40.00 |

# TABLE LXXXVIII. ARGUMENT 4.

Equation = 88″.9 + 48″.9 sin $z$.

| Days. | 280 | 290 | 300 | 310 | 320 | 330 | 340 | 350 | 360 |
|---|---|---|---|---|---|---|---|---|---|
| Days. | ″ | ″ | ″ | ″ | ″ | ″ | ″ | ″ | ″ |
| 5.0 | 79.96 | 71.87 | 64.27 | 57.40 | 51.47 | 46.63 | 43.05 | 40.82 | 40.00 |
| 5.1 | 79.87 | 71.79 | 64.19 | 57.33 | 51.41 | 46.58 | 43.02 | 40.80 | 40.00 |
| 5.2 | 79.79 | 71.71 | 64.12 | 57.27 | 51.36 | 46.54 | 42.99 | 40.79 | 40.00 |
| 5.3 | 79.71 | 71.63 | 64.05 | 57.20 | 51.30 | 46.50 | 42.96 | 40.77 | 40.00 |
| 5.4 | 79.63 | 71.55 | 63.98 | 57.14 | 51.25 | 46.46 | 42.93 | 40.76 | 40.00 |
| 5.5 | 79.55 | 71.47 | 63.91 | 57.07 | 51.19 | 46.42 | 42.90 | 40.74 | 40.00 |
| 5.6 | 79.46 | 71.39 | 63.83 | 57.01 | 51.14 | 46.38 | 42.87 | 40.73 | 40.00 |
| 5.7 | 79.38 | 71.31 | 63.76 | 56.95 | 51.09 | 46.34 | 42.84 | 40.71 | 40.00 |
| 5.8 | 79.30 | 71.23 | 63.69 | 56.88 | 51.03 | 46.30 | 42.81 | 40.70 | 40.00 |
| 5.9 | 79.22 | 71.15 | 63.62 | 56.82 | 50.98 | 46.26 | 42.78 | 40.69 | 40.00 |
| 6.0 | 79.14 | 71.08 | 63.55 | 56.76 | 50.93 | 46.22 | 42.76 | 40.67 | 40.00 |
| 6.1 | 79.05 | 71.00 | 63.47 | 56.69 | 50.87 | 46.17 | 42.73 | 40.65 | 40.00 |
| 6.2 | 78.97 | 70.92 | 63.40 | 56.63 | 50.82 | 46.13 | 42.70 | 40.64 | 40.00 |
| 6.3 | 78.89 | 70.84 | 63.33 | 56.57 | 50.77 | 46.09 | 42.67 | 40.63 | 40.00 |
| 6.4 | 78.80 | 70.76 | 63.26 | 56.51 | 50.71 | 46.05 | 42.65 | 40.62 | 40.00 |
| 6.5 | 78.72 | 70.69 | 63.19 | 56.45 | 50.66 | 46.01 | 42.62 | 40.60 | 40.00 |
| 6.6 | 78.64 | 70.61 | 63.11 | 56.38 | 50.61 | 45.97 | 42.59 | 40.59 | 40.00 |
| 6.7 | 78.55 | 70.53 | 63.04 | 56.32 | 50.55 | 45.93 | 42.57 | 40.58 | 40.00 |
| 6.8 | 78.47 | 70.45 | 62.97 | 56.26 | 50.50 | 45.89 | 42.54 | 40.56 | 40.01 |
| 6.9 | 78.39 | 70.37 | 62.90 | 56.20 | 50.45 | 45.85 | 42.51 | 40.55 | 40.01 |
| 7.0 | 78.31 | 70.30 | 62.83 | 56.14 | 50.40 | 45.81 | 42.49 | 40.54 | 40.01 |
| 7.1 | 78.22 | 70.22 | 62.75 | 56.07 | 50.34 | 45.77 | 42.46 | 40.52 | 40.01 |
| 7.2 | 78.14 | 70.14 | 62.68 | 56.01 | 50.29 | 45.73 | 42.43 | 40.51 | 40.01 |
| 7.3 | 78.06 | 70.06 | 62.61 | 55.95 | 50.24 | 45.69 | 42.41 | 40.50 | 40.02 |
| 7.4 | 77.98 | 69.98 | 62.54 | 55.89 | 50.19 | 45.65 | 42.38 | 40.49 | 40.02 |
| 7.5 | 77.90 | 69.91 | 62.47 | 55.83 | 50.14 | 45.61 | 42.35 | 40.48 | 40.02 |
| 7.6 | 77.81 | 69.83 | 62.40 | 55.76 | 50.09 | 45.57 | 42.33 | 40.46 | 40.02 |
| 7.7 | 77.73 | 69.75 | 62.33 | 55.70 | 50.04 | 45.53 | 42.30 | 40.45 | 40.03 |
| 7.8 | 77.65 | 69.67 | 62.26 | 55.64 | 49.99 | 45.49 | 42.28 | 40.44 | 40.03 |
| 7.9 | 77.57 | 69.59 | 62.19 | 55.58 | 49.94 | 45.45 | 42.25 | 40.43 | 40.03 |
| 8.0 | 77.49 | 69.52 | 62.12 | 55.52 | 49.89 | 45.42 | 42.23 | 40.42 | 40.04 |
| 8.1 | 77.40 | 69.44 | 62.05 | 55.45 | 49.84 | 45.38 | 42.20 | 40.41 | 40.04 |
| 8.2 | 77.32 | 69.36 | 61.98 | 55.39 | 49.79 | 45.34 | 42.18 | 40.40 | 40.04 |
| 8.3 | 77.24 | 69.28 | 61.91 | 55.33 | 49.74 | 45.30 | 42.15 | 40.39 | 40.05 |
| 8.4 | 77.16 | 69.21 | 61.84 | 55.27 | 49.69 | 45.26 | 42.13 | 40.38 | 40.05 |
| 8.5 | 77.08 | 69.13 | 61.77 | 55.21 | 49.64 | 45.23 | 42.10 | 40.37 | 40.06 |
| 8.6 | 77.00 | 69.05 | 61.70 | 55.15 | 49.59 | 45.19 | 42.08 | 40.36 | 40.06 |
| 8.7 | 76.92 | 68.98 | 61.63 | 55.09 | 49.54 | 45.15 | 42.06 | 40.35 | 40.07 |
| 8.8 | 76.84 | 68.90 | 61.56 | 55.03 | 49.49 | 45.11 | 42.03 | 40.34 | 40.07 |
| 8.9 | 76.76 | 68.82 | 61.49 | 54.97 | 49.44 | 45.07 | 42.01 | 40.33 | 40.08 |
| 9.0 | 76.68 | 68.75 | 61.42 | 54.91 | 49.39 | 45.04 | 41.99 | 40.32 | 40.08 |
| 9.1 | 76.59 | 68.67 | 61.35 | 54.85 | 49.34 | 45.00 | 41.96 | 40.31 | 40.09 |
| 9.2 | 76.51 | 68.59 | 61.28 | 54.79 | 49.29 | 44.96 | 41.94 | 40.30 | 40.09 |
| 9.3 | 76.43 | 68.52 | 61.21 | 54.73 | 49.24 | 44.93 | 41.92 | 40.29 | 40.10 |
| 9.4 | 76.35 | 68.44 | 61.14 | 54.67 | 49.19 | 44.89 | 41.89 | 40.28 | 40.10 |
| 9.5 | 76.27 | 68.37 | 61.07 | 54.61 | 49.14 | 44.85 | 41.87 | 40.27 | 40.11 |
| 9.6 | 76.19 | 68.29 | 61.00 | 54.55 | 49.09 | 44.82 | 41.85 | 40.26 | 40.11 |
| 9.7 | 76.11 | 68.21 | 60.93 | 54.49 | 49.04 | 44.78 | 41.82 | 40.25 | 40.12 |
| 9.8 | 76.03 | 68.14 | 60.86 | 54.43 | 48.99 | 44.75 | 41.80 | 40.24 | 40.12 |
| 9.9 | 75.95 | 68.06 | 60.79 | 54.37 | 48.94 | 44.71 | 41.78 | 40.23 | 40.13 |
| 10.0 | 75.87 | 67.99 | 60.73 | 54.31 | 48.90 | 44.68 | 41.76 | 40.23 | 40.14 |

# TABLES LXXXIX. XC.

| Tables | LXXXIX. | | | | XC. | | | | |
|---|---|---|---|---|---|---|---|---|---|
| Arguments | 4. | | | | 5. | | | | |
| Days. | 0 | 100 | 200 | 300 | 0 | 100 | 200 | 300 | 400 |
| 0 | 6.64″ | 5.34″ | 7.00″ | 7.81″ | 9.11″ | 0.46″ | 8.75″ | 0.88″ | 8.26″ |
| 01 | 6.61 | 5.34 | 7.02 | 7.80 | 9.16 | 0.40 | 8.82 | 0.80 | 8.35 |
| 02 | 6.59 | 5.34 | 7.04 | 7.79 | 9.20 | 0.34 | 8.89 | 0.72 | 8.44 |
| 03 | 6.57 | 5.35 | 7.07 | 7.78 | 9.24 | 0.29 | 8.95 | 0.65 | 8.53 |
| 04 | 6.54 | 5.35 | 7.09 | 7.77 | 9.27 | 0.24 | 9.01 | 0.58 | 8.61 |
| 05 | 6.52 | 5.36 | 7.11 | 7.76 | 9.30 | 0.20 | 9.07 | 0.51 | 8.69 |
| 06 | 6.50 | 5.37 | 7.13 | 7.75 | 9.33 | 0.16 | 9.12 | 0.45 | 8.76 |
| 07 | 6.48 | 5.37 | 7.15 | 7.73 | 9.35 | 0.13 | 9.17 | 0.39 | 8.83 |
| 08 | 6.46 | 5.38 | 7.17 | 7.72 | 9.37 | 0.10 | 9.21 | 0.33 | 8.90 |
| 09 | 6.43 | 5.39 | 7.19 | 7.71 | 9.38 | 0.07 | 9.25 | 0.28 | 8.96 |
| 10 | 6.41 | 5.40 | 7.21 | 7.69 | 9.39 | 0.05 | 9.28 | 0.23 | 9.02 |
| 11 | 6.39 | 5.40 | 7.23 | 7.68 | 9.40 | 0.03 | 9.31 | 0.19 | 9.07 |
| 12 | 6.37 | 5.41 | 7.25 | 7.67 | 9.40 | 0.02 | 9.33 | 0.15 | 9.12 |
| 13 | 6.35 | 5.42 | 7.27 | 7.65 | 9.40 | 0.01 | 9.35 | 0.12 | 9.17 |
| 14 | 6.32 | 5.42 | 7.29 | 7.64 | 9.39 | 0.00 | 9.37 | 0.09 | 9.21 |
| 15 | 6.30 | 5.43 | 7.31 | 7.62 | 9.38 | 0.00 | 9.38 | 0.06 | 9.25 |
| 16 | 6.28 | 5.44 | 7.33 | 7.61 | 9.36 | 0.01 | 9.39 | 0.04 | 9.28 |
| 17 | 6.26 | 5.45 | 7.35 | 7.59 | 9.34 | 0.02 | 9.40 | 0.02 | 9.31 |
| 18 | 6.24 | 5.46 | 7.37 | 7.58 | 9.31 | 0.03 | 9.40 | 0.01 | 9.33 |
| 19 | 6.22 | 5.47 | 7.39 | 7.56 | 9.28 | 0.05 | 9.39 | 0.00 | 9.35 |
| 20 | 6.20 | 5.48 | 7.41 | 7.55 | 9.25 | 0.07 | 9.38 | 0.00 | 9.37 |
| 21 | 6.18 | 5.49 | 7.43 | 7.53 | 9.21 | 0.09 | 9.37 | 0.00 | 9.38 |
| 22 | 6.16 | 5.50 | 7.45 | 7.52 | 9.17 | 0.12 | 9.35 | 0.01 | 9.39 |
| 23 | 6.14 | 5.51 | 7.46 | 7.50 | 9.12 | 0.15 | 9.33 | 0.02 | 9.40 |
| 24 | 6.12 | 5.52 | 7.48 | 7.49 | 9.07 | 0.19 | 9.30 | 0.03 | 9.40 |
| 25 | 6.10 | 5.53 | 7.50 | 7.47 | 9.01 | 0.23 | 9.27 | 0.05 | 9.40 |
| 26 | 6.08 | 5.54 | 7.51 | 7.45 | 8.95 | 0.28 | 9.24 | 0.07 | 9.39 |
| 27 | 6.06 | 5.56 | 7.53 | 7.43 | 8.89 | 0.33 | 9.20 | 0.10 | 9.38 |
| 28 | 6.04 | 5.57 | 7.55 | 7.41 | 8.82 | 0.39 | 9.16 | 0.13 | 9.36 |
| 29 | 6.02 | 5.58 | 7.56 | 7.40 | 8.75 | 0.45 | 9.11 | 0.16 | 9.33 |
| 30 | 6.00 | 5.60 | 7.58 | 7.38 | 8.68 | 0.51 | 9.06 | 0.20 | 9.30 |
| 31 | 5.98 | 5.61 | 7.59 | 7.36 | 8.60 | 0.58 | 9.00 | 0.24 | 9.27 |
| 32 | 5.96 | 5.62 | 7.61 | 7.34 | 8.52 | 0.65 | 8.94 | 0.29 | 9.24 |
| 33 | 5.94 | 5.64 | 7.62 | 7.32 | 8.43 | 0.72 | 8.88 | 0.34 | 9.20 |
| 34 | 5.92 | 5.65 | 7.64 | 7.30 | 8.34 | 0.80 | 8.81 | 0.40 | 9.16 |
| 35 | 5.90 | 5.67 | 7.65 | 7.28 | 8.25 | 0.88 | 8.74 | 0.46 | 9.11 |
| 36 | 5.88 | 5.68 | 7.66 | 7.26 | 8.15 | 0.97 | 8.67 | 0.52 | 9.06 |
| 37 | 5.86 | 5.70 | 7.68 | 7.24 | 8.05 | 1.06 | 8.59 | 0.59 | 9.00 |
| 38 | 5.85 | 5.71 | 7.69 | 7.22 | 7.95 | 1.15 | 8.51 | 0.66 | 8.94 |
| 39 | 5.83 | 5.73 | 7.70 | 7.20 | 7.85 | 1.25 | 8.42 | 0.74 | 8.88 |
| 40 | 5.81 | 5.75 | 7.72 | 7.18 | 7.74 | 1.35 | 8.33 | 0.82 | 8.81 |
| 41 | 5.79 | 5.76 | 7.73 | 7.16 | 7.63 | 1.45 | 8.24 | 0.90 | 8.74 |
| 42 | 5.77 | 5.78 | 7.74 | 7.14 | 7.52 | 1.56 | 8.14 | 0.99 | 8.66 |
| 43 | 5.76 | 5.80 | 7.75 | 7.12 | 7.40 | 1.67 | 8.04 | 1.08 | 8.58 |
| 44 | 5.74 | 5.81 | 7.76 | 7.10 | 7.28 | 1.78 | 7.94 | 1.17 | 8.50 |
| 45 | 5.73 | 5.83 | 7.77 | 7.08 | 7.16 | 1.89 | 7.84 | 1.26 | 8.41 |
| 46 | 5.71 | 5.85 | 7.78 | 7.06 | 7.04 | 2.01 | 7.73 | 1.36 | 8.32 |
| 47 | 5.70 | 5.87 | 7.79 | 7.04 | 6.91 | 2.13 | 7.62 | 1.46 | 8.23 |
| 48 | 5.68 | 5.89 | 7.80 | 7.02 | 6.78 | 2.25 | 7.51 | 1.57 | 8.13 |
| 49 | 5.67 | 5.91 | 7.81 | 7.00 | 6.65 | 2.37 | 7.39 | 1.68 | 8.03 |
| 50 | 5.65 | 5.93 | 7.82 | 6.98 | 6.52 | 2.49 | 7.27 | 1.79 | 7.93 |

# TABLES LXXXIX. XC.

| Tables | LXXXIX. | | | | XC. | | | | |
|---|---|---|---|---|---|---|---|---|---|
| Arguments | 4. | | | | 5. | | | | |
| Days. | 0 | 100 | 200 | 300 | 0 | 100 | 200 | 300 | 400 |
| 50 | ″5.65 | ″5.93 | ″7.82 | ″6.98 | ″6.52 | ″2.49 | ″7.27 | ″1.79 | ″7.93 |
| 51 | 5.64 | 5.95 | 7.83 | 6.96 | 6.39 | 2.62 | 7.15 | 1.90 | 7.83 |
| 52 | 5.62 | 5.97 | 7.84 | 6.94 | 6.26 | 2.75 | 7.03 | 2.02 | 7.72 |
| 53 | 5.61 | 5.99 | 7.84 | 6.91 | 6.12 | 2.88 | 6.90 | 2.14 | 7.61 |
| 54 | 5.59 | 6.01 | 7.85 | 6.89 | 5.98 | 3.01 | 6.77 | 2.26 | 7.49 |
| 55 | 5.58 | 6.03 | 7.86 | 6.87 | 5.84 | 3.15 | 6.64 | 2.38 | 7.37 |
| 56 | 5.57 | 6.05 | 7.87 | 6.85 | 5.70 | 3.29 | 6.51 | 2.51 | 7.25 |
| 57 | 5.55 | 6.07 | 7.87 | 6.83 | 5.56 | 3.43 | 6.38 | 2.64 | 7.13 |
| 58 | 5.54 | 6.09 | 7.88 | 6.80 | 5.42 | 3.57 | 6.25 | 2.77 | 7.01 |
| 59 | 5.53 | 6.11 | 7.89 | 6.78 | 5.28 | 3.71 | 6.11 | 2.90 | 6.88 |
| 60 | 5.51 | 6.13 | 7.89 | 6.76 | 5.14 | 3.85 | 5.97 | 3.03 | 6.75 |
| 61 | 5.50 | 6.15 | 7.90 | 6.74 | 4.99 | 3.99 | 5.83 | 3.17 | 6.62 |
| 62 | 5.49 | 6.17 | 7.91 | 6.72 | 4.85 | 4.13 | 5.69 | 3.30 | 6.49 |
| 63 | 5.48 | 6.19 | 7.91 | 6.69 | 4.71 | 4.27 | 5.55 | 3.44 | 6.36 |
| 64 | 5.47 | 6.21 | 7.91 | 6.67 | 4.56 | 4.41 | 5.41 | 3.58 | 6.23 |
| 65 | 5.46 | 6.23 | 7.92 | 6.65 | 4.42 | 4.55 | 5.26 | 3.72 | 6.09 |
| 66 | 5.45 | 6.25 | 7.92 | 6.62 | 4.28 | 4.70 | 5.12 | 3.86 | 5.95 |
| 67 | 5.44 | 6.27 | 7.92 | 6.60 | 4.14 | 4.84 | 4.98 | 4.00 | 5.81 |
| 68 | 5.44 | 6.30 | 7.92 | 6.58 | 3.99 | 4.98 | 4.84 | 4.14 | 5.67 |
| 69 | 5.43 | 6.32 | 7.92 | 6.55 | 3.85 | 5.13 | 4.69 | 4.28 | 5.53 |
| 70 | 5.42 | 6.34 | 7.93 | 6.53 | 3.71 | 5.27 | 4.55 | 4.42 | 5.39 |
| 71 | 5.41 | 6.36 | 7.93 | 6.51 | 3.57 | 5.41 | 4.41 | 4.57 | 5.25 |
| 72 | 5.40 | 6.38 | 7.93 | 6.49 | 3.43 | 5.55 | 4.26 | 4.71 | 5.11 |
| 73 | 5.40 | 6.41 | 7.93 | 6.47 | 3.29 | 5.69 | 4.12 | 4.86 | 4.96 |
| 74 | 5.39 | 6.43 | 7.93 | 6.44 | 3.15 | 5.83 | 3.98 | 5.01 | 4.82 |
| 75 | 5.38 | 6.45 | 7.93 | 6.42 | 3.02 | 5.97 | 3.84 | 5.15 | 4.68 |
| 76 | 5.38 | 6.47 | 7.93 | 6.40 | 2.89 | 6.11 | 3.70 | 5.29 | 4.53 |
| 77 | 5.37 | 6.49 | 7.93 | 6.38 | 2.76 | 6.25 | 3.56 | 5.43 | 4.39 |
| 78 | 5.37 | 6.52 | 7.93 | 6.36 | 2.63 | 6.39 | 3.42 | 5.57 | 4.25 |
| 79 | 5.36 | 6.54 | 7.93 | 6.33 | 2.50 | 6.52 | 3.28 | 5.71 | 4.11 |
| 80 | 5.36 | 6.56 | 7.92 | 6.31 | 2.37 | 6.65 | 3.14 | 5.85 | 3.96 |
| 81 | 5.35 | 6.58 | 7.92 | 6.29 | 2.25 | 6.78 | 3.01 | 5.99 | 3.82 |
| 82 | 5.35 | 6.60 | 7.92 | 6.27 | 2.13 | 6.91 | 2.88 | 6.13 | 3.68 |
| 83 | 5.34 | 6.63 | 7.92 | 6.25 | 2.01 | 7.03 | 2.75 | 6.27 | 3.54 |
| 84 | 5.34 | 6.65 | 7.92 | 6.23 | 1.89 | 7.15 | 2.62 | 6.40 | 3.40 |
| 85 | 5.34 | 6.67 | 7.91 | 6.21 | 1.78 | 7.27 | 2.49 | 6.53 | 3.26 |
| 86 | 5.34 | 6.69 | 7.91 | 6.19 | 1.67 | 7.39 | 2.36 | 6.66 | 3.12 |
| 87 | 5.34 | 6.71 | 7.90 | 6.17 | 1.56 | 7.51 | 2.24 | 6.79 | 2.99 |
| 88 | 5.33 | 6.74 | 7.90 | 6.15 | 1.46 | 7.62 | 2.12 | 6.92 | 2.86 |
| 89 | 5.33 | 6.76 | 7.89 | 6.13 | 1.36 | 7.73 | 2.00 | 7.05 | 2.73 |
| 90 | 5.33 | 6.78 | 7.88 | 6.11 | 1.26 | 7.84 | 1.88 | 7.17 | 2.60 |
| 91 | 5.33 | 6.80 | 7.88 | 6.09 | 1.16 | 7.95 | 1.77 | 7.29 | 2.47 |
| 92 | 5.33 | 6.82 | 7.87 | 6.07 | 1.07 | 8.05 | 1.66 | 7.41 | 2.34 |
| 93 | 5.33 | 6.85 | 7.86 | 6.05 | 0.98 | 8.15 | 1.55 | 7.52 | 2.22 |
| 94 | 5.33 | 6.87 | 7.86 | 6.03 | 0.89 | 8.25 | 1.45 | 7.63 | 2.10 |
| 95 | 5.33 | 6.89 | 7.85 | 6.01 | 0.81 | 8.34 | 1.35 | 7.74 | 1.98 |
| 96 | 5.33 | 6.91 | 7.84 | 5.99 | 0.73 | 8.43 | 1.25 | 7.85 | 1.87 |
| 97 | 5.33 | 6.93 | 7.83 | 5.97 | 0.66 | 8.52 | 1.15 | 7.96 | 1.76 |
| 98 | 5.34 | 6.96 | 7.82 | 5.95 | 0.59 | 8.60 | 1.06 | 8.06 | 1.65 |
| 99 | 5.34 | 6.98 | 7.82 | 5.93 | 0.52 | 8.68 | 0.97 | 8.16 | 1.54 |
| 100 | 5.34 | 7.00 | 7.81 | 5.91 | 0.46 | 8.75 | 0.88 | 8.26 | 1.44 |

# TABLES XCI. XCII.

| Tables | XCI. | XCII. |
|---|---|---|
| Arguments | **5.** | **78.** |

**Table XCI.**

| Days. | **0** | **100** | **200** | **300** | **400** |
|---|---|---|---|---|---|
| Days. | " | " | " | " | " |
| 0 | 1.57 | 1.85 | 0.50 | 0.11 | 1.42 |
| 01 | 1.58 | 1.84 | 0.49 | 0.12 | 1.43 |
| 02 | 1.60 | 1.83 | 0.47 | 0.12 | 1.45 |
| 03 | 1.61 | 1.82 | 0.46 | 0.13 | 1.46 |
| 04 | 1.62 | 1.81 | 0.45 | 0.14 | 1.47 |
| 05 | 1.63 | 1.80 | 0.44 | 0.15 | 1.49 |
| 06 | 1.64 | 1.79 | 0.43 | 0.16 | 1.50 |
| 07 | 1.66 | 1.78 | 0.41 | 0.16 | 1.51 |
| 08 | 1.67 | 1.77 | 0.40 | 0.17 | 1.53 |
| 09 | 1.68 | 1.76 | 0.39 | 0.18 | 1.54 |
| 10 | 1.69 | 1.75 | 0.38 | 0.19 | 1.55 |
| 11 | 1.70 | 1.74 | 0.37 | 0.20 | 1.56 |
| 12 | 1.71 | 1.73 | 0.35 | 0.20 | 1.58 |
| 13 | 1.72 | 1.72 | 0.34 | 0.21 | 1.59 |
| 14 | 1.73 | 1.71 | 0.33 | 0.23 | 1.60 |
| 15 | 1.74 | 1.70 | 0.32 | 0.24 | 1.61 |
| 16 | 1.75 | 1.69 | 0.31 | 0.25 | 1.62 |
| 17 | 1.76 | 1.68 | 0.30 | 0.26 | 1.63 |
| 18 | 1.77 | 1.67 | 0.29 | 0.27 | 1.65 |
| 19 | 1.78 | 1.66 | 0.28 | 0.28 | 1.66 |
| 20 | 1.79 | 1.65 | 0.27 | 0.29 | 1.67 |
| 21 | 1.80 | 1.63 | 0.26 | 0.30 | 1.68 |
| 22 | 1.81 | 1.62 | 0.25 | 0.31 | 1.69 |
| 23 | 1.82 | 1.61 | 0.24 | 0.32 | 1.70 |
| 24 | 1.83 | 1.60 | 0.23 | 0.33 | 1.71 |
| 25 | 1.84 | 1.59 | 0.22 | 0.34 | 1.72 |
| 26 | 1.84 | 1.57 | 0.21 | 0.36 | 1.73 |
| 27 | 1.85 | 1.56 | 0.20 | 0.37 | 1.74 |
| 28 | 1.86 | 1.55 | 0.19 | 0.38 | 1.75 |
| 29 | 1.87 | 1.54 | 0.18 | 0.39 | 1.76 |
| 30 | 1.88 | 1.53 | 0.17 | 0.40 | 1.77 |
| 31 | 1.88 | 1.51 | 0.16 | 0.42 | 1.78 |
| 32 | 1.89 | 1.50 | 0.15 | 0.43 | 1.79 |
| 33 | 1.90 | 1.48 | 0.14 | 0.44 | 1.80 |
| 34 | 1.90 | 1.47 | 0.13 | 0.45 | 1.81 |
| 35 | 1.91 | 1.46 | 0.12 | 0.46 | 1.82 |
| 36 | 1.91 | 1.44 | 0.12 | 0.48 | 1.83 |
| 37 | 1.92 | 1.43 | 0.11 | 0.49 | 1.84 |
| 38 | 1.92 | 1.41 | 0.10 | 0.50 | 1.84 |
| 39 | 1.93 | 1.40 | 0.10 | 0.52 | 1.85 |
| 40 | 1.93 | 1.39 | 0.09 | 0.53 | 1.86 |
| 41 | 1.94 | 1.37 | 0.09 | 0.55 | 1.87 |
| 42 | 1.94 | 1.36 | 0.08 | 0.56 | 1.88 |
| 43 | 1.95 | 1.34 | 0.08 | 0.57 | 1.88 |
| 44 | 1.95 | 1.33 | 0.07 | 0.59 | 1.89 |
| 45 | 1.96 | 1.32 | 0.07 | 0.60 | 1.90 |
| 46 | 1.96 | 1.30 | 0.06 | 0.62 | 1.90 |
| 47 | 1.96 | 1.29 | 0.06 | 0.63 | 1.91 |
| 48 | 1.97 | 1.27 | 0.05 | 0.64 | 1.91 |
| 49 | 1.97 | 1.26 | 0.05 | 0.66 | 1.92 |
| 50 | 1.97 | 1.25 | 0.04 | 0.67 | 1.92 |

**Table XCII.**

| Days. | **0** | **10** | **20** | **30** | **40** | **50** | Days |
|---|---|---|---|---|---|---|---|
| Days. | " | " | " | " | " | " | Days. |
| 0.0 | 0.31 | 0.15 | 1.72 | 4.85 | 9.18 | 14.25 | 10.0 |
| 0.1 | 0.30 | 0.16 | 1.74 | 4.89 | 9.23 | 14.30 | 9.9 |
| 0.2 | 0.29 | 0.17 | 1.77 | 4.93 | 9.28 | 14.35 | 9.8 |
| 0.3 | 0.28 | 0.17 | 1.79 | 4.96 | 9.32 | 14.41 | 9.7 |
| 0.4 | 0.27 | 0.18 | 1.82 | 5.00 | 9.37 | 14.46 | 9.6 |
| 0.5 | 0.26 | 0.19 | 1.84 | 5.04 | 9.42 | 14.51 | 9.5 |
| 0.6 | 0.25 | 0.20 | 1.87 | 5.08 | 9.47 | 14.56 | 9.4 |
| 0.7 | 0.24 | 0.21 | 1.89 | 5.12 | 9.52 | 14.61 | 9.3 |
| 0.8 | 0.23 | 0.21 | 1.92 | 5.15 | 9.56 | 14.67 | 9.2 |
| 0.9 | 0.22 | 0.22 | 1.94 | 5.19 | 9.61 | 14.72 | 9.1 |
| 1.0 | 0.21 | 0.23 | 1.97 | 5.23 | 9.66 | 14.77 | 9.0 |
| 1.1 | 0.20 | 0.24 | 2.00 | 5.27 | 9.71 | 14.82 | 8.9 |
| 1.2 | 0.19 | 0.25 | 2.02 | 5.31 | 9.76 | 14.88 | 8.8 |
| 1.3 | 0.19 | 0.26 | 2.05 | 5.35 | 9.81 | 14.93 | 8.7 |
| 1.4 | 0.18 | 0.27 | 2.07 | 5.39 | 9.86 | 14.99 | 8.6 |
| 1.5 | 0.17 | 0.28 | 2.10 | 5.43 | 9.91 | 15.04 | 8.5 |
| 1.6 | 0.16 | 0.29 | 2.13 | 5.47 | 9.96 | 15.09 | 8.4 |
| 1.7 | 0.15 | 0.30 | 2.15 | 5.51 | 10.01 | 15.14 | 8.3 |
| 1.8 | 0.15 | 0.31 | 2.18 | 5.55 | 10.05 | 15.20 | 8.2 |
| 1.9 | 0.14 | 0.32 | 2.20 | 5.59 | 10.10 | 15.25 | 8.1 |
| 2.0 | 0.13 | 0.33 | 2.23 | 5.63 | 10.15 | 15.30 | 8.0 |
| 2.1 | 0.12 | 0.34 | 2.26 | 5.67 | 10.20 | 15.35 | 7.9 |
| 2.2 | 0.12 | 0.35 | 2.29 | 5.71 | 10.25 | 15.40 | 7.8 |
| 2.3 | 0.11 | 0.36 | 2.31 | 5.75 | 10.30 | 15.46 | 7.7 |
| 2.4 | 0.11 | 0.37 | 2.34 | 5.79 | 10.35 | 15.51 | 7.6 |
| 2.5 | 0.10 | 0.38 | 2.37 | 5.83 | 10.40 | 15.56 | 7.5 |
| 2.6 | 0.09 | 0.39 | 2.40 | 5.87 | 10.45 | 15.61 | 7.4 |
| 2.7 | 0.09 | 0.40 | 2.43 | 5.91 | 10.50 | 15.67 | 7.3 |
| 2.8 | 0.08 | 0.42 | 2.45 | 5.96 | 10.55 | 15.72 | 7.2 |
| 2.9 | 0.08 | 0.43 | 2.48 | 6.00 | 10.60 | 15.78 | 7.1 |
| 3.0 | 0.07 | 0.44 | 2.51 | 6.04 | 10.65 | 15.83 | 7.0 |
| 3.1 | 0.07 | 0.45 | 2.54 | 6.08 | 10.70 | 15.88 | 6.9 |
| 3.2 | 0.06 | 0.47 | 2.57 | 6.12 | 10.75 | 15.93 | 6.8 |
| 3.3 | 0.06 | 0.48 | 2.59 | 6.17 | 10.80 | 15.99 | 6.7 |
| 3.4 | 0.05 | 0.50 | 2.62 | 6.21 | 10.85 | 16.04 | 6.6 |
| 3.5 | 0.05 | 0.51 | 2.65 | 6.25 | 10.90 | 16.09 | 6.5 |
| 3.6 | 0.05 | 0.52 | 2.68 | 6.29 | 10.95 | 16.14 | 6.4 |
| 3.7 | 0.04 | 0.54 | 2.71 | 6.33 | 11.00 | 16.19 | 6.3 |
| 3.8 | 0.04 | 0.55 | 2.74 | 6.38 | 11.05 | 16.25 | 6.2 |
| 3.9 | 0.03 | 0.57 | 2.77 | 6.42 | 11.10 | 16.30 | 6.1 |
| 4.0 | 0.03 | 0.58 | 2.80 | 6.46 | 11.15 | 16.35 | 6.0 |
| 4.1 | 0.03 | 0.59 | 2.83 | 6.50 | 11.20 | 16.40 | 5.9 |
| 4.2 | 0.03 | 0.61 | 2.86 | 6.54 | 11.25 | 16.46 | 5.8 |
| 4.3 | 0.02 | 0.62 | 2.89 | 6.59 | 11.30 | 16.51 | 5.7 |
| 4.4 | 0.02 | 0.64 | 2.92 | 6.63 | 11.35 | 16.57 | 5.6 |
| 4.5 | 0.02 | 0.65 | 2.95 | 6.67 | 11.40 | 16.62 | 5.5 |
| 4.6 | 0.02 | 0.67 | 2.98 | 6.71 | 11.45 | 16.67 | 5.4 |
| 4.7 | 0.02 | 0.68 | 3.01 | 6.76 | 11.50 | 16.72 | 5.3 |
| 4.8 | 0.01 | 0.70 | 3.05 | 6.80 | 11.56 | 16.78 | 5.2 |
| 4.9 | 0.01 | 0.71 | 3.08 | 6.85 | 11.61 | 16.83 | 5.1 |
| 5.0 | 0.01 | 0.73 | 3.11 | 6.89 | 11.66 | 16.88 | 5.0 |
| Days. | **190** | **180** | **170** | **160** | **150** | **140** | Days. |

# TABLES XCI. XCII.

| TABLES | XCI. | XCII. |
|---|---|---|
| ARGUMENTS | 5. | 78. |

| Days. | 0 | 100 | 200 | 300 | 400 |
|---|---|---|---|---|---|
| 50 | 1.97 | 1.25 | 0.04 | 0.67 | 1.92 |
| 51 | 1.98 | 1.23 | 0.04 | 0.69 | 1.93 |
| 52 | 1.98 | 1.22 | 0.03 | 0.70 | 1.93 |
| 53 | 1.98 | 1.20 | 0.03 | 0.71 | 1.94 |
| 54 | 1.98 | 1.19 | 0.03 | 0.73 | 1.94 |
| 55 | 1.99 | 1.17 | 0.02 | 0.74 | 1.95 |
| 56 | 1.99 | 1.15 | 0.02 | 0.76 | 1.95 |
| 57 | 1.99 | 1.14 | 0.02 | 0.77 | 1.96 |
| 58 | 1.99 | 1.12 | 0.01 | 0.78 | 1.96 |
| 59 | 1.99 | 1.11 | 0.01 | 0.80 | 1.96 |
| 60 | 2.00 | 1.10 | 0.01 | 0.81 | 1.97 |
| 61 | 2.00 | 1.08 | 0.01 | 0.83 | 1.97 |
| 62 | 2.00 | 1.07 | 0.01 | 0.84 | 1.97 |
| 63 | 2.00 | 1.05 | 0.00 | 0.86 | 1.98 |
| 64 | 2.00 | 1.04 | 0.00 | 0.87 | 1.98 |
| 65 | 2.00 | 1.02 | 0.00 | 0.89 | 1.98 |
| 66 | 2.00 | 1.00 | 0.00 | 0.91 | 1.98 |
| 67 | 2.00 | 0.99 | 0.00 | 0.92 | 1.99 |
| 68 | 2.00 | 0.97 | 0.00 | 0.94 | 1.99 |
| 69 | 1.99 | 0.96 | 0.00 | 0.95 | 1.99 |
| 70 | 1.99 | 0.94 | 0.00 | 0.97 | 1.99 |
| 71 | 1.99 | 0.92 | 0.00 | 0.99 | 1.99 |
| 72 | 1.99 | 0.91 | 0.01 | 1.00 | 2.00 |
| 73 | 1.99 | 0.89 | 0.01 | 1.02 | 2.00 |
| 74 | 1.98 | 0.88 | 0.01 | 1.03 | 2.00 |
| 75 | 1.98 | 0.87 | 0.01 | 1.04 | 2.00 |
| 76 | 1.98 | 0.85 | 0.01 | 1.06 | 2.00 |
| 77 | 1.97 | 0.84 | 0.02 | 1.07 | 2.00 |
| 78 | 1.97 | 0.82 | 0.02 | 1.09 | 2.00 |
| 79 | 1.97 | 0.80 | 0.02 | 1.11 | 2.00 |
| 80 | 1.96 | 0.79 | 0.02 | 1.13 | 2.00 |
| 81 | 1.96 | 0.77 | 0.02 | 1.14 | 1.99 |
| 82 | 1.96 | 0.76 | 0.03 | 1.16 | 1.99 |
| 83 | 1.95 | 0.74 | 0.03 | 1.17 | 1.99 |
| 84 | 1.95 | 0.73 | 0.03 | 1.18 | 1.99 |
| 85 | 1.94 | 0.72 | 0.04 | 1.20 | 1.99 |
| 86 | 1.94 | 0.70 | 0.04 | 1.21 | 1.98 |
| 87 | 1.93 | 0.69 | 0.04 | 1.23 | 1.98 |
| 88 | 1.93 | 0.67 | 0.05 | 1.24 | 1.98 |
| 89 | 1.92 | 0.66 | 0.05 | 1.26 | 1.97 |
| 90 | 1.92 | 0.65 | 0.06 | 1.28 | 1.97 |
| 91 | 1.91 | 0.63 | 0.06 | 1.29 | 1.97 |
| 92 | 1.91 | 0.61 | 0.07 | 1.31 | 1.96 |
| 93 | 1.90 | 0.60 | 0.07 | 1.32 | 1.96 |
| 94 | 1.90 | 0.59 | 0.08 | 1.33 | 1.96 |
| 95 | 1.89 | 0.57 | 0.08 | 1.35 | 1.95 |
| 96 | 1.88 | 0.56 | 0.09 | 1.36 | 1.95 |
| 97 | 1.88 | 0.54 | 0.09 | 1.38 | 1.94 |
| 98 | 1.87 | 0.53 | 0.10 | 1.39 | 1.94 |
| 99 | 1.86 | 0.52 | 0.10 | 1.40 | 1.93 |
| 100 | 1.85 | 0.50 | 0.11 | 1.42 | 1.93 |

| Days. | 0 | 10 | 20 | 30 | 40 | 50 | Days |
|---|---|---|---|---|---|---|---|
| 5.0 | 0.01 | 0.73 | 3.11 | 6.89 | 11.66 | 16.88 | 5.0 |
| 5.1 | 0.01 | 0.75 | 3.14 | 6.93 | 11.71 | 16.93 | 4.9 |
| 5.2 | 0.01 | 0.76 | 3.17 | 6.98 | 11.76 | 16.98 | 4.8 |
| 5.3 | 0.00 | 0.78 | 3.21 | 7.02 | 11.81 | 17.04 | 4.7 |
| 5.4 | 0.00 | 0.79 | 3.24 | 7.07 | 11.86 | 17.09 | 4.6 |
| 5.5 | 0.00 | 0.81 | 3.27 | 7.11 | 11.91 | 17.14 | 4.5 |
| 5.6 | 0.00 | 0.83 | 3.30 | 7.15 | 11.96 | 17.19 | 4.4 |
| 5.7 | 0.00 | 0.84 | 3.33 | 7.20 | 12.01 | 17.24 | 4.3 |
| 5.8 | 0.00 | 0.86 | 3.37 | 7.24 | 12.07 | 17.30 | 4.2 |
| 5.9 | 0.00 | 0.87 | 3.40 | 7.29 | 12.12 | 17.35 | 4.1 |
| 6.0 | 0.00 | 0.89 | 3.43 | 7.33 | 12.17 | 17.40 | 4.0 |
| 6.1 | 0.00 | 0.91 | 3.46 | 7.37 | 12.22 | 17.45 | 3.9 |
| 6.2 | 0.00 | 0.93 | 3.49 | 7.42 | 12.27 | 17.51 | 3.8 |
| 6.3 | 0.00 | 0.94 | 3.53 | 7.46 | 12.32 | 17.56 | 3.7 |
| 6.4 | 0.00 | 0.96 | 3.56 | 7.51 | 12.37 | 17.62 | 3.6 |
| 6.5 | 0.00 | 0.98 | 3.59 | 7.55 | 12.42 | 17.67 | 3.5 |
| 6.6 | 0.00 | 1.00 | 3.62 | 7.60 | 12.47 | 17.72 | 3.4 |
| 6.7 | 0.00 | 1.02 | 3.66 | 7.64 | 12.52 | 17.77 | 3.3 |
| 6.8 | 0.01 | 1.03 | 3.69 | 7.69 | 12.58 | 17.83 | 3.2 |
| 6.9 | 0.01 | 1.05 | 3.73 | 7.73 | 12.63 | 17.88 | 3.1 |
| 7.0 | 0.01 | 1.07 | 3.76 | 7.78 | 12.68 | 17.93 | 3.0 |
| 7.1 | 0.01 | 1.09 | 3.79 | 7.83 | 12.73 | 17.98 | 2.9 |
| 7.2 | 0.01 | 1.11 | 3.83 | 7.87 | 12.78 | 18.03 | 2.8 |
| 7.3 | 0.02 | 1.13 | 3.86 | 7.92 | 12.84 | 18.09 | 2.7 |
| 7.4 | 0.02 | 1.15 | 3.90 | 7.96 | 12.89 | 18.14 | 2.6 |
| 7.5 | 0.02 | 1.17 | 3.93 | 8.01 | 12.94 | 18.19 | 2.5 |
| 7.6 | 0.02 | 1.19 | 3.97 | 8.06 | 12.99 | 18.24 | 2.4 |
| 7.7 | 0.03 | 1.21 | 4.00 | 8.10 | 13.04 | 18.29 | 2.3 |
| 7.8 | 0.03 | 1.23 | 4.04 | 8.15 | 13.10 | 18.35 | 2.2 |
| 7.9 | 0.04 | 1.25 | 4.07 | 8.19 | 13.15 | 18.40 | 2.1 |
| 8.0 | 0.04 | 1.27 | 4.11 | 8.24 | 13.20 | 18.45 | 2.0 |
| 8.1 | 0.04 | 1.29 | 4.15 | 8.29 | 13.25 | 18.50 | 1.9 |
| 8.2 | 0.05 | 1.31 | 4.18 | 8.33 | 13.30 | 18.55 | 1.8 |
| 8.3 | 0.05 | 1.34 | 4.22 | 8.38 | 13.36 | 18.61 | 1.7 |
| 8.4 | 0.06 | 1.36 | 4.25 | 8.42 | 13.41 | 18.66 | 1.6 |
| 8.5 | 0.06 | 1.38 | 4.29 | 8.47 | 13.46 | 18.71 | 1.5 |
| 8.6 | 0.07 | 1.40 | 4.33 | 8.52 | 13.51 | 18.76 | 1.4 |
| 8.7 | 0.07 | 1.42 | 4.36 | 8.57 | 13.56 | 18.81 | 1.3 |
| 8.8 | 0.08 | 1.45 | 4.40 | 8.61 | 13.62 | 18.87 | 1.2 |
| 8.9 | 0.08 | 1.47 | 4.43 | 8.66 | 13.67 | 18.92 | 1.1 |
| 9.0 | 0.09 | 1.49 | 4.47 | 8.71 | 13.72 | 18.97 | 1.0 |
| 9.1 | 0.10 | 1.51 | 4.51 | 8.76 | 13.77 | 19.02 | 0.9 |
| 9.2 | 0.10 | 1.53 | 4.55 | 8.80 | 13.82 | 19.07 | 0.8 |
| 9.3 | 0.11 | 1.56 | 4.58 | 8.85 | 13.88 | 19.13 | 0.7 |
| 9.4 | 0.11 | 1.58 | 4.62 | 8.89 | 13.93 | 19.18 | 0.6 |
| 9.5 | 0.12 | 1.60 | 4.66 | 8.94 | 13.98 | 19.23 | 0.5 |
| 9.6 | 0.13 | 1.62 | 4.70 | 8.99 | 14.03 | 19.28 | 0.4 |
| 9.7 | 0.13 | 1.65 | 4.74 | 9.04 | 14.09 | 19.33 | 0.3 |
| 9.8 | 0.14 | 1.67 | 4.77 | 9.08 | 14.14 | 19.39 | 0.2 |
| 9.9 | 0.14 | 1.70 | 4.81 | 9.13 | 14.20 | 19.44 | 0.1 |
| 10.0 | 0.15 | 1.72 | 4.85 | 9.18 | 14.25 | 19.49 | 0.0 |
| Days. | 190 | 180 | 170 | 160 | 150 | 140 | Days. |

| Tables | XCII. |
|---|---|
| Arguments | **78.** |

| Days. | **60** | **70** | **80** | **90** | Days. |
|---|---|---|---|---|---|
| Days. | ″ | ″ | ″ | ″ | Days. |
| 0.0 | 19.49 | 24.31 | 28.21 | 30.73 | 10.0 |
| 0.1 | 19.54 | 24.35 | 28.24 | 30.75 | 9.9 |
| 0.2 | 19.59 | 24.40 | 28.27 | 30.76 | 9.8 |
| 0.3 | 19.64 | 24.44 | 28.31 | 30.78 | 9.7 |
| 0.4 | 19.69 | 24.49 | 28.34 | 30.79 | 9.6 |
| 0.5 | 19.74 | 24.53 | 28.37 | 30.81 | 9.5 |
| 0.6 | 19.79 | 24.57 | 28.40 | 30.83 | 9.4 |
| 0.7 | 19.84 | 24.62 | 28.43 | 30.84 | 9.3 |
| 0.8 | 19.90 | 24.66 | 28.47 | 30.86 | 9.2 |
| 0.9 | 19.95 | 24.71 | 28.50 | 30.87 | 9.1 |
| 1.0 | 20.00 | 24.75 | 28.53 | 30.89 | 9.0 |
| 1.1 | 20.05 | 24.79 | 28.56 | 30.91 | 8.9 |
| 1.2 | 20.10 | 24.84 | 28.59 | 30.92 | 8.8 |
| 1.3 | 20.15 | 24.88 | 28.62 | 30.94 | 8.7 |
| 1.4 | 20.20 | 24.93 | 28.65 | 30.95 | 8.6 |
| 1.5 | 20.25 | 24.97 | 28.68 | 30.97 | 8.5 |
| 1.6 | 20.30 | 25.01 | 28.71 | 30.98 | 8.4 |
| 1.7 | 20.35 | 25.05 | 28.74 | 31.00 | 8.3 |
| 1.8 | 20.40 | 25.10 | 28.77 | 31.01 | 8.2 |
| 1.9 | 20.45 | 25.14 | 28.80 | 31.03 | 8.1 |
| 2.0 | 20.50 | 25.18 | 28.83 | 31.04 | 8.0 |
| 2.1 | 20.55 | 25.22 | 28.86 | 31.05 | 7.9 |
| 2.2 | 20.60 | 25.26 | 28.89 | 31.07 | 7.8 |
| 2.3 | 20.65 | 25.31 | 28.92 | 31.08 | 7.7 |
| 2.4 | 20.70 | 25.35 | 28.95 | 31.10 | 7.6 |
| 2.5 | 20.75 | 25.39 | 28.98 | 31.11 | 7.5 |
| 2.6 | 20.80 | 25.43 | 29.01 | 31.12 | 7.4 |
| 2.7 | 20.85 | 25.47 | 29.04 | 31.13 | 7.3 |
| 2.8 | 20.90 | 25.52 | 29.06 | 31.15 | 7.2 |
| 2.9 | 20.95 | 25.56 | 29.09 | 31.16 | 7.1 |
| 3.0 | 21.00 | 25.60 | 29.12 | 31.17 | 7.0 |
| 3.1 | 21.05 | 25.64 | 29.15 | 31.18 | 6.9 |
| 3.2 | 21.10 | 25.68 | 29.18 | 31.19 | 6.8 |
| 3.3 | 21.15 | 25.73 | 29.20 | 81.21 | 6.7 |
| 3.4 | 21.20 | 25.77 | 29.23 | 31.22 | 6.6 |
| 3.5 | 21.25 | 25.81 | 29.26 | 31.23 | 6.5 |
| 3.6 | 21.30 | 25.85 | 29.29 | 31.24 | 6.4 |
| 3.7 | 21.35 | 25.89 | 29.32 | 31.25 | 6.3 |
| 3.8 | 21.40 | 25.93 | 29.34 | 31.26 | 6.2 |
| 3.9 | 21.45 | 25.97 | 29.37 | 31.27 | 6.1 |
| 4.0 | 21.50 | 26.01 | 29.40 | 31.28 | 6.0 |
| 4.1 | 21.55 | 26.05 | 29.43 | 31.29 | 5.9 |
| 4.2 | 21.60 | 26.09 | 29.45 | 31.30 | 5.8 |
| 4.3 | 21.64 | 26.13 | 29.48 | 31.31 | 5.7 |
| 4.4 | 21.69 | 26.17 | 29.50 | 31.32 | 5.6 |
| 4.5 | 21.74 | 26.21 | 29.53 | 31.33 | 5.5 |
| 4.6 | 21.79 | 26.25 | 29.56 | 31.34 | 5.4 |
| 4.7 | 21.84 | 26.29 | 29.58 | 31.35 | 5.3 |
| 4.8 | 21.89 | 26.33 | 29.61 | 31.36 | 5.2 |
| 4.9 | 21.94 | 26.37 | 29.63 | 31.37 | 5.1 |
| 5.0 | 21.99 | 26.41 | 29.66 | 31.38 | 5.0 |
| Days. | **130** | **120** | **110** | **100** | Days. |

| Tables | XCIII. |
|---|---|
| Arguments | **73.** |

| Days. | **0** | **100** | **200** | **300** | **400** | **500** | Days. |
|---|---|---|---|---|---|---|---|
| Days. | ″ | ″ | ″ | ″ | ″ | ″ | Days. |
| 0 | 7.80 | 8.33 | 10.00 | 12.66 | 16.10 | 20.04 | 100 |
| 01 | 7.80 | 8.34 | 10.02 | 12.69 | 16.13 | 20.08 | 99 |
| 02 | 7.80 | 8.35 | 10.04 | 12.72 | 16.17 | 20.12 | 98 |
| 03 | 7.80 | 8.36 | 10.06 | 12.75 | 16.21 | 20.16 | 97 |
| 04 | 7.80 | 8.37 | 10.08 | 12.78 | 16.25 | 20.20 | 96 |
| 05 | 7.80 | 8.39 | 10.11 | 12.81 | 16.29 | 20.24 | 95 |
| 06 | 7.80 | 8.40 | 10.13 | 12.84 | 16.32 | 20.28 | 94 |
| 07 | 7.80 | 8.41 | 10.15 | 12.87 | 16.36 | 20.32 | 93 |
| 08 | 7.80 | 8.42 | 10.17 | 12.90 | 16.40 | 20.36 | 92 |
| 09 | 7.80 | 8.43 | 10.19 | 12.93 | 16.44 | 20.40 | 91 |
| 10 | 7.80 | 8.45 | 10.22 | 12.97 | 16.48 | 20.45 | 90 |
| 11 | 7.80 | 8.46 | 10.24 | 13.00 | 16.51 | 20.49 | 89 |
| 12 | 7.80 | 8.47 | 10.26 | 13.03 | 16.55 | 20.53 | 88 |
| 13 | 7.80 | 8.48 | 10.29 | 13.06 | 16.59 | 20.57 | 87 |
| 14 | 7.80 | 8.50 | 10.31 | 13.09 | 16.63 | 20.61 | 86 |
| 15 | 7.81 | 8.51 | 10.33 | 13.13 | 16.67 | 20.65 | 85 |
| 16 | 7.81 | 8.52 | 10.36 | 13.16 | 16.70 | 20.69 | 84 |
| 17 | 7.81 | 8.54 | 10.38 | 13.19 | 16.74 | 20.73 | 83 |
| 18 | 7.81 | 8.55 | 10.41 | 13.22 | 16.78 | 20.77 | 82 |
| 19 | 7.81 | 8.56 | 10.43 | 13.25 | 16.82 | 20.81 | 81 |
| 20 | 7.81 | 8.58 | 10.46 | 13.29 | 16.86 | 20.86 | 80 |
| 21 | 7.82 | 8.59 | 10.48 | 13.32 | 16.90 | 20.90 | 79 |
| 22 | 7.82 | 8.60 | 10.50 | 13.35 | 16.93 | 20.94 | 78 |
| 23 | 7.82 | 8.62 | 10.53 | 13.38 | 16.97 | 20.98 | 77 |
| 24 | 7.82 | 8.63 | 10.55 | 13.42 | 17.01 | 21.02 | 76 |
| 25 | 7.82 | 8.64 | 10.58 | 13.45 | 17.05 | 21.06 | 75 |
| 26 | 7.83 | 8.66 | 10.60 | 13.48 | 17.09 | 21.10 | 74 |
| 27 | 7.83 | 8.67 | 10.62 | 13.52 | 17.13 | 21.14 | 73 |
| 28 | 7.83 | 8.69 | 10.65 | 13.55 | 17.17 | 21.18 | 72 |
| 29 | 7.83 | 8.70 | 10.67 | 13.58 | 17.21 | 21.22 | 71 |
| 30 | 7.84 | 8.72 | 10.70 | 13.62 | 17.25 | 21.27 | 70 |
| 31 | 7.84 | 8.73 | 10.72 | 13.65 | 17.28 | 21.31 | 69 |
| 32 | 7.84 | 8.75 | 10.75 | 13.68 | 17.32 | 21.35 | 68 |
| 33 | 7.84 | 8.76 | 10.77 | 13.72 | 17.36 | 21.39 | 67 |
| 34 | 7.85 | 8.78 | 10.80 | 13.75 | 17.40 | 21.43 | 66 |
| 35 | 7.85 | 8.79 | 10.82 | 13.78 | 17.44 | 21.48 | 65 |
| 36 | 7.85 | 8.81 | 10.85 | 13.82 | 17.48 | 21.52 | 64 |
| 37 | 7.86 | 8.82 | 10.87 | 13.85 | 17.52 | 21.56 | 63 |
| 38 | 7.86 | 8.84 | 10.90 | 13.89 | 17.56 | 21.60 | 62 |
| 39 | 7.86 | 8.85 | 10.92 | 13.92 | 17.60 | 21.64 | 61 |
| 40 | 7.87 | 8.87 | 10.95 | 13.96 | 17.64 | 21.69 | 60 |
| 41 | 7.87 | 8.88 | 10.97 | 13.99 | 17.67 | 21.73 | 59 |
| 42 | 7.88 | 8.90 | 11.00 | 14.02 | 17.71 | 21.77 | 58 |
| 43 | 7.88 | 8.91 | 11.03 | 14.06 | 17.75 | 21.81 | 57 |
| 44 | 7.89 | 8.93 | 11.05 | 14.09 | 17.79 | 21.85 | 56 |
| 45 | 7.89 | 8.94 | 11.08 | 14.13 | 17.83 | 21.89 | 55 |
| 46 | 7.90 | 8.96 | 11.11 | 14.16 | 17.87 | 21.94 | 54 |
| 47 | 7.90 | 8.98 | 11.13 | 14.19 | 17.91 | 21.98 | 53 |
| 48 | 7.91 | 9.00 | 11.16 | 14.23 | 17.95 | 22.02 | 52 |
| 49 | 7.91 | 9.01 | 11.19 | 14.26 | 17.99 | 22.06 | 51 |
| 50 | 7.92 | 9.03 | 11.22 | 14.30 | 18.03 | 22.10 | 50 |
| Days. | **2100** | **2000** | **1900** | **1800** | **1700** | **1600** | Days. |

# TABLES XCII. XCIII.

Tables XCII. — Arguments 78.

| Days. | 60 | 70 | 80 | 90 | Days. |
|---|---|---|---|---|---|
| Days. | ″ | ″ | ″ | ″ | Days. |
| 5.0 | 21.99 | 26.41 | 29.66 | 31.38 | 5.0 |
| 5.1 | 22.04 | 26.45 | 29.68 | 31.39 | 4.9 |
| 5.2 | 22.09 | 26.49 | 29.71 | 31.40 | 4.8 |
| 5.3 | 22.13 | 26.52 | 29.73 | 31.40 | 4.7 |
| 5.4 | 22.18 | 26.56 | 29.76 | 31.41 | 4.6 |
| 5.5 | 22.23 | 26.60 | 29.78 | 31.42 | 4.5 |
| 5.6 | 22.28 | 26.64 | 29.80 | 31.43 | 4.4 |
| 5.7 | 22.33 | 26.68 | 29.83 | 31.44 | 4.3 |
| 5.8 | 22.37 | 26.71 | 29.85 | 31.44 | 4.2 |
| 5.9 | 22.42 | 26.75 | 29.88 | 31.45 | 4.1 |
| 6.0 | 22.47 | 26.79 | 29.90 | 31.46 | 4.0 |
| 6.1 | 22.52 | 26.83 | 29.92 | 31.47 | 3.9 |
| 6.2 | 22.57 | 26.87 | 29.95 | 31.47 | 3.8 |
| 6.3 | 22.61 | 26.90 | 29.97 | 31.48 | 3.7 |
| 6.4 | 22.66 | 26.94 | 30.00 | 31.48 | 3.6 |
| 6.5 | 22.71 | 26.98 | 30.02 | 31.49 | 3.5 |
| 6.6 | 22.76 | 27.02 | 30.04 | 31.50 | 3.4 |
| 6.7 | 22.80 | 27.06 | 30.06 | 31.50 | 3.3 |
| 6.8 | 22.85 | 27.09 | 30.09 | 31.51 | 3.2 |
| 6.9 | 22.89 | 27.13 | 30.11 | 31.51 | 3.1 |
| 7.0 | 22.94 | 27.17 | 30.13 | 31.52 | 3.0 |
| 7.1 | 22.99 | 27.21 | 30.15 | 31.53 | 2.9 |
| 7.2 | 23.04 | 27.24 | 30.17 | 31.53 | 2.8 |
| 7.3 | 23.08 | 27.28 | 30.20 | 31.54 | 2.7 |
| 7.4 | 23.13 | 27.31 | 30.22 | 31.54 | 2.6 |
| 7.5 | 23.18 | 27.35 | 30.24 | 31.55 | 2.5 |
| 7.6 | 23.23 | 27.39 | 30.26 | 31.55 | 2.4 |
| 7.7 | 23.27 | 27.42 | 30.28 | 31.56 | 2.3 |
| 7.8 | 23.32 | 27.46 | 30.31 | 31.56 | 2.2 |
| 7.9 | 23.36 | 27.49 | 30.33 | 31.57 | 2.1 |
| 8.0 | 23.41 | 27.53 | 30.35 | 31.57 | 2.0 |
| 8.1 | 23.46 | 27.56 | 30.37 | 31.57 | 1.9 |
| 8.2 | 23.50 | 27.60 | 30.39 | 31.57 | 1.8 |
| 8.3 | 23.55 | 27.63 | 30.41 | 31.58 | 1.7 |
| 8.4 | 23.59 | 27.67 | 30.43 | 31.58 | 1.6 |
| 8.5 | 23.64 | 27.70 | 30.45 | 31.58 | 1.5 |
| 8.6 | 23.69 | 27.73 | 30.47 | 31.58 | 1.4 |
| 8.7 | 23.73 | 27.77 | 30.49 | 31.58 | 1.3 |
| 8.8 | 23.78 | 27.80 | 30.51 | 31.59 | 1.2 |
| 8.9 | 23.82 | 27.84 | 30.53 | 31.59 | 1.1 |
| 9.0 | 23.87 | 27.87 | 30.55 | 31.59 | 1.0 |
| 9.1 | 23.91 | 27.90 | 30.57 | 31.59 | 0.9 |
| 9.2 | 23.96 | 27.94 | 30.59 | 31.59 | 0.8 |
| 9.3 | 24.00 | 27.97 | 30.60 | 31.59 | 0.7 |
| 9.4 | 24.05 | 28.01 | 30.62 | 31.60 | 0.6 |
| 9.5 | 24.09 | 28.04 | 30.64 | 31.60 | 0.5 |
| 9.6 | 24.13 | 28.07 | 30.66 | 31.60 | 0.4 |
| 9.7 | 24.18 | 28.11 | 30.68 | 31.60 | 0.3 |
| 9.8 | 24.22 | 28.14 | 30.69 | 31.60 | 0.2 |
| 9.9 | 24.27 | 28.18 | 30.71 | 31.60 | 0.1 |
| 10.0 | 24.31 | 28.21 | 30.73 | 31.60 | 0.0 |
| Days. | 130 | 120 | 110 | 100 | Days. |

Tables XCIII. — Arguments 73.

| Days. | 0 | 100 | 200 | 300 | 400 | 500 | Days. |
|---|---|---|---|---|---|---|---|
| Days. | ″ | ″ | ″ | ″ | ″ | ″ | Days. |
| 50 | 7.92 | 9.03 | 11.22 | 14.30 | 18.03 | 22.10 | 50 |
| 51 | 7.92 | 9.04 | 11.24 | 14.33 | 18.07 | 22.14 | 49 |
| 52 | 7.93 | 9.06 | 11.27 | 14.37 | 18.11 | 22.18 | 48 |
| 53 | 7.93 | 9.08 | 11.30 | 14.40 | 18.15 | 22.22 | 47 |
| 54 | 7.94 | 9.09 | 11.32 | 14.44 | 18.19 | 22.26 | 46 |
| 55 | 7.94 | 9.11 | 11.35 | 14.47 | 18.23 | 22.31 | 45 |
| 56 | 7.95 | 9.13 | 11.38 | 14.51 | 18.27 | 22.35 | 44 |
| 57 | 7.96 | 9.14 | 11.40 | 14.54 | 18.31 | 22.39 | 43 |
| 58 | 7.96 | 9.16 | 11.43 | 14.58 | 18.35 | 22.43 | 42 |
| 59 | 7.97 | 9.18 | 11.46 | 14.61 | 18.39 | 22.47 | 41 |
| 60 | 7.98 | 9.20 | 11.49 | 14.65 | 18.43 | 22.51 | 40 |
| 61 | 7.98 | 9.22 | 11.51 | 14.68 | 18.47 | 22.55 | 39 |
| 62 | 7.99 | 9.23 | 11.54 | 14.72 | 18.51 | 22.60 | 38 |
| 63 | 8.00 | 9.25 | 11.57 | 14.75 | 18.55 | 22.64 | 37 |
| 64 | 8.00 | 9.27 | 11.60 | 14.79 | 18.59 | 22.68 | 36 |
| 65 | 8.01 | 9.29 | 11.63 | 14.82 | 18.63 | 22.72 | 35 |
| 66 | 8.02 | 9.31 | 11.65 | 14.86 | 18.67 | 22.76 | 34 |
| 67 | 8.02 | 9.33 | 11.68 | 14.89 | 18.71 | 22.81 | 33 |
| 68 | 8.03 | 9.35 | 11.71 | 14.93 | 18.75 | 22.85 | 32 |
| 69 | 8.04 | 9.37 | 11.74 | 14.96 | 18.79 | 22.89 | 31 |
| 70 | 8.05 | 9.39 | 11.77 | 15.00 | 18.83 | 22.93 | 30 |
| 71 | 8.05 | 9.40 | 11.80 | 15.03 | 18.87 | 22.97 | 29 |
| 72 | 8.06 | 9.42 | 11.82 | 15.07 | 18.91 | 23.01 | 28 |
| 73 | 8.07 | 9.44 | 11.85 | 15.10 | 18.95 | 23.06 | 27 |
| 74 | 8.08 | 9.46 | 11.88 | 15.14 | 18.99 | 23.10 | 26 |
| 75 | 8.09 | 9.48 | 11.91 | 15.17 | 19.03 | 23.14 | 25 |
| 76 | 8.09 | 9.50 | 11.94 | 15.21 | 19.07 | 23.18 | 24 |
| 77 | 8.10 | 9.52 | 11.97 | 15.25 | 19.11 | 23.22 | 23 |
| 78 | 8.11 | 9.54 | 12.00 | 15.28 | 19.15 | 23.26 | 22 |
| 79 | 8.12 | 9.56 | 12.03 | 15.32 | 19.19 | 23.30 | 21 |
| 80 | 8.13 | 9.58 | 12.06 | 15.36 | 19.23 | 23.34 | 20 |
| 81 | 8.14 | 9.60 | 12.09 | 15.39 | 19.27 | 23.38 | 19 |
| 82 | 8.15 | 9.62 | 12.12 | 15.43 | 19.31 | 23.43 | 18 |
| 83 | 8.16 | 9.64 | 12.15 | 15.47 | 19.35 | 23.47 | 17 |
| 84 | 8.17 | 9.66 | 12.18 | 15.50 | 19.39 | 23.51 | 16 |
| 85 | 8.18 | 9.68 | 12.21 | 15.54 | 19.43 | 23.55 | 15 |
| 86 | 8.19 | 9.70 | 12.24 | 15.58 | 19.47 | 23.59 | 14 |
| 87 | 8.20 | 9.72 | 12.27 | 15.61 | 19.51 | 23.63 | 13 |
| 88 | 8.21 | 9.74 | 12.30 | 15.65 | 19.55 | 23.67 | 12 |
| 89 | 8.22 | 9.76 | 12.33 | 15.69 | 19.59 | 23.71 | 11 |
| 90 | 8.23 | 9.78 | 12.36 | 15.73 | 19.64 | 23.75 | 10 |
| 91 | 8.24 | 9.80 | 12.39 | 15.76 | 19.68 | 23.80 | 09 |
| 92 | 8.25 | 9.82 | 12.42 | 15.80 | 19.72 | 23.84 | 08 |
| 93 | 8.26 | 9.84 | 12.45 | 15.84 | 19.76 | 23.88 | 07 |
| 94 | 8.27 | 9.86 | 12.48 | 15.87 | 19.80 | 23.92 | 06 |
| 95 | 8.28 | 9.89 | 12.51 | 15.91 | 19.84 | 23.96 | 05 |
| 96 | 8.29 | 9.91 | 12.54 | 15.95 | 19.88 | 24.00 | 04 |
| 97 | 8.30 | 9.93 | 12.57 | 15.98 | 19.92 | 24.04 | 03 |
| 98 | 8.31 | 9.95 | 12.60 | 16.02 | 19.96 | 24.08 | 02 |
| 99 | 8.32 | 9.97 | 12.63 | 16.06 | 20.00 | 24.12 | 01 |
| 100 | 8.33 | 10.00 | 12.66 | 16.10 | 20.04 | 24.16 | 00 |
| Days. | 2100 | 2000 | 1900 | 1800 | 1700 | 1600 | Days. |

# TABLES XCIII.-XCV.

| TABLES | XCIII. | | | | | XCIV. | | XCV. | | | |
|---|---|---|---|---|---|---|---|---|---|---|---|
| ARGUMENTS | 73. | | | | | 12‴. | | 79. | | | |
| Days. | **600** | **700** | **800** | **900** | **1000** | **0** | **100** | **0** | **100** | **200** | Days. |
| Days 00 | 24.16 | 28.12 | 31.59 | 34.29 | 36.01 | 1.13 | 0.74 | 0.28 | 0.39 | 0.17 | Days. 100 |
| 01 | 24.20 | 28.16 | 31.63 | 34.32 | 36.03 | 1.13 | 0.73 | 0.28 | 0.39 | 0.17 | 99 |
| 02 | 24.24 | 28.20 | 31.66 | 34.34 | 36.04 | 1.14 | 0.72 | 0.28 | 0.39 | 0.17 | 98 |
| 03 | 24.28 | 28.24 | 31.69 | 34.36 | 36.05 | 1.14 | 0.71 | 0.29 | 0.39 | 0.17 | 97 |
| 04 | 24.32 | 28.27 | 31.72 | 34.38 | 36.06 | 1.15 | 0.70 | 0.29 | 0.39 | 0.16 | 96 |
| 05 | 24.36 | 28.31 | 31.75 | 34.40 | 36.07 | 1.15 | 0.69 | 0.29 | 0.39 | 0.16 | 95 |
| 06 | 24.40 | 28.35 | 31.78 | 34.43 | 36.08 | 1.15 | 0.68 | 0.30 | 0.38 | 0.16 | 94 |
| 07 | 24.44 | 28.38 | 31.81 | 34.45 | 36.09 | 1.16 | 0.67 | 0.30 | 0.38 | 0.15 | 93 |
| 08 | 24.48 | 28.42 | 31.84 | 34.47 | 36.10 | 1.16 | 0.66 | 0.30 | 0.38 | 0.15 | 92 |
| 09 | 24.52 | 28.46 | 31.87 | 34.49 | 36.11 | 1.16 | 0.65 | 0.30 | 0.38 | 0.15 | 91 |
| 10 | 24.57 | 28.49 | 31.90 | 34.51 | 36.12 | 1.17 | 0.64 | 0.31 | 0.38 | 0.14 | 90 |
| 11 | 24.61 | 28.53 | 31.93 | 34.53 | 36.13 | 1.17 | 0.63 | 0.31 | 0.38 | 0.14 | 89 |
| 12 | 24.65 | 28.57 | 31.96 | 34.56 | 36.14 | 1.17 | 0.62 | 0.31 | 0.38 | 0.14 | 88 |
| 13 | 24.69 | 28.61 | 31.99 | 34.58 | 36.15 | 1.18 | 0.61 | 0.31 | 0.38 | 0.14 | 87 |
| 14 | 24.73 | 28.64 | 32.02 | 34.60 | 36.16 | 1.18 | 0.60 | 0.31 | 0.38 | 0.14 | 86 |
| 15 | 24.77 | 28.68 | 32.05 | 34.62 | 36.17 | 1.18 | 0.59 | 0.32 | 0.38 | 0.13 | 85 |
| 16 | 24.81 | 28.72 | 32.08 | 34.64 | 36.18 | 1.19 | 0.58 | 0.32 | 0.37 | 0.13 | 84 |
| 17 | 24.85 | 28.75 | 32.11 | 34.66 | 36.19 | 1.19 | 0.57 | 0.32 | 0.37 | 0.13 | 83 |
| 18 | 24.89 | 28.79 | 32.14 | 34.68 | 36.20 | 1.19 | 0.56 | 0.32 | 0.37 | 0.13 | 82 |
| 19 | 24.93 | 28.83 | 32.17 | 34.70 | 36.21 | 1.19 | 0.55 | 0.32 | 0.37 | 0.13 | 81 |
| 20 | 24.97 | 28.86 | 32.20 | 34.72 | 36.22 | 1.20 | 0.53 | 0.33 | 0.37 | 0.12 | 80 |
| 21 | 25.01 | 28.90 | 32.23 | 34.74 | 36.23 | 1.20 | 0.52 | 0.33 | 0.37 | 0.12 | 79 |
| 22 | 25.05 | 28.94 | 32.26 | 34.76 | 36.24 | 1.20 | 0.51 | 0.33 | 0.37 | 0.12 | 78 |
| 23 | 25.09 | 28.97 | 32.29 | 34.78 | 36.25 | 1.20 | 0.50 | 0.33 | 0.36 | 0.12 | 77 |
| 24 | 25.13 | 29.01 | 32.32 | 34.80 | 36.26 | 1.20 | 0.49 | 0.33 | 0.36 | 0.11 | 76 |
| 25 | 25.17 | 29.05 | 32.35 | 34.82 | 36.27 | 1.20 | 0.48 | 0.34 | 0.36 | 0.11 | 75 |
| 26 | 25.21 | 29.08 | 32.38 | 34.84 | 36.28 | 1.20 | 0.47 | 0.34 | 0.36 | 0.11 | 74 |
| 27 | 25.25 | 29.12 | 32.41 | 34.86 | 36.29 | 1.20 | 0.46 | 0.34 | 0.36 | 0.10 | 73 |
| 28 | 25.29 | 29.15 | 32.44 | 34.88 | 36.30 | 1.20 | 0.45 | 0.34 | 0.36 | 0.10 | 72 |
| 29 | 25.33 | 29.19 | 32.47 | 34.90 | 36.31 | 1.20 | 0.44 | 0.34 | 0.35 | 0.10 | 71 |
| 30 | 25.38 | 29.22 | 32.49 | 34.92 | 36.31 | 1.20 | 0.42 | 0.35 | 0.35 | 0.09 | 70 |
| 31 | 25.42 | 29.26 | 32.52 | 34.94 | 36.32 | 1.20 | 0.41 | 0.35 | 0.35 | 0.09 | 69 |
| 32 | 25.46 | 29.30 | 32.55 | 34.96 | 36.33 | 1.20 | 0.40 | 0.35 | 0.35 | 0.09 | 68 |
| 33 | 25.50 | 29.33 | 32.58 | 34.98 | 36.34 | 1.19 | 0.39 | 0.35 | 0.35 | 0.09 | 67 |
| 34 | 25.54 | 29.37 | 32.61 | 35.00 | 36.35 | 1.19 | 0.38 | 0.35 | 0.35 | 0.09 | 66 |
| 35 | 25.58 | 29.41 | 32.64 | 35.02 | 36.35 | 1.19 | 0.37 | 0.36 | 0.34 | 0.08 | 65 |
| 36 | 25.62 | 29.44 | 32.67 | 35.04 | 36.36 | 1.19 | 0.36 | 0.36 | 0.34 | 0.08 | 64 |
| 37 | 25.66 | 29.48 | 32.70 | 35.06 | 36.37 | 1.19 | 0.35 | 0.36 | 0.34 | 0.08 | 63 |
| 38 | 25.70 | 29.51 | 32.73 | 35.08 | 36.38 | 1.18 | 0.34 | 0.36 | 0.34 | 0.08 | 62 |
| 39 | 25.74 | 29.55 | 32.76 | 35.10 | 36.39 | 1.18 | 0.33 | 0.36 | 0.34 | 0.08 | 61 |
| 40 | 25.78 | 29.58 | 32.78 | 35.11 | 36.39 | 1.18 | 0.32 | 0.37 | 0.33 | 0.07 | 60 |
| 41 | 25.82 | 29.62 | 32.81 | 35.13 | 36.40 | 1.18 | 0.31 | 0.37 | 0.33 | 0.07 | 59 |
| 42 | 25.86 | 29.65 | 32.84 | 35.15 | 36 41 | 1.17 | 0.30 | 0.37 | 0.33 | 0.07 | 58 |
| 43 | 25.90 | 29.69 | 32.87 | 35.17 | 36.41 | 1.17 | 0.29 | 0.37 | 0.33 | 0.07 | 57 |
| 44 | 25.94 | 29.72 | 32.89 | 35.19 | 36.42 | 1.17 | 0.28 | 0.37 | 0.33 | 0.07 | 56 |
| 45 | 25.98 | 29.76 | 32.92 | 35.20 | 36.42 | 1.17 | 0.27 | 0.37 | 0.32 | 0.06 | 55 |
| 46 | 26.02 | 29.79 | 32.95 | 35.22 | 36.43 | 1.16 | 0.26 | 0.37 | 0.32 | 0.06 | 54 |
| 47 | 26.06 | 29.83 | 32.97 | 35.24 | 36.43 | 1.16 | 0.25 | 0 38 | 0.32 | 0.06 | 53 |
| 48 | 26.10 | 29.86 | 33.00 | 35.26 | 36.44 | 1.16 | 0.24 | 0.38 | 0.32 | 0.06 | 52 |
| 49 | 26.14 | 29.90 | 33.03 | 35.28 | 36.44 | 1.15 | 0.23 | 0.38 | 0.32 | 0.06 | 51 |
| 50 | 26.18 | 29.93 | 33.05 | 35.29 | 36.45 | 1.15 | 0.23 | 0.38 | 0.31 | 0.05 | 50 |
| Days. | **1500** | **1400** | **1300** | **1200** | **1100** | **300** | **200** | **500** | **400** | **300** | Days. |

NOTE. — Arg. 12‴ = Arg. 12 — 20.00.

# TABLES XCIII. - XCV.

| Tables | XCIII. | | | | | XCIV. | | XCV. | | | |
|---|---|---|---|---|---|---|---|---|---|---|---|
| Arguments | **73.** | | | | | **12‴.** | | **79.** | | | |
| Days. | **600** | **700** | **800** | **900** | **1000** | **0** | **100** | **0** | **100** | **200** | Days. |
| Days | " | " | " | " | " | " | " | " | " | " | Days. |
| 50 | 26.18 | 29.93 | 33.05 | 35.29 | 36.45 | 1.15 | 0.23 | 0.38 | 0.31 | 0.05 | 50 |
| 51 | 26.22 | 29.97 | 33.08 | 35.31 | 36.45 | 1.14 | 0.22 | 0.38 | 0.31 | 0.05 | 49 |
| 52 | 26.26 | 30.00 | 33.11 | 35.33 | 36.46 | 1.14 | 0.21 | 0.38 | 0.31 | 0.05 | 48 |
| 53 | 26.30 | 30.04 | 33.14 | 35.34 | 36.46 | 1.13 | 0.20 | 0.38 | 0.31 | 0.05 | 47 |
| 54 | 26.34 | 30.07 | 33.16 | 35.36 | 36.47 | 1.13 | 0.19 | 0.38 | 0.30 | 0.05 | 46 |
| 55 | 26.38 | 30.11 | 33.19 | 35.38 | 36.48 | 1.12 | 0.19 | 0.38 | 0.30 | 0.04 | 45 |
| 56 | 26.42 | 30.14 | 33.22 | 35.39 | 36.48 | 1.11 | 0.18 | 0.39 | 0.30 | 0.04 | 44 |
| 57 | 26.46 | 30.18 | 33.24 | 35.41 | 36.49 | 1.11 | 0.17 | 0.39 | 0.29 | 0.04 | 43 |
| 58 | 26.50 | 30.21 | 33.27 | 35.42 | 36.49 | 1.10 | 0.16 | 0.39 | 0.29 | 0.04 | 42 |
| 59 | 26.54 | 30.25 | 33.30 | 35.44 | 36.50 | 1.10 | 0.15 | 0.39 | 0.29 | 0.04 | 41 |
| 60 | 26.57 | 30.28 | 33.32 | 35.45 | 36.51 | 1.09 | 0.15 | 0.39 | 0.28 | 0.03 | 40 |
| 61 | 26.61 | 30.32 | 33.35 | 35.47 | 36.51 | 1.09 | 0.14 | 0.39 | 0.28 | 0.03 | 39 |
| 62 | 26.65 | 30.35 | 33.38 | 35.49 | 36.52 | 1.08 | 0.13 | 0.39 | 0.28 | 0.03 | 38 |
| 63 | 26.69 | 30.39 | 33.40 | 35.50 | 36.52 | 1.08 | 0.13 | 0.39 | 0.28 | 0.03 | 37 |
| 64 | 26.73 | 30.42 | 33.43 | 35.52 | 36.53 | 1.07 | 0.12 | 0.39 | 0.28 | 0.03 | 36 |
| 65 | 26.77 | 30.46 | 33.46 | 35.54 | 36.53 | 1.06 | 0.12 | 0.39 | 0.27 | 0.03 | 35 |
| 66 | 26.81 | 30.49 | 33.48 | 35.55 | 36.54 | 1.06 | 0.11 | 0.40 | 0.27 | 0.03 | 34 |
| 67 | 26.85 | 30.52 | 33.51 | 35.57 | 36.54 | 1.05 | 0.11 | 0.40 | 0.27 | 0.02 | 33 |
| 68 | 26.89 | 30.56 | 33.53 | 35.58 | 36.54 | 1.04 | 0.10 | 0.40 | 0.27 | 0.02 | 32 |
| 69 | 26.93 | 30.59 | 33.56 | 35.60 | 36.55 | 1.03 | 0.10 | 0.40 | 0.27 | 0.02 | 31 |
| 70 | 26.96 | 30.62 | 33.58 | 35.61 | 36.55 | 1.02 | 0.09 | 0.40 | 0.26 | 0.02 | 30 |
| 71 | 27.00 | 30.66 | 33.61 | 35.63 | 36.55 | 1.02 | 0.09 | 0.40 | 0.26 | 0.02 | 29 |
| 72 | 27.04 | 30.69 | 33.63 | 35.64 | 36.56 | 1.01 | 0.08 | 0.40 | 0.26 | 0.02 | 28 |
| 73 | 27.08 | 30.72 | 33.66 | 35.66 | 36.56 | 1.00 | 0.08 | 0.40 | 0.26 | 0.02 | 27 |
| 74 | 27.12 | 30.76 | 33.68 | 35.67 | 36.56 | 0.99 | 0.07 | 0.40 | 0.25 | 0.02 | 26 |
| 75 | 27.16 | 30.79 | 33.71 | 35.69 | 36.56 | 0.98 | 0.07 | 0.40 | 0.25 | 0.01 | 25 |
| 76 | 27.20 | 30.82 | 33.73 | 35.70 | 36.57 | 0.98 | 0.06 | 0.40 | 0.25 | 0.01 | 24 |
| 77 | 27.24 | 30.86 | 33.76 | 35.71 | 36.57 | 0.97 | 0.06 | 0.40 | 0.24 | 0.01 | 23 |
| 78 | 27.28 | 30.89 | 33.78 | 35.73 | 36.57 | 0.96 | 0.05 | 0.40 | 0.24 | 0.01 | 22 |
| 79 | 27.32 | 30.92 | 33.81 | 35.74 | 36.57 | 0.95 | 0.05 | 0.40 | 0.24 | 0.01 | 21 |
| 80 | 27.35 | 30.95 | 33.83 | 35.75 | 36.58 | 0.94 | 0.04 | 0.40 | 0.23 | 0.01 | 20 |
| 81 | 27.39 | 30.99 | 33.86 | 35.77 | 36.58 | 0.94 | 0.04 | 0.40 | 0.23 | 0.01 | 19 |
| 82 | 27.43 | 31.02 | 33.88 | 35.78 | 36.58 | 0.93 | 0.04 | 0.40 | 0.23 | 0.01 | 18 |
| 83 | 27.47 | 31.05 | 33.91 | 35.80 | 36.58 | 0.92 | 0.03 | 0.40 | 0.23 | 0.01 | 17 |
| 84 | 27.51 | 31.08 | 33.93 | 35.81 | 36.58 | 0.91 | 0.03 | 0.40 | 0.22 | 0.01 | 16 |
| 85 | 27.55 | 31.11 | 33.96 | 35.83 | 36.59 | 0.90 | 0.03 | 0.40 | 0.22 | 0.01 | 15 |
| 86 | 27.59 | 31.15 | 33.98 | 35.84 | 36.59 | 0.89 | 0.02 | 0.40 | 0.22 | 0.00 | 14 |
| 87 | 27.63 | 31.18 | 34.00 | 35.85 | 36.59 | 0.88 | 0.02 | 0.40 | 0.21 | 0.00 | 13 |
| 88 | 27.67 | 31.21 | 34.03 | 35.87 | 36.59 | 0.87 | 0.02 | 0.40 | 0.21 | 0.00 | 12 |
| 89 | 27.71 | 31.24 | 34.05 | 35.88 | 36.59 | 0.86 | 0.02 | 0.40 | 0.21 | 0.00 | 11 |
| 90 | 27.74 | 31.27 | 34.07 | 35.89 | 36.59 | 0.85 | 0.01 | 0.40 | 0.20 | 0.00 | 10 |
| 91 | 27.78 | 31.31 | 34.10 | 35.91 | 36.59 | 0.84 | 0.01 | 0.40 | 0.20 | 0.00 | 09 |
| 92 | 27.82 | 31.34 | 34.12 | 35.92 | 36.59 | 0.83 | 0.01 | 0.40 | 0.20 | 0.00 | 08 |
| 93 | 27.86 | 31.37 | 34.14 | 35.93 | 36.60 | 0.82 | 0.01 | 0.40 | 0.20 | 0.00 | 07 |
| 94 | 27.90 | 31.40 | 34.16 | 35.94 | 36.60 | 0.81 | 0.01 | 0.40 | 0.19 | 0.00 | 06 |
| 95 | 27.94 | 31.43 | 34.18 | 35.95 | 36.60 | 0.80 | 0.00 | 0.40 | 0.19 | 0.00 | 05 |
| 96 | 27.97 | 31.47 | 34.21 | 35.97 | 36.60 | 0.79 | 0.00 | 0.39 | 0.19 | 0.00 | 04 |
| 97 | 28.01 | 31.50 | 34.23 | 35.98 | 36.60 | 0.78 | 0.00 | 0.39 | 0.18 | 0.00 | 03 |
| 98 | 28.05 | 31.53 | 34.25 | 35.99 | 36.60 | 0.77 | 0.00 | 0.39 | 0.18 | 0.00 | 02 |
| 99 | 28.09 | 31.56 | 34.27 | 36.00 | 36.60 | 0.76 | 0.00 | 0.39 | 0.18 | 0.00 | 01 |
| 100 | 28.12 | 31.59 | 34.29 | 36.01 | 36.60 | 0.74 | 0.00 | 0.39 | 0.17 | 0.00 | 00 |
| Days. | **1500** | **1400** | **1300** | **1200** | **1100** | **300** | **200** | **500** | **400** | **300** | Days. |

**Note.** — Arg. 12‴ = Arg. 12 — 20.00.

# TABLES XCVI. - CI.

| Tables | XCVI. | | XCVII. | | XCVIII. | | XCIX. | | C. | CI. | | |
|---|---|---|---|---|---|---|---|---|---|---|---|---|
| Arguments | **80.** | | **81.** | | **82.** | | **83.** | | **84.** | **48.** | | |
| Days. | **0** | **100** | **0** | Days. | Days. | **0** | **0** | **10** | **0** | **0** | **10** | Days. |
| Days. | ″ | ″ | ″ | Days. | Days. | ″ | ″ | ″ | ″ | ″ | ″ | Days. |
| 00 | 0.16 | 0.14 | 0.93 | 100 | 0.0 | 0.96 | 0.00 | 0.68 | 0.02 | 0.75 | 0.75 | 10.0 |
| 01 | 0.16 | 0.14 | 0.90 | 99 | 0.1 | 0.89 | 0.00 | 0.69 | 0.02 | 0.76 | 0.75 | 9.9 |
| 02 | 0.16 | 0.14 | 0.87 | 98 | 0.2 | 0.82 | 0.00 | 0.70 | 0.01 | 0.77 | 0.74 | 9.8 |
| 03 | 0.16 | 0.14 | 0.83 | 97 | 0.3 | 0.76 | 0.00 | 0.71 | 0.01 | 0.78 | 0.73 | 9.7 |
| 04 | 0.16 | 0.14 | 0.80 | 96 | 0.4 | 0.70 | 0.00 | 0.72 | 0.00 | 0.79 | 0.72 | 9.6 |
| 05 | 0.17 | 0.13 | 0.77 | 95 | 0.5 | 0.64 | 0.00 | 0.73 | 0.00 | 0.79 | 0.71 | 9.5 |
| 06 | 0.17 | 0.13 | 0.73 | 94 | 0.6 | 0.58 | 0.00 | 0.74 | 0.00 | 0.80 | 0.70 | 9.4 |
| 07 | 0.17 | 0.13 | 0.70 | 93 | 0.7 | 0.53 | 0.00 | 0.75 | 0.01 | 0.81 | 0.69 | 9.3 |
| 08 | 0.17 | 0.13 | 0.66 | 92 | 0.8 | 0.48 | 0.00 | 0.76 | 0.02 | 0.82 | 0.68 | 9.2 |
| 09 | 0.17 | 0.13 | 0.63 | 91 | 0.9 | 0.43 | 0.00 | 0.77 | 0.03 | 0.83 | 0.67 | 9.1 |
| 10 | 0.18 | 0.12 | 0.59 | 90 | 1.0 | 0.38 | 0.00 | 0.79 | 0.04 | 0.83 | 0.66 | 9.0 |
| 11 | 0.18 | 0.12 | 0.56 | 89 | 1.1 | 0.34 | 0.00 | 0.80 | 0.06 | 0.84 | 0.65 | 8.9 |
| 12 | 0.18 | 0.12 | 0.52 | 88 | 1.2 | 0.30 | 0.00 | 0.81 | 0.08 | 0.85 | 0.63 | 8.8 |
| 13 | 0.18 | 0.12 | 0.49 | 87 | 1.3 | 0.26 | 0.01 | 0.82 | 0.10 | 0.86 | 0.62 | 8.7 |
| 14 | 0.18 | 0.12 | 0.45 | 86 | 1.4 | 0.22 | 0.01 | 0.83 | 0.12 | 0.86 | 0.61 | 8.6 |
| 15 | 0.18 | 0.11 | 0.42 | 85 | 1.5 | 0.18 | 0.01 | 0.84 | 0.14 | 0.87 | 0.60 | 8.5 |
| 16 | 0.18 | 0.11 | 0.39 | 84 | 1.6 | 0.15 | 0.01 | 0.85 | 0.17 | 0.88 | 0.59 | 8.4 |
| 17 | 0.18 | 0.11 | 0.36 | 83 | 1.7 | 0.12 | 0.01 | 0.87 | 0.20 | 0.89 | 0.58 | 8.3 |
| 18 | 0.19 | 0.11 | 0.33 | 82 | 1.8 | 0.09 | 0.01 | 0.88 | 0.23 | 0.89 | 0.57 | 8.2 |
| 19 | 0.19 | 0.11 | 0.30 | 81 | 1.9 | 0.07 | 0.02 | 0.89 | 0.26 | 0.90 | 0.56 | 8.1 |
| 20 | 0.19 | 0.10 | 0.27 | 80 | 2.0 | 0.05 | 0.02 | 0.90 | 0.29 | 0.90 | 0.55 | 8.0 |
| 21 | 0.19 | 0.10 | 0.24 | 79 | 2.1 | 0.03 | 0.02 | 0.91 | 0.32 | 0.91 | 0.54 | 7.9 |
| 22 | 0.19 | 0.10 | 0.22 | 78 | 2.2 | 0.02 | 0.02 | 0.92 | 0.35 | 0.92 | 0.53 | 7.8 |
| 23 | 0.19 | 0.10 | 0.19 | 77 | 2.3 | 0.01 | 0.03 | 0.93 | 0.39 | 0.92 | 0.52 | 7.7 |
| 24 | 0.19 | 0.10 | 0.17 | 76 | 2.4 | 0.00 | 0.03 | 0.94 | 0.43 | 0.93 | 0.51 | 7.6 |
| 25 | 0.20 | 0.09 | 0.15 | 75 | 2.5 | 0.00 | 0.03 | 0.95 | 0.47 | 0.93 | 0.50 | 7.5 |
| 26 | 0.20 | 0.09 | 0.13 | 74 | 2.6 | 0.00 | 0.04 | 0.96 | 0.51 | 0.94 | 0.49 | 7.4 |
| 27 | 0.20 | 0.09 | 0.11 | 73 | 2.7 | 0.01 | 0.04 | 0.97 | 0.55 | 0.94 | 0.48 | 7.3 |
| 28 | 0.20 | 0.09 | 0.09 | 72 | 2.8 | 0.01 | 0.05 | 0.98 | 0.59 | 0.95 | 0.47 | 7.2 |
| 29 | 0.20 | 0.09 | 0.08 | 71 | 2.9 | 0.02 | 0.05 | 0.99 | 0.63 | 0.95 | 0.46 | 7.1 |
| 30 | 0.20 | 0.08 | 0.06 | 70 | 3.0 | 0.03 | 0.06 | 1.00 | 0.67 | 0.96 | 0.45 | 7.0 |
| 31 | 0.20 | 0.08 | 0.05 | 69 | 3.1 | 0.05 | 0.06 | 1.01 | 0.71 | 0.96 | 0.44 | 6.9 |
| 32 | 0.20 | 0.08 | 0.04 | 68 | 3.2 | 0.07 | 0.07 | 1.02 | 0.75 | 0.96 | 0.43 | 6.8 |
| 33 | 0.20 | 0.08 | 0.03 | 67 | 3.3 | 0.09 | 0.07 | 1.03 | 0.79 | 0.97 | 0.42 | 6.7 |
| 34 | 0.20 | 0.08 | 0.02 | 66 | 3.4 | 0.11 | 0.08 | 1.04 | 0.83 | 0.97 | 0.41 | 6.6 |
| 35 | 0.20 | 0.07 | 0.01 | 65 | 3.5 | 0.14 | 0.08 | 1.05 | 0.86 | 0.97 | 0.40 | 6.5 |
| 36 | 0.20 | 0.07 | 0.01 | 64 | 3.6 | 0.17 | 0.09 | 1.06 | 0.90 | 0.98 | 0.39 | 6.4 |
| 37 | 0.20 | 0.07 | 0.00 | 63 | 3.7 | 0.20 | 0.09 | 1.07 | 0.93 | 0.98 | 0.38 | 6.3 |
| 38 | 0.20 | 0.07 | 0.00 | 62 | 3.8 | 0.24 | 0.10 | 1.08 | 0.96 | 0.98 | 0.37 | 6.2 |
| 39 | 0.20 | 0.07 | 0.00 | 61 | 3.9 | 0.28 | 0.10 | 1.09 | 0.99 | 0.98 | 0.36 | 6.1 |
| 40 | 0.20 | 0.06 | 0.00 | 60 | 4.0 | 0.32 | 0.11 | 1.10 | 1.02 | 0.99 | 0.35 | 6.0 |
| 41 | 0.20 | 0.06 | 0.01 | 59 | 4.1 | 0.37 | 0.11 | 1.11 | 1.05 | 0.99 | 0.34 | 5.9 |
| 42 | 0.20 | 0.06 | 0.02 | 58 | 4.2 | 0.42 | 0.12 | 1.12 | 1.08 | 0.99 | 0.33 | 5.8 |
| 43 | 0.20 | 0.06 | 0.03 | 57 | 4.3 | 0.47 | 0.12 | 1.13 | 1.10 | 0.99 | 0.32 | 5.7 |
| 44 | 0.20 | 0.06 | 0.04 | 56 | 4.4 | 0.52 | 0.13 | 1.14 | 1.12 | 0.99 | 0.31 | 5.6 |
| 45 | 0.20 | 0.06 | 0.05 | 55 | 4.5 | 0.57 | 0.14 | 1.15 | 1.14 | 1.00 | 0.30 | 5.5 |
| 46 | 0.20 | 0.06 | 0.06 | 54 | 4.6 | 0.63 | 0.14 | 1.16 | 1.16 | 1.00 | 0.29 | 5.4 |
| 47 | 0.20 | 0.05 | 0.07 | 53 | 4.7 | 0.69 | 0.15 | 1.17 | 1.17 | 1.00 | 0.28 | 5.3 |
| 48 | 0.20 | 0.05 | 0.09 | 52 | 4.8 | 0.75 | 0.16 | 1.18 | 1.18 | 1.00 | 0.27 | 5.2 |
| 49 | 0.20 | 0.05 | 0.11 | 51 | 4.9 | 0.81 | 0.17 | 1.19 | 1.19 | 1.00 | 0.26 | 5.1 |
| 50 | 0.20 | 0.05 | 0.13 | 50 | 5.0 | 0.87 | 0.18 | 1.19 | 1.19 | 1.00 | 0.25 | 5.0 |
| Days. | **300** | **200** | **100** | Days. | Days. | **10** | **30** | **20** | **10** | **30** | **20** | Days. |

# TABLES XCVI. - CI.

| Tables | XCVI. | | XCVII. | | XCVIII. | | XCIX. | | C. | CI. | | |
|---|---|---|---|---|---|---|---|---|---|---|---|---|
| Arguments | **80.** | | **81.** | | **82.** | | **83.** | | **84.** | **48.** | | |
| Days. | **0** | **100** | **0** | Days. | Days. | **0** | **0** | **10** | **0** | **0** | **10** | Days. |
| Days. | " | " | " | Days. | Days. | " | " | " | " | " | " | Days. |
| 50 | 0.20 | 0.05 | 0.13 | 50 | 5.0 | 0.87 | 0.18 | 1.19 | 1.19 | 1.00 | 0.25 | 5.0 |
| 51 | 0.20 | 0.05 | 0.15 | 49 | 5.1 | 0.94 | 0.18 | 1.20 | 1.20 | 1.00 | 0.24 | 4.9 |
| 52 | 0.20 | 0.05 | 0.17 | 48 | 5.2 | 1.01 | 0.19 | 1.21 | 1.20 | 1.00 | 0.23 | 4.8 |
| 53 | 0.20 | 0.04 | 0.20 | 47 | 5.3 | 1.08 | 0.20 | 1.22 | 1.20 | 1.00 | 0.22 | 4.7 |
| 54 | 0.20 | 0.04 | 0.22 | 46 | 5.4 | 1.15 | 0.21 | 1.22 | 1.20 | 1.00 | 0.21 | 4.6 |
| 55 | 0.20 | 0.04 | 0.25 | 45 | 5.5 | 1.22 | 0.22 | 1.23 | 1.19 | 0.99 | 0.21 | 4.5 |
| 56 | 0.19 | 0.04 | 0.28 | 44 | 5.6 | 1.29 | 0.22 | 1.24 | 1.18 | 0.99 | 0.20 | 4.4 |
| 57 | 0.19 | 0.04 | 0.30 | 43 | 5.7 | 1.36 | 0.23 | 1.24 | 1.17 | 0.99 | 0.19 | 4.3 |
| 58 | 0.19 | 0.04 | 0.33 | 42 | 5.8 | 1.44 | 0.24 | 1.25 | 1.16 | 0.99 | 0.18 | 4.2 |
| 59 | 0.19 | 0.03 | 0.36 | 41 | 5.9 | 1.51 | 0.25 | 1.26 | 1.14 | 0.99 | 0.17 | 4.1 |
| 60 | 0.19 | 0.03 | 0.39 | 40 | 6.0 | 1.59 | 0.26 | 1.26 | 1.12 | 0.99 | 0.17 | 4.0 |
| 61 | 0.19 | 0.03 | 0.42 | 39 | 6.1 | 1.66 | 0.27 | 1.27 | 1.10 | 0.98 | 0.16 | 3.9 |
| 62 | 0.19 | 0.03 | 0.46 | 38 | 6.2 | 1.74 | 0.28 | 1.27 | 1.08 | 0.98 | 0.15 | 3.8 |
| 63 | 0.19 | 0.03 | 0.49 | 37 | 6.3 | 1.81 | 0.29 | 1.28 | 1.06 | 0.98 | 0.14 | 3.7 |
| 64 | 0.19 | 0.03 | 0.53 | 36 | 6.4 | 1.89 | 0.30 | 1.29 | 1.03 | 0.98 | 0.14 | 3.6 |
| 65 | 0.19 | 0.03 | 0.56 | 35 | 6.5 | 1.97 | 0.31 | 1.29 | 1.00 | 0.97 | 0.13 | 3.5 |
| 66 | 0.19 | 0.03 | 0.60 | 34 | 6.6 | 2.05 | 0.32 | 1.30 | 0.97 | 0.97 | 0.12 | 3.4 |
| 67 | 0.19 | 0.02 | 0.63 | 33 | 6.7 | 2.12 | 0.33 | 1.30 | 0.94 | 0.97 | 0.12 | 3.3 |
| 68 | 0.19 | 0.02 | 0.67 | 32 | 6.8 | 2.20 | 0.34 | 1.31 | 0.91 | 0.96 | 0.11 | 3.2 |
| 69 | 0.19 | 0.02 | 0.70 | 31 | 6.9 | 2.27 | 0.35 | 1.31 | 0.87 | 0.96 | 0.10 | 3.1 |
| 70 | 0.19 | 0.02 | 0.74 | 30 | 7.0 | 2.34 | 0.36 | 1.32 | 0.83 | 0.96 | 0.10 | 3.0 |
| 71 | 0.18 | 0.02 | 0.77 | 29 | 7.1 | 2.41 | 0.37 | 1.32 | 0.80 | 0.95 | 0.09 | 2.9 |
| 72 | 0.18 | 0.02 | 0.81 | 28 | 7.2 | 2.48 | 0.38 | 1.33 | 0.76 | 0.95 | 0.08 | 2.8 |
| 73 | 0.18 | 0.02 | 0.84 | 27 | 7.3 | 2.55 | 0.39 | 1.33 | 0.72 | 0.94 | 0.08 | 2.7 |
| 74 | 0.18 | 0.02 | 0.88 | 26 | 7.4 | 2.62 | 0.40 | 1.34 | 0.68 | 0.94 | 0.07 | 2.6 |
| 75 | 0.18 | 0.02 | 0.91 | 25 | 7.5 | 2.69 | 0.41 | 1.34 | 0.64 | 0.93 | 0.07 | 2.5 |
| 76 | 0.18 | 0.01 | 0.94 | 24 | 7.6 | 2.76 | 0.42 | 1.34 | 0.61 | 0.93 | 0.06 | 2.4 |
| 77 | 0.18 | 0.01 | 0.98 | 23 | 7.7 | 2.82 | 0.43 | 1.35 | 0.57 | 0.92 | 0.06 | 2.3 |
| 78 | 0.17 | 0.01 | 1.01 | 22 | 7.8 | 2.88 | 0.44 | 1.35 | 0.53 | 0.92 | 0.05 | 2.2 |
| 79 | 0.17 | 0.01 | 1.04 | 21 | 7.9 | 2.94 | 0.45 | 1.35 | 0.49 | 0.91 | 0.05 | 2.1 |
| 80 | 0.17 | 0.01 | 1.07 | 20 | 8.0 | 3.00 | 0.46 | 1.36 | 0.45 | 0.91 | 0.04 | 2.0 |
| 81 | 0.17 | 0.01 | 1.10 | 19 | 8.1 | 3.05 | 0.47 | 1.36 | 0.41 | 0.90 | 0.04 | 1.9 |
| 82 | 0.17 | 0.01 | 1.13 | 18 | 8.2 | 3.10 | 0.48 | 1.36 | 0.37 | 0.90 | 0.04 | 1.8 |
| 83 | 0.17 | 0.01 | 1.16 | 17 | 8.3 | 3.15 | 0.49 | 1.37 | 0.33 | 0.89 | 0.03 | 1.7 |
| 84 | 0.17 | 0.01 | 1.18 | 16 | 8.4 | 3.20 | 0.50 | 1.37 | 0.30 | 0.88 | 0.03 | 1.6 |
| 85 | 0.17 | 0.00 | 1.21 | 15 | 8.5 | 3.25 | 0.51 | 1.37 | 0.27 | 0.88 | 0.03 | 1.5 |
| 86 | 0.16 | 0.00 | 1.23 | 14 | 8.6 | 3.29 | 0.52 | 1.38 | 0.24 | 0.87 | 0.02 | 1.4 |
| 87 | 0.16 | 0.00 | 1.25 | 13 | 8.7 | 3.33 | 0.53 | 1.38 | 0.21 | 0.87 | 0.02 | 1.3 |
| 88 | 0.16 | 0.00 | 1.27 | 12 | 8.8 | 3.37 | 0.54 | 1.38 | 0.18 | 0.86 | 0.02 | 1.2 |
| 89 | 0.16 | 0.00 | 1.29 | 11 | 8.9 | 3.41 | 0.55 | 1.38 | 0.15 | 0.85 | 0.02 | 1.1 |
| 90 | 0.16 | 0.00 | 1.31 | 10 | 9.0 | 3.44 | 0.57 | 1.39 | 0.12 | 0.84 | 0.01 | 1.0 |
| 91 | 0.16 | 0.00 | 1.33 | 09 | 9.1 | 3.47 | 0.58 | 1.39 | 0.10 | 0.84 | 0.01 | 0.9 |
| 92 | 0.15 | 0.00 | 1.34 | 08 | 9.2 | 3.50 | 0.59 | 1.39 | 0.08 | 0.83 | 0.01 | 0.8 |
| 93 | 0.15 | 0.00 | 1.36 | 07 | 9.3 | 3.52 | 0.60 | 1.39 | 0.06 | 0.82 | 0.01 | 0.7 |
| 94 | 0.15 | 0.00 | 1.37 | 06 | 9.4 | 3.54 | 0.61 | 1.39 | 0.04 | 0.81 | 0.00 | 0.6 |
| 95 | 0.15 | 0.00 | 1.38 | 05 | 9.5 | 3.56 | 0.62 | 1.40 | 0.03 | 0.80 | 0.00 | 0.5 |
| 96 | 0.15 | 0.00 | 1.39 | 04 | 9.6 | 3.58 | 0.63 | 1.40 | 0.02 | 0.79 | 0.00 | 0.4 |
| 97 | 0.14 | 0.00 | 1.39 | 03 | 9.7 | 3.59 | 0.64 | 1.40 | 0.01 | 0.78 | 0.00 | 0.3 |
| 98 | 0.14 | 0.00 | 1.40 | 02 | 9.8 | 3.60 | 0.65 | 1.40 | 0.00 | 0.77 | 0.00 | 0.2 |
| 99 | 0.14 | 0.00 | 1.40 | 01 | 9.9 | 3.60 | 0.66 | 1.40 | 0.00 | 0.76 | 0.00 | 0.1 |
| 100 | 0.14 | 0.00 | 1.40 | 0 | 10.0 | 3.60 | 0.68 | 1.40 | 0.00 | 0.75 | 0.00 | 0.0 |
| Days. | **300** | **200** | **100** | Days. | Days. | **10** | **30** | **20** | **10** | **30** | **20** | Days. |

# TABLES CII. - CVII.

| Tables | CII. | | CIII. | | CIV. | CV. | CVI. | CVII. | | |
|---|---|---|---|---|---|---|---|---|---|---|
| Arguments | **85.** | | **86.** | | **87.** | **88.** | **89.** | **90.** | | |
| Days. | **0** | **10** | **0** | **10** | **0** | **0** | **0** | **0** | **10** | Days. |
| Days. 0.0 | ″ 0.64 | ″ 0.04 | ″ 0.01 | ″ 0.28 | ″ 0.37 | ″ 0.12 | ″ 0.40 | ″ 0.35 | ″ 0.27 | Days. 10.0 |
| 0.1 | 0.63 | 0.05 | 0.01 | 0.28 | 0.36 | 0.11 | 0.40 | 0.35 | 0.27 | 9.9 |
| 0.2 | 0.62 | 0.05 | 0.00 | 0.29 | 0.35 | 0.10 | 0.40 | 0.35 | 0.27 | 9.8 |
| 0.3 | 0.61 | 0.06 | 0.00 | 0.29 | 0.33 | 0.09 | 0.40 | 0.35 | 0.26 | 9.7 |
| 0.4 | 0.60 | 0.07 | 0.00 | 0.30 | 0.32 | 0.08 | 0.40 | 0.35 | 0.26 | 9.6 |
| 0.5 | 0.59 | 0.07 | 0.00 | 0.30 | 0.30 | 0.08 | 0.40 | 0.36 | 0.26 | 9.5 |
| 0.6 | 0.58 | 0.08 | 0.00 | 0.31 | 0.29 | 0.07 | 0.40 | 0.36 | 0.26 | 9.4 |
| 0.7 | 0.57 | 0.09 | 0.00 | 0.31 | 0.27 | 0.06 | 0.39 | 0.36 | 0.25 | 9.3 |
| 0.8 | 0.56 | 0.09 | 0.00 | 0.32 | 0.26 | 0.06 | 0.39 | 0.36 | 0.25 | 9.2 |
| 0.9 | 0.55 | 0.10 | 0.00 | 0.32 | 0.24 | 0.05 | 0.39 | 0.36 | 0.25 | 9.1 |
| 1.0 | 0.54 | 0.11 | 0.00 | 0.33 | 0.22 | 0.05 | 0.38 | 0.37 | 0.24 | 9.0 |
| 1.1 | 0.53 | 0.12 | 0.00 | 0.33 | 0.21 | 0.04 | 0.38 | 0.37 | 0.24 | 8.9 |
| 1.2 | 0.52 | 0.13 | 0.00 | 0.34 | 0.19 | 0.03 | 0.37 | 0.37 | 0.24 | 8.8 |
| 1.3 | 0.51 | 0.13 | 0.00 | 0.35 | 0.17 | 0.03 | 0.37 | 0.37 | 0.23 | 8.7 |
| 1.4 | 0.50 | 0.14 | 0.00 | 0.35 | 0.15 | 0.02 | 0.36 | 0.37 | 0.23 | 8.6 |
| 1.5 | 0.49 | 0.15 | 0.00 | 0.36 | 0.13 | 0.02 | 0.35 | 0.38 | 0.23 | 8.5 |
| 1.6 | 0.48 | 0.16 | 0.00 | 0.36 | 0.11 | 0.02 | 0.34 | 0.38 | 0.22 | 8.4 |
| 1.7 | 0.47 | 0.17 | 0.00 | 0.37 | 0.10 | 0.02 | 0.33 | 0.38 | 0.22 | 8.3 |
| 1.8 | 0.46 | 0.17 | 0.01 | 0.37 | 0.08 | 0.01 | 0.32 | 0.38 | 0.21 | 8.2 |
| 1.9 | 0.45 | 0.18 | 0.01 | 0.38 | 0.07 | 0.01 | 0.31 | 0.38 | 0.21 | 8.1 |
| 2.0 | 0.44 | 0.19 | 0.01 | 0.38 | 0.06 | 0.01 | 0.29 | 0.39 | 0.20 | 8.0 |
| 2.1 | 0.43 | 0.20 | 0.01 | 0.38 | 0.05 | 0.01 | 0.28 | 0.39 | 0.20 | 7.9 |
| 2.2 | 0.42 | 0.21 | 0.01 | 0.39 | 0.04 | 0.00 | 0.27 | 0.39 | 0.20 | 7.8 |
| 2.3 | 0.41 | 0.22 | 0.01 | 0.39 | 0.03 | 0.00 | 0.26 | 0.39 | 0.19 | 7.7 |
| 2.4 | 0.40 | 0.23 | 0.01 | 0.40 | 0.02 | 0.00 | 0.25 | 0.39 | 0.19 | 7.6 |
| 2.5 | 0.38 | 0.24 | 0.02 | 0.40 | 0.01 | 0.00 | 0.23 | 0.39 | 0.18 | 7.5 |
| 2.6 | 0.37 | 0.25 | 0.02 | 0.40 | 0.01 | 0.00 | 0.22 | 0.39 | 0.18 | 7.4 |
| 2.7 | 0.36 | 0.26 | 0.02 | 0.41 | 0.00 | 0.00 | 0.21 | 0.40 | 0.18 | 7.3 |
| 2.8 | 0.35 | 0.27 | 0.02 | 0.41 | 0.00 | 0.00 | 0.20 | 0.40 | 0.17 | 7.2 |
| 2.9 | 0.34 | 0.28 | 0.02 | 0.41 | 0.00 | 0.00 | 0.18 | 0.40 | 0.17 | 7.1 |
| 3.0 | 0.33 | 0.29 | 0.02 | 0.42 | 0.00 | 0.00 | 0.17 | 0.40 | 0.16 | 7.0 |
| 3.1 | 0.32 | 0.30 | 0.02 | 0.42 | 0.00 | 0.00 | 0.16 | 0.40 | 0.16 | 6.9 |
| 3.2 | 0.31 | 0.31 | 0.02 | 0.43 | 0.01 | 0.00 | 0.15 | 0.40 | 0.16 | 6.8 |
| 3.3 | 0.30 | 0.32 | 0.02 | 0.43 | 0.01 | 0.00 | 0.14 | 0.40 | 0.15 | 6.7 |
| 3.4 | 0.29 | 0.33 | 0.03 | 0.43 | 0.02 | 0.01 | 0.12 | 0.40 | 0.15 | 6.6 |
| 3.5 | 0.28 | 0.34 | 0.03 | 0.44 | 0.03 | 0.01 | 0.11 | 0.40 | 0.14 | 6.5 |
| 3.6 | 0.27 | 0.35 | 0.03 | 0.44 | 0.04 | 0.01 | 0.10 | 0.40 | 0.14 | 6.4 |
| 3.7 | 0.26 | 0.36 | 0.03 | 0.45 | 0.05 | 0.02 | 0.09 | 0.40 | 0.14 | 6.3 |
| 3.8 | 0.25 | 0.37 | 0.03 | 0.45 | 0.06 | 0.02 | 0.08 | 0.40 | 0.13 | 6.2 |
| 3.9 | 0.24 | 0.38 | 0.03 | 0.45 | 0.07 | 0.02 | 0.07 | 0.40 | 0.13 | 6.1 |
| 4.0 | 0.23 | 0.39 | 0.04 | 0.46 | 0.09 | 0.03 | 0.06 | 0.40 | 0.12 | 6.0 |
| 4.1 | 0.22 | 0.40 | 0.04 | 0.46 | 0.10 | 0.03 | 0.05 | 0.40 | 0.12 | 5.9 |
| 4.2 | 0.21 | 0.41 | 0.04 | 0.47 | 0.12 | 0.04 | 0.04 | 0.40 | 0.12 | 5.8 |
| 4.3 | 0.20 | 0.42 | 0.04 | 0.47 | 0.13 | 0.04 | 0.03 | 0.40 | 0.11 | 5.7 |
| 4.4 | 0.19 | 0.43 | 0.05 | 0.47 | 0.15 | 0.05 | 0.02 | 0.40 | 0.11 | 5.6 |
| 4.5 | 0.18 | 0.44 | 0.05 | 0.48 | 0.17 | 0.06 | 0.02 | 0.40 | 0.11 | 5.5 |
| 4.6 | 0.17 | 0.45 | 0.05 | 0.48 | 0.18 | 0.06 | 0.01 | 0.40 | 0.10 | 5.4 |
| 4.7 | 0.17 | 0.46 | 0.06 | 0.49 | 0.20 | 0.07 | 0.01 | 0.40 | 0.10 | 5.3 |
| 4.8 | 0.16 | 0.47 | 0.06 | 0.49 | 0.22 | 0.07 | 0.00 | 0.40 | 0.10 | 5.2 |
| 4.9 | 0.15 | 0.48 | 0.06 | 0.49 | 0.24 | 0.08 | 0.00 | 0.40 | 0.10 | 5.1 |
| 5.0 | 0.14 | 0.49 | 0.07 | 0.50 | 0.26 | 0.09 | 0.00 | 0.40 | 0.09 | 5.0 |
| Days. | **30** | **20** | **30** | **20** | **10** | **10** | **10** | **30** | **20** | Days. |

# TABLES CII.-CVII.

| Tables | CII. | | CIII. | | CIV. | CV. | CVI. | CVII. | | |
|---|---|---|---|---|---|---|---|---|---|---|
| Arguments | **85.** | | **86.** | | **87.** | **88.** | **89.** | **90.** | | |
| Days. | **0** | **10** | **0** | **10** | **0** | **0** | **0** | **0** | **10** | Days. |
| 5.0 | 0.14 | 0.49 | 0.07 | 0.50 | 0.26 | 0.09 | 0.00 | 0.40 | 0.09 | 5.0 |
| 5.1 | 0.13 | 0.50 | 0.07 | 0.50 | 0.28 | 0.09 | 0.00 | 0.40 | 0.09 | 4.9 |
| 5.2 | 0.12 | 0.51 | 0.07 | 0.51 | 0.29 | 0.10 | 0.00 | 0.40 | 0.09 | 4.8 |
| 5.3 | 0.12 | 0.52 | 0.07 | 0.51 | 0.31 | 0.11 | 0.00 | 0.39 | 0.08 | 4.7 |
| 5.4 | 0.11 | 0.53 | 0.08 | 0.51 | 0.32 | 0.12 | 0.00 | 0.39 | 0.08 | 4.6 |
| 5.5 | 0.10 | 0.54 | 0.08 | 0.52 | 0.33 | 0.13 | 0.00 | 0.39 | 0.08 | 4.5 |
| 5.6 | 0.10 | 0.55 | 0.08 | 0.52 | 0.34 | 0.13 | 0.01 | 0.39 | 0.07 | 4.4 |
| 5.7 | 0.09 | 0.56 | 0.09 | 0.53 | 0.35 | 0.14 | 0.01 | 0.39 | 0.07 | 4.3 |
| 5.8 | 0.08 | 0.57 | 0.09 | 0.53 | 0.36 | 0.15 | 0.02 | 0.38 | 0.07 | 4.2 |
| 5.9 | 0.08 | 0.58 | 0.09 | 0.53 | 0.37 | 0.16 | 0.02 | 0.38 | 0.07 | 4.1 |
| 6.0 | 0.07 | 0.59 | 0.10 | 0.54 | 0.38 | 0.17 | 0.03 | 0.38 | 0.06 | 4.0 |
| 6.1 | 0.07 | 0.60 | 0.10 | 0.54 | 0.38 | 0.17 | 0.03 | 0.38 | 0.06 | 3.9 |
| 6.2 | 0.06 | 0.61 | 0.10 | 0.54 | 0.39 | 0.18 | 0.04 | 0.38 | 0.06 | 3.8 |
| 6.3 | 0.06 | 0.62 | 0.11 | 0.54 | 0.39 | 0.19 | 0.05 | 0.38 | 0.05 | 3.7 |
| 6.4 | 0.05 | 0.63 | 0.11 | 0.54 | 0.40 | 0.20 | 0.06 | 0.38 | 0.05 | 3.6 |
| 6.5 | 0.05 | 0.64 | 0.11 | 0.55 | 0.40 | 0.21 | 0.07 | 0.37 | 0.05 | 3.5 |
| 6.6 | 0.04 | 0.65 | 0.12 | 0.55 | 0.40 | 0.22 | 0.08 | 0.37 | 0.04 | 3.4 |
| 6.7 | 0.04 | 0.65 | 0.12 | 0.55 | 0.40 | 0.23 | 0.09 | 0.37 | 0.04 | 3.3 |
| 6.8 | 0.03 | 0.66 | 0.13 | 0.55 | 0.39 | 0.24 | 0.10 | 0.37 | 0.04 | 3.2 |
| 6.9 | 0.03 | 0.67 | 0.13 | 0.55 | 0.39 | 0.25 | 0.11 | 0.37 | 0.04 | 3.1 |
| 7.0 | 0.02 | 0.68 | 0.14 | 0.56 | 0.38 | 0.26 | 0.13 | 0.36 | 0.03 | 3.0 |
| 7.1 | 0.02 | 0.69 | 0.14 | 0.56 | 0.37 | 0.27 | 0.14 | 0.36 | 0.03 | 2.9 |
| 7.2 | 0.02 | 0.69 | 0.14 | 0.56 | 0.36 | 0.28 | 0.15 | 0.36 | 0.03 | 2.8 |
| 7.3 | 0.01 | 0.70 | 0.15 | 0.56 | 0.35 | 0.29 | 0.16 | 0.36 | 0.03 | 2.7 |
| 7.4 | 0.01 | 0.70 | 0.15 | 0.56 | 0.34 | 0.30 | 0.17 | 0.36 | 0.03 | 2.6 |
| 7.5 | 0.01 | 0.71 | 0.16 | 0.57 | 0.32 | 0.30 | 0.19 | 0.35 | 0.03 | 2.5 |
| 7.6 | 0.01 | 0.72 | 0.16 | 0.57 | 0.31 | 0.31 | 0.20 | 0.35 | 0.02 | 2.4 |
| 7.7 | 0.00 | 0.72 | 0.16 | 0.57 | 0.29 | 0.32 | 0.21 | 0.35 | 0.02 | 2.3 |
| 7.8 | 0.00 | 0.73 | 0.17 | 0.57 | 0.28 | 0.32 | 0.22 | 0.35 | 0.02 | 2.2 |
| 7.9 | 0.00 | 0.73 | 0.17 | 0.57 | 0.26 | 0.33 | 0.23 | 0.35 | 0.02 | 2.1 |
| 8.0 | 0.00 | 0.74 | 0.18 | 0.58 | 0.24 | 0.33 | 0.25 | 0.34 | 0.02 | 2.0 |
| 8.1 | 0.00 | 0.74 | 0.18 | 0.58 | 0.23 | 0.34 | 0.26 | 0.34 | 0.01 | 1.9 |
| 8.2 | 0.00 | 0.75 | 0.19 | 0.58 | 0.21 | 0.35 | 0.27 | 0.34 | 0.01 | 1.8 |
| 8.3 | 0.00 | 0.75 | 0.19 | 0.58 | 0.19 | 0.35 | 0.28 | 0.34 | 0.01 | 1.7 |
| 8.4 | 0.00 | 0.76 | 0.20 | 0.58 | 0.17 | 0.36 | 0.30 | 0.33 | 0.01 | 1.6 |
| 8.5 | 0.00 | 0.76 | 0.20 | 0.59 | 0.15 | 0.36 | 0.31 | 0.33 | 0.01 | 1.5 |
| 8.6 | 0.00 | 0.77 | 0.21 | 0.59 | 0.13 | 0.36 | 0.32 | 0.33 | 0.01 | 1.4 |
| 8.7 | 0.01 | 0.77 | 0.21 | 0.59 | 0.11 | 0.37 | 0.33 | 0.32 | 0.00 | 1.3 |
| 8.8 | 0.01 | 0.77 | 0.22 | 0.59 | 0.10 | 0.37 | 0.34 | 0.32 | 0.00 | 1.2 |
| 8.9 | 0.01 | 0.78 | 0.22 | 0.59 | 0.08 | 0.38 | 0.35 | 0.32 | 0.00 | 1.1 |
| 9.0 | 0.01 | 0.78 | 0.23 | 0.60 | 0.07 | 0.38 | 0.36 | 0.31 | 0.00 | 1.0 |
| 9.1 | 0.01 | 0.78 | 0.23 | 0.60 | 0.06 | 0.38 | 0.37 | 0.31 | 0.00 | 0.9 |
| 9.2 | 0.02 | 0.79 | 0.24 | 0.60 | 0.05 | 0.39 | 0.38 | 0.31 | 0.00 | 0.8 |
| 9.3 | 0.02 | 0.79 | 0.24 | 0.60 | 0.04 | 0.39 | 0.38 | 0.30 | 0.00 | 0.7 |
| 9.4 | 0.02 | 0.79 | 0.25 | 0.60 | 0.03 | 0.39 | 0.39 | 0.30 | 0.00 | 0.6 |
| 9.5 | 0.03 | 0.79 | 0.25 | 0.60 | 0.02 | 0.40 | 0.39 | 0.30 | 0.00 | 0.5 |
| 9.6 | 0.03 | 0.79 | 0.26 | 0.60 | 0.01 | 0.40 | 0.39 | 0.29 | 0.00 | 0.4 |
| 9.7 | 0.03 | 0.80 | 0.26 | 0.60 | 0.01 | 0.40 | 0.40 | 0.29 | 0.00 | 0.3 |
| 9.8 | 0.04 | 0.80 | 0.27 | 0.60 | 0.00 | 0.40 | 0.40 | 0.28 | 0.00 | 0.2 |
| 9.9 | 0.04 | 0.80 | 0.27 | 0.60 | 0.00 | 0.40 | 0.40 | 0.28 | 0.00 | 0.1 |
| 10.0 | 0.04 | 0.80 | 0.28 | 0.60 | 0.00 | 0.40 | 0.40 | 0.27 | 0.00 | 0.0 |
| Days. | **30** | **20** | **30** | **20** | **10** | **10** | **10** | **30** | **20** | Days. |

# TABLE CVIII. ARGUMENT 77.

Equation = 6″.2 — 6″.18 sin. 3$\bar{y}$.

| $\bar{y}$ | 210° 90 330 | 211° 91 331 | 212° 92 332 | 213° 93 333 | 214° 94 334 | 215° 95 335 | 216° 96 336 | 217° 97 337 | 218° 98 338 | 219° 99 339 | $\bar{y}$ |
|---|---|---|---|---|---|---|---|---|---|---|---|
| 0″ | 12″.38 | 12″.37 | 12″.35 | 12″.30 | 12″.24 | 12″.17 | 12″.08 | 11″.97 | 11″.85 | 11″.71 | 3600″ |
| 100 | 12.38 | 12.37 | 12.35 | 12.30 | 12.24 | 12.17 | 12.08 | 11.97 | 11.85 | 11.71 | 3500 |
| 200 | 12.38 | 12.37 | 12.35 | 12.30 | 12.24 | 12.17 | 12.08 | 11.97 | 11.85 | 11.71 | 3400 |
| 300 | 12.38 | 12.37 | 12.35 | 12.30 | 12.24 | 12.17 | 12.07 | 11.96 | 11.84 | 11.70 | 3300 |
| 400 | 12.38 | 12.37 | 12.35 | 12.30 | 12.24 | 12.16 | 12.07 | 11.96 | 11.84 | 11.70 | 3200 |
| 500 | 12.38 | 12.37 | 12.34 | 12.30 | 12.24 | 12.16 | 12.07 | 11.96 | 11.83 | 11.69 | 3100 |
| 600 | 12.38 | 12.37 | 12.34 | 12.30 | 12.23 | 12.16 | 12.06 | 11.95 | 11.83 | 11.69 | 3000 |
| 700 | 12.38 | 12.37 | 12.34 | 12.30 | 12.23 | 12.16 | 12.06 | 11.95 | 11.83 | 11.69 | 2900 |
| 800 | 12.38 | 12.37 | 12.34 | 12.29 | 12.23 | 12.15 | 12.06 | 11.95 | 11.82 | 11.68 | 2800 |
| 900 | 12.38 | 12.37 | 12.34 | 12.29 | 12.23 | 12.15 | 12.05 | 11.94 | 11.82 | 11.68 | 2700 |
| 1000 | 12.38 | 12.37 | 12.34 | 12.29 | 12.23 | 12.15 | 12.05 | 11.94 | 11.81 | 11.67 | 2600 |
| 1100 | 12.38 | 12.36 | 12.34 | 12.29 | 12.23 | 12.15 | 12.05 | 11.94 | 11.81 | 11.67 | 2500 |
| 1200 | 12.38 | 12.36 | 12 33 | 12.29 | 12.22 | 12.14 | 12.04 | 11.93 | 11.80 | 11.66 | 2400 |
| 1300 | 12.38 | 12.36 | 12.33 | 12.29 | 12.22 | 12.14 | 12.04 | 11.93 | 11.80 | 11.66 | 2300 |
| 1400 | 12.38 | 12.36 | 12.33 | 12.29 | 12.22 | 12.14 | 12.04 | 11.93 | 11.80 | 11.66 | 2200 |
| 1500 | 12.38 | 12.36 | 12.33 | 12.28 | 12.22 | 12.14 | 12.04 | 11.92 | 11.79 | 11.65 | 2100 |
| 1600 | 12.38 | 12.36 | 12.33 | 12.28 | 12.22 | 12.13 | 12.03 | 11.92 | 11.79 | 11.65 | 2000 |
| 1700 | 12.38 | 12.36 | 12.33 | 12.28 | 12.21 | 12.13 | 12.03 | 11.92 | 11.78 | 11.64 | 1900 |
| 1800 | 12.38 | 12.36 | 12.33 | 12.28 | 12.21 | 12.13 | 12.03 | 11.91 | 11.78 | 11.64 | 1800 |
| 1900 | 12.38 | 12.36 | 12.33 | 12.28 | 12.21 | 12.13 | 12.03 | 11.91 | 11.77 | 11.64 | 1700 |
| 2000 | 12.38 | 12.36 | 12.33 | 12.28 | 12.21 | 12.12 | 12.02 | 11.91 | 11.77 | 11.63 | 1600 |
| 2100 | 12.38 | 12.36 | 12.32 | 12.28 | 12.21 | 12.12 | 12.02 | 11.90 | 11.77 | 11.63 | 1500 |
| 2200 | 12.38 | 12.36 | 12.32 | 12.27 | 12.20 | 12.12 | 12.02 | 11.90 | 11.76 | 11.62 | 1400 |
| 2300 | 12.38 | 12.36 | 12.32 | 12.27 | 12.20 | 12.12 | 12.02 | 11.90 | 11.76 | 11.62 | 1300 |
| 2400 | 12.38 | 12.36 | 12.32 | 12.27 | 12.20 | 12.11 | 12.01 | 11.89 | 11.75 | 11.61 | 1200 |
| 2500 | 12.38 | 12.36 | 12.32 | 12.27 | 12.20 | 12.11 | 12.01 | 11.89 | 11.75 | 11.61 | 1100 |
| 2600 | 12.38 | 12.36 | 12.32 | 12.27 | 12.20 | 12.11 | 12.01 | 11.89 | 11.75 | 11.60 | 1000 |
| 2700 | 12.38 | 12.36 | 12.32 | 12.26 | 12.19 | 12.11 | 12.00 | 11.88 | 11.74 | 11.60 | 900 |
| 2800 | 12.38 | 12.36 | 12.32 | 12.26 | 12.19 | 12.10 | 12.00 | 11.88 | 11.74 | 11.59 | 800 |
| 2900 | 12.38 | 12.36 | 12.32 | 12.26 | 12.19 | 12.10 | 12.00 | 11.88 | 11.74 | 11.59 | 700 |
| 3000 | 12.37 | 12.36 | 12.31 | 12.26 | 12.19 | 12.10 | 11.99 | 11.87 | 11.73 | 11.58 | 600 |
| 3100 | 12.37 | 12.35 | 12.31 | 12.25 | 12.18 | 12.10 | 11.99 | 11.87 | 11.73 | 11.58 | 500 |
| 3200 | 12.37 | 12.35 | 12.31 | 12.25 | 12.18 | 12.09 | 11.99 | 11.87 | 11.73 | 11.57 | 400 |
| 3300 | 12.37 | 12.35 | 12.31 | 12.25 | 12.18 | 12.09 | 11.98 | 11.86 | 11.72 | 11.57 | 300 |
| 3400 | 12.37 | 12.35 | 12.31 | 12.25 | 12.18 | 12.09 | 11.98 | 11.86 | 11.72 | 11.56 | 200 |
| 3500 | 12.37 | 12.35 | 12.31 | 12.25 | 12.17 | 12.09 | 11.98 | 11.86 | 11.72 | 11.56 | 100 |
| 3600 | 12.37 | 12.35 | 12.30 | 12.24 | 12.17 | 12.08 | 11.97 | 11.85 | 11.71 | 11.55 | 0 |
| $\bar{y}$ | 89° 209 329 | 88° 208 328 | 87° 207 327 | 86° 206 326 | 85° 205 325 | 84° 204 324 | 83° 203 323 | 82° 202 322 | 81° 201 321 | 80° 200 320 | $\bar{y}$ |

# TABLE CVIII. ARGUMENT 77.

Equation $= 6''.2 - 6''.18 \sin. 3\bar{y}$.

| $\bar{y}$ | 220° | 221° | 222° | 223° | 224° | 225° | 226° | 227° | 228° | 229° | $\bar{y}$ |
|---|---|---|---|---|---|---|---|---|---|---|---|
| | 100 | 101 | 102 | 103 | 104 | 105 | 106 | 107 | 108 | 109 | |
| | 340 | 341 | 342 | 343 | 344 | 345 | 346 | 347 | 348 | 349 | |
| 0″ | 11″.55 | 11″.38 | 11″.20 | 11″.00 | 10″.79 | 10″.57 | 10″.33 | 10″.09 | 9″.83 | 9″.57 | 3600″ |
| 100 | 11.55 | 11.38 | 11.20 | 11.00 | 10.79 | 10.57 | 10.33 | 10.09 | 9.83 | 9.57 | 3500 |
| 200 | 11.55 | 11.37 | 11.19 | 10.99 | 10.78 | 10.56 | 10.32 | 10.08 | 9.82 | 9.56 | 3400 |
| 300 | 11.54 | 11.37 | 11.19 | 10.99 | 10.78 | 10.55 | 10.31 | 10.07 | 9.81 | 9.55 | 3300 |
| 400 | 11.53 | 11.36 | 11.18 | 10.98 | 10.77 | 10.55 | 10.31 | 10.06 | 9.80 | 9.54 | 3200 |
| 500 | 11.53 | 11.36 | 11.18 | 10.98 | 10.77 | 10.54 | 10.30 | 10.06 | 9.80 | 9.53 | 3100 |
| 600 | 11.52 | 11.35 | 11.17 | 10.97 | 10.76 | 10.53 | 10.29 | 10.05 | 9.79 | 9.53 | 3000 |
| 700 | 11.52 | 11.35 | 11.17 | 10.96 | 10.75 | 10.53 | 10.29 | 10.04 | 9.78 | 9.52 | 2900 |
| 800 | 11.51 | 11.34 | 11.16 | 10.96 | 10.75 | 10.52 | 10.28 | 10.03 | 9.78 | 9.51 | 2800 |
| 900 | 11.51 | 11.34 | 11.16 | 10.95 | 10.74 | 10.51 | 10.27 | 10.03 | 9.77 | 9.50 | 2700 |
| 1000 | 11.50 | 11.33 | 11.15 | 10.95 | 10.74 | 10.51 | 10.27 | 10.02 | 9.76 | 9.49 | 2600 |
| 1100 | 11.50 | 11.33 | 11.15 | 10.94 | 10.73 | 10.50 | 10.26 | 10.01 | 9.75 | 9.48 | 2500 |
| 1200 | 11.49 | 11.32 | 11.14 | 10.93 | 10.72 | 10.49 | 10.25 | 10.00 | 9.74 | 9.47 | 2400 |
| 1300 | 11.49 | 11.32 | 11.14 | 10.93 | 10.72 | 10.49 | 10.25 | 10.00 | 9.74 | 9.47 | 2300 |
| 1400 | 11.49 | 11.31 | 11.13 | 10.92 | 10.71 | 10.48 | 10.24 | 9.99 | 9.73 | 9.46 | 2200 |
| 1500 | 11.48 | 11.31 | 11.13 | 10.92 | 10.71 | 10.47 | 10.23 | 9.98 | 9.72 | 9.45 | 2100 |
| 1600 | 11.48 | 11.30 | 11.12 | 10.91 | 10.70 | 10.47 | 10.23 | 9.98 | 9.72 | 9.44 | 2000 |
| 1700 | 11.47 | 11.30 | 11.12 | 10.91 | 10.70 | 10.46 | 10.22 | 9.97 | 9.71 | 9.44 | 1900 |
| 1800 | 11.47 | 11.29 | 11.11 | 10.90 | 10.69 | 10.45 | 10.21 | 9.96 | 9.70 | 9.43 | 1800 |
| 1900 | 11.46 | 11.29 | 11.10 | 10.89 | 10.68 | 10.45 | 10.21 | 9.96 | 9.70 | 9.42 | 1700 |
| 2000 | 11.46 | 11.28 | 11.10 | 10.89 | 10.68 | 10.44 | 10.20 | 9.95 | 9.69 | 9.41 | 1600 |
| 2100 | 11.46 | 11.28 | 11.09 | 10.88 | 10.67 | 10.43 | 10.19 | 9.94 | 9.68 | 9.40 | 1500 |
| 2200 | 11.45 | 11.27 | 11.09 | 10.88 | 10.67 | 10.43 | 10.19 | 9.94 | 9.68 | 9.40 | 1400 |
| 2300 | 11.45 | 11.27 | 11.08 | 10.87 | 10.66 | 10.42 | 10.18 | 9.93 | 9.67 | 9.39 | 1300 |
| 2400 | 11.44 | 11.26 | 11.07 | 10.86 | 10.65 | 10.41 | 10.17 | 9.92 | 9.66 | 9.38 | 1200 |
| 2500 | 11.44 | 11.26 | 11.07 | 10.86 | 10.65 | 10.41 | 10.17 | 9.92 | 9.66 | 9.38 | 1100 |
| 2600 | 11.43 | 11.25 | 11.06 | 10.85 | 10.64 | 10.40 | 10.16 | 9.91 | 9.65 | 9.37 | 1000 |
| 2700 | 11.43 | 11.25 | 11.06 | 10.85 | 10.63 | 10.39 | 10.15 | 9.90 | 9.64 | 9.36 | 900 |
| 2800 | 11.42 | 11.24 | 11.05 | 10.84 | 10.63 | 10.39 | 10.15 | 9.89 | 9.63 | 9.35 | 800 |
| 2900 | 11.42 | 11.24 | 11.04 | 10.84 | 10.62 | 10.38 | 10.14 | 9.89 | 9.63 | 9.34 | 700 |
| 3000 | 11.41 | 11.23 | 11.04 | 10.83 | 10.61 | 10.37 | 10.13 | 9.88 | 9.62 | 9.34 | 600 |
| 3100 | 11.41 | 11.23 | 11.03 | 10.82 | 10.61 | 10.37 | 10.13 | 9.87 | 9.61 | 9.33 | 500 |
| 3200 | 11.40 | 11.22 | 11.03 | 10.82 | 10.60 | 10.36 | 10.12 | 9.86 | 9.60 | 9.32 | 400 |
| 3300 | 11.40 | 11.22 | 11.02 | 10.81 | 10.59 | 10.35 | 10.11 | 9.86 | 9.60 | 9.31 | 300 |
| 3400 | 11.39 | 11.21 | 11.02 | 10.81 | 10.59 | 10.35 | 10.11 | 9.85 | 9.59 | 9.31 | 200 |
| 3500 | 11.39 | 11.21 | 11.01 | 10.80 | 10.58 | 10.34 | 10.10 | 9.84 | 9.58 | 9.30 | 100 |
| 3600 | 11.38 | 11.20 | 11.00 | 10.79 | 10.57 | 10.33 | 10.09 | 9.83 | 9.57 | 9.29 | 0 |
| | 79° | 78° | 77° | 76° | 75° | 74° | 73° | 72° | 71° | 70° | |
| $\bar{y}$ | 199 | 198 | 197 | 196 | 195 | 194 | 193 | 192 | 191 | 190 | $\bar{y}$ |
| | 319 | 318 | 317 | 316 | 315 | 314 | 313 | 312 | 311 | 310 | |

# TABLE CVIII. ARGUMENT 77.

Equation = 6″.2 — 6″.18 sin. 3$\bar{y}$.

| $\bar{y}$ | 230° 110 350 | 231° 111 351 | 232° 112 352 | 233° 113 353 | 234° 114 354 | 235° 115 355 | 236° 116 356 | 237° 117 357 | 238° 118 358 | 239° 119 359 | $\bar{y}$ |
|---|---|---|---|---|---|---|---|---|---|---|---|
| 0″ | 9.29″ | 9.01″ | 8.71″ | 8.41″ | 8.11″ | 7.80″ | 7.48″ | 7.17″ | 6.85″ | 6.52″ | 3600 |
| 100 | 9.29 | 9.01 | 8.71 | 8.41 | 8.11 | 7.80 | 7.48 | 7.17 | 6.85 | 6.52 | 3500 |
| 200 | 9.28 | 9.00 | 8.70 | 8.40 | 8.10 | 7.79 | 7.47 | 7.16 | 6.84 | 6.51 | 3400 |
| 300 | 9.27 | 8.99 | 8.69 | 8.39 | 8.09 | 7.78 | 7.46 | 7.15 | 6.83 | 6.50 | 3300 |
| 400 | 9.26 | 8.98 | 8.68 | 8.38 | 8.08 | 7.77 | 7.45 | 7.14 | 6.82 | 6.49 | 3200 |
| 500 | 9.26 | 8.97 | 8.67 | 8.37 | 8.07 | 7.76 | 7.44 | 7.13 | 6.81 | 6.48 | 3100 |
| 600 | 9.25 | 8.96 | 8.66 | 8.36 | 8.06 | 7.75 | 7.43 | 7.12 | 6.80 | 6.47 | 3000 |
| 700 | 9.24 | 8.96 | 8.66 | 8.36 | 8.06 | 7.74 | 7.42 | 7.11 | 6.79 | 6.47 | 2900 |
| 800 | 9.23 | 8.95 | 8.65 | 8.35 | 8.05 | 7.73 | 7.42 | 7.10 | 6.78 | 6.46 | 2800 |
| 900 | 9.23 | 8.94 | 8.64 | 8.34 | 8.04 | 7.72 | 7.41 | 7.09 | 6.77 | 6.45 | 2700 |
| 1000 | 9.22 | 8.93 | 8.63 | 8.33 | 8.03 | 7.71 | 7.40 | 7.08 | 6.76 | 6.44 | 2600 |
| 1100 | 9.21 | 8.92 | 8.62 | 8.32 | 8.02 | 7.70 | 7.39 | 7.07 | 6.75 | 6.43 | 2500 |
| 1200 | 9.20 | 8.91 | 8.61 | 8.31 | 8.01 | 7.69 | 7.38 | 7.06 | 6.74 | 6.42 | 2400 |
| 1300 | 9.20 | 8.91 | 8.61 | 8.31 | 8.01 | 7.69 | 7.37 | 7.06 | 6.74 | 6.42 | 2300 |
| 1400 | 9.19 | 8.90 | 8.60 | 8.30 | 8.00 | 7.68 | 7.36 | 7.05 | 6.73 | 6.41 | 2200 |
| 1500 | 9.18 | 8.89 | 8.59 | 8.29 | 7.99 | 7.67 | 7.35 | 7.04 | 6.72 | 6.40 | 2100 |
| 1600 | 9.17 | 8.88 | 8.58 | 8.28 | 7.98 | 7.66 | 7.35 | 7.03 | 6.71 | 6.39 | 2000 |
| 1700 | 9.16 | 8.87 | 8.57 | 8.27 | 7.97 | 7.65 | 7.34 | 7.02 | 6.70 | 6.38 | 1900 |
| 1800 | 9.15 | 8.86 | 8.56 | 8.26 | 7.96 | 7.64 | 7.33 | 7.01 | 6.69 | 6.37 | 1800 |
| 1900 | 9.15 | 8.86 | 8.56 | 8.26 | 7.95 | 7.63 | 7.32 | 7.00 | 6.68 | 6.36 | 1700 |
| 2000 | 9.14 | 8.85 | 8.55 | 8.25 | 7.94 | 7.63 | 7.31 | 6.99 | 6.67 | 6.35 | 1600 |
| 2100 | 9.13 | 8.84 | 8.54 | 8.24 | 7.93 | 7.62 | 7.30 | 6.98 | 6.66 | 6.34 | 1500 |
| 2200 | 9.12 | 8.83 | 8.53 | 8.23 | 7.92 | 7.61 | 7.29 | 6.97 | 6.65 | 6.33 | 1400 |
| 2300 | 9.11 | 8.82 | 8.52 | 8.22 | 7.91 | 7.60 | 7.28 | 6.96 | 6.64 | 6.32 | 1300 |
| 2400 | 9.10 | 8.81 | 8.51 | 8.21 | 7.90 | 7.59 | 7.27 | 6.95 | 6.63 | 6.31 | 1200 |
| 2500 | 9.10 | 8.81 | 8.51 | 8.21 | 7.90 | 7.58 | 7.27 | 6.95 | 6.63 | 6.31 | 1100 |
| 2600 | 9.09 | 8.80 | 8.50 | 8.20 | 7.89 | 7.57 | 7.26 | 6.94 | 6.62 | 6.30 | 1000 |
| 2700 | 9.08 | 8.79 | 8.49 | 8.19 | 7.88 | 7.57 | 7.25 | 6.93 | 6.61 | 6.29 | 900 |
| 2800 | 9.07 | 8.78 | 8.48 | 8.18 | 7.87 | 7.56 | 7.24 | 6.92 | 6.60 | 6.28 | 800 |
| 2900 | 9.07 | 8.77 | 8.47 | 8-17 | 7.86 | 7.55 | 7.23 | 6.91 | 6.59 | 6.27 | 700 |
| 3000 | 9.06 | 8.76 | 8.46 | 8.16 | 7.85 | 7.54 | 7.22 | 6.90 | 6.58 | 6.26 | 600 |
| 3100 | 9.05 | 8.76 | 8.46 | 8.16 | 7.85 | 7.53 | 7.22 | 6.90 | 6.57 | 6.25 | 500 |
| 3200 | 9.04 | 8.75 | 8.45 | 8.15 | 7.84 | 7.52 | 7.21 | 6.89 | 6.56 | 6.24 | 400 |
| 3300 | 9.04 | 8.74 | 8.44 | 8.14 | 7.83 | 7.51 | 7.20 | 6.88 | 6.55 | 6.23 | 300 |
| 3400 | 9.03 | 8.73 | 8.43 | 8.13 | 7.82 | 7.50 | 7.19 | 6.87 | 6.54 | 6.22 | 200 |
| 3500 | 9.02 | 8.72 | 8.42 | 8.12 | 7.81 | 7.49 | 7.18 | 6.86 | 6.53 | 6.21 | 100 |
| 3600 | 9.01 | 8.71 | 8.41 | 8.11 | 7.80 | 7.48 | 7.17 | 6.85 | 6.52 | 6.20 | 0 |
| $\bar{y}$ | 69° 189 309 | 68° 188 308 | 67° 187 307 | 66° 186 306 | 65° 185 305 | 64° 184 304 | 63° 183 303 | 62° 182 302 | 61° 181 301 | 60° 180 300 | $\bar{y}$ |

# TABLE CVIII. ARGUMENT 77.

Equation $= 6''.2 - 6''.18 \sin 3\bar{y}$.

| $\bar{y}$ | 240° | 241° | 242° | 243° | 244° | 245° | 246° | 247° | 248° | 249° | $\bar{y}$ |
|---|---|---|---|---|---|---|---|---|---|---|---|
| | 120 | 121 | 122 | 123 | 124 | 125 | 126 | 127 | 128 | 129 | |
| | 0 | 1 | 2 | 3 | 4 | 5 | 6 | 7 | 8 | 9 | |
| 0″ | 6″.20 | 5″.88 | 5″.55 | 5″.23 | 4″.92 | 4″.60 | 4″.29 | 3″.99 | 3″.69 | 3″.39 | 3600″ |
| 100 | 6.19 | 5.87 | 5.54 | 5.22 | 4.91 | 4.59 | 4.28 | 3.98 | 3.68 | 3.38 | 3500 |
| 200 | 6.18 | 5.86 | 5.53 | 5.21 | 4.90 | 4.58 | 4.27 | 3.97 | 3.67 | 3.37 | 3400 |
| 300 | 6.17 | 5.85 | 5.52 | 5.20 | 4.89 | 4.57 | 4.26 | 3.96 | 3.66 | 3.36 | 3300 |
| 400 | 6.16 | 5.84 | 5.51 | 5.19 | 4.88 | 4.56 | 4.25 | 3.95 | 3.65 | 3.36 | 3200 |
| 500 | 6.15 | 5.83 | 5.50 | 5.18 | 4.87 | 4.55 | 4.24 | 3.94 | 3.64 | 3.35 | 3100 |
| 600 | 6.14 | 5.82 | 5.50 | 5.18 | 4.86 | 4.55 | 4.24 | 3.94 | 3.64 | 3.34 | 3000 |
| 700 | 6.13 | 5.81 | 5.49 | 5.17 | 4.85 | 4.54 | 4.23 | 3.93 | 3.63 | 3.33 | 2900 |
| 800 | 6.12 | 5.80 | 5.48 | 5.16 | 4.84 | 4.53 | 4.22 | 3.92 | 3.62 | 3.33 | 2800 |
| 900 | 6.11 | 5.79 | 5.47 | 5.15 | 4.83 | 4.52 | 4.21 | 3.91 | 3.61 | 3.32 | 2700 |
| 1000 | 6.10 | 5.78 | 5.46 | 5.14 | 4.82 | 4.51 | 4.20 | 3.90 | 3.60 | 3.31 | 2600 |
| 1100 | 6.09 | 5.77 | 5.45 | 5.13 | 4.81 | 4.50 | 4.19 | 3.89 | 3.59 | 3.30 | 2500 |
| 1200 | 6.09 | 5.77 | 5.45 | 5.13 | 4.81 | 4.50 | 4.19 | 3.89 | 3.59 | 3.30 | 2400 |
| 1300 | 6.08 | 5.76 | 5.44 | 5.12 | 4.80 | 4.49 | 4.18 | 3.88 | 3.58 | 3.29 | 2300 |
| 1400 | 6.07 | 5.75 | 5.43 | 5.11 | 4.79 | 4.48 | 4.17 | 3.87 | 3.57 | 3.28 | 2200 |
| 1500 | 6.06 | 5.74 | 5.42 | 5.10 | 4.78 | 4.47 | 4.16 | 3.86 | 3.56 | 3.27 | 2100 |
| 1600 | 6.05 | 5.73 | 5.41 | 5.09 | 4.77 | 4.46 | 4.15 | 3.85 | 3.55 | 3.26 | 2000 |
| 1700 | 6.04 | 5.72 | 5.40 | 5.08 | 4.76 | 4.45 | 4.14 | 3.84 | 3.54 | 3.25 | 1900 |
| 1800 | 6.03 | 5.71 | 5.39 | 5.07 | 4.76 | 4.44 | 4.14 | 3.84 | 3.54 | 3.25 | 1800 |
| 1900 | 6.02 | 5.70 | 5.38 | 5.06 | 4.75 | 4.43 | 4.13 | 3.83 | 3.53 | 3.24 | 1700 |
| 2000 | 6.01 | 5.69 | 5.37 | 5.05 | 4.74 | 4.42 | 4.12 | 3.82 | 3.52 | 3.23 | 1600 |
| 2100 | 6.00 | 5.68 | 5.36 | 5.04 | 4.73 | 4.41 | 4.11 | 3.81 | 3.51 | 3.22 | 1500 |
| 2200 | 5.99 | 5.67 | 5.35 | 5.03 | 4.72 | 4.40 | 4.10 | 3.80 | 3.50 | 3.21 | 1400 |
| 2300 | 5.98 | 5.66 | 5.34 | 5.02 | 4.71 | 4.39 | 4.09 | 3.79 | 3.49 | 3.20 | 1300 |
| 2400 | 5.98 | 5.66 | 5.34 | 5.02 | 4.71 | 4.39 | 4.09 | 3.79 | 3.49 | 3.20 | 1200 |
| 2500 | 5.97 | 5.65 | 5.33 | 5.01 | 4.70 | 4.38 | 4.08 | 3.78 | 3.48 | 3.19 | 1100 |
| 2600 | 5.96 | 5.64 | 5.32 | 5.00 | 4.69 | 4.37 | 4.07 | 3.77 | 3.47 | 3.18 | 1000 |
| 2700 | 5.95 | 5.63 | 5.31 | 4.99 | 4.68 | 4.36 | 4.06 | 3.76 | 3.46 | 3.17 | 900 |
| 2800 | 5.94 | 5.62 | 5.30 | 4.98 | 4.67 | 4.35 | 4.05 | 3.75 | 3.45 | 3.17 | 800 |
| 2900 | 5.93 | 5.61 | 5.29 | 4.97 | 4.66 | 4.34 | 4.04 | 3.74 | 3.44 | 3.16 | 700 |
| 3000 | 5.93 | 5.60 | 5.28 | 4.97 | 4.65 | 4.34 | 4.04 | 3.74 | 3.44 | 3.15 | 600 |
| 3100 | 5.92 | 5.59 | 5.27 | 4.96 | 4.64 | 4.33 | 4.03 | 3.73 | 3.43 | 3.14 | 500 |
| 3200 | 5.91 | 5.58 | 5.26 | 4.95 | 4.63 | 4.32 | 4.02 | 3.72 | 3.42 | 3.14 | 400 |
| 3300 | 5.90 | 5.57 | 5.25 | 4.94 | 4.62 | 4.31 | 4.01 | 3.71 | 3.41 | 3.13 | 300 |
| 3400 | 5.89 | 5.56 | 5.24 | 4.93 | 4.61 | 4.30 | 4.00 | 3.70 | 3.40 | 3.12 | 200 |
| 3500 | 5.88 | 5.55 | 5.23 | 4.92 | 4.60 | 4.29 | 3.99 | 3.69 | 3.39 | 3.11 | 100 |
| 3600 | 5.88 | 5.55 | 5.23 | 4.92 | 4.60 | 4.29 | 3.99 | 3.69 | 3.39 | 3.11 | 0 |
| $\bar{y}$ | 59° | 58° | 57° | 56° | 55° | 54° | 53° | 52° | 51° | 50° | $\bar{y}$ |
| | 179 | 178 | 177 | 176 | 175 | 174 | 173 | 172 | 171 | 170 | |
| | 299 | 298 | 297 | 296 | 295 | 294 | 293 | 292 | 291 | 290 | |

# TABLE CVIII. ARGUMENT 77.

Equation = $6''.2 - 6''.18 \sin 3g$.

| g | 250° 130 10 | 251° 131 11 | 252° 132 12 | 253° 133 13 | 254° 134 14 | 255° 135 15 | 256° 136 16 | 257° 137 17 | 258° 138 18 | 259° 139 19 | g |
|---|---|---|---|---|---|---|---|---|---|---|---|
| 0″ | 3.11″ | 2.83″ | 2.57″ | 2.31″ | 2.07″ | 1.83″ | 1.61″ | 1.40″ | 1.20″ | 1.02″ | 3600″ |
| 100 | 3.10 | 2.82 | 2.56 | 2.30 | 2.06 | 1.82 | 1.60 | 1.39 | 1.20 | 1.02 | 3500 |
| 200 | 3.09 | 2.81 | 2.55 | 2.29 | 2.05 | 1.81 | 1.60 | 1.39 | 1.19 | 1.01 | 3400 |
| 300 | 3.08 | 2.80 | 2.54 | 2.29 | 2.05 | 1.81 | 1.59 | 1.38 | 1.19 | 1.01 | 3300 |
| 400 | 3.08 | 2.80 | 2.54 | 2.28 | 2.04 | 1.80 | 1.59 | 1.38 | 1.18 | 1.00 | 3200 |
| 500 | 3.07 | 2.79 | 2.53 | 2.27 | 2.03 | 1.79 | 1.58 | 1.37 | 1.18 | 1.00 | 3100 |
| 600 | 3.06 | 2.78 | 2.52 | 2.27 | 2.03 | 1.79 | 1.58 | 1.37 | 1.17 | 0.99 | 3000 |
| 700 | 3.05 | 2.77 | 2.51 | 2.26 | 2.02 | 1.78 | 1.57 | 1.36 | 1.17 | 0.99 | 2900 |
| 800 | 3.05 | 2.77 | 2.51 | 2.25 | 2.01 | 1.77 | 1.56 | 1.35 | 1.16 | 0.98 | 2800 |
| 900 | 3.04 | 2.76 | 2.50 | 2.25 | 2.01 | 1.77 | 1.56 | 1.35 | 1.16 | 0.98 | 2700 |
| 1000 | 3.03 | 2.75 | 2.49 | 2.24 | 2.00 | 1.76 | 1.55 | 1.34 | 1.15 | 0.97 | 2600 |
| 1100 | 3.02 | 2.74 | 2.48 | 2.23 | 1.99 | 1.75 | 1.55 | 1.34 | 1.15 | 0.97 | 2500 |
| 1200 | 3.02 | 2.74 | 2.48 | 2.23 | 1.99 | 1.75 | 1.54 | 1.33 | 1.14 | 0.96 | 2400 |
| 1300 | 3.01 | 2.73 | 2.47 | 2.22 | 1.98 | 1.74 | 1.53 | 1.32 | 1.14 | 0.96 | 2300 |
| 1400 | 3.00 | 2.72 | 2.46 | 2.21 | 1.97 | 1.73 | 1.53 | 1.32 | 1.13 | 0.95 | 2200 |
| 1500 | 2.99 | 2.72 | 2.46 | 2.21 | 1.97 | 1.73 | 1.52 | 1.31 | 1.13 | 0.95 | 2100 |
| 1600 | 2.99 | 2.71 | 2.45 | 2.20 | 1.96 | 1.72 | 1.52 | 1.31 | 1.12 | 0.94 | 2000 |
| 1700 | 2.98 | 2.70 | 2.44 | 2.19 | 1.95 | 1.72 | 1.51 | 1.30 | 1.12 | 0.94 | 1900 |
| 1800 | 2.97 | 2.70 | 2.44 | 2.19 | 1.95 | 1.71 | 1.51 | 1.30 | 1.11 | 0.93 | 1800 |
| 1900 | 2.96 | 2.69 | 2.43 | 2.18 | 1.94 | 1.71 | 1.50 | 1.29 | 1.11 | 0.93 | 1700 |
| 2000 | 2.96 | 2.68 | 2.42 | 2.17 | 1.93 | 1.70 | 1.49 | 1.28 | 1.10 | 0.93 | 1600 |
| 2100 | 2.95 | 2.68 | 2.42 | 2.17 | 1.93 | 1.70 | 1.49 | 1.28 | 1.10 | 0.92 | 1500 |
| 2200 | 2.94 | 2.67 | 2.41 | 2.16 | 1.92 | 1.69 | 1.48 | 1.27 | 1.09 | 0.92 | 1400 |
| 2300 | 2.93 | 2.66 | 2.40 | 2.15 | 1.91 | 1.69 | 1.48 | 1.27 | 1.09 | 0.91 | 1300 |
| 2400 | 2.93 | 2.66 | 2.40 | 2.15 | 1.91 | 1.68 | 1.47 | 1.26 | 1.08 | 0.91 | 1200 |
| 2500 | 2.92 | 2.65 | 2.39 | 2.14 | 1.90 | 1.67 | 1.46 | 1.26 | 1.08 | 0.91 | 1100 |
| 2600 | 2.91 | 2.64 | 2.38 | 2.13 | 1.89 | 1.67 | 1.46 | 1.25 | 1.07 | 0.90 | 1000 |
| 2700 | 2.90 | 2.63 | 2.37 | 2.13 | 1.89 | 1.66 | 1.45 | 1.25 | 1.07 | 0.90 | 900 |
| 2800 | 2.89 | 2.63 | 2.37 | 2.12 | 1.88 | 1.66 | 1.45 | 1.24 | 1.06 | 0.89 | 800 |
| 2900 | 2.88 | 2.62 | 2.36 | 2.11 | 1.87 | 1.65 | 1.44 | 1.24 | 1.06 | 0.89 | 700 |
| 3000 | 2.88 | 2.61 | 2.35 | 2.11 | 1.87 | 1.64 | 1.43 | 1.23 | 1.05 | 0.88 | 600 |
| 3100 | 2.87 | 2.60 | 2.34 | 2.10 | 1.86 | 1.64 | 1.43 | 1.23 | 1.05 | 0.88 | 500 |
| 3200 | 2.86 | 2.60 | 2.34 | 2.09 | 1.85 | 1.63 | 1.42 | 1.22 | 1.04 | 0.87 | 400 |
| 3300 | 2.85 | 2.59 | 2.33 | 2.09 | 1.85 | 1.63 | 1.42 | 1.22 | 1.04 | 0.87 | 300 |
| 3400 | 2.84 | 2.58 | 2.32 | 2.08 | 1.84 | 1.62 | 1.41 | 1.21 | 1.03 | 0.86 | 200 |
| 3500 | 2.83 | 2.57 | 2.31 | 2.07 | 1.83 | 1.62 | 1.41 | 1.21 | 1.03 | 0.86 | 100 |
| 3600 | 2.83 | 2.57 | 2.31 | 2.07 | 1.83 | 1.61 | 1.40 | 1.20 | 1.02 | 0.85 | 0 |
| g | 49° 169 289 | 48° 168 288 | 47° 167 287 | 46° 166 286 | 45° 165 285 | 44° 164 284 | 43° 163 283 | 42° 162 282 | 41° 161 281 | 40° 160 280 | g |

# TABLE CVIII. ARGUMENT 77.

Equation $= 6''.2 - 6''.18 \sin 3\bar{y}$.

| $\bar{y}$ | 260° 140 20 | 261° 141 21 | 262° 142 22 | 263° 143 23 | 264° 144 24 | 265° 145 25 | 266° 146 26 | 267° 147 27 | 268° 148 28 | 269° 149 29 | $\bar{y}$ |
|---|---|---|---|---|---|---|---|---|---|---|---|
| 0″ | 0.85″ | 0.69″ | 0.55″ | 0.43″ | 0.32″ | 0.23″ | 0.16″ | 0.10″ | 0.05″ | 0.03″ | 3600″ |
| 100 | 0.85 | 0.69 | 0.55 | 0.43 | 0.32 | 0.23 | 0.16 | 0.10 | 0.05 | 0.03 | 3500 |
| 200 | 0.84 | 0.68 | 0.55 | 0.43 | 0.32 | 0.23 | 0.16 | 0.10 | 0.05 | 0.03 | 3400 |
| 300 | 0.84 | 0.68 | 0.54 | 0.42 | 0.32 | 0.23 | 0.16 | 0.10 | 0.05 | 0.03 | 3300 |
| 400 | 0.83 | 0.68 | 0.54 | 0.42 | 0.31 | 0.22 | 0.15 | 0.09 | 0.05 | 0.03 | 3200 |
| 500 | 0.83 | 0.67 | 0.54 | 0.42 | 0.31 | 0.22 | 0.15 | 0.09 | 0.05 | 0.03 | 3100 |
| 600 | 0.82 | 0.67 | 0.53 | 0.41 | 0.31 | 0.22 | 0.15 | 0.09 | 0.05 | 0.03 | 3000 |
| 700 | 0.82 | 0.67 | 0.53 | 0.41 | 0.31 | 0.22 | 0.15 | 0.09 | 0.05 | 0.03 | 2900 |
| 800 | 0.81 | 0.66 | 0.53 | 0.41 | 0.30 | 0.21 | 0.14 | 0.09 | 0.05 | 0.03 | 2800 |
| 900 | 0.81 | 0.66 | 0.52 | 0.40 | 0.30 | 0.21 | 0.14 | 0.09 | 0.05 | 0.02 | 2700 |
| 1000 | 0.80 | 0.66 | 0.52 | 0.40 | 0.30 | 0.21 | 0.14 | 0.09 | 0.04 | 0.02 | 2600 |
| 1100 | 0.80 | 0.65 | 0.52 | 0.40 | 0.30 | 0.21 | 0.14 | 0.09 | 0.04 | 0.02 | 2500 |
| 1200 | 0.79 | 0.65 | 0.51 | 0.39 | 0.29 | 0.20 | 0.13 | 0.08 | 0.04 | 0.02 | 2400 |
| 1300 | 0.79 | 0.65 | 0.51 | 0.39 | 0.29 | 0.20 | 0.13 | 0.08 | 0.04 | 0.02 | 2300 |
| 1400 | 0.78 | 0.64 | 0.51 | 0.39 | 0.29 | 0.20 | 0.13 | 0.08 | 0.04 | 0.02 | 2200 |
| 1500 | 0.78 | 0.64 | 0.50 | 0.39 | 0.29 | 0.20 | 0.13 | 0.08 | 0.04 | 0.02 | 2100 |
| 1600 | 0.77 | 0.63 | 0.50 | 0.38 | 0.28 | 0.20 | 0.13 | 0.08 | 0.04 | 0.02 | 2000 |
| 1700 | 0.77 | 0.63 | 0.50 | 0.38 | 0.28 | 0.20 | 0.13 | 0.08 | 0.04 | 0.02 | 1900 |
| 1800 | 0.77 | 0.63 | 0.49 | 0.38 | 0.28 | 0.19 | 0.12 | 0.08 | 0.04 | 0.02 | 1800 |
| 1900 | 0.76 | 0.62 | 0.49 | 0.38 | 0.28 | 0.19 | 0.12 | 0.08 | 0.04 | 0.02 | 1700 |
| 2000 | 0.76 | 0.62 | 0.49 | 0.37 | 0.27 | 0.19 | 0.12 | 0.07 | 0.04 | 0.02 | 1600 |
| 2100 | 0.75 | 0.61 | 0.48 | 0.37 | 0.27 | 0.19 | 0.12 | 0.07 | 0.04 | 0.02 | 1500 |
| 2200 | 0.75 | 0.61 | 0.48 | 0.37 | 0.27 | 0.19 | 0.12 | 0.07 | 0.04 | 0.02 | 1400 |
| 2300 | 0.74 | 0.61 | 0.48 | 0.37 | 0.27 | 0.19 | 0.12 | 0.07 | 0.04 | 0.02 | 1300 |
| 2400 | 0.74 | 0.60 | 0.47 | 0.36 | 0.26 | 0.18 | 0.11 | 0.07 | 0.04 | 0.02 | 1200 |
| 2500 | 0.73 | 0.60 | 0.47 | 0.36 | 0.26 | 0.18 | 0.11 | 0.07 | 0.04 | 0.02 | 1100 |
| 2600 | 0.73 | 0.59 | 0.47 | 0.36 | 0.26 | 0.18 | 0.11 | 0.07 | 0.04 | 0.02 | 1000 |
| 2700 | 0.73 | 0.59 | 0.46 | 0.35 | 0.26 | 0.18 | 0.11 | 0.07 | 0.04 | 0.02 | 900 |
| 2800 | 0.72 | 0.59 | 0.46 | 0.35 | 0.25 | 0.18 | 0.11 | 0.06 | 0.03 | 0.02 | 800 |
| 2900 | 0.72 | 0.58 | 0.46 | 0.35 | 0.25 | 0.18 | 0.11 | 0.06 | 0.03 | 0.02 | 700 |
| 3000 | 0.71 | 0.58 | 0.45 | 0.34 | 0.25 | 0.17 | 0.11 | 0.06 | 0.03 | 0.02 | 600 |
| 3100 | 0.71 | 0.57 | 0.45 | 0.34 | 0.25 | 0.17 | 0.11 | 0.06 | 0.03 | 0.02 | 500 |
| 3200 | 0.70 | 0.57 | 0.45 | 0.34 | 0.24 | 0.17 | 0.11 | 0.06 | 0.03 | 0.02 | 400 |
| 3300 | 0.70 | 0.56 | 0.44 | 0.33 | 0.24 | 0.17 | 0.10 | 0.06 | 0.03 | 0.02 | 300 |
| 3400 | 0.70 | 0.56 | 0.44 | 0.33 | 0.24 | 0.17 | 0.10 | 0.06 | 0.03 | 0.02 | 200 |
| 3500 | 0.69 | 0.56 | 0.44 | 0.33 | 0.24 | 0.17 | 0.10 | 0.06 | 0.03 | 0.02 | 100 |
| 3600 | 0.69 | 0.55 | 0.43 | 0.32 | 0.23 | 0.16 | 0.10 | 0.05 | 0.03 | 0.02 | 0 |
| $\bar{y}$ | 39° 159 279 | 38° 158 278 | 37° 157 277 | 36° 156 276 | 35° 155 275 | 34° 154 274 | 33° 153 273 | 32° 152 272 | 31° 151 271 | 30° 150 270 | $\bar{y}$ |

# TABLE CIX.

Equation $= 9''.1 + 2''.17 \cos. \bar{u} - 8''.80 \sin. \bar{u}$.

| | 0° | 10° | 20° | 30° | 40° | 50° | 60° | 70° | 80° |
|---|---|---|---|---|---|---|---|---|---|
| 0° 0" | 11".27 | 9".71 | 8".13 | 6".58 | 5".10 | 3".75 | 2".56 | 1".57 | 0".81 |
| 0 1000 | 11.23 | 9.67 | 8.09 | 6.54 | 5.06 | 3.71 | 2.53 | 1.54 | 0.79 |
| 0 2000 | 11.19 | 9.62 | 8.05 | 6.50 | 5.02 | 3.68 | 2.50 | 1.52 | 0.77 |
| 0 3000 | 11.14 | 9.58 | 8.00 | 6.45 | 4.98 | 3.64 | 2.47 | 1.50 | 0.75 |
| 1 400 | 11.10 | 9.54 | 7.96 | 6.41 | 4.94 | 3.61 | 2.44 | 1.47 | 0.73 |
| 1 1400 | 11.06 | 9.49 | 7.91 | 6.37 | 4.90 | 3.57 | 2.42 | 1.45 | 0.72 |
| 1 2400 | 11.02 | 9.45 | 7.87 | 6.33 | 4.86 | 3.54 | 2.39 | 1.43 | 0.70 |
| 1 3400 | 10.97 | 9.41 | 7.82 | 6.28 | 4.82 | 3.51 | 2.36 | 1.40 | 0.68 |
| 2 800 | 10.93 | 9.36 | 7.78 | 6.24 | 4.78 | 3.47 | 2.33 | 1.38 | 0.66 |
| 2 1800 | 10.89 | 9.32 | 7.73 | 6.20 | 4.75 | 3.44 | 2.30 | 1.36 | 0.65 |
| 2 2800 | 10.85 | 9.28 | 7.69 | 6.16 | 4.71 | 3.40 | 2.27 | 1.33 | 0.63 |
| 3 200 | 10.80 | 9.23 | 7.65 | 6.12 | 4.67 | 3.37 | 2.24 | 1.31 | 0.62 |
| 3 1200 | 10.76 | 9.19 | 7.61 | 6.07 | 4.63 | 3.34 | 2.21 | 1.29 | 0.60 |
| 3 2200 | 10.72 | 9.15 | 7.56 | 6.03 | 4.59 | 3.30 | 2.18 | 1.27 | 0.59 |
| 3 3200 | 10.67 | 9.10 | 7.52 | 5.99 | 4.56 | 3.27 | 2.15 | 1.24 | 0.57 |
| 4 600 | 10.63 | 9.06 | 7.48 | 5.95 | 4.52 | 3.24 | 2.13 | 1.22 | 0.56 |
| 4 1600 | 10.58 | 9.01 | 7.44 | 5.91 | 4.48 | 3.20 | 2.10 | 1.20 | 0.55 |
| 4 2600 | 10.54 | 8.97 | 7.39 | 5.87 | 4.44 | 3.17 | 2.07 | 1.18 | 0.53 |
| 5 0 | 10.49 | 8.92 | 7.35 | 5.83 | 4.41 | 3.14 | 2.04 | 1.16 | 0.52 |
| 5 1000 | 10.45 | 8.88 | 7.31 | 5.78 | 4.37 | 3.10 | 2.01 | 1.14 | 0.50 |
| 5 2000 | 10.40 | 8.84 | 7.27 | 5.74 | 4.33 | 3.07 | 1.98 | 1.12 | 0.49 |
| 5 3000 | 10.36 | 8.79 | 7.22 | 5.70 | 4.30 | 3.04 | 1.96 | 1.10 | 0.48 |
| 6 400 | 10.32 | 8.75 | 7.18 | 5.66 | 4.26 | 3.00 | 1.93 | 1.08 | 0.46 |
| 6 1400 | 10.27 | 8.70 | 7.14 | 5.62 | 4.22 | 2.97 | 1.90 | 1.06 | 0.45 |
| 6 2400 | 10.23 | 8.66 | 7.09 | 5.58 | 4.19 | 2.94 | 1.88 | 1.04 | 0.44 |
| 6 3400 | 10.18 | 8.61 | 7.05 | 5.54 | 4.15 | 2.90 | 1.85 | 1.02 | 0.42 |
| 7 800 | 10.14 | 8.57 | 7.01 | 5.50 | 4.11 | 2.87 | 1.82 | 1.00 | 0.41 |
| 7 1800 | 10.10 | 8.52 | 6.96 | 5.46 | 4.08 | 2.84 | 1.80 | 0.98 | 0.40 |
| 7 2800 | 10.06 | 8.48 | 6.92 | 5.42 | 4.04 | 2.81 | 1.77 | 0.96 | 0.39 |
| 8 200 | 10.01 | 8.44 | 6.88 | 5.38 | 4.00 | 2.77 | 1.74 | 0.94 | 0.37 |
| 8 1200 | 9.97 | 8.39 | 6.83 | 5.34 | 3.97 | 2.74 | 1.72 | 0.92 | 0.36 |
| 8 2200 | 9.93 | 8.35 | 6.79 | 5.30 | 3.93 | 2.71 | 1.69 | 0.90 | 0.35 |
| 8 3200 | 9.88 | 8.31 | 6.75 | 5.26 | 3.89 | 2.68 | 1.67 | 0.88 | 0.34 |
| 9 600 | 9.84 | 8.26 | 6.71 | 5.22 | 3.86 | 2.65 | 1.64 | 0.86 | 0.33 |
| 9 1600 | 9.79 | 8.22 | 6.67 | 5.18 | 3.82 | 2.62 | 1.62 | 0.84 | 0.32 |
| 9 2600 | 9.75 | 8.18 | 6.62 | 5.14 | 3.78 | 2.59 | 1.59 | 0.82 | 0.31 |
| 10 0 | 9.71 | 8.13 | 6.58 | 5.10 | 3.75 | 2.56 | 1.57 | 0.81 | 0.30 |

# TABLE CIX.

Equation $= 9''.1 + 2''.17 \cos. \bar{u} - 8''.80 \sin. \bar{u}$.

| | 90° | 100° | 110° | 120° | 130° | 140° | 150° | 160° | 170° |
|---|---|---|---|---|---|---|---|---|---|
| 0° 0″ | 0″.30 | 0″.05 | 0″.09 | 0″.39 | 0″.97 | 1″.79 | 2″.82 | 4″.05 | 5″.44 |
| 0 1000 | 0.29 | 0.05 | 0.09 | 0.40 | 0.98 | 1.81 | 2.85 | 4.08 | 5.48 |
| 0 2000 | 0.28 | 0.05 | 0.10 | 0.41 | 1.00 | 1.84 | 2.88 | 4.12 | 5.52 |
| 0 3000 | 0.27 | 0.05 | 0.10 | 0.43 | 1.02 | 1.86 | 2.92 | 4.16 | 5.56 |
| 1 400 | 0.26 | 0.05 | 0.11 | 0.44 | 1.04 | 1.89 | 2.95 | 4.19 | 5.60 |
| 1 1400 | 0.25 | 0.04 | 0.11 | 0.46 | 1.06 | 1.91 | 2.98 | 4.23 | 5.64 |
| 1 2400 | 0.24 | 0.04 | 0.12 | 0.47 | 1.08 | 1.94 | 3.02 | 4.27 | 5.68 |
| 1 3400 | 0.23 | 0.04 | 0.12 | 0.49 | 1.10 | 1.96 | 3.05 | 4.30 | 5.72 |
| 2 800 | 0.22 | 0.04 | 0.13 | 0.50 | 1.12 | 1.99 | 3.08 | 4.34 | 5.76 |
| 2 1800 | 0.21 | 0.04 | 0.14 | 0.52 | 1.14 | 2.02 | 3.12 | 4.38 | 5.80 |
| 2 2800 | 0.20 | 0.04 | 0.14 | 0.53 | 1.16 | 2.04 | 3.15 | 4.41 | 5.84 |
| 3 200 | 0.19 | 0.04 | 0.15 | 0.54 | 1.18 | 2.07 | 3.18 | 4.45 | 5.88 |
| 3 1200 | 0.18 | 0.04 | 0.16 | 0.56 | 1.21 | 2.10 | 3.22 | 4.49 | 5.92 |
| 3 2200 | 0.17 | 0.04 | 0.16 | 0.57 | 1.23 | 2.13 | 3.25 | 4.53 | 5.96 |
| 3 3200 | 0.17 | 0.04 | 0.17 | 0.59 | 1.25 | 2.15 | 3.28 | 4.57 | 6.00 |
| 4 600 | 0.16 | 0.04 | 0.18 | 0.60 | 1.28 | 2.18 | 3.32 | 4.60 | 6.04 |
| 4 1600 | 0.15 | 0.04 | 0.18 | 0.62 | 1.30 | 2.21 | 3.35 | 4.64 | 6.08 |
| 4 2600 | 0.14 | 0.04 | 0.19 | 0.63 | 1.32 | 2.24 | 3.38 | 4.68 | 6.12 |
| 5 0 | 0.14 | 0.04 | 0.20 | 0.65 | 1.35 | 2.27 | 3.42 | 4.72 | 6.17 |
| 5 1000 | 0.13 | 0.04 | 0.20 | 0.66 | 1.37 | 2.30 | 3.45 | 4.76 | 6.21 |
| 5 2000 | 0.13 | 0.04 | 0.21 | 0.68 | 1.39 | 2.33 | 3.48 | 4.80 | 6.25 |
| 5 3000 | 0.12 | 0.05 | 0.22 | 0.70 | 1.42 | 2.36 | 3.52 | 4.84 | 6.29 |
| 6 400 | 0.12 | 0.05 | 0.23 | 0.71 | 1.44 | 2.39 | 3.55 | 4.88 | 6.33 |
| 6 1400 | 0.11 | 0.05 | 0.24 | 0.73 | 1.47 | 2.42 | 3.59 | 4.92 | 6.38 |
| 6 2400 | 0.11 | 0.05 | 0.25 | 0.75 | 1.49 | 2.45 | 3.62 | 4.96 | 6.42 |
| 6 3400 | 0.10 | 0.05 | 0.26 | 0.76 | 1.52 | 2.48 | 3.66 | 5.00 | 6.46 |
| 7 800 | 0.10 | 0.06 | 0.27 | 0.78 | 1.54 | 2.51 | 3.69 | 5.04 | 6.50 |
| 7 1800 | 0.09 | 0.06 | 0.28 | 0.80 | 1.57 | 2.54 | 3.73 | 5.08 | 6.55 |
| 7 2800 | 0.09 | 0.06 | 0.29 | 0.82 | 1.59 | 2.57 | 3.76 | 5.12 | 6.59 |
| 8 200 | 0.08 | 0.06 | 0.30 | 0.83 | 1.61 | 2.60 | 3.80 | 5.16 | 6.63 |
| 8 1200 | 0.08 | 0.07 | 0.31 | 0.85 | 1.64 | 2.63 | 3.83 | 5.20 | 6.67 |
| 8 2200 | 0.07 | 0.07 | 0.32 | 0.87 | 1.66 | 2.66 | 3.87 | 5.24 | 6.72 |
| 8 3200 | 0.07 | 0.07 | 0.34 | 0.89 | 1.69 | 2.69 | 3.90 | 5.28 | 6.76 |
| 9 600 | 0.06 | 0.08 | 0.35 | 0.91 | 1.71 | 2.72 | 3.94 | 5.32 | 6.80 |
| 9 1600 | 0.06 | 0.08 | 0.36 | 0.93 | 1.74 | 2.75 | 3.97 | 5.36 | 6.84 |
| 9 2600 | 0.06 | 0.08 | 0.37 | 0.95 | 1.76 | 2.78 | 4.01 | 5.40 | 6.88 |
| 10 0 | 0.05 | 0.09 | 0.39 | 0.97 | 1.79 | 2.82 | 4.05 | 5.44 | 6.93 |

# TABLE CIX.

Equation $= 9''.1 + 2''.17 \cos. \bar{u} - 8''.80 \sin. \bar{u}$.

| | 180° | 190° | 200° | 210° | 220° | 230° | 240° | 250° | 260° |
|---|---|---|---|---|---|---|---|---|---|
| 0° 0'' | 6''.93 | 8''.49 | 10''.07 | 11''.62 | 13''.10 | 14''.45 | 15''.64 | 16''.63 | 17''.39 |
| 0 1000 | 6.97 | 8.53 | 10.11 | 11.67 | 13.14 | 14.49 | 15.67 | 16.66 | 17.41 |
| 0 2000 | 7.01 | 8.57 | 10.15 | 11.71 | 13.18 | 14.52 | 15.70 | 16.68 | 17.43 |
| 0 3000 | 7.05 | 8.62 | 10.20 | 11.75 | 13.22 | 14.56 | 15.73 | 16.70 | 17.45 |
| 1 400 | 7.09 | 8.66 | 10.24 | 11.79 | 13.26 | 14.59 | 15.76 | 16.73 | 17.47 |
| 1 1400 | 7.14 | 8.70 | 10.29 | 11.84 | 13.30 | 14.63 | 15.79 | 16.75 | 17.48 |
| 1 2400 | 7.18 | 8.75 | 10.33 | 11.88 | 13.34 | 14.66 | 15.82 | 16.77 | 17.50 |
| 1 3400 | 7.22 | 8.79 | 10.38 | 11.92 | 13.38 | 14.70 | 15.85 | 16.80 | 17.52 |
| 2 800 | 7.26 | 8.83 | 10.42 | 11.96 | 13.42 | 14.73 | 15.88 | 16.82 | 17.54 |
| 2 1800 | 7.31 | 8.88 | 10.47 | 12.00 | 13.45 | 14.76 | 15.90 | 16.84 | 17.55 |
| 2 2800 | 7.35 | 8.92 | 10.52 | 12.05 | 13.49 | 14.80 | 15.93 | 16.87 | 17.57 |
| 3 200 | 7.39 | 8.96 | 10.56 | 12.09 | 13.53 | 14.83 | 15.96 | 16.89 | 17.58 |
| 3 1200 | 7.44 | 9.01 | 10.60 | 12.13 | 13.57 | 14.86 | 15.99 | 16.91 | 17.60 |
| 3 2200 | 7.48 | 9.05 | 10.64 | 12.17 | 13.61 | 14.90 | 16.02 | 16.93 | 17.61 |
| 3 3200 | 7.53 | 9.10 | 10.68 | 12.21 | 13.64 | 14.93 | 16.05 | 16.96 | 17.63 |
| 4 600 | 7.57 | 9.14 | 10.73 | 12.25 | 13.68 | 14.96 | 16.08 | 16.98 | 17.64 |
| 4 1600 | 7.62 | 9.19 | 10.77 | 12.29 | 13.72 | 15.00 | 16.11 | 17.00 | 17.66 |
| 4 2600 | 7.66 | 9.23 | 10.81 | 12.33 | 13.76 | 15.03 | 16.14 | 17.02 | 17.67 |
| 5 0 | 7.71 | 9.28 | 10.85 | 12.37 | 13.79 | 15.06 | 16.16 | 17.04 | 17.68 |
| 5 1000 | 7.75 | 9.32 | 10.90 | 12.41 | 13.83 | 15.10 | 16.19 | 17.06 | 17.70 |
| 5 2000 | 7.79 | 9.37 | 10.94 | 12.46 | 13.87 | 15.13 | 16.22 | 17.08 | 17.71 |
| 5 3000 | 7.84 | 9.41 | 10.98 | 12.50 | 13.90 | 15.16 | 16.24 | 17.10 | 17.72 |
| 6 400 | 7.88 | 9.46 | 11.03 | 12.54 | 13.94 | 15.20 | 16.27 | 17.12 | 17.74 |
| 6 1400 | 7.92 | 9.50 | 11.07 | 12.58 | 13.98 | 15.23 | 16.30 | 17.14 | 17.75 |
| 6 2400 | 7.97 | 9.55 | 11.11 | 12.62 | 14.01 | 15.26 | 16.32 | 17.16 | 17.76 |
| 6 3400 | 8.01 | 9.59 | 11.16 | 12.66 | 14.05 | 15.30 | 16.35 | 17.18 | 17.78 |
| 7 800 | 8.05 | 9.64 | 11.20 | 12.70 | 14.09 | 15.33 | 16.38 | 17.20 | 17.79 |
| 7 1800 | 8.10 | 9.68 | 11.24 | 12.74 | 14.12 | 15.36 | 16.40 | 17.22 | 17.80 |
| 7 2800 | 8.14 | 9.72 | 11.29 | 12.78 | 14.16 | 15.39 | 16.43 | 17.24 | 17.81 |
| 8 200 | 8.18 | 9.77 | 11.33 | 12.82 | 14.20 | 15.43 | 16.46 | 17.26 | 17.83 |
| 8 1200 | 8.23 | 9.81 | 11.37 | 12.86 | 14.23 | 15.46 | 16.48 | 17.28 | 17.84 |
| 8 2200 | 8.27 | 9.85 | 11.41 | 12.90 | 14.27 | 15.49 | 16.51 | 17.30 | 17.85 |
| 8 3200 | 8.31 | 9.90 | 11.46 | 12.94 | 14.31 | 15.52 | 16.53 | 17.32 | 17.86 |
| 9 600 | 8.36 | 9.94 | 11.50 | 12.98 | 14.34 | 15.55 | 16.56 | 17.34 | 17.87 |
| 9 1600 | 8.40 | 9.99 | 11.54 | 13.02 | 14.38 | 15.58 | 16.58 | 17.36 | 17.88 |
| 9 2600 | 8.44 | 10.03 | 11.58 | 13.06 | 14.42 | 15.61 | 16.61 | 17.38 | 17.89 |
| 10 0 | 8.49 | 10.07 | 11.62 | 13.10 | 14.45 | 15.64 | 16.63 | 17.39 | 17.90 |

# TABLE CIX.

Equation $= 9''.1 + 2''.17 \cos \tilde{u} - 8''.80 \sin \tilde{u}$.

| | 270° | 280° | 290° | 300° | 310° | 320° | 330° | 340° | 350° |
|---|---|---|---|---|---|---|---|---|---|
| 0° 0″ | 17″.90 | 18″.15 | 18″.11 | 17″.81 | 17″.23 | 16″.41 | 15″.38 | 14″.15 | 12″.76 |
| 0 1000 | 17.91 | 18.15 | 18.11 | 17.80 | 17.22 | 16.39 | 15.35 | 14.12 | 12.72 |
| 0 2000 | 17.92 | 18.15 | 18.10 | 17.79 | 17.20 | 16.36 | 15.32 | 14.08 | 12.68 |
| 0 3000 | 17.93 | 18.15 | 18.10 | 17.77 | 17.18 | 16.34 | 15.28 | 14.04 | 12.64 |
| 1 400 | 17.94 | 18.16 | 18.09 | 17.76 | 17.16 | 16.31 | 15.25 | 14.01 | 12.60 |
| 1 1400 | 17.95 | 18.16 | 18.09 | 17.74 | 17.14 | 16.29 | 15.22 | 13.97 | 12.56 |
| 1 2400 | 17.96 | 18.16 | 18.08 | 17.73 | 17.12 | 16.26 | 15.18 | 13.93 | 12.52 |
| 1 3400 | 17.97 | 18.16 | 18.08 | 17.71 | 17.10 | 16.24 | 15.15 | 13.90 | 12.48 |
| 2 800 | 17.98 | 18.16 | 18.07 | 17.70 | 17.08 | 16.21 | 15.12 | 13.86 | 12.44 |
| 2 1800 | 17.99 | 18.16 | 18.06 | 17.68 | 17.06 | 16.18 | 15.08 | 13.82 | 12.40 |
| 2 2800 | 18.00 | 18.16 | 18.06 | 17.67 | 17.04 | 16.16 | 15.05 | 13.79 | 12.36 |
| 3 200 | 18.01 | 18.16 | 18.05 | 17.66 | 17.02 | 16.13 | 15.02 | 13.75 | 12.32 |
| 3 1200 | 18.02 | 18.16 | 18.04 | 17.64 | 16.99 | 16.10 | 14.98 | 13.71 | 12.28 |
| 3 2200 | 18.03 | 18.16 | 18.04 | 17.63 | 16.97 | 16.07 | 14.95 | 13.67 | 12.24 |
| 3 3200 | 18.03 | 18.16 | 18.03 | 17.61 | 16.95 | 16.05 | 14.92 | 13.64 | 12.20 |
| 4 600 | 18.04 | 18.16 | 18.02 | 17.60 | 16.92 | 16.02 | 14.88 | 13.60 | 12.16 |
| 4 1600 | 18.05 | 18.16 | 18.02 | 17.58 | 16.90 | 15.99 | 14.85 | 13.56 | 12.12 |
| 4 2600 | 18.06 | 18.16 | 18.01 | 17.56 | 16.88 | 15.96 | 14.82 | 13.52 | 12.08 |
| 5 0 | 18.06 | 18.16 | 18.00 | 17.55 | 16.85 | 15.93 | 14.78 | 13.48 | 12.03 |
| 5 1000 | 18.07 | 18.16 | 18.00 | 17.54 | 16.83 | 15.90 | 14.75 | 13.44 | 11.99 |
| 5 2000 | 18.08 | 18.16 | 17.99 | 17.52 | 16.81 | 15.87 | 14.72 | 13.40 | 11.95 |
| 5 3000 | 18.08 | 18.15 | 17.98 | 17.50 | 16.78 | 15.84 | 14.68 | 13.36 | 11.91 |
| 6 400 | 18.09 | 18.15 | 17.97 | 17.49 | 16.76 | 15.81 | 14.65 | 13.32 | 11.87 |
| 6 1400 | 18.09 | 18.15 | 17.96 | 17.47 | 16.73 | 15.78 | 14.61 | 13.28 | 11.82 |
| 6 2400 | 18.10 | 18.15 | 17.95 | 17.45 | 16.71 | 15.75 | 14.58 | 13.24 | 11.78 |
| 6 3400 | 18.10 | 18.15 | 17.94 | 17.44 | 16.68 | 15.72 | 14.54 | 13.20 | 11.74 |
| 7 800 | 18.11 | 18.14 | 17.93 | 17.42 | 16.66 | 15.69 | 14.51 | 13.16 | 11.70 |
| 7 1800 | 18.11 | 18.14 | 17.92 | 17.40 | 16.63 | 15.66 | 14.47 | 13.12 | 11.65 |
| 7 2800 | 18.12 | 18.14 | 17.91 | 17.38 | 16.61 | 15.63 | 14.44 | 13.08 | 11.61 |
| 8 200 | 18.12 | 18.14 | 17.90 | 17.37 | 16.59 | 15.60 | 14.40 | 13.04 | 11.57 |
| 8 1200 | 18.13 | 18.13 | 17.89 | 17.35 | 16.56 | 15.57 | 14.37 | 13.00 | 11.53 |
| 8 2200 | 18.13 | 18.13 | 17.88 | 17.33 | 16.54 | 15.54 | 14.33 | 12.96 | 11.49 |
| 8 3200 | 18.14 | 18.13 | 17.86 | 17.31 | 16.51 | 15.51 | 14.30 | 12.92 | 11.44 |
| 9 600 | 18.14 | 18.12 | 17.85 | 17.29 | 16.49 | 15.48 | 14.26 | 12.88 | 11.40 |
| 9 1600 | 18.14 | 18.12 | 17.84 | 17.27 | 16.46 | 15.45 | 14.23 | 12.84 | 11.36 |
| 9 2600 | 18.15 | 18.12 | 17.83 | 17.25 | 16.44 | 15.42 | 14.19 | 12.80 | 11.32 |
| 10 0 | 18.15 | 18.11 | 17.81 | 17.23 | 16.41 | 15.38 | 14.15 | 12.76 | 11.27 |

# TABLE CX. ARGUMENT 1″.

Equation $= 348''.0 + 186''.8 \cos x + 10''.3 \cos 2x + 0''.6 \cos 3x$.

| Days. | 0 | | 1 | | 2 | | 3 | | 4 | | 5 | |
|---|---|---|---|---|---|---|---|---|---|---|---|---|
| Days. | Equation. | Diff. | Equation. | Diff. | Equation. | Diff. | Equation. | Diff. | Equation. | Diff. | Equation. | Diff. |
| d. .00 | 338″.66 | .42 | 297″.79 | .39 | 260″.80 | .35 | 229″.06 | .29 | 203″.60 | .22 | 185″.13 | .15 |
| .01 | 338.24 | .42 | 297.40 | .39 | 260.45 | .35 | 228.77 | .29 | 203.38 | .22 | 184.98 | .14 |
| .02 | 337.82 | .42 | 297.01 | .39 | 260.10 | .34 | 228.48 | .29 | 203.16 | .22 | 184.84 | .15 |
| .03 | 337.40 | .43 | 296.62 | .39 | 259.76 | .35 | 228.19 | .28 | 202.94 | .22 | 184.69 | .14 |
| .04 | 336.97 | .42 | 296.23 | .39 | 259.41 | .34 | 227.91 | .29 | 202.72 | .22 | 184.55 | .15 |
| .05 | 336.55 | .42 | 295.84 | .39 | 259.07 | .34 | 227.62 | .28 | 202.50 | .22 | 184.40 | .14 |
| .06 | 336.13 | .42 | 295.45 | .39 | 258.73 | .34 | 227.34 | .28 | 202.28 | .21 | 184.26 | .14 |
| .07 | 335.71 | .42 | 295.06 | .39 | 258.39 | .34 | 227.06 | .28 | 202.07 | .22 | 184.12 | .14 |
| .08 | 335.29 | .42 | 294.67 | .39 | 258.05 | .34 | 226.78 | .28 | 201.85 | .21 | 183.98 | .14 |
| .09 | 334.87 | .42 | 294.28 | .39 | 257.71 | .34 | 226.50 | .28 | 201.64 | .21 | 183.84 | .14 |
| .10 | 334.45 | .42 | 293.89 | .39 | 257.37 | .34 | 226.22 | .28 | 201.43 | .22 | 183.70 | .14 |
| .11 | 334.03 | .42 | 293.50 | .39 | 257.03 | .34 | 225.94 | .28 | 201.21 | .21 | 183.56 | .14 |
| .12 | 333.61 | .42 | 293.11 | .39 | 256.69 | .34 | 225.66 | .28 | 201.00 | .21 | 183.42 | .14 |
| .13 | 333.19 | .42 | 292.72 | .39 | 256.35 | .34 | 225.38 | .28 | 200.79 | .21 | 183.28 | .14 |
| .14 | 332.77 | .42 | 292.33 | .39 | 256.01 | .34 | 225.10 | .28 | 200.58 | .21 | 183.14 | .14 |
| .15 | 332.35 | .41 | 291.94 | .38 | 255.67 | .34 | 224.82 | .28 | 200.37 | .21 | 183.00 | .13 |
| .16 | 331.94 | .42 | 291.56 | .38 | 255.33 | .34 | 224.54 | .27 | 200.16 | .21 | 182.87 | .14 |
| .17 | 331.52 | .42 | 291.18 | .38 | 254.99 | .33 | 224.27 | .28 | 199.95 | .21 | 182.73 | .13 |
| .18 | 331.10 | .42 | 290.80 | .38 | 254.66 | .34 | 223.99 | .27 | 199.74 | .21 | 182.60 | .14 |
| .19 | 330.68 | .42 | 290.42 | .38 | 254.32 | .33 | 223.72 | .28 | 199.53 | .21 | 182.46 | .13 |
| 20 | 330.26 | .42 | 290.04 | .39 | 253.99 | .34 | 223.44 | .27 | 199.32 | .21 | 182.33 | .13 |
| .21 | 329.84 | .42 | 289.65 | .39 | 253.65 | .33 | 223.17 | .28 | 199.11 | .20 | 182.20 | .13 |
| .22 | 329.42 | .42 | 289.26 | .38 | 253.32 | .34 | 222.89 | .27 | 198.91 | .21 | 182.07 | .13 |
| .23 | 329.00 | .42 | 288.88 | .38 | 252.98 | .33 | 222.62 | .28 | 198.70 | .20 | 181.94 | .13 |
| .24 | 328.58 | .42 | 288.50 | .38 | 252.65 | .33 | 222.34 | .27 | 198.50 | .21 | 181.81 | .13 |
| .25 | 328.16 | .42 | 288.12 | .38 | 252.32 | .33 | 222.07 | .27 | 198.29 | .20 | 181.68 | .13 |
| .26 | 327.74 | .42 | 287.74 | .38 | 251.99 | .33 | 221.80 | .27 | 198.09 | .20 | 181.55 | .13 |
| .27 | 327.32 | .41 | 287.36 | .38 | 251.66 | .33 | 221.53 | .27 | 197.89 | .20 | 181.42 | .13 |
| .28 | 326.91 | .41 | 286.98 | .38 | 251.33 | .33 | 221.26 | .27 | 197.69 | .20 | 181.29 | .12 |
| .29 | 326.50 | .41 | 286.60 | .38 | 251.00 | .33 | 220.99 | .27 | 197.49 | .20 | 181.17 | .13 |
| .30 | 326.09 | .41 | 286.22 | .38 | 250.67 | .33 | 220.72 | .27 | 197.29 | .20 | 181.04 | .12 |
| .31 | 325.68 | .41 | 285.84 | .38 | 250.34 | .33 | 220.45 | .27 | 197.09 | .20 | 180.92 | .13 |
| .32 | 325.27 | .42 | 285.46 | .38 | 250.01 | .33 | 220.18 | .27 | 196.89 | .20 | 180.79 | .12 |
| .33 | 324.85 | .42 | 285.08 | .38 | 249.68 | .33 | 219.91 | .27 | 196.69 | .20 | 180.67 | .13 |
| .34 | 324.43 | .41 | 284.70 | .38 | 249.35 | .33 | 219.64 | .27 | 196.49 | .20 | 180.54 | .12 |
| .35 | 324.02 | .41 | 284.32 | .38 | 249.02 | .32 | 219.37 | .26 | 196.29 | .19 | 180.42 | .12 |
| .36 | 323.61 | .41 | 283.94 | .38 | 248.70 | .32 | 219.11 | .27 | 196.10 | .19 | 180.30 | .12 |
| .37 | 323.20 | .41 | 283.56 | .37 | 248.38 | .32 | 218.84 | .26 | 195.91 | .19 | 180.18 | .12 |
| .38 | 322.79 | .42 | 283.19 | .37 | 248.06 | .32 | 218.58 | .26 | 195.72 | .19 | 180.06 | .12 |
| .39 | 322.37 | .42 | 282.82 | .37 | 247.74 | .32 | 218.32 | .25 | 195.53 | .19 | 179.94 | .12 |
| .40 | 321.95 | .42 | 282.45 | .38 | 247.42 | .33 | 218.07 | .26 | 195.34 | .19 | 179.82 | .12 |
| .41 | 321.53 | .41 | 282.07 | .38 | 247.09 | .32 | 217.81 | .26 | 195.15 | .19 | 179.70 | .11 |
| .42 | 321.12 | .41 | 281.69 | .38 | 246.77 | .32 | 217.55 | .26 | 194.96 | .19 | 179.59 | .12 |
| .43 | 320.71 | .41 | 281.31 | .37 | 246.45 | .32 | 217.29 | .26 | 194.77 | .19 | 179.47 | .11 |
| .44 | 320.30 | .41 | 280.94 | .37 | 246.13 | .32 | 217.03 | .26 | 194.58 | .19 | 179.36 | .12 |
| .45 | 319.89 | .41 | 280.57 | .37 | 245.81 | .32 | 216.77 | .26 | 194.39 | .19 | 179.24 | .11 |
| .46 | 319.48 | .41 | 280.20 | .37 | 245.49 | .32 | 216.51 | .26 | 194.20 | .18 | 179.13 | .11 |
| .47 | 319.07 | .41 | 279.83 | .37 | 245.17 | .32 | 216.25 | .25 | 194.02 | .19 | 179.02 | .11 |
| .48 | 318.66 | .41 | 279.46 | .37 | 244.85 | .32 | 216.00 | .26 | 193.83 | .18 | 178.91 | .11 |
| .49 | 318.25 | .41 | 279.09 | .37 | 244.53 | .33 | 215.74 | .25 | 193.65 | .19 | 178.80 | .11 |
| .50 | 317.84 | .41 | 278.72 | .37 | 244.20 | .32 | 215.49 | .25 | 193.46 | .18 | 178.69 | .11 |

NOTE. — Arg. 1″ = Arg. 1 + 13.77728.

# TABLES

# OF THE MOON'S PARALLAX.

---

THESE tables are constructed from the formulæ given by WALKER in a report to Prof. BACHE, the Superintendent of the Coast Survey, and printed on the 114th page of the *Coast Survey Report for* 1848; and from those given by ADAMS on the 263d page of Volume XIII. of the *Proceedings of the Royal Astronomical Society* of London. They are substituted for the Tables given in the first edition of this work.

The following is the formula for the Horizontal Parallax.

| EQUATION. sin Moon's Equatorial Horizontal Parallax = | AUTHORITY. | ARGUMENT. | TABLE. | EQUATION. Moon's Equatorial Horizontal Parallax, continued. | AUTHORITY. | ARGUMENT. | TABLE. |
|---|---|---|---|---|---|---|---|
| 3000″. | A. | | | — 0″.31 cos [120] | W. & A. | 15 | 121 |
| + 345.58 | A. | | 110 | + 0.39 | A. | | 122 |
| + 186.51 cos [1] | A. | 1 | 110 | — 0.11 cos [11] | A. | 16 | 122 |
| + 10.17 cos [2] | A. | | 110 | + 0.28 cos [22] | A. | | 122 |
| + 0.63 cos [3] | A. | | 110 | + 0.14 | A. | | 123 |
| + 0.04 cos [4] | A. | | 110 | + 0.14 cos [110] | A. | 17 | 123 |
| + 29.44 | A. | | 111 | + 0.22 | A. | | 124 |
| — 0.95 cos [10] | A. | 3 | 111 | + 0.22 cos [1′21] | A. | 18 | 124 |
| + 28.23 cos [20] | A. | | 111 | + 0.12 | A. | | 125 |
| + 0.26 cos [40] | A. | | 111 | — 0.12 cos [2′3] | A. | 19 | 125 |
| + 34.67 | A. | | 112 | + 0.12 | A. | | 126 |
| + 34.30 cos [21′] | A. | 2 | 112 | + 0.12 cos [1′02] | A. | 20 | 126 |
| + 0.37 cos [42′] | A. | | 112 | + 0.09 | A. | | 127 |
| + 1.45 | W. & A. | | 113 | + 0.09 cos [2′20] | A. | 22 | 127 |
| + 1.45 cos [1′21′] | W. & A. | 6 | 113 | + 0.09 | A. | | 128 |
| + 3.09 | A. | | 114 | — 0.09 cos [202′1] | A. | 23 | 128 |
| + 3.09 cos [21] | A. | 7 | 114 | + 0.10 | A. | | 129 |
| + 1.92 | W. & A. | | 115 | — 0.10 cos [102] | A. | 24 | 129 |
| + 1.92 cos [1′20] | W. & A. | 8 | 115 | + 0.05 | A. | | 130 |
| + 1.16 | A. | | 116 | + 0.05 cos [2′21′] | A. | 28 | 130 |
| + 1.16 cos [1′01] | A. | 9 | 116 | + 0.06 | A. | | 131 |
| + 0.95 | A. | | 117 | + 0.06 cos [1′41′] | A. | 30 | 131 |
| — 0.95 cos [101] | A. | 10 | 117 | + 0.40 | A. | | 132 |
| + 0.71 | A. | | 118 | — 0.40 cos [100] | A. | 4 | 132 |
| — 0.71 cos [2001′] | A. | 11 | 118 | + 0.32 | A. | | 133 |
| + 0.60 | A. | | 119 | + 0.01 cos [1′1] | A. | 5 | 133 |
| + 0.60 cos [41′] | A. | 13 | 119 | — 0.31 cos [2′2] | A. | | 133 |
| + 0.23 | W. & A. | | 120 | + 0.11 | A. | | 134 |
| — 0.23 cos [121′] | W. & A. | 14 | 120 | — 0.11 cos [202′0] | A. | 12′ | 134 |
| + 0.31 | W. & A. | | 121 | | | | |

Table 135 contains the excess of the Moon's Horizontal Parallax above its sine.

# TABLE CX. ARGUMENT 1.

Equation $= 345''.58 + 186''.51 \cos x + 10''.17 \cos 2x + 0''.63 \cos 3x + 0''.04 \cos 4x$.

| Days. | 0 | | 1 | | 2 | | 3 | | 4 | | 5 | |
|---|---|---|---|---|---|---|---|---|---|---|---|---|
| Days. | Equation. | Diff. | Equation. | Diff. | Equation. | Diff. | Equation. | Diff. | Equation. | Diff. | Equation. | Diff. |
| d. | ″ | | ″ | | ″ | | ″ | | ″ | | ″ | |
| .00 | 334.49 | .42 | 377.26 | .43 | 419.92 | .42 | 459.95 | .38 | 494.63 | .31 | 521.36 | .22 |
| .01 | 334.91 | .42 | 377.69 | .43 | 420.34 | .42 | 460.33 | .37 | 494.94 | .31 | 521.58 | .21 |
| .02 | 335.33 | .43 | 378.12 | .43 | 420.76 | .41 | 460.70 | .38 | 495.25 | .31 | 521.79 | .22 |
| .03 | 335.76 | .42 | 378.55 | .43 | 421.17 | .42 | 461.08 | .37 | 495.56 | .31 | 522.01 | .21 |
| .04 | 336.18 | .42 | 378.98 | .43 | 421.59 | .42 | 461.45 | .38 | 495.87 | .31 | 522.22 | .22 |
| .05 | 336.60 | .42 | 379.41 | .43 | 422.01 | .42 | 461.83 | .37 | 496.18 | .30 | 522.44 | .21 |
| .06 | 337.02 | .42 | 379.84 | .43 | 422.43 | .41 | 462.20 | .38 | 496.48 | .31 | 522.65 | .21 |
| .07 | 337.44 | .43 | 380.27 | .44 | 422.84 | .42 | 462.58 | .37 | 496.79 | .30 | 522.86 | .22 |
| .08 | 337.87 | .42 | 380.71 | .43 | 423.26 | .41 | 462.95 | .38 | 497.09 | .31 | 523.08 | .21 |
| .09 | 338.29 | .42 | 381.14 | .43 | 423.67 | .42 | 463.33 | .37 | 497.40 | .30 | 523.29 | .21 |
| .10 | 338.71 | .42 | 381.57 | .43 | 424.09 | .41 | 463.70 | .37 | 497.70 | .30 | 523.50 | .21 |
| .11 | 339.13 | .42 | 382.00 | .43 | 424.50 | .42 | 464.07 | .37 | 498.00 | .30 | 523.71 | .20 |
| .12 | 339.55 | .43 | 382.43 | .43 | 424.92 | .41 | 464.44 | .38 | 498.30 | .31 | 523.91 | .21 |
| .13 | 339.98 | .42 | 382.86 | .43 | 425.33 | .42 | 464.82 | .37 | 498.61 | .30 | 524.12 | .20 |
| .14 | 340.40 | .42 | 383.29 | .43 | 425.75 | .41 | 465.19 | .37 | 498.91 | .30 | 524.32 | .21 |
| .15 | 340.82 | .42 | 383.72 | .43 | 426.16 | .41 | 465.56 | .37 | 499.21 | .30 | 524.53 | .20 |
| .16 | 341.24 | .43 | 384.15 | .43 | 426.57 | .41 | 465.93 | .37 | 499.51 | .29 | 524.73 | .20 |
| .17 | 341.67 | .42 | 384.58 | .43 | 426.98 | .42 | 466.30 | .36 | 499.80 | .30 | 524.93 | .21 |
| .18 | 342.09 | .43 | 385.01 | .43 | 427.40 | .41 | 466.66 | .37 | 500.10 | .29 | 525.14 | .20 |
| .19 | 342.52 | .42 | 385.44 | .43 | 427.81 | .41 | 467.03 | .37 | 500.39 | .30 | 525.34 | .20 |
| .20 | 342.94 | .42 | 385.87 | .43 | 428.22 | .41 | 467.40 | .36 | 500.69 | .29 | 525.54 | .20 |
| .21 | 343.36 | .43 | 386.30 | .43 | 428.63 | .41 | 467.76 | .37 | 500.98 | .30 | 525.74 | .19 |
| .22 | 343.79 | .42 | 386.73 | .44 | 429.04 | .42 | 468.13 | .36 | 501.28 | .29 | 525.93 | .20 |
| .23 | 344.21 | .43 | 387.17 | .43 | 429.46 | .41 | 468.49 | .37 | 501.57 | .30 | 526.13 | .19 |
| .24 | 344.64 | .42 | 387.60 | .43 | 429.87 | .41 | 468.86 | .36 | 501.87 | .29 | 526.32 | .20 |
| .25 | 345.06 | .43 | 388.03 | .43 | 430.28 | .41 | 469.22 | .36 | 502.16 | .29 | 526.52 | .19 |
| .26 | 345.49 | .42 | 388.46 | .43 | 430.69 | .41 | 469.58 | .37 | 502.45 | .29 | 526.71 | .19 |
| .27 | 345.91 | .43 | 388.89 | .43 | 431.10 | .41 | 469.95 | .36 | 502.74 | .28 | 526.90 | .19 |
| .28 | 346.34 | .42 | 389.32 | .43 | 431.51 | .41 | 470.31 | .37 | 503.02 | .29 | 527.09 | .19 |
| .29 | 346.76 | .43 | 389.75 | .43 | 431.92 | .41 | 470.68 | .36 | 503.31 | .29 | 527.28 | .19 |
| .30 | 347.19 | .43 | 390.18 | .43 | 432.33 | .41 | 471.04 | .36 | 503.60 | .28 | 527.47 | .19 |
| .31 | 347.62 | .43 | 390.61 | .43 | 432.74 | .41 | 471.40 | .36 | 503.88 | .28 | 527.66 | .18 |
| .32 | 348.05 | .42 | 391.04 | .42 | 433.15 | .40 | 471.76 | .35 | 504.16 | .29 | 527.84 | .19 |
| .33 | 348.47 | .43 | 391.46 | .43 | 433.55 | .41 | 472.11 | .36 | 504.45 | .28 | 528.03 | .18 |
| .34 | 348.90 | .43 | 391.89 | .43 | 433.96 | .41 | 472.47 | .36 | 504.73 | .28 | 528.21 | .19 |
| .35 | 349.33 | .43 | 392.32 | .43 | 434.37 | .41 | 472.83 | .36 | 505.01 | .28 | 528.40 | .18 |
| .36 | 349.76 | .42 | 392.75 | .43 | 434.78 | .40 | 473.19 | .35 | 505.29 | .28 | 528.58 | .18 |
| .37 | 350.18 | .43 | 393.18 | .43 | 435.18 | .41 | 473.54 | .36 | 505.57 | .28 | 528.76 | .18 |
| .38 | 350.61 | .42 | 393.61 | .43 | 435.59 | .40 | 473.90 | .35 | 505.85 | .28 | 528.94 | .18 |
| .39 | 351.03 | .43 | 394.04 | .43 | 435.99 | .41 | 474.25 | .36 | 506.13 | .28 | 529.12 | .18 |
| .40 | 351.46 | .43 | 394.47 | .43 | 436.40 | .40 | 474.61 | .35 | 506.41 | .28 | 529.30 | .17 |
| .41 | 351.89 | .43 | 394.90 | .43 | 436.80 | .41 | 474.96 | .36 | 506.69 | .27 | 529.47 | .18 |
| .42 | 352.32 | .42 | 395.33 | .42 | 437.21 | .40 | 475.32 | .35 | 506.96 | .28 | 529.65 | .17 |
| .43 | 352.74 | .43 | 395.75 | .43 | 437.61 | .41 | 475.67 | .36 | 507.24 | .27 | 529.82 | .18 |
| .44 | 353.17 | .43 | 396.18 | .43 | 438.02 | .40 | 476.03 | .35 | 507.51 | .28 | 530.00 | .17 |
| .45 | 353.60 | .43 | 396.61 | .43 | 438.42 | .40 | 476.38 | .35 | 507.79 | .27 | 530.17 | .17 |
| .46 | 354.03 | .43 | 397.04 | .43 | 438.82 | .40 | 476.73 | .35 | 508.06 | .27 | 530.34 | .17 |
| .47 | 354.46 | .42 | 397.47 | .42 | 439.22 | .41 | 477.08 | .35 | 508.33 | .27 | 530.51 | .17 |
| .48 | 354.88 | .43 | 397.89 | .43 | 439.63 | .40 | 477.43 | .35 | 508.60 | .27 | 530.68 | .17 |
| .49 | 355.31 | .43 | 398.32 | .43 | 440.03 | .40 | 477.78 | .35 | 508.87 | .27 | 530.85 | .17 |
| .50 | 355.74 | .43 | 398.75 | .43 | 440.43 | .40 | 478.13 | .35 | 509.14 | .27 | 531.02 | .16 |

# TABLE CX. ARGUMENT 1.

Equation $= 345''.58 + 186''.51 \cos x + 10''.17 \cos 2x + 0''.63 \cos 3x + 0''.04 \cos 4x.$

| Days. | 0 | | 1 | | 2 | | 3 | | 4 | | 5 | |
|---|---|---|---|---|---|---|---|---|---|---|---|---|
| Days. | Equation. | Diff. | Equation. | Diff. | Equation. | Diff. | Equation. | Diff. | Equation | Diff. | Equation. | Diff |
| d. | ″ | | ″ | | ″ | | ″ | | ″ | | ″ | |
| .50 | 355.74 | .43 | 398.75 | .43 | 440.43 | .40 | 478.13 | .35 | 509.14 | .27 | 531.02 | .16 |
| .51 | 356.17 | .43 | 399.18 | .43 | 440.83 | .40 | 478.48 | .34 | 509.41 | .26 | 531.18 | .17 |
| .52 | 356.60 | .43 | 399.61 | .42 | 441.23 | .40 | 478.82 | .35 | 509.67 | .27 | 531.35 | .16 |
| .53 | 357.03 | .43 | 400.03 | .43 | 441.63 | .40 | 479.17 | .34 | 509.94 | .26 | 531.51 | .17 |
| .54 | 357.46 | .43 | 400.46 | .43 | 442.03 | .40 | 479.51 | .35 | 510.20 | .27 | 531.68 | .16 |
| .55 | 357.89 | .43 | 400.89 | .43 | 442.43 | .40 | 479.86 | .34 | 510.47 | .26 | 531.84 | .16 |
| .56 | 358.32 | .43 | 401.32 | .42 | 442.83 | .40 | 480.20 | .34 | 510.73 | .26 | 532.00 | .16 |
| .57 | 358.75 | .42 | 401.74 | .43 | 443.23 | .40 | 480.54 | .35 | 510.99 | .27 | 532.16 | .15 |
| .58 | 359.17 | .43 | 402.17 | .42 | 443.63 | .40 | 480.89 | .34 | 511.26 | .26 | 532.31 | .16 |
| .59 | 359.60 | .43 | 402.59 | .43 | 444.03 | .40 | 481.23 | .34 | 511.52 | .26 | 532.47 | .16 |
| .60 | 360.03 | .43 | 403.02 | .43 | 444.43 | .40 | 481.57 | .34 | 511.78 | .26 | 532.63 | .15 |
| .61 | 360.46 | .43 | 403.45 | .42 | 444.83 | .39 | 481.91 | .34 | 512.04 | .25 | 532.78 | .15 |
| .62 | 360.89 | .43 | 403.87 | .43 | 445.22 | .40 | 482.25 | .34 | 512.29 | .26 | 532.93 | .16 |
| .63 | 361.32 | .43 | 404.30 | .42 | 445.62 | .39 | 482.59 | .34 | 512.55 | .25 | 533.09 | .15 |
| .64 | 361.75 | .43 | 404.72 | .43 | 446.01 | .40 | 482.93 | .34 | 512.80 | .26 | 533.24 | .15 |
| .65 | 362.18 | .43 | 405.15 | .43 | 446.41 | .39 | 483.27 | .34 | 513.06 | .25 | 533.39 | .15 |
| .66 | 362.61 | .43 | 405.58 | .42 | 446.80 | .40 | 483.61 | .33 | 513.31 | .25 | 533.54 | .14 |
| .67 | 363.04 | .43 | 406.00 | .43 | 447.20 | .39 | 483.94 | .34 | 513.56 | .26 | 533.68 | .15 |
| .68 | 363.47 | .43 | 406.43 | .42 | 447.59 | .40 | 484.28 | .33 | 513.82 | .25 | 533.83 | .14 |
| .69 | 363.90 | .43 | 406.85 | .43 | 447.99 | .39 | 484.61 | .34 | 514.07 | .25 | 533.97 | .15 |
| .70 | 364.33 | .43 | 407.28 | .42 | 448.38 | .39 | 484.95 | .33 | 514.32 | .25 | 534.12 | .14 |
| .71 | 364.76 | .43 | 407.70 | .43 | 448.77 | .39 | 485.28 | .33 | 514.57 | .24 | 534.26 | .14 |
| .72 | 365.19 | .43 | 408.13 | .42 | 449.16 | .40 | 485.61 | .34 | 514.81 | .25 | 534.40 | .14 |
| .73 | 365.62 | .43 | 408.55 | .43 | 449.56 | .39 | 485.95 | .33 | 515.06 | .24 | 534.54 | .14 |
| .74 | 366.05 | .43 | 408.98 | .42 | 449.95 | .39 | 486.28 | .33 | 515.30 | .25 | 534.68 | .14 |
| .75 | 366.48 | .43 | 409.40 | .42 | 450.34 | .39 | 486.61 | .33 | 515.55 | .24 | 534.82 | .14 |
| .76 | 366.91 | .43 | 409.82 | .42 | 450.73 | .39 | 486.94 | .33 | 515.79 | .24 | 534.96 | .13 |
| .77 | 367.34 | .44 | 410.24 | .43 | 451.12 | .38 | 487.27 | .32 | 516.03 | .25 | 535.09 | .14 |
| .78 | 367.78 | .43 | 410.67 | .42 | 451.50 | .39 | 487.59 | .33 | 516.28 | .24 | 535.23 | .13 |
| .79 | 368.21 | .43 | 411.09 | .42 | 451.89 | .39 | 487.92 | .33 | 516.52 | .24 | 535.36 | .14 |
| .80 | 368.64 | .43 | 411.51 | .42 | 452.28 | .39 | 488.25 | .33 | 516.76 | .24 | 535.50 | .13 |
| .81 | 369.07 | .43 | 411.93 | .42 | 452.67 | .39 | 488.58 | .32 | 517.00 | .24 | 535.63 | .13 |
| .82 | 369.50 | .43 | 412.35 | .43 | 453.06 | .38 | 488.90 | .33 | 517.24 | .23 | 535.76 | .13 |
| .83 | 369.93 | .43 | 412.78 | .42 | 453.44 | .39 | 489.23 | .32 | 517.47 | .24 | 535.89 | .13 |
| .84 | 370.36 | .43 | 413.20 | .42 | 453.83 | .39 | 489.55 | .33 | 517.71 | .24 | 536.02 | .13 |
| .85 | 370.79 | .43 | 413.62 | .42 | 454.22 | .38 | 489.88 | .32 | 517.95 | .23 | 536.15 | .12 |
| .86 | 371.22 | .43 | 414.04 | .42 | 454.60 | .39 | 490.20 | .32 | 518.18 | .23 | 536.27 | .13 |
| .87 | 371.65 | .44 | 414.46 | .43 | 454.99 | .38 | 490.52 | .32 | 518.41 | .24 | 536.40 | .12 |
| .88 | 372.09 | .43 | 414.89 | .42 | 455.37 | .39 | 490.84 | .32 | 518.65 | .23 | 536.52 | .13 |
| .89 | 372.52 | .43 | 415.31 | .42 | 455.76 | .38 | 491.16 | .32 | 518.88 | .23 | 536.65 | .12 |
| .90 | 372.95 | .43 | 415.73 | .42 | 456.14 | .38 | 491.48 | .32 | 519.11 | .23 | 536.77 | .12 |
| .91 | 373.38 | .43 | 416.15 | .42 | 456.52 | .38 | 491.80 | .32 | 519.34 | .23 | 536.89 | .12 |
| .92 | 373.81 | .43 | 416.57 | .42 | 456.90 | .39 | 492.12 | .32 | 519.57 | .22 | 537.01 | .11 |
| .93 | 374.24 | .43 | 416.99 | .42 | 457.29 | .38 | 492.43 | .32 | 519.79 | .23 | 537.12 | .12 |
| .94 | 374.67 | .43 | 417.41 | .42 | 457.67 | .38 | 492.75 | .32 | 520.02 | .23 | 537.24 | .12 |
| .95 | 375.10 | .43 | 417.83 | .42 | 458.05 | .38 | 493.07 | .31 | 520.25 | .22 | 537.36 | .11 |
| .96 | 375.53 | .43 | 418.25 | .42 | 458.43 | .38 | 493.38 | .31 | 520.47 | .22 | 537.47 | .11 |
| .97 | 375.96 | .44 | 418.67 | .41 | 458.81 | .38 | 493.69 | .32 | 520.69 | .23 | 537.58 | .12 |
| .98 | 376.40 | .43 | 419.08 | .42 | 459.19 | .38 | 494.01 | .31 | 520.92 | .22 | 537.70 | .11 |
| .99 | 376.83 | .43 | 419.50 | .42 | 459.57 | .38 | 494.32 | .31 | 521.14 | .22 | 537.81 | .11 |
| 1.00 | 377.26 | .43 | 419.92 | .43 | 459.95 | .38 | 494.63 | .31 | 521.36 | .22 | 537.92 | .11 |

# TABLE CX. ARGUMENT i.

Equation $= 345''.58 + 186''.51 \cos x + 10''.17 \cos 2x + 0''.63 \cos 3x + 0''.04 \cos 4x$.

| Days. | 6 | | 7 | | 8 | | 9 | | 10 | | 11 | |
|---|---|---|---|---|---|---|---|---|---|---|---|---|
| Days. | Equation. | Diff. | Equation. | Diff. | Equation. | Diff. | Equation. | Diff. | Equation. | Diff. | Equation. | Diff. |
| d. | ″ | | ″ | | ″ | | ″ | | ″ | | ″ | |
| .00 | 537.92 | .11 | 542.88 | .01 | 535.80 | .13 | 517.31 | .24 | 488.99 | .33 | 453.16 | .39 |
| .01 | 538.03 | .10 | 542.87 | .01 | 535.67 | .13 | 517.07 | .24 | 488.66 | .32 | 452.77 | .39 |
| .02 | 538.13 | .11 | 542.86 | .02 | 535.54 | .14 | 516.83 | .24 | 488.34 | .33 | 452.38 | .38 |
| .03 | 538.24 | .10 | 542.84 | .01 | 535.40 | .13 | 516.59 | .24 | 488.01 | .32 | 452.00 | .39 |
| .04 | 538.34 | .11 | 542.83 | .01 | 535.27 | .13 | 516.35 | .24 | 487.69 | .33 | 451.61 | .39 |
| .05 | 538.45 | .10 | 542.82 | .02 | 535.14 | .14 | 516.11 | .25 | 487.36 | .33 | 451.22 | .39 |
| .06 | 538.55 | .10 | 542.80 | .02 | 535.00 | .14 | 515.86 | .24 | 487.03 | .33 | 450.83 | .39 |
| .07 | 538.65 | .10 | 542.78 | .02 | 534.86 | .13 | 515.62 | .25 | 486.70 | .33 | 450.44 | .39 |
| .08 | 538.75 | .10 | 542.76 | .02 | 534.73 | .14 | 515.37 | .24 | 486.37 | .33 | 450.05 | .39 |
| .09 | 538.85 | .10 | 542.74 | .02 | 534.59 | .14 | 515.13 | .25 | 486.04 | .33 | 449.66 | .39 |
| .10 | 538.95 | .09 | 542.72 | .03 | 534.45 | .14 | 514.88 | .25 | 485.71 | .33 | 449.27 | .39 |
| .11 | 539.04 | .10 | 542.69 | .02 | 534.31 | .15 | 514.63 | .25 | 485.38 | .34 | 448.88 | .40 |
| .12 | 539.14 | .09 | 542.67 | .03 | 534.16 | .14 | 514.38 | .25 | 485.04 | .33 | 448.48 | .39 |
| .13 | 539.23 | .10 | 542.64 | .02 | 534.02 | .15 | 514.13 | .25 | 484.71 | .34 | 448.09 | .40 |
| .14 | 539.33 | .09 | 542.62 | .03 | 533.87 | .14 | 513.88 | .25 | 484.37 | .33 | 447.69 | .39 |
| .15 | 539.42 | .09 | 542.59 | .03 | 533.73 | .15 | 513.63 | .25 | 484.04 | .34 | 447.30 | .39 |
| .16 | 539.51 | .09 | 542.56 | .03 | 533.58 | .15 | 513.38 | .26 | 483.70 | .34 | 446.91 | .40 |
| .17 | 539.60 | .09 | 542.53 | .04 | 533.43 | .15 | 513.12 | .25 | 483.36 | .33 | 446.51 | .39 |
| .18 | 539.69 | .09 | 542.49 | .03 | 533.28 | .15 | 512.87 | .26 | 483.03 | .34 | 446.12 | .40 |
| .19 | 539.78 | .09 | 542.46 | .03 | 533.13 | .15 | 512.61 | .25 | 482.69 | .34 | 445.72 | .39 |
| .20 | 539.87 | .08 | 542.43 | .04 | 532.98 | .16 | 512.36 | .26 | 482.35 | .34 | 445.33 | .40 |
| .21 | 539.95 | .08 | 542.39 | .04 | 532.82 | .15 | 512.10 | .26 | 482.01 | .34 | 444.93 | .40 |
| .22 | 540.03 | .09 | 542.35 | .03 | 532.67 | .16 | 511.84 | .25 | 481.67 | .35 | 444.53 | .39 |
| .23 | 540.12 | .08 | 542.32 | .04 | 532.51 | .15 | 511.59 | .26 | 481.32 | .34 | 444.14 | .40 |
| .24 | 540.20 | .08 | 542.28 | .04 | 532.36 | .16 | 511.33 | .26 | 480.98 | .34 | 443.74 | .40 |
| .25 | 540.28 | .08 | 542.24 | .04 | 532.20 | .16 | 511.07 | .26 | 480.64 | .34 | 443.34 | .40 |
| .26 | 540.36 | .08 | 542.20 | .05 | 532.04 | .16 | 510.81 | .27 | 480.30 | .35 | 442.94 | .40 |
| .27 | 540.44 | .07 | 542.15 | .04 | 531.88 | .17 | 510.54 | .26 | 479.95 | .34 | 442.54 | .40 |
| .28 | 540.51 | .08 | 542.11 | .05 | 531.71 | .16 | 510.28 | .27 | 479.61 | .35 | 442.14 | .40 |
| .29 | 540.59 | .08 | 542.06 | .04 | 531.55 | .16 | 510.01 | .26 | 479.26 | .34 | 441.74 | .40 |
| .30 | 540.67 | .07 | 542.02 | .05 | 531.39 | .17 | 509.75 | .27 | 478.92 | .35 | 441.34 | .40 |
| .31 | 540.74 | .07 | 541.97 | .05 | 531.22 | .16 | 509.48 | .27 | 478.57 | .35 | 440.94 | .40 |
| .32 | 540.81 | .07 | 541.92 | .05 | 531.06 | .17 | 509.21 | .26 | 478.22 | .34 | 440.54 | .40 |
| .33 | 540.88 | .07 | 541.87 | .05 | 530.89 | .16 | 508.95 | .27 | 477.88 | .35 | 440.14 | .40 |
| .34 | 540.95 | .07 | 541.82 | .05 | 530.73 | .17 | 508.68 | .27 | 477.53 | .35 | 439.74 | .40 |
| .35 | 541.02 | .07 | 541.77 | .06 | 530.56 | .17 | 508.41 | .27 | 477.18 | .35 | 439.34 | .40 |
| .36 | 541.09 | .06 | 541.71 | .05 | 530.39 | .17 | 508.14 | .28 | 476.83 | .35 | 438.94 | .41 |
| .37 | 541.15 | .07 | 541.66 | .06 | 530.22 | .18 | 507.86 | .27 | 476.48 | .36 | 438.53 | .40 |
| .38 | 541.22 | .06 | 541.60 | .05 | 530.04 | .17 | 507.59 | .28 | 476.12 | .35 | 438.13 | .41 |
| .39 | 541.28 | .07 | 541.55 | .06 | 529.87 | .17 | 507.31 | .27 | 475.77 | .35 | 437.72 | .40 |
| .40 | 541.35 | .06 | 541.49 | .06 | 529.70 | .18 | 507.04 | .28 | 475.42 | .35 | 437.32 | .41 |
| .41 | 541.41 | .06 | 541.43 | .06 | 529.52 | .18 | 506.76 | .27 | 475.07 | .36 | 436.91 | .40 |
| .42 | 541.47 | .05 | 541.37 | .07 | 529.34 | .17 | 506.49 | .28 | 474.71 | .35 | 436.51 | .41 |
| .43 | 541.52 | .06 | 541.30 | .06 | 529.17 | .18 | 506.21 | .27 | 474.36 | .36 | 436.10 | .40 |
| .44 | 541.58 | .06 | 541.24 | .06 | 528.99 | .18 | 505.94 | .28 | 474.00 | .35 | 435.70 | .41 |
| .45 | 541.64 | .05 | 541.18 | .07 | 528.81 | .18 | 505.66 | .28 | 473.65 | .36 | 435.29 | .41 |
| .46 | 541.69 | .05 | 541.11 | .07 | 528.63 | .18 | 505.38 | .28 | 473.29 | .36 | 434.88 | .40 |
| .47 | 541.74 | .06 | 541.04 | .07 | 528.45 | .19 | 505.10 | .29 | 472.93 | .35 | 434.48 | .41 |
| .48 | 541.80 | .05 | 540.97 | .07 | 528.26 | .18 | 504.81 | .28 | 472.58 | .36 | 434.07 | .40 |
| .49 | 541.85 | .05 | 540.90 | .07 | 528.08 | .18 | 504.53 | .28 | 472.22 | .36 | 433.67 | .41 |
| .50 | 541.90 | .05 | 540.83 | .07 | 527.90 | .19 | 504.25 | .29 | 471.86 | .36 | 433.26 | .41 |

# TABLE CX. ARGUMENT 1.

$$\text{Equation} = 345''.58 + 186''.51 \cos x + 10''.17 \cos 2x + 0''.63 \cos 3x + 0''.04 \cos 4x.$$

| Days. | 6 | | 7 | | 8 | | 9 | | 10 | | 11 | |
|---|---|---|---|---|---|---|---|---|---|---|---|---|
| Days. | Equation. | Diff. | Equation. | Diff. | Equation. | Diff. | Equation. | Diff. | Equation | Diff. | Equation. | Diff. |
| d. .50 | 541.90″ | .05 | 540.83″ | .07 | 527.90″ | .19 | 504.25″ | .29 | 471.86″ | .36 | 433.26″ | .41 |
| .51 | 541.95 | .05 | 540.76 | .08 | 527.71 | .19 | 503.96 | .29 | 471.50 | .36 | 432.85 | .41 |
| .52 | 542.00 | .04 | 540.68 | .07 | 527.52 | .18 | 503.67 | .28 | 471.14 | .37 | 432.44 | .41 |
| .53 | 542.04 | .05 | 540.61 | .08 | 527.34 | .19 | 503.39 | .29 | 470.77 | .36 | 432.03 | .41 |
| .54 | 542.09 | .05 | 540.53 | .07 | 527.15 | .19 | 503.10 | .29 | 470.41 | .36 | 431.62 | .41 |
| .55 | 542.14 | .04 | 540.46 | .08 | 526.96 | .19 | 502.81 | .29 | 470.05 | .36 | 431.21 | .41 |
| .56 | 542.18 | .04 | 540.38 | .08 | 526.77 | .20 | 502.52 | .29 | 469.69 | .37 | 430.80 | .41 |
| .57 | 542.22 | .04 | 540.30 | .08 | 526.57 | .19 | 502.23 | .29 | 469.32 | .36 | 430.39 | .41 |
| .58 | 542.26 | .04 | 540.22 | .08 | 526.38 | .20 | 501.94 | .29 | 468.96 | .37 | 429.98 | .41 |
| .59 | 542.30 | .04 | 540.14 | .08 | 526.18 | .19 | 501.65 | .29 | 468.59 | .36 | 429.57 | .41 |
| .60 | 542.34 | .04 | 540.06 | .09 | 525.99 | .20 | 501.36 | .29 | 468.23 | .37 | 429.16 | .41 |
| .61 | 542.38 | .03 | 539.97 | .08 | 525.79 | .20 | 501.07 | .30 | 467.86 | .37 | 428.75 | .41 |
| .62 | 542.41 | .04 | 539.89 | .09 | 525.59 | .20 | 500.77 | .29 | 467.49 | .36 | 428.34 | .42 |
| .63 | 542.45 | .03 | 539.80 | .08 | 525.39 | .20 | 500.48 | .30 | 467.13 | .37 | 427.92 | .41 |
| .64 | 542.48 | .04 | 539.72 | .09 | 525.19 | .20 | 500.18 | .29 | 466.76 | .37 | 427.51 | .41 |
| .65 | 542.52 | .03 | 539.63 | .09 | 524.99 | .20 | 499.89 | .30 | 466.39 | .37 | 427.10 | .41 |
| .66 | 542.55 | .03 | 539.54 | .09 | 524.79 | .21 | 499.59 | .30 | 466.02 | .37 | 426.69 | .42 |
| .67 | 542.58 | .02 | 539.45 | .10 | 524.58 | .20 | 499.29 | .30 | 465.65 | .37 | 426.27 | .41 |
| .68 | 542.60 | .03 | 539.35 | .09 | 524.38 | .21 | 498.99 | .30 | 465.28 | .37 | 425.86 | .42 |
| .69 | 542.63 | .03 | 539.26 | .09 | 524.17 | .20 | 498.69 | .30 | 464.91 | .37 | 425.44 | .41 |
| .70 | 542.66 | .02 | 539.17 | .10 | 523.97 | .21 | 498.39 | .30 | 464.54 | .37 | 425.03 | .42 |
| .71 | 542.68 | .02 | 539.07 | .10 | 523.76 | .21 | 498.09 | .30 | 464.17 | .37 | 424.61 | .41 |
| .72 | 542.70 | .03 | 538.97 | .09 | 523.55 | .21 | 497.79 | .31 | 463.80 | .38 | 424.20 | .42 |
| .73 | 542.73 | .02 | 538.88 | .10 | 523.34 | .21 | 497.48 | .30 | 463.42 | .37 | 423.78 | .41 |
| .74 | 542.75 | .02 | 538.78 | .10 | 523.13 | .21 | 497.18 | .30 | 463.05 | .37 | 423.37 | .42 |
| .75 | 542.77 | .02 | 538.68 | .10 | 522.92 | .21 | 496.88 | .31 | 462.68 | .38 | 422.95 | .42 |
| .76 | 542.79 | .02 | 538.58 | .11 | 522.71 | .22 | 496.57 | .31 | 462.30 | .37 | 422.53 | .41 |
| .77 | 542.81 | .01 | 538.47 | .10 | 522.49 | .21 | 496.26 | .30 | 461.93 | .38 | 422.12 | .42 |
| .78 | 542.82 | .02 | 538.37 | .11 | 522.28 | .22 | 495.96 | .31 | 461.55 | .37 | 421.70 | .41 |
| .79 | 542.84 | .02 | 538.26 | .10 | 522.06 | .21 | 495.65 | .31 | 461.18 | .38 | 421.29 | .42 |
| .80 | 542.86 | .01 | 538.16 | .11 | 521.85 | .22 | 495.34 | .31 | 460.80 | .38 | 420.87 | .42 |
| .81 | 542.87 | .01 | 538.05 | .11 | 521.63 | .22 | 495.03 | .31 | 460.42 | .38 | 420.45 | .42 |
| .82 | 542.88 | .01 | 537.94 | .10 | 521.41 | .22 | 494.72 | .32 | 460.04 | .37 | 420.03 | .41 |
| .83 | 542.89 | .01 | 537.84 | .11 | 521.19 | .22 | 494.40 | .31 | 459.67 | .38 | 419.62 | .42 |
| .84 | 542.90 | .01 | 537.73 | .11 | 520.97 | .22 | 494.09 | .31 | 459.29 | .38 | 419.20 | .42 |
| .85 | 542.91 | .00 | 537.62 | .12 | 520.75 | .22 | 493.78 | .31 | 458.91 | .38 | 418.78 | .42 |
| .86 | 542.91 | .01 | 537.50 | .11 | 520.53 | .23 | 493.47 | .32 | 458.53 | .38 | 418.36 | .42 |
| .87 | 542.92 | .00 | 537.39 | .12 | 520.30 | .22 | 493.15 | .31 | 458.15 | .38 | 417.94 | .42 |
| .88 | 542.92 | .01 | 537.27 | .11 | 520.08 | .23 | 492.84 | .32 | 457.77 | .38 | 417.52 | .42 |
| .89 | 542.93 | .00 | 537.16 | .12 | 519.85 | .22 | 492.52 | .31 | 457.39 | .38 | 417.10 | .42 |
| .90 | 542.93 | .00 | 537.04 | .12 | 519.63 | .23 | 492.21 | .32 | 457.01 | .38 | 416.68 | .42 |
| .91 | 542.93 | .00 | 536.92 | .12 | 519.40 | .23 | 491.89 | .32 | 456.63 | .39 | 416.26 | .42 |
| .92 | 542.93 | .01 | 536.80 | .13 | 519.17 | .23 | 491.57 | .32 | 456.24 | .38 | 415.84 | .42 |
| .93 | 542.92 | .00 | 536.67 | .12 | 518.94 | .23 | 491.25 | .32 | 455.86 | .39 | 415.42 | .42 |
| .94 | 542.92 | .00 | 536.55 | .12 | 518.71 | .23 | 490.93 | .32 | 455.47 | .38 | 415.00 | .42 |
| .95 | 542.92 | .01 | 536.43 | .13 | 518.48 | .23 | 490.61 | .32 | 455.09 | .39 | 414.58 | .42 |
| 96 | 542.91 | .01 | 536.30 | .12 | 518.25 | .24 | 490.29 | .33 | 454.70 | .38 | 414.16 | .42 |
| .97 | 542.90 | .00 | 536.18 | .13 | 518.01 | .23 | 489.96 | .32 | 454.32 | .39 | 413.74 | .43 |
| .98 | 542.90 | .01 | 536.05 | .12 | 517.78 | .24 | 489.64 | .33 | 453.93 | .38 | 413.31 | .42 |
| .99 | 542.89 | .01 | 535.93 | .13 | 517.54 | .23 | 489.31 | .32 | 453.55 | .39 | 412.89 | .42 |
| 1.00 | 542.88 | .01 | 535.80 | .13 | 517.31 | .24 | 488.99 | .33 | 453.16 | .39 | 412.47 | .42 |

# TABLE CX. ARGUMENT 1.

$$\text{Equation} = 345''.58 + 186''.51 \cos x + 10''.17 \cos 2x + 0''.63 \cos 3x + 0''.04 \cos 4x.$$

| Days. | 12 | | 13 | | 14 | | 15 | | 16 | | 17 | |
|---|---|---|---|---|---|---|---|---|---|---|---|---|
| Days. | Equation. | Diff. | Equation. | Diff. | Equation. | Diff. | Equation. | Diff. | Equation. | Diff. | Equation. | Diff. |
| d. | ″ | | ″ | | ″ | | ″ | | ″ | | ″ | |
| .00 | 412.47 | .42 | 369.62 | .43 | 327.07 | .42 | 286.97 | .38 | 251.04 | .33 | 220.59 | .27 |
| .01 | 412.05 | .42 | 369.19 | .43 | 326.65 | .41 | 286.59 | .38 | 250.71 | .33 | 220.32 | .27 |
| .02 | 411.63 | .43 | 368.76 | .44 | 326.24 | .42 | 286.21 | .38 | 250.38 | .34 | 220.05 | .28 |
| .03 | 411.20 | .42 | 368.32 | .43 | 325.82 | .41 | 285.83 | .38 | 250.04 | .33 | 219.77 | .27 |
| .04 | 410.78 | .42 | 367.89 | .43 | 325.41 | .42 | 285.45 | .38 | 249.71 | .33 | 219.50 | .27 |
| .05 | 410.36 | .42 | 367.46 | .43 | 324.99 | .41 | 285.07 | .38 | 249.38 | .33 | 219.23 | .27 |
| .06 | 409.94 | .43 | 367.03 | .43 | 324.58 | .42 | 284.69 | .38 | 249.05 | .33 | 218.96 | .27 |
| .07 | 409.51 | .42 | 366.60 | .43 | 324.16 | .41 | 284.31 | .38 | 248.72 | .33 | 218.69 | .26 |
| .08 | 409.09 | .43 | 366.17 | .43 | 323.75 | .42 | 283.93 | .38 | 248.39 | .33 | 218.43 | .27 |
| .09 | 408.66 | .42 | 365.74 | .43 | 323.33 | .41 | 283.55 | .38 | 248.06 | .33 | 218.16 | .27 |
| .10 | 408.24 | .42 | 365.31 | .43 | 322.92 | .41 | 283.17 | .38 | 247.73 | .33 | 217.89 | .27 |
| .11 | 407.82 | .43 | 364.88 | .43 | 322.51 | .41 | 282.79 | .38 | 247.40 | .33 | 217.62 | .26 |
| .12 | 407.39 | .42 | 364.45 | .43 | 322.10 | .42 | 282.41 | .37 | 247.07 | .32 | 217.36 | .27 |
| .13 | 406.97 | .43 | 364.02 | .43 | 321.68 | .41 | 282.04 | .38 | 246.75 | .33 | 217.09 | .26 |
| .14 | 406.54 | .42 | 363.59 | .43 | 321.27 | .41 | 281.66 | .38 | 246.42 | .33 | 216.83 | .27 |
| .15 | 406.12 | .43 | 363.16 | .43 | 320.86 | .41 | 281.28 | .37 | 246.09 | .32 | 216.56 | .26 |
| .16 | 405.69 | .42 | 362.73 | .43 | 320.45 | .41 | 280.91 | .38 | 245.77 | .33 | 216.30 | .26 |
| .17 | 405.27 | .43 | 362.30 | .43 | 320.04 | .42 | 280.53 | .37 | 245.44 | .32 | 216.04 | .27 |
| .18 | 404.84 | .42 | 361.87 | .43 | 319.62 | .41 | 280.16 | .38 | 245.12 | .33 | 215.77 | .26 |
| .19 | 404.42 | .43 | 361.44 | .43 | 319.21 | .41 | 279.78 | .37 | 244.79 | .32 | 215.51 | .26 |
| .20 | 403.99 | .43 | 361.01 | .43 | 318.80 | .41 | 279.41 | .37 | 244.47 | .32 | 215.25 | .26 |
| .21 | 403.56 | .42 | 360.58 | .43 | 318.39 | .41 | 279.04 | .38 | 244.15 | .32 | 214.99 | .26 |
| .22 | 403.14 | .43 | 360.15 | .43 | 317.98 | .42 | 278.66 | .37 | 243.83 | .32 | 214.73 | .25 |
| .23 | 402.71 | .42 | 359.72 | .43 | 317.56 | .41 | 278.29 | .38 | 243.51 | .32 | 214.48 | .26 |
| .24 | 402.29 | .43 | 359.29 | .43 | 317.15 | .41 | 277.91 | .37 | 243.19 | .32 | 214.22 | .26 |
| .25 | 401.86 | .43 | 358.86 | .43 | 316.74 | .41 | 277.54 | .37 | 242.87 | .32 | 213.96 | .26 |
| .26 | 401.43 | .43 | 358.43 | .43 | 316.33 | .41 | 277.17 | .37 | 242.55 | .32 | 213.70 | .25 |
| .27 | 401.00 | .42 | 358.00 | .42 | 315.92 | .40 | 276.80 | .37 | 242.23 | .32 | 213.45 | .26 |
| .28 | 400.58 | .43 | 357.58 | .43 | 315.52 | .41 | 276.43 | .37 | 241.91 | .32 | 213.19 | .25 |
| .29 | 400.15 | .43 | 357.15 | .43 | 315.11 | .41 | 276.06 | .37 | 241.59 | .32 | 212.94 | .26 |
| .30 | 399.72 | .43 | 356.72 | .43 | 314.70 | .41 | 275.69 | .37 | 241.27 | .31 | 212.68 | .25 |
| .31 | 399.29 | .42 | 356.29 | .43 | 314.29 | .41 | 275.32 | .37 | 240.96 | .32 | 212.43 | .25 |
| .32 | 398.87 | .43 | 355.86 | .42 | 313.88 | .40 | 274.95 | .36 | 240.64 | .31 | 212.18 | .26 |
| .33 | 398.44 | .42 | 355.44 | .43 | 313.48 | .41 | 274.59 | .37 | 240.33 | .32 | 211.92 | .25 |
| .34 | 398.02 | .43 | 355.01 | .43 | 313.07 | .41 | 274.22 | .37 | 240.01 | .31 | 211.67 | .25 |
| .35 | 397.59 | .43 | 354.58 | .43 | 312.66 | .41 | 273.85 | .37 | 239.70 | .31 | 211.42 | .25 |
| .36 | 397.16 | .43 | 354.15 | .43 | 312.25 | .40 | 273.48 | .36 | 239.39 | .31 | 211.17 | .25 |
| .37 | 396.73 | .43 | 353.72 | .42 | 311.85 | .41 | 273.12 | .37 | 239.08 | .32 | 210.92 | .24 |
| .38 | 396.30 | .43 | 353.30 | .43 | 311.44 | .40 | 272.75 | .36 | 238.76 | .31 | 210.68 | .25 |
| .39 | 395.87 | .43 | 352.87 | .43 | 311.04 | .41 | 272.39 | .37 | 238.45 | .31 | 210.43 | .25 |
| .40 | 395.44 | .43 | 352.44 | .43 | 310.63 | .40 | 272.02 | .36 | 238.14 | .31 | 210.18 | .25 |
| .41 | 395.01 | .43 | 352.01 | .43 | 310.23 | .41 | 271.66 | .37 | 237.83 | .31 | 209.93 | .24 |
| .42 | 394.58 | .42 | 351.58 | .42 | 309.82 | .40 | 271.29 | .36 | 237.52 | .31 | 209.69 | .25 |
| .43 | 394.16 | .43 | 351.16 | .43 | 309.42 | .41 | 270.93 | .37 | 237.21 | .31 | 209.44 | .24 |
| .44 | 393.73 | .43 | 350.73 | .43 | 309.01 | .40 | 270.56 | .36 | 236.90 | .31 | 209.20 | .25 |
| .45 | 393.30 | .43 | 350.30 | .43 | 308.61 | .40 | 270.20 | .36 | 236.59 | .31 | 208.95 | .24 |
| .46 | 392.87 | .43 | 349.87 | .42 | 308.21 | .40 | 269.84 | .36 | 236.28 | .30 | 208.71 | .24 |
| .47 | 392.44 | .43 | 349.45 | .43 | 307.81 | .41 | 269.48 | .37 | 235.98 | .31 | 208.47 | .25 |
| .48 | 392.01 | .43 | 349.02 | .42 | 307.40 | .40 | 269.11 | .36 | 235.67 | .30 | 208.22 | .24 |
| .49 | 391.58 | .43 | 348.60 | .43 | 307.00 | .40 | 268.75 | .36 | 235.37 | .31 | 207.98 | .24 |
| .50 | 391.15 | .43 | 348.17 | .43 | 306.60 | .40 | 268.39 | .36 | 235.06 | .30 | 207.74 | .24 |

# TABLE CX. ARGUMENT 1.

Equation = $345''.58 + 186''.51 \cos x + 10''.17 \cos 2x + 0''.63 \cos 3x + 0''.04 \cos 4x$.

| Days. | 12 | | 13 | | 14 | | 15 | | 16 | | 17 | |
|---|---|---|---|---|---|---|---|---|---|---|---|---|
| Days. | Equation. | Diff. | Equation. | Diff. | Equation | Diff. | Equation. | Diff. | Equation | Diff. | Equation. | Diff. |
| d. | " | | " | | " | | " | | " | | " | |
| .50 | 391.15 | .43 | 348.17 | .43 | 306.60 | .40 | 268.39 | .36 | 235.06 | .30 | 207.74 | .24 |
| .51 | 390.72 | .43 | 347.74 | .42 | 306.20 | .40 | 268.03 | .36 | 234.76 | .31 | 207.50 | .24 |
| .52 | 390.29 | .43 | 347.32 | .43 | 305.80 | .40 | 267.67 | .35 | 234.45 | .30 | 207.26 | .23 |
| .53 | 389.86 | .43 | 346.89 | .42 | 305.40 | .40 | 267.32 | .36 | 234.15 | .31 | 207.03 | .24 |
| .54 | 389.43 | .43 | 346.47 | .43 | 305.00 | .40 | 266.96 | .36 | 233.84 | .30 | 206.79 | .24 |
| .55 | 389.00 | .43 | 346.04 | .43 | 304.60 | .40 | 266.60 | .36 | 233.54 | .30 | 206.55 | .23 |
| .56 | 388.57 | .43 | 345.61 | .42 | 304.20 | .40 | 266.24 | .35 | 233.24 | .30 | 206.32 | .24 |
| .57 | 388.14 | .43 | 345.19 | .43 | 303.80 | .40 | 265.89 | .36 | 232.94 | .30 | 206.08 | .23 |
| .58 | 387.71 | .43 | 344.76 | .42 | 303.40 | .40 | 265.53 | .35 | 232.64 | .30 | 205.85 | .24 |
| .59 | 387.28 | .43 | 344.34 | .43 | 303.00 | .40 | 265.18 | .36 | 232.34 | .30 | 205.61 | .23 |
| .60 | 386.85 | .43 | 343.91 | .42 | 302.60 | .40 | 264.82 | .35 | 232.04 | .30 | 205.38 | .23 |
| .61 | 386.42 | .43 | 343.49 | .43 | 302.20 | .40 | 264.47 | .36 | 231.74 | .30 | 205.15 | .23 |
| .62 | 385.99 | .43 | 343.06 | .42 | 301.80 | .39 | 264.11 | .35 | 231.44 | .29 | 204.92 | .24 |
| .63 | 385.56 | .43 | 342.64 | .43 | 301.41 | .40 | 263.76 | .36 | 231.15 | .30 | 204.68 | .23 |
| .64 | 385.13 | .43 | 342.21 | .42 | 301.01 | .40 | 263.40 | .35 | 230.85 | .30 | 204.45 | .23 |
| .65 | 384.70 | .43 | 341.79 | .42 | 300.61 | .39 | 263.05 | .35 | 230.55 | .29 | 204.22 | .23 |
| .66 | 384.27 | .43 | 341.37 | .43 | 300.22 | .40 | 262.70 | .35 | 230.26 | .30 | 203.99 | .23 |
| .67 | 383.84 | .43 | 340.94 | .42 | 299.82 | .39 | 262.35 | .35 | 229.96 | .29 | 203.76 | .22 |
| .68 | 383.41 | .43 | 340.52 | .43 | 299.43 | .40 | 262.00 | .35 | 229.67 | .30 | 203.54 | .23 |
| .69 | 382.98 | .43 | 340.09 | .42 | 299.03 | .39 | 261.65 | .35 | 229.37 | .29 | 203.31 | .23 |
| .70 | 382.55 | .43 | 339.67 | .42 | 298.64 | .39 | 261.30 | .35 | 229.08 | .29 | 203.08 | .22 |
| .71 | 382.12 | .43 | 339.25 | .42 | 298.25 | .40 | 260.95 | .35 | 228.79 | .29 | 202.86 | .23 |
| .72 | 381.69 | .44 | 338.83 | .43 | 297.85 | .39 | 260.60 | .35 | 228.50 | .29 | 202.63 | .22 |
| .73 | 381.25 | .43 | 338.40 | .42 | 297.46 | .40 | 260.25 | .35 | 228.21 | .29 | 202.41 | .23 |
| .74 | 380.82 | .43 | 337.98 | .42 | 297.06 | .39 | 259.90 | .35 | 227.92 | .29 | 202.18 | .22 |
| .75 | 380.39 | .43 | 337.56 | .42 | 296.67 | .39 | 259.55 | .35 | 227.63 | .29 | 201.96 | .22 |
| .76 | 379.96 | .43 | 337.14 | .42 | 296.28 | .39 | 259.20 | .34 | 227.34 | .29 | 201.74 | .22 |
| .77 | 379.53 | .43 | 336.72 | .43 | 295.89 | .40 | 258.86 | .35 | 227.05 | .28 | 201.52 | .23 |
| .78 | 379.10 | .43 | 336.29 | .42 | 295.49 | .39 | 258.51 | .34 | 226.77 | .29 | 201.29 | .22 |
| .79 | 378.67 | .43 | 335.87 | .42 | 295.10 | .39 | 258.17 | .35 | 226.48 | .29 | 201.07 | .22 |
| .80 | 378.24 | .43 | 335.45 | .42 | 294.71 | .39 | 257.82 | .34 | 226.19 | .29 | 200.85 | .22 |
| .81 | 377.81 | .43 | 335.03 | .42 | 294.32 | .39 | 257.48 | .34 | 225.90 | .28 | 200.63 | .22 |
| .82 | 377.38 | .44 | 334.61 | .42 | 293.93 | .39 | 257.14 | .35 | 225.62 | .29 | 200.41 | .21 |
| .83 | 376.94 | .43 | 334.19 | .42 | 293.54 | .39 | 256.79 | .34 | 225.33 | .28 | 200.20 | .22 |
| .84 | 376.51 | .43 | 333.77 | .42 | 293.15 | .39 | 256.45 | .34 | 225.05 | .29 | 199.98 | .22 |
| .85 | 376.08 | .43 | 333.35 | .42 | 292.76 | .39 | 256.11 | .34 | 224.76 | .28 | 199.76 | .21 |
| .86 | 375.65 | .43 | 332.93 | .42 | 292.37 | .39 | 255.77 | .34 | 224.48 | .28 | 199.55 | .22 |
| .87 | 375.22 | .43 | 332.51 | .42 | 291.98 | .38 | 255.43 | .35 | 224.20 | .28 | 199.33 | .21 |
| .88 | 374.79 | .43 | 332.09 | .42 | 291.60 | .39 | 255.08 | .34 | 223.92 | .28 | 199.12 | .22 |
| .89 | 374.36 | .43 | 331.67 | .42 | 291.21 | .39 | 254.74 | .34 | 223.64 | .28 | 198.90 | .21 |
| .90 | 373.93 | .43 | 331.25 | .42 | 290.82 | .39 | 254.40 | .34 | 223.36 | .28 | 198.69 | .21 |
| .91 | 373.50 | .43 | 330.83 | .42 | 290.43 | .38 | 254.06 | .34 | 223.08 | .28 | 198.48 | .21 |
| .92 | 373.07 | .44 | 330.41 | .41 | 290.05 | .39 | 253.72 | .33 | 222.80 | .28 | 198.27 | .21 |
| .93 | 372.63 | .43 | 330.00 | .42 | 289.66 | .38 | 253.39 | .34 | 222.52 | .28 | 198.06 | .21 |
| .94 | 372.20 | .43 | 329.58 | .42 | 289.28 | .39 | 253.05 | .34 | 222.24 | .28 | 197.85 | .21 |
| .95 | 371.77 | .43 | 329.16 | .42 | 288.89 | .38 | 252.71 | .33 | 221.96 | .27 | 197.64 | .21 |
| .96 | 371.34 | .43 | 328.74 | .42 | 288.51 | .39 | 252.38 | .34 | 221.69 | .28 | 197.43 | .20 |
| .97 | 370.91 | .43 | 328.32 | .41 | 288.12 | .38 | 252.04 | .33 | 221.41 | .27 | 197.23 | .21 |
| .98 | 370.48 | .43 | 327.91 | .42 | 287.74 | .39 | 251.71 | .34 | 221.14 | .28 | 197.02 | .20 |
| .99 | 370.05 | .43 | 327.49 | .42 | 287.35 | .38 | 251.37 | .33 | 220.86 | .27 | 196.82 | .21 |
| 1.00 | 369.62 | .43 | 327.07 | .42 | 286.97 | .38 | 251.04 | .33 | 220.59 | .27 | 196.61 | .20 |

# TABLE CX. ARGUMENT 1.

Equation $= 345''.58 + 186''.51 \cos x + 10''.17 \cos 2x + 0''.63 \cos 3x + 0''.04 \cos 4x$.

| | 18 | | 19 | | 20 | | 21 | | 22 | |
|---|---|---|---|---|---|---|---|---|---|---|
| Days. | Equation. | Diff. | Equation. | Diff. | Equation. | Diff. | Equation. | Diff. | Equation. | Diff. |
| d. | ″ | | ″ | | ″ | | ″ | | ″ | |
| .00 | 196.61 | .20 | 179.77 | .13 | 170.51 | .05 | 169.03 | .03 | 175.37 | .10 |
| .01 | 196.41 | .21 | 179.64 | .13 | 170.46 | .05 | 169.06 | .02 | 175.47 | .11 |
| .02 | 196.20 | .20 | 179.51 | .12 | 170.41 | .06 | 169.08 | .03 | 175.58 | .10 |
| .03 | 196.00 | .21 | 179.39 | .13 | 170.35 | .05 | 169.11 | .02 | 175.68 | .11 |
| .04 | 195.79 | .20 | 179.26 | .13 | 170.30 | .05 | 169.13 | .03 | 175.79 | .10 |
| .05 | 195.59 | .20 | 179.13 | .13 | 170.25 | .05 | 169.16 | .03 | 175.89 | .11 |
| .06 | 195.39 | .20 | 179.00 | .12 | 170.20 | .05 | 169.19 | .03 | 176.00 | .11 |
| .07 | 195.19 | .20 | 178.88 | .13 | 170.15 | .04 | 169.22 | .03 | 176.11 | .10 |
| .08 | 194.99 | .20 | 178.75 | .12 | 170.11 | .05 | 169.25 | .03 | 176.21 | .11 |
| .09 | 194.79 | .20 | 178.63 | .13 | 170.06 | .05 | 169.28 | .03 | 176.32 | .11 |
| .10 | 194.59 | .20 | 178.50 | .12 | 170.01 | .04 | 169.31 | .03 | 176.43 | .11 |
| .11 | 194.39 | .19 | 178.38 | .12 | 169.97 | .05 | 169.34 | .04 | 176.54 | .11 |
| .12 | 194.20 | .20 | 178.26 | .13 | 169.92 | .04 | 169.38 | .03 | 176.65 | .12 |
| .13 | 194.00 | .19 | 178.13 | .12 | 169.88 | .05 | 169.41 | .04 | 176.77 | .11 |
| .14 | 193.81 | .20 | 178.01 | .12 | 169.83 | .04 | 169.45 | .03 | 176.88 | .11 |
| .15 | 193.61 | .19 | 177.89 | .12 | 169.79 | .04 | 169.48 | .04 | 176.99 | .12 |
| .16 | 193.42 | .19 | 177.77 | .12 | 169.75 | .04 | 169.52 | .04 | 177.11 | .11 |
| .17 | 193.23 | .20 | 177.65 | .11 | 169.71 | .04 | 169.56 | .03 | 177.22 | .12 |
| .18 | 193.03 | .19 | 177.54 | .12 | 169.67 | .04 | 169.59 | .04 | 177.34 | .11 |
| .19 | 192.84 | .19 | 177.42 | .12 | 169.63 | .04 | 169.63 | .04 | 177.45 | .12 |
| .20 | 192.65 | .19 | 177.30 | .11 | 169.59 | .04 | 169.67 | .04 | 177.57 | .12 |
| .21 | 192.46 | .19 | 177.19 | .11 | 169.55 | .04 | 169.71 | .04 | 177.69 | .12 |
| .22 | 192.27 | .18 | 177.08 | .12 | 169.51 | .03 | 169.75 | .05 | 177.81 | .12 |
| .23 | 192.09 | .19 | 176.96 | .11 | 169.48 | .04 | 169.80 | .04 | 177.93 | .12 |
| .24 | 191.90 | .19 | 176.85 | .11 | 169.44 | .04 | 169.84 | .04 | 178.05 | .12 |
| .25 | 191.71 | .18 | 176.74 | .11 | 169.40 | .03 | 169.88 | .05 | 178.17 | .12 |
| .26 | 191.53 | .19 | 176.63 | .11 | 169.37 | .03 | 169.93 | .04 | 178.29 | .12 |
| .27 | 191.34 | .18 | 176.52 | .11 | 169.34 | .04 | 169.97 | .05 | 178.41 | .13 |
| .28 | 191.16 | .19 | 176.41 | .11 | 169.30 | .03 | 170.02 | .04 | 178.54 | .12 |
| .29 | 190.97 | .18 | 176.30 | .11 | 169.27 | .03 | 170.06 | .05 | 178.66 | .12 |
| .30 | 190.79 | .18 | 176.19 | .11 | 169.24 | .03 | 170.11 | .05 | 178.78 | .13 |
| .31 | 190.61 | .18 | 176.08 | .11 | 169.21 | .03 | 170.16 | .05 | 178.91 | .13 |
| .32 | 190.43 | .19 | 175.97 | .10 | 169.18 | .02 | 170.21 | .05 | 179.04 | .12 |
| .33 | 190.24 | .18 | 175.87 | .11 | 169.16 | .03 | 170.26 | .05 | 179.16 | .13 |
| .34 | 190.06 | .18 | 175.76 | .11 | 169.13 | .03 | 170.31 | .05 | 179.29 | .13 |
| .35 | 189.88 | .18 | 175.65 | .10 | 169.10 | .02 | 170.36 | .05 | 179.42 | .13 |
| .36 | 189.70 | .18 | 175.55 | .10 | 169.08 | .03 | 170.41 | .06 | 179.55 | .13 |
| .37 | 189.52 | .17 | 175.45 | .11 | 169.05 | .02 | 170.47 | .05 | 179.68 | .13 |
| .38 | 189.35 | .18 | 175.34 | .10 | 169.03 | .03 | 170.52 | .06 | 179.81 | .13 |
| .39 | 189.17 | .18 | 175.24 | .10 | 169.00 | .02 | 170.58 | .05 | 179.94 | .13 |
| .40 | 188.99 | .17 | 175.14 | .10 | 168.98 | .02 | 170.63 | .06 | 180.07 | .13 |
| .41 | 188.82 | .18 | 175.04 | .10 | 168.96 | .02 | 170.69 | .06 | 180.20 | .14 |
| .42 | 188.64 | .17 | 174.94 | .09 | 168.94 | .03 | 170.75 | .05 | 180.34 | .13 |
| .43 | 188.47 | .18 | 174.85 | .10 | 168.91 | .02 | 170.80 | .06 | 180.47 | .14 |
| .44 | 188.29 | .17 | 174.75 | .10 | 168.89 | .02 | 170.86 | .06 | 180.61 | .13 |
| .45 | 188.12 | .17 | 174.65 | .09 | 168.87 | .02 | 170.92 | .06 | 180.74 | .14 |
| .46 | 187.95 | .17 | 174.56 | .10 | 168.85 | .01 | 170.98 | .06 | 180.88 | .14 |
| .47 | 187.78 | .17 | 174.46 | .09 | 168.84 | .02 | 171.04 | .07 | 181.02 | .14 |
| .48 | 187.61 | .17 | 174.37 | .10 | 168.82 | .01 | 171.11 | .06 | 181.16 | .14 |
| .49 | 187.44 | .17 | 174.27 | .09 | 168.81 | .02 | 171.17 | .06 | 181.30 | .14 |
| .50 | 187.27 | .17 | 174.18 | .09 | 168.79 | .01 | 171.23 | .06 | 181.44 | .14 |

# TABLE CX. ARGUMENT 1.

Equation $= 345''.58 + 186''.51 \cos x + 10''.17 \cos 2x + 0''.63 \cos 3x + 0''.04 \cos 4x$.

| | 18 | | 19 | | 20 | | 21 | | 22 | |
|---|---|---|---|---|---|---|---|---|---|---|
| Days. | Equation. | Diff. | Equation. | Diff. | Equation | Diff. | Equation. | Diff. | Equation. | Diff. |
| d. | ″ | | ″ | | ″ | | ″ | | ″ | |
| .50 | 187.27 | .17 | 174.18 | .09 | 168.79 | .01 | 171.23 | .06 | 181.44 | .14 |
| .51 | 187.10 | .17 | 174.09 | .09 | 168.78 | .01 | 171.29 | .07 | 181.58 | .14 |
| .52 | 186.93 | .16 | 174.00 | .10 | 168.77 | .02 | 171.36 | .06 | 181.72 | .15 |
| .53 | 186.77 | .17 | 173.90 | .09 | 168.75 | .01 | 171.42 | .07 | 181.87 | .14 |
| .54 | 186.60 | .17 | 173.81 | .09 | 168.74 | .01 | 171.49 | .06 | 182.01 | .14 |
| .55 | 186.43 | .16 | 173.72 | .09 | 168.73 | .01 | 171.55 | .07 | 182.15 | .15 |
| .56 | 186.27 | .16 | 173.63 | .08 | 168.72 | .01 | 171.62 | .07 | 182.30 | .14 |
| .57 | 186.11 | .17 | 173.55 | .09 | 168.71 | .01 | 171.69 | .07 | 182.44 | .15 |
| .58 | 185.94 | .16 | 173.46 | .08 | 168.70 | .01 | 171.76 | .07 | 182.59 | .14 |
| .59 | 185.78 | .16 | 173.38 | .09 | 168.69 | .01 | 171.83 | .07 | 182.73 | .15 |
| .60 | 185.62 | .16 | 173.29 | .08 | 168.68 | .01 | 171.90 | .07 | 182.88 | .15 |
| .61 | 185.46 | .16 | 173.21 | .09 | 168.67 | .00 | 171.97 | .07 | 183.03 | .15 |
| .62 | 185.30 | .16 | 173.12 | .08 | 168.67 | .01 | 172.04 | .08 | 183.18 | .15 |
| .63 | 185.14 | .16 | 173.04 | .09 | 168.66 | .00 | 172.12 | .07 | 183.33 | .15 |
| .64 | 184.98 | .16 | 172.95 | .08 | 168.66 | .01 | 172.19 | .07 | 183.48 | .15 |
| .65 | 184.82 | .16 | 172.87 | .08 | 168.65 | .00 | 172.26 | .08 | 183.63 | .15 |
| .66 | 184.66 | .15 | 172.79 | .08 | 168.65 | .01 | 172.34 | .08 | 183.78 | .16 |
| .67 | 184.51 | .16 | 172.71 | .07 | 168.64 | .00 | 172.42 | .07 | 183.94 | .15 |
| .68 | 184.35 | .15 | 172.64 | .08 | 168.64 | .00 | 172.49 | .08 | 184.09 | .16 |
| .69 | 184.20 | .16 | 172.56 | .08 | 168.64 | .01 | 172.57 | .08 | 184.25 | .15 |
| .70 | 184.04 | .15 | 172.48 | .08 | 168.65 | .00 | 172.65 | .08 | 184.40 | .16 |
| .71 | 183.89 | .15 | 172.40 | .07 | 168.65 | .00 | 172.73 | .08 | 184.56 | .15 |
| .72 | 183.74 | .16 | 172.33 | .08 | 168.65 | .01 | 172.81 | .09 | 184.71 | .16 |
| .73 | 183.58 | .15 | 172.25 | .07 | 168.66 | .00 | 172.90 | .08 | 184.87 | .15 |
| .74 | 183.43 | .15 | 172.18 | .08 | 168.66 | .00 | 172.98 | .08 | 185.02 | .16 |
| .75 | 183.28 | .15 | 172.10 | .07 | 168.66 | .01 | 173.06 | .08 | 185.18 | .16 |
| .76 | 183.13 | .14 | 172.03 | .07 | 168.67 | .01 | 173.14 | .09 | 185.34 | .16 |
| .77 | 182.99 | .15 | 171.96 | .08 | 168.68 | .00 | 173.23 | .08 | 185.50 | .17 |
| .78 | 182.84 | .14 | 171.88 | .07 | 168.68 | .01 | 173.31 | .09 | 185.67 | .16 |
| .79 | 182.70 | .15 | 171.81 | .07 | 168.69 | .01 | 173.40 | .08 | 185.83 | .16 |
| .80 | 182.55 | .15 | 171.74 | .07 | 168.70 | .01 | 173.48 | .09 | 185.99 | .16 |
| .81 | 182.40 | .14 | 171.67 | .07 | 168.71 | .01 | 173.57 | .09 | 186.15 | .17 |
| .82 | 182.26 | .15 | 171.60 | .06 | 168.72 | .01 | 173.66 | .09 | 186.32 | .16 |
| .83 | 182.11 | .14 | 171.54 | .07 | 168.73 | .01 | 173.75 | .09 | 186.48 | .17 |
| .84 | 181.97 | .15 | 171.47 | .07 | 168.74 | .01 | 173.84 | .09 | 186.65 | .16 |
| .85 | 181.82 | .14 | 171.40 | .06 | 168.75 | .01 | 173.93 | .09 | 186.81 | .17 |
| .86 | 181.68 | .14 | 171.34 | .06 | 168.76 | .02 | 174.02 | .09 | 186.98 | .17 |
| .87 | 181.54 | .14 | 171.28 | .07 | 168.78 | .01 | 174.11 | .10 | 187.15 | .16 |
| .88 | 181.40 | .14 | 171.21 | .06 | 168.79 | .02 | 174.21 | .09 | 187.31 | .17 |
| .89 | 181.26 | .14 | 171.15 | .06 | 168.81 | .01 | 174.30 | .09 | 187.48 | .17 |
| .90 | 181.12 | .14 | 171.09 | .06 | 168.82 | .02 | 174.39 | .10 | 187.65 | .17 |
| .91 | 180.98 | .13 | 171.03 | .06 | 168.84 | .02 | 174.49 | .09 | 187.82 | .17 |
| .92 | 180.85 | .14 | 170.97 | .06 | 168.86 | .02 | 174.58 | .10 | 187.99 | .18 |
| .93 | 180.71 | .13 | 170.91 | .06 | 168.88 | .02 | 174.68 | .09 | 188.17 | .17 |
| .94 | 180.58 | .14 | 170.85 | .06 | 168.90 | .02 | 174.77 | .10 | 188.34 | .17 |
| .95 | 180.44 | .13 | 170.79 | .06 | 168.92 | .02 | 174.87 | .10 | 188.51 | .18 |
| .96 | 180.31 | .14 | 170.73 | .05 | 168.94 | .02 | 174.97 | .10 | 188.69 | .17 |
| .97 | 180.17 | .13 | 170.68 | .06 | 168.96 | .03 | 175.07 | .10 | 188.86 | .18 |
| .98 | 180.04 | .14 | 170.62 | .05 | 168.99 | .02 | 175.17 | .10 | 189.04 | .17 |
| .99 | 179.90 | .13 | 170.57 | .06 | 169.01 | .02 | 175.27 | .10 | 189.21 | .18 |
| 1.00 | 179.77 | .13 | 170.51 | .05 | 169.03 | .03 | 175.37 | .10 | 189.39 | .18 |

# TABLE CX. ARGUMENT 1.

Equation $= 345''.58 + 186''.51 \cos x + 10''.17 \cos 2x + 0''.63 \cos 3x + 0''.04 \cos 4x$.

| | 23 | | 24 | | 25 | | 26 | | 27 | |
|---|---|---|---|---|---|---|---|---|---|---|
| Days. | Equation. | Diff. | Equation. | Diff. | Equation. | Diff. | Equation. | Diff. | Equation. | Diff. |
| d. | ″ | | ″ | | ″ | | ″ | | ″ | |
| .00 | 189.39 | .18 | 210.74 | .25 | 238.84 | .31 | 272.85 | .37 | 311.56 | .41 |
| .01 | 189.57 | .18 | 210.99 | .25 | 239.15 | .32 | 273.22 | .36 | 311.97 | .40 |
| .02 | 189.75 | .18 | 211.24 | .25 | 239.47 | .31 | 273.58 | .37 | 312.37 | .41 |
| .03 | 189.93 | .18 | 211.49 | .25 | 239.78 | .32 | 273.95 | .36 | 312.78 | .40 |
| .04 | 190.11 | .18 | 211.74 | .25 | 240.10 | .31 | 274.31 | .37 | 313.18 | .41 |
| .05 | 190.29 | .18 | 211.99 | .25 | 240.41 | .32 | 274.68 | .37 | 313.59 | .41 |
| .06 | 190.47 | .18 | 212.24 | .26 | 240.73 | .32 | 275.05 | .37 | 314.00 | .41 |
| .07 | 190.65 | .19 | 212.50 | .25 | 241.05 | .31 | 275.42 | .37 | 314.41 | .40 |
| .08 | 190.84 | .18 | 212.75 | .26 | 241.36 | .32 | 275.79 | .37 | 314.81 | .41 |
| .09 | 191.02 | .18 | 213.01 | .25 | 241.68 | .32 | 276.16 | .37 | 315.22 | .41 |
| .10 | 191.20 | .19 | 213.26 | .26 | 242.00 | .32 | 276.53 | .37 | 315.63 | .41 |
| .11 | 191.39 | .19 | 213.52 | .25 | 242.32 | .32 | 276.90 | .37 | 316.04 | .41 |
| .12 | 191.58 | .18 | 213.77 | .26 | 242.64 | .31 | 277.27 | .38 | 316.45 | .41 |
| .13 | 191.76 | .19 | 214.03 | .25 | 242.95 | .32 | 277.65 | .37 | 316.86 | .41 |
| .14 | 191.95 | .19 | 214.28 | .26 | 243.27 | .32 | 278.02 | .37 | 317.27 | .41 |
| .15 | 192.14 | .19 | 214.54 | .26 | 243.59 | .32 | 278.39 | .37 | 317.68 | .41 |
| .16 | 192.33 | .19 | 214.80 | .26 | 243.91 | .33 | 278.76 | .38 | 318.09 | .41 |
| .17 | 192.52 | .19 | 215.06 | .26 | 244.24 | .32 | 279.14 | .37 | 318.50 | .41 |
| .18 | 192.71 | .19 | 215.32 | .26 | 244.56 | .33 | 279.51 | .38 | 318.91 | .41 |
| .19 | 192.90 | .19 | 215.58 | .26 | 244.89 | .32 | 279.89 | .37 | 319.32 | .41 |
| .20 | 193.09 | .19 | 215.84 | .26 | 245.21 | .32 | 280.26 | .38 | 319.73 | .41 |
| .21 | 193.28 | .20 | 216.10 | .27 | 245.53 | .33 | 280.64 | .37 | 320.14 | .42 |
| .22 | 193.48 | .19 | 216.37 | .26 | 245.86 | .32 | 281.01 | .38 | 320.56 | .41 |
| .23 | 193.67 | .20 | 216.63 | .27 | 246.18 | .33 | 281.39 | .37 | 320.97 | .42 |
| .24 | 193.87 | .19 | 216.90 | .26 | 246.51 | .32 | 281.76 | .38 | 321.39 | .41 |
| .25 | 194.06 | .20 | 217.16 | .27 | 246.83 | .33 | 282.14 | .38 | 321.80 | .41 |
| .26 | 194.26 | .20 | 217.43 | .27 | 247.16 | .33 | 282.52 | .38 | 322.21 | .42 |
| .27 | 194.46 | .19 | 217.70 | .26 | 247.49 | .32 | 282.90 | .37 | 322.63 | .41 |
| .28 | 194.65 | .20 | 217.96 | .27 | 247.81 | .33 | 283.27 | .38 | 323.04 | .42 |
| .29 | 194.85 | .20 | 218.23 | .27 | 248.14 | .33 | 283.65 | .38 | 323.46 | .41 |
| .30 | 195.05 | .20 | 218.50 | .27 | 248.47 | .33 | 284.03 | .38 | 323.87 | .41 |
| .31 | 195.25 | .20 | 218.77 | .27 | 248.80 | .33 | 284.41 | .38 | 324.28 | .42 |
| .32 | 195.45 | .20 | 219.04 | .27 | 249.13 | .34 | 284.79 | .38 | 324.70 | .41 |
| .33 | 195.65 | .20 | 219.31 | .27 | 249.47 | .33 | 285.17 | .38 | 325.11 | .42 |
| .34 | 195.85 | .20 | 219.58 | .27 | 249.80 | .33 | 285.55 | .38 | 325.53 | .41 |
| .35 | 196.05 | .21 | 219.85 | .27 | 250.13 | .33 | 285.93 | .38 | 325.94 | .42 |
| .36 | 196.26 | .20 | 220.12 | .27 | 250.46 | .34 | 286.31 | .39 | 326.36 | .41 |
| .37 | 196.46 | .21 | 220.39 | .28 | 250.80 | .33 | 286.70 | .38 | 326.77 | .42 |
| .38 | 196.67 | .20 | 220.67 | .27 | 251.13 | .34 | 287.08 | .39 | 327.19 | .41 |
| .39 | 196.87 | .21 | 220.94 | .27 | 251.47 | .33 | 287.47 | .38 | 327.60 | .42 |
| .40 | 197.08 | .21 | 221.21 | .28 | 251.80 | .34 | 287.85 | .38 | 328.02 | .42 |
| .41 | 197.29 | .21 | 221.49 | .28 | 252.14 | .33 | 288.23 | .39 | 328.44 | .42 |
| .42 | 197.50 | .20 | 221.77 | .27 | 252.47 | .34 | 288.62 | .38 | 328.86 | .41 |
| .43 | 197.70 | .21 | 222.04 | .28 | 252.81 | .33 | 289.00 | .39 | 329.27 | .42 |
| .44 | 197.91 | .21 | 222.32 | .28 | 253.14 | .34 | 289.39 | .38 | 329.69 | .42 |
| .45 | 198.12 | .21 | 222.60 | .28 | 253.48 | .34 | 289.77 | .39 | 330.11 | .42 |
| .46 | 198.33 | .21 | 222.88 | .28 | 253.82 | .34 | 290.16 | .38 | 330.53 | .42 |
| .47 | 198.54 | .22 | 223.16 | .28 | 254.16 | .33 | 290.54 | .39 | 330.95 | .41 |
| .48 | 198.76 | .21 | 223.44 | .28 | 254.49 | .34 | 290.93 | .38 | 331.36 | .42 |
| .49 | 198.97 | .21 | 223.72 | .28 | 254.83 | .34 | 291.31 | .39 | 331.78 | .42 |
| .50 | 199.18 | .22 | 224.00 | .28 | 255.17 | .34 | 291.70 | .39 | 332.20 | .42 |

# TABLE CX. ARGUMENT 1.

Equation $= 345''.58 + 186''.51 \cos x + 10''.17 \cos 2x + 0''.63 \cos 3x + 0''.04 \cos 4x$.

| | 23 | | 24 | | 25 | | 26 | | 27 | |
|---|---|---|---|---|---|---|---|---|---|---|
| Days. | Equation. | Diff. | Equation. | Diff. | Equation. | Diff. | Equation. | Diff. | Equation. | Diff. |
| d. | " | | " | | " | | " | | " | |
| .50 | 199.18 | .22 | 224.00 | .28 | 255.17 | .34 | 291.70 | .39 | 332.20 | .42 |
| .51 | 199.40 | .21 | 224.28 | .28 | 255.51 | .34 | 292.09 | .39 | 332.62 | .42 |
| .52 | 199.61 | .22 | 224.56 | .29 | 255.85 | .35 | 292.48 | .39 | 333.04 | .42 |
| .53 | 199.83 | .21 | 224.85 | .28 | 256.20 | .34 | 292.87 | .39 | 333.46 | .42 |
| .54 | 200.04 | .22 | 225.13 | .28 | 256.54 | .34 | 293.26 | .39 | 333.88 | .42 |
| .55 | 200.26 | .22 | 225.41 | .29 | 256.88 | .35 | 293.65 | .39 | 334.30 | .42 |
| .56 | 200.48 | .22 | 225.70 | .28 | 257.23 | .34 | 294.04 | .39 | 334.72 | .42 |
| .57 | 200.70 | .21 | 225.98 | .29 | 257.57 | .35 | 294.43 | .39 | 335.14 | .43 |
| .58 | 200.91 | .22 | 226.27 | .28 | 257.92 | .34 | 294.82 | .39 | 335.57 | .42 |
| .59 | 201.13 | .22 | 226.55 | .29 | 258.26 | .35 | 295.21 | .39 | 335.99 | .42 |
| .60 | 201.35 | .22 | 226.84 | .29 | 258.61 | .35 | 295.60 | .39 | 336.41 | .42 |
| .61 | 201.57 | .22 | 227.13 | .29 | 258.96 | .34 | 295.99 | .39 | 336.83 | .42 |
| .62 | 201.79 | .23 | 227.42 | .29 | 259.30 | .35 | 296.38 | .40 | 337.25 | .43 |
| .63 | 202.02 | .22 | 227.71 | .29 | 259.65 | .34 | 296.78 | .39 | 337.68 | .42 |
| .64 | 202.24 | .22 | 228.00 | .29 | 259.99 | .35 | 297.17 | .39 | 338.10 | .42 |
| .65 | 202.46 | .23 | 228.29 | .29 | 260.34 | .35 | 297.56 | .39 | 338.52 | .42 |
| .66 | 202.69 | .22 | 228.58 | .29 | 260.69 | .35 | 297.95 | .40 | 338.94 | .42 |
| .67 | 202.91 | .23 | 228.87 | .30 | 261.04 | .35 | 298.35 | .39 | 339.36 | .43 |
| .68 | 203.14 | .22 | 229.17 | .29 | 261.39 | .35 | 298.74 | .40 | 339.79 | .42 |
| .69 | 203.36 | .23 | 229.46 | .29 | 261.74 | .35 | 299.14 | .39 | 340.21 | .42 |
| .70 | 203.59 | .23 | 229.75 | .30 | 262.09 | .35 | 299.53 | .40 | 340.63 | .42 |
| .71 | 203.82 | .23 | 230.05 | .29 | 262.44 | .35 | 299.93 | .40 | 341.05 | .43 |
| .72 | 204.05 | .23 | 230.34 | .30 | 262.79 | .36 | 300.33 | .39 | 341.48 | .42 |
| .73 | 204.28 | .23 | 230.64 | .29 | 263.15 | .35 | 300.72 | .40 | 341.90 | .43 |
| .74 | 204.51 | .23 | 230.93 | .30 | 263.50 | .35 | 301.12 | .40 | 342.33 | .42 |
| .75 | 204.74 | .23 | 231.23 | .30 | 263.85 | .36 | 301.52 | .40 | 342.75 | .42 |
| .76 | 204.97 | .24 | 231.53 | .30 | 264.21 | .35 | 301.92 | .40 | 343.17 | .43 |
| .77 | 205.21 | .23 | 231.83 | .29 | 264.56 | .36 | 302.32 | .39 | 343.60 | .42 |
| .78 | 205.44 | .24 | 232.12 | .30 | 264.92 | .35 | 302.71 | .40 | 344.02 | .43 |
| .79 | 205.68 | .23 | 232.42 | .30 | 265.27 | .36 | 303.11 | .40 | 344.45 | .42 |
| .80 | 205.91 | .24 | 232.72 | .30 | 265.63 | .36 | 303.51 | .40 | 344.87 | .43 |
| .81 | 206.15 | .23 | 233.02 | .30 | 265.99 | .35 | 303.91 | .40 | 345.30 | .42 |
| .82 | 206.38 | .24 | 233.32 | .31 | 266.34 | .36 | 304.31 | .40 | 345.72 | .43 |
| .83 | 206.62 | .23 | 233.63 | .30 | 266.70 | .35 | 304.71 | .40 | 346.15 | .42 |
| .84 | 206.85 | .24 | 233.93 | .30 | 267.05 | .36 | 305.11 | .40 | 346.57 | .43 |
| .85 | 207.09 | .24 | 234.23 | .30 | 267.41 | .36 | 305.51 | .40 | 347.00 | .43 |
| .86 | 207.33 | .24 | 234.53 | .31 | 267.77 | .36 | 305.91 | .40 | 347.43 | .42 |
| .87 | 207.57 | .24 | 234.84 | .30 | 268.13 | .36 | 306.31 | .41 | 347.85 | .43 |
| .88 | 207.81 | .24 | 235.14 | .31 | 268.49 | .36 | 306.72 | .40 | 348.28 | .42 |
| .89 | 208.05 | .24 | 235.45 | .30 | 268.85 | .36 | 307.12 | .40 | 348.70 | .43 |
| .90 | 208.29 | .24 | 235.75 | .31 | 269.21 | .36 | 307.52 | .40 | 349.13 | .43 |
| .91 | 208.53 | .25 | 236.06 | .31 | 269.57 | .36 | 307.92 | .40 | 349.56 | .43 |
| .92 | 208.78 | .24 | 236.37 | .30 | 269.93 | .37 | 308.32 | .41 | 349.99 | .42 |
| .93 | 209.02 | .25 | 236.67 | .31 | 270.30 | .36 | 308.73 | .40 | 350.41 | .43 |
| .94 | 209.27 | .24 | 236.98 | .31 | 270.66 | .36 | 309.13 | .40 | 350.84 | .43 |
| .95 | 209.51 | .25 | 237.29 | .31 | 271.02 | .37 | 309.53 | .41 | 351.27 | .43 |
| .96 | 209.76 | .24 | 237.60 | .31 | 271.39 | .36 | 309.94 | .40 | 351.70 | .43 |
| .97 | 210.00 | .25 | 237.91 | .31 | 271.75 | .37 | 310.34 | .41 | 352.13 | .42 |
| .98 | 210.25 | .24 | 238.22 | .31 | 272.12 | .36 | 310.75 | .40 | 352.55 | .43 |
| .99 | 210.49 | .25 | 238.53 | .31 | 272.48 | .37 | 311.15 | .41 | 352.98 | .43 |
| 1.00 | 210.74 | .25 | 238.84 | .31 | 272.85 | .37 | 311.56 | .41 | 353.41 | .43 |

# TABLE CXI. ARGUMENT 3.

Equation $= 29''.44 - 0''.95 \cos t + 28''.23 \cos 2t + 0''.26 \cos 4t.$

| Days. | 0 | 1 | 2 | 3 | 4 | 5 | 6 | 7 | 8 | 9 | Days. |
|---|---|---|---|---|---|---|---|---|---|---|---|
| Days. .00 | 58″.73 | 57″.33 | 50″.97 | 40″.89 | 28″.95 | 17″.33 | 8″.01 | 2″.53 | 1″.75 | 5″.78 | Days. 1.00 |
| .01 | 58.74 | 57.29 | 50.89 | 40.78 | 28.83 | 17.22 | 7.93 | 2.50 | 1.77 | 5.84 | .99 |
| .02 | 58.75 | 57.25 | 50.80 | 40.66 | 28.71 | 17.11 | 7.86 | 2.47 | 1.79 | 5.91 | .98 |
| .03 | 58.77 | 57.20 | 50.72 | 40.55 | 28.58 | 17.01 | 7.78 | 2.43 | 1.80 | 5.97 | .97 |
| .04 | 58.78 | 57.16 | 50.63 | 40.43 | 28.46 | 16.90 | 7.71 | 2.40 | 1.82 | 6.04 | .96 |
| .05 | 58.79 | 57.12 | 50.55 | 40.32 | 28.34 | 16.79 | 7.63 | 2.37 | 1.84 | 6.10 | .95 |
| .06 | 58.80 | 57.08 | 50.46 | 40.20 | 28.22 | 16.68 | 7.56 | 2.34 | 1.86 | 6.17 | .94 |
| .07 | 58.81 | 57.03 | 50.37 | 40.09 | 28.10 | 16.58 | 7.49 | 2.31 | 1.88 | 6.23 | .93 |
| .08 | 58.81 | 56.99 | 50.29 | 39.97 | 27.98 | 16.47 | 7.41 | 2.29 | 1.90 | 6.30 | .92 |
| .09 | 58.82 | 56.94 | 50.20 | 39.86 | 27.86 | 16.37 | 7.34 | 2.26 | 1.92 | 6.36 | .91 |
| .10 | 58.83 | 56.90 | 50.11 | 39.74 | 27.74 | 16.26 | 7.27 | 2.23 | 1.94 | 6.43 | .90 |
| .11 | 58.84 | 56.85 | 50.02 | 39.62 | 27.62 | 16.16 | 7.20 | 2.20 | 1.96 | 6.50 | .89 |
| .12 | 58.84 | 56.81 | 49.93 | 39.51 | 27.50 | 16.05 | 7.13 | 2.18 | 1.99 | 6.57 | .88 |
| .13 | 58.85 | 56.76 | 49.84 | 39.39 | 27.37 | 15.95 | 7.05 | 2.15 | 2.01 | 6.63 | .87 |
| .14 | 58.85 | 56.72 | 49.75 | 39.28 | 27.25 | 15.84 | 6.98 | 2.13 | 2.04 | 6.70 | .86 |
| .15 | 58.86 | 56.67 | 49.66 | 39.16 | 27.13 | 15.74 | 6.91 | 2.10 | 2.06 | 6.77 | .85 |
| .16 | 58.86 | 56.62 | 49.57 | 39.04 | 27.01 | 15.64 | 6.84 | 2.08 | 2.08 | 6.84 | .84 |
| .17 | 58.87 | 56.57 | 49.48 | 38.93 | 26.89 | 15.53 | 6.77 | 2.05 | 2.11 | 6.91 | .83 |
| .18 | 58.87 | 56.53 | 49.38 | 38.81 | 26.77 | 15.43 | 6.71 | 2.03 | 2.13 | 6.98 | .82 |
| .19 | 58.88 | 56.48 | 49.29 | 38.70 | 26.65 | 15.32 | 6.64 | 2.00 | 2.16 | 7.05 | .81 |
| .20 | 58.88 | 56.43 | 49.20 | 38.58 | 26.53 | 15.22 | 6.57 | 1.98 | 2.18 | 7.12 | .80 |
| .21 | 58.88 | 56.38 | 49.11 | 38.46 | 26.41 | 15.12 | 6.50 | 1.96 | 2.21 | 7.19 | .79 |
| .22 | 58.88 | 56.33 | 49.02 | 38.34 | 26.29 | 15.02 | 6.43 | 1.94 | 2.24 | 7.26 | .78 |
| .23 | 58.88 | 56.27 | 48.92 | 38.23 | 26.17 | 14.91 | 6.37 | 1.92 | 2.26 | 7.34 | .77 |
| .24 | 58.88 | 56.22 | 48.83 | 38.11 | 26.05 | 14.81 | 6.30 | 1.90 | 2.29 | 7.41 | .76 |
| .25 | 58.88 | 56.17 | 48.74 | 37.99 | 25.93 | 14.71 | 6.23 | 1.88 | 2.32 | 7.48 | .75 |
| .26 | 58.88 | 56.12 | 48.64 | 37.87 | 25.81 | 14.61 | 6.17 | 1.86 | 2.35 | 7.55 | .74 |
| .27 | 58.88 | 56.06 | 48.55 | 37.75 | 25.69 | 14.51 | 6.10 | 1.84 | 2.38 | 7.63 | .73 |
| .28 | 58.87 | 56.01 | 48.45 | 37.64 | 25.57 | 14.41 | 6.04 | 1.82 | 2.41 | 7.70 | .72 |
| .29 | 58.87 | 55.95 | 48.36 | 37.52 | 25.45 | 14.31 | 5.97 | 1.80 | 2.44 | 7.78 | .71 |
| .30 | 58.87 | 55.90 | 48.26 | 37.40 | 25.33 | 14.21 | 5.91 | 1.78 | 2.47 | 7.85 | .70 |
| .31 | 58.87 | 55.84 | 48.16 | 37.28 | 25.21 | 14.11 | 5.85 | 1.76 | 2.50 | 7.93 | .69 |
| .32 | 58.86 | 55.79 | 48.07 | 37.16 | 25.09 | 14.01 | 5.78 | 1.75 | 2.53 | 8.00 | .68 |
| .33 | 58.86 | 55.73 | 47.97 | 37.05 | 24.97 | 13.91 | 5.72 | 1.73 | 2.57 | 8.08 | .67 |
| .34 | 58.85 | 55.68 | 47.88 | 36.93 | 24.85 | 13.81 | 5.65 | 1.72 | 2.60 | 8.15 | .66 |
| .35 | 58.85 | 55.62 | 47.78 | 36.81 | 24.73 | 13.71 | 5.59 | 1.70 | 2.63 | 8.23 | .65 |
| .36 | 58.84 | 55.56 | 47.68 | 36.69 | 24.61 | 13.61 | 5.53 | 1.69 | 2.67 | 8.31 | .64 |
| .37 | 58.83 | 55.50 | 47.58 | 36.57 | 24.50 | 13.51 | 5.47 | 1.67 | 2.70 | 8.38 | .63 |
| .38 | 58.83 | 55.45 | 47.49 | 36.45 | 24.38 | 13.42 | 5.41 | 1.66 | 2.74 | 8.46 | .62 |
| .39 | 58.82 | 55.39 | 47.39 | 36.33 | 24.27 | 13.32 | 5.35 | 1.64 | 2.77 | 8.53 | .61 |
| .40 | 58.81 | 55.33 | 47.29 | 36.21 | 24.15 | 13.22 | 5.29 | 1.63 | 2.81 | 8.61 | .60 |
| .41 | 58.80 | 55.27 | 47.19 | 36.08 | 24.03 | 13.12 | 5.23 | 1.62 | 2.85 | 8.69 | .59 |
| .42 | 58.79 | 55.21 | 47.09 | 35.97 | 23.91 | 13.03 | 5.17 | 1.61 | 2.88 | 8.77 | .58 |
| .43 | 58.78 | 55.15 | 46.99 | 35.86 | 23.80 | 12.93 | 5.12 | 1.59 | 2.92 | 8.85 | .57 |
| .44 | 58.77 | 55.09 | 46.89 | 35.74 | 23.68 | 12.84 | 5.06 | 1.58 | 2.95 | 8.93 | .56 |
| .45 | 58.76 | 55.03 | 46.79 | 35.62 | 23.56 | 12.74 | 5.00 | 1.57 | 2.99 | 9.01 | .55 |
| .46 | 58.75 | 54.97 | 46.69 | 35.50 | 23.44 | 12.65 | 4.94 | 1.56 | 3.03 | 9.09 | .54 |
| .47 | 58.73 | 54.90 | 46.59 | 35.38 | 23.32 | 12.55 | 4.89 | 1.55 | 3.07 | 9.17 | .53 |
| .48 | 58.72 | 54.84 | 46.49 | 35.26 | 23.21 | 12.46 | 4.83 | 1.55 | 3.11 | 9.26 | .52 |
| .49 | 58.70 | 54.77 | 46.39 | 35.14 | 23.09 | 12.36 | 4.78 | 1.54 | 3.15 | 9.34 | .51 |
| .50 | 58.69 | 54.71 | 46.29 | 35.02 | 22.97 | 12.27 | 4.72 | 1.53 | 3.19 | 9.42 | .50 |
| Days. | 29 | 28 | 27 | 26 | 25 | 24 | 23 | 22 | 21 | 20 | Days. |

# TABLE CXI. ARGUMENT 3.

Equation $= 29''.44 - 0''.95 \cos t + 28''.23 \cos 2t + 0''.26 \cos 4t$.

| Days. | 0 | 1 | 2 | 3 | 4 | 5 | 6 | 7 | 8 | 9 | Days. |
|---|---|---|---|---|---|---|---|---|---|---|---|
| Days. | | | | | | | | | | | Days. |
| .50 | 58.69 | 54.71 | 46.29 | 35.02 | 22.97 | 12.27 | 4.72 | 1.53 | 3.19 | 9.42 | .50 |
| .51 | 58.67 | 54.65 | 46.19 | 34.90 | 22.85 | 12.18 | 4.67 | 1.52 | 3.23 | 9.50 | .49 |
| .52 | 58.66 | 54.58 | 46.09 | 34.78 | 22.73 | 12.08 | 4.61 | 1.52 | 3.27 | 9.58 | .48 |
| .53 | 58.64 | 54.52 | 45.98 | 34.65 | 22.62 | 11.99 | 4.56 | 1.51 | 3.32 | 9.67 | .47 |
| .54 | 58.63 | 54.45 | 45.88 | 34.53 | 22.50 | 11.89 | 4.50 | 1.51 | 3.36 | 9.75 | .46 |
| .55 | 58.61 | 54.39 | 45.78 | 34.41 | 22.38 | 11.80 | 4.45 | 1.50 | 3.40 | 9.83 | .45 |
| .56 | 58.59 | 54.32 | 45.68 | 34.29 | 22.26 | 11.71 | 4.40 | 1.50 | 3.44 | 9.92 | .44 |
| .57 | 58.57 | 54.25 | 45.57 | 34.17 | 22.15 | 11.62 | 4.35 | 1.49 | 3.49 | 10.00 | .43 |
| .58 | 58.56 | 54.19 | 45.47 | 34.05 | 22.03 | 11.53 | 4.29 | 1.49 | 3.53 | 10.09 | .42 |
| .59 | 58.54 | 54.12 | 45.36 | 33.93 | 21.92 | 11.44 | 4.24 | 1.48 | 3.58 | 10.17 | .41 |
| .60 | 58.52 | 54.05 | 45.26 | 33.81 | 21.80 | 11.35 | 4.19 | 1.48 | 3.62 | 10.26 | .40 |
| .61 | 58.50 | 53.98 | 45.15 | 33.69 | 21.69 | 11.26 | 4.14 | 1.48 | 3.67 | 10.35 | .39 |
| .62 | 58.48 | 53.91 | 45.05 | 33.57 | 21.57 | 11.17 | 4.09 | 1.48 | 3.71 | 10.43 | .38 |
| .63 | 58.46 | 53.84 | 44.94 | 33.44 | 21.46 | 11.08 | 4.04 | 1.47 | 3.76 | 10.52 | .37 |
| .64 | 58.44 | 53.77 | 44.84 | 33.32 | 21.34 | 10.99 | 3.99 | 1.47 | 3.80 | 10.60 | .36 |
| .65 | 58.42 | 53.70 | 44.73 | 33.20 | 21.23 | 10.90 | 3.94 | 1.47 | 3.85 | 10.69 | .35 |
| .66 | 58.40 | 53.63 | 44.62 | 33.08 | 21.12 | 10.81 | 3.89 | 1.47 | 3.90 | 10.78 | .34 |
| .67 | 58.37 | 53.56 | 44.52 | 32.96 | 21.00 | 10.72 | 3.84 | 1.47 | 3.95 | 10.87 | .33 |
| .68 | 58.35 | 53.48 | 44.41 | 32.84 | 20.89 | 10.64 | 3.80 | 1.47 | 3.99 | 10.95 | .32 |
| .69 | 58.32 | 53.41 | 44.31 | 32.72 | 20.77 | 10.55 | 3.75 | 1.47 | 4.04 | 11.04 | .31 |
| .70 | 58.30 | 53.34 | 44.20 | 32.60 | 20.66 | 10.46 | 3.70 | 1.47 | 4.09 | 11.13 | .30 |
| .71 | 58.27 | 53.27 | 44.09 | 32.48 | 20.55 | 10.37 | 3.65 | 1.47 | 4.14 | 11.22 | .29 |
| .72 | 58.25 | 53.19 | 43.98 | 32.36 | 20.43 | 10.29 | 3.61 | 1.48 | 4.19 | 11.31 | .28 |
| .73 | 58.22 | 53.12 | 43.88 | 32.23 | 20.32 | 10.20 | 3.57 | 1.48 | 4.25 | 11.40 | .27 |
| .74 | 58.20 | 53.04 | 43.77 | 32.11 | 20.20 | 10.12 | 3.52 | 1.49 | 4.30 | 11.49 | .26 |
| .75 | 58.17 | 52.97 | 43.66 | 31.99 | 20.09 | 10.03 | 3.48 | 1.49 | 4.35 | 11.58 | .25 |
| .76 | 58.14 | 52.89 | 43.55 | 31.87 | 19.98 | 9.95 | 3.44 | 1.50 | 4.40 | 11.67 | .24 |
| .77 | 58.11 | 52.82 | 43.44 | 31.75 | 19.87 | 9.86 | 3.39 | 1.50 | 4.45 | 11.76 | .23 |
| .78 | 58.09 | 52.74 | 43.34 | 31.62 | 19.75 | 9.78 | 3.35 | 1.51 | 4.51 | 11.86 | .22 |
| .79 | 58.06 | 52.67 | 43.23 | 31.50 | 19.64 | 9.69 | 3.30 | 1.51 | 4.56 | 11.95 | .21 |
| .80 | 58.03 | 52.59 | 43.12 | 31.38 | 19.53 | 9.61 | 3.26 | 1.52 | 4.61 | 12.04 | .20 |
| .81 | 58.00 | 52.51 | 43.01 | 31.26 | 19.42 | 9.53 | 3.22 | 1.53 | 4.67 | 12.13 | .19 |
| .82 | 57.97 | 52.43 | 42.90 | 31.14 | 19.31 | 9.44 | 3.18 | 1.54 | 4.72 | 12.22 | .18 |
| .83 | 57.93 | 52.36 | 42.79 | 31.02 | 19.19 | 9.36 | 3.14 | 1.54 | 4.78 | 12.32 | .17 |
| .84 | 57.90 | 52.28 | 42.68 | 30.90 | 19.08 | 9.27 | 3.10 | 1.55 | 4.83 | 12.41 | .16 |
| .85 | 57.87 | 52.20 | 42.57 | 30.78 | 18.97 | 9.19 | 3.06 | 1.56 | 4.89 | 12.50 | .15 |
| .86 | 57.84 | 52.12 | 42.46 | 30.66 | 18.86 | 9.11 | 3.02 | 1.57 | 4.95 | 12.59 | .14 |
| .87 | 57.80 | 52.04 | 42.35 | 30.54 | 18.75 | 9.03 | 2.98 | 1.58 | 5.00 | 12.69 | .13 |
| .88 | 57.77 | 51.96 | 42.23 | 30.41 | 18.64 | 8.95 | 2.95 | 1.59 | 5.06 | 12.78 | .12 |
| .89 | 57.73 | 51.88 | 42.12 | 30.29 | 18.53 | 8.87 | 2.91 | 1.60 | 5.11 | 12.88 | .11 |
| .90 | 57.70 | 51.80 | 42.01 | 30.17 | 18.42 | 8.79 | 2.87 | 1.61 | 5.17 | 12.97 | .10 |
| .91 | 57.66 | 51.72 | 41.90 | 30.05 | 18.31 | 8.71 | 2.84 | 1.62 | 5.23 | 13.07 | .09 |
| .92 | 57.63 | 51.64 | 41.79 | 29.93 | 18.20 | 8.63 | 2.80 | 1.63 | 5.29 | 13.16 | .08 |
| .93 | 57.59 | 51.55 | 41.67 | 29.80 | 18.09 | 8.55 | 2.77 | 1.65 | 5.35 | 13.26 | .07 |
| .94 | 57.56 | 51.47 | 41.56 | 29.68 | 17.98 | 8.47 | 2.73 | 1.66 | 5.41 | 13.35 | .06 |
| .95 | 57.52 | 51.39 | 41.45 | 29.56 | 17.87 | 8.39 | 2.70 | 1.67 | 5.47 | 13.45 | .05 |
| .96 | 57.48 | 51.31 | 41.34 | 29.44 | 17.76 | 8.31 | 2.67 | 1.69 | 5.53 | 13.55 | .04 |
| .97 | 57.44 | 51.22 | 41.23 | 29.32 | 17.65 | 8.24 | 2.63 | 1.70 | 5.59 | 13.65 | .03 |
| .98 | 57.41 | 51.14 | 41.11 | 29.19 | 17.55 | 8.16 | 2.60 | 1.72 | 5.66 | 13.74 | .02 |
| .99 | 57.37 | 51.05 | 41.00 | 29.07 | 17.44 | 8.09 | 2.56 | 1.73 | 5.72 | 13.84 | .01 |
| 1.00 | 57.33 | 50.97 | 40.89 | 28.95 | 17.33 | 8.00 | 2.53 | 1.75 | 5.78 | 13.94 | .00 |
| Days. | 29 | 28 | 27 | 26 | 25 | 24 | 23 | 22 | 21 | 20 | Days. |

| Tables | CXI. | CXII. |
|---|---|---|
| Arguments | **3.** | **2.** |

**Table CXI.**

| Days. | **10** | **11** | **12** | **13** | **14** | Days. |
|---|---|---|---|---|---|---|
| Days. | ″ | ″ | ″ | ″ | ″ | Days. |
| .00 | 13.94 | 24.87 | 36.65 | 47.15 | 54.39 | 1.00 |
| .01 | 14.04 | 24.99 | 36.76 | 47.24 | 54.44 | .99 |
| .02 | 14.14 | 25.10 | 36.88 | 47.33 | 54.49 | .98 |
| .03 | 14.24 | 25.22 | 36.99 | 47.42 | 54.54 | .97 |
| .04 | 14.34 | 25.33 | 37.11 | 47.51 | 54.59 | .96 |
| .05 | 14.44 | 25.45 | 37.22 | 47.60 | 54.64 | .95 |
| .06 | 14.54 | 25.57 | 37.33 | 47.69 | 54.69 | .94 |
| .07 | 14.64 | 25.69 | 37.45 | 47.78 | 54.74 | .93 |
| .08 | 14.74 | 25.80 | 37.56 | 47.86 | 54.78 | .92 |
| .09 | 14.84 | 25.92 | 37.68 | 47.95 | 54.83 | .91 |
| .10 | 14.94 | 26.04 | 37.79 | 48.04 | 54.88 | .90 |
| .11 | 15.04 | 26.16 | 37.90 | 48.13 | 54.92 | .89 |
| .12 | 15.14 | 26.28 | 38.02 | 48.22 | 54.97 | .88 |
| .13 | 15.25 | 26.39 | 38.13 | 48.30 | 55.01 | .87 |
| .14 | 15.35 | 26.51 | 38.25 | 48.39 | 55.06 | .86 |
| .15 | 15.45 | 26.63 | 38.36 | 48.48 | 55.10 | .85 |
| .16 | 15.55 | 26.75 | 38.47 | 48.57 | 55.14 | .84 |
| .17 | 15.65 | 26.87 | 38.58 | 48.65 | 55.18 | .83 |
| .18 | 15.76 | 26.98 | 38.70 | 48.74 | 55.23 | .82 |
| .19 | 15.86 | 27.10 | 38.81 | 48.82 | 55.27 | .81 |
| .20 | 15.96 | 27.22 | 38.92 | 48.91 | 55.31 | .80 |
| .21 | 16.06 | 27.34 | 39.03 | 48.99 | 55.35 | .79 |
| .22 | 16.17 | 27.46 | 39.14 | 49.08 | 55.39 | .78 |
| .23 | 16.27 | 27.57 | 39.26 | 49.16 | 55.43 | .77 |
| .24 | 16.38 | 27.69 | 39.37 | 49.25 | 55.47 | .76 |
| .25 | 16.48 | 27.81 | 39.48 | 49.33 | 55.51 | .75 |
| .26 | 16.59 | 27.93 | 39.59 | 49.41 | 55.55 | .74 |
| .27 | 16.69 | 28.05 | 39.70 | 49.49 | 55.59 | .73 |
| .28 | 16.80 | 28.16 | 39.81 | 49.58 | 55.62 | .72 |
| .29 | 16.90 | 28.28 | 39.92 | 49.66 | 55.66 | .71 |
| .30 | 17.01 | 28.40 | 40.03 | 49.74 | 55.70 | .70 |
| .31 | 17.12 | 28.52 | 40.14 | 49.82 | 55.74 | .69 |
| .32 | 17.22 | 28.64 | 40.25 | 49.90 | 55.77 | .68 |
| .33 | 17.33 | 28.76 | 40.36 | 49.98 | 55.81 | .67 |
| .34 | 17.43 | 28.88 | 40.47 | 50.06 | 55.84 | .66 |
| .35 | 17.54 | 29.00 | 40.58 | 50.14 | 55.88 | .65 |
| .36 | 17.65 | 29.12 | 40.69 | 50.22 | 55.91 | .64 |
| .37 | 17.76 | 29.24 | 40.80 | 50.30 | 55.94 | .63 |
| .38 | 17.86 | 29.35 | 40.90 | 50.37 | 55.98 | .62 |
| .39 | 17.97 | 29.47 | 41.01 | 50.45 | 56.01 | .61 |
| .40 | 18.08 | 29.59 | 41.12 | 50.53 | 56.04 | .60 |
| .41 | 18.19 | 29.71 | 41.23 | 50.61 | 56.07 | .59 |
| .42 | 18.30 | 29.83 | 41.34 | 50.68 | 56.10 | .58 |
| .43 | 18.40 | 29.95 | 41.44 | 50.76 | 56.13 | .57 |
| .44 | 18.51 | 30.07 | 41.55 | 50.83 | 56.16 | .56 |
| .45 | 18.62 | 30.19 | 41.66 | 50.91 | 56.19 | .55 |
| .46 | 18.73 | 30.31 | 41.77 | 50.98 | 56.22 | .54 |
| .47 | 18.84 | 30.43 | 41.87 | 51.06 | 56.24 | .53 |
| .48 | 18.95 | 30.54 | 41.98 | 51.13 | 56.26 | .52 |
| .49 | 19.06 | 30.66 | 42.08 | 51.21 | 56.29 | .51 |
| .50 | 19.17 | 30.78 | 42.19 | 51.28 | 56.32 | .50 |
| Days. | **19** | **18** | **17** | **16** | **15** | Days. |

**Table CXII.**

| Days. | **0** | | **10** | |
|---|---|---|---|---|
| Days. | Equation. | Diff. | Equation. | Diff. |
| Days | ″ | | ″ | |
| 0.0 | 33.66 | .68 | 66.71 | .27 |
| 0.1 | 34.34 | .68 | 66.44 | .28 |
| 0.2 | 35.02 | .68 | 66.16 | .30 |
| 0.3 | 35.70 | .67 | 65.86 | .31 |
| 0.4 | 36.37 | .68 | 65.55 | .32 |
| 0.5 | 37.05 | .68 | 65.23 | .33 |
| 0.6 | 37.73 | .67 | 64.90 | .35 |
| 0.7 | 38.40 | .68 | 64.55 | .35 |
| 0.8 | 39.08 | .68 | 64.20 | .37 |
| 0.9 | 39.76 | .67 | 63.83 | .39 |
| 1.0 | 40.43 | .67 | 63.44 | .39 |
| 1.1 | 41.10 | .67 | 63.05 | .40 |
| 1.2 | 41.77 | .66 | 62.65 | .41 |
| 1.3 | 42.43 | 67 | 62.24 | .43 |
| 1.4 | 43.10 | .66 | 61.81 | .44 |
| 1.5 | 43.76 | .66 | 61.37 | .44 |
| 1.6 | 44.42 | .65 | 60.93 | .46 |
| 1.7 | 45.07 | .65 | 60.47 | .47 |
| 1.8 | 45.72 | .65 | 60.00 | .47 |
| 1.9 | 46.37 | .64 | 59.53 | .49 |
| 2.0 | 47.01 | .64 | 59.04 | .50 |
| 2.1 | 47.65 | .63 | 58.54 | .50 |
| 2.2 | 48.28 | .63 | 58.04 | .52 |
| 2.3 | 48.91 | .62 | 57.52 | .52 |
| 2.4 | 49.53 | .62 | 57.00 | .53 |
| 2.5 | 50.15 | .61 | 56.47 | .54 |
| 2.6 | 50.76 | .60 | 55.93 | .55 |
| 2.7 | 51.36 | .60 | 55.38 | .56 |
| 2.8 | 51.96 | .60 | 54.82 | .56 |
| 2.9 | 52.56 | .58 | 54.26 | .57 |
| 3.0 | 53.14 | .58 | 53.69 | .58 |
| 3.1 | 53.72 | .57 | 53.11 | .59 |
| 3.2 | 54.29 | .57 | 52.52 | .59 |
| 3.3 | 54.86 | .55 | 51.93 | .60 |
| 3.4 | 55.41 | .55 | 51.33 | .61 |
| 3.5 | 55.96 | .54 | 50.72 | .61 |
| 3.6 | 56.50 | .53 | 50.11 | .62 |
| 3.7 | 57.03 | .52 | 49.49 | .62 |
| 3.8 | 57.55 | .52 | 48.87 | .63 |
| 3.9 | 58.07 | .50 | 48.24 | .63 |
| 4.0 | 58.57 | .50 | 47.61 | .64 |
| 4.1 | 59.07 | .48 | 46.97 | .64 |
| 4.2 | 59.55 | .48 | 46.33 | .65 |
| 4.3 | 60.03 | .47 | 45.68 | .65 |
| 4.4 | 60.50 | .45 | 45.03 | .65 |
| 4.5 | 60.95 | .45 | 44.38 | .66 |
| 4.6 | 61.40 | .43 | 43.72 | .66 |
| 4.7 | 61.83 | .43 | 43.06 | .67 |
| 4.8 | 62.26 | .41 | 42.39 | .66 |
| 4.9 | 62.67 | .41 | 41.73 | .67 |
| 5.0 | 63.08 | .39 | 41.06 | .67 |

| TABLES | CXI. | CXII. |
|---|---|---|
| ARGUMENTS | 3. | 2. |

**Table CXI.**

| Days. | 10 | 11 | 12 | 13 | 14 | Days. |
|---|---|---|---|---|---|---|
| .50 | 19.17″ | 30.78″ | 42.19″ | 51.28″ | 56.32″ | .50 |
| .51 | 19.28 | 30.90 | 42.30 | 51.35 | 56.35 | .49 |
| .52 | 19.39 | 31.02 | 42.40 | 51.42 | 56.37 | .48 |
| .53 | 19.50 | 31.13 | 42.51 | 51.50 | 56.40 | .47 |
| .54 | 19.61 | 31.25 | 42.61 | 51.57 | 56.42 | .46 |
| .55 | 19.72 | 31.37 | 42.72 | 51.64 | 56.45 | .45 |
| .56 | 19.83 | 31.49 | 42.82 | 51.71 | 56.47 | .44 |
| .57 | 19.94 | 31.61 | 42.93 | 51.78 | 56.49 | .43 |
| .58 | 20.05 | 31.73 | 43.03 | 51.85 | 56.52 | .42 |
| .59 | 20.16 | 31.85 | 43.14 | 51.92 | 56.54 | .41 |
| .60 | 20.27 | 31.97 | 43.24 | 51.99 | 56.56 | .40 |
| .61 | 20.38 | 32.09 | 43.34 | 52.06 | 56.58 | .39 |
| .62 | 20.50 | 32.21 | 43.44 | 52.13 | 56.60 | .38 |
| .63 | 20.61 | 32.32 | 43.55 | 52.19 | 56.62 | .37 |
| .64 | 20.73 | 32.44 | 43.65 | 52.26 | 56.64 | .36 |
| .65 | 20.84 | 32.56 | 43.75 | 52.33 | 56.66 | .35 |
| .66 | 20.95 | 32.68 | 43.85 | 52.40 | 56.68 | .34 |
| .67 | 21.06 | 32.80 | 43.95 | 52.46 | 56.69 | .33 |
| .68 | 21.18 | 32.91 | 44.06 | 52.53 | 56.71 | .32 |
| .69 | 21.29 | 33.03 | 44.16 | 52.59 | 56.72 | .31 |
| .70 | 21.40 | 33.15 | 44.26 | 52.66 | 56.74 | .30 |
| .71 | 21.51 | 33.27 | 44.36 | 52.72 | 56.75 | .29 |
| .72 | 21.63 | 33.39 | 44.46 | 52.79 | 56.77 | .28 |
| .73 | 21.74 | 33.50 | 44.56 | 52.85 | 56.78 | .27 |
| .74 | 21.86 | 33.62 | 44.66 | 52.92 | 56.80 | .26 |
| .75 | 21.97 | 33.74 | 44.76 | 52.98 | 56.81 | .25 |
| .76 | 22.09 | 33.86 | 44.86 | 53.04 | 56.82 | .24 |
| .77 | 22.20 | 33.97 | 44.96 | 53.10 | 56.83 | .23 |
| .78 | 22.32 | 34.09 | 45.05 | 53.16 | 56.85 | .22 |
| .79 | 22.43 | 34.20 | 45.15 | 53.22 | 56.86 | .21 |
| .80 | 22.55 | 34.32 | 45.25 | 53.28 | 56.87 | .20 |
| .81 | 22.66 | 34.44 | 45.35 | 53.34 | 56.88 | .19 |
| .82 | 22.78 | 34.56 | 45.45 | 53.40 | 56.89 | .18 |
| .83 | 22.89 | 34.67 | 45.54 | 53.46 | 56.90 | .17 |
| .84 | 23.01 | 34.79 | 45.64 | 53.52 | 56.91 | .16 |
| .85 | 23.12 | 34.91 | 45.74 | 53.58 | 56.92 | .15 |
| .86 | 23.24 | 35.03 | 45.84 | 53.64 | 56.93 | .14 |
| .87 | 23.35 | 35.14 | 45.93 | 53.69 | 56.93 | .13 |
| .88 | 23.47 | 35.26 | 46.03 | 53.75 | 56.94 | .12 |
| .89 | 23.58 | 35.37 | 46.12 | 53.80 | 56.94 | .11 |
| .90 | 23.70 | 35.49 | 46.22 | 53.86 | 56.95 | .10 |
| .91 | 23.82 | 35.61 | 46.31 | 53.91 | 56.95 | .09 |
| .92 | 23.93 | 35.72 | 46.41 | 53.97 | 56.96 | .08 |
| .93 | 24.05 | 35.84 | 46.50 | 54.02 | 56.96 | .07 |
| .94 | 24.16 | 35.95 | 46.60 | 54.08 | 56.97 | .06 |
| .95 | 24.28 | 36.07 | 46.69 | 54.13 | 56.97 | .05 |
| .96 | 24.40 | 36.19 | 46.78 | 54.18 | 56.97 | .04 |
| .97 | 24.52 | 36.30 | 46.87 | 54.23 | 56.97 | .03 |
| .98 | 24.63 | 36.42 | 46.97 | 54.29 | 56.98 | .02 |
| .99 | 24.75 | 36.53 | 47.06 | 54.34 | 56.98 | .01 |
| 1.00 | 24.87 | 36.65 | 47.15 | 54.39 | 56.98 | .00 |
| Days. | 19 | 18 | 17 | 16 | 15 | Days. |

**Table CXII.**

| Days. | 0 | | 10 | |
|---|---|---|---|---|
| Days. | Equation. | Diff. | Equation. | Diff. |
| 5.0 | 63.08″ | .39 | 41.06″ | .67 |
| 5.1 | 63.47 | .38 | 40.39 | .68 |
| 5.2 | 63.85 | .37 | 39.71 | .67 |
| 5.3 | 64.22 | .35 | 39.04 | .68 |
| 5.4 | 64.57 | .35 | 38.36 | .67 |
| 5.5 | 64.92 | .33 | 37.69 | .68 |
| 5.6 | 65.25 | .32 | 37.01 | .68 |
| 5.7 | 65.57 | .31 | 36.33 | .67 |
| 5.8 | 65.88 | .30 | 35.66 | .68 |
| 5.9 | 66.18 | .28 | 34.98 | .68 |
| 6.0 | 66.46 | .27 | 34.30 | .68 |
| 6.1 | 66.73 | .27 | 33.62 | .67 |
| 6.2 | 67.00 | .23 | 32.95 | .68 |
| 6.3 | 67.23 | 23 | 32.27 | .67 |
| 6.4 | 67.46 | .22 | 31.60 | .68 |
| 6.5 | 67.68 | .21 | 30.92 | .67 |
| 6.6 | 67.89 | .19 | 30.25 | .66 |
| 6.7 | 68.08 | .18 | 29.59 | .67 |
| 6.8 | 68.26 | .16 | 28.92 | .66 |
| 6.9 | 68.42 | .16 | 28.26 | .66 |
| 7.0 | 68.58 | .14 | 27.60 | .66 |
| 7.1 | 68.72 | .12 | 26.94 | .65 |
| 7.2 | 68.84 | .11 | 26.29 | .66 |
| 7.3 | 68.95 | .10 | 25.63 | .64 |
| 7.4 | 69.05 | .08 | 24.99 | .64 |
| 7.5 | 69.13 | .07 | 24.35 | .64 |
| 7.6 | 69.20 | .06 | 23.71 | .63 |
| 7.7 | 69.26 | .04 | 23.08 | .63 |
| 7.8 | 69.30 | .03 | 22.45 | .62 |
| 7.9 | 69.33 | .01 | 21.83 | .62 |
| 8.0 | 69.34 | .00 | 21.21 | .61 |
| 8.1 | 69.34 | .02 | 20.60 | .61 |
| 8.2 | 69.32 | .03 | 19.99 | .60 |
| 8.3 | 69.29 | .04 | 19.39 | .59 |
| 8.4 | 69.25 | .05 | 18.80 | .59 |
| 8.5 | 69.20 | .08 | 18.21 | .58 |
| 8.6 | 69.12 | .08 | 17.63 | .58 |
| 8.7 | 69.04 | .10 | 17.05 | .56 |
| 8.8 | 68.94 | .11 | 16.49 | .56 |
| 8.9 | 68.83 | .12 | 15.93 | .55 |
| 9.0 | 68.71 | .14 | 15.38 | .55 |
| 9.1 | 68.57 | .15 | 14.83 | .53 |
| 9.2 | 68.42 | .17 | 14.30 | .53 |
| 9.3 | 68.25 | .18 | 13.77 | .52 |
| 9.4 | 68.07 | .19 | 13.25 | .52 |
| 9.5 | 67.88 | .21 | 12.73 | .50 |
| 9.6 | 67.67 | .22 | 12.23 | .49 |
| 9.7 | 67.45 | .23 | 11.74 | .49 |
| 9.8 | 67.22 | .25 | 11.25 | .48 |
| 9.9 | 66.97 | .26 | 10.77 | .46 |
| 10.0 | 66.71 | .27 | 10.31 | .46 |

# TABLES CXII.-CXV.

| TABLES | CXII. | CXIII. | CXIV. | CXV. |
|---|---|---|---|---|
| ARGUMENTS | 2. | 6. | 7. | 8. |

**Table CXII.**

| Days. | 20 Equation. | 20 Diff. | 30 Equation. | 30 Diff. |
|---|---|---|---|---|
| 0.0 | 10.31″ | .46 | 21.79″ | .62 |
| 0.1 | 9.85 | .45 | 22.41 | .63 |
| 0.2 | 9.40 | .44 | 23.04 | .63 |
| 0.3 | 8.96 | .42 | 23.67 | .64 |
| 0.4 | 8.54 | .42 | 24.31 | .64 |
| 0.5 | 8.12 | .41 | 24.95 | .65 |
| 0.6 | 7.71 | .40 | 25.60 | .65 |
| 0.7 | 7.31 | .38 | 26.25 | .65 |
| 0.8 | 6.93 | .38 | 26.90 | .66 |
| 0.9 | 6.55 | .36 | 27.56 | .66 |
| 1.0 | 6.19 | .36 | 28.22 | .66 |
| 1.1 | 5.83 | .34 | 28.88 | .67 |
| 1.2 | 5.49 | .33 | 29.55 | .67 |
| 1.3 | 5.16 | .32 | 30.22 | .67 |
| 1.4 | 4.84 | .31 | 30.89 | .67 |
| 1.5 | 4.53 | .30 | 31.56 | .67 |
| 1.6 | 4.23 | .29 | 32.23 | .68 |
| 1.7 | 3.94 | .27 | 32.91 | .67 |
| 1.8 | 3.67 | .27 | 33.58 | .68 |
| 1.9 | 3.40 | .25 | 34.26 | .68 |
| 2.0 | 3.15 | .23 | 34.94 | .67 |
| 2.1 | 2.92 | .23 | 35.61 | .68 |
| 2.2 | 2.69 | .22 | 36.29 | .68 |
| 2.3 | 2.47 | .20 | 36.97 | .68 |
| 2.4 | 2.27 | .19 | 37.65 | .67 |
| 2.5 | 2.08 | .17 | 38.32 | .68 |
| 2.6 | 1.91 | .17 | 39.00 | .67 |
| 2.7 | 1.74 | .15 | 39.67 | .68 |
| 2.8 | 1.59 | .14 | 40.35 | .67 |
| 2.9 | 1.45 | .13 | 41.02 | .67 |
| 3.0 | 1.32 | .12 | 41.69 | .66 |
| 3.1 | 1.20 | .10 | 42.35 | .67 |
| 3.2 | 1.10 | .09 | 43.02 | .66 |
| 3.3 | 1.01 | .07 | 43.68 | .66 |
| 3.4 | 0.94 | .07 | 44.34 | .65 |
| 3.5 | 0.87 | .05 | 44.99 | .65 |
| 3.6 | 0.82 | .04 | 45.64 | .65 |
| 3.7 | 0.78 | .02 | 46.29 | .64 |
| 3.8 | 0.76 | .02 | 46.93 | .64 |
| 3.9 | 0.74 | .00 | 47.57 | .63 |
| 4.0 | 0.74 | .01 | 48.20 | .63 |
| 4.1 | 0.75 | .03 | 48.83 | .63 |
| 4.2 | 0.78 | .04 | 49.46 | .61 |
| 4.3 | 0.82 | .05 | 50.07 | .61 |
| 4.4 | 0.87 | .06 | 50.68 | .61 |
| 4.5 | 0.93 | .08 | 51.29 | .60 |
| 4.6 | 1.01 | .09 | 51.89 | .59 |
| 4.7 | 1.10 | .10 | 52.48 | .58 |
| 4.8 | 1.20 | .11 | 53.06 | .58 |
| 4.9 | 1.31 | .13 | 53.64 | .57 |
| 5.0 | 1.44 | .14 | 54.21 | .57 |

**Tables CXIII., CXIV., CXV.**

| Days. | CXIII. 0 | CXIII. 10 | CXIII. 20 | CXIII. 30 | CXIV. 0 | CXV. 0 | CXV. 10 |
|---|---|---|---|---|---|---|---|
| 0.0 | 1.30″ | 2.89″ | 0.94″ | 0.25″ | 2.70″ | 1.68″ | 0.52″ |
| 0.1 | 1.33 | 2.88 | 0.92 | 0.27 | 2.91 | 1.76 | 0.47 |
| 0.2 | 1.35 | 2.88 | 0.89 | 0.28 | 3.11 | 1.84 | 0.42 |
| 0.3 | 1.38 | 2.87 | 0.87 | 0.30 | 3.31 | 1.91 | 0.38 |
| 0.4 | 1.40 | 2.87 | 0.84 | 0.31 | 3.51 | 1.99 | 0.33 |
| 0.5 | 1.43 | 2.86 | 0.82 | 0.33 | 3.71 | 2.07 | 0.28 |
| 0.6 | 1.46 | 2.85 | 0.80 | 0.35 | 3.90 | 2.15 | 0.24 |
| 0.7 | 1.48 | 2.85 | 0.77 | 0.36 | 4.09 | 2.23 | 0.21 |
| 0.8 | 1.51 | 2.84 | 0.75 | 0.38 | 4.28 | 2.30 | 0.17 |
| 0.9 | 1.53 | 2.84 | 0.72 | 0.39 | 4.47 | 2.38 | 0.14 |
| 1.0 | 1.56 | 2.83 | 0.70 | 0.41 | 4.65 | 2.46 | 0.11 |
| 1.1 | 1.59 | 2.82 | 0.68 | 0.43 | 4.82 | 2.53 | 0.09 |
| 1.2 | 1.61 | 2.81 | 0.66 | 0.45 | 4.98 | 2.61 | 0.07 |
| 1.3 | 1.64 | 2.81 | 0.64 | 0.47 | 5.14 | 2.68 | 0.05 |
| 1.4 | 1.66 | 2.80 | 0.62 | 0.49 | 5.28 | 2.75 | 0.03 |
| 1.5 | 1.69 | 2.79 | 0.60 | 0.51 | 5.42 | 2.82 | 0.02 |
| 1.6 | 1.72 | 2.78 | 0.58 | 0.53 | 5.55 | 2.89 | 0.01 |
| 1.7 | 1.74 | 2.77 | 0.56 | 0.55 | 5.67 | 2.95 | 0.01 |
| 1.8 | 1.77 | 2.75 | 0.53 | 0.57 | 5.77 | 3.02 | 0.00 |
| 1.9 | 1.79 | 2.74 | 0.51 | 0.59 | 5.87 | 3.08 | 0.00 |
| 2.0 | 1.82 | 2.73 | 0.49 | 0.61 | 5.95 | 3.14 | 0.00 |
| 2.1 | 1.84 | 2.72 | 0.47 | 0.63 | 6.02 | 3.20 | 0.01 |
| 2.2 | 1.87 | 2.70 | 0.45 | 0.65 | 6.08 | 3.26 | 0.02 |
| 2.3 | 1.89 | 2.69 | 0.44 | 0.68 | 6.12 | 3.31 | 0.03 |
| 2.4 | 1.92 | 2.67 | 0.42 | 0.70 | 6.15 | 3.37 | 0.05 |
| 2.5 | 1.94 | 2.66 | 0.40 | 0.72 | 6.17 | 3.42 | 0.07 |
| 2.6 | 1.96 | 2.65 | 0.38 | 0.74 | 6.18 | 3.46 | 0.10 |
| 2.7 | 1.99 | 2.63 | 0.36 | 0.77 | 6.17 | 3.51 | 0.12 |
| 2.8 | 2.01 | 2.62 | 0.35 | 0.79 | 6.15 | 3.55 | 0.15 |
| 2.9 | 2.04 | 2.60 | 0.33 | 0.82 | 6.12 | 3.59 | 0.18 |
| 3.0 | 2.06 | 2.59 | 0.31 | 0.84 | 6.07 | 3.63 | 0.21 |
| 3.1 | 2.08 | 2.57 | 0.30 | 0.86 | 6.01 | 3.66 | 0.25 |
| 3.2 | 2.11 | 2.55 | 0.28 | 0.89 | 5.94 | 3.69 | 0.29 |
| 3.3 | 2.13 | 2.54 | 0.27 | 0.91 | 5.86 | 3.72 | 0.33 |
| 3.4 | 2.16 | 2.52 | 0.25 | 0.94 | 5.76 | 3.74 | 0.38 |
| 3.5 | 2.18 | 2.50 | 0.24 | 0.96 | 5.66 | 3.77 | 0.42 |
| 3.6 | 2.20 | 2.48 | 0.23 | 0.98 | 5.54 | 3.79 | 0.47 |
| 3.7 | 2.22 | 2.46 | 0.21 | 1.01 | 5.41 | 3.81 | 0.53 |
| 3.8 | 2.24 | 2.44 | 0.20 | 1.03 | 5.27 | 3.82 | 0.59 |
| 3.9 | 2.26 | 2.42 | 0.18 | 1.06 | 5.12 | 3.83 | 0.64 |
| 4.0 | 2.28 | 2.40 | 0.17 | 1.08 | 4.97 | 3.84 | 0.70 |
| 4.1 | 2.30 | 2.38 | 0.16 | 1.11 | 4.80 | 3.84 | 0.76 |
| 4.2 | 2.32 | 2.36 | 0.15 | 1.13 | 4.63 | 3.84 | 0.82 |
| 4.3 | 2.35 | 2.34 | 0.13 | 1.16 | 4.45 | 3.83 | 0.89 |
| 4.4 | 2.37 | 2.32 | 0.12 | 1.18 | 4.27 | 3.83 | 0.95 |
| 4.5 | 2.39 | 2.30 | 0.11 | 1.21 | 4.08 | 3.82 | 1.02 |
| 4.6 | 2.41 | 2.28 | 0.10 | 1.24 | 3.89 | 3.81 | 1.09 |
| 4.7 | 2.43 | 2.26 | 0.09 | 1.26 | 3.69 | 3.79 | 1.16 |
| 4.8 | 2.45 | 2.24 | 0.09 | 1.29 | 3.49 | 3.77 | 1.24 |
| 4.9 | 2.47 | 2.22 | 0.08 | 1.31 | 3.29 | 3.75 | 1.31 |
| 5.0 | 2.49 | 2.20 | 0.07 | 1.34 | 3.09 | 3.73 | 1.38 |

# TABLES CXII.-CXV.

| Tables | CXII. | | | | |
|---|---|---|---|---|---|
| Arguments | 2. | | | | |
| Days. | 20 | | 30 | | |
| Days. | Equation. | Diff. | Equation. | Diff. | |

| Days. | 20 Equation. | 20 Diff. | 30 Equation. | 30 Diff. |
|---|---|---|---|---|
| 5.0 | 1.44″ | .14 | 54.21″ | .57 |
| 5.1 | 1.58 | .15 | 54.78 | .56 |
| 5.2 | 1.73 | .17 | 55.34 | .55 |
| 5.3 | 1.90 | .17 | 55.89 | .54 |
| 5.4 | 2.07 | .19 | 56.43 | .54 |
| 5.5 | 2.26 | .20 | 56.97 | .53 |
| 5.6 | 2.46 | .22 | 57.50 | .52 |
| 5.7 | 2.68 | .22 | 58.02 | .50 |
| 5.8 | 2.90 | .24 | 58.52 | .49 |
| 5.9 | 3.14 | .25 | 59.01 | .48 |
| 6.0 | 3.39 | .26 | 59.49 | .47 |
| 6.1 | 3.65 | .27 | 59.96 | .47 |
| 6.2 | 3.92 | .29 | 60.43 | .46 |
| 6.3 | 4.21 | .30 | 60.89 | .45 |
| 6.4 | 4.51 | .31 | 61.34 | .44 |
| 6.5 | 4.82 | .32 | 61.78 | .43 |
| 6.6 | 5.14 | .33 | 62.21 | .42 |
| 6.7 | 5.47 | .34 | 62.63 | .41 |
| 6.8 | 5.81 | .35 | 63.04 | .39 |
| 6.9 | 6.16 | .37 | 63.43 | .38 |
| 7.0 | 6.53 | .37 | 63.81 | .37 |
| 7.1 | 6.90 | .39 | 64.18 | .36 |
| 7.2 | 7.29 | .40 | 64.54 | .34 |
| 7.3 | 7.69 | .40 | 64.88 | .33 |
| 7.4 | 8.09 | .42 | 65.21 | .32 |
| 7.5 | 8.51 | .43 | 65.53 | .31 |
| 7.6 | 8.94 | .44 | 65.84 | .30 |
| 7.7 | 9.38 | .44 | 66.14 | .29 |
| 7.8 | 9.82 | .46 | 66.43 | .28 |
| 7.9 | 10.28 | .47 | 66.71 | .26 |
| 8.0 | 10.75 | .47 | 66.97 | .25 |
| 8.1 | 11.22 | .49 | 67.22 | .23 |
| 8.2 | 11.71 | .49 | 67.45 | .22 |
| 8.3 | 12.20 | .50 | 67.67 | .20 |
| 8.4 | 12.70 | .51 | 67.87 | .19 |
| 8.5 | 13.21 | .52 | 68.06 | .18 |
| 8.6 | 13.73 | .53 | 68.24 | .17 |
| 8.7 | 14.26 | .54 | 68.41 | .15 |
| 8.8 | 14.80 | .54 | 68.56 | .14 |
| 8.9 | 15.34 | .56 | 68.70 | .13 |
| 9.0 | 15.90 | .56 | 68.83 | .11 |
| 9.1 | 16.46 | .56 | 68.94 | .10 |
| 9.2 | 17.02 | .58 | 69.04 | .08 |
| 9.3 | 17.60 | .58 | 69.12 | .07 |
| 9.4 | 18.18 | .58 | 69.19 | .06 |
| 9.5 | 18.76 | .60 | 69.25 | .04 |
| 9.6 | 19.36 | .60 | 69.29 | .03 |
| 9.7 | 19.96 | .60 | 69.32 | .02 |
| 9.8 | 20.56 | .61 | 69.34 | .00 |
| 9.9 | 21.17 | .62 | 69.34 | .00 |
| 10.0 | 21.79 | .62 | 69.34 | .00 |

| Tables | CXIII. | | | | CXIV. | CXV. | |
|---|---|---|---|---|---|---|---|
| Arguments | 6. | | | | 7. | 8. | |
| Days. | 0 | 10 | 20 | 30 | 0 | 0 | 10 |
| 5.0 | 2.49″ | 2.20″ | 0.07″ | 1.34″ | 3.09″ | 3.73″ | 1.38″ |
| 5.1 | 2.51 | 2.18 | 0.06 | 1.37 | 2.89 | 3.70 | 1.46 |
| 5.2 | 2.52 | 2.15 | 0.06 | 1.39 | 2.69 | 3.67 | 1.54 |
| 5.3 | 2.54 | 2.13 | 0.05 | 1.42 | 2.49 | 3.63 | 1.61 |
| 5.4 | 2.55 | 2.10 | 0.05 | 1.44 | 2.29 | 3.60 | 1.69 |
| 5.5 | 2.57 | 2.08 | 0.04 | 1.47 | 2.10 | 3.56 | 1.77 |
| 5.6 | 2.58 | 2.06 | 0.03 | 1.50 | 1.91 | 3.51 | 1.85 |
| 5.7 | 2.60 | 2.03 | 0.03 | 1.52 | 1.73 | 3.47 | 1.93 |
| 5.8 | 2.62 | 2.01 | 0.02 | 1.55 | 1.55 | 3.42 | 2.00 |
| 5.9 | 2.63 | 1.98 | 0.02 | 1.57 | 1.38 | 3.37 | 2.08 |
| 6.0 | 2.65 | 1.96 | 0.01 | 1.60 | 1.21 | 3.32 | 2.16 |
| 6.1 | 2.66 | 1.94 | 0.01 | 1.63 | 1.06 | 3.26 | 2.24 |
| 6.2 | 2.68 | 1.91 | 0.01 | 1.65 | 0.91 | 3.20 | 2.31 |
| 6.3 | 2.69 | 1.89 | 0.00 | 1.68 | 0.77 | 3.14 | 2.39 |
| 6.4 | 2.71 | 1.86 | 0.00 | 1.70 | 0.64 | 3.08 | 2.46 |
| 6.5 | 2.72 | 1.84 | 0.00 | 1.73 | 0.52 | 3.02 | 2.54 |
| 6.6 | 2.73 | 1.81 | 0.00 | 1.76 | 0.42 | 2.95 | 2.61 |
| 6.7 | 2.74 | 1.79 | 0.00 | 1.78 | 0.32 | 2.89 | 2.69 |
| 6.8 | 2.76 | 1.76 | 0.00 | 1.81 | 0.24 | 2.82 | 2.76 |
| 6.9 | 2.77 | 1.74 | 0.00 | 1.83 | 0.17 | 2.75 | 2.83 |
| 7.0 | 2.78 | 1.71 | 0.00 | 1.86 | 0.11 | 2.68 | 2.90 |
| 7.1 | 2.79 | 1.68 | 0.00 | 1.88 | 0.06 | 2.61 | 2.96 |
| 7.2 | 2.80 | 1.66 | 0.00 | 1.91 | 0.03 | 2.53 | 3.03 |
| 7.3 | 2.81 | 1.63 | 0.01 | 1.93 | 0.01 | 2.46 | 3.09 |
| 7.4 | 2.82 | 1.61 | 0.01 | 1.96 | 0.00 | 2.38 | 3.15 |
| 7.5 | 2.83 | 1.58 | 0.01 | 1.98 | 0.01 | 2.31 | 3.21 |
| 7.6 | 2.84 | 1.55 | 0.02 | 2.01 | 0.03 | 2.23 | 3.26 |
| 7.7 | 2.84 | 1.53 | 0.02 | 2.03 | 0.06 | 2.15 | 3.32 |
| 7.8 | 2.85 | 1.50 | 0.03 | 2.05 | 0.10 | 2.08 | 3.37 |
| 7.9 | 2.85 | 1.48 | 0.03 | 2.08 | 0.16 | 2.00 | 3.42 |
| 8.0 | 2.86 | 1.45 | 0.04 | 2.10 | 0.23 | 1.92 | 3.47 |
| 8.1 | 2.86 | 1.42 | 0.05 | 2.12 | 0.31 | 1.84 | 3.51 |
| 8.2 | 2.87 | 1.40 | 0.05 | 2.14 | 0.41 | 1.76 | 3.55 |
| 8.3 | 2.87 | 1.37 | 0.06 | 2.17 | 0.51 | 1.69 | 3.59 |
| 8.4 | 2.88 | 1.35 | 0.06 | 2.19 | 0.63 | 1.61 | 3.63 |
| 8.5 | 2.88 | 1.32 | 0.07 | 2.21 | 0.76 | 1.53 | 3.67 |
| 8.6 | 2.88 | 1.29 | 0.08 | 2.23 | 0.90 | 1.45 | 3.70 |
| 8.7 | 2.89 | 1.27 | 0.09 | 2.25 | 1.04 | 1.38 | 3.73 |
| 8.8 | 2.89 | 1.24 | 0.10 | 2.27 | 1.20 | 1.30 | 3.75 |
| 8.9 | 2.90 | 1.22 | 0.11 | 2.29 | 1.36 | 1.23 | 3.77 |
| 9.0 | 2.90 | 1.19 | 0.12 | 2.31 | 1.53 | 1.16 | 3.79 |
| 9.1 | 2.90 | 1.16 | 0.13 | 2.33 | 1.71 | 1.09 | 3.81 |
| 9.2 | 2.90 | 1.14 | 0.14 | 2.35 | 1.90 | 1.02 | 3.82 |
| 9.3 | 2.90 | 1.11 | 0.15 | 2.37 | 2.09 | 0.96 | 3.83 |
| 9.4 | 2.90 | 1.09 | 0.17 | 2.39 | 2.28 | 0.89 | 3.84 |
| 9.5 | 2.90 | 1.06 | 0.18 | 2.41 | 2.47 | 0.82 | 3.84 |
| 9.6 | 2.90 | 1.04 | 0.19 | 2.43 | 2.67 | 0.76 | 3.84 |
| 9.7 | 2.90 | 1.01 | 0.21 | 2.45 | 2.87 | 0.70 | 3.83 |
| 9.8 | 2.89 | 0.99 | 0.22 | 2.47 | 3.07 | 0.64 | 3.83 |
| 9.9 | 2.89 | 0.96 | 0.24 | 2.49 | 3.27 | 0.58 | 3.82 |
| 10.0 | 2.89 | 0.94 | 0.25 | 2.51 | 3.48 | 0.52 | 3.81 |

# TABLES CXVI. - CXIX.

| Tables | CXVI. | | | CXVII. | | | CXVIII. | | | CXIX. |
|---|---|---|---|---|---|---|---|---|---|---|
| Arguments | **9.** | | | **10.** | | | **11.** | | | **13.** |
| Days. | **0** | **10** | **20** | **0** | **10** | **20** | **0** | **10** | **20** | **0** |
| Days. | " | " | " | " | " | " | " | " | " | " |
| 0.0 | 1.14 | 2.16 | 0.15 | 0.99 | 0.31 | 1.89 | 0.80 | 0.14 | 1.41 | 0.26 |
| 0.1 | 1.16 | 2.15 | 0.14 | 0.97 | 0.33 | 1.89 | 0.78 | 0.15 | 1.41 | 0.29 |
| 0.2 | 1.19 | 2.14 | 0.13 | 0.95 | 0.35 | 1.88 | 0.77 | 0.16 | 1.41 | 0.32 |
| 0.3 | 1.21 | 2.12 | 0.12 | 0.92 | 0.36 | 1.88 | 0.75 | 0.17 | 1.42 | 0.35 |
| 0.4 | 1.24 | 2.11 | 0.11 | 0.90 | 0.38 | 1.87 | 0.74 | 0.18 | 1.42 | 0.39 |
| 0.5 | 1.26 | 2.10 | 0.10 | 0.88 | 0.40 | 1.87 | 0.72 | 0.19 | 1.42 | 0.42 |
| 0.6 | 1.28 | 2.08 | 0.09 | 0.86 | 0.42 | 1.86 | 0.70 | 0.20 | 1.42 | 0.46 |
| 0.7 | 1.31 | 2.07 | 0.08 | 0.83 | 0.44 | 1.85 | 0.69 | 0.21 | 1.42 | 0.50 |
| 0.8 | 1.33 | 2.06 | 0.07 | 0.81 | 0.46 | 1.85 | 0.67 | 0.23 | 1.42 | 0.54 |
| 0.9 | 1.36 | 2.04 | 0.06 | 0.78 | 0.48 | 1.84 | 0.66 | 0.24 | 1.42 | 0.58 |
| 1.0 | 1.38 | 2.03 | 0.05 | 0.76 | 0.50 | 1.83 | 0.64 | 0.25 | 1.42 | 0.62 |
| 1.1 | 1.40 | 2.01 | 0.04 | 0.74 | 0.52 | 1.82 | 0.62 | 0.26 | 1.42 | 0.66 |
| 1.2 | 1.43 | 1.99 | 0.04 | 0.72 | 0.54 | 1.81 | 0.61 | 0.28 | 1.42 | 0.70 |
| 1.3 | 1.45 | 1.98 | 0.03 | 0.69 | 0.57 | 1.80 | 0.59 | 0.29 | 1.41 | 0.73 |
| 1.4 | 1.48 | 1.96 | 0.03 | 0.67 | 0.59 | 1.79 | 0.58 | 0.31 | 1.41 | 0.77 |
| 1.5 | 1.50 | 1.94 | 0.02 | 0.65 | 0.61 | 1.78 | 0.56 | 0.32 | 1.41 | 0.80 |
| 1.6 | 1.52 | 1.92 | 0.02 | 0.63 | 0.63 | 1.77 | 0.54 | 0.33 | 1.41 | 0.83 |
| 1.7 | 1.54 | 1.90 | 0.02 | 0.61 | 0.65 | 1.75 | 0.53 | 0.35 | 1.40 | 0.87 |
| 1.8 | 1.57 | 1.89 | 0.01 | 0.58 | 0.68 | 1.74 | 0.51 | 0.36 | 1.40 | 0.90 |
| 1.9 | 1.59 | 1.87 | 0.01 | 0.56 | 0.70 | 1.72 | 0.50 | 0.38 | 1.39 | 0.93 |
| 2.0 | 1.61 | 1.85 | 0.01 | 0.54 | 0.72 | 1.71 | 0.48 | 0.39 | 1.39 | 0.96 |
| 2.1 | 1.63 | 1.83 | 0.00 | 0.52 | 0.74 | 1.70 | 0.46 | 0.41 | 1.38 | 0.99 |
| 2.2 | 1.65 | 1.81 | 0.00 | 0.50 | 0.76 | 1.68 | 0.45 | 0.42 | 1.38 | 1.02 |
| 2.3 | 1.68 | 1.78 | 0.00 | 0.48 | 0.79 | 1.67 | 0.43 | 0.44 | 1.37 | 1.04 |
| 2.4 | 1.70 | 1.76 | 0.00 | 0.46 | 0.81 | 1.65 | 0.42 | 0.45 | 1.37 | 1.07 |
| 2.5 | 1.72 | 1.74 | 0.00 | 0.44 | 0.83 | 1.64 | 0.40 | 0.47 | 1.36 | 1.09 |
| 2.6 | 1.74 | 1.72 | 0.00 | 0.42 | 0.85 | 1.62 | 0.39 | 0.49 | 1.35 | 1.11 |
| 2.7 | 1.76 | 1.70 | 0.00 | 0.40 | 0.88 | 1.60 | 0.37 | 0.50 | 1.34 | 1.12 |
| 2.8 | 1.79 | 1.67 | 0.01 | 0.39 | 0.90 | 1.59 | 0.36 | 0.52 | 1.34 | 1.14 |
| 2.9 | 1.81 | 1.65 | 0.01 | 0.37 | 0.93 | 1.57 | 0.34 | 0.53 | 1.33 | 1.15 |
| 3.0 | 1.83 | 1.63 | 0.01 | 0.35 | 0.95 | 1.55 | 0.33 | 0.55 | 1.32 | 1.17 |
| 3.1 | 1.85 | 1.61 | 0.01 | 0.33 | 0.97 | 1.53 | 0.32 | 0.57 | 1.31 | 1.18 |
| 3.2 | 1.87 | 1.59 | 0.02 | 0.31 | 1.00 | 1.51 | 0.30 | 0.58 | 1.30 | 1.19 |
| 3.3 | 1.88 | 1.56 | 0.02 | 0.30 | 1.02 | 1.50 | 0.29 | 0.60 | 1.29 | 1.19 |
| 3.4 | 1.90 | 1.54 | 0.03 | 0.28 | 1.05 | 1.48 | 0.27 | 0.61 | 1.28 | 1.20 |
| 3.5 | 1.92 | 1.52 | 0.03 | 0.26 | 1.07 | 1.46 | 0.26 | 0.63 | 1.27 | 1.20 |
| 3.6 | 1.94 | 1.50 | 0.04 | 0.25 | 1.09 | 1.44 | 0.25 | 0.65 | 1.26 | 1.20 |
| 3.7 | 1.96 | 1.47 | 0.04 | 0.23 | 1.11 | 1.42 | 0.24 | 0.66 | 1.25 | 1.19 |
| 3.8 | 1.97 | 1.45 | 0.05 | 0.22 | 1.14 | 1.40 | 0.22 | 0.68 | 1.24 | 1.19 |
| 3.9 | 1.99 | 1.42 | 0.05 | 0.20 | 1.16 | 1.38 | 0.21 | 0.69 | 1.23 | 1.18 |
| 4.0 | 2.01 | 1.40 | 0.06 | 0.19 | 1.18 | 1.36 | 0.20 | 0.71 | 1.22 | 1.17 |
| 4.1 | 2.03 | 1.38 | 0.07 | 0.18 | 1.20 | 1.34 | 0.19 | 0.73 | 1.21 | 1.15 |
| 4.2 | 2.04 | 1.35 | 0.08 | 0.16 | 1.22 | 1.32 | 0.18 | 0.74 | 1.20 | 1.14 |
| 4.3 | 2.06 | 1.33 | 0.09 | 0.15 | 1.25 | 1.29 | 0.17 | 0.76 | 1.18 | 1.12 |
| 4.4 | 2.07 | 1.30 | 0.10 | 0.13 | 1.27 | 1.27 | 0.16 | 0.77 | 1.17 | 1.10 |
| 4.5 | 2.09 | 1.28 | 0.11 | 0.12 | 1.29 | 1.25 | 0.15 | 0.79 | 1.16 | 1.08 |
| 4.6 | 2.10 | 1.26 | 0.12 | 0.11 | 1.31 | 1.23 | 0.14 | 0.81 | 1.15 | 1.05 |
| 4.7 | 2.12 | 1.23 | 0.13 | 0.10 | 1.33 | 1.21 | 0.13 | 0.82 | 1.13 | 1.03 |
| 4.8 | 2.13 | 1.21 | 0.14 | 0.09 | 1.36 | 1.18 | 0.12 | 0.84 | 1.12 | 1.00 |
| 4.9 | 2.15 | 1.18 | 0.15 | 0.08 | 1.38 | 1.16 | 0.11 | 0.85 | 1.10 | 0.98 |
| 5.0 | 2.16 | 1.16 | 0.16 | 0.07 | 1.40 | 1.14 | 0.10 | 0.87 | 1.09 | 0.95 |

# TABLES CXVI.-CXIX.

| Tables | CXVI. | | | CXVII. | | | CXVIII. | | | CXIX. |
|---|---|---|---|---|---|---|---|---|---|---|
| Arguments | **9.** | | | **10.** | | | **11.** | | | **13.** |
| Days. | **0** | **10** | **20** | **0** | **10** | **20** | **0** | **10** | **20** | **0** |
| Days | ″ | ″ | ″ | ″ | ″ | ″ | ″ | ″ | ″ | ″ |
| 5.0 | 2.16 | 1.16 | 0.16 | 0.07 | 1.40 | 1.14 | 0.10 | 0.87 | 1.09 | 0.95 |
| 5.1 | 2.17 | 1.14 | 0.17 | 0.06 | 1.42 | 1.12 | 0.09 | 0.89 | 1.08 | 0.92 |
| 5.2 | 2.18 | 1.11 | 0.19 | 0.05 | 1.44 | 1.09 | 0.08 | 0.90 | 1.06 | 0.88 |
| 5.3 | 2.19 | 1.09 | 0.20 | 0.05 | 1.46 | 1.07 | 0.08 | 0.92 | 1.05 | 0.85 |
| 5.4 | 2.20 | 1.06 | 0.22 | 0.04 | 1.48 | 1.04 | 0.07 | 0.93 | 1.03 | 0.81 |
| 5.5 | 2.21 | 1.04 | 0.23 | 0.03 | 1.50 | 1.02 | 0.06 | 0.95 | 1.02 | 0.78 |
| 5.6 | 2.22 | 1.02 | 0.25 | 0.03 | 1.52 | 1.00 | 0.05 | 0.97 | 1.00 | 0.74 |
| 5.7 | 2.23 | 0.99 | 0.26 | 0.02 | 1.54 | 0.98 | 0.05 | 0.98 | 0.99 | 0.71 |
| 5.8 | 2.24 | 0.97 | 0.28 | 0.02 | 1.55 | 0.95 | 0.04 | 1.00 | 0.97 | 0.67 |
| 5.9 | 2.25 | 0.94 | 0.29 | 0.01 | 1.57 | 0.93 | 0.04 | 1.01 | 0.96 | 0.64 |
| 6.0 | 2.26 | 0.92 | 0.31 | 0.01 | 1.59 | 0.91 | 0.03 | 1.03 | 0.94 | 0.60 |
| 6.1 | 2.27 | 0.90 | 0.33 | 0.01 | 1.61 | 0.89 | 0.03 | 1.04 | 0.92 | 0.56 |
| 6.2 | 2.27 | 0.87 | 0.35 | 0.01 | 1.62 | 0.86 | 0.02 | 1.06 | 0.91 | 0.53 |
| 6.3 | 2.28 | 0.85 | 0.36 | 0.00 | 1.64 | 0.84 | 0.02 | 1.07 | 0.89 | 0.49 |
| 6.4 | 2.28 | 0.82 | 0.38 | 0.00 | 1.65 | 0.81 | 0.01 | 1.09 | 0.88 | 0.46 |
| 6.5 | 2.29 | 0.80 | 0.40 | 0.00 | 1.67 | 0.79 | 0.01 | 1.10 | 0.86 | 0.42 |
| 6.6 | 2.29 | 0.78 | 0.42 | 0.00 | 1.68 | 0.77 | 0.01 | 1.11 | 0.84 | 0.39 |
| 6.7 | 2.30 | 0.76 | 0.44 | 0.00 | 1.70 | 0.75 | 0.01 | 1.13 | 0.83 | 0.35 |
| 6.8 | 2.30 | 0.73 | 0.45 | 0.00 | 1.71 | 0.72 | 0.00 | 1.14 | 0.81 | 0.32 |
| 6.9 | 2.31 | 0.71 | 0.47 | 0.00 | 1.73 | 0.70 | 0.00 | 1.16 | 0.80 | 0.28 |
| 7.0 | 2.31 | 0.69 | 0.49 | 0.01 | 1.74 | 0.68 | 0.00 | 1.17 | 0.78 | 0.25 |
| 7.1 | 2.31 | 0.67 | 0.51 | 0.01 | 1.75 | 0.66 | 0.00 | 1.18 | 0.76 | 0.22 |
| 7.2 | 2.31 | 0.65 | 0.53 | 0.01 | 1.76 | 0.64 | 0.00 | 1.19 | 0.75 | 0.20 |
| 7.3 | 2.32 | 0.62 | 0.56 | 0.01 | 1.78 | 0.61 | 0.00 | 1.21 | 0.73 | 0.17 |
| 7.4 | 2.32 | 0.60 | 0.58 | 0.02 | 1.79 | 0.59 | 0.00 | 1.22 | 0.72 | 0.15 |
| 7.5 | 2.32 | 0.58 | 0.60 | 0.02 | 1.80 | 0.57 | 0.00 | 1.23 | 0.70 | 0.12 |
| 7.6 | 2.32 | 0.56 | 0.62 | 0.03 | 1.81 | 0.55 | 0.00 | 1.24 | 0.68 | 0.10 |
| 7.7 | 2.32 | 0.54 | 0.64 | 0.04 | 1.82 | 0.53 | 0.00 | 1.25 | 0.67 | 0.08 |
| 7.8 | 2.32 | 0.51 | 0.67 | 0.04 | 1.82 | 0.51 | 0.01 | 1.26 | 0.65 | 0.07 |
| 7.9 | 2.32 | 0.49 | 0.69 | 0.05 | 1.83 | 0.49 | 0.01 | 1.27 | 0.64 | 0.05 |
| 8.0 | 2.31 | 0.47 | 0.71 | 0.06 | 1.84 | 0.47 | 0.01 | 1.28 | 0.62 | 0.04 |
| 8.1 | 2.31 | 0.45 | 0.73 | 0.07 | 1.85 | 0.45 | 0.01 | 1.29 | 0.60 | 0.03 |
| 8.2 | 2.31 | 0.43 | 0.75 | 0.08 | 1.86 | 0.43 | 0.02 | 1.30 | 0.59 | 0.02 |
| 8.3 | 2.30 | 0.42 | 0.78 | 0.08 | 1.86 | 0.41 | 0.02 | 1.31 | 0.57 | 0.01 |
| 8.4 | 2.30 | 0.40 | 0.80 | 0.09 | 1.87 | 0.39 | 0.03 | 1.32 | 0.56 | 0.01 |
| 8.5 | 2.30 | 0.38 | 0.82 | 0.10 | 1.88 | 0.37 | 0.03 | 1.33 | 0.54 | 0.00 |
| 8.6 | 2.29 | 0.36 | 0.84 | 0.11 | 1.88 | 0.35 | 0.04 | 1.34 | 0.52 | 0.00 |
| 8.7 | 2.29 | 0.34 | 0.87 | 0.12 | 1.88 | 0.33 | 0.04 | 1.34 | 0.50 | 0.01 |
| 8.8 | 2.28 | 0.33 | 0.89 | 0.14 | 1.89 | 0.32 | 0.05 | 1.35 | 0.49 | 0.01 |
| 8.9 | 2.28 | 0.31 | 0.92 | 0.15 | 1.89 | 0.30 | 0.05 | 1.35 | 0.48 | 0.02 |
| 9.0 | 2.27 | 0.29 | 0.94 | 0.16 | 1.89 | 0.28 | 0.06 | 1.36 | 0.46 | 0.03 |
| 9.1 | 2.26 | 0.27 | 0.96 | 0.17 | 1.90 | 0.26 | 0.07 | 1.37 | 0.44 | 0.04 |
| 9.2 | 2.25 | 0.26 | 0.99 | 0.19 | 1.90 | 0.25 | 0.07 | 1.37 | 0.43 | 0.06 |
| 9.3 | 2.24 | 0.24 | 1.01 | 0.20 | 1.90 | 0.23 | 0.08 | 1.38 | 0.41 | 0.07 |
| 9.4 | 2.23 | 0.23 | 1.04 | 0.22 | 1.90 | 0.22 | 0.08 | 1.38 | 0.40 | 0.09 |
| 9.5 | 2.22 | 0.22 | 1.06 | 0.23 | 1.90 | 0.20 | 0.09 | 1.39 | 0.38 | 0.11 |
| 9.6 | 2.21 | 0.20 | 1.08 | 0.25 | 1.90 | 0.19 | 0.10 | 1.39 | 0.37 | 0.13 |
| 9.7 | 2.20 | 0.19 | 1.11 | 0.26 | 1.90 | 0.18 | 0.11 | 1.40 | 0.35 | 0.16 |
| 9.8 | 2.18 | 0.17 | 1.13 | 0.28 | 1.89 | 0.16 | 0.12 | 1.40 | 0.34 | 0.18 |
| 9.9 | 2.17 | 0.16 | 1.16 | 0.29 | 1.89 | 0.15 | 0.13 | 1.41 | 0.32 | 0.21 |
| 10.0 | 2.16 | 0.15 | 1.18 | 0.31 | 1.89 | 0.14 | 0.14 | 1.41 | 0.31 | 0.24 |

# TABLES CXX.-CXXIV.

| Tables | CXX. | | | CXXI. | | CXXII. | | CXXIII. | | | CXXIV. |
|---|---|---|---|---|---|---|---|---|---|---|---|
| Arguments | **14.** | | | **15.** | | **16.** | | **17.** | | | **18.** |
| Days. | **0** | **10** | **20** | **0** | **10** | **0** | **10** | **0** | **10** | **20** | **0** |
| Days 0.0 | ″ 0.25 | ″ 0.03 | ″ 0.43 | ″ 0.43 | ″ 0.55 | ″ 0.64 | ″ 0.15 | ″ 0.13 | ″ 0.25 | ″ 0.00 | ″ 0.21 |
| 0.1 | 0.25 | 0.03 | 0.43 | 0.42 | 0.56 | 0.61 | 0.17 | 0.13 | 0.25 | 0.00 | 0.23 |
| 0.2 | 0.24 | 0.03 | 0.43 | 0.40 | 0.57 | 0.59 | 0.18 | 0.14 | 0.25 | 0.00 | 0.24 |
| 0.3 | 0.24 | 0.04 | 0.44 | 0.39 | 0.57 | 0.56 | 0.20 | 0.14 | 0.24 | 0.00 | 0.25 |
| 0.4 | 0.23 | 0.04 | 0.44 | 0.37 | 0.58 | 0.54 | 0.22 | 0.15 | 0.24 | 0.00 | 0.27 |
| 0.5 | 0.23 | 0.04 | 0.44 | 0.36 | 0.59 | 0.51 | 0.24 | 0.15 | 0.24 | 0.00 | 0.28 |
| 0.6 | 0.22 | 0.04 | 0.44 | 0.35 | 0.59 | 0.48 | 0.26 | 0.15 | 0.24 | 0.00 | 0.29 |
| 0.7 | 0.22 | 0.05 | 0.44 | 0.34 | 0.60 | 0.45 | 0.29 | 0.15 | 0.24 | 0.00 | 0.30 |
| 0.8 | 0.21 | 0.05 | 0.45 | 0.32 | 0.60 | 0.43 | 0.31 | 0.16 | 0.23 | 0.00 | 0.32 |
| 0.9 | 0.21 | 0.06 | 0.45 | 0.31 | 0.61 | 0.40 | 0.34 | 0.16 | 0.23 | 0.00 | 0.33 |
| 1.0 | 0.20 | 0.06 | 0.45 | 0.30 | 0.61 | 0.37 | 0.37 | 0.16 | 0.23 | 0.00 | 0.34 |
| 1.1 | 0.19 | 0.06 | 0.45 | 0.29 | 0.61 | 0.34 | 0.40 | 0.17 | 0.23 | 0.00 | 0.35 |
| 1.2 | 0.19 | 0.06 | 0.45 | 0.27 | 0.61 | 0.31 | 0.43 | 0.17 | 0.23 | 0.00 | 0.36 |
| 1.3 | 0.18 | 0.07 | 0.46 | 0.26 | 0.62 | 0.29 | 0.45 | 0.17 | 0.22 | 0.00 | 0.37 |
| 1.4 | 0.18 | 0.07 | 0.46 | 0.24 | 0.62 | 0.26 | 0.48 | 0.18 | 0.22 | 0.00 | 0.38 |
| 1.5 | 0.17 | 0.07 | 0.46 | 0.23 | 0.62 | 0.24 | 0.51 | 0.18 | 0.22 | 0.00 | 0.39 |
| 1.6 | 0.17 | 0.07 | 0.46 | 0.22 | 0.62 | 0.22 | 0.54 | 0.18 | 0.21 | 0.00 | 0.40 |
| 1.7 | 0.16 | 0.08 | 0.46 | 0.21 | 0.62 | 0.20 | 0.56 | 0.18 | 0.21 | 0.00 | 0.41 |
| 1.8 | 0.16 | 0.08 | 0.46 | 0.19 | 0.61 | 0.18 | 0.59 | 0.19 | 0.21 | 0.00 | 0.42 |
| 1.9 | 0.15 | 0.09 | 0.46 | 0.18 | 0.61 | 0.17 | 0.61 | 0.19 | 0.20 | 0.00 | 0.42 |
| 2.0 | 0.15 | 0.09 | 0.46 | 0.17 | 0.61 | 0.15 | 0.64 | 0.19 | 0.20 | 0.00 | 0.43 |
| 2.1 | 0.15 | 0.09 | 0.46 | 0.16 | 0.61 | 0.14 | 0.66 | 0.20 | 0.20 | 0.01 | 0.43 |
| 2.2 | 0.14 | 0.10 | 0.46 | 0.15 | 0.60 | 0.13 | 0.68 | 0.20 | 0.20 | 0.01 | 0.43 |
| 2.3 | 0.14 | 0.10 | 0.46 | 0.13 | 0.60 | 0.12 | 0.70 | 0.20 | 0.19 | 0.01 | 0.44 |
| 2.4 | 0.13 | 0.11 | 0.46 | 0.12 | 0.59 | 0.12 | 0.71 | 0.21 | 0.19 | 0.01 | 0.44 |
| 2.5 | 0.13 | 0.11 | 0.46 | 0.11 | 0.59 | 0.11 | 0.73 | 0.21 | 0.19 | 0.01 | 0.44 |
| 2.6 | 0.13 | 0.11 | 0.46 | 0.10 | 0.58 | 0.11 | 0.74 | 0.21 | 0.18 | 0.01 | 0.44 |
| 2.7 | 0.12 | 0.12 | 0.46 | 0.09 | 0.58 | 0.11 | 0.75 | 0.21 | 0.18 | 0.01 | 0.44 |
| 2.8 | 0.12 | 0.12 | 0.46 | 0.08 | 0.57 | 0.11 | 0.76 | 0.22 | 0.18 | 0.02 | 0.43 |
| 2.9 | 0.11 | 0.13 | 0.46 | 0.07 | 0.57 | 0.12 | 0.77 | 0.22 | 0.17 | 0.02 | 0.43 |
| 3.0 | 0.11 | 0.13 | 0.46 | 0.06 | 0.56 | 0.12 | 0.78 | 0.22 | 0.17 | 0.02 | 0.43 |
| 3.1 | 0.11 | 0.14 | 0.46 | 0.05 | 0.55 | 0.13 | 0.78 | 0.22 | 0.17 | 0.02 | 0.42 |
| 3.2 | 0.10 | 0.14 | 0.46 | 0.05 | 0.54 | 0.14 | 0.78 | 0.22 | 0.17 | 0.02 | 0.42 |
| 3.3 | 0.10 | 0.15 | 0.45 | 0.04 | 0.53 | 0.15 | 0.77 | 0.23 | 0.16 | 0.02 | 0.41 |
| 3.4 | 0.09 | 0.15 | 0.45 | 0.04 | 0.52 | 0.16 | 0.77 | 0.23 | 0.16 | 0.02 | 0.41 |
| 3.5 | 0.09 | 0.16 | 0.45 | 0.03 | 0.51 | 0.17 | 0.76 | 0.23 | 0.16 | 0.03 | 0.40 |
| 3.6 | 0.09 | 0.16 | 0.45 | 0.03 | 0.50 | 0.19 | 0.75 | 0.23 | 0.15 | 0.03 | 0.39 |
| 3.7 | 0.08 | 0.17 | 0.45 | 0.02 | 0.49 | 0.21 | 0.74 | 0.23 | 0.15 | 0.03 | 0.38 |
| 3.8 | 0.08 | 0.17 | 0.44 | 0.02 | 0.48 | 0.23 | 0.72 | 0.24 | 0.15 | 0.03 | 0.37 |
| 3.9 | 0.07 | 0.18 | 0.44 | 0.01 | 0.47 | 0.25 | 0.71 | 0.24 | 0.14 | 0.03 | 0.36 |
| 4.0 | 0.07 | 0.18 | 0.44 | 0.01 | 0.46 | 0.27 | 0.69 | 0.24 | 0.14 | 0.04 | 0.35 |
| 4.1 | 0.07 | 0.19 | 0.44 | 0.01 | 0.45 | 0.29 | 0.67 | 0.24 | 0.14 | 0.04 | 0.34 |
| 4.2 | 0.06 | 0.19 | 0.44 | 0.01 | 0.43 | 0.31 | 0.65 | 0.24 | 0.13 | 0.04 | 0.33 |
| 4.3 | 0.06 | 0.20 | 0.43 | 0.00 | 0.42 | 0.33 | 0.63 | 0.24 | 0.13 | 0.04 | 0.32 |
| 4.4 | 0.05 | 0.20 | 0.43 | 0.00 | 0.40 | 0.35 | 0.60 | 0.25 | 0.13 | 0.05 | 0.30 |
| 4.5 | 0.05 | 0.21 | 0.43 | 0.00 | 0.39 | 0.37 | 0.58 | 0.25 | 0.12 | 0.05 | 0.29 |
| 4.6 | 0.05 | 0.21 | 0.43 | 0.00 | 0.38 | 0.39 | 0.55 | 0.25 | 0.12 | 0.05 | 0.28 |
| 4.7 | 0.05 | 0.22 | 0.43 | 0.00 | 0.36 | 0.41 | 0.53 | 0.25 | 0.12 | 0.05 | 0.26 |
| 4.8 | 0.04 | 0.22 | 0.42 | 0.01 | 0.35 | 0.43 | 0.50 | 0.26 | 0.11 | 0.06 | 0.25 |
| 4.9 | 0.04 | 0.23 | 0.42 | 0.01 | 0.33 | 0.45 | 0.47 | 0.26 | 0.11 | 0.06 | 0.23 |
| 5.0 | 0.04 | 0.23 | 0.42 | 0.01 | 0.32 | 0.47 | 0.44 | 0.26 | 0.11 | 0.06 | 0.22 |

# TABLES CXX.-CXXIV.

| Tables | CXX. | | | CXXI. | | CXXII. | | CXXIII. | | | CXXIV. |
|---|---|---|---|---|---|---|---|---|---|---|---|
| Arguments | **14.** | | | **15.** | | **16.** | | **17.** | | | **18.** |
| Days. | **0** | **10** | **20** | **0** | **10** | **0** | **10** | **0** | **10** | **20** | **0** |
| Days 5.0 | ″ 0.04 | ″ 0.23 | ″ 0.42 | ″ 0.01 | ″ 0.32 | ″ 0.47 | ″ 0.44 | ″ 0.26 | ″ 0.11 | ″ 0.06 | ″ 0.22 |
| 5.1 | 0.04 | 0.23 | 0.42 | 0.01 | 0.31 | 0.48 | 0.41 | 0.26 | 0.10 | 0.06 | 0.21 |
| 5.2 | 0.04 | 0.24 | 0.42 | 0.02 | 0.29 | 0.50 | 0.39 | 0.26 | 0.10 | 0.06 | 0.19 |
| 5.3 | 0.03 | 0.24 | 0.41 | 0.02 | 0.28 | 0.51 | 0.36 | 0.27 | 0.10 | 0.07 | 0.18 |
| 5.4 | 0.03 | 0.25 | 0.41 | 0.03 | 0.26 | 0.52 | 0.34 | 0.27 | 0.09 | 0.07 | 0.16 |
| 5.5 | 0.03 | 0.25 | 0.41 | 0.03 | 0.25 | 0.53 | 0.31 | 0.27 | 0.09 | 0.07 | 0.15 |
| 5.6 | 0.03 | 0.26 | 0.41 | 0.04 | 0.24 | 0.54 | 0.29 | 0.27 | 0.09 | 0.07 | 0.14 |
| 5.7 | 0.03 | 0.26 | 0.40 | 0.05 | 0.23 | 0.55 | 0.26 | 0.27 | 0.09 | 0.08 | 0.13 |
| 5.8 | 0.02 | 0.27 | 0.40 | 0.05 | 0.21 | 0.55 | 0.24 | 0.27 | 0.08 | 0.08 | 0.11 |
| 5.9 | 0.02 | 0.27 | 0.39 | 0.06 | 0.20 | 0.56 | 0.21 | 0.27 | 0.08 | 0.08 | 0.10 |
| 6.0 | 0.02 | 0.28 | 0.39 | 0.07 | 0.19 | 0.56 | 0.19 | 0.28 | 0.08 | 0.09 | 0.09 |
| 6.1 | 0.02 | 0.28 | 0.39 | 0.08 | 0.18 | 0.56 | 0.17 | 0.28 | 0.08 | 0.09 | 0.08 |
| 6.2 | 0.02 | 0.29 | 0.38 | 0.09 | 0.17 | 0.55 | 0.16 | 0.28 | 0.07 | 0.09 | 0.07 |
| 6.3 | 0.01 | 0.29 | 0.38 | 0.10 | 0.15 | 0.55 | 0.14 | 0.28 | 0.07 | 0.10 | 0.06 |
| 6.4 | 0.01 | 0.30 | 0.37 | 0.11 | 0.14 | 0.54 | 0.13 | 0.28 | 0.07 | 0.10 | 0.05 |
| 6.5 | 0.01 | 0.30 | 0.37 | 0.12 | 0.13 | 0.53 | 0.12 | 0.28 | 0.06 | 0.10 | 0.04 |
| 6.6 | 0.01 | 0.31 | 0.37 | 0.13 | 0.12 | 0.52 | 0.12 | 0.28 | 0.06 | 0.11 | 0.03 |
| 6.7 | 0.01 | 0.31 | 0.36 | 0.14 | 0.11 | 0.51 | 0.11 | 0.28 | 0.06 | 0.11 | 0.03 |
| 6.8 | 0.00 | 0.32 | 0.36 | 0.16 | 0.10 | 0.50 | 0.11 | 0.28 | 0.05 | 0.11 | 0.02 |
| 6.9 | 0.00 | 0.32 | 0.35 | 0.17 | 0.09 | 0.48 | 0.11 | 0.28 | 0.05 | 0.12 | 0.02 |
| 7.0 | 0.00 | 0.33 | 0.35 | 0.18 | 0.08 | 0.47 | 0.11 | 0.28 | 0.05 | 0.12 | 0.01 |
| 7.1 | 0.00 | 0.33 | 0.35 | 0.19 | 0.07 | 0.45 | 0.12 | 0.28 | 0.05 | 0.12 | 0.01 |
| 7.2 | 0.00 | 0.34 | 0.34 | 0.20 | 0.06 | 0.43 | 0.12 | 0.28 | 0.05 | 0.13 | 0.01 |
| 7.3 | 0.00 | 0.34 | 0.34 | 0.22 | 0.05 | 0.41 | 0.13 | 0.28 | 0.04 | 0.13 | 0.00 |
| 7.4 | 0.00 | 0.35 | 0.33 | 0.23 | 0.05 | 0.39 | 0.13 | 0.28 | 0.04 | 0.13 | 0.00 |
| 7.5 | 0.00 | 0.35 | 0.33 | 0.24 | 0.04 | 0.37 | 0.14 | 0.28 | 0.04 | 0.14 | 0.00 |
| 7.6 | 0.00 | 0.35 | 0.33 | 0.25 | 0.03 | 0.35 | 0.15 | 0.28 | 0.04 | 0.14 | 0.00 |
| 7.7 | 0.00 | 0.36 | 0.32 | 0.27 | 0.03 | 0.33 | 0.16 | 0.28 | 0.04 | 0.14 | 0.00 |
| 7.8 | 0.00 | 0.36 | 0.32 | 0.28 | 0.02 | 0.31 | 0.18 | 0.28 | 0.03 | 0.15 | 0.01 |
| 7.9 | 0.00 | 0.37 | 0.31 | 0.30 | 0.02 | 0.29 | 0.20 | 0.28 | 0.03 | 0.15 | 0.01 |
| 8.0 | 0.00 | 0.37 | 0.31 | 0.31 | 0.01 | 0.27 | 0.22 | 0.28 | 0.03 | 0.15 | 0.01 |
| 8.1 | 0.00 | 0.37 | 0.31 | 0.32 | 0.01 | 0.25 | 0.24 | 0.28 | 0.03 | 0.16 | 0.02 |
| 8.2 | 0.00 | 0.38 | 0.30 | 0.34 | 0.01 | 0.23 | 0.26 | 0.28 | 0.03 | 0.16 | 0.02 |
| 8.3 | 0.00 | 0.38 | 0.30 | 0.35 | 0.00 | 0.21 | 0.28 | 0.27 | 0.02 | 0.16 | 0.03 |
| 8.4 | 0.00 | 0.39 | 0.29 | 0.37 | 0.00 | 0.19 | 0.30 | 0.27 | 0.02 | 0.17 | 0.04 |
| 8.5 | 0.00 | 0.39 | 0.29 | 0.38 | 0.00 | 0.17 | 0.32 | 0.27 | 0.02 | 0.17 | 0.05 |
| 8.6 | 0.00 | 0.39 | 0.29 | 0.39 | 0.00 | 0.16 | 0.34 | 0.27 | 0.02 | 0.17 | 0.06 |
| 8.7 | 0.00 | 0.39 | 0.28 | 0.40 | 0.00 | 0.15 | 0.36 | 0.27 | 0.02 | 0.17 | 0.07 |
| 8.8 | 0.01 | 0.40 | 0.28 | 0.42 | 0.00 | 0.14 | 0.38 | 0.27 | 0.01 | 0.18 | 0.08 |
| 8.9 | 0.01 | 0.40 | 0.27 | 0.43 | 0.00 | 0.13 | 0.40 | 0.27 | 0.01 | 0.18 | 0.09 |
| 9.0 | 0.01 | 0.40 | 0.27 | 0.44 | 0.00 | 0.12 | 0.42 | 0.27 | 0.01 | 0.18 | 0.10 |
| 9.1 | 0.01 | 0.40 | 0.26 | 0.45 | 0.01 | 0.12 | 0.44 | 0.27 | 0.01 | 0.19 | 0.11 |
| 9.2 | 0.01 | 0.41 | 0.25 | 0.46 | 0.01 | 0.11 | 0.46 | 0.27 | 0.01 | 0.19 | 0.12 |
| 9.3 | 0.02 | 0.41 | 0.25 | 0.48 | 0.01 | 0.11 | 0.48 | 0.26 | 0.01 | 0.19 | 0.14 |
| 9.4 | 0.02 | 0.42 | 0.24 | 0.49 | 0.02 | 0.11 | 0.49 | 0.26 | 0.01 | 0.20 | 0.15 |
| 9.5 | 0.02 | 0.42 | 0.23 | 0.50 | 0.02 | 0.11 | 0.51 | 0.26 | 0.01 | 0.20 | 0.16 |
| 9.6 | 0.02 | 0.42 | 0.23 | 0.51 | 0.03 | 0.12 | 0.52 | 0.26 | 0.01 | 0.20 | 0.17 |
| 9.7 | 0.02 | 0.42 | 0.22 | 0.52 | 0.03 | 0.12 | 0.53 | 0.26 | 0.01 | 0.20 | 0.19 |
| 9.8 | 0.03 | 0.43 | 0.22 | 0.53 | 0.04 | 0.13 | 0.54 | 0.25 | 0.00 | 0.21 | 0.20 |
| 9.9 | 0.03 | 0.43 | 0.21 | 0.54 | 0.04 | 0.14 | 0.54 | 0.25 | 0.00 | 0.21 | 0.22 |
| 10.0 | 0.03 | 0.43 | 0.21 | 0.55 | 0.05 | 0.15 | 0.55 | 0.25 | 0.00 | 0.21 | 0.23 |

# TABLES CXXV.-CXXVIII.

| Tables | CXXV. | | | CXXVI. | | CXXVII. | | | | CXXVIII. | | |
|---|---|---|---|---|---|---|---|---|---|---|---|---|
| Arguments | **19.** | | | **20.** | | **22.** | | | | **23.** | | |
| Days. | **0** | **10** | **20** | **0** | **10** | **0** | **10** | **20** | **30** | **0** | **10** | **20** |
| Days. 0.0 | 0″.15 | 0″.04 | 0″.24 | 0″.08 | 0″.03 | 0″.09 | 0″.03 | 0″.18 | 0″.02 | 0″.09 | 0″.05 | 0″.17 |
| 0.1 | 0.15 | 0.04 | 0.24 | 0.08 | 0.03 | 0.09 | 0.02 | 0.18 | 0.03 | 0.09 | 0.05 | 0.17 |
| 0.2 | 0.14 | 0.04 | 0.24 | 0.09 | 0.02 | 0.10 | 0.02 | 0.18 | 0.03 | 0.09 | 0.05 | 0.17 |
| 0.3 | 0.14 | 0.05 | 0.23 | 0.09 | 0.02 | 0.10 | 0.02 | 0.18 | 0.03 | 0.08 | 0.05 | 0.16 |
| 0.4 | 0.13 | 0.05 | 0.23 | 0.10 | 0.01 | 0.11 | 0.02 | 0.18 | 0.04 | 0.08 | 0.05 | 0.16 |
| 0.5 | 0.13 | 0.05 | 0.23 | 0.10 | 0.01 | 0.11 | 0.01 | 0.18 | 0.04 | 0.08 | 0.06 | 0.16 |
| 0.6 | 0.13 | 0.05 | 0.23 | 0.11 | 0.01 | 0.11 | 0.01 | 0.18 | 0.04 | 0.08 | 0.06 | 0.16 |
| 0.7 | 0.12 | 0.05 | 0.23 | 0.11 | 0.01 | 0.12 | 0.01 | 0.18 | 0.04 | 0.08 | 0.06 | 0.16 |
| 0.8 | 0.12 | 0.06 | 0.23 | 0.12 | 0.00 | 0.12 | 0.01 | 0.17 | 0.05 | 0.07 | 0.07 | 0.15 |
| 0.9 | 0.11 | 0.06 | 0.23 | 0.12 | 0.00 | 0.13 | 0.01 | 0.17 | 0.05 | 0.07 | 0.07 | 0.15 |
| 1.0 | 0.11 | 0.06 | 0.23 | 0.13 | 0.00 | 0.13 | 0.01 | 0.17 | 0.05 | 0.07 | 0.07 | 0.15 |
| 1.1 | 0.11 | 0.07 | 0.23 | 0.13 | 0.00 | 0.13 | 0.01 | 0.17 | 0.05 | 0.07 | 0.07 | 0.15 |
| 1.2 | 0.11 | 0.07 | 0.23 | 0.14 | 0.00 | 0.13 | 0.01 | 0.17 | 0.06 | 0.07 | 0.07 | 0.15 |
| 1.3 | 0.10 | 0.07 | 0.22 | 0.14 | 0.00 | 0.14 | 0.00 | 0.17 | 0.06 | 0.06 | 0.08 | 0.14 |
| 1.4 | 0.10 | 0.08 | 0.22 | 0.15 | 0.00 | 0.14 | 0.00 | 0.17 | 0.06 | 0.06 | 0.08 | 0.14 |
| 1.5 | 0.10 | 0.08 | 0.22 | 0.15 | 0.00 | 0.14 | 0.00 | 0.17 | 0.07 | 0.06 | 0.08 | 0.14 |
| 1.6 | 0.10 | 0.08 | 0.22 | 0.16 | 0.00 | 0.14 | 0.00 | 0.16 | 0.07 | 0.06 | 0.08 | 0.14 |
| 1.7 | 0.09 | 0.08 | 0.22 | 0.16 | 0.00 | 0.14 | 0.00 | 0.16 | 0.08 | 0.06 | 0.08 | 0.14 |
| 1.8 | 0.09 | 0.09 | 0.21 | 0.17 | 0.00 | 0.15 | 0.00 | 0.16 | 0.08 | 0.05 | 0.09 | 0.13 |
| 1.9 | 0.08 | 0.09 | 0.21 | 0.17 | 0.00 | 0.15 | 0.00 | 0.16 | 0.09 | 0.05 | 0.09 | 0.13 |
| 2.0 | 0.08 | 0.09 | 0.21 | 0.18 | 0.00 | 0.15 | 0.00 | 0.15 | 0.09 | 0.05 | 0.09 | 0.13 |
| 2.1 | 0.08 | 0.09 | 0.21 | 0.18 | 0.00 | 0.16 | 0.00 | 0.15 | 0.09 | 0.05 | 0.09 | 0.13 |
| 2.2 | 0.08 | 0.09 | 0.21 | 0.19 | 0.00 | 0.16 | 0.00 | 0.15 | 0.10 | 0.05 | 0.09 | 0.13 |
| 2.3 | 0.07 | 0.10 | 0.20 | 0.19 | 0.01 | 0.16 | 0.00 | 0.15 | 0.10 | 0.04 | 0.10 | 0.12 |
| 2.4 | 0.07 | 0.10 | 0.20 | 0.20 | 0.01 | 0.16 | 0.00 | 0.14 | 0.11 | 0.04 | 0.10 | 0.12 |
| 2.5 | 0.07 | 0.10 | 0.20 | 0.20 | 0.01 | 0.17 | 0.00 | 0.14 | 0.11 | 0.04 | 0.10 | 0.12 |
| 2.6 | 0.07 | 0.11 | 0.19 | 0.20 | 0.01 | 0.17 | 0.00 | 0.14 | 0.11 | 0.04 | 0.10 | 0.12 |
| 2.7 | 0.07 | 0.11 | 0.19 | 0.21 | 0.01 | 0.17 | 0.00 | 0.14 | 0.11 | 0.04 | 0.10 | 0.12 |
| 2.8 | 0.06 | 0.11 | 0.19 | 0.21 | 0.02 | 0.17 | 0.01 | 0.13 | 0.12 | 0.03 | 0.11 | 0.11 |
| 2.9 | 0.06 | 0.12 | 0.18 | 0.22 | 0.02 | 0.17 | 0.01 | 0.13 | 0.12 | 0.03 | 0.11 | 0.11 |
| 3.0 | 0.06 | 0.12 | 0.18 | 0.22 | 0.02 | 0.17 | 0.01 | 0.13 | 0.12 | 0.03 | 0.11 | 0.11 |
| 3.1 | 0.06 | 0.12 | 0.18 | 0.22 | 0.03 | 0.17 | 0.01 | 0.12 | 0.12 | 0.03 | 0.11 | 0.11 |
| 3.2 | 0.05 | 0.13 | 0.18 | 0.22 | 0.03 | 0.17 | 0.01 | 0.12 | 0.13 | 0.03 | 0.12 | 0.11 |
| 3.3 | 0.05 | 0.13 | 0.17 | 0.23 | 0.03 | 0.18 | 0.02 | 0.12 | 0.13 | 0.02 | 0.12 | 0.10 |
| 3.4 | 0.04 | 0.13 | 0.17 | 0.23 | 0.04 | 0.18 | 0.02 | 0.11 | 0.13 | 0.02 | 0.12 | 0.10 |
| 3.5 | 0.04 | 0.14 | 0.17 | 0.23 | 0.04 | 0.18 | 0.02 | 0.11 | 0.14 | 0.02 | 0.12 | 0.10 |
| 3.6 | 0.04 | 0.14 | 0.17 | 0.23 | 0.04 | 0.18 | 0.02 | 0.11 | 0.14 | 0.02 | 0.13 | 0.10 |
| 3.7 | 0.04 | 0.14 | 0.17 | 0.23 | 0.05 | 0.18 | 0.02 | 0.10 | 0.14 | 0.02 | 0.13 | 0.10 |
| 3.8 | 0.03 | 0.15 | 0.16 | 0.24 | 0.05 | 0.18 | 0.03 | 0.10 | 0.14 | 0.01 | 0.13 | 0.09 |
| 3.9 | 0.03 | 0.15 | 0.16 | 0.24 | 0.06 | 0.18 | 0.03 | 0.09 | 0.15 | 0.01 | 0.13 | 0.09 |
| 4.0 | 0.03 | 0.15 | 0.16 | 0.24 | 0.06 | 0.18 | 0.03 | 0.09 | 0.15 | 0.01 | 0.13 | 0.09 |
| 4.1 | 0.03 | 0.15 | 0.15 | 0.24 | 0.07 | 0.18 | 0.03 | 0.09 | 0.15 | 0.01 | 0.14 | 0.09 |
| 4.2 | 0.03 | 0.15 | 0.15 | 0.24 | 0.07 | 0.18 | 0.03 | 0.08 | 0.15 | 0.01 | 0.14 | 0.08 |
| 4.3 | 0.02 | 0.16 | 0.15 | 0.24 | 0.08 | 0.18 | 0.04 | 0.08 | 0.15 | 0.01 | 0.14 | 0.08 |
| 4.4 | 0.02 | 0.16 | 0.14 | 0.24 | 0.08 | 0.18 | 0.04 | 0.07 | 0.16 | 0.01 | 0.14 | 0.08 |
| 4.5 | 0.02 | 0.16 | 0.14 | 0.24 | 0.09 | 0.18 | 0.04 | 0.07 | 0.16 | 0.01 | 0.14 | 0.08 |
| 4.6 | 0.02 | 0.17 | 0.14 | 0.24 | 0.09 | 0.18 | 0.04 | 0.07 | 0.16 | 0.01 | 0.15 | 0.07 |
| 4.7 | 0.02 | 0.17 | 0.13 | 0.24 | 0.10 | 0.18 | 0.05 | 0.07 | 0.16 | 0.01 | 0.15 | 0.07 |
| 4.8 | 0.01 | 0.17 | 0.13 | 0.24 | 0.10 | 0.17 | 0.05 | 0.06 | 0.16 | 0.00 | 0.15 | 0.07 |
| 4.9 | 0.01 | 0.18 | 0.13 | 0.24 | 0.11 | 0.17 | 0.05 | 0.06 | 0.17 | 0.00 | 0.15 | 0.06 |
| 5.0 | 0.01 | 0.18 | 0.12 | 0.24 | 0.11 | 0.17 | 0.06 | 0.06 | 0.17 | 0.00 | 0.15 | 0.06 |

# TABLES CXXV.-CXXVIII.

| Tables | CXXV. | | | CXXVI. | | CXXVII. | | | | CXXVIII. | | |
|---|---|---|---|---|---|---|---|---|---|---|---|---|
| Arguments | **19.** | | | **20.** | | **22.** | | | | **23.** | | |
| Days. | **0** | **10** | **20** | **0** | **10** | **0** | **10** | **20** | **30** | **0** | **10** | **20** |
| Days. 5.0 | ″0.01 | ″0.18 | ″0.12 | ″0.24 | ″0.11 | ″0.17 | ″0.06 | ″0.06 | ″0.17 | ″0.00 | ″0.15 | ″0.06 |
| 5.1 | 0.01 | 0.18 | 0.12 | 0.24 | 0.12 | 0.17 | 0.06 | 0.06 | 0.17 | 0.00 | 0.15 | 0.06 |
| 5.2 | 0.01 | 0.18 | 0.12 | 0.24 | 0.12 | 0.17 | 0.06 | 0.05 | 0.17 | 0.00 | 0.16 | 0.06 |
| 5.3 | 0.01 | 0.19 | 0.11 | 0.23 | 0.13 | 0.16 | 0.07 | 0.05 | 0.17 | 0.00 | 0.16 | 0.05 |
| 5.4 | 0.01 | 0.19 | 0.11 | 0.23 | 0.13 | 0.16 | 0.07 | 0.05 | 0.18 | 0.00 | 0.16 | 0.05 |
| 5.5 | 0.01 | 0.19 | 0.11 | 0.23 | 0.14 | 0.16 | 0.07 | 0.04 | 0.18 | 0.00 | 0.16 | 0.05 |
| 5.6 | 0.01 | 0.19 | 0.10 | 0.23 | 0.14 | 0.16 | 0.08 | 0.04 | 0.18 | 0.00 | 0.16 | 0.05 |
| 5.7 | 0.01 | 0.19 | 0.10 | 0.22 | 0.15 | 0.16 | 0.08 | 0.04 | 0.18 | 0.00 | 0.16 | 0.05 |
| 5.8 | 0.00 | 0.20 | 0.10 | 0.22 | 0.15 | 0.15 | 0.08 | 0.04 | 0.18 | 0.00 | 0.17 | 0.04 |
| 5.9 | 0.00 | 0.20 | 0.09 | 0.21 | 0.16 | 0.15 | 0.09 | 0.03 | 0.18 | 0.00 | 0.17 | 0.04 |
| 6.0 | 0.00 | 0.20 | 0.09 | 0.21 | 0.16 | 0.15 | 0.09 | 0.03 | 0.18 | 0.00 | 0.17 | 0.04 |
| 6.1 | 0.00 | 0.20 | 0.09 | 0.21 | 0.17 | 0.15 | 0.09 | 0.03 | 0.18 | 0.00 | 0.17 | 0.04 |
| 6.2 | 0.00 | 0.20 | 0.09 | 0.20 | 0.17 | 0.15 | 0.10 | 0.03 | 0.18 | 0.00 | 0.17 | 0.04 |
| 6.3 | 0.00 | 0.21 | 0.08 | 0.20 | 0.18 | 0.14 | 0.10 | 0.03 | 0.18 | 0.00 | 0.17 | 0.03 |
| 6.4 | 0.00 | 0.21 | 0.08 | 0.19 | 0.18 | 0.14 | 0.10 | 0.02 | 0.18 | 0.00 | 0.17 | 0.03 |
| 6.5 | 0.00 | 0.21 | 0.08 | 0.19 | 0.19 | 0.14 | 0.11 | 0.02 | 0.18 | 0.00 | 0.17 | 0.03 |
| 6.6 | 0.00 | 0.21 | 0.07 | 0.19 | 0.19 | 0.14 | 0.11 | 0.02 | 0.18 | 0.00 | 0.17 | 0.03 |
| 6.7 | 0.00 | 0.21 | 0.07 | 0.18 | 0.20 | 0.13 | 0.11 | 0.02 | 0.18 | 0.00 | 0.17 | 0.03 |
| 6.8 | 0.00 | 0.21 | 0.07 | 0.18 | 0.20 | 0.13 | 0.12 | 0.02 | 0.17 | 0.00 | 0.18 | 0.03 |
| 6.9 | 0.00 | 0.22 | 0.06 | 0.17 | 0.21 | 0.13 | 0.12 | 0.01 | 0.17 | 0.00 | 0.18 | 0.02 |
| 7.0 | 0.00 | 0.22 | 0.06 | 0.17 | 0.21 | 0.12 | 0.12 | 0.01 | 0.17 | 0.00 | 0.18 | 0.02 |
| 7.1 | 0.00 | 0.22 | 0.06 | 0.17 | 0.21 | 0.12 | 0.13 | 0.01 | 0.17 | 0.00 | 0.18 | 0.02 |
| 7.2 | 0.00 | 0.22 | 0.06 | 0.16 | 0.21 | 0.12 | 0.13 | 0.01 | 0.17 | 0.00 | 0.18 | 0.02 |
| 7.3 | 0.00 | 0.22 | 0.05 | 0.16 | 0.22 | 0.11 | 0.13 | 0.01 | 0.17 | 0.01 | 0.18 | 0.02 |
| 7.4 | 0.00 | 0.22 | 0.05 | 0.15 | 0.22 | 0.11 | 0.14 | 0.00 | 0.17 | 0.01 | 0.18 | 0.02 |
| 7.5 | 0.00 | 0.23 | 0.05 | 0.15 | 0.22 | 0.11 | 0.14 | 0.00 | 0.17 | 0.01 | 0.18 | 0.02 |
| 7.6 | 0.00 | 0.23 | 0.05 | 0.14 | 0.22 | 0.11 | 0.14 | 0.00 | 0.16 | 0.01 | 0.18 | 0.02 |
| 7.7 | 0.00 | 0.23 | 0.05 | 0.14 | 0.22 | 0.10 | 0.14 | 0.00 | 0.16 | 0.01 | 0.18 | 0.02 |
| 7.8 | 0.01 | 0.23 | 0.04 | 0.13 | 0.23 | 0.10 | 0.15 | 0.00 | 0.16 | 0.01 | 0.18 | 0.01 |
| 7.9 | 0.01 | 0.23 | 0.04 | 0.13 | 0.23 | 0.10 | 0.15 | 0.00 | 0.16 | 0.01 | 0.18 | 0.01 |
| 8.0 | 0.01 | 0.23 | 0.04 | 0.12 | 0.23 | 0.09 | 0.15 | 0.00 | 0.16 | 0.01 | 0.18 | 0.01 |
| 8.1 | 0.01 | 0.23 | 0.04 | 0.11 | 0.23 | 0.09 | 0.15 | 0.00 | 0.15 | 0.01 | 0.18 | 0.01 |
| 8.2 | 0.01 | 0.23 | 0.04 | 0.11 | 0.23 | 0.08 | 0.16 | 0.00 | 0.15 | 0.01 | 0.18 | 0.01 |
| 8.3 | 0.01 | 0.24 | 0.03 | 0.10 | 0.23 | 0.08 | 0.16 | 0.00 | 0.15 | 0.02 | 0.18 | 0.01 |
| 8.4 | 0.01 | 0.24 | 0.03 | 0.10 | 0.24 | 0.07 | 0.16 | 0.00 | 0.14 | 0.02 | 0.18 | 0.01 |
| 8.5 | 0.01 | 0.24 | 0.03 | 0.09 | 0.24 | 0.07 | 0.16 | 0.00 | 0.14 | 0.02 | 0.18 | 0.01 |
| 8.6 | 0.01 | 0.24 | 0.03 | 0.09 | 0.24 | 0.07 | 0.17 | 0.00 | 0.14 | 0.02 | 0.18 | 0.01 |
| 8.7 | 0.01 | 0.24 | 0.03 | 0.08 | 0.24 | 0.06 | 0.17 | 0.00 | 0.14 | 0.02 | 0.18 | 0.01 |
| 8.8 | 0.02 | 0.24 | 0.02 | 0.08 | 0.24 | 0.06 | 0.17 | 0.01 | 0.13 | 0.02 | 0.18 | 0.00 |
| 8.9 | 0.02 | 0.24 | 0.02 | 0.07 | 0.24 | 0.05 | 0.17 | 0.01 | 0.13 | 0.03 | 0.18 | 0.00 |
| 9.0 | 0.02 | 0.24 | 0.02 | 0.07 | 0.24 | 0.05 | 0.17 | 0.01 | 0.13 | 0.03 | 0.18 | 0.00 |
| 9.1 | 0.02 | 0.24 | 0.02 | 0.07 | 0.24 | 0.05 | 0.17 | 0.01 | 0.13 | 0.03 | 0.18 | 0.00 |
| 9.2 | 0.02 | 0.24 | 0.02 | 0.06 | 0.23 | 0.05 | 0.17 | 0.01 | 0.12 | 0.03 | 0.18 | 0.00 |
| 9.3 | 0.03 | 0.24 | 0.01 | 0.06 | 0.23 | 0.04 | 0.18 | 0.01 | 0.12 | 0.03 | 0.17 | 0.00 |
| 9.4 | 0.03 | 0.24 | 0.01 | 0.05 | 0.23 | 0.04 | 0.18 | 0.01 | 0.12 | 0.03 | 0.17 | 0.00 |
| 9.5 | 0.03 | 0.24 | 0.01 | 0.05 | 0.23 | 0.04 | 0.18 | 0.01 | 0.11 | 0.04 | 0.17 | 0.00 |
| 9.6 | 0.03 | 0.24 | 0.01 | 0.05 | 0.23 | 0.04 | 0.18 | 0.01 | 0.11 | 0.04 | 0.17 | 0.00 |
| 9.7 | 0.03 | 0.24 | 0.01 | 0.04 | 0.23 | 0.04 | 0.18 | 0.02 | 0.10 | 0.04 | 0.17 | 0.00 |
| 9.8 | 0.04 | 0.24 | 0.01 | 0.04 | 0.22 | 0.03 | 0.18 | 0.02 | 0.10 | 0.04 | 0.17 | 0.00 |
| 9.9 | 0.04 | 0.24 | 0.01 | 0.03 | 0.22 | 0.03 | 0.18 | 0.02 | 0.09 | 0.04 | 0.17 | 0.00 |
| 10.0 | 0.04 | 0.24 | 0.01 | 0.03 | 0.22 | 0.03 | 0.18 | 0.02 | 0.09 | 0.05 | 0.17 | 0.00 |

# TABLES CXXIX. - CXXXII.

| Tables | CXXIX. | | CXXX. | | | | CXXXI. | | | CXXXII. | | | |
|---|---|---|---|---|---|---|---|---|---|---|---|---|---|
| Arguments | **24.** | | **28.** | | | | **30.** | | | **4.** | | | |
| Days. | **0** | **10** | **0** | **10** | **20** | **30** | **0** | **10** | Days. | **0** | **100** | **200** | **300** |
| Days. 0.0 | ″ 0.12 | ″ 0.20 | ″ 0.04 | ″ 0.10 | ″ 0.05 | ″ 0.00 | ″ 0.05 | ″ 0.06 | Days. 0 | ″ 0.41 | ″ 0.01 | ″ 0.51 | ″ 0.76 |
| 0.1 | 0.11 | 0.20 | 0.04 | 0.10 | 0.05 | 0.00 | 0.05 | 0.06 | 1 | 0.40 | 0.01 | 0.52 | 0.76 |
| 0.2 | 0.11 | 0.20 | 0.04 | 0.10 | 0.05 | 0.00 | 0.04 | 0.05 | 2 | 0.40 | 0.01 | 0.52 | 0.75 |
| 0.3 | 0.10 | 0.20 | 0.05 | 0.10 | 0.05 | 0.00 | 0.04 | 0.05 | 3 | 0.39 | 0.01 | 0.53 | 0.75 |
| 0.4 | 0.10 | 0.20 | 0.05 | 0.10 | 0.05 | 0.00 | 0.03 | 0.05 | 4 | 0.38 | 0.01 | 0.54 | 0.75 |
| 0.5 | 0.09 | 0.20 | 0.05 | 0.10 | 0.05 | 0.00 | 0.03 | 0.04 | 5 | 0.37 | 0.01 | 0.54 | 0.74 |
| 0.6 | 0.09 | 0.20 | 0.05 | 0.10 | 0.05 | 0.00 | 0.03 | 0.04 | 6 | 0.37 | 0.02 | 0.55 | 0.74 |
| 0.7 | 0.08 | 0.20 | 0.05 | 0.10 | 0.05 | 0.00 | 0.03 | 0.04 | 7 | 0.36 | 0.02 | 0.56 | 0.73 |
| 0.8 | 0.08 | 0.20 | 0.05 | 0.10 | 0.04 | 0.00 | 0.02 | 0.03 | 8 | 0.35 | 0.02 | 0.56 | 0.73 |
| 0.9 | 0.07 | 0.20 | 0.05 | 0.10 | 0.04 | 0.00 | 0.02 | 0.03 | 9 | 0.35 | 0.02 | 0.57 | 0.73 |
| 1.0 | 0.07 | 0.20 | 0.05 | 0.10 | 0.04 | 0.00 | 0.02 | 0.03 | 10 | 0.34 | 0.02 | 0.58 | 0.72 |
| 1.1 | 0.07 | 0.19 | 0.05 | 0.10 | 0.04 | 0.00 | 0.02 | 0.03 | 11 | 0.33 | 0.03 | 0.58 | 0.72 |
| 1.2 | 0.06 | 0.19 | 0.05 | 0.10 | 0.04 | 0.00 | 0.02 | 0.02 | 12 | 0.33 | 0.03 | 0.59 | 0.71 |
| 1.3 | 0.06 | 0.19 | 0.06 | 0.10 | 0.04 | 0.00 | 0.01 | 0.02 | 13 | 0.32 | 0.03 | 0.60 | 0.71 |
| 1.4 | 0.05 | 0.19 | 0.06 | 0.10 | 0.04 | 0.00 | 0.01 | 0.02 | 14 | 0.31 | 0.03 | 0.60 | 0.70 |
| 1.5 | 0.05 | 0.19 | 0.06 | 0.10 | 0.04 | 0.00 | 0.01 | 0.01 | 15 | 0.30 | 0.04 | 0.61 | 0.70 |
| 1.6 | 0.05 | 0.18 | 0.06 | 0.10 | 0.04 | 0.00 | 0.01 | 0.01 | 16 | 0.30 | 0.04 | 0.61 | 0.69 |
| 1.7 | 0.04 | 0.18 | 0.06 | 0.10 | 0.04 | 0.00 | 0.01 | 0.01 | 17 | 0.29 | 0.04 | 0.62 | 0.69 |
| 1.8 | 0.04 | 0.18 | 0.06 | 0.10 | 0.03 | 0.00 | 0.00 | 0.01 | 18 | 0.28 | 0.05 | 0.62 | 0.68 |
| 1.9 | 0.03 | 0.17 | 0.06 | 0.10 | 0.03 | 0.00 | 0.00 | 0.00 | 19 | 0.28 | 0.05 | 0.63 | 0.68 |
| 2.0 | 0.03 | 0.17 | 0.06 | 0.10 | 0.03 | 0.00 | 0.00 | 0.00 | 20 | 0.27 | 0.05 | 0.63 | 0.67 |
| 2.1 | 0.03 | 0.17 | 0.06 | 0.10 | 0.03 | 0.00 | 0.00 | 0.00 | 21 | 0.26 | 0.06 | 0.64 | 0.67 |
| 2.2 | 0.03 | 0.16 | 0.06 | 0.10 | 0.03 | 0.00 | 0.00 | 0.00 | 22 | 0.26 | 0.06 | 0.64 | 0.66 |
| 2.3 | 0.02 | 0.16 | 0.06 | 0.10 | 0.03 | 0.00 | 0.00 | 0.00 | 23 | 0.25 | 0.06 | 0.65 | 0.66 |
| 2.4 | 0.02 | 0.15 | 0.06 | 0.10 | 0.03 | 0.00 | 0.00 | 0.00 | 24 | 0.25 | 0.07 | 0.65 | 0.65 |
| 2.5 | 0.02 | 0.15 | 0.06 | 0.10 | 0.03 | 0.00 | 0.00 | 0.00 | 25 | 0.24 | 0.07 | 0.66 | 0.65 |
| 2.6 | 0.01 | 0.15 | 0.06 | 0.10 | 0.03 | 0.00 | 0.00 | 0.00 | 26 | 0.24 | 0.07 | 0.66 | 0.64 |
| 2.7 | 0.01 | 0.14 | 0.06 | 0.10 | 0.03 | 0.01 | 0.00 | 0.00 | 27 | 0.23 | 0.08 | 0.67 | 0.64 |
| 2.8 | 0.01 | 0.14 | 0.07 | 0.10 | 0.03 | 0.01 | 0.01 | 0.00 | 28 | 0.23 | 0.08 | 0.67 | 0.63 |
| 2.9 | 0.01 | 0.13 | 0.07 | 0.10 | 0.03 | 0.01 | 0.01 | 0.00 | 29 | 0.22 | 0.09 | 0.68 | 0.63 |
| 3.0 | 0.01 | 0.13 | 0.07 | 0.10 | 0.03 | 0.01 | 0.01 | 0.00 | 30 | 0.21 | 0.09 | 0.68 | 0.62 |
| 3.1 | 0.00 | 0.13 | 0.07 | 0.10 | 0.03 | 0.01 | 0.01 | 0.00 | 31 | 0.21 | 0.09 | 0.69 | 0.62 |
| 3.2 | 0.00 | 0.12 | 0.07 | 0.09 | 0.03 | 0.01 | 0.01 | 0.00 | 32 | 0.20 | 0.10 | 0.69 | 0.61 |
| 3.3 | 0.00 | 0.12 | 0.07 | 0.09 | 0.02 | 0.01 | 0.02 | 0.01 | 33 | 0.19 | 0.10 | 0.70 | 0.61 |
| 3.4 | 0.00 | 0.11 | 0.07 | 0.09 | 0.02 | 0.01 | 0.02 | 0.01 | 34 | 0.19 | 0.11 | 0.70 | 0.60 |
| 3.5 | 0.00 | 0.11 | 0.07 | 0.09 | 0.02 | 0.01 | 0.02 | 0.01 | 35 | 0.18 | 0.11 | 0.71 | 0.60 |
| 3.6 | 0.00 | 0.10 | 0.07 | 0.09 | 0.02 | 0.01 | 0.02 | 0.01 | 36 | 0.18 | 0.12 | 0.71 | 0.59 |
| 3.7 | 0.00 | 0.10 | 0.07 | 0.09 | 0.02 | 0.01 | 0.02 | 0.01 | 37 | 0.17 | 0.12 | 0.72 | 0.59 |
| 3.8 | 0.00 | 0.09 | 0.07 | 0.09 | 0.02 | 0.01 | 0.03 | 0.02 | 38 | 0.17 | 0.13 | 0.72 | 0.58 |
| 3.9 | 0.00 | 0.09 | 0.07 | 0.09 | 0.02 | 0.01 | 0.03 | 0.02 | 39 | 0.16 | 0.13 | 0.73 | 0.58 |
| 4.0 | 0.00 | 0.08 | 0.07 | 0.09 | 0.02 | 0.01 | 0.03 | 0.02 | 40 | 0.16 | 0.14 | 0.73 | 0.57 |
| 4.1 | 0.00 | 0.08 | 0.08 | 0.09 | 0.02 | 0.01 | 0.03 | 0.02 | 41 | 0.15 | 0.14 | 0.73 | 0.56 |
| 4.2 | 0.00 | 0.07 | 0.08 | 0.09 | 0.02 | 0.01 | 0.04 | 0.03 | 42 | 0.15 | 0.15 | 0.74 | 0.56 |
| 4.3 | 0.01 | 0.07 | 0.08 | 0.09 | 0.02 | 0.01 | 0.04 | 0.03 | 43 | 0.14 | 0.15 | 0.74 | 0.55 |
| 4.4 | 0.01 | 0.06 | 0.08 | 0.09 | 0.02 | 0.02 | 0.05 | 0.03 | 44 | 0.14 | 0.16 | 0.74 | 0.54 |
| 4.5 | 0.01 | 0.06 | 0.08 | 0.09 | 0.02 | 0.02 | 0.05 | 0.04 | 45 | 0.13 | 0.16 | 0.75 | 0.54 |
| 4.6 | 0.01 | 0.06 | 0.08 | 0.09 | 0.02 | 0.02 | 0.05 | 0.04 | 46 | 0.13 | 0.17 | 0.75 | 0.53 |
| 4.7 | 0.01 | 0.05 | 0.08 | 0.09 | 0.02 | 0.02 | 0.06 | 0.04 | 47 | 0.12 | 0.17 | 0.75 | 0.52 |
| 4.8 | 0.02 | 0.05 | 0.08 | 0.09 | 0.01 | 0.02 | 0.06 | 0.05 | 48 | 0.12 | 0.18 | 0.76 | 0.52 |
| 4.9 | 0.02 | 0.04 | 0.08 | 0.09 | 0.01 | 0.02 | 0.07 | 0.05 | 49 | 0.11 | 0.18 | 0.76 | 0.51 |
| 5.0 | 0.02 | 0.04 | 0.08 | 0.09 | 0.01 | 0.02 | 0.07 | 0.05 | 50 | 0.11 | 0.19 | 0.76 | 0.50 |

# TABLES CXXIX. - CXXXII.

| Tables | CXXIX. | | CXXX. | | | | CXXXI. | | | CXXXII. | | | |
|---|---|---|---|---|---|---|---|---|---|---|---|---|---|
| Arguments | **24.** | | **28.** | | | | **30.** | | | **4.** | | | |
| Days. | **0** | **10** | **0** | **10** | **20** | **30** | **0** | **10** | Days. | **0** | **100** | **200** | **300** |
| 5.0 | 0.02 | 0.04 | 0.08 | 0.09 | 0.01 | 0.02 | 0.07 | 0.05 | 50 | 0.11 | 0.19 | 0.76 | 0.50 |
| 5.1 | 0.03 | 0.04 | 0.08 | 0.09 | 0.01 | 0.02 | 0.07 | 0.05 | 51 | 0.10 | 0.19 | 0.77 | 0.50 |
| 5.2 | 0.03 | 0.03 | 0.08 | 0.09 | 0.01 | 0.02 | 0.07 | 0.06 | 52 | 0.10 | 0.20 | 0.77 | 0.49 |
| 5.3 | 0.03 | 0.03 | 0.08 | 0.08 | 0.01 | 0.02 | 0.08 | 0.06 | 53 | 0.09 | 0.20 | 0.77 | 0.48 |
| 5.4 | 0.03 | 0.02 | 0.08 | 0.08 | 0.01 | 0.02 | 0.08 | 0.07 | 54 | 0.09 | 0.21 | 0.77 | 0.48 |
| 5.5 | 0.04 | 0.02 | 0.08 | 0.08 | 0.01 | 0.02 | 0.08 | 0.07 | 55 | 0.08 | 0.22 | 0.77 | 0.47 |
| 5.6 | 0.04 | 0.02 | 0.09 | 0.08 | 0.01 | 0.02 | 0.08 | 0.07 | 56 | 0.08 | 0.22 | 0.78 | 0.46 |
| 5.7 | 0.04 | 0.02 | 0.09 | 0.08 | 0.01 | 0.02 | 0.09 | 0.08 | 57 | 0.07 | 0.23 | 0.78 | 0.46 |
| 5.8 | 0.05 | 0.01 | 0.09 | 0.08 | 0.01 | 0.02 | 0.09 | 0.08 | 58 | 0.07 | 0.24 | 0.78 | 0.45 |
| 5.9 | 0.05 | 0.01 | 0.09 | 0.08 | 0.01 | 0.02 | 0.10 | 0.09 | 59 | 0.07 | 0.24 | 0.78 | 0.44 |
| 6.0 | 0.06 | 0.01 | 0.09 | 0.08 | 0.01 | 0.03 | 0.10 | 0.09 | 60 | 0.06 | 0.25 | 0.78 | 0.44 |
| 6.1 | 0.06 | 0.01 | 0.09 | 0.08 | 0.01 | 0.03 | 0.10 | 0.09 | 61 | 0.06 | 0.26 | 0.79 | 0.43 |
| 6.2 | 0.06 | 0.01 | 0.09 | 0.08 | 0.01 | 0.03 | 0.10 | 0.09 | 62 | 0.05 | 0.26 | 0.79 | 0.42 |
| 6.3 | 0.07 | 0.00 | 0.09 | 0.08 | 0.01 | 0.03 | 0.11 | 0.10 | 63 | 0.05 | 0.27 | 0.79 | 0.42 |
| 6.4 | 0.07 | 0.00 | 0.09 | 0.08 | 0.01 | 0.03 | 0.11 | 0.10 | 64 | 0.05 | 0.27 | 0.79 | 0.41 |
| 6.5 | 0.08 | 0.00 | 0.09 | 0.08 | 0.01 | 0.03 | 0.11 | 0.10 | 65 | 0.04 | 0.28 | 0.79 | 0.40 |
| 6.6 | 0.08 | 0.00 | 0.09 | 0.08 | 0.01 | 0.03 | 0.11 | 0.10 | 66 | 0.04 | 0.28 | 0.79 | 0.40 |
| 6.7 | 0.09 | 0.00 | 0.09 | 0.08 | 0.01 | 0.03 | 0.11 | 0.10 | 67 | 0.04 | 0.29 | 0.79 | 0.39 |
| 6.8 | 0.09 | 0.00 | 0.09 | 0.07 | 0.00 | 0.03 | 0.12 | 0.11 | 68 | 0.03 | 0.30 | 0.80 | 0.38 |
| 6.9 | 0.10 | 0.00 | 0.09 | 0.07 | 0.00 | 0.03 | 0.12 | 0.11 | 69 | 0.03 | 0.30 | 0.80 | 0.37 |
| 7.0 | 0.10 | 0.00 | 0.09 | 0.07 | 0.00 | 0.03 | 0.12 | 0.11 | 70 | 0.03 | 0.31 | 0.80 | 0.37 |
| 7.1 | 0.10 | 0.00 | 0.09 | 0.07 | 0.00 | 0.03 | 0.12 | 0.11 | 71 | 0.02 | 0.31 | 0.80 | 0.36 |
| 7.2 | 0.11 | 0.00 | 0.09 | 0.07 | 0.00 | 0.03 | 0.12 | 0.11 | 72 | 0.02 | 0.32 | 0.80 | 0.35 |
| 7.3 | 0.11 | 0.00 | 0.09 | 0.07 | 0.00 | 0.04 | 0.12 | 0.12 | 73 | 0.02 | 0.33 | 0.80 | 0.35 |
| 7.4 | 0.12 | 0.00 | 0.09 | 0.07 | 0.00 | 0.04 | 0.12 | 0.12 | 74 | 0.02 | 0.33 | 0.80 | 0.34 |
| 7.5 | 0.12 | 0.00 | 0.09 | 0.07 | 0.00 | 0.04 | 0.12 | 0.12 | 75 | 0.02 | 0.34 | 0.80 | 0.33 |
| 7.6 | 0.12 | 0.00 | 0.09 | 0.07 | 0.00 | 0.04 | 0.12 | 0.12 | 76 | 0.01 | 0.34 | 0.80 | 0.33 |
| 7.7 | 0.13 | 0.00 | 0.09 | 0.07 | 0.00 | 0.04 | 0.12 | 0.12 | 77 | 0.01 | 0.35 | 0.80 | 0.32 |
| 7.8 | 0.13 | 0.01 | 0.10 | 0.07 | 0.00 | 0.04 | 0.12 | 0.12 | 78 | 0.01 | 0.36 | 0.80 | 0.31 |
| 7.9 | 0.14 | 0.01 | 0.10 | 0.07 | 0.00 | 0.04 | 0.12 | 0.12 | 79 | 0.01 | 0.36 | 0.80 | 0.31 |
| 8.0 | 0.14 | 0.01 | 0.10 | 0.07 | 0.00 | 0.04 | 0.12 | 0.12 | 80 | 0.01 | 0.37 | 0.80 | 0.30 |
| 8.1 | 0.15 | 0.01 | 0.10 | 0.07 | 0.00 | 0.04 | 0.12 | 0.12 | 81 | 0.01 | 0.38 | 0.80 | 0.29 |
| 8.2 | 0.15 | 0.01 | 0.10 | 0.07 | 0.00 | 0.04 | 0.11 | 0.12 | 82 | 0.00 | 0.39 | 0.80 | 0.29 |
| 8.3 | 0.16 | 0.02 | 0.10 | 0.06 | 0.00 | 0.04 | 0.11 | 0.12 | 83 | 0.00 | 0.40 | 0.80 | 0.28 |
| 8.4 | 0.16 | 0.02 | 0.10 | 0.06 | 0.00 | 0.04 | 0.11 | 0.11 | 84 | 0.00 | 0.40 | 0.80 | 0.28 |
| 8.5 | 0.16 | 0.02 | 0.10 | 0.06 | 0.00 | 0.04 | 0.11 | 0.11 | 85 | 0.00 | 0.41 | 0.80 | 0.27 |
| 8.6 | 0.17 | 0.03 | 0.10 | 0.06 | 0.00 | 0.04 | 0.11 | 0.11 | 86 | 0.00 | 0.42 | 0.79 | 0.26 |
| 8.7 | 0.17 | 0.03 | 0.10 | 0.06 | 0.00 | 0.04 | 0.10 | 0.11 | 87 | 0.00 | 0.42 | 0.79 | 0.26 |
| 8.8 | 0.18 | 0.03 | 0.10 | 0.06 | 0.00 | 0.05 | 0.10 | 0.11 | 88 | 0.00 | 0.43 | 0.79 | 0.25 |
| 8.9 | 0.18 | 0.04 | 0.10 | 0.06 | 0.00 | 0.05 | 0.10 | 0.10 | 89 | 0.00 | 0.44 | 0.79 | 0.24 |
| 9.0 | 0.18 | 0.04 | 0.10 | 0.06 | 0.00 | 0.05 | 0.09 | 0.10 | 90 | 0.00 | 0.44 | 0.79 | 0.24 |
| 9.1 | 0.18 | 0.04 | 0.10 | 0.06 | 0.00 | 0.05 | 0.09 | 0.10 | 91 | 0.00 | 0.45 | 0.78 | 0.23 |
| 9.2 | 0.19 | 0.05 | 0.10 | 0.06 | 0.00 | 0.05 | 0.09 | 0.10 | 92 | 0.00 | 0.46 | 0.78 | 0.22 |
| 9.3 | 0.19 | 0.05 | 0.10 | 0.05 | 0.00 | 0.05 | 0.08 | 0.09 | 93 | 0.00 | 0.47 | 0.78 | 0.22 |
| 9.4 | 0.19 | 0.06 | 0.10 | 0.05 | 0.00 | 0.05 | 0.08 | 0.09 | 94 | 0.00 | 0.47 | 0.78 | 0.21 |
| 9.5 | 0.19 | 0.06 | 0.10 | 0.05 | 0.00 | 0.05 | 0.08 | 0.09 | 95 | 0.00 | 0.48 | 0.77 | 0.20 |
| 9.6 | 0.19 | 0.06 | 0.10 | 0.05 | 0.00 | 0.05 | 0.08 | 0.09 | 96 | 0.00 | 0.48 | 0.77 | 0.20 |
| 9.7 | 0.19 | 0.07 | 0.10 | 0.05 | 0.00 | 0.05 | 0.07 | 0.08 | 97 | 0.00 | 0.49 | 0.77 | 0.19 |
| 9.8 | 0.20 | 0.07 | 0.10 | 0.05 | 0.00 | 0.06 | 0.07 | 0.08 | 98 | 0.01 | 0.50 | 0.77 | 0.18 |
| 9.9 | 0.20 | 0.08 | 0.10 | 0.05 | 0.00 | 0.06 | 0.06 | 0.07 | 99 | 0.01 | 0.50 | 0.76 | 0.18 |
| 10.0 | 0.20 | 0.09 | 0.10 | 0.05 | 0.00 | 0.06 | 0.06 | 0.07 | 100 | 0.01 | 0.51 | 0.76 | 0.17 |

# TABLES CXXXIII.-CXXXV.

| Tables | CXXXIII. | | | | | CXXXIV. | | CXXXV. | |
|---|---|---|---|---|---|---|---|---|---|
| Arguments | 5. | | | | | 12′. | | Hor. Par. | |
| Days. | 0 | 100 | 200 | 300 | 400 | 0 | 100 | Hor. Par. | 0″ |
| Days. | ″ | ″ | ″ | ″ | ″ | ″ | ″ | Seconds. | ″ |
| 0 | 0.20 | 0.46 | 0.17 | 0.50 | 0.11 | 0.10 | 0.07 | 3000 | 0.11 |
| 1 | 0.21 | 0.45 | 0.18 | 0.49 | 0.12 | 0.10 | 0.07 | 3010 | 0.11 |
| 2 | 0.22 | 0.44 | 0.19 | 0.48 | 0.13 | 0.11 | 0.06 | 3020 | 0.11 |
| 3 | 0.23 | 0.43 | 0.20 | 0.47 | 0.14 | 0.11 | 0.06 | 3030 | 0.11 |
| 4 | 0.24 | 0.43 | 0.20 | 0.46 | 0.14 | 0.12 | 0.05 | 3040 | 0.11 |
| 5 | 0.25 | 0.42 | 0.21 | 0.45 | 0.15 | 0.12 | 0.05 | 3050 | 0.11 |
| 6 | 0.26 | 0.41 | 0.22 | 0.44 | 0.16 | 0.12 | 0.05 | 3060 | 0.11 |
| 7 | 0.27 | 0.40 | 0.23 | 0.43 | 0.17 | 0.12 | 0.05 | 3070 | 0.11 |
| 8 | 0.28 | 0.39 | 0.24 | 0.42 | 0.18 | 0.13 | 0.04 | 3080 | 0.11 |
| 9 | 0.29 | 0.38 | 0.25 | 0.42 | 0.18 | 0.13 | 0.04 | 3090 | 0.12 |
| 10 | 0.30 | 0.37 | 0.26 | 0.41 | 0.19 | 0.13 | 0.04 | 3100 | 0.12 |
| 11 | 0.31 | 0.36 | 0.27 | 0.40 | 0.20 | 0.14 | 0.03 | 3110 | 0.12 |
| 12 | 0.32 | 0.35 | 0.28 | 0.39 | 0.21 | 0.14 | 0.03 | 3120 | 0.12 |
| 13 | 0.33 | 0.34 | 0.29 | 0.38 | 0.22 | 0.14 | 0.03 | 3130 | 0.12 |
| 14 | 0.34 | 0.33 | 0.29 | 0.37 | 0.22 | 0.15 | 0.02 | 3140 | 0.12 |
| 15 | 0.35 | 0.32 | 0.30 | 0.36 | 0.23 | 0.15 | 0.02 | 3150 | 0.12 |
| 16 | 0.36 | 0.31 | 0.31 | 0.35 | 0.24 | 0.15 | 0.02 | 3160 | 0.12 |
| 17 | 0.37 | 0.30 | 0.32 | 0.34 | 0.25 | 0.16 | 0.02 | 3170 | 0.12 |
| 18 | 0.38 | 0.29 | 0.33 | 0.33 | 0.26 | 0.16 | 0.01 | 3180 | 0.12 |
| 19 | 0.38 | 0.29 | 0.34 | 0.33 | 0.27 | 0.17 | 0.01 | 3190 | 0.13 |
| 20 | 0.39 | 0.28 | 0.35 | 0.32 | 0.28 | 0.17 | 0.01 | 3200 | 0.13 |
| 21 | 0.40 | 0.27 | 0.36 | 0.31 | 0.29 | 0.17 | 0.01 | 3210 | 0.13 |
| 22 | 0.41 | 0.26 | 0.37 | 0.30 | 0.30 | 0.18 | 0.01 | 3220 | 0.13 |
| 23 | 0.42 | 0.25 | 0.38 | 0.29 | 0.31 | 0.18 | 0.00 | 3230 | 0.13 |
| 24 | 0.43 | 0.24 | 0.39 | 0.28 | 0.31 | 0.19 | 0.00 | 3240 | 0.13 |
| 25 | 0.44 | 0.23 | 0.40 | 0.27 | 0.32 | 0.19 | 0.00 | 3250 | 0.14 |
| 26 | 0.45 | 0.22 | 0.41 | 0.26 | 0.33 | 0.19 | 0.00 | 3260 | 0.14 |
| 27 | 0.46 | 0.21 | 0.42 | 0.25 | 0.34 | 0.19 | 0.00 | 3270 | 0.14 |
| 28 | 0.47 | 0.20 | 0.43 | 0.24 | 0.35 | 0.20 | 0.00 | 3280 | 0.14 |
| 29 | 0.47 | 0.20 | 0.43 | 0.23 | 0.36 | 0.20 | 0.00 | 3290 | 0.14 |
| 30 | 0.48 | 0.19 | 0.44 | 0.22 | 0.37 | 0.20 | 0.00 | 3300 | 0.14 |
| 31 | 0.49 | 0.18 | 0.45 | 0.21 | 0.38 | 0.20 | 0.00 | 3310 | 0.14 |
| 32 | 0.50 | 0.17 | 0.46 | 0.20 | 0.39 | 0.20 | 0.00 | 3320 | 0.14 |
| 33 | 0.51 | 0.16 | 0.47 | 0.19 | 0.40 | 0.20 | 0.00 | 3330 | 0.15 |
| 34 | 0.51 | 0.16 | 0.47 | 0.19 | 0.41 | 0.21 | 0.00 | 3340 | 0.15 |
| 35 | 0.52 | 0.15 | 0.48 | 0.18 | 0.42 | 0.21 | 0.00 | 3350 | 0.15 |
| 36 | 0.53 | 0.14 | 0.49 | 0.17 | 0.43 | 0.21 | 0.00 | 3360 | 0.15 |
| 37 | 0.54 | 0.13 | 0.50 | 0.16 | 0.44 | 0.21 | 0.00 | 3370 | 0.15 |
| 38 | 0.54 | 0.13 | 0.51 | 0.15 | 0.45 | 0.21 | 0.00 | 3380 | 0.15 |
| 39 | 0.55 | 0.12 | 0.51 | 0.15 | 0.45 | 0.21 | 0.00 | 3390 | 0.15 |
| 40 | 0.55 | 0.12 | 0.52 | 0.14 | 0.46 | 0.21 | 0.01 | 3400 | 0.15 |
| 41 | 0.56 | 0.11 | 0.53 | 0.13 | 0.47 | 0.21 | 0.01 | 3410 | 0.15 |
| 42 | 0.57 | 0.10 | 0.54 | 0.12 | 0.48 | 0.21 | 0.01 | 3420 | 0.16 |
| 43 | 0.57 | 0.10 | 0.54 | 0.11 | 0.49 | 0.22 | 0.01 | 3430 | 0.16 |
| 44 | 0.58 | 0.09 | 0.55 | 0.11 | 0.49 | 0.22 | 0.01 | 3440 | 0.16 |
| 45 | 0.58 | 0.09 | 0.55 | 0.10 | 0.50 | 0.22 | 0.01 | 3450 | 0.16 |
| 46 | 0.59 | 0.08 | 0.56 | 0.09 | 0.51 | 0.22 | 0.01 | 3460 | 0.16 |
| 47 | 0.59 | 0.07 | 0.57 | 0.09 | 0.52 | 0.22 | 0.01 | 3470 | 0.16 |
| 48 | 0.60 | 0.07 | 0.57 | 0.08 | 0.53 | 0.22 | 0.02 | 3480 | 0.17 |
| 49 | 0.60 | 0.06 | 0.58 | 0.08 | 0.53 | 0.22 | 0.02 | 3490 | 0.17 |
| 50 | 0.61 | 0.06 | 0.58 | 0.07 | 0.54 | 0.22 | 0.02 | 3500 | 0.17 |

# TABLES CXXXIII. - CXXXV.

| Tables | CXXXIII. | | | | | CXXXIV. | | CXXXV. | |
|---|---|---|---|---|---|---|---|---|---|
| Arguments | 5. | | | | | 12'. | | Hor. Par. | |
| Days. | **0** | **100** | **200** | **300** | **400** | **0** | **100** | Hor. Par. | **0''** |
| Days | " | " | " | " | " | " | " | Seconds. | " |
| 50 | 0.61 | 0.06 | 0.58 | 0.07 | 0.54 | 0.22 | 0.02 | 3500 | 0.17 |
| 51 | 0.61 | 0.05 | 0.59 | 0.07 | 0.55 | 0.22 | 0.02 | 3510 | 0.17 |
| 52 | 0.61 | 0.05 | 0.59 | 0.06 | 0.56 | 0.22 | 0.02 | 3520 | 0.17 |
| 53 | 0.61 | 0.04 | 0.60 | 0.05 | 0.56 | 0.22 | 0.03 | 3530 | 0.17 |
| 54 | 0.62 | 0.04 | 0.60 | 0.05 | 0.57 | 0.22 | 0.03 | 3540 | 0.17 |
| 55 | 0.62 | 0.03 | 0.61 | 0.04 | 0.57 | 0.22 | 0.03 | 3550 | 0.17 |
| 56 | 0.62 | 0.03 | 0.61 | 0.03 | 0.58 | 0.22 | 0.03 | 3560 | 0.18 |
| 57 | 0.62 | 0.03 | 0.61 | 0.03 | 0.58 | 0.22 | 0.04 | 3570 | 0.18 |
| 58 | 0.62 | 0.03 | 0.61 | 0.03 | 0.59 | 0.21 | 0.04 | 3580 | 0.18 |
| 59 | 0.63 | 0.02 | 0.62 | 0.02 | 0.59 | 0.21 | 0.04 | 3590 | 0.18 |
| 60 | 0.63 | 0.02 | 0.62 | 0.02 | 0.60 | 0.21 | 0.05 | 3600 | 0.18 |
| 61 | 0.63 | 0.02 | 0.62 | 0.02 | 0.60 | 0.21 | 0.05 | 3610 | 0.18 |
| 62 | 0.63 | 0.02 | 0.62 | 0.02 | 0.60 | 0.20 | 0.05 | 3620 | 0.18 |
| 63 | 0.63 | 0.02 | 0.62 | 0.02 | 0.61 | 0.20 | 0.06 | 3630 | 0.19 |
| 64 | 0.63 | 0.02 | 0.63 | 0.01 | 0.61 | 0.20 | 0.06 | 3640 | 0.19 |
| 65 | 0.63 | 0.02 | 0.63 | 0.01 | 0.62 | 0.19 | 0.06 | 3650 | 0.19 |
| 66 | 0.63 | 0.02 | 0.63 | 0.01 | 0.62 | 0.19 | 0.06 | 3660 | 0.19 |
| 67 | 0.63 | 0.02 | 0.63 | 0.00 | 0.62 | 0.19 | 0.07 | 3670 | 0.19 |
| 68 | 0.63 | 0.02 | 0.63 | 0.00 | 0.62 | 0.18 | 0.07 | 3680 | 0.19 |
| 69 | 0.62 | 0.02 | 0.63 | 0.00 | 0.63 | 0.18 | 0.08 | 3690 | 0.20 |
| 70 | 0.62 | 0.02 | 0.63 | 0.00 | 0.63 | 0.18 | 0.08 | 3700 | 0.20 |
| 71 | 0.62 | 0.02 | 0.63 | 0.00 | 0.63 | 0.18 | 0.08 | 3710 | 0.20 |
| 72 | 0.62 | 0.02 | 0.63 | 0.00 | 0.63 | 0.17 | 0.09 | 3720 | 0.20 |
| 73 | 0.62 | 0.02 | 0.63 | 0.00 | 0.63 | 0.17 | 0.09 | 3730 | 0.20 |
| 74 | 0.61 | 0.03 | 0.62 | 0.00 | 0.63 | 0.17 | 0.10 | 3740 | 0.20 |
| 75 | 0.61 | 0.03 | 0.62 | 0.00 | 0.63 | 0.17 | 0.10 | 3750 | 0.21 |
| 76 | 0.61 | 0.03 | 0.62 | 0.00 | 0.63 | 0.16 | 0.10 | 3760 | 0.21 |
| 77 | 0.61 | 0.03 | 0.62 | 0.00 | 0.63 | 0.16 | 0.11 | 3770 | 0.21 |
| 78 | 0.60 | 0.04 | 0.62 | 0.00 | 0.63 | 0.16 | 0.11 | 3780 | 0.21 |
| 79 | 0.60 | 0.04 | 0.61 | 0.01 | 0.63 | 0.15 | 0.12 | 3790 | 0.21 |
| 80 | 0.59 | 0.05 | 0.61 | 0.01 | 0.63 | 0.15 | 0.12 | 3800 | 0.21 |
| 81 | 0.59 | 0.05 | 0.61 | 0.01 | 0.62 | 0.15 | 0.12 | 3810 | 0.21 |
| 82 | 0.58 | 0.06 | 0.61 | 0.01 | 0.62 | 0.14 | 0.13 | 3820 | 0.22 |
| 83 | 0.58 | 0.06 | 0.60 | 0.02 | 0.62 | 0.14 | 0.13 | 3830 | 0.22 |
| 84 | 0.57 | 0.07 | 0.60 | 0.02 | 0.62 | 0.13 | 0.14 | 3840 | 0.22 |
| 85 | 0.57 | 0.07 | 0.59 | 0.03 | 0.61 | 0.13 | 0.14 | 3850 | 0.22 |
| 86 | 0.56 | 0.08 | 0.59 | 0.03 | 0.61 | 0.13 | 0.14 | 3860 | 0.22 |
| 87 | 0.55 | 0.09 | 0.58 | 0.03 | 0.61 | 0.12 | 0.15 | 3870 | 0.23 |
| 88 | 0.55 | 0.09 | 0.58 | 0.04 | 0.61 | 0.12 | 0.15 | 3880 | 0.23 |
| 89 | 0.54 | 0.10 | 0.57 | 0.04 | 0.60 | 0.11 | 0.16 | 3890 | 0.23 |
| 90 | 0.54 | 0.10 | 0.57 | 0.05 | 0.60 | 0.11 | 0.16 | 3900 | 0.23 |
| 91 | 0.53 | 0.11 | 0.56 | 0.05 | 0.60 | 0.11 | 0.16 | 3910 | 0.23 |
| 92 | 0.52 | 0.12 | 0.55 | 0.06 | 0.59 | 0.10 | 0.17 | 3920 | 0.23 |
| 93 | 0.51 | 0.12 | 0.55 | 0.06 | 0.59 | 0.10 | 0.17 | 3930 | 0.24 |
| 94 | 0.51 | 0.13 | 0.54 | 0.07 | 0.58 | 0.09 | 0.18 | 3940 | 0.24 |
| 95 | 0.50 | 0.13 | 0.54 | 0.07 | 0.58 | 0.09 | 0.18 | 3950 | 0.24 |
| 96 | 0.49 | 0.14 | 0.53 | 0.08 | 0.57 | 0.09 | 0.18 | 3960 | 0.24 |
| 97 | 0.48 | 0.15 | 0.52 | 0.09 | 0.56 | 0.08 | 0.18 | 3970 | 0.24 |
| 98 | 0.47 | 0.16 | 0.51 | 0.10 | 0.56 | 0.08 | 0.19 | 3980 | 0.25 |
| 99 | 0.47 | 0.17 | 0.51 | 0.10 | 0.55 | 0.07 | 0.19 | 3990 | 0.25 |
| 100 | 0.46 | 0.17 | 0.50 | 0.11 | 0.55 | 0.07 | 0.19 | 4000 | 0.25 |

# TABLE CXXXVI.

Argument, *Horizontal Parallax.*

| Hor. Par. | 0″ | 1000″ | 2000″ | 3000″ | Hor. Par. | 0″ | 1000″ | 2000″ | 3000″ |
|---|---|---|---|---|---|---|---|---|---|
| ″ 0 | ″ 0.00 | ″ 272.27 | ″ 544.55 | ″ 816.82 | ″ 500 | ′ 136.14 | ″ 408.41 | ″ 680.69 | ″ 952.96 |
| 10 | 2.72 | 274.99 | 547.27 | 819.54 | 510 | 138.86 | 411.13 | 683.41 | 955.68 |
| 20 | 5.45 | 277.72 | 549.99 | 822.27 | 520 | 141.58 | 413.85 | 686.13 | 958.40 |
| 30 | 8.17 | 280.44 | 552.72 | 824.99 | 530 | 144.31 | 416.58 | 688.86 | 961.13 |
| 40 | 10.89 | 283.17 | 555.44 | 827.72 | 540 | 147.03 | 419.30 | 691.58 | 963.85 |
| 50 | 13.61 | 285.89 | 558.16 | 830.44 | 550 | 149.75 | 422.02 | 694.30 | 966.57 |
| 60 | 16.33 | 288.61 | 560.88 | 833.16 | 560 | 152.47 | 424.74 | 697.02 | 969.29 |
| 70 | 19.06 | 291.33 | 563.60 | 835.88 | 570 | 155.19 | 427.47 | 699.74 | 972.02 |
| 80 | 21.78 | 294.06 | 566.33 | 838.61 | 580 | 157.92 | 430.19 | 702.47 | 974.74 |
| 90 | 24.51 | 296.78 | 569.05 | 841.33 | 590 | 160.64 | 432.92 | 705.19 | 977.47 |
| 100 | 27.23 | 299.50 | 571.77 | 844.05 | 600 | 163.36 | 435.64 | 707.91 | 980.19 |
| 110 | 29.95 | 302.22 | 574.49 | 846.77 | 610 | 166.08 | 438.36 | 710.63 | 982.91 |
| 120 | 32.67 | 304.95 | 577.22 | 849.49 | 620 | 168.81 | 441.08 | 713.36 | 985.63 |
| 130 | 35.40 | 307.67 | 579.94 | 852.22 | 630 | 171.53 | 443.81 | 716.08 | 988.36 |
| 140 | 38.12 | 310.40 | 582.67 | 854.94 | 640 | 174.26 | 446.53 | 718.81 | 991.08 |
| 150 | 40.84 | 313.12 | 585.39 | 857.66 | 650 | 176.98 | 449.25 | 721.53 | 993.80 |
| 160 | 43.56 | 315.84 | 588.11 | 860.38 | 660 | 179.70 | 451.97 | 724.25 | 996.52 |
| 170 | 46.28 | 318.56 | 590.83 | 863.11 | 670 | 182.42 | 454.70 | 726.97 | 999.24 |
| 180 | 49.01 | 321.29 | 593.56 | 865.83 | 680 | 185.15 | 457.42 | 729.70 | 1001.97 |
| 190 | 51.73 | 324.01 | 596.28 | 868.56 | 690 | 187.87 | 460.15 | 732.42 | 1004.69 |
| 200 | 54.45 | 326.73 | 599.00 | 871.28 | 700 | 190.59 | 462.87 | 735.14 | 1007.41 |
| 210 | 57.17 | 329.45 | 601.72 | 874.00 | 710 | 193.31 | 465.59 | 737.86 | 1010.13 |
| 220 | 59.90 | 322.17 | 604.45 | 876.72 | 720 | 196.04 | 468.31 | 740.58 | 1012.86 |
| 230 | 62.62 | 334.90 | 607.17 | 879.45 | 730 | 198.76 | 471.04 | 743.31 | 1015.58 |
| 240 | 65.35 | 337.62 | 609.90 | 882.17 | 740 | 201.49 | 473.76 | 746.03 | 1018.31 |
| 250 | 68.07 | 340.34 | 612.62 | 884.89 | 750 | 204.21 | 476.48 | 748.75 | 1021.03 |
| 260 | 70.79 | 343.06 | 615.34 | 887.61 | 760 | 206.93 | 479.20 | 751.47 | 1023.75 |
| 270 | 73.51 | 345.79 | 618.06 | 890.33 | 770 | 209.65 | 481.92 | 754.20 | 1026.47 |
| 280 | 76.24 | 348.51 | 620.79 | 893.06 | 780 | 212.38 | 484.65 | 756.92 | 1029.20 |
| 290 | 78.96 | 351.24 | 623.51 | 895.78 | 790 | 215.10 | 487.37 | 759.65 | 1031.92 |
| 300 | 81.68 | 353.96 | 626.23 | 898.50 | 800 | 217.82 | 490.09 | 762.37 | 1034.64 |
| 310 | 84.40 | 356.68 | 628.95 | 901.22 | 810 | 220.54 | 492.81 | 765.09 | 1037.36 |
| 320 | 87.13 | 359.40 | 631.67 | 903.95 | 820 | 223.26 | 495.54 | 767.81 | 1040.08 |
| 330 | 89.85 | 362.13 | 634.40 | 906.67 | 830 | 225.99 | 498.26 | 770.54 | 1042.81 |
| 340 | 92.58 | 364.85 | 637.12 | 909.40 | 840 | 228.71 | 500.99 | 773.26 | 1045.53 |
| 350 | 95.30 | 367.57 | 639.84 | 912.12 | 850 | 231.43 | 503.71 | 775.98 | 1048.25 |
| 360 | 98.02 | 370.29 | 642.56 | 914.84 | 860 | 234.15 | 506.43 | 778.70 | 1050.97 |
| 370 | 100.74 | 373.01 | 645.29 | 917.56 | 870 | 236.88 | 509.15 | 781.42 | 1053.70 |
| 380 | 103.47 | 375.74 | 648.01 | 920.29 | 880 | 239.60 | 511.88 | 784.15 | 1056.42 |
| 390 | 106.19 | 378.46 | 650.74 | 923.01 | 890 | 242.33 | 514.60 | 786.87 | 1059.15 |
| 400 | 108.91 | 381.18 | 653.46 | 925.73 | 900 | 245.05 | 517.32 | 789.59 | 1061.87 |
| 410 | 111.63 | 383.90 | 656.18 | 928.45 | 910 | 247.77 | 520.04 | 792.31 | 1064.59 |
| 420 | 114.35 | 386.63 | 658.90 | 931.18 | 920 | 250.49 | 522.76 | 795.04 | 1067.31 |
| 430 | 117.08 | 389.35 | 661.63 | 933.90 | 930 | 253.22 | 525.49 | 797.76 | 1070.04 |
| 440 | 119.80 | 392.08 | 664.35 | 936.63 | 940 | 255.94 | 528.21 | 800.49 | 1072.76 |
| 450 | 122.52 | 394.80 | 667.07 | 939.35 | 950 | 258.66 | 530.93 | 803.21 | 1075.48 |
| 460 | 125.24 | 397.52 | 669.79 | 942.07 | 960 | 261.38 | 533.65 | 805.93 | 1078.20 |
| 470 | 127.97 | 400.24 | 672.52 | 944.79 | 970 | 264.10 | 536.38 | 808.65 | 1080.93 |
| 480 | 130.69 | 402.97 | 675.24 | 947.52 | 980 | 266.83 | 539.10 | 811.38 | 1083.65 |
| 490 | 133.42 | 405.69 | 677.97 | 950.24 | 990 | 269.55 | 541.83 | 814.10 | 1086.38 |
| 500 | 136.14 | 408.41 | 680.69 | 952.96 | 1000 | 272.27 | 544.55 | 816.82 | 1089.10 |

The Latitude $= A \sin \bar{y} + B \cos \bar{y} + C$, as given on page 12, Introduction, may be put in the form,

$$\text{Latitude} = 18500'' \sin \bar{y} + A' \sin \bar{y} + B \cos \bar{y} + C,$$

in which $A'$ only differs from $A$ in that the constant $900''$ is subtracted instead of the constant $17600''$ added. Compute $18500'' \sin \bar{y}$ for each noon and midnight from Table CXXXVII.; compute $A' \sin \bar{y} + B \cos \bar{y} + C$ for each noon, using five place decimals, and interpolate to midnight. In Table CXXXVII., the columns headed P. P. are the proportional parts for the seconds of $\bar{y}$.

# TABLE CXXXVII. ARGUMENT 77.

Equation = 18500″ sin $\bar{y}$.

| $\bar{y}$ | 180°— 0°+ | | 181°— 1°+ | | 182°— 2°+ | | 183°— 3°+ | | 184°— 4°+ | | 185°— 5°+ | | $\bar{y}$ |
|---|---|---|---|---|---|---|---|---|---|---|---|---|---|
| | Equation. | P. P. | Equation. | P. P. | Equation. | P. P. | Equation. | P. P. | Equation. | P. P. | Equation. | P. P. | |
| ′ | ° ′ ″ | ″ | ° ′ ″ | ″ | ° ′ ″ | ″ | ° ′ ″ | ″ | ° ′ ″ | ″ | ° ′ ″ | ″ | ′ |
| 0 | 0 0 0.00 | 0.00 | 0 5 22.87 | 0.00 | 0 10 45.64 | 0.00 | 0 16 8.22 | 0.00 | 0 21 30.49 | 0.00 | 0 26 52.38 | 0.00 | 60 |
| 1 | 0 5.38 | 0.09 | 5 28.25 | 0.09 | 10 51.02 | 0.09 | 16 13 60 | 0.09 | 21 35.86 | 0.09 | 26 57.74 | 0.09 | 59 |
| 2 | 0 10.76 | 0.18 | 5 33.63 | 0.18 | 10 56.40 | 0.18 | 16 18.98 | 0.18 | 21 41.23 | 0.18 | 27 3.10 | 0.18 | 58 |
| 3 | 0 16.14 | 0.27 | 5 39.01 | 0.27 | 11 1.78 | 0.27 | 16 24.35 | 0.27 | 21 46.60 | 0.27 | 27 8.46 | 0.27 | 57 |
| 4 | 0 21.52 | 0.36 | 5 44.39 | 0.36 | 11 7.16 | 0.36 | 16 29.72 | 0.36 | 21 51.97 | 0.36 | 27 13.82 | 0.36 | 56 |
| 5 | 0 26.90 | 0.45 | 5 49.77 | 0.45 | 11 12.53 | 0.45 | 16 35.09 | 0.45 | 21 57.33 | 0.45 | 27 19.18 | 0.45 | 55 |
| 6 | 0 0 32.28 | 0.54 | 0 5 55.15 | 0.54 | 0 11 17.91 | 0.54 | 0 16 40.47 | 0.54 | 0 22 2.70 | 0.53 | 0 27 24.54 | 0.53 | 54 |
| 7 | 0 37.66 | 0.63 | 6 0.53 | 0.63 | 11 23.29 | 0.63 | 16 45.85 | 0.63 | 22 8.07 | 0.62 | 27 29.90 | 0.62 | 53 |
| 8 | 0 43.04 | 0.72 | 6 5.91 | 0.72 | 11 28.67 | 0.72 | 16 51.22 | 0.72 | 22 13.44 | 0.71 | 27 35.26 | 0.71 | 52 |
| 9 | 0 48.42 | 0.81 | 6 11.29 | 0.81 | 11 34.05 | 0.81 | 16 56.59 | 0.81 | 22 18.80 | 0.80 | 27 40.62 | 0.80 | 51 |
| 10 | 0 53.81 | 0.90 | 6 16.67 | 0.90 | 11 39.42 | 0.90 | 17 1.96 | 0.90 | 22 24.17 | 0.89 | 27 45.98 | 0.89 | 50 |
| 11 | 0 0 59.19 | 0.99 | 0 6 22.05 | 0.99 | 0 11 44.80 | 0.99 | 0 17 7.34 | 0.99 | 0 22 29.54 | 0.98 | 0 27 51.34 | 0.98 | 49 |
| 12 | 1 4.57 | 1.08 | 6 27.43 | 1.08 | 11 50.18 | 1.08 | 17 12.71 | 1.08 | 22 34.91 | 1.07 | 27 56.70 | 1.07 | 48 |
| 13 | 1 9.95 | 1.17 | 6 32.81 | 1.17 | 11 55.56 | 1.17 | 17 18.08 | 1.17 | 22 40.28 | 1.16 | 28 52.06 | 1 16 | 47 |
| 14 | 1 15.33 | 1.26 | 6 38.19 | 1.26 | 12 00.94 | 1.26 | 17 23.45 | 1.26 | 22 45.64 | 1.25 | 28 57.42 | 1.25 | 46 |
| 15 | 1 20.72 | 1.35 | 6 43.57 | 1.35 | 12 6.31 | 1.35 | 17 28.82 | 1.35 | 22 51.00 | 1.34 | 28 12.78 | 1.34 | 45 |
| 16 | 0 1 26.10 | 1.44 | 0 6 48.95 | 1.44 | 0 12 11.69 | 1.44 | 0 17 34.20 | 1.44 | 0 22 56.37 | 1.43 | 0 28 18.14 | 1.42 | 44 |
| 17 | 1 31.48 | 1.53 | 6 54.33 | 1.53 | 12 17.07 | 1.53 | 17 39.57 | 1.53 | 23 1.74 | 1.52 | 28 23.50 | 1.51 | 43 |
| 18 | 1 36.86 | 1.62 | 6 59.71 | 1.62 | 12 22.45 | 1.62 | 17 44.94 | 1.62 | 23 7.11 | 1.61 | 28 28.86 | 1.60 | 42 |
| 19 | 1 42.24 | 1.71 | 7 5.09 | 1.72 | 12 27.83 | 1.71 | 17 50.31 | 1.71 | 23 12.47 | 1.70 | 28 34.22 | 1.69 | 41 |
| 20 | 1 47.63 | 1.79 | 7 10.47 | 1.79 | 12 33.20 | 1.79 | 17 55.68 | 1.79 | 23 17.83 | 1.79 | 28 39.57 | 1.78 | 40 |
| 21 | 0 1 53.01 | 1.88 | 0 7 15.85 | 1.88 | 0 12 38.58 | 1.88 | 0 18 1.06 | 1.88 | 0 23 23.20 | 1.88 | 0 28 44.93 | 1.87 | 39 |
| 22 | 1 58.39 | 1.97 | 7 21.23 | 1.97 | 12 43.96 | 1.97 | 18 6.43 | 1.97 | 23 28.57 | 1.97 | 28 50.29 | 1.96 | 38 |
| 23 | 2 3.77 | 2.06 | 7 26.61 | 2.06 | 12 49.34 | 2.06 | 18 11.80 | 2.06 | 23 33.94 | 2.06 | 28 55.65 | 2.05 | 37 |
| 24 | 2 9.15 | 2.15 | 7 31.99 | 2.15 | 12 54.71 | 2.15 | 18 17.17 | 2.15 | 23 39.30 | 2.15 | 29 1.01 | 2.14 | 36 |
| 25 | 2 14.54 | 2.24 | 7 37.37 | 2.24 | 13 0.08 | 2.24 | 18 22.54 | 2.24 | 23 44.66 | 2.24 | 29 6.36 | 2.23 | 35 |
| 26 | 0 2 19.92 | 2.33 | 0 7 42.75 | 2.33 | 0 13 5.46 | 2.33 | 0 18 27.92 | 2.33 | 0 23 50.03 | 2.32 | 0 29 11.72 | 2.32 | 34 |
| 27 | 2 25.30 | 2.42 | 7 48.13 | 2.42 | 13 10.84 | 2.42 | 18 33.29 | 2.42 | 23 55.40 | 2.41 | 29 17.08 | 2.41 | 33 |
| 28 | 2 30.68 | 2.51 | 7 53.51 | 2.51 | 13 16.22 | 2.51 | 18 38.66 | 2.51 | 24 0.77 | 2.50 | 29 22.44 | 2.50 | 32 |
| 29 | 2 36.06 | 2.60 | 7 58.89 | 2.60 | 13 21.59 | 2.60 | 18 44.03 | 2.60 | 24 6.13 | 2.59 | 29 27.80 | 2.59 | 31 |
| 30 | 2 41.44 | 2.69 | 8 4.27 | 2.69 | 13 26.96 | 2.69 | 18 49.40 | 2.69 | 24 11.49 | 2.68 | 29 33.15 | 2.68 | 30 |
| 31 | 0 2 46.82 | 2.78 | 0 8 9.65 | 2.78 | 0 13 32.34 | 2.78 | 0 18 54.78 | 2.78 | 0 24 16.86 | 2.77 | 0 29 38.51 | 2.77 | 29 |
| 32 | 2 52.20 | 2.87 | 8 15.03 | 2.87 | 13 37.72 | 2.87 | 19 0.15 | 2.87 | 24 22.23 | 2.86 | 29 43.87 | 2.86 | 28 |
| 33 | 2 57.58 | 2.96 | 8 20.41 | 2.96 | 13 43.10 | 2.96 | 19 5.52 | 2.96 | 24 27.60 | 2.95 | 29 49.23 | 2.95 | 27 |
| 34 | 3 2.97 | 3.05 | 8 25.79 | 3.05 | 13 48.47 | 3.05 | 19 10.89 | 3.05 | 24 32.96 | 3.04 | 29 54.58 | 3.04 | 26 |
| 35 | 3 8.36 | 3.14 | 8 31.17 | 3.14 | 13 53.84 | 3.14 | 19 16.26 | 3.14 | 24 38.32 | 3.13 | 29 59.93 | 3.13 | 25 |
| 36 | 0 3 13.74 | 3.23 | 0 8 36.55 | 3.23 | 0 13 59.22 | 3.23 | 0 19 21.63 | 3.23 | 0 24 43.69 | 3.22 | 0 30 5.29 | 3.21 | 24 |
| 37 | 3 19.12 | 3.32 | 8 41.93 | 3.32 | 14 4.60 | 3.32 | 19 27.00 | 3.32 | 24 49.06 | 3.31 | 30 10.65 | 3.30 | 23 |
| 38 | 3 24.50 | 3.41 | 8 47.31 | 3.41 | 14 9.98 | 3.41 | 19 32.37 | 3.41 | 24 54.42 | 3.40 | 30 16.01 | 3.39 | 22 |
| 39 | 3 29.88 | 3.50 | 8 52.69 | 3.50 | 14 15.35 | 3.50 | 19 37.74 | 3.50 | 24 59.78 | 3.49 | 30 21.36 | 3.48 | 21 |
| 40 | 3 35.26 | 3.59 | 8 58.07 | 3.59 | 14 20.72 | 3.59 | 19 43.11 | 3.58 | 25 5.14 | 3.58 | 30 26.71 | 3.57 | 20 |
| 41 | 0 3 40.64 | 3.68 | 0 9 3.45 | 3.68 | 0 14 26.10 | 3.68 | 0 19 48.48 | 3.67 | 0 25 10.51 | 3.67 | 0 30 32.07 | 3.66 | 19 |
| 42 | 3 46.02 | 3.77 | 9 8.83 | 3.77 | 14 31.48 | 3.77 | 19 53.85 | 3.76 | 25 15.87 | 3.76 | 30 37.43 | 3.75 | 18 |
| 43 | 3 51.40 | 3.86 | 9 14.21 | 3.86 | 14 36.86 | 3.86 | 19 59.22 | 3.85 | 25 21.23 | 3.85 | 30 47.78 | 3.84 | 17 |
| 44 | 3 56.78 | 3.95 | 9 19.59 | 3.95 | 14 42.23 | 3.95 | 20 4.59 | 3.94 | 25 26.59 | 3.94 | 30 48.13 | 3.93 | 16 |
| 45 | 4 2.16 | 4.04 | 9 24.96 | 4.04 | 14 47.60 | 4.04 | 20 9.96 | 4.03 | 25 31.95 | 4.03 | 30 53.48 | 4.02 | 15 |
| 46 | 0 4 7.54 | 4.13 | 0 9 30.34 | 4.13 | 0 14 52.98 | 4.13 | 0 20 15.33 | 4.12 | 0 25 37.32 | 4.11 | 0 30 58.84 | 4.10 | 14 |
| 47 | 4 12.92 | 4.22 | 9 35.72 | 4.22 | 14 58.36 | 4.22 | 20 20.70 | 4.21 | 25 42.68 | 4.20 | 31 4 20 | 4.19 | 13 |
| 48 | 4 18.30 | 4.31 | 9 41.10 | 4.31 | 15 3.74 | 4.31 | 20 26.07 | 4.30 | 25 48.04 | 4.29 | 31 9.55 | 4.28 | 12 |
| 49 | 4 23.68 | 4.40 | 9 46.48 | 4.40 | 15 9.11 | 4.40 | 20 31.44 | 4.39 | 25 53.40 | 4.38 | 31 14.90 | 4.37 | 11 |
| 50 | 4 29.07 | 4.48 | 9 51.86 | 4.48 | 15 14.48 | 4.48 | 20 36.81 | 4.47 | 25 58.76 | 4.47 | 31 20.25 | 4.46 | 10 |
| 51 | 0 4 34.45 | 4.57 | 0 9 57.24 | 4.57 | 0 15 19.86 | 4.57 | 0 20 42.18 | 4.56 | 0 26 4.13 | 4.56 | 0 31 25.61 | 4.55 | 9 |
| 52 | 4 39.83 | 4.66 | 10 2.62 | 4.66 | 15 25.24 | 4.66 | 20 47.55 | 4.65 | 26 9.49 | 4.65 | 31 30.97 | 4.64 | 8 |
| 53 | 4 45.21 | 4.75 | 10 8.00 | 4.75 | 15 30.61 | 4.75 | 20 52.92 | 4.74 | 26 14.85 | 4.74 | 31 36.32 | 4.73 | 7 |
| 54 | 4 50.59 | 4.84 | 10 13.38 | 4.84 | 15 35.98 | 4.84 | 20 58.29 | 4.83 | 26 20.21 | 4.83 | 31 41.67 | 4 82 | 6 |
| 55 | 4 55.97 | 4.93 | 10 18.75 | 4.93 | 15 41.35 | 4.93 | 21 3.65 | 4.92 | 26 25.57 | 4.92 | 31 47.02 | 4.91 | 5 |
| 56 | 0 5 1.35 | 5.02 | 0 10 24.13 | 5.02 | 0 15 46.73 | 5.02 | 0 21 9.02 | 5.01 | 0 26 30.94 | 5.01 | 0 31 52.38 | 5.00 | 4 |
| 57 | 5 6.73 | 5.11 | 10 29.51 | 5.11 | 15 52.11 | 5.11 | 21 14.39 | 5.10 | 26 36.30 | 5.10 | 31 57.73 | 5.09 | 3 |
| 58 | 5 12.11 | 5.20 | 10 34.89 | 5.20 | 15 57.48 | 5.20 | 21 19.76 | 5.19 | 26 41.66 | 5.19 | 32 3.08 | 5.18 | 2 |
| 59 | 5 17.49 | 5.29 | 10 40.27 | 5.29 | 16 2.85 | 5.29 | 21 25.13 | 5.28 | 26 47.02 | 5.28 | 32 8.45 | 5.27 | 1 |
| 60 | 5 22.87 | 5.38 | 10 45.64 | 5.38 | 16 8.22 | 5.38 | 21 30.49 | 5.37 | 26 52.38 | 5.37 | 32 13.78 | 5.36 | 0 |
| $\bar{y}$ | 179°+ 359°— | | 178°+ 358°— | | 177°+ 357°— | | 176°+ 356°— | | 175°+ 355°— | | 174°+ 354°— | | $\bar{y}$ |

# TABLE CXXXVII. ARGUMENT 77.

Equation = 18500″ sin $\bar{y}$.

| $\bar{y}$ | 186°— 6°+ Equation. | P. P. | 187°— 7°+ Equation. | P. P. | 188°— 8°+ Equation. | P. P. | 189°— 9°+ Equation. | P. P. | 190°— 10°+ Equation. | P. P. | 191°— 11°+ Equation. | P. P. | $\bar{y}$ |
|---|---|---|---|---|---|---|---|---|---|---|---|---|---|
| ′ | ° ′ ″ | ″ | ° ′ ″ | ″ | ° ′ ″ | ″ | ° ′ ″ | ″ | ° ′ ″ | ″ | ° ′ ″ | ″ | ′ |
| 0 | 0 32 13.78 | 0.00 | 0 37 34.58 | 0.00 | 0 42 54.70 | 0.00 | 0 48 14.03 | 0.00 | 0 53 32.49 | 0.00 | 0 58 49.97 | 0.00 | 60 |
| 1 | 32 19.14 | 0.09 | 37 39.92 | 0.09 | 43 0.03 | 0.09 | 48 19.35 | 0.09 | 53 37.79 | 0.09 | 58 55.26 | 0.09 | 59 |
| 2 | 32 24.49 | 0.18 | 37 45.26 | 0.18 | 43 5.36 | 0.18 | 48 24.67 | 0.18 | 53 43.09 | 0.18 | 59 0.54 | 0.18 | 58 |
| 3 | 32 29.84 | 0.27 | 37 50.60 | 0.27 | 43 10.69 | 0.27 | 48 29.98 | 0.27 | 53 48.39 | 0.27 | 59 5.82 | 0.27 | 57 |
| 4 | 32 35.19 | 0.36 | 37 55.94 | 0.36 | 43 16.02 | 0.36 | 48 35.29 | 0.36 | 53 53.69 | 0.36 | 59 11.10 | 0.36 | 56 |
| 5 | 32 40.54 | 0.45 | 38 1.28 | 0.45 | 43 21.34 | 0.45 | 48 40.60 | 0.45 | 53 58.99 | 0.45 | 59 16.38 | 0.44 | 55 |
| 6 | 0 32 45.89 | 0.53 | 0 38 6.62 | 0.53 | 0 43 26.67 | 0.53 | 0 48 45.92 | 0.53 | 0 54 4.29 | 0.53 | 0 59 21.66 | 0.53 | 54 |
| 7 | 32 51.24 | 0.62 | 38 11.96 | 0.62 | 43 32.00 | 0.62 | 48 51.24 | 0.62 | 54 9.59 | 0.62 | 59 26.94 | 0.62 | 53 |
| 8 | 32 56.59 | 0.71 | 38 17.30 | 0.71 | 43 37.33 | 0.71 | 48 56.55 | 0.71 | 54 14.89 | 0.71 | 59 32.22 | 0.71 | 52 |
| 9 | 33 1.94 | 0.80 | 38 22.64 | 0.80 | 43 42.66 | 0.80 | 49 1.86 | 0.80 | 54 20.19 | 0.80 | 59 37.50 | 0.79 | 51 |
| 10 | 33 7.29 | 0.89 | 38 27.98 | 0.89 | 43 47.98 | 0.89 | 49 7.17 | 0.89 | 54 25.48 | 0.88 | 59 42.78 | 0.88 | 50 |
| 11 | 0 33 12.64 | 0.98 | 0 38 33.32 | 0.98 | 0 43 53.31 | 0.98 | 0 49 12.49 | 0.98 | 0 54 30.78 | 0.97 | 0 59 48.06 | 0.97 | 49 |
| 12 | 33 17.99 | 1.07 | 38 38.66 | 1.07 | 43 58.64 | 1.07 | 49 17.80 | 1.07 | 54 36.08 | 1.06 | 59 53.34 | 1.06 | 48 |
| 13 | 33 23.34 | 1.16 | 38 44.00 | 1.16 | 44 3.97 | 1.16 | 49 23.11 | 1.16 | 54 41.38 | 1.15 | 59 58.62 | 1.15 | 47 |
| 14 | 33 28.69 | 1.25 | 38 49.34 | 1.25 | 44 9.29 | 1.25 | 49 28.42 | 1.25 | 54 46.67 | 1.24 | 1 0 3.90 | 1.23 | 46 |
| 15 | 33 34.04 | 1.34 | 38 54.68 | 1.34 | 44 14.61 | 1.34 | 49 33.73 | 1.34 | 54 51.96 | 1.33 | 0 9.18 | 1.32 | 45 |
| 16 | 0 33 39.39 | 1.42 | 0 39 0.02 | 1.42 | 0 44 19.94 | 1.42 | 0 49 39.04 | 1.42 | 0 54 57.26 | 1.41 | 1 0 14.46 | 1.41 | 44 |
| 17 | 33 44.74 | 1.51 | 39 5.36 | 1.51 | 44 25.27 | 1.51 | 49 44.35 | 1.51 | 55 2.56 | 1.50 | 0 19.74 | 1.50 | 43 |
| 18 | 33 50.09 | 1.60 | 39 10.70 | 1.60 | 44 30.60 | 1.60 | 49 49.66 | 1.60 | 55 7.85 | 1.59 | 0 25.02 | 1.58 | 42 |
| 19 | 33 55.44 | 1.69 | 39 16.04 | 1.69 | 44 35.92 | 1.69 | 49 54.97 | 1.69 | 55 13.14 | 1.68 | 0 30.29 | 1.67 | 41 |
| 20 | 34 0.78 | 1.78 | 39 21.37 | 1.78 | 44 41.24 | 1.77 | 50 0.28 | 1.77 | 55 18.43 | 1.76 | 0 35.56 | 1.76 | 40 |
| 21 | 0 34 6.23 | 1.87 | 0 39 26.71 | 1.87 | 0 44 46.57 | 1.86 | 0 50 5.55 | 1.86 | 0 55 23.73 | 1.85 | 1 0 40.84 | 1.85 | 39 |
| 22 | 34 11.58 | 1.96 | 39 32.05 | 1.96 | 44 51.90 | 1.95 | 50 10.90 | 1.95 | 55 29.03 | 1.94 | 0 46.12 | 1.94 | 38 |
| 23 | 34 16.93 | 2.05 | 39 37.39 | 2.05 | 44 57.22 | 2.04 | 50 16.21 | 2.04 | 55 34.32 | 2.03 | 0 51.40 | 2.03 | 37 |
| 24 | 34 22.28 | 2.14 | 39 42.72 | 2.14 | 45 2.54 | 2.13 | 50 21.52 | 2.13 | 55 39.61 | 2.12 | 0 56.67 | 2.11 | 36 |
| 25 | 34 27.52 | 2.23 | 39 48.05 | 2.23 | 45 7.86 | 2.22 | 50 26.83 | 2.22 | 55 44.90 | 2.21 | 1 1.94 | 2.20 | 35 |
| 26 | 0 34 32.88 | 2.31 | 0 39 53.39 | 2.31 | 0 45 13.19 | 2.30 | 0 50 32.14 | 2.30 | 0 55 50.20 | 2.29 | 1 1 7.22 | 2.29 | 34 |
| 27 | 34 38.23 | 2.40 | 39 58.73 | 2.40 | 45 18.51 | 2.39 | 50 37.45 | 2.39 | 55 55.49 | 2.38 | 1 12.50 | 2.38 | 33 |
| 28 | 34 43.58 | 2.49 | 40 4.07 | 2.49 | 45 23.83 | 2.48 | 50 42.76 | 2.48 | 56 0.78 | 2.47 | 1 17.77 | 2.46 | 32 |
| 29 | 34 48.92 | 2.58 | 40 9.40 | 2.58 | 45 29.15 | 2.57 | 50 48.07 | 2.57 | 56 6.07 | 2.56 | 1 23.04 | 2.55 | 31 |
| 30 | 34 54.26 | 2.67 | 40 14.73 | 2.67 | 45 34.47 | 2.66 | 50 53.37 | 2.66 | 56 11.36 | 2.65 | 1 28.31 | 2.64 | 30 |
| 31 | 0 34 59.61 | 2.76 | 0 40 20.07 | 2.76 | 0 45 39.80 | 2.75 | 0 50 58.68 | 2.75 | 0 56 16.65 | 2.74 | 1 1 33.59 | 2.73 | 29 |
| 32 | 35 4.96 | 2.85 | 40 25.41 | 2.85 | 45 45.12 | 2.84 | 51 3.99 | 2.84 | 56 21.94 | 2.83 | 1 38.86 | 2.82 | 28 |
| 33 | 35 10.31 | 2.94 | 40 30.75 | 2.94 | 45 50.44 | 2.93 | 51 9.30 | 2.93 | 56 27.23 | 2.92 | 1 44 13 | 2.91 | 27 |
| 34 | 35 15.65 | 3.03 | 40 36 08 | 3.03 | 45 55.76 | 3.02 | 51 14.61 | 3.02 | 56 32.52 | 3.01 | 1 49.40 | 3.00 | 26 |
| 35 | 35 20.99 | 3.12 | 40 41.41 | 3.12 | 46 1.08 | 3.11 | 51 19.91 | 3.11 | 56 37.81 | 3.10 | 1 54.67 | 3.09 | 25 |
| 36 | 0 35 26.34 | 3.21 | 0 40 46.75 | 3.20 | 0 46 6.40 | 3.19 | 0 51 25.22 | 3.19 | 0 56 43.10 | 3.19 | 1 1 59.95 | 3.18 | 24 |
| 37 | 35 31.69 | 3.30 | 40 52.09 | 3.29 | 46 11.72 | 3.28 | 51 30.53 | 3.27 | 56 48.39 | 3.27 | 2 5 22 | 3.27 | 23 |
| 38 | 35 37.04 | 3.39 | 40 57.42 | 3.38 | 46 17.04 | 3.37 | 51 35.84 | 3.36 | 56 53.68 | 3.36 | 2 10.49 | 3.35 | 22 |
| 39 | 35 42.38 | 3.48 | 41 2.75 | 3.47 | 46 22.36 | 3.46 | 51 41.14 | 3.45 | 56 58.97 | 3.45 | 2 15.76 | 3.43 | 21 |
| 40 | 35 47.72 | 3.57 | 41 8.08 | 3.56 | 46 27.68 | 3.55 | 51 46.44 | 3.54 | 57 4.26 | 3.53 | 2 21.03 | 3.51 | 20 |
| 41 | 0 35 53.07 | 3.66 | 0 41 13.42 | 3.65 | 0 46 33.00 | 3.64 | 0 51 51.75 | 3.63 | 0 57 9.55 | 3.62 | 1 2 26.30 | 3.60 | 19 |
| 42 | 35 58.42 | 3.75 | 41 18.75 | 3.74 | 46 38.32 | 3.73 | 51 57.06 | 3.72 | 57 14.84 | 3.71 | 2 31.57 | 3.69 | 18 |
| 43 | 36 3.76 | 3.84 | 41 24.08 | 3.83 | 46 43.64 | 3.82 | 52 2.36 | 3.81 | 57 20.13 | 3.79 | 2 36.84 | 3.57 | 17 |
| 44 | 36 9.10 | 3.93 | 41 29.41 | 3.92 | 46 48.96 | 3.91 | 52 7.66 | 3.90 | 57 25.42 | 3.68 | 2 42.11 | 3.66 | 16 |
| 45 | 36 14.44 | 4.02 | 41 34.74 | 4.01 | 46 54.28 | 4.00 | 52 12.96 | 3.99 | 57 30.70 | 3.97 | 2 47.38 | 3.95 | 15 |
| 46 | 0 36 19.79 | 4.10 | 0 41 40.08 | 4.09 | 0 46 59.60 | 4.08 | 0 52 18.27 | 4.07 | 0 57 35.91 | 4.05 | 1 2 52.65 | 4.04 | 14 |
| 47 | 36 25.14 | 4.19 | 41 45.41 | 4.18 | 47 4.92 | 4.17 | 52 23.58 | 4.16 | 57 41.28 | 4.14 | 2 57.92 | 4.13 | 13 |
| 48 | 36 30.48 | 4.28 | 41 50.74 | 4.27 | 47 10.24 | 4.26 | 52 28.88 | 4.25 | 57 46.57 | 4.23 | 3 3.19 | 4.22 | 12 |
| 49 | 36 35.82 | 4.37 | 41 56.07 | 4.36 | 47 15.56 | 4.35 | 52 34.18 | 4.34 | 57 51.85 | 4.32 | 3 8.46 | 4.31 | 11 |
| 50 | 36 41.16 | 4.46 | 42 1.40 | 4.45 | 47 20.87 | 4.43 | 52 39.48 | 4.43 | 57 57.13 | 4.41 | 3 13.72 | 4.39 | 10 |
| 51 | 0 36 46.51 | 4.55 | 0 42 6.73 | 4.54 | 0 47 26.19 | 4.52 | 0 52 44.79 | 4.52 | 0 58 2.42 | 4.50 | 1 3 18.99 | 4.48 | 9 |
| 52 | 36 51.85 | 4.64 | 42 12.06 | 4.63 | 47 31.51 | 4.61 | 52 50.09 | 4.61 | 58 7.71 | 4.59 | 3 24.26 | 4.57 | 8 |
| 53 | 36 57.19 | 4.73 | 42 17.39 | 4.72 | 47 36.83 | 4.70 | 52 55.39 | 4.70 | 58 12.99 | 4.68 | 3 29.53 | 4.65 | 7 |
| 54 | 37 2.53 | 4.82 | 42 22.72 | 4.81 | 47 42.14 | 4.79 | 53 0.69 | 4.79 | 58 18.27 | 4.77 | 3 34.79 | 4.74 | 6 |
| 55 | 37 7.87 | 4.91 | 42 28.05 | 4.90 | 47 47.45 | 4.88 | 53 5.99 | 4.88 | 58 23.55 | 4.85 | 3 40.05 | 4.83 | 5 |
| 56 | 0 37 13.22 | 4.99 | 0 42 33.38 | 4.98 | 0 47 52.77 | 4.96 | 0 53 11.29 | 4.96 | 0 58 28.84 | 4.94 | 1 3 45.32 | 4.92 | 4 |
| 57 | 37 18.56 | 5.08 | 42 38.71 | 5.07 | 47 58.09 | 5.05 | 53 16.59 | 5.05 | 58 34.13 | 5.03 | 3 50.59 | 5.01 | 3 |
| 58 | 37 23.90 | 5.17 | 42 44.04 | 5.16 | 48 3.41 | 5.14 | 53 21.89 | 5.14 | 58 39.41 | 5.12 | 3 55.85 | 5.09 | 2 |
| 59 | 37 29.24 | 5.26 | 42 49.37 | 5.25 | 48 8.72 | 5.23 | 53 27.19 | 5.23 | 58 44.69 | 5.20 | 4 1.11 | 5.18 | 1 |
| 60 | 37 34.58 | 5.35 | 42 54.70 | 5.34 | 48 14.03 | 5.32 | 53 32.49 | 5.31 | 58 49.97 | 5.29 | 4 6.37 | 5.27 | 0 |
| $\bar{y}$ | 173°+ 353°— | | 172°+ 352°— | | 171°+ 351°— | | 170°+ 350°— | | 169°+ 349°— | | 168°+ 348°— | | $\bar{y}$ |

# TABLE CXXXVII. ARGUMENT 77.

Equation = 18500″ sin $\bar{y}$.

| $\bar{y}$ | 192°– 12°+ Equation. | P. P. | 193°– 13°+ Equation. | P. P. | 194°– 14°+ Equation. | P. P. | 195°– 15°+ Equation. | P. P. | 196°– 16°+ Equation. | P. P. | 197°– 17°+ Equation. | P. P. | $\bar{y}$ |
|---|---|---|---|---|---|---|---|---|---|---|---|---|---|
| ′ | ° ′ ″ | ″ | ° ′ ″ | ″ | ° ′ ″ | ″ | ° ′ ″ | ″ | ° ′ ″ | ″ | ° ′ ″ | ″ | ′ |
| 0 | 1 4 6.37 | 0.00 | 1 9 21.59 | 0.00 | 1 14 35.55 | 0.00 | 1 19 48.17 | 0.00 | 1 24 59.29 | 0.00 | 1 30 8.88 | 0.00 | 60 |
| 1 | 4 11.64 | 0.09 | 9 26.84 | 0.09 | 14 40.77 | 0.09 | 19 53.37 | 0.09 | 25 4.47 | 0.09 | 30 14.03 | 0.09 | 59 |
| 2 | 4 16.90 | 0.18 | 9 32.08 | 0.18 | 14 45.99 | 0.18 | 19 58.57 | 0.18 | 25 9.64 | 0.18 | 30 19.18 | 0.18 | 58 |
| 3 | 4 22.16 | 0.27 | 9 37.32 | 0.26 | 14 51.21 | 0.26 | 20 3.77 | 0.26 | 25 14.81 | 0.26 | 30 24.32 | 0.26 | 57 |
| 4 | 4 27.42 | 0.36 | 9 42.56 | 0.35 | 14 56.43 | 0.34 | 20 8.97 | 0.35 | 25 19.98 | 0.34 | 30 29.46 | 0.34 | 56 |
| 5 | 4 32.68 | 0.44 | 9 47.80 | 0.43 | 15 1.65 | 0.43 | 20 14.16 | 0.43 | 25 25.15 | 0.43 | 30 34.60 | 0.43 | 55 |
| 6 | 1 4 37.95 | 0.53 | 1 9 53.04 | 0.52 | 1 15 6.87 | 0.51 | 1 20 19.36 | 0.52 | 1 25 30.32 | 0.52 | 1 30 39.75 | 0.52 | 54 |
| 7 | 4 43.21 | 0.62 | 9 58.28 | 0.61 | 15 12.09 | 0.60 | 20 24.56 | 0.61 | 25 35.49 | 0.61 | 30 44.89 | 0.60 | 53 |
| 8 | 4 48.47 | 0.71 | 10 3.52 | 0.69 | 15 17.31 | 0.69 | 20 29.75 | 0.69 | 25 40.66 | 0.69 | 30 50.03 | 0.69 | 52 |
| 9 | 4 53.73 | 0.79 | 10 8.76 | 0.78 | 15 22.53 | 0.78 | 20 34.94 | 0.77 | 25 45.83 | 0.77 | 30 55.17 | 0.78 | 51 |
| 10 | 4 58.99 | 0.88 | 10 14.00 | 0.87 | 15 27.74 | 0.87 | 20 40.13 | 0.86 | 25 51.00 | 0.86 | 31 0.31 | 0.86 | 50 |
| 11 | 1 5 4.25 | 0.97 | 1 10 19.24 | 0.96 | 1 15 32.96 | 0.96 | 1 20 45.32 | 0.94 | 1 25 56.17 | 0.94 | 1 31 5.45 | 0.94 | 49 |
| 12 | 5 9.51 | 1.06 | 10 24.48 | 1.05 | 15 38.18 | 1.04 | 20 50.51 | 1.03 | 26 1.34 | 1.03 | 31 10.59 | 1.02 | 48 |
| 13 | 5 14.77 | 1.15 | 10 29.72 | 1.14 | 15 43.40 | 1.13 | 20 55.70 | 1.12 | 26 6.51 | 1.12 | 31 15.73 | 1.11 | 47 |
| 14 | 5 20.03 | 1.33 | 10 34.96 | 1.23 | 15 48.62 | 1.22 | 21 0.89 | 1.21 | 26 11.67 | 1.20 | 31 20.87 | 1.20 | 46 |
| 15 | 5 25.29 | 1.32 | 10 40.20 | 1.31 | 15 53.83 | 1.30 | 21 6.08 | 1.30 | 26 16.83 | 1.29 | 31 26.01 | 1.28 | 45 |
| 16 | 1 5 30.55 | 1.41 | 1 10 45.44 | 1.40 | 1 15 59.05 | 1.38 | 1 21 11.27 | 1.39 | 1 26 22.00 | 1.38 | 1 31 31.15 | 1.36 | 44 |
| 17 | 5 35.81 | 1.49 | 10 50.68 | 1.48 | 16 4.27 | 1.47 | 21 16.46 | 1.47 | 26 27.17 | 1.46 | 31 36.29 | 1.45 | 43 |
| 18 | 5 41.07 | 1.58 | 10 55.92 | 1.57 | 16 9.49 | 1.56 | 21 21.65 | 1.56 | 26 32.33 | 1.54 | 31 41.45 | 1.53 | 42 |
| 19 | 5 46.33 | 1.67 | 11 1.16 | 1.66 | 16 14.70 | 1.65 | 21 26.84 | 1.65 | 26 37.49 | 1.63 | 31 46.57 | 1 62 | 41 |
| 20 | 5 51.58 | 1.75 | 11 6.39 | 1.74 | 16 19.91 | 1.74 | 21 32.03 | 1.73 | 26 42.65 | 1.72 | 31 51.70 | 1.71 | 40 |
| 21 | 1 5 50.84 | 1.84 | 1 11 11.63 | 1.82 | 1 16 25.13 | 1.82 | 1 21 37.22 | 1.82 | 1 26 47.82 | 1.80 | 1 31 56.84 | 1.80 | 39 |
| 22 | 6 2.10 | 1.93 | 11 16.87 | 1.91 | 16 30.35 | 1.90 | 21 42.41 | 1.90 | 26 52.99 | 1.89 | 32 1.98 | 1.88 | 38 |
| 23 | 6 7.36 | 2.01 | 11 22.11 | 2.00 | 16 35.56 | 1.99 | 21 47.60 | 1.99 | 26 58.15 | 1.97 | 32 7.12 | 1.97 | 37 |
| 24 | 6 12.61 | 2.10 | 11 27.34 | 2.09 | 16 40.77 | 2.07 | 21 52.79 | 2.07 | 27 3.31 | 2.06 | 32 12.25 | 2.06 | 36 |
| 25 | 6 17.86 | 2.19 | 11 32.57 | 2.18 | 16 45.98 | 2.16 | 21 57.97 | 2.16 | 27 8.47 | 2.15 | 32 17.38 | 2.14 | 35 |
| 26 | 1 6 23.12 | 2.28 | 1 11 37.81 | 2.26 | 1 16 51.19 | 2.25 | 1 22 3.16 | 2.24 | 1 27 13.64 | 2.23 | 1 32 22.52 | 2.23 | 34 |
| 27 | 6 28.38 | 2.37 | 11 43.04 | 2.35 | 16 56.40 | 2.33 | 22 8.45 | 2.33 | 27 18.80 | 2.32 | 32 27.66 | 2.32 | 33 |
| 28 | 6 33.63 | 2.45 | 11 48.27 | 2.44 | 17 1.61 | 2.42 | 22 13.54 | 2.42 | 27 23.96 | 2.41 | 32 32.80 | 2.40 | 32 |
| 29 | 6 38.88 | 2.54 | 11 53.50 | 2.53 | 17 6.82 | 2.51 | 22 18.73 | 2.51 | 27 29.12 | 2.49 | 32 37.93 | 2.49 | 31 |
| 30 | 6 44.13 | 2.63 | 11 58.73 | 2.62 | 17 12.03 | 2.60 | 22 23.91 | 2.59 | 27 34.28 | 2.58 | 32 43.06 | 2.57 | 30 |
| 31 | 1 6 49.39 | 2.72 | 1 12 3.96 | 2.70 | 1 17 17.24 | 2.68 | 1 22 29.10 | 2.67 | 1 27 39.44 | 2.66 | 1 32 48.20 | 2.66 | 29 |
| 32 | 6 54.64 | 2.81 | 12 9.19 | 2.79 | 17 22.45 | 2.77 | 22 34.29 | 2.76 | 27 44.60 | 2.75 | 32 53.33 | 2.75 | 28 |
| 33 | 6 59.89 | 2.90 | 12 14.42 | 2.87 | 17 27.66 | 2.86 | 22 39.48 | 2.84 | 27 49.76 | 2.84 | 32 58.46 | 2.84 | 27 |
| 34 | 7 5.14 | 2.99 | 12 19.65 | 2.96 | 17 32.87 | 2.95 | 22 44.66 | 2.93 | 27 54.92 | 2.92 | 33 3.59 | 2.92 | 26 |
| 35 | 7 10.39 | 3.07 | 12 24.88 | 3.04 | 17 38.07 | 3.03 | 22 49.84 | 3.02 | 28 0.07 | 3.01 | 33 8.72 | 3.00 | 25 |
| 36 | 1 7 15.65 | 3.16 | 1 12 30.11 | 3.13 | 1 17 43.28 | 3.12 | 1 22 55.03 | 3.11 | 1 28 5.23 | 3.09 | 1 33 13.85 | 3.09 | 24 |
| 37 | 7 20.90 | 3.25 | 12 35.34 | 3.22 | 17 48.49 | 3.21 | 23 0.21 | 3.19 | 28 10.39 | 3.18 | 33 18.98 | 3.18 | 23 |
| 38 | 7 26.15 | 3.33 | 12 40.57 | 3.31 | 17 53.70 | 3.30 | 23 5.39 | 3.28 | 28 15.55 | 3.26 | 33 24.11 | 3.26 | 22 |
| 39 | 7 31.40 | 3.41 | 12 45.80 | 3.40 | 17 58.91 | 3.39 | 23 10.57 | 3.36 | 28 20.70 | 3.35 | 33 29.24 | 3.34 | 21 |
| 40 | 7 36.65 | 3.50 | 12 51.03 | 3.49 | 18 4.11 | 3.47 | 23 15.75 | 3.45 | 28 25.85 | 3.44 | 33 34.36 | 3.42 | 20 |
| 41 | 1 7 41.90 | 3.59 | 1 12 56.26 | 3.58 | 1 18 9.32 | 3.55 | 1 23 20.93 | 3.54 | 1 28 31.01 | 3.52 | 1 33 39.49 | 3.50 | 19 |
| 42 | 7 47.15 | 3.68 | 13 1.49 | 3.66 | 18 14.53 | 3.64 | 23 26.11 | 3.62 | 28 36.17 | 3.61 | 33 44.62 | 3.59 | 18 |
| 43 | 7 52.40 | 3.76 | 13 6.72 | 3.75 | 18 19.74 | 3.73 | 23 31.29 | 3.69 | 28 41.33 | 3.70 | 33 49.75 | 3.68 | 17 |
| 44 | 7 57.65 | 3.85 | 13 11.95 | 3.84 | 18 24.94 | 3.82 | 23 36.47 | 3.77 | 28 46.48 | 3.78 | 33 54.87 | 3.77 | 16 |
| 45 | 8 2.90 | 3.94 | 13 17.18 | 3.92 | 18 30.14 | 3.91 | 23 41.65 | 3.86 | 28 51.63 | 3.87 | 33 59.99 | 3.85 | 15 |
| 46 | 1 8 8.15 | 4.03 | 1 13 22.41 | 4.01 | 1 18 35.35 | 3.99 | 1 23 46.83 | 3.95 | 1 28 56.79 | 3.96 | 1 34 5.12 | 3.94 | 14 |
| 47 | 8 13.40 | 4.11 | 13 27.64 | 4.09 | 18 40.56 | 4.08 | 23 52.01 | 4.04 | 29 1.95 | 4.04 | 34 10.25 | 4.02 | 13 |
| 48 | 8 18.65 | 4.20 | 13 32.87 | 4.18 | 18 45.76 | 4.17 | 23 57.19 | 4.13 | 29 7.10 | 4.13 | 34 15.37 | 4.11 | 12 |
| 49 | 8 23.90 | 4.29 | 13 38.10 | 4.27 | 18 50.96 | 4.26 | 24 2.37 | 4.22 | 29 12.25 | 4.21 | 34 20.49 | 4.20 | 11 |
| 50 | 8 29.14 | 4.38 | 13 43.32 | 4.36 | 18 56.16 | 4.34 | 24 7.54 | 4.31 | 29 17.40 | 4.30 | 34 25.61 | 4.28 | 10 |
| 51 | 1 8 34.39 | 4.47 | 1 13 48.55 | 4.44 | 1 19 1.37 | 4.42 | 1 24 12.72 | 4.40 | 1 29 22.55 | 4.39 | 1 34 30.74 | 4.37 | 9 |
| 52 | 8 39.64 | 4.55 | 13 53.78 | 4.53 | 19 6.57 | 4.51 | 24 17.90 | 4.49 | 29 27.70 | 4.48 | 34 35.86 | 4.45 | 8 |
| 53 | 8 44.89 | 4.64 | 13 59.00 | 4.62 | 19 11.77 | 4.60 | 24 23.08 | 4.58 | 29 32.85 | 4.57 | 34 40.98 | 4.54 | 7 |
| 54 | 8 50.13 | 4.73 | 14 4.22 | 4.70 | 19 16.97 | 4.68 | 24 28.25 | 4.66 | 29 38.00 | 4.66 | 34 46.10 | 4.62 | 6 |
| 55 | 8 55.37 | 4.81 | 14 9.44 | 4.78 | 19 22.17 | 4.77 | 24 33.42 | 4.75 | 29 43.15 | 4.74 | 34 51.22 | 4.71 | 5 |
| 56 | 1 9 0.62 | 4.90 | 1 14 14.67 | 4.87 | 1 19 27.37 | 4.86 | 1 24 38.60 | 4.84 | 1 29 48.30 | 4.83 | 1 34 56.34 | 4.79 | 4 |
| 57 | 9 5.87 | 4.98 | 14 19.89 | 4.96 | 19 32.57 | 4.94 | 24 43.78 | 4.92 | 29 53.45 | 4.92 | 35 1.46 | 4.88 | 3 |
| 58 | 9 11.11 | 5.07 | 14 24.11 | 5.05 | 19 37.77 | 5.03 | 24 48.95 | 5.00 | 29 58.60 | 5.00 | 35 6.58 | 4.97 | 2 |
| 59 | 9 16.35 | 5.16 | 14 29.33 | 5.14 | 19 42.97 | 5.12 | 24 54.12 | 5.09 | 30 3.74 | 5.08 | 35 11.70 | 5.05 | 1 |
| 60 | 9 21.59 | 5.25 | 14 35.55 | 5.23 | 19 48.16 | 5.21 | 24 59.29 | 5.18 | 30 8.88 | 5.16 | 35 16.81 | 5.13 | 0 |
| $\bar{y}$ | 167°+ 347°– | | 166°+ 346°– | | 165°+ 345°– | | 164°+ 344°– | | 163°+ 343°– | | 162°+ 342°– | | $\bar{y}$ |

# TABLE CXXXVII. ARGUMENT 77.

Equation = 18500″ sin $\bar{y}$.

| $\bar{y}$ | 198°− 18°+ Equation. | P. P. | 199°− 19°+ Equation. | P. P. | 200°− 20°+ Equation. | P. P. | 201°− 21°+ Equation. | P. P. | 202°− 22°+ Equation. | P. P. | 203°− 23°+ Equation. | P. P. | $\bar{y}$ |
|---|---|---|---|---|---|---|---|---|---|---|---|---|---|
| 0′ | 1° 35′ 16.81″ | 0.00″ | 1° 40′ 24.01″ | 0.00″ | 1° 45′ 27.38″ | 0.00″ | 1° 50′ 29.81″ | 0.00″ | 1° 55′ 30.23″ | 0.00″ | 2° 0′ 28.52″ | 0.00″ | 60′ |
| 1 | 35 21.93 | 0.09 | 40 28.10 | 0.08 | 45 32.44 | 0.08 | 50 34.84 | 0.08 | 55 35.21 | 0.08 | 0 33.48 | 0.08 | 59 |
| 2 | 35 27.05 | 0.18 | 40 33.19 | 0.17 | 45 37.00 | 0.17 | 50 39.86 | 0.16 | 55 40.20 | 0.16 | 0 38.44 | 0.16 | 58 |
| 3 | 35 32.17 | 0.25 | 40 38.28 | 0.26 | 45 42.55 | 0.25 | 50 44.88 | 0.25 | 55 45.19 | 0.25 | 0 43.39 | 0.24 | 57 |
| 4 | 35 37.28 | 0.34 | 40 43.36 | 0.34 | 45 47.60 | 0.33 | 50 49.90 | 0.34 | 55 50.18 | 0.33 | 0 48.34 | 0.32 | 56 |
| 5 | 35 42.39 | 0.43 | 40 48.44 | 0.42 | 45 52.65 | 0.42 | 50 54.92 | 0.42 | 55 55.17 | 0.41 | 0 53.29 | 0.41 | 55 |
| 6 | 1 35 47.51 | 0.52 | 1 40 53.53 | 0.50 | 1 45 57.71 | 0.50 | 1 50 59.94 | 0.50 | 1 56 0.15 | 0.48 | 2 0 58.24 | 0.49 | 54 |
| 7 | 35 52.63 | 0.60 | 40 58.62 | 0.59 | 46 2.76 | 0.59 | 51 4.96 | 0.59 | 56 5.13 | 0.56 | 1 3.19 | 0.58 | 53 |
| 8 | 35 57.74 | 0.69 | 41 3.70 | 0.67 | 46 7.81 | 0.67 | 51 9.98 | 0.67 | 56 10.11 | 0.65 | 1 8.14 | 0.66 | 52 |
| 9 | 36 2.85 | 0.77 | 41 8.78 | 0.76 | 46 12.86 | 0.75 | 51 15.00 | 0.75 | 56 15.10 | 0.74 | 1 13.09 | 0.74 | 51 |
| 10 | 36 7.96 | 0.85 | 41 13.86 | 0.85 | 46 17.91 | 0.89 | 51 20.02 | 0.87 | 56 20.09 | 0.83 | 1 18.04 | 0.82 | 50 |
| 11 | 1 36 13.08 | 0.94 | 1 41 18.95 | 0.93 | 1 46 22.97 | 0.92 | 1 51 25.04 | 0.92 | 1 56 25.07 | 0.91 | 2 1 22.99 | 0.90 | 49 |
| 12 | 36 18.19 | 1.02 | 41 24.04 | 1.02 | 46 28.02 | 1.00 | 51 30.06 | 1.00 | 56 30.05 | 1.00 | 1 27.94 | 0.98 | 48 |
| 13 | 36 23.30 | 1.11 | 41 29.12 | 1.10 | 46 33.07 | 1.09 | 51 35.08 | 1.08 | 56 35.03 | 1.08 | 1 32.88 | 1.07 | 47 |
| 14 | 36 28.41 | 1.19 | 41 34.20 | 1.19 | 46 38.12 | 1.17 | 51 40.10 | 1.16 | 56 40.01 | 1.16 | 1 37.82 | 1.15 | 46 |
| 15 | 36 33.52 | 1.27 | 41 39.28 | 1.27 | 46 43.17 | 1.26 | 51 45.11 | 1.25 | 56 45.00 | 1.24 | 1 42.76 | 1.23 | 45 |
| 16 | 1 36 38.63 | 1.35 | 1 41 44.36 | 1.35 | 1 46 48.22 | 1.34 | 1 51 50.13 | 1.34 | 1 56 49.98 | 1.32 | 2 1 47.71 | 1.31 | 44 |
| 17 | 36 43.74 | 1.44 | 41 49.44 | 1.44 | 46 53.27 | 1.43 | 51 55.15 | 1.42 | 56 54.96 | 1.41 | 1 52.65 | 1.39 | 43 |
| 18 | 36 48.85 | 1.52 | 41 54.52 | 1.52 | 46 58.32 | 1.51 | 52 0.16 | 1.50 | 56 59.93 | 1.50 | 1 57.59 | 1.48 | 42 |
| 19 | 36 53.96 | 1.61 | 41 59.60 | 1.60 | 47 3.37 | 1.60 | 52 5.17 | 1.59 | 57 4.91 | 1.58 | 2 2.53 | 1.56 | 41 |
| 20 | 36 59.07 | 1.70 | 42 4.68 | 1.69 | 47 8.41 | 1.68 | 52 10.18 | 1.67 | 57 9.89 | 1.66 | 2 7.47 | 1.65 | 40 |
| 21 | 1 37 4.18 | 1.79 | 1 42 9.76 | 1.78 | 1 47 13.40 | 1.76 | 1 52 15.20 | 1.76 | 1 57 14.87 | 1.74 | 2 2 12.41 | 1.73 | 39 |
| 22 | 37 9.29 | 1.87 | 42 14.84 | 1.86 | 47 18.51 | 1.85 | 52 20.21 | 1.84 | 57 19.85 | 1.82 | 2 17.35 | 1.81 | 38 |
| 23 | 37 14.41 | 1.96 | 42 19.92 | 1.95 | 47 23.55 | 1.93 | 52 25.22 | 1.92 | 57 24.83 | 1.90 | 2 22.29 | 1.90 | 37 |
| 24 | 37 19.51 | 2.05 | 42 24.99 | 2.04 | 47 28.59 | 2.01 | 52 30.23 | 2.01 | 57 29.80 | 1.98 | 2 27.23 | 1.98 | 36 |
| 25 | 37 24.61 | 2.14 | 42 30.06 | 2.13 | 47 33.63 | 2.10 | 52 35.24 | 2.10 | 57 34.77 | 2.06 | 2 32.17 | 2.06 | 35 |
| 26 | 1 37 29.72 | 2.23 | 1 42 35.14 | 2.21 | 1 47 38.68 | 2.18 | 1 52 40.25 | 2.18 | 1 57 39.75 | 2.15 | 2 2 37.11 | 2.14 | 34 |
| 27 | 37 34.83 | 2.31 | 42 40.22 | 2.29 | 47 43.72 | 2.26 | 52 45.26 | 2.26 | 57 44.73 | 2.23 | 2 42.05 | 2.22 | 33 |
| 28 | 37 39.93 | 2.39 | 42 45.29 | 2.37 | 47 48.76 | 2.35 | 52 50.27 | 2.34 | 57 49.70 | 2.31 | 2 46.99 | 2.30 | 32 |
| 29 | 37 45.03 | 2.47 | 42 50.36 | 2.45 | 47 53.80 | 2.44 | 52 55.27 | 2.42 | 57 54.67 | 2.40 | 2 51.93 | 2.38 | 31 |
| 30 | 37 50.13 | 2.55 | 42 55.43 | 2.53 | 47 58.84 | 2.52 | 53 0.28 | 2.50 | 57 59.64 | 2.48 | 2 56.86 | 2.47 | 30 |
| 31 | 1 37 55.24 | 2.64 | 1 43 0.51 | 2.61 | 1 48 3.88 | 2.60 | 1 53 5.29 | 2.58 | 1 58 4.62 | 2.56 | 2 3 1.80 | 2.55 | 29 |
| 32 | 38 0.34 | 2.72 | 43 5.58 | 2.70 | 48 8.92 | 2.69 | 53 10.29 | 2.66 | 58 9.59 | 2.65 | 3 6.74 | 2.63 | 28 |
| 33 | 38 5.44 | 2.81 | 43 10 65 | 2.78 | 48 13.96 | 2.77 | 53 15.30 | 2.74 | 58 14.56 | 2.74 | 3 11 67 | 2.71 | 27 |
| 34 | 38 10.54 | 2.90 | 43 15.72 | 2.87 | 48 19.00 | 2.86 | 53 20.30 | 2.82 | 58 19.53 | 2.82 | 3 10.60 | 2.79 | 26 |
| 35 | 38 15.64 | 2.98 | 43 20.79 | 2.95 | 48 24.04 | 2.94 | 53 25.30 | 2.91 | 58 24.50 | 2.90 | 3 21.53 | 2.88 | 25 |
| 36 | 1 38 20.74 | 3.07 | 1 43 25.86 | 3.04 | 1 48 29.08 | 3.03 | 1 53 30.30 | 3.00 | 1 58 29.47 | 2.98 | 2 3 26.46 | 2.96 | 24 |
| 37 | 38 25.84 | 3.15 | 43 30.93 | 3.12 | 48 34.12 | 3.11 | 53 35.30 | 3.09 | 58 34.44 | 3.06 | 3 31.39 | 3.04 | 23 |
| 38 | 38 30.94 | 3.24 | 43 36.00 | 3.21 | 48 39.16 | 3.20 | 53 40.31 | 3.18 | 58 39.41 | 3.14 | 3 36.32 | 3.12 | 22 |
| 39 | 38 36.04 | 3.32 | 43 41.07 | 3.30 | 48 44.19 | 3.28 | 53 45.31 | 3.26 | 58 44.38 | 3.22 | 3 41.25 | 3.20 | 21 |
| 40 | 38 41.14 | 3.40 | 43 46.14 | 3.38 | 48 49.22 | 3.36 | 53 50.31 | 3.34 | 58 49.34 | 3.31 | 3 46.18 | 3.29 | 20 |
| 41 | 1 38 46.24 | 3.49 | 1 43 51.21 | 3.46 | 1 48 54.26 | 3.44 | 1 53 55.31 | 3.42 | 1 58 54.31 | 3.40 | 2 3 51.11 | 3.37 | 19 |
| 42 | 38 51.34 | 3.58 | 43 56.28 | 3.55 | 48 59.30 | 3.53 | 54 0.31 | 3.50 | 58 59.27 | 3.48 | 3 56.04 | 3.46 | 18 |
| 43 | 38 56.44 | 3.66 | 44 1.35 | 3.63 | 49 4.33 | 3.61 | 54 5.31 | 3.59 | 59 4.23 | 3.56 | 4 0.97 | 3.54 | 17 |
| 44 | 39 1.54 | 3.75 | 44 6.41 | 3.72 | 49 9.36 | 3.70 | 54 10.31 | 3.67 | 59 9.19 | 3.65 | 4 5.90 | 3.62 | 16 |
| 45 | 39 6.63 | 3.84 | 44 11.47 | 3.80 | 49 14.39 | 3.78 | 54 15.31 | 3.75 | 59 14.15 | 3.73 | 4 10.82 | 3.70 | 15 |
| 46 | 1 39 11.73 | 3.92 | 1 44 16.54 | 3.89 | 1 49 19.42 | 3.87 | 1 54 20.31 | 3.84 | 1 59 19.11 | 3.82 | 2 4 15.75 | 3.79 | 14 |
| 47 | 39 16.83 | 4. 0 | 44 21.61 | 3.96 | 49 24.45 | 3.95 | 54 25.31 | 3.91 | 59 24.07 | 3.90 | 4 20.68 | 3.87 | 13 |
| 48 | 39 21.92 | 4. 8 | 44 26.67 | 4.04 | 49 29.48 | 4.03 | 54 30.30 | 4.00 | 59 29.03 | 3.98 | 4 25.60 | 3.95 | 12 |
| 49 | 39 27.01 | 4.16 | 44 31.73 | 4.13 | 49 34.51 | 4.11 | 54 35.30 | 4.09 | 59 33.99 | 4.06 | 4 30.52 | 4.03 | 11 |
| 50 | 39 32.11 | 4.25 | 44 36.79 | 4.22 | 49 39.54 | 4.20 | 54 40.30 | 4.18 | 59 38.95 | 4.14 | 4 35.44 | 4.12 | 10 |
| 51 | 1 39 37.21 | 4.33 | 1 44 41.85 | 4.30 | 1 49 44.57 | 4.28 | 1 54 45.30 | 4.26 | 1 59 43.91 | 4.22 | 2 4 40.36 | 4.21 | 9 |
| 52 | 39 42.30 | 4.42 | 44 46.91 | 4.39 | 49 49.60 | 4.37 | 54 50.29 | 4.35 | 59 48.87 | 4.31 | 4 45.28 | 4.29 | 8 |
| 53 | 39 47.39 | 4.50 | 44 51.97 | 4.47 | 49 54.63 | 4.45 | 54 55.29 | 4.44 | 59 53.83 | 4.39 | 4 50.20 | 4.37 | 7 |
| 54 | 39 52.48 | 4.59 | 44 57.03 | 4.56 | 49 59.66 | 4.54 | 55 0.28 | 4.52 | 59 58.79 | 4.47 | 4 55.12 | 4.45 | 6 |
| 55 | 39 57.57 | 4.68 | 45 2.09 | 4.64 | 50 4.68 | 4.62 | 55 5.27 | 4.60 | 2 0 3.74 | 4.55 | 5 0.04 | 4.53 | 5 |
| 56 | 1 40 2.66 | 4.76 | 1 45 7.15 | 4.73 | 1 50 9.71 | 4.70 | 1 55 10.26 | 4.68 | 2 0 8.70 | 4.64 | 2 5 4.96 | 4.61 | 4 |
| 57 | 40 7.75 | 4.85 | 45 12.21 | 4.82 | 50 14.74 | 4.79 | 55 15.25 | 4.76 | 0 13.66 | 4.72 | 5 9.88 | 4.69 | 3 |
| 58 | 40 12.84 | 4.93 | 45 17.27 | 4.90 | 50 19.77 | 4.87 | 55 20.24 | 4.85 | 0 18.62 | 4.80 | 5 14.80 | 4.77 | 2 |
| 59 | 40 17.93 | 5.02 | 45 22.33 | 4.99 | 50 24.79 | 4.96 | 55 25.24 | 4.93 | 0 23.57 | 4.88 | 5 19.72 | 4.85 | 1 |
| 60 | 40 23.01 | 5.10 | 45 27.38 | 5.07 | 50 29.81 | 5.04 | 55 30.23 | 5.01 | 0 28.52 | 4.97 | 5 24.63 | 4.94 | 0 |
| $\bar{y}$ | 161°+ 341°− | | 160°+ 340°− | | 159°+ 339°− | | 158°+ 338°− | | 157°+ 337°− | | 156°+ 336°− | | $\bar{y}$ |

# TABLE CXXXVII. ARGUMENT 77.

Equation = 18500″ sin ȳ.

| ȳ | 204°— 24°+ Equation. | P. P. | 205°— 25°+ Equation. | P. P. | 206°— 26°+ Equation. | P. P. | 207°— 27°+ Equation. | P. P. | 208°— 28°+ Equation. | P. P. | 209°— 29°+ Equation. | P. P. | ȳ |
|---|---|---|---|---|---|---|---|---|---|---|---|---|---|
| ′ 0 | ° ′ ″ 2 5 24.63 | ″ 0.00 | ° ′ ″ 2 10 18.46 | ″ 0.00 | ° ′ ″ 2 15 9.87 | ″ 0.00 | ° ′ ″ 2 19 58.82 | ″ 0.00 | ° ′ ″ 2 24 45.22 | ″ 0.00 | ° ′ ″ 2 29 28.98 | ″ 0.00 | ′ 60 |
| 1 | 5 29.55 | 0.08 | 10 23.34 | 0.08 | 15 14.71 | 0.08 | 20 3.62 | 0.08 | 24 49.97 | 0.08 | 29 33.69 | 0.08 | 59 |
| 2 | 5 34.47 | 0.16 | 10 28.21 | 0.16 | 15 19.55 | 0.16 | 20 8.42 | 0.16 | 24 54.72 | 0.16 | 29 38.40 | 0.16 | 58 |
| 3 | 5 39.38 | 0.24 | 10 33.08 | 0.24 | 15 24.38 | 0.24 | 20 13.21 | 0.24 | 24 59.47 | 0.24 | 29 43.11 | 0.24 | 57 |
| 4 | 5 44.29 | 0.32 | 10 37.75 | 0.32 | 15 29.21 | 0.32 | 20 18.00 | 0.32 | 25 4.22 | 0.32 | 29 47.81 | 0.32 | 56 |
| 5 | 5 49.20 | 0.41 | 10 42.82 | 0.40 | 15 34.04 | 0.40 | 20 22.79 | 0.40 | 25 8.97 | 0.40 | 29 52.51 | 0.40 | 55 |
| 6 | 2 5 54.12 | 0.49 | 2 10 47.70 | 0.48 | 2 15 38.88 | 0.48 | 2 20 27.58 | 0.48 | 2 25 13.72 | 0.48 | 2 29 57.22 | 0.48 | 54 |
| 7 | 5 59.03 | 0.57 | 10 52.57 | 0.56 | 15 43.71 | 0.56 | 20 32.37 | 0.56 | 25 18.47 | 0.56 | 30 1.92 | 0.56 | 53 |
| 8 | 6 3.94 | 0.65 | 10 57.44 | 0.64 | 15 48.54 | 0.64 | 20 37.16 | 0.64 | 25 23.22 | 0.64 | 30 6.62 | 0.64 | 52 |
| 9 | 6 8.85 | 0.73 | 11 2.31 | 0.72 | 15 53.37 | 0.72 | 20 41.95 | 0.72 | 25 27.97 | 0.72 | 30 11.32 | 0.71 | 51 |
| 10 | 6 13.76 | 0.82 | 11 7.18 | 0.81 | 15 58.20 | 0.80 | 20 46.74 | 0.80 | 25 32.72 | 0.79 | 30 16.02 | 0.78 | 50 |
| 11 | 2 6 18.67 | 0.90 | 2 11 12.05 | 0.89 | 2 16 3.03 | 0.88 | 2 20 51.53 | 0.88 | 2 25 37.46 | 0.87 | 2 30 20.72 | 0.86 | 49 |
| 12 | 6 23.58 | 0.98 | 11 16.92 | 0.97 | 16 7.86 | 0.96 | 20 56.32 | 0.96 | 25 42.20 | 0.95 | 30 25.42 | 0.94 | 48 |
| 13 | 6 28.49 | 1.06 | 11 21.79 | 1.05 | 16 12.69 | 1.04 | 21 1.10 | 1.04 | 25 46.94 | 1.03 | 30 30.11 | 1.02 | 47 |
| 14 | 6 33.40 | 1.14 | 11 26.66 | 1.13 | 16 17.52 | 1.12 | 21 5.88 | 1.12 | 25 51.68 | 1.11 | 30 34.80 | 1.10 | 46 |
| 15 | 6 38.30 | 1.22 | 11 31.53 | 1.21 | 16 22.34 | 1.20 | 21 10.66 | 1.20 | 25 56.41 | 1.19 | 30 39.50 | 1.18 | 45 |
| 16 | 2 6 43.21 | 1.30 | 2 11 36.40 | 1.29 | 2 16 27.17 | 1.28 | 2 21 15.45 | 1.28 | 2 26 1.15 | 1.27 | 2 30 44.20 | 1.26 | 44 |
| 17 | 6 48.12 | 1.38 | 11 41.27 | 1.37 | 16 32.00 | 1.36 | 21 20.23 | 1.36 | 26 5.89 | 1.35 | 30 48.90 | 1.34 | 43 |
| 18 | 6 53.02 | 1.46 | 11 46.14 | 1.45 | 16 36.82 | 1.44 | 21 25.01 | 1.44 | 26 10.63 | 1.43 | 30 53.90 | 1.42 | 42 |
| 19 | 6 57.92 | 1.54 | 11 51.00 | 1.53 | 16 41.64 | 1.52 | 21 29.79 | 1.52 | 26 15.37 | 1.51 | 30 58.28 | 1.49 | 41 |
| 20 | 7 2.82 | 1.63 | 11 55.86 | 1.62 | 16 46.46 | 1.61 | 21 34.57 | 1.59 | 26 20.10 | 1.58 | 31 2.97 | 1.56 | 40 |
| 21 | 2 7 7.73 | 1.71 | 2 12 0.73 | 1.70 | 2 16 51.29 | 1.69 | 2 21 39.35 | 1.67 | 2 26 24.84 | 1.66 | 2 31 7.66 | 1.64 | 39 |
| 22 | 7 12.63 | 1.80 | 12 5.59 | 1.78 | 16 56.11 | 1.77 | 21 44.13 | 1.75 | 26 29.58 | 1.74 | 31 12.35 | 1.72 | 38 |
| 23 | 7 17.53 | 1.88 | 12 10.45 | 1.86 | 17 0.93 | 1.85 | 21 48.91 | 1.83 | 26 34.31 | 1.82 | 31 17.04 | 1.80 | 37 |
| 24 | 7 22.43 | 1.96 | 12 15.31 | 1.94 | 17 5.75 | 1.93 | 21 53.69 | 1.91 | 26 39.04 | 1.90 | 31 21.73 | 1.88 | 36 |
| 25 | 7 27.33 | 2.04 | 12 20.17 | 2.02 | 17 10.57 | 2.01 | 21 58.46 | 1.99 | 26 43.77 | 1.98 | 31 26.42 | 1.96 | 35 |
| 26 | 2 7 32.23 | 2.12 | 2 12 25.03 | 2.10 | 2 17 15.39 | 2.09 | 2 22 3.24 | 2.07 | 2 26 48.51 | 2.06 | 2 31 31.11 | 2.04 | 34 |
| 27 | 7 37.13 | 2.20 | 12 29.89 | 2.18 | 17 20.21 | 2.17 | 22 8.02 | 2.15 | 26 53.24 | 2.14 | 31 35.80 | 2.12 | 33 |
| 28 | 7 42.03 | 2.28 | 12 34.75 | 2.26 | 17 25.03 | 2.25 | 22 12.79 | 2.23 | 26 57.97 | 2.22 | 31 40.48 | 2.20 | 32 |
| 29 | 7 46.93 | 2.36 | 12 39.61 | 2.34 | 17 29.85 | 2.33 | 22 17.57 | 2.31 | 27 2.70 | 2.29 | 31 45.16 | 2.27 | 31 |
| 30 | 7 51.83 | 2.45 | 12 44.46 | 2.42 | 17 34.66 | 2.41 | 22 22.34 | 2.39 | 27 7.43 | 2.36 | 31 49.84 | 2.34 | 30 |
| 31 | 2 7 56.73 | 2.53 | 2 12 49.32 | 2.50 | 2 17 39.48 | 2.49 | 2 22 27.11 | 2.47 | 2 27 12.16 | 2.44 | 2 31 54.53 | 2.42 | 29 |
| 32 | 8 1.63 | 2.62 | 12 54.18 | 2.58 | 17 44.30 | 2.57 | 22 31.88 | 2.55 | 27 16.89 | 2.52 | 31 59.21 | 2.50 | 28 |
| 33 | 8 6.53 | 2.70 | 12 59.03 | 2.66 | 17 49.11 | 2.65 | 22 36.65 | 2.63 | 27 21.62 | 2.60 | 32 3.89 | 2.58 | 27 |
| 34 | 8 11.42 | 2.78 | 13 3.88 | 2.74 | 17 53.92 | 2.73 | 22 41.42 | 2.71 | 27 26.35 | 2.68 | 32 8.57 | 2.66 | 26 |
| 35 | 8 16.31 | 2.87 | 13 8.73 | 2.82 | 17 58.73 | 2.81 | 22 46.20 | 2.79 | 27 31.07 | 2.76 | 32 13.25 | 2.74 | 25 |
| 36 | 2 8 21.21 | 2.95 | 2 13 13.59 | 2.90 | 2 18 3.54 | 2.89 | 2 22 50.97 | 2.87 | 2 27 35.80 | 2.84 | 2 32 17.93 | 2.82 | 24 |
| 37 | 8 26.10 | 3.03 | 13 18.44 | 2.98 | 18 8.35 | 2.97 | 22 55.74 | 2.95 | 27 40.53 | 2.92 | 32 22.61 | 2.90 | 23 |
| 38 | 8 30.99 | 3.11 | 13 23.29 | 3.06 | 18 13.16 | 3.05 | 23 0.51 | 3.03 | 27 45.25 | 3.00 | 32 27.29 | 2.98 | 22 |
| 39 | 8 35.88 | 3.19 | 13 28.14 | 3.14 | 18 17.97 | 3.13 | 23 5.28 | 3.11 | 27 50.97 | 3.08 | 32 31.96 | 3.05 | 21 |
| 40 | 8 40.77 | 3.26 | 13 32.99 | 3.23 | 18 22.78 | 3.21 | 23 10.04 | 3.19 | 27 54.69 | 3.15 | 32 36.64 | 3.12 | 20 |
| 41 | 2 8 45.66 | 3.34 | 2 13 37.84 | 3.31 | 2 18 27.59 | 3.29 | 2 23 14.81 | 3.27 | 2 27 59.41 | 3.23 | 2 32 41.32 | 3.20 | 19 |
| 42 | 8 50.55 | 3.42 | 13 42.69 | 3.39 | 18 32.40 | 3.37 | 23 19.58 | 3.35 | 28 4.13 | 3.31 | 32 46.60 | 3.28 | 18 |
| 43 | 8 55.44 | 3.50 | 13 47.54 | 3.47 | 18 37.21 | 3.45 | 23 24.34 | 3.43 | 28 8.85 | 3.39 | 32 50.67 | 3.36 | 17 |
| 44 | 9 0.33 | 3.58 | 13 52.39 | 3.55 | 18 42.02 | 3.53 | 23 29.10 | 3.51 | 28 13.57 | 3.47 | 32 55.34 | 3.44 | 16 |
| 45 | 9 5.21 | 3.66 | 13 57.24 | 3.63 | 18 46.82 | 3.61 | 23 33.86 | 3.59 | 28 18.29 | 3.55 | 33 0.01 | 3.52 | 15 |
| 46 | 2 9 10.10 | 3.75 | 2 14 2.09 | 3.71 | 2 18 51.63 | 3.69 | 2 23 38.63 | 3.67 | 2 28 23.01 | 3.63 | 2 33 4.68 | 3.60 | 14 |
| 47 | 9 14.99 | 3.83 | 14 6.94 | 3.79 | 18 56.44 | 3.77 | 23 43.39 | 3.75 | 28 27.73 | 3.71 | 33 9.35 | 3.68 | 13 |
| 48 | 9 19.87 | 3.91 | 14 11.79 | 3.87 | 19 1.24 | 3.85 | 23 48.15 | 3.83 | 28 32.45 | 3.79 | 33 14.02 | 3.76 | 12 |
| 49 | 9 24.75 | 4.00 | 14 16.63 | 3.95 | 19 6.04 | 3.94 | 23 52.91 | 3.91 | 28 37.16 | 3.87 | 33 18.69 | 3.83 | 11 |
| 50 | 9 29.63 | 4.08 | 14 21.47 | 4.04 | 19 10.84 | 4.01 | 23 57.67 | 3.99 | 28 41.87 | 3.74 | 33 23.36 | 3.90 | 10 |
| 51 | 2 9 34.52 | 4.16 | 2 14 26.32 | 4.12 | 2 19 15.64 | 4.09 | 2 24 2.43 | 4.07 | 2 28 46.59 | 4.02 | 2 33 28.03 | 3.98 | 9 |
| 52 | 9 39.40 | 4.24 | 14 31.16 | 4.20 | 19 20.44 | 4.17 | 24 7.19 | 4.15 | 28 51.30 | 4.10 | 33 32.70 | 4.06 | 8 |
| 53 | 9 44.28 | 4.32 | 14 36.00 | 4.28 | 19 25.24 | 4.25 | 24 11.95 | 4.23 | 28 56.01 | 4.18 | 33 37.37 | 4.14 | 7 |
| 54 | 9 49.16 | 4.40 | 14 40.84 | 4.36 | 19 30.04 | 4.33 | 24 16.71 | 4.31 | 29 0.72 | 4.26 | 33 42.04 | 4.22 | 6 |
| 55 | 9 54.05 | 4.49 | 14 45.68 | 4.44 | 19 34.84 | 4.41 | 24 20.46 | 4.39 | 29 5.43 | 4.34 | 33 46.69 | 4.30 | 5 |
| 56 | 2 9 58.94 | 4.57 | 2 14 50.52 | 4.52 | 2 19 39.64 | 4.49 | 2 24 26.22 | 4.47 | 2 29 10.14 | 4.42 | 2 33 51.36 | 4.38 | 4 |
| 57 | 10 3.82 | 4.65 | 14 55.36 | 4.60 | 19 44.44 | 4.57 | 24 30.97 | 4.55 | 29 14.85 | 4.50 | 33 56 02 | 4.46 | 3 |
| 58 | 10 8.70 | 4.73 | 15 0.20 | 4.68 | 19 49.24 | 4.65 | 24 35.72 | 4.63 | 29 19.56 | 4.58 | 34 0.68 | 4.54 | 2 |
| 59 | 10 13.58 | 4.81 | 15 5.04 | 4.74 | 19 54.03 | 4.73 | 24 40.47 | 4.71 | 29 23.27 | 4.66 | 34 5.34 | 4.61 | 1 |
| 60 | 10 18.46 | 4.90 | 15 9.87 | 4.85 | 19 58.82 | 4.82 | 24 45.22 | 4.78 | 29 28.98 | 4.73 | 34 10.00 | 4.68 | 0 |
| ȳ | 155°+ 335°— | | 154°+ 334°— | | 153°+ 333°— | | 152°+ 332°— | | 151°+ 331°— | | 150°+ 330°— | | ȳ |

# TABLE CXXXVII. ARGUMENT 77.

Equation = 18500″ sin $\bar{y}$.

| $\bar{y}$ | 210°— 30°+ Equation. | P. P. | 211°— 31°+ Equation. | P. P. | 212°— 32°+ Equation. | P. P. | 213°— 33°+ Equation. | P. P. | 214°— 34°+ Equation. | P. P. | 215°— 35°+ Equation. | P. P. | $\bar{y}$ |
|---|---|---|---|---|---|---|---|---|---|---|---|---|---|
| ′ | ° ′ ″ | ″ | ° ′ ″ | ″ | ° ′ ″ | ″ | ° ′ ″ | ″ | ° ′ ″ | ″ | ° ′ ″ | ″ | ′ |
| 0 | 2 34 10.00 | 0.00 | 2 38 48.20 | 0.00 | 2 43 23.51 | 0.00 | 2 47 55.82 | 0.00 | 2 52 25.07 | 0.00 | 2 56 51.16 | 0.00 | 60 |
| 1 | 34 14.66 | 0.08 | 38 52.82 | 0.08 | 43 28.08 | 0.08 | 48 0.34 | 0.08 | 52 29.53 | 0.08 | 56 55.57 | 0.08 | 59 |
| 2 | 34 19.32 | 0.16 | 38 57.43 | 0.16 | 43 32.64 | 0.16 | 48 4.86 | 0.16 | 52 33.99 | 0.16 | 56 59.98 | 0.16 | 58 |
| 3 | 34 23.98 | 0.24 | 39 2.04 | 0.24 | 43 37.20 | 0.24 | 48 9.37 | 0.24 | 52 38.45 | 0.24 | 57 4.39 | 0.24 | 57 |
| 4 | 34 28.64 | 0.32 | 39 6.65 | 0.32 | 43 41.76 | 0.32 | 48 13.88 | 0.32 | 52 42.91 | 0.32 | 57 8.79 | 0.31 | 56 |
| 5 | 34 33.29 | 0.40 | 39 11.26 | 0.40 | 43 46.32 | 0.40 | 48 18.39 | 0.40 | 52 47.37 | 0.39 | 57 13.19 | 0.38 | 55 |
| 6 | 2 34 37.95 | 0.48 | 2 39 15.87 | 0.48 | 2 43 50.88 | 0.48 | 2 48 22.90 | 0.47 | 2 52 51.83 | 0.46 | 2 57 17.60 | 0.45 | 54 |
| 7 | 34 42.61 | 0.56 | 39 20.48 | 0.56 | 43 55.44 | 0.55 | 48 27.41 | 0.54 | 52 56.29 | 0.52 | 57 22.00 | 0.52 | 53 |
| 8 | 34 47.26 | 0.63 | 39 25.09 | 0.63 | 44 0.00 | 0.62 | 48 31.92 | 0.61 | 53 0.74 | 0.60 | 57 26.40 | 0.59 | 52 |
| 9 | 34 51.91 | 0.70 | 39 29.69 | 0.70 | 44 4.56 | 0.69 | 48 36.43 | 0.68 | 53 5.19 | 0.67 | 57 30.80 | 0.66 | 51 |
| 10 | 34 56.56 | 0.77 | 39 34.29 | 0.77 | 44 9.11 | 0.76 | 48 40.93 | 0.75 | 53 9.64 | 0.74 | 57 35.20 | 0.73 | 50 |
| 11 | 2 35 1.22 | 0.85 | 2 39 38.90 | 0.85 | 2 44 13.67 | 0.84 | 2 48 45.43 | 0.83 | 2 53 14.09 | 0.82 | 2 57 39.60 | 0.81 | 49 |
| 12 | 35 5.87 | 0.93 | 39 43.50 | 0.93 | 44 18.22 | 0.92 | 48 49.93 | 0.91 | 53 18.54 | 0.90 | 57 44.00 | 0.89 | 48 |
| 13 | 35 10.52 | 1.01 | 39 48.10 | 1.01 | 44 22.77 | 1.00 | 48 54.43 | 0.99 | 53 22.99 | 0.98 | 57 48.40 | 0.97 | 47 |
| 14 | 35 15.17 | 1.09 | 39 52.70 | 1.09 | 44 27.32 | 1.08 | 48 58.93 | 1.07 | 53 27.44 | 1.06 | 57 52.79 | 1.04 | 46 |
| 15 | 35 19.82 | 1.17 | 39 57.30 | 1.17 | 44 31.87 | 1.16 | 49 3.43 | 1.15 | 53 31.89 | 1.13 | 57 57.18 | 1.11 | 45 |
| 16 | 2 35 24.47 | 1.25 | 2 40 1.90 | 1.25 | 2 44 36.42 | 1.23 | 2 49 7.93 | 1.22 | 2 53 36.34 | 1.20 | 2 58 1.58 | 1.18 | 44 |
| 17 | 35 29.12 | 1.33 | 40 6.50 | 1.32 | 44 40.97 | 1.30 | 49 12.43 | 1.29 | 53 40.79 | 1.27 | 58 5.97 | 1.25 | 43 |
| 18 | 35 33.77 | 1.41 | 40 11.10 | 1.39 | 44 45.52 | 1.37 | 49 16.93 | 1.36 | 53 45.24 | 1.34 | 58 10.36 | 1.32 | 42 |
| 19 | 35 38.42 | 1.48 | 40 15.70 | 1.46 | 44 50.07 | 1.44 | 49 21.42 | 1.44 | 53 49.68 | 1.41 | 58 14.75 | 1.39 | 41 |
| 20 | 35 43.06 | 1.55 | 40 20.29 | 1.53 | 44 54.61 | 1.50 | 49 25.91 | 1.50 | 53 54.12 | 1.48 | 58 19.14 | 1.46 | 40 |
| 21 | 2 35 47.71 | 1.63 | 2 40 24.89 | 1.61 | 2 44 59.16 | 1.59 | 2 49 30.41 | 1.58 | 2 53 58.57 | 1.56 | 2 58 23.53 | 1.54 | 39 |
| 22 | 35 52.35 | 1.71 | 40 29.49 | 1.69 | 45 3.71 | 1.67 | 49 34.91 | 1.66 | 54 3.01 | 1.64 | 58 27.92 | 1.62 | 38 |
| 23 | 35 56.99 | 1.79 | 40 34.08 | 1.77 | 45 8.25 | 1.75 | 49 39.00 | 1.74 | 54 7.45 | 1.72 | 58 32.31 | 1.70 | 37 |
| 24 | 36 1.63 | 1.87 | 40 38.67 | 1.85 | 45 12.79 | 1.83 | 49 43.89 | 1.82 | 54 11.89 | 1.80 | 58 36.70 | 1.77 | 36 |
| 25 | 36 6.27 | 1.95 | 40 43.26 | 1.93 | 45 17.33 | 1.91 | 49 48.38 | 1.89 | 54 16.33 | 1.87 | 58 41.08 | 1.84 | 35 |
| 26 | 2 36 10.91 | 2.03 | 2 40 47.86 | 2.01 | 2 45 21.88 | 1.99 | 2 49 52.88 | 1.96 | 2 54 20.77 | 1.94 | 2 58 45.47 | 1.91 | 34 |
| 27 | 36 15.55 | 2.11 | 40 52.45 | 2.09 | 45 26.42 | 2.06 | 49 57.37 | 2.03 | 54 25.21 | 2.01 | 58 49.86 | 1.98 | 33 |
| 28 | 36 20.19 | 2.18 | 40 57.04 | 2.16 | 45 30.96 | 2.13 | 50 1.86 | 2.10 | 54 29.65 | 2.08 | 58 54.24 | 2.05 | 32 |
| 29 | 36 24.83 | 2.25 | 41 1.63 | 2.23 | 45 35.50 | 2.20 | 50 6.35 | 2.17 | 54 34.08 | 2.15 | 58 58.62 | 2.12 | 31 |
| 30 | 36 29.46 | 2.32 | 41 6.22 | 2.30 | 45 40.04 | 2.27 | 50 10.84 | 2.24 | 54 38.51 | 2.22 | 59 3.00 | 2.19 | 30 |
| 31 | 2 36 34.10 | 2.40 | 2 41 10.81 | 2.38 | 2 45 44.58 | 2.35 | 2 50 15.33 | 2.32 | 2 54 42.95 | 2.30 | 2 59 7.38 | 2.27 | 29 |
| 32 | 36 38.74 | 2.48 | 41 15.40 | 2.46 | 45 49.12 | 2.43 | 50 19.82 | 2.40 | 54 47.38 | 2.38 | 59 11.76 | 2.35 | 28 |
| 33 | 36 43.37 | 2.56 | 41 19.99 | 2.54 | 45 53.66 | 2.51 | 50 24.31 | 2.48 | 54 51.81 | 2.46 | 59 16.14 | 2.43 | 27 |
| 34 | 36 48.00 | 2.64 | 41 24.58 | 2.62 | 45 58.20 | 2.59 | 50 28.49 | 2.56 | 54 56.24 | 2.54 | 59 20.52 | 2.50 | 26 |
| 35 | 36 52.63 | 2.72 | 41 29.16 | 2.70 | 46 2.73 | 2.67 | 50 33.27 | 2.64 | 55 0.67 | 2.61 | 59 24.90 | 2.57 | 25 |
| 36 | 2 36 57.26 | 2.80 | 2 41 33.75 | 2.78 | 2 46 7.27 | 2.74 | 2 50 37.75 | 2.71 | 2 55 5.10 | 2.68 | 2 59 29.28 | 2.64 | 24 |
| 37 | 37 1.89 | 2.88 | 41 38.33 | 2.85 | 46 11.80 | 2.81 | 50 42.23 | 2.78 | 55 9.53 | 2.75 | 59 33.66 | 2.71 | 23 |
| 38 | 37 6.52 | 2.96 | 41 42.91 | 2.92 | 46 16.33 | 2.88 | 50 46.71 | 2.85 | 55 13.96 | 2.82 | 59 38.03 | 2.78 | 22 |
| 39 | 37 11.15 | 3.02 | 41 47.49 | 2.98 | 46 20.86 | 2.95 | 50 51.19 | 2.92 | 55 18.39 | 2.89 | 59 42.40 | 2.85 | 21 |
| 40 | 37 15.78 | 3.09 | 41 52.07 | 3.06 | 46 25.39 | 3.02 | 50 55.67 | 2.99 | 55 22.81 | 2.96 | 59 46.77 | 2.92 | 20 |
| 41 | 2 37 20.41 | 3.17 | 2 41 56.65 | 3.14 | 2 46 29.92 | 3.10 | 2 51 0.15 | 3.07 | 2 55 27.24 | 3.04 | 2 59 51.14 | 3.00 | 19 |
| 42 | 37 25.04 | 3.24 | 42 1.23 | 3.22 | 46 32.45 | 3.18 | 51 4.63 | 3.15 | 55 31.67 | 3.12 | 59 55.51 | 3.08 | 18 |
| 43 | 37 29.67 | 3.33 | 42 5.81 | 3.30 | 46 38.98 | 3.26 | 51 8.11 | 3.23 | 55 36.10 | 3.20 | 59 59.88 | 3.16 | 17 |
| 44 | 37 34.30 | 3.41 | 42 10.39 | 3.38 | 46 43.50 | 3.34 | 51 13.58 | 3.31 | 55 40.52 | 3.28 | 3 0 4.25 | 3.23 | 16 |
| 45 | 37 38.92 | 3.49 | 42 14.96 | 3.46 | 46 48.02 | 3.42 | 51 18.05 | 3.39 | 55 44.94 | 3.36 | 0 8.61 | 3.30 | 15 |
| 46 | 2 37 43.54 | 3.57 | 2 42 19.54 | 3.54 | 2 46 52.55 | 3.49 | 2 51 22.53 | 3.46 | 2 55 49.36 | 3.43 | 3 0 12.98 | 3.37 | 14 |
| 47 | 37 48.16 | 3.65 | 42 24.12 | 3.62 | 46 57.07 | 3.56 | 51 27.00 | 3.53 | 55 53.78 | 3.50 | 0 17.35 | 3.44 | 13 |
| 48 | 37 52.78 | 3.73 | 42 28.69 | 3.69 | 47 1.59 | 3.63 | 51 31.47 | 3.60 | 55 58.20 | 3.57 | 0 21.71 | 3.51 | 12 |
| 49 | 37 57.40 | 3.80 | 42 33.26 | 3.76 | 47 6.11 | 3.70 | 51 35.94 | 3.67 | 56 2.62 | 3.64 | 0 26.07 | 3.58 | 11 |
| 50 | 38 2.03 | 3.87 | 42 37.83 | 3.83 | 47 10.63 | 3.77 | 51 40.41 | 3.74 | 56 7.04 | 3.70 | 0 30.43 | 3.65 | 10 |
| 51 | 2 38 6.65 | 3.95 | 2 42 42.40 | 3.91 | 2 47 15.15 | 3.85 | 2 51 44.88 | 3.82 | 2 56 11.46 | 3.78 | 3 0 34.79 | 3.73 | 9 |
| 52 | 38 11.27 | 4.03 | 42 46.97 | 3.99 | 47 19.67 | 3.93 | 51 49.35 | 3.90 | 56 15.88 | 3.86 | 0 39.15 | 3.81 | 8 |
| 53 | 38 15.89 | 4.11 | 42 51.54 | 4.07 | 47 24.19 | 4.01 | 51 53.82 | 3.98 | 56 20.29 | 3.94 | 0 43.51 | 3.89 | 7 |
| 54 | 38 20.51 | 4.19 | 42 56.11 | 4.15 | 47 28.71 | 4.09 | 51 58.29 | 4.06 | 56 24.70 | 4.02 | 0 47.87 | 3.96 | 6 |
| 55 | 38 25.12 | 4.27 | 43 0.68 | 4.23 | 47 33.23 | 4.17 | 52 2.75 | 4.14 | 56 29.11 | 4.09 | 0 52.23 | 4.03 | 5 |
| 56 | 2 38 29.74 | 4.35 | 2 43 5.25 | 4.31 | 2 47 37.75 | 4.25 | 2 52 7.22 | 4.21 | 2 56 33.52 | 4.16 | 3 0 56.59 | 4.10 | 4 |
| 57 | 38 34.36 | 4.43 | 43 9.82 | 4.38 | 47 42.27 | 4.32 | 52 11.69 | 4.28 | 56 37.93 | 4.23 | 1 0.96 | 4.17 | 3 |
| 58 | 38 38.98 | 4.50 | 43 14.39 | 4.45 | 47 46.79 | 4.39 | 52 16.15 | 4.35 | 56 42.34 | 4.30 | 1 5.32 | 4.24 | 2 |
| 59 | 38 43.59 | 4.57 | 43 18.95 | 4.52 | 47 51.31 | 4.46 | 52 20.61 | 4.42 | 56 46.75 | 4.37 | 1 9.68 | 4.31 | 1 |
| 60 | 38 48.20 | 4.64 | 43 23.51 | 4.59 | 47 55.82 | 4.53 | 52 25.07 | 4.49 | 56 51.16 | 4.44 | 1 14.02 | 4.38 | 0 |
| $\bar{y}$ | 149°+ 329°— | | 148°+ 328°— | | 147°+ 327°— | | 146°+ 326°— | | 145°+ 325°— | | 144°+ 324°— | | $\bar{y}$ |

# TABLE CXXXVII. ARGUMENT 77.

Equation $= 18500'' \sin \bar{y}$.

| $\bar{y}$ | 216°− 36°+ Equation. | P. P. | 217°− 37°+ Equation. | P. P. | 218°− 38°+ Equation. | P. P. | 219°− 39°+ Equation. | P. P. | 220°− 40°+ Equation. | P. P. | 221°− 41°+ Equation. | P. P. | $\bar{y}$ |
|---|---|---|---|---|---|---|---|---|---|---|---|---|---|
| ′ | ° ′ ″ | ″ | ° ′ ″ | ″ | ° ′ ″ | ″ | ° ′ ″ | ″ | ° ′ ″ | ″ | ° ′ ″ | ″ | ′ |
| 0 | 3 1 14.02 | 0.00 | 3 5 33.58 | 0.00 | 3 9 49.76 | 0.00 | 3 14 2.42 | 0.00 | 3 18 11.57 | 0.00 | 3 22 17.09 | 0.00 | 60 |
| 1 | 1 18.38 | 0.08 | 5 37.88 | 0.08 | 9 53.98 | 0.07 | 14 6 60 | 0.07 | 18 15.69 | 0.07 | 22 21.15 | 0.07 | 59 |
| 2 | 1 22.74 | 0.16 | 5 42.18 | 0.15 | 9 58.22 | 0.14 | 14 10.78 | 0.14 | 18 19.81 | 0.14 | 22 25.21 | 0.13 | 58 |
| 3 | 1 27.09 | 0.23 | 5 46.48 | 0.22 | 10 2.46 | 0.21 | 14 14.96 | 0.21 | 18 23.93 | 0.21 | 22 29.27 | 0.20 | 57 |
| 4 | 1 31.44 | 0.30 | 5 50.77 | 0.29 | 10 6.70 | 0.28 | 14 19.14 | 0.28 | 18 28.05 | 0.28 | 22 33.33 | 0.26 | 56 |
| 5 | 1 35.79 | 0.37 | 5 55.06 | 0.36 | 10 10.94 | 0.35 | 14 23.32 | 0.35 | 18 32.17 | 0.34 | 22 37.38 | 0.33 | 55 |
| 6 | 3 1 40.14 | 0.44 | 3 5 59.35 | 0.43 | 3 10 15.18 | 0.42 | 3 14 27.50 | 0.42 | 3 18 36.29 | 0.41 | 3 22 41.44 | 0.39 | 54 |
| 7 | 1 44.49 | 0.51 | 6 3.64 | 0.50 | 10 19.42 | 0.49 | 14 31.68 | 0.49 | 18 40.41 | 0.48 | 22 45.50 | 0.46 | 53 |
| 8 | 1 48.84 | 0.58 | 6 7.93 | 0.57 | 10 23.65 | 0.56 | 14 35.85 | 0.56 | 18 44.52 | 0.54 | 22 49.55 | 0.53 | 52 |
| 9 | 1 53.19 | 0.65 | 6 12.22 | 0.64 | 10 27.88 | 0.63 | 14 40.02 | 0.63 | 18 48.63 | 0.61 | 22 53.60 | 0.60 | 51 |
| 10 | 1 57.53 | 0.72 | 6 16.51 | 0.71 | 10 32.11 | 0.70 | 14 44.19 | 0.69 | 18 52.74 | 0.68 | 22 57.65 | 0.67 | 50 |
| 11 | 3 2 1.87 | 0.80 | 3 6 20.80 | 0.79 | 3 10 36.34 | 0.77 | 3 14 48.36 | 0.76 | 3 18 56.85 | 0.75 | 3 23 1.70 | 0.74 | 49 |
| 12 | 2 6.21 | 0.88 | 6 25.09 | 0.86 | 10 40.57 | 0.84 | 14 52.53 | 0.83 | 19 0.96 | 0.82 | 23 5.75 | 0.81 | 48 |
| 13 | 2 10.55 | 0.95 | 6 29.38 | 0.93 | 10 44.80 | 0.91 | 14 56.70 | 0.90 | 19 5.07 | 0.90 | 23 9.80 | 0.88 | 47 |
| 14 | 2 14.89 | 1.02 | 6 33.66 | 1.00 | 10 49.02 | 0.98 | 15 0.87 | 0.97 | 19 9.18 | 0.97 | 23 13.85 | 0.94 | 46 |
| 15 | 2 19.23 | 1.09 | 6 37.94 | 1.07 | 10 53.24 | 1.05 | 15 5.04 | 1.04 | 19 13.29 | 1.04 | 23 17.90 | 1.01 | 45 |
| 16 | 3 2 23.57 | 1.16 | 3 6 42.23 | 1.14 | 3 10 57.47 | 1.12 | 3 15 9.21 | 1.11 | 3 19 17.40 | 1.11 | 3 23 21.95 | 1. 8 | 44 |
| 17 | 2 27.91 | 1.23 | 6 46.51 | 1.21 | 11 1.69 | 1.19 | 15 13.38 | 1.18 | 19 21.51 | 1.18 | 23 26.00 | 1.14 | 43 |
| 18 | 2 32.25 | 1.30 | 6 50.79 | 1.28 | 11 5.91 | 1.26 | 15 17.55 | 1.25 | 19 25.62 | 1.24 | 23 30.04 | 1.21 | 42 |
| 19 | 2 36.58 | 1.37 | 6 55.07 | 1.35 | 11 10.13 | 1.33 | 15 21.71 | 1.32 | 19 29.72 | 1.30 | 23 34.08 | 1.28 | 41 |
| 20 | 2 40.91 | 1.44 | 6 59.35 | 1.42 | 11 14.35 | 1.40 | 15 25.87 | 1.38 | 19 33.82 | 1.36 | 23 38.12 | 1.34 | 40 |
| 21 | 3 2 45.25 | 1.52 | 3 7 3.63 | 1.50 | 3 11 18.57 | 1.48 | 3 15 30.03 | 1.45 | 3 19 37.92 | 1.43 | 3 23 42.16 | 1.41 | 39 |
| 22 | 2 49.59 | 1.60 | 7 7.91 | 1.58 | 11 22.79 | 1.55 | 15 34.19 | 1.52 | 19 42.02 | 1.50 | 23 46.20 | 1.48 | 38 |
| 23 | 2 53.92 | 1.68 | 7 12.19 | 1.65 | 11 27.01 | 1.62 | 15 38.35 | 1.59 | 19 46.12 | 1.57 | 23 50.24 | 1.55 | 37 |
| 24 | 2 58.25 | 1.75 | 7 16.46 | 1.72 | 11 31.23 | 1.69 | 15 42.51 | 1.66 | 19 50.22 | 1.64 | 23 54.28 | 1.62 | 36 |
| 25 | 3 2.58 | 1.82 | 7 20.73 | 1.79 | 11 35.44 | 1.76 | 15 46.67 | 1.73 | 19 54.32 | 1.71 | 23 58.31 | 1.69 | 35 |
| 26 | 3 3 6.91 | 1.89 | 3 7 25.01 | 1.86 | 3 11 39.66 | 1.83 | 3 15 50.83 | 1.80 | 3 19 58.42 | 1.78 | 3 24 2.35 | 1.75 | 34 |
| 27 | 3 11.24 | 1.96 | 7 29.28 | 1.93 | 11 43.88 | 1.90 | 15 54.99 | 1.87 | 20 2.52 | 1.85 | 24 6.38 | 1.82 | 33 |
| 28 | 3 15.57 | 2.03 | 7 33.55 | 2.00 | 11 48.10 | 1.97 | 15 59.14 | 1.94 | 20 6.61 | 1.92 | 24 10.41 | 1.88 | 32 |
| 29 | 3 19.90 | 2.10 | 7 37.82 | 2.07 | 11 52.31 | 2.04 | 16 3.29 | 2.01 | 20 10.70 | 1.99 | 24 14.44 | 1.95 | 31 |
| 30 | 3 24.23 | 2.17 | 7 42.09 | 2.14 | 11 56.52 | 2.11 | 16 7.44 | 2.08 | 20 14.79 | 2.05 | 24 18.47 | 2.02 | 30 |
| 31 | 3 3 28.56 | 2.25 | 3 7 46.36 | 2.22 | 3 12 0.73 | 2.18 | 3 16 11.59 | 2.15 | 3 20 18.88 | 2.12 | 3 24 22.50 | 2.09 | 29 |
| 32 | 3 32.89 | 2.33 | 7 50.63 | 2.29 | 12 4.94 | 2.25 | 16 15.74 | 2.22 | 20 22.97 | 2.19 | 24 26.53 | 2.16 | 28 |
| 33 | 3 37.21 | 2.40 | 7 54.90 | 2.36 | 12 9.15 | 2.32 | 16 19.89 | 2.29 | 20 27.06 | 2.25 | 24 30.56 | 2.23 | 27 |
| 34 | 3 41.53 | 2.47 | 7 59.17 | 2.43 | 12 13.36 | 2.39 | 16 24.04 | 2.36 | 20 31.15 | 2.32 | 24 34.58 | 2.30 | 26 |
| 35 | 3 45.85 | 2.54 | 8 3.44 | 2.50 | 12 17.57 | 2.46 | 16 28.19 | 2.43 | 20 35.23 | 2.39 | 24 38.60 | 2.36 | 25 |
| 36 | 3 3 50.17 | 2.61 | 3 8 7.71 | 2.57 | 3 12 21.78 | 2.53 | 3 16 32.34 | 2.50 | 3 20 39.32 | 2.46 | 3 24 42.63 | 2.42 | 24 |
| 37 | 3 54.49 | 2.68 | 8 11.97 | 2.64 | 12 25.99 | 2.60 | 16 36.49 | 2.57 | 20 43.41 | 2.53 | 24 46.65 | 2.49 | 23 |
| 38 | 3 58.81 | 2.75 | 8 16.23 | 2.71 | 12 30.19 | 2.67 | 16 40.64 | 2.64 | 20 47.49 | 2.59 | 24 50.67 | 2.56 | 22 |
| 39 | 4 3.13 | 2.82 | 8 20.49 | 2.78 | 12 34.39 | 2.74 | 16 44.78 | 2.71 | 20 51.57 | 2.66 | 24 54.69 | 2.63 | 21 |
| 40 | 4 7.44 | 2.89 | 8 24.75 | 2.85 | 12 38.59 | 2.81 | 16 48.92 | 2.77 | 20 55.65 | 2.73 | 24 58.71 | 2.69 | 20 |
| 41 | 3 4 11.76 | 2.97 | 3 8 29.01 | 2.93 | 3 12 42.79 | 2.88 | 3 16 53.06 | 2.84 | 3 20 59.74 | 2.80 | 3 25 2.73 | 2.76 | 19 |
| 42 | 4 16.08 | 3.05 | 8 33.27 | 3.00 | 12 46.99 | 2.95 | 16 57.20 | 2.91 | 21 3.82 | 2.87 | 25 6.75 | 2.82 | 18 |
| 43 | 4 20.39 | 3.12 | 8 37.52 | 3.07 | 12 51.19 | 3.02 | 17 1.34 | 2.98 | 21 7.90 | 2.95 | 25 10.77 | 2.89 | 17 |
| 44 | 4 24.70 | 3.19 | 8 41.77 | 3.14 | 12 55.39 | 3.09 | 17 5.48 | 3.05 | 21 11.98 | 3.01 | 25 14.79 | 2.96 | 16 |
| 45 | 4 29.01 | 3.26 | 8 46.02 | 3.21 | 12 59.58 | 3.16 | 17 9.62 | 3.12 | 21 16.06 | 3.08 | 25 18.81 | 3.03 | 15 |
| 46 | 3 4 33.32 | 3.33 | 3 8 50.27 | 3.28 | 3 13 3.78 | 3.23 | 3 17 13.76 | 3.19 | 3 21 20.14 | 3.15 | 3 25 22.83 | 3.10 | 14 |
| 47 | 4 37.63 | 3.40 | 8 54.52 | 3.35 | 13 7.98 | 3.30 | 17 17.90 | 3.26 | 21 24.22 | 3.22 | 25 26.85 | 3.16 | 13 |
| 48 | 4 41.94 | 3.47 | 8 58.77 | 3.42 | 13 12.17 | 3.37 | 17 22.03 | 3.33 | 21 28.30 | 3.29 | 25 30.86 | 3.23 | 12 |
| 49 | 4 46.25 | 3.54 | 9 3.02 | 3.49 | 13 16.36 | 3.44 | 17 26.16 | 3.40 | 21 32.37 | 3.35 | 25 34.87 | 3.30 | 11 |
| 50 | 4 50.56 | 3.61 | 9 7.27 | 3.56 | 13 20.55 | 3.51 | 17 30.29 | 3.46 | 21 36.44 | 3.41 | 25 38.88 | 3.36 | 10 |
| 51 | 3 4 54.87 | 3.69 | 3 9 11.52 | 3.64 | 3 13 24.74 | 3.58 | 3 17 34.42 | 3.53 | 3 21 40.51 | 3.48 | 3 25 42.89 | 3.43 | 9 |
| 52 | 4 59.18 | 3.77 | 9 15.77 | 3.71 | 13 28.93 | 3.65 | 17 38.55 | 3.60 | 21 44.58 | 3.55 | 25 46.90 | 3.50 | 8 |
| 53 | 5 3.48 | 3.84 | 9 20.02 | 3.78 | 13 33.12 | 3.72 | 17 42.68 | 3.63 | 21 48.65 | 3.62 | 25 50.91 | 3.57 | 7 |
| 54 | 5 7.78 | 3.91 | 9 24.27 | 3.85 | 13 37.31 | 3.79 | 17 46.81 | 3.74 | 21 52.72 | 3.69 | 25 54.92 | 3.64 | 6 |
| 55 | 5 12.08 | 3.98 | 9 28.51 | 3.92 | 13 41.50 | 3.86 | 17 50.94 | 3.81 | 21 56.78 | 3.75 | 25 58.92 | 3.70 | 5 |
| 56 | 3 5 16.38 | 4.05 | 3 9 32.76 | 3.99 | 3 13 45.69 | 3.93 | 3 17 55.07 | 3.88 | 3 22 0.85 | 3.82 | 3 26 2.92 | 3.77 | 4 |
| 57 | 5 20.68 | 4.12 | 9 37.01 | 4.06 | 13 49.88 | 4.00 | 17 59.20 | 3.95 | 22 4.91 | 3.89 | 26 6 92 | 3.84 | 3 |
| 58 | 5 24.98 | 4.19 | 9 41.26 | 4.13 | 13 54.06 | 4.07 | 18 3.33 | 4.02 | 22 8.97 | 3.95 | 26 10.92 | 3.90 | 2 |
| 59 | 5 29.28 | 4.26 | 9 45.50 | 4.20 | 13 58.24 | 4.14 | 18 7.45 | 4.09 | 22 13.03 | 4.02 | 26 14.92 | 3.96 | 1 |
| 60 | 5 33.58 | 4.33 | 9 49.74 | 4.27 | 14 2.42 | 4.21 | 18 11.57 | 4.15 | 22 17.09 | 4.09 | 26 18.92 | 4.03 | 0 |
| $\bar{y}$ | 143°+ 323°− | | 142°+ 322°− | | 141°+ 321°− | | 140°+ 320°− | | 139°+ 319°− | | 138°+ 318°− | | $\bar{y}$ |

# TABLE CXXXVII. ARGUMENT 77.

Equation = 18500″ sin $\bar{y}$.

| $\bar{y}$ | 222°— 42°+ | | 223°— 43°+ | | 224°— 44°+ | | 225°— 45°+ | | 226°— 46°+ | | 227°— 47°+ | | $\bar{y}$ |
|---|---|---|---|---|---|---|---|---|---|---|---|---|---|
| ′ | Equation. | P. P. | Equation. | P. P. | Equation. | P. P. | Equation. | P. P. | Equation. | P. P. | Equation. | P. P. | ′ |
| 0 | 3 26 18.92 | 0.00 | 3 30 16.97 | 0.00 | 3 34 11.18 | 0.00 | 3 38 1.47 | 0.00 | 3 41 47.78 | 0.00 | 3 45 30.04 | 0.00 | 60 |
| 1 | 26 22.92 | 0.07 | 30 20.91 | 0.06 | 34 15.05 | 0.06 | 38 5.27 | 0.06 | 41 51.52 | 0.06 | 45 33.71 | 0.06 | 59 |
| 2 | 26 26.91 | 0.13 | 30 24.85 | 0.12 | 34 18.92 | 0.12 | 38 9.07 | 0.12 | 41 55.26 | 0.12 | 45 37.38 | 0.12 | 58 |
| 3 | 26 30.91 | 0.20 | 30 28.78 | 0.18 | 34 22.79 | 0.18 | 38 12.87 | 0.18 | 41 59.00 | 0.18 | 45 41.05 | 0.18 | 57 |
| 4 | 26 34.90 | 0.26 | 30 32.71 | 0.24 | 34 26.66 | 0.24 | 38 16.67 | 0.24 | 42 2.73 | 0.24 | 45 44.72 | 0.24 | 56 |
| 5 | 26 38.90 | 0.33 | 30 36.64 | 0.30 | 34 30.55 | 0.30 | 38 20.47 | 0.30 | 42 6.46 | 0.30 | 45 48.38 | 0.30 | 55 |
| 6 | 3 26 42.89 | 0.40 | 3 30 40.57 | 0.37 | 3 34 34.39 | 0.37 | 3 38 24.27 | 0.37 | 3 42 10.19 | 0.36 | 3 45 52.05 | 0.36 | 54 |
| 7 | 26 46.88 | 0.47 | 30 44.50 | 0.44 | 34 38.25 | 0.44 | 38 28.07 | 0.42 | 42 13.92 | 0.42 | 45 55.71 | 0.42 | 53 |
| 8 | 26 50.87 | 0.54 | 30 48.43 | 0.51 | 34 42.11 | 0.51 | 38 31.87 | 0.49 | 42 17.65 | 0.48 | 45 59.37 | 0.48 | 52 |
| 9 | 26 54.86 | 0.60 | 30 52.36 | 0.58 | 34 45.97 | 0.57 | 38 35.66 | 0.56 | 42 21.38 | 0.55 | 46 2.03 | 0.54 | 51 |
| 10 | 26 58.86 | 0.66 | 30 56.28 | 0.65 | 34 49.83 | 0.64 | 38 39.45 | 0.63 | 42 25.11 | 0.62 | 46 6.69 | 0.61 | 50 |
| 11 | 3 27 2.85 | 0.73 | 3 31 0.21 | 0.72 | 3 34 53.69 | 0.71 | 3 38 43.25 | 0.70 | 3 42 28.84 | 0.68 | 3 46 10.35 | 0.67 | 49 |
| 12 | 27 6.84 | 0.79 | 31 4.13 | 0.79 | 34 57.55 | 0.78 | 38 47.05 | 0.76 | 42 32.57 | 0.74 | 46 14.01 | 0.73 | 48 |
| 13 | 27 10.83 | 0.86 | 31 8.05 | 0.86 | 35 1.41 | 0.84 | 38 50.84 | 0.83 | 42 36.29 | 0.80 | 46 17.66 | 0.79 | 47 |
| 14 | 27 14.81 | 0.92 | 31 11.97 | 0.92 | 35 5.27 | 0.91 | 38 54.63 | 0.90 | 42 40.01 | 0.86 | 46 21.31 | 0.85 | 46 |
| 15 | 27 18.79 | 0.98 | 31 15.89 | 0.99 | 35 9.12 | 0.98 | 38 58.42 | 0.96 | 42 43.73 | 0.93 | 46 24.96 | 0.91 | 45 |
| 16 | 3 27 22.78 | 1.05 | 3 31 19.81 | 1.06 | 3 35 12.98 | 1.04 | 3 39 2.21 | 1.02 | 3 42 47.45 | 0.99 | 3 46 28.61 | 0.97 | 44 |
| 17 | 27 26.76 | 1.12 | 31 23.73 | 1.12 | 35 16.83 | 1.10 | 39 6.00 | 1.08 | 42 51.17 | 1.05 | 46 32.26 | 1.03 | 43 |
| 18 | 27 30.74 | 1.19 | 31 27.65 | 1.18 | 35 20.68 | 1.16 | 39 9.79 | 1.14 | 42 54.89 | 1.11 | 46 35.91 | 1.09 | 42 |
| 19 | 27 34.72 | 1.26 | 31 31.57 | 1.24 | 35 24.53 | 1.22 | 39 13.58 | 1.20 | 42 58.61 | 1.17 | 46 39.56 | 1.15 | 41 |
| 20 | 27 38.70 | 1.33 | 31 35.48 | 1.30 | 35 28.38 | 1.28 | 39 17.36 | 1.26 | 43 2.32 | 1.24 | 46 43.20 | 1.21 | 40 |
| 21 | 3 27 42.68 | 1.40 | 3 31 39.40 | 1.37 | 3 35 32.23 | 1.35 | 3 39 21.14 | 1.32 | 3 43 6.04 | 1.30 | 3 46 46.85 | 1.27 | 39 |
| 22 | 27 46.66 | 1.47 | 31 43.31 | 1.44 | 35 36.08 | 1.41 | 39 24.92 | 1.38 | 43 9.75 | 1.36 | 46 50.50 | 1.33 | 38 |
| 23 | 27 50.64 | 1.53 | 31 47.22 | 1.50 | 35 39.93 | 1.47 | 39 28.70 | 1.45 | 43 13.46 | 1.42 | 46 54.14 | 1.39 | 37 |
| 24 | 27 54.61 | 1.60 | 31 51.13 | 1.57 | 35 43.77 | 1.54 | 39 32.48 | 1.51 | 43 17.17 | 1.48 | 46 57.78 | 1.45 | 36 |
| 25 | 27 58.58 | 1.67 | 31 55.04 | 1.64 | 35 47.61 | 1.60 | 39 36.26 | 1.57 | 43 20.88 | 1.54 | 47 1.42 | 1.51 | 35 |
| 26 | 3 28 2.55 | 1.73 | 3 31 58.95 | 1.71 | 3 35 51.46 | 1.66 | 3 39 40.04 | 1.64 | 3 43 24.59 | 1.60 | 3 47 5.06 | 1.57 | 34 |
| 27 | 28 6.52 | 1.80 | 32 2.86 | 1.77 | 35 55.30 | 1.73 | 39 43.82 | 1.70 | 43 28.30 | 1.66 | 47 8.70 | 1.63 | 33 |
| 28 | 28 10.49 | 1.86 | 32 6.76 | 1.84 | 35 59.14 | 1.80 | 39 47.59 | 1.76 | 43 32.01 | 1.72 | 47 12.34 | 1.69 | 32 |
| 29 | 28 14.46 | 1.92 | 32 10.66 | 1.90 | 36 2.98 | 1.86 | 39 51.36 | 1.82 | 43 35.72 | 1.78 | 47 15.98 | 1.75 | 31 |
| 30 | 28 18.42 | 1.99 | 32 14.56 | 1.96 | 36 6.82 | 1.92 | 39 55.13 | 1.88 | 43 39.42 | 1.85 | 47 19.62 | 1.82 | 30 |
| 31 | 3 28 22.39 | 2.06 | 3 32 18.46 | 2.03 | 3 36 10.66 | 1.98 | 3 39 58.90 | 1.94 | 3 43 43.13 | 1.91 | 3 47 23.26 | 1.88 | 29 |
| 32 | 28 26.36 | 2.12 | 32 22.36 | 2.10 | 36 14.50 | 2.05 | 40 2.67 | 2.00 | 43 46.83 | 1.97 | 47 26.90 | 1.94 | 28 |
| 33 | 28 30.32 | 2.19 | 32 26.26 | 2.17 | 36 18.34 | 2.11 | 40 6.00 | 2.07 | 43 50.57 | 2.03 | 47 30.53 | 2.00 | 27 |
| 34 | 28 34.28 | 2.25 | 32 30.16 | 2.24 | 36 22.17 | 2.18 | 40 10.21 | 2.13 | 43 54.23 | 2.09 | 47 34.16 | 2.06 | 26 |
| 35 | 28 38.24 | 2.32 | 32 34.06 | 2.30 | 36 26.00 | 2.25 | 40 13.97 | 2.19 | 43 57.93 | 2.15 | 47 37.79 | 2.12 | 25 |
| 36 | 3 28 42.20 | 2.39 | 3 32 37.96 | 2.37 | 3 36 29.83 | 2.31 | 3 40 17.74 | 2.25 | 3 44 1.63 | 2.21 | 3 47 41.42 | 2.18 | 24 |
| 37 | 28 46.16 | 2.46 | 32 41.86 | 2.43 | 36 33.66 | 2.38 | 40 21.51 | 2.32 | 44 0.00 | 2.28 | 47 45.05 | 2.24 | 23 |
| 38 | 28 50.12 | 2.53 | 32 45.76 | 2.49 | 36 37.49 | 2.44 | 40 25.27 | 2.38 | 44 9.03 | 2.34 | 47 48.68 | 2.30 | 22 |
| 39 | 28 54.08 | 2.59 | 32 49.65 | 2.55 | 36 41.32 | 2.50 | 40 29.03 | 2.44 | 44 12.72 | 2.40 | 47 52.31 | 2.36 | 21 |
| 40 | 28 58.04 | 2.65 | 32 53.54 | 2.60 | 36 45.15 | 2.56 | 40 32.79 | 2.51 | 44 16.40 | 2.47 | 47 55.93 | 2.42 | 20 |
| 41 | 3 29 2.00 | 2.72 | 3 32 57.43 | 2.68 | 3 36 48.98 | 2.63 | 3 40 36.55 | 2.58 | 3 44 20.09 | 2.53 | 3 47 59.56 | 2.48 | 19 |
| 42 | 29 5.96 | 2.79 | 33 1.32 | 2.74 | 36 52.81 | 2.70 | 40 40.31 | 2.64 | 44 23.78 | 2.69 | 48 3.18 | 2.54 | 18 |
| 43 | 29 9.91 | 2.86 | 33 5.21 | 2.81 | 36 56.63 | 2.76 | 40 44.07 | 2.70 | 44 27.47 | 2.66 | 48 6.80 | 2.60 | 17 |
| 44 | 29 13.86 | 2.92 | 33 9.10 | 2.87 | 37 0.45 | 2.83 | 40 47.83 | 2.77 | 44 31.16 | 2.72 | 48 10.42 | 2.66 | 16 |
| 45 | 29 17.81 | 2.99 | 33 12.99 | 2.94 | 37 4.27 | 2.90 | 40 51.58 | 2.83 | 44 34.85 | 2.78 | 48 14.04 | 2.72 | 15 |
| 46 | 3 29 21.76 | 3.06 | 3 33 16.88 | 3.00 | 3 37 8.09 | 2.96 | 3 40 55.34 | 2.90 | 3 44 38.54 | 2.84 | 3 48 17.66 | 2.78 | 14 |
| 47 | 29 25.71 | 3.13 | 33 20.77 | 3.06 | 37 11.91 | 3.02 | 40 59.09 | 2.96 | 44 42.22 | 2.90 | 48 21.28 | 2.84 | 13 |
| 48 | 29 29.66 | 3.19 | 33 24.65 | 3.13 | 37 15.73 | 3.08 | 41 2.84 | 3.02 | 44 45.90 | 2.96 | 48 24.90 | 2.90 | 12 |
| 49 | 29 33.61 | 3.25 | 33 28.53 | 3.19 | 37 19.55 | 3.14 | 41 6.59 | 3.08 | 44 49.58 | 3.02 | 48 28.51 | 2.96 | 11 |
| 50 | 29 37.55 | 3.32 | 33 32.41 | 3.26 | 37 23.37 | 3.20 | 41 10.34 | 3.14 | 44 53.26 | 3.09 | 48 32.12 | 3.03 | 10 |
| 51 | 3 29 41.50 | 3.39 | 3 33 36.29 | 3.33 | 3 37 27.19 | 3.27 | 3 41 14.09 | 3.20 | 3 44 56.95 | 3.15 | 3 48 35.73 | 3.09 | 9 |
| 52 | 29 45.45 | 3.46 | 33 40.17 | 3.40 | 37 31.01 | 3.33 | 41 17.84 | 3.27 | 45 0.63 | 3.21 | 48 39.34 | 3.15 | 8 |
| 53 | 29 49.39 | 3.53 | 33 44.05 | 3.46 | 37 34.82 | 3.40 | 41 21.59 | 3.33 | 45 4.31 | 3.27 | 48 42.95 | 3.21 | 7 |
| 54 | 29 53.33 | 3.60 | 33 47.93 | 3.52 | 37 38.63 | 3.46 | 41 25.33 | 3.39 | 45 7.99 | 3.34 | 48 46.56 | 3.27 | 6 |
| 55 | 29 57.27 | 3.66 | 33 51.81 | 3.59 | 37 42.44 | 3.53 | 41 29.07 | 3.45 | 45 11.67 | 3.40 | 48 50.17 | 3.33 | 5 |
| 56 | 3 30 1.21 | 3.73 | 3 33 55.69 | 3.65 | 3 37 46.25 | 3.59 | 3 41 32.82 | 3.52 | 3 45 15.34 | 3.46 | 3 48 53.78 | 3.39 | 4 |
| 57 | 30 5.15 | 3.80 | 33 59.57 | 3.72 | 37 50.06 | 3.65 | 41 36.56 | 3.58 | 45 19.01 | 3.52 | 48 57.38 | 3.45 | 3 |
| 58 | 30 9.09 | 3.86 | 34 3.44 | 3.79 | 37 53.87 | 3.72 | 41 40.30 | 3.64 | 45 22.68 | 3.58 | 49 0.98 | 3.51 | 2 |
| 59 | 30 13.03 | 3.92 | 34 7.31 | 3.85 | 37 57.67 | 3.78 | 41 44.04 | 3.71 | 45 26.36 | 3.64 | 49 4.58 | 3.57 | 1 |
| 60 | 30 16.97 | 3.98 | 34 11.18 | 3.90 | 38 1.47 | 3.84 | 41 47.78 | 3.77 | 45 30.04 | 3.71 | 49 8.18 | 3.63 | 0 |
| $\bar{y}$ | 137°+ 317°— | | 136°+ 316°— | | 135°+ 315°— | | 134°+ 314°— | | 133°+ 313°— | | 132°+ 312°— | | $\bar{y}$ |

# TABLE CXXXVII. ARGUMENT 77.

Equation = 18500″ sin $\bar{y}$.

| $\bar{y}$ | 228°— 48°+ Equation. | P. P. | 229°— 49°+ Equation. | P. P. | 230°— 50°+ Equation. | P. P. | 231°— 51°+ Equation. | P. P. | 232°— 52°+ Equation. | P. P. | 233°— 53°+ Equation. | P. P. | $\bar{y}$ |
|---|---|---|---|---|---|---|---|---|---|---|---|---|---|
| 0′ | 3° 49′ 8.18″ | 0.00″ | 3° 52′ 42.13″ | 0.00″ | 3° 56′ 11.82″ | 0.00″ | 3° 59′ 37.20″ | 0.00″ | 4° 2′ 58.18″ | 0.00″ | 4° 6′ 14.76″ | 0.00″ | 60′ |
| 1 | 49 11.78 | 0.06 | 52 45.66 | 0.06 | 56 15.28 | 0.06 | 59 40.59 | 0.06 | 3 1.49 | 0.06 | 6 18.00 | 0.06 | 59 |
| 2 | 49 15.38 | 0.12 | 52 49.19 | 0.12 | 56 18.74 | 0.12 | 59 43.98 | 0.12 | 3 4.80 | 0.11 | 6 21.24 | 0.11 | 58 |
| 3 | 49 18.98 | 0.18 | 52 52.72 | 0.18 | 56 22.20 | 0.18 | 59 47.36 | 0.18 | 3 8.11 | 0.17 | 6 24.48 | 0.16 | 57 |
| 4 | 49 22.57 | 0.24 | 52 56.24 | 0.24 | 56 25.65 | 0.24 | 59 50.74 | 0.24 | 3 11.42 | 0.22 | 6 27.71 | 0.22 | 56 |
| 5 | 49 26.16 | 0.30 | 52 59.76 | 0.30 | 56 29.10 | 0.29 | 59 54.12 | 0.29 | 3 14.73 | 0.28 | 6 30.94 | 0.27 | 55 |
| 6 | 3 49 29.76 | 0.36 | 3 53 3.29 | 0.36 | 3 56 32.55 | 0.35 | 3 59 57.50 | 0.34 | 4 3 18.04 | 0.33 | 4 6 34.13 | 0.32 | 54 |
| 7 | 49 33.35 | 0.42 | 53 6.81 | 0.42 | 56 36.00 | 0.40 | 4 0 0.88 | 0.40 | 3 21.35 | 0.39 | 6 37.40 | 0.38 | 53 |
| 8 | 49 36.94 | 0.48 | 53 10.33 | 0.48 | 56 39.45 | 0.46 | 0 4.26 | 0.46 | 3 24.65 | 0.45 | 6 40.63 | 0.43 | 52 |
| 9 | 49 40.53 | 0.54 | 53 13.85 | 0.53 | 56 42.90 | 0.52 | 0 7.64 | 0.51 | 3 27.95 | 0.50 | 6 43.86 | 0.48 | 51 |
| 10 | 49 44.12 | 0.59 | 53 17.37 | 0.58 | 56 46.35 | 0.57 | 0 11.01 | 0.56 | 3 31.25 | 0.55 | 6 47.09 | 0.53 | 50 |
| 11 | 3 49 47.71 | 0.65 | 3 53 20.89 | 0.64 | 3 56 49.80 | 0.63 | 4 0 14.38 | 0.62 | 4 3 34.56 | 0.61 | 4 6 50.32 | 0.59 | 49 |
| 12 | 49 56.30 | 0.71 | 53 24.41 | 0.70 | 56 53.25 | 0.68 | 0 17.75 | 0.67 | 3 37.86 | 0.66 | 6 53.54 | 0.64 | 48 |
| 13 | 49 54.89 | 0.77 | 53 27.93 | 0.76 | 56 56.69 | 0.74 | 0 21.12 | 0.73 | 3 41.16 | 0.72 | 6 56.76 | 0.70 | 47 |
| 14 | 49 58.48 | 0.83 | 53 31.44 | 0.82 | 57 0.13 | 0.80 | 0 24.49 | 0.78 | 3 44.46 | 0.78 | 6 59.98 | 0.76 | 46 |
| 15 | 50 2.06 | 0.89 | 53 34.95 | 0.88 | 57 3.57 | 0.85 | 0 27.86 | 0.84 | 3 47.76 | 0.83 | 7 3.20 | 0.81 | 45 |
| 16 | 3 50 5.65 | 0.95 | 3 53 38.46 | 0.94 | 3 57 7.01 | 0.91 | 4 0 31.23 | 0.89 | 4 3 51.06 | 0.89 | 4 7 6.42 | 0.86 | 44 |
| 17 | 50 9.23 | 1.01 | 53 41.97 | 1.00 | 57 10.45 | 0.96 | 0 34.60 | 0.95 | 3 54.36 | 0.94 | 7 9.64 | 0.91 | 43 |
| 18 | 50 12.81 | 1.07 | 53 45.48 | 1.06 | 57 13.89 | 1.02 | 0 37.97 | 1.00 | 3 57.65 | 0.99 | 7 12.86 | 0.97 | 42 |
| 19 | 50 16.39 | 1.13 | 53 48.99 | 1.12 | 57 17.33 | 1.08 | 0 41.33 | 1.05 | 4 0.94 | 1.04 | 7 16.07 | 1.02 | 41 |
| 20 | 50 19.97 | 1.19 | 53 52.50 | 1.17 | 57 20.76 | 1.14 | 0 44.69 | 1.11 | 4 4.23 | 1.09 | 7 19.28 | 1.07 | 40 |
| 21 | 3 50 23.55 | 1.25 | 3 53 56.01 | 1.23 | 3 57 24.20 | 1.20 | 4 0 48.05 | 1.17 | 4 4 7.52 | 1.14 | 4 7 22.49 | 1.13 | 39 |
| 22 | 50 27.13 | 1.31 | 53 59.52 | 1.29 | 57 27.63 | 1.26 | 0 51.41 | 1.22 | 4 10.81 | 1.20 | 7 25.70 | 1.18 | 38 |
| 23 | 50 30.70 | 1.37 | 54 3.02 | 1.35 | 57 31.06 | 1.31 | 0 54.77 | 1.28 | 4 14.10 | 1.26 | 7 28.91 | 1.23 | 37 |
| 24 | 50 33.27 | 1.43 | 54 6.52 | 1.41 | 57 34.49 | 1.37 | 0 58.13 | 1.32 | 4 17.38 | 1.31 | 7 32.12 | 1.28 | 36 |
| 25 | 50 37.84 | 1.49 | 54 10.02 | 1.47 | 57 37.92 | 1.42 | 1 1.49 | 1.38 | 4 20.66 | 1.37 | 7 35.33 | 1.34 | 35 |
| 26 | 3 50 41.41 | 1.55 | 3 54 13.52 | 1.52 | 3 57 41.35 | 1.48 | 4 1 4.85 | 1.43 | 4 4 23.94 | 1.42 | 4 7 38.54 | 1.40 | 34 |
| 27 | 50 44.98 | 1.61 | 54 17.02 | 1.58 | 57 44.78 | 1.54 | 1 8.20 | 1.49 | 4 27.22 | 1.48 | 7 41.75 | 1.45 | 33 |
| 28 | 50 49.55 | 1.67 | 54 20.52 | 1.64 | 57 48.21 | 1.60 | 1 11.55 | 1.55 | 4 30.50 | 1.54 | 7 44.96 | 1.50 | 32 |
| 29 | 50 52.12 | 1.73 | 54 24.02 | 1.69 | 57 51.63 | 1.66 | 1 14.90 | 1.61 | 4 33.78 | 1.59 | 7 48.16 | 1.55 | 31 |
| 30 | 50 55.68 | 1.78 | 54 27.51 | 1.75 | 57 55.05 | 1.72 | 1 18.25 | 1.67 | 4 37.05 | 1.64 | 7 51.36 | 1.60 | 30 |
| 31 | 3 50 59.25 | 1.84 | 3 54 31.01 | 1.81 | 3 57 58.47 | 1.78 | 4 1 21.60 | 1.73 | 4 4 40.33 | 1.70 | 4 7 54.56 | 1.66 | 29 |
| 32 | 51 2.81 | 1.90 | 54 34.50 | 1.87 | 58 1.89 | 1.83 | 1 24.95 | 1.79 | 4 43.60 | 1.75 | 7 57.76 | 1.72 | 28 |
| 33 | 51 6.37 | 1.96 | 54 37.99 | 1.93 | 58 5.31 | 1.89 | 1 28.30 | 1.85 | 4 46.87 | 1.81 | 8 0.96 | 1.78 | 27 |
| 34 | 51 9.93 | 2.02 | 54 41.48 | 1.99 | 58 8.73 | 1.95 | 1 31.64 | 1.91 | 4 50.14 | 1.87 | 8 4.16 | 1.84 | 26 |
| 35 | 51 13.49 | 2.08 | 54 44.97 | 2.05 | 58 12.15 | 2.01 | 1 34.98 | 1.97 | 4 53.41 | 1.92 | 8 7.36 | 1.89 | 25 |
| 36 | 3 51 17.05 | 2.14 | 3 54 48.46 | 2.10 | 3 58 15.57 | 2.06 | 4 1 38.32 | 2.03 | 4 4 56.68 | 1.98 | 4 8 10.56 | 1.94 | 24 |
| 37 | 51 20.61 | 2.20 | 54 51.95 | 2.16 | 58 18.99 | 2.12 | 1 41.66 | 2.08 | 4 59.95 | 2.03 | 8 13.75 | 1.99 | 23 |
| 38 | 51 24.17 | 2.26 | 54 55.44 | 2.22 | 58 22.40 | 2.18 | 1 44.98 | 2.13 | 5 3.32 | 2.09 | 8 16.94 | 2.04 | 22 |
| 39 | 51 27.73 | 2.32 | 54 58.92 | 2.27 | 58 25.81 | 2.24 | 1 48.32 | 2.18 | 5 6.48 | 2.14 | 8 20.13 | 2.09 | 21 |
| 40 | 51 31.28 | 2.37 | 55 2.40 | 2.33 | 58 29.22 | 2.29 | 1 51.68 | 2.23 | 5 9.74 | 2.19 | 8 23.32 | 2.13 | 20 |
| 41 | 3 51 34.84 | 2.43 | 3 55 5.88 | 2.39 | 3 58 32.63 | 2.35 | 4 1 55.02 | 2.29 | 4 5 13.00 | 2.25 | 4 8 26.51 | 2.19 | 19 |
| 42 | 51 38.39 | 2.49 | 55 9.36 | 2.45 | 58 36.04 | 2.41 | 1 58.36 | 2.34 | 5 16.26 | 2.30 | 8 29.69 | 2.25 | 18 |
| 43 | 51 41.94 | 2.55 | 55 12.84 | 2.51 | 58 39.45 | 2.47 | 2 1.69 | 2.40 | 5 19.52 | 2.36 | 8 32.87 | 2.31 | 17 |
| 44 | 51 45.49 | 2.61 | 55 16.32 | 2.56 | 58 42.86 | 2.52 | 2 5.02 | 2.46 | 5 22.78 | 2.41 | 8 36.05 | 2.36 | 16 |
| 45 | 51 49.04 | 2.67 | 55 19.80 | 2.62 | 58 46.26 | 2.58 | 2 8.35 | 2.51 | 5 26.04 | 2.46 | 8 39.23 | 2.42 | 15 |
| 46 | 3 51 52.59 | 2.73 | 3 55 23.28 | 2.68 | 3 58 49.67 | 2.64 | 4 2 11.68 | 2.57 | 4 5 29.30 | 2.52 | 4 8 42.41 | 2.46 | 14 |
| 47 | 51 56.14 | 2.79 | 55 26.76 | 2.74 | 58 53.07 | 2.70 | 2 15.01 | 2.63 | 5 32.56 | 2.58 | 8 45.59 | 2.51 | 13 |
| 48 | 51 59.69 | 2.85 | 55 30.23 | 2.80 | 58 56.47 | 2.76 | 2 18.34 | 2.69 | 5 35.81 | 2.64 | 8 48.77 | 2.56 | 12 |
| 49 | 52 3.23 | 2.91 | 55 33.70 | 2.86 | 58 59.87 | 2.81 | 2 21.67 | 2.74 | 5 39.06 | 2.69 | 8 51.95 | 2.61 | 11 |
| 50 | 52 6.77 | 2.97 | 55 37.17 | 2.92 | 59 3.27 | 2.86 | 2 24.99 | 2.79 | 5 42.31 | 2.74 | 8 55.11 | 2.66 | 10 |
| 51 | 3 52 10.31 | 3.03 | 3 55 40.64 | 2.98 | 3 59 6.67 | 2.92 | 4 2 28.32 | 2.85 | 4 5 45.56 | 2.79 | 4 8 58.29 | 2.72 | 9 |
| 52 | 52 13.85 | 3.09 | 55 44.11 | 3.04 | 59 10.07 | 2.98 | 2 31.64 | 2.90 | 5 48.81 | 2.84 | 9 1.46 | 2.77 | 8 |
| 53 | 52 17.39 | 3.15 | 55 47.58 | 3.10 | 59 13.47 | 3.04 | 2 34.96 | 2.96 | 5 52.06 | 2.89 | 9 4.63 | 2.82 | 7 |
| 54 | 52 20.93 | 3.21 | 55 51.05 | 3.16 | 59 16.86 | 3.09 | 2 38.28 | 3.02 | 5 55.31 | 2.95 | 9 7.80 | 2.87 | 6 |
| 55 | 52 24.47 | 3.27 | 55 54.51 | 3.22 | 59 20.25 | 3.15 | 2 41.60 | 3.08 | 5 58.55 | 3.01 | 9 10.97 | 2.93 | 5 |
| 56 | 3 52 28.01 | 3.33 | 3 55 57.98 | 3.28 | 3 59 23.64 | 3.21 | 4 2 44.92 | 3.14 | 4 6 1.80 | 3.07 | 4 9 14.14 | 2.98 | 4 |
| 57 | 52 31.54 | 3.39 | 56 1.44 | 3.33 | 59 27.03 | 3.27 | 2 48.24 | 3.19 | 6 5.04 | 3.12 | 9 17.32 | 3.04 | 3 |
| 58 | 52 35.07 | 3.45 | 56 4.90 | 3.38 | 59 30.42 | 3.32 | 2 51.57 | 3.24 | 6 8.28 | 3.18 | 9 20.49 | 3.10 | 2 |
| 59 | 52 38.60 | 3.51 | 56 7.36 | 3.44 | 59 33.81 | 3.38 | 2 54.87 | 3.29 | 6 11.52 | 3.23 | 9 23.66 | 3.15 | 1 |
| 60 | 52 42.13 | 3.56 | 56 11.82 | 3.50 | 59 37.20 | 3.43 | 2 58.18 | 3.34 | 6 14.70 | 3.28 | 9 26.82 | 3.20 | 0 |
| $\bar{y}$ | 131°+ 311°— | | 130°+ 310°— | | 129°+ 309°— | | 128°+ 308°— | | 127°+ 307°— | | 126°+ 306°— | | $\bar{y}$ |

# TABLE CXXXVII. ARGUMENT 77.

Equation = 18500″ sin $\bar{y}$.

| $\bar{y}$ | 234°— 54°+ Equation. | P. P. | 235°— 55°+ Equation. | P. P. | 236°— 56°+ Equation. | P. P. | 237°— 57°+ Equation. | P. P. | 238°— 58°+ Equation. | P. P. | 239°— 59°+ Equation. | P. P. | $\bar{y}$ |
|---|---|---|---|---|---|---|---|---|---|---|---|---|---|
| 0′ | 4° 9′ 26.82″ | 0.00″ | 4° 12′ 34.31″ | 0.00″ | 4° 15′ 37.19″ | 0.00″ | 4° 18′ 35.40″ | 0.00″ | 4° 21′ 28.89″ | 0.00″ | 4° 24′ 17.59″ | 0.00″ | 60′ |
| 1 | 9 29.99 | 0.05 | 12 37.40 | 0.05 | 15 40.20 | 0.05 | 18 38.33 | 0.05 | 21 31.74 | 0.05 | 24 20.36 | 0.05 | 59 |
| 2 | 9 33.15 | 0.10 | 12 40.49 | 0.10 | 15 43.21 | 0.10 | 18 41.26 | 0.10 | 21 34.59 | 0.10 | 24 23.13 | 0.10 | 58 |
| 3 | 9 36.31 | 0.15 | 12 43.57 | 0.15 | 15 46.22 | 0.15 | 18 44.19 | 0.15 | 21 37.44 | 0.15 | 24 25.90 | 0.14 | 57 |
| 4 | 9 39.47 | 0.20 | 12 46.65 | 0.20 | 15 49.22 | 0.20 | 18 47.12 | 0.20 | 21 40.29 | 0.20 | 24 28.67 | 0.18 | 56 |
| 5 | 9 42.63 | 0.26 | 12 49.73 | 0.25 | 15 52.22 | 0.25 | 18 50.04 | 0.25 | 21 43.14 | 0.25 | 24 31.43 | 0.23 | 55 |
| 6 | 4 9 45.79 | 0.31 | 4 12 52.81 | 0.30 | 4 15 55.22 | 0.30 | 4 18 52.97 | 0.30 | 4 21 45.99 | 0.29 | 4 24 34.20 | 0.28 | 54 |
| 7 | 9 48.95 | 0.36 | 12 55.00 | 0.35 | 15 58.22 | 0.35 | 18 55.89 | 0.35 | 21 48.83 | 0.34 | 24 36.96 | 0.32 | 53 |
| 8 | 9 52.10 | 0.42 | 12 58.97 | 0.40 | 16 1.22 | 0.40 | 18 58.81 | 0.40 | 21 51.67 | 0.38 | 24 39.72 | 0.37 | 52 |
| 9 | 9 55.25 | 0.47 | 13 2.04 | 0.45 | 16 4.22 | 0.45 | 19 1.73 | 0.44 | 21 54.51 | 0.42 | 24 42.48 | 0.42 | 51 |
| 10 | 9 58.40 | 0.52 | 13 5.11 | 0.51 | 16 7.22 | 0.50 | 19 4.65 | 0.48 | 21 57.35 | 0.47 | 24 45.24 | 0.46 | 50 |
| 11 | 4 10 1.55 | 0.58 | 4 13 8.18 | 0.56 | 4 16 10.22 | 0.55 | 4 19 7.57 | 0.53 | 4 22 0.19 | 0.52 | 4 24 48.00 | 0.51 | 49 |
| 12 | 10 4.70 | 0.63 | 13 11.25 | 0.61 | 16 13.21 | 0.60 | 19 10.49 | 0.57 | 22 3.03 | 0.57 | 24 50.76 | 0.56 | 48 |
| 13 | 10 7.84 | 0.69 | 13 14.32 | 0.66 | 16 16.20 | 0.65 | 19 13.40 | 0.62 | 22 5.86 | 0.61 | 24 53.52 | 0.60 | 47 |
| 14 | 10 10.96 | 0.74 | 13 17.39 | 0.71 | 16 19.19 | 0.70 | 19 16.31 | 0.67 | 22 8.69 | 0.66 | 24 56.27 | 0.65 | 46 |
| 15 | 10 14.12 | 0.79 | 13 20.46 | 0.76 | 16 22.18 | 0.75 | 19 19.22 | 0.72 | 22 11.52 | 0.70 | 24 59.02 | 0.70 | 45 |
| 16 | 4 10 17.26 | 0.84 | 4 13 23.53 | 0.81 | 4 16 25.17 | 0.80 | 4 19 22.13 | 0.77 | 4 22 14.35 | 0.75 | 4 25 1.78 | 0.74 | 44 |
| 17 | 10 20.40 | 0.89 | 13 26.60 | 0.86 | 16 28.16 | 0.85 | 19 25.04 | 0.82 | 22 17.18 | 0.80 | 25 4.53 | 0.79 | 43 |
| 18 | 10 23.54 | 0.94 | 13 29.66 | 0.91 | 16 31.15 | 0.90 | 19 27.95 | 0.87 | 22 20.01 | 0.85 | 25 7.28 | 0.83 | 42 |
| 19 | 10 26.68 | 0.99 | 13 32.72 | 0.96 | 16 34.13 | 0.95 | 19 30.86 | 0.92 | 22 22.84 | 0.89 | 25 10.03 | 0.87 | 41 |
| 20 | 10 29.82 | 1.04 | 13 35.78 | 1.02 | 16 37.11 | 0.99 | 19 33.76 | 0.96 | 22 25.66 | 0.94 | 25 12.76 | 0.91 | 40 |
| 21 | 4 10 32.96 | 1.10 | 4 13 38.84 | 1.07 | 4 16 40.09 | 1.04 | 4 19 36.67 | 1.01 | 4 22 28.49 | 0.99 | 4 25 15.51 | 0.96 | 39 |
| 22 | 10 36.10 | 1.15 | 13 41.90 | 1.12 | 16 43.07 | 1.09 | 19 39.57 | 1.05 | 22 31.31 | 1.03 | 25 18.25 | 1.00 | 38 |
| 23 | 10 39.23 | 1.20 | 13 44.96 | 1.17 | 16 46.05 | 1.14 | 19 42.47 | 1.10 | 22 34.13 | 1.08 | 25 20.99 | 1.05 | 37 |
| 24 | 10 42.36 | 1.26 | 13 48.02 | 1.22 | 16 49.03 | 1.19 | 19 45.37 | 1.15 | 22 36.95 | 1.12 | 25 23.73 | 1.10 | 36 |
| 25 | 10 45.49 | 1.31 | 13 51.07 | 1.27 | 16 52.01 | 1.24 | 19 48.27 | 1.20 | 22 39.77 | 1.17 | 25 26.47 | 1.14 | 35 |
| 26 | 4 10 48.62 | 1.36 | 4 13 54.13 | 1.32 | 4 16 54.99 | 1.29 | 4 19 51.17 | 1.25 | 4 22 42.59 | 1.22 | 4 25 29.21 | 1.19 | 34 |
| 27 | 10 51.75 | 1.41 | 13 57.18 | 1.37 | 16 57.97 | 1.34 | 19 54.07 | 1.30 | 22 45.41 | 1.26 | 25 31.95 | 1.24 | 33 |
| 28 | 10 54.88 | 1.46 | 14 0.23 | 1.42 | 17 0.94 | 1.39 | 19 56.96 | 1.35 | 22 48.23 | 1.30 | 25 34.68 | 1.28 | 32 |
| 29 | 10 58.01 | 1.51 | 14 3.28 | 1.47 | 17 3.91 | 1.44 | 19 59.85 | 1.40 | 22 51.04 | 1.35 | 25 37.41 | 1.33 | 31 |
| 30 | 11 1.14 | 1.57 | 14 6.33 | 1.52 | 17 6.88 | 1.49 | 20 2.74 | 1.45 | 22 53.85 | 1.40 | 25 40.14 | 1.37 | 30 |
| 31 | 4 11 4.27 | 1.63 | 4 14 9.38 | 1.57 | 4 17 9.85 | 1.54 | 4 20 5.63 | 1.50 | 4 22 56.66 | 1.45 | 4 25 42.87 | 1.42 | 29 |
| 32 | 11 7.40 | 1.68 | 14 12.43 | 1.62 | 17 12.82 | 1.59 | 20 8.52 | 1.55 | 22 59.47 | 1.50 | 25 45.60 | 1.46 | 28 |
| 33 | 11 10.52 | 1.74 | 14 15.48 | 1.67 | 17 15.79 | 1.64 | 20 11.41 | 1.60 | 23 2.28 | 1.55 | 25 48.33 | 1.51 | 27 |
| 34 | 11 13.64 | 1.80 | 14 18.52 | 1.72 | 17 18.76 | 1.69 | 20 14.30 | 1.65 | 23 5.09 | 1.59 | 25 51.06 | 1.56 | 26 |
| 35 | 11 16.76 | 1.85 | 14 21.56 | 1.77 | 17 21.72 | 1.74 | 20 17.18 | 1.70 | 23 7.89 | 1.64 | 25 53.78 | 1.60 | 25 |
| 36 | 4 11 19.88 | 1.90 | 4 14 24.60 | 1.82 | 4 17 24.68 | 1.79 | 4 20 20.07 | 1.74 | 4 23 10.70 | 1.68 | 4 25 56.51 | 1.65 | 24 |
| 37 | 11 23.00 | 1.95 | 14 27.64 | 1.87 | 17 27.64 | 1.84 | 20 22.95 | 1.79 | 23 13.50 | 1.73 | 25 59.23 | 1.69 | 23 |
| 38 | 11 26.12 | 2.00 | 14 30.68 | 1.92 | 17 30.60 | 1.89 | 20 25.83 | 1.84 | 23 16.30 | 1.77 | 26 1.95 | 1.74 | 22 |
| 39 | 11 29.23 | 2.05 | 14 33.72 | 1.97 | 17 33.56 | 1.94 | 20 28.71 | 1.88 | 23 19.10 | 1.82 | 26 4.67 | 1.78 | 21 |
| 40 | 11 32.34 | 2.09 | 14 36.75 | 2.03 | 17 36.52 | 1.98 | 20 31.59 | 1.93 | 23 21.90 | 1.87 | 26 7.39 | 1.82 | 20 |
| 41 | 4 11 35.45 | 2.14 | 4 14 39.79 | 2.08 | 4 17 39.48 | 2.03 | 4 20 34.47 | 1.98 | 4 23 24.70 | 1.92 | 4 26 10.11 | 1.87 | 19 |
| 42 | 11 38.56 | 2.19 | 14 42.82 | 2.13 | 17 42.44 | 2.08 | 20 37.35 | 2.02 | 23 27.50 | 1.96 | 26 12.83 | 1.91 | 18 |
| 43 | 11 41.67 | 2.25 | 14 45.85 | 2.18 | 17 45.39 | 2.13 | 20 40.22 | 2.07 | 23 30.29 | 2.01 | 26 15.54 | 1.96 | 17 |
| 44 | 11 44.77 | 2.30 | 14 48.88 | 2.23 | 17 48.34 | 2.18 | 20 43.09 | 2.12 | 23 33.08 | 2.06 | 26 18.25 | 2.00 | 16 |
| 45 | 11 47.89 | 2.35 | 14 51.91 | 2.28 | 17 51.29 | 2.23 | 20 45.96 | 2.17 | 23 35.87 | 2.10 | 26 20.96 | 2.05 | 15 |
| 46 | 4 11 50.98 | 2.40 | 4 14 54.95 | 2.33 | 4 17 54.24 | 2.28 | 4 20 48.83 | 2.21 | 4 23 38.66 | 2.15 | 4 26 23.67 | 2.09 | 14 |
| 47 | 11 54.08 | 2.45 | 14 57.97 | 2.38 | 17 57.19 | 2.33 | 20 51.70 | 2.26 | 23 41.45 | 2.20 | 26 26.38 | 2.14 | 13 |
| 48 | 11 57.18 | 2.50 | 15 1.00 | 2.43 | 18 0.14 | 2.38 | 20 54.57 | 2.31 | 23 44.24 | 2.24 | 26 29.09 | 2.18 | 12 |
| 49 | 12 0.28 | 2.55 | 15 4.02 | 2.48 | 18 3.09 | 2.43 | 20 57.44 | 2.36 | 23 47.03 | 2.29 | 26 31.79 | 2.23 | 11 |
| 50 | 12 3.38 | 2.61 | 15 7.04 | 2.54 | 18 6.03 | 2.48 | 21 0.30 | 2.41 | 23 49.81 | 2.34 | 26 34.49 | 2.28 | 10 |
| 51 | 4 12 6.48 | 2.67 | 4 15 10.06 | 2.59 | 4 18 8.97 | 2.53 | 4 21 3.17 | 2.46 | 4 23 52.60 | 2.39 | 4 26 37.19 | 2.32 | 9 |
| 52 | 12 9.58 | 2.72 | 15 13.08 | 2.64 | 18 11.91 | 2.58 | 21 6.04 | 2.50 | 23 55.38 | 2.43 | 26 39.89 | 2.36 | 8 |
| 53 | 12 12.68 | 2.77 | 15 16.10 | 2.69 | 18 14.85 | 2.63 | 21 8.89 | 2.55 | 23 58.16 | 2.48 | 26 42.59 | 2.41 | 7 |
| 54 | 12 15.77 | 2.82 | 15 19.12 | 2.74 | 18 17.79 | 2.68 | 21 11.75 | 2.60 | 24 0.94 | 2.52 | 26 45.29 | 2.46 | 6 |
| 55 | 12 18.86 | 2.87 | 15 22.13 | 2.79 | 18 20.73 | 2.73 | 21 14.61 | 2.65 | 24 3.72 | 2.56 | 26 47.99 | 2.50 | 5 |
| 56 | 4 12 21.95 | 2.92 | 4 15 25.15 | 2.84 | 4 18 23.67 | 2.78 | 4 21 17.47 | 2.70 | 4 24 6.50 | 2.61 | 4 26 50.69 | 2.54 | 4 |
| 57 | 12 25.04 | 2.97 | 15 28.16 | 2.89 | 18 26.61 | 2.83 | 21 20.33 | 2.75 | 24 9.28 | 2.66 | 26 53.39 | 2.58 | 3 |
| 58 | 12 28.13 | 3.02 | 15 31.17 | 2.94 | 18 29.54 | 2.88 | 21 23.19 | 2.80 | 24 12.05 | 2.71 | 26 56.09 | 2.63 | 2 |
| 59 | 12 31.22 | 3.08 | 15 34.18 | 2.99 | 18 32.47 | 2.93 | 21 26.04 | 2.85 | 24 14.82 | 2.76 | 26 58.78 | 2.68 | 1 |
| 60 | 12 34.31 | 3.13 | 15 37.19 | 3.05 | 18 35.40 | 2.98 | 21 28.89 | 2.89 | 24 17.59 | 2.81 | 27 1.48 | 2.73 | 0 |
| $\bar{y}$ | 125°+ 305°— | | 124°+ 304°— | | 123°+ 303°— | | 122°+ 302°— | | 121°+ 301°— | | 120°+ 300°— | | $\bar{y}$ |

# TABLE CXXXVII. ARGUMENT 77.

Equation = 18500″ sin $\bar{y}$.

| $\bar{y}$ | 240°— 60°+ | | 241°— 61°+ | | 242°— 62°+ | | 243°— 63°+ | | 244°— 64°+ | | 245°— 65°+ | | $\bar{y}$ |
|---|---|---|---|---|---|---|---|---|---|---|---|---|---|
| | Equation. | P. P. | Equation. | P. P. | Equation. | P. P. | Equation. | P. P. | Equation. | P. P. | Equation. | P. P. | |
| 0′ | 4° 27′ 1″.47 | 0″.00 | 4° 29′ 40″.47 | 0″.00 | 4° 32′ 14″.53 | 0″.00 | 4° 34′ 43″62 | 0″.00 | 4° 37′ 7″.68 | 0″.00 | 4° 39′ 26″.69 | 0″.00 | 60′ |
| 1 | 27 4.16 | 0.05 | 29 43.08 | 0.05 | 32 17.06 | 0.04 | 34 46.06 | 0.04 | 37 10.04 | 0.04 | 39 28.96 | 0.04 | 59 |
| 2 | 27 6.85 | 0.10 | 29 45.69 | 0.10 | 32 19.59 | 0.08 | 34 48.50 | 0.08 | 37 12.39 | 0.08 | 39 31.23 | 0.08 | 58 |
| 3 | 27 9.54 | 0.14 | 29 48.30 | 0.14 | 32 22.11 | 0.12 | 34 50.94 | 0.12 | 37 14.74 | 0.12 | 39 33.50 | 0.12 | 57 |
| 4 | 27 12.23 | 0.18 | 29 50.90 | 0.19 | 32 24.63 | 0.16 | 34 53.38 | 0.16 | 37 17.09 | 0.16 | 39 35.77 | 0.16 | 56 |
| 5 | 27 14.91 | 0.22 | 29 53.50 | 0.23 | 32 27.15 | 0.20 | 34 55.81 | 0.20 | 37 19.45 | 0.20 | 39 38.04 | 0.20 | 55 |
| 6 | 4 27 17.59 | 0.27 | 4 29 56.10 | 0.27 | 4 32 29.67 | 0.25 | 4 34 58.25 | 0.24 | 4 37 21.80 | 0.24 | 4 39 40.31 | 0.23 | 54 |
| 7 | 27 20.27 | 0.32 | 29 58.70 | 0.31 | 32 32.19 | 0.29 | 35 0.68 | 0.28 | 37 24.15 | 0.28 | 39 42.58 | 0.27 | 53 |
| 8 | 27 22.95 | 0.36 | 30 1.30 | 0.35 | 32 34.71 | 0.33 | 35 3.11 | 0.32 | 37 26.50 | 0.32 | 39 44.84 | 0.30 | 52 |
| 9 | 27 25.63 | 0.40 | 30 3.90 | 0.39 | 32 37.22 | 0.38 | 35 5.54 | 0.36 | 37 28.85 | 0.36 | 39 47.10 | 0.34 | 51 |
| 10 | 27 28.31 | 0.44 | 30 6.49 | 0.43 | 32 39.73 | 0.42 | 35 7.97 | 0.40 | 37 31.19 | 0.39 | 39 49.36 | 0.37 | 50 |
| 11 | 4 27 30.99 | 0.48 | 4 30 9.09 | 0.47 | 4 32 42.24 | 0.46 | 4 35 10.40 | 0.44 | 4 37 33.54 | 0.43 | 4 39 51.62 | 0.40 | 49 |
| 12 | 27 33.67 | 0.52 | 30 11.68 | 0.52 | 32 44.75 | 0.50 | 35 12.83 | 0.48 | 37 35.89 | 0.47 | 39 53.88 | 0.44 | 48 |
| 13 | 27 36.34 | 0.57 | 30 14.27 | 0.56 | 32 47.26 | 0.54 | 35 15.26 | 0.52 | 37 38.23 | 0.51 | 39 56.14 | 0.48 | 47 |
| 14 | 27 39.01 | 0.61 | 30 16.86 | 0.60 | 32 49.77 | 0.58 | 35 17.69 | 0.56 | 37 40.57 | 0.55 | 39 58.40 | 0.52 | 46 |
| 15 | 27 41.68 | 0.66 | 30 19.45 | 0.64 | 32 52.27 | 0.62 | 35 20.11 | 0.60 | 37 42.91 | 0.59 | 40 0.65 | 0.55 | 45 |
| 16 | 4 27 44.35 | 0.70 | 4 30 22.04 | 0.68 | 4 32 54.78 | 0.66 | 4 35 22.53 | 0.64 | 4 37 45.25 | 0.63 | 4 40 2.90 | 0.59 | 44 |
| 17 | 27 47.02 | 0.74 | 30 24.63 | 0.73 | 32 57.28 | 0.70 | 35 24.95 | 0.68 | 37 47.59 | 0.67 | 40 5.15 | 0.63 | 43 |
| 18 | 27 49.69 | 0.78 | 30 27.22 | 0.78 | 32 59.78 | 0.74 | 35 27.37 | 0.72 | 37 49.93 | 0.70 | 40 7.40 | 0 66 | 42 |
| 19 | 27 52.35 | 0.83 | 30 29.80 | 0.82 | 33 2.28 | 0.78 | 35 29.79 | 0.76 | 37 52.26 | 0.74 | 40 9.65 | 0.70 | 41 |
| 20 | 27 55.01 | 0.88 | 30 32.38 | 0.86 | 33 4.78 | 0.83 | 35 32.21 | 0.80 | 37 54.59 | 0.77 | 40 11.90 | 0.74 | 40 |
| 21 | 4 27 57.67 | 0.93 | 4 30 34.96 | 0.90 | 4 33 7.28 | 0.87 | 4 35 34.63 | 0.84 | 4 37 56.92 | 0.81 | 4 40 14.15 | 0.78 | 39 |
| 22 | 28 0.33 | 0.97 | 30 37.54 | 0.94 | 33 9.78 | 0.91 | 35 37.04 | 0.88 | 37 59.25 | 0.85 | 40 16.39 | 0.82 | 38 |
| 23 | 28 2.99 | 1.02 | 30 40.12 | 0.98 | 33 12.28 | 0.96 | 35 39.45 | 0.92 | 38 1.58 | 0.89 | 40 18.63 | 0.85 | 37 |
| 24 | 28 5.65 | 1.07 | 30 42.70 | 1.03 | 33 14.77 | 1.00 | 35 41.86 | 0.96 | 38 3.91 | 0.93 | 40 20.87 | 0.89 | 36 |
| 25 | 28 8.31 | 1.11 | 30 45.27 | 1.08 | 33 17.26 | 1.04 | 35 44.27 | 1.00 | 38 6.23 | 0.97 | 40 23.11 | 0.93 | 35 |
| 26 | 4 28 10.97 | 1.16 | 4 30 47.84 | 1.12 | 4 33 19.75 | 1.08 | 4 35 46.68 | 1.04 | 4 38 8.55 | 1.01 | 4 40 25.35 | 0.97 | 34 |
| 27 | 28 13.63 | 1.20 | 30 50.41 | 1.16 | 33 22.24 | 1.12 | 35 49.08 | 1.08 | 38 10.87 | 1.05 | 40 27.59 | 1.00 | 33 |
| 28 | 28 16.28 | 1.25 | 30 52.98 | 1.20 | 33 24.73 | 1.16 | 35 51.48 | 1.12 | 38 13.19 | 1.09 | 40 29.83 | 1.04 | 32 |
| 29 | 28 18.93 | 1.29 | 30 55.55 | 1.24 | 33 27.22 | 1.20 | 35 53.88 | 1.16 | 38 15.51 | 1.13 | 40 31.06 | 1.08 | 31 |
| 30 | 28 21.58 | 1.33 | 30 58.12 | 1.28 | 33 29.70 | 1.25 | 35 56.28 | 1.20 | 38 17.82 | 1.16 | 40 34.29 | 1.12 | 30 |
| 31 | 4 28 24.23 | 1.38 | 4 31 0.69 | 1.32 | 4 33 32.19 | 1.31 | 4 35 58.68 | 1.24 | 4 38 20.14 | 1.20 | 4 40 36.62 | 1.16 | 29 |
| 32 | 28 26.88 | 1.43 | 31 3.26 | 1.36 | 33 34.67 | 1.35 | 36 1.08 | 1.28 | 38 22.45 | 1.24 | 40 38.85 | 1.20 | 28 |
| 33 | 28 29.53 | 1.47 | 31 5.82 | 1.41 | 33 37.15 | 1.39 | 36 3.48 | 1.32 | 38 24.76 | 1.28 | 40 41.08 | 1.23 | 27 |
| 34 | 28 32.18 | 1.52 | 31 8.38 | 1.46 | 33 39.63 | 1.43 | 36 5.87 | 1.36 | 38 27.07 | 1.32 | 40 43.31 | 1.27 | 26 |
| 35 | 28 34.82 | 1.56 | 31 10.94 | 1.50 | 33 42.11 | 1.47 | 36 8.26 | 1.40 | 38 29.38 | 1.36 | 40 45.43 | 1.30 | 25 |
| 36 | 4 28 37.46 | 1.61 | 4 31 13.50 | 1.54 | 4 33 44.59 | 1.51 | 4 36 10.65 | 1.44 | 4 38 31.69 | 1.40 | 4 40 47.65 | 1.34 | 24 |
| 37 | 28 40.10 | 1.65 | 31 16.06 | 1.58 | 33 47.07 | 1.55 | 36 13.04 | 1.48 | 38 34.00 | 1.44 | 40 49.87 | 1.38 | 23 |
| 38 | 28 42.74 | 1.69 | 31 18.62 | 1.63 | 33 49.54 | 1.59 | 36 15.43 | 1.52 | 38 36.31 | 1.48 | 40 52.09 | 1.41 | 22 |
| 39 | 28 45.38 | 1.73 | 31 21.18 | 1.67 | 33 51.81 | 1.63 | 36 17.82 | 1.56 | 38 38.61 | 1.52 | 40 54.31 | 1.45 | 21 |
| 40 | 28 48.02 | 1.77 | 31 23.73 | 1.71 | 33 54.48 | 1.66 | 36 20.21 | 1.60 | 38 40.91 | 1.55 | 40 56.53 | 1.49 | 20 |
| 41 | 4 28 50.66 | 1.82 | 4 31 26.28 | 1.75 | 4 33 56.95 | 1.70 | 4 36 22.60 | 1.64 | 4 38 43.21 | 1.59 | 4 40 58.75 | 1.53 | 19 |
| 42 | 28 53.29 | 1.86 | 31 28.83 | 1.80 | 33 59.42 | 1.74 | 36 24.99 | 1.68 | 38 45.51 | 1.63 | 41 0.97 | 1.57 | 18 |
| 43 | 28 55.92 | 1.91 | 31 31.38 | 1.84 | 34 1.89 | 1.78 | 36 27.38 | 1.72 | 38 47.81 | 1.67 | 41 3.18 | 1.60 | 17 |
| 44 | 28 58.55 | 1.96 | 31 33.93 | 1.88 | 34 4.36 | 1.82 | 36 29.76 | 1.76 | 38 50.11 | 1.71 | 41 5.39 | 1.64 | 16 |
| 45 | 29 1.18 | 2.00 | 31 36.48 | 1.92 | 34 6.82 | 1.86 | 36 32.14 | 1.80 | 38 52.41 | 1.75 | 41 7.60 | 1.68 | 15 |
| 46 | 4 29 3.81 | 2.04 | 4 31 39.03 | 1.96 | 4 34 9.29 | 1.92 | 4 36 34.52 | 1.84 | 4 38 54.71 | 1.79 | 4 41 9.81 | 1.71 | 14 |
| 47 | 29 6.44 | 2.09 | 31 41.58 | 2.01 | 34 11.75 | 1.96 | 36 36.90 | 1.88 | 38 57.01 | 1.83 | 41 12.02 | 1.74 | 13 |
| 48 | 29 9.07 | 2.13 | 31 44.12 | 2.06 | 34 14.21 | 2.00 | 36 39.28 | 1.92 | 38 59.30 | 1.87 | 41 14.23 | 1.78 | 12 |
| 49 | 29 11.69 | 2.17 | 31 46.66 | 2.10 | 34 16.67 | 2.04 | 36 41.66 | 1.96 | 39 1.59 | 1.91 | 41 16.43 | 1.82 | 11 |
| 50 | 29 14.31 | 2.21 | 31 49.20 | 2.14 | 34 19.13 | 2.08 | 36 44.03 | 2.00 | 39 3.88 | 1.94 | 41 18.63 | 1.86 | 10 |
| 51 | 4 29 16.93 | 2.26 | 4 31 51.74 | 2.19 | 4 34 21.59 | 2.12 | 4 36 46.40 | 2.04 | 4 39 6.17 | 1.98 | 4 41 20.83 | 1.90 | 9 |
| 52 | 29 19.55 | 2.30 | 31 54.28 | 2.23 | 34 24.05 | 2.16 | 36 48.77 | 2.08 | 39 8.46 | 2.02 | 41 23.03 | 1.93 | 8 |
| 53 | 29 22.13 | 2.35 | 31 56 82 | 2.27 | 34 26.50 | 2.20 | 36 51.14 | 2.12 | 39 10.75 | 2.06 | 41 25.23 | 1.97 | 7 |
| 54 | 29 24.79 | 2.39 | 31 59.35 | 2.32 | 34 28.95 | 2.24 | 36 53.51 | 2.16 | 39 13.03 | 2.10 | 41 27.43 | 2.00 | 6 |
| 55 | 29 27.41 | 2.44 | 32 1.88 | 2.36 | 34 31.40 | 2.28 | 36 55.88 | 2.20 | 39 15.31 | 2.14 | 41 29.63 | 2.04 | 5 |
| 56 | 4 29 30.03 | 2.48 | 4 32 4.41 | 2.40 | 4 34 33.85 | 2.32 | 4 36 58.24 | 2.24 | 4 39 17.59 | 2.18 | 4 41 31.83 | 2.08 | 4 |
| 57 | 29 32.64 | 2.54 | 32 6.94 | 2.44 | 34 36.30 | 2.36 | 37 0.60 | 2.28 | 39 19.87 | 2.22 | 41 34.02 | 2.12 | 3 |
| 58 | 29 35.25 | 2.58 | 32 9.43 | 2.48 | 34 38.74 | 2.40 | 37 2.96 | 2.32 | 39 22.15 | 2.25 | 41 36.21 | 2.16 | 2 |
| 59 | 29 37.86 | 2.62 | 32 12.00 | 2.52 | 34 41.18 | 2.44 | 37 5.32 | 2.36 | 39 24.42 | 2.29 | 41 38.40 | 2.20 | 1 |
| 60 | 29 40.47 | 2.65 | 32 14.53 | 2.57 | 34 43.62 | 2.49 | 37 7.68 | 2.40 | 39 26.69 | 2.32 | 41 40.59 | 2.23 | 0 |
| $\bar{y}$ | 119°+ 299°— | | 118°+ 298°— | | 117°+ 297°— | | 116°+ 296°— | | 115°+ 295°— | | 114°+ 294°— | | $\bar{y}$ |

# TABLE CXXXVII. ARGUMENT 77.

Equation = 18500″ sin $\bar{y}$.

| $\bar{y}$ | 246°− 66°+ Equation. | P. P. | 247°− 67°+ Equation. | P. P. | 248°− 68°+ Equation. | P. P. | 249°− 69°+ Equation. | P. P. | 250°− 70°+ Equation. | P. P. | 251°− 71°+ Equation. | P. P. | $\bar{y}$ |
|---|---|---|---|---|---|---|---|---|---|---|---|---|---|
| ′ | ° ′ ″ | ″ | ° ′ ″ | ″ | ° ′ ″ | ″ | ° ′ ″ | ″ | ° ′ ″ | ″ | ° ′ ″ | ″ | ′ |
| 0 | 4 41 40.59 | 0.00 | 4 43 49.34 | 0.00 | 4 45 52.90 | 0.00 | 4 47 51.23 | 0.00 | 4 49 44.31 | 0.00 | 4 51 32.10 | 0.00 | 60 |
| 1 | 41 42.78 | 0.04 | 43 51.44 | 0.04 | 45 54.92 | 0.03 | 47 53.16 | 0.03 | 49 46.15 | 0.03 | 51 33.85 | 0.03 | 59 |
| 2 | 41 44.97 | 0.08 | 43 53.54 | 0.08 | 45 56.93 | 0.06 | 47 55.09 | 0.06 | 49 47.99 | 0.06 | 51 35.60 | 0.06 | 58 |
| 3 | 41 47.16 | 0.12 | 43 55.64 | 0.11 | 45 58.94 | 0.09 | 47 57.01 | 0.09 | 49 49.83 | 0.09 | 51 37.35 | 0.09 | 57 |
| 4 | 41 49.34 | 0.15 | 43 57.74 | 0.14 | 46 0.95 | 0.12 | 47 58.93 | 0.12 | 49 51.66 | 0.12 | 51 39.09 | 0.12 | 56 |
| 5 | 41 51.52 | 0.18 | 43 59.84 | 0.18 | 46 2.96 | 0.16 | 48 0.85 | 0.15 | 49 53.49 | 0.15 | 51 40.83 | 0.15 | 55 |
| 6 | 4 41 53.70 | 0.22 | 4 44 1.94 | 0.21 | 4 46 4.97 | 0.20 | 4 48 2.77 | 0.18 | 4 49 55.32 | 0.18 | 4 51 42.57 | 0.18 | 54 |
| 7 | 41 55.88 | 0.25 | 44 4.03 | 0.25 | 46 6.98 | 0.23 | 48 4.69 | 0.21 | 49 57.15 | 0.21 | 51 44.31 | 0.21 | 53 |
| 8 | 41 58.06 | 0.29 | 44 6.12 | 0.28 | 46 8.98 | 0.26 | 48 6.61 | 0.24 | 49 58.98 | 0.24 | 51 46.05 | 0.24 | 52 |
| 9 | 42 0.24 | 0.33 | 44 8.21 | 0.31 | 46 10.98 | 0.30 | 48 8.53 | 0.28 | 50 0.81 | 0.27 | 51 47.79 | 0.27 | 51 |
| 10 | 42 2.41 | 0.36 | 44 10.30 | 0.34 | 46 12.98 | 0.33 | 48 10.44 | 0.32 | 50 2.64 | 0.30 | 51 49.53 | 0.29 | 50 |
| 11 | 4 42 4.58 | 0.40 | 4 44 12.39 | 0.38 | 4 46 14.98 | 0.36 | 4 48 12.35 | 0.35 | 4 50 4.47 | 0.33 | 4 51 51.27 | 0.32 | 49 |
| 12 | 42 6.75 | 0.43 | 44 14.48 | 0.41 | 46 16.98 | 0.40 | 48 14.26 | 0.38 | 50 6.30 | 0.36 | 51 53.00 | 0.35 | 48 |
| 13 | 42 8.92 | 0.47 | 44 16.56 | 0.44 | 46 18.98 | 0.43 | 48 16.17 | 0.41 | 50 8.12 | 0.39 | 51 54.73 | 0.38 | 47 |
| 14 | 42 11.09 | 0.51 | 44 18.64 | 0.48 | 46 20.97 | 0.47 | 48 18.08 | 0.44 | 50 9.94 | 0.42 | 51 56.46 | 0.41 | 46 |
| 15 | 42 13.26 | 0.54 | 44 20.72 | 0.52 | 46 22.97 | 0.50 | 48 19.99 | 0.47 | 50 11.76 | 0.45 | 51 58.19 | 0.43 | 45 |
| 16 | 4 42 15.43 | 0.58 | 4 44 22.80 | 0.55 | 4 46 24.97 | 0.53 | 4 48 21.90 | 0.50 | 4 50 13.58 | 0.48 | 4 51 59.92 | 0.46 | 44 |
| 17 | 42 17.60 | 0.62 | 44 24.88 | 0.58 | 46 26.96 | 0.56 | 48 23.81 | 0.53 | 50 15.40 | 0.51 | 52 1.65 | 0.49 | 43 |
| 18 | 42 19.76 | 0.66 | 44 26.96 | 0.61 | 46 28.95 | 0.60 | 48 25.71 | 0.56 | 50 17.22 | 0.54 | 52 3.38 | 0.51 | 42 |
| 19 | 42 21.92 | 0.69 | 44 29.04 | 0.65 | 46 30.94 | 0.63 | 48 27.61 | 0.60 | 50 19.03 | 0.57 | 52 5.10 | 0.54 | 41 |
| 20 | 42 24.08 | 0.72 | 44 31.11 | 0.69 | 46 32.93 | 0.66 | 48 29.51 | 0.63 | 50 20.84 | 0.60 | 52 6.82 | 0.57 | 40 |
| 21 | 4 42 26.24 | 0.76 | 4 44 33.18 | 0.72 | 4 46 34.92 | 0.69 | 4 48 31.41 | 0.66 | 4 50 22.65 | 0.63 | 4 52 8.54 | 0.60 | 39 |
| 22 | 42 28.40 | 0.80 | 44 35.25 | 0.76 | 46 36.91 | 0.73 | 48 33.31 | 0.69 | 50 24.46 | 0.66 | 52 10.26 | 0.63 | 38 |
| 23 | 42 30.56 | 0.83 | 44 37.32 | 0.80 | 46 38.89 | 0.76 | 48 35.21 | 0.72 | 50 26.27 | 0.69 | 52 11.98 | 0.66 | 37 |
| 24 | 42 32.71 | 0.86 | 44 39.39 | 0.83 | 46 40.87 | 0.80 | 48 37.10 | 0.75 | 50 28.08 | 0.72 | 52 13.70 | 0.69 | 36 |
| 25 | 42 34.86 | 0.90 | 44 41.46 | 0.87 | 46 42.85 | 0.83 | 48 38.99 | 0.78 | 50 29.88 | 0.75 | 52 15.42 | 0.72 | 35 |
| 26 | 4 42 37.01 | 0.94 | 4 44 43.53 | 0.90 | 4 46 44.83 | 0.86 | 4 48 40.88 | 0.81 | 4 50 31.68 | 0.78 | 4 52 17.14 | 0.75 | 34 |
| 27 | 42 39.16 | 0.98 | 44 45.59 | 0.94 | 46 46.81 | 0.90 | 48 42.77 | 0.84 | 50 33.48 | 0.81 | 52 18.86 | 0.78 | 33 |
| 28 | 42 41.31 | 1.01 | 44 47.65 | 0.97 | 46 48.78 | 0.93 | 48 44.66 | 0.88 | 50 35.28 | 0.84 | 52 20.57 | 0.81 | 32 |
| 29 | 42 43.46 | 1.04 | 44 49.71 | 1.00 | 46 50.75 | 0.96 | 48 46.54 | 0.91 | 50 37.08 | 0.87 | 52 22.28 | 0.84 | 31 |
| 30 | 42 45.61 | 1.07 | 44 51.77 | 1.03 | 46 52.72 | 0.99 | 48 48.42 | 0.95 | 50 38.87 | 0.90 | 52 23.99 | 0.86 | 30 |
| 31 | 4 42 47.76 | 1.11 | 4 44 53.83 | 1.07 | 4 46 54.69 | 1.02 | 4 48 50.30 | 0.98 | 4 50 40.67 | 0.93 | 4 52 25.70 | 0.89 | 29 |
| 32 | 42 49.91 | 1.14 | 44 55.89 | 1.11 | 46 56.66 | 1.06 | 48 52.18 | 1.01 | 50 42.46 | 0.96 | 52 27.41 | 0.92 | 28 |
| 33 | 42 52.05 | 1.18 | 44 57.95 | 1.14 | 46 58.63 | 1.09 | 48 54.06 | 1.04 | 50 44.25 | 0.99 | 52 29.12 | 0.94 | 27 |
| 34 | 42 54.19 | 1.22 | 45 0.00 | 1.17 | 47 0.60 | 1.12 | 48 55.94 | 1.07 | 50 46.04 | 1.02 | 52 30.82 | 0.97 | 26 |
| 35 | 42 56.33 | 1.25 | 45 2.05 | 1.20 | 47 2.56 | 1.16 | 48 57.82 | 1.10 | 50 47.83 | 1.05 | 52 32.52 | 1.00 | 25 |
| 36 | 4 42 58.47 | 1.28 | 4 45 4.10 | 1.24 | 4 47 4.53 | 1.19 | 4 48 59.70 | 1.13 | 4 50 49.62 | 1.08 | 4 52 34.22 | 1.03 | 24 |
| 37 | 43 0.61 | 1.32 | 45 6.15 | 1.27 | 47 6.49 | 1.23 | 49 1.58 | 1.16 | 50 51.41 | 1.11 | 52 35.92 | 1.06 | 23 |
| 38 | 43 2.75 | 1.36 | 45 8.20 | 1.30 | 47 8.45 | 1.26 | 49 3.45 | 1.19 | 50 53.20 | 1.14 | 52 37.62 | 1.09 | 22 |
| 39 | 43 4.88 | 1.39 | 45 10.25 | 1.33 | 47 10.41 | 1.29 | 49 5.32 | 1.22 | 50 54.98 | 1.17 | 52 39.31 | 1.11 | 21 |
| 40 | 43 7.01 | 1.43 | 45 12.29 | 1.37 | 47 12.37 | 1.32 | 49 7.19 | 1.26 | 50 56.76 | 1.20 | 52 41.00 | 1.14 | 20 |
| 41 | 4 43 9.14 | 1.47 | 4 45 14.34 | 1.40 | 4 47 14.33 | 1.35 | 4 49 9.06 | 1.29 | 4 50 58.54 | 1.23 | 4 52 42.69 | 1.17 | 19 |
| 42 | 43 11.27 | 1.50 | 45 16.38 | 1.44 | 47 16.29 | 1.38 | 49 10.93 | 1.32 | 51 0.32 | 1.26 | 52 44.38 | 1.20 | 18 |
| 43 | 43 13.40 | 1.54 | 45 18.42 | 1.47 | 47 18.24 | 1.42 | 49 12.80 | 1.35 | 51 2.10 | 1.29 | 52 46.07 | 1.22 | 17 |
| 44 | 43 15.52 | 1.57 | 45 20.46 | 1.50 | 47 20.19 | 1.45 | 49 14.67 | 1.38 | 51 3.87 | 1.32 | 52 47.75 | 1.25 | 16 |
| 45 | 43 17.64 | 1.60 | 45 22.50 | 1.54 | 47 22.14 | 1.48 | 49 16.53 | 1.41 | 51 5.05 | 1.35 | 52 49.93 | 1.28 | 15 |
| 46 | 4 43 19.76 | 1.63 | 4 45 24.54 | 1.58 | 4 47 24.09 | 1.51 | 4 49 18.39 | 1.44 | 4 51 7.43 | 1.38 | 4 52 51.11 | 1.31 | 14 |
| 47 | 43 21.88 | 1.67 | 45 26.58 | 1.61 | 47 26.04 | 1.54 | 49 20.25 | 1.47 | 51 9.20 | 1.41 | 52 52.79 | 1.34 | 13 |
| 48 | 43 24.00 | 1.71 | 45 28.61 | 1.64 | 47 27.99 | 1.57 | 49 22.11 | 1.50 | 51 10.97 | 1.44 | 52 54.47 | 1.37 | 12 |
| 49 | 43 26.12 | 1.75 | 45 30.64 | 1.68 | 47 29.93 | 1.61 | 49 23.87 | 1.53 | 51 12.74 | 1.47 | 52 56.15 | 1.40 | 11 |
| 50 | 43 28.24 | 1.79 | 45 32.67 | 1.72 | 47 31.87 | 1.65 | 49 25.83 | 1.57 | 51 14.51 | 1.50 | 52 57.83 | 1.43 | 10 |
| 51 | 4 43 30.36 | 1.83 | 4 45 34.70 | 1.76 | 4 47 33.81 | 1.68 | 4 49 27.69 | 1.60 | 4 51 16.28 | 1.53 | 4 52 59.51 | 1.46 | 9 |
| 52 | 43 32.48 | 1.86 | 45 36.73 | 1.79 | 47 35.75 | 1.72 | 49 29.54 | 1.63 | 51 18.05 | 1.56 | 53 1.19 | 1.49 | 8 |
| 53 | 43 34.59 | 1.90 | 45 38.76 | 1.83 | 47 37.69 | 1.75 | 49 31.39 | 1.66 | 51 19.81 | 1.59 | 53 2.86 | 1.52 | 7 |
| 54 | 43 36.70 | 1.94 | 45 40.78 | 1.86 | 47 39.63 | 1.79 | 49 33.24 | 1.69 | 51 21.57 | 1.62 | 53 4.53 | 1.54 | 6 |
| 55 | 43 38.81 | 1.98 | 45 42.80 | 1.90 | 47 41.57 | 1.81 | 49 35.09 | 1.72 | 51 23.33 | 1.65 | 53 6.20 | 1.57 | 5 |
| 56 | 4 43 40.92 | 2.01 | 4 45 44.82 | 1.93 | 4 47 43.51 | 1.84 | 4 49 36.04 | 1.75 | 4 51 25.00 | 1.68 | 4 53 7.87 | 1.60 | 4 |
| 57 | 43 43.03 | 2.05 | 45 46.84 | 1.97 | 47 45.44 | 1.87 | 49 38.79 | 1.78 | 51 26.85 | 1.71 | 53 9.54 | 1.63 | 3 |
| 58 | 43 45.14 | 2.09 | 45 48.86 | 2.00 | 47 47.37 | 1.90 | 49 40.63 | 1.82 | 51 28.60 | 1.74 | 53 11.21 | 1.66 | 2 |
| 59 | 43 47.24 | 2.12 | 45 50.88 | 2.03 | 47 49.30 | 1.94 | 49 42.47 | 1.85 | 51 30.35 | 1.77 | 53 12.88 | 1.69 | 1 |
| 60 | 43 49.34 | 2.15 | 45 52.90 | 2.06 | 47 51.23 | 1.98 | 49 44.31 | 1.89 | 51 32.10 | 1.80 | 53 14.54 | 1.71 | 0 |
| $\bar{y}$ | 113°+ 293°− | | 112°+ 292°− | | 111°+ 291°− | | 110°+ 290°− | | 109°+ 289°− | | 108°+ 288°− | | $\bar{y}$ |

# TABLE CXXXVII. ARGUMENT 77.

Equation = 18500″ sin $\bar{y}$.

| $\bar{y}$ | 252°– 72°+ Equation. | P. P. | 253°– 73°+ Equation. | P. P. | 254°– 74°+ Equation. | P. P. | 255°– 75°+ Equation. | P. P. | 256°– 76°+ Equation. | P. P. | 257°– 77°+ Equation. | P. P. | $\bar{y}$ |
|---|---|---|---|---|---|---|---|---|---|---|---|---|---|
| 0′ | 4° 53′ 14″.54 | 0″.00 | 4° 54′ 51″.64 | 0″.00 | 4° 56′ 23″.35 | 0″.00 | 4° 57′ 49″.63 | 0″.00 | 4° 59′ 10″.47 | 0″.00 | 5° 0′ 25″.84 | 0″.00 | 60′ |
| 1 | 53 16.20 | 0.03 | 54 53.21 | 0.03 | 56 24.83 | 0.03 | 57 51.02 | 0.02 | 59 11.77 | 0.02 | 0 27.04 | 0.02 | 59 |
| 2 | 53 17.86 | 0.06 | 54 54.78 | 0.06 | 56 26.31 | 0.06 | 57 52.41 | 0.04 | 59 13.07 | 0.04 | 0 28.25 | 0.04 | 58 |
| 3 | 53 19.52 | 0.09 | 54 56.35 | 0.09 | 56 27.79 | 0.08 | 57 53.80 | 0.07 | 59 14.37 | 0.06 | 0 29.46 | 0.06 | 57 |
| 4 | 53 21.18 | 0.12 | 54 57.92 | 0.12 | 56 29.27 | 0.11 | 57 55.19 | 0.09 | 59 15.67 | 0.08 | 0 30.67 | 0.08 | 56 |
| 5 | 53 22.84 | 0.15 | 54 59.49 | 0.14 | 56 30.75 | 0.13 | 57 56.58 | 0.12 | 59 16.96 | 0.10 | 0 31.88 | 0.10 | 55 |
| 6 | 4 53 24.50 | 0.17 | 4 55 1.06 | 0.17 | 4 56 32.23 | 0.15 | 4 57 57.97 | 0.14 | 4 59 18.25 | 0.12 | 5 0 33.08 | 0.12 | 54 |
| 7 | 53 26.15 | 0.20 | 55 2.62 | 0.20 | 56 33.70 | 0.18 | 57 59.35 | 0.17 | 59 19.54 | 0.14 | 0 34.28 | 0.14 | 53 |
| 8 | 53 27.80 | 0.23 | 55 4.18 | 0.22 | 56 35.17 | 0.20 | 58 0.73 | 0.19 | 59 20.83 | 0.17 | 0 35.48 | 0.16 | 52 |
| 9 | 53 29.45 | 0.25 | 55 5.74 | 0.24 | 56 36.64 | 0.22 | 58 2.11 | 0.21 | 59 22.12 | 0.19 | 0 36.68 | 0.18 | 51 |
| 10 | 53 31.10 | 0.27 | 55 7.30 | 0.26 | 56 38.11 | 0.24 | 58 3.49 | 0.23 | 59 23.41 | 0.21 | 0 37.88 | 0.19 | 50 |
| 11 | 4 53 32.75 | 0.30 | 4 55 8.86 | 0.28 | 4 56 39.58 | 0.27 | 4 58 4.87 | 0.25 | 4 59 24.70 | 0.23 | 5 0 39.07 | 0.21 | 49 |
| 12 | 53 34.40 | 0.32 | 55 10.42 | 0.31 | 56 41.05 | 0.30 | 58 6.24 | 0.27 | 59 25.99 | 0.25 | 0 40.26 | 0.23 | 48 |
| 13 | 53 36.04 | 0.35 | 55 11.97 | 0.34 | 56 42.51 | 0.32 | 58 7.61 | 0.30 | 59 27.27 | 0.27 | 0 41.45 | 0.25 | 47 |
| 14 | 53 37.68 | 0.37 | 55 13.52 | 0.36 | 56 43.97 | 0.34 | 58 8.98 | 0.32 | 59 28.55 | 0.29 | 0 42.64 | 0.27 | 46 |
| 15 | 53 39.32 | 0.40 | 55 15.07 | 0.38 | 56 45.43 | 0.36 | 58 10.35 | 0.34 | 59 29.83 | 0.32 | 0 43.83 | 0.29 | 45 |
| 16 | 4 53 40.96 | 0.43 | 4 55 16.62 | 0.41 | 4 56 46.89 | 0.38 | 4 58 11.72 | 0.37 | 4 59 31.11 | 0.34 | 5 0 45.02 | 0.31 | 44 |
| 17 | 53 42.60 | 0.45 | 55 18.17 | 0.43 | 56 48.35 | 0.41 | 58 13.09 | 0.39 | 59 32.39 | 0.36 | 0 46.21 | 0.33 | 43 |
| 18 | 53 44.24 | 0.48 | 55 19.72 | 0.45 | 56 49.81 | 0.43 | 58 14.45 | 0.41 | 59 33.67 | 0.38 | 0 47.39 | 0.35 | 42 |
| 19 | 53 45.88 | 0.51 | 55 21.26 | 0.48 | 56 51.27 | 0.45 | 58 15.81 | 0.43 | 59 34.94 | 0.40 | 0 48.57 | 0.37 | 41 |
| 20 | 53 47.51 | 0.54 | 55 22.80 | 0.51 | 56 52.72 | 0.48 | 58 17.17 | 0.45 | 59 36.21 | 0.42 | 0 49.75 | 0.39 | 40 |
| 21 | 4 53 49.14 | 0.57 | 4 55 24.34 | 0.54 | 4 56 54.17 | 0.51 | 4 58 18.53 | 0.47 | 4 59 37.48 | 0.44 | 5 0 50.93 | 0.41 | 39 |
| 22 | 53 50.77 | 0.60 | 55 25.88 | 0.57 | 56 55.62 | 0.53 | 58 19.89 | 0.49 | 59 38.75 | 0.46 | 0 52.11 | 0.43 | 38 |
| 23 | 53 52.40 | 0.63 | 55 27.42 | 0.60 | 56 57.07 | 0.56 | 58 21.25 | 0.52 | 59 40.02 | 0.48 | 0 53.29 | 0.45 | 37 |
| 24 | 53 54.03 | 0.65 | 55 28.96 | 0.62 | 56 58.52 | 0.58 | 58 22.61 | 0.54 | 59 41.29 | 0.50 | 0 54.46 | 0.47 | 36 |
| 25 | 53 55.66 | 0.68 | 55 30.50 | 0.65 | 56 59.97 | 0.60 | 58 23.96 | 0.56 | 59 42.55 | 0.53 | 0 55.63 | 0.49 | 35 |
| 26 | 4 53 57.28 | 0.71 | 4 55 32.04 | 0.68 | 4 57 1.41 | 0.63 | 4 58 25.32 | 0.59 | 4 59 43.81 | 0.55 | 5 0 56.80 | 0.51 | 34 |
| 27 | 53 58.90 | 0.73 | 55 33.58 | 0.70 | 57 2.85 | 0.65 | 58 26.68 | 0.61 | 59 45.97 | 0.57 | 0 57.97 | 0.53 | 33 |
| 28 | 54 0.52 | 0.76 | 55 35.11 | 0.72 | 57 4.29 | 0.68 | 58 28.03 | 0.63 | 59 46.33 | 0.59 | 0 59.14 | 0.55 | 32 |
| 29 | 54 2.14 | 0.79 | 55 36.64 | 0.74 | 57 5.73 | 0.70 | 58 29.38 | 0.65 | 59 47.5[illegible] | 0.61 | 1 0.31 | 0.57 | 31 |
| 30 | 54 3.76 | 0.81 | 55 38.17 | 0.76 | 57 7.17 | 0.72 | 58 30.73 | 0.68 | 59 48.84 | 0.63 | 1 1.47 | 0.58 | 30 |
| 31 | 4 54 5.38 | 0.84 | 4 55 39.70 | 0.79 | 4 57 8.61 | 0.75 | 4 58 32.08 | 0.70 | 4 59 50.17 | 0.65 | 5 1 2.63 | 0.60 | 29 |
| 32 | 54 7.00 | 0.86 | 55 41.23 | 0.81 | 57 10.05 | 0.77 | 58 33.43 | 0.72 | 59 51.35 | 0.67 | 1 3.79 | 0.62 | 28 |
| 33 | 54 8.61 | 0.89 | 55 42.76 | 0.84 | 57 11.48 | 0.80 | 58 34.78 | 0.75 | 59 52.60 | 0.69 | 1 4.95 | 0.64 | 27 |
| 34 | 54 10.22 | 0.92 | 55 44.28 | 0.86 | 57 12.91 | 0.82 | 58 36.12 | 0.77 | 59 53.85 | 0.72 | 1 6.11 | 0.66 | 26 |
| 35 | 54 11.83 | 0.95 | 55 45.80 | 0.88 | 57 14.34 | 0.84 | 58 37.46 | 0.79 | 59 55.10 | 0.74 | 1 7.27 | 0.68 | 25 |
| 36 | 4 54 13.44 | 0.97 | 4 55 47.32 | 0.91 | 4 57 15.77 | 0.87 | 4 58 38.80 | 0.81 | 4 59 56.35 | 0.76 | 5 1 8.43 | 0.70 | 24 |
| 37 | 54 15.05 | 1.00 | 55 48.84 | 0.94 | 57 17.20 | 0.90 | 58 40.14 | 0.83 | 59 57.60 | 0.78 | 1 9.59 | 0.72 | 23 |
| 38 | 54 16.66 | 1.03 | 55 50.36 | 1.97 | 57 18.63 | 0.92 | 58 41.48 | 0.85 | 59 58.84 | 0.80 | 1 10.74 | 0.74 | 22 |
| 39 | 54 18.27 | 1.06 | 55 51.88 | 1.00 | 57 20.05 | 0.94 | 58 42.81 | 0.87 | 5 0 0.08 | 0.82 | 1 11.89 | 0.76 | 21 |
| 40 | 54 19.87 | 1.08 | 55 53.39 | 1.02 | 57 21.47 | 0.96 | 58 44.14 | 0.90 | 0 1.32 | 0.84 | 1 13.04 | 0.77 | 20 |
| 41 | 4 54 21.47 | 1.11 | 4 55 54.90 | 1.05 | 4 57 22.89 | 0.98 | 4 58 45.47 | 0.92 | 5 0 2.56 | 0.86 | 5 1 14.19 | 0.79 | 19 |
| 42 | 54 23.07 | 1.14 | 55 56.41 | 1.07 | 57 24.31 | 1.00 | 58 46.80 | 0.94 | 0 3.80 | 0.88 | 1 15.34 | 0.81 | 18 |
| 43 | 54 24.67 | 1.16 | 55 57.92 | 1.10 | 57 25.73 | 1.03 | 58 48.13 | 0.97 | 0 5.04 | 0.90 | 1 16.49 | 0.83 | 17 |
| 44 | 54 26.27 | 1.19 | 55 59.43 | 1.12 | 57 27.15 | 1.05 | 58 49.45 | 0.99 | 0 6.28 | 0.93 | 1 17.63 | 0.85 | 16 |
| 45 | 54 27.87 | 1.21 | 56 0.93 | 1.14 | 57 28.57 | 1.08 | 58 50.77 | 1.01 | 0 7.51 | 0.95 | 1 18.77 | 0.87 | 15 |
| 46 | 4 54 29.47 | 1.24 | 4 56 1.44 | 1.17 | 4 57 29.98 | 1.10 | 4 58 52.09 | 1.04 | 5 0 8.74 | 0.97 | 5 1 19.91 | 0.89 | 14 |
| 47 | 54 31.06 | 1.27 | 56 3.94 | 1.19 | 57 31.39 | 1.12 | 58 53.41 | 1.06 | 0 9.97 | 0.99 | 1 21.05 | 0.91 | 13 |
| 48 | 54 32.65 | 1.29 | 56 5.44 | 1.22 | 57 32.80 | 1.15 | 58 54.73 | 1.09 | 0 11.20 | 1.01 | 1 22.19 | 0.93 | 12 |
| 49 | 54 34.24 | 1.32 | 56 6.94 | 1.25 | 57 33.21 | 1.18 | 58 56.05 | 1.11 | 0 12.43 | 1.03 | 1 23.33 | 0.95 | 11 |
| 50 | 54 35.83 | 1.35 | 56 8.44 | 1.28 | 57 35.62 | 1.20 | 58 57.37 | 1.13 | 0 13.66 | 1.05 | 1 24.46 | 0.97 | 10 |
| 51 | 4 54 37.42 | 1.38 | 4 56 9.94 | 1.31 | 4 57 37.03 | 1.23 | 4 58 58.69 | 1.15 | 5 0 14.89 | 1.07 | 5 1 25.59 | 0.99 | 9 |
| 52 | 54 39.01 | 1.40 | 56 11.44 | 1.33 | 57 38.44 | 1.25 | 59 0.01 | 1.17 | 0 16.11 | 1.09 | 1 26.72 | 1.01 | 8 |
| 53 | 54 40.59 | 1.43 | 56 12.93 | 1.36 | 57 39.84 | 1.28 | 59 1.32 | 1.20 | 0 17.33 | 1.11 | 1 27.85 | 1.03 | 7 |
| 54 | 54 42.17 | 1.46 | 56 14.42 | 1.38 | 57 41.24 | 1.30 | 59 2.63 | 1.22 | 0 18.55 | 1.14 | 1 28.98 | 1.05 | 6 |
| 55 | 54 43.75 | 1.48 | 56 15.91 | 1.40 | 57 42.64 | 1.32 | 59 3.94 | 1.24 | 0 19.77 | 1.16 | 1 30.11 | 1.07 | 5 |
| 56 | 4 54 45.33 | 1.51 | 4 56 17.40 | 1.43 | 4 57 44.04 | 1.34 | 4 59 5.25 | 1.27 | 5 0 20.99 | 1.18 | 5 1 31.24 | 1.09 | 4 |
| 57 | 54 46.91 | 1.53 | 56 18.89 | 1.45 | 57 45.44 | 1.36 | 59 6.56 | 1.29 | 0 22.21 | 1.20 | 1 32.37 | 1.11 | 3 |
| 58 | 54 48.49 | 1.56 | 56 20.38 | 1.48 | 57 46.84 | 1.38 | 59 7.87 | 1.31 | 0 23.42 | 1.22 | 1 33.49 | 1.13 | 2 |
| 59 | 54 50.07 | 1.59 | 56 21.87 | 1.51 | 57 48.24 | 1.40 | 59 9.17 | 1.33 | 0 24.63 | 1.24 | 1 34.61 | 1.15 | 1 |
| 60 | 54 51.64 | 1.62 | 56 23.35 | 1.53 | 57 49.63 | 1·44 | 59 10.47 | 1.35 | 0 25.84 | 1.26 | 1 35.73 | 1.16 | 0 |
| $\bar{y}$ | 107°+ 287°– | | 106°+ 286°– | | 105°+ 285°– | | 104°+ 284°– | | 103°+ 283°– | | 102°+ 282°– | | $\bar{y}$ |

# TABLE CXXXVII. ARGUMENT 77.

Equation = 18500″ sin $\bar{y}$.

| $\bar{y}$ | 258°− 78°+ Equation. | P. P. | 259°− 79°+ Equation. | P. P. | 260°− 80°+ Equation. | P. P. | 261°− 81°+ Equation. | P. P. | 262°− 82°+ Equation. | P. P. | 263°− 83°+ Equation. | P. P. | $\bar{y}$ |
|---|---|---|---|---|---|---|---|---|---|---|---|---|---|
| ′ 0 | ° ′ ″ 5 1 35.73 | ″ 0.00 | ° ′ ″ 5 2 40.10 | ″ 0.00 | ° ′ ″ 5 3 38.94 | ″ 0.00 | ° ′ ″ 5 4 32.23 | ″ 0.00 | ° ′ ″ 5 5 19.96 | ″ 0.00 | ° ′ ″ 5 6 2.10 | ″ 0.00 | ′ 60 |
| 1 | 1 36.85 | 0.02 | 2 41.13 | 0.02 | 3 39.87 | 0.01 | 4 33.07 | 0.01 | 5 20.71 | 0.01 | 6 2.75 | 0.01 | 59 |
| 2 | 1 37.97 | 0.04 | 2 42.16 | 0.04 | 3 40.80 | 0.03 | 4 33.91 | 0.02 | 5 21.46 | 0.02 | 6 3.40 | 0.02 | 58 |
| 3 | 1 39.09 | 0.05 | 2 43.18 | 0.05 | 3 41.73 | 0.04 | 4 34.75 | 0.04 | 5 22.21 | 0.03 | 6 4.05 | 0.03 | 57 |
| 4 | 1 40.20 | 0.07 | 2 44.20 | 0.07 | 3 42.66 | 0.06 | 4 35.58 | 0.05 | 5 22.95 | 0.04 | 6 4.70 | 0.04 | 56 |
| 5 | 1 41.31 | 0.09 | 2 45.22 | 0.08 | 3 43.59 | 0.07 | 4 36.41 | 0.06 | 5 23.69 | 0.05 | 6 5.35 | 0.05 | 55 |
| 6 | 5 1 42.42 | 0.11 | 5 2 46.24 | 0.10 | 5 3 44.52 | 0.09 | 5 4 37.24 | 0.07 | 5 5 24.43 | 0.07 | 5 6 6.00 | 0.06 | 54 |
| 7 | 1 43.53 | 0.12 | 2 47.26 | 0.12 | 3 45.44 | 0.10 | 4 38.00 | 0.09 | 5 25.17 | 0.08 | 6 6.65 | 0.07 | 53 |
| 8 | 1 44.64 | 0.14 | 2 48.28 | 0.13 | 3 46.36 | 0.11 | 4 38.90 | 0.10 | 5 25.90 | 0.09 | 6 7.29 | 0.08 | 52 |
| 9 | 1 45.75 | 0.16 | 2 49.29 | 0.14 | 3 47.28 | 0.13 | 4 39.73 | 0.11 | 5 26.63 | 0.10 | 6 7.93 | 0.09 | 51 |
| 10 | 1 46.85 | 0.18 | 2 50.30 | 0.16 | 3 48.20 | 0.15 | 4 40.56 | 0.13 | 5 27.36 | 0.12 | 6 8.57 | 0.10 | 50 |
| 11 | 5 1 47.95 | 0.20 | 5 2 51.31 | 0.17 | 5 3 49.12 | 0.16 | 5 4 41.39 | 0.14 | 5 5 28.10 | 0.13 | 5 6 9.21 | 0.11 | 49 |
| 12 | 1 49.05 | 0.22 | 2 52.32 | 0.18 | 3 50.04 | 0.18 | 4 42.22 | 0.15 | 5 28.83 | 0.14 | 6 9.85 | 0.12 | 48 |
| 13 | 1 50.15 | 0.23 | 2 53.33 | 0.20 | 3 50.96 | 0.19 | 4 43.04 | 0.17 | 5 29.56 | 0.15 | 6 10.49 | 0.13 | 47 |
| 14 | 1 51.25 | 0.25 | 2 54.33 | 0.22 | 3 51.87 | 0.21 | 4 43.86 | 0.18 | 5 30.29 | 0.16 | 6 11.13 | 0.14 | 46 |
| 15 | 1 52.34 | 0.27 | 2 55.33 | 0.23 | 3 52.78 | 0.22 | 4 44.68 | 0.19 | 5 31.02 | 0.18 | 6 11.76 | 0.15 | 45 |
| 16 | 5 1 53.43 | 0.28 | 5 2 56.33 | 0.25 | 5 3 53.69 | 0.24 | 5 4 45.50 | 0.21 | 5 5 31.74 | 0.19 | 5 6 12.39 | 0.16 | 44 |
| 17 | 1 54.52 | 0.30 | 2 57.33 | 0.27 | 3 54.60 | 0.25 | 4 46.32 | 0.22 | 5 32.46 | 0.20 | 6 13.02 | 0.17 | 43 |
| 18 | 1 55.61 | 0.32 | 2 58.33 | 0.00 | 3 55.51 | 0.26 | 4 47.14 | 0.23 | 5 33.18 | 0.21 | 6 13.65 | 0.18 | 42 |
| 19 | 1 56.70 | 0.34 | 2 59.33 | 0.30 | 3 56.42 | 0.28 | 4 47.95 | 0.25 | 5 33.90 | 0.22 | 6 14.28 | 0.19 | 41 |
| 20 | 1 57.79 | 0.36 | 3 0.33 | 0.33 | 3 57.32 | 0.29 | 4 48.76 | 0.26 | 5 34.62 | 0.23 | 6 14.90 | 0.20 | 40 |
| 21 | 5 1 58.88 | 0.38 | 5 3 1.33 | 0.35 | 5 3 58.22 | 0.30 | 5 4 49.57 | 0.27 | 5 5 35.34 | 0.24 | 5 6 15.53 | 0.21 | 39 |
| 22 | 1 59.97 | 0.40 | 3 2.32 | 0.37 | 3 59.12 | 0.32 | 4 50.38 | 0.29 | 5 36.06 | 0.25 | 6 16.15 | 0.22 | 38 |
| 23 | 2 1.05 | 0.41 | 3 3.31 | 0.38 | 4 0.02 | 0.33 | 4 51.19 | 0.30 | 5 36.77 | 0.26 | 6 16.77 | 0.23 | 37 |
| 24 | 2 2.13 | 0.43 | 3 4.30 | 0.40 | 4 0.92 | 0.35 | 4 51.99 | 0.31 | 5 37.48 | 0.27 | 6 17.39 | 0.24 | 36 |
| 25 | 2 3.21 | 0.45 | 3 5.29 | 0.41 | 4 1.82 | 0.36 | 4 52.79 | 0.33 | 5 38.19 | 0.29 | 6 18.01 | 0.25 | 35 |
| 26 | 5 2 4.29 | 0.46 | 5 3 6.28 | 0.43 | 5 4 2.72 | 0.37 | 5 4 53.59 | 0.34 | 5 5 38.90 | 0.30 | 5 6 18.63 | 0.26 | 34 |
| 27 | 2 5.37 | 0.48 | 3 7.27 | 0.44 | 4 3.61 | 0.39 | 4 54.39 | 0.35 | 5 39.61 | 0.31 | 6 19.24 | 0.27 | 33 |
| 28 | 2 6.45 | 0.50 | 3 8.25 | 0.46 | 4 4.50 | 0.40 | 4 55.19 | 0.37 | 5 40.32 | 0.32 | 6 19.85 | 0.28 | 32 |
| 29 | 2 7.53 | 0.52 | 3 9.23 | 0.47 | 4 5.39 | 0.42 | 4 55.99 | 0.38 | 5 41.03 | 0.33 | 6 20.46 | 0.29 | 31 |
| 30 | 2 8.61 | 0.54 | 3 10.21 | 0.48 | 4 6.28 | 0.44 | 4 56.79 | 0.40 | 5 41.73 | 0.35 | 6 21.07 | 0.30 | 30 |
| 31 | 5 2 9.68 | 0.56 | 5 3 11.19 | 0.51 | 5 4 7.17 | 0.45 | 5 4 57.59 | 0.41 | 5 5 42.43 | 0.36 | 5 6 21.68 | [illegible] | 29 |
| 32 | 2 10.75 | 0.58 | 3 12.17 | 0.52 | 4 8.06 | 0.47 | 4 58.38 | 0.42 | 5 43.13 | 0.37 | 6 22.29 | 0.32 | 28 |
| 33 | 2 11.82 | 0.59 | 3 13.15 | 0.54 | 4 8.94 | 0.48 | 4 59.17 | 0.44 | 5 43.83 | 0.38 | 6 22.89 | 0.33 | 27 |
| 34 | 2 12.89 | 0.61 | 3 14.12 | 0.55 | 4 9.82 | 0.50 | 4 59.96 | 0.45 | 5 44.53 | 0.40 | 6 23.49 | 0.34 | 26 |
| 35 | 2 13.96 | 0.63 | 3 15.09 | 0.57 | 4 10.70 | 0.51 | 5 0.75 | 0.46 | 5 45.22 | 0.41 | 6 24.09 | 0.35 | 25 |
| 36 | 5 2 15.03 | 0.65 | 5 3 16.06 | 0.59 | 5 4 11.58 | 0.53 | 5 5 1.54 | 0.48 | 5 5 45.91 | 0.42 | 5 6 24.69 | 0.36 | 24 |
| 37 | 2 16.09 | 0.66 | 3 17.03 | 0.60 | 4 12.46 | 0.54 | 5 2.33 | 0.49 | 5 46.60 | 0.44 | 6 25.29 | 0.37 | 23 |
| 38 | 2 17.15 | 0.68 | 3 18.00 | 0.62 | 4 13.34 | 0.56 | 5 3.11 | 0.50 | 5 47.29 | 0.45 | 6 25.89 | 0.38 | 22 |
| 39 | 2 18.20 | 0.70 | 3 18.97 | 0.64 | 4 14.21 | 0.57 | 5 3.89 | 0.51 | 5 47.98 | 0.46 | 6 26.49 | 0.39 | 21 |
| 40 | 2 19.27 | 0.72 | 3 19.94 | 0.65 | 4 15.08 | 0.59 | 5 4.67 | 0.53 | 5 48.67 | 0.47 | 6 27.08 | 0.40 | 20 |
| 41 | 5 2 20.33 | 0.74 | 5 3 20.91 | 0.66 | 5 4 15.95 | 0.60 | 5 5 5.45 | 0.54 | 5 5 49.36 | 0.48 | 5 6 27.67 | 0.41 | 19 |
| 42 | 2 21.38 | 0.76 | 3 21.87 | 0.68 | 4 16.82 | 0.62 | 5 6.23 | 0.55 | 5 50.05 | 0.49 | 6 28.26 | 0.42 | 18 |
| 43 | 2 22.43 | 0.77 | 3 22.83 | 0.70 | 4 17.69 | 0.63 | 5 7.01 | 0.57 | 5 50.73 | 0.50 | 6 28.83 | 0.43 | 17 |
| 44 | 2 23.48 | 0.79 | 3 23.79 | 0.71 | 4 18.56 | 0.65 | 5 7.78 | 0.58 | 5 51.41 | 0.52 | 6 29.44 | 0.44 | 16 |
| 45 | 2 24.53 | 0.81 | 3 24.75 | 0.73 | 4 19.43 | 0.66 | 5 8.55 | 0.59 | 5 52.09 | 0.53 | 6 30.03 | 0.45 | 15 |
| 46 | 5 2 25.58 | 0.83 | 5 3 25.76 | 0.74 | 5 4 20.30 | 0.68 | 5 5 9.32 | 0.61 | 5 5 52.77 | 0.54 | 5 6 30.62 | 0.46 | 14 |
| 47 | 2 26.63 | 0.84 | 3 26.67 | 0.76 | 4 21.16 | 0.69 | 5 10.09 | 0.62 | 5 53.45 | 0.55 | 6 31.20 | 0.47 | 13 |
| 48 | 2 27.67 | 0.86 | 3 27.62 | 0.78 | 4 22.02 | 0.70 | 5 10.86 | 0.63 | 5 54.13 | 0.57 | 6 31.78 | 0.48 | 12 |
| 49 | 2 28.71 | 0.88 | 3 28.57 | 0.80 | 4 22.88 | 0.72 | 5 11.63 | 0.65 | 5 54.80 | 0.58 | 6 32.36 | 0.49 | 11 |
| 50 | 2 29.75 | 0.90 | 3 29.52 | 0.82 | 4 23.74 | 0.74 | 5 12.39 | 0.66 | 5 55.47 | 0.59 | 6 32.94 | 0.50 | 10 |
| 51 | 5 2 30.79 | 0.92 | 5 3 30.47 | 0.84 | 5 4 24.60 | 0.75 | 5 5 13.15 | 0.68 | 5 5 56.13 | 0.60 | 5 6 33.52 | 0.51 | 9 |
| 52 | 2 31.83 | 0.94 | 3 31.42 | 0.86 | 4 25.46 | 0.77 | 5 13.91 | 0.69 | 5 56.80 | 0.61 | 6 34.10 | 0.52 | 8 |
| 53 | 2 32.87 | 0.95 | 3 32.37 | 0.87 | 4 26.31 | 0.78 | 5 14.67 | 0.70 | 5 57.47 | 0.62 | 6 34.67 | 0.53 | 7 |
| 54 | 2 33.91 | 0.97 | 3 33.31 | 0.89 | 4 27.16 | 0.80 | 5 15.43 | 0.72 | 5 58.14 | 0.63 | 6 35.24 | 0.54 | 6 |
| 55 | 2 34.94 | 0.99 | 3 34.25 | 0.91 | 4 28.01 | 0.81 | 5 16.19 | 0.73 | 5 58.81 | 0.64 | 6 35.81 | 0.55 | 5 |
| 56 | 5 2 35.98 | 1.01 | 5 3 35.19 | 0.92 | 5 4 28.86 | 0.83 | 5 5 16.95 | 0.75 | 5 5 59.47 | 0.65 | 5 6 36.38 | 0.56 | 4 |
| 57 | 2 37.01 | 1.02 | 3 36.13 | 0.93 | 4 29.71 | 0.84 | 5 17.71 | 0.76 | 6 0.13 | 0.66 | 6 36.95 | 0.57 | 3 |
| 58 | 2 38.04 | 1.04 | 3 37.07 | 0.95 | 4 30.55 | 0.86 | 5 18.46 | 0.77 | 6 0.79 | 0.67 | 6 37.52 | 0.58 | 2 |
| 59 | 2 39.07 | 1.06 | 3 38.01 | 0.96 | 4 31.39 | 0.87 | 5 19.21 | 0.78 | 6 1.45 | 0.68 | 6 38.09 | 0.59 | 1 |
| 60 | 2 40.10 | 1.08 | 3 38.94 | 0.98 | 4 32.23 | 0.88 | 5 19.96 | 0.79 | 6 2.10 | 0.70 | 6 38.65 | 0.60 | 0 |
| $\bar{y}$ | 101°+ 281°− | | 100°+ 280°− | | 99°+ 279°− | | 98°+ 278°− | | 97°+ 277°− | | 96°+ 276°− | | $\bar{y}$ |

# TABLE CXXXVII. ARGUMENT 77.

Equation = 18500″ sin $\bar{y}$.

| $\bar{y}$ | 264°— 84°+ | | 265°— 85°+ | | 266°— 86°+ | | 267°— 87°+ | | 268°— 88°+ | | 269°— 89°+ | | $\bar{y}$ |
|---|---|---|---|---|---|---|---|---|---|---|---|---|---|
| | Equation. | P. P. | Equation. | P. P. | Equation. | P. P. | Equation. | P. P. | Equation. | P. P. | Equation. | P. P. | |
| 0′ | 5° 6′ 38″.65 | 0″.00 | 5° 7′ 9″.60 | 0″.00 | 5° 7′ 34″.92 | 0″.00 | 5° 7′ 54″.65 | 0″.00 | 5° 8′ 8″.73 | 0″.00 | 5° 8′ 17″.18 | 0″.00 | 60′ |
| 1 | 6 39.21 | 0.01 | 7 10.07 | 0.01 | 7 35.29 | 0.01 | 7 54.93 | 0.00 | 8 8.92 | 0.00 | 8 17.27 | 0.00 | 59 |
| 2 | 6 39.77 | 0.02 | 7 10.54 | 0.01 | 7 35.66 | 0.01 | 7 55.21 | 0.01 | 8 9.11 | 0.00 | 8 17.36 | 0.00 | 58 |
| 3 | 6 40.33 | 0.03 | 7 11.01 | 0.02 | 7 36.03 | 0.02 | 7 55.49 | 0.01 | 8 9.29 | 0.01 | 8 17.45 | 0.00 | 57 |
| 4 | 6 40.89 | 0.04 | 7 11.47 | 0.02 | 7 36.40 | 0.02 | 7 55.76 | 0.01 | 8 9.47 | 0.01 | 8 17.54 | 0.00 | 56 |
| 5 | 6 41.45 | 0.05 | 7 11.93 | 0.03 | 7 36.77 | 0.03 | 7 56.03 | 0.02 | 8 9.65 | 0.01 | 8 17.62 | 0.00 | 55 |
| 6 | 5 6 42.01 | 0.06 | 5 7 12.39 | 0.04 | 5 7 37.14 | 0.03 | 5 7 56.30 | 0.02 | 5 8 9.83 | 0.01 | 5 8 17.71 | 0.01 | 54 |
| 7 | 6 42.56 | 0.07 | 7 12.85 | 0.04 | 7 37.51 | 0.04 | 7 56.57 | 0.03 | 8 10.01 | 0.02 | 8 17.78 | 0.01 | 53 |
| 8 | 6 43.11 | 0.08 | 7 13.81 | 0.05 | 7 37.87 | 0.04 | 7 56.84 | 0.03 | 8 10.19 | 0.02 | 8 17.87 | 0.01 | 52 |
| 9 | 6 43.66 | 0.09 | 7 13.77 | 0.06 | 7 38.23 | 0.05 | 7 57.11 | 0.04 | 8 10.36 | 0.02 | 8 17.95 | 0.01 | 51 |
| 10 | 6 44.21 | 0.09 | 7 14.22 | 0.07 | 7 38.59 | 0.05 | 7 57.38 | 0.04 | 8 10.53 | 0.02 | 8 18.03 | 0.01 | 50 |
| 11 | 5 6 44.76 | 0.10 | 5 7 14.67 | 0.07 | 5 7 38.95 | 0.06 | 5 7 57.65 | 0.04 | 5 8 10.70 | 0.02 | 5 8 18.11 | 0.01 | 49 |
| 12 | 6 45.30 | 0.11 | 7 15.12 | 0.08 | 7 39.31 | 0.06 | 7 57.92 | 0.04 | 8 10.87 | 0.02 | 8 18.19 | 0.01 | 48 |
| 13 | 6 45.84 | 0.12 | 7 15.57 | 0.09 | 7 39.67 | 0.07 | 7 58.18 | 0.05 | 8 11.04 | 0.02 | 8 18.27 | 0.02 | 47 |
| 14 | 6 46.38 | 0.12 | 7 16.02 | 0.10 | 7 40.03 | 0.07 | 7 58.44 | 0.05 | 8 11.21 | 0.03 | 8 18.34 | 0.02 | 46 |
| 15 | 6 46.92 | 0.13 | 7 16.46 | 0.10 | 7 40.38 | 0.08 | 7 58.70 | 0.05 | 8 11.37 | 0.03 | 8 18.41 | 0.02 | 45 |
| 16 | 5 6 47.46 | 0.14 | 5 7 16.91 | 0.11 | 5 7 40.73 | 0.08 | 5 7 58.96 | 0.06 | 5 8 11.53 | 0.03 | 5 8 18.48 | 0.02 | 44 |
| 17 | 6 48.00 | 0.15 | 7 17.35 | 0.12 | 7 41.68 | 0.09 | 7 59.22 | 0.06 | 8 11.69 | 0.03 | 8 18.55 | 0.02 | 43 |
| 18 | 6 48.54 | 0.16 | 7 17.79 | 0.12 | 7 41.43 | 0.09 | 7 59.48 | 0.06 | 8 11.85 | 0.04 | 8 18.62 | 0.02 | 42 |
| 19 | 6 49.07 | 0.17 | 7 18.23 | 0.13 | 7 41.78 | 0.10 | 7 59.73 | 0.07 | 8 12.01 | 0.04 | 8 18.69 | 0.02 | 41 |
| 20 | 6 49.60 | 0.17 | 7 18.67 | 0.14 | 7 42.13 | 0.11 | 7 59.98 | 0.07 | 8 12.17 | 0.05 | 8 18.75 | 0.02 | 40 |
| 21 | 5 6 50.13 | 0.18 | 5 7 19.11 | 0.15 | 5 7 42.47 | 0.12 | 5 8 0.23 | 0.07 | 5 8 12.33 | 0.05 | 5 8 18.81 | 0.02 | 39 |
| 22 | 6 50.66 | 0.19 | 7 19.55 | 0.15 | 7 42.81 | 0.12 | 8 0.48 | 0.07 | 8 12.48 | 0.05 | 8 18.87 | 0.02 | 38 |
| 23 | 6 51.19 | 0.20 | 7 19.98 | 0.16 | 7 43.15 | 0.13 | 8 0.73 | 0.08 | 8 12.63 | 0.05 | 8 18.93 | 0.02 | 37 |
| 24 | 6 51.72 | 0.20 | 7 20.41 | 0.17 | 7 43.49 | 0.13 | 8 0.97 | 0.08 | 8 12.78 | 0.06 | 8 18.99 | 0.02 | 36 |
| 25 | 6 52.24 | 0.21 | 7 20.84 | 0.18 | 7 43.83 | 0.14 | 8 1.21 | 0.08 | 8 12.93 | 0.06 | 8 19.04 | 0.02 | 35 |
| 26 | 5 6 52.76 | 0.22 | 5 7 21.27 | 0.18 | 5 7 44.17 | 0.14 | 5 8 1.45 | 0.09 | 5 8 13.08 | 0.06 | 5 8 19.09 | 0.02 | 34 |
| 27 | 6 53.28 | 0.23 | 7 21.70 | 0.19 | 7 44.50 | 0.15 | 8 1.69 | 0.09 | 8 13.23 | 0.06 | 8 19.14 | 0.02 | 33 |
| 28 | 6 53.80 | 0.24 | 7 22.12 | 0.20 | 7 44.83 | 0.15 | 8 1.93 | 0.10 | 8 13.38 | 0.07 | 8 19.19 | 0.02 | 32 |
| 29 | 6 54.32 | 0.25 | 7 22.54 | 0.20 | 7 45.16 | 0.16 | 8 2.17 | 0.10 | 8 13.52 | 0.07 | 8 19.24 | 0.02 | 31 |
| 30 | 6 54.83 | 0.26 | 7 22.96 | 0.21 | 7 45.49 | 0.16 | 8 2.40 | 0.11 | 8 13.66 | 0.07 | 8 19.29 | 0.02 | 30 |
| 31 | 5 6 55.34 | 0.27 | 5 7 23.38 | 0.22 | 5 7 45.82 | 0.16 | 5 8 2.63 | 0.11 | 5 8 13.80 | 0.07 | 5 8 19.34 | 0.02 | 29 |
| 32 | 6 55.85 | 0.28 | 7 23.80 | 0.23 | 7 46.15 | 0.17 | 8 2.86 | 0.12 | 8 13.94 | 0.08 | 8 19.38 | 0.02 | 28 |
| 33 | 6 56.36 | 0.29 | 7 24.22 | 0.23 | 7 46.47 | 0.17 | 8 3.09 | 0.12 | 8 14.08 | 0.08 | 8 19.42 | 0.02 | 27 |
| 34 | 6 56.87 | 0.29 | 7 24.63 | 0.24 | 7 46.79 | 0.18 | 8 3.32 | 0.13 | 8 14.22 | 0.08 | 8 19.46 | 0.03 | 26 |
| 35 | 6 57.38 | 0.30 | 7 25.04 | 0.25 | 7 47.11 | 0.18 | 8 3.55 | 0.13 | 8 14.35 | 0.09 | 8 19.50 | 0.03 | 25 |
| 36 | 5 6 57.89 | 0.31 | 5 7 25.45 | 0.25 | 5 7 47.43 | 0.19 | 5 8 3.78 | 0.13 | 5 8 14.48 | 0.09 | 5 8 19.54 | 0.03 | 24 |
| 37 | 6 58.40 | 0.32 | 7 25.86 | 0.26 | 7 47.75 | 0.19 | 8 4.00 | 0.14 | 8 14.61 | 0.09 | 8 19.58 | 0.03 | 23 |
| 38 | 6 58.90 | 0.33 | 7 26.27 | 0.27 | 7 48.07 | 0.20 | 8 4.22 | 0.14 | 8 14.74 | 0.09 | 8 19.62 | 0.03 | 22 |
| 39 | 6 59.40 | 0.33 | 7 26.68 | 0.27 | 7 48.39 | 0.20 | 8 4.44 | 0.14 | 8 14.87 | 0.09 | 8 19.65 | 0.03 | 21 |
| 40 | 6 59.90 | 0.34 | 7 27.09 | 0.28 | 7 48.70 | 0.21 | 8 4.66 | 0.15 | 8 15.00 | 0.09 | 8 19.68 | 0.03 | 20 |
| 41 | 5 7 0.40 | 0.35 | 5 7 27.50 | 0.28 | 5 7 49.01 | 0.21 | 5 8 4.88 | 0.15 | 5 8 15.12 | 0.09 | 5 8 19.71 | 0.03 | 19 |
| 42 | 7 0.90 | 0.36 | 7 27.91 | 0.29 | 7 49.32 | 0.22 | 8 5.10 | 0.15 | 8 15.24 | 0.10 | 8 19.74 | 0.03 | 18 |
| 43 | 7 1.40 | 0.37 | 7 28.31 | 0.30 | 7 49.63 | 0.22 | 8 5.32 | 0.15 | 8 15.36 | 0.10 | 8 19.77 | 0.03 | 17 |
| 44 | 7 1.90 | 0.38 | 7 28.71 | 0.31 | 7 49.94 | 0.23 | 8 5.53 | 0.16 | 8 15.48 | 0.10 | 8 19.80 | 0.04 | 16 |
| 45 | 7 2.39 | 0.38 | 7 29.11 | 0.31 | 7 50.25 | 0.23 | 8 5.74 | 0.16 | 8 15.60 | 0.11 | 8 19.82 | 0.04 | 15 |
| 46 | 5 7 2.88 | 0.39 | 5 7 29.51 | 0.32 | 5 7 50.56 | 0.24 | 5 8 5.95 | 0.17 | 5 8 15.72 | 0.11 | 5 8 19.84 | 0.04 | 14 |
| 47 | 7 3.37 | 0.40 | 7 29.91 | 0.33 | 7 50.86 | 0.24 | 8 6.16 | 0.17 | 8 15.84 | 0.11 | 8 19.86 | 0.04 | 13 |
| 48 | 7 3.86 | 0.41 | 7 30.31 | 0.34 | 7 51.16 | 0.25 | 8 6.37 | 0.17 | 8 15.95 | 0.11 | 8 19.88 | 0.04 | 12 |
| 49 | 7 4.35 | 0.42 | 7 30.70 | 0.34 | 7 51.46 | 0.26 | 8 6.58 | 0.18 | 8 16.06 | 0.12 | 8 19.90 | 0.04 | 11 |
| 50 | 7 4.84 | 0.43 | 7 31.09 | 0.35 | 7 51.76 | 0.27 | 8 6.78 | 0.18 | 8 16.17 | 0.12 | 8 19.92 | 0.04 | 10 |
| 51 | 5 7 5.32 | 0.44 | 5 7 31.48 | 0.36 | 5 7 52.06 | 0.27 | 5 8 6.98 | 0.18 | 5 8 16.28 | 0.12 | 5 8 19.94 | 0.04 | 9 |
| 52 | 7 5.80 | 0.45 | 7 31.87 | 0.36 | 7 52.36 | 0.28 | 8 7.18 | 0.19 | 8 16.39 | 0.12 | 8 19.95 | 0.04 | 8 |
| 53 | 7 6.28 | 0.46 | 7 32.26 | 0.37 | 7 52.65 | 0.28 | 8 7.38 | 0.19 | 8 16.50 | 0.13 | 8 19.96 | 0.04 | 7 |
| 54 | 7 6.76 | 0.47 | 7 32.65 | 0.38 | 7 52.94 | 0.29 | 8 7.58 | 0.19 | 8 16.60 | 0.13 | 8 19.97 | 0.05 | 6 |
| 55 | 7 7.24 | 0.47 | 7 33.03 | 0.39 | 7 53.23 | 0.29 | 8 7.78 | 0.20 | 8 16.70 | 0.13 | 8 19.98 | 0.05 | 5 |
| 56 | 5 7 7.72 | 0.48 | 5 7 33.41 | 0.39 | 5 7 53.52 | 0.30 | 5 8 7.97 | 0.20 | 5 8 16.80 | 0.14 | 5 8 19.98 | 0.05 | 4 |
| 57 | 7 8.19 | 0.49 | 7 33.79 | 0.40 | 7 53.81 | 0.30 | 8 8.16 | 0.21 | 8 16.90 | 0.14 | 8 19.99 | 0.05 | 3 |
| 58 | 7 8.66 | 0.50 | 7 34.17 | 0.41 | 7 54.09 | 0.31 | 8 8.35 | 0.21 | 8 17.00 | 0.14 | 8 19.99 | 0.05 | 2 |
| 59 | 7 9.13 | 0.51 | 7 34.55 | 0.41 | 7 54.37 | 0.31 | 8 8.54 | 0.22 | 8 17.09 | 0.14 | 8 20.00 | 0.05 | 1 |
| 60 | 7 9.60 | 0.51 | 7 34.92 | 0.42 | 7 54.65 | 0.32 | 8 8.73 | 0.22 | 8 17.18 | 0.14 | 8 20.00 | 0.05 | 0 |
| $\bar{y}$ | 95°+ 275°— | | 94°+ 274°— | | 93°+ 273°— | | 92°+ 272°— | | 91°+ 271°— | | 90°+ 270°— | | $\bar{y}$ |

www.ingramcontent.com/pod-product-compliance
Lightning Source LLC
LaVergne TN
LVHW010204110826
845151LV00002B/599

* 9 7 8 1 4 2 5 5 3 5 5 2 0 *